FUZZY SETS, FUZZY LOGIC, AND FUZZY SYSTEMS

Selected Papers by Lotfi A. Zadeh

ADVANCES IN FUZZY SYSTEMS — APPLICATIONS AND THEORY

Vol. 1: Between Mind and Computer: Fuzzy Science and Engineering
(*Eds. P.-Z. Wang and K.-F. Loe*)

Vol. 2: Industrial Applications of Fuzzy Technology in the World
(*Eds. K. Hirota and M. Sugeno*)

Vol. 3: Comparative Approaches to Medical Reasoning
(*Eds. M. E. Cohen and D. L. Hudson*)

Vol. 4: Fuzzy Logic and Soft Computing
(*Eds. B. Bouchon-Meunier, R. R. Yager and L. A. Zadeh*)

Vol. 5: Fuzzy Sets, Fuzzy Logic, Applications
(*G. Bojadziev and M. Bojadziev*)

Vol. 6: Fuzzy Sets, Fuzzy Logic, and Fuzzy Systems: Selected Papers by Lotfi A. Zadeh
(*Eds. G. J. Klir and B. Yuan*)

Vol. 8: Foundations and Applications of Possibility Theory
(*Eds. G. de Cooman, D. Ruan and E. E. Kerre*)

Forthcoming volumes:

Vol. 7: Genetic Algorithms and Fuzzy Logic Systems: Soft Computing Perspectives
(*Eds. E. Sanchez, T. Shibata and L. A. Zadeh*)

Advances in Fuzzy Systems — Applications and Theory Vol. 6

FUZZY SETS, FUZZY LOGIC, AND FUZZY SYSTEMS

Selected Papers by Lotfi A. Zadeh

Editors

George J. Klir & Bo Yuan

Center for Intelligent Systems and Department of Systems Science & Industrial Engineering
T. J. Watson School of Engineering and Applied Science
Binghamton University–SUNY, Binghamton, New York, USA

World Scientific
Singapore • New Jersey • London • Hong Kong

Published by

World Scientific Publishing Co Pte Ltd
P O Box 128, Farrer Road, Singapore 912805
USA office: Suite 1B, 1060 Main Street, River Edge, NJ 07661
UK office: 57 Shelton Street, Covent Garden, London WC2H 9HE

Library of Congress Cataloging-in-Publication
Zadeh, Lotfi Asker.
Fuzzy sets, fuzzy logic, and fuzzy systems : selected papers / by Lotfi A. Zadeh; edited by George J. Klir & Bo Yuan.
p. cm. -- (Advances in fuzzy systems ; vol. 6)
Includes bibliographical references and indexes.
ISBN 9810224214. -- ISBN 9810224222 (pbk.)
1. Fuzzy sets. 2. Fuzzy logic. 3. Fuzzy systems. I. Klir, George J., 1932– . II. Yuan, Bo. III. Title. IV. Series.
QA248.5.Z33 1996
511.3'22--dc20 96-11991
CIP

British Library Cataloguing-in-Publication Data
A catalogue record for this book is available from the British Library.

Printed in Singapore by Uto-Print

LOTFI A. ZADEH

When useful fuzzy concepts
Are used in many contexts,
They have a host of varied meanings,
As recognized by human beings.

When Lotfi Zadeh's gifted mind,
Turned to the concepts of this kind,
A great discovery was made,
That's not going to fade.

George J. Klir

模稜寓萬事
黑白交融，似清非清
廣流通，指理深
自古人間瞭若燈

慧眼識邏輯
查德大師，卓見創新
撥雲霧，拔舊根
此道綿綿欣欣生

Translated by Iris J. Chang

CONTENTS

PREFACE

This book is the second volume of Collected Papers by Lotfi A. Zadeh. The first volume, entitled *Fuzzy Sets and Applications*, was published in 1987 by John Wiley. Its editors, Ronald R. Yager, Sergei Ovchinnikov, Richard M. Tong, and Hung T. Ngugen, describe in the Preface to the book their motivation to undertake the project:

> At the beginning of 1985 the four of us decided that the 20th anniversary of the publication of the first paper on fuzzy sets would be a good time to undertake the project that resulted in this collection of papers. Our original conception was to be a personal tribute to Professor Zadeh who had in each case been instrumental in encouraging our efforts in the area of fuzzy sets. However, we soon realized that a selection of Professor Zadeh's papers would be of interest to a wide audience, and so by degrees our small project evolved into this volume.

The editors' judgment has turned out to be right. The book has proved to be of great utility to anyone interested in fuzzy set theory and its applications. For us, it has consistently been one of the most frequently used books. However, it was always somewhat frustrating when a needed paper by Lotfi Zadeh was not in the book. With passage of time, the number of Zadeh's papers not included in the book was steadily increasing, and so was the need for a second volume. In early 1995, we felt that the 30th anniversary of the publication of the first paper on fuzzy sets was an excellent occasion on which to publish such a needed book. Since we did not know of anyone else being interested in pursuing this project, we eventually decided to undertake it ourselves.

We felt that the book would fit well into the book series on *Advances in Fuzzy Systems—Applications and Theory* published by World Scientific. Our proposal to include the book in this book series was enthusiastically accepted by the publisher. Lotfi Zadeh not only endorsed the project, but provided us also with all information and documents we needed. We are very grateful for his help.

Our principal aim in defining the content of this book was to select, from among all papers by Lotfi Zadeh not included in the previous volume, those papers on fuzzy sets, fuzzy logic, and fuzzy systems whose easy accessibility would likely be of benefit to those working in these areas. From any group of papers on the same topic, we attempted to select the most comprehensive one. Some papers were chosen for their historical significance. This includes the first paper on fuzzy sets, published in 1965, which is the only paper in this volume that is also included in the previous volume.

In addition to his papers, also included in this book is an *Introduction*, in which we present a short biography of Lotfi Zadeh, an overview of his principal scholarly contributions, focusing primarily on his contributions to fuzzy set theory, fuzzy logic, and fuzzy systems, and a complete bibliography of his papers. The bibliography is divided into two parts: A. Papers on Fuzzy Set Theory and Related Subjects; and B. Other Papers.

Most papers included in this book are reprinted in their original form. New typesetting was employed only for papers whose original forms were not of sufficiently high quality. In a few papers, we had to make minor adjustments to avoid confusion caused by taking the papers out of their contexts. For readers' convenience, we prepared a Subject Index.

The purpose of this book is twofold. Firstly, it is intended as a reference for those working in the field. Secondly, it is expected to play a useful role in higher education, as a rich source of supplementary readings in relevant courses and seminars. We hope that the book will serve its purpose well.

George J. Klir and Bo Yuan
Binghamton, New York
December 1995

Lotfi A. Zadeh (middle) with the Editors,
Bo Yuan (left) and George J. Klir (right).

NOTE TO THE READER

Papers in this book are presented in the order in which they were published. Bibliography of Papers by Lotfi A. Zadeh is divided into two parts: **Part A**. *Papers on Fuzzy Set Theory and Related Subjects*; and **Part B**. *Other Papers*. In Part A of the Bibliography (pp. 7–12), papers identified by bold numbers and the asterisks are included in this book, while those identified only by bold numbers are included in the previous book of Collected Papers by Lotfi A. Zadeh (*Fuzzy Sets and Applications*, ed. by R. R. Yager *et al.*, John Wiley, 1987). For a quick identification of a special subject, the reader is advised to use Subject Index.

ACKNOWLEDGMENTS

This book consists of 44 reprinted papers. The following is the list of relevant copyright owners whose permissions to reproduce the papers in this book are gratefully acknowledged (the numbers refer to papers listed in Part A of the Bibliography):

Academic Press [1,3,5,26,34]
American Association for Artificial Intelligence [77]
American Society of Mechanical Engineers [15]
American Statistical Society [103]
Association for Computing Machinery [99]
Brockmeyer [52]
Elsevier [8,40,54,70,88]
Institute of Electrical and Electronics Engineers [20,95,102]
John Wiley [84]
Kluwer Academic Publishers [27,30,33,49,65,80,85]
Marcel Dekker [38]
Plenum Publishing Corporation [29]
S. Karger Publishers [18]
Springer Verlag [79]
The Research Council of Norway [100]
Vandenhoeck & Ruprecht [24]
Westview Press [50]
W. H. Freeman [21]

INTRODUCTION

Lotfi A. Zadeh was born in 1921 in Baku, the former Soviet Azerbaijan, where he lived only until 1931. The next 13 years, he lived in Tehran, Iran. He studied at Aborz College (an American Presbyterian Missionary School) and, later, at the University of Tehran, where he received in 1942 a B.S. degree in electrical engineering. In 1944, he came to the United States for graduate studies at MIT, where he received the S.M. degree in electrical engineering in 1946. The same year, he joined Columbia University as an instructor in electrical engineering and was also admitted to the doctoral program. He received his Ph.D. degree in 1949 and served on the Electrical Engineering Faculty of Columbia University until 1959.

During his 13 years at Columbia University, Zadeh made several important contributions to electrical engineering, including a new direction in frequency analysis of time-varying networks, an extension of Wiener's theory of prediction, and a new way of analyzing sampled-data systems, which led to the well-known and widely used z-transformation. He taught courses in circuit analysis, system theory, electromagnetic theory, finite-state machines, and information theory. During this period, he also became interested in the emerging computer technology, whose significance he quickly recognized.

In 1959, Zadeh left Columbia University and joined the Electrical Engineering Department of the University of California at Berkeley. During his early years at Berkeley, he worked on various problems emerging from system theory, including problems of optimal control, time-varying systems, and system identification. Some of this work resulted in a monograph *Linear System Theory: The State Space Approach* (McGraw-Hill, 1963), which he co-authored with Charles Desoer. His papers during this period, as well as his earlier papers written at Columbia University, are listed in Part B of our Bibliography.

In 1963, Zadeh was appointed Chairman of the Department of Electrical Engineering and held the position for five years. In this position, he emphasized the growing importance of computer technology and managed to transform the department into the Department of Electrical Engineering and Computer Science. Since 1965, when he introduced the concept of a fuzzy set, Zadeh's research has almost exclusively been oriented to the development of fuzzy set theory and related areas. His work in these areas, which is the subject of this book, is characterized in more detail later in this biographical overview.

During his academic career, Zadeh also held visiting positions at other institutions, including the Princeton Advanced Study Institute (1956), Electrical Engineering Department of MIT (1962 and 1968), IBM Research Laboratory in San Jose (1968, 1973, and 1977), Artificial Intelligence Laboratory of the Stanford Research Institute at Menlo Park, California (1981), and the Center for the Study of Language and Information of Stanford University (1988). After 1991, when he became Professor Emeritus, he has continued to be active in teaching and research as the Director of the Berkeley Initiative in Soft Computing.

For his enormous contributions to science and engineering, Zadeh has received numerous awards and honors. In 1995, he received the IEEE Medal of Honor, the highest honor given by IEEE, for his "pioneering development of fuzzy logic and its many diverse applications." Among his other awards are the Honda Prize (1989), the IEEE Education Medal (1958), the IEEE Centennial Medal (1984), the IEEE Richard W. Hamming Medal (1992), the ASME Rudolf Olderburger Medal (1993), the Kampe de Feriet Medal (1993), the Grigore Moisil Prize (1993), and several honorary doctoral degrees. He is also a member of the National Academy of Engineering, a foreign member of the Russian Academy of Natural Sciences, and a Fellow of IEEE, AAAS, ACM, and AAAI.

In this book, we are interested only in Zadeh's contributions to fuzzy set theory and related areas. To facilitate our examination of these contributions and to introduce his papers included in this book, we utilize Part A of our Bibliography. This part of the Bibliography contains all papers by Zadeh published in the period 1965–95 that deal with fuzzy set theory and related areas; Zadeh's other papers are listed in Part B of the Bibliography. For convenience of the reader, reference numbers of papers that are included in the two volumes of Collected Papers by Lotfi A. Zadeh (see Preface) are printed in bold, and those included in this volume are identified by the asterisks.

As is well known, fuzzy set theory began its existence in 1965, when Lotfi Zadeh introduced the concept of a fuzzy set in his seminal paper [1]. However, Zadeh is not only the founder of fuzzy set theory, but he has also been one of the most important contributors to the theory during its thirty-year existence. Indeed, he has originated most of the key ideas associated with the theory and conceived of many of its applications. He often developed his new ideas only to some degree, and let others to develop them further.

It is significant, but less known, that Zadeh recognized the need for fuzzy mathematics a few years before he published the seminal paper on fuzzy sets. This recognition, which emerged from his work on system theory, is expressed, for example, in the following quote from his 1962 paper "From Circuit Theory to System Theory" [56] (in Part B of Bibliography):

> ... there is a fairly wide gap between what might be regarded as "animate" system theorists and "inanimate" system theorists at the present time, and it is not at all certain that this gap will be narrowed, much less closed, in the near future. There are some who feel this gap reflects the fundamental inadequacy of the conventional mathematics—the mathematics of precisely-defined points, functions, sets, probability measures, etc.—for coping with the analysis of biological system, and that to deal effectively with such systems, which are generally orders of magnitude more complex than man-made system, we need a radically different kind of mathematics, the mathematics of fuzzy or cloudy quantities which are not described in terms of probability distributions. Indeed, the need for such mathematics is becoming increasingly apparent even in the realm of inanimate systems, for in most practical cases the *a priori* data as well as the criteria by which the performance of a man-made system is judged are far from being precisely specified or having accurately known probability distributions.

In the rest of this overview, we intend to trace the development of Zadeh's ideas pertaining to fuzzy sets, fuzzy logic, and fuzzy systems via his papers. To capture this development, we decided to present the papers in this book in the order in which they were published.

After careful reading of the seminal paper [1], in which Zadeh introduced the notion of fuzzy sets, one can easily recognize that the paper is rich source of ideas that played a fundamental role in the evolution of fuzzy set theory. Some of these ideas were further developed by Zadeh himself in his other papers, some were later developed by others. Let us examine these ideas.

First, it is quite significant that fuzzy complementation, intersection, and union are defined in the paper by operations that are usually referred to as *standard fuzzy set operations*. As is now well known, these specific operations possess several significant properties. Among all possible fuzzy complements, for example, the standard fuzzy complement is the only linear one. Among all possible fuzzy intersections (t-norms) and fuzzy unions (t-conorms), the standard operations are the only operations that are *idempotent*, and also the only operations that are *cutworthy* (i.e., they are preserved in all α-cuts of the fuzzy sets involved). Moreover, the standard fuzzy intersection is the largest fuzzy intersection, while the standard fuzzy union is the smallest fuzzy union. Although Zadeh was apparently aware that fuzzy counterparts of classical set operations are not unique, and mentioned examples of other possible operations in the paper, his remarkable insight allowed him to recognize the significance of the standard operations. He also recognized the existence of aggregation operations whose outcomes are fuzzy sets that contain the standard fuzzy intersection and are contained in the standard fuzzy union. Operations of this kind, which have no counterparts in classical set theory, are now referred to as *averaging operations*. It is significant that the standard fuzzy intersection and standard fuzzy union may also be viewed as the smallest and greatest averaging operations, respectively.

Second, the paper introduces the concept of a *fuzzy relation* and the notion of a *composition* of two binary fuzzy relations that are compatible. For fuzzy relations defined on the n-dimensional Euclidean spaces ($n \geq 2$), it also introduces the concept of *shadows* (or *projections*) on various hyperplanes. The subject of fuzzy relations was further developed by Zadeh in his later papers, especially papers [4] and [12]. In [4], he elaborates on properties of shadows of fuzzy relations on n-dimensional Euclidean spaces. In [12], he introduces fuzzy counterparts of the classical properties of *reflexivity*, *symmetry*, *transitivity*, and *antisymmetry* of binary relations. Using these fuzzy properties, he examines various types of fuzzy relations, such as *fuzzy equivalence*, *compatibility*, and *ordering relations*. All the defined properties and the various types of fuzzy relations based on them are cutworthy.

Third, the paper contains the first formulation of the *extension principle*, even though Zadeh did not use the term "extension principle" in the paper. The principle is introduced in the paper under the heading "fuzzy sets induced by mappings." The term "extension principle" was introduced by Zadeh in [28], where the principle and its utility are thoroughly explained.

Fourth, the paper introduces the notion of *convexity* of fuzzy sets and examines some of its properties. It also introduces the notion of boundedness of fuzzy sets. Both of these notions, which are defined in the paper as cutworthy concepts, were later instrumental in formulating the concept of a fuzzy number and fuzzy arithmetic.

Fifth, although the paper deals with membership functions whose range is the unit interval [0,1], it was recognized by Zadeh that "the range of the membership function can be taken to be a suitable partially ordered set P." He thus anticipated the existence of fuzzy sets that are now referred to as *L-fuzzy sets*.

Sixth, the concept of an α-cut is introduced in the paper and, as previously mentioned, it is utilized for defining convexity and boundedness of fuzzy sets. The *α-cut representation* of fuzzy sets is not explicitly included in the paper; it was formulated by Zadeh a few years later in [12].

Seventh, an extension of the *separation theorem* for classical convex sets to fuzzy sets is introduced in the paper, and the utility of this extension for dealing with the problem of pattern discrimination is discussed. The use of fuzzy sets to pattern discrimination and data clustering, which is only hinted at in the paper, is further examined in [3] (whose early version appeared as RAND Memorandum RM-4307-PR in October 1964) and, more extensively, in [34].

In addition to the seminal paper, which we just discussed, Zadeh also published in 1965 another paper [2], less known but also significant. In this paper, he introduces the concept of a *fuzzy system* and discusses the problem of optimizing crisp systems under fuzzy constraints. Zadeh's interest in fuzzy systems has remained strong, as documented by several other papers he has published on the subject [10, 21, 22, 24, 49, 100]. He also introduced various new ideas regarding fuzzy sets in these papers. In [10], for example, he introduced two important ideas, the idea of a fuzzy graph and the idea of representing fuzzy sets by *n*-dimensional unit hypercubes. The notion of *fuzzy control* was introduced for the first time in papers [15] and [20]. The concept of a *fuzzy finite-state machine* was introduced in [10].

In one of his early papers on fuzzy sets [5], Zadeh introduced the concept of a *fuzzy algorithm* and the associated concept of a *fuzzy Turing machine*. In another paper [16], he introduced the concept of a *fuzzy Markoff algorithm*. Although he addressed various issues regarding fuzzy algorithms in other papers (e.g., [10, 14, 22, 28]), this subject is still rather underdeveloped.

Another important concept recognized by Zadeh in his early papers [8, 11, 14, 18] is the concept of a *fuzzy language*. Although he did not develop fuzzy languages beyond their coverage in these four papers, they were further developed by other researchers and applied to pattern recognition and other areas.

It is easy to recognize that the important and broad area of *fuzzy decision making* was initiated by a key paper [9], which Lotfi Zadeh co-authored with Richard Bellman. The paper is a rich source of ideas regarding fuzzy decision making, including *fuzzy dynamic programming*. Zadeh presented further ideas concerning fuzzy decision making and *fuzzy optimization* a few year later in another paper [29].

A very important contribution by Zadeh was his introduction of *possibility theory* as a measure-theoretic calculus for dealing with information expressed by fuzzy propositions [36]. He also demonstrated the great utility of possibility theory in several other papers, including [35, 37, 44, 46, 48, 50, 52, 53]. In [37], he formulates a meaning representational language PRUF (an acronym for Possibilistic Relational Universal Fuzzy) for natural languages, which is based on possibility theory. In [52, 65], he shows how PRUF can be employed for determining the meaning of linguistic terms of natural language by possibility distributions.

Another important idea due to Zadeh is the concept of a *linguistic variable*, introduced initially in [22]. This paper is also a source of many other basic ideas that underlie most of the current applications of fuzzy logic. Among these are the calculus of fuzzy if-then rules and fuzzy algorithmic description of dependencies and commands. This paper and the 1965 paper on fuzzy sets [1] have been cited by the Citation Index as "Citation Classics." In addition, paper [22] has been identified by the Citation Index as the most frequently cited paper among all papers that have been published in the *IEEE Transactions on Systems, Man and Cybernetics.*

The concept of linguistic variables was fully developed by Zadeh later, in a significant, three-part paper [28]. Virtually all material covered in this extensive paper is directly applicable to *fuzzy logic* in its broad sense, as a system of concepts, principles, and methods for dealing with modes of reasoning that are approximate rather than exact. The paper also introduces the intriguing concept of a *fuzzy theorem*, a potentially very important concept, which still remains totally undeveloped.

Fuzzy logic in its broad sense was addressed by Zadeh in a paper presented at the 1974 IFIP Congress [25]. It is basically viewed as an application of tools developed within fuzzy set theory to approximate reasoning. These tools include aggregation operations on fuzzy sets, fuzzy numbers and fuzzy arithmetic, fuzzy relations and fuzzy relation equations, α-cut representations of fuzzy sets, the extension principle, and the like.

The development of basic ideas (principles, methods, etc.) of *approximate reasoning*, which has occupied Zadeh since the mid 1970s, is another of his principal contributions. In addition to the mentioned paper [28], in which a connection is established between approximate reasoning and linguistic variables, he wrote several broad papers on approximate reasoning focusing on different issues [26, 27, 30, 43, 64, 72, 89, 98]. He also explored the role of approximate reasoning in *expert systems* [58, 79, 95]. Some of his papers deal with special aspects of approximate reasoning, such as *reasoning with dispositions* [60, 66, 69, 76, 84, 86, 88], the concepts of *usuality* [74, 76, 80, 85], *information granularity* [40], *fuzzy quantifiers* [28, 55], or *the calculus of fuzzy if-then rules* [98]. More recently, Zadeh proposed the notion of *soft computing* [99, 102], whose aim is to exploit the tolerance for uncertainty to achieve tractability, robustness, and low cost. In soft computing, fuzzy logic is employed in conjunction with other tools, such as neural networks, genetic algorithms, and theories of imprecise probabilities.

In several papers published in the late 1970s and early 1980s, Zadeh addressed the issue of determining the right representation of linguistic terms (in given contexts) by fuzzy sets or, in other words, the issue of constructing appropriate membership functions. In addition to the three already mentioned papers that describe the use of the representational language PRUF for this purpose [37, 52, 65], at least the following papers belong to this category [32, 54, 57, 59, 63, 79, 81].

One additional subject initiated by Zadeh should be mentioned, the joint use of fuzziness and probability. In one of his early papers [6], he introduced the concept of *probability measures of fuzzy events*. Later, he introduced the concept of *fuzzy probabilities* [51, 70]. He also showed, in his various papers on approximate reasoning, how these concepts can be utilized for dealing with probability-qualified fuzzy propositions. He also published debate papers [47, 62, 78], in which he attempts to clarify the various misconceptions regarding the relationship between fuzzy set theory and probability theory.

At the time of publication of this book, Zadeh's primary interest is in developing a methodology in which words are used in place of numbers for computing and reasoning. This subject, which he refers to as "computing with words," is a further extension of approximate reasoning.

Although our overview of Lotfi Zadeh's work on fuzzy set theory and related subjects is not fully comprehensive, we hope that it will help the reader to get sufficiently oriented to comprehend the enormous contribution to this field by one of the most outstanding scholars of this century.

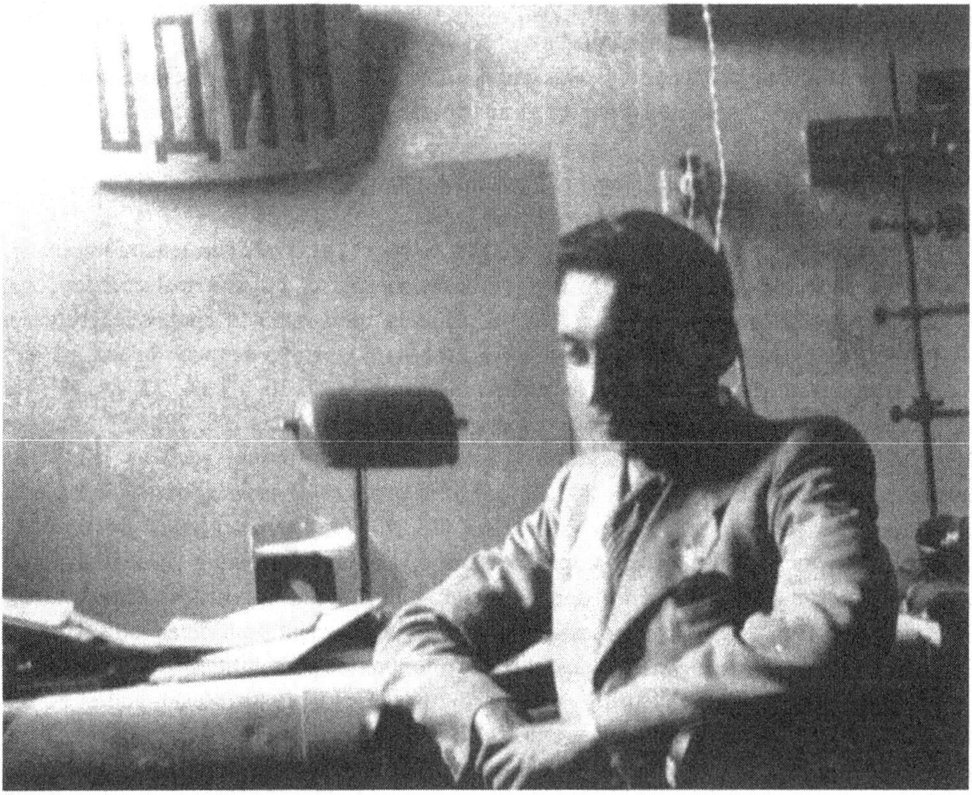

Lotfi Zadeh during his student years in Tehran in the early 1940s (the large Russian sign ODIN, which means "alone," was his early proclamation of independence).

BIBLIOGRAPHY OF PAPERS BY LOTFI A. ZADEH

Part A. Papers on Fuzzy Set Theory and Related Subjects

1* "Fuzzy sets." *Information and Control*, **8**(3), pp. 338–353, 1965.

2* "Fuzzy sets and systems." In: Fox, J., ed., *System Theory*. Polytechnic Press, Brooklyn, New York, pp. 29–39, 1965.

3* "Abstraction and pattern classification." *J. of Math. Analysis and Applications*, **13**(1), pp. 1–7, 1966 (with Bellman, R. and R. Kalaba).

4* "Shadows of fuzzy sets." *Prob. in Trans. of Information 2*, Moscow, pp. 37–44, 1966.

5* "Fuzzy algorithms." *Information and Control*, **12**(2), pp. 94–102, 1968.

6 "Probability measures and fuzzy events." *J. of Math. Analysis and Applications*, **23**(2), pp. 421–427, 1968.

7 "Biological application of the theory of fuzzy sets and systems." Proctor, L. D., ed., *Proc. of the Symp. on the Biocybernetics of the Higher Nervous System*. Little, Brown and Co., Boston, pp. 199–206, 1969.

8* "Note on fuzzy languages." *Information Sciences*, **1**(4), pp. 421–434, 1969 (with Lee, E. T.).

9 "Decision-making in a fuzzy environment." *Management Science*, **17**(4), pp. 141–164, 1970 (with Bellman, R. E.).

10* "Towards a theory of fuzzy systems." In: Kalman, R. E. and R. N. DeClairis, eds., *Aspects of Networks and Systems Theory*. Holt, Rinehart & Winston, New York, pp. 469–490, 1971.

11* "Quantitative fuzzy semantics." *Information Sciences*, **3**(2), pp. 159–176, 1971.

12 "Similarity relations and fuzzy orderings." *Information Sciences*, **3**(2), pp. 177–200, 1971.

13 "Human intelligence vs. machine intelligence." *Proc. of Intern. Congress on Science and Society, Belgrade*, pp. 127–133, 1971.

14 "Toward fuzziness in computer systems-fuzzy algorithms and languages." In: Boulaye, G., ed., *Architecture and Design of Digital Computers*. Dunod, Paris, pp. 9–18, 1971.

15* "A rationale for fuzzy control." *J. of Dynamical Systems, Measurement, and Control (Trans. ASME. Ser. G)*, **94**(1), pp. 3–4, 1972.

16* "On fuzzy algorithms." ERL Memorandum M-325, *University of California, Berkeley*, 1972.

17 "A fuzzy-set-theoretic interpretation of linguistic hedges." *J. of Cybernetics*, **2**(3), pp. 4–34, 1972.

18* "Fuzzy languages and their relation to human and machine intelligence." *Proc. of Intern. Conf. on Man and Computer, Bordeaux, France*, pp. 130–165, 1972.

19 "Linguistic cybernetics." *Proc. of the Intern. Symp. on System Science and Cybernetics, Oxford University*, pp. 1607–1617, 1972.

20* "On fuzzy mapping and control." *IEEE Trans. on Systems, Man, and Cybernetics*, **2**(1), pp. 30–34, 1972 (with Chang, S. S. L.).

21* "A system-theoretic view of behavior modification." In: Wheeler, H., ed., *Beyond the Punitive Society*. W. H. Freeman, San Francisco, pp. 160–169, 1973.

22 "Outline of a new approach to the analysis of complex systems and decision processes." *IEEE Trans. on Systems, Man, and Cybernetics*, **1**(1), pp. 28–44, 1973.

23 "Numerical vs. linguistic variables." *Newsletter of the Circuit and Systems Society*, **7**, pp. 3–4, 1974.

24* "On the analysis of large-scale systems." In: Gottinger, H., ed., *Systems Approaches and Environment Problems*. Vandenhoeck and Ruprecht, Gottingen, pp. 23–37, 1974.

25 "Fuzzy logic and its application to approximate reasoning." *Information Processing*, **74**, pp. 591–594, 1974.

26* "Calculus of fuzzy restrictions." In: Zadeh, L. A., K. S. Fu, K. Tanaka and M. Shimura, eds., *Fuzzy Sets and Their Applications to Cognitive and Decision Processes*. Academic Press, New York, pp. 1–39, 1975.

27* "Fuzzy logic and approximate reasoning." *Synthese*, **30**, pp. 407–428, 1975.

28 "The concept of a linguistic variable and its application to approximate reasoning I, II, III." *Information Sciences*, **8**(3), pp. 199–251, (4) 301–357; **9**, pp. 43–80, 1975.

29* "The linguistic approach and its application to decision analysis." In: Ho, Y. C. and S. K. Mitter, eds., *Directions in Large Scale Systems*. Plenum Press, New York, pp. 339–370, 1976.

30* "Local and fuzzy logics." In: Dunn, J. M. and G. Epstein, eds., *Modern Uses of Multiple-Valued Logic*. D. Reidel, Boston, pp. 105–165, 1977. (with Bellman, R. E.).

31 "Sematic inference from fuzzy premises." *Proc. Sixth Intern. Symp. on Multiple-Valued Logic, Utah State University at Logan*, pp. 217–218, 1976.

32 "A fuzzy-algorithmic approach to the definition of complex or imprecise concepts." *Intern. J. of Man-Machine Studies*, **8**(3), pp. 249–291, 1976.

33* "Linguistic characterization of preference relations as a basis for choice in social systems." *Erkenntnis*, **11**(3), pp. 383–410, 1977.

34* "Fuzzy sets and their application to pattern classification and clustering analysis." In: Van Ryzin, J., ed., *Classification and Clustering*. Academic Press, New York, pp. 251–299, 1977.

35 "Possibility theory and its application to information analysis." *Proc. Intern. Colloq. on Information Theory*, C.N.R.S. Paris, pp. 173–182, 1978.

36 "Fuzzy sets as a basis for a theory of possibility." *Fuzzy Sets and Systems*, **1**(1), pp. 3–28, 1978.

37 "PRUF—a meaning representation language for nature languages." *Intern. J. of Man-Machine Studies*, **10**(4), pp. 395–460, 1978.

38* "Fuzzy sets." In: Holzman, A. G., ed., *Operations Research Support Methodology*. Marcel Dekker, New York, pp. 569-606, 1979.

39 "On the validity of Dempster's rule of combination of evidence." ERL Memorandum M79/24, University of California, Berkeley. 1979.

40* "Fuzzy sets and information granularity." In: Gupta, M. M., R. K. Ragade and R. R. Yager, eds., *Advances in Fuzzy Set Theory and Applications*. North-Holland, New York, pp. 3–18, 1979.

41* "Liar's paradox and truth-qualification principle." ERL Memorandum M79/34, University of California, Berkeley1979.

42 "Approximate reasoning based on fuzzy logic." *Proc. Sixth Intern. Conf. on Artificial Intelligence, Tokyo*, Japan, pp. 1004–1010, 1979.

43 "A theory of approximate reasoning." In: Hayes, J., D. Michie and L. I. Mikulich, eds., *Machine Intelligence*, Vol. 9. Halstead Press, New York, pp. 149–194, 1979.

44 "Possibility theory and its application to the representation and manipulation of uncertain data." In: Kahane, R., ed., *Proc. of the Workshop on Image Understanding, NESC, Washington, D.C.*, pp. 36–60, 1979.

45 "Inference in fuzzy logic." *Proc. of the Tenth Intern. Symp. on Multiple-Valued Logic, Northwestern University, Evanston, Illinois*, pp. 124–131, 1980.

46 "Possibility theory as a basis for information processing and knowledge representation." *Proc. of the Computer Software and Application Conference, Chicago*, 1980.

47 "Fuzzy sets vs. probability." *Proc. IEEE*, **68**, pp. 421, 1980.

48 "Possibility theory as a basis for a mathematical model of human communication." *Proc. of the Intern. Symp. on Human Communication, UNESCO, Vienna*, 1980.

49* "Fuzzy systems theory: A framework for the analysis of humanistic systems." In: Cavallo, R. E., ed., *Recent Developments in Systems Methodology in Social Science Research*. Kluwer, Boston, pp. 25–41, 1981.

50* "Possibility theory and soft data analysis." In: Cobb, L. and R. M. Thrall, eds., *Mathematical Frontiers of the Social and Policy Sciences*. Westview Press, Boulder, Colorado, pp. 69–129, 1981.

51 "Fuzzy probabilites and their role in decision analysis." *Proc. MIT/ONR Workshop on C3, MIT, Cambridge, MA*, 1981.

52* "Test-score semantics for natural languages and meaning representation via PRUF." In: Rieger, B., ed., *Empirical Semantics*. Brockmeyer, Bochum, Germany, pp. 281–349, 1982.

53 "Possibility theory as a basis for representation of meaning." *Proc. of the Sixth Wittgenstein Symp., Kirchberg, Austria*, pp. 253–261, 1982.

54* "A note on prototype theory and fuzzy sets." *Cognition*, **12**(3), pp. 291–297, 1982.

55 "A computational approach to fuzzy quantifiers in natural languages." *Computers and Mathematics with Applications*, **9**(1), pp. 149–184, 1983. Abridged version in the *Proc. of the Fourth Conference of the Canadian Conference for Computational Studies of Intelligence*, Saskatoon, 116–120, 1982.

56 "Linguistic variables and approximate reasoning." *Proc. of the Sixth Annual Symp. on Computer Applications in Medical Care, Washington, D.C.*, pp. 787–791, 1982.

57 "Test-score semantics for the natural languages." *Proc. of the Ninth Intern. Conf. on Computational Linguistics, Prague*, pp. 425–430, 1982.

58 "The role of fuzzy logic in the management of uncertainty in expert systems." *Fuzzy Sets and Systems*, **11**(3), pp. 199–228, 1983.

59* "A fuzzy-set-theoretic approach to the compositionality of meaning: Propositions, dispositions and canonical forms." *J. of Semantics*, **2**(3/4), pp. 253–272, 1983.

60 "Linguistic variables, approximate reasoning and dispositions." *Medical Information*, **8**, pp. 173–186, 1983.

61 "Commonsense knowledge representation based on fuzzy logic." *IEEE Computer Magazine*, **16**, pp. 61–65, 1983.

62 "Is possibility different from probability?" *Human Systems Mangement*, **3**(2), pp. 253–254, 1983.

63 "Test-score semantics as a basis for a computational approach to the representation of meaning." *Proc. of the Tenth Annual Conf. of the Association for Literary and Linguistic Computing*, 1983.

64 "A theory of commonsense knowledge." In: Skala, H. J., S. Termini and E. Trillas, eds., *Aspects of Vagueness*. D. Reidel, Dordrecht and Boston, pp. 257–296, 1984.

65* "Precisiation of meaning via translation into PRUF." In: Vaina, L. and J. Hintikka, eds., *Cognitive Constraints on Communication*. D. Reidel, Boston, pp. 373–402, 1984.

66 "Syllogistic reasoning in fuzzy logic and its application to reasoning with dispositions." *Proc. of 1984 Intern. Symp. on Multiple-Valued Logic, Winnipeg, Canada*, pp. 148–153, 1984.

67 "A simple view of the Dempster–Shafer theory of evidence." *Berkeley Cognitive Science Report* 27, 1984.

68 "Making computers think like people." *IEEE Spectrum*, **21**, pp. 26–32, 1984.

69 "A computational theory of dispositions." *Proc. of the 1984 Intern. Conf. on Computational Linguistics, Stanford, CA*, pp. 312–318, 1984.

70* "*Fuzzy probabilities.*" *Information Processing and Management*, **20**(3), pp. 363–372, 1984.

71 "The role of fuzzy sets in dealing with uncertainty." *Newsletter of the ORSA/TIMS, Applied Probability Group*, pp. 2–4, 1984.

72 "Fuzzy sets and commonsense reasoning." *Institute of Cognitive Studies Report*, **21**, 1984.

73* "A formalization of commonsense reasoning based on fuzzy logic." *Proc. of GI Congress 1985, Knowledge-based Systems, Munich*, pp. 398–402, 1985.

74 "Fuzzy sets, usuality and commonsense reasoning." *Institute of Cognitive Studies Report 32* (*an expanded version of Institute of Cognitive Studies Report 21*), 1985.

75* "Management of uncertainty in expert systems." *Proc. of the Federal Emergency Agency Symp. on Expert Systems in Emergency Management, Washington, D.C.*, 1985.

76 "Syllogistic reasoning in fuzzy logic and its application to usuality and reasoning with dispositions." *IEEE Trans. on Systems, Man, and Cybernetics*, **15**(6), pp. 754–765, 1985.

77* "A simple view of the Dempster–Shafer theory of evidence and its implication for the rule of combination." *AI Magazine*, **7**(2), pp. 85–90, 1986.

78 "Is probability theory sufficient for dealing with uncertainty in AI: A negative view." In: Kanal, L. N. and J. F. Lemmer, eds., *Uncertainty in Artificial Intelligence*. North-Holland, Amsterdam, 1986.

79* "Outline of a computational approach to meaning and knowledge representation based on the concept of a generalized assignment statement." In: Thoma, M. and W. Wyner, eds., *Proc. of the Intern. Seminar on AI and Man-Machine Systems*. Springer-Verlag, Heidelberg, pp. 198-211, 1986.

80* "Outline of a theory of usuality based on fuzzy logic." In: Jones, A., A. Kaufmann and H. J. Zimmermann, eds., *Fuzzy Sets Theory and Applications*. Reidel, Dordrecht, pp. 79–97, 1986.

81 "Test-score semantics as a basis for a computational approach to the representation of meaning." *Literary and Linguistic Computing*, **1**(1), pp. 24–35, 1986.

82 "On the combinability of evidence in the Dempster–Shafer theory." *Proc. of the Workshop on Uncertainty in AI, Philadelphia, PA*, pp. 347–349, 1986. (with Ralescu, A.).

83 "Commonsense reasoning based on fuzzy logic." In: Wilson, J. and J. Henriksen, eds, *Proc. of the Winter Simulation Conf.*, pp. 445–447, 1986.

84* "A computational theory of dispositions." *Intern. J. of Intelligent Systems*, **2**(1), pp. 39–63, 1987.

85* "Fuzzy sets, usuality and commonsense reasoning." In: Vaina, L. M., ed., *Matters of Intelligence*. D. Reidel Publishing Company, Dordrecht, pp. 289–309, 1987.

86 "Dispositional logic and commonsense reasoning." *Proc. of the Second Annual Artificial Intelligence Forum, NASA Ames Research Center, Moutain View, CA.*, pp. 375–389, 1987.

87 "Nonmontonic reasoning in a possibilistic setting." *AI Magazine*, **8**(4), pp. 18–19, 1987.

88* "Dispositional logic." *Appl. Math. Lett.*, **1**, pp. 95–99, 1988.

89 "Fuzzy logic." *IEEE Computer Magazine*, **1**(4), pp. 83–93, 1988.

90 "Dispositional logic and commonsense reasoning." In: Ramadge, P. J. and S. Verdu, eds., *Proc. of the 1988 Princeton Conf. on Information Sciences and Systems*. Princeton University Press, Princeton, pp. 517–520, 1988.

91 "An inquiry into computer understanding: a partial dissent." *Computational Intelligence*, **4**(1), pp. 126–128, 1988.

92 "On the treatment of uncertianty in AI." *The Knowledge Engineering Review*, **2**(1), pp. 81–85, 1988.

93 "Fuzzy logic in knowledge-based systems and control." *Proc. of the Intern. Workshop on Fuzzy System Applications, Kyushu Inst. of Technology, Iizuka, Japan*, pp. 1–2, 1988.

94 "QSA/FL-Qualitative systems analysis based on fuzzy logic." *Stanford AAAI Symp. on Limited Rationality*, Stanford, CA, pp. 111–114, 1989.

95* "Knowledge representation in fuzzy logic." *IEEE Trans. on Knowledge and Data Engineering*, **1**(1), pp. 89–100, 1989.

96 "The birth and evolution of fuzzy logic." *Intern. J. of General Systems*, **17**(2–3), pp. 95–105, 1990.

97 "Fuzzy logic and the calculus of fuzzy If-Then rules." *Proc. of SYNAPSE '91, Tokyo*, 1991.

98 "The calculus of fuzzy If–Then rules." *AI Expert*, **7**(3), pp. 23–27, 1992.

99* "Fuzzy logic, neural networks and soft computing." *Communications of the ACM*, **37**(3), pp. 77–84, 1994.

100* "The role of fuzzy logic in modeling, identification and control." *Modeling Identification and Control*, **15**(3), pp. 191–203, 1994.

101 "Why the success of fuzzy logic is not paradoxical." *IEEE Expert*, **9**(4), pp. 43–45, 1994.

102* "Soft computing and fuzzy logic." *IEEE Software*, **11**(6), pp. 48–56, 1994.

103* "Probability theory and fuzzy logic are complementary rather than competitive." *Technometrics*, **37**(3), pp. 271–276, 1995.

104* "The birth and evolution of fuzzy logic, soft computing, and computing with words: A personal perspective."

Part B. Other Papers

1 "Probability criterion for the design of servomechanisms." *J. Appl. Phys.*, **20**(2), pp. 141–144, 1949 (with J. R. Ragazzini).

2 "Thinking machines–a new field in electrical engineering." *Columbia Engineering Quarterly*, **3**, pp. 12–13, 30, 31, 1950.

3 "A wide band audio phasemeter." *Review Scientific Instruments*, **21**, pp. 145–148, 1950 (with J. R. Ragazzini).

4 "Frequency analysis of variable networks." *Proc. IRE*, **38**(3), pp. 291–299, 1950.

5 "Circuit analysis of linear varying-parameter networks." *J. Appl. Phys.*, **21**(11), pp. 1171–1177, 1950.

6 "The determination of the impulsive response of variable networks." *J. Appl. Phys.*, **21**(7), pp. 642–645, 1950.

7 "An extension of Wiener's theory of prediction." *J. Appl. Phys.*, **21**(7), pp. 645–655, 1950 (with J. R. Ragazzini).

8 "Band-pass low-pass transformation in variable networks." *Proc. IRE*, **38**(11), pp. 1339–1341, 1950.

9 "Correlation functions and power spectra in variable networks." *Proc. IRE*, **38**(11), pp. 1342–1345, 1950.

10 "On stability of linear varying-parameter systems." *J. Appl. Phys.*, **22**(4), pp. 402–405, 1951.

11 "Correlation functions and spectra of phase- and delay-modulated signals." *Proc. IRE*, **39**(4), pp. 425–428, 1951.

12 "Constant-resistant networks of the linear varying-parameter type." *Proc. IRE*, **39**(6), pp. 688–691, 1951.

13 "Initial conditions in linear varying-parameter systems." *J. Appl. Phys.*, **22**(6), pp. 782–786, 1951.

14 "A note on the initial excitation of linear systems." *J. Appl. Phys.*, **22**(9), pp. 1216–1217, 1951.

15 "Time-dependent heaviside operators." *J. Math. and Phys.*, **30**, pp. 73–78, 1951.

16 "Some applications of matrix and tensor methods in the analysis and synthesis of variable systems." *Matrix and Tensor Quarterly*, **2**, pp. 13–18, 1951.

17 "General input-output relations for linear networks." *Proc. IRE*, **40**(1), pp. 103, 1952.

18 "Generalized ideal filters." *J. Appl. Phys.*, **23**(2), pp. 223–228, 1952.

19 "On the theory of filtration of signals." *Zeit. Angew. Math. Phys.*, **3**(2), pp. 149–156, 1952.

20 "Some basis problems in communication of information." *Trans. N.Y. Acad. Sci.*, **14**, pp. 201–204, 1952.

21 "Continuous matrices and their applications." *Matrix and Tensor Quarterly*, **2**, pp. 8–14, 1952.

22 "A general theory of linear signal transmission systems." *J. Franklin Institute*, **253**, pp. 293–312, 1952.

23 "Operational analysis of variable-delay systems." *Proc. IRE*, **40**(5), pp. 564–568, 1952.

24 "Matrix formulation of the filtering process." *Matrix and Tensor Quarterly*, **2**, pp. 7–13, 1952.

25 "Fundamental aspects of linear multiplexing." *Proc. IRE*, **40**(9), pp. 1091–1097, 1952 (with K. S. Miller).

26 "Optimum filters for the detection of signals in noise." *Proc. IRE*, **40**(10), pp. 1223–1231, 1952 (with J. R. Ragazzini).

27 "The analysis of sampled-data systems." *Applications and Industry (AIEE)*, 1, pp. 224–234, 1952 (with J. R. Ragazzini).

28 Optimum nonlinear filters, *J. Appl. Phys.* **24**, 396–404, 1953.

29 "On a class of stochastic operators." *J. Math. and Phys.*, **32**, pp. 48–53, 1953.

30 "Optimum nonlinear filters for the extraction and detection of signals." *Convention Record of the IRE*, , pp. 57–65, 1953.

31 "Nonlinear multipoles." *Proc. Natl. Acad. Sci. USA*, **39**, pp. 274–280, 1953.

32 "A contribution to the theory of nonlinear systems." *J. Franklin Institute*, **255**, pp. 387–408, 1953.

33 "A note on the analysis of vacuum tube and transistor circuits." *Proc. IRE*, **41**, pp. 989–992, 1953.

34 "Theory of filtering." *SIAM J. on Applied Mathematics*, **1**(1), pp. 35–51, 1953.

35 "System theory." *Cloumbia Engineering Quarterly*, **8**, pp. 16–19, 1954.

36 "General filters for separation of signals and noise." *Proc. Symp. Information Networks, P.I.B., New York*, pp. 31–49, 1955.

37 "Applications of time-variable network theory." *Proc. Symp. Circuit Theory University of Illinois*, pp. 6.11–6.14, 1955.

38 "Generalized Fourier integrals." *Trans. PGCT*, **CT-2**, pp. 256–260, 1955 (with K. S. Miller).

39 "On passive and active networks and generalized Norton's and Thevenin's theorems." *Proc. IRE*, **44**(3), pp. 378, 1956.

40 "Solution of an integral equation occuring in the theories of prediction and detection." *IRE Trans. on Information Theory*, **IT-2.2**, pp. 72–75, 1956.

41 "On the identification problem." *IRE Trans. on Circuit Theory*, **CT-3**, pp. 277–281, 1956.

42 "On the representation of nonlinear operators." *1957 WESCON Convention Record*, pp. 105–113, 1957.

43 "Multipole analysis of active networks." *IRE Trans. on Circuit Theory*, **CT-4**, pp. 97–105, 1957.

44 "Signal-flow graphs and random signals." *Proc. IRE*, **45**(10), pp. 1413–1414, 1957.

45 "What is optimal." *IRE Trans. on Information Theory*, **IT-4**, pp. 3, 1958.

46 "Toward an institute for research in communication sciences." *IRE Trans. on Information Theory*, **IT-6**, pp. 2, 1960.

47 "Note on an integral equation occuring in the prediction, detection and analysis of multiple time series." *IRE Trans. on Information Theory*, **IT-7**, pp. 118–120, 1961 (with J. B. Thomas).

48 "Optimal control problems in discrete-time systems." *Computer Control Systems Technology*. McGraw-Hill, New York, pp. 389–414, 1961.

49 "Progress in information theory in the U.S.A. , 1957-1960: Prediction and filtering." *IRE Trans. on Information Theory*, **IT-7**, pp. 139–144, 1961.

50 "An extended definition of linearity." *Proc. IRE*, **49**, pp. 1452–1453, 1961.

51 "Time-varying networks I." *Proc. IRE*, **49**, pp. 1488–1503, 1961.

52 "Remark on the paper by Bellman and Kalaba." *Information Control*, **4**, pp. 350–352, 1961.

53 "On the extended definition of linearity." *Proc. IRE*, **50**, pp. 200–201, 1962.

54 "Optimal pursuit strategies in discrete-state probabilistic systems." *J. Basic Engineering*, **84**(Series D), pp. 23–29, 1962 (with J. H. Eaton).

55 "A critical view of our research in automatic control." *IRE Trans. on Automatic Control*, **7**(3), pp. 74–75, 1962.

56 "From circuit theory to systems theory." *IRE Proc.*, **50**, pp. 856–865, 1962.

57 "An introduction to state space techniques." *Proc. JACC*, , pp. 101–105, 1962.

58 "On optimal control and linear programming." *IEEE Trans. on Automatic Control*, **7**(4), pp. 45–46, 1962 (with B. Whalen).

59 "Optimality and non-scalar-valued performance criteria." *IEEE Trans. on Automatic Control*, **8**(1), pp. 59–60, 1963.

60 "On the definition of adaptivity." *Proc. IEEE*, **51**, pp. 469–470, 1963.

61 "An alternation principle for improved control." *Automatika i Telemehanika*, **24**, pp. 328–330, 1963 (with J. H. Eaton).

62 "Stochastic finite-systems in control theory." *Proc. Symp. on Optimal Control and Nonlinear Systems, Faculte des Sciences de Paris*, pp. 123–143, 1963.

63 "The general identification problem." *Proc. Princeton University Conf. on Identification Problems in Communication and Control Systems*, pp. 1–17, 1963.

64 *Linear System Theory-The State Space Approach*. McGraw-Hill, New York. 1963. (with C. A. Desoer).

65 "Report on progress in information theory in USA: 1960–1963." *IEEE Trans. Prof. Group on Information Theory*, pp. 179, 1963.

66 "The concept of state in system theory." *Proc. of the Second Systems Symp., Case Institute of Technology*. John Wiley, New York, pp. 39–50, 1964.

67 "Electrical engineering at the crossroads." *IEEE Trans. on Education*, **8**, pp. 30–33, 1965.

68 "Practice experience and engineering education." *IEEE Spectrum*, pp. 60–67, 1967 (with E. Weber, J. Herbert Hollomon, T. F. Jones and R. H. Lyon).

69 "Computer sciences as a discipline." *J. Eng. Ed.*, **58**, pp. 913–916, 1968.

70 "The dilemma of computer sciences." In: Finerman, A., ed., *University Education in Computing Sciences*. Academic Press, New York1968.

71 "The conept of state in system theory." In: *Network and Switching Theory*. Academic Press, New York, pp. 21–26, 1968.

72 "Education in computer sciences." *Proc. Fourth National Congress on Data Processing, Hebrew University*, 1968.

73 *System Theory*. McGraw-Hill, New York. 1968.(with E. Polak).

74 "The concepts of system, aggregate and state in system theory." In: Zadeh, L. A. and E. Polak, eds., *System Theory*. McGraw-Hill, New York, pp. 3–42, 1968.

75 *Computing Methods in Optimization Problems*. Academic Press, New York. 1969. (with L. W. Neustadt and A. V. Balakrishnan).

76 "Mathematics—a call for reorientation." *Newsletter of the Conf. Board on Mathematical Sciences*, **7**, pp. 1–3, 1972.

77 "The drop in engineering enrollments—a transient or a trend." *Newsletter of IEEE Circuit Theory Group*, **6**, pp. 6, 11, 1972.

78 "A new approach to system analysis." In: Marois, M., ed., *Man and Computer*. North-Holland, New York, pp. 55–94, 1974.

Selected Papers by Lotfi A. Zadeh

Fuzzy Sets*

L. A. Zadeh

Department of Electrical Engineering and Electronics Research Laboratory, University of California, Berkeley, California

A fuzzy set is a class of objects with a continuum of grades of membership. Such a set is characterized by a membership (characteristic) function which assigns to each object a grade of membership ranging between zero and one. The notions of inclusion, union, intersection, complement, relation, convexity, etc., are extended to such sets, and various properties of these notions in the context of fuzzy sets are established. In particular, a separation theorem for convex fuzzy sets is proved without requiring that the fuzzy sets be disjoint.

I. INTRODUCTION

More often than not, the classes of objects encountered in the real physical world do not have precisely defined criteria of membership. For example, the class of animals clearly includes dogs, horses, birds, etc. as its members, and clearly excludes such objects as rocks, fluids, plants, etc. However, such objects as starfish, bacteria, etc. have an ambiguous status with respect to the class of animals. The same kind of ambiguity arises in the case of a number such as 10 in relation to the "class" of all real numbers which are much greater than 1.

Clearly, the "class of all real numbers which are much greater than 1," or "the class of beautiful women," or "the class of tall men," do not constitute classes or sets in the usual mathematical sense of these terms. Yet, the fact remains that such imprecisely defined "classes" play an important role in human thinking, particularly in the domains of pattern recognition, communication of information, and abstraction.

The purpose of this note is to explore in a preliminary way some of the basic properties and implications of a concept which may be of use in

* This work was supported in part by the Joint Services Electronics Program (U.S. Army, U.S. Navy and U.S. Air Force) under Grant No. AF-AFOSR-139-64 and by the National Science Foundation under Grant GP-2413.

Reprinted, with permission, from *Information and Control*, 8(3), pp. 338–353.

dealing with "classes" of the type cited above. The concept in question is that of a *fuzzy set*,[1] that is, a "class" with a continuum of grades of membership. As will be seen in the sequel, the notion of a fuzzy set provides a convenient point of departure for the construction of a conceptual framework which parallels in many respects the framework used in the case of ordinary sets, but is more general than the latter and, potentially, may prove to have a much wider scope of applicability, particularly in the fields of pattern classification and information processing. Essentially, such a framework provides a natural way of dealing with problems in which the source of imprecision is the absence of sharply defined criteria of class membership rather than the presence of random variables.

We begin the discussion of fuzzy sets with several basic definitions.

II. DEFINITIONS

Let X be a space of points (objects), with a generic element of X denoted by x. Thus, $X = \{x\}$.

A *fuzzy set (class)* A in X is characterized by a *membership (characteristic) function* $f_A(x)$ which associates with each point[2] in X a real number in the interval [0, 1],[3] with the value of $f_A(x)$ at x representing the "grade of membership" of x in A. Thus, the nearer the value of $f_A(x)$ to unity, the higher the grade of membership of x in A. When A is a set in the ordinary sense of the term, its membership function can take on only two values 0 and 1, with $f_A(x) = 1$ or 0 according as x does or does not belong to A. Thus, in this case $f_A(x)$ reduces to the familiar characteristic function of a set A. (When there is a need to differentiate between such sets and fuzzy sets, the sets with two-valued characteristic functions will be referred to as *ordinary sets* or simply *sets*.)

Example. Let X be the real line R^1 and let A be a fuzzy set of numbers

[1] An application of this concept to the formulation of a class of problems in pattern classification is described in RAND Memorandum RM-4307-PR, "Abstraction and Pattern Classification," by R. Bellman, R. Kalaba and L. A. Zadeh, October, 1964.

[2] More generally, the domain of definition of $f_A(x)$ may be restricted to a subset of X.

[3] In a more general setting, the range of the membership function can be taken to be a suitable partially ordered set P. For our purposes, it is convenient and sufficient to restrict the range of f to the unit interval. If the values of $f_A(x)$ are interpreted as truth values, the latter case corresponds to a multivalued logic with a continuum of truth values in the interval [0, 1].

which are much greater than 1. Then, one can give a precise, albeit subjective, characterization of A by specifying $f_A(x)$ as a function on R^1. Representative values of such a function might be: $f_A(0) = 0$; $f_A(1) = 0$; $f_A(5) = 0.01$; $f_A(10) = 0.2$; $f_A(100) = 0.95$; $f_A(500) = 1$.

It should be noted that, although the membership function of a fuzzy set has some resemblance to a probability function when X is a countable set (or a probability density function when X is a continuum), there are essential differences between these concepts which will become clearer in the sequel once the rules of combination of membership functions and their basic properties have been established. In fact, the notion of a fuzzy set is completely nonstatistical in nature.

We begin with several definitions involving fuzzy sets which are obvious extensions of the corresponding definitions for ordinary sets.

A fuzzy set is *empty* if and only if its membership function is identically zero on X.

Two fuzzy sets A and B are *equal*, written as $A = B$, if and only if $f_A(x) = f_B(x)$ for all x in X. (In the sequel, instead of writing $f_A(x) = f_B(x)$ for all x in X, we shall write more simply $f_A = f_B$.)

The *complement* of a fuzzy set A is denoted by A' and is defined by

$$f_{A'} = 1 - f_A . \tag{1}$$

As in the case of ordinary sets, the notion of containment plays a central role in the case of fuzzy sets. This notion and the related notions of union and intersection are defined as follows.

Containment. A is *contained in* B (or, equivalently, A is a *subset of* B, or A is *smaller than or equal to* B) if and only if $f_A \leqq f_B$. In symbols

$$A \subset B \Leftrightarrow f_A \leqq f_B . \tag{2}$$

Union. The *union* of two fuzzy sets A and B with respective membership functions $f_A(x)$ and $f_B(x)$ is a fuzzy set C, written as $C = A \cup B$, whose membership function is related to those of A and B by

$$f_C(x) = \text{Max}\,[f_A(x), f_B(x)], \qquad x \in X \tag{3}$$

or, in abbreviated form

$$f_C = f_A \vee f_B . \tag{4}$$

Note that $\cup$ has the associative property, that is, $A \cup (B \cup C) = (A \cup B) \cup C$.

Comment. A more intuitively appealing way of defining the union is the following: The union of A and B is the smallest fuzzy set containing both A and B. More precisely, if D is any fuzzy set which contains both A and B, then it also contains the union of A and B.

To show that this definition is equivalent to (3), we note, first, that C as defined by (3) contains both A and B, since

$$\operatorname{Max}[f_A, f_B] \geqq f_A$$

and

$$\operatorname{Max}[f_A, f_B] \geqq f_B .$$

Furthermore, if D is any fuzzy set containing both A and B, then

$$f_D \geqq f_A$$

$$f_D \geqq f_B$$

and hence

$$f_D \geqq \operatorname{Max}[f_A, f_B] = f_C$$

which implies that $C \subset D$. Q.E.D.

The notion of an intersection of fuzzy sets can be defined in an analogous manner. Specifically:

Intersection. The *intersection* of two fuzzy sets A and B with respective membership functions $f_A(x)$ and $f_B(x)$ is a fuzzy set C, written as $C = A \cap B$, whose membership function is related to those of A and B by

$$f_C(x) = \operatorname{Min}[f_A(x), f_B(x)], \qquad x \in X, \tag{5}$$

or, in abbreviated form

$$f_C = f_A \wedge f_B . \tag{6}$$

As in the case of the union, it is easy to show that the intersection of A and B is the *largest* fuzzy set which is contained in both A and B. As in the case of ordinary sets, A and B are *disjoint* if $A \cap B$ is empty. Note that $\cap$, like $\cup$, has the associative property.

The intersection and union of two fuzzy sets in R^1 are illustrated in Fig. 1. The membership function of the union is comprised of curve segments 1 and 2; that of the intersection is comprised of segments 3 and 4 (heavy lines).

Comment. Note that the notion of "belonging," which plays a fundamental role in the case of ordinary sets, does not have the same role in

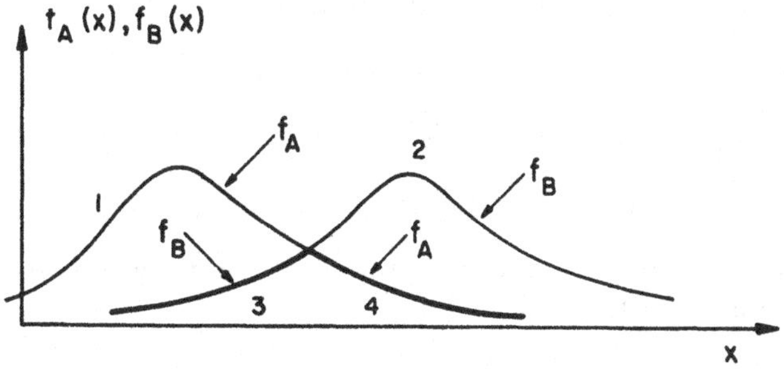

FIG. 1. Illustration of the union and intersection of fuzzy sets in R^1

the case of fuzzy sets. Thus, it is not meaningful to speak of a point x "belonging" to a fuzzy set A except in the trivial sense of $f_A(x)$ being positive. Less trivially, one can introduce two levels α and β ($0 < \alpha < 1$, $0 < \beta < 1$, $\alpha > \beta$) and agree to say that (1) "x belongs to A" if $f_A(x) \geqq \alpha$; (2) "x does not belong to A" if $f_A(x) \leqq \beta$; and (3) "x has an indeterminate status relative to A" if $\beta < f_A(x) < \alpha$. This leads to a three-valued logic (Kleene, 1952) with three truth values: T ($f_A(x) \geqq \alpha$), F ($f_A(x) \leqq \beta$), and U ($\beta < f_A(x) < \alpha$).

III. SOME PROPERTIES OF $\cup$, $\cap$, AND COMPLEMENTATION

With the operations of union, intersection, and complementation defined as in (3), (5), and (1), it is easy to extend many of the basic identities which hold for ordinary sets to fuzzy sets. As examples, we have

$$\left.\begin{aligned}(A \cup B)' &= A' \cap B' \\ (A \cap B)' &= A' \cup B'\end{aligned}\right\}\text{De Morgan's laws} \qquad \begin{aligned}(7)\\(8)\end{aligned}$$

$$C \cap (A \cup B) = (C \cap A) \cup (C \cap B) \qquad \text{Distributive laws.} \qquad (9)$$

$$C \cup (A \cap B) = (C \cup A) \cap (C \cup B) \qquad (10)$$

These and similar equalities can readily be established by showing that the corresponding relations for the membership functions of A, B, and C are identities. For example, in the case of (7), we have

$$1 - \text{Max}\,[f_A, f_B] = \text{Min}\,[1 - f_A, 1 - f_B] \qquad (11)$$

which can be easily verified to be an identity by testing it for the two possible cases: $f_A(x) > f_B(x)$ and $f_A(x) < f_B(x)$.

Similarly, in the case of (10), the corresponding relation in terms of f_A, f_B, and f_C is:

$$\text{Max}\,[f_C, \text{Min}\,[f_A, f_B] = \text{Min}\,[\text{Max}\,[f_C, f_A], \text{Max}\,[f_C, f_B]] \quad (12)$$

which can be verified to be an identity by considering the six cases:

$$f_A(x) > f_B(x) > f_C(x), f_A(x) > f_C(x) > f_B(x), f_B(x) > f_A(x) > f_C(x),$$

$$f_B(x) > f_C(x) > f_A(x), f_C(x) > f_A(x) > f_B(x), f_C(x) > f_B(x) > f_A(x).$$

Essentially, fuzzy sets in X constitute a distributive lattice with a 0 and 1 (Birkhoff, 1948).

An Interpretation for Unions and Intersections

In the case of ordinary sets, a set C which is expressed in terms of a family of sets $A_1, \cdots, A_i, \cdots, A_n$ through the connectives $\cup$ and $\cap$, can be represented as a network of switches $\alpha_1, \cdots, \alpha_n$, with $A_i \cap A_j$ and $A_i \cup A_j$ corresponding, respectively, to series and parallel combinations of α_i and α_j. In the case of fuzzy sets, one can give an analogous interpretation in terms of sieves. Specifically, let $f_i(x)$, $i = 1, \cdots, n$, denote the value of the membership function of A_i at x. Associate with $f_i(x)$ a sieve $S_i(x)$ whose meshes are of size $f_i(x)$. Then, $f_i(x) \vee f_j(x)$ and $f_i(x) \wedge f_j(x)$ correspond, respectively, to parallel and series combinations of $S_i(x)$ and $S_j(x)$, as shown in Fig. 2.

More generally, a well-formed expression involving $A_1, \cdots, A_n$, $\cup$, and $\cap$ corresponds to a network of sieves $S_1(x), \cdots, S_n(x)$ which can be found by the conventional synthesis techniques for switching circuits. As a very simple example,

$$C = [(A_1 \cup A_2) \cap A_3] \cup A_4 \quad (13)$$

corresponds to the network shown in Fig. 3.
Note that the mesh sizes of the sieves in the network depend on x and that the network as a whole is equivalent to a single sieve whose meshes are of size $f_C(x)$.

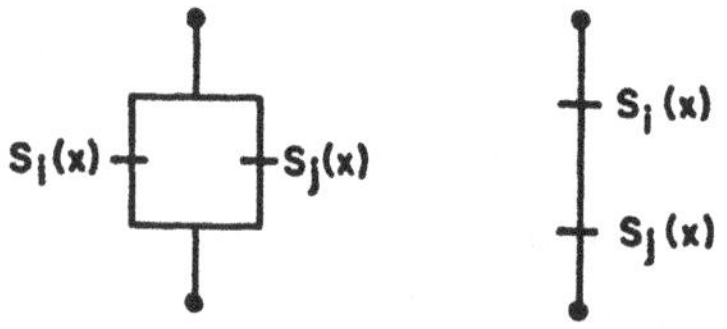

FIG. 2. Parallel and series connection of sieves simultating $\cup$ and $\cap$

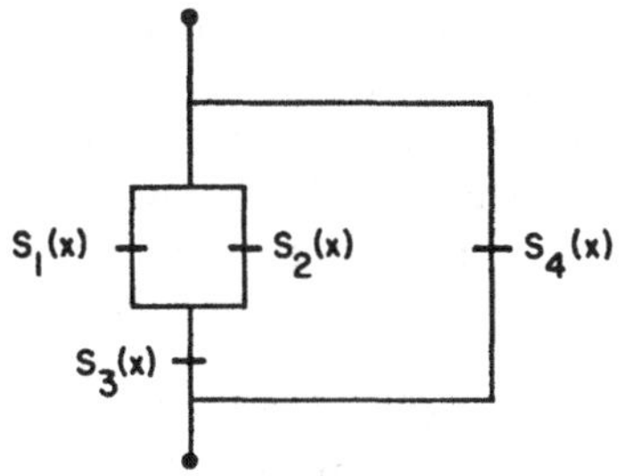

FIG. 3. A network of sieves simultating $\{[f_1(x) \vee f_2(x)] \wedge f_3(x)\} \vee f_4(x)$

IV. ALGEBRAIC OPERATIONS ON FUZZY SETS

In addition to the operations of union and intersection, one can define a number of other ways of forming combinations of fuzzy sets and relating them to one another. Among the more important of these are the following.

Algebraic product. The *algebraic product* of A and B is denoted by AB and is defined in terms of the membership functions of A and B by the relation

$$f_{AB} = f_A f_B . \tag{14}$$

Clearly,

$$AB \subset A \cap B. \tag{15}$$

Algebraic sum.[4] The *algebraic sum* of A and B is denoted by $A + B$ and is defined by

$$f_{A+B} = f_A + f_B \tag{16}$$

provided the sum $f_A + f_B$ is less than or equal to unity. Thus, unlike the algebraic product, the algebraic sum is meaningful only when the condition $f_A(x) + f_B(x) \leqq 1$ is satisfied for all x.

Absolute difference. The *absolute difference* of A and B is denoted by $|A - B|$ and is defined by

$$f_{|A-B|} = |f_A - f_B|.$$

Note that in the case of ordinary sets $|A - B|$ reduces to the relative complement of $A \cap B$ in $A \cup B$.

[4] The dual of the algebraic product is the *sum* $A \oplus B = (A'B')' = A + B - AB$. (This was pointed out by T. Cover.) Note that for ordinary sets $\cap$ and the algebraic product are equivalent operations, as are $\cup$ and $\oplus$.

Convex combination. By a convex combination of two vectors f and g is usually meant a linear combination of f and g of the form $\lambda f + (1 - \lambda)g$, in which $0 \leqq \lambda \leqq 1$. This mode of combining f and g can be generalized to fuzzy sets in the following manner.

Let A, B, and Λ be arbitrary fuzzy sets. The *convex combination of* A, B, *and* Λ is denoted by $(A, B; \Lambda)$ and is defined by the relation

$$(A, B; \Lambda) = \Lambda A + \Lambda' B \tag{17}$$

where Λ' is the complement of Λ. Written out in terms of membership functions, (17) reads

$$f_{(A,B;\Lambda)}(x) = f_\Lambda(x) f_A(x) + [1 - f_\Lambda(x)] f_B(x), \qquad x \in X. \tag{18}$$

A basic property of the convex combination of A, B, and Λ is expressed by

$$A \cap B \subset (A, B; \Lambda) \subset A \cup B \qquad \text{for all } \Lambda. \tag{19}$$

This property is an immediate consequence of the inequalities

$$\begin{aligned}\text{Min}\,[f_A(x), f_B(x)] &\leqq \lambda f_A(x) + (1 - \lambda) f_B(x) \\ &\leqq \text{Max}\,[f_A(x), f_B(x)], \qquad x \in X\end{aligned} \tag{20}$$

which hold for all λ in $[0, 1]$. It is of interest to observe that, given any fuzzy set C satisfying $A \cap B \subset C \subset A \cup B$, one can always find a fuzzy set Λ such that $C = (A, B; \Lambda)$. The membership function of this set is given by

$$f_\Lambda(x) = \frac{f_C(x) - f_B(x)}{f_A(x) - f_B(x)}, \qquad x \in X. \tag{21}$$

Fuzzy relation. The concept of a *relation* (which is a generalization of that of a *function*) has a natural extension to fuzzy sets and plays an important role in the theory of such sets and their applications—just as it does in the case of ordinary sets. In the sequel, we shall merely define the notion of a fuzzy relation and touch upon a few related concepts.

Ordinarily, a relation is defined as a set of ordered pairs (Halmos, 1960); e.g., the set of all ordered pairs of real numbers x and y such that $x \geqq y$. In the context of fuzzy sets, a *fuzzy relation in* X is a fuzzy set in the product space $X \times X$. For example, the relation denoted by $x \gg y$, $x, y \in R^1$, may be regarded as a fuzzy set A in R^2, with the membership function of A, $f_A(x, y)$, having the following (subjective) representative values: $f_A(10, 5) = 0$; $f_A(100, 10) = 0.7$; $f_A(100, 1) = 1$; etc.

More generally, one can define an *n-ary fuzzy relation* in X as a fuzzy set A in the product space $X \times X \times \cdots \times X$. For such relations, the membership function is of the form $f_A(x_1, \cdots, x_n)$, where $x_i \in X$, $i = 1, \cdots, n$.

In the case of binary fuzzy relations, the *composition* of two fuzzy relations A and B is denoted by $B \circ A$ and is defined as a fuzzy relation in X whose membership function is related to those of A and B by

$$f_{B \circ A}(x, y) = \text{Sup}_v \text{ Min } [f_A(x, v), f_B(v, y)].$$

Note that the operation of composition has the associative property

$$A \circ (B \circ C) = (A \circ B) \circ C.$$

Fuzzy sets induced by mappings. Let T be a mapping from X to a space Y. Let B be a fuzzy set in Y with membership function $f_B(y)$. The inverse mapping T^{-1} induces a fuzzy set A in X whose membership function is defined by

$$f_A(x) = f_B(y), \qquad y \in Y \tag{22}$$

for all x in X which are mapped by T into y.

Consider now a converse problem in which A is a given fuzzy set in X, and T, as before, is a mapping from X to Y. The question is: What is the membership function for the fuzzy set B in Y which is induced by this mapping?

If T is not one-one, then an ambiguity arises when two or more distinct points in X, say x_1 and x_2, with different grades of membership in A, are mapped into the same point y in Y. In this case, the question is: What grade of membership in B should be assigned to y?

To resolve this ambiguity, we agree to assign the larger of the two grades of membership to y. More generally, the membership function for B will be defined by

$$f_B(y) = \text{Max}_{x \in T^{-1}(y)} f_A(x), \qquad y \in Y \tag{23}$$

where $T^{-1}(y)$ is the set of points in X which are mapped into y by T.

V. CONVEXITY

As will be seen in the sequel, the notion of convexity can readily be extended to fuzzy sets in such a way as to preserve many of the properties which it has in the context of ordinary sets. This notion appears to be particularly useful in applications involving pattern classification, optimization and related problems.

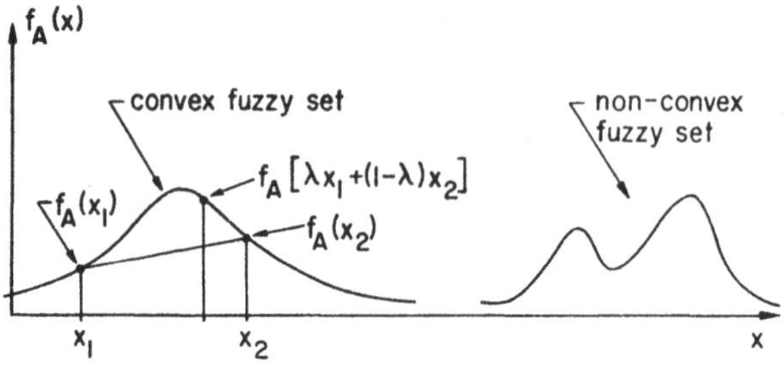

FIG. 4. Convex and nonconvex fuzzy sets in E^1

In what follows, we assume for concreteness that X is a real Euclidean space E^n.

DEFINITIONS

Convexity. A fuzzy set A is *convex* if and only if the sets Γ_α defined by

$$\Gamma_\alpha = \{x \mid f_A(x) \geqq \alpha\} \tag{24}$$

are convex for all α in the interval (0, 1].

An alternative and more direct definition of convexity is the following[5]: A is *convex* if and only if

$$f_A[\lambda x_1 + (1 - \lambda)x_2] \geqq \text{Min}\,[f_A(x_1), f_A(x_2)] \tag{25}$$

for all x_1 and x_2 in X and all λ in [0, 1]. Note that this definition does not imply that $f_A(x)$ must be a convex function of x. This is illustrated in Fig. 4 for $n = 1$.

To show the equivalence between the above definitions note that if A is convex in the sense of the first definition and $\alpha = f_A(x_1) \leqq f_A(x_2)$, then $x_2 \in \Gamma_\alpha$ and $\lambda x_1 + (1 - \lambda)x_2 \in \Gamma_\alpha$ by the convexity of Γ_α. Hence

$$f_A[\lambda x_1 + (1 - \lambda)x_2] \geqq \alpha = f_A(x_1) = \text{Min}\,[f_A(x_1), f_A(x_2)].$$

Conversely, if A is convex in the sense of the second definition and $\alpha = f_A(x_1)$, then Γ_α may be regarded as the set of all points x_2 for which $f_A(x_2) \geqq f_A(x_1)$. In virtue of (25), every point of the form $\lambda x_1 + (1 - \lambda)x_2$, $0 \leqq \lambda \leqq 1$, is also in Γ_α and hence Γ_α is a convex set. Q.E.D.

A basic property of convex fuzzy sets is expressed by the

THEOREM. *If A and B are convex, so is their intersection.*

[5] This way of expressing convexity was suggested to the writer by his colleague, E. Berlekamp.

Proof: Let $C = A \cap B$. Then

$$f_C[\lambda x_1 + (1 - \lambda)x_2] = \text{Min}\,[f_A[\lambda x_1 + (1 - \lambda)x_2], f_B[\lambda x_1 + (1 - \lambda)x_2]]. \quad (26)$$

Now, since A and B are convex

$$f_A[\lambda x_1 + (1 - \lambda)x_2] \geqq \text{Min}\,[f_A(x_1), f_A(x_2)]$$
$$f_B[\lambda x_1 + (1 - \lambda)x_2] \geqq \text{Min}\,[f_B(x_1), f_B(x_2)] \quad (27)$$

and hence

$$f_C[\lambda x_1 + (1 - \lambda)x_2] \geqq \text{Min}\,[\text{Min}\,[f_A(x_1), f_A(x_2)], \text{Min}\,[f_B(x_1), f_B(x_2)]] \quad (28)$$

or equivalently

$$f_C[\lambda x_1 + (1 - \lambda)x_2] \geqq \text{Min}\,[\text{Min}\,[f_A(x_1), f_B(x_1)], \text{Min}\,[f_A(x_2), f_B(x_2)]] \quad (29)$$

and thus

$$f_C[\lambda x_1 + (1 - \lambda)x_2] \geqq \text{Min}\,[f_C(x_1), f_C(x_2)]. \quad \text{Q. E. D.} \quad (30)$$

Boundedness. A fuzzy set A is *bounded* if and only if the sets $\Gamma_\alpha = \{x \mid f_A(x) \geqq \alpha\}$ are bounded for all $\alpha > 0$; that is, for every $\alpha > 0$ there exists a finite $R(\alpha)$ such that $\| x \| \leqq R(\alpha)$ for all x in Γ_α.

If A is a bounded set, then for each $\epsilon > 0$ then exists a hyperplane H such that $f_A(x) \leqq \epsilon$ for all x on the side of H which does not contain the origin. For, consider the set $\Gamma_\epsilon = \{x \mid f_A(x) \geqq \epsilon\}$. By hypothesis, this set is contained in a sphere S of radius $R(\epsilon)$. Let H be any hyperplane supporting S. Then, all points on the side of H which does not contain the origin lie outside or on S, and hence for all such points $f_A(x) \leqq \epsilon$.

LEMMA. *Let A be a bounded fuzzy set and let $M = \text{Sup}_x f_A(x)$. (M will be referred to as the* maximal grade *in A.) Then there is at least one point x_0 at which M is essentially attained in the sense that, for each $\epsilon > 0$, every spherical neighborhood of x_0 contains points in the set $Q(\epsilon) = \{x \mid f_A(x) \geqq M - \epsilon\}$.*

Proof.[6] Consider a nested sequence of bounded sets $\Gamma_1, \Gamma_2, \cdots$, where $\Gamma_n = \{x \mid f_A(x) \geqq M - M/(n + 1)\}$, $n = 1, 2, \cdots$. Note that

[6] This proof was suggested by A. J. Thomasian.

Γ_n is nonempty for all finite n as a consequence of the definition of M as $M = \text{Sup}_x f_A(x)$. (We assume that $M > 0$.)

Let x_n be an arbitrarily chosen point in Γ_n, $n = 1, 2, \cdots$. Then, $x_1, x_2, \cdots$, is a sequence of points in a closed bounded set Γ_1. By the Bolzano-Weierstrass theorem, this sequence must have at least one limit point, say x_0, in Γ_1. Consequently, every spherical neighborhood of x_0 will contain infinitely many points from the sequence $x_1, x_2, \cdots$, and, more particularly, from the subsequence $x_{N+1}, x_{N+2}, \cdots$, where $N \geqq M/\epsilon$. Since the points of this subsequence fall within the set $Q(\epsilon) = \{x \mid f_A(x) \geqq M - \epsilon\}$, the lemma is proved.

Strict and strong convexity. A fuzzy set A is *strictly convex* if the sets Γ_α, $0 < \alpha \leqq 1$ are strictly convex (that is, if the midpoint of any two distinct points in Γ_α lies in the interior of Γ_α). Note that this definition reduces to that of strict convexity for ordinary sets when A is such a set.

A fuzzy set A is *strongly convex* if, for any two distinct points x_1 and x_2, and any λ in the open interval $(0, 1)$

$$f_A[\lambda x_1 + (1 - \lambda)x_2] > \text{Min}\,[f_A(x_1), f_A(x_2)].$$

Note that strong convexity does not imply strict convexity or vice-versa. Note also that if A and B are bounded, so is their union and intersection. Similarly, if A and B are strictly (strongly) convex, their intersection is strictly (strongly) convex.

Let A be a convex fuzzy set and let $M = \text{Sup}_x f_A(x)$. If A is bounded, then, as shown above, either M is attained for some x, say x_0, or there is at least one point x_0 at which M is essentially attained in the sense that, for each $\epsilon > 0$, every spherical neighborhood of x_0 contains points in the set $Q(\epsilon) = \{x \mid M - f_A(x) \leqq \epsilon\}$. In particular, if A is strongly convex and x_0 is attained, then x_0 is unique. For, if $M = f_A(x_0)$ and $M = f_A(x_1)$, with $x_1 \neq x_0$, then $f_A(x) > M$ for $x = 0.5x_0 + 0.5x_1$, which contradicts $M = \text{Max}_x f_A(x)$.

More generally, let $C(A)$ be the set of all points in X at which M is essentially attained. This set will be referred to as the *core* of A. In the case of convex fuzzy sets, we can assert the following property of $C(A)$.

THEOREM. *If A is a convex fuzzy set, then its core is a convex set.*

Proof: It will suffice to show that if M is essentially attained at x_0 and x_1, $x_1 \neq x_0$, then it is also essentially attained at all x of the form $x = \lambda x_0 + (1 - \lambda)x_1$, $0 \leqq \lambda \leqq 1$.

To the end, let P be a cylinder of radius ϵ with the line passing through x_0 and x_1 as its axis. Let x_0' be a point in a sphere of radius ϵ centering on x_0 and x_1' be a point in a sphere of radius ϵ centering on x_1 such that $f_A(x_0') \geqq M - \epsilon$ and $f_A(x_1') \geqq M - \epsilon$. Then, by the convexity of A, for any point u on the segment $x_0'x_1'$, we have $f_A(u) \geqq M - \epsilon$. Furthermore, by the convexity of P, all points on $x_0'x_1'$ will lie in P.

Now let x be any point in the segment x_0x_1. The distance of this point from the segment $x_0'x_1'$ must be less than or equal to ϵ, since $x_0'x_1'$ lies in P. Consequently, a sphere of radius ϵ centering on x will contain at least one point of the segment $x_0'x_1'$ and hence will contain at least one point, say w, at which $f_A(w) \geqq M - \epsilon$. This establishes that M is essentially attained at x and thus proves the theorem.

COROLLARY. *If $X = E^1$ and A is strongly convex, then the point at which M is essentially attained is unique.*

Shadow of a fuzzy set. Let A be a fuzzy set in E^n with membership function $f_A(x) = f_A(x_1, \cdots, x_n)$. For notational simplicity, the notion of the *shadow* (projection) of A on a hyperplane H will be defined below for the special case where H is a coordinate hyperplane, e.g., $H = \{x \mid x_1 = 0\}$.

Specifically, the *shadow* of A on $H = \{x \mid x_1 = 0\}$ is defined to be a fuzzy set $S_H(A)$ in E^{n-1} with $f_{S_H(A)}(x)$ given by

$$f_{S_H(A)}(x) = f_{S_H(A)}(x_2, \cdots, x_n) = \text{Sup}_{x_1} f_A(x_1, \cdots, x_n).$$

Note that this definition is consistent with (23).

When A is a convex fuzzy set, the following property of $S_H(A)$ is an immediate consequence of the above definition: If A is a convex fuzzy set, then its shadow on any hyperplane is also a convex fuzzy set.

An interesting property of the shadows of two convex fuzzy sets is expressed by the following implication

$$S_H(A) = S_H(B) \text{ for all } H \Rightarrow A = B.$$

To prove this assertion,[7] it is sufficient to show that if there exists a point, say x_0, such that $f_A(x_0) \neq f_B(x_0)$, then their exists a hyperplane H such that $f_{S_H(A)}(x_0^*) \neq f_{S_H(B)}(x_0^*)$, where x_0^* is the projection of x_0 on H.

Suppose that $f_A(x_0) = \alpha > f_B(x_0) = \beta$. Since B is a convex fuzzy set, the set $\Gamma_\beta = \{x \mid f_B(x) > \beta\}$ is convex, and hence there exists a hyperplane F supporting Γ_β and passing through x_0. Let H be a hyperplane orthogonal to F, and let x_0^* be the projection of x_0 on H. Then, since

[7] This proof is based on an idea suggested by G. Dantzig for the case where A and B are ordinary convex sets.

$f_B(x) \leqq \beta$ for all x on F, we have $f_{S_H(B)}(x_0^*) \leqq \beta$. On the other hand, $f_{S_H(A)}(x_0^*) \geqq \alpha$. Consequently, $f_{S_H(B)}(x_0^*) \neq f_{S_H(A)}(x_0^*)$, and similarly for the case where $\alpha < \beta$.

A somewhat more general form of the above assertion is the following: Let A, but not necessarily B, be a convex fuzzy set, and let $S_H(A) = S_H(B)$ for all H. Then $A = \text{conv } B$, where conv B is the convex hull of B, that is, the smallest convex set containing B. More generally, $S_H(A) = S_H(B)$ for all H implies $\text{conv } A = \text{conv } B$.

Separation of convex fuzzy sets. The classical separation theorem for ordinary convex sets states, in essence, that if A and B are disjoint convex sets, then there exists a separating hyperplane H such that A is on one side of H and B is on the other side.

It is natural to inquire if this theorem can be extended to convex fuzzy sets, without requiring that A and B be disjoint, since the condition of disjointness is much too restrictive in the case of fuzzy sets. It turns out, as will be seen in the sequel, that the answer to this question is in the affirmative.

As a preliminary, we shall have to make a few definitions. Specifically, let A and B be two bounded fuzzy sets and let H be a hypersurface in E^n defined by an equation $h(x) = 0$, with all points for which $h(x) \geqq 0$ being on one side of H and all points for which $h(x) \leqq 0$ being on the other side.[8] Let K_H be a number dependent on H such that $f_A(x) \leqq K_H$ on one side of H and $f_B(x) \leqq K_H$ on the other side. Let M_H be Inf K_H. The number $D_H = 1 - M_H$ will be called the *degree of separation of A and B by H.*

In general, one is concerned not with a given hypersurface H, but with a family of hypersurfaces $\{H_\lambda\}$, with λ ranging over, say, E^m. The problem, then, is to find a member of this family which realizes the highest possible degree of separation.

A special case of this problem is one where the H_λ are hyperplanes in E^n, with λ ranging over E^n. In this case, we define the *degree of separability* of A and B by the relation

$$D = 1 - \bar{M} \tag{31}$$

where

$$\bar{M} = \text{Inf}_H M_H \tag{32}$$

with the subscript λ omitted for simplicity.

[8] Note that the sets in question have H in common.

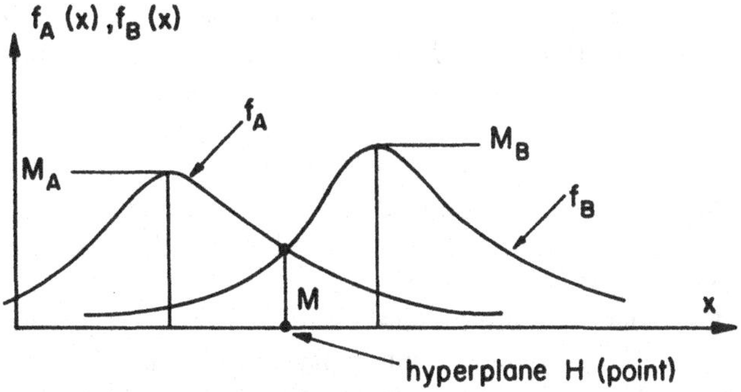

FIG. 5. Illustration of the separation theorem for fuzzy sets in E^1

Among the various assertions that can be made concerning D, the following statement[9] is, in effect, an extension of the separation theorem to convex fuzzy sets.

THEOREM. *Let A and B be bounded convex fuzzy sets in* E^n, *with maximal grades* M_A *and* M_B, *respectively* [$M_A = \text{Sup}_x f_A(x)$, $M_B = \text{Sup}_x f_B(x)$]. *Let M be the maximal grade for the intersection* $A \cap B$ ($M = \text{Sup}_x \text{Min} \cdot [f_A(x), f_B(x)]$). *Then* $D = 1 - M$.

Comment. In plain words, the theorem states that the highest degree of separation of two convex fuzzy sets A and B that can be achieved with a hyperplane in E^n is one minus the maximal grade in the intersection $A \cap B$. This is illustrated in Fig. 5 for $n = 1$.

Proof: It is convenient to consider separately the following two cases: (1) $M = \text{Min}(M_A, M_B)$ and (2) $M < \text{Min}(M_A, M_B)$. Note that the latter case rules out $A \subset B$ or $B \subset A$.

Case 1. For concreteness, assume that $M_A < M_B$, so that $M = M_A$. Then, by the property of bounded sets already stated there exists a hyperplane H such that $f_B(x) \leqq M$ for all x on one side of H. On the other side of H, $f_A(x) \leqq M$ because $f_A(x) \leqq M_A = M$ for all x.

It remains to be shown that there do not exist an $M' < M$ and a hyperplane H' such that $f_A(x) \leqq M'$ on one side of H' and $f_B(x) \leqq M'$ on the other side.

This follows at once from the following observation. Suppose that such H' and M' exist, and assume for concreteness that the core of A (that is, the set of points at which $M_A = M$ is essentially attained) is on the plus side of H'. This rules out the possibility that $f_A(x) \leqq M'$

[9] This statement is based on a suggestion of E. Berlekamp.

for all x on the plus side of H', and hence necessitates that $f_A(x) \leqq M'$ for all x on the minus side of H', and $f_B(x) \leqq M'$ for all x on the plus side of H'. Consequently, over all x on the plus side of H'

$$\text{Sup}_x \text{ Min } [f_A(x), f_B(x)] \leqq M'$$

and likewise for all x on the minus side of H'. This implies that, over all x in X, $\text{Sup}_x \text{ Min } [f_A(x), f_B(x)] \leqq M'$, which contradicts the assumption that $\text{Sup}_x \text{ Min } [f_A(x), f_B(x)] = M > M'$.

Case 2. Consider the convex sets $\Gamma_A = \{x \mid f_A(x) > M\}$ and $\Gamma_B = \{x \mid f_B(x) > M\}$. These sets are nonempty and disjoint, for if they were not there would be a point, say u, such that $f_A(u) > M$ and $f_B(u) > M$, and hence $f_{A \cap B}(u) > M$, which contradicts the assumption that $M = \text{Sup}_x f_{A \cap B}(x)$.

Since Γ_A and Γ_B are disjoint, by the separation theorem for ordinary convex sets there exists a hyperplane H such that Γ_A is on one side of H (say, the plus side) and Γ_B is on the other side (the minus side). Furthermore, by the definitions of Γ_A and Γ_B, for all points on the minus side of $H, f_A(x) \leqq M$, and for all points on the plus side of $H, f_B(x) \leqq M$.

Thus, we have shown that there exists a hyperplane H which realizes $1 - M$ as the degree of separation of A and B. The conclusion that a higher degree of separation of A and B cannot be realized follows from the argument given in Case 1. This concludes the proof of the theorem.

The separation theorem for convex fuzzy sets appears to be of particular relevance to the problem of pattern discrimination. Its application to this class of problems as well as to problems of optimization will be explored in subsequent notes on fuzzy sets and their properties.

Received: November 30, 1964

References

Birkhoff, G. (1948), "Lattice Theory," Am. Math. Soc. Colloq. Publ., Vol. 25, New York.

Halmos, P. R. (1960), "Naive Set Theory." Van Nostrand, New York.

Kleene, S. C. (1952), "Introduction to Metamathematics," p. 334. Van Nostrand, New York.

FUZZY SETS AND SYSTEMS*

L. A. Zadeh

Department of Electrical Engineering, University of California, Berkeley, California

The notion of fuzziness as defined in this paper relates to situations in which the source of imprecision is not a random variable or a stochastic process, but rather a class or classes which do not possess sharply defined boundaries, e.g., the "class of bald men," or the "class of numbers which are much greater than 10," or the "class of adaptive systems," etc.

A basic concept which makes it possible to treat fuzziness in a quantitative manner is that of a fuzzy set, that is, a class in which there may be grades of membership intermediate between full membership and non-membership. Thus, a fuzzy set is characterized by a membership function which assigns to each object its grade of membership (a number lying between 0 and 1) in the fuzzy set.

After a review of some of the relevant properties of fuzzy sets, the notions of a fuzzy system and a fuzzy class of systems are introduced and briefly analyzed. The paper closes with a section dealing with optimization under fuzzy constraints in which an approach to problems of this type is briefly sketched.

1. INTRODUCTION

This paper constitutes a very preliminary attempt at introducing into system theory several concepts which provide a way of treating fuzziness in a quantitative manner. Essentially, these concepts relate to situations in which the source of imprecision is not a random variable or a stochastic process but rather a class or classes which do not possess sharply defined boundaries. An example of such a "class" is the "class" of adaptive systems. A simpler example is the "class" of real numbers which are much larger than, say, 10. Still another example is the "class" of bald men. Clearly, such classes are not classes or sets in the usual mathematical sense of these terms, since they do not dichotomize all objects into those that belong to the class and those that do not.

One way of dealing with classes in which there may be intermediate grades of membership was described in a recent paper.[1] The approach in question is based on the use of the concept of a "fuzzy set," that is, a class in which there may be a continuous infinity of grades of membership, with the grade of membership of an object x in a fuzzy set A represented by a number $\mu_A(x)$ in the interval [0, 1]. Thus, a fuzzy set A in a space of objects $X = \{x\}$ is characterized by a membership function μ_A which is defined on X and takes values in the interval [0, 1],

*This text is an abbreviated version of a paper presented at the Symposium under the title of "A New View of System Theory." The work described here was supported in part by the National Science Foundation under Grant GP-2413.

Presented at the Symposium on System Theory
Polytechnic Institute of Brooklyn, April 20, 21, 22, 1965

such that the nearer the value of $\mu_A(x)$ to unity, the higher the grade of membership of x in A. As a simple example, let A be the fuzzy set of real numbers which are much greater than 10. In this case, a set of representative values of $\mu_A(x)$ may be: $\mu_A(10) = 0$; $\mu_A(50) = 0.6$; $\mu_A(100) = 0.9$; $\mu_A(500) = 1$; etc. In general, the values of $\mu_A(x)$ would be specified on a subjective rather than an objective basis.

2. CONCEPTS RELATING TO FUZZY SETS

As a preliminary to sketching a possible role for fuzzy sets in system theory, it will be helpful to summarize some of their main properties.* To begin with, it is clear that when there is no fuzziness in the definition of a class A, A is a set or a class in the ordinary sense of this term,** and its membership function reduces to the familiar two-valued characteristic (indicator) function for A, with $\mu_A(x)$ being one or zero according as x belongs or does not belong to A.

The notion of a fuzzy set provides a convenient way of defining *abstraction*—a process which plays a basic role in human thinking and communication. Specifically, suppose that A is a fuzzy set with an unknown membership function μ_A. Furthermore, suppose that one is given a set of n samples from A of the form $(x_1, \mu_A(x_1)), \ldots, (x_N, \mu_A(x_N))$, where x_i, $i = 1, \ldots, N$, is an object in X and $\mu_A(x_i)$ is its grade of membership in A. Then, by abstraction on these samples is meant the formation of an estimate, $\tilde{\mu}_A$, of the membership function of A in terms of the specified values of $\mu_A(x)$ at the points $x_1, \ldots, x_N$.

Many of the problems in pattern classification involve abstraction in the sense defined above. For example, suppose that we are concerned with devising a test for differentiating between handwritten letters O and D. One approach to this problem would be to give a set of handwritten letters and indicate their grades of membership in the fuzzy sets O and D. On performing abstraction on these samples, one obtains the estimates $\tilde{\mu}_O$ and $\tilde{\mu}_D$ of μ_O and μ_D, respectively. Then, given any letter x which is not one of the given samples, one can calculate its grades of membership in O and D, and, if O and D have no overlap, classify x in O or D.

To make abstraction mathematically meaningful, it is necessary to have enough a priori information about the membership function μ_A to make it possible to assess or at least place bounds on the error in the estimate of μ_A. As stated in reference 2, a disconcerting aspect of the problem of abstraction is that the human mind can perform abstraction very effectively even when the problems involved are not mathematically well defined. It is this lack of understanding of the way in which humans can abstract in mathematically ill-defined situations and our consequent inability to devise abstracting devices which can perform even remotely as well as the human mind, that lie at the root of many unresolved problems in heuristic programming, pattern recognition and related problem areas.

*A more detailed exposition of fuzzy sets and their properties is given in references 1 and 2.

**When it is necessary to emphasize the distinction between fuzzy sets and ordinary sets, T. Cover has suggested that the latter be referred to as *crisp* sets. We shall follow his suggestion in this paper.

There are several concepts relating to fuzzy sets which will be needed in later discussions. These are:

Equality. Two fuzzy sets A and B in a space X are *equal*, written $A = B$, if and only if $\mu_A(x) = \mu_B(x)$ for all x in X. (In the sequel, to simplify the notation we shall follow the convention of suppressing an argument to indicate that an equality or inequality holds for all values of that argument.)

Containment. A fuzzy set A is *contained* in a fuzzy set B, written as $A \subset B$, if and only if $\mu_A \leq \mu_B$. In this sense, the fuzzy set of "very tall men" is contained in the fuzzy set of "tall men." Similarly, the fuzzy set of real numbers which are "much greater than 10" is contained in the crisp set of real numbers which are "greater than 10."

Complementation. A fuzzy set A' is the *complement* of A if and only if $\mu_A' = 1 - \mu_A$.

Union. The *union* of two fuzzy sets A and B is denoted by $A \cup B$ and is defined as the smallest fuzzy set containing both A and B. An immediate consequence of this definition is that the membership function of $A \cup B$ is given by

$$\mu_{A \cup B}(x) = \text{Max}\,[\mu_A(x), \mu_B(x)]. \tag{1}$$

Thus, if at a point x, $\mu_A(x) = 0.8$, say, and $\mu_B(x) = 0.5$, then at that point, $\mu_{A \cup B}(x) = 0.8$.

Intersection. The intersection of two fuzzy sets A and B is denoted by $A \cap B$ and is defined as the largest fuzzy set contained in both A and B. The membership function of $A \cap B$ is given by

$$\mu_{A \cap B}(x) = \text{Min}\,[\mu_A(x), \mu_B(x)] \tag{2}$$

In this case, if $\mu_A(x) = 0.8$ and $\mu_B(x) = 0.5$, then $\mu_{A \cap B}(x) = 0.5$.

So far, we have not made any restrictive assumptions either about X or μ_A (other than $0 \leq \mu_A(x) \leq 1$ everywhere on X). In what follows, we shall assume for concreteness that $X = E^n$ (Euclidean n-space) and define a few more notions* relating to fuzzy sets which will be of use at later points.

Shadow. Consider a fuzzy set A in E^n which is characterized by a membership function $\mu_A(x_1, \ldots, x_n)$, with $x = (x_1, \ldots, x_n)$. Let H be a hyperplane in E^n. Then, the *orthogonal shadow* (or simply *shadow*) of A on H is a fuzzy set $S_H(A)$ in H which is related to A in the following manner.

Let L be a line orthogonal to H and let h be its point of intersection with H. Then,

$$\mu_{S_H(A)}(h) = \sup_{x \in L} \mu_A(x) \tag{3}$$

and

$$\mu_{S_H(A)}(x) = 0 \text{ for } x \notin H.$$

The fuzzy set $S_H(A)$ is called a shadow of A because it is suggestive of a shadow cast by a cloud on a plane.

If H_1 is a coordinate hyperplane $H_1 = \{x \mid x_1 = 0\}$, then the membership func-

*The notions of shadow, convexity, concavity, etc., can be defined, of course, in the context of more general spaces than E^n. For our purposes, however, it is sufficient to assume that $X = E^n$.

tion of the shadow of A on H_1 is given by

$$\mu_{S_{H_1}(A)}(x_2, \ldots, x_n) = \operatorname*{Sup}_{x_1} \mu_A(x_1, \ldots, x_n), \quad x_1 = 0$$
$$= 0, \quad x_1 \neq 0. \tag{4}$$

Note that $\mu_{S_{H_1}(A)}$ is analogous to a marginal distribution of a probability distribution in E^n. However, whereas in the case of a marginal distribution, an argument of a distribution is eliminated by integration, in the case of a shadow the elimination occurs through taking the supremum of the membership function.

Let $S_H^*(A)$ denote a cylindrical fuzzy set defined by

$$\mu_{S^*_{H_1}(A)}(x) = \mu_{S_{H_1}(A)}(x_2, \ldots, x_n), \quad x \in E^n. \tag{5}$$

Then, clearly, $A \subset S^*_{H_1}(A)$. Thus, if $H_i = \{x \mid x_i = 0\}, i = 1, \ldots, n$, then A is bounded from above by the intersection of $S^*_{H_1}(A), \ldots, S^*_{H_n}(A)$. In symbols,

$$A \subset \bigcap_{i=1}^{n} S^*_{H_i}(A). \tag{6}$$

Complementary shadow. The *complementary shadow* of A on H is denoted by $C_H(A)$ and is defined as the complement (on H) of the shadow of the complement of A. More specifically,

$$\mu_{C_H(A)}(h) = \operatorname*{Inf}_{x \in L} \mu_A(x), \quad x \in H \tag{7}$$
$$= 0, \quad x \notin H.$$

In terms of complementary shadow, A is bounded from below by the union of the cylindrical fuzzy sets $C^*_{H_1}(A), \ldots, C^*_{H_n}(A)$. Thus,

$$\bigcup_{i=1}^{n} C^*_{H_i}(A) \subset A \subset \bigcap_{i=1}^{n} S^*_{H_i}(A) \tag{8}$$

As will be seen later, these bounds are of some use in problems involving optimization under fuzzy constraints.

Convexity. A fuzzy set A is *convex* if and only if the sets $\Gamma_\alpha = \{x \mid \mu_A(x) \geq \alpha\}$ are convex for all α in the interval (0, 1]. Equivalently, A is convex if and only if for any pair of points x_1 and x_2 in E^n and any λ in [0, 1], we have

$$\mu_A(\lambda x_1 + (1 - \lambda)x_2) \geq \operatorname{Min}[\mu_A(x_1), \mu_A(x_2)]. \tag{9}$$

For example, the fuzzy set of real numbers which are "approximately equal to 1" is a convex fuzzy set in E^1. The membership function of this set is depicted in Fig. 1. In the same figure, μ_B is the membership function of a non-convex fuzzy set in E^1.

Concavity. A fuzzy set A is *concave* if and only if its complement A' is convex. The notions of convexity and concavity are duals of one another, as are A and A', union and intersection, $\supset$ and $\subset$, shadow and complementary shadow, etc.

This concludes our brief introduction to some of the basic notions pertaining to fuzzy sets. In the following, we shall merely indicate a few of the possible applications of these notions in system theory, without any attempt at detailed analysis or exploration.

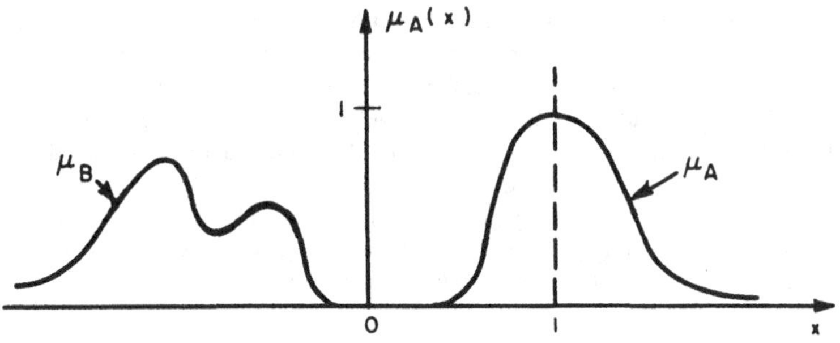

Fig. 1. Convex and non-convex sets in E^1.

3. FUZZY SYSTEMS

We begin with the notion of a fuzzy system, by which we mean the following. Let S be a system, with the input, output and state of S at time t denoted by $u(t)$, $y(t)$, and $x(t)$, respectively. Then S is a *fuzzy system* if $u(t)$ or $y(t)$ or $x(t)$ or any combination of them ranges over fuzzy sets. For example, if the input† to S at time t is specified to be "considerably in excess of 5," then this input is a fuzzy set and a system which can act on such imprecisely defined inputs is a fuzzy system. Similarly, if the states of S are described by such fuzzy adjectives as light, heavy, not very heavy, very light, etc., that is, if they are fuzzy sets, then S is a fuzzy system.

Assuming for simplicity that S is a discrete time system, with t ranging over the integers, we can characterize S by the usual state equations

$$x_{t+1} = f(x_t, u_t) \tag{10}$$

$$y_t = g(x_t, u_t) \tag{11}$$

where u_t, y_t and x_t denote, respectively, the input, output and state of S at time t, and f and g are functions of the indicated arguments. The difference between fuzzy and non-fuzzy systems, then, lies in the nature of the ranges of the variables, u_t, y_t and x_t. Thus, in the case of a fuzzy system, one or more of these variables range over spaces where elements are fuzzy sets. Since a fuzzy set is characterized by a scalar-valued membership function, that is, by a functional, this implies in effect that, in the case of a fuzzy system, the values of one or more of the variables u_t, y_t and x_t are functionals.

The situation described above is similar to that encountered in the case of stochastic systems which can be described as deterministic systems in terms of the probability distribution of the input, output and state variables.[3] In the case of such a system, a relation such as (10) would signify that the probability distribution of the states at time $t + 1$ is uniquely determined by the probability distribution of the states at time t and the probability distribution of the inputs at time t.

The difference between a stochastic and a fuzzy system is that in the latter the source of imprecision is nonstatistical in nature and has to do with the lack of

†It should be recognized, of course, that such inputs admit of precise definition in terms of fuzzy sets.

sharp boundaries of the classes entering into the descriptions of the input, output or state. Mathematically, however, these two types of systems are substantially similar and present comparable and, unfortunately, great difficulties in their analyses. These difficulties stem from the fact that, at present, we do not possess effective computational techniques for dealing with functionals, so that equations such as (10) and (11) are easy to write in symbolic form but difficult to translate into explicit computer programs when the variables involved in them are functionals rather than points in spaces of fairly low dimensionality—which is usually the case with conventional non-fuzzy systems.

4. FUZZY CLASSES OF SYSTEMS

A notion which is related to and yet distinct from that of a fuzzy system is that of a *fuzzy class* of systems. For instance, the "class" of systems which are "approximately equivalent" to a given system S is a fuzzy class of systems; so is the "class" of systems which are "approximately linear"; and so is the "class" of systems which are "adaptive." In fact, one may argue that most of the adjectives used in system theory to describe various types of systems, such as: linear, nonlinear, adaptive, time-invariant, stable, etc., are in reality names for fuzzy classes of systems. If one accepts this point of view, then one is freed from the necessity of defining these terms in a way that dichotomizes the class of all systems into two classes, e.g., systems that are linear and systems that are nonlinear. More realistically, then, one would regard, say, the "class" of adaptive systems as a fuzzy class, with each system having a grade of membership in it which may range from zero to one.

How can a fuzzy class of systems be characterized? The answer to this question depends on the mode of characterization of the systems which form a fuzzy class. More specifically, if one starts with the definition of a system as a set of input-output pairs— which is the point of departure in reference 4—then a fuzzy class of systems would be a fuzzy set in the product space $U \times Y$, where U is the space of inputs and Y is the space of outputs.

To illustrate this point, suppose that a system designer wishes to give a precise, albeit subjective, characterization of the fuzzy class, A, of time-invariant, approximately linear, systems. He could do this, at least in principle, by associating with each input-output pair (u, y) a number in the interval $[0, 1]$, representing its grade of membership in A. For example, he may assign the grade 0.8 to an input-output pair $(t, t + 0.001\, t^2)$, $0 \leq t \leq 100$; the grade 0.3 to $(t, 0.1 + t)$, $0 \leq t \leq 100$; and so forth. In this way, A would be characterized as a fuzzy set in the product space of input-output pairs. In practice, of course, the designer could assign grades of membership to only a finite number of input-output pairs (u, y). Thus, in general, one would have to estimate the membership function $\mu_A(u, y)$ from the values of this function over a finite set of sample input-output pairs $(u_1, y_1), (u_2, y_2), \ldots, (u_N, y_N)$. As was pointed out in the beginning of this paper, this is a problem in abstraction—a problem for which we do not possess as yet effective general methods of solution.

Alternatively, if one starts with a characterization of a system in terms of its input-output-state relation or state equations, and if each system is indexed by a parameter λ taking values in a space Λ, then a fuzzy class of systems may be characterized as a fuzzy set in Λ. For example, consider a family of discrete-time systems characterized by the state equations

$$x_{t+1} = f_\lambda(x_t, u_t) \tag{12}$$

$$y_t = g_\lambda(x_t, u_t) \tag{13}$$

in which λ is a real non-negative number. Then a fuzzy class, say A, of such systems would be defined by a fuzzy set, say B, in the parameter space $[0, \infty]$, with the grade of membership of the system with index λ in A being given by the grade of membership of λ in B, that is, by $\mu_B(\lambda)$.

One of the basic problems in the case of non-fuzzy (crisp) systems is that of deriving an input-output-state relation or, equivalently, state equations for a system which is defined by a set of input-output pairs. Recently, a solution to this problem in the context of finite-state automata was described by Tal.[5,6] The same basic, although much more difficult problem presents itself in the case of fuzzy classes of systems. More specifically, suppose that a fuzzy class of discrete-time systems, say A, is defined as a fuzzy set of input-output pairs (u, y) in the product space $U \times Y$. Then, the problem is to find a representation for this fuzzy class in the form of a family of state equations (12) and (13) and a fuzzy set B in the parameter Λ. It hardly needs saying that, in general, this would be an extremely difficult problem—a problem concerning which we know practically nothing at this time.

5. OPTIMIZATION UNDER FUZZY CONSTRAINTS

In the previous two sections, we focused our attention on ways in which fuzziness can enter into the definition of a system or a class of systems. In this section, we briefly touch on a different facet of fuzziness in system theory, namely, the optimization of crisp systems under fuzzy constraints.

Our consideration of this problem is motivated by the fact that in many practical optimization problems, particularly these involving man-machine systems, the constraints on variables are seldom sharply defined. Thus, in many instances the constraints are fuzzy or "soft," in the sense that the variables which they involve are only approximately—rather than precisely—constrained to fall within specified sets. For example, a constraint on a variable x may have fuzzy forms such as "x should not be significantly larger than 5," or "x should be close to 10," or "x should be approximately between 5 and 10," etc.

A standard approach to problems of this type is to idealize a fuzzy constraint by replacing it with an approximating "hard" (that is, crisp) constraint. For obvious reasons, this approach and its variants do not constitute a satisfactory way of handling problems in which the constraints are intrinsically fuzzy, and do not lend themselves to satisfactory approximation with hard constraints. In such cases, it is more natural—and perhaps more efficient computationwise—to deal with fuzzy constraints in the manner sketched below.

As a preliminary, consider the standard problem of maximizing a non-negative objective function $f(x_1, \ldots, x_n)$ over a crisp constraint set A in E^n, that is, subject to the condition that $x \in A$.

Let $\mu_A(x)$ denote the characteristic function of A ($\mu_A(x) = 1$ for $x \in A$ and $\mu_A(x) = 0$ for $x \notin A$). Then, it is clear that the above problem is equivalent to the maximization of the modified objective function†

$$f^*(x) = f(x)\, \mu_A(x) \tag{14}$$

without any side conditions. This suggests that, when A is a fuzzy set and hence it is not meaningful to speak of x being constrained to A, the maximization of f over a fuzzy constraint set A be interpreted to mean the maximization of the modified objective function (14) over E^n. In this way, the maximization of $f(x)$, subject to a fuzzy constraint represented by a fuzzy set A, reduces to an unconstrained maximization of the function,

$$f^*(x_1, \ldots, x_n) = f(x_1, \ldots, x_n)\, \mu_A(x_1, \ldots, x_n). \tag{15}$$

In many optimal control problems, the constraints on x have the form $x_1 \in A_1$, $x_2 \in A_2, \ldots, x_n \in A_n$, where $A_1, \ldots, A_n$ are specified crisp sets in E^n. In such cases, the constraints in question can be replaced by the single constraint on x: $x \in A$, where A is the direct product of $A_1, \ldots, A_n$, that is, $A = A_1 \times A_2 \ldots \times A_n$. Note that the crisp sets $A_1, \ldots, A_n$ may be regarded as the shadows of the crisp set A on the coordinate axes.‡

A natural question that suggests itself at this point is: what if $A_1, \ldots, A_n$ are fuzzy sets? How can we derive A from $A_1, \ldots, A_n$, if the latter are taken to be shadows of A on the coordinate axes?

In the case of fuzzy sets, these questions do not have a unique answer, since A is not uniquely determined by its shadows.§ However, as in (6), one can bound A from above by the intersection of the cylindrical fuzzy sets $A_1^*, \ldots, A_n^*$, where the membership function of A_i^*, $i = 1, \ldots, n$, is given by

$$\mu_{A_i}^*(x) = \operatorname*{Sup}_{x_2} \operatorname*{Sup}_{x_3} \ldots \operatorname*{Sup}_{x_n} \mu_A(x_1, \ldots, x_n) = \mu_i(x_i) \tag{16}$$

More specifically

$$A \subset \bigcap_{i=1}^{n} \mu_i(x'_i) \tag{17}$$

or equivalently,

$$\mu_A(x) \leq \text{Min}\,[\mu_1(x_1), \ldots, \mu_n(x_n)]. \tag{18}$$

Then, if—as an approximation—$\mu_A(x)$ is identified with the right member of (18), the modified objective function becomes

$$f^*(x_1, \ldots, x_n) = f(x_1, \ldots, x_n)\, \text{Min}\,[\mu_1(x_1), \ldots, \mu_n(x_n)]. \tag{19}$$

†More generally, the modified objective function can be taken to be $f^*(x) = f(x)\,[\mu_A(x)]^k$, where k is any positive real number. For our purposes, it will suffice to let $k = 1$.

‡The membership functions of the shadow of A on the axis $0x_1$ is given by $\mu_{A_1}(x) = \operatorname*{Sup}_{x_2} \operatorname*{Sup}_{x_3} \ldots \operatorname*{Sup}_{x_n} \mu_A(x_1, \ldots, x_n)$ on the axis; $\mu_{A_1}(x) = 0$ elsewhere; and similarly for other axes.

§As shown in references 1 and 2, a convex fuzzy set is uniquely determined by the totality of its shadows on all hyperplanes in E^n. Dually, a concave fuzzy set is uniquely determined by the totality of its complementary shadows.

In many practical situations, this approximation may be quite adequate. Unfortunately, no sharper estimates of A can be made when all we know about A are its shadows on coordinate axes.

The subject of optimization under fuzzy constraints has numerous additional ramifications, a few of which are now in process of exploration. Preliminary results seem to indicate that, in some cases, it may actually be advantageous to approximate to hard constraints by fuzzy constraints and employ steepest ascent techniques or other methods to maximize the modified objective functions. There are many other cases, however, in which optimization under fuzzy constraints is ineffective or computationally infeasible as an alternative to conventional optimization methods for dealing with problems involving crisp constraints.

CONCLUDING REMARKS

In the foregoing sections, we have not attempted to do more than merely touch upon the concept of fuzziness and point to some of its implications in system theory. Whether the particular concepts defined in this paper will prove to be of value in system design or analysis remains to be seen. It is clear, though, that in one form or another, the notion of fuzziness will come to play an important role in pattern classification, control, system optimization and other fields, since fuzziness is a basic and all-pervasive part of life that cannot be avoided merely because it is difficult to deal with precisely.

REFERENCES

1. L. A. Zadeh, "Fuzzy Sets," *Information and Control*, 8, 338-353, (June, 1965).
2. L. A. Zadeh, "Shadows of Fuzzy Sets," to appear in *Problems of Information Transmission*, June, 1966.
3. J. W. Carlyle, "Equivalent Stochastic Sequential Machines," Tech. Report No. 415, ERL, Univ. of California, Berkeley, 1961.
4. L. A. Zadeh and C. A. Desoer, *Linear System Theory--The State Space Approach*, (New York: McGraw-Hill, 1963).
5. A. Tal, "Questionnaire Language and Abstract Synthesis of Minimal Sequential Machines," *Automatika i Telemechanika*, 25, 946-962 (June, 1964).
6. A. Tal, "Abstract Synthesis of Sequential Machines by Answers to Questions of First Type in Questionnaire Language," Automatika i Telemechanika, 26, 676-682 (April, 1965).

Abstraction and Pattern Classification

R. Bellman, R. Kalaba, and L. Zadeh

The RAND Corporation, Santa Monica, California

1. Introduction

This note deals in a preliminary way with several concepts and ideas which have a bearing on the problem of pattern classification—a problem which plays an important role in communication and control theories.

There are two basic operations: abstraction and generalization, which appear under various guises is most of the schemes employed for classifying patterns into a finite number of categories. Although abstraction and generalization can be defined in terms of operations on sets of patterns, a more natural as well as more general framework for dealing with these concepts can be constructed around the notion of a "fuzzy" set—a notion which extends the concept of membership in a set to situations in which there are many, possibly a continuum of, grades of membership.

To be more specific, a *fuzzy set* A in a space $\Omega = \{x\}$ is represented by a characteristic function f which is defined on Ω and takes values in the interval [0, 1], with the value of f at $x, f(x)$, representing the "grade of membership" of x in A. Thus, if A is a set in the usual sense, $f(x)$ is 1 or 0 according as x belongs or does not belong to A. When A is a fuzzy set, then the nearer the value of $f(x)$ to 0, the more tenuous is the membership of x in A, with the "degree of belonging" increasing with increase in $f(x)$. In some cases it may be convenient to concretize the belonging of a point to a fuzzy set A by selecting two levels ϵ_1 and ϵ_2 ($\epsilon_1, \epsilon_2 \in [0, 1]$) and agreeing that (a) a point x "*belongs*" to A if $f(x) \geqslant 1 - \epsilon_1$; (b) *does not belong* to A if $f(x) \leqslant \epsilon_2$; and (c) x is *indeterminate relative to* A if $\epsilon_2 < f(x) < 1 - \epsilon_1$. In effect, this amounts to using a three-valued characteristic function, with $f(x) = 1$ if $x \in A$; $f(x) = 1/2$, say, if x is indeterminate relative to A; and $f(x) = 0$ if $x \notin A$.

Let A and B be two fuzzy sets in the sense defined above, with f_A and f_B denoting their respective characteristic functions. The *union* of A and B will be denoted in the usual way as

$$C = A \cup B, \tag{1}$$

Reprinted, with permission, from *J. of Math. Analysis and Applications*, **13**(1), pp. 1–7.

with the characteristic function of C defined by

$$f_C(x) = \text{Max}(f_A(x), f_B(x)). \tag{2}$$

For brevity, the relation expressed by (2) will be written as

$$f_C = f_A \vee f_B . \tag{3}$$

Note that when A and B are sets, (2) reduces to the definition of "or."

In a similar fashion, the *intersection* of two fuzzy sets A and B will be denoted by

$$C = A \cap B \tag{4}$$

with the characteristic function of C defined by

$$f_C(x) = \text{Min}(f_A(x), f_B(x)), \tag{5}$$

which for brevity will be written as

$$f_C = f_A \wedge f_B . \tag{6}$$

In the case of the intersection, when A and B are sets (5) reduces to the definition of "and." When the characteristic functions are three-valued, (2) and (5) lead to the three-valued logic of Kleene [1].

2. Abstraction and Generalization

Let $x^1, \ldots, x^n$ be given members of a set A in Ω. In informal terms, by abstraction on $x^1, \ldots, x^n$ is meant the identification of those properties of $x^1, \ldots, x^n$ which they have in common and which, in aggregate, define the set A.

The notion of a fuzzy set provides a natural as well as convenient way of giving a more concrete meaning to the notion of *abstraction*. Specifically, let f^i denote the value of the characteristic function, f, of a fuzzy set A at a point x^i in Ω. A collection of pairs $\{(x^1, f^1), \ldots, (x^n, f^n)\}$ or, for short $\{(x^i, f^i)\}^n$, will be called a collection of *samples* or *observations* from A. By an abstraction on the collection $\{(x^i, f^i)\}^n$, we mean the estimation of the characteristic function of A from the samples $(x^1, f^1), \ldots, (x^n, f^n)$. Once an estimate of f has been constructed, we perform a *generalization* on the collection $\{(x^i, f^i)\}^n$ when we use the estimate in question to compute the values of f at points other than $x^1, \ldots, x^n$.

An estimate of f employing the given samples $(x^1, f^1), \ldots, (x^n, f^n)$ will be denoted by $\hat{f}$ or, more explicitly, by $\hat{f}(x; \{x^i, f^i)\}^n)$,and will be referred to as an abstracting function. Clearly, the problem of determining an abstracting function is essentially one of reconstructing a function from the knowledge of its values over a finite set of points. To make this problem meaningful, one must have some a priori information about the class of functions to which f belongs, such that this information in combination with the samples from A would be sufficient to enable one to construct a "good" estimate of f. As in interpolation theory, this approach involves choosing—usually on purely heuristic grounds—a class of estimates of f: $\tilde{F} = \{\tilde{f}(x; \lambda) \mid \lambda \in R^l\}$ and finding that member of this family which fits, or fits "best" (in some specified sense of "best"), the given samples $(x^1, f^1), ..., (x^n, f^n)$. A special case of this procedure which applies to ordinary rather than fuzzy sets is the widely used technique for distinguishing between two sets of patterns via a separating hyperplane. Stated in terms of a single set of patterns, the problem in question is essentially that of finding, if it exists, a hyperplane L passing through the origin of $R^l(\Omega = R^l$, by assumption) such that the given points $x^1, ..., x^n$ belonging to a set A are all on the same side of the hyperplane. (Note that, since A is a set, $f^1 = f^2 = \cdots = f^n = 1$.) In effect, in this case $\tilde{f}(x; \lambda)$ is of the form

$$\begin{aligned} \tilde{f}(x; \lambda) &= 1 \qquad \text{for} \quad \langle x, \lambda \rangle \geqslant 0, \\ \tilde{f}(x; \lambda) &= 0 \qquad \text{for} \quad \langle x, \lambda \rangle < 0, \end{aligned} \tag{7}$$

where $\langle x, \lambda \rangle$ denotes the scalar product of x and λ, and the problem is to find a λ in R^l such that

$$\langle x^i, \lambda \rangle \geqslant 0 \qquad \text{for} \quad i = 1, ..., n.$$

Any $\tilde{f}(x; \lambda)$ whose λ satisfies (8) will qualify as an abstracting function, and the corresponding generalization on $(x^1, 1), ..., (x^n, 1)$ will take the form of the statement "Any x satisfying $\langle x, \lambda \rangle \geqslant 0$ belongs to the same set as the samples $x^1, ..., x^n$." If one is not content with just satisfying (8) but wishes, in addition, to maximize the distance between L and the set of points $x^1, ..., x^n$ (in the sense of maximizing $\text{Min}\langle x^i, \lambda \rangle$), $\| \lambda \| = 1$, then the determination of the corresponding abstracting function requires the solution of a quadratic program, as was shown by Rosen [2] in connection with a related problem in pattern recognition.

In most practical situations, the a priori information about the characteristic function of a fuzzy set is not sufficient to construct an estimate of $f(x)$ which is "optimal" in a meaningful sense. Thus, in most instances one is forced to resort to a heuristic rule for estimating $f(x)$, with the only means of judging the "goodness" of the estimate yielded by such a rule lying in experimentation. In the sequel, we shall describe one such rule for pattern classification and show that a special case of it is equivalent to the "minimum-distance" principle which is frequently employed in signal discrimination and pattern recognition.

3. Pattern Classification

For purposes of our discussion, a *pattern* is merely another name for a point in Ω, and a *category of patterns* is a (possibly fuzzy) set in Ω. When we speak of *pattern classification*, we have in mind a class of problems which can be subsumed under the following formulation and its variants.

Let A and B denote two[1] disjoint sets in Ω representing two categories of patterns. Suppose that we are given n points (patterns) $\alpha^1, ..., \alpha^n$ which are known to belong to A, and m points $\beta^1, ..., \beta^m$ which are known to belong to B. The problem is to construct estimates of the characteristic functions of A and B based on the knowledge of the samples $\alpha^1, ..., \alpha^n$ from A and $\beta^1, ..., \beta^m$ from B.

Clearly, one can attempt to estimate f_A without making any use of the β^j, $j = 1, ..., m$. However, in general, such an estimate would not be as good as one employing both α's and β's. This is a consequence of an implied or explicit dependence between A and B (e.g., the disjointness of A and B), through which the knowledge of β's contributes some information about f_A. The same applies to the estimation of f_B.

The heuristic rule suggested in the sequel is merely a way of constructing estimates of f_A and f_B, given $\alpha^1, ..., \alpha^n$, and $\beta^1, ..., \beta^m$, in terms of estimates of f_A and f_B, given a single pair of samples α^i and β^j. Specifically, suppose that with every $\alpha \in A$ and every $\beta \in B$ are associated two sets $\tilde{A}(\alpha; \beta)$ and $\tilde{B}(\beta; \alpha)$ representing the estimates of A and B, given α and β. (In effect, $\tilde{A}(\alpha; \beta)$ defines the set of points in Ω over which the estimate $\tilde{f}_A(\alpha; \beta)$ of f_A is unity, and likewise for $\tilde{f}_B(\beta; \alpha)$ and $\tilde{B}(\beta; \alpha)$. Points in Ω which are neither in $\tilde{A}(\alpha; \beta)$ nor in $\tilde{B}(\beta; \alpha)$ have indeterminate status relative to these sets.)

In terms of the sets in question, the estimates of A and B (or, equivalently, f_A and f_B), given $\alpha^1, ..., \alpha^n$ and $\beta^1, ..., \beta^m$, are constructed as follows

$$\tilde{A} = \bigcap_{j=1}^{m} \bigcup_{i=1}^{n} \tilde{A}(\alpha^i; \beta^j), \tag{9}$$

$$\tilde{B} = \bigcap_{i=1}^{n} \bigcup_{j=1}^{m} \tilde{B}(\beta^j; \alpha^i). \tag{10}$$

Thus, under the rule expressed by (9) and (10), we generalize on $\alpha^1, ..., \alpha^n$

[1] The restriction to two sets serves merely to simplify the analysis and does not entail any essential loss in generality.

and $\beta^1, \ldots, \beta^m$ by identifying A with $\tilde{A}$ and B with $\tilde{B}$. Note that this rule is consistent in the sense that if α is known to belong to A then $\alpha \in \tilde{A}$, and likewise for a point belonging to B. However, the consistency of this rule does not extend to fuzzy sets. Thus, if (9) and (10) were applied to the estimation of f_A and f_B when A and B are fuzzy sets, it would not necessarily be true that $f_A(\alpha) = \tilde{f}_A(\alpha)$ for all given α in A.

In essence, the rule expressed by (9) and (10) implies that a point x is classified as a member of A if and only if for all β^j there exists an α^i such that x lies in $\tilde{A}(\alpha^i, \beta^j)$. For this reason, the rule in question will be referred to as the "rule of complete dominance."

To illustrate the rule of complete dominance and indicate its connection with the "minimum-distance" principle which is frequently employed in signal discrimination, consider the simple case where Ω is R^l and $\tilde{A}(\alpha; \beta)$ and $\tilde{B}(\beta; \alpha)$ are defined as follows:

$$\tilde{A}(\alpha; \beta) = \left\{ x \,\middle|\, \left\langle x - \frac{(\alpha + \beta)}{2}, \alpha - \beta \right\rangle \geqslant 0 \right\}, \tag{11}$$

$$\tilde{B}(\beta; \alpha) = \left\{ x \,\middle|\, \left\langle x - \frac{(\alpha + \beta)}{2}, \alpha - \beta \right\rangle < 0 \right\}. \tag{12}$$

In effect, $\tilde{A}(\alpha; \beta)$ is the set of all points which are nearer to α than to β or are equidistant from α and β, while $\tilde{B}(\beta; \alpha)$ is the complement of this set with respect to R^l.

Now consider the following "minimum-distance" decision rule. Let A^* and B^* denote the sets of samples $\alpha^1, \ldots, \alpha^n$ and $\beta^1, \ldots, \beta^m$, respectively. Define the distance of a point x in Ω from A^* to be $\text{Min}_i \| x - \alpha^i \|$, where $\| \;\|$ denotes the Euclidean norm and $i = 1, \ldots, n$; do likewise for B^*. Then, given a point x in Ω, decide that $x \in A$ if and only if the distance of x from A^* is less than or equal to the distance of x from B^*.

It is easy to show that this decision rule is a special case of (9) and (10). Specifically, with $\tilde{A}(\alpha; \beta)$ and $\tilde{B}(\beta; \alpha)$ defined by (11) and (12), respectively, the decision rule in question can be expressed as follows:

$$x \in \tilde{A} \Leftrightarrow \forall \beta^j \, \exists \, \alpha^i \{ \| x - \alpha^i \| \leqslant \| x - \beta^j \| \}, \qquad \begin{array}{l} i = 1, \ldots, n, \\ j = 1, \ldots, m. \end{array} \tag{13}$$

Now

$$\tilde{A}(\alpha^i; \beta^j) = \{ x \mid \| x - \alpha^i \| \leqslant \| x - \beta^j \| \} \tag{14}$$

and consequently (13) defines the set

$$\tilde{A} = \{ x \mid \forall \beta^j \, \exists \, \alpha^i (x \in \tilde{A}(\alpha^i; \beta^j)) \}. \tag{15}$$

Clearly, (15) is equivalent to

$$\tilde{A} = \bigcap_{j=1}^{m} \bigcup_{i=1}^{n} \tilde{A}(\alpha^i; \beta^j), \tag{16}$$

and similarly for B. Q.E.D.

In the foregoing discussion of the minimum-distance decision rule, we identified Ω with R^l and used the Euclidean metric in R^l to measure the distance between two patterns in Ω. However, in many cases of practical interest, Ω is a set of line patterns in R^2 such as letters, numerals, etc., to which the Euclidean metric is not applicable. In this case, the distance between two line patterns in R^2, say L_0 and L_1, can be defined by

$$d(L_0, L_1) = \operatorname*{Max}_{y_0 \in L_0} \operatorname*{Min}_{y_1 \in L_1} \| y_0 - y_1 \|, \tag{17}$$

where $\| \ \|$ is the Euclidean norm in R^2, and y_0 and y_1 are points in R^2 belonging to L_0 and L_1, respectively.

Now suppose that we agree to regard two patterns L_0 and L_1 as equivalent if one can be obtained from the other through translation, rotation, contraction (or dilation) or any combination of these operations. Thus, let T_δ denote the translation $y \to y + \delta$, where $y, \delta \in R^2$; let T_θ denote the rotation through an angle θ around the origin of R^2; and let T_ρ denote the contraction (or dilation) $x \to \rho x$ where $\rho \in R^1$. Then, we define the *reduced* distance of L_1 from L_0 by the relation

$$d^*(L_1 ; L_0) = \operatorname*{Min}_{T_\delta} \operatorname*{Min}_{T_\theta} \operatorname*{Min}_{T_\rho} d(L_0, T_\delta T_\theta T_\rho L_1), \tag{18}$$

where $T_\delta T_\theta T_\rho L_1$ denotes the image of L_1 under the operation $T_\delta T_\theta T_\rho$, and $d(L_0, T_\delta T_\theta T_\rho L_1)$ is the distance between L_0 and $T_\delta T_\theta T_\rho L_1$ in the sense of (17). Clearly, it is the reduced distance in the sense of (18) rather than the distance in the sense of (17) that should be used in applying the minimum-distance decision rule to the case where Ω is a set of line patterns in R^2.

To conclude our discussion of pattern classification, we shall indicate how the formulation given in the beginning of this section can be extended to fuzzy sets. Thus, let A and B denote two such sets in Ω, with f_A and f_B denoting their respective characteristic functions. Suppose that we are given n sample triplets $(x^1, f_A^{\ 1}, f_B^{\ 1}), \ldots, (x^n, f_A^{\ n}, f_B^{\ n})$, with $(x^i, f_A^{\ i}, f_B^{\ i})$ representing a sample consisting of x^i and the values of f_A and f_B at x^i. The problem of pattern classification in this context is essentially that of estimating the characteristic functions f_A and f_B from the given collection of samples. Clearly, this formulation of the problem includes as a special case the pattern-classification problem stated earlier for the case where A and B are sets in Ω.

References

1. S. C. Kleene, "Introduction to Metamathematics," p. 334. D. Van Nostrand Co., Inc., New York, 1952.
2. J. B. Rosen, "Pattern Recognition by Convex Programming," Tech. Rept. No. 30 (Stanford University, June 1963).

SHADOWS OF FUZZY SETS*

L. A. ZADEH

Department of Electrical Engineering,
University of California, Berkeley, California

In information theory as well as in many other fields of science it is customary to treat uncertainty and imprecision through the concepts and methods of probability theory. The almost exclusive reliance on probability theory for this purpose obscures the fact that there are many situations in which the source of imprecision is not a random variable but a class or classes which do not possess sharply defined boundaries. For example, the "class" of real number which are much greater than 10 is clearly not a precisely defined set of objects. The same is true of the "class" of good strategies in a game, the "class" of handwritten characters representing the letter A, the "class" of intelligent men, the "class" of systems which are approximately equivalent to a specified system, etc. In fact, on closer examination it appears that most of the classes of objects encountered in the real world are of this fuzzy, not sharply defined, type. In such classes, an object need not necessarily either belong or not belong to a class; there may be intermediate grades of membership. Thus, to describe the degree of belonging to such a class requires the use of a multivalued logic with a possibly continuous infinity of truth values.

In a recent paper,[1] a conceptual framework for dealing with classes in which there may be grades of membership intermediate between full membership and non-membership was outlined. A central concept in this framework is that of a fuzzy set, i.e., a "class" with a possibly continuous infinity of grades of membership in it. More specifically, let X be a collection of objects (points) with a generic object (point) denoted by x. Thus, $x = \{x\}$. Then, a *fuzzy set* A in X is characterized by a membership function, $\mu_A(x)$ (or simply μ_A), which assigns to each x a number in the interval [0, 1], which represents the grade of membership of x in A. Thus, the nearer the value of $\mu_A(x)$ to unity, the higher the grade of membership of x in A; and conversely, the smaller the value of $\mu_A(x)$, the lower the grade of membership of x in A.

*This work was supported in part by the National Science Foundation under Grant GP-2413.

Consider, for example, the fuzzy set in $E^1 : A = \{x \,|\, x \gg 10\}$. In this case, A may be characterized — subjectively, of course — by a membership function μ_A whose typical values may be: $\mu_A(10) = 0$; $\mu_A(50) = 0.3$; $\mu_A(100) = 0.9$; $\mu_A(200) = 1$, etc.

The concept of a fuzzy set provides a natural way of formulating the problem of abstraction — a problem which plays a central role in pattern classification, heuristic programming and many other fields.[2] Specifically, assume that we are given a finite number of samples from a fuzzy set A, e.g., N pairs of the form $(x_1, \mu_A(x_1)), \ldots, (x_N, \mu_A(x_N))$, where x_i is a point in X and $\mu_A(x_i)$ is its grade of membership in A. Then, an abstraction on this set of samples consists in estimating the membership function μ_A of A from the sample values $(x_1, \mu_A(x_1)), \ldots, (x_N, \mu_A(x_N))$. In the form stated, this is of course, not a mathematically well-posed problem, since there is no provision for assessing the goodness of the estimate of μ_A. To make abstraction mathematically meaningful, it is necessary to have some *a priori* information about the class of functions to which μ_A belongs and have some way of comparing μ_A with its estimate. What is disconcerting about the problem of abstraction is that the human mind can perform abstraction very effectively even when the problems involved are not mathematically well defined. It is this lack of understanding of abstraction processes and our consequent inability to instruct machines on how to perform them that is at the center of many unresolved problems in heuristic programming, pattern classification and related problem areas.

It should be noted that, from the point of view of fuzzy sets, when one says, for example, "Eugene is a tall man," one gives a pair (Eugene, μ_A) where A is the fuzzy set of tall men and μ_A is its membership function. Usually, $\mu_A(x)$ would be known only for a finite set of sample men and thus, in general, one would have to perform an abstraction to estimate μ_A.

As a first step toward the development of systematic techniques for performing abstraction on finite samples from fuzzy sets, it is necessary to construct a mathematical framework for manipulating fuzzy sets and studying their properties. In this note, we shall concern ourselves with one particular aspect of such sets, namely, the notion of a shadow of a fuzzy set and certain properties related to the dual notions of convexity and concavity. Although the theory of fuzzy sets appears to have considerable relevance to problems in pattern classification, optimization under fuzzy constraints and transmission of information, we shall not touch upon these and other applications in the present discussion.

In order to make our discussion self-contained, we summarize below some of the basic definitions relating to fuzzy sets.

1. Two fuzzy sets A and B are *equal*, written as $A = B$, if and only if $\mu_A(x) = \mu_B(x)$ for all x. In the sequel, this relation will be written as $\mu_A = \mu_B$, with the understanding that the suppression of x indicates that the equality holds for all

x. The same convention will be used in all cases where an equality or inequality holds for all x.

2. The *complement* of a fuzzy set A is a fuzzy set A' whose membership function is expressed by
$$\mu_{A'} = 1 - \mu_A\,. \tag{1}$$
3. A fuzzy set A is *contained* in a fuzzy set B, written as $A \subset B$, if and only if
$$\mu_A \leq \mu_B\,. \tag{2}$$
4. The *union* of two fuzzy sets A and B is denoted by $A \cup B$ and is defined as the smallest fuzzy set containing both A and B. The membership function of $A \cup B$ is given by
$$\mu_{A\cup B}(x) = \mathrm{Max}[\,\mu_A(x), \mu_B(x)]\,. \tag{3}$$
5. Similarly, the intersection of two fuzzy sets A and B is denoted by $A \cap B$ and is defined as the largest fuzzy set contained in both A and B. The membership function of $A \cap B$ is expressed by
$$\mu_{A\cap B}(x) = \mathrm{Min}[\,\mu_A(x), \mu_B(x)]\,. \tag{4}$$
6. The union and intersection of A and B are special cases of the *convex combination* of A, B and a third fuzzy set Λ. Specifically, the membership function of the convex combination — denoted by $(A, B; \Lambda)$ — of A, B and Λ is expressed by
$$\mu_{(A,B;\Lambda)}(x) = \mu_\Lambda(x)\mu_A(x) + (1 - \mu_\Lambda(x))\mu_B(x)\,. \tag{5}$$

In what follows, we assume for concreteness that X is a real Euclidean n-space E^n. In such a space, a fuzzy set A is *convex* if and only if the sets $\Gamma_\alpha = \{x \mid \mu_A(x) \geq \alpha\}$ are convex for all $\alpha > 0$. Equivalently, A is convex if and only if the inequality
$$\mu_A(\lambda x_1 + (1 - \lambda)x_2) \geq \mathrm{Min}[\,\mu_A(x_1), \mu_A(x_2)] \tag{6}$$
holds for all x_1, x_2 in E^n and all λ in the interval [0, 1].

A fuzzy set A is *concave* if A is the complement of a convex set. This implies that for a concave set the inequality (6) is replaced by the dual inequality
$$\mu_A(\lambda x_1 + (1 - \lambda)x_2) \leq \mathrm{Max}[\,\mu_A(x_1), \mu_A(x_2)]\,. \tag{7}$$

It is easy to show[1] that convexity is preserved under intersections. Dually, concavity is preserved under unions.

The *convex hull* of A is denoted by conv A and is defined as the smallest convex fuzzy set containing A. Similarly, the *concave core* of A is denoted by conc A and is defined as the largest concave fuzzy set contained in A.

We are now ready to define the notion of a shadow of a fuzzy set and examine some of its basic properties.

Let p_0 and H be, respectively, a point and a hyperplane in E^n. Then, a *point-shadow* of A on H is a fuzzy set $S(A)$ in H whose membership function $\mu_{S(A)}(x)$ is defined as follows: Let L be a line passing through p_0, with L intersecting H at a point h. Then,

$$\begin{aligned} \mu_{S(A)}(h) &= \operatorname*{Sup}_{x \in L} \mu_A(x), \quad h \in H \\ \mu_{S(A)}(x) &= 0, \quad x \notin H . \end{aligned} \tag{8}$$

Note that we use the suggestive term "point-shadow" to describe this fuzzy set because it bears resemblance to the shadow thrown by a cloud A on a plane H, with p_0 acting as a point source of light.

Dual to the notion of a point-shadow is that of a *complementary point-shadow*, $C(A)$, which is defined as the complement of $S(A')$ on H, where A' is the complement of A. More explicitly,

$$\begin{aligned} \mu_{C(A)}(h) &= \operatorname*{Inf}_{x \in L} \mu_A(x), \quad h \in H \\ \mu_{C(A)}(x) &= 0, \quad x \notin H . \end{aligned} \tag{9}$$

The transformation S which takes A into $S(A)$ will be referred to as *point-projection* of A on H *with respect to* p_0. In the special case where p_0 is a point at infinity and the lines L are orthogonal to H, we shall refer to $S(A)$ and S as *orthogonal shadow* and *orthogonal projection*, respectively. For example, if H is the coordinate plane $H_1 = \{x \mid x_1 = 0\}, x = (x_1, \ldots, x_n)$, then the orthogonal shadow of A on H_1 is characterized by the membership function

$$\begin{aligned} \mu_{S(A)}(0, x_2, \ldots, x_n) &= \operatorname*{Sup}_{x_1} \mu_A(x_1, \ldots, x_n), \quad x \in H_1 \\ &= 0, \quad x \notin H_1 . \end{aligned} \tag{10}$$

In the sequel, we shall frequently use the terms shadow and projection without the adjectives "point" or "orthogonal," relying on the context to indicate the specific meaning in which these terms should be understood.

We proceed to establish several basic properties of shadows and complementary shadows of fuzzy sets. Most of these properties are immediate consequences of the defining relations (8) and (9).

Homogeneity. Let kA denote a fuzzy set whose membership function is given by

$$\mu_{kA}(x) = k\mu_A(x) \tag{11}$$

where k is a constant, $0 \leq k \leq 1$. Then clearly

$$S(kA) = kS(A) . \tag{12}$$

Monotonicity. This property is expressed by the relation

$$A \subset B \Longrightarrow S(A) \subset S(B) \tag{13}$$

and is an immediate consequence of

$$(\forall_x)[\mu_A(x) \leq \mu_B(x)] \Longrightarrow \operatorname*{Sup}_{x \in L} \mu_A(x) \leq \sup_{x \in L} \mu_B(x) \tag{14}$$

Distributivity. For any fuzzy sets A and B, we have

$$S(A \cup B) = S(A) \cup S(B) \tag{15}$$

which implies that S is distributive with respect to $\cup$. This follows at once from the identity

$$\operatorname*{Sup}_{x \in L} \operatorname{Max}[\mu_A(x), \mu_B(x)] = \operatorname{Max}\left[\operatorname*{Sup}_{x \in L} \mu_A(x), \operatorname*{Sup}_{x \in L} \mu_B(x)\right]. \tag{16}$$

In connection with (15), it is natural to raise the question: Is S distributive with respect to $\cap$, i.e., is it true that

$$S(A \cap B) = S(A) \cap S(B). \tag{17}$$

In this case, the corresponding relation in terms of membership functions reads

$$\operatorname*{Sup}_{x \in L} \operatorname{Min}[\mu_A(x), \mu_B(x)] = \operatorname{Min}\left[\operatorname*{Sup}_{x \in L} \mu_A(x), \operatorname*{Sup}_{x \in L} \mu_B(x)\right]. \tag{18}$$

This equality does not hold for arbitrary μ_A and μ_B. However, it can be made valid by suitably restricting $\mu_A(x)$ and $\mu_B(x)$, as in the minimax theorem.[3] For arbitrary μ_A and μ_B, one can assert that

$$S(A \cap B) \subset S(A) \cap S(B) \tag{19}$$

since (see (43) *et seq.*)

$$\operatorname*{Sup}_{x \in L} \operatorname{Min}[\mu_A(x), \mu_B(x)] \leq \operatorname{Min}\left[\operatorname*{Sup}_{x \in L} \mu_A(x), \operatorname*{Sup}_{x \in L} \mu_B(x)\right]. \tag{20}$$

Note that by combining (11) and (15), we have for any constants k_1 and k_2 in [0, 1],

$$S(k_1 A \cup k_2 B) = k_1 S(A) \cup k_2 S(B). \tag{21}$$

This identity indicates that S is a linear transformation, with the restriction that k_1, $k_2 \in [0,1]$. Note also that S is idempotent, i.e.,

$$S^2(A) = S(S(A)) = S(A).$$

Invariance of convexity and concavity under projections. Let A be a convex fuzzy set in E^n and let $S(A)$ be an orthogonal shadow of A on a hyperplane H.

Then, $S(A)$ is a convex fuzzy set in H. Dually, if A is concave, then so is $C(A)$ (complementary shadow of A).

Proof. It will suffice to prove the assertion relating to convexity. To this end, let h_1 and h_2 be two arbitrary points in H and let h be any point in H defined by

$$h = \lambda\, h_1 + (1-\lambda)\, h_2 \tag{22}$$

with $\lambda \in [0,1]$. Let L_1, L_2 and L be lines orthogonal to H and passing through h_1, h_2 and h, respectively.

By the definition of Sup, for every $\varepsilon > 0$ there will be at least two points x_1 and x_2 in L_1 and L_2 such that

$$\operatorname*{Sup}_{x\in L_1} \mu_A(x) - \mu_A(x_1) \le \varepsilon \tag{23}$$

$$\operatorname*{Sup}_{x\in L_2} \mu_A(x) - \mu_A(x_2) \le \varepsilon \tag{24}$$

Now, since A is a convex fuzzy set, we have

$$\mu_A(\lambda x_1 + (1-\lambda)x_2) \ge \operatorname{Min}[\mu_A(x_1), \mu_A(x_2)]\,, \tag{25}$$

which in view of (23) and (24) implies

$$\mu_A(\lambda x_1 + (1-\lambda)\, x_2) \ge \operatorname{Min}\left[\operatorname*{Sup}_{x\in L_1} \mu_A(x), \operatorname*{Sup}_{x\in L_2} \mu_A(x)\right] - \varepsilon\,. \tag{26}$$

Noting that

$$\mu_{S(A)}(h) = \operatorname*{Sup}_{x\in L} \mu_A(x) \ge \mu_A(\lambda x_1 + (1-\lambda)\, x_2) \tag{27}$$

and

$$\mu_{S(A)}(h_1) = \operatorname*{Sup}_{x\in L_1} \mu_A(x) \tag{28}$$

$$\mu_{S(A)}(h_2) = \operatorname*{Sup}_{x\in L_2} \mu_A(x) \tag{29}$$

we can infer from (26)

$$\mu_{S(A)}(h) \ge \operatorname{Min}[\mu_{S(A)}(h_1), \mu_{S(A)}(h_2)] - \varepsilon \tag{30}$$

for all $\varepsilon > 0$, and hence

$$\mu_{S(A)}(h) \ge \operatorname{Min}[\mu_{S(A)}(h_1)\,, \mu_{S(A)}(h_2)], \tag{31}$$

which demonstrates that $S(A)$ is a convex fuzzy set in H. Q.E.D.

Bounds in terms of shadows and complementary shadows. The shadows and complementary shadows of A on a set of hyperplanes provide an obvious means of placing upper and lower bounds on A. Such bounds are useful when A has to be estimated from the knowledge of its shadows, as is frequently the case in problems involving optimization under fuzzy constraints.

Specifically, let A be a fuzzy set in E^n with membership function $\mu_A(x_1, \ldots, x_n)$ and let H_i denote the ith coordinate hyperplane $H_i = \{x \mid x_i = 0\}, i = 1, \ldots, n$. Let S_i and C_i denote, respectively, the shadow and complementary shadow of A on H_i, with the membership functions of S_i and C_i given by

$$\begin{aligned}\mu_{S_i}(x) &= \operatorname*{Sup}_{x_i} \mu_A(x_1, \ldots, x_n), \quad x \in H_i \\ &= 0, \quad x \notin H_i . \end{aligned} \tag{32}$$

$$\begin{aligned}\mu_{C_i}(x) &= \operatorname*{Inf}_{x_i} \mu_A(x_1, \ldots, x_n), \quad x \in H_i \\ &= 0, \quad x \notin H_i . \end{aligned} \tag{33}$$

Consider now cylindrical fuzzy sets $\bar{S}_i$ and $\bar{C}_i$ generated by S_i and C_i via the membership functions

$$\mu_{\bar{S}_i}(x) = \operatorname*{Sup}_{x_i} \mu_A(x_1, \ldots, x_n) \tag{34}$$

$$\mu_{\bar{C}_i}(x) = \operatorname*{Inf}_{x_i} \mu_A(x_1, \ldots, x_n) . \tag{35}$$

In terms of these cylindrical fuzzy sets, A can be bounded from above and below by the intersection of the $\bar{S}_i$ and the union of the $\bar{C}_i$, $i = 1, \ldots, n$. Thus

$$\bigcup_{i=1}^{n} \bar{C}_i \subset A \subset \bigcap_{i=1}^{n} \bar{S}_i . \tag{36}$$

This relation is an immediate consequence of the inequalities

$$\operatorname*{Inf}_{x_i} \mu_A(x_1, \ldots, x_n) \le \mu_A(x_1, \ldots, x_n) \le \operatorname*{Sup}_{x_i} \mu_A(x_1, \ldots, x_n), i = 1, \ldots, n . \tag{37}$$

When A is a convex or concave fuzzy set and $\{H\}$ constitute the set of all hyperplanes in E^n, the inequalities in (36) can be replaced by equalities. More concretely, we can assert that: If A and B are convex sets and $S(A) = S(B)$ for all p_0 (and a fixed H), then $A = B$. (Dually, the same conclusion holds for concave sets and complementary shadows.)

Proof. It will be sufficient to show that if $A \neq B$, then there exists a p_0 such that $S(A) \neq S(B)$.

Assuming that $A \neq B$, let x_0 be a point at which $\mu_A(x_0) \neq \mu_B(x_0)$, e.g., for concreteness, $\mu_A(x_0) = \alpha > \mu_B(x_0) = \beta$. Since B is a convex set, the set $\Gamma_\beta = \{x \mid \mu_B(x) > \beta\}$ is a convex set and hence there exists a hyperplane F supporting Γ_β and passing through x_0. In relation to F, we have $\mu_B(x) \le \beta$ for all x on F and on the side of F not containing Γ_β.

Now let p_0 be an arbitrarily chosen point on F, and let L be a line passing through p_0 and x_0. At the intersection, h, of this line with H (which may be at infinity), we have

$$\mu_{S(B)}(h) \leq \beta$$

but on the other hand $\mu_{S(A)}(h) \geq \alpha$ since $\mu_A(x_0) = \alpha$. Consequently, $\mu_{S(A)}(h) \neq \mu_{S(B)}(h)$. Q.E.D.

In the case of orthogonal shadows, the statement of the property in question becomes: If A and B are convex sets and $S(A) = S(B)$ for all H, then $A = B$. More generally, if A and B are not necessarily convex, then the conclusion $A = B$ would be replaced by the weaker equality conv $A =$ conv B, where conv A and conv B denote the convex hulls of A and B, respectively.

Degree of separability. In Ref. 1, the classical separation theorem for convex sets was generalized to convex fuzzy sets in the following manner: Let A and B be two convex fuzzy sets in E^n and let M be the maximal grade in the intersection of A and B, i.e.,

$$M = \operatorname*{Sup}_{x} \operatorname{Min}[\mu_A(x), \ \mu_B(x)]. \tag{38}$$

Then, (a) there exists a hyperplane H such that $\mu_A(x) \leq M$ for all x on one side of H and $\mu_B(x) \leq M$ for all x on the other side of H; and (b) there does not exist a number $M' < M$ for which this is true. For this reason, the number $D = 1 - M$ is called the degree of separability of A and B.

In connection with applications to pattern classification, it is of interest to inquire if the degree of separability can be increased by projecting A and B on a hyperplane. The answer to this question can readily be shown to be in the negative.

For simplicity, let $n = 2$ and consider the shadows of convex fuzzy sets A and B on the hyperplane $\{x \mid x_2 = 0\}$. By (10), the membership functions of these convex shadows on the hyperplane $\{x \mid x_2 = 0\}$ are given by

$$\mu_{S(A)}(x_1) = \operatorname*{Sup}_{x_2} \mu_A(x_1, x_2) \tag{39}$$

$$\mu_{S(B)}(x_1) = \operatorname*{Sup}_{x_2} \mu_B(x_1, x_2). \tag{40}$$

Now the degree of separability for A and B can be expressed as

$$D = 1 - \operatorname*{Sup}_{x_1} \operatorname*{Sup}_{x_2} \operatorname{Min}[\mu_A(x_1, x_2), \mu_B(x_1, x_2)] \tag{41}$$

whereas the degree of separability for $S(A)$ and $S(B)$ is given by

$$D_s = 1 - \operatorname*{Sup}_{x_1} \operatorname{Min}\left[\operatorname*{Sup}_{x_2} \mu_A(x_1, x_2), \operatorname*{Sup}_{x_2} \mu_B(x_1, x_2)\right]. \tag{42}$$

Thus, to show that $D_s \leq D$ it suffices to show that, for all x_1,

$$\operatorname*{Sup}_{x_2} \operatorname{Min}[\mu_A(x_1,x_2),\mu_B(x_1,x_2)] \leq \operatorname{Min}\left[\operatorname*{Sup}_{x_2} \mu_A(x_1,x_2), \operatorname*{Sup}_{x_2} \mu_B(x_1,x_2)\right]. \quad (43)$$

This inequality follows at once by noting that the inequalities

$$\operatorname*{Sup}_{x_2} \mu_A(x_1,x_2) \geq \mu_A(x_1,x_2) \qquad \text{for all } x_1 \quad (44)$$

and

$$\operatorname*{Sup}_{x_2} \mu_B(x_1,x_2) \geq \mu_B(x_1,x_2) \qquad \text{for all } x_1 \quad (45)$$

imply that for all x_1

$$\operatorname{Min}\left[\operatorname*{Sup}_{x_2} \mu_A(x_1,x_2), \operatorname*{Sup}_{x_2} \mu_B(x_1,x_2)\right] \geq \operatorname{Min}\left[\mu_A(x_1,x_2),\mu_B(x_1,x_2)\right] \quad (46)$$

and hence imply (43).

Concluding Remarks

Essentially, the notion of the shadow of a fuzzy set plays the same role in the theory of fuzzy sets as the notion of a marginal distribution plays in the theory of probability. In this note, we touched only upon some of the more elementary properties of shadows of fuzzy sets and did not concern ourselves with applications. Although work on these is still in its preliminary stages, it appears that the concept of a shadow along with some of the other notions sketched in this note may have useful applications in several areas, particularly in pattern classification and optimization under fuzzy constraints.

References

1. L. A. Zadeh, "Fuzzy Sets," *Information and Control* **8** (1965), pp. 338–353.
2. R. Bellman, R. Kalaba and L. A. Zadeh, "Abstraction and Pattern Classification," *J. Math. Analysis and Applications* **13** (1966), pp. 1–7.
3. S. Karlin, *Mathematical Methods and Theory in Games, Programming and Economics* (Addison-Wesley, Reading, Mass.), p. 28 *et seq.*

Fuzzy Algorithms

L. A. ZADEH*

Department of Electrical Engineering and Project MAC, Massachusetts Institute of Technology, Cambridge, Massachusetts 02139

I. INTRODUCTION

Unlike most papers in *Information and Control*, our note contains no theorems and no proofs. Essentially, its purpose is to introduce a basic concept which, though fuzzy rather than precise in nature, may eventually prove to be of use in a wide variety of problems relating to information processing, control, pattern recognition, system identification, artificial intelligence and, more generally, decision processes involving incomplete or uncertain data.

The concept in question will be called a *fuzzy algorithm* because it may be viewed as a generalization, through the process of fuzzification, of the conventional (nonfuzzy) conception of an algorithm.

More specifically, unlike a nonfuzzy deterministic or nondeterministic algorithm (Floyd, 1967), a fuzzy algorithm may contain fuzzy statements, that is, statements containing names of fuzzy sets (Zadeh, 1965), by which we mean classes in which there may be grades of membership intermediate between full membership and nonmembership.

To illustrate, fuzzy algorithms may contain fuzzy instructions such as:

(a) "Set y *approximately equal to 10* if x is *approximately equal to 5*,"

or

(b) "If x is *large*, increase y by *several* units,"

or

(c) "If x is *large*, increase y by *several* units; if x is *small*, decrease y by *several* units; otherwise keep y unchanged."

* Permanent address: Department of Electrical Engineering and Computer Sciences, Electronics Research Laboratory, University of California, Berkeley, California. Research sponsored by the National Aeronautics and Space Administration under Grant NSG-354, Suppl. 4.

The sources of fuzziness in these instructions are fuzzy sets which are identified by their underlined names.

Familiar examples of fuzzy algorithms drawn from everyday experience are cooking recipes, directions for repairing a TV set, instructions on how to treat a disease, instructions for parking a car, etc. Generally, such instructions are not dignified with the name "algorithm." From our point of view, however, they may be regarded as very crude forms of fuzzy algorithms.

A fuzzy instruction which is a part of a fuzzy algorithm can be assigned a precise meaning by making use of the concept of the membership function of a fuzzy set. For example, in (a) the class of numbers which are approximately equal to 5 is a fuzzy set, say A, in the space of real numbers, R^1. Similarly, the class of numbers which are approximately equal to 10 is a fuzzy set, say B, in R^1. These sets can be defined precisely by their respective membership functions $\mu_A(x)$ [1] and $\mu_B(y)$ which associate with each x and y in R^1 their grades of membership in the fuzzy sets A and B. The grades of membership may be numbers in the interval [0, 1] or, more generally, points in a lattice (Goguen, 1967) or even a more general type of space. Clearly, such specifications are subjective in nature and, in general, reflect the context in which the problem is viewed.

Thus, the meaning of (a) can be made precise by specifying the membership functions of A and B. More generally, a statement such as (a) may be regarded as a binary fuzzy relation, say C, in R^2, which is characterized by a bivariate membership function $\mu_C(x, y)$. From this point of view, the fuzzy sets A and B are the shadows (Zadeh, 1965, 1966) of C on the coordinate axes $0x$ and $0y$, respectively.

To gain a better understanding of the significance of C, it is helpful to visualize (a) as a fuzzified version of a statement such as

(a′) "Choose y in the interval [9.9, 10.1] if x is in the interval [4.9, 5.1]."

In this case, A is the nonfuzzy set [4.9, 5.1], B is the nonfuzzy set [9.9, 10.1] and C is the two-dimensional interval $[4.9, 5.1] \times [9.9, 10.1]$ in R^2 whose projections on $0x$ and $0y$ are the intervals A and B, respectively.

Clearly, nonfuzzy instructions such as that cited above and its simpler

[1] We use the symbol μ rather than f, as in Zadeh (1965), to denote a membership function. With this exception the notation and terminology used in this note follow that of Zadeh (1965).

version:

(a″) "Set y equal to 10 if x is equal to 5,"

convey no information on what should be done if x is not in [4.9, 5.1] or $x \neq 5$. To provide such in formation in the latter case, for example, we must have a set of instructions like (a″) covering all possible values of x. Thus, if the domain of x is an interval, say Γ, then we must specify the pairs (x, y) for all $x \in \Gamma$. The result will be a graph, G, in R^2 which is the union of the ordered pairs (x, y), with x ranging over Γ.

Similarly, in the fuzzy case an instruction such as (a) may be regarded as a member, say C_x, of an indexed family of fuzzy sets $\{C_x\}$, with x ranging over a nonfuzzy set Γ. Then, the analog of the nonfuzzy graph G will be a fuzzy graph (relation), G, expressed by

$$G = \bigcup_x C_x \tag{1}$$

where the union [2] is taken over $x \in \Gamma$. This fuzzy graph may be visualized as a fuzzified version of the curve which depicts y as a function of x in the nonfuzzy case.

II. EXECUTION OF FUZZY INSTRUCTIONS

The above examples illustrate how a precise meaning may be assigned to a fuzzy instruction or to a family of such instructions by the use of the membership functions of the fuzzy sets which enter into such instructions. However, the assignment of a precise meaning to a fuzzy instruction does not in itself resolve the ambiguity of how it should be executed. The same is true, of course, of nonfuzzy instructions in a nondeterministic algorithm, in which the sources of ambiguity are statements of the form "Choose any x in a set A."

To illustrate the nature of the ambiguity of execution of a fuzzy instruction, consider the simple example of an unconditional instruction "Move *several steps* forward." Suppose that the membership function of A, the fuzzy set named "several steps," is specified as follows: $\mu_A(0) = \mu_A(1) = \mu_A(2) = \mu_A(3) = 0$; $\mu_A(4) = 0.8$; $\mu_A(5) = \mu_A(6) = \mu_A(7) = 1$; $\mu_A(8) = 0.7$; $\mu_A(x) = 0$ for $x \geqslant 9$. What would a human being do given $\mu_A(x)$ and instructed to move several steps forward, assuming that his actions are not influenced by any external factors such as the expenditure of energy involved in taking n steps, etc?

[2] The union of two fuzzy sets A and B is the smallest fuzzy set which contains both A and B. The membership function of $A \cup B$ is given by $\mu_{A \cup B}(x) = \text{Max}\,[\mu_A(x), \mu_B(x)]$.

Needless to say, our consideration of the response of a human being to a fuzzy instruction is intended merely to provide an intuitive basis for formulating as a convention the way or ways in which such instructions should be executed. With this understanding, we are led to considering the following modes of execution.

I. PROBABILISTIC EXECUTION

In this case, we assume that if a possible outcome x is assigned a grade of membership $\mu_A(x)$, then it should be chosen with a probability proportional to $\mu_A(x)$. Thus, in the above example, 0, 1, 2 and 3 would be chosen with probability 0; 4 with probability 0.8/4.5; 5, 6 and 7 with probability 1/4.5; 8 with probability 0.7/4.5; and 9, 10, $\cdots$ with probability 0.

A variant of this mode of execution is one where a threshold α is set and all x's whose grade of membership is less than α are executed with probability 0. For example, if $\alpha = 0.8$, then 4 would be chosen with probability 0.8/3.8; 5, 6, and 7 with probability 1/3.8; and the rest with probability 0.

II. NONDETERMINISTIC EXECUTION WITH THRESHOLD

In this case, let A_α be the set of all x's such that $\mu_A(x) \geqslant \alpha$, where α denotes a specified threshold. Then, as in a nondeterministic algorithm, any x in A_α would constitute a permissible choice.

A special case of this mode of execution is one where α has the largest possible value, with the constraint that A_α be nonempty. In this case, A_α is the *core* of A, that is, the set of points which have maximal grade of membership in A.

The above modes of execution apply also to conditional fuzzy instructions such as

(b) "If x is *large*, increase y by *several* units."

In this case, assume that x and y range over nonnegative integers and that the fuzzy set, B, of "large x" is characterized by the membership function

$$\mu_B(x) = \left(1 + \left(\frac{x}{100}\right)^{-2}\right)^{-1}.$$

Let α be a specified threshold, say $\alpha = 0.9$, and let B_α be the set of all x such that $\mu_B(x) \geqslant 0.9$. Then, for each x in B_α, the instruction "Increase y by several units" will be executed as an unconditional instruction in the manner of (I) or (II). For x not in B_α, no execution will take place since the instruction does not cover this contingency.

Now suppose that instead of having a single instruction like (b), which is conditioned on a fuzzy set, we have a family of such instructions giving rise to the graph G defined by (1). In this case, if the grade of membership of each x in the shadow of G on $0x$ is unity, the execution will always take place. Furthermore, there is no need to set a threshold, since the instructions may be regarded as being indexed by x rather than conditioned on fuzzy sets.

Clearly, the several particular cases considered above by no means provide definitive answers to the questions relating to the execution of fuzzy instructions. The problem of execution of such instructions is many-faceted and complex, and our brief discussion of it in this note is intended merely to draw attention to the problem and suggest in very tentative terms a few ways of approaching it.

III. FUZZY ALGORITHMS AND FUZZY TURING MACHINES

Up to this point, we have employed the term "algorithm" in the very broad and somewhat vague sense of a set of numbered instructions. Actually, just as the notion of a conventional (nonfuzzy) algorithm can be defined precisely in the context of countable sets by placing it in one–one correspondence with a Turing machine (Aizerman, 1963; Korfhage, 1966), so can the notion of a fuzzy algorithm be given a precise, although restricted, meaning by placing it in one–one correspondence with a fuzzy Turing machine. The latter differs from a nonfuzzy Turing machine mainly in the way in which its state at time $n + 1$ depends on the state at time n and the input symbol at time n. Specifically, let $Q = \{q_0, q_1, \cdots, q_r\}$ be the set of states of a Turing machine and $U = \{u_0, u_1, \cdots, u_m\}$ be its set of tape symbols. Now, in the case of a nonfuzzy deterministic Turing machine, the state at time $n + 1$ is a function of the state at time n and the tape symbol at time n, i.e.,

$$q^{n+1} = f(q^n, u^n) \tag{2}$$

where f is a function from $Q \times U$ to Q and q^n and u^n are variables ranging over Q and U, respectively.

In the case of a nonfuzzy nondeterministic Turing machine, f in (2) is a multi-valued rather than a single-valued function. This is equivalent to saying that the dependence of q^{n+1} on q^n and u^n is described by a relation

$$R = \{(q^{n+1}, q^n, u^n)\} \tag{3}$$

where R is a subset of the product space $Q \times Q \times U$, rather than by a function, as in (2). It should be noted that a *nondeterministic* algorithm (Floyd, 1967) corresponds to a nonfuzzy nondeterministic Turing machine.

Now in the case of a fuzzy Turing machine, the relation (3) is a fuzzy rather than a nonfuzzy subset of the product space $Q \times Q \times U$. Such a fuzzy subset would be characterized by a membership function $\mu_R(q^{n+1}, q^n, u^n)$ which associates with each triplet (q^{n+1}, q^n, u^n) a grade of membership in the fuzzy relation R. Thus, a nonfuzzy nondeterministic Turing machine may be regarded as a special case of a fuzzy Turing machine in which $\mu_R(q^{n+1}, q^n, u^n)$ can take only two values, 1 or 0, according as (q^{n+1}, q^n, u^n) does or does not belong to R. From a more general point of view, a fuzzy Turing machine may be regarded as a special case of a fuzzy system (Zadeh, 1965).

In short, an algorithm corresponds to a Turing machine, a nondeterministic algorithm corresponds to a nondeterministic Turing machine, and a fuzzy algorithm corresponds to a fuzzy Turing machine. It should be noted, however, that the identification of an algorithm with a Turing machine restricts the applicability of the notion of an algorithm, whether fuzzy or not, to those situations in which the variables entering into the algorithm range over finite, or, at most, countable sets. Actually, it is common practice to use the term "algorithm" in a broader and more loose sense to describe recursive procedures in which the variables may range over continua, e.g., the simplex algorithm of linear programming, rather than just finite or countable sets. In this sense, an algorithm is a fuzzy algorithm when its variables range over fuzzy sets, regardless of whether they are finite sets or continua.

IV. RATIONALE FOR FUZZY ALGORITHMS

It is a truism that precision is respectable and fuzziness is not. However, in our quest for ever greater degree of precision in pure and applied science, we have perhaps tended to lose sight of one basic fact, namely, that the class of nontrivial problems for which one can find precise algorithmic solutions is quite limited. Unfortunately, most realistic problems tend to be complex, and many complex problems are either algorithmically unsolvable or, if solvable in principle, are computationally infeasible. For example, it is well known that, in principle, there is an optimal strategy for playing chess. In reality, however, it is completely beyond the capability of any conceivable computer to trace the decision tree of all possible moves and, using backward or forward iteration, decide on the best move at each stage of the game. Thus in chess, as in many other complex situations, fuzzy local goals must be substituted for the precisely specified terminal objective, and what on the surface appears to be a precise problem turns out to be a very fuzzy one.

Another illustration of a situation in which complexity rules out a precise algorithmic solution is provided by a problem drawn from everyday experience, namely, the problem of parking a car C in a space available between two cars parked at a curb.

A control theorist would formulate this problem as follows: Let w denote the position of a fixed reference point in C (e.g., the center of a rectangle which approximates to C) and let θ denote the orientation of C. Then the state of C can be identified with the vector $x = (w, \theta)$ and the differential equation of motion of C can be expressed in the form

$$\dot{x} = f(x, u) \tag{4}$$

where the control vector u is assumed to have two components, u_1 and u_2, representing respectively the angle of the front wheels and the speed of C. u_1 is a bounded variable and u_2 is assumed for simplicity to be capable of taking only three values α (in the forward direction), β (in the reverse direction), and zero.

The space available between the two cars defines a set of allowable terminal states Γ, and the two cars define a constraint set Ω from which x is excluded. The problem of parking the car, then, may be regarded as that of finding a strategy $u(x)$ for transferring a specified initial state x^0 into Γ subject to the prescribed constraints on u and x.

When formulated in this precise form, the problem in question is too complex for solution even with the aid of large scale computers. Thus, for all practical purposes, the stated problem does not have a precise algorithmic solution. On the other hand, we know that by following a set of instructions of the type one gets in a driving school (instructions which may be regarded as a crude form of a fuzzy algorithm) an inexperienced driver can park his car in the available space without having precise information concerning the differential equation characterizing C, the constraint set Ω or the set of allowable terminal states Γ. Thus, by treating the parking problem as a fuzzy rather than a precise problem, one can formulate a fuzzy algorithm for solving it.

The crux of such an algorithm is the observation that the reference point w in C can be transferred in a lateral direction by performing the following maneuver: First, while the car is moving forward, the wheels are turned to the right and then to the left; and second, the direction of motion is reversed and the wheels are turned first to the right and then to the left. By repeating this maneuver as many times as necessary, C can be moved in a lateral direction by any desired amount.

If we were not familiar with how to park a car, the finding of a fuzzy algorithm for solving the problem would not be entirely trivial. The development of systematic procedures for finding fuzzy algorithms and the recognition that in many realistic problems it is not practicable to search for nonfuzzy algorithms may in time confer upon fuzzy algorithms the respectability which they lack at present.

It should be noted that, in order to lead to a fuzzy solution of a problem such as that of parking a car, a fuzzy algorithm must be robust in the sense that its success should not depend on the knowledge of the precise meaning of its instructions, that is, on the precise specification of the membership functions of the fuzzy sets entering into such instructions. Indeed, the property of robustness in the above sense constitutes an essential characteristic of a fuzzy algorithm.

It is of interest to note that, in addition to providing a possible way of approaching complex control problems, fuzzy algorithms might be useful in defining fuzzy sets of objects such as, for example, the class of handwritten versions of the script letter $\mathcal{A}$ or the cardiograms associated with a particular disease of the heart. In such cases, the algorithm would serve as a fuzzy algorithmic definition of a fuzzy set of objects, just as the differential equation $\ddot{x} + w^2x = 0$ serves as a nonfuzzy algorithmic definition of the nonfuzzy class of sine waves of the form $a \cos (wt + \theta)$, where a and θ range over scalars.

What is the relationship between a fuzzy algorithm and a heuristic program? In effect, a heuristic program is a nonfuzzy approximation, expressed in a computer language, to a fuzzy algorithm. We have to employ such programs in implementing a fuzzy algorithm on a computer because present day computers cannot operate on fuzzy sets. It would be an advance of vast importance when we learn how to design machines that can understand fuzzy concepts in much the same way as human beings are capable of doing.

What we have said here about fuzzy algorithms is very preliminary in nature. Although it may be premature to say so at this juncture, this writer believes that the domain of applicability of systematic reasoning might be enlarged by the acceptance of fuzzy algorithmic solutions to both precise and imprecise problems. Clearly, there are many obvious questions about fuzzy algorithms that we have not posed, much less attempted to answer in this note. It is possible to prove theorems about fuzzy algorithms. But the real challenge is to discover those, possibly fuzzy, properties of such algorithms which do not depend on the precise specification of the fuzzy sets which enter into their fuzzy instructions, nor on the precise manner in which such instructions should be executed.

RECEIVED: January 22, 1968.

REFERENCES

AIZERMAN, M. A., GUSEV, L. A., ROZONOER, L. I., SMIRNOVA, I. M., AND TAL, A. A., (1963). "Logic, Automata and Algorithms," Fizmatgiz, Moscow.

FLOYD, R. W., (1967). Nondeterministic Algorithms, *J. Assoc. Comp. Mach.* **14,** 636–644.

GOGUEN, J. A., (1967). *L*-Fuzzy Sets. *J. Math. Anal. Appl.* **18,** 145–174.

KORFHAGE, R. R., (1966). "Logic and Algorithms," Wiley, New York.

ZADEH, L. A., (1965), Fuzzy Sets, *Inform. Control* **8,** 338–353.

ZADEH, L. A., (1965). Fuzzy Sets and Systems, *Proc. Symp. System Theory,* Polytechnic Institute of Brooklyn, 29–37.

ZADEH, L. A., (1966). Shadows of Fuzzy Sets, *Probl. Trans. Information,* **2,** 37–44.

Note on Fuzzy Languages†

E. T. LEE

AND L. A. ZADEH
Department of Electrical Engineering and Computer Sciences
University of California, Berkeley, California

ABSTRACT

A fuzzy language is defined to be a fuzzy subset of the set of strings over a finite alphabet. The notions of union, intersection, concatenation, Kleene closure, and grammar for such languages are defined as extensions of the corresponding notions in the theory of formal languages. An explicit expression for the membership function of the language $L(G)$ generated by a fuzzy grammar G is given, and it is shown that any context-sensitive fuzzy grammar is recursive. For fuzzy context-free grammars, procedures for constructing the Chomsky and Greibach normal forms are outlined and illustrated by examples.

1. INTRODUCTION

The precision of formal languages contrasts rather sharply with the imprecision of natural languages. To reduce the gap between them, it is natural to introduce randomness into the structure of formal languages, thus leading to the concept of stochastic languages [1–3]. Another possibility lies in the introduction of fuzziness. This leads to what might be called *fuzzy languages*.

It appears that much of the existing theory of formal languages can be extended quite readily to fuzzy languages. In this preliminary note, we shall merely sketch how this can be done for a few basic concepts and results. More detailed exposition of the theory of fuzzy languages will be presented in subsequent papers.

Our notation, terminology, and reasoning parallel closely the presentation of the theory of formal languages in Hopcroft and Ullman [4].

† This work was supported in part by the Army Research Office, Durham, DAHCO-4-69-0024.

Reprinted, with permission, from *Information Sciences*, 1(4), pp. 421–434.

2. BASIC DEFINITIONS

As usual, we denote by V_T a set of terminals; by V_N a set of non-terminals, with $V_T \cap V_N = \phi$; by $V_T{}^*$ the set of finite strings composed of elements of V_T; and by $(V_T \cup V_N)^*$ the set of finite strings composed of the elements of V_T or V_N. A generic string in $V_T{}^*$ is denoted by x or, more generally, by a lowercase letter near the end of the Latin alphabet.

Fuzzy language

A *fuzzy language*, L, is a fuzzy set† in $V_T{}^*$. Thus, L is a set of ordered pairs

$$L = \{(x, \mu_L(x))\}, \qquad x \in V_T{}^*, \tag{1}$$

where $\mu_L(x)$ is the grade of membership of x in L. We assume that $\mu_L(x)$ is a number in the interval [0, 1].

A trivial example of a fuzzy language is the fuzzy set

$$L = \{(0, 1.0), (1, 1.0), (00, 0.8), (01, 0.7), (10, 0.6), (11, 0.5)\}$$

in $(0, 1)^*$. It is understood that all strings in $(0, 1)^*$ other than those listed have the grade of membership 0 in L.

Union, intersection, concatenation, and Kleene closure

Let L_1 and L_2 be two fuzzy languages in $V_T{}^*$. The *union* of L_1 and L_2 is a fuzzy language denoted by $L_1 + L_2$ and defined by

$$\mu_{L_1+L_2}(x) = \max(\mu_{L_1}(x), \mu_{L_2}(x)), \qquad x \in V_T{}^*. \tag{2}$$

In effect, $L_1 + L_2$ is the union of the fuzzy sets L_1 and L_2. Employing $\vee$ as an infix operator instead of max and omitting the argument x, we can write (2) more simply as

$$\mu_{L_1+L_2} = \mu_{L_1} \vee \mu_{L_2}. \tag{3}$$

The *intersection* of L_1 and L_2 is a fuzzy language denoted by $L_1 \cap L_2$ and defined by

$$\mu_{L_1 \cap L_2}(x) = \min(\mu_{L_1}(x), \mu_{L_2}(x)), \qquad x \in V_T{}^*, \tag{4}$$

† Intuitively, a fuzzy set is a class with unsharp boundaries, that is, a class in which the transition from membership to non-membership may be gradual rather than abrupt. More concretely, a fuzzy set A in a space $X = \{x\}$ is a set of ordered pairs $\{(x, \mu_A(x))\}$, where $\mu_A(x)$ is termed the *grade of membership* of x in A. (See [5] and [6] for more detailed discussion.) We shall assume that $\mu_A(x)$ is a number in the interval [0, 1]; more generally, it can be a point in a lattice [7, 8]. The *union* of two fuzzy sets A and B is defined by $\mu_{A \cup B}(x) = \max(\mu_A(x), \mu_B(x))$. The *intersection* of A and B is defined by $\mu_{A \cap B}(x) = \min(\mu_A(x), \mu_B(x))$. Containment is defined by $A \subset B \Leftrightarrow \mu_A(x) \leq \mu_B(x)$ for all x. Equality is defined by $A = B \Leftrightarrow \mu_A(x) = \mu_B(x)$ for all x.

or, employing $\wedge$ instead of min,

$$\mu_{L_1 \cap L_2} = \mu_{L_1} \wedge \mu_{L_2}. \tag{5}$$

The *concatenation* of L_1 and L_2 is a fuzzy language denoted by $L_1 L_2$ and defined as follows. Let a string x in $V_T{}^*$ be expressed as a concatenation of a prefix string u and a suffix string v, that is, $x = uv$. Then

$$\mu_{L_1 L_2}(x) = \sup_u \min(\mu_{L_1}(u), \mu_{L_2}(v)), \tag{6}$$

where the supremum is taken over all prefixes u of x. Using $\vee$ and $\wedge$ in place of sup and min, we may express (6) in the somewhat simpler form

$$\mu_{L_1 L_2}(x) = \bigvee_u (\mu_{L_1}(u) \wedge \mu_{L_2}(v)). \tag{7}$$

It is of interest to note that (7) takes on the appearance of a convolution when v is expressed as $x - u$, with $\vee$ corresponding to the sum (integral) and $\wedge$ to the product:

$$\mu_{L_1 L_2}(x) = \bigvee_u (\mu_{L_1}(u) \wedge \mu_{L_2}(x - u)).$$

Note also that (7) implies—by virtue of the distributivity of $\vee$ and $\wedge$—that concatenation has the associative property.

Having defined the union and concatenation, we can readily extend the notion of *Kleene closure* to fuzzy languages. Specifically, denoting the Kleene closure of L by L^*, we have as the definition of L^*,

$$L^* = \epsilon + L + LL + LLL + LLLL + \cdots, \tag{8}$$

where ϵ is the null string. Note that the meaning of the multiple concatenations LLL, LLLL, ... is unambiguous because of the associativity of concatenation.

Fuzzy grammar

Informally, a *fuzzy grammar* may be viewed as a set of rules for generating the elements of a fuzzy set.† More concretely, a *fuzzy grammar*, or simply a *grammar*, is a quadruple $G = (V_N, V_T, P, S)$ in which V_T is a set of terminals, V_N is a set of non-terminals ($V_T \cap V_N = \phi$), P is a set of fuzzy productions, and $S \in V_N$. Essentially, the elements of V_N are labels for certain fuzzy subsets of $V_T{}^*$ called *fuzzy syntactic categories*, with S being the label for the syntactic category "sentence." The elements of P define conditioned fuzzy sets‡ in $(V_T \cup V_N)^*$.

More specifically, the elements of P are expressions of the form

$$\mu(\alpha \to \beta) = \rho, \qquad \rho > 0, \tag{9}$$

where α and β are strings in $(V_T \cup V_N)^*$ and ρ is the grade of membership of

† Note that an element of a fuzzy set, L, is an ordered pair of the form $(x, \mu_A(x))$.

‡ A fuzzy set conditioned on α is a fuzzy set whose membership function depends on α as a parameter.

β given α. Where convenient, we shall abbreviate $\mu(\alpha \to \beta) = \rho$ to $\alpha \overset{\rho}{\to} \beta$ or, more simply, $\alpha \to \beta$.

As in the case of non-fuzzy grammars, the expression $\alpha \to \beta$ represents a rewriting rule. Thus, if $\alpha \overset{\rho}{\to} \beta$ and γ and δ are arbitrary strings in $(V_T \cup V_N)^*$, then

$$\gamma\alpha\delta \overset{\rho}{\to} \gamma\beta\delta \tag{10}$$

and $\gamma\beta\delta$ is said to be *directly derivable from* $\gamma\alpha\delta$.

If $\alpha_1, \ldots, \alpha_m$ are strings in $(V_T \cup V_N)^*$ and $\alpha_1 \overset{\rho_2}{\to} \alpha_2, \ldots, \alpha_{m-1} \overset{\rho_m}{\to} \alpha_m$, $\rho_2, \ldots, \rho_m > 0$, then α_1 is said to *derive* α_m in grammar G, or, equivalently, α_m is *derivable* from α_1 in grammar G. This is expressed by $\alpha_1 \underset{G}{\Rightarrow} \alpha_m$ or simply $\alpha_1 \Rightarrow \alpha_m$. The expression

$$\alpha_1 \overset{\rho_2}{\to} \alpha_2 \cdots \alpha_{m-1} \overset{\rho_m}{\to} \alpha_m \tag{11}$$

will be referred to as a *derivation chain from* α_1 *to* α_m.

A fuzzy grammar G generates a fuzzy language $L(G)$ in the following manner. A string of terminals x is said to be *in* $L(G)$ if and only if x is derivable from S. The grade of membership of x in $L(G)$ is given by

$$\mu_G(x) = \sup \min(\mu(S \to \alpha_1), \mu(\alpha_1 \to \alpha_2), \ldots, \mu(\alpha_m \to x)), \tag{12}$$

where $\mu_G(x)$ is an abbreviation for $\mu_{L(G)}(x)$ and the supremum is taken over all derivation chains from S to x. Thus, (12) defines $L(G)$ as a fuzzy set in $(V_T \cup V_N)^*$. If $L(G_1) = L(G_2)$ in the sense of equality of fuzzy sets, then the grammars G_1 and G_2 are said to be *equivalent*.

It is helpful to observe that if a production $\alpha \overset{\rho}{\to} \beta$ is visualized as a chain link of strength ρ, then the strength of a derivation chain $\alpha_1 \overset{\rho_2}{\to} \alpha_2 \cdots \overset{\rho_m}{\to} \alpha_m$ is the strength of its weakest link, that is $\min(\rho_2, \ldots, \rho_m)$. Then, the defining equation (12) may be expressed in words as:

$\mu_G(x)$ = grade of membership of x in the language generated by grammar G

= strength of the strongest derivation chain from S to x.

Let $\mu(S \to \alpha_1) = \rho_1$, $\mu(\alpha_1 \to \alpha_2) = \rho_2$, $\ldots$, $\mu(\alpha_m \to x) = \rho_{m+1}$. Then, on writing (12) in the form

$$\mu_G(x) = \vee(\rho_1 \wedge \rho_2 \cdots \wedge \rho_{m+1}) \tag{13}$$

it follows at once from the associativity of $\wedge$ that (12) is equivalent to a more general expression in which the successive α's are derivable from their immediate predecessors rather than *directly* derivable from them, as in (12).

Example. Suppose that $V_T = \{0,1\}$, $V_N = \{A,B,S\}$, and P is given by

$$\mu(S \to AB) = 0.5 \qquad \mu(A \to 0) = 0.5$$
$$\mu(S \to A) = 0.8 \qquad \mu(A \to 1) = 0.6$$
$$\mu(S \to B) = 0.8 \qquad \mu(B \to A) = 0.4$$
$$\mu(AB \to BA) = 0.4 \qquad \mu(B \to 0) = 0.2.$$

Consider the terminal string $x = 0$. The possible derivation chains for this string are $S \overset{0.8}{\to} A \overset{0.5}{\to} 0$, $S \overset{0.8}{\to} B \overset{0.2}{\to} 0$, and $S \overset{0.8}{\to} B \overset{0.4}{\to} A \overset{0.5}{\to} 0$. Hence

$$\mu_L(0) = \max(\min(0.8, 0.5),\ \min(0.8, 0.2),\ \min(0.8, 0.4, 0.5)) = 0.5.$$

Similarly, the possible derivation chains for the terminal string $x = 01$ are $S \overset{0.5}{\to} AB \overset{0.5}{\to} 0B \overset{0.4}{\to} 0A \overset{0.6}{\to} 01$, $S \overset{0.5}{\to} AB \overset{0.4}{\to} AA \overset{0.5}{\to} 0A \overset{0.6}{\to} 01$, $S \overset{0.5}{\to} AB \overset{0.4}{\to} BA \overset{0.2}{\to} 0A \overset{0.6}{\to} 01$, and $S \overset{0.5}{\to} AB \overset{0.4}{\to} BA \overset{0.4}{\to} AA \overset{0.5}{\to} 0A \overset{0.6}{\to} 01$. Hence,

$$\mu_G(01) = \max(0.4, 0.4, 0.2, 0.4) = 0.4.$$

Given a grammar G, an important question which arises in connection with the definition of $L(G)$ is whether or not there exists an algorithm for computing $\mu_G(x)$ by the use of the defining equation (12). If such an algorithm exists, then G is said to be *recursive*.

3. TYPES OF GRAMMARS

Paralleling the standard classification of non-fuzzy grammars, we can distinguish four principal types of fuzzy grammars.

Type 0 grammar

In this case, productions are of the general form $\alpha \overset{\rho}{\to} \beta$, $\rho > 0$, where α and β are strings in $(V_T \cup V_N)^*$.

Type 1 grammar (context-sensitive)

Here the productions are of the form $\alpha_1 A \alpha_2 \overset{\rho}{\to} \alpha_1 \beta \alpha_2$, $\rho > 0$, with α_1, α_2, and β in $(V_T \cup V_N)^*$, A in V_N, and $\beta \neq \epsilon$. In addition, the production $S \to \epsilon$ is allowed.

Type 2 grammar (context-free)

The allowable productions are of the form $A \overset{\rho}{\to} \beta$, $\rho > 0$, $A \in V_N$, $\beta \in (V_T \cup V_N)^*$, $\beta \neq \epsilon$, and $S \to \epsilon$.

Type 3 grammar (regular)

In this case the allowable productions are of the form $A \overset{\rho}{\to} aB$ or $A \overset{\rho}{\to} a$, $\rho > 0$, where $a \in V_T$, $A, B \in V_N$. In addition, $S \to \epsilon$ is allowed.

In what follows, we shall focus our attention on context-free grammars. However, there is one basic property of context-sensitive grammars that needs stating at this point. Specifically, in defining $L(G)$ we have mentioned that G is recursive if there exists an algorithm for computing $\mu_G(x)$. It is easy to demonstrate that context-sensitive—and hence also context-free and regular—grammars are recursive. This can be stated as an extension of Theorem 2.2 in Hopcroft and Ullman [4].

THEOREM. *If* $G = (V_N, V_T, P, S)$ *is a fuzzy context-sensitive grammar, then* G *is recursive.*

Proof. First we show that for any type of grammar the supremum in (12) may be taken over a subset of the set of all derivation chains from S to x, namely, the subset of all *loop-free* derivation chains. These are chains in which no α_i, $i = 1, \ldots, m$, occurs more than once.

For suppose that in a derivation chain C,

$$C = S \xrightarrow{\rho_1} \alpha_1 \xrightarrow{\rho_2} \alpha_2 \cdots \xrightarrow{\rho_m} \alpha_m \xrightarrow{\rho_{m+1}} x,$$

α_i, say, is the same as α_j, $j > i$. Now consider the chain C' resulting from replacing the subchain $\alpha_i \xrightarrow{\rho_{i+1}} \cdots \xrightarrow{\rho_j} \alpha_j \xrightarrow{\rho_{j+1}} \alpha_{j+1}$ in C by $\alpha_i \xrightarrow{\rho_{j+1}} \alpha_{j+1}$. Clearly, if C is a derivation chain from S to x, so is C'. But

$$\min(\rho_1, \ldots, \rho_i, \rho_{i+1}, \ldots, \rho_{j+1}, \ldots, \rho_{m+1}) \leqslant \min(\rho_1, \ldots, \rho_i, \rho_{j+1}, \ldots, \rho_{m+1})$$

and hence C may be deleted without affecting the supremum in (12). Consequently, we can replace the definition (12) for $\mu_L(x)$ by

$$\mu_G(x) = \sup \min(\mu(S \to \alpha_1), \mu(\alpha_1 \to \alpha_2), \ldots, \mu(\alpha_m \to x)), \tag{14}$$

where the supremum is taken over all loop-free derivation chains from S to x.

Next we show that for context-sensitive grammars the set over which the supremum is taken in (14) can be further restricted to derivation chains of bounded length l_0, where l_0 depends on $|x|$ (length of x) and the number of symbols in $V_T \cup V_N$.

Specifically, if G is context-sensitive, then because of the non-contracting character of productions in P, we have

$$|\alpha_j| \geqslant |\alpha_i| \qquad \text{if } j > i. \tag{15}$$

Now let k be the number of symbols in $V_T \cup V_N$. Since there are at most k^l distinct strings in $(V_T \cup V_N)^*$ of length l, and since the derivation chain is loop-free, (15) implies that the total length of the chain is bounded by

$$l_0 = 1 + k + \cdots + k^{|x|}.$$

To complete the proof, we have to exhibit a way for generating all finite derivation chains from S to x of length $\leqslant l_0$. For this purpose, we start with S

and using P generate the set Q_1 of all strings in $(V_T \cup V_N)^*$ of length $\leqslant |x|$ which are derivable from S in one step (that is, are directly derivable from S). Then, we construct Q_2—the set of all strings in $(V_T \cup V_N)^*$ of length $\leqslant |x|$ which are derivable from S in two steps—by noting that Q_2 is identical with the set of all strings in $(V_T \cup V_N)^*$ of length $\leqslant |x|$ which are directly derivable from strings in Q_1. Continuing this process, we construct consecutively Q_3, $Q_4, \ldots, Q_r$ until $r = l_0$ or $Q_r = \phi$, whichever happens first. Since the Q_λ, $\lambda = 1, \ldots, r$, are finite sets, their knowledge enables us to find in a finite number of steps all loop-free derivation chains from S to x of length $\leqslant l_0$ and thus to compute $\mu_G(x)$ by the use of (14). This, then, constitutes an algorithm—though not necessarily an efficient one—for the computation of $\mu_G(x)$. Consequently, G is recursive.

4. FUZZY CONTEXT-FREE GRAMMARS

As was stated in the introduction, many of the basic results in the theory of formal languages can readily be extended to fuzzy languages. As an illustration, we shall sketch—without giving proofs—such extensions in the case of the Chomsky and Greibach normal forms for context-free languages.

Chomsky normal form for fuzzy context-free languages

Let G be a fuzzy context-free grammar. Then, any such grammar is equivalent to a grammar G_c in which all productions are of the form $A \xrightarrow{\rho} BC$ or $A \xrightarrow{\rho} a$, where $\rho > 0$; A, B, C are non-terminals, and a is a terminal.

It is convenient to effect the construction of G_c in three stages, as follows.

First, we construct a grammar G_1 equivalent to G in which there are no productions of the form $A \to B$, $A, B \in V_N$.

Thus, suppose that in G we have productions of the form $A \to B$, which lead to derivation chains of the form

$$A \xrightarrow{\rho_1} B_1 \xrightarrow{\rho_2} B_2 \cdots B_m \xrightarrow{\rho_{m+1}} B \xrightarrow{\rho_{m+2}} \alpha,$$

where $\alpha \notin V_N$. Then we replace all such productions: $A \xrightarrow{\rho_1} B_1$, $B_1 \xrightarrow{\rho_2} B_2, \ldots,$ $B_m \xrightarrow{\rho_{m+1}} B$ in G by single productions of the form $A \xrightarrow{\rho} \alpha$, in which

$$\rho = \min(\mu(A \Rightarrow B), \mu(B \to \alpha)) \tag{16}$$

where

$$\mu(A \Rightarrow B) = \sup \min(\mu(A \to B_1), \ldots, \mu(B_m \to B)) \tag{17}$$

with the supremum taken over all loop-free derivation chains from A to B. It can readily be shown that the resultant grammar, G_1, is equivalent to G.

Second, we construct a grammar G_2 equivalent to G_1 in which there are no productions of the form $A \xrightarrow{\rho} B_1 B_2 \cdots B_m$, $\rho > 0$, $m > 2$, in which one or more of the B's are terminals. Thus, suppose that B_i, say, is a terminal a. Then B_i in $B_1 B_2 \cdots B_m$ is replaced by a new non-terminal C_i which does not appear on the right-hand side of any other production, and we set

$$\mu(A \to B_1 B_2 \cdots B_i \cdots B_m) = \mu(A \to B_1 B_2 \cdots C_i \cdots B_m) \tag{18}$$

Furthermore, we add to the productions of G the production $C_i \xrightarrow{1} a$. On doing this for all terminals in $B_1 \cdots B_m$ in all productions of the form $A \to B_1 \cdots B_m$, we arrive at a grammar G_2 in which all productions are of the form $A \to a$ or $A \to B_1 \cdots B_m$, $m \geqslant 2$, where all the B's are non-terminals. It is evident that G_2 is equivalent to G_1.

Third, we construct a grammar G_3 equivalent to G_2 in which all productions are of the form $A \to a$ or $A \to BC$, $A,B,C \in V_N$, $a \in V_T$. To this end, consider a typical production in G_2 of the form $A \xrightarrow{\rho} B_1 \cdots B_m$, $\rho > 0$, $m > 2$. Replace this production by the productions

$$\begin{aligned} A &\xrightarrow{\rho} B_1 D_1 \\ D_1 &\xrightarrow{1} B_2 D_2 \\ D_{m-2} &\xrightarrow{1} B_{m-1} B_m, \end{aligned} \tag{19}$$

where the D's are new non-terminals which do not appear on the right-hand side of any production in G_2. On performing such replacements for all productions in G_2 of the form $A \xrightarrow{\rho} B_1 \cdots B_m$, we obtain a grammar G_3 which is equivalent to G_2. This establishes that G_3—which is in Chomsky normal form—is equivalent to G.

Example. Consider the following fuzzy grammar in which $V_T = \{a, b\}$ and $V_n = \{A, B, S\}$.

$$\begin{array}{ll} S \xrightarrow{0.8} bA & B \xrightarrow{0.4} b \\ S \xrightarrow{0.6} aB & A \xrightarrow{0.3} bSA \\ A \xrightarrow{0.2} a & B \xrightarrow{0.5} aSB. \end{array}$$

To find the equivalent grammar in Chomsky normal form, we proceed as follows.

First, $S \xrightarrow{0.8} bA$ is replaced by $S \xrightarrow{0.8} C_1 A$, $C_1 \xrightarrow{1} b$. Similarly, $S \xrightarrow{0.6} aB$ is replaced by $S \xrightarrow{0.6} C_2 B$ and $C_2 \xrightarrow{1} a$. Also $A \xrightarrow{0.3} bSA$ is replaced by $A \xrightarrow{0.3} C_3 SA$, $C_3 \xrightarrow{1} b$; $B \xrightarrow{0.5} aSB$ is replaced by $B \xrightarrow{0.5} C_4 SB$ and $C_4 \xrightarrow{1} a$.

Second, the production $A \xrightarrow{0.3} C_3 SA$ is replaced by $A \xrightarrow{0.3} C_3 D_1$, $D_1 \xrightarrow{1} SA$; and the production $B \xrightarrow{0.5} C_4 SB$ is replaced by $B \xrightarrow{0.5} C_4 D_2$, $D_2 \xrightarrow{1} SB$. Thus, the productions in the equivalent Chomsky normal form read:

$$
\begin{array}{ll}
S \xrightarrow{0.8} C_1 A & A \xrightarrow{0.3} C_3 D_1 \\
C_1 \xrightarrow{1} b & D_1 \xrightarrow{1} SA \\
S \xrightarrow{0.6} C_2 B & C_3 \xrightarrow{1} b \\
C_2 \xrightarrow{1} a & B \xrightarrow{0.5} C_4 D_2 \\
A \xrightarrow{0.2} a & D_2 \xrightarrow{1} SB \\
B \xrightarrow{0.4} b & C_4 \xrightarrow{1} a.
\end{array}
$$

Greibach normal form

As in the case of the Chomsky normal form, let G be any fuzzy context-free grammar. Then G is equivalent to a fuzzy grammar G_G in which all productions are of the form $A \to a\alpha$, where A is a non-terminal, a is a terminal and α is a string in V_N^*. The fuzzy grammar G_G is in *Greibach normal form.*

Paralleling the approach used in Ullman and Hopcroft, it is convenient to state two lemmas which are of use in constructing G_G. We shall omit proofs of these lemmas since their validity is reasonably evident and their detailed proofs fairly long.

LEMMA 1. *Let G be a fuzzy context-free grammar. Let $A \to \alpha_1 B \alpha_2$ be a production in P, $A, B \in V_N$, and $\alpha_1, \alpha_2 \in (V_T \cup V_N)^*$. Furthermore, let $B \to \beta_1, \ldots, B \to \beta_r$ be the set of all B-productions (that is, all productions with B on the left-hand side). Let G_1 be the grammar resulting from the replacement of each of the productions of the form $A \to \alpha_1 B \alpha_2$ with the productions $A \to \alpha_1 \beta_1 \alpha_2, \ldots, A \to \alpha_1 \beta_r \alpha_2$, in which*

$$\mu(A \to \alpha_1 \beta_i \alpha_2) = \min(\mu(A \to \alpha_1 B\alpha_2), \mu(B \to \beta_i)), \qquad i = 1, \ldots, r. \quad (20)$$

Then G_1 is equivalent to G.

LEMMA 2. *Let G be a fuzzy context-free grammar. Let $A \to A\alpha_i$, $i = 1, \ldots, r$, be the set of A-productions for which A is also the leftmost symbol on the right-hand side. Furthermore, let $A \to \beta_j$, $j = 1, \ldots, s$ be the remaining A-productions,* *with $\alpha_i, \beta_j \in (V_T \cup V_N)^*$, $i = 1, \ldots, r, j = 1, \ldots, s$. Let G_2 be the grammar resulting from the replacement of the $A \to A\alpha_i$ in G with the productions:*

$$A \to \beta_j Z, \qquad j = 1, \ldots, s \tag{21}$$

$$Z \to \alpha_i, Z \to \alpha_i Z, \qquad i = 1, \ldots, r, \tag{22}$$

where

$$\begin{aligned} \mu(A \to \beta_j Z) &= \mu(A \to \beta_j), \qquad i = 1, \ldots, r \\ \mu(Z \to \alpha_i) &= \mu(A \to A\alpha_i) \\ \mu(Z \to \alpha_i Z) &= \mu(A \to A\alpha_i). \end{aligned} \tag{23}$$

Making use of these lemmas, the Greibach normal form for G can be derived as follows.

First, G is put into the Chomsky normal form. Let the non-terminals in this form be denoted by $A_1, \ldots, A_m$.

Second, the productions of the form $A_i \to A_j\gamma$, $\gamma \in (V_T \cup V_N)^*$, are modified in such a way that for all such productions $j \geqslant i$. This is done in stages. Thus, suppose that it has been done for $i \leqslant k$, that is, if

$$A_i \to A_j \gamma \tag{24}$$

is a production with $i \leqslant k$, then $j > i$. To extend this to A_{k+1}-productions suppose that $A_{k+1} \to A_j\gamma$ is any production with $j < k + 1$. Using Lemma 1 and substituting for A_j the right-hand side of each A_j-production, we obtain by repeated substitution productions of the form

$$A_{k+1} \to A_l \gamma, \qquad l \geqslant k + 1. \tag{25}$$

In (25), those productions in which l is equal to $k + 1$ are replaced by the application of Lemma 2, resulting in a new non-terminal Z_{k+1}. Then, by repetition of this process all productions are put into the form

$$A_k \to A_l \gamma, \qquad l > k, \gamma \in (V_N \cup \{Z_1, \ldots, Z_n\})^* \tag{26}$$

$$A_k \to a\gamma, \qquad a \in V_T \tag{27}$$

$$Z_k \to \gamma \tag{28}$$

with membership grades given by Lemmas 1 and 2.

In view of (26) and (27), the leftmost symbol on the right-hand side of any production for A_m must be a terminal. Similarly, for A_{m-1}, the leftmost symbol on the right-hand side must be either A_m or a terminal. Substituting for A_m by Lemma 1, we obtain productions whose right-hand sides start with terminals. Repeating this process for $A_{m-2}, \ldots, A_1$, we eventually put all productions for the A_i, $i = 1, \ldots, m$, into a form where their right-hand sides start with terminals.

At this stage, only the productions in (28) may not be in the desired form.

We observe that the leftmost symbol in γ in (28) may be either a terminal or one of the A_i, $i = 1, \ldots, m$. If it is the latter, application of Lemma 1 to each Z_i production results in productions of the desired form and thus completes the construction.

Example. As a simple illustration, we shall convert into the Greibach normal form a fuzzy grammar G in which $V_T = \{a, b\}$, $V_N = \{A_1, A_2, A_3\}$ and the productions are in the Chomsky normal form:

$$A_1 \xrightarrow{0.8} A_2 A_3 \qquad A_3 \xrightarrow{0.2} A_1 A_2$$
$$A_2 \xrightarrow{0.7} A_3 A_1 \qquad A_3 \xrightarrow{0.5} a.$$
$$A_2 \xrightarrow{0.6} b$$

Step 1. Since the right-hand sides of the productions for A_1 and A_2 start with terminals or higher-numbered variables, we begin with the production $A_3 \rightarrow A_1 A_2$ and substitute $A_2 A_3$ for A_1. Note that $A_1 \rightarrow A_2 A_3$ is the only production with A_1 on the left.

The resulting set of productions is

$$A_1 \xrightarrow{0.8} A_2 A_3 \qquad A_2 \xrightarrow{0.7} A_3 A_1$$
$$A_2 \xrightarrow{0.6} b \qquad A_3 \xrightarrow{0.2} A_2 A_3 A_2$$
$$A_3 \xrightarrow{0.5} a$$

Note that in $A_3 \xrightarrow{0.2} A_2 A_3 A_2$, 0.2 is $0.8 \wedge 0.2$.

Since the right-hand side of the production $A_3 \rightarrow A_2 A_3 A_2$ begins with a lower-numbered variable, we substitute for the first occurrence of A_2 either $A_3 A_1$ or b.

The new set is

$$A_1 \xrightarrow{0.8} A_2 A_3 \qquad A_2 \xrightarrow{0.7} A_3 A_1$$
$$A_2 \xrightarrow{0.6} b \qquad A_3 \xrightarrow{0.2} A_3 A_1 A_3 A_2.$$
$$A_3 \xrightarrow{0.2} b A_3 A_2 \qquad A_3 \xrightarrow{0.5} a$$

We now apply Lemma 2 to the productions $A_1 \rightarrow A_3 A_1 A_3 A_2$, $A_3 \rightarrow b A_3 A_2$, and $A_3 \rightarrow a$. We introduce Z_3 and replace the production $A_3 \rightarrow A_3 A_1 A_3 A_2$ by $A_3 \rightarrow b A_3 A_2 Z_3$, $A_3 \rightarrow a Z_3$, $Z_3 \rightarrow A_1 A_3 A_2$, and $Z_3 \rightarrow A_1 A_3 A_2 Z_3$.

The resulting set is

$$A_1 \overset{0.8}{\rightarrow} A_2 A_3 \qquad A_2 \overset{0.7}{\rightarrow} A_3 A_1 \qquad A_3 \overset{0.2}{\rightarrow} bA_3 A_2 Z_3.$$

$$A_2 \overset{0.6}{\rightarrow} b \qquad A_3 \overset{0.2}{\rightarrow} bA_3 A_2$$

$$A_3 \overset{0.5}{\rightarrow} a \qquad A_3 \overset{0.5}{\rightarrow} aZ_3$$

$$Z_3 \overset{0.2}{\rightarrow} A_1 A_3 A_2 Z_3 \qquad Z_3 \overset{0.2}{\rightarrow} A_1 A_3 A_2$$

Step 2. Now all productions with A_3 on the left have right-hand sides that start with terminals. These are used to replace A_3 in the production $A_2 \rightarrow A_3 A_1$ and then the productions with A_2 on the left are used to replace A_2 in the production $A_1 \rightarrow A_2 A_3$. The resulting set is

$$A_3 \overset{0.2}{\rightarrow} bA_3 A_2 \qquad A_3 \overset{0.2}{\rightarrow} bA_3 A_2 Z_3$$

$$A_3 \overset{0.5}{\rightarrow} a \qquad A_3 \overset{0.5}{\rightarrow} aZ_3$$

$$A_2 \overset{0.2}{\rightarrow} bA_3 A_2 A_1 \qquad A_2 \overset{0.2}{\rightarrow} bA_3 A_2 Z_3 A_1$$

$$A_2 \overset{0.5}{\rightarrow} aA_1 \qquad A_2 \overset{0.5}{\rightarrow} aZ_3 A_1$$

$$A_2 \overset{0.6}{\rightarrow} b \qquad A_1 \overset{0.2}{\rightarrow} bA_3 A_2 A_1 A_3$$

$$A_1 \overset{0.2}{\rightarrow} bA_3 A_2 Z_3 A_1 A_3 \qquad A_1 \overset{0.5}{\rightarrow} aA_1 A_3$$

$$A_1 \overset{0.6}{\rightarrow} bA_3 \qquad Z_3 \overset{0.2}{\rightarrow} A_1 A_3 A_2 Z_3.$$

$$Z_3 \overset{0.2}{\rightarrow} A_1 A_3 A_2$$

Note that in $A_2 \overset{0.2}{\rightarrow} bA_3 A_2 A_1$, 0.2 is $0.7 \wedge 0.2$. Likewise, in $A_1 \overset{0.5}{\rightarrow} aA_1 A_3$, 0.5 is $0.5 \wedge 0.8$. The same holds for the way in which the membership grades of other productions are determined (by the use of Lemmas 1 and 2).

Step 3. The two Z_3 productions, $Z_3 \overset{0.2}{\rightarrow} A_1 A_3 A_2$ and $Z_3 \overset{0.2}{\rightarrow} A_1 A_3 A_2 Z_3$, are converted to desired form by substituting the right-hand side of each of the five productions with A_1 on the left for the first occurrence of A_1. Thus, $Z_3 \overset{0.2}{\rightarrow} A_1 A_3 A_2$ is replaced by

$$Z_3 \overset{0.2}{\rightarrow} bA_3 A_3 A_2 \qquad Z_3 \overset{0.2}{\rightarrow} bA_3 A_2 A_1 A_3 A_3 A_2$$

$$Z_3 \overset{0.2}{\rightarrow} aA_1 A_3 A_3 A_2 \qquad Z_3 \overset{0.2}{\rightarrow} bA_3 A_2 Z_3 A_1 A_3 A_3 A_2.$$

$$Z_3 \overset{0.2}{\rightarrow} aZ_3 A_1 A_3 A_3 A_2$$

The other production for Z_3 is converted similarly. The final set of productions reads

$$A_3 \overset{0.2}{\rightarrow} bA_3A_2 \qquad A_3 \overset{0.2}{\rightarrow} bA_3A_2Z_3$$

$$A_3 \overset{0.5}{\rightarrow} a \qquad A_3 \overset{0.5}{\rightarrow} aZ_3$$

$$A_2 \overset{0.2}{\rightarrow} bA_3A_2A_1 \qquad A_2 \overset{0.2}{\rightarrow} bA_3A_2Z_3A_1$$

$$A_2 \overset{0.5}{\rightarrow} aA_1 \qquad A_2 \overset{0.5}{\rightarrow} aZ_3A_1$$

$$A_2 \overset{0.6}{\rightarrow} a \qquad A_1 \overset{0.2}{\rightarrow} bA_3A_2A_1A_3$$

$$A_1 \overset{0.2}{\rightarrow} bA_3A_2Z_3A_1A_3 \qquad A_1 \overset{0.5}{\rightarrow} aA_1A_3$$

$$A_1 \overset{0.5}{\rightarrow} aZ_3A_1A_3 \qquad A_1 \overset{0.6}{\rightarrow} bA_3$$

$$Z_3 \overset{0.2}{\rightarrow} bA_3A_3A_2 \qquad Z_3 \overset{0.2}{\rightarrow} bA_3A_3A_2Z_3$$

$$Z_3 \overset{0.2}{\rightarrow} bA_3A_2A_1A_3A_3A_2 \qquad Z_3 \overset{0.2}{\rightarrow} bA_3A_2A_1A_3A_3A_2Z_3$$

$$Z_3 \overset{0.2}{\rightarrow} aA_1A_3A_3A_2 \qquad Z_3 \overset{0.2}{\rightarrow} aA_1A_3A_3A_2Z_3$$

$$Z_3 \overset{0.2}{\rightarrow} bA_3A_2Z_3A_1A_3A_3A_2 \qquad Z_3 \overset{0.2}{\rightarrow} bA_3A_2Z_3A_1A_3A_3A_2Z_3$$

$$Z_3 \overset{0.2}{\rightarrow} aZ_3A_1A_3A_3A_2 \qquad Z_3 \overset{0.2}{\rightarrow} aZ_3A_1A_3A_3A_2Z_3.$$

This concludes our brief description of the construction of the Chomsky and Greibach normal forms for a fuzzy context-free grammar.

As was stated in the introduction, the purpose of the present note is merely to illustrate by a few examples how some of the basic concepts and results in the theory of formal languages can be extended to fuzzy languages. As the reader can see, the extensions are, for the most part, quite straightforward and require hardly any modifications in the statements of lemmas and theorems. The proofs, however, are generally somewhat longer since they involve not just the positivity of membership functions but their values in the interval [0, 1].

The theory of fuzzy languages offers what appears to be a fertile field for further study. It may prove to be of relevance in the construction of better models for natural languages and may contribute to a better understanding of the role of fuzzy algorithms and fuzzy automata in decision making, pattern recognition, and other processes involving the manipulation of fuzzy data.

REFERENCES

1 P. Turakainen, On stochastic languages, *Information and Control*, **12** (April 1968), 304–313.
2 M. M. Kherts, Entropy of languages generated by automated or context-free grammars with a single-valued deduction, *Nauchno-Tekhnicheskaya Informatsya*, Ser. 2, No. 1 (1968).
3 K. S. Fu and T. J. Li, On stochastic automata and languages, *3rd Conference on Information and System Sciences, Princeton University*, 1969, pp. 338–377.
4 J. E. Hopcroft and J. D. Ullman, *Formal Languages and Their Relation to Automata*, Addison-Wesley, Reading, Mass., 1969.
5 L. A. Zadeh, Fuzzy sets, *Information and Control*, **8** (June 1965), 338–353.
6 L. A. Zadeh, Toward a Theory of Fuzzy Systems, *ERL Rept.* No. 69-2, *Electronics Research Laboratories, University of California*, Berkeley, June 1969.
7 J. Goguen, L-fuzzy sets, *J. Math. Anal. Appl.*, **18** (April 1967), 145–174.
8 J. G. Brown, Fuzzy sets on Boolean lattices, *Rept.* No. 1957, *Ballistic Research Laboratories*, Aberdeen, Md., Jan. 1969.

Received August 11, 1969

Toward a Theory of Fuzzy Systems

L. A. Zadeh

INTRODUCTION

Many of the advances in network theory and system theory during the past three decades are traceable to the influence and contributions of Ernst Guillemin, Norbert Wiener, Richard Bellman, Rudolph Kalman, and their students. In sum, we now possess an impressive armanentarium of techniques for the analysis and synthesis of linear and nonlinear systems of various types—techniques that are particularly effective in dealing with systems characterized by ordinary differential or difference equations of moderately high order such as those encountered in network theory, control theory, and related fields.

What we still lack, and lack rather acutely, are methods for dealing with systems which are too complex or too ill-defined to admit of precise analysis. Such systems pervade life sciences, social sciences, philosophy, economics, phychology and many other "soft" fields. Furthermore, they are encountered in what are normally regarded as "nonsoft" fields when the complexity of a system rules out the possibility of analyzing it by

NOTE: This work was supported in part by the National Aeronautics and Space Administration under Grant NsG-354(S-5), and while the author was on leave as Guggenheim Fellow and Visiting Professor of Electrical Engineering, Project MAC, Massachusetts Institute of Technology, Cambridge, Mass.

Reprinted, with permission, from *Aspects of Networks and Systems Theory*, edited by R. E. Kalman and R. N. De Claris, pp. 469–490.

conventional mathematical means, whether with or without the aid of computers. Many examples of such systems are found among large-scale traffic control systems, pattern-recognition systems, machine translators, large-scale information-processing systems, large-scale power-distribution networks, neural networks, and games such as chess and checkers.

Perhaps the major reason for the ineffectiveness of classical mathematical techniques in dealing with systems of high order of complexity lies in their failure to come to grips with the issue of fuzziness, that is, with imprecision that stems not from randomness but from a lack of sharp transition from membership in a class to nonmembership in it. It is this type of imprecision that arises when one speaks, for example, of the class of real numbers much larger than 10, since the real numbers can not be divided dichotomously into those that are much larger than 10 and those that are not. The same applies to classes such as "tall men," "good strategies for playing chess," "pairs of numbers that are approximately equal to one another," "systems that are approximately linear," and so forth. Actually, most of the classes encountered in the real world are of this fuzzy, imprecisely defined kind. What sets such classes apart from classes that are well-defined in the conventional mathematical sense is the fuzziness of their boundaries. In effect, in the case of a class with a fuzzy boundary, an object may have a grade of membership in it that lies somewhere between full membership and nonmembership.

A class that admits of the possibility of partial membership in it is called a fuzzy set.[1] In this sense, the class of tall men, for example, is a fuzzy set, as is the class of real numbers that are much larger than 10. We make a *fuzzy statement* or assertion when some of the words appearing in the statement or assertion in question are names for fuzzy sets. This is true, for example, of such statements as "John is *tall*," "x is *approximately* equal to 5," "y is *much larger than* 10." In these statements, the sources of fuzziness are the italicized words, which, in effect, are labels for fuzzy sets.

Why is fuzziness so relevant to complexity? Because no matter what the nature of a system is, when its complexity exceeds a certain threshold it becomes impractical or computationally infeasible to make precise assertions about it. For example, in the case of chess the size of the decision tree is so large that it is impossible, in general, to find a precise algorithmic solution to the following problem: Given the position of pieces on the board, determine an optimal next move. Similarly, in the case of a large-scale traffic-control system, the complexity of the system precludes the possibility of precise evaluation of its performance. Thus, any significant assertion about the performance of such a system must necessarily be fuzzy in nature, with the degree of fuzziness increasing with the complexity of the system.

How can fuzziness be made a part of system theory? A tentative step in this direction was taken in recent papers[2],[3] in which the notions of a fuzzy system[1] and fuzzy algorithm were introduced. In what follows, we shall proceed somewhat further in this direction, focusing our attention on the definition of a fuzzy system and its state. It should be emphasized, however, that the task of constructing a complete theory of fuzzy systems is one of very considerable magnitude, and that what we shall have to say about fuzzy systems in the sequel is merely a first step toward devising a conceptual framework for dealing with such systems in both qualitative and quantitative ways.

ELEMENTARY PROPERTIES OF FUZZY SETS

The concept of a fuzzy system is intimately related to that of a fuzzy set. In order to make our discussion self-contained, it will be helpful to begin with a brief summary of some of the basic definitions pertaining to such sets.[2]

Definition of a Fuzzy Set

Let $X = \{x\}$ denote a space of points (objects), with x denoting a generic element of X. Then a *fuzzy set* A in X is a set of ordered pairs

$$A = \{[x, \mu_A(x)]\} \qquad x \in X \tag{1}$$

where $\mu_A(x)$ is termed the *grade of membership* of x in A. Thus, if $\mu_A(x)$ takes values in a space M—termed the *membership space*—then A is essentially a function from X to M. The function $\mu_A: X \rightarrow M$, which defines A, is called the *membership function* of A. When M contains only two points 0 and 1, A is nonfuzzy and its membership function reduces to the conventional characteristic function of a nonfuzzy set.

Intuitively, a fuzzy set A in X is a class without sharply defined boundaries—that is, a class in which a point (object) x may have a grade of membership intermediate between full membership and nonmembership. The important point to note is that such a fuzzy set can be defined *precisely* by associating with each x its grade of membership in A. In what follows, we shall assume for simplicity that M is the interval [0, 1], with the grades 0 and 1 representing, respectively, nonmembership and full membership in a fuzzy set. (More generally, M can be a partially ordered set or, more particularly, a lattice.[6]) Thus, our basic assumption

[1] The maximin automata of Wee and Santos[4],[5] may be regarded as instances of fuzzy systems.

[2] More detailed discussions of fuzzy sets and their properties may be found in the references listed at the end of this chapter.

will be that a fuzzy set A in X, though lacking in sharply defined boundaries, can be precisely characterized by a membership function that associates with each x in X a number in the interval [0, 1] representing the grade of membership of x in A.

Example

Let $A = \{x | x \gg 1\}$ (that is, A is the fuzzy set of real numbers that are much larger than 1). Such a set may be defined subjectively by a membership function such as:

$$\begin{aligned} \mu_A(x) &= 0 && \text{for } x \leq 1 \\ &= [1 + (x-1)^{-2}]^{-1} && \text{for } x > 1 \end{aligned} \qquad (2)$$

It is important to note that in the case of a fuzzy set it is not meaningful to speak of an object as belonging or not belonging to that set, except for objects whose grade of membership in the set is unity or zero. Thus, if A is the fuzzy set of tall men, then the statement "John is tall" should not be interpreted as meaning that John belongs to A. Rather, such a statement should be interpreted as an association of John with the fuzzy set A—an association which will be denoted by John $\underset{\sim}{\in}$ A to distinguish it from an assertion of belonging in the usual nonfuzzy sense—that is, John $\in A$, which is meaningful only when A is nonfuzzy.[3]

Containment

Let A and B be fuzzy sets in X. Then A *is contained in* B (or A is a *subset* of B) written as $A \subset B$, if and only if $\mu_A(x) \leq \mu_B(x)$ for all x in X. (In the sequel, to simplify the notation we shall omit x when an equality or inequality holds for all values of x in X.)

Example

If $\mu_A = \mu_B^2$, then $A \subset B$.

Equality

Two fuzzy sets are *equal*, written as $A = B$, if and only if $\mu_A = \mu_B$.

Complementation

A fuzzy set A' is the *complement* of a fuzzy set A if and only if $\mu_{A'} = 1 - \mu_A$.

[3] Here and elsewhere in this chapter we shall employ the convention of underscoring a symbol with a wavy bar to represent a fuzzified version of the meaning of that symbol. For example, $x \underset{\sim}{=} y$ will denote a fuzzy equality of x and y; $x \underset{\sim}{\Rightarrow} y$ will denote fuzzy implication, etc.

Example

The fuzzy sets $A = \{x|x \gg 1\}$ and $A' = \{x|x \text{ not} \gg 1\}$ are complements of one another.

Union

The *union* of A and B is denoted by $A \cup B$ and is defined as the smallest fuzzy set containing both A and B. The membership function of $A \cup B$ is given by $\mu_{A \cup B} = \text{Max}\,[\mu_A, \mu_B]$. Thus, if at a point x, $\mu_A(x) = 0.9$, say, and $\mu_B(x) = 0.4$, then at that point $\mu_{A \cup B}(x) = 0.9$.

As in the case of nonfuzzy sets, the notion of the union is closely related to that of the connective "or." Thus, if A is a class of tall men, B is a class of fat men and "John is tall" or "John is fat," then John is associated with the union of A and B. More generally, expressed in symbols we have

$$x \underset{\sim}{\in} A \quad \text{or} \quad x \underset{\sim}{\in} B \Rightarrow x \underset{\sim}{\in} A \cup B \tag{3}$$

Intersection

The *intersection* of A and B is denoted by $A \cap B$ and is defined as the largest fuzzy set contained in both A and B. The membership function of $A \cap B$ is given by $\mu_{A \cap B} = \text{Min}\,[\mu_A, \mu_B]$. It is easy to verify that $A \cap B = (A' \cup B')'$. The relation between the connective "and" and $\cap$ is expressed by

$$x \underset{\sim}{\in} A \quad \text{and} \quad x \underset{\sim}{\in} B \Rightarrow x \underset{\sim}{\in} A \cap B \tag{4}$$

Algebraic Product

The *algebraic product of* A and B is denoted by AB and is defined by $\mu_{AB} = \mu_A \mu_B$. Note that the product distributes over the union but not vice-versa.

Algebraic Sum

The algebraic sum of A and B is denoted by $A \oplus B$ and is defined by $\mu_{A \oplus B} = \mu_A + \mu_B - \mu_{AB}$. It is trivial to verify that $A \oplus B = (A'B')'$.

Relation

A *fuzzy relation*, R, in the product space $X \times Y = \{(x, y)\}$, $x \in X$, $y \in Y$, is a fuzzy set in $X \times Y$ characterized by a membership function μ_R that associates with each ordered pair (x, y) a grade of membership $\mu_R(x, y)$ in R. More generally, an n-ary fuzzy relation in a product space $X = X^1 \times X^2 \times \cdots \times X^n$ is a fuzzy set in X characterized by an

n-variate membership function $\mu_R(x_1, \cdots, x_n)$, $x_i \in X^i$, for $i = 1, \cdots, n$.

Example

Let $X = R \times R$, where R is the real line $(-\infty, \infty)$. Then $x \gg y$ is a fuzzy relation in R^2. A subjective expression for μ_R in this case might be

$$\mu_R(x, y) = 0 \text{ for } x \leq y$$

$$\mu_R(x, y) = \left[1 + \left(1 - \frac{x}{y}\right)^{-2}\right]^{-1} \qquad \text{for } x > y$$

Composition of Relations

If R_1 and R_2 are two fuzzy relations in X^2, then by the *composition* of R_1 and R_2 is meant a fuzzy relation in X^2 which is denoted by $R_1 \circ R_2$ and is defined by

$$\mu_{R_1 \circ R_2}(x, y) = \operatorname*{Sup}_v \operatorname{Min}\,[R_1(x, v),\ R_2(v, y)] \tag{5}$$

where the supremum is taken over all v in X.

Fuzzy Sets Induced by Mappings

Let f: $X \rightarrow Y$ be a mapping from X to Y, with the image of x under f denoted by $y = f(x)$. Let A be a fuzzy set in X. Then the mapping f induces a fuzzy set B in Y whose membership function is given by

$$\mu_B(y) = \operatorname*{Sup}_{x \in f^{-1}(y)} \mu_A(x) \tag{6}$$

where $f^{-1}(y)$ denotes the set of points in X which are mapped by f into y.

Shadow of a Fuzzy Set

Let A be a fuzzy set in $X \times Y$, and let f denote the mapping that takes (x, y) into x. The fuzzy set in X that is induced by this mapping is called the *shadow*[7] (projection) of A on X and is denoted by $S_X(A)$. In consequence of (6), the membership function of $S_X(A)$ is given by

$$\mu_{S_X(A)}(x) = \operatorname*{Sup}_y \mu_A(x, y) \tag{7}$$

where $\mu_A(x, y)$ is the membership function of A.

Conditioned Fuzzy Sets

A fuzzy set $B(x)$ in Y will be said to be *conditioned on* x if its membership function depends on x as a parameter. To place this dependence in evidence, we shall denote the membership function of $B(x)$ as $\mu_B(y|x)$ or—when B can be omitted with no risk of confusion—as $\mu(y|x)$.

Now suppose that the parameter x ranges over a space X. Then, the function $\mu_B(y|x)$ defines a mapping from X to the space of fuzzy sets defined on Y. Through this mapping, a fuzzy set A in X induces a fuzzy set B in Y, which is defined by

$$\mu_B(y) = \operatorname*{Sup}_{x\in X} \text{Min}\,[\mu_A(x), \mu_B(y|x)] \tag{8}$$

where μ_A and μ_B denote the membership functions of A and B, respectively. In effect, (8) is a special case of the composition of relations (5).

The notion of a conditioned fuzzy set bears some resemblance to the notion of a conditional probability distribution. Thus, (8) is the counterpart of the familiar identity

$$p_B(y) = \int_X p_B(y|x)p_A(x)\,dx \tag{9}$$

where, for simplicity, x and y are assumed to be real-valued, $p_A(x)$ denotes the probability density of x, $p_B(y|x)$ denotes the conditional probability density of y given x and $p_B(y)$ denotes the probability density of y.[4] It is worthy of note that, in this as well as many other instances involving fuzziness on the one hand and probability on the other, the corresponding formulas differ from one another in that to the operations of summation and integration involving probabilities corresponds the operation of taking the supremum (or maximum) of membership functions, and to the operation of multiplication of probabilities corresponds the operation of taking the infimum (or minimum) of membership functions. To make this correspondence more evident, it is convenient to use the symbols $\vee$ and $\wedge$ for the supremum and infimum, respectively. Then, (9) becomes

$$\mu_B(y) = \bigvee_x [\mu_A(x) \wedge \mu_B(y|x)] \tag{10}$$

Similarly, (7) becomes

$$\mu_B(y) = \bigvee_{x\in f^{-1}(y)} \mu_A(x) \tag{11}$$

for which its probabilitistic counterpart reads

$$p_B(y) = \sum_{x\in f^{-1}(y)} p_A(x) \tag{12}$$

where x and y are assumed to range over finite sets and $p_A(x)$ and $p_B(y)$ denote probabilities rather than probability densities as in (9).

This concludes our brief summary of some of the basic concepts relating to fuzzy sets. In what follows, we shall employ these concepts

[4] To simplify the notation, we use the same symbol to denote a random variable and a generic value of that variable.

in defining a fuzzy system and explore some of the elementary properties of such systems.

SYSTEM, AGGREGATE, AND STATE

For simplicity, we shall restrict our attention to time-invariant discrete-time systems in which t, time, ranges over integers, and the input and output at time t are real-valued.

In the theory of nonfuzzy discrete-time systems, it is customary to introduce the notion of state at the very outset by defining a system A through its state equations:

$$\begin{aligned} x_{t+1} &= f(x_t, u_t) \qquad t = \cdots, -1, 0, 1, \cdots \\ y_t &= g(x_t, u_t) \end{aligned} \tag{13}$$

where u_t denotes the *input* at time t, y_t is the *output* at time t and x_t is the *state* at time t, with the ranges of u_t, y_t, and x_t denoted by U, Y, and X, respectively. In this way, A is characterized by two mappings, $f: X \times U \to X$ and $g: X \times U \to Y$. The space X is called the *state space* of A, and a point α in X is called a *state* of A.

Let u denote an input sequence starting at, say, $t = 0$. Thus, $u = u_0u_1 \cdots u_l$, where $u_t \in U$, $t = 0, 1, \cdots, l$, and l is a nonnegative integer. The set of all sequences whose elements are drawn from U will be denoted by U^*.

Now, to each state α in X and each input sequence $u = u_0u_1 \cdots u_l$ in U^* will correspond an output sequence $y = y_0y_1 \cdots y_l$ in Y^*. The pair of sequences (u, y) is called an *input–output* pair of length $l + 1$. The totality of input–output pairs (u, y) of varying lengths that correspond to a particular state α in X will be referred to as an *aggregate* of input–output pairs, or simply an *aggregate*, $A(\alpha)$, with α playing the role of a label for this aggregate. The union

$$A = \bigcup_{\alpha \in X} A(\alpha)$$

represents the totality of input–output pairs that correspond to all the states of A. It is this totality of input–output pairs that we shall equate with A.

The fact that a state is merely a label for an aggregate suggests that the concept of an aggregate be accorded a central place among the basic concepts of system theory. This is done implicitly in Refs. [8] and [9], and explicitly in [10]. The point of departure in the theory developed in Ref. [8] is the definition of a system as a collection of input–output pairs. An aggregate, then, may be defined as a subset of input–output pairs which satisfy certain consistency conditions, with a state playing the role of a name for an aggregate.

In what follows, we shall first generalize to fuzzy systems the conventional approach in which a system is described through its state equations. Then we shall indicate a connection between the notion of a fuzzy algorithm and a fuzzy system. Finally, we shall present in a summary form some of the basic definitions relating to the notion of an aggregate and briefly touch upon their generalization to fuzzy systems.

STATE EQUATIONS FOR FUZZY SYSTEMS

Let u_t, y_t, and x_t denote, respectively, the input, output and state of a system A at time t. Such a system is said to be *deterministic* if it is characterized by state equations of the form

$$x_{t+1} = f(x_t, u_t) \qquad t = -1, 0, 1, 2, \cdots \tag{14}$$

$$y_t = g(x_t, u_t) \tag{15}$$

in which f and g are mappings from $X \times U$ to X and Y, respectively.

A is said to be *nondeterministic* if x_{t+1} and/or y_t are not uniquely determined by x_t and u_t. Let $X^{t+1}(x_t, u_t)$ and $Y^t(x_t, u_t)$ or X^{t+1} and Y^t, for short, denote the sets of possible values of x_{t+1} and y_t, respectively, given x_t and u_t. Then (14) and (15) can be replaced by equations of the form

$$X^{t+1} = F(x_t, u_t) \tag{16}$$

$$Y^t = G(x_t, u_t) \tag{17}$$

where F and G are mappings from $X \times U$ into the space of subsets of X and Y, respectively. Thus, a nondeterministic system is characterized by equations of the form (16) and (17), in which X^{t+1} and Y^t are subsets of X and Y, respectively.

The next step in the direction of further generalization is to assume that X^{t+1} and Y^t are fuzzy rather than nonfuzzy sets in X and Y, respectively. In this case, we shall say that A is a *fuzzy* discrete-time system. Clearly, such a system reduces to a nondeterministic system when X^{t+1} and Y^t are nonfuzzy sets. In turn, a nondeterministic system reduces to a deterministic system when X^{t+1} and Y^t are single points (singletons) in their respective spaces.

Let $\mu_X(x_{t+1}|x_t, u_t)$ and $\mu_Y(y_t|x_t, u_t)$ denote the membership functions of X^{t+1} and Y^t, respectively, given x_t and u_t. Then we can say that A is *characterized* by the two membership functions $\mu_X(x_{t+1}|x_t, u_t)$ and $\mu_Y(y_t|x_t, u_t)$, which define conditioned fuzzy sets in X and Y, respectively, involving x_t and u_t as parameters.

To illustrate, suppose that $X = R^3$. Then A is a fuzzy system if its characterization contains statements such as: "If an input $u_t = 5$ is applied to A in state $x_t = (3, 5, 1)$ at time t, then the state of A at time

$t + 1$ will be in the *vicinity* of the point (7, 3, 5)." Here the set of points in X that lie in the vicinity of a given point α is a fuzzy set in X. Such a set may be characterized by a membership function such as

$$\mu(x) = \exp\left(-\frac{1}{k}\|x - \alpha\|\right) \tag{18}$$

where x is a point in X, $\|x - \alpha\|$ denotes a norm of the vector $x - \alpha$, and k is a positive constant.

By analogy with nonfuzzy systems, a fuzzy system A will be said to be *memoryless* if the fuzzy set Y^t is independent of x_t—that is, if its membership function is of the form $\mu_Y(y_t|u_t)$. Just as a nonfuzzy memoryless system is characterized by a graph $y_t = g(u_t)$, $u_t \in U$, so a fuzzy memoryless system is characterized by a fuzzy graph that is a family of fuzzy sets $\{Y^t(u_t), u_t \in U\}$.

In the case of a memoryless system, to each point u_t in U corresponds a fuzzy set $Y^t(u_t)$, or Y^t for short, in Y. Thus, we can write

$$Y^t = G(u_t) \qquad t = \cdots, -1 \;\; 0, 1, 2, \cdots \tag{19}$$

where G is a function from R^1 to the space of fuzzy sets in Y. Now as a consequence of equation (8), this implies that if U^t is a fuzzy set in U characterized by a membership function $\mu_U(u_t)$, then to U^t will correspond the fuzzy set Y^t defined by the membership function

$$\mu_Y(y_t) = \bigvee_{u_t} (\mu_U(u_t) \wedge \mu_Y(y_t|u_t)) \tag{20}$$

where $\vee$ and $\wedge$ denote the supremum and minimum, respectively. Thus, (20) establishes a relation between U^t and Y^t which can be expressed as

$$Y^t = G_0(U^t) \qquad t = \cdots, -1, 0, 1, 2, \cdots \tag{21}$$

where G_0 is a function from the space of fuzzy sets in U to the space of fuzzy sets in Y.

The important point to be noted here is that equation (19), which expresses Y^t as a function of u_t, induces equation (21), which expresses Y^t as a function of U^t. As should be expected, (21) reduces to (19) when U^t is taken to be the singleton $\{u_t\}$.

Intuitively, equations (19) and (21) may be interpreted as follows. If A is a fuzzy memoryless system, then to every nonfuzzy input u_t at time t corresponds a unique fuzzy output, which is represented by a conditioned fuzzy set Y^t in Y. The membership function of this fuzzy set is given by $\mu_Y(y_t|u_t)$.

If the input to A is fuzzy—that is, if it is a fuzzy set U^t in U—then the corresponding fuzzy output Y^t is given uniquely by (21). The membership function for Y^t is expressed by (20).

As a very simple example, suppose that U and Y are finite sets: $U = \{1, 2, 3\}$ and $Y = \{1, 2, 3\}$. Furthermore, suppose that if the input

u_t is 1, then the output is a fuzzy set described verbally as "y_t is approximately equal to 1." Similarly, if $u_t = 2$ then y_t is approximately equal to 2, and if $u_t = 3$ then y_t is approximately equal to 3. More concretely, we assume that $\mu_Y(y_t|u_t)$ is defined by the table:

$$\begin{array}{lll} \mu_Y(1|1) = 1 & \mu_Y(2|1) = 0.3 & \mu_Y(3|1) = 0.1 \\ \mu_Y(1|2) = 0.2 & \mu_Y(2|2) = 1 & \mu_Y(3|2) = 0.2 \\ \mu_Y(1|3) = 0.1 & \mu_Y(2|3) = 0.2 & \mu_Y(3|3) = 1 \end{array}$$

Now assume that the input is a fuzzy set described verbally as "u_t is close to 1," and characterized by the membership function

$$\mu_U(1) = 1 \qquad \mu_U(2) = 0.2 \qquad \mu_U(3) = 0.1$$

Then, by using (20), the response to this fuzzy input is found to be a fuzzy set defined by the membership function

$$\mu_Y(1) = 1 \qquad \mu_Y(2) = 0.2 \qquad \mu_Y(3) = 0.2$$

It is convenient to regard (21) as a mapping from names of fuzzy sets in U to names of fuzzy sets in Y. In many cases of practical interest such a mapping can be adequately characterized by a finite, and perhaps even fairly small, number of points [ordered pairs (U, Y)] on the graph of G_0. For example, G_0 might be characterized approximately by a table such as shown below. (For simplicity we suppress the subscript t in u_t and y_t.)

U^t	Y^t
$\underset{\sim}{1}$	$\underset{\sim}{1}$
$\underset{\sim}{1.1}$	$\underset{\sim}{1.3}$
$\underset{\sim}{1.2}$	$\underset{\sim}{1.6}$
$\underset{\sim}{1.3}$	$\underset{\sim}{2}$
$\underset{\sim}{1.4}$	$\underset{\sim}{2.5}$
$\underset{\sim}{1.5}$	$\underset{\sim}{2.9}$
$\underset{\sim}{1.6}$	$\underset{\sim}{2.5}$
$\underset{\sim}{1.7}$	$\underset{\sim}{2.1}$
$\underset{\sim}{1.8}$	$\underset{\sim}{1.8}$
$\underset{\sim}{1.9}$	$\underset{\sim}{1.6}$
$\underset{\sim}{2}$	$\underset{\sim}{1.5}$
$\underset{\sim}{2.1}$	$\underset{\sim}{1.5}$
.	.
.	.
.	. .
$\underset{\sim}{3}$	1.5

where $\underset{\sim}{x}$, $x \in R$, is the name for the fuzzy set of real numbers that are approximately equal to x. Such a set may be characterized quantitatively by a membership function. In many practical situations a very approximate description of this membership function would be sufficient. In this way, equation (21) can serve the purpose of an approximate characterization of a fuzzy memoryless system.

Turning to nonmemoryless fuzzy systems, consider a system A which is characterized by state equations of the form

$$X^{t+1} = F(x_t, u_t) \tag{22}$$
$$Y^t = G(x_t, u_t) \tag{23}$$

where F is a function from the product space $X \times U$ to the space of fuzzy sets in X, G is a function from $X \times U$ to the space of fuzzy sets in Y, X^{t+1} denotes a fuzzy set in X that is conditioned on x_t and u_t, and Y^t denotes a fuzzy set in Y that, like X^{t+1}, is conditioned on x_t and u_t. X^t and Y^t represent, respectively, the fuzzy state and output of A at time t and are defined by the membership functions $\mu_X(x_{t+1}|x_t, u_t)$ and $\mu_Y(y_t|x_t, u_t)$.

Equations (22) and (23) relate the fuzzy state at time $t + 1$ and the fuzzy output at time t to the nonfuzzy state and nonfuzzy input at time t. As in the case of a memoryless system, we can deduce from these equations—by repeated application of (8)—the state equations for A for the case where the state at time t or the input at time t, or both, are fuzzy.

Specifically, let us assume that the state at time t is a fuzzy set characterized by a membership function $\mu_X(x_t)$. Then, by applying (8), we deduce from (22) and (23)

$$\mu_X(x_{t+1}) = \bigvee_{x_t} (\mu_X(x_t) \wedge \mu_X(x_{t+1}|x_t, u_t)) \tag{24}$$
$$\mu_Y(y_t) = \bigvee_{x_t} (\mu_X(x_t) \wedge \mu_Y(y_t|x_t, u_t)) \tag{25}$$

which in symbolic form may be expressed as

$$X^{t+1} = F_0(X^t, u_t) \tag{26}$$
$$Y^t = G_0(X^t, u_t) \tag{27}$$

In what follows, to simplify the appearance of equations such as (24) and (25) we shall omit the subscripts X and Y in membership functions.

By n-fold iteration of (26) and (27), we can obtain expressions for X^{t+n+1} and Y^{t+n}, for $n = 1, 2, 3, \cdots$, in terms of X^t and $u_t, \cdots, u_{t+n}$. For example, for $n = 1$, we have

$$X^{t+2} = F_0(F_0(X^t, u_t), u_{t+1}) \tag{28}$$
$$Y^{t+1} = G_0(F_0(X^t, u_t), u_{t+1}) \tag{29}$$

or, more compactly,

$$X^{t+2} = F_1(X^t, u_t, u_{t+1}) \tag{30}$$
$$Y^{t+1} = G_1(X^t, u_t, u_{t+1}) \tag{31}$$

To express (30) and (31) in terms of membership functions, we note that on replacing t with $t + 1$ in (24) and (25), we obtain

$$\mu(x_{t+2}) = \bigvee_{x_{t+1}} (\mu(x_{t+1}) \wedge \mu(x_{t+2}|x_{t+1}, u_{t+1})) \quad (32)$$

$$\mu(y_{t+1}) = \bigvee_{x_{t+1}} (\mu(x_{t+1}) \wedge \mu(y_{t+1}|x_{t+1}, u_{t+1})) \quad (33)$$

Then, on substituting $\mu(x_{t+1})$ from (24) into (32) and (33), we get

$$\mu(x_{t+2}) = \bigvee_{x_{t+1}} (\bigvee_{x_t} (\mu(x_t) \wedge \mu(x_{t+1}|x_t, u_t)) \wedge \mu(x_{t+2}|x_{t+1}, u_{t+1})) \quad (34)$$

and

$$\mu(y_{t+1}) = \bigvee_{x_{t+1}} (\bigvee_{x_t} (\mu(x_t) \wedge \mu(x_{t+1}|x_t, u_t)) \wedge \mu(y_{t+1}|x_{t+1}, u_{t+1})) \quad (35)$$

which by virtue of the distributivity of $\vee$ and $\wedge$ may be expressed as

$$\mu(x_{t+2}) = \bigvee_{x_{t+1}} \bigvee_{x_t} (\mu(x_t) \wedge \mu(x_{t+1}|x_t, u_t) \wedge \mu(x_{t+2}|x_{t+1}, u_{t+1})) \quad (36)$$

$$\mu(y_{t+1}) = \bigvee_{x_{t+1}} \bigvee_{x_t} (\mu(x_t) \wedge \mu(x_{t+1}|x_t, u_t) \wedge \mu(y_{t+1}|x_{t+1}, u_{t+1})) \quad (37)$$

and likewise for larger values of n. It should be noted that these relations are fuzzy counterparts of the corresponding expressions for stochastic systems,[11] with $\wedge$ and $\vee$ replacing product and sum, respectively, and membership functions replacing probability functions [see (19) and the equations following it].

In the above analysis, we have assumed that the successive inputs $u_t, \cdots, u_{t+n}$ are nonfuzzy. On this basis, we can obtain expressions for $X^{t+1}, \cdots, X^{t+n+1}$ and $Y^t, \cdots, Y^{t+n}$ in terms of X^t and $u_t, \cdots, u_{t+n}$. It is natural to raise the question of what the corresponding expressions for $X^{t+1}, \cdots, X^{t+n+1}$ and $Y^t \cdots Y^{t+n}$ are when the successive inputs are fuzzy.

First, let us focus our attention on the state equations (16) and (17), in which F and G are functions from $X \times U$ to fuzzy sets in X and Y, respectively. Suppose that both the input at time t and the state at time t are fuzzy. What would be the expressions for the membership functions of X^{t+1} and Y^t in this simple case?

Let $\mu(x_t, u_t)$ denote the membership function of the fuzzy set whose elements are ordered pairs (x_t, u_t).[5] Then, using equation (8) we can express the membership functions of X^{t+1} and Y^t as follows:

$$\mu(x_{t+1}) = \bigvee_{x_t} \bigvee_{u_t} (\mu(x_t, u_t) \wedge \mu(x_{t+1}|x_t, u_t)) \quad (38)$$

$$\mu(y_t) = \bigvee_{x_t} \bigvee_{u_t} (\mu(x_t, u_t) \wedge \mu(y_t|x_t, u_t)) \quad (39)$$

[5] The probabilistic counterpart of this membership function is the joint probability of x and u.

These formulas assume a simpler form when $\mu(x_t, u_t)$ can be expressed as

$$\mu(x_t, u_t) = \mu(x_t) \wedge \mu(u_t) \tag{40}$$

where $\mu(x_t)$ and $\mu(u_t)$ denote, respectively, the membership functions of the fuzzy state and the fuzzy input at time t. In this case, we shall say that the fuzzy sets X^t and U^t are *noninteracting*. Essentially, the notion of noninteraction of fuzzy sets corresponds to the notion of independence of random variables.

The assumption that X^t and U^t are noninteracting fuzzy sets is a reasonable one to make in many cases of practical interest. Under this assumption, (38) and (39) reduce to

$$\mu(x_{t+1}) = \bigvee_{x_t} \bigvee_{u_t} (\mu(x_t) \wedge \mu(u_t) \wedge \mu(x_{t+1}|x_t, u_t)) \tag{41}$$

$$\mu(y_t) = \bigvee_{x_t} \bigvee_{u_t} (\mu(x_t) \wedge \mu(u_t) \wedge \mu(y_t|x_t, u_t)) \tag{42}$$

It should be noted that the same expressions can be obtained by applying (8) to (26) and (27), with the input at time t assumed to be a fuzzy set characterized by $\mu(u_t)$.

In symbolic form, (41) and (42) can be expressed as

$$X^{t+1} = F_{00}(X^t, U^t) \tag{43}$$

$$Y^t = G_{00}(X^t, U^t) \tag{44}$$

where F_{00} and G_{00} are, respectively, functions from the product space of fuzzy sets in X and fuzzy sets in U to the space of fuzzy sets in X and fuzzy sets in Y. Thus, equation (43) expresses the fuzzy state at time $t + 1$ as a function of the fuzzy state at time t and the fuzzy input at time t. Similarly, equation (44) expresses the fuzzy output at time t as a function of the fuzzy state at time t and the fuzzy input at time t. Note that (43) is induced via (8) by (22), which expresses the fuzzy state at time $t + 1$ as a function of the nonfuzzy state at time t and the nonfuzzy input at time t. The same is true of (44) and (23).

When X, U and Y are finite sets, the above equations can be written more compactly by expressing the membership functions in matrix or vector form. Specifically, suppose that X, for example, is a finite set $X = \{x^1, \cdots, x^m\}$. For each input u_t, let $M(u_t)$ denote a matrix whose (i, j)th element is given by

$$M_{ij}(u_t) = \mu(x^i|x^j, u_t)$$

Also, let $\bar{x}_{t+1}$ and $\bar{x}_t$ be column vectors whose ith elements are $\mu(x_{t+1})$ and $\mu(x_t)$, respectively, evaluated at x_{t+1} and x_t equal to x^i, $i = 1, \cdots,$ m. Then, (24) and (25) may be written in matrix form as

$$\bar{x}_{t+1} = M(u_t)\bar{x}_t$$

where the right-hand member should be interpreted as the matrix product of $M(u_t)$ and $\bar{x}_t$, with + replaced by $\vee$ and product by $\wedge$. Similarly, (36) and (37) become

$$\bar{x}_{t+2} = M(u_{t+1})M(u_t)\bar{x}_t$$
$$\bar{y}_{t+1} = M_Y(u_{t+1})M(u_t)\bar{x}_t$$

where $M_Y(u_{t+1})$ is defined in the same way as $M(u_t)$, with y_{t+1} replacing x_{t+1} in the definition of the latter, and likewise for $\bar{y}_{t+1}$. More generally, for $n = 1, 2, \cdots$, we can write

$$\bar{x}_{t+n+1} = M(u_{t+n}) \cdots M(u_t)\bar{x}_t$$
$$\bar{y}_{t+n} = M_Y(u_{t+n})M(u_{t+n-1}) \cdots M(u_t)\bar{x}_t$$

When both x_t and u_t are fuzzy, we can no longer employ the matrix notation to simplify expressions such as (24) and (25). However, some notational simplification, particularly in the case of expressions like (36) and (37), may be achieved by the use of the tensor notation or the notation commonly employed in dealing with bilinear forms.

A simple numerical example will serve to illustrate the use of the formulas derived above. Specifically, let us consider a fuzzy system with binary input and output, $U = Y = \{0, 1\}$, and finite state space $X = \{\alpha, \beta, \gamma\}$. Suppose that the membership functions $\mu(x_{t+1}|x_t, u_t)$ and $\mu(y_t|x_t, u_t)$ for this system are characterized by the following tables

$\mu(x_{t+1} | x_t, U_t)$:

	$u_t = 0$			$u_t = 1$		
x_t \ x_{t+1}	α	β	γ	α	β	γ
α	1	0.8	0.6	0.8	0.5	1
β	0.7	0.2	1	0.2	1	0.6
γ	0.3	0.3	0.4	0.9	0.7	1

$\mu(y_t | x_t, u_t)$:

	$u_t = 0$		$u_t = 1$	
x_t \ y_t	0	1	0	1
α	0.8	0.3	0.6	0.3
β	1	0.1	0.5	1
γ	0.8	0.7	0.3	0.2

Further, assume that X^t and U^t are characterized by the membership functions

$$\mu(\alpha) = 1 \qquad \mu(\beta) = 0.8 \qquad \mu(\gamma) = 0.4$$
$$\mu(0) = 1 \qquad \mu(1) = 0.3$$

Then, using (41) and (42) and employing matrix multiplication (with the operations $\vee$ and $\wedge$ replacing sum and product), we can readily compute the values of the membership functions of X^{t+1} and Y^t at the points α, β, γ, 0, and 1, respectively. These values are

$$\mu(\alpha) = 1 \qquad \mu(\beta) = 0.8 \qquad \mu(\gamma) = 0.8$$
$$\mu(0) = 0.8 \qquad \mu(1) = 0.4$$

It should be noted that, as in the case of a memoryless fuzzy system’ (43) and (44) can be used to provide an approximate characterization of a nonmemoryless fuzzy system. To illustrate, let us employ the convention introduced earlier, namely, using the symbol $\underset{\sim}{x}$ to denote the name of a fuzzy set of real numbers that are approximately equal to x. Then, viewed as relations between names of fuzzy sets, (43), and (44) may take the appearance of tables such as shown below:

X^{t+1}:

$U^t \backslash X^t$	$\underset{\sim}{1}$	$\underset{\sim}{2}$	$\underset{\sim}{3}$	$\underset{\sim}{4}$
$\underset{\sim}{0}$	$\underset{\sim}{2}$	$\underset{\sim}{1}$	$\underset{\sim}{4}$	$\underset{\sim}{3}$
$\underset{\sim}{1}$	$\underset{\sim}{3}$	$\underset{\sim}{4}$	$\underset{\sim}{1}$	$\underset{\sim}{3}$

Y^{t+1}:

$U^t \backslash X^t$	$\underset{\sim}{1}$	$\underset{\sim}{2}$	$\underset{\sim}{3}$	$\underset{\sim}{4}$
$\underset{\sim}{0}$	$\underset{\sim}{0}$	$\underset{\sim}{1}$	$\underset{\sim}{1}$	$\underset{\sim}{0}$
$\underset{\sim}{1}$	$\underset{\sim}{1}$	$\underset{\sim}{0}$	$\underset{\sim}{1}$	$\underset{\sim}{1}$

where for simplicity we restricted x and u to integral values. More generally, the entries in these tables would be names for fuzzy sets in X, U, and Y, and only a *finite* number of such names would be used as representative samples (paradigms) of the fuzzy sets in their respective spaces.

So far, we have restricted our attention to the case where a single fuzzy input U^t is applied to A in state X^t. For this case, we found expressions for X^{t+1} and Y^t in terms of X^t and U^t. The same approach can readily be extended, however, to the case in which the input is a sequence of noninteracting fuzzy inputs $U^t U^{t+1} \cdots U^{t+n}$, for $n \geq 1$. The assumption of noninteraction implies that

$$\mu(u_t, \cdots, u_{t+n}) = \mu(u_t) \wedge \mu(u_{t+1}) \wedge \cdots \wedge \mu(u_{t+n}) \tag{45}$$

To illustrate, let $n = 1$. Then by applying (8) to (36) and (37), we obtain

$$\mu(x_{t+2}) = \bigvee_{x_{t+1}} \bigvee_{x_t} \bigvee_{u_t} \bigvee_{u_{t+1}} (\mu(x_t) \wedge \mu(x_{t+1}|x_t, u_t) \wedge \mu(x_{t+2}|x_{t+1}, u_{t+1}) \wedge \mu(u_t) \wedge \mu(u_{t+1})) \tag{46}$$

$$\mu(y_{t+1}) = \bigvee_{x_{t+1}} \bigvee_{x_t} \bigvee_{u_t} \bigvee_{u_{t+1}} (\mu(x_t) \wedge \mu(x_{t+1}|x_t, u_t) \wedge \mu(y_{t+1}|x_{t+1}, u_{t+1}) \wedge \mu(u_t) \wedge \mu(u_{t+1})) \tag{47}$$

As in the case of (36 and (37), for higher values of n such relations can be expressed more compactly through the use of vector and tensor notation. For our purposes, the simple case $n = 1$ considered above suffices to illustrate the main features of the method which can be used to compute the fuzzy state and fuzzy output of a system at the end of a finite sequence of noninteracting fuzzy inputs.

FUZZY SYSTEMS AND FUZZY ALGORITHMS

As was shown in a recent note,[3] the notion of a fuzzy system bears a close relation to that of a fuzzy algorithm.

Roughly speaking, a fuzzy algorithm is an algorithm in which some of the instructions are fuzzy in nature. Examples of such instructions are: (a) Increase x *slightly* if y is *slightly* larger than 10; (b) Decrease u until it becomes *much smaller* than v; (c) *Reduce* speed if the road is *slippery*. The sources of fuzziness in these instructions are the underlined words.

More generally, we may view a fuzzy algorithm as a fuzzy system A characterized by equations of the form:

$$X^{t+1} = F(X^t, U^t) \tag{48}$$

$$U^t = H(X^t) \tag{49}$$

where X^t is a fuzzy state of A at time t, U^t is a fuzzy input (representing a fuzzy instruction) at time t, and X^{t+1} is the fuzzy state at time $t + 1$ resulting from the execution of the fuzzy instruction represented by U^t. As seen from (48) and (49), the function F defines the dependence of the fuzzy state at time $t + 1$ on the fuzzy state at time t and the fuzzy input at time t, whereas the function H describes the dependence of the fuzzy input at time t on the fuzzy state at time t.

To illustrate (48) and (49), we shall consider a very simple example. Suppose that X is a fuzzy subset of a finite set $X = \{\alpha_1, \alpha_2, \alpha_3, \alpha_4\}$ and

U^t is a fuzzy subset of a finite set $U = \{\beta_1, \beta_2\}$. Since the membership functions of X^t and U^t are mappings from, respectively, X and U to the unit interval, these functions can be represented as points in unit hypercubes in R^4 and R^2, which we shall denote for convenience by C^4 and C^2. Thus, E may be defined by a mapping from $C^4 \times C^2$ to C^4 and H by a mapping from C^4 to C^2. For example, if the membership function of X^t is represented by the vector (0.5, 0.8, 1, 0.6) and that of U^t by the vector (1, 0.2), then the membership function of X^{t+1} would be defined by F as a vector—say (0.2, 1, 0.8, 0.4)—whereas that of U^t would be defined by H as a vector (0.3, 1), say.

It is clear that even in the very simple case where X and U are small finite sets, it is impracticable to attempt to characterize F with any degree of precision as a mapping from a product of unit hypercubes to a unit hypercube. Thus, in general, it would be necessary to resort to an approximate definition of F and H through the process of exemplification, as was done in the case of the relation between Y^t and U^t in the previous section 9: see (21) and subsequent equations. This amounts to selecting a finite number of sample fuzzy sets in X and U, and tabulating finite approximations to F and H as mappings from and to the names of these fuzzy sets. In this light, an instruction such as "Reduce speed if the road is slippery" may be viewed as an ordered pair in H involving the names of fuzzy sets: "Reduce speed" and "Road is slippery."

Consider now the following situation. One is given an instruction of the form: "If x is much larger than 1 make y equal to 2. Otherwise make y equal to 1." Furthermore, the membership function of the class of numbers that are much larger than 1 is specified to be

$$\begin{aligned} \mu_E(x) &= 0 && \text{for } x < 1 \\ &= [1 + (x-1)^{-2}]^{-1} && \text{for } x \geq 1 \end{aligned} \tag{50}$$

where E denotes the class in question and μ_E is its membership function.

Now suppose that $x = 3$. How should the above instruction be executed? Note that $\mu_E(3) = 0.8$.

The answer to this question is that the given instruction does not cover this contingency or, for that matter, any situation in which x is a number such that $\mu_E(x) > 0$. Specifically, the instruction in question tells us only that if the input is a fuzzy set characterized by the membership function (50), then $y = 2$; and if the input is characterized by the membership function $1 - \mu_E(x)$, then $y = 1$. Now when x is specified to be equal to 3, the input may be regarded as a fuzzy set whose membership function is equal to 1 for $x = 3$ and vanishes elsewhere. This fuzzy set is not in the domain of the instruction—if we view the instruction as a function defined on a collection of fuzzy sets.

In some cases, it may be permissible to extend the domain of definition of a fuzzy instruction by an appropriate interpretation of its intent. For example, in the case considered above it may be reasonable to assume that $y = 2$ not just for the fuzzy set of numbers that are much larger than 1, but also for all fuzzy subsets of this set whose maximal grade of membership exceeds or is equal to a prescribed threshold; or, it may be reasonable to assume that $y = 2$ for all x whose grade of membership in E is greater than or equal to a threshold α. Alternatively, the domain of the instruction can be extended by employing randomized execution—that is, by choosing $y = 2$ and $y = 1$ for a given x with probabilities $\mu_E(x)$ and $1 - \mu_E(x)$, respectively. These and other ways of extending the domain of fuzzy instructions make the specification of F and H a problem that, though nontrivial, is well within the range of computational feasibility in many cases of practical interest.

Actually, crude forms of fuzzy algorithms are employed quite extensively in everyday practice. A food recipe is an example of an algorithm of this type. So is the set of instructions for parking a car or repairing a TV set. The effectiveness of such algorithms depends in large measure on the existence of a fuzzy feedback which makes it possible to observe the output and apply a corrective input. Indeed, this is implicit in equation (50), except that in practice the H function is itself quite ill-defined.

The foregoing discussion of the notion of a fuzzy algorithm was intended primarily to point to a close connection between this notion and that of a fuzzy system. It may well turn out, however, that many of the complex problems (such as machine translation of languages) that so far have eluded all attempts to solve them by conventional techniques cannot be properly formulated, much less solved, without the use, in one form or another, of a broader conceptual framework in which the notion of a fuzzy algorithm plays a basic role.

THE CONCEPT OF AGGREGATE

As was pointed out in a previous section, the state of a system may be viewed as a name for an aggregate of input–output pairs. In what follows, we shall summarize some of the principal notions relating to the concept of an aggregate, but will leave open the question of how these notions can be extended to fuzzy systems.

As in that section, let u and y denote a pair of sequences $u = u_0u_1 \cdots u_t$ and $y = y_0y_1 \cdots y_t$ of length $t + 1$, where, for simplicity, t is assumed to range over nonnegative integers. If $u = u_0u_1 \cdots u_\tau$ and $v = v_{\tau+1} \cdots v_t$, then the concatenation of u and v is denoted by uv and is defined by $uv = u_0v_1 \cdots u_\tau v_{\tau+1} \cdots v_t$.

Definition of a System

A *system (discrete-time system)* A is defined as a collection of ordered pairs of time functions (u, y) satisfying the condition of *closure under segmentation*, or CUS for short. Thus

$$A = \{(u, y)\} \qquad u \in U^*, y \in Y^*$$

where u and y are, respectively, the *input* and *output* of A, and (u, y) is an *input–output pair* belonging to A. The expression for the CUS condition is:

If $u = vv'$ and $y = ww'$ (that is, u is a concatenation of time functions v and v', and y is a concatenation of w and w') and $(u, y) \in A$, then $(v, w) \in A$ and $(v', w') \in A$. In effect, this condition requires that every segment of an input–output pair of A be an input–output pair of A.

Comment

When we define a system as a collection of input–output pairs, we are in effect identifying a physical system or a mathematical model of it with the totality of observations that can be made of its input and output time functions. Furthermore, we tacitly assume that we have as many copies of the system as there are different initial states, and that each u is applied to all these copies, so that to each u correspond as many y's as there are copies of the system.

To characterize A as a collection of input–output pairs it is usually more expedient to employ an algorithm for generating input–output pairs belonging to A than to list them. From this point of view, a differential or difference equation relating the output of a system to its input may be viewed as a compact way of specifying the collection of input–output pairs that defines A. An algorithm or an equation that serves this purpose is called an *input–output relation.*

Definition of an Aggregate

Let $A(t_0)$ denote a subset of A comprising those input–output pairs that start at time t_0. Now suppose we group together those input–output pairs in $A(t_0)$ that have some property in common, and call such groups *bundles* of input–output pairs. As we shall see presently, the *aggregates* of A are bundles of input–output pairs with certain special properties, defined in such a way as to make a state of A merely a name or a label for an aggregate of A.

It is convenient to state the properties in question as a set of four conditions defining aggregates of A. These conditions are as follows:

1. *Covering condition.* Let a generic bundle of input–output pairs in $A(t_0)$ be denoted by $A_{\alpha_0}(t_0)$, with α_0 serving as an identifying tag for a bundle. A collection of such bundles will be denoted by $\{A_{\alpha_0}(t_0)\}$, $\alpha_0 \in \Sigma_{t_0}$,

where Σ_{t_0} is the range of values that can be assumed by α_0 at t_0. Anticipating that α_0 will play the role of a state of A, Σ_{t_0} will be referred to as the *state space* of A at time t_0. Note that t_0 is a variable ranging over the integers 0, 1, 2, $\cdots$.

The covering condition requires that the collection $\{A_{\alpha_0}(t_0)\}$, $\alpha_0 \in \Sigma_{t_0}$, be a covering for $A(t_0)$; that is,

$$\bigcup_{\alpha_0} A_{\alpha_0}(t_0) = A(t_0) \qquad \text{for all } t_0 \text{ in } \{0, 1, \cdots\} \tag{51}$$

In effect, this condition requires that every input–output pair in $A(t_0)$ be included in some bundle in the collection $\{A_{\alpha_0}(t_0)\}$, $\alpha_0 \in \Sigma_{t_0}$.

2. *Uniqueness condition.* The uniqueness condition is expressed by

$$(u, y) \in A_{\alpha_0}(t_0) \text{ and } (u, y') \in A_{\alpha_0}(t_0) \Rightarrow y = y' \tag{52}$$

In other words, to each input u in the domain of the relation $A_{\alpha_0}(t_0)$ corresponds a unique output y. (Note that the sequences u and y are assumed to be of the same length.)

3. *Prefix condition.* Consider an input–output pair (uu', yy') in $A_{\alpha_0}(t_0)$, which is a concatenation of the input–output pairs (u, y) and (u', y'). The expression for the condition is

$$(uu', yy') \in A_{\alpha_0}(t_0) \Rightarrow (u, y) \in A_{\alpha_0}(t_0) \tag{53}$$

Thus, this condition requires that any prefix [that is, (u, y)] of an input–output pair in $A_{\alpha_0}(t_0)$ also be an input–output pair in $A_{\alpha_0}(t_0)$.

4. *Continuation condition.* As in the preceding condition, let (uu', yy') be an input–output pair in $A_{\alpha_0}(t_0)$, with (u', y') starting at, say, t_1. The continuation condition may be expressed as

$$\{(u', y') | (uu', yy') \in A_{\alpha_0}(t_0)\} = A_{\alpha_1}(t_1) \tag{54}$$

where $A_{\alpha_1}(t_1)$ denotes a bundle of input–output pairs starting at t_1, with the understanding that $A_{\alpha_1}(t_1)$ is a member of the collection of bundles $\{A_{\alpha_0}(t_0)\}$, $\alpha_0 \in \Sigma_{t_0}$, $t_0 = 0, 1, 2, \cdots$, and that α_1 ranges over Σ_{t_1}.

Informally, the continuation condition merely asserts that a state α_0 at time t_0 is transferred by input u into a state α_1 at time t_1.

In terms of the four conditions stated above, the aggregates and states of a system can be defined as follows:

Definition

The *aggregates* of A are bundles of input–output pairs of A satisfying the covering, uniqueness, prefix, and continuation conditions. The *states* of A are names (or tags) of the aggregates of A. The set of names of the aggregates of input–output pairs starting at t_0 is the *state space* of A at time t_0. Usually, the state space Σ_{t_0} is assumed to be independent of t_0.

With the above definitions as a point of departure, one can deduce all of the properties of the states and state equations of a system that, in the classical approach, are assumed at the outset. The way in which this can be done is described in Ref. [8] and, more explicitly though in lesser detail, in Ref. [9].

In a previous section, we showed how the conventional approach in which the point of departure is the definition of a system through its state equations (14) and (15), can be generalized to fuzzy systems. This naturally gives rise to the question: How can the approach sketched above in which the starting point is (a) the definition of a system as a collection of input–output pairs, (b) the definition of an aggregate as a bundle of input–output pairs satisfying certain conditions, and (c) the definition of a state as a name for an aggregate, be similarly generalized to fuzzy systems?

If we could find an answer to this basic question, we might, perhaps, be able to develop effective techniques for the approximate analysis of complex systems for which state equations cannot be postulated at the outset. We state this question as an open problem because its solution can be perceived only dimly at this rudimentary stage of the development of the theory of fuzzy systems.

REFERENCES

[1] Zadeh, L. A., "Fuzzy sets," *Information and Control*, vol. 8, pp. 338–353, June 1965.

[2] Zadeh, L. A., "Fuzzy sets and systems," *Proc. Symp. System Theory*, Polytech. Inst. of Brooklyn, pp. 29–39, Apr. 1965.

[3] Zadeh, L. A., "Fuzzy algorithms," *Information and Control*, vol. 12, pp. 99–102, Feb. 1968.

[4] Santos, E. S., and W. G. Wee, "General formulation of sequential machines," *Information and Control*, vol. 12, pp. 5–10, 1968.

[5] Santos, E. S., "Maximin automata," *Information and Control*, vol. 13, pp. 363–377, Oct. 1968.

[6] Goguen, J., "L-fuzzy sets," *J. Math. Anal. Appl.*, vol. 18, pp. 145–174, Apr. 1967.

[7] Zadeh, L. A., "Shadows of fuzzy sets," *Problems in Transmission of Information* (in Russian), vol. 2, pp. 37–44, Mar. 1966.

[8] Zadeh, L. A., and C. A. Desoer, *Linear System Theory—The State Space Approach*. New York: McGraw-Hill, 1963.

[9] Zadeh, L. A., "The concept of state in system theory," in *Network and Switching Theory*, G. Biorci, ed. New York: Academic Press, 1968.

[10] Zadeh, L. A., "The concepts of system, aggregate and state in system theory," in *System Theory*, L. A. Zadeh and E. Polak, eds. New York: McGraw-Hill, 1969.

[11] Carlyle, J. W., "Reduced forms for stochastic sequential machines," *J. Math. Anal. Appl.*, vol. 7, pp. 167–175, 1963.

Quantitative Fuzzy Semantics†

L. A. ZADEH

Department of Electrical Engineering and Computer Sciences and Electronics Research Laboratory, University of California, Berkeley, California

ABSTRACT

The point of departure in this paper is the definition of a language, L, as a fuzzy relation from a set of terms, $T = \{x\}$, to a universe of discourse, $U = \{y\}$. As a fuzzy relation, L is characterized by its membership function $\mu_L: T \times U \to [0,1]$, which associates with each ordered pair (x,y) its grade of membership, $\mu_L(x,y)$, in L.

Given a particular x in T, the membership function $\mu_L(x,y)$ defines a fuzzy set, $M(x)$, in U whose membership function is given by $\mu_{M(x)}(y) = \mu_L(x,y)$. The fuzzy set $M(x)$ is defined to be the *meaning* of the term x, with x playing the role of a name for $M(x)$.

If a term x in T is a concatenation of other terms in T, that is, $x = x_1 \cdots x_n$, $x_i \in T$, $i = 1,\ldots,n$, then the meaning of x can be expressed in terms of the meanings of $x_1,\ldots,x_n$ through the use of a lambda-expression or by solving a system of equations in the membership functions of the x_i which are deduced from the syntax tree of x. The use of this approach is illustrated by examples.

1. INTRODUCTION

Few concepts are as basic to human thinking and yet as elusive of precise definition as the concept of "meaning." Innumerable papers and books in the fields of philosophy, psychology, and linguistics[1] have dealt at length with the question of what is the meaning of "meaning" without coming up with any definitive answers. In recent years, however, a number of fairly successful attempts at the formalization of semantics—the study of meaning—have been made by theoretical linguists [1–20] on the one side, and workers in the fields of programming languages and compilers [21–32] on the other.

† This work was supported in part by a grant from the Army Research Office, Durham, DAHCO-4-69-0024.
ABSTRACT

[1] Authoritative accounts of the development and foundations of semantics may be found in the books by Black [1], Lyons [2], Quine [3], Linsky [4], Abraham and Kiefer [5], Bar-Hillel [6], Carnap [7], Chomsky [8], Fodor and Katz [9], Harris [10], Katz [11], Ullmann [12], Shaumjan [13], and others.

Reprinted, with permission, from *Information Sciences*, 3(2), pp. 159–176.

These attempts reflect, above all, the acute need for a better understanding of the semantics of both natural and artificial languages—a need brought about by the rapidly growing availability of large-scale computers for automated information processing.

One of the basic aspects of the notion of "meaning" which has received considerable attention in the literature of linguistics, but does not appear to have been dealt with from a quantitative point of view, is that of the *fuzziness* of meaning. Thus, a word like "green" is a name for a class whose boundaries are not sharply defined, that is, a fuzzy class in which the transition from membership to non-membership is gradual rather than abrupt. The same is true of phrases such as "beautiful women," "tall buildings," "large integers," etc. In fact, it may be argued that in the case of natural languages, most of the words occurring in a sentence are names of fuzzy rather than non-fuzzy sets, with the sentence as a whole constituting a composite name for a fuzzy subset of the universe of discourse.

Can the fuzziness of meaning be treated quantitatively, at least in principle? The purpose of the present paper is to suggest a possible approach to this problem based on the theory of fuzzy sets [33–42]. It should be stressed, however, that our ideas, as described in the sequel, are rather tentative at this stage of their development and have no pretense at providing a working framework for a quantitative theory of the semantics of natural languages. Thus, our intent is merely to point to the possibility of treating the fuzziness of meaning in a quantitative way and suggest a basis for what might be called *quantitative fuzzy semantics*. Such semantics might be of some relevance to natural languages and may find perhaps some practical applications in the construction of fuzzy query languages for information retrieval systems. It may also be of use in dealing with problems relating to pattern recognition, fuzzy algorithms, and the description of the behavior of large-scale systems which are too complex to admit of characterization in precise terms.

2. PRELIMINARY DEFINITIONS AND NOTATION

Kernel Space

Our initial goal is to formalize the notion of "meaning" by equating it with a fuzzy subset of a "universe of discourse." To this end, we shall have to make several preliminary definitions, with our point of departure being a collection of objects which will be referred to as the *kernel space*.

A kernel space, $K=\{w\}$, with generic elements denoted by w, can be any prescribed set of objects or constructs. For example:

(a) $K=$ set of stationary objects in a room.
(b) $K=$ set of stationary as well as moving objects in a room.

(c) K = a finite set of lines which can be arbitrarily placed in a plane.
(d) K = the set of non-negative integers.
(e) K = a set of objects that one has seen, is seeing or can visualize.
(f) K = a set of smells.
(g) K = a set of objects with which one can interact through the sense of taction.

Note that we assume that K may include functions of time, e.g., moving cars, growing plants, running men, etc.

Let A be a fuzzy subset[2] of K, e.g., in the case of (d), the subset of large integers. Such a subset can be characterized by its membership function μ_A which associates with each element w of K its grade of membership, $\mu_A(w)$, in K. We assume that $\mu_A(w)$ is a number in the interval [0,1], with 1 and 0 representing, respectively, full membership and non-membership in A. For example, for the subset of large integers, μ_A can be defined subjectively by the expression:

$$\mu_A(w) = (1 + (w - 100)^{-2})^{-1}, \qquad \text{for } w \geqslant 100,$$
$$= 0, \qquad \text{for } w < 100.$$

As an additional illustration, let K be the set of integers from 0 to 100 representing the ages of individuals in a group. Then a fuzzy subset, labeled "middle-aged," may be characterized by a table of its membership function, e.g.,

w(=age)	40	41	42	43	44	45	46	47	48	49	50	51	52	53
$\mu_A(w)$	0.3	0.5	0.8	0.9	1	1	1	1	1	0.9	0.8	0.7	0.5	0.3

where only those pairs $(w, \mu_A(w))$ in which $\mu_A(w)$ is positive are tabulated.

Note that μ_A can be defined in a variety of ways; in particular, (a) by a formula, (b) by a table, (c) by an algorithm (recursively), and (d) in terms of other membership functions (as in a dictionary). In many practical situations μ_A has to be estimated from partial information about it, such as the values which $\mu_A(w)$ takes over a finite set of sample points $w_1, \ldots, w_N$. When a fuzzy

[2] Intuitively, a fuzzy set is a class with unsharp boundaries, that is, a class in which the transition from membership to non-membership may be gradual rather than abrupt. More concretely, a fuzzy set A in a space $X = \{x\}$ is a set of ordered pairs $\{(x, \mu_A(x))\}$, where $\mu_A(x)$ is termed the *grade of membership* of x in A. (See [33] for a more detailed discussion.) We shall assume that $\mu_A(x)$ is a number in the interval [0,1]; more generally, it can be a point in a lattice [36, 42]. The *union* of two fuzzy sets A and B is defined by $\mu_{A \cup B}(x) = \max(\mu_A(x), \mu_B(x))$. The *intersection* of A and B is defined by $\mu_{A \cap B}(x) = \min(\mu_A(x), \mu_B(x))$. Containment is defined by $A \subset B \Leftrightarrow \mu_A(x) \leqslant \mu_B(x)$ for all x. Equality is defined by $A = B \Leftrightarrow \mu_A(x) = \mu_B(x)$ for all x. Complementation is defined by $\mu_{A'}(x) = 1 - \mu_A(x)$ for all x. The symbols $\vee$ and $\wedge$ stand for max and min in infix form. Note that a membership function may be regarded as a predicate in a multivalued logic in which the truth values range over [0,1].

set A is defined incompletely—and hence only approximately—in this fashion, we shall say that A is partially defined by *exemplification*.[3] The problem of estimating μ_A from the set of pairs $\{(w_1,\mu_A(w_1)),\ldots,(w_N,\mu_A(w_N))\}$ is the problem of *abstraction*—a problem that plays a central role in pattern recognition [34]. We shall not concern ourselves with this problem in the present paper and will assume throughout that $\mu_A(w)$ is given or can be computed for all w in K.

Universe of Discourse

As was indicated earlier, our goal is to formalize the concept of meaning by equating it with a fuzzy subset of a certain collection of objects. In general, this collection has to be richer than K, the kernel space, because the concepts we may wish to define may involve not only the elements of K, but also ordered n-tuples of elements of K and, more generally, collections of fuzzy subsets of K. For example, if K is the set of non-negative integers, then the relation of approximate equality, $\approx$, is a fuzzy subset of K^2 ($K^2 =$ space of ordered pairs (w_1,w_2), with $w_1 \in K$ and $w_2 \in K$) rather than K. Similarly, if K is the collection of integers from 0 to 100 representing the ages of individuals in a group, then "middle-aged" may be regarded as a label for a fuzzy subset of K, while "much older than" is a label for a fuzzy subset of K^2.

Informally, the "universe of discourse" is a collection of objects, U, that is rich enough to make it possible to identify any concept, within a specified set of concepts, with a fuzzy subset of U.

One way of constructing such a collection is to start with a kernel space K and generate other collections by forming unions, direct products, and collections of fuzzy subsets. Thus, let $A+B$ (rather than $A \cup B$) denote the union of A and B; let $A \times B$ denote the direct product of A and B; and let $\mathscr{F}(A)$ denote the collection of all fuzzy (as well as non-fuzzy) subsets of A. Then, with K as a generating element, we can formally construct expressions such as[4]

$$
\begin{aligned}
&E = K + K^2 + \cdots + K^r, \qquad (1)\\
&E = K + K^2 + \mathscr{F}(K),\\
&E = K + K^2 + K \times \mathscr{F}(K),\\
&E = K + K^2 + \mathscr{F}(\mathscr{F}(K)),\\
&E = K + K^2 + (\mathscr{F}(K))^2,\\
&\text{etc.}
\end{aligned}
$$

[3] Definition by exemplification is somewhat similar to the notion of an ostensive definition in linguistics.

[4] Note that $\mathscr{P}(K)$, the power set of A, is a subset of $\mathscr{F}(K)$. Note also that K is an element of $\mathscr{P}(K)$ (as well as $\mathscr{F}(K)$), rather than a subset of $\mathscr{F}(K)$. Hence $K + \mathscr{F}(K) \neq \mathscr{F}(K)$. $\mathscr{F}(K)$ is a fuzzy set of type $n+1$ if K is a set of type n. Essentially, $\mathscr{F}(K)$ is the collection of functions from K to the unit interval.

More generally, E can be any expression which can be generated from K by a finite application of the operations $+$, $\times$, and $\mathscr{F}$, and which contains K as a summand.

The set expressed by E will, in general, contain many subsets which are of no interest. Thus, the universe of discourse will, in general, be a subset of E. This leads us to the following definition, which summarizes the foregoing discussion:

Definition 1. Let K be a given collection of objects termed the *kernel space*. Let E be a set which contains K and which is generated from K by a finite application of the operations $+$ (union), $\times$ (direct product), and $\mathscr{F}$ (collection of fuzzy subsets). Then, a *universe of discourse*, $U(K)$, or simply U, is a designated (not necessarily proper) subset of E.

Example 2. Let K be the set of integers from 0 to 100 representing the possible ages of a population. Let $E = K + K^2$ and let U be the subset of E in which K is restricted to the range 20–55. Then, such terms as "young," "middle-aged," and "close to middle age" may be regarded as labels for specified fuzzy subsets of K (see Figure 1). Similarly, "much older than"

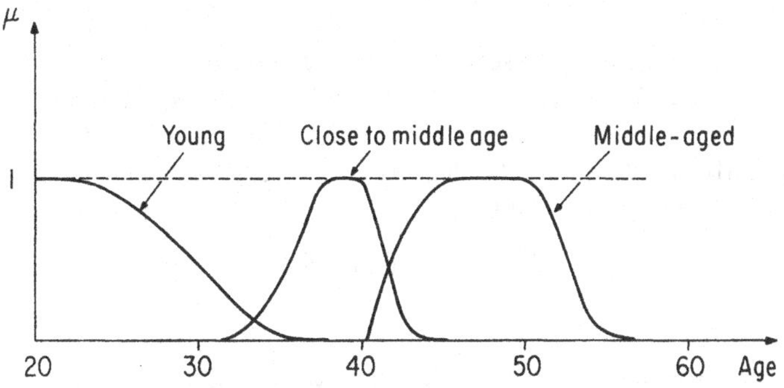

FIGURE 1. Characterization of "young," "close to middle-age" and "middle-aged" as fuzzy sets in U.

may be regarded as a label for a fuzzy relation, that is, a fuzzy subset of K^2. As a more specific illustration, consider an element of K such as 32. This element of K might be assigned the grade of membership of 0.2 in the fuzzy set labeled "young"; 0.1 in the fuzzy set labeled "close to middle age"; and 0 in the fuzzy set labeled "middle-aged." Similarly, a pair such as (44, 28) might be assigned the grade of membership 1 in the fuzzy set labeled "much older than," while the pair (44, 38) might be assigned the grade of membership 0.4 in the same fuzzy set.

Example 3. Let K have the same meaning as in Example 2, and assume that $U = K$. As in Example 2, we can define such terms as "young," "old," "middle-aged," "very young," "very very old," etc. as labels for specified subsets of U. However, if we were to attempt to define the term "very" in this fashion, we would fail because "very" is a function from $\mathscr{F}(K)$ to $\mathscr{F}(K)$, that is, it is an operation which transforms a fuzzy subset of K into a fuzzy subset of itself (see Figure 2). Thus, "very" has to be defined as a collection

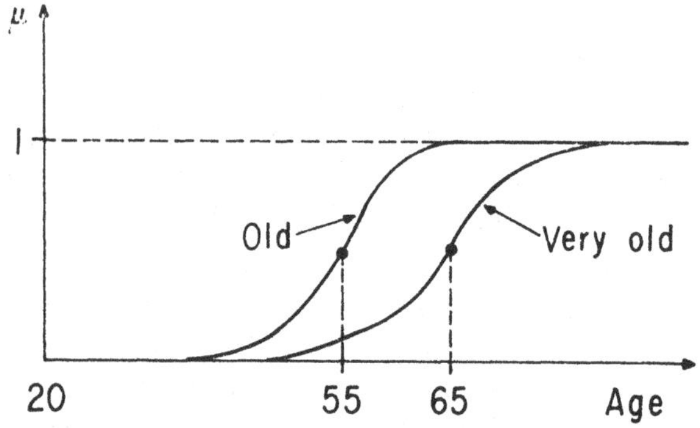

FIGURE 2. Representation of "very" as a function from $\mathscr{F}(K)$ to $\mathscr{F}(K)$.

of ordered pairs of fuzzy subsets of K, with a typical pair being of the form ("old," "very old"). In other words, "very" may be equated with a subset of $\mathscr{F}(K) \times \mathscr{F}(K)$ but not with a subset of K. This implies that: (a) $U = K$ is not sufficiently rich to allow the definition of "very" as a fuzzy subset of the universe of discourse; and (b) that

$$U = K + \mathscr{F}(K) \times \mathscr{F}(K) \tag{2}$$

is sufficiently rich for this purpose.

Comment 4. The above example illustrates an important point, namely, that the problem of finding an appropriate universe of discourse, U, given a set of terms which we wish to define as fuzzy subsets of U, may in general be quite non-trivial. We shall encounter further instances of this problem in Sections 3 and 4.

The concept of the universe of discourse provides us with a basis for formalizing certain aspects of the notion of meaning. A way in which this can be done is sketched in the following section.

3. MEANING

Consider two spaces: (a) a universe of discourse, U, and (b) a set of terms, T, which play the roles of names of fuzzy subsets of U. Let the generic elements of T and U be denoted by x and y, respectively. Our definition of the meaning of x may be stated as follows.

Definition 5. Let x be a term in T. Then the *meaning* of x, denoted by $M(x)$, is a fuzzy[5] subset of U characterized by a membership function $\mu(y|x)$ which is conditioned on x [40]. $\mu(y|x)$ may be specified in various ways, e.g., by a table, or by a formula, or by an algorithm, or by exemplification, or in terms of other membership functions.

Example 6. Let U be the universe of objects which we can see. Let T be the set of terms *white*, *gray*, *green*, *blue*, *yellow*, *red*, *black*. Then each of these terms, e.g., *red*, may be regarded as a name for a fuzzy subset of elements of U which are red in color. Thus, the meaning of *red*, $M(red)$, is a specified fuzzy subset of U.

Example 7. Let K be the set of integers from 0 to 100 representing the ages of individuals in a population, and let the universe of discourse be defined by $U = K$. Furthermore, let the set of terms be $T = \{$*young*, *old*, *middle-aged*, *not old*, *not young*, *not middle-aged*, *young or old*, *not young and not old*$\}$.

Consider the term $x = young$. The meaning of x is a fuzzy subset of U denoted by $M(young)$. Suppose that the membership function of $M(young)$ is subjectively specified to be

$$\begin{aligned}\mu(y|young) &= 1, \qquad \text{for } y < 25,\\ &= \left(1 + \left(\frac{y-25}{5}\right)^2\right)^{-1}, \qquad \text{for } y \geqslant 25,\end{aligned}$$

and similarly

$$\begin{aligned}\mu(y|old) &= 0, \qquad \text{for } y < 50,\\ &= \left(1 + \left(\frac{y-50}{5}\right)^{-2}\right)^{-1}, \qquad \text{for } y \geqslant 50,\end{aligned}$$

and

$$\begin{aligned}\mu(y|middle\text{-}aged) &= 0, \qquad \text{for } 0 \leqslant y < 35,\\ &= \left(1 + \left(\frac{y-45}{4}\right)^4\right)^{-1}, \qquad \text{for } 35 \leqslant y < 45,\\ &= \left(1 + \left(\frac{y-45}{5}\right)^2\right)^{-1}, \qquad \text{for } y \geqslant 45.\end{aligned}$$

The meaning of the remaining elements of T can be defined in terms of *young*, *old*, and *middle-aged* by interpreting "not" as the operation of com-

[5] It is understood, of course, that, as a special case, $M(x)$ may be non-fuzzy.

plementation, (or, equivalently, negation), "and" as the operation of intersection, and "or" as the operation of union in U. More specifically,

$$\begin{aligned}
&\mu(y|\textit{not old}) = 1 - \mu(y|\textit{old}),\\
&\mu(y|\textit{not young}) = 1 - \mu(y|\textit{young}),\\
&\mu(y|\textit{not middle-aged}) = 1 - \mu(y|\textit{middle-aged}),\\
&\mu(y|\textit{young or old}) = \mu(y|\textit{young}) \vee \mu(y|\textit{old}),\\
&\mu(y|\textit{not young and not old}) = (1 - \mu(y|\textit{young})) \wedge (1 - \mu(y|\textit{old})),
\end{aligned}$$

where the symbols $\wedge$ and $\vee$ stand for min and max, respectively. Thus, for $y = 57$, for example,

$$\begin{aligned}
&\mu(57|\textit{old}) = 0.66,\\
&\mu(57|\textit{not old}) = 1 - 0.66 = 0.34,\\
&\mu(57|\textit{young}) = 0.024,\\
&\mu(57|\textit{young or old}) = 0.66 \vee 0.024 = 0.66,\\
&\mu(57|\textit{not young and not old}) = (1 - 0.024) \wedge (1 - 0.66)\\
&\qquad = 0.976 \wedge 0.34\\
&\qquad = 0.34.
\end{aligned}$$

Note that the operations "not," "and," "or" are not elements of T and hence need not be defined in the same way as "young," "old," etc. However, if these operations were listed as elements of T, then we would need the space $\mathscr{F}(K) \times \mathscr{F}(K)$ to define "not" (which is a function from $\mathscr{F}(K)$ to $\mathscr{F}(K)$) as a subset of $\mathscr{F}(K) \times \mathscr{F}(K)$; and we would need the space $\mathscr{F}(K) \times \mathscr{F}(K) \times \mathscr{F}(K)$ to define "or" and "and" (which are functions from $\mathscr{F}(K) \times \mathscr{F}(K)$ to $\mathscr{F}(K)$) as subsets of $\mathscr{F}(K) \times \mathscr{F}(K) \times \mathscr{F}(K)$.

With Definition 5 as a starting point, we can define a number of notions which are related to the notion of meaning. In particular:

Definition 8. A *fuzzy concept*, or simply a *concept*, is a fuzzy subset of the universe of discourse. In this sense, a *term*, that is, an element of T, may be regarded as a name for a subset of U. Thus, if x is a term, then its meaning, $M(x)$, is a concept.

Although x and $M(x)$ are entirely different entities, it is expedient to abbreviate $M(x)$ to x, relying on the context for the determination of whether x stands for a term or for its meaning, $M(x)$. This is what we usually do in everyday discourse, because in such discourse it is rarely necessary to differentiate between x and $M(x)$. On the other hand, it is important to differentiate —or at least to understand the difference—between x and $M(x)$ in the case of programming languages, machine translation of languages, and other areas in which ambiguity of interpretation can lead to serious errors.

It is convenient to classify terms and concepts according to their *level* (or *type*), which is a rough measure of the complexity of characterization of a concept. More specifically:

Definition 9. Let K be the kernel space of U, the universe of discourse. Then a term x and the corresponding concept $M(x)$ are at *level* 1 if $M(x)$ is a subset of K or, more generally, K^n, $n = 1,2,\ldots$, for some finite n; x and $M(x)$ are at level 2 if $M(x)$ is a subset of $\mathscr{F}(K)$ or $(\mathscr{F}(K))^n$ for some finite n; and, more generally, x and $M(x)$ are at level l if $M(x)$ is a subset of $(\mathscr{F}^{l-1}(K))^n$ for some finite n, where $\mathscr{F}^{l-1}(K)$ stands for $\mathscr{F}(\cdots\mathscr{F}(\mathscr{F}(K)))$, with $l-1$ $\mathscr{F}$'s in the expression. Equivalently, and recursively, we can say that $M(x)$ is a concept at level l if $M(x)$ is a collection of concepts at level $l-1$.

Example 10. Suppose that K is the set of objects which can be seen or visualized. Then the concepts labeled "white," "yellow," "green," "red," "black," etc. are at level 1 because they can be represented as fuzzy subsets of K. Likewise, the concepts labeled "redder than," "darker than," etc., are at level 1 because they can be represented as fuzzy subsets of K^2. (For example, if y_1 and y_2 are objects in K, then with the ordered pair (y_1,y_2) we can associate a grade of membership $\mu(y_1,y_2)$ in a fuzzy set in K^2 labeled "darker than.")

Consider, on the other hand, the concept labeled "color." This concept is essentially a collection of the concepts $M(white)$, $M(yellow)$, $M(green),\ldots$, $M(black)$, and as such is a subset of $\mathscr{F}(K)$. Thus, "color" is a name for a concept at level 2.

Still higher on the scale is the concept labeled "visual attribute." In this case, we may view "visual attribute," as a collection of concepts labeled "color," "shape," "size," etc. each of which is at level 2. Hence, "visual attribute," is a label for a concept at level 3.

Clearly, concepts at level higher than 1 are generally harder to define by exemplification than concepts at level 1. It is for this reason that in teaching a natural language to one who does not know any other language, e.g., a child, we usually begin by defining via exemplification a set of primitive concepts at level 1 which form a basic vocabulary, and then build up on this vocabulary by defining other concepts on level 1 as well as concepts on levels higher than 1 in terms of the concepts already defined.

One of the basic aspects of the notion of meaning which we have not mentioned so far is that of context-dependence. Clearly, the meaning of "tall building" is quite different in New York from what it is in Washington, D.C. Thus, in identifying the meaning of a term x with a fuzzy subset M of the universe of discourse, it is tacitly understood that M depends not only on x but also on the context in which x occurs. Depending on the nature of context-dependence, this may or may not seriously complicate the association of a meaning with a composite term—a subject discussed in the following section.

4. LANGUAGE

In the preceding section we defined the meaning of a term $x \in T$ as a fuzzy subset, $M(x)$, of the universe of discourse U, with the understanding that $M(x)$ is characterized by a conditioned membership function $\mu(y|x)$.

In this spirit, it is natural to regard a *language* as a fuzzy correspondence between the elements of T and U. More specifically:

Definition 11. A *language*, L, is a fuzzy binary relation[6] from a set of terms, T, to a universe of discourse, U. As a fuzzy relation, L is characterized by a membership function μ_L: $T \times U \to [0,1]$ which associates with each ordered pair $(x,y), x \in T, y \in U$, its grade of membership $\mu_L(x,y)$ in L, with $0 \leqslant \mu_L(x,y) \leqslant 1$.

The fuzzy relation L induces a correspondence between the elements of T and the fuzzy subsets of U. Thus, to a term x_0 in T corresponds a fuzzy subset $M(x_0)$, that is, the *meaning* of x_0, whose membership function is defined in terms of $\mu_L(x,y)$ by

$$\mu_{M(x_0)}(y) = \mu_L(x_0,y), \qquad y \in U, \tag{3}$$

which implies that $\mu_L(x,y)$ may be equated with $\mu(y|x)$.

Note that, if we consider a particular element of U, say y_0, then $\mu_L(x,y_0)$ defines a fuzzy set, $D(y_0)$, in T in which a term x has the grade of membership

$$\mu_{D(y_0)}(x) = \mu_L(x,y_0).$$

Intuitively, this fuzzy set, to which we shall refer as a *descriptor* set, serves to characterize the extent to which each term in T describes a given element of U.

In summary, a *language*, L, is a fuzzy relation from T to U characterized by a membership function $\mu_L(x,y)$. As a relation, L associates with each term x_0 in T its *meaning*, $M(x_0)$, which is a fuzzy set in U defined by $\mu_{M(x_0)}(y) = \mu_L(x_0,y)$. Furthermore, L associates with each element y_0 of U a fuzzy *descriptor set*, $D(y_0)$, defined by $\mu_{D(y_0)}(x) = \mu_L(x,y_0)$.

Comment 12. Our definition of a language as a fuzzy relation is closer in spirit to the traditional conception of language in linguistics than to its definition in the theory of formal languages. In the latter, a language is defined as a subset of strings over a finite alphabet—a definition which fails to reflect

---

[6] A fuzzy binary relation R from $X = \{x\}$ to $Y = \{y\}$ is a fuzzy subset of $X \times Y$. Let $\mu_R(x,y)$ denote the membership of an ordered pair (x,y) in R. The domain of R is denoted by dom R and is defined by $\mu_{\text{dom}\,R}(x) = \vee_y \mu_R(x,y)$, where $\vee_y$ denotes the supremum over Y. A fuzzy relation from X to X is *reflexive* iff $\mu_R(x,x) = 1$ for all x in X. R is *symmetric* iff $\mu_R(x,y) = \mu_R(y,x)$ for all x, y in X; and R is *transitive* iff $R \supset R \circ R$, where the composition, $R \circ Q$, of relations R and Q is defined by $\mu_{R \circ Q}(x,y) = \vee \mu_R(x,z) \wedge \mu_Q(z,y)$. Further details may be found in [39].

the essential role of a language as a *correspondence* between a set of strings and a set of objects. As we shall see presently, if one adopts as a starting point the definition of a language L as a fuzzy relation from T to U, then a language in the sense of the theory of formal languages may be regarded as the *domain* of L.

Example 13. As a very simple illustration at this point, consider the case in which $U = K =$ set of integers from 60 to 80 representing the heights of individuals in a population, and T consists of the terms "short," "average," "tall," "very tall." Suppose that the membership function of a language L from T to U is defined as follows:

$$\mu_L(short, y) = \left(1 + \left(\frac{y-60}{8}\right)^2\right)^{-1},$$

$$\mu_L(average, y) = \left(1 + \left(\frac{y-68}{4}\right)^2\right)^{-1},$$

$$\mu_L(tall, y) = 0, \qquad \text{for } 60 \leqslant y < 66,$$

$$\mu_L(tall, y) = \left(1 + \left(\frac{y-66}{2}\right)^{-2}\right)^{-1}, \qquad \text{for } 66 \leqslant y \leqslant 80,$$

$$\mu_L(very\ tall, y) = (\mu_L(tall, y))^2.$$

Assume $y_0 = 68$. The corresponding fuzzy descriptor set may be expressed as

$$D(y_0) = \{(short, 0.5), (average, 1), (tall, 0.5), (very\ tall, 0.25)\}.$$

Domain of a Language

If L is a fuzzy language from T to U, then its *domain*, $D(L)$, is a fuzzy set in T which is the "shadow"[7] of L on T. The expression for the membership function of $D(L)$ is

$$\mu_{D(L)}(x) = \bigvee_y \mu_L(x,y), \tag{5}$$

where the supremum $\bigvee_y$ is taken over all y in U.

If T is a set of strings over a finite alphabet, then $D(L)$ is a fuzzy subset of T. In this sense, $D(L)$ corresponds to the notion of a fuzzy language described in [41].

Intuitively, $D(L)$ serves to indicate, in a sense, the degree of *meaningfulness*

[7] If A is fuzzy set in $X = X_1 \times X_2 \times \cdots \times X_n$, $X_i = \{x_i\}$, $i = 1,\ldots,n$, with membership function $\mu(x_1,\ldots,x_n)$, then the *shadow* of A on $X_2 \times \cdots \times X_n$ is a fuzzy set in $X_2 \times \cdots \times X_n$ whose membership function, μ_1, is given by $\mu_1(x_2,\ldots,x_n) = \bigvee_{x_1} \mu(x_1,\ldots,x_n)$. Additional details may be found in [35].

of each term in T. We include the qualification "in a sense" in this statement because the concept of meaningfulness has many aspects which are not covered by the above interpretation of $D(L)$.

From the definition of $D(L)$ it follows at once that if each term x in T is *fully meaningful* in the sense that its meaning, $M(x)$, is a normal[8] fuzzy subset of U, then the domain of L coincides with T. For, we can write

$$\mu_{D(L)}(x) = \bigvee_y \mu_L(x,y) = 1, \qquad x \in T,$$

and hence $D(L) = T$.

Another simple consequence of (5) is the following. Assume that each x in T is fully meaningful. Let $M(x_0)$ denote the normal fuzzy subset of U which is the meaning of a term x_0 in T. This subset induces,[9] via the relation L, a fuzzy subset $\bar{M}(x_0)$ of T whose membership function is given by

$$\mu_{\bar{M}(x_0)}(x) = \bigvee_y \mu_L(x,y) \wedge \mu_{M(x_0)}(y)$$

or

$$\mu_{\bar{M}(x_0)}(x) = \bigvee_y \mu_L(x,y) \wedge \mu_L(x_0,y).$$

Clearly,

$$\mu_{\bar{M}(x_0)}(x_0) = \bigvee_y \mu_L(x_0,y) = 1$$

by the normality of $M(x_0)$. Thus, as should be expected on the grounds of consistency, the term x_0 has unity grade of membership in $M(x_0)$.

Computation of $\mu_L(x,y)$

So long as the number of elements in T is small and U is a reasonable simple space in relation to the information processing capabilities of the system employing L as a language, it may be practicable to define L by tabulating its membership function $\mu_L(x,y)$.

In most cases, however, the storage capacity of a system is not adequate for a tabulation of $\mu_L(x,y)$. This makes it necessary, in general, to characterize $\mu_L(x,y)$ in part by a table and in part by a procedure which makes it possible to compute the values of $\mu_L(x,y)$ for a given x rather than look them up in a table.

The same limitations make it necessary, in general, to characterize T by a grammar, G_T, rather than by a listing of its elements. Typically, then, the

---

[8] A fuzzy set A in X is *normal* iff $\bigvee_x \mu_A(x) = 1$ and *subnormal* iff $\bigvee_x \mu_A(x) < 1$. Thus, in Example 13, the fuzzy sets $M(\textit{short})$ and $M(\textit{average})$ are normal while the fuzzy set $M(\textit{short and average})$ is subnormal.

[9] If R is a fuzzy relation from $X = \{x\}$ to $Y = \{y\}$, then a fuzzy set A in X induces a fuzzy set B in Y whose membership function is expressed by $\mu_B(y) = \bigvee_x \mu_R(x,y) \wedge \mu_A(x)$. (See [40] for additional details.)

elements of T are strings of words separated by spaces, with the grammar G_T providing a set of rules for the generation of all such strings which represent the terms of T. Thus, a term in T is either a word or a concatenation of words. These two types of terms will be referred to as *simple terms* and *composite terms*, respectively, when there is a need for differentiating between them.

As in classical semantics, a central problem in quantitative semantics is that of devising a procedure for computing the meaning, $M(x)$, of a composite term x in T from the knowledge of the meanings of the simple terms $x_1, x_2, \ldots, x_N$ whose concatenation forms x. The converse problem, namely, the problem of *description*, is that of (a) determining a term x in T whose meaning, $M(x)$, is a specified fuzzy subset of U, or (b) determining the descriptor set in T corresponding to a given element y in U. In general, (a) is a more complicated problem than (b) because in most cases it involves an approximation to the given fuzzy subset by one which corresponds to a term in T. We shall not consider either (a) or (b) in the present paper.

The problem of the computation of $\mu_L(x,y)$ for composite terms is a relatively simple one when x may be represented as an N-tuple of parameters for a given program or, alternatively, as an N-tuple of arguments for a lambda-expression. A more difficult problem is that of constructing a program for computing $\mu_L(x,y)$, with x as a parameter, given the grammar G_T for generating the terms in T.

As an illustration of these problems consider first the case in which x is an N-tuple $(x_1, x_2, \ldots, x_N)$ in which each x_i is a simple term that has a specified meaning in U characterized by a membership function $\mu_i(y) = \mu_L(x_i, y)$. For example, the x_i could be the attributes of a record in a file reading (*old, tall, 15, very, fat*). Thus, $x_1 = old$, $x_2 = tall$, $x_3 = 15$, $x_4 = very$, $x_5 = fat$. Assuming for simplicity that U is the real half-line, the procedure for computation of $\mu_L(x,y)$ as a function of y could have the following form for each $y \geqslant x_3$. Expressed in plain words:

1. If $x_4 = very$ set $z_1 = (\mu_5(y))^2$. Else if $x_4 = blank$ set $z_1 = \mu_5(y)$.
2. Set $z_2 = z_1 \vee \mu_2(y)$.
3. Set $z_3 = \mu_1(y) \wedge z_2$.
4. Set $\mu_L(x,y) = z_3\,(1 + (y - x_3)^2)^{-1}$.

Equivalently, the computations to be performed on the given attributes may be expressed in the form of a lambda-expression [43]. For the example under consideration, assume for simplicity that $r(x_4) = 1$ if $x_4 = blank$ and $r(x_4) = 2$ if $x_4 = very$. Then

$$\mu_L(x,y) = \lambda(x_1,x_2,x_3,x_4,x_5)\,[(\mu_L(x_1,y) \wedge (\mu_L(x_2,y) \vee (\mu_L(x_5,y))^{r(x_4)}))$$
$$(1 + (y - x_3)^2)^{-1}]\,[old,\ tall,\ 15,\ very,\ fat]. \quad (6)$$

In this expression, the factor $\lambda(x_1,\ldots,x_5)$ signifies that the arguments *old, tall, 15, very, fat* should be substituted, respectively, for the bound variables x_1, x_2, x_3, x_4, x_5 in the bracketed expression.

As a simple illustration of the case in which T is characterized by a grammar, assume that the simple terms of T are the following: *young, old, very, not, and, or* and that the composite terms of T are generated by the production system P defined below, in which S, A, B, C, O and Y are non-terminals. (The parentheses serve as markers.)

$$\begin{array}{ll} S \to A & C \to O \\ S \to S \text{ or } A & C \to Y \\ A \to B & O \to \text{very } O \\ A \to A \text{ and } B & Y \to \text{very } Y \\ B \to C & O \to \text{old} \\ B \to \text{not } C & Y \to \text{young} \\ C \to (S) & \end{array}$$

Typical terms generated by this grammar are:

not very young
not very young and not very old
young and not old
old or not very very young
young and (old or not young)

To compute $\mu_L(x,y)$ when x is a composite term, we shall use an approach similar to that described by Knuth in [32]. Specifically, suppose that we are given $\mu_L(young, y)$ and $\mu_L(old, y)$. The remaining simple terms are regarded as functions on $\mathscr{F}(K)$ or $\mathscr{F}(K) \times \mathscr{F}(K)$ (in the sense of Example 7) which are defined by the following rules associated with those productions in P in which they occur. Employing the subscripts L and R to differentiate between the terminal symbols on the left- and right-hand sides of a production and using $\mu(E)$ as an abbreviation for $\mu_L(E,y)$, where E is a terminal or non-terminal symbol, the rules in question can be expressed as

$$\begin{array}{lll} S \to A & \Rightarrow & \mu(S_L) = \mu(A_R) \\ A \to B & \Rightarrow & \mu(A_L) = \mu(B_R) \\ B \to C & \Rightarrow & \mu(B_L) = \mu(C_R) \\ S \to S \text{ or } A & \Rightarrow & \mu(S_L) = \mu(S_R) \vee \mu(A_R) \\ A \to A \text{ and } B & \Rightarrow & \mu(A_L) = \mu(A_R) \wedge \mu(B_R) \\ B \to \text{not } C & \Rightarrow & \mu(B_L) = 1 - \mu(C_R) \\ O \to \text{very } O & \Rightarrow & \mu(O_L) = (\mu(O_R))^2 \\ Y \to \text{very } Y & \Rightarrow & \mu(Y_L) = (\mu(Y_R))^2 \\ C \to O & \Rightarrow & \mu(C_L) = \mu(O_R) \\ C \to Y & \Rightarrow & \mu(C_L) = \mu(Y_R) \end{array} \tag{7}$$

$$C \to (S) \quad \Rightarrow \mu(C_L) = \mu(S_R)$$
$$O \to old \quad \Rightarrow \mu(O_L) = \mu(old)$$
$$Y \to young \quad \Rightarrow \mu(Y_L) = \mu(young)$$

Now consider a composite term such as

$$x = \textit{not very young and not very old.} \tag{8}$$

In this simple case the expression for the membership function of $M(x)$ can be written by inspection. Thus,

$$\mu_L(x,y) = (1 - \mu_L{}^2(young,y)) \wedge (1 - \mu_L{}^4(old,y)). \tag{9}$$

More generally, as a first step in the computation of $\mu_L(x,y)$ it is necessary to construct the syntax tree of x. For the composite term under consideration, the syntax tree is readily found to be that shown in Figure 3. (The subscripts in this figure serve the purpose of numbering the nodes.)

Proceeding from bottom to top and employing the relations of (7) for the computation of the membership function at each node, we obtain the system of non-linear equations:

$$\begin{aligned}
\mu(Y_7) &= \mu_L(young, y) \\
\mu(Y_6) &= \mu^2(Y_7) \\
\mu(C_5) &= \mu(Y_6) \\
\mu(B_4) &= 1 - \mu(C_5) \\
\mu(A_3) &= \mu(B_4) \\
\mu(O_{12}) &= \mu_L(old, y) \\
\mu(O_{11}) &= \mu^2(O_{12}) \\
\mu(O_{10}) &= \mu^2(O_{11}) \\
\mu(C_9) &= \mu(O_{10}) \\
\mu(B_8) &= 1 - \mu(C_9) \\
\mu(A_2) &= \mu(A_3) \wedge \mu(B_8) \\
\mu_L(x,y) &= \mu(S_1) = \mu(A_2)
\end{aligned} \tag{10}$$

In virtue of the tree structure of the syntax tree this system of equations can readily be solved by successive substitutions, yielding the result expressed by (9).

The simplicity of the above example owes much, of course, to the assumption that T can be generated by a context-free grammar. The problem of computation of $\mu_L(x,y)$ may become considerably more complicated when this assumption cannot be made. And, needless to say, it becomes far more complex in the setting of natural languages, in which both the semantics and syntax are intrinsically fuzzy in character.

When we speak of the fuzziness of syntax in the case of natural languages, we mean that, for such languages, the notion of grammaticality is a fuzzy concept. For example, the set of sentences in English is a fuzzy subset, E, of the set of all strings over the alphabet $\{A, B, \ldots, Z, \text{blank}\}$. Thus, if x

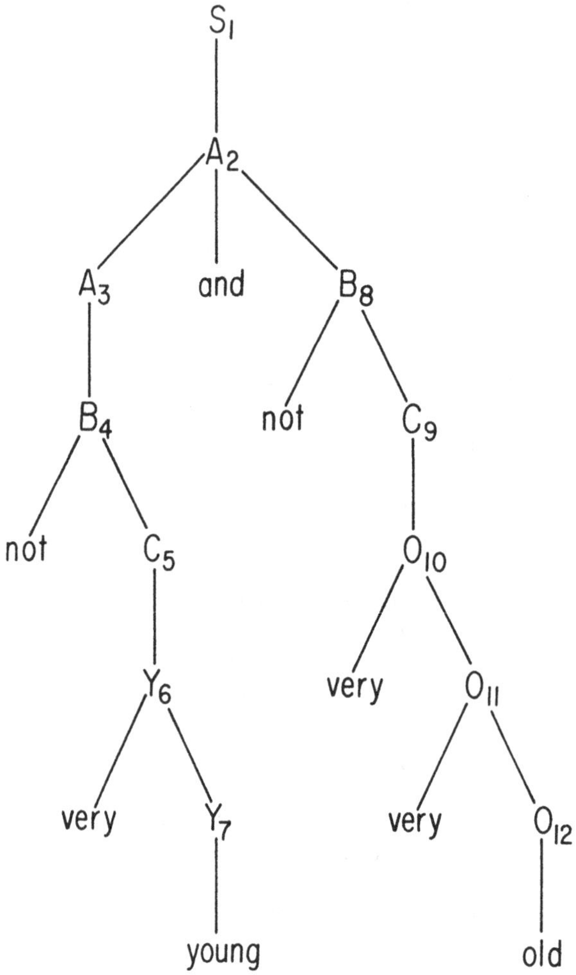

FIGURE 3. Syntax tree for x = *not very young and not very very old.*

is a sentence, then $\mu_E(x)$, the grade of membership of x in E, may be regarded as the degree of grammaticality of x.

A fuzzy set of strings may be generated by a fuzzy grammar in which a typical production is of the form $\alpha \xrightarrow{\rho} \beta$, where α and β are sentential forms and ρ is the grade of membership of β in a fuzzy set conditioned on α (i.e., the consequent is a fuzzy set conditioned on the antecedent—see [41] for additional details). This does not imply, however, that a fuzzy grammar of this nature can provide an adequate model for the fuzziness of the syntax of a natural language. Indeed, it appears that we are still quite far from being able to construct such a model for natural languages and use it as a basis for machine translation or other applications in which the semantics of natural languages plays an essential role.

CONCLUDING REMARKS

In the foregoing discussion we have addressed ourselves to but a few of the many basic issues involved in the construction of a conceptual framework for a quantitative theory of fuzzy semantics. Our limited aim has been to suggest the possibility of constructing such a theory for artificial languages whose terms have fuzzy meaning, and, indirectly, to contribute to a clarification of the concept of meaning in the case of natural languages.

At this early stage of its development, our approach appears to have potential applicability to the construction of fuzzy query languages for purposes of information retrieval, and, possibly, to the formulation and implementation of fuzzy algorithms and programs. Eventually, it may contribute, perhaps, to a better understanding of the semantic structure of natural languages.

REFERENCES

1 M. Black, *The Labyrinth of Language*, Mentor Books, New York, 1968.
2 J. Lyons, *Introduction to Theoretical Linguistics*, Cambridge University Press, Cambridge, 1968.
3 W. Quine, *Word and Object*, MIT Press, Cambridge, Mass., 1960.
4 L. Linsky (ed.), *Semantics and the Philosophy of Language*, University of Illinois Press, Urbana, Ill., 1952.
5 S. Abraham and F. Kiefer, *A Theory of Structural Semantics*, Mouton, The Hague, 1965.
6. Y. Bar-Hillel, *Language and Information*, Addison-Wesley, Reading, Mass., 1964.
7 R. Carnap, *Meaning and Necessity*, University of Chicago Press, Chicago, 1956.
8 N. Chomsky, *Cartesian Linguistics*, Harper & Row, New York, 1966.
9 J. A. Fodor and J. J. Katz (eds.), *The Structure of Language*, Prentice-Hall, Englewood Cliffs, N. J., 1964.
10 Z. Harris, *Mathematical Structures of Language*, Interscience, New York, 1968.
11 J. J. Katz, *The Philosophy of Language*, Harper & Row, New York, 1966.
12 S. Ullmann, *Semantics: An Introduction to the Science of Meaning*, Blackwell, Oxford, 1962.
13 S. K. Shaumjan, *Structural Linguistics*, Nauka, Moscow, 1965.
14 S. K. Shaumjan (ed.), *Problems of Structural Linguistics*, Nauka, Moscow, 1967.
15 F. Kiefer, *Mathematical Linguistics in Eastern Europe*, American Elsevier, New York, 1968.
16 N. Chomsky, *Current Issues in Linguistic Theory*, Mouton, The Hague, 1965.
17 R. Jacobson (ed.), *On the Structure of Language and its Mathematical Aspects*, American Mathematical Society, Providence, R. I., 1961.

18 J. J. Katz, Recent issues in semantic theory, *Found. Language* **3** (1967), 124–194.
19 P. Ziff, *Semantic Analysis*, Cornell University Press, Ithaca, N. Y., 1960.
20 B. Altmann and W. A. Riessler, *Linguistic Problems and Outline of a Prototype Test*, TR-1392, Harry Diamond Laboratories, Washington, D. C., 1968.
21 C. Strachey, Towards a formal semantics. *Formal Language Description Languages for Computer Programming*, T. B. Steel, Jr. (ed.), North-Holland, Amsterdam, 1966.
22 D. G. Hays, *Introduction to Computational Linguistics*, American Elsevier, New York, 1967.
23 E. T. Irons, A syntax directed compiler for ALGOL 60, *Comm. ACM*, **4** (1961), 51–55.
24 E. T. Irons, Toward more versatile mechanical translators, *Amer. Math. Soc., Proc. Symp. Appl. Math.* **18** (1963), 41–50.
25 J. W. de Bakker, Formal definition of programming languages, with an application to the definition of ALGOL 60, *Math. Centrum Amsterdam* **18** (1967).
26 C. Böhm, The CUCH as a formal and description language, *Formal Language Description Languages for Computer Programming*, North-Holland, Amsterdam, 1966, pp. 266–294.
27 J. McCarthy, A formal definition of a subset of ALGOL, *Formal Language Description Languages for Computer Programming*, North-Holland, Amsterdam, 1966, pp. 1–12.
28 N. Wirth and H. Weber, Euler: A generalization of ALGOL and its formal definition, *Comm. ACM*, **9** (1966), 11–23, 89–99, 878.
29 C. C. Elgot, Machine species and their computation languages, *Formal Language Description Languages for Computer Programming*, North-Holland, Amsterdam, 1966, pp. 160–179.
30 P. J. Landin, A correspondence between ALGOL 60 and Church's *lambda notation*, *Comm. ACM* **8** (1965), 89–101, 158–165.
31 PL/1 Definition Group of the Vienna Laboratory, *Formal Definition of* PL/1, *IBM Tech. Report* TR25.071, Vienna, 1966.
32 D. E. Knuth, Semantics of context-free languages, *Math. Systems Theory* **2** (1968) 127–145.
33 L. A. Zadeh, Fuzzy sets, *Information and Control* **8** (1965), 338–353.
34 R. E. Bellman, R. Kalaba, and L. A. Zadeh, Abstraction and pattern classification, *J. Math. Anal. Appl.* **13** (1966), 1–7.
35 L. A. Zadeh, Shadows of fuzzy sets, *Problems of Information Transmission* (in Russian), **2** (March 1966), 37–44.
36 J. Goguen, *L*-Fuzzy sets, *J. Math. Anal. Appl.* **18** (1967), 145–174.
37 L. A. Zadeh, Fuzzy algorithms, *Information and Control* **12** (1968), 99–102.
38 C. L. Chang, Fuzzy topological spaces, *J. Math. Anal. Appl.* **24** (1968), 182–190.
39 L. A. Zadeh, *Similarity Relations and Fuzzy Orderings*, Memo No. ERL-M277, July 1970, Electronics Research Laboratory, University of California, Berkeley, Calif. (to appear in *Information Sciences*).
40 L. A. Zadeh, *Toward a Theory of Fuzzy Systems*, Report No. 69–2, June 1969, Electronics Research Laboratory, University of California, Berkeley, Calif.
41 E. T. Lee and L. A. Zadeh, Note on fuzzy languages, *Information Sciences* **1** (1969), 421–434.
42 J. G. Brown, Fuzzy Sets on Boolean Lattices, Report No. 1957, January 1969, Ballistic Research Laboratories, Aberdeen, Maryland.
43 A. Church, *The Calculi of Lambda-Conversion*, Princeton University Press, Princeton, N. J., 1941.

Received September 2, 1970; revised September 10, 1970

A RATIONALE FOR FUZZY CONTROL*,†

L. A. ZADEH

Department of Electrical Engineering and Computer Sciences,
and Electronics Research Laboratory,
University of California
Berkeley, California

The past decade has witnessed a rapidly growing mathematization of control theory, with the result that the relation between the theory and its application has become more tenuous than ever.

Looking backward, in the years following World War II when the theory of control systems was still in its infancy, much of the control literature centered on the steady-state or transient analysis of time-invariant linear systems. The level of mathematical sophistication of the theory was relatively low, and only a few papers contained theorems and their proofs.

The advent of the space age in 1957 had a dramatic effect on the orientation and character of control theory. The sudden elevation in its importance attracted to control theory a number of prominent mathematicians, most notably L. S. Pontryagin. As a result, starting in 1960 the level of mathematical sophistication of the theory began to grow very rapidly, swinging the pendulum all the way from the low-brow imprecision of the forties to the high-brow mathematical formalism of the seventies.

Today, no respectable paper in any high-class periodical dealing with control theory can fail to contain at least a few theorems and their proofs. In one respect, this deserves applause. Certainly, the theorem–proof type of exposition forces the author to state his assumptions and conclusions very precisely and use rigorous reasoning to establish the validity of his assertions. On the other hand, the quest for precision frequently tends to overshadow other, perhaps more important goals, such as the invention of new types of control systems or the discovery of results which, though not of mathematical interest, are of high relevance to real world problems. Indeed, one very visible consequence of the preoccupation with precision is that much of the literature of control theory has become farther and farther

*This work was supported in part by the Navy Electronic Systems Command, Contract N00039-71-C-0255.

removed from reality, and less and less capable to contribute to the solution of the complex large-scale man–machine systems problems which are at the root of the many crises confronting modern society.

In short, I believe that excessive concern with precision has become a stultifying influence in control and system theory, largely because it tends to focus the research in these fields on those, and only those, problems which are susceptible of exact solution. As a result, the many classes of important problems in which the data, the objectives, and the constraints are too complex or too ill-defined to admit of precise mathematical analysis have been and are being avoided on the grounds of mathematical intractability.

To be able to say something that is significant about problems of this type, we have to abandon our insistence on precision and admit answers that are somewhat fuzzy or uncertain. For example, we may have to be satisfied with a fuzzy as well as uncertain assertion such as "It is *very likely* that x will be in the *neighborhood* of 0.3 if y is increased by 5 percent," rather than with a precise but uncertain assertion like "If y is increased by 5 percent, then with probability 0.9 x will be in the interval [0.28, 0.32]."

The essence of the difference between the fuzzy assertion, on the one hand, and the precise assertion, on the other, is that the former contains names of fuzzy sets (denoted by italicized words), i.e., *very likely*, and *neighborhood.* These fuzzy sets can be defined precisely via their respective membership functions, e.g.,

$$\mu\ (\mathit{neighborhood},\ x) = \left(1 + (50(x - 0.3))^2\right)^{-1} \tag{1}$$

and

$$\mu\ (\mathit{very\ likely},\ p) = p^2\,, \quad 0 \le p \le 1 \tag{2}$$

where p denotes probability.

Thus, (1) implies that the value $x = 0.32$ has the grade of membership μ (neighborhood, 0.32) $= 0.5$ in the fuzzy subset of real numbers labeled "neighborhood of 0.3." Similarly, (2) implies that $p = 0.8$ has the grade of membership μ (*very likely*, 0.8) $= 0.64$ in the fuzzy subset of the interval [0, 1] labeled "*very likely.*"

In this way we can make precise, but not certain,[a] a fuzzy assertion. What is much more significant, however, is the possibility of constructing fuzzy algorithms[b] in which the existence of fuzzy feedback makes it unnecessary to specify the membership functions of fuzzy sets in precise quantitative terms. By providing approximate (fuzzy) solutions to complex problems, such algorithms could vastly enlarge the applicability of control theory to real world problems, particularly in the realm of large-scale man–machine systems.

[a] An assertion is not *certain* if it contains probabilistic statements. Thus a fuzzy assertion can be precise without being certain if the membership functions of the fuzzy sets appearing in the assertion are defined precisely.

[b] Bellman, R. L. and Zadeh, L. A., "Decision-Making in a Fuzzy Environment," *Management Science*, Vol. 17, Dec. 1970, pp. B-141–B-164.

Fuzzy algorithms underlie much of human thinking. In fact, we employ them all the time, both consciously and subconsciously. Thus, we use fuzzy algorithms when we walk, eat, drive, or park a car, tie a knot, cook food, recognize patterns and make a decision. Our use of these algorithms, however, is for the most part intuitive and qualitative rather than systematic and quantitative. Thus, in many instances we would not be able to specify the steps in an algorithm for performing a familiar task, such as tying a necktie of recognizing a visual or aural pattern. Indeed, one of the basic problems of artificial intelligence is that of identifying the fuzzy algorithms which human beings use subconsciously and yet so successfully in abstraction, pattern recognition, and decision making.

The key to the success of a fuzzy algorithm is fuzzy feedback, that is, a mechanism for (*a*) observing—not necessarily precisely—the result of execution of a fuzzy instruction; and (*b*) executing a new instruction based on the result or results of preceding instructions. Generally, the fuzzy feedback must have the property that the degree of fuzziness in observations decreases as the system under control approaches its goal.

To illustrate this point, consider the following simple control problem. Suppose that we wish to transfer a blind-folded subject A from an initial position x in a room with no obstacles to a final position y. Furthermore, suppose that the fuzzy instructions are limited to the following set: (1) Turn counter-clockwise by approximately α degrees, with α being a multiple of, say, 15; (2) Take a step; (3) Take a small step; and (4) Take a very small step.

Under these assumptions, a simple fuzzy algorithm for guiding A from x to y may be stated as follows. (It is understood that after A executes an instruction, his new position and orientation are observed fuzzily by the experimenter, who then chooses that instruction from the algorithm which fits most closely the last observation.)

1 If A is facing y then go to 2 or else go to 5.
2 If A is close to y go to 3 or else go to 7.
3 If A is very close to y go to 4 or else go to 8.
4 If A is very very close to y then stop.
5 Ask A to turn counterclockwise by an amount needed to make him face y. Go to 1.
6 Ask A to take a step. Go to 1.
7 Ask A to take a small step. Go to 1.
8 Ask A to take a very small step. Go to 1.

Will this algorithm work? If yes, how well? A basic characteristic of fuzzy algorithms is that questions of this type cannot, in general, be answered precisely. Thus, one must be content with fuzzy answers such as "The algorithm will work reasonably well so long as the degree of fuzziness in observations in relatively small and the subject executes the instructions in a way that is consistent with the expectation of the experimenter." Needless to say, such vague assertions would not be acceptable to those who expect the convergence properties of an algorithm to be expressible as a provable theorem. Unfortunately, unpalatable as it may be, there may be no alternative to accepting much lower standards of precision if we wish to be able to devise approximate (that is, fuzzy) solutions to the many complex and ill-defined problems which arise in the analysis of large-scale man–machine or man-like systems.

In conclusion, I believe that in the years ahead fuzzy algorithms and control policies will gain increasing though perhaps grudging acceptance. They will have to be accepted and accorded some measure of respectability because the conventional nonfuzzy algorithms cannot, in general, cope with the complexity and ill-definedness of large-scale systems.

I also believe that, in order to provide a hospitable environment for the development of fuzzy algorithms, control theory must become less preoccupied with mathematical rigor and precision, and more concerned with the development of qualitative or approximate solutions to pressing real world problems. Such a theory may well turn out to be far richer and far more exciting than control theory is today.

ON FUZZY ALGORITHMS

L. A. Zadeh*

ABSTRACT

A fuzzy algorithm is an ordered set of fuzzy instructions which upon execution yield an approximate solution to a given problem.

Two unrelated aspects of fuzzy algorithms are considered in this paper. The first is concerned with the problem of maximization of a reward function. It is argued that the conventional notion of a maximizing value for a function is not sufficiently informative and that a more useful notion is that of a maximizing set. Essentially, a maximizing set serves to provide information not only concerning the point or points at which a function is maximized, but also about the extent to which the values of the reward function approximate to its supremum at other points in its range.

The second is concerned with the formalization of the notion of a fuzzy algorithm. In this connection, the notion of a fuzzy Markoff algorithm is introduced and illustrated by an example. It is shown that the generation of strings by a fuzzy Markoff algorithm bears a resemblance to a birth-and-death process and that the execution of the algorithm terminates when no more "live" strings are left.

---

*Department of Electrical Engineering and Computer Sciences, and the Electronics Research Laboratory, University of California, Berkeley, California 94720.

This work was supported in part by the Navy Electronic Systems Command, Contract N00039-71-C-0255.

I. Introduction

Roughly speaking, a fuzzy algorithm [1] is an ordered set of fuzzy instructions which upon execution yield an approximate solution to a given problem. As in the case of non-fuzzy algorithms, a fuzzy algorithm is usually expected to be capable of providing an approximate solution to any problem in a specified class of problems rather than to a single problem.

Simple examples of fuzzy algorithms which occur in everyday experience are cooking recipes, instructions for parking a car, instructions for tying a knot, etc. As a more concrete example, consider the following simple control problem. Suppose that we wish to transfer a blind-folded subject A from an initial position x in a room with no obstacles to a final position y. Furthermore, suppose that the fuzzy instructions are limited to the following set: 1) Turn counter-clockwise by approximately α degrees, with α being a multiple of, say, 15; 2) Take a step; 3) Take a small step; and 4) Take a very small step.

Under these assumptions, a simple fuzzy algorithm for guiding A from x to y may be stated as follows. (It is understood that after A executes an instruction, his new position and orientation are observed fuzzily by the experimenter, who then chooses that instruction from the algorithm which fits most closely the last observation.)

1. If A is facing y then go to 2 else go to 5.
2. If A is close to y go to 3 else go to 7.
3. If A is very close to y go to 4 else go to 8.
4. If A is very very close to y then stop.

5. Ask A to turn counterclockwise by an amount needed to make him face y. Go to 1.

6. Ask A to take a step. Go to 1.

7. Ask A to take a small step. Go to 1.

8. Ask A to take a very small step. Go to 1.

Will this algorithm work? If yes, how well? A basic characteristic of fuzzy algorithms is that questions of this type cannot, in general, be answered precisely. Thus, one must be content with fuzzy answers such as "The algorithm will work reasonably well so long as the degree of fuzziness in observations is relatively small and the subject executes the instructions in a way that is consistent with the expectation of the experimenter." Needless to say, such vague assertions would not be acceptable to those who expect the convergence properties of an algorithm to be expressible as a provable theorem. Unfortunately, unpalatable as it may be, there may be no alternative to accepting much lower standards of precision if we wish to be able to devise approximate (that is, fuzzy) solutions to the many complex and ill-defined problems which arise in the analysis of large-scale man-machine and man-like systems [2].

Fuzzy algorithms and fuzzy algorithmic definitions may well prove to be of considerable practical importance once we learn more about their properties and how to construct them for specific purposes. In what follows, we shall focus our attention on a few concepts which may contribute to this objective.

2. The Concept of a Maximizing Set

Consider a real-valued function f on X = {x}, with f(x) representing the reward associated with an action x, $x \in X$. We assume that f is bounded both from above and from below, that is, $-\infty < \text{Inf } f \leq \text{Sup } f < \infty$, where Sup f and Inf f represent, respectively, the supremum and infimum of f over X.

Suppose that we wish to maximize the reward and pose the question: For what value of x does f attain its maximum value? A conventional answer to this question might be "At $x = x_o$," say. It is clear, however, that such an answer does not provide sufficient information about the value that should be assigned to x because what matters is not only that f is maximized at $x = x_o$, but also how it behaves in the neighborhood of x_o. Thus, if f is quite flat around x_o, then the solution $x = x_o$ is a robust one and hence it is not essential that x be exactly equal to x_o. The opposite is true, of course, if f is sharply peaked around x_o.

The inadequacy of the concept of a maximizing value suggests the introduction of a more general concept, namely, the concept of a *maximizing set*. Intuitively, a maximizing set M(f), or simply M, for a function f on X is a fuzzy subset of X such that the grade of membership of a point x in M represents the degree to which f(x) approximates to Sup f in some specified sense. For example, suppose for simplicity that X is the finite set X = {1,2,3,4,5,6,7,8} and that f(1) = 5, f(2) = 6, f(3) = 8, f(4) = 10, f(5) = 9, f(6) = 2, f(7) = 6 and f(8) = 1. Further, suppose that the grade of membership of x in M is defined by

$$(1) \qquad \mu_M(x) = \left[\frac{f(x)}{\text{Sup } f}\right]^2 \qquad \text{if } \mu_M(x) > 0.5$$

$$= 0 \qquad \text{if } \mu_M(x) \leq 0.5$$

Then $\mu_M(3) = 0.64$, $\mu_M(4) = 1$, $\mu_M(5) = 0.81$, with all other points having zero grade of membership in M.

In the case under consideration, the maximizing value of x is $x_o = 4$ and the maximizing set for f is the fuzzy set M = {(3,0.64),(4,1.0),(5,0.81)}. Clearly, since the maximizing set provides essential information about the effect of choosing values of x other than x_o on the values of the reward function f, it would be very desirable, in general, to know M - and not just x_o - in situations involving a decision on the value to assign to x in order to maximize a reward function. For example, if the maximizing set M for a reward function defined on the interval [0,10] is of the form

$$\mu_M(x) = 0.9 \qquad \text{for } 0 \leq x \leq 5$$

$$\mu_M(x) = 0.2 \qquad \text{for } 5 < x < 6$$

$$\mu_M(x) = 1.0 \qquad \text{for } x = 6$$

$$\mu_M(x) = 0.1 \qquad \text{for } 6 < x \leq 10$$

then the maximizing value for the reward is $x_o = 6$. However, inasmuch as the values of the reward function in the immediate neighborhood of $x_o = 6$ are very low, it would be very risky to set x = 6. Obviously, it would be much better to set x = 3, say, since μ_M is flat and close to unity in the neighborhood of 3. Although contrived to illustrate the point, the example clearly shows the inadequacy of the notion of the maximizing value for dealing with realistic decision problems - problems in which the sensitivity of the solution to perturbations is almost always an important issue.

An equation such as (1) serves to "calibrate" the definition of a maximizing set. It would be unreasonable to expect that a universal definition be applicable to all situations. However, the following calibrating definition can frequently be used as a starting point from which other definitions, if necessary, may be obtained by modification.

Definition of a maximizing set

Assume that a real-valued reward function f is defined over a domain X and that $-\infty < \text{Inf } f \leq \text{Sup } f < \infty$, that is, f is bounded both from above and from below. To define a maximizing set for f it is expedient to consider separately three cases, as follows.

Case 1. A reward function f will be said to be positive-definite if it is non-negative for all x in X, that is, if $\text{Inf } f \geq 0$ (Fig. 1). In this case the membership function of the maximizing set is defined by

$$(2) \qquad \mu_M(x) = \frac{f(x)}{\text{Sup } f}, \qquad x \in X .$$

Case 2. A reward function f is non-definite if $\text{Inf } f \leq 0$ and $\text{Sup } f \geq 0$ (Fig. 2). In this case, the defining relation (2) is applied to a translate of f expressed by

$$(3) \qquad f^* = f - \text{Inf } f$$

Thus, for a non-definite reward function, the membership function of the maximizing set is defined by

(4) $$\mu_M(x) = \frac{f - \text{Inf } f}{\text{Sup } f - \text{Inf } f}$$

Case 3. A reward function f is negative-definite if it is non-positive for all x in X, that is, Sup $f \leq 0$. In this case, (2) is applied to a translate of f expressed by

(5) $$f^* = f - \text{Sup } f - \text{Inf } f$$

yielding the definition

(6) $$\mu_M(x) = \frac{\text{Sup } f + \text{Inf } f - f}{\text{Inf } f}$$

Taken together, (2), (4) and (6) constitute a general definition of the maximizing set for a reward function which is bounded both from above and from below.

The following properties of the maximizing set are immediate consequences of the above definition.

1. The maximizing set for f is unique.
2. The maximizing set for f is invariant under linear scaling. In other words

(7) $$M(kf) = M(f)$$

where k is any real constant.

3. The maximizing set for f is not invariant under translation. Thus, if $f \not\equiv 0$ and α = constant $\neq 0$, then in general

$$M(f + \alpha) \neq M(f).$$

More specifically, for any fixed x, the dependence of $\mu_M(x)$ on α is of the form

$$\mu_M(x) = \frac{a + \alpha}{b + \alpha}$$

where a and b are constants. This implies that, as the magnitude of α increases, the membership function tends to unity.

4. For $X = R^n$ the maximizing set is convex if and only if the reward function is quasi-concave.

By definition, a fuzzy subset A of R^n (linear vector space of n-tuples of real numbers) is convex [3] iff all of its level sets are convex, that is, iff the sets

(8) $$A_\alpha = \{x \mid \mu_A(x) \geq \alpha\}, \qquad 0 < \alpha \leq '$$

are convex in R^n. Equivalently, A is convex iff μ_A satisfies

(9) $$\mu_A(\lambda x_1 + (1-\lambda)x_2) \geq \text{Min}\,(\mu_A(x_1), \mu_A(x_2))$$

for all λ in [0,1] and all x_1, x_2 in R^n.

Also by definition, a function f on R^n is quasi-concave iff all of the level sets

$$f_\alpha = \{x \mid f(x) \geq \alpha\}$$

are convex for all finite α in $(-\infty, \infty)$.

Now the definition of μ_M in terms of f implies that if f is quasi-concave, so is μ_M. This in turn implies the convexity of M. Thus, if f is quasi-concave then M is convex and vice-versa.

Example. The maximizing sets for the reward functions shown in Figs. 1, 2 and 3 are convex.

Comment It should be observed that a concave reward function can be transformed into a quasi-concave function which is bounded both from above and from below by an order-preserving transformation.

The fuzzy maximum

The concept of a maximizing set is, in effect, a fuzzification of the concept of a maximizing value. From this point of view it is natural to ask the question: What is the fuzzy counterpart of the notion of the maximum of a function? To put it another way: If x_o is a maximizing value for f then the maximum value of f is $f(x_o)$, that is, the image of x_o under the mapping f. What is the corresponding image of the maximizing set M?

To answer this question we note that if f is a function from $X = \{x\}$ to $Y = \{y\}$, with $y = f(x)$, then, as defined in [3], a fuzzy set A in X induces a fuzzy set B in Y whose membership function is given by

$$\mu_B(y) = \operatorname*{Sup}_{x \in f^{-1}(y)} \mu_A(x) \tag{10}$$

where $f^{-1}(y)$ is the preimage of y, that is

$$f^{-1}(y) = \{x \mid y = f(x)\} \tag{11}$$

If we identify A with the maximizing set in X, then B may be interpreted as the <u>fuzzy maximum</u> of f, which is a fuzzy subset of Y (Y = range of f). Denoting this fuzzy subset of Y by MM, it follows from the definition of M that the value of $\mu_M(x)$ for each point in the preimage of f is the same, namely, $\mu_M(f^{-1}(y))$. Consequently, from (10) we can infer that the membership function of the fuzzy maximum of f is given by

$$\begin{aligned} \mu_{MM}(y) &= \mu_M(f^{-1}(y)) \qquad \text{if } f^{-1}(y) \text{ exists} \\ &= 0 \quad \text{otherwise.} \end{aligned} \tag{12}$$

<u>Example</u>. Suppose that $X = [0,10]$ and f has the form shown in Fig. 1. More specifically,

$$f(x) = x + 2 \quad , \quad 0 \le x \le 2$$

$$f(x) = -x + 6 \quad , \quad 2 < x \le 3$$

$$f(x) = 3 \qquad , \qquad x > 3$$

The maximizing set for f is given by

$$\mu_M(x) = \frac{x+2}{4} \qquad , \qquad 0 \le x \le 2$$

$$\mu_M(x) = \frac{6-x}{4} \qquad , \qquad 2 < x \le 3$$

$$\mu_M(x) = \frac{3}{4} \qquad , \qquad x > 3$$

Correspondingly, the fuzzy maximum of f is given by

$$\mu_{MM}(y) = \frac{y}{4} \qquad , \qquad 2 \le y \le 4$$

$$= 0 \qquad \text{elsewhere.}$$

The minimizing set

So far we have focused our attention on the concept of the maximizing set for f - denoted by M(f) or simply M. In terms of M, the minimizing set for f (denoted by m(f) or simply m) may be defined by

(13) Minimizing set for f = Maximizing set for -f.

By using the expressions for μ_M given by (2), (4), and (6), it can readily be shown that the sum of μ_M and μ_m is a constant. Thus

(14) $\mu_M(x) + \mu_m(x) = \frac{\text{Sup } f + \text{Inf } f}{\text{Sup } f}$ for positive-definite f

(15) $\mu_M(x) + \mu_m(x) = 1$ for non-definite f

and

(16) $\mu_M(x) + \mu_m(x) = \frac{\text{Sup } f + \text{Inf } f}{\text{Inf } f}$ for negative-definite f.

The constancy of the sum of $\mu_M(x)$ and $\mu_m(x)$ implies that $\mu_M(x)$ is large where $\mu_m(x)$ is small and vice-versa. (Fuzzy sets which are related to one another in this way are weakly complementary.) In particular, if f is non-definite, then by (15) M and m are complementary fuzzy subsets of X - a property which is in accord with our intuition.

The maximizing and minimizing sets of a reward function contain the type of information which is usually provided by a sensitivity analysis. In practice, these sets would usually be defined by exemplification, that is, by associating approximate grades of membership with a finite set of representative points in X.

3. Fuzzy Markoff Algorithms

In the preceding section, we were concerned with the formalization of the notion of an approximate maximizing value, which led us to the concept of a maximizing set.

In this section, our concern is with the formalization of the notion of a fuzzy algorithm. As was pointed out in [1], a fuzzy algorithm may be equated with a fuzzy Turing machine. In [4], both the fuzzy Turing machine and the fuzzy Markoff algorithm are defined and their equivalence is demonstrated. Here, we shall give a simpler definition of a fuzzy Markoff algorithm which is a natural extension of the conventional way in which a Markoff algorithm is defined [5], [6]. In effect, our definition of a fuzzy Markoff algorithm is intended mainly to make more precise the concept of a fuzzy algorithm in the same sense that a Markoff algorithm formalizes the concept of a non-fuzzy algorithm.

Let A^* denote the set of all finite strings over a finite alphabet A. For our purposes, it will be convenient to represent a finite fuzzy subset, L, of A^* in the form of a linear combination

(17) $$L = \mu_1\alpha_1 + \mu_2\alpha_2 + \ldots + \mu_n\alpha_n$$

where the α_i, $i = 1,\ldots,n$, denote strings in A^* and the μ_i represent their respective grades of membership in L.

Example. Let $A = \{a,b\}$. Then

$$L = 0.3\ aab + 0.8\ bba + 1.0\ aa + 0.3\ ba$$

is equivalent to expressing L as the collection of ordered pairs

$$L = \{(0.3,aab),\ (0.8,bba),\ (1.0,aa),\ (0.3,ba)\}$$

When expressed in the form (17), the concatenation of two fuzzy sets of strings

$$L = \mu_1\alpha_1 + \ldots + \mu_n\alpha_n$$

and

$$L' = \mu_1'\alpha_1' + \ldots + \mu_m'\alpha_m'$$

where $\alpha_1,\ldots,\alpha_n$ and $\alpha_1',\ldots,\alpha_m'$ are strings in A^*, can readily be obtained by term by term multiplication and addition, with the understanding that

(18) $$\mu_i\mu_j' = \mu_i \wedge \mu_j' = \text{Min}\ (\mu_1,\mu_j')$$

(19) $$\mu_1 + \mu_j' = \mu_i \vee \mu_j' = \text{Max}\ (\mu_i,\mu_j')$$

and

(20) $$\alpha_i\alpha_j' = \text{concatenation of } \alpha_i \text{ and } \alpha_j'.$$

Example.

$$L = 0.3\ aa + 0.5\ aba$$

$$L' = 0.2\ ab + 0.9\ ba$$

Then

$$LL' = 0.2\ aaab + 0.2\ abaab + 0.3\ aaba + 0.5\ ababa$$

A non-fuzzy Markoff algorithm M is a function from A^* to A^* which is characterized by a finite sequence of productions $P_1, \ldots, P_n$ of the general form

$$\alpha \rightarrow \beta \text{ or } \alpha \rightarrow \beta \, . \tag{21}$$

where α (the antecedent) and β (the consequent) are strings in A^* and the arrow signifies that if α occurs as a substring in a string x, then the leftmost occurrence of α in x may be replaced by β . The presence of the period indicates that the production is terminal in the sense that the execution of the algorithm terminates after a terminal production is applied.

A typical very simple problem in the theory of Markoff algorithms is the following. Suppose $A = \{a,b,c\}$ and let x be any string in A^* . Find a Markoff algorithm which removes the first three occurrences of c from x. E.g., acabbcabcc is transformed into aabbabc.

A fuzzy version of this problem would be: Find a fuzzy Markoff algorithm which removes the first *few* occurrences of c from x. In this case, if we define *few* as the fuzzy set

$$\underline{few} = \{(1,1.0),\ (2,1.0),\ (3,0.8),\ (4,0.6)\}$$

then the result of applying this fuzzy Markoff algorithm to x = acabbabcc would be a fuzzy set rather than a single string. Thus, denoting the fuzzy algorithm by FM, we have in symbols

$$FM(acabbcabcc) = 1.0 \text{ aabbcabcc} + 1.0 \text{ aabbabcc} + 0.8 \text{ aabbabc} + 0.6 \text{ aabbab}$$

More generally, let $\mathcal{F}(A^*)$ denote the set of all fuzzy subsets of A^* . Then a *fuzzy Markoff algorithm*, FM, may be regarded as a function from A^* to $\mathcal{F}(A^*)$ which satisfies certain conditions and is characterized in a particular way which will be described presently.

Specifically, let L be a finite fuzzy subset of A^*

(22) $L = \mu_1\alpha_1 + \ldots + \mu_n\alpha_n , \alpha_i \in A^* , i = 1, \ldots, n .$

Then we postulate that the image of L under FM is given by

$$(23) \quad FM(L) = FM(\mu_1\alpha_1 + \ldots + \mu_n\alpha_n) = \mu_1 FM(\alpha_1) + \ldots + \mu_n FM(\alpha_n)$$

which implies that FM is a linear operator in A^* . In consequence of (23), the operation of FM on a fuzzy set of strings can be described in terms of its operation on individual strings. This basic property of fuzzy Markoff algorithms plays an important role in the description of their execution.

In contrast to the form of a production in a non-fuzzy Markoff algorithm, a typical production, P_i, in a fuzzy Markoff algorithm has the appearance

$$(24) \quad P_i : \alpha \to \mu_1\beta_1 + \ldots + \mu_k\beta_k + \mu_{k+1}\beta_{k+1} \bullet + \ldots + \mu_n\beta_n \bullet$$

where the β's ε A^* , the μ's are numbers in the interval [0,1], and the terms ending with a period are the <u>terminating</u> components in the consequent of P_i. The important point is that the consequent of P_i is a fuzzy set of strings rather than a single string.

Now suppose that a string x can be expressed as x = u α v, where u,α, v ε A^* and α is not a substring of u. (I.e., α in u α v represents its leftmost occurrence.) Then, on substituting the consequent of P_i for α in x, we obtain the fuzzy set of strings represented by

$$(25) \quad u\,\alpha\,v = u\,(\mu_1\beta_1 + \ldots + \mu_k\beta_k + \mu_{k+1}\beta_{k+1} \bullet + \ldots + \mu_n\beta_n \bullet)v$$

$$= \mu_1 u\beta_1 v + \ldots + \mu_k u\beta_k v + \mu_{k+1} u\beta_{k+1} v \bullet + \ldots + \mu_n u\beta_n v \bullet$$

Furthermore, if ρ is a number in [0,1], then

$$(26) \quad \rho\, u\, \alpha\, v = \rho\, \mu_1 u\beta_1 v + \ldots + \rho\, \mu_k u\beta_k v + \rho\, \mu_{k+1} u\beta_k v \bullet + \ldots + \rho\, \mu_n u\beta_n v \bullet$$

where $\rho\, \mu_i = \rho \wedge u_i$, $i = 1, \ldots, n$.

<u>Example.</u> Suppose x = abbabbb and

ba → 0.3 ab + 0.9 a •

Then

abbabbb = 0.3 ababbbb + 0.9 ababbb.

and

0.4 abbabbb = 0.3 ababbbb + 0.4 ababbb.

In summary, a production P_i is applicable to a string x if its antecedent is a substring of x. The result of applying of P_i to x is expressed by (25) and (26). (Note that the substitution is made in the leftmost occurrence in x of the antecedent of P_i.)

We are now ready to define the execution of a fuzzy Markoff algorithm in terms of (23) and the rewriting rules (25) and (26).

<u>Definition of a fuzzy Markoff algorithm</u>

A fuzzy Markoff algorithm, FM, is a function from A^* to $\mathcal{F}(A^*)$ which satisfies (23) and is characterized by (a) a finite alphabet A; (b) possibly a finite auxiliary alphabet A' (comprising various markers which may be needed for bookkeeping purposes); and (c) a finite sequence of productions $P_1, \ldots, P_n$ of the form (24), with P_n: $\Lambda \rightarrow \Lambda$. ($\Lambda$ = null string).

It is convenient to describe the operation of FM on a string x in A^* in terms of a subalgorithm $\overline{FM}$ which is defined on $\mathcal{F}(A^*)$. Thus, if L is a fuzzy set of strings in A^*, e.g.,

$$L = \mu_1 v_1 + \ldots + \mu_r v_r \quad , \quad v_i \in A^* \quad , \quad i = 1, \ldots , r$$

then, as in (23)

$$(27) \qquad \overline{FM}(L) = \mu_1 \overline{FM}(v_1) + \ldots + \mu_r \overline{FM}(v_r)$$

To compute $\overline{FM}(v_i)$, $v_i \in A^*$, $i = 1, \ldots, r$, we proceed as follows:

Apply the first applicable production in the sequence $P_1, \ldots, P_n$ to v_i and call the result $\overline{FM}(v_i)$. (Note that P_n will always be applicable since v_i may be written as Λv_i.) Set

(28) $D(v_i)$ = sum of terms in $\overline{FM}(v_i)$ which terminate in a period

(29) $B(v_i)$ = sum of the remaining terms in $\overline{FM}(v_i)$

and

$$(30) \qquad D(L) = \mu_1 D(v_1) + \ldots + \mu_r D(v_r)$$

$$(31) \qquad B(L) = \mu_1 B(v_1) + \ldots + \mu_r B(v_r)$$

The result of operating with $\overline{FM}$ on L is defined to be the sum of the fuzzy sets of strings D(L) and B(L). Thus

$$(32) \qquad \overline{FM}(L) = D(L) + B(L)$$

In terms of $\overline{FM}$, the computation of FM(x), where $x \in A^*$, is carried out as follows.

1. Set L = x = initial string
2. Set FM(x) = θ (empty set)

3. Apply $\overline{FM}$ to L and compute $\overline{FM}(L) = B(L) + D(L)$.

4. Set

$$FM(x) = FM(x) + D(L) \tag{33}$$

5. If B(L) is empty, terminate the execution of FM.

6. If B(L) is not empty, set L = B(L). Go to 3.

The execution of the algorithm is actually quite straightforward and simple in principle. The following example will serve as an illustration. (No auxiliary alphabet used.)

<u>Example.</u> Assume $A = \{a,b\}$ and

P_1: ab $\rightarrow$ 0.3 bb + 0.6 a + 0.9 ab.

P_2: ba $\rightarrow$ 0.8 a. + 1.0 bb.

P_3: b $\rightarrow$ 0.6 a.

Λ $\rightarrow$ 1.0 Λ.

Let the initial string be x = abba. Applying $\overline{FM}$ to L = x, we note that the first applicable production is P_1. It yields for L = x

$\overline{FM}(L)$ = 0.3 bbba + 0.6 aba + 0.9 abba.

D(L) = 0.9 abba.

B(L) = 0.3 bbba + 0.6 aba

and

FM(x) = 0.9 abba.

Since B(L) is non-empty, we apply $\overline{FM}$ to L = B(L) yielding

$\overline{FM}$ (0.3 bbba + 0.6 aba) = 0.3 $\overline{FM}$ (bbba) + 0.6 $\overline{FM}$ (aba)

Now, applying P_2 to bbba we get

$\overline{FM}$ (bbba) = 0.8 bbba. + 1.0 bbbb.

and applying P_1 to aba we have

$$\overline{FM}\,(aba) = 0.3\ bba + 0.6\ aa + 0.6\ aba.$$

Thus

$$FM(L) = 0.3\ bba + 0.6\ aa + 0.6\ aba. + 0.3\ bba. + 0.3\ bbbb.$$

$$D(L) = 0.6\ aba. + 0.3\ bba. + 0.3\ bbbb.$$

$$B(L) = 0.3\ bba + 0.6\ aa$$

and

$$FM(x) = 0.9\ abba. + 0.6\ aba. + 0.3\ bba. + 0.3\ bbbb.$$

Since B(L) is non-empty, we apply $\overline{FM}$ to L = B(L), obtaining

$$\overline{FM}\,(0.3\ bba + 0.6\ aa) = 0.3\ \overline{FM}\,(bba) + 0.6\ \overline{FM}\,(aa).$$

Next, applying P_2 to bba, we get

$$\overline{FM}\,(bba) = 0.8\ ba. + 1.0\ bbb.$$

and applying P_3 co aa, we obtain

$$\overline{FM}\,(aa) = 1.0\ aa.$$

thus

$$\overline{FM}(L) = 0.3\ ba. + 0.3\ bbb. + 0.6\ aa.$$

$$D'(L) = 0.3\ ba. + 0.3\ bbb. + 0.6\ aa.$$

$$B(L) = \theta$$

and finally

$$FM(x) = 0.9\ abba. + 0.6\ aba. + 0.3\ bba. + 0.3\ bbbb.$$
$$+ 0.3\ ba. + 0.3\ bbb. + 0.6\ aa.$$

At this point the execution of the algorithm terminates because B(L) = θ.

The execution of a fuzzy Markoff algorithm may be likened to a birth-and-death process in which the operation with $\overline{FM}$ on a string v_i gives rise to the birth of new strings, represented by $B(v_i)$, and the death of others, represented by $D(v_i)$. In the same sense, B(L) and D(L) represent the "newly born" and the "dead" strings resulting from operating with $\overline{FM}$ on a "live" fuzzy set of strings L. Finally, F(x) plays the role of the population of the dead in a cemetery, with (33) representing the addition of the newly deceased to that population.

As in a birth-and-death process, the population of "live" strings can grow explosively if the productions $P_1, \ldots, P_n$ are such that each execution of $\overline{FM}$ results in significantly more "births" than "deaths." This rather interesting aspect of fuzzy Markoff algorithms is not present in conventional Markoff algorithms.

In the foregoing discussion, we have restricted ourselves to formulating what appears to be a natural extension of the notion of a Markoff algorithm. Exploration of the properties of such algorithms will be pursued in subsequent papers on this subject.

References

1. L. A. Zadeh, "Fuzzy Algorithms," Information and Control, vol. 12, pp. 99-102, February 1968.
2. S. S. L. Chang and L. A. Zadeh, "Fuzzy Mapping and Control," Trans. on Systems, Man and Cybernetics, vol. SMC-2, pp. 30-34, January 1972.
3. L. A. Zadeh, "Fuzzy Sets," Information and Control, vol. 8, pp. 338-353, June 1965.
4. E. Santos, "Fuzzy Algorithms," Information and Control, vol. 17, pp. 326-339, November 1970.
5. A. T. Berztiss, "Data Structures," Mc Graw-Hill Book Co., New York, 1971.
6. H. Galler and A. Perlis, " A View of Programming Languages," Addison Wesley, Reading, Mass., 1970.

$$\mu_M(x) = \frac{f(x)}{\sup f}$$

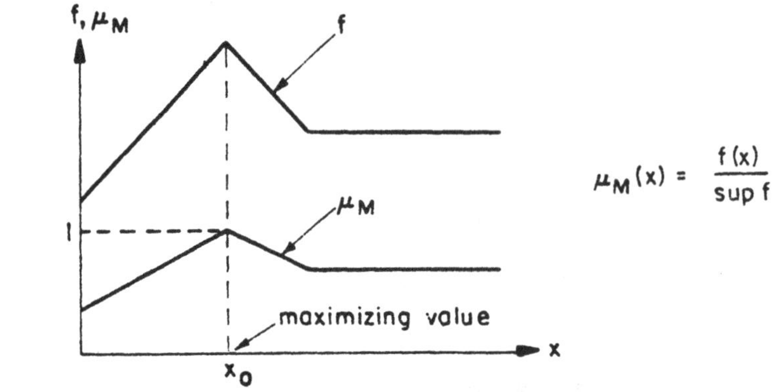

Fig. 1.   The maximizing set for a positive-definite
reward function.

$$\mu_M(x) = \frac{\text{Sup } f + \text{Inf} - f(x)}{\text{Inf } f}$$

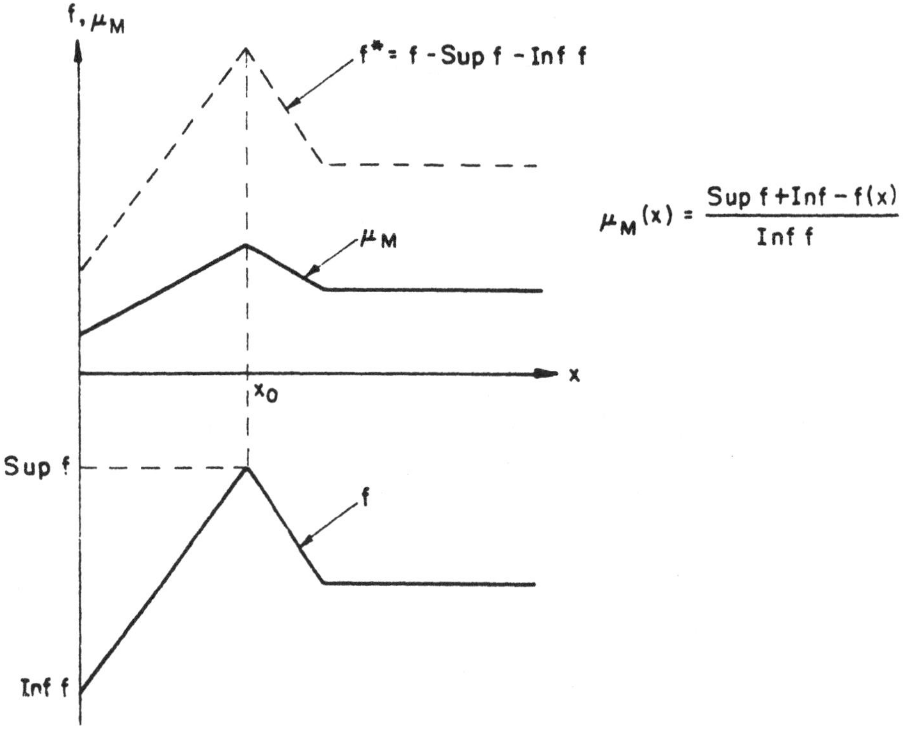

Fig. 2.   The maximizing set for a non-definite reward
function.

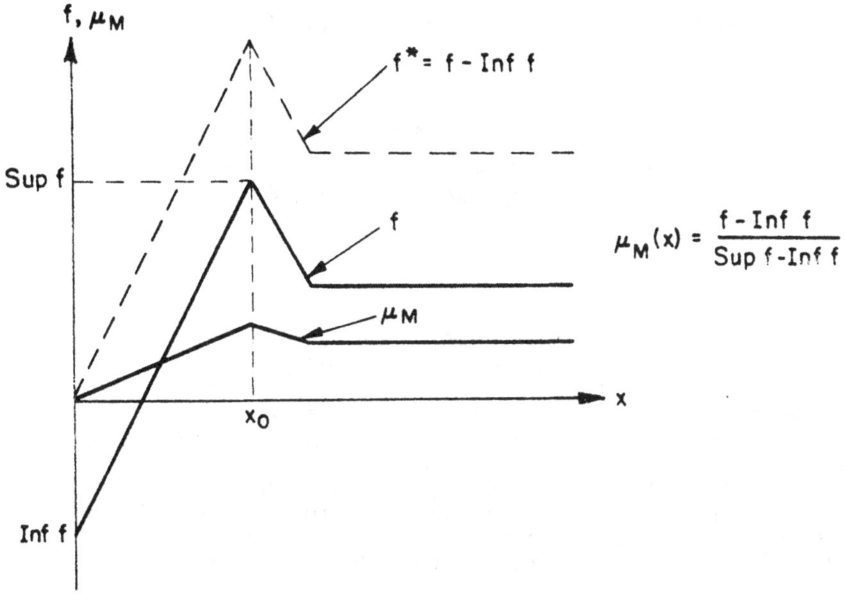

Fig. 3. The maximizing set for a negative-definite reward function.

FUZZY LANGUAGES AND THEIR RELATION TO HUMAN AND MACHINE INTELLIGENCE*

L. A. ZADEH

Electronics Research Laboratory, College of Engineering,
University of California, Berkeley, 94720

ABSTRACT

A *fuzzy language* as defined in this paper is a quadruple $L = (U, T, E, N)$ in which U is a non-fuzzy *universe of discourse*; T (called *term set*) is a fuzzy set of terms which serve as names of fuzzy subsets of U; E (called an *embedding set* for T) is a collection of symbols and their combinations from which the terms are drawn, i.e., T is a fuzzy subset of E; and N is a fuzzy relation from E (or the support of T) to U called a *naming relation*.

As a fuzzy subset of E, T is characterized by a membership function $\mu_T : E \to [0,1]$, with $\mu_T(x)$ representing the grade of membership of a term x in T. Similarly, the naming relation N is characterized by a bivariate membership function $\mu_N : E \times U \to [0,1]$ in which $\mu_N(x,y)$ represents the strength of the relation between a term x and an object y in U.

The *syntax* and *semantics* of L are viewed as collections of rules for the computation of μ_T and μ_N, respectively. The *meaning* of a term x is defined to be a fuzzy subset, $M(x)$, of U, whose membership function is given by $\mu_{M(x)}(y) = \mu_N(x,y)$.

Various concepts relating to fuzzy languages are introduced and their relevance to natural languages and human intelligence is pointed out. In particular, it is suggested that the theory of fuzzy languages may have the potential of providing better models for natural languages than is possible within the framework of the classical theory of formal languages.

1. Introduction

The question of whether or not machines can think has been the subject of many discussions and debates during the past two decades.[1–10] As computers become more powerful and thus more influential in human affairs, the philosophical aspects of this question become increasingly overshadowed by the practical need to develop an operational understanding of the limitations of machine judgment and decision-making ability. Can computers be relied upon to match people; decide on promotions and dismissals; make medical diagnoses; prescribe treatments; act as teachers;

*This is the text of a paper presented at the Conference on Man and Computer, Bordeaux, France, June 22–26. 1970. (Organized by Institut de la Vie, Paris.) The work described was supported in part by the National Science Foundation, Grant GK-10656X and the Joint Services Electronics Program, Contract F44620-71-C-0087.

formulate business, political and military strategies; and, more generally, perform intellectual tasks of high complexity which in the past required expert human judgment? Clearly, this is already a pressing issue which is certain to grow in importance in the years ahead.

A thesis advanced in this paper is that there is indeed a very basic difference between human and machine intelligence which may well prove to be a very difficult obstacle in the path of designing machines that can outperform humans in the realm of cognitive processes involving concept formation, abstraction, pattern recognition, and decision-making under uncertainty. The difference in question lies in the ability of the human brain — an ability which present day digital computers do not possess — to think and reason in imprecise, non-quantitative, terms. Thus, a human being can understand and execute imprecise instructions such as "increase x a *little* if y is *much larger than* 5," "rise *slowly*," "reduce speed if the road is *slippery*," and so forth. He can maneuver his car through dense traffic and park it in a tight spot. He can decipher sloppy handwriting, understand distorted speech and untie a complicated knot. By contrast, the manipulative ability of digital computers is limited to precise instructions such as "add x to y," "if $x = 5$ then $z = 3$ else $z = 7$," "stop if x is non-negative," etc. In addition, a digital computer can accept digitized analog data and produce printed text, line drawings and the like under digital control. In all these cases, the input to the computer must be precisely defined.

The type of imprecision which is exemplified by the italicized words in the above instructions may be characterized as *fuzziness*, since it relates to the use of words such as *little*, *slowly*, *slippery*, etc., which in effect are labels for fuzzy sets,[a] classes which admit of grades of membership intermediate between full membership and non-membership. For example, the class of integers which are *much larger than* 5 is a fuzzy set in which an integer such as 25 may be assigned a partial grade of membership, say 0.8, with 0 and 1 representing the extremes of non-membership and full membership, respectively. The same applies to classes characterized by words such as *green*, *tall*, *several*, *young*, *sparse*, *oval*, etc. Indeed, it may be argued that much, perhaps most, of human thinking and interaction with the outside world involves classes without sharply defined boundaries in which the transition from membership to non-membership is gradual rather than abrupt.

[a] A fuzzy set is a class with fuzzy boundaries, i.e., a class in which the transition from membership to non-membership is gradual rather than abrupt. More precisely, if $X = \{x\}$ is a collection of objects denoted generically by x, then a fuzzy subset of X, A, is a set of ordered pairs $\{(x, \mu_A(x))\}$, $x \in X$, where $\mu_A(x)$ is the *grade of membership* of x in A and μ_A is the *membership function*. Unless stated to the contrary, it will be assumed that $\mu_A(x)$ is a number in the interval [0,1], with 0 and 1 representing non-membership and full membership, respectively; more generally, $\mu_A(x)$ can be a point in a lattice. If A and B are fuzzy subsets of X, then A is a *subset* of B, written as $A \subset B$, iff $\mu_A(x) \leq \mu_B(x)$ for all x in X. The *union* of A and B is denoted by $A \cup B$ (or $A + B$ when no confusion can arise) and is defined by $\mu_{A \cap B}(x) = \mu_A(x) \vee \mu_B(x)$, $x \in X$, where $a \vee b$ denotes Max(a, b). The *intersection* of A and B is denoted by $A \cap B$ and is defined by $\mu_{A \cap B}(x) = \mu_A(x) \wedge \mu_B(x)$, $x \in X$, where $a \wedge b$ denotes Min(a, b). The *complement*, A', of A is defined by $\mu_{A'}(x) = 1 - \mu_A(x)$, $x \in X$. It should be noted that a membership function may be regarded as a predicate in a multivalued logic in which the truth values range over [0,1]. More detailed discussion of fuzzy sets and their properties may be found in Refs. 11–20.

The ability of a human brain, weighing only a few hundred grams, to manipulate complicated fuzzy concepts and act on a multi-dimensional fuzzy sensory inputs endows it with a capability to solve rather easily a wide variety of problems which, if formulated in precise quantitative terms, would exceed the computing power of the most powerful and sophisticated digital computer in existence. The explanation for this apparent paradox is that, in many instances, the solution to a problem need not be exact, so that a considerable measure of fuzziness in its formulation and results may be tolerable. The human brain is designed to take advantage of this tolerance for imprecision whereas a digital computer, with its need for precise data and instructions, is not. It is primarily for this reason that a problem which would be regarded as simple by a mentally retarded adult, might well be computationally infeasible for a machine equipped with a very large memory and operating at very high speed. A commonplace example of such a problem is that of parking a car. Humans can park a car very easily and without making any use of quantitative measurements so long as the terminal position of the car is specified fuzzily rather than precisely. On the other hand, to program a computer to park a car in a specified location would be a very difficult problem involving precise quantitative data on the position of the car, its dimensions, dynamics and the parking space.

In general, complexity and precision bear an inverse relation to one another in the sense that, as the complexity of a problem increases, the possibility of analyzing it in precise terms diminishes. Thus it is a truism that the class of problems which are susceptible of exact solution is much smaller than that which can be solved approximately. From this point of view, the capacity of a human brain to manipulate fuzzy concepts and non-quantitative sensory inputs may well be one of its most important assets. Thus, "fuzzy thinking" may not be deplorable, after all, if it makes possible the solution of problems which are much too complex for precise analysis. For example, in the case of chess the choice of moves at an intermediate stage of the game is determined by subgoals, such as winning a piece or strengthening the center, which are fuzzily related to the ultimate goal — to win the game. Consequently, even though there is no imprecision or randomness in the rules of chess, the ability to play chess well depends in an essential way on the facility of the player in manipulating fuzzy concepts and relationships. The impressive performance of some chess-playing computer programs is not inconsistent with this assertion because the programs in question incorporate strategies which are arrived at through the ability of the programmer to operate on fuzzy sets and relations between them.

Although present day computers are not designed to accept fuzzy data or execute fuzzy instructions, they can be programmed to do so indirectly by treating a fuzzy set as a data-type which can be encoded as an array.[21] Granted that this is not a fully satisfactory approach to the endowment of a computer with an ability to manipulate fuzzy concepts, it is at least a step in the direction of enhancing the ability of machines to emulate human thought processes. It is quite possible, however, that truly significant advances in artificial intelligence will have to await the development of machines that can reason in fuzzy and non-quantitative terms in much the same manner as a human being.

A good illustration[b] of a problem which is far beyond the power of any existing computer is that of preparing a summary of a given document or book. The reason for this, in the first place, is that the notion of a summary is a fuzzy concept which cannot be defined in conventional terms for machine use. Second, and more important, the words in a natural language usually have fuzzy meaning, with the result that it is very difficult to devise an algorithm for constructing the meaning of a sentence, much less that of a concatenation of sentences, from the specification of the fuzzy meaning of individual words and the context in which they occur. Thus, to solve the problem of summarization, it would be necessary to develop a far better understanding of how to manipulate fuzzy concepts and relations than we possess at present.

An essential step in this direction requires the construction of a conceptual framework for languages in which the syntax or semantics or both are fuzzy in nature. Such languages, which may appropriately be called *fuzzy languages*, could provide a significantly better approximation to natural languages than is possible within the framework of the classical theory of formal languages in which no provision is made for fuzziness in either syntax or semantics.

In what follows, we shall outline some of the basic aspects of the syntax and semantics of fuzzy languages, with the understanding that the theory of such languages is still in an embryonic stage at this juncture and our discussion of it will touch upon only a few of its many facets.

2. Fuzzy Languages

In the theory of formal languages,[22-30] a language is defined as a set of strings over a finite alphabet. Such a definition is too narrow for many purposes because it fails to reflect the primary function of a language as a system of correspondences between strings of words and sets of objects or constructs which are described by these strings.

By contrast, in the definition of fuzzy languages given below, the correspondence between strings of words and sets of objects enters in an explicit fashion. Furthermore, the correspondence between words and objects is allowed to be fuzzy, as it is in the case of natural languages. In this way, the concept of a fuzzy language becomes much broader and more general than that of a formal language in its conventional sense.

Definition 1. A *fuzzy language* L is a quadruple

$$L = (U, T, E, N) \tag{1}$$

[b]This example was suggested by Dr. M. Senko, Information Sciences Department, IBM, San Jose California.

in which U is non-fuzzy *universe of discourse*; T (called the *term set*) is a fuzzy set of terms which serve as names of fuzzy subsets of U; E (called an *embedding set* for T) is a collection of symbols and their combinations from which the terms are drawn, i.e., T is a fuzzy subset of E; and N is a fuzzy relation[c] from E (or, more specifically, the support of T) to U which will be referred to as a *naming relation.*

The first component of L is a universe of discourse, U, which may be any set of objects, actions, relations, concepts, etc. For example, U may be the set of integers; or the set of objects in a room; or the set of objects in a room together with the set of relations between them; or the set of colors; or the union of the set of integers and the set of functions from integers to integers; etc. In essence, U, as its name implies, is the collection of objects or constructs which form the subject of discourse in L.

The second component of L, T, is a set of terms which serve as names of fuzzy subsets of U. The elements of T may have a variety of forms, e.g., they can be sounds, pictures, strings of letters, etc. In what follows, the terms will usually have the form of strings of letters or words drawn from a finite alphabet, with each word having a blank symbol (space) at its right end. For example, in the case of English, T would be the set of all English words and their well-formed concatenations.

The term set, T, is assumed to be a fuzzy subset of E, the embedding set for T, which in most cases is a collection of combinations of symbols drawn from an alphabet A. For example, in the case of English, A is the set of alpha-numeric characters and E might be taken to be the collection of all finite strings of these characters. In the case of a formal language, A is usually denoted by V_T (set of terminals) and E is identified with V_T^* (the Kleene closure of V_T), which is the set of all finite strings over V_T.

A term may be *atomic* or *composite.* An atomic term is defined as a string which has no term as a substring. A *composite* term is a concatenation of atomic terms. For example, words such as *red,* and *barn* are atomic terms, while their concatenation *red barn* is a composite term.

Since the term set, T, is assumed to be a fuzzy subset of E, it is characterized by a membership function $\mu_T : E \to [0,1]$ which associates with each[d] term $x \in E$ its grade of membership, $\mu_T(x)$, in T. For example, if E is the set of all finite strings over the alphabet $A = \{a, b, +\}$, then the grades of membership of some of

[c]A fuzzy relation R from $X = \{x\}$ to $Y = \{y\}$ is a fuzzy subset of the cartesian product $X \times Y = \{(x,y)\}$. For example, if $x = y = R =$ real line, then $\gg$ (much larger than) is a fuzzy relation from R to R (or, more simply, a fuzzy relation *in* R). For a given ordered pair (x,y), the grade of membership $\mu_R(x,y)$ of (x,y) in R will be referred to as the *strength* of the relation between x and y. The *domain* of R is a fuzzy set in X denoted by dom(R) and defined by $\mu_{\text{dom}(R)}(x) = \vee_y \mu_R(x,y)$, where $\vee_y$ denotes the supremum over $Y = \{y\}$. Similarly, the *range* of R is a fuzzy set in Y denoted by ran(R) and defined by $\mu_{ran(R)}(y) = \vee_x \mu_R(x,y)$. (See Refs. 17 and 20 for additional details.)

The *support* of a fuzzy subset A of X is non-fuzzy subset Supp(A) defined by Supp(A) $= \{x | \mu_A(x) > 0\}$. The *cardinality* of a fuzzy subset A with a finite support is denoted by $|A|$ and is defined by $|A| = \Sigma_i \mu_A(x_i)$, $x_i \in$ Supp(A). Essentially, the cardinality of a fuzzy set is a generalization of the notion of the number of members of a non-fuzzy set.

[d]More generally, μ_T may be a partial function, i.e., $\mu_T(x)$ may be undefined for some x in E.

the representative strings in T might be:

$$\mu_T(a\ +\ b) = 1.0 \qquad \mu_T(a\ +\ b\ +\ b) = 1.0$$
$$\mu_T(+\ a) = 0.8 \qquad \mu_T(+\ a\ +\ b) = 0.8$$
$$\mu_T(+\ +\ a) = 0.1 \qquad \mu_T(a\ +\ +\ b) = 0.1\,.$$

The grade of membership, $\mu_T(x)$, may be used to represent the degree of *well-formedness* or *grammaticality* of x. For example, if T is the fuzzy set of words and phrases in English, then μ_T (John went home yesterday) = 1.0; μ_T (John yesterday went home) = 0.8; and μ_T (John home went yesterday) = 0.2. The important point to note is that in the model under discussion, the set of terms need not have a sharply defined boundary which separates these terms which belong to T from those that do not. Thus, the model allows a term to have a grade of membership in T which may lie somewhere between full membership on one end, and non-membership, on the other.

The fourth component of L is the fuzzy naming relation, N, from E to U. This relation is characterized by a bivariate membership function $\mu_N : \text{Supp}(T) \times U \to [0,1]$, which associates with each[e] ordered pair $(x, y), x \in T$,[f] $y \in U$, the grade of membership $\mu_N(x, y)$, of (x, y) in N. In effect, $\mu_N(x, y)$ may be interpreted as the degree to which a term x fits an element y of U, and vice-versa. For example, if U is the set of ages from 1 to 100, x is the term *young* and $y = 35$ years, we may have μ_N (*young*, 35) = 0.2 while μ_N(*old*, 35) = 0 and μ_N(*middle-aged*, 35) = 0.02. Similarly, if y denotes the height, we may have

$$\mu_N\ (\textit{tall},\ 5'8'') = 0.6$$
$$\mu_N\ (\textit{tall},\ 5'10'') = 0.8$$
$$\mu_N\ (\textit{tall},\ 6') = 1.0$$
$$\mu_N\ (\textit{tall},\ 6'2'') = 1.0$$

and likewise for other values of y.

The relationship between U, T, E and N is illustrated in Fig. 1.

Comment 2. In the above examples, the values of $\mu_N(x, y)$ are given for only a few representative values of x and y. To define a language completely, μ_N must be tabulated for all x in T and all y in U. In many practical situations, however, both μ_T and μ_N have to be estimated from partial information about them, such as the values which μ_T and μ_N take at a finite number of sample points in their respective domains of definition. When a fuzzy set is defined incompletely—and hence only approximately—in this fashion, it is said to be defined by *exemplification*.[g]

[e] As in the case of μ_T, μ_N may be a partial function over $\text{Supp}(T) \times U$.

[f] Here and elsewhere in this paper, $x \in T$ should be interpreted as $x \in \text{Supp}(T)$.

[g] The definition of a fuzzy set by exemplification is an extension of the familiar linguistic notion of ostensive definition.

The problem of estimating the membership function of a fuzzy set in X from the knowledge of its values over a finite set of points in X is the problem of *abstraction*, which plays a central role in pattern recognition.[31,32] We shall not concern ourselves with this problem in the sequel and will assume throughout that μ_T and μ_N are either given or can be computed. It should be noted that the values assigned to $\mu_N(x, y)$ need not have an objective basis since they represent a subjective and, generally, context-dependent definition of a correspondence between the terms in T and elements of the universe of discourse.

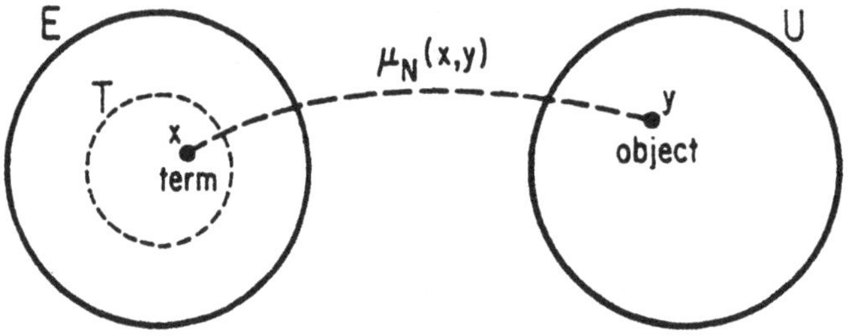

Fig. 1. The components of a fuzzy language: U = universe of discourse; T = term set; E = embedding set for T; N = naming relation from E to U; x = term; y = object in U; $\mu_N(x, y)$ = strength of the relation between x and y; $\mu_T(x)$ = grade of membership of x in T.

When T and U are sets with a small number of elements, it may be practicable to define the naming relation N by a tabulation of $\mu_N(x, y)$. In general, however, both T and U are infinite sets, with the consequence that the characterization of T and N requires that they be endowed with a structure allowing the computation of $\mu_T(x)$ and $\mu_N(x, y)$ rather than a table look-up of their values. This is the rationale for the following definition of a *structured fuzzy language*.

Definition 3. A *structured fuzzy language* L is a quadruple

$$L = (U, S_T, E, S_N) \tag{2}$$

in which U is a universe of discourse; E is an embedding set for the term set T; S_T is a set of rules, called the *syntactic* rules of L, which collectively provide an algorithm for computing the membership function, μ_T, of the term set T; and S_N is a set of rules, called the *semantic* rules of L, which collectively provide an algorithm for computing the membership function, μ_N, of the fuzzy naming relation N.[h] The collection of syntactic and semantic rules of L constitute, respectively, the *syntax* and *semantics* of L.

[h] As will be seen in Sec. 5, the semantic rules are used in the main to compute $\mu_N(x, y)$ when x is a composite term. For atomic terms, $\mu_N(x, y)$ will be assumed to be given as a function on U.

Comment 4. Note that the only basic difference between Definition 1 and Definition 3 is that, in the case of an unstructured language, the set of terms T and the relation N are assumed to be defined explicitly by a tabulation of their respective membership functions or some equivalent means, whereas in the case of a structured language T and N are assumed to have an underlying structure which makes it possible to compute μ_T and μ_N through the use of syntactic and semantic rules, respectively.

It should be noted that when T is non-fuzzy, a procedure for computing μ_T reduces to a procedure for determining whether or not a given string x is an element of T, which in turn is equivalent to a procedure for generating elements of T.[i] Similarly, when N is non-fuzzy, a procedure for computing μ_N reduces to a procedure for determining whether or not a given ordered pair (x, y) belongs to N, which in turn is equivalent to a procedure for generating the ordered pairs (x, y) which are in N.

A language, whether structured or unstructured, will be said to be *fuzzy* if T or N or both are fuzzy. Consequently, a non-fuzzy language is one in which both T and N are non-fuzzy. In particular, a non-fuzzy structured language is a language with both non-fuzzy syntax and non-fuzzy semantics.

From this point of view, programming languages are non-fuzzy structured languages in which the *compiler* embodies the rules for computing the two-valued membership functions for the term set T and the naming relation N. Thus, by the use of syntactic rules, the compiler can determine whether or not a given string x is a term in T. If x is in T, then by the use of semantic rules the compiler can compute $\mu_N(x, y)$, $y \in U$ = set of machine language terms, and thus can determine a machine language instruction which corresponds to x.

In contrast to programming languages, natural languages have both fuzzy syntax and fuzzy semantics. The fuzziness of syntax manifests itself in the possibility that a sentence in, say, English, may have a degree of grammaticality[j] intermediate between complete correctness and incorrectness, e.g., μ_T(John yesterday went home) = 0.8. In most cases however, the degree of grammaticality of a sentence is either zero or one, so that the set of terms in a natural language has a fairly sharply defined boundary between grammatical and ungrammatical sentences.

The fuzziness of semantics, on the other hand, is a far more pronounced and pervasive characteristic of natural languages. For example, as was pointed out earlier, if the universe of discourse is identified with the set of ages from 1 to 100, then the atomic terms *young* and *old* do not correspond to sharply defined subsets of U. The same applies to composite terms such as *not very young, not very young and not very old*, etc. In effect, most of the terms in a natural language correspond to fuzzy rather than non-fuzzy subsets of the universe of discourse.

[i] We are tacitly assuming that T and N are recursively enumerable. See Ref. 30, pp. 5–7.
[j] For a discussion of grammaticality see Refs. 25 and 28.

Our observation that natural languages are generally characterized by slightly fuzzy syntax and rather fuzzy semantics does not necessarily hold true when T is associated with an infinite rather than finite alphabet. Thus, when the terms of a language have the form of sounds, pictures, handwritten characters, etc., the fuzziness of its syntax may be quite pronounced. For example, the class of handwritten characters (or sounds) which correspond to a single letter, say R, is rather fuzzy, and this is even more true of concatenations of handwritten characters (or sounds).

3. The Meaning of Meaning

With the notion of a fuzzy language $L = (U, T, E, N)$ as a point of departure, it becomes possible to give a concrete definition for the otherwise elusive concept of *meaning*. Specifically, let $\mu_N : \text{Supp}(T) \times U \to [0,1]$ be the membership function characterizing N, with $\mu_N(x, y)$ representing the strength of the relation between a term x in T and an object y in U. Then, the definition of the *meaning* of x can be stated as follows[34]:

Definition 5. The *meaning* of a term x in T is a fuzzy subset $M(x)$ of U in which the grade of membership of an element y of U is given by

$$\mu_{M(x)}(y) = \mu_N(x, y). \tag{3}$$

Thus, $M(x)$ is a fuzzy subset of U which is conditioned on x as a parameter and which is a *section* of N in the sense that its membership function, $\mu_{M(x)} : U \to [0,1]$, is obtained by assigning a particular value, x, to the first argument in the membership function of N.

Example 6. As a very simple illustration of this definition, consider an unstructured language $L = (U, T, E, N)$ in which among the elements of T are the terms *young, old* and *middle-aged*; U is the set of ages from 1 to 100; and N is a fuzzy naming relation from E to U defined by

$$\begin{aligned} \mu_N(\textit{young},\ y) &= 1\,, \quad \text{for } y < 25 \\ &= \left[1 + \left(\frac{y-25}{5}\right)^2\right]^{-1}, \quad \text{for } y \geq 25 \end{aligned} \tag{4}$$

$$\begin{aligned} \mu_N(\textit{old},\ y) &= 0\,, \quad \text{for } y < 50 \\ &= \left[1 + \left(\frac{y-50}{5}\right)^{-2}\right]^{-1}, \quad \text{for } y \geq 50 \end{aligned} \tag{5}$$

$$\mu_N(\textit{middle-aged},\ y) = 0\ , \quad \text{for } 1 \le y < 35$$
$$= \left[1 + \left(\frac{y-45}{4}\right)^4\right]^{-1}, \quad \text{for } 35 \le y < 45$$
$$= \left[1 + \left(\frac{y-45}{5}\right)^2\right]^{-1}, \quad \text{for } y \ge 45 \qquad (6)$$

for $1 \le y \le 100$.

Then the meaning of the term *young* is the fuzzy subset, $M(\textit{young})$, of $U = [1, 100]$ whose membership function is given by

$$\mu_{M(\textit{young})}(y) = 1\ , \quad \text{for } y < 25$$
$$= \left[1 + \left(\frac{y-25}{5}\right)^2\right]^{-1}, \quad \text{for } y \le 25 \qquad (7)$$

and similarly for the meanings of *old* and *middle-aged*. (See Fig. 2)

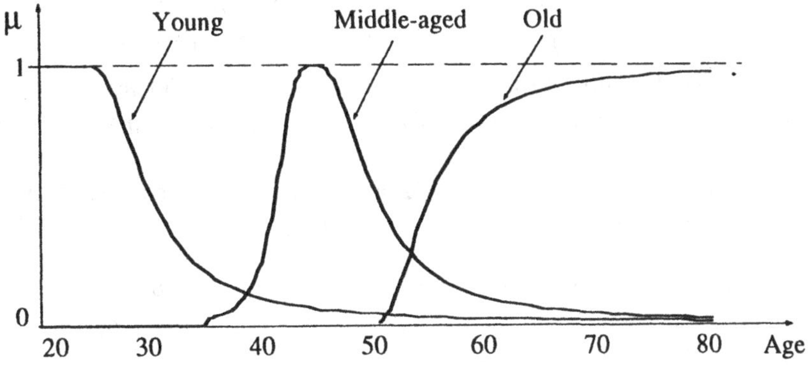

Fig. 2. Membership functions of the fuzzy sets $M(\textit{young})$, $M(\textit{middle-aged})$ and $M(\textit{old})$.

As another simple example, consider a fuzzy term such as *several*. If the universe of discourse is taken to be the set of non-negative integers, then *several* can be viewed as a name for a fuzzy subset $M(\textit{several})$ of U given by the collection of ordered pairs

$$M(\textit{several}) = \{(3, 0.4),\ (4, 0.8),\ (5, 1.0),\ (6, 1.0),\ (7, 1.0),\ (8, 0.4)\} \qquad (8)$$

in which we list only those pairs in which the grade of membership is positive.

In short, a term x, whether atomic or composite, is a name of a fuzzy subset of U. This subset, $M(x)$, constitutes the meaning of x. The membership function of $M(x)$ is given by (3), where μ_N is the naming relation in the language in which x is a term.

If N is a fuzzy naming relation from E to U, then its *domain* $D(N)$ is a fuzzy set in T which is the *shadow*[k] of N on E. The membership function of $D(N)$ is given by

$$\mu_{D(N)}(x) = \vee_y \mu_N(x,y) \tag{9}$$

where the supremum $\vee_y$ is taken over all y in U.

The grade of membership of x in $D(N)$ may be interpreted as the *degree of meaningfulness* of x. Thus, x is *fully meaningful* if $M(x)$ is a *normal*[l] fuzzy set, that is

$$\mu_{D(N)}(x) = \vee_y \; \mu_N(x,y) = 1\,. \tag{10}$$

Essentially, this implies that x is fully meaningful if there exists a y such that $\mu_N(x,y) = 1$. Conversely, x is *meaningless* if $M(x)$ is an empty set, that is, $\mu_N(x,y) = 0$ for all y in U.

Example 7. Suppose that U is the set of integers $U = \{1, 2, \ldots, 10\}$ and the terms *small, large, not small and not large, large and small,* are defined as the following fuzzy subsets of U.

$$\begin{aligned} M(small) &= \{(1,1.0),\ (2,1.0),\ (3,0.8),\ (4,0.2)\} \\ M(large) &= \{(7,0.2),\ (8,0.8),\ (9,1.0),\ (10,1.0)\} \\ M(not\ small\ and\ not\ large) &= M'(small) \cap M'(large) \\ M(large\ and\ small) &= M(large) \cap M(small) \end{aligned}$$

where M' denotes the complement of M and $\cap$ stands for the intersection (see footnote a). From the definition of complement and intersection, it follows that

$$\begin{aligned} M(not\ small\ and\ not\ large) = \{&(3,0.2),\ (4,0.8),\ (5,1.0)\,, \\ &(6,1.0),\ (7,0.8),\ (8,0.2)\} \end{aligned}$$

and

$$M(large\ and\ small) = empty\ set\,.$$

Thus, *not small and not large* is fully meaningful, while *large and small* is meaningless.

An important aspect of meaning is its context — dependence. Thus, in general, the meaning of a term x when it is a component of a composite term depends on the context in which x occurs. To illustrate, in example 6, the terms *young, old*

[k]If A is a fuzzy set in $X = X_1 \times X_2 \times \cdots \times X_n$, $X_i = \{x_i\}$, $i = 1, \ldots, n$, with membership function $\mu(x_1, \ldots, x_n)$, then the *shadow* of A on $X_2 \times \ldots X_n$ is a fuzzy set in $X_2 \times \ldots \times X_n$ whose membership function, μ_1, is given by $\mu_1(x_2, \ldots, x_n) = \vee_{x_1} \mu(x_1, \ldots, x_n)$. (Additional details may be found in Refs. 11 and 12.

[l]A fuzzy set A in X is *normal* iff $\vee_x \mu_A(x) = 1$; otherwise A is subnormal. If A has a finite support, this implies that A is normal iff there exists an x whose grade of membership in A is unity.

and *middle-aged* were defined with a tacit understanding that they are adjectives applying to *man*. Clearly, the same adjectives when applied to, say, *dog*, would correspond to fuzzy sets in U quite different from those defined by (4), (5) and (6).

Can the terms like *young, old, tall*, etc. be defined in such a way as to make them relatively insensitive to the context in which they occur? One possibility lies in defining such terms on the basis of percentiles. Specifically, consider the term *tall* and assume that the tallness of an object y in a subset of U named z is measured in terms of its height, $h(y)$. Further, let h_{50} denote the median of $h(y)$ over z and h_r denote the r-percentile of $h(y)$ over z, that is, a value of h such that 100-r percent of the number of members of z have height greater than or equal to h_r. Then, we would assign the grade of membership 0.5 in the fuzzy set labeled *tall* z to an object whose height is h_{50}, and the grade of membership $\mu_{tall\ z}(y) = \frac{r}{100}$ to an object y whose height is h_r. More generally, the grade of membership of an object whose height is h_r might be related to r not linearly, as in $\frac{r}{100}$, but through an S-shaped function which takes the value 0.5 at $r = 50$ and tends to 0 and 1, respectively, as r approaches 0 and 100.

As a simple illustration, assume that U is the set of buildings in a city and z is the subset of hotels in that city. Suppose that the height of a particular hotel y is 150 feet and that this height represents the 75 percentile of the heights of hotels in the city. Then, the grade of membership of the hotel in question in the class named *tall hotel* in that city would be 0.75.

It should be noted that, in the case of natural languages, the context-dependence of meaning plays an important role in the resolution of ambiguities. Thus, if $x_1x_2x_3$ is a composite term and x_2 has two possible meanings, say $M^1(x_2)$ and $M^2(x_2)$, then x_2 would be assigned that meaning which maximizes the degree of meaningfulness of $x_1x_2x_3$. More generally, the rule governing the resolution of ambiguity may be stated informally as follows: If a component of a composite term has more than one meaning, assign that meaning to the component which maximizes the meaningfulness of the composite term in the context in which the latter occurs.

One of the most important aspects of the concept of meaning has to do with the semantic rules which make it possible to determine the meaning of a composite term from the knowledge of the meanings of its atomic components. This question will be considered in Sec. 5. As a preliminary, we shall turn our attention to some of the basic concepts underlying the syntax of fuzzy languages.

4. Syntax of Fuzzy Languages

As pointed out in Ref. 33, it is quite easy to generalize much of the theory of formal languages to the case where T is a fuzzy, rather than non-fuzzy, subset of strings over a finite alphabet. However, the resulting theory still falls far short of providing an adequate model for the syntax of natural languages for the case where the grade of membership of a composite term in T is equated with the degree of its grammaticality.

In what follows, we shall summarize and extend some of the main results of Refs. 33 and 34, and point to a connection between fuzzy term sets and non-fuzzy languages.

Following the standard notation of the theory of formal languages,[30] let V_T be a finite alphabet of terminal symbols (e.g., alpha-numeric characters in English) and let V_T^* denote the set of all finite strings composed of elements of V_T. Furthermore, let V_N denote a set of non-terminals, that is, a set of labels for the elements of a finite collection of fuzzy subsets of V_T^* called *syntactic categories*. For example, in the case of English, the elements of V_N would include N, standing for the syntactic category Noun; V, standing for Verb; NP, standing for Noun Phrase, etc. It is assumed that V_T and V_N are disjoint.

In the case of a fuzzy structured language $L = (U, S_T, V_T^*, S_N)$, the term set, T, is assumed to be a fuzzy subset of V_T^* characterized by a membership function $\mu_T : V_T^* \to [0, 1]$ which associates with each string x in V_T^* its grade of membership, $\mu_T(x)$, in T, $0 \leq \mu_T(x) \leq 1$. The support of T is the set of all finite strings in V_T^* which have positive grades of membership in T.

It is convenient to represent T in the form of a power series (in the sense of Ref. 29)

$$T = \mu_1 x_1 + \mu_2 x_2 + \ldots \tag{11}$$

where the x_i denote elements of the support of T and the μ_i are their respective grades of membership in T. Then, if the concatenation of two strings x and x' is denoted by xx', the concatenation of T with another fuzzy set of strings T'

$$T' = \mu_1' x_1' + \mu_2' x_2' + \ldots \tag{12}$$

is denoted by TT' and is defined by

$$TT' = \sum_i \sum_j (\mu_i \wedge \mu_j') x_i x_j' \tag{13}$$

where

$$\mu_i \mu_j' = \mu_i \wedge \mu_j' = \mathrm{Min}(\mu_i, \mu_j') \tag{14}$$

and

$$\mu_i + \mu_j' = \mu_i \vee \mu_j = \mathrm{Max}(\mu_i, \mu_j') \,. \tag{15}$$

Thus, (13), (14) and (15) imply that the grade of membership of the string $v = x_i x_j'$ in the fuzzy set TT' is given by

$$\mu_{TT'}(v) = \vee_{x_i, x_j'} (\mu_T(x_i) \wedge \mu_{T'}(x_j'))$$

where the supremum is taken over all x_i, x_j' such that $x_i x_j' = v$.

Example 8. As a very simple illustration, suppose that $V_T = \{a, b\}$ and

$$T = 0.2\, a + 0.3\, ab + 1.0\, aba$$

and

$$T' = 0.3\, a + 0.8\, aba + 1.0\, \varepsilon$$

where ε is the nullstring. Then

$$\begin{aligned} TT' = {} & (0.2 \wedge 0.3)\, aa + (0.3 \wedge 0.3)\, aba + (0.3 \wedge 1.0)\, abaa \\ & + (0.2 \wedge 0.8)\, aaba + (0.3 \wedge 0.8)\, ababa + (1.0 \wedge 0.8)\, abaaba \\ & + (0.2 \wedge 1)\, a + (0.3 \wedge 1.0)\, ab + (1.0 \wedge 1.0)\, aba \end{aligned}$$

which upon simplification becomes

$$\begin{aligned} TT' = {} & 0.2\, aa + 1.0\, aba + 0.3\, abaa + 0.2\, aaba + 0.3\, ababa \\ & + 0.8\, abaaba + 0.2\, a + 0.3\, ab\,. \end{aligned}$$

The associativity of the concatenation of fuzzy sets of strings makes it possible to define the *Kleene closure* of T by the expression

$$T^* = \varepsilon + T + T^2 + T^3 + \cdots \tag{16}$$

where + stands for union and T^n, $n = 2, 3, \ldots$, denotes an n-fold concatenation of T with itself. As will be seen presently, the notions of concatenation and Kleene closure of fuzzy sets of strings play significant roles in the definition of the syntax of T.

The function of the syntax, S_T, of L is to provide a set of rules for generating strings in the support of T together with their grades of membership in T. Such a set of syntactic rules constitutes a *fuzzy grammar* for L.

A particular form of fuzzy grammar can be obtained by generalizing the notion of a phrase-structure grammar.[24] Specifically, a fuzzy phrase-structure grammar or, simply, *fuzzy grammar*,[33] is a quadruple

$$G = (V_T, V_N, S, P)$$

in which $S \in V_N$ is a starting symbol standing for the syntactic category "sentence" and P is a finite set of fuzzy productions of the form

$$\alpha \xrightarrow{\rho} \beta \tag{17}$$

where α and β are strings composed of elements of $V_T + V_N$ (except that $\alpha \neq \varepsilon$), and $0 < \rho \leq 1$. Thus, if $\alpha \xrightarrow{\rho} \beta$ and γ and δ are arbitrary strings in $(V_T + V_N)^*$, then

$$\gamma\alpha\delta \xrightarrow{\rho} \gamma\beta\delta \tag{18}$$

and $\gamma\beta\delta$ is said to be *directly derivable* from $\gamma\alpha\delta$. Note that α, β, γ and δ are, in effect, labels for fuzzy subsets of strings in V_T^*, and $\gamma\alpha\delta$ and $\gamma\beta\delta$ represent concatenations of these subsets in the sense of (13).

If u and v are two strings in $(V_T + V_N)^*$ and there exist strings $\alpha_1, \alpha_2, \ldots, \alpha_{n-1}$ in $(V_T + V_N)^*$ such that

$$u \xrightarrow{\rho_1} \alpha_1 \xrightarrow{\rho_2} \alpha_2 \cdots \xrightarrow{\rho_{n-1}} \alpha_{n-1} \xrightarrow{\rho_n} v \tag{19}$$

then v is said to be *derivable from u via the derivation chain* $(u, \alpha_1, \alpha_2, \ldots, \alpha_{n-1}, v)$. The *strength* of this chain is defined to be the strength of its weakest link, i.e.,

$$\begin{aligned} \text{strength of } (u, \alpha_1, \alpha_2, \ldots, \alpha_{n-1}, v) &= \text{Min}(\rho_1, \ldots, \rho_n) \\ &= \rho_1 \wedge \rho_2 \wedge \cdots \wedge \rho_n . \end{aligned} \tag{20}$$

The *strength, ρ, of the relation between* u and v is defined to be the strength of the strongest chain between u and v. Thus,

$$\rho = \text{Sup Min}(\rho_1, \ldots, \rho_n), \tag{21}$$

where Sup is taken over all derivation chains for u to v.

If v is derivable from u and the strength of the relation between u and v is ρ, then we write

$$u \overset{\rho}{\Longrightarrow} v . \tag{22}$$

The generation of T by G is governed by the definition:

Definition 9. A fuzzy grammar G generates a fuzzy term set T, or more explicitly, $T(G)$, in the following way. A terminal string[m] x is in $T(G)$ (i.e., in the support of $T(G)$) if x is derivable from S. The grade of membership of x in $T(G)$, $\mu_T(x)$, is given by the strength of the relation between S and x.

Example 10. Suppose that $V_T = \{0, 1\}$, $V_N = \{A, B, S\}$, and P is given by

$$\begin{array}{rlrl} P: S &\xrightarrow{0.5} AB & A &\xrightarrow{0.5} a \\ S &\xrightarrow{0.8} A & A &\xrightarrow{0.6} b \\ S &\xrightarrow{0.8} B & B &\xrightarrow{0.4} A \\ AB &\xrightarrow{0.4} BA & B &\xrightarrow{0.2} a . \end{array}$$

Consider the terminal string $x = a$. The possible derivation chains for this string are $S \overset{0.8}{\to} A \overset{0.5}{\to} a$, $S \overset{0.8}{\to} B \overset{0.2}{\to} a$, and $S \overset{0.8}{\to} B \overset{0.4}{\to} A \overset{0.5}{\to} a$. Hence

$$\mu_T(a) = (0.8 \wedge 0.5) \vee (0.8 \wedge 0.2) \vee (0.8 \wedge 0.4 \wedge 0.5) = 0.5 .$$

[m] A *terminal* string is a concatenation of terminals. A *sentential form* is a concatenation of terminals and non-terminals which is derivable from S.

Similarly, the possible derivation chains for the terminal string $x = ab$ are $S \overset{0.5}{\to} AB \overset{0.5}{\to} aB \overset{0.4}{\to} aA \overset{0.6}{\to} ab$, $S \overset{0.5}{\to} AB \overset{0.4}{\to} AA \overset{0.5}{\to} aA \overset{0.6}{\to} ab$, $S \overset{0.5}{\to} AB \overset{0.4}{\to} BA \overset{0.2}{\to} aA \overset{0.6}{\to} ab$, and $S \overset{0.5}{\to} AB \overset{0.4}{\to} BA \overset{0.4}{\to} AA \overset{0.5}{\to} aA \overset{0.6}{\to} ab$. Hence,

$$\mu_T(ab) = 0.4 \vee 0.4 \vee 0.2 \vee 0.4 = 0.4\,.$$

Two fuzzy grammars G_1 and G_2 are *equivalent* if they generate the same fuzzy set of strings, i.e.,

$$T(G_1) = T(G_2)\,.$$

For example, it is easy to verify that with G defined as in Example 10, the grammars $G = (\{0,1\},\ \{A, B, S\}, S,\ P)$ and $G' = (\{0,1\},\ \{A, B, C, S\},\ S,\ P')$, in which

$$\begin{aligned} P' : S &\xrightarrow{0.5} AB \qquad & A &\xrightarrow{0.5} a \\ S &\xrightarrow{0.8} A & A &\xrightarrow{0.6} b \\ S &\xrightarrow{0.8} B & B &\xrightarrow{0.4} A \\ AB &\xrightarrow{0.4} AC & B &\xrightarrow{0.2} a \\ AC &\xrightarrow{1.0} BC & & \\ BC &\xrightarrow{1.0} BA & & \end{aligned} \tag{23}$$

are equivalent.

For many purposes, it is convenient to express the productions in P in an algebraic notation which is similar in appearance to — but more general than — that used in connection with non-fuzzy languages.[35] The basic ingredients of this notation are: (a) the representation of a fuzzy set of strings in the power series form (11)

$$T = \mu_1 x_1 + \mu_2 x_2 + \cdots \tag{24}$$

where μ_i, $i = 1, 2, \ldots$, is the grade of membership of the string x_i in T; (b) the definition of concatenation of fuzzy sets of strings (13); and (c) the definition of the expression γT[n] (in which $0 < \gamma \leq 1$) as a fuzzy set in which a generic string x has the grade of membership given by

$$\mu_{\gamma T}(x) = \gamma \wedge \mu_T(x)\,. \tag{25}$$

With this understanding, a production of the form

$$\alpha \xrightarrow{\rho} \beta$$

[n]Note that an expression of the form γT in which $0 < \gamma \leq 1$ and T is a fuzzy set of strings may be regarded as a degenerate form of the concatenation $T'T$ in which $T' = \gamma\varepsilon$, $\varepsilon =$ nullstring. Then (25) follows from (13).

in which α and β are labels for fuzzy subsets of V_T^*, may be replaced by the equation

$$\alpha = \rho\beta \tag{26}$$

in which $\rho\beta$ is a fuzzy set of strings defined by (25), i.e.,

$$\mu_{\rho\beta}(x) = \rho \wedge \mu_\beta(x), \qquad x \in V_T^* . \tag{27}$$

Furthermore, if P contains the productions

$$\alpha \xrightarrow{\rho_1} \beta_1 \tag{28}$$

and

$$\alpha \xrightarrow{\rho_2} \beta_2 \tag{29}$$

then (28) and (29) give rise to the equation

$$\alpha = \rho_1\beta_1 + \rho_2\beta_2 . \tag{30}$$

Example 11. Written in algebraic form, the production system of Example 10 reads

$$S = 0.5\,AB + 0.8\,A + 0.8\,B \tag{31}$$

$$AB = 0.4\,BA \tag{32}$$

$$A = 0.5\,a + 0.6\,b \tag{33}$$

$$B = 0.4\,A + 0.2\,a . \tag{34}$$

The fuzzy set of strings generated by this grammar can be obtained by solving the system of equations (31)–(34) for S. Thus, on substituting (33) in (34) and using (13) and (25) we find

$$B = 0.4\,a + 0.4\,b$$

and hence

$$\begin{aligned} AB &= (0.5\,a + 0.6\,b)(0.4\,a + 0.4\,b) \\ &= 0.4\,aa + 0.4\,ba + 0.4\,ab + 0.4\,bb . \end{aligned}$$

Similar substitutions finally yield

$$T(G) = S = 0.5\,a + 0.6\,b + 0.4\,(aa + ba + ab + bb) . \tag{35}$$

In solving a system of algebraic equations representing the production system of a fuzzy grammar, one frequently encounters linear equations of the form

$$u = \alpha u + \beta \tag{36}$$

in which u, α and β are fuzzy sets of strings over a finite alphabet, and + and the product denote the union and concatenation, respectively. A straightforward extension of Arden's theorem[37] to (36) yields the following proposition.

Proposition 12. If α does not contain the nullstring, then (36) has a unique solution for u which is given by

$$u = \alpha^* \beta \tag{37}$$

where α^* is the Kleene closure of α (in the sense of (16)).

Example 13. The solution of

$$u = (0.3\,a + 0.5\,b)u + 0.4\,a$$

is given by

$$u = (0.3\,a + 0.5\,b)^* 0.4\,a$$

which in expanded form reads

$$u = 0.4\,a + 0.3\,aa + 0.4\,ba + 0.3\,aaa + 0.3\,aba$$
$$+ 0.3\,baa + 0.4\,bba + \cdots .$$

A basic question in the theory of formal languages is whether or not there exists an algorithm for determining if a given terminal string x is in the language $L(G)$ generated by a given G. The counterpart of this question in the case of fuzzy languages is the existence of an algorithm for computing the membership function μ_T for the fuzzy term set $T(G)$ generated by a given fuzzy grammar G. If such an algorithm exists, then G is said to be *recursive.* In this sense, the grammar of Example 10 is recursive.

As in the case of non-fuzzy languages, it is convenient to classify the grammars of fuzzy languages into four principal categories, which in order of decreasing generality are:

Type 0 grammars

In this case, productions are of the general form

$$\alpha \xrightarrow{\rho} \beta \tag{38}$$

where α and β are strings in $(V_T + V_N)^*$, with $\alpha \neq \varepsilon$.

Example 14. Assume that V_T and V_N are as in Example 10. Then (38) is exemplified by $AB \overset{0.3}{\to} BA$, $ABa \overset{0.6}{\to} Bb$, $A \overset{0.8}{\to} b$.

Type 1 grammars (*context-sensitive*)

Here the productions are of the form

$$\alpha \xrightarrow{\rho} \beta \tag{39}$$

where α and β are strings in $(V_T + V_N)^*$, with $\alpha \neq \varepsilon$ and $|\beta| \geq |\alpha|$, i.e., the length of the right-hand side (the consequent) must be at least as great as that of the left-hand aside (the antecedent).

Example 15. (39) is exemplified by $AB \overset{0.5}{\rightarrow} BA$, $A \overset{0.8}{\rightarrow} bb$, but not by $BA \overset{0.9}{\rightarrow} B$.

If G is a context-sensitive grammar in the sense defined above, then it can readily be shown that there exists an equivalent grammar G' in which the productions are of the form

$$\beta A\gamma \xrightarrow{\rho} \beta\alpha\gamma \tag{40}$$

where $A \in V_N$, and $\alpha,\ \beta,\ \gamma \in (V_T + V_N)^*$, $\alpha \neq \varepsilon$. However, $S \xrightarrow{\rho} \varepsilon$ is allowed if S does not appear in any consequent. (40) implies that the nonterminal A can be replaced by α provided it occurs in the context (β, γ), i.e., is preceded on the left by β and on the right by γ.

Example 16. (40) is exemplified by $aAb \overset{0.8}{\rightarrow} abb$, $Ab \overset{0.3}{\rightarrow} bbb$, but not by $AB \overset{0.3}{\rightarrow} BA$. However, by introducing a new nonterminal C, the latter production can be replaced by the following three productions of the form (40), with the resulting grammar being equivalent to the original one.

$$AB \xrightarrow{0.3} AC$$
$$AC \xrightarrow{1.0} BC$$
$$BC \xrightarrow{1.0} BA\,.$$

An important property of context-sensitive grammars which is established in Ref. 33 is their recursiveness. This implies that, if the productions in a grammar G are of the form (40), there exists an algorithm for computing the grade of membership in $T(G)$ of any terminal string x.

Type 2 grammars (*context-free*)
Here the allowable productions are of the form

$$A \xrightarrow{\rho} \alpha \tag{41}$$

where $A \in V_N$, $\alpha \in (V_T + V_N)^*$, and $S \xrightarrow{\rho} \varepsilon$ is allowed. Thus, in the case of a context-free grammar, A can be replaced by α regardless of the context in which A occurs.

In the case of non-fuzzy languages, context-free grammars are important because they can be used to generate, with some exceptions, well-formed strings in programming languages. Their relevance to natural languages, however, is not as great because context-sensitivity is a pervasive characteristic of such languages.

Type 3 grammars (*regular*)
In this case the allowable productions are of the form

$$A \xrightarrow{\rho} aB$$
$$A \xrightarrow{\rho} Ba$$
$$A \xrightarrow{\rho} a$$
$$S \xrightarrow{\rho} \varepsilon$$

where $A,\ B \in V_N$ and $a \in V_T$.

Comment 17. The algebraic notation which was described earlier is particularly useful in the case of context-free grammars. Thus if the nonterminals in V_N are denoted by $X_1, \ldots, X_n$, and $X = (X_1, \ldots, X_n)$, with $X_1 = S$, then the production system P can be put into the form

$$X = f(X) \tag{42}$$

where f is an n-vector whose components are multinomials in the X_i, $i = 1, \ldots, n$. In this way, the determination of the fuzzy set of string generated by the grammar reduces to finding a fixed point of the function f. In this connection, it can really be shown that if we set $X' = \theta =$ empty set and form the iterates

$$X^{k+1} = f(X^k)\,,\ X^0 = \theta\,,\quad k = 1, 2, 3, \ldots \tag{43}$$

then, for each k, X^k is a fuzzy subset of the solution of (42).

Decomposition of a fuzzy grammar into non-fuzzy grammars

An important connection between fuzzy and non-fuzzy grammars relates to the possibility of decomposing a fuzzy grammar — in the sense defined below — into non-fuzzy grammars of the same type.

This possibility stems from a basic property of fuzzy sets which is stated below.

Let A be a fuzzy set in a space $X = \{x\}$, where x denotes a generic element of X. For λ in (0,1], define a λ-*level-set* or simply, a *level set*[11] of A as a non-fuzzy set A_λ comprising all elements of X whose grade of membership in A is greater than or equal to λ, i.e.,

$$A_\lambda = \{x | \mu_A(x) \geq \lambda\}\,. \tag{44}$$

Clearly, the A_λ form a nested collection of subsets of X, with

$$\lambda \geq \lambda' \Longrightarrow A_\lambda \subset A_{\lambda'}\,. \tag{45}$$

As shown in Ref. 20, A admits of the resolution expressed by

$$A = \sum_\lambda \lambda A_\lambda\,, \quad 0 < \lambda \leq 1 \tag{46}$$

where Σ stands for the union of fuzzy sets and λA_λ denotes a fuzzy set with a two-valued membership function defined by[o]

$$\begin{aligned} \mu_{\lambda A_\lambda}(x) &= \lambda\,, \quad \text{for } x \in A_\lambda \\ &= 0\,, \quad \text{elsewhere}\,. \end{aligned} \tag{47}$$

[o]More generally, if A is a fuzzy set in $X = \{x\}$, with μ_A denoting the grade of membership of x in A, then λA is a fuzzy set in X such that the grade of membership of x in λA is $\lambda \wedge \mu_A(x)$. Thus, if A is expressed in power series from as $A = \mu_1 x_1 + \mu_2 x_2 + \ldots$, then $\lambda A = (\lambda \wedge \mu_1)x_1 + (\lambda \wedge \mu_2)x_2 + \ldots$. Note that this is consistent with (25).

To illustrate, let $X = \{x_1, x_2, x_3, x_4, x_5, x_6\}$ and assume that A, expressed as a power series, is given by

$$A = 0.3\, x_1 + 0.5\, x_2 + 0.6\, x_3 + 0.8\, x_4 + 1.0\, x_5 + 1.0\, x_6\,. \tag{48}$$

Then

$$\begin{aligned} A_{1.0} &= \{x_5, x_6\} \\ A_{0.8} &= \{x_4, x_5, x_6\} \\ A_{0.6} &= x_3, x_4, x_5, x_6 \\ A_{0.5} &= x_2, x_3, x_4, x_5, x_6 \\ A_{0.3} &= x_1, x_2, x_3, x_4, x_5, x_6 \end{aligned}$$

and the resolution of A reads

$$A = 0.3\, A_{0.3} + 0.5\, A_{0.5} + 0.6\, A_{0.6} + 0.8\, A_{0.8} + 1.0\, A_{1.0} \tag{49}$$

where + denotes the union of fuzzy sets. A straightforward way of verifying the equivalence of (48) and (49) is to substitute the power series expressions for $A_{0.3}, \ldots, A_{1.0}$ into (49), yielding

$$\begin{aligned} A = 0.3\, &(x_1 + x_2 + x_3 + x_4 + x_5 + x_6) + 0.5\, (x_2 + x_3 + x_4 + x_5 + x_6) \\ &+ 0.6\, (x_3 + x_4 + x_5 + x_6) + 0.8\, (x_4 + x_5 + x_6) + 1.0\, (x_5 + x_6)\,. \end{aligned}$$

Then, on noting that, by the definition of +,

$$\lambda x_i + \lambda' x_i = (\lambda \vee \lambda')x_i, \quad i = 1, \ldots, 6$$

we obtain (48).

To illustrate the application of the resolution expressed by (46) to fuzzy grammars, it will be convenient to focus our attention on context-free grammars, with the understanding that the same conclusions apply as well to grammars of type 0, 1, and 3.

Specifically, consider a fuzzy context-free grammar $G = (V_T, V_N, S, P)$ and let P_λ be the subset of productions in P such that if $\alpha \xrightarrow{\rho} \beta$, with $\rho \geq \lambda$, is in P, then $\alpha \xrightarrow{1.0} \beta$ (or simply $\alpha \to \beta$) is in P_λ. Further, let

$$G_\lambda = (V_T, V_N, S, P_\lambda) \tag{50}$$

be a non-fuzzy grammar with the production system P_λ.

The non-fuzzy grammar G_λ generates a non-fuzzy context-free term set $T(G_\lambda)$. As we shall see presently, $T(G)$ can be resolved into the $T(G_\lambda)$ just as a fuzzy set A can be resolved into its level sets A_λ. More specifically, we can assert the following proposition.

Proposition 18. If $G(V_T, V_N, S, P)$ is a fuzzy context-free grammar and the G_λ, $0 < \lambda \leq 1$, are non-fuzzy context-free grammars defined by (50), then

$$T(G) = \sum_\lambda \lambda T(G_\lambda)\,, \quad \lambda = \text{values of } \rho \text{ in } P \tag{51}$$

where $T(G)$ and $T(G_\lambda)$ are the fuzzy context-free and non-fuzzy context-free term sets generated by G and G_λ, respectively, and $\lambda T(G_\lambda)$ is a fuzzy set of terms such that[p]

$$\mu_{\lambda T(G_\lambda)}(x) = \lambda \;\wedge\; \mu_{T(G_\lambda)}(x)\,. \tag{52}$$

To prove (51) it is sufficient to note that (51) would be a special case of the resolution of a fuzzy set (see (46)) if the $T(G_\lambda)$ were the level sets of $T(G)$. Thus, all that is necessary to show is that $T(G_\lambda)$, which is the fuzzy set of terms generated by G_λ, is a λ-level set of $T(G)$. To this end, let x be a terminal string in $T(G_\lambda)$. Since the ρ of all productions in G_λ is greater than or equal to λ, it follows from the definitions of $\mu_{T(G)}(x)$ and $\mu_{T(G_\lambda)}(x)$ (see definition 9) that $\mu_{T(G)}(x) \geq \mu_{T(G_\lambda)}(x) \geq \lambda$ and hence that x belongs to the λ-level set of $T(G)$. Conversely, let x be a terminal string in the λ-level set of $T(G)$. Then $\mu_{T(G)}(x) \geq \lambda$ and by definition 9 it follows that x derivable from S via a derivation chain which uses only those productions in G in which $\rho \geq \lambda$. Consequently, x belongs to $T(G_\lambda)$. Thus, both

$$T(G_\lambda) \subset \lambda - \text{level set of } T(G)$$

and

$$\lambda - \text{level set of } T(G) \subset T(G_\lambda)$$

are true, and hence

$$T(G_\lambda) = \lambda - \text{level set of } T(G) \tag{53}$$

which is what we set out to establish.

Example 19. Consider the fuzzy grammar

$$G = (\{a, b\},\ \{A, B, S\},\ S,\ P)$$

in which

$$\begin{aligned} P: S &\xrightarrow{0.8} bA \qquad & B &\xrightarrow{1.0} b \\ S &\xrightarrow{0.6} aB & A &\xrightarrow{0.3} bSA \\ A &\xrightarrow{1.0} a & B &\xrightarrow{0.3} aSB\,. \end{aligned}$$

[p]Note that (52) is consistent with (25) as well as with the definition given in footnote o.

In this case, the non-fuzzy production systems P_λ are given by

$$\begin{array}{lll} P_{1.0}: & A \to a & B \to b \\ P_{0.8}: & A \to a & B \to b \\ & S \to bA & \\ P_{0.6}: & A \to a & B \to b \\ & S \to bA & S \to aB \\ P_{0.3}: & A \to a & B \to b \\ & S \to bA & S \to aB \\ & A \to bSA & B \to aSB \end{array}$$

and the non-fuzzy context-free term sets generated by the corresponding grammars $G_{1.0}, G_{0.8}, G_{0.6}$ and $G_{0.3}$ are $T(G_{1.0}), T(G_{0.8}), T(G_{0.6})$ and $T(G_{0.3})$. In terms of these, the fuzzy term set generated by G is given by the resolution

$$T(G) = 0.3\,T(G_{0.3}) + 0.6\,T(G_{0.6}) + 0.8\,T(G_{0.8}) + T(G_{1.0})\,. \tag{54}$$

It is easy to show that the converse of proposition 18 also holds true. Thus, if the G_λ, $0 < \lambda \leq 1$, constitute a nested sequence of non-fuzzy context-free grammars such that

$$\lambda \geq \lambda' \Longrightarrow P_\lambda \subset P_{\lambda'} \tag{55}$$

then the expression

$$\sum_\lambda \lambda T(G_\lambda) \tag{56}$$

will represent a fuzzy term set which can be generated by a fuzzy context-free grammar.

As pointed out in Ref. 33, many of the basic results in the theory of non-fuzzy formal languages can readily be extended to fuzzy term sets defined by fuzzy grammars. For example, it is easy to show, both directly[33] and by making use of the resolution of fuzzy term sets,[q] that a fuzzy context-free term set can be put into the Chomsky and Greibach normal forms. Similarly, it can readily be shown[36] that a fuzzy context-free term set is accepted by a fuzzy push-down automaton. We shall not discuss these and other extensions[r] in the present paper and instead will turn our attention to the semantics of fuzzy languages.

5. Semantics of Fuzzy Languages

Consider a structured fuzzy language $L = (U, S_T, E, S_N)$ in which S_T is a set of syntactic rules defining a term set $T \subset E$, U is a universe of discourse, and S_N is a

[q] The possibility of establishing the validity of the Chomsky and Greibach normal forms for fuzzy context-free grammars by making use of the resolutions of fuzzy term sets was suggested to the author by Professor R. Karp.

[r] A number of interesting results may be found in Ref. 39.

set of semantic rules defining a fuzzy naming relation N from E to U. To simplify our discussion, we shall assume that T is a non-fuzzy subset of E which can be generated by a context-free grammar.

As was stated previously, the central problem of semantics is that of specifying a set of semantic rules, S_N, which can serve as an algorithm for computing the meaning of a composite term in T from the knowledge of the meanings of its components. In the case of an artificial language, especially a programming language, the semantic rules can be set by the designer of the language. In the case of natural languages, on the other hand, the semantic rules must be deduced from a partial knowledge of the membership function, $\mu_N : \text{Supp}(T) \times U \to [0,1]$, of the naming relation N. More specifically, S_N must be deduced from a finite set of ordered pairs $\{((x_i, y_j),\ \mu_N(x_i, y_j))\}$, $i = 1, \ldots, k$, $j = 1, \ldots, m$, in which the x_i and y_j are examples (i.e., sample points) in T and U, respectively, and $\mu_N(x_i, y_j)$ is the strength of the relation between x_i and y_j. From this point of view, the deduction of S_N constitutes a problem in abstraction — which, as was pointed out earlier — plays a central role in the field of pattern recognition.[31,32s]

At present, there are no systematic techniques for solving the problem of abstraction and thus the deduction of S_T and S_N for natural languages must be carried out in an *ad hoc* fashion. Indeed, the complexity of natural languages is so great that it is not even clear, at this juncture, what the form of the rules in S_N should be.

To make at least a modest beginning toward the development of a quantitative theory of semantics within the conceptual framework we have constructed so far, it is expedient to start with a few relatively simple special cases involving fragments of natural or artificial languages. In such cases, we can give explicit quantitative rules for determining the meaning of a composite term from the knowledge of the meanings of its components. The following simple examples are intended to illustrate the manner in which this can be done.

Example 20. Suppose the terms *young and old* are defined as in Example 6, that is, as fuzzy subsets of the set of integers $K = [0, 100]$, characterized respectively by the membership functions

$$\begin{aligned}\mu_N(\textit{young},\ y) &= 1, \quad \text{for } y < 25 \\ &= \left(1 + \left(\frac{y-25}{5}\right)^2\right)^{-1}, \quad \text{for } y \geq 25\end{aligned}$$

and

$$\begin{aligned}\mu_N(\textit{old},\ y) &= 0, \quad \text{for } y < 50 \\ &= \left(1 + \left(\frac{y-50}{5}\right)^{-2}\right)^{-1}, \quad \text{for } y \geq 50\,.\end{aligned}$$

[s] For a discussion of grammatical inference see [40] and [41].

We wish to define also the modifiers *not* and *very* and the connectives *or* and *and.* To this end, let $\mathcal{F}(K)$ denote the fuzzy power set of K, i.e., the set of all fuzzy subsets of K. Then, the modifier *not* can be regarded as a function from $\mathcal{F}(K)$ to $\mathcal{F}(K)$ defined by

$$\mu_N(not\ x, y) = 1 - \mu_N(x, y)\,, \qquad y \in K \tag{57}$$

where the term x is a label for a fuzzy subset of K and *not* x is a composite term consisting of a concatenation of *not* and x. Thus,

$$\mu_N(not\ young, y) = 1 - \mu_N(young, y)\,, \quad y \in K$$

and

$$\mu_N(not\ old, y) = 1 - \mu_N(old, y)$$

with *not* acting as a *complementer.*

Similarly, the term *very* can be regarded as a function from $\mathcal{F}(K)$ to $\mathcal{F}(K)$ defined by, say

$$\mu_N(very\ x, y) = \mu_N^2(x, y), \quad y \in K \tag{58}$$

which has the effect of concentrating the membership function of x around its maximum value. Thus,

$$\mu_N(very\ young, y) = \mu_N^2(young, y), \quad y \in K$$

and

$$\mu_N(very\ old, y) = \mu_N^2(old, y)\,.$$

The effect of concentration on the term *old* is illustrated in Fig. 3. To place in evidence this property of the term *very*, it will be referred to as a *concentrator.*

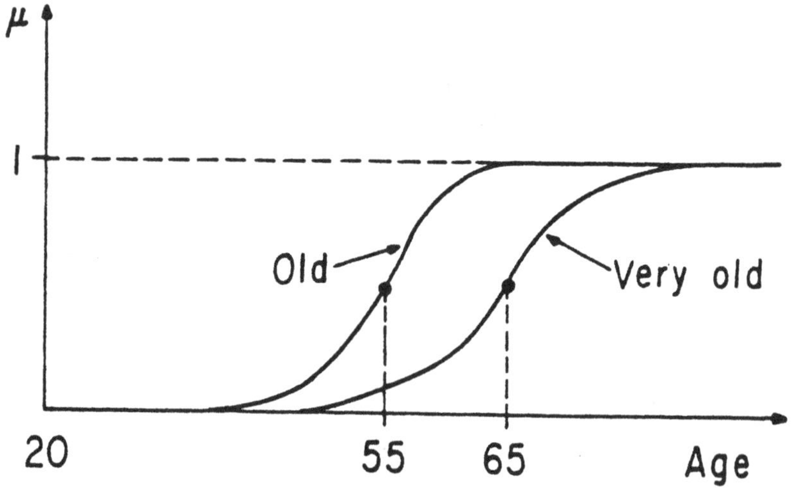

Fig. 3. The effect of the concentrator *very* on the fuzzy set $M(old)$.

The connective *or* is a function from $\mathcal{F}(K) \times \mathcal{F}(K)$ to $\mathcal{F}(K)$ which serves to generate the union of its arguments. Thus, if x_1 and x_2 are terms, then the meaning of the composite term x_1 *or* x_2 is defined by

$$M(x_1 \text{ or } x_2) = M(x_1) \cup M(x_2) \tag{59}$$

or, in terms of membership functions,

$$\mu_N(x_1 \text{ or } x_2, y) = \mu_N(x_1, y) \vee \mu_N(x_2, y) . \tag{60}$$

Similarly, the connective *and* is a function from $\mathcal{F}(K) \times \mathcal{F}(K)$ to $\mathcal{F}(K)$ which serves to generate the intersection of its arguments. Thus,

$$M(x_1 \text{ and } x_2) = M(x_1) \cap M(x_2) \tag{61}$$

or, more explicitly,

$$\mu_N(x_1 \text{ and } x_2, y) = \mu_N(x_1, y) \wedge \mu_N(x_2, y), \quad y \in K \tag{62}$$

It should be noted that, whereas the meaning of x_1 *and* x_2 is a fuzzy subset of K defined by (62), the meaning of *and* is a fuzzy subset of $\mathcal{F}(K) \times \mathcal{F}(K) \times \mathcal{F}(K)$ rather than K. Consequently, to define the terms *young, old, not, or* and *and* as fuzzy subsets of the universe of discourse, K must be augmented[t] with the collections $\mathcal{F}(K) \times \mathcal{F}(K)$ and $\mathcal{F}(K) \times \mathcal{F}(K) \times \mathcal{F}(K)$, resulting in the expression

$$U = K + \mathcal{F}(K) \times \mathcal{F}(K) + \mathcal{F}(K) \times \mathcal{F}(K) \times \mathcal{F}(K) \tag{63}$$

where $+$ stands for union and $\times$ for the cartesian product.

Another point that should be noted is that, in English, the connective *and* may be used in a sense other than that defined above. For example, in the sentence "The box contains nuts *and* bolts," *and* serves to define a set of objects consisting of the union rather than the intersection of its arguments. As was pointed out earlier, this type of context-dependence is characteristic of natural languages.

To facilitate the determination of the meaning of a composite term, it is convenient to construct a covering of the term set T with a collection of *syntactic categories* which are non-fuzzy subsets of T. For example, in the case of English the syntactic category "noun" would contain such term as *dog, cat, door, car*, etc., while the syntactic category "adjective" would contain *red, tall, young, old, narrow*, etc.

Now suppose that x_1 is an adjective, i.e., $x_1 \in$ adjective, and x_2 is a noun. Then, if $M(x_1)$ and $M(x_2)$ are the fuzzy subsets of U representing, respectively, the meanings of x_1 and x_2, the meaning of the composite term x_1x_2 is defined as the intersection of $M(x_1)$ and $M(x_2)$, i.e.,

$$M(x_1x_2) = M(x_1) \cap M(x_2) . \tag{64}$$

[t]This point is discussed more fully in Ref. 34.

For example, if U consists of the totality of objects in a room and $x_1 = red$ and $x_2 = chair$, then $M(x_1)$ is the fuzzy set of red objects in the room, $M(x_2)$ is the set of chairs in the room, and $M(x_1x_2)$ is the fuzzy subset of *red chairs* in the room. According to (62), if the grade of membership of an object in the fuzzy set of *red* objects is 0.8, say, while its grade of membership in the set of *chairs* is 1.0, then its grade of membership in the fuzzy set of *red chairs* is $0.8 \wedge 1.0 = 0.8$.

In the above example, $M(x_1x_2)$, with $x_1 \in$ Adjective and $x_2 \in$ Noun, is a subset of both $M(x_1)$ and $M(x_2)$. This would not necessarily be the case if x_1 were a member of a syntactic category other than adjective. For example, if x_1 were a verb, e.g., $x_1 = ran$, and $x_2 = home$, then $M(x_1)$ would be a fuzzy subset of a set of actions, say A, while $M(x_2)$ is a fuzzy subset of a set of object, say Q. In this case, $M(ran\ home)$ would be a fuzzy subset of the cartesian product $A \times Q$, rather than a subset of either A or Q. However, if $M(x_1)$ and $M(x_2)$ are interpreted as cylindrical[u] fuzzy subsets of $A \times Q$, then $M(x_1x_2)$ may be taken to be the intersection of $M(x_1)$ and $M(x_2)$.

In the cases considered so far, the semantic rules governing the construction of the meaning of a composite term are quite simple, e.g.,

$$M(x_1 \text{ or } x_2) = M(x_1) \cup M(x_2) \tag{65}$$

and

$$x_1 \in \text{adjective and } x_2 \in \text{noun} \Longrightarrow M(x_1x_2) = M(x_1) \cap M(x_2)\,.^{\text{v}} \tag{66}$$

In a more complex example which is described in Ref. 34, the atomic terms in T are: *young, old, very, not, and,* (,), and the composite terms in T are generated by a grammar G in which S, A, B, C, D and Y are nonterminals and the production system is given by

$$\begin{array}{ll} S \longrightarrow A & C \longrightarrow O \\ S \longrightarrow S \text{ or } A & C \longrightarrow Y \\ A \longrightarrow B & O \longrightarrow \textit{very } O \\ A \longrightarrow A \textit{ and } B & Y \longrightarrow \textit{very } Y\,. \\ B \longrightarrow C & O \longrightarrow \textit{old} \\ B \longrightarrow \textit{not } C & Y \longrightarrow \textit{young} \\ C \longrightarrow (S) & \end{array} \tag{67}$$

[u] A fuzzy subset of a product space $X_1 \times X_2 \times \cdots \times X_n$, $X_i = \{x_i\}$, $i = 1, \ldots, n$, is *cylindrical* if it is characterized by a membership function whose arguments form a proper subset of $\{x_1, \ldots, x_n\}$. E.g., for $i = 2$, a fuzzy set where membership function is a function of x_1 alone is a cylindrical fuzzy subset of $X_1 \times X_2$.

[v] A rule such as (66) is much too simple to hold for all adjectives and all nouns in a natural language. In general, the usual syntactic categories, e.g. adjective, noun, etc., are too broad for rules like (66), necessitating the use of a finer covering of T than is provided by the syntactic categories in question. Thus, in the case of English, it should be understood that the validity of (66) is restricted to certain subcategories of the syntactic categories adjective and noun.

Typical terms generated by this grammar are:

not very young

not very young and not very old

young and not old

old or not very very young

young and (old or not young).

To compute $\mu_N(x, y)$ when x is a composite term, one can use an approach similar to that described by Knuth in Ref. 38. Specifically, suppose that we are given $\mu_N(young, y)$ and $\mu_N(old, y)$. The remaining atomic terms are regarded as functions on $\mathcal{F}(K)$ or $\mathcal{T}(K) \times \mathcal{F}(K)$ which are defined by the following rules associated with those productions in P in which they occur.

Employing the subscripts L and R to differentiate between the terminal symbols on the left- and right-hand sides of a production and using $\mu(H)$ as an abbreviation for $\mu_N(H, y)$, where H is a terminal or non-terminal symbol, the rules in question can be expressed as

$$
\begin{array}{ll}
S \longrightarrow A & \Longrightarrow \mu(S_L) = \mu(A_R) \\
A \longrightarrow B & \Longrightarrow \mu(A_L) = \mu(B_R) \\
B \longrightarrow C & \Longrightarrow \mu(B_L) = \mu(C_R) \\
S \longrightarrow S \text{ or } A & \Longrightarrow \mu(S_L) = \mu(S_R) \vee \mu(A_R) \\
A \longrightarrow A \text{ and } B & \Longrightarrow \mu(A_L) = \mu(A_R) \wedge \mu(B_R) \\
B \longrightarrow \text{not } C & \Longrightarrow \mu(B_L) = 1 - \mu(C_R) \\
O \longrightarrow \text{very } O & \Longrightarrow \mu(O_L) = (\mu(O_R))^2 \\
Y \longrightarrow \text{very } Y & \Longrightarrow \mu(Y_L) = (\mu(Y_R))^2 \\
C \longrightarrow O & \Longrightarrow \mu(C_L) = \mu(O_R) \\
C \longrightarrow Y & \Longrightarrow \mu(C_L) = \mu(Y_R) \\
C \longrightarrow (S) & \Longrightarrow \mu(C_L) = \mu(S_R) \\
O \longrightarrow \text{old} & \Longrightarrow \mu(O_L) = \mu(\text{old}) \\
Y \longrightarrow \text{young} & \Longrightarrow \mu(Y_L) = \mu(\text{young}) \,.
\end{array}
\tag{68}
$$

Now consider a composite term such as

$$x = \textit{not very young and not very very old}\,.$$

In this sample case the expression for the membership function of $M(x)$ can be written by inspection. Thus,

$$\mu_N(x, y) = (1 - \mu_N^2(young, y)) \wedge (1 - \mu_N^4(old, y))\,. \tag{69}$$

More generally, as a first step in the computation of $\mu_N(x, y)$ it is necessary to construct the syntax tree of x. For the composite term under consideration, the syntax tree is readily found to be that shown in Fig. 4. (The subscripts in this figure serve the purpose of numbering the nodes.)

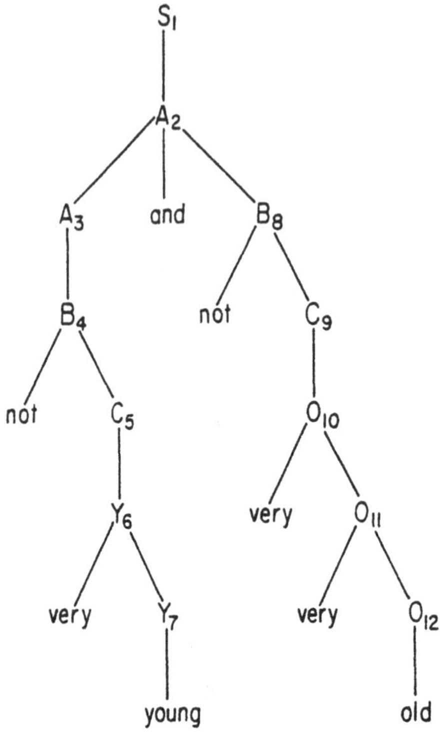

Fig. 4. Syntax tree for x = *not very young and not very very old.*

Proceeding from bottom to top and employing the relations (68) for the computation of the membership function at each node, we obtain the system of non-linear equations:

$$\begin{aligned}
\mu(Y_7) &= \mu_N(young, y) \\
\mu(Y_6) &= \mu^2(Y_7) \\
\mu(C_5) &= \mu(Y_6) \\
\mu(B_4) &= 1 - \mu(C_5) \\
\mu(A_3) &= \mu(B_4) \\
\mu(O_{12}) &= \mu_N(old, y) \\
\mu(O_{11}) &= \mu^2(O_{12}) \\
\mu(O_{10}) &= \mu^2(O_{11}) \\
\mu(C_9) &= \mu(O_{10}) \\
\mu(B_8) &= 1 - \mu(C_9) \\
\mu(A_2) &= \mu(A_3) \wedge \mu(B_8) \\
\mu_N(x, y) &= \mu(S_1) = \mu(A_2)\,.
\end{aligned} \tag{70}$$

In virtue of the tree structure of the syntax tree this system of equations can readily be solved by successive substitutions, yielding the result expressed by (69).

The basic idea underlying the approach sketched above is the following: The semantic rules governing the computation of the meaning of a composite term x are induced by the syntactic rules by which x is generated from S in the grammar G defining the term set T. In particular, each production in G induces a relation between the membership functions of the fuzzy sets whose labels appear in the production in question.

Approaches such as this can be of use in the construction of query languages for information retrieval systems. It appears that they also have the potential for providing reasonably good models for the semantics of subsets of natural languages. Such models will be described in a subsequent paper.

Concluding Remarks

The concept of a fuzzy language differs from that of a formal language in two important respects. First, it incorporates a naming relation, N, which serves to define a correspondence between a set of terms, T, and a universe of discourse, U; and second, it allows both the set of terms and the naming relation to be fuzzy.

With the concept of a fuzzy language as a point of departure, the notions of syntax and semantics can be given a precise meaning as algorithms serving to compute the membership functions of T and N, respectively. From this point of view, the central problem in semantics may be regarded as that of computing the meaning of a composite term $x_1, x_2, \ldots, x_n$ from the knowledge of the meanings of its components, $x_1, x_2, \ldots, x_n$.

At present, the theory of fuzzy languages is in an embryonic stage. Eventually, it may serve to provide considerably better models for natural languages than is possible within the restricted framework of the classical theory of formal languages.

References

1. N. Rashevsky, "The logical mechanisms of logical thinking," *Bull. Math. Biophysics* **8** (1946).
2. A. M. Turing, "Computing machinery and intelligence," *Mind* **59** (1950), pp. 433–460 also in *Computers and Thought*, eds. E. Feigenbaum and J. Feldman (McGraw-Hill, 1963), pp. 11–35.
3. J. von Neumann, *The Computer and the Brain* (Yale Univ. Press, 1958).
4. W. R. Ashby, *Design for a Brain* (J. Wiley, 1960).
5. J. Pfeiffer, *Thinking Machine* (Lippincott, 1962).
6. M. Minsky, "Matter, mind and models," *Proc. IFIP Congress* (1965), pp. 45–49.
7. H. L. Dreyfus, "Alchemy and artificial intelligence," Rand Paper P-3244 (Rand Corp., Santa Monica, Calif., 1965).
8. S. Papert, "The artificial intelligence of Hubert L. Dreyfus: A budget of fallacies," Memorandum 154, Project MAC (MIT, January, 1968).
9. H. L. Dreyfus, *A Critique of Artificial Reasoning* (Harper and Row, 1971).
10. R. E. Bellman, "Man, society and the computer," *Proceedings of the Conference on Man and Computer* (Institut de la vie), Bordeaux, France, 1970.

11. L. A. Zadeh, "Fuzzy sets," *Information and Control* **8** (June 1965), pp. 338–353.
12. L. A. Zadeh, "Shadows of fuzzy sets," *Problems in Transmission of Information* (in Russian) **2** (March 1966), pp. 37–44.
13. J. Goguen, "L-fuzzy sets," *Jour. Math. Anal. and Appl.* **18** (April 1967), pp. 145–174.
14. C. L. Chang, "Fuzzy topological spaces," *Jour. Math. Analysis and Applications* **24** (1968), pp. 182–190.
15. E. J. Santos, "Maximum automata," *Information and Control* **13** (October 1968), pp. 363–377.
16. M. Mizumoto, J. Toyoda, and K. Tanaka, "Some considerations on fuzzy automata," *Jour. of Computer and System Sciences* **3** (November 1969), pp. 409–422.
17. S. Tamura, S. Niguchi and K. Tanaka, "Pattern classification based on fuzzy relations," *Systems, Man and Cybernetics* **SMC-1** (January 1971), pp. 61–66.
18. J. G. Brown, "A note on fuzzy sets," *Information and Control* **18** (February 1971), pp. 32–39.
19. L. A. Zadeh, "Toward a theory of fuzzy systems," in *Aspects of Network and System Theory*, eds. R. E. Kalman and N. Declaris (Holt, Rinehart and Winston, 1971).
20. L. A. Zadeh, "Similarity relations and fuzzy orderings," *Information Sciences* **3** (April 1971), pp. 177–200.
21. S. K. Chang, "Fuzzy Programs — Theory and Applications," in *Proc. Polytechnic Institute of Brooklyn Conference on Computers and Automata*, Brooklyn, New York (1971).
22. R. Carnap, *The Logical Syntax of Language* (Harcourt, Brace and Co., New York, 1937).
23. N. Chomsky, *Syntactic Structures* (Mouton, The Hague, 1957).
24. Y. Bar-Hillel, M. Perles, and E. Shamir, "On formal properties of simple phrase-structure grammars," *Z. Phonetic, Sprachwiss. Kommunikationsforch* **14** (1961), pp. 143–172.
25. H. Hiz, "Congrammaticality, batteries of transformations, and grammatical categories," in *Proc. Symp. in Applied Math.* (American Math. Soc., 1961), pp. 43–50.
26. N. Chomsky, *Aspects of the Theory of Syntax* (MIT Press, 1965).
27. S. Ginsburg, *The Mathematical Theory of Context-Free Languages* (McGraw-Hill, 1966).
28. Z. Harris, *Mathematical Structures of Language* (Interscience Publishers, 1968).
29. E. Shamir, "Algebraic, rational, and context-free power series in noncommuting variables," in *Algebraic Theory of Machines, Languages and Semigroups*, ed. M. Arbib (Academic Press, 1968), pp. 329–341.
30. J. E. Hopcroft and J. D. Ullman, *Formal Languages and Their Relation to Automata* (Addison-Wesley, 1969).
31. R. E. Bellman, R. Kalaba and L. A. Zadeh, "Abstraction and pattern classification," *Jour. Math. Analysis and Applications* **13** (1966), pp. 1–7.
32. S. M. Watanabe, "Methodologies of pattern recognition," in *Proc. of the International Conference on Methodologies of Pattern Recognition*, Univ. of Hawaii, 1968 (Academic Press, 1969).
33. E. T. Lee and L. A. Zadeh, "Note on fuzzy languages," *Information Sciences* **1** (October 1969), pp. 421–434.
34. L. A. Zadeh, "Quantitative fuzzy semantics," *Information Sciences* **3** (April 1971), pp. 159–176.
35. D. J. Rosenkrantz, "Matrix equation and normal forms for context-free grammars," *Jour. Assoc. for Computing Machinery* **14** (1967), pp. 501–507.

36. E. T. Lee and L. A. Zadeh, "Fuzzy languages and their acceptance by automata," in *Proc. 4th Princeton Conference on Information Sciences and Systems* (Princeton University, 1970), p. 399.
37. J. A. Brzozowski, "Regular expressions for linear sequential circuits," *IEEE Trans. on Electronic Computers* **EC-14** (1965), pp. 148–156.
38. K. Knuth, "Semantics of context-free languages," *Math. Systems Theory* **2** (1968), pp. 127–145.
39. M. Mizumoto, "Fuzzy automata and fuzzy grammars," Ph.D. thesis, Faculty of Engineering Science, Osaka University, February 1971.
40. J. Feldman, J. Horning, J. Grips, and S. Reder, "Grammatical complexity and inference," Artificial Intelligence Laboratory, Stanford University, AI 89, June 1969.
41. A. Koutsoudas, *Writing Transformational Grammars* (McGraw-Hill, 1966).

On Fuzzy Mapping and Control

SHELDON S. L. CHANG, FELLOW, IEEE, AND LOFTI A. ZADEH, FELLOW, IEEE

Abstract—A fuzzy mapping from X to Y is a fuzzy set on $X \times Y$. The concept is extended to fuzzy mappings of fuzzy sets on X to Y, fuzzy function and its inverse, fuzzy parametric functions, fuzzy observation, and control. Set theoretical relations are obtained for fuzzy mappings, fuzzy functions, and fuzzy parametric functions. It is shown that under certain conditions a precise control goal can be attained with fuzzy observation and control as long as the observations become sufficiently precise when the goal is approached.

I. Introduction

SINCE its introduction, the concept of fuzziness has been extended to algorithms, learning theory, automata, formal languages, pattern classification, probability theory, and the decision making process [1], [16]. The present extension to fuzzy mapping is pertinent to the study of social and economic systems, some decision making processes, and control systems of incompletely specified processes. In social and economic studies, one often discusses functions of a certain type without explicit expression or even an exact definition. For instance, in economic studies the demand function of a merchandize is defined as the number of units which will be consumed as a function of its price. Implicit in this definition is that the purchasing power of the prospective consumers are known or fixed. However in a closed economy, sale and production of the very merchandize causes a change in associated industries (suppliers, etc.) and affects the purchasing power of the prospective consumers through many chains of interaction. If one neglects these interactions, the demand function is not very useful, or at least it is not the pertinent one for optimum price and production determination. If one includes these interactions, the demand function can only be fuzzily defined. It is no wonder many outstanding economists confine their studies to trends or abstract models and avoid using exact mathematical descriptions.

Going the other extreme, control engineers tend to treat their mathematical models of physical systems as exact and precise though they know that the models are neither. They obtain an optimum solution for the nominal model with possibly an added criterion of minimum sensitivity. However no one can be sure how the system performs if it deviates from the nominal model in some finite way.

It is desirable in both cases to have fuzzy mathematics which represent exactly the inexact state of knowledge. For economics and social studies it may be desirable to have some quantitative measure of the trends so that if there exist two or more opposing trends, the result is not completely unpredictable. For the control of physical systems with uncertainty, it may be desirable to have a "robust" control, robust in the sense that the controller is simple and gives guaranteed performance within the uncertain range. A first step in this direction is the introduction of fuzzy functions. The notion of fuzzy mapping clarifies conceptually what one means by fuzzy function and its inverse. It is consistent with prior work in that the set theoretical relations of union and intersection are treated in the same way as [1]. Nonfuzzy mappings and fuzzy parametric functions are then treated as special classes of fuzzy mappings and functions.

Two related concepts are introduced: fineness and observation. The degree of exactitude in our knowledge is represented by the fineness of the fuzzy set or fuzzy mapping. If our knowledge improves, the fuzzy set representing the state or the fuzzy function representing the system becomes finer. If our knowledge becomes exact, the fuzzy set representing the state becomes a point (membership function equals 1 at the point and 0 elsewhere), and the fuzzy function representing the system becomes an ordinary function. Observation is represented by the observation operator. Since our knowledge on the state is improved by observation, the effect of an observation operator on a set is to make it finer.

In the subsequent sections, the lower case letters represent elements or points in space represented by the corresponding upper case letters. The sign $\wedge$ means taking the minimum of two numbers and the sign $\vee$ means taking the maximum of two numbers. The greek letter μ represents membership function. Other symbols are defined as they are introduced.

II. Fuzzy Mapping and Fuzzy Function

Definition: A fuzzy mapping f from X to Y is a fuzzy set on $X \times Y$ with membership function $\mu_f(x,y)$. A fuzzy function $f(x)$ is a fuzzy set on Y with membership function

$$\mu_{f(x)}(y) = \mu_f(x,y). \tag{1}$$

Its inverse $f^{-1}(y)$ is a fuzzy set on X with

$$\mu_{f^{-1}(y)}(x) = \mu_f(x,y). \tag{2}$$

A fuzzy function f is said to be finer than a fuzzy function g if

$$\mu_{f(x)}(y) \le \mu_{g(x)}(y), \qquad \forall x,y \in X,Y. \tag{3}$$

Theorem 1: If f is finer than g, f^{-1} is finer than g^{-1}.

Proof: $\mu_{f^{-1}(y)}(x) = \mu_f(x,y) \le \mu_g(x,y) \le \mu_{g^{-1}(y)}(x)$.

III. Fuzzy Mapping of Set

Let A be a fuzzy set on X. The fuzzy set $f(A)$ is defined as

$$\mu_{f(A)}(y) \equiv \sup_{x \in X} (\mu_A(x) \wedge \mu_f(x,y)). \tag{4}$$

Manuscript received April 9, 1971; revised August 31, 1971. This work was supported in part by NSF Grant GK-16017.

S. S. L. Chang is with the Department of Electrical Sciences, State University of New York, Stony Brook, N.Y. 11790.

L. A. Zadeh is with the Department of Electrical Engineering and Computer Sciences, University of California, Berkeley, Calif. 94720.

Theorem 2: Let A, B be two fuzzy sets on X. Then

$$\text{if } A \supseteq B, \quad f(A) \supseteq f(B) \tag{5}$$

$$f(A \cup B) = f(A) \cup f(B) \tag{6}$$

$$f(A \cap B) \subseteq f(A) \cap f(B) \tag{7}$$

$$\text{if } f \text{ is finer than } g, \quad \text{then } f(A) \subseteq g(A). \tag{8}$$

Proof of (6): Let $C = A \cup B$

$$\begin{aligned}\mu_{f(C)}(y) &= \sup_{x \in X} (\mu_C(x) \wedge \mu_f(x,y)) \\ &= \sup_{x \in X} ((\mu_A(x) \vee \mu_B(x)) \wedge \mu_f(x,y)) \\ &= \sup_{x \in X} [(\mu_A(x) \wedge \mu_f(x,y)) \vee (\mu_B(x) \wedge \mu_f(x,y))] \\ &= \sup_{x \in X} (\mu_A(x) \wedge \mu_f(x,y)) \vee \sup_{x \in X} (\mu_B(x) \wedge \mu_f(x,y)).\end{aligned}$$

Proof of (7): Let $D = A \cap B$, then

$$\begin{aligned}\mu_{f(D)}(y) &= \sup_{x \in X} (\mu_D(x) \wedge \mu_f(x,y)) \\ &= \sup_{x \in X} (\mu_A(x) \wedge \mu_B(x) \wedge \mu_f(x,y)) \\ &\leq \sup_{x \in X} (\mu_A(x) \wedge \mu_f(x,y)) \wedge \sup_{x \in X} (\mu_B(x) \wedge \mu_f(x,y)) \\ &= \mu_{f(A)}(y) \wedge \mu_{f(B)}(y).\end{aligned}$$

The proofs of (5) and (8) are trivial and omitted.

IV. Fuzzy Parametric Function

One special class of fuzzy mapping according to (4) is the *fuzzy parametric function*. Let A denote a fuzzy set on the parametric space R. Let Z denote the product space $X \times R$. The fuzzy set (x,A) on Z is defined by its membership function:

$$\mu_{(x_0,A)}(x,r) = \Delta(x - x_0)\mu_A(r) \tag{9}$$

where the function Δ is defined by

$$\Delta(0) = 1$$
$$\Delta(x) = 0, \qquad \forall x \neq 0. \tag{10}$$

Let f be a fuzzy mapping from Z to Y with its membership function given as

$$\mu_f((x,r),y) = \Delta(y - \psi(x,r)) \tag{11}$$

where ψ is an ordinary mapping from $X \times R$ to Y. According to (4)

$$\begin{aligned}\mu_{f(x_0,A)}(y) &= \sup_{x,r} \{\mu_{(x_0,A)}(x,r) \wedge \mu_f((x,r),y)\} \\ &= \sup_{x,r} \{\Delta(x - x_0)\mu_A(r) \wedge \Delta(y - \psi(x,r))\} \\ &= \sup_{r} \{\mu_A(r) \wedge \Delta(y - \psi(x_0,r))\}.\end{aligned} \tag{12}$$

Equation (12) may be interpreted as a membership function $\mu_A(r)$ on the equality relation

$$y = \psi(x_0,r). \tag{13}$$

The function $\psi(x,r)$ is a fuzzy parametric function with fuzzy parameter r. If, given x_0 and y, (13) is satisfied by more than one value of r, (12) gives the membership of (13) as the largest of $\mu_A(r)$ with r satisfying (13).

The function $f(\ ,A)$ is a fuzzy mapping from X to Y with membership function $\mu_{f(\ ,A)}(x_0,y)$ given by (12). However it has the additional property that derivatives and integrals can be defined:

$$\mu_{f_x(x,A)}(y) \equiv \sup_r \{\mu_A(r)\,\Delta(y - \psi_x(x,r))\} \tag{14}$$

$$\mu_{f^{(-1)}(x,A)}(y) \equiv \sup_r \{\mu_A(r)\,\Delta(y - \psi^{(-1)}(x,r)\} \tag{15}$$

where $f^{(-1)}(x,A) = \int_{x_1}^{x} f(t,A)\,dt$ and $\psi^{(-1)}$ is similarly defined.

The following corollary is a direct result of Theorem 2.

Corollary: Let A, B be two fuzzy sets on R, and $f(\ ,A)$, $f(\ ,B)$ be two fuzzy mappings from X to Y with membership functions given by (12).

If $A \subseteq B$, then $f(\ ,A) \subseteq f(\ ,B)$ and $f(\ ,A)$ is said to be finer than $f(\ ,B)$, and

$$f(\ ,A \cup B) = f(\ ,A) \cup f(\ ,B) \tag{16}$$

$$f(\ ,A \cap B) \subseteq f(\ ,A) \cap f(\ ,B). \tag{17}$$

V. Support of Fuzzy Set

The support of a fuzzy set A is a nonfuzzy set defined as $S_A = \{x \mid \mu_A(x) \neq 0\}$.

Theorem 3: A and B are fuzzy sets on X. Then

$$\text{if } A \supseteq B, \quad S_A \supseteq S_B \tag{18}$$

$$S_{A \cup B} = S_A \cup S_B \tag{19}$$

$$S_{A \cap B} = S_A \cap S_B. \tag{20}$$

VI. Fuzzy Control System

Let $X = E^n$ represent the state space. Let $U \subset E^m$ represent the set of allowed controls. The state of the system is a fuzzy set $p(t)$ on X. The dynamic system is represented by a fuzzy mapping from $X \times U$ into X

$$f\colon\ X \times U \to X$$

$$\mu_{p(t+1)}(x(t+1)) = \mu_f(x(t),u;\, x(t+1)).$$

The control f, U is said to be *finer* than the control g, V if

$$\forall v \in V, \quad \exists u \in U \text{ subject to } f(x(t),u) \subseteq g(x(t),v), \quad \text{for all } x(t). \tag{21}$$

VII. Observation Operator

Definition: An observation on p is a renormalization of a subset of p. Let q be a subset of p and $\bar{q}$ denote the renormalized q. Then:

$$\mu_q(x) < \mu_p(x)$$

$$\mu_{\bar{q}}(x) = \frac{\mu_q(x)}{\sup_{x \in X} \mu_q(x)}. \tag{22}$$

It follows from the definition of S and (22), that $S_A = S_{\bar{A}}$ for any A.

An instrument or means of observation is represented by an operator O. Given O and p, the fuzzy set $\bar{q}$ representing the observed state is not unique. The set of possible $\bar{q}$ given O and p is represented by $O \circ p$. Therefore, by definition,

$$\bar{q} \in O \circ p. \tag{23}$$

After the observation, the state of the system becomes $\bar{q}$. An observation operator O satisfies:

$$O \circ A \subseteq O \circ B, \qquad \text{for all } A \subseteq B. \tag{24}$$

The observation operator is characterized by its indefiniteness. An observation on a fuzzy set p may yield any element from the set $O \circ p$. For every element $\bar{q}$ from the set $O \circ p$, there is a q so that (22) is satisfied. But the converse is not true. A $\bar{q}$ satisfying (22) may not belong to $O \circ p$.

In the subsequent sections, the overhead bar on a symbol representing the observed state will be dropped.

Theorem 4: Let A, B be two fuzzy sets on X such that

$$A \subset O \circ B$$

then

$$S_A \subset S_B. \tag{25}$$

Definition: Let O_1 and O_2 be two observation operators in X, and p be an arbitrary fuzzy set on X. We say that O_2 is *more definite* than O_1 if for each

$$q_2 \in O_2 \circ p, \qquad \exists q_1 \in O_1 \circ p \quad \text{subject to} \quad q_2 \subseteq q_1.$$

VIII. Fuzzy Feedback Control System

A fuzzy feedback control system consists of the following: 1) a fuzzy mapping f such that $f: X \times U \to X$; 2) an observation operator O; 3) a goal set G on X; and 4) a control policy η which maps the observed state to a control u such that $\eta: Q \to U$, where Q is the set of observed fuzzy sets $Q = \{q \mid q \in O \circ p, p = \text{fuzzy set on } X\}$.

The feedback control system works as follows. 1) The initial state is a fuzzy set $p(0)$ on X. 2) An observation is made, and the state of the system becomes $q(0)$ such that $q(0) \in O \circ p(0)$. 3) $u(0) = \eta \circ q(0)$. 4) Since the fuzzy mapping $\mu_f(x(0),u(0); x(1))$ representing the controlled dynamic system is given, $\mu_f(q(0),u(0); x(1))$ is obtained from (4), and $p(1)$ is the fuzzy set with membership function

$$\mu_{p(1)}(x) = \mu_f(q(0),u(0); x). \tag{26}$$

5) $p(1)$ becomes the initial state, and steps 2), 3), 4) are repeated with the time variable increased by 1.

As previously described, the control problem is represented by the set of objects f, O, G, and the feedback control system is represented by f, O, η. The goal G is said to be attainable if there is an η such that $q(t) \subseteq G(t)$, for some t, which may or may not be specified.

Theorem 5: Let $P_1(f_1,O_1,G)$ and $P_2(f_2,O_2,G)$ be two control problems such that f_2 is finer than f_1 and O_2 is more definite than O_1. Then G is attainable in P_2 if it is attainable in P_1.

Remarks: Under the assumption of the theorem, there is policy η_1

$$\eta_1: (O_1 \circ p_1) \to U_1 \tag{27}$$

such that for some t_a

$$q_1(t_a) \subseteq G. \tag{28}$$

The existence of η_2 will be proved by induction. Assume that given $p_2(t)$ there is a possible $p_1(t)$ satisfying

$$p_2(t) \subseteq p_1(t) \tag{29}$$

and $p_1(t)$ is obtained from $p(0)$ by following η_1. It will be shown that there exists a policy η_2 such that for every possible $p_2(t+1)$ as a result of following η_2 there exists a $p_1(t+1)$ which is obtainable by following η_1 and

$$p_2(t+1) \subseteq p_1(t+1) \tag{30}$$

$$q_2(t_a) \subseteq G. \tag{31}$$

Since (29) is valid at $t = 0$, the theorem is then proved.

Lemma 1: Given $q_2(t) \in O_2 \circ p_2(t)$, there is a $q_1(t) \in O_1 \circ p_1(t)$ such that

$$q_2(t) \subseteq q_1(t). \tag{32}$$

Proof: Since O_2 is more definite than O_1 there exists q_1 such that

$$q_1 \in O_1 \circ p_2(t) \tag{33}$$

$$q_2(t) \subseteq q_1. \tag{34}$$

From (24) and (29)

$$O_1 \circ p_2(t) \subseteq O_1 \circ p_1(t)$$

and therefore $q_1 \in O_1 \circ p_1(t)$. Q.E.D.

The control policy η_2 is formulated as follows. Given $\hat{q}_2(t)$, there is a corresponding $\hat{q}_1(t)$ subject to (32) is valid. Using η_1, $\hat{u}_1$ is selected: $\hat{u}_1 = \eta_1 \circ \hat{q}_1(t)$. Since f_2 is finer than f_1, there is a control $\hat{u}_2 \in U_2$ such that (21) $f_2(x(t),\hat{u}_2) \subseteq f_1(x(t),\hat{u}_1)$. This $\hat{u}_2$ is then the selected $\hat{u}_2$

$$\hat{u}_2 \equiv \eta_2 \circ \hat{q}_2(t). \tag{35}$$

It will now be shown that the policy η_2 as formulated gives the desirable results (30) and (31).

From (32) and (5)

$$f_1(q_2(t),\hat{u}_1) \subseteq f_1(q_1(t),\hat{u}_1) = p_1(t+1). \tag{36}$$

From (21)

$$f_2(\hat{q}_2(t),\hat{u}_2) \subseteq f_1(\hat{q}_2(t),\hat{u}_1). \tag{37}$$

Noting that $p_2(t+1) = f_2(\hat{q}_2(t),\hat{u}_2)$, (37) and (36) give (30). Repeating the preceding steps, eventually $p_2(t_a) \subseteq p_1(t_a)$ and Lemma 1 gives $q_2(t_a) \subseteq q_1(t_a) \subseteq G$. Q.E.D.

The preceding theorem shows that if a control goal can be attained with a given control and observation, it can be attained with finer controls and more definite observations. The power of the feedback concept is demonstrated by showing that a precise goal can be attained with rather sloppy control and observation, except that as the goal is approached the observation must be precise. The last required condition is necessary because otherwise one cannot tell whether the goal is attained or not.

IX. Example

Consider a one-dimensional control problem as follows. 1) The membership function of the state $p(t)$ is not known, except that its support set is $[\xi_1(t),\xi_2(t)]$. 2) The set of control U has only three members $\{-1,0,1\}$. 3) The fuzzy control f is only partially known:

$$u = -1, \qquad -a < \dot{\xi}_1 < \dot{\xi}_2 < -b < 0 \tag{38}$$

$$u = 0, \qquad \dot{\xi}_1 = \dot{\xi}_2 = 0 \tag{39}$$

$$u = 1, \qquad 0 < b < \dot{\xi}_1 < \dot{\xi}_2 < a. \tag{40}$$

In plain words, the state moves in the selected direction at a speed no lower than b and no higher than a. 4) The goal set is

$$\mu_G(x) = \begin{cases} 1, & g_1 \le x \le g_2 \\ 0, & x < g_1 \text{ or } x > g_2. \end{cases}$$

5) The observation O satisfies the following condition: Let $[K_1,K_2]$ denote the support of q. There exist $m > 0$ such that

$$K_2 - K_1 < g_2 - g_1 - m, \qquad \text{if } q \cap G \neq \phi. \tag{41}$$

The significance of (41) is as follows. It does not matter if the observation is quite inaccurate at a distance, as long as it is sufficiently precise when the goal is approached so that the condition $q \subset G$ can be satisfied with some margin m.

A. Continuous Time Case

The interval τ for applying u can be selected at will before another observation is made. The following control policy is used. 1) If $K_2 < g_2$, and $K_1 < g_1$ choose $u = 1$ for an interval

$$\tau = \frac{g_2 - K_2}{a}. \tag{42}$$

2) If $K_1 > g_1$, and $K_2 > g_2$, choose $u = -1$ for an interval,

$$\frac{K_1 - g_1}{a}.$$

3) If $K_2 < g_2$, and $K_1 > g_1$, choose $u = 0$. Condition 3) represents a system having arrived at its goal.

Assuming that the system is in condition 1) at $t = 0$, the preceding control policy gives:

$$\xi_1(\tau) \ge K_1(0) + b\tau \ge K_1(0) + \frac{bm}{a} \tag{43}$$

$$\xi_2(\tau) \le K_2(0) + a\tau = g_2. \tag{44}$$

Subsequent observation yields

$$K_1(\tau) \ge \xi_1(\tau) \ge K_1(0) + \frac{bm}{a} \tag{45}$$

$$K_2(\tau) \le \xi_2(\tau) \le g_2. \tag{46}$$

As the preceding processes are repeated, K_2 is always less or equal to g_2 and K_1 is increased by at least bm/a at each observation. Therefore 3) is eventually arrived.

B. Discrete Time Case

If the interval τ for each application of u is fixed, the goal is attainable if $\tau \le m/a$. If $\tau > m/a$, there is a possibility of the observed system hunting about its goal set indefinitely.

X. Noisy Observation

Let q be an observed fuzzy set on X and w be a random vector in x space with zero mean, $\overline{w^2} = \sigma^2$, and w_k, for $k = 1,2,\cdots$ are independent. A noisy observation q' is a translation of the fuzzy set q by a distance w:

$$\mu_{q'}(x + w) = \mu_q(x). \tag{47}$$

XI. Example of System with Noisy Observation

The following modifications are made on the system of Section IX. 1) It has noisy observation O':

$$\mu_q'(x + w) = \mu_q(x).$$

2) The observed state q has a constant support interval

$$K_2 - K_1 = \text{constant} < g_2 - g_1. \tag{48}$$

The support sets of q' and q are related by

$$K_{1,2}' = K_{1,2} + w. \tag{49}$$

Let S and S' denote the actual and observed errors, respectively,

$$S = \tfrac{1}{2}(K_1 + K_2 - g_1 - g_2) \tag{50}$$

$$S' = \tfrac{1}{2}(K_1' + K_2' - g_1 - g_2). \tag{51}$$

Let S_n and S_n' denote the values of S and S' at the nth observation. The proposed control policy is

$$u_n = -\operatorname{sgn} S_n' \tag{52}$$

for an interval

$$\tau_n = a_n|S_n'|. \tag{53}$$

From (38), (40), and (48)–(53):

$$S_{n+1} = -a_n v_n S_n' + S_n \tag{54}$$

where $v_n \in [a,b]$.

Theorem 6: As $n \to \infty$, $S_n \to 0$ in probability, if the following conditions are satisfied by the sequence $\{a_i\}$,

$$a_i > 0, \qquad i = 0,1,2,\cdots. \tag{55}$$

As $n \to \infty$

$$a_n \to 0 \tag{56}$$

$$\sum_{i=0}^{i=n} a_i \to \infty \tag{57}$$

$$\sum_{i=0}^{i=n} (a_i)^2 < C \tag{58}$$

where C is a constant.

Lemma 2: Given any sequence $\{a_i\}$ satisfying (55)–(58), then

$$\prod_{i=m}^{i=\infty} (1 - a_i) = 0, \qquad \text{for any finite } m. \tag{59}$$

Let A_i be defined inductively,

$$A_0 = a_0^2, \qquad A_i = a_i^2 + (1 - a_i)^2 A_{i-1}. \tag{60}$$

Then

$$\lim_{n\to\infty} A_n = 0. \tag{61}$$

Proof (of (61)): From (56), for sufficiently large m,

$$\prod_{i=m}^{i=m'} (1 - a_i)(1 + a_i) = \prod_{i=m}^{i=m'} (1 - a_i^2) < 1. \tag{62}$$

Since

$$\prod_{i=m}^{i=m'} (1 + a_i) = 1 + \sum_{i=m}^{i=m'} a_i + \text{positive terms}$$

$$> \sum_{i=m}^{i=m'} a_i.$$

From (57) given any $\varepsilon > 0$, $\exists M$ such that for all $m' > M$

$$\prod_{i=m}^{i=m'} (1 + a_i) > \frac{1}{\varepsilon}. \tag{63}$$

From (62) and (63)

$$\prod_{i=m}^{i=m'} (1 - a_i) < \frac{1}{1/\varepsilon} = \varepsilon. \tag{64}$$

The limit (59) is proved.

From (58), given any ε, $\exists$ an m such that

$$\sum_{i=m}^{i=\infty} (a_i)^2 < \frac{\varepsilon}{2}.$$

From (59), $\exists$ an M such that

$$\prod_{i=m}^{i=M} (1 - a_i)^2 A_{m-1} < \frac{\varepsilon}{2}.$$

For all $m' > M$

$$A_{m'} = \sum_{k=m}^{k=m'} \prod_{i=k+1}^{i=m'} (1 - a_i)^2 a_k^2 + \prod_{i=m}^{i=m'} (1 - a_i)^2 A_{m-1}$$

$$< \sum_{k=m}^{k=m'} a_k^2 + \frac{\varepsilon}{2} < \varepsilon.$$

Equation (61) is proved.

Proof of Theorem 6: Equation (54) can be written as

$$S_{n+1} = (1 - a_n v_n) S_n - a_n v_n w_n. \tag{65}$$

Reducing n by 1 and substituting the resulting expression for S_n in (65)

$$S_{n+1} = (1 - a_n v_n)(1 - a_{n-1} v_{n-1}) S_{n-1} - (1 - a_n v_n) a_{n-1} v_{n-1} w_{n-1} - a_n v_n w_n.$$

Repeated substitution gives

$$S_n = S_n' + S_n'' \tag{66}$$

where S_n' is a fixed component and S_n'' is a random component

$$S_n' = S_0 \prod_{i=0}^{i=n-1} (1 - a_i v_i) \tag{67}$$

$$S_n'' = -\sum_{k=0}^{k=n-1} \left[\prod_{i=k+1}^{i=n-1} (1 - a_i v_i) \right] a_k v_k w_k. \tag{68}$$

The expected value of $S_n''^2$ is

$$E[S_n''^2] = \sum_{k=0}^{k=n-1} \left[\prod_{i=k+1}^{i=n-1} (1 - a_i v_i) \right]^2 a_k^2 v_k^2 w^2. \tag{69}$$

Since $b \le v_n \le a$, the conditions (55)–(58) are satisfied by taking $(a_i v_i)$ as a_i. Equation (69) becomes

$$E[S_n''^2] = A_{n+1} w^2. \tag{70}$$

From (59), (61), (67), and (69):

$$\lim_{n\to\infty} S_n' \to 0, \qquad \lim_{n\to\infty} E[S_n''^2] \to 0.$$

Q.E.D.

References

[1] L. A. Zadeh, "Fuzzy sets," *Inform. Contr.*, vol. 8, pp. 338–353, June, 1965.
[2] ——, "Toward a theory of fuzzy systems," Electronics Res. Lab., Univ. California, Berkeley, ERL Rep. No. 69-2, June, 1969.
[3] ——, "Fuzzy algorithms," *Inform. Contr.*, vol. 12, pp. 99–102, Feb. 1968.
[4] S. S. L. Chang, "Fuzzy dynamic programming and the decision making process," in *Proc. 3rd Princeton Conf. Information Sciences and Systems*, pp. 200–203, 1969.
[5] K. S. Fu and T. J. Li, "On the behavior of learning automata and its applications," Purdue Univ., Lafayette, Ind., Tech. Rep. TR-EE 68-20, Aug. 1968.
[6] J. Goguen, "L-fuzzy sets," *J. Math. Anal. Appl.*, vol. 18, pp. 145–174, Apr. 1967.
[7] J. G. Brown, "Fuzzy sets on Boolean lattices," Ballistic Res. Lab., Aberdeen, Md., Rep. 1957, Jan. 1969.
[8] R. Bellman, R. Kalaba, and L. A. Zadeh, "Abstraction and pattern classification," *J. Math. Anal. Appl.*, vol. 13, pp. 1–7, Jan. 1966.
[9] W. G. Wee, "On generalization of adaptive algorithms and application of the fuzzy set concept to pattern classification," Purdue Univ., Lafayette, Ind., Tech. Rep. TR-EE-67-7, July, 1967.
[10] L. A. Zadeh, "Probability measures of fuzzy events," *J. Math. Anal. Appl.*, vol. 10, pp. 421–427, Aug. 1968.
[11] H. M. Wagner, *Principles of Operations Research.* Englewood Cliffs, N.J.: Prentice-Hall, 1969.
[12] L. A. Zadeh, "Probability measures of fuzzy events," *J. Math. Anal. Appl.*, vol. 10, pp. 421–427, Aug. 1968.
[13] J. H. Eaton and L. A. Zadeh, "Optimal pursuit strategies in discrete-state probablistic systems," *Trans. ASME, J. Basic Eng.*, vol. 84, Series D, pp. 23–29, Mar. 1962.
[14] R. E. Bellman and L. A. Zadeh, "Decision-making in a fuzzy environment," *Manag. Sci.*
[15] M. Mizumoto, J. Toyoda, and K. Tanaka, *J. Comput. Syst. Sci.*, vol. 3, pp. 409–422, 1969.
[16] E. T. Lee and L. A. Zadeh, "Note on fuzzy languages," Electronic Res. Lab. Univ. California, Berkeley, ERL Rep. 69-7, Nov. 1969.

A System-Theoretic View of Behavior Modification

L. A. Zadeh

L. A. Zadeh, professor of electrical engineering and computer sciences at the University of California, Berkeley, is co-author of Linear System Theory *and editor of the* Journal of Computer and System Sciences.

This evaluation is of special value in that it considers Skinnerian behaviorism from a mathematical point of view. Zadeh employs the formalism of the theory of "fuzzy sets" that he developed in evaluating operant conditioning. He concludes that "the time is coming, if it has not come already, when the society will have much more effective means at its disposal for manipulating . . . its members." Zadeh concludes that operant conditioning lends itself to formulation in a mathematical model, which would facilitate computer analysis.

The work on this paper was supported, in part, by National Science Foundation Grant GK-10656X.

To someone like myself, steeped in the quantitative analyses of inanimate systems, the principal ideas in Skinner's *Beyond Freedom and Dignity* are difficult to translate into assertions that are capable of proof or refutation. Nevertheless, I find them highly interesting and thought-provoking.

It is a truism that human behavior is vastly more complex than the behavior of man-conceived systems. This is reflected in the fact that

From *Beyond the Punitive Society*, edited by H. Wheeler, pp. 160–169.

such basic concepts as control, reinforcement, feedback, goal, constraint, decision, strategy, adaptation, and environment, which are central to the discussion of human behavior, are much better understood and more clearly defined in system theory—which deals with abstract systems from an axiomatic point of view—than in psychology or philosophy. Unfortunately, high precision is rarely compatible with high complexity. Thus, the precision and determinism of system theory have the effect of severely restricting its capability to deal with the complexities of human behavior.

Essentially, inanimate systems are amenable to quantitative analysis because their behavior is sufficiently simple to admit of characterization by equations containing numerical variables (that is, scalars or vectors whose components are real or complex numbers). Typically, the state of an inanimate system S at time[1] t, $t = 0, 1, 2, \ldots$, is an n-vector, x_t, of low or moderate dimensionality, whose components are real numbers. For example, if S is a point of mass m moving in a three-dimensional space, then its state has six components, of which the first three define its position and the last three its velocity.

If S is subjected to a sequence of inputs, $u_0, u_1, u_2, \ldots$, each of which is a numerical variable, then the behavior of S is usually characterized by two equations:

$$x_{t+1} = f(x_t, u_t), \tag{1}$$

$$y_t = g(x_t, u_t). \tag{2}$$

The first equation defines the next state (that is, the state at time $t + 1$) as a function of the present state, x_t, and the present input, u_t. The second equation defines the present output, y_t, as a function of the present state and the present input. Thus, the behavior of a deterministic discrete-time system may be characterized by two functions f and g, which define, respectively, the next state and the output of the system.

In the past, attempts to describe human behavior by equations of the form of (1) and (2) have met with little success because human behavior, in general, is much too complex to admit of description by numerical variables. However, as suggested by Zadeh (1971) and Bellman and Zadeh (1970), a possible way of dealing with the problem of complexity is to employ *fuzzy* variables—in place of numerical variables—in (1) and (2). The values of such variables are not numbers but labels of fuzzy sets[2]—that is, names of classes that do not have sharply defined

[1]For simplicity, we assume that time varies discretely. Dependence on t will frequently be assumed but not exhibited explicitly.

[2]Roughly speaking, a fuzzy set is a class with unsharp boundaries. More precisely, a fuzzy set A in a space $X = \{x\}$ is a collection of ordered pairs $A = \{[x, \mu_A(x)]\}$, in which $\mu_A(x)$ is the *grade of membership* of x in A, with $0 \leq \mu_A(x) \leq 1$. A more detailed discussion of fuzzy sets may be found in Zadeh (1971) and Bellman and Zadeh (1970).

boundaries. For example, the terms *green*, *big*, *tired*, *happy*, *young*, *bald*, and *oval* may be viewed as labels for classes in which the transition from membership to nonmembership is gradual rather than abrupt. Thus, a man aged 32 may have partial membership—represented by a number, say, 0.6—in the class of *young* men. The class of young men, then, would be characterized by a membership function $\mu_{\text{young}}(x)$ that associates with each man x his grade of membership in the class of young men. For simplicity, membership functions are assumed to take values in the interval [0, 1], with 0 and 1 representing nonmembership and full membership, respectively.

The use of fuzzy variables to describe human behavior is, in effect, a retreat into imprecision in the face of complexity. This, of course, is what has been done all along in psychology and philosophy. However, the use of fuzzy variables in conjunction with equations such as (1) and (2) may make it possible to deal with human behavior in a more systematic and somewhat more precise fashion than is customary in psychology and related fields.

In what follows, I shall sketch the rudiments of this approach and relate it, in part, to human behavior modification. In my brief discussion of the equations characterizing human behavior, I shall not attempt to specify the functions of fuzzy variables that enter into these equations, nor shall I concretize the meaning of the variables representing state, input, environment, and so on. Thus, my very limited aim in this paper is merely to suggest that some of the aspects of behavior modification discussed by Skinner may be formulated, perhaps more systematically, through the use of equations and functions employing fuzzy, rather than numerically-valued, variables. It should be understood, of course, that the detailed task of characterizing the functions entering into these equations by tables or flow charts of labels of fuzzy sets would normally require a great deal of psychological testing and data analysis.

Our point of departure is the assumption that the behavior of a human —who, for convenience, will be referred to as H—can be represented, in part, by the following two pairs of equations:

$$x_{t+1} = h_1(x_t, u_t, e_t, t), \tag{3}$$

$$y_t = h_2(x_t, u_t, e_t, t); \tag{4}$$

$$s_{t+1} = g_1(s_t, u_t, y_t, t), \tag{5}$$

$$e_t = g_2(s_t, u_t, y_t, t); \tag{6}$$

in which

x_t = state of H at time t, $t = 0, 1, 2, \ldots,$

u_t = action taken by H at time t, with u_t chosen from a constrained (possibly fuzzy) set of alternatives,
e_t = input representing the effect of the external influences not under the control of H (for example, the effect of the environment, both physical and social),
y_t = response of H to action u_t and external influences e_t,
s_t = state of environment at time t, and
h_1, h_2, g_1, g_2 = fuzzy and, possibly, random functions.

It is understood that some or all of the variables in the above equations are fuzzy, which means that their values are labels of fuzzy sets (for example, x_t = tired, u_t = taking a nap, e_t = hot and humid, and so on). Thus, a typical entry in a table characterizing (3), say, would read: If, at time t, the state of H is a fuzzy set described by a label α (for example, α = tired), the effect of the environment is a fuzzy set described by a label β, and the action by H is a fuzzy set labeled γ, then, with high likelihood, the next state of H will be a fuzzy set labeled δ, and possibly, but much less likely, the next state will be ϵ.

In effect, the first pair of equations, (3) and (4), serves to describe, in a very approximate (and yet systematic) fashion, the response of H (or some particular aspect of the response of H, represented by y_t) to the external influences (represented by e_t) and the action taken by H (represented by u_t). In a similar fashion, the second pair (5) and (6), describes the effect of the behavior of H on the environment. Generally, the effect of H on the environment is much smaller than the effect of the environment on H. This is not true, however, in the case of operant conditioning, where the changes in environment serve to reinforce a particular mode of behavior of H.

To make the description of the behavior of H more explicit, we need an additional equation that describes the decision principle employed by H in selecting an action u_t from a constrained set of alternatives. To this end, it is expedient to make use of the notion of the *maximizing set* of a function, which is an approximation to—or, in our terminology, a fuzzification of—the notion of a maximizing value.

Suppose that $f(x)$ is a real-valued function that is bounded both from below and from above, with x ranging over a domain X. The maximizing set of f is a fuzzy set, M, in X, such that the grade of membership, $\mu_M(x)$, of x in M represents the degree to which $f(x)$ is close to the maximum value of f over X, that is, $\sup f$ ($\sup f$ = supremum of $f(x)$ over X.) For example, if $\mu_M(x_1) = 0.8$ at $x = x_1$, then the value of $f(x)$ at $x_1 = x_1$ is about 80% of its maximum value with respect to some reference point. In effect, then, the maximizing set of a function f serves to grade the points in the domain of f according to the degree to which $f(x)$ approximates $\sup f$.[3]

Now let $R_t(u_t)$ denote the estimated total reward[4] associated with action u_t at time t, with the negative values of R_t representing loss, pain, discomfort, and so forth. Then we postulate that the decision principle employed by H is the following: For each t at which a decision has to be made, H chooses the u_t that is the maximizing set for the estimated reward. It is understood that, if the membership function of this set does not peak sharply around some particular action, then H first narrows his choice to those actions that have a high grade of membership in u_t and then uses some random or arbitrary rule to select one among them.

To gain better insight into the operation of the decision principle, it is advantageous to decompose the estimated reward function into two components, one representing an immediate reward or gratification and the other representing estimate future reward (or penalty, if the reward is negative). More specifically, we assume that R_t is a function of two arguments: immediate reward function $IR_t(u_t)$ and estimated future reward function $FR_t(u_t)$. Thus, in symbols,

$$R_t(u_t) = G_t[IR_t(u_t), FR_t(u_t)], \tag{7}$$

where G_t represents a function[5] of IR_t and FR_t, playing a role analogous to that of an objective function in control theory. Note that implicit in

---

[3]In more precise terms, the membership function of the maximizing set of a real-valued function $f(x)$, $x \in X$, is defined by the following equations (in which $\inf f$ = infimum of $f(x)$ over X):

$$\mu_M(x) = \frac{f(x)}{\sup f},$$

if $\inf f \geq 0$;

$$\mu_M(x) = \frac{\sup f + \inf f - f}{\inf f},$$

if $\sup f \leq 0$; and

$$\mu_M(x) = \frac{f - \sup f}{\sup f - \inf f},$$

if $\inf f \leq 0$ and $\sup f \geq 0$. If f is a fuzzy function—that is, if, for each $x \in X$, $f(x)$ is a fuzzy set with membership function $\mu_f(x,y)$—then the maximizing set for $f(x)$ is defined by the preceding equations with $f(x)$ replaced by $\sup_y \mu_f(x,y)$. Although the definitions given are precise, it should be understood that, in dealing with fuzzy variables, maximization and other operations performed on functions of such variables are highly approximate in nature.

[4]It should be understood that expressing the total reward as a function of u_t alone is intended merely to single out the dependence of R_t on u_t. In general, R_t will depend, in addition, on the strategy used by H as well as on x_t, s_t, y_t, e_t, and, possibly, other variables.

[5]As in the case of R_t, it is tacitly understood that G_t may depend on x_t, s_t, y_t, t, and, possibly, other variables.

FR_t is a goal (or subgoals) in terms of which the consequence of choosing u_t may be estimated.

We are now in a position to make the description of the behavior of H more explicit by adding to (3), (4), (5), and (6) the equation

$$u_t = \text{maximizing set for } G_t(IR_t, FR_t). \tag{8}$$

In words, this equation means that H chooses the action u_t that maximizes a specified combination of the immediate reward IR_t and the estimated future reward FR_t, with IR_t and FR_t understood to be known functions of the actions. It should be remarked that the description of the behavior of H by (3), (4), (5), (6), and (8) is consistent with the point of view taken in Skinner's work.

If the variables appearing in equations (3), (4), (5), (6), and (8) were assumed to be numerically valued, the task of characterizing the functions h_1, h_2, g_1, g_2, IR_t, FR_t, and G would be impossibly complex. The crux of this idea is to regard the variables in question as fuzzy variables ranging over labels of appropriate fuzzy sets.[6] Equations (3)–(8), then, would represent approximate (that is, fuzzy) relations between fuzzy variables. These relations could be characterized by (a) tables in which the entries are labels of fuzzy sets, or (b) algorithmically—that is, by a set of fuzzy rules (like a computer program with fuzzy instructions) for generating a fuzzy set from other fuzzy sets. In this way, the description of the relations between the variables characterizing human behavior could be greatly simplified—at the cost, of course, of a commensurate loss in precision. In this perspective, the approach sketched above may be viewed as a systematization of the conventional verbal characterizations of human behavior (Zadeh, 1973).

When human behavior is described by equations of the form (3), (4), (5), (6), and (8), a modification in human behavior may be viewed as a change in the functions h_1, h_2, G_t, IR_t, and FR_t. Of these, the changes in G, IR_t, and FR_t play a particularly important role because they influence, in a direct way, the choice of actions taken by H. Thus, in terms of these functions, Skinner's operant conditioning may be regarded as a form of modification of behavior resulting largely from a manipulation of IR_t through its dependence on the environment.

To clarify the role played by FR_t in relation to IR_t, it will be convenient to make a very rough approximation to G_t by a numerically valued convex linear combination,

---

[6]It is understood that the fuzzy sets in question would, in general, be defined in an approximate fashion by exemplification (that is, ostensively). For example, the fuzzy set *very likely* would be defined by a collection of examples of probability values together with their grades of membership—for example, {(1, 1.0), (0.9, 0.9), (0.8, 0.7), (0.7, 0.4), (0.6, 0.1)}—in which the first element is a probability value and the second element is its grade of membership in the fuzzy set *very likely*.

$$R_t = \alpha\, IR_t + (1 - \alpha)FR_t, \tag{9}$$

in which α is a weighting coefficient, $0 \leq \alpha \leq 1$. Thus, (9) signifies that the reward at time t is a weighted linear combination of the immediate reward and the estimated future reward at time t, with the latter multiplied by the factor $\rho = (1 - \alpha)/\alpha$ in relation to the former.

Though not a constant, the *anticipation coefficient* ρ constitutes an important personality parameter of an individual. In this connection, it should be noted that, in a given individual, ρ will be small when the uncertainty in the estimate FR_t is large. To put it another way, the influence of the immediate reward tends to be predominant when there is considerable uncertainty about the future consequences of an action.

As an individual matures and learns from his own experience as well as that of others, his knowledge of the IR_t and FR_t functions improves and his anticipation coefficient trends to increase—that is, he tends to become more far-sighted. Nevertheless, it is probably true that, judged over a long period of time, the ρ of most individuals is not as large as it should be for their own good, as well as for the good of others. The acceptance of this premise naturally raises the troublesome question: To what extent should society attempt to coerce its members to increase their anticipation coefficient if they are unwilling to do so on their own volition? Obviously, it is this question that is at the heart of problems relating to such practices as smoking, drinking, and drug-taking.

It is important to observe that the effect of increasing ρ (for negative FR_t) can also be achieved, for fixed ρ, by decreasing IR_t. In other words, if an individual tends not to give sufficient weight to long-term harmful consequences of an action that gives him immediate pleasure, then one way of inducing him to modify his behavior is to make IR_t sufficiently negative by adding to it an immediate penalty. For example, one possible way of controlling affinity for excessive drinking might be to implant an electronic monitor in a person who is in need of external reinforcement of his will power. Such a monitor could be programmed to produce an acute sensation of pain or some other form of discomfort when the level of alcohol in blood reaches a predetermined threshold. In this way, the immediate pleasure derived from having one or more drinks would be offset by the nearly simultaneous feeling of pain, with the net immediate reward becoming negative when the amount of alcohol consumed exceeds a set limit.

Behavior-modifying monitors of this type are within the reach of modern electronic technology. Clearly, the potential for abuse of such devices is rather high: through remote signalling, they could be used by a totalitarian government as a highly effective means of punishment and control.

The *temporal* decomposition of the reward function into two components, one representing the immediate reward and the other representing the estimated future reward, serves to exhibit an important facet of the decision-making process—namely, the way in which an individual, H, balances short-term gains against long-term losses. In a similar way, we can perform what might be referred to as a *relational* decomposition of the reward function into components that represent the rewards to other members of a group of individuals who interact with H. Specifically, suppose that we have a group of N individuals $H^i, \ldots, H^N$, with the reward function and action associated with H^i denoted by $R_t^i(u_t^i)$ and u_t^i, respectively.

As a very rough approximation, we assume that $R_t^i(u_t^i)$ admits of the following decomposition:[7]

$$R_t^i(u_t^i) = w_{i1}\, R_t^{i1}(u_t^i) + w_{i2}\, R_t^{i2}(u_t^i) + \ldots + w_{iN}\, R_t^{iN}(u_t^i), \quad (10)$$

in which

$R_t^{ij}(u_t^i)$ = reward accruing to H^j at time t as a result of action u_t^i taken by H^i,

w^{ij} = weight attached by H^i to the reward accruing to H^j as a result of action u_t^i, with $w_{i1} + w_{i2} + \ldots + w_{iN} = 1, 0 \leq w_{ij} \leq 1$, and

$R_t^{ii}(u_t^i)$ = self-reward = reward accruing to H^i at time t as a result of the action u_t^i taken by H^i.

The basic assumption underlying (10) is that the behavior of H^i is governed not only by the self-reward function R_t^{ii}, but also by a weighted combination of the rewards accruing to other members of the group as a result of the action taken by H^i. More precisely, this implies that when H^i is faced with a decision, he chooses the u_t^i that maximizes R_t^i, as expressed by (10), rather than the u_t^i that maximizes R_t^{ii}.

As in the case of the anticipation coefficient ρ, the relational coefficients $w_1, \ldots, w_N$ constitute important parameters of an individual's behavior and personality. In what way does an individual weigh the reward to himself in relation to the rewards to his family, close relatives, friends, enemies, coworkers, members of the same religion, residents of his community, fellow countrymen, and so on? Clearly, the answer to this question would be very different for a typical member of a primitive society than for a person of high level of culture and enlightenment. Indeed, the evolution of a society is directly related to the changes in the relational coefficients of its members, with an individual learning from his own experience, as well as from that of others, that it is in his

---

[7]As in the case of (7), implicit in $R_t^i(u_t^i)$ is the possibility that R_t^i may depend on other variables and actions in addition to u_t^i.

long-term self-interest to assign greater weight to the interests of others—not only those who are close to him, but also those who are remote.

In essence, then, once the reward functions IR_t, FR_t and R_t^{ij} have been identified, the behavior modification would involve, in the main, changes in the anticipation coefficient ρ and the relational coefficients w. In the past, changes in ρ and w were induced primarily by experience, education, religious training, political indoctrination, and other environmental influences. As implied by Skinner, the time is coming, if it has not come already, when the society will have much more effective means at its disposal for manipulating the ρ and w of its members, perhaps electronically or through systematic psychological conditioning on a mass scale.

To give a simple example of electronic manipulation in a small group, consider a group comprising just two members: H^1 = husband and H^2 = wife. Suppose that each has a device with a push-button such that, when the button is pressed, the other party experiences acute pain or discomfort induced by a probe implanted in or attached to the body. Thus, if H^1, say, takes an action that makes H^2 unhappy, then H^2 can retaliate by pressing her button, and vice versa. To limit the extent of retaliation, both H^1 and H^2 have a quota that varies from day to day in a random fashion and is not made known to H^1 or H^2. This rule is intended to induce H^1 and H^2 to use their push-buttons rather sparingly.

The point of this example is that the availability of means of retaliation is likely to have the effect of increasing the values of relational coefficients w_{12} and w_{21} in the reward equations

$$R_t^1(u_t^1) = w_{11}\, R_t^{11}(u_t^1) + w_{12}\, R_t^{12}(u_t^1) \tag{11}$$

and

$$R_t^2(u_t^2) = w_{21}\, R_t^{21}(u_t^2) + w_{22}\, R_t^{22}(u_t^2), \tag{12}$$

which govern the behavior of H^1 and H^2. However, excessive retaliatory capability or its misuse may, of course, result in a rupture of the relationship between H^1 and H^2.

The use of electronic means (rather than some other means) of retaliation in the preceding example is intended merely to make retaliation more convenient to apply and, hence, more effective as a modifier of behavior. The basic point, however, is that, whether in small groups or in large ones, the threat of retaliation plays an essential role in tending to increase the values of those relational coefficients that would be small in the absence of retaliatory capability. This is particularly true of the modern technologically based society, in which the degree of communication and interdependence between distant individuals and groups is far greater than it was in the past.

It has been experimentally observed of inanimate systems that, as the degree of interaction (feedback) between the constituents of a system increases, the system eventually becomes unstable. The same phenomenon may well be at the root of the many crises confronting modern society, particularly in race relations, pollution, mass transit, health care, power distribution, monetary systems, employment, and education. These crises seem to grow in number and intensity as technology—in the form of TV, radio, telephone, communication satellites, computers, data banks, jumbo jets, and the automobile—rapidly increases the degree of interaction between individuals, groups, organizations, societies, and countries. The "culprit" may well be the very basic and universal human desire for freedom, which makes it distasteful for most of us to accept the degree of control and discipline that is needed to maintain societal and interpersonal equilibrium in the face of rapid growth in the degree of interdependence brought about by technological progress. Thus, we are witnessing what may be called the *crisis of under-coordination*—a crisis that, in the main, is a manifestation of insufficient planning and control in relation to the extent of interaction between the constituents of our society.

We may be faced with the necessity to curtail our freedoms—perhaps rather extensively—in order to achieve survival in a technologically based, highly interdependent world of tomorrow. Perhaps this is the crux of Skinner's thesis in *Beyond Freedom and Dignity*.

In conclusion, it is quite possible that deliberate, systematic, mass-scale behavior modification employing Skinnerian techniques of operant conditioning, electronic monitors, computers, devices to alter brain function, and other paraphernalia of modern technology may become a reality in the near future. I, for one, do not look forward to that day.

*Lotfi A. Zadeh**

On the Analysis of Large-Scale Systems

ABSTRACT

In recent years, systems analysis has become a widely used technique for dealing with problems relating to the design, management and operation of large-scale systems.
A thesis advanced in this paper is that the conventional techniques of systems analysis are of limited applicability to societal systems, because such systems are, in general, much too complex and much too ill-defined to be amenable to quantitative analyses. It is suggested that the applicability of systems analysis may be enhanced through the use of the so-called *linguistic approach*, in which words rather than numbers serve as values of variables. The basic elements of this approach are outlined and illustrated by examples.

1. Introduction

One of the most significant concomitants of technological progress has been — and continues to be — the accelerating growth in the degree of inter-dependence both within and across all strata of modern society.
This phenomenon — which is becoming increasingly pervasive in its manifestations — affects individuals, groups, organizations, industrial enterprises, cities, countries and continents. Thus, the events in Kuwait may have a profound impact on the jobs of workers in Detroit and Dodge City; the strike of copper miners in Chile may curtail the production of electric motors in Schenectady; and the latest developments in Washington may be the subject of informed discussions in the cafes of Teheran, Vienna and Rio de Janeiro.
Reduced to its basic factors, the growth in the degree of interdependence in modern society may be viewed as a confluence of several distinct and yet interrelated developments: (a) The major advances in our ability to communicate information at high speed, low cost and over long distances; (b) the decline in cost combined with the increase in speed of transportation of raw materials and manufactured products; (c) the growing mobility of people brought about by the enhancement in speed, comfort and economy of traveling; (d) the sharing of energy and information resources through power distribution networks, oil pipelines, radio and television networks, data banks, computer networks, etc.; (e) the drive toward greater efficiency which impels a centralization of decision-making and exerts pervasive pressure to merge small units into bigger ones; (f) and last, but not least important, the growth in population density, especially in the vicinity of urban centers.

* Computer Science Division, University of California, Berkeley, Calif. 94720.
This work was supported in part by NESC Contract N00039-71-C-0255.

In the case of physical systems, it is a well-known empirical fact that unrestrained increase in the degree of feedback between the components of a system leads to instability, oscillations and, eventually, catastrophic failures. There is a warning in this that cannot be ignored: our societal systems, too, are likely to become unstable if the growth in the degree of interdependance within them is not accompanied by better planning, coordination, and — what might be much less palatable — restraints on our freedoms.[1] Indeed, in some of the advanced societies with libertarian traditions — in which there is an understandable aversion to planning and control — we are already witnessing the manifestations of what might be diagnosed as the *crisis of undercoordination:* vehicular and air traffic congestion, deterioration in the quality of municipal services, decay of urban centers, power blackouts, air and water pollution, shortages of energy, unemployment, etc. And these may well be the precursors of far more serious stresses and strains which lie ahead — stresses which may test to the limit the endurance of our democratic institutions.

Does it follow that the price of survival is the loss of the large measure of freedom which we enjoy today in deciding on where to live, for whom to work, where to travel, etc.? Hopefully, the answer is in the negative. But it is clear that in order to be able to survive without a significant erosion of our freedoms, it will be necessary to develop a much better understanding of the forces which shape — and the dynamics which govern — the evolution of the highly interdependent large-scale system which constitutes our modern society. For, it is only through such understanding that we may be able to achieve that degree of coordination which might be needed to preserve the equilibrium of our societal structures without creating an oppressive environment in which an individual has few of the freedoms which we take for granted at present.

Although we have made a great deal of progress during the past two decades in our ability to analyze the behavior of small-scale systems whose behavior is governed by differential, difference or integral equations, there are still many difficult problems which stand in the way of our ability to comprehend, much less predict, the behavior of large-scale societal systems. In part, the difficulties in question relate to the fact that societal systems are orders of magnitude more complex than the well-structured mechanistic systems which constitute the major part of the domain of applicability of classical system theory. More importantly, we still have a far from adequate understanding of the basic issues relating to conflict resolution, aggregation of preferences, choice of time-horizons, decision-making under uncertainty, and many other problems which arise when we deal not with machines — as in classical system theory — but with human judgements, perceptions and emotions.

To make system theory more relevant to societal problems, we may have to make radical changes in our basic approaches to systems analysis. In particular, we may have to accept what to some may be a rather unpalatable conclusion, namely, that in the case of societal systems relevance is incompatible with

1 This is implicit in Skinner's controversial book "Beyond Freedom and Dignity" [1]. See also H. Wheeler's "Beyond the Punitive Society" [2].

precision. In more specific terms, this means that we may have to accept much lower standards of rigor and precision in our analyses of societal systems than those which prevail in system theory — if we wish our analyses to have substantial relevance to real-life problems.

In retreating from precision in the face of the overpowering complexity of societal systems, it is natural to explore the use of what might be called *linguistic* variables, that is, variables whose values are not numbers, but words or sentences in a natural or artificial language. The motivation for the use of such variables is that, in general, verbal characterizations are less precise than numerical ones, and thus serve the function of providing a means of approximate description of phenomena which are too complex or too ill-defined to admit of analysis in conventional quantitative terms. Actually, we use such variables in ordinary discourse, e.g., when we assert that "Paris is *very beautiful*", „David is a *highly intelligent* man", "Harry *loves* Ann", "The economy is in a state of *recession*", "*Reduce* speed if the road is *slippery*", etc. In these assertions, the italicized words may be viewed as the values of linguistic variables, with each such value representing a label of a fuzzy subset of a universe of discourse. In this sense, a statement such as "Stella is *young*", may be interpreted as the assignment of a linguistic value *young* to a linguistic variable named *Age*, and a collection of such statements constitutes a system of assignment equations from which other assignment equations may be deduced by a process of logical inference.

What we suggest is that in the case of societal systems the use of linguistic variables may offer a more realistic — if less precise — means of systems analysis than the conventional approaches based on the use of quantified variables. In effect, our contention is that the classical techniques of systems analysis — which were conceived and developed for dealing with systems which have well-structured mathematical models — are unsuitable for the analysis of the behavior of societal systems. To cope with such systems, we must forsake our veneration of precision and be content with answers which are linguistic rather than numerical in nature. This, in essence, is the spirit of what might be called the *linguistic approach* — an approach in which the concept of a linguistic variable is employed both as a means of approximate characterization of system behavior and as a basis for approximate reasoning involving the use of a fuzzy logic with linguistic truth-values.

In what follows, we shall present in a summarized form some of the basic concepts which play a central role in the linguistic approach. More detailed expositions of these concepts may be found in [3] and [4].

2. Elements of the Linguistic Approach

As was stated in the Introduction, linguistic variables serve as a means of approximate characterization of phenomena which are too complex or too ill-defined to be amenable to description in numerical terms. More concretely, a linguistic variable is characterized by a quintuple $(\mathfrak{X}, T(\mathfrak{X}), U, G, M)$ in which $\mathfrak{X}$ is the name of the variable; $T(\mathfrak{X})$ is the *term-set* of $\mathfrak{X}$, that is, the set of names, X, of *linguistic values* of $\mathfrak{X}$; U is a universe of discourse; G is a *syntactic rule* for generating the names, X, of values of $\mathfrak{X}$; and M is a *semantic rule* for associating a *meaning*, M(X), with each name (linguistic value) in $T(\mathfrak{X})$. Generally, M(X) will be assumed to be a fuzzy subset of U.

As an illustration, consider a linguistic variable named *Age*. The term-set, T(*Age*), or simply T, of *Age* may be represented as follows

(1) *Age* = *young* + *very young* + *not young* + *very very young* + *not very young* + ... + *old* + *very old* + *not old* + ... + *not very young and not very old* + ... *extremely young* + ... + *more or less young* + ...

in which + denotes the union rather than the arithmetic sum.

The universe of discourse for *Age* may be taken to be the interval [0,100], with the numerical variable u which ranges over U = [0,100] constituting the *base variable* for *Age*. Then, a value of *Age*, e.g., *young* may be viewed as a name of a fuzzy subset of U which is characterized by its *compatibility function* $c : U \rightarrow [0,1]$, with c(u) representing the *compatibility* of a numerical age u with the label *young*.[2] For example, the compatibilities of the numerical ages 22, 28, and 35 with *young* might be 1, 0.7 and 0.2, respectively. The meaning of *young*, then, would be represented by a graph of the form shown in Fig. 1, which is a plot of the compatibility function of *young* with respect to the base variable u.

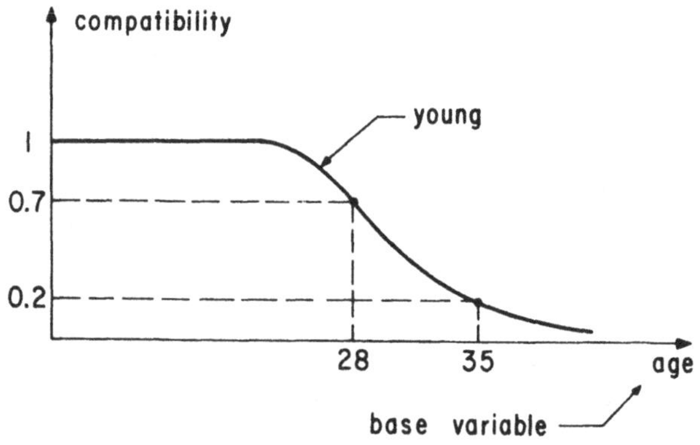

Fig. 1: Plot of the compatibility function of *young*

A typical linguistic value in (1) contains one or more *primary terms*, e.g., *young*, *old*, whose meaning is both subjective and context-dependent and hence must be defined a priori; connectives such as *and* and *or*; the negation *not*; and linguistic hedges such as *very*, *more or less*, *extremely*, *quite*, etc. The syntactic rule may be represented as a context-free grammar which generates the terms (linguistic values) in T(*Age*) (see [3]), while the semantic rule is a procedure for computing the meaning of a linguistic value from the knowledge of the meanings of its components. Thus, if *very* is defined to be an operator which squares the compatibility function of its operand, then the compatibility function of *very young* may be expressed as (see Fig. 2)

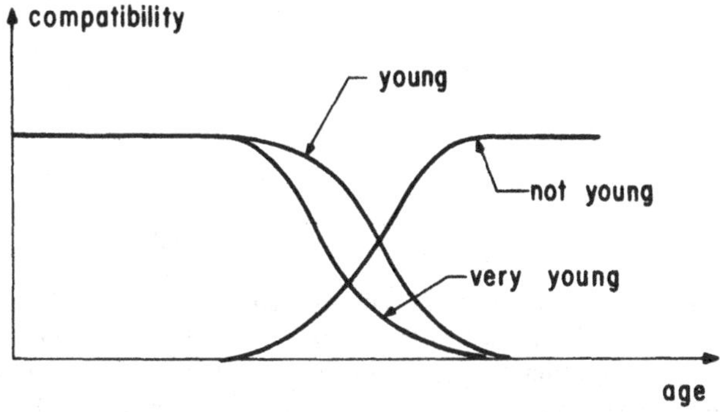

Fig. 2: Compatibility functions of *young*, *not young* and *very young*

(2) $c_{very\ young}(u) = (c_{young}(u))^2$

Similarly, if *more or less* X, where X is a primary term, is defined by

(3) $c_{more\ or\ less\ X}(u) = (c_X(u))^{\frac{1}{2}}$

then

(4) $c_{more\ or\ less\ young}(u) = (c_{young}(u))^{\frac{1}{2}}$

The negation and the connectives are defined by the relations

(5) $c_{not\ X}(u) = 1 - c_X(u)$

(6) $c_{X\ and\ Y}(u) = c_X(u) \wedge c_Y(u)$

(7) $c_{X\ or\ Y}(u) = c_X(u) \vee c_Y(u)$

where X and Y are labels of fuzzy subsets of U, and $\vee$ and $\wedge$ stand for Max and Min, respectively. As an illustration, if

2 The compatibility of u with *young* is identical with the grade of membership of u in the fuzzy set labeled *young*.

(8) $c_{young}(35) = 0.2$

(9) $c_{old}(35) = 0.1$

then

(10) $c_{very\ young}(35) = 0.04$

(11) $c_{very\ old}(35) = 0.01$

(12) $c_{not\ very\ young}(35) = 0.96$

(13) $c_{not\ very\ old}(35) = 0.99$

and

(14) $c_{not\ very\ young\ and\ not\ very\ old}(35) = 0.96 \wedge 0{,}99 = 0.96$

What this example shows is that once we have defined the meaning of *and*, *or*, *not* and the linguistic hedges, the meaning of any value of the linguistic variable which can be generated by the syntactic rule, can be computed from the knowledge of the meaning of the primary terms. In effect, it is this structured nature of linguistic variables that makes them so convenient to use in the approximate characterization of complex phenomena.

Another point that helps to clarify the significance of a linguistic variable is that if the values of a conventional variable are represented as points in a plane, then the values of a linguistic variable may be likened to ball-parks with fuzzy boundaries. Furthermore, the compatibility function which defines the meaning of a linguistic value may be regarded as the membership function of a fuzzy *restriction* on the values of the base variable. This implies that a linguistic variable has a hierarchical structure which is illustrated in Fig. 3.

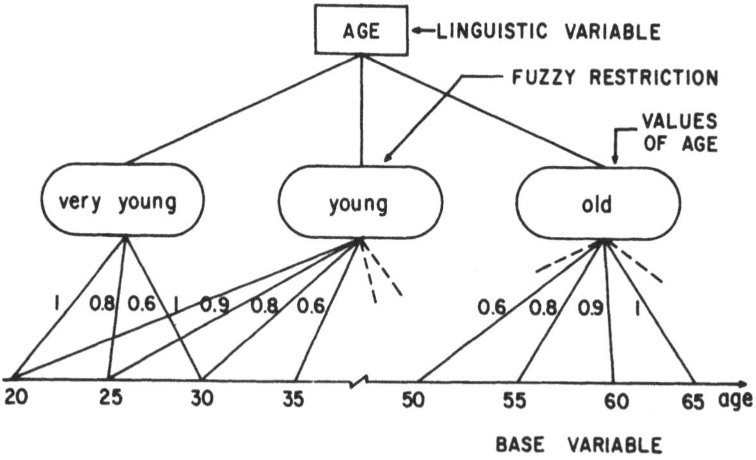

Fig. 3: Hierarchical structure of the linguistic variable *Age*

If $\mathfrak{X}$ and $\mathcal{Y}$ are linguistic variables with respective universes of discourse U and V, then a *linguistic function* from U to V is defined to be a function from $T(\mathfrak{X})$ to $T(\mathcal{Y})$. To illustrate, suppose that $U = V = (-\infty, \infty)$ and the function from $T(\mathfrak{X})$ to $T(\mathcal{Y})$ is defined by the table

X	Y
very small	*very very small*
small and not very small	*very small*
not small and not large	*small*
large	*not very small*

Then the *fuzzy graph*, f, of the function in question is the union of the cartesian products[3]

(15) f = *very small* x *very very small* + *small and not very small* x *very small* + *not small and not large* x *small* + *large* x *not very small*

As an additional illustration, suppose that $\mathfrak{X}$ and $\mathcal{Y}$ represent, respectively, the input and output of a memoryless system which is characterized by a linguistic input-output function, f, whose table has the form shown below

X	Y
"u_1"	"v_1"
"u_2"	"v_2"
—	—
"u_n"	"v_n"

where "u_i", $i = 1, \ldots, n$, denotes a fuzzy subset of $(-\infty, \infty)$ labeled *approximately* u_i, and likewise for "v_i". In more concrete terms, "u_i" may be defined by an expression such as

$$\text{(16)} \qquad \text{“}u_i\text{”} = \int_{-\infty}^{\infty} \left(1 + \left(\frac{u - u_i}{a}\right)^2\right)^{-1} / u$$

in which $\left(1 + \left(\frac{u - u_i}{a}\right)^2\right)^{-1}$ is the compatibility function of "u_i", with a being a parameter which may depend on u. (The notation

$$\text{(17)} \qquad A = \int_U \mu(u)/u$$

3 The *cartesian product* of a fuzzy subset A of U and a fuzzy subset B of V is a fuzzy subset A×B of U×V whose compatibility function is related to those of A and B by $c_{A \times B}(u, v) = c_A(u) \wedge c_B(v)$. The *union* of A and B is denoted by A+B (or, more conventionally, by A∪B) and is defined by $c_{A \cup B}(u) = c_A(u) \vee c_B(u)$.

means that A is a fuzzy subset of U which may be represented as the union of fuzzy singletons $\mu(u)/u$. Thus, the integral sign in (17) denotes the union; u is the base variable; and $\mu(u)$ is the grade of membership of u in A or, equivalently, the compatibility of u with A.)

In the case under consideration, the graph of f is given by (Fig. 4)

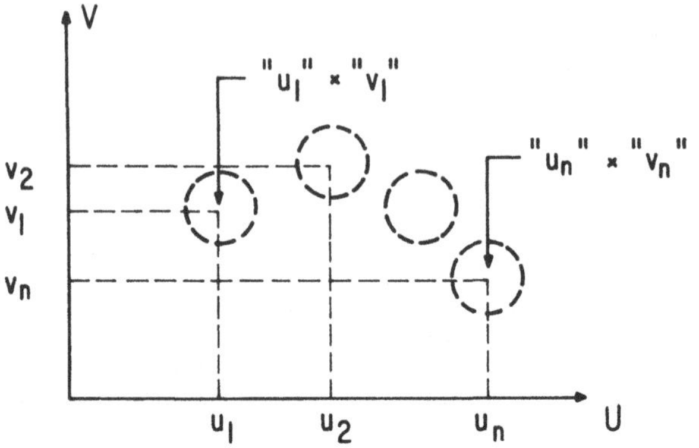

Fig. 4: Graph of a fuzzy function

(18) $$f = \text{“}u_1\text{”} \times \text{“}v_1\text{”} + \ldots + \text{“}u_n\text{”} \times \text{“}v_n\text{”}$$

where "u_i" × "v_i", $i = 1, \ldots, n$, denotes the cartesian product of the fuzzy sets "u_i" and "v_i". More generally, in the case of a system with memory, the dependence of s^{t+1}, the state at time t+1, on s^t, the state at time t, and u^t, the input at time t, may be expressed approximately as a fuzzy graph g

(19) $$g = \sum_i \text{“}s_i^{t+1}\text{”} \times \text{“}s_i^{t}\text{”} \times \text{“}u_i^{t}\text{”}$$

where s_i^t is a point in the state space of the system; "s_i^t" is a fuzzy subset of the state space labeled *approximately* s_i^t; u_i^t is a point in the input space; "u_i^t" is a fuzzy subset of the input space labeled *approximately* u_i^t; and Σ denotes the union rather than the arithmetic sum.

Among the various concepts that can be dealt with linguistically, there are two that are of particular relevance to the analysis of societal systems, namely, *Truth* and *Probability*. In the case of *Truth*, its term-set may be assumed to be (compare with (1))

(20) *Truth* = *true* + *very true* + *not true* + *very very true* + *not very true* + ... + *false* + *very false* + ... + *not very false and not very true* + ... *more or less true* + ...

while that of *Probability* might be

(21) *Probability* = *likely* + *very likely* + *not likely* + *very very likely* + *unlikely* + *very unlikely* + ... + *more or less likely* + "0" + "0.1" + ... + "1" + ...

The primary term in *Truth* is *true*, which is defined to be a fuzzy subset of the unit interval [0,1]. A convenient approximation to the compatibility function of *true* is provided by the expression

$$c_{true}(v) = 0 \quad \text{for} \quad 0 \leqslant v \leqslant a$$

(22)
$$= 2\left(\frac{v-a}{1-a}\right)^2 \quad \text{for } a \leqslant v \leqslant \frac{a+1}{2}$$

$$= 1 - \left(\frac{v-1}{1-a}\right)^2 \quad \text{for } \frac{a+1}{2} \leqslant v \leqslant 1$$

which has $v = \frac{1+a}{2}$ as its *crossover point* (i.e., the point at which c(v) = 0.5). Correspondingly, the compatibility function of *false* is given by (see Fig. 5)

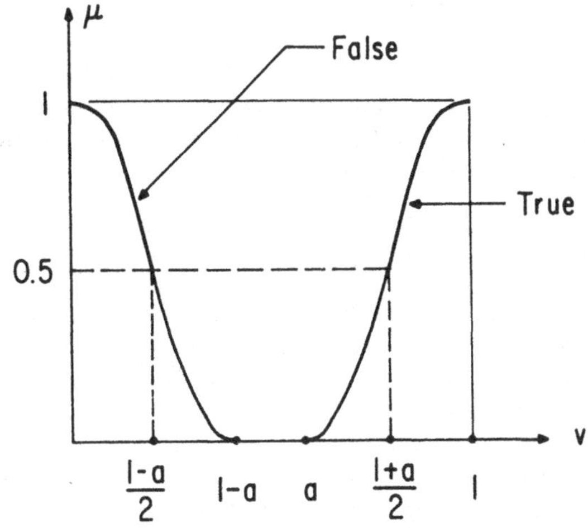

Fig. 5: Compatibility functions of *true* and *false*

(23) $$c_{false}(v) = c_{true}(1-v), \quad 0 \leqslant v \leqslant 1$$

The same applies to *Probability*, with *likely* and *unlikely* being analogous to *true* and *false*, respectively.

The linguistic truth-values in (21) serve the function of providing an approximate assessment of the truth of a possibly fuzzy assertion. As an illustration, consider the proposition "*George is very intelligent*", which, as pointed out earlier, may be interpreted as an assignment of the linguistic value *very intelligent* to the intelligence of George. Now, the assignment of a truth-value, say *very true*, to the proposition in question results in the composite proposition

" '*George is very intelligent*' is *very true*"

As shown in [4], such a proposition may be approximated by a simple proposition of the form

"George is X"

where X is a linguistic value of *Intelligence* which depends on the compatibility functions of the primary terms *intelligent* and *true*.
In the case of a societal system, S, we would usually be concerned with a collection of propositions such as:

A_1: "S is *quite stable*"
A_2: "S is *highly mobile*"
A_3: "S is *experiencing rapid growth*"

A_n: "S is *in a state of depression*"

Suppose that the propositions $A_1, \ldots, A_n$ are assigned the linguistic truth-values $T_1, \ldots, T_n$, respectively. The collection of possible truth-values that can be assigned to $A_1, \ldots, A_n$ is called a *truth-value distribution*. For example, for n = 3, we may have the truth-value distribution

(24) T = (*true, quite true, very true*) + (*false, false, true*) + (*very true, more or less true, not true*) + (*true, true, false*)

which means that there are four possible assignments of truth-values to A_1, A_2, A_3 expressed by the terms of (24). These assignments reflect the relationships between the truth-values of A_1, A_2, A_3, which are induced by the underlying dependencies between the propositions in question.
The use of linguistic truth-values leads to a *fuzzy logic* in which not only the truth-values but also the rules of inference are fuzzy in nature. A simple example of such inference is the following: (x and y are real numbers)

premiss:	x is small
premiss:	x and y are approximately equal
approximate conclusion:	y is more or less small

The difference between fuzzy logic and the classical two-valued logic is illustrated by the familiar syllogism:

premiss:	All men are mortal
premiss:	Socrates is a man
conclusion:	Socrates is mortal

In fuzzy logic, an analogous syllogism would be

premiss:	Most men shave
premiss:	Lakoff is a man
approximate probabilistic conclusion:	It is very likely that Lakoff shaves

The idea here is that *most* and *likely* may be defined as fuzzy subsets of the unit interval (Fig. 6). Thus, if the compatibility function of *very likely* is an acceptable approximation to that of *most*, we can assume that the conclusion "it is very likely that Lakoff shaves", follows approximately from the premisses "most men shave" and "Lakoff is a man".

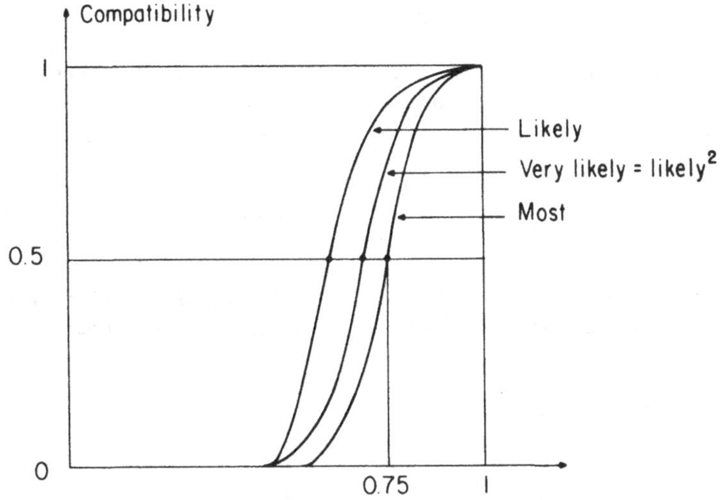

Fig. 6: Compatibility function of *very likely* as an approximation to *most*

A basic rule of inference in fuzzy logic is the compositional rule [3]. In a simplified form, this rule may be stated as follows. Let A: "u is P" be a proposition in which P is a value of a linguistic variable, e.g., "u is *small*". Let B: "u and v are Q" be another proposition in which Q is a fuzzy relation expressed in linguistic terms, e.g., "u and v are *approximately equal*". Then, from A and B we can infer C:

A:	u is P
B:	u and v are Q
C:	v is $P \cdot Q$

where P · Q is the composition[4] of the unary relation P with the binary relation Q.

As a simple illustration of this rule assume that we have

A: u is *small*

B: u and v are *approximately equal*

where *small* is defined as a fuzzy subset of the universe of discourse (+ means union)

(25) U = 1 + 2 + 3 + 4

which is expressed as

(26) *small* = 1/1 + 0.6/2 + 0.2/3

where a term of the form μ/u signifies that the grade of membership of u in *small* (or, equivalently, the compatibility of u with *small*) is μ. Similarly, *approximately equal* is defined as a fuzzy relation by

$$\textit{approximately equal} = 1/(1,1) + 1/(2,2) + 1/(3,3) + 1/(4,4) + 0.5/(1,2) + 0.5/(2,1) + 0.5/(2,3) + 0.5/(3,2) + 0.5/(3,4) + 0.5/(4,3) \quad (27)$$

To compute the composition *small* · *approximately equal* it is sufficient to form the max-min matrix product of *small* and *approximately equal* as shown below

$$[1 \quad 0.6 \quad 0.2 \quad 1] \begin{bmatrix} 1 & 0.5 & 0 & 0 \\ 0.5 & 1 & 0.5 & 0 \\ 0 & 0.5 & 1 & 0.5 \\ 0 & 0 & 0.5 & 1 \end{bmatrix} = [1 \quad 0.6 \quad 0.5 \quad 0.2]$$

Thus,

(29) *small* · *approximately equal* = 1/1 + 0.6/2 + 0.5/3 + 0.2/4

which may be approximated linguistically as *more or less small.* It is this result that provides the basis for the statement made earlier to the effect that from A and B we can infer (approximately) that v is *more or less small.*

A special and yet important case of the compositional rule of inference is one where the proposition B has the form

B: If u is R then v is S

4 The compatibility function of the composition of P and Q is given by $c_{P \cdot Q}(u, v) = \vee_u (c_P(u) \wedge c_Q(u, v))$, where $\vee_u$ denotes "maximum over u".

where R and S are values of linguistic variables, e.g., "If u is *small* then v is *very large*". It can be shown [4], that in this case B may be replaced by the equivalent proposition

B*: u and v are Q

where (+ denotes the union and V is the universe of discourse associated with S)

(30) $Q = R \times S + \textit{not}\ R \times V$

Then, the application of the compositional rule of inference to A and B* yields what might be called the *generalized modus ponens:*

A: u is P
B: If u is R then v is S

C: v is P · (R x S + *not* R x V)

Examples of the application of this rule may be found in [3] and [4].
Just as linguistic truth-values can be used to provide a basis for the assignment of approximate truths to assertions about a complex system, so can linguistic probabilities be employed to assert approximate likelihoods of various events. For example, in response to the question "What is the probability that there will be a recession next year", we may respond with a fuzzy ball-park estimate *very likely*, with the understanding that *very likely* is a linguistic probability-value whose meaning can be computed once the compatibility function of *likely* has been defined. The way in which this can be done as well as the techniques for computing with linguistic probabilities are discussed in greater detail in [4].

3. Concluding Remarks

Our main objective in the foregoing discussion was to outline some of the basic aspects of the concept of a linguistic variable and suggest that the "ball-park" nature of the values of linguistic variables may make them an appropriate tool for the analysis of societal systems. Clearly, the task of applying the linguistic approach to the solution of specific problems relating to the behavior of societal systems is certain to be nontrivial. Nevertheless, the ideas immanent in the linguistic approach appear to be of sufficient relevance to the analysis of societal systems to justify further exploration of their utility in the characterization of the behavior of large-scale systems.

REFERENCES

B. Skinner, *Beyond Freedom and Dignity*, A. Knopf, New York, 1971.
H. Wheeler, ed., *Beyond the Punitive Society*, W. H. Freeman Co., San Francisco, 1973.
L. A. Zadeh, "Outline of a New Approach to the Analysis of Complex Systems and Decision Processes", *IEEE Trans. on Systems, Man and Cybernetics*, vol. SMC-3, pp.28-44, January 1973.
L. A. Zadeh, "The Concept of a Linguistic Variable and Its Application to Approximate Reasoning", Memorandum M 411, Electronics Research Laboratory, University of California, Berkeley, October 1973.

DISCUSSION

R. L. Keeney
Could you discuss some of your experiences in empirically assessing the membership functions. In particular, what types of questions do you find appropriate, what difficulties have you encountered, how did you overcome these, and how do you check for consistenca, that is, the internal consistency of the respondant.

P. H. Sonntag
1. You act as if "very young = young^2?" It occurs not to be a more particular assumption to call your numbers assumed probabilities. That is exactly what you do, you calculate as if the numbers were probabilities. The limit of interpretation is a different problem.
2. As an application of your method I suggest a refinement of the content analysis (not just let the computer look for one word in a text) or documentation (look for certain combinations of items). Does it make sense to you, or do you envisage a different kind of application?

D. L. DeHaven
In the context of a modelling situation where an equality (or inequality) constraint is applied and it is known that there are relative values associated with the degree of constraint satisfaction ... does this application fall within the fuzzy set concept where relative value distributions are subjective according to persons involved?

R. Rosen
1. It seems to me that there is a relation between fuzzy concepts and what the modeller often calls robust ones. That is, if we take a quantitative mathematical effect, then "fuzzifying" the cause (and/or the *model*) must result in the "fuzzification" of the original effect. Unless this kind of continuity, or stability, obtains, the notion of fuzziness seems inapplicable, even in ordinary language. But if it does obtain, then we can certainly use quantitative models, in which fuzzy concepts are given a precise numerical representation, to develop some feeling or intuition about relations in the general case. Indeed, I would suggest that the only way in which we can develop such intuitions is by this means.
2. What is really needed is a "fuzzy" theory of dynamics and control. Could you comment on the way in which you would see such a theory developing?

N. Müller
How do you get the items like long hair, etc. in the hippie-example empirically and how do you get the curves?

On the Analysis of Large-Scale Systems **37**

By the way, am I right in assuming that the structure of curves of fuzzy isolated concepts like old, tall, etc., that is out of compounded concepts for instance not old and not young, is of a special type.
And if that is all right, is it empirically proved? The functions for "old" and "not old" are symmetric around a line. May I conclude from this, that negation is not a fuzzy concept?

Answer from L. A. Zadeh
In response to the questions posed by R. L. Keeney and D. L. De Haven, it should be underscored that the grade of an object x in a fuzzy set A is a subjective matter. Thus, if Hans, say, states that the grade of membership of Maribel in the class of *intelligent* women is 0.9, than 0.9 is merely the degree to which Maribel fits (or is compatible with) Hans' conception of intelligent women. Then, given Hans' membership function of the fuzzy set of intelligent women, one can compute — by the use of a semantic rule — the grade of membership of Maribel in the class of *very intelligent* women, *more or less intelligent* women, etc. Thus, what matters in the case of fuzzy sets is the relative consistency of their membership functions as well as their behavior under mappings. In this connection, the experimental studies which have been reported by Professors M. Kochen and McVicar-Whalen are worthy of note.
With reference to the comment made by P.H. Sonntag, I should like to reiterate that fuzziness and randomness are distinct phenomena which call for different modes of tratment. To clarify this point, it is helpful to draw on what might be called the *valise analogy*. Specifically, consider a soft valise, X, into which one can put different objects $x_1, \ldots, x_n$. With each x_i we can associate two numbers, $\mu(x_i)$ and $p(x_i)$, $0 \leqslant \mu(x_i) \leqslant 1$, $0 \leqslant p(x_i) \leqslant 1$, which represent, respectively, the degree of ease with x_i can be put into X and the probability that x_i is put in X. The μ_i define the *restriction* associated with the *fuzzy* variable X whereas the p_i define the probability distribution associated with the *random* variable X. It should be noted that the μ_i and the p_i not only have distinct interpretations, but also obey different rules of combination.
The point made by R. Rosen is certainly a valid one. As regards a fuzzy theory of dynamics and control, I have touched upon this subject in my earlier papers on fuzzy systems. More recently, I have been doing some work on systems in which time is a fuzzy variable. There is no doubt in my mind that there will be many advances in the development of a theory of fuzzy systems within the next several years.
In response to N. Müller, the meaning of a composite term such as *not very young and not very old* may be defined in terms of the meaning assigned to the primary terms *young* and *old*, as described in greater detail in [4]. The operation of negation may be viewed as a nonfuzzy mapping from the space of fuzzy sets to itself. However, it is possible to fuzzify the notion of negation in such a way that *not* A is a fuzzy set when A is a nonfuzzy set. This does happen in ordinary discourse, especially when *not* is used in a loose sense.

CALCULUS OF FUZZY RESTRICTIONS

L. A. ZADEH*

Department of Electrical Engineering and Computer Sciences, University of California, Berkeley, California 94720, USA

ABSTRACT

A fuzzy restriction may be visualized as an elastic constraint on the values that may be assigned to a variable. In terms of such restrictions, the meaning of a proposition of the form "x is P," where x is the name of an object and P is a fuzzy set, may be expressed as a relational assignment equation of the form $R(A(x)) = P$, where $A(x)$ is an implied attribute of x, R is a fuzzy restriction on x, and P is the unary fuzzy relation which is assigned to R. For example, "Stella is *young*," where *young* is a fuzzy subset of the real line, translates into $R(\text{Age}(\text{Stella})) = young$.

The calculus of fuzzy restrictions is concerned, in the main, with (a) translation of propositions of various types into relational assignment equations, and (b) the study of transformations of fuzzy restrictions which are induced by linguistic modifiers, truth-functional modifiers, compositions, projections and other operations. An important application of the calculus of fuzzy restrictions relates to what might be called *approximate reasoning*, that is, a type of reasoning which is neither very exact nor very inexact. The main ideas behind this application are outlined and illustrated by examples.

1. Introduction

During the past decade, the theory of fuzzy sets has developed in a variety of directions, finding applications in such diverse fields as taxonomy, topology, linguistics, automata theory, logic, control theory, game theory, information theory, psychology, pattern recognition, medicince, law, decision analysis, system theory and information retrieval.

A common thread that runs through most of the applications of the theory of fuzzy sets relates to the concept of a *fuzzy restriction* — that is, a fuzzy relation which acts as an elastic constraint on the values that may be assigned to a variable. Such restrictions appear to play an important role in human cognition, especially in situations involving concept formation, pattern recognition, and decision-making in fuzzy or uncertain environments.

As its name implies, the *calculus of fuzzy restrictions* is essentially a body of concepts and techniques for dealing with fuzzy restrictions in a systematic fashion.

*This work was supported in part by the Naval Electronics Systems Command, Contract N00039-75-0034, The Army Research Office, Grant DAHC04-75-G-0056, and the National Science Foundation, Grant GK-43024X.

As such, it may be viewed as a branch of the theory of fuzzy relations, in which it plays a role somewhat analogous to that of the calculus of probabilities in probability theory. However, a more specific aim of the calculus of fuzzy restrictions is to furnish a conceptual basis for fuzzy logic and what might be called *approximate reasoning*,[1] i.e. a type of reasoning which is neither very exact nor very inexact. Such reasoning plays a basic role in human decision-making because it provides a way of dealing with problems which are too complex for precise solution. However, approximate reasoning is more than a method of last recourse for coping with insurmountable complexities. It is, also, a way of simplifying the performance of tasks in which a high degree of precision is neither needed nor required. Such tasks pervade much of what we do on both conscious and subconscious levels.

What is a fuzzy restriction? To illustrate its meaning in an informal fashion, consider the following propositions (in which italicized words represent fuzzy concepts):

Tosi is *young* (1.1)

Ted has *gray hair* (1.2)

Sakti and Kapali are *approximately equal* in height. (1.3)

Starting with (1.1), let Age (Tosi) denote a numerically-valued variable which ranges over the interval $[0, 100]$. With this interval regarded as our universe of discourse U, *young* may be interpreted as the label of a fuzzy subset[a] of U which is characterized by a *compatibility function*, μ_{young}, of the form shown in Fig. 1.1. Thus, the degree to which a numerical age, say $u = 28$, is compatible with the concept of *young* is 0.7, while the compatibilities of 30 and 35 with *young* are 0.5 and 0.2, respectively. (The age at which the compatibility takes the value 0.5 is the *crossover point* of *young*.) Equivalently, the function μ_{young} may be viewed as the *membership function* of the fuzzy set *young*, with the value of μ_{young} at u representing the grade of membership of u in *young*.

Since *young* is a fuzzy set with no sharply defined boundaries, the conventional interpretation of the proposition "Tosi is *young*," namely, "Tosi is a member of the class of *young* men," is not meaningful if membership in a set is interpreted in its usual mathematical sense. To circumvent this difficulty, we shall view (1.1) as an assertion of a restriction on the possible values of Tosi's age rather than as an assertion concerning the membership of Tosi in a class of individuals. Thus, on denoting the restriction on the age of Tosi by $R(\text{Age(Tosi)})$, (1.1) may be expressed as an assignment equation

$$R(\text{Age(Tosi)}) = young \tag{1.4}$$

in which the fuzzy set *young* (or, equivalently, the unary fuzzy relation *young*) is assigned to the restriction on the variable Age(Tosi). In this instance, the restriction $R(\text{Age(Tosi)})$ is a *fuzzy restriction* by virtue of the fuzziness of the set *young*.

[a] A summary of the basic properties of fuzzy sets is presented in the Appendix.

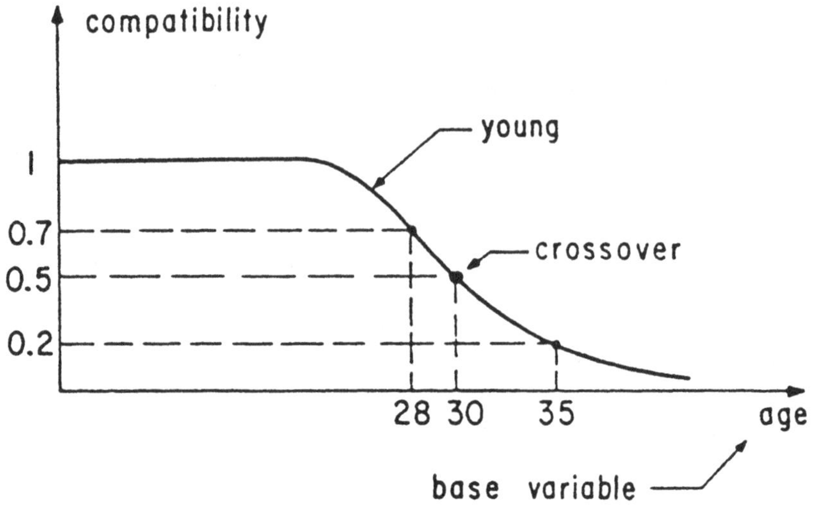

Fig. 1.1. Compatibility Function of *young*.

Using the same point of view, (1.2) may be expressed as

$$R(\text{color}(\text{Hair}(\text{Ted}))) = \textit{gray}\,. \tag{1.5}$$

Thus, in this case, the fuzzy set *gray* is assigned as a value to the fuzzy restriction on the variable Color(Hair(Ted)).

In the case of (1.1) and (1.2), the fuzzy restriction has the form of a fuzzy set or, equivalently, a unary fuzzy relation. In the case of (1.3), we have two variables to consider, namely, Height(Sakti) and Height(Kapali). Thus, in this instance, the assignment equation takes the form

$$R(\text{Height}(\text{Sakti}), \text{Height}(\text{Kapali})) = \textit{approximately equal} \tag{1.6}$$

in which *approximately equal* is a binary fuzzy relation characterized by a compatibility matrix $\mu_{approximately\ equal}(u, v)$ such as shown in Table. 1.2.

Table 1.2. Compatibility matrix of the fuzzy relation *approximately equal*.

$u\backslash v$	5′6	5′8	5′10	6	6′2	6′4
5′6	1	0.8	0.6	0.2	0	0
5′8	0.8	1	0.9	0.7	0.3	0
5′10	0.6	0.9	1	0.9	0.7	0
6	0.2	0.7	0.9	1	0.9	0.8
6′2	0	0.3	0.7	0.9	1	0.9
6′4	0	0	0	0.8	0.9	1

Thus, if Sakti's height is 5′8 and Kapali's is 5′10, then the degree to which they are approximately equal is 0.9.

The restrictions involved in (1.1), (1.2) and (1.3) are unrelated in the sense that the restriction on the age of Tosi has no bearing on the color of Ted's hair or the height of Sakti and Kapali. More generally, however, the restrictions may be interrelated, as in the following example.

$$u \text{ is } \textit{small} \tag{1.7}$$

$$u \text{ and } v \text{ are } \textit{approximately equal}\,. \tag{1.8}$$

In terms of the fuzzy restrictions on u and v, (1.7) and (1.8) translate into the assignment equations

$$R(u) = \textit{small} \tag{1.9}$$

$$R(u,v) = \textit{approximately equal} \tag{1.10}$$

where $R(u)$ and $R(u,v)$ denote the restrictions on u and (u,v), respectively.

As will be shown in Sec. 2, from the knowledge of a fuzzy restriction on u and a fuzzy restriction on (u,v) we can deduce a fuzzy restriction on v. Thus, in the case of (1.9) and (1.10), we can assert that

$$R(v) = R(u) \circ R(u,v) = \textit{small} \circ \textit{approximately equal} \tag{1.11}$$

where $\circ$ denotes the composition[b] of fuzzy relations.

The rule by which (1.11) is inferred from (1.9) and (1.10) is called the *compositional rule of inference*. As will be seen in the sequel, this rule is a special case of a more general method for deducing a fuzzy restriction on a variable from the knowledge of fuzzy restrictions on related variables.

In what follows, we shall outline some of the main ideas which form the basis for the calculus of fuzzy restrictions and sketch its application to approximate reasoning. For convenient reference, a summary of those aspects of the theory of fuzzy sets which are relevant to the calculus of fuzzy restrictions is presented in the Appendix.

2. Calculus of Fuzzy Restrictions

The point of departure for our discussion of the calculus of fuzzy restrictions is the paradigmatic proposition[c]

$$p \triangleq x \text{ is } P \tag{2.1}$$

[b]If A is a unary fuzzy relation in U and B is a binary fuzzy relation in $U \times V$, the membership function of the composition of A and B is expressed by $\mu_{A \circ B}(v) = \vee_u(\mu_A(u) \wedge \mu_B(u,v))$, where $\vee_u$ denotes the supremum over $u \in U$. A more detailed discussion of the composition of fuzzy relations may be found in Refs. 2 and 3.

[c]The symbol $\triangleq$ stands for "denotes" or "is defined to be."

which is exemplified by

$$x \text{ is a positive integer} \tag{2.2}$$

$$\text{Soup is } \textit{hot} \tag{2.3}$$

$$\text{Elvira is } \textit{blond} \tag{2.4}$$

If P is a label of a nonfuzzy set, e.g., $p \triangleq$ set of positive integers, then "x is P," may be interpreted as "x belongs to P," or, equivalently, as "x is a member of P." In (2.3) and (2.4), however, P is a label of a fuzzy set, i.e., $P \triangleq$ *hot* and $P \triangleq$ *blond*. In such cases, the interpretation of "x is P" will be assumed to be characterized by what will be referred to as a *relational assignment equation.* More specifically, we have:

Definition 2.5. The meaning of the proposition

$$p \triangleq x \text{ is } P \tag{2.6}$$

where x is a name of an object (or a construct) and P is a label of a fuzzy subset of a universe of discourse U, is expressed by the *relational assignment equation*

$$R(A(x)) = P \tag{2.7}$$

where A is an *implied attribute* of x, i.e., an attribute which is implied by x and P; and R denotes a fuzzy restriction on $A(x)$ to which the value P is assigned by (2.7). In other words, (2.7) implies that the attribute $A(x)$ takes values in U and that $R(A(x))$ is a fuzzy restriction on the values that $A(x)$ may take, with $R(A(x))$ equated to P by the relational assignment equation.

As an illustration, consider the proposition "Soup is *hot*." In this case, the implied attribute is Temperature and (2.3) becomes

$$R(\text{Temperature (Soup)}) = \textit{hot} \tag{2.8}$$

with *hot* being a subset of the interval $[0, 212]$ defined by, say, a compatibility function of the form (see Appendix)

$$\mu_{hot}(u) = S(u;\ 32, 100,\ 200) \tag{2.9}$$

Thus, if the temperature of the soup is $u = 100°$, then the degree to which it is compatible with the fuzzy restriction *hot* is 0.5, whereas the compatibility of 200° with *hot* is unity. It is in this sense that R(Temperature(Soup)) plays the role of a fuzzy restriction on the soup temperature which is assigned the value *hot*, with the compatibility function of *hot* serving to define the compatibilities of the numerical values of soup temperature with the fuzzy restriction *hot*.

In the case of (2.4), the implied attribute is Color(Hair), and the relational assignemnt equation takes the from

$$R(\text{Color (Hair (Elvira))}) = \textit{blond}\,. \tag{2.10}$$

There are two important points that are brought out by this example. First, the implied attribute of x may have a nested structure, i.e., may be of the general form

$$A_k(A_{k-1}(\ldots A_2(A_1(x)) \ldots)); \tag{2.11}$$

and second, the fuzzy set which is assigned to the fuzzy restriction (i.e., *blond*) may not have a numerically-valued *base variable,* that is, the variable ranging over the universe of discourse U. In such cases, we shall assume that P is defined by exemplification, that is, by pointing to specific instances of x and indicating the degree (either numerical or linguistic) to which that instance is compatible with P. For example, we may have μ_{blond} (June) $= 0.2$, μ_{blond} (Jurata) $=$ *very high*, etc. In this way, the fuzzy set *blond* is defined in an approximate fashion as a fuzzy subset of a universe of discourse comprised of a collection of individuals $U = \{x\}$, with the restriction $R(x)$ playing the role of a fuzzy restriction on the values of x rather than on the values of an implied attribute $A(x)$.[d] (In the sequel, we shall write $R(x)$ and speak of the restriction on x rather than on $A(x)$ not only in those cases in which P is defined by exemplification but also when the implied attribute is not identified in an explicit fashion.)

So far, we have confined our attention to fuzzy restrictions which are defined by a single proposition of the form "x is P." In a more general setting, we may have n constituent propositions of the form

$$x_i \text{ is } P_i\,,\ i = 1, \ldots, n \tag{2.12}$$

in which P_i is a fuzzy subset of U_i, $i = 1, \ldots, n$. In this case, the propositions "x_i is P_i," $i = 1, \ldots, n$, collectively define a fuzzy restriction on the n-ary object $(x_1, \ldots, x_n)$. The way in which this restriction depends on the P_i is discussed in the following.

The rules of implied conjunction and maximal restriction

For simplicity we shall assume that $n = 2$, with the constituent propositions having the form

$$x \text{ is } P \tag{2.13}$$

$$y \text{ is } Q \tag{2.14}$$

where P and Q are fuzzy subsets of U and V, respectively. For example,

Georgia is *very warm* (2.15)

George is *highly intelligent* (2.16)

or, if $x = y$,

Georgia is *very warm* (2.17)

Georgia is *highly intelligent*. (2.18)

[d] A more detailed discussion of this and related issues may be found in Refs. 3–5.

The *rule of implied conjunction* asserts that, in the absence of additional information concerning the constituent propositions, (2.13) and (2.14) taken together imply the composite proposition "x is P and y is Q"; i.e.,

$$\{x \text{ is } P\,,\ y \text{ is } Q\} \Longrightarrow x \text{ is } P \text{ and } y \text{ is } Q\,. \tag{2.19}$$

Under the same assumption, the *rule of maximal restriction* asserts that

$$x \text{ is } P \text{ and } y \text{ is } Q \Longrightarrow (x\,,\ y) \text{ is } P \times Q \tag{2.20}$$

and, if $x = y$,

$$x \text{ is } P \text{ and } x \text{ is } Q \Longrightarrow x \text{ is } P \cap Q \tag{2.21}$$

where $P \times Q$ and $P \cap Q$ denote, respectively, the cartesian product and the intersection of P and Q.[e]

The rule of maximal restriction is an instance of a more general principle which is based on the following properties of n-ary fuzzy restrictions.

Let R be a n-ary fuzzy relation in $U_1 \times \cdots \times U_n$ which is characterized by its membership (compatibility) function $\mu_R(u_1, \ldots, u_n)$. Let $q = (i_1, \ldots, i_k)$ be a subsequence of the index sequence $(1, \ldots, n)$ and let q' denote the complementary subsequence $(j_1, \ldots, j_\ell)$. (E.g., if $n = 5$ and $q = (2, 4, 5)$, then $q' = (1, 3)$.) Then, the *projection of R on* $U_{(q)} \triangleq U_{i_1} \times \cdots \times U_{i_k}$ is a fuzzy relation, R_q, in $U_{(q)}$ whose membership function is related to that of R by the expression

$$\mu_{R_q}(u_{i_1}, \ldots, u_{i_k}) = \vee_{U_{(q')}}\ \mu_R(u_1, \ldots, u_n) \tag{2.22}$$

where the right-hand member represents the supremum of $\mu_R(u_1, \ldots, u_n)$ over the u's which are in $U_{(q')}$.

If R is interpreted as a fuzzy restriction on $(u_1, \ldots, u_n)$ in $U_1 \times \cdots \times U_n$, then its projection on $U_{i_1} \times \cdots \times U_{i_k}$, R_q, constitutes a *marginal restriction* which is induced by R in $U_{(q)}$. Conversely, given a fuzzy restriction R_q in $U_{(q)}$, there exist fuzzy restrictions in $U_1 \times \cdots \times U_n$ whose projection on $U_{(q)}$ is R_q. From (2.22), it follows that the largest[f] of these restrictions is the *cylindrical extension* of R_q, denoted by $\bar{R}_q$, whose membership function is given by

$$\mu_{\bar{R}_q}(u_1, \ldots, u_n) = \mu_{R_q}(u_{i_1}, \ldots, u_{i_k}) \tag{2.23}$$

and whose *base* is R_q. ($\bar{R}_q$ is referred to as the cylindrical extension of R_q because the value of $\mu_{\bar{R}_q}$ at any point $(u'_1, \ldots, u'_n)$ is the same as at the point $(u_1, \ldots, u_n)$ so long as $u'_{i_1} = u_{i_1}, \ldots, u'_{i_k} = u_{i_k}$.)

Since $\bar{R}_q$ is the largest restriction in $U_1 \times \cdots \times U_n$ whose base is R_q, it follows that

$$R \subset \bar{R}_q \tag{2.24}$$

[e]The *cartesian product* of P and Q is a fuzzy subset of $U \times V$ whose membership function is expressed by $\mu_{P \times Q}(u, v) = \mu_P(u) \wedge \mu_Q(v)$. The membership function of $P \cap Q$ is given by $\mu_{P \cap Q}(u) = \mu_P(u) \wedge \mu_Q(u)$. The symbol $\wedge$ stands for min. (See the Appendix for more details.)
[f]A fuzzy relation R in U is *larger* than S (in U) iff $\mu_R(u) \geq \mu_S(u)$ for all u in U.

for all q, and hence that R satisfies the *containment relation*

$$R \subset \bar{R}_{q_1} \cap \bar{R}_{q_2} \cap \cdots \cap \bar{R}_{q_r} \tag{2.25}$$

which holds for arbitrary index subsequences $q_1, \ldots, q_r$. Thus, if we are given the marginal restrictions $R_{q_1}, \ldots, R_{q_r}$, then the restriction

$$R_{\mathrm{MAX}}(R_{q_1}, \ldots, R_{q_r}) \triangleq \bar{R}_{q_1} \cap \cdots \cap \bar{R}_{q_r} \tag{2.26}$$

is the *maximal* (i.e., least restrictive) restriction which is consistent with the restrictions $R_{q_1}, \ldots, R_{q_r}$. It is this choice of R_{MAX} given $R_{q_1}, \ldots, R_{q_r}$ that constitutes a general selection principle of which the rule of maximal restriction is a special case.[g]

By applying the same approach to the disjunction of two propositions, we are led to the rule

$$x \text{ is } P \text{ or } y \text{ is } Q \Longrightarrow (x, y) \text{ is } \bar{P} + \bar{Q} \tag{2.27}$$

or, equivalently,

$$x \text{ is } P \text{ or } y \text{ is } Q \Longrightarrow (x, y) \text{ is } (P' \times Q')' \tag{2.28}$$

where P' and Q' are the complements of P and Q, respectively, and $+$ denotes the union.[h]

As a simple illustration of (2.27), assume that

$$U = 1 + 2 + 3 + 4$$

and that

$$P \triangleq \mathit{small} \triangleq 1/1 + 0.6/2 + 0.2/3 \tag{2.29}$$

$$\mathit{large} \triangleq 0.2/2 + 0.6/3 + 1/4 \tag{2.30}$$

$$Q \triangleq \mathit{very\ large} = 0.04/2 + 0.36/3 + 1/4 \tag{2.31}$$

Then

$$\begin{aligned} P' &= 0.4/2 + 0.8/3 + 1/4 \\ Q' &= 1/1 + 0.96/2 + 0.64/3 \end{aligned} \tag{2.32}$$

and

[g] A somewhat analogous role in the case of probability distributions is played by the maximum entropy principle of E. Jaynes and M. Tribus.[6,7]

[h] The membership function of P' is related to that of P by $\mu_{P'}(u) = 1 - \mu_P(u)$. The membership function of the union of P and Q is expressed by $\mu_{P+Q}(u) = \mu_P(u) \vee \mu_Q(u)$, where $\vee$ denotes max.

$$\bar{P}+\bar{Q} = (P' \times Q')' = 1/((1,\ 1)+(1,\ 2)+(1,\ 3)+(1,\ 4)$$
$$+(2,\ 4)+(3,\ 4)+(4,4))$$
$$+0.6/((2,\ 1)+(2,\ 2)+(2,\ 3))$$
$$+0.3/(3,\ 1)+(3,\ 2))+0.36/((3,\ 3)$$
$$+(4,\ 3))+0.04/(4,2) \qquad (2.33)$$

Conditional propositions

In the case of conjunctions and disjunctions, our intuition provides a reasonably reliable guide for defining the form of the dependence of $R(x, y)$ on $R(x)$ and $R(y)$. This is less true, however, of conditional propositions of the form

$$p \triangleq \text{If } x \text{ is } P \text{ then } y \text{ is } Q \text{ else } y \text{ } is \text{ } S \qquad (2.34)$$

and

$$q \triangleq \text{If } x \text{ is } P \text{ then } y \text{ is } Q \qquad (2.35)$$

where P is a fuzzy subset of U, while Q and S are fuzzy subsets of V.

With this qualification, two somewhat different definition for the restrictions induced by p and q suggest themselves. The first, to which we shall refer as the *maximin rule of conditional propositions*, is expressed by:

$$\text{If } x \text{ is } P \text{ then } y \text{ is } Q \text{ else } y \text{ is } S \Longrightarrow (x,y) \text{ is } P \times Q + P' \times S\,, \qquad (2.36)$$

which implies that the meaning of P is expressed by the relational assignment equation

$$R(x,y) = P \times Q + P' \times S\,. \qquad (2.37)$$

The conditional proposition (2.35) may be interpreted as a special case of (2.34) corresponding to $S = V$. Under this assumption, we have

$$\text{If } x \text{ is } P \text{ then } y \text{ is } Q \Longrightarrow (x,y) \text{ is } P \times Q + P' \times V\,. \qquad (2.38)$$

As an illustration, consider the conditional proposition

$$p \triangleq \text{If Maya is } tall \text{ then Turkan is } very\ tall\,. \qquad (2.39)$$

Using (2.38), the fuzzy restriction induced by p is defined by the relational assignment equation

$$R(\text{Height (Maya), Height (Turkan)}) = tall \times very\ tall + not\ tall \times V$$

where V might be taken to be the interval [150, 200] (in centimeters), and *tall* and *very tall* are fuzzy subsets of V defined by their respective compatibility functions (see Appendix)

$$\mu_{tall} = S(160,\ 170,\ 180) \qquad (2.40)$$

and

$$\mu_{very\ tall} = S^2(160,\ 170,\ 180) \tag{2.41}$$

in which the argument u is suppressed for simplicity.

An alternative definition, to which we shall refer as the *arithmetic rule of conditional propositions*, is expressed by

$$\text{If } x \text{ is } P \text{ then } y \text{ is } Q \text{ else } y \text{ is } S \Longrightarrow (x,y) \text{ is } ((P \times V \ominus U \times Q) + (P' \times V \ominus U \times S))' \tag{2.42}$$

or, equivalently and more simply,

$$\text{If } x \text{ is } P \text{ then } y \text{ is } Q \text{ else } y \text{ is } S \Longrightarrow (x,y) \text{ is } (\bar{P}' \oplus \bar{Q}) \cap (\bar{P} \oplus \bar{S}) \tag{2.43}$$

where $\oplus$ and $\ominus$ denote the *bounded-sum* and *bounded-difference* operations,[i] respectively; $\bar{P}$ and $\bar{Q}$ are the cylindrical extensions of P and Q; and $+$ is the union. This definition may be viewed as an adaptation to fuzzy sets of Lukasiewicz's definition of material implication in L_{aleph_1} logic, namely[8]

$$v(r \longrightarrow s) \triangleq \min(1,\ 1 - v(r) + v(s)) \tag{2.44}$$

where $v(r)$ and $v(s)$ denote the truth-values of r and s, respectively, with $0 \leq v(r) \leq 1,\ 0 \leq v(s) \leq 1$. In particular, if S is equated to V, then (2.43) reduces to

$$\text{If } x \text{ is } P \text{ then } y \text{ is } Q \Longrightarrow (x,y) \text{ is } (\bar{P}' \oplus \bar{Q})\,. \tag{2.45}$$

Note that in (2.42), $P \times V$ and $U \times Q$ are the cylindrical extensions, $\bar{P}$ and $\bar{Q}$, of P and Q, respectively.

Of the two definitions stated above, the first is somewhat easier to manipulate but the second seems to be in closer accord with our intuition. Both yield the same result when P, Q and S are nonfuzzy sets.

As an illustration, in the special case where $x = y$ and $P = Q$, (2.45) yields

$$\text{If } x \text{ is } P \text{ then } x \text{ is } P \Longrightarrow x \text{ is } (P' \oplus P)\,, \tag{2.46}$$

which implies, as should be expected, that the proposition in question induces no restriction on x. The same holds true, more generally, when $P \subset Q$.

Modification of fuzzy restrictions

Basically, there are three distinct ways in which a fuzzy restriction which is induced by a proposition of the form

$$P \triangleq x \text{ is } P$$

may be modified.

[i]The membership functions of the bounded-sum and -difference of P and Q are defined by $\mu_{P \oplus Q}(u) = \min(1, \mu_P(u) + \mu_Q(u))$ and $\mu_{P \ominus Q}(u) = \max(0, \mu_P(u) - \mu_Q(u))$, $u \in U$, where $+$ denotes the arithmetic sum.

First, by a combination with other restrictions, as in

$$r \triangleq x \text{ is } P \text{ and } x \text{ is } Q \tag{2.47}$$

which transforms P into $P \cap Q$.

Second, by the application of a modifier m to P, as in

$$\text{Hans is } \textit{very kind} \tag{2.48}$$

$$\text{Maribel is } \textit{highly temperamental} \tag{2.49}$$

$$\text{Lydia is } \textit{more or less happy} \tag{2.50}$$

in which the operators *very, highly* and *more or less* modify the fuzzy restrictions represented by the fuzzy sets *kind, temperamental* and *happy*, respectively.

And third, by the use of truth-values, as in

$$(\text{Sema is } \textit{young}) \text{ is } \textit{very true} \tag{2.51}$$

in which *very true* is a fuzzy restriction on the truth-value of the proposition "Sema is *young*."

The effect of modifiers such as *very, highly, extremely, more or less*, etc., is discussed in greater detail in Refs. 9–11. For the purposes of the present discussion, it will suffice to observe that the effect of *very* and *more or less* may be approximated very roughly by the operations CON (standing for CONCENTRATION) and DIL (standing for DILATION) which are defined respectively by

$$\text{CON}(A) = \int_U (\mu_A(u))^2/u \tag{2.52}$$

and

$$\text{DIL}(A) = \int_U (\mu_A(u))^{0.5}/u \tag{2.53}$$

where A is a fuzzy set in U with membership function μ_A, and

$$A = \int_U \mu_A(u)/u \tag{2.54}$$

is the integral representation of A. (See the Appendix.) Thus, as an approximation, we assume that

$$\textit{very } A = \text{CON}(A) \tag{2.55}$$

and

$$\textit{more or less } A = \text{DIL}(A)\,. \tag{2.56}$$

For example, if

$$\textit{young} = \int_0^{100} \left(1 + \left(\frac{u}{30}\right)^2\right)^{-1} \Big/ u \tag{2.57}$$

then

$$very\ young = \int_0^{100} \left(1 + \left(\frac{u}{30}\right)^2\right)^{-2} \Big/ u \tag{2.58}$$

and

$$more\ or\ less\ young = \int_0^{100} \left(1 + \left(\frac{u}{30}\right)^2\right)^{-0.5} \Big/ u\,. \tag{2.59}$$

The process by which a fuzzy restriction is modified by a fuzzy truth-value is significantly different from the point transformations expressed by (2.55) and (2.56). More specifically, the *rule of truth-functional modification*, which defines the transformation in question, may be stated in symbols as

$$(x \text{ is } Q) \text{ is } \tau \Longrightarrow x \text{ is } \mu_Q^{-1} \circ \tau \tag{2.60}$$

where τ is a linguistic truth-value (e.g., *true, very true, false, not very true, more or less true,* etc.); μ_Q^{-1} is a relation inverse to the compatibility function of A, and $\mu_Q^{-1} \circ \tau$ is the composition of the nonfuzzy relation μ_Q^{-1} with the unary fuzzy relation τ. (See footnote b in Sec. 1 for the definition of composition.)

As an illustration, the application of this rule to the proposition

$$(\text{Sema is } young) \text{ is } very\ true \tag{2.61}$$

yields

$$\text{Sema is } \mu_{young}^{-1} \circ very\ true\,. \tag{2.62}$$

Thus, if the compatibility functions of *young* and *very true* have the form of the curves labeled μ_{young_1} and $\mu_{very\ true}$ in Fig. 2.1, then the compatibility function of $\mu_{young} \circ very\ true$ is represented by the curve μ_{young_2}. The ordinates of μ_{young_2} can readily be determined by the graphical procedure illustrated in Fig. 2.1.

The important point brought out by the foregoing discussion is that the association of a truth-value with a proposition does not result in a proposition of a new type; rather, it merely modifies the fuzzy restriction induced by that proposition in accordance with the rule expressed by (2.60). The same applies, more generally, to nested propositions of the form

$$(\ldots(((x \text{ is } P_1) \text{ is } \tau_1) \text{ is } \tau_2)\ldots \text{is } \tau_n) \tag{2.63}$$

in which $\tau_1, \ldots, \tau_n$ are linguistic or numerical truth-values. It can be shown[j] that the restriction on x which is induced by a proposition of this form may be expressed as

$$x \text{ is } P_{n+1}$$

[j] A more detailed discussion of this and related issues may be found in Ref. 4.

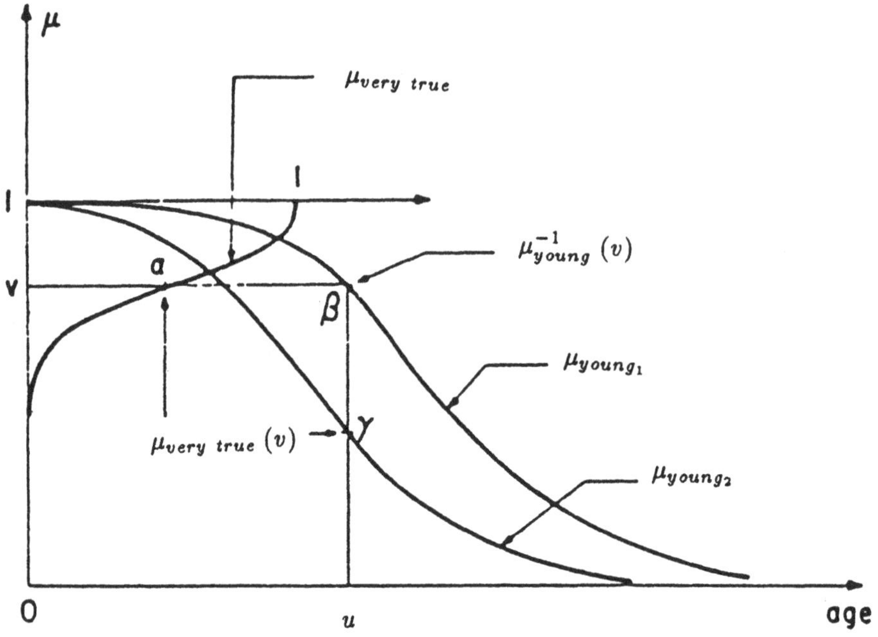

Fig. 2.1. Illustration of Truth-Functional Modification.

where

$$P_{k+1} = \mu_{P_k}^{-1} \circ \tau_k \ , \ k = 1,\ 2,\ \ldots,\ n \tag{2.64}$$

3. Approximate Reasoning (AR)

The calculus of fuzzy restrictions provides a basis for a systematic approach to approximate reasoning (or AR, for short) by interpreting such reasoning as the process of approximate solution of a system of relational assignment equations. In what follows, we shall present a brief sketch of some of the main ideas behind this interpretation.

Specifically, let us assume that we have a collection of objects $x_1, \ldots, x_n$, a collection of universes of discourse $U_1, \ldots, U_n$, and a collection, $\{P_r\}$, of propositions of the form

$$p_r \triangleq (x_{r_1}, x_{r_2}, \ldots, x_{r_k}) \text{ is } P_r,\ r = 1, \ldots, N \tag{3.1}$$

in which P_r is a fuzzy relation in $U_{r_1} \times \cdots \times U_{r_k}$.[k] For example,

$$p_1 \triangleq x_1 \text{ is } \mathit{small} \tag{3.2}$$

$$p_2 \triangleq x_1 \text{ and } x_2 \text{ are } \mathit{approximately\ equal} \tag{3.3}$$

[k]In some cases, the proposition "$(x_{r_1}, \ldots, x_{r_k})$ is P_r," may be expressed more naturally in English as "x_{r_1} and $\ldots x_{r_k}$ are P_r."

in which $U_1 = U_2 \triangleq (-\infty, \infty)$; *small* is a fuzzy subset of the real line $(-\infty, \infty)$; and *approximately equal* is a fuzzy binary relation in $(-\infty, \infty) \times (-\infty, \infty)$.

As stated in Sec. 2, each p_r in $\{p_r\}$ may be translated into a relational assignment equation of the form

$$R(A_{r_1}(x_{r_1}), \ldots, A_{r_k}(x_{r_k})) = P_r, \; r = 1, \ldots, N \tag{3.4}$$

where A_{r_i} is an implied attribute of $x_{r_i}, i = 1, \ldots, k$, (with k dependent on r). Thus, the collection of propositions $\{p_r\}$ may be represented as a system of relational assignment equation (3.4).

Let $\bar{P}_r$ be the cylindrical extension of P_r, i.e.,

$$\bar{P}_r = P_r \times U_{s_1} \times \cdots \times U_{s_\ell} \tag{3.5}$$

where the index sequence $(s_1, \ldots, s_\ell)$ is the complement of the index sequence $(r_1, \ldots, r_k)$ (i.e., if $n = 5$, for example, and $(r_1, r_2, r_3) = (2,4,5)$, then $(s_1, s_2) = (1,3)$).

By the rule of the implied conjunction, the collection of propositions $\{p_r\}$ induces a relational assignment equation of the form

$$R(A_1(x_1), \ldots, A_n(x_n)) = \bar{P}_1 \cap \cdots \cap \bar{P}_N \tag{3.6}$$

which subsumes the system of assignment equations (3.4). It is this equation that forms the basis for approximate inferences from the given propositions $p_1, \ldots, p_N$.

Specifically, by an *inference about* $(x_{r_1}, \ldots, x_{r_k})$ *from* $\{p_r\}$, we mean the fuzzy restriction resulting from the projection of $p \triangleq \bar{P}_1 \cap \cdots \cap \bar{P}_N$ on $U_{r_1} \times \cdots \times U_{r_k}$. Such an inference will, in general, be approximate in nature because of (a) approximations in the computation of the projection of P; and/or (b) linguistic approximation to the projection of P by variables whose values are linguistic rather than numerical.[1]

As a simple illustration of (3.6), consider the propositions

$$x_1 \text{ is } P_1 \tag{3.7}$$

$$x_1 \text{ and } x_2 \text{ are } P_2 \,. \tag{3.8}$$

In this case, (3.6) becomes

$$R(A(x_1), \; A(x_2)) = \bar{P}_1 \cap P_2 \tag{3.9}$$

and the projection of $\bar{P}_1 \cap P_2$ on U_2 reduces to the composition of P_1 and P_2. In this way, we are led to the *compositional rule of inference* which may be expressed in symbols as

[1]A linguistic variable is a variable whose values are words or sentences in a natural or artificial language. For example, age is a linguistic variable if its values are assumed to be *young, not young, very young, more or less young,* etc. A more detailed discussion of linguistic variables may be found in Refs. 3, 4, 11. (See also Appendix.)

$$\begin{array}{l} x_1 \text{ is } P_1 \\ x_1 \text{ and } x_2 \text{ are } P_2 \\ \hline x_2 \text{ is } P_1 \circ P_2 \end{array} \tag{3.10}$$

or, more generally,

$$\begin{array}{l} x_1 \text{ and } x_2 \text{ are } P_1 \\ x_2 \text{ and } x_3 \text{ are } P_2 \\ \hline x_1 \text{ and } x_3 \text{ are } P_1 \circ P_2 \end{array} \tag{3.11}$$

in which the respective inferences are shown below the horizontal line. As a more concrete example, consider the propositions

$$x_1 \text{ is } \mathit{small} \tag{3.12}$$

$$x_1 \text{ and } x_2 \text{ are } \mathit{approximately\ equal} \tag{3.13}$$

where

$$U_1 = U_2 \triangleq 1 + 2 + 3 + 4 \tag{3.14}$$

$$\mathit{small} \triangleq 1/1 + 0.6/2 + 0.2/3 \tag{3.15}$$

and

$$\begin{aligned} \mathit{approximately\ equal} = {} & 1/((1,1) + (2,2) + (3,3) + (4,4)) \\ & + 0.5/((1,2) + (2,1) + (2,3) \\ & + (3,2) + (3,4) + (4,3) . \end{aligned} \tag{3.16}$$

In this case, the composition *small* $\circ$ *approximately equal* may be expressed as the max–min product of the relation matrices of *small* and *approximately equal*. Thus

$$\begin{aligned} \mathit{small} \circ \mathit{approximately\ equal} &= [1 \quad 0.6 \quad 0.2 \quad 0] \circ \begin{bmatrix} 1 & 0.5 & 0 & 0 \\ 0.5 & 1 & 0.5 & 0 \\ 0 & 0.5 & 1 & 0.5 \\ 0 & 0 & 0.5 & 1 \end{bmatrix} \\ &= [1 \quad 0.6 \quad 0.5 \quad 0.2] \end{aligned} \tag{3.17}$$

and hence the fuzzy restriction on x_2 is given by

$$R(x_2) = 1/1 + 0.6/2 + 0.5/3 + 0.2/4 . \tag{3.18}$$

Using the definition of *more or less* (see (2.56)), a rough linguistic approximation to (3.18) may be expressed as

$$\mathrm{LA}(1/1 + 0.6/2 + 0.5/3 + 0.2/4) = \textit{more or less small} \tag{3.19}$$

where LA stands for the operation of linguistic approximation. In this way, from (3.12) and (3.13) we can deduce the approximate conclusion

$$x_2 \text{ is } \textit{more or less small} \tag{3.20}$$

which may be regarded as an approximate solution of the relational assignment equations

$$R(x_1) = \textit{small} \tag{3.21}$$

and

$$R(x_1, x_2) = \textit{approximately equal}\,. \tag{3.22}$$

Proceeding in a similar fashion in various special cases, one can readily derive one or more approximate conclusions from a given set of propositions, with the understanding that the degree of approximation in each case depends on the definition of the fuzzy restrictions which are induced by the propositions in question. Among the relatively simple examples of such approximate inferences are the following:

x_1 is *close* to x_2
x_2 is *close* to x_3 (3.23)

---

x_1 is *more or less close* to x_3

Most Swedes are *tall*
Nils is a Swede (3.24)

It is *very likely* that Nils is *tall*

Most Swedes are *tall*
Most tall Swedes are *blond*
Karl is a Swedes (3.25)

It is *very likely* that Karl is *tall* and it is
more or less (*very likely*) that Karl is *blond*.

It should be noted that the last two examples involve a fuzzy quantifier, *most*, and fuzzy linguistic probabilities *very likely* and *more or less* (*very likely*). By defining *most* as a fuzzy subset of the unit interval, and *tall* as a fuzzy subset of the interval [150, 200], the proposition $p \triangleq$ *Most* Swedes are *tall* induces a fuzzy restriction on the distribution of heights of Swedes, from which the conclusion "It is *very likely* that Nils is *tall*," follows as a linguistic approximation. The same applies to the last example, except that the probability *very likely* is dilated in the consequent proposition because of the double occurrence of the quantifier *most* among the antecedent propositions. The goodness of the linguistic approximation in these examples depends essentially on the degree to which *very likely* approximates to most.

A more general rule of inference which follows at once from (2.45) and (3.10) may be viewed as a generalization of the classical rule of *modus ponens*. This rule, which will be referred to as the *compositional modus ponens*, is expressed by

$$\begin{array}{l} x \text{ is } P \\ \text{If } x \text{ is } Q \text{ then } y \text{ is } S \\ \hline y \text{ is } P \circ (\bar{Q}' \oplus \bar{S}) \end{array} \tag{3.26}$$

where $\oplus$ is the bounded-sum operation, $\bar{Q}'$ is the cylindrical extension of the complement of Q, and $\bar{S}$ is the cylindrical extension of S. Alternatively, using the maximin rule for conditional propositions (see (2.36)), we obtain

$$\begin{array}{l} x \text{ is } P \\ \text{If } x \text{ is } Q \text{ then } y \text{ is } S \\ \hline y \text{ is } P \circ (Q \times S + \bar{Q}') \end{array} \tag{3.27}$$

where $+$ is the union and $\bar{Q}' \triangleq Q' \times V$.

Note 3.28. If $P = Q$ and P and S are nonfuzzy, both (3.26) and (3.27) reduce to the classical *modus ponens*

$$\begin{array}{l} x \text{ is } P \\ \text{If } x \text{ is } P \text{ then } y \text{ is } S \\ \hline y \text{ is } S\,. \end{array} \tag{3.29}$$

However, if $P = Q$ and P is fuzzy, we do not obtain (3.29) because of the *interference effect* of the implied part of the conditional proposition "If x is P then y is S," namely "If x is P' then y is V." As a simple illustration of this effect, let $U = 1 + 2 + 3 + 4$ and assume that

$$P = 0.6/2 + 1/3 + 0.5/4 \tag{3.30}$$

and

$$S = 1/2 + 0.6/3 + 0.2/4\,. \tag{3.31}$$

In this case,

$$\bar{P}' \oplus \bar{S} = \begin{bmatrix} 1 & 1 & 1 & 1 \\ 0.4 & 1 & 1 & 0.6 \\ 0 & 1 & 0.6 & 0.6 \\ 0.5 & 1 & 1 & 0.7 \end{bmatrix} \tag{3.32}$$

$$P \times S + \bar{P}' = \begin{bmatrix} 1 & 1 & 1 & 1 \\ 0.4 & 0.6 & 0.6 & 0.6 \\ 0 & 1 & 0.6 & 0.2 \\ 0.5 & 0.5 & 0.5 & 0.5 \end{bmatrix} \tag{3.33}$$

and both (3.26) and (3.27) yield

$$y = 0.5/1 + 1/2 + 0.6/3 + 0.6/4 \tag{3.34}$$

which differs from S at those points at which $\mu_S(v)$ is below 0.5.

The compositional form of the *modus ponens* is of use in the formulation of fuzzy algorithms and the execution of fuzzy instructions.[11] The paper by S. K. Chang[12] and the recent theses by Fellinger[13] and LeFaiver[14] present a number of interesting concepts relating to such instructions and contain many illustrative examples.

Concluding Remarks

In the foregoing discussion, we have attempted to convery some of the main ideas behind the calculus of fuzzy restrictions and its application to approximate reasoning. Although our understanding of the processes of approximate reasoning is quite fragmentary at this juncture, it is very likely that, in time, approximate reasoning will become an important area of study and research in artificial intelligence, psychology and related fields.

References

1. L. A. Zadeh, "Fuzzy logic and approximate reasoning," *Synthese* **30** (1975), pp. 407–428.
2. L. A. Zadeh, "Similarity relations and fuzzy orderings," *Inf. Sci.* **3** (1971), pp. 177–200.
3. L. A. Zadeh, "The concept of a linguistic variable and its application to approximate reasoning," *Information Sciences* **8** (1975), pp. 199–249, 301–357 & **9** (1975), pp. 43–80.
4. L. A. Zadeh, "A fuzzy-algorithmic approach to the definition of complex or imprecise concepts," ERL Memorandum M-474, October 1974.
5. R. E. Bellman, R. Kalaba and L. A. Zadeh, "Abstraction and pattern classification," *Jour. Math. Analysis and Appl.* **13** (1966), pp. 1–7.
6. E. T. Jaynes, "Maximum entropy for hypothesis formulation," *Annals. of Math. Stat.* **34** (1963), pp. 911–930.
7. M. Tribus, *Rational Descriptions, Decisions and Designs* (Pergamon Press, New York and Oxford, 1969).
8. N. Rescher, *Many-Valued Logic* (McGraw-Hill, New York, 1969).
9. L. A. Zadeh, "A fuzzy-set-theoretic interpretation of linguistic hedges," *Jour. of Cybernetics* **2** (1972), pp. 4–34.
10. G. Lakoff, "Hedges: A study of meaning criteria and the logic of fuzzy concepts," *Jour. of Philosophical Logic* **2** (1973), pp. 458–508.
11. L. A. Zadeh, "Outline of a new approach to the analysis of complex systems and decision processes," *IEEE Trans. on Systems, Man and Cybernetics* **SMC-3** (1973), pp. 28–44.

12. S. K. Chang, "On the execution of fuzzy programs using finite state machines," *IEEE Trans. Elec. Comp.* **C-21** (1972), pp. 241–253.
13. W. L. Fellinger, "Specifications for a fuzzy system modeling language," Ph.D. thesis, Oregon State University, 1974.
14. R. LeFaivre, "Fuzzy problem solving," Tech. Report 37, Madison Academic Computing Center, University of Wisconsin, August 1974.
15. J. Goguen, "L-fuzzy sets," *Jour. Math. Analysis and Appl.* **18** (1967), pp. 145–174.
16. J. G. Brown, "A note on fuzzy sets," *Inf. Control* **18** (1971), pp. 32–39.
17. A. De Luca and S. Termini, "Algebraic properties of fuzzy sets," *Jour. Math. Analysis and Appl.* **40** (1972), pp. 373–386.

Appendix

Fuzzy sets — notation, terminology and basic properties

The symbols $U, V, W, \ldots$, with or without subscripts, are generally used to denote specific universes of discourse, which may be arbitrary collections of objects, concepts or mathematical constructs. For example, U may denote the set of all real numbers; the set of all residents in a city; the set of all sentences in a book; the set of all colors that can be perceived by the human eye, etc.

Conventionally, if A is a subset of U whose elements are $u_1, \ldots, u_n$, then A is expressed as

$$A = \{u_1, \ldots, u_n\}. \tag{A.1}$$

For our purposes, however, it is more convenient to express A as

$$A = u_1 + \cdots + u_n \tag{A.2}$$

or

$$A = \sum_{i=1}^{n} u_i \tag{A.3}$$

with the understanding that, for all i, j,

$$u_i + u_j = u_j + u_i \tag{A.4}$$

and

$$u_i + u_i = u_i\,. \tag{A.5}$$

As an extension of this notation, a finite *fuzzy* subset of U is expressed as

$$F = \mu_1 u_1 + \cdots + \mu_n u_n \tag{A.6}$$

or, equivalently, as

$$F = \mu_1/u_1 + \cdots + \mu_n/u_n \tag{A.7}$$

where the μ_i, $i = 1, \ldots, n$, represent the *grades of membership* of the u_i in F. Unless stated to the contrary, the μ_i are assumed to lie in the interval $[0, 1]$, with 0 and 1 denoting *no* membership and *full* membership, respectively.

Consistent with the representation of a finite fuzzy set as a linear form in the u_i, an arbitrary fuzzy subset of U may be expressed in the form of an integral

$$F = \int_U \mu_F(u)/u \tag{A.8}$$

in which $\mu_F : U \to [0,1]$ is the *membership* or, equivalently, the *compatibility function* of F; and the integral $\int_U$ denotes the union (defined by (A.28)) of *fuzzy singletons* $\mu_F(u)/u$ over the universe of discourse U.

The points in U at which $\mu_F(u) > 0$ constitute the *support* of F. The points at which $\mu_F(u) = 0.5$ are the *crossover* points of F.

Example A.9. Assume

$$U = a + b + c + d\,. \tag{A.10}$$

Then, we may have

$$A = a + b + d \tag{A.11}$$

and

$$F = 0.3a + 0.9b + d \tag{A.12}$$

as nonfuzzy and fuzzy subsets of U, respectively.

If

$$U = 0 + 0.1 + 0.2 + \cdots + 1 \tag{A.13}$$

then a fuzzy subset of U would be expressed as, say,

$$F = 0.3/0.5 + 0.6/0.7 + 0.8/0.9 + 1/1 \tag{A.14}$$

If $U = [0,1]$, then F might be expressed as

$$F = \int_0^1 \frac{1}{1+u^2} \Big/ u \tag{A.15}$$

which means that F is a fuzzy subset of the unit interval [0, 1] whose membership function is defined by

$$\mu_F(u) = \frac{1}{1+u^2}\,. \tag{A.16}$$

In many cases, it is convenient to express the membership function of a fuzzy subset of the real line in terms of a standard function whose parameters may be adjusted to fit a specified membership function in an approximate fashion. Two such functions, of the form shown in Fig. A.1, are defined below.

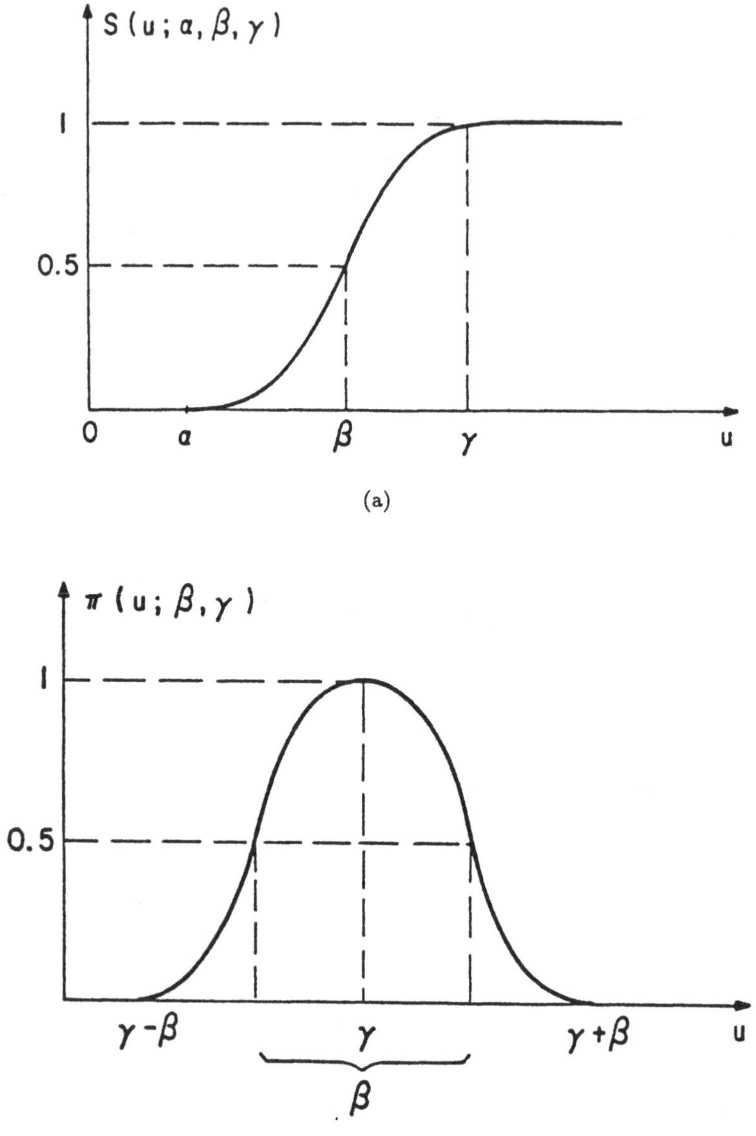

(b)

Fig. A.1. Plots of S and π Functions.

$$
\begin{aligned}
S(u;\alpha,\beta,\gamma) &= 0 && \text{for } u \le \alpha \\
&= 2\left(\frac{u-\alpha}{\gamma-\alpha}\right)^2 && \text{for } \alpha \le u \le \beta \\
&= 1-2\left(\frac{u-\gamma}{\gamma-\alpha}\right)^2 && \text{for } \beta \le u \le \gamma \\
&= 1 && \text{for } u \ge \gamma
\end{aligned}
\tag{A.17}
$$

$$
\begin{aligned}
\pi(u;\ \beta,\ \gamma) &= S\left(u;\gamma-\beta,\gamma-\frac{\beta}{2},\gamma\right) && \text{for } u \le \gamma \\
&= 1 - s\left(u;\gamma,\gamma+\frac{\beta}{2},\gamma+\beta\right) && \text{for } u \ge \gamma\,.
\end{aligned}
\tag{A.18}
$$

In $S(u;\alpha,\beta,\gamma)$, the parameter $\beta, \beta = \frac{\alpha+\gamma}{2}$, is the crossover point. In $\pi(u;\beta,\gamma), \beta$ is the bandwidth, i.e., the separation between the crossover points of π, while γ is the point at which π is unity.

In some cases, the assumption that μ_F is a mapping from U to $[0,1]$ may be too restrictive, and it may be desirable to allow μ_F to take values in a lattice or, more particulary, in a Boolean algebra.[15-17] For most purposes, however, it is sufficient to deal with the first two of the following hierarchy of fuzzy sets.

Definition A.19. A fuzzy subset, F, of U is of *type* 1 if its membership function, μ_F, is a mapping from U to $[0,1]$; and F is of type n, $n = 2,3,\ldots$, if μ_F is a mapping from U to the set of fuzzy subsets of type $n-1$. For simplicity, it will always be understood that F is of type 1 if it is not specified to be of a higher type.

Example A.20. Suppose that U is the set of all nonnegative integers and F is a fuzzy subset of U labeled *small integers*. Then F is of type 1 if the grade of membership of a generic element u in F is a number in the interval $[0,1]$, e.g.,

$$\mu_{small\ integers}(u) = \left(1+\left(\frac{u}{5}\right)^2\right)^{-1} \qquad u = 0,1,2,\ldots\,. \tag{A.21}$$

On the other hand, F is of type 2 if for each u in U, $\mu_F(u)$ is a fuzzy subset of $[0,1]$ of type 1, e.g., for $u = 10$,

$$\mu_{small\ integers}(10) = low \tag{A.22}$$

where *low* is a fuzzy subset of $[0,1]$ whose membership function is defined by, say,

$$\mu_{low}(v) = 1 - S(v;0,0.25,0.5), \quad v \in [0,1] \tag{A.23}$$

which implies that

$$low = \int_0^1 (1 - S(v;0,0.25,0.5))/v\,. \tag{A.24}$$

If F is a fuzzy subset of U, then its *α-level-set*, F_α, is a nonfuzzy subset of U defined by[18]

$$F_\alpha = \{u \mid \mu_F(u) \geq \alpha\} \tag{A.25}$$

for $0 < \alpha \leq 1$.

If u is a linear vector space, the F is *convex* iff for all $\lambda \in [0, 1]$ and all u_1, u_2 in U,

$$\mu_F(\lambda u_1 + (1-\lambda)u_2) \geq \min(\mu_F(u_1),\ \mu_F(u_2))\,. \tag{A.26}$$

In terms of the level-sets of F, F is convex iff the F_α are convex for all $\alpha \in [0, 1]$.[m]

The relation of containment for fuzzy subsets F and G of U is defined by

$$F \subset G \Longleftrightarrow \mu_F(u) \leq \mu_G(u), \quad u \in U\,. \tag{A.27}$$

Thus, F is a fuzzy subset of G if (A.27) holds for all u in U.

Operations on fuzzy sets

If F and G are fuzzy subsets of U, their *union*, $F \cup G$, *intersection*, $F \cap G$, *bounded-sum*, $F \oplus G$, and *bounded-difference*, $F \ominus G$, are fuzzy subsets of U defined by

$$F \cup G \triangleq \int_U \mu_F(u) \vee \mu_G(u)/u \tag{A.28}$$

$$F \cup G = \int_U \mu_F(u) \wedge \mu_G(u)/u \tag{A.29}$$

$$F \oplus G = \int_U 1 \wedge (\mu_F(u) + \mu_G(u))/u \tag{A.30}$$

$$F \ominus G = \int_U 0 \vee (\mu_F(u) - \mu_G(u))/u \tag{A.31}$$

where $\wedge$ and $\vee$ denote max and min, respectively. The *complement* of F is defined by

$$F' = \int_U (1 - \mu_F(u))/u \tag{A.32}$$

or, equivalently,

$$F' = U \ominus F\,. \tag{A.33}$$

It can readily be shown that F and G satisfy the identities

$$(F \cap G)' = F' \cup G' \tag{A.34}$$

$$(F \cup G)' = F' \cap G' \tag{A.35}$$

$$(F \oplus G)' = F' \ominus G \tag{A.36}$$

$$(F \ominus G)' = F' \oplus G \tag{A.37}$$

[m]This definition of convexity can readily be extended to fuzzy sets of type 2 by applying the extension principle (see (A.75)) to (A.26).

and that F satisfies the resolution identity[2]

$$F = \int_0^1 \alpha F_\alpha \tag{A.38}$$

where F_α is the α-level-set of F; αF_α is a set whose membership function is $\mu_{\alpha F_\alpha} = \alpha\mu_{F_\alpha}$, and $\int_0^1$ denotes the union of the αF, with $\alpha \in (0, 1]$.

Although it is traditional to use the symbol $\cup$ to denote the union of nonfuzzy sets, in the case of fuzzy sets it is advantageous to use the symbol $+$ in place of $\cup$ where no confusion with the arithmetic sum can result. This convention is employed in the following example, which is intended to illustrate (A.28), (A.29), (A.30), (A.31) and (A.32).

Example A.39. For U defined by (A.10) and F and G expressed by

$$F = 0.4a + 0.9b + d \tag{A.40}$$

$$G = 0.6a + 0.5b \tag{A.41}$$

we have

$$F + G = 0.6a + 0.9b + d \tag{A.42}$$

$$F \cap G = 0.4a + 0.5b \tag{A.43}$$

$$F \oplus G = a + b + d \tag{A.44}$$

$$F \ominus G = 0.4b + d \tag{A.45}$$

$$F' = 0.6a + 0.1b + c \tag{A.46}$$

The linguistic connectives *and* (conjunction) and *or* (disjunction) are identified with $\cap$ and $+$, respectively. Thus,

$$F \textit{ and } G \triangleq F \cap G \tag{A.47}$$

and

$$F \textit{ or } G \triangleq F + G\,. \tag{A.48}$$

As defined by (A.47) and (A.48), *and* and *or* are implied to be *noninteractive* in the sense that there is no "trade-off" between their operands. When this is not the case, *and* and *or* are denoted by $\langle \textit{and} \rangle$ and $\langle \textit{or} \rangle$, respectively, and are defined in a way that reflects the nature of the trade-off. For example, we may have

$$F \langle \textit{and} \rangle G \triangleq \int_U \mu_F(u)\mu_G(u)/u \tag{A.49}$$

$$F \langle \textit{or} \rangle G \triangleq \int_U (\mu_F(u) + \mu_G(u) - \mu_F(u)\mu_G(u))/u \tag{A.50}$$

whose + denotes the arithmetic sum. In general, the interactive versions of *and* and *or* do not possess the simplifying properties of the connectives defined by (A.47) and (A.48), e.g., associativity, distributivity, etc. (See Ref. 4.)

If α is a real number, then F^α is defined by

$$F^\alpha \triangleq \int_U (\mu_F(u))^\alpha / u \,. \tag{A.51}$$

For example, for the fuzzy set defined by (A.40), we have

$$F^2 = 0.16a + 0.81b + d \tag{A.52}$$

and

$$F^{1/2} = 0.63a + 0.95b + d \,. \tag{A.53}$$

These operations may be used to approximate, very roughly, to the effect of the linguistic modifiers *very* and *more or less.* Thus,

$$\textit{very}\ F \triangleq F^2 \tag{A.54}$$

and

$$\textit{more or less}\ F \triangleq F^{1/2} \,. \tag{A.55}$$

If $F_1, \ldots, F_n$ are fuzzy subsets of $U_1, \ldots, U_n$ then the *cartesian product* of $F_1, \ldots,$ F_n is a fuzzy subset of $U_1 \times \cdots \times U_n$ defined by

$$F_1 \times \cdots \times F_n = \int_{U_1 \times \cdots \times U_n} (\mu_{F_1}(u_1) \wedge \cdots \wedge \mu_{F_n}(u_n))/(u_1, \ldots, u_n) \,. \tag{A.56}$$

As an illustration, for the fuzzy sets defined by (A.40) and (A.41), we have

$$\begin{aligned} F \times G &= (0.4a + 0.9b + d) \times (0.6a + 0.5b) \\ &= 0.4/(a,a) + 0.4/(a,b) + 0.6/(b,a) \\ &\quad + 0.5/(b,b) + 0.6/(d,a) + 0.5/(d,b) \end{aligned} \tag{A.57}$$

which is a fuzzy subset of $(a + b + c + d) \times (a + b + c + d)$.

Fuzzy relations

An n-ary *fuzzy relation* R in $U_1 \times \cdots \times U_n$ is a fuzzy subset of $U_1 \times \cdots \times U_n$. The *projection of* R *on* $U_{i_1} \times \cdots \times U_{i_k}$, where $(i_1, \ldots, i_k)$ is a subsequence of $(1, \ldots, n)$, is a relation in $U_{i_1} \times \cdots \times U_{i_k}$ defined by

$$\text{Proj } R \text{ on } U_{i_1} \times \cdots \times U_{i_k} \triangleq \int_{U_{i_1} \times \cdots \times U_{i_k}} \vee_{u_{j_1}, \ldots, u_{j_\ell}} \mu_R(u_1, \ldots, u_n)/(u_1, \ldots, u_n) \tag{A.58}$$

where $(j_1, \ldots, j_\ell)$ is the sequence complementary to $(i_1, \ldots, i_k)$ (e.g., if $n = 6$ then (1, 3, 6) is complementary to (2, 4, 5)), and $\vee_{u_{j_1}, \ldots, u_{j_\ell}}$ denotes the supremum over $U_{j_1} \times \cdots \times U_{j_\ell}$.

If R is a fuzzy subset of $U_{i_1}, \ldots, U_{i_k}$, then its *cylindrical extension* in $U_1 \times \cdots \times U_n$ is a fuzzy subset of $U_1 \times \cdots \times U_n$ defined by

$$\bar{R} = \int_{U_1 \times \cdots \times U_n} \mu_R(u_{i_1}, \ldots, u_{i_k})/(u_1, \ldots, u_n) \,. \tag{A.59}$$

In terms of their cylindrical extensions, the *composition* of two binary relations R and S (in $U_1 \times U_2$ and $U_2 \times U_3$, respectively) is expressed by

$$R \circ S = \text{Proj } \bar{R} \cap \bar{S} \text{ on } U_1 \times U_3 \tag{A.60}$$

where $\bar{R}$ and $\bar{S}$ are the cylindrical extensions of R and S in $U_1 \times U_2 \times U_3$. Similarly, if R is a binary relation in $U_1 \times U_2$ and S is a unary relation in U_2, their composition is given by

$$R \circ S = \text{Proj } R \cap \bar{S} \text{ on } U_1 \,. \tag{A.61}$$

Example A.62. Let R be defined by the right-hand member of (A.57) and

$$S = 0.4a + b + 0.8d \,. \tag{A.63}$$

Then

$$\text{Proj } R \text{ on } U_1 (\triangleq \; a + b + c + d) = 0.4a + 0.6b + 0.6d \tag{A.64}$$

and

$$R \circ S = 0.4a + 0.5b + 0.5d \tag{A.65}$$

Linguistic variables

Informally, a linguistic variable, $\mathcal{X}$, is a variable whose values are words or sentences in a natural or artificial language. For example, if *age* is interpreted as a linguistic variable, then its *term-set*, $T(\mathcal{X})$, that is, the set of its linguistic values, might be

$$\begin{aligned} T(\textit{age}) &= \textit{young} + \textit{old} + \textit{very young} + \textit{not young} \\ &\quad + \textit{very old} + \textit{very very young} \\ &\quad + \textit{rather young} + \textit{more or less young} + \ldots \,. \end{aligned} \tag{A.66}$$

where each of the terms in $T(\textit{age})$ is a label of a fuzzy subset of a universe of discourse, say $U = [0, 100]$.

A linguistic variable is associated with two rules: (a) a *syntactic rule*, which defines the well-formed sentences in $T(\mathcal{X})$; and (b) a *semantic rule*, by which the meaning of the terms in $T(\mathcal{X})$ may be determined. If x is a term in $T(\mathcal{X})$, then its *meaning* (in a denotational sense) is a subset of U. A *primary term* in $T(\mathcal{X})$ is a term whose meaning is a *primary fuzzy set*, that is, a term whose meaning must be defined *a priori*, and which serves as a basis for the computation of the meaning of the nonprimary terms in $T(\mathcal{X})$. For example, the primary terms in (A.66) are *young* and *old*, whose meaning might be defined by their respective compatibility functions μ_{young} and μ_{old}. From these, then, the meaning — or, equivalently, the compatibility functions — of the non-primary terms in (A.66) may be computed by the application of a semantic rule. For example, employing (A.54) and (A.55), we have

$$\mu_{very\ young} = (\mu_{young})^2 \tag{A.67}$$

$$\mu_{more\ or\ less\ old} = (\mu_{old})^{1/2} \tag{A.68}$$

$$\mu_{not\ very\ young} = 1 - (\mu_{young})^2 . \tag{A.69}$$

For illustration, plots of the compatibility functions of these terms are shown in Fig. A.2.

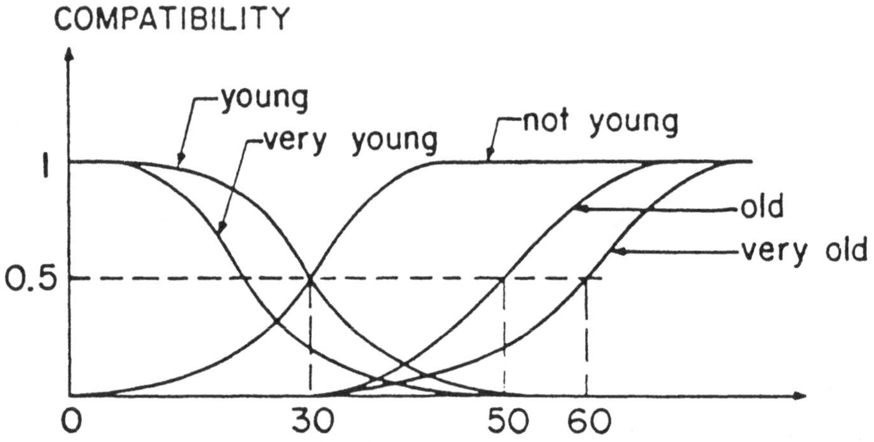

Fig. A.2. Compatibility Function of *young* and its Modifications.

The extension principle

Let f be a mapping from U to V. Thus,

$$v = f(u) \tag{A.70}$$

where u and v are generic elements of U and V, respectively.

Let F be a fuzzy subset of U expressed as

$$F = \mu_1 u_1 + \cdots + \mu_n u_n \tag{A.71}$$

or, more generally,

$$F = \int_U \mu_F(u)/u . \tag{A.72}$$

By the extension principle,[3] the image of F under f is given by

$$f(F) = \mu_1 f(u_1) + \cdots + \mu_n f(u_n) \tag{A.73}$$

or, more generally,

$$f(F) = \int_U \mu_F(u)/f(u) \tag{A.74}$$

Similarly, if f is a mapping from $U \times V$ to W, and F and G are fuzzy subsets of U and V, respectively, then

$$f(F,\ G) = \int_W (\mu_F(u) \wedge \mu_G(v))/f(u,v)\,. \tag{A.75}$$

Example A.76. Assume that f is the operation of squaring. Then, for the set defined by (A.14), we have

$$f(0.3/0.5+0.6/0.7+0.8/0.9+1/1) = 0.3/0.25+0.6/0.49+0.8/0.81+1/1\,. \tag{A.77}$$

Similarly, for the binary operation $\vee$ ($\triangleq$ max), we have

$$(0.9/0.1 + 0.2/0.5 + 1/1) \vee (0.3/0.2 + 0.8/0.6) = 0.3/0.2 + 0.2/0.5 + 0.8/1 + 0.8/0.6 + 0.2/0.6\,. \tag{A.78}$$

It should be noted that the operation of squaring in (A.77) is different from that of (A.51) and (A.52).

L. A. ZADEH*

FUZZY LOGIC AND APPROXIMATE REASONING

(In Memory of Grigore Moisil)

ABSTRACT. The term *fuzzy logic* is used in this paper to describe an imprecise logical system, FL, in which the truth-values are fuzzy subsets of the unit interval with linguistic labels such as *true, false, not true, very true, quite true, not very true and not very false*, etc. The truth-value set, $\mathcal{T}$, of FL is assumed to be generated by a context-free grammar, with a semantic rule providing a means of computing the meaning of each linguistic truth-value in $\mathcal{T}$ as a fuzzy subset of [0, 1].

Since $\mathcal{T}$ is not closed under the operations of negation, conjunction, disjunction and implication, the result of an operation on truth-values in $\mathcal{T}$ requires, in general, a linguistic approximation by a truth-value in $\mathcal{T}$. As a consequence, the truth tables and the rules of inference in fuzzy logic are (i) inexact and (ii) dependent on the meaning associated with the primary truth-value *true* as well as the modifiers *very, quite, more or less*, etc.

Approximate reasoning is viewed as a process of approximate solution of a system of relational assignment equations. This process is formulated as a compositional rule of inference which subsumes *modus ponens* as a special case. A characteristic feature of approximate reasoning is the fuzziness and nonuniqueness of consequents of fuzzy premisses. Simple examples of approximate reasoning are: (a) *Most* men are *vain*; Socrates is a man; therefore, it is *very likely* that Socrates is *vain*. (b) x is *small*; x and y are *approximately equal*; therefore y is *more or less small*, where italicized words are labels of fuzzy sets.

1. INTRODUCTION

It is a truism that much of human reasoning is approximate rather than precise in nature. As a case in point, we reason in approximate terms when we decide on how to cross a traffic intersection, which route to take to a desired destination, how much to bet in poker and what approach to use in proving a theorem. Indeed, it could be argued, rather convincingly, that only a small fraction of our thinking could be categorized as precise in either logical or quantitative terms.

Perhaps the simplest way of characterizing fuzzy logic is to say that it is a logic of approximate reasoning. As such, it is a logic whose distinguishing features are (i) fuzzy truth-values expressed in linguistic terms, e.g., *true, very true, more or less true, rather true, not true, false, not very true and not very false,* etc.; (ii) imprecise truth tables; and (iii) rules of inference whose validity is approximate rather than exact. In these respects, fuzzy logic differs significantly from standard logical systems ranging from

Reprinted, with permission, from *Synthese*, **30**, pp. 407–428.

the classical Aristotelian logic [1] to inductive logics [2] and many-valued logics with set-valued truth-values [3].

An elementary example of approximate reasoning in fuzzy logic is the following variation on a familiar Aristotelian syllogism.

A_1 : *Most* men are *vain* (1.1)
A_2 : Socrates is a man

A_3 : It is *likely* that Socrates is *vain*

or

A_3' : It is *very likely* that Socrates is *vain*

In this example, both A_3 and A_3' are admissible approximate consequents of A_1 and A_2, with the degree of approximation depending on the definitions of the terms *most, likely* and *very* as fuzzy subsets of their respective universes of discourse. For example, assume that *most* and *likely* are defined as fuzzy subsets of the unit interval by compatibility functions[1] of the form shown in Figure 1, and let *very* be defined as a modifier which squares the compatibility function of its operand. Then A_3' is a better approximation than A_3 to the exact consequent of A_1 and

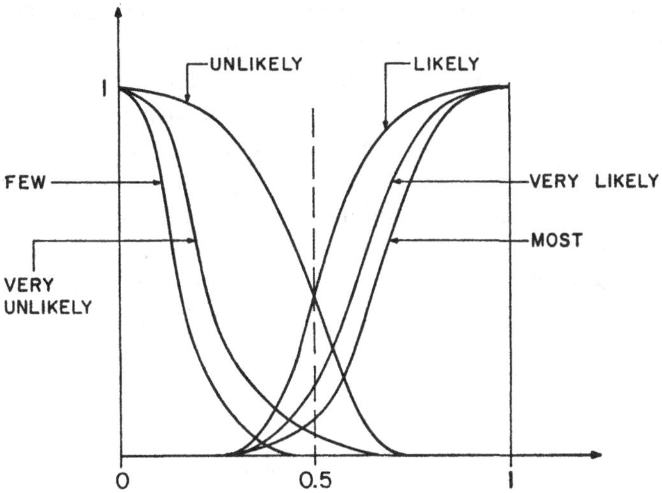

Fig. 1. Compatibility functions (not to scale) of *most, likely, very likely, unlikely, few* and *very unlikely*. Note that *unlikely* and *likely* are symmetric with respect to u=0.5; *very likely* is the square of *likely*; and *very unlikely* is the square of *unlikely*.

A_2 provided *very likely*, as a fuzzy subset of [0, 1], is a better approximation than *likely* to the fuzzy subset *most*. This is assumed to be the case in Figure 1.

Additional examples of approximate reasoning in fuzzy logic are the following. (u_1 and u_2 are numbers.)

$$\frac{\begin{array}{l} A_1 : u_1 \text{ is } \textit{small} \\ A_2 : u_1 \text{ and } u_2 \text{ are } \textit{approximately equal} \end{array}}{A_3 : u_2 \text{ is } \textit{more or less small}} \tag{1.2}$$

$$\frac{\begin{array}{l} A_1 : (u_1 \text{ is } \textit{small}) \text{ is } \textit{very true} \\ A_2 : (u_1 \text{ and } u_2 \text{ are } \textit{approximately equal}) \text{ is } \textit{very true} \end{array}}{A_3 : (u_2 \text{ is } \textit{more or less small}) \text{ is } \textit{true}} \tag{1.3}$$

The italicized words in these examples represent labels of fuzzy sets. Thus, a fuzzy proposition of the form 'u_1 is *small*', represents the assignment of a fuzzy set (or, equivalently, a unary fuzzy relation) labeled *small* as a value of u_1. Similarly, the fuzzy proposition 'u_1 and u_2 are *approximately equal*', represents the assignment of a binary fuzzy relation *approximately equal* to the ordered pair (u_1, u_2). And, the nested fuzzy proposition '(u_1 is *small*) is *very true*', represents the assignment of a fuzzy truth-value *very true* to the fuzzy proposition (u_1 is *small*).

As will be seen in Section 3, the above examples may be viewed as special instances of a model of reasoning in which the process of inference involves the solution of a system of relational assignment equations. Thus, in terms of this model, *approximate* reasoning may be viewed as the determination of an *approximate* solution of a system of relational assignment equations in which the assigned relations are generally, but not necessarily, fuzzy rather than nonfuzzy subsets of a universe of discourse.

In what follows, we shall outline in greater detail some of the main ideas which form the basis for fuzzy logic and approximate reasoning. Our presentation will be informal in nature.

2. Fuzzy logic

A fuzzy logic, FL, may be viewed, in part, as a fuzzy extension of a nonfuzzy multi-valued logic which constitutes a *base* logic for FL. For our purposes, it will be convenient to use as a base logic for FL the standard Łukasiewicz logic L_1 (abbreviated from L_{Aleph_1}) in which the truth-values are real numbers in the interval [0, 1] and [2]

$$v(\neg p) \triangleq 1 - v(p) \tag{2.1}$$

$$v(p \vee q) \triangleq \max(v(p), v(q)) \tag{2.2}$$

$$v(p \wedge q) = \min(v(p), v(q)) \tag{2.3}$$

$$v(p \Rightarrow q) = \min(1, 1 - v(p) + v(q)) \tag{2.4}$$

where $v(p)$ denotes the truth-value of a proposition p, $\neg$ is the negation, $\wedge$ is the conjunction, $\vee$ is the disjunction and $\Rightarrow$ is the implication. In what follows, however, it will be more convenient to denote the negation, conjunction and disjunction by *not*, *and* and *or*, respectively, reserving the symbols $\neg$, $\wedge$ and $\vee$ to denote operations on truth-values, with $\wedge \triangleq \min$ and $\vee \triangleq \max$.

The truth-value set of FL

The truth-value set of FL is assumed to be a countable set $\mathscr{T}$ of the form

$$\mathscr{T} = \{\textit{true}, \textit{false}, \textit{not true}, \textit{very true}, \textit{not very true}, \textit{more or less true}, \textit{rather true}, \textit{not very true and not very false}, \ldots\} \tag{2.5}$$

Each element of this set represents a fuzzy subset of the truth-value set of L_1, i.e., [0, 1]. Thus, the *meaning* of a linguistic truth-value, τ, in $\mathscr{T}$ is assumed to be a fuzzy subset of [0, 1].

More specifically, let μ_τ: [0, 1] → [0, 1] denote the compatibility (or membership) function of τ. Then the meaning of τ, as a fuzzy subset of [0, 1], is expressed by

$$\tau = \int_0^1 \mu_\tau(v)/v \tag{2.6}$$

where the integral sign denotes the union of fuzzy singletons $\mu_\tau(v)/v$, with $\mu_\tau(v)/v$ signifying that the compatibility of the numerical truth-value v with the linguistic truth-value τ is $\mu_\tau(v)$, or, equivalently, that the grade of membership of v in the fuzzy set labeled τ is $\mu_\tau(v)$.

If the support[3] of τ is a finite subset $\{v_1, \dots, v_n\}$ of [0, 1], τ may be expressed as

$$\tau = \mu_1/v_1 + \cdots + \mu_n/v_n \tag{2.7}$$

or more simply as

$$\tau = \mu_1 v_1 + \cdots + \mu_n v_n \tag{2.8}$$

when no confusion between μ_i and v_i in a term of the form $\mu_i v_i$ can arise. Note that + in (2.7) plays the role of the union rather than the arithmetic sum.

As a simple illustration, suppose that the meaning of *true* is defined by

$$\begin{aligned} \mu_{true}(v) &= 0 && \text{for } 0 \leqslant v \leqslant \alpha \\ &= 2\left(\frac{v-\alpha}{1-\alpha}\right)^2 && \text{for } \alpha \leqslant v \leqslant \frac{\alpha+1}{2} \\ &= 1 - 2\left(\frac{v-1}{1-\alpha}\right)^2 && \text{for } \frac{\alpha+1}{2} \leqslant v \leqslant 1 \end{aligned} \tag{2.9}$$

where α is a point in [0, 1].

Then, we may write

$$true \triangleq \int_{\alpha}^{\frac{1}{2}(\alpha+1)} 2\left(\frac{v-\alpha}{1-\alpha}\right)^2 \Big/ v + \int_{\frac{1}{2}(\alpha+1)}^{1} \left(1 - 2\left(\frac{v-1}{1-\alpha}\right)^2\right) \Big/ v \tag{2.10}$$

If $v_1 = 0, v_2 = 0.1, \dots, v_{11} = 1$, then *true* might be defined by, say,

$$true = 0.3/0.6 + 0.5/0.7 + 0.7/0.8 + 0.9/0.9 + 1/1 \tag{2.11}$$

In terms of the meaning of *true*, the truth-value *false* may be defined as

$$false \triangleq \int_0^1 \mu_{true}(1-v)/v \tag{2.12}$$

while *not true* is given by

$$not\ true = \int_0^1 (1 - \mu_{true}(v))/v \tag{2.13}$$

Thus, as a fuzzy set, *not true* is the complement of *true* whereas *false* is the truth-value of the proposition *not p*, if *true* is the truth-value of *p*. In the case of (2.11), this implies that

$$\textit{false} \triangleq \neg\, \textit{true} = 1/0 + 0.9/0.1 + 0.7/0.2 + 0.5/0.3 + 0.3/0.4$$

and (2.14)

$$\textit{not true} \triangleq \textit{true}' = 1/(0 + 0.1 + 0.2 + 0.3 + 0.4 + 0.5) + 0.7/0.6 + 0.5/0.7 + 0.3/0.8 + 0.1/0.9 \quad (2.15)$$

where $\neg$ stands for negation and $'$ denotes the complement (see note 5).

More generally, the truth-value set of FL is characterized by two rules: (i) a *syntactic rule*, which we shall assume to have the form of a context-free grammar G such that

$$\mathcal{T} = \mathrm{L(G)} \quad (2.16)$$

that is, $\mathcal{T}$ is the language generated by G; and (ii) a *semantic rule*, which is an algorithmic procedure for computing the meaning of the elements of $\mathcal{T}$. Generally, we shall assume that $\mathcal{T}$ contains one or more *primary terms* (e.g., *true*) whose meaning is specified *a priori* and which form the basis for the computation of the meaning of the other terms in $\mathcal{T}$. The truth-values in $\mathcal{T}$ are referred to as *linguistic* truth-values in order to differentiate them from the numerical truth-values of L_1.

Example 2.17. As a simple illustration, suppose that $\mathcal{T}$ is of the form

$$\mathcal{T} = \{\textit{true}, \textit{false}, \textit{not true}, \textit{very true}, \textit{very very true}, \textit{not very true}, \textit{not true and not false}, \textit{true and (not false or not true)}, \ldots\} \quad (2.18)$$

It can readily be verified that $\mathcal{T}$ can be generated by a context-free grammar G whose production system is given by

$$\begin{array}{ll}
\mathrm{T} \to \mathrm{A} & \mathrm{C} \to \mathrm{D} \\
\mathrm{T} \to \mathrm{T}\ \textit{or}\ \mathrm{A} & \mathrm{C} \to \mathrm{E} \\
\mathrm{A} \to \mathrm{B} & \mathrm{D} \to \textit{very}\ \mathrm{D} \\
\mathrm{A} \to \mathrm{A}\ \textit{and}\ \mathrm{B} & \mathrm{E} \to \textit{very}\ \mathrm{E} \\
\mathrm{B} \to \mathrm{C} & \mathrm{D} \to \textit{true} \\
\mathrm{B} \to \textit{not}\ \mathrm{C} & \mathrm{E} \to \textit{false} \\
\mathrm{C} \to (\mathrm{T}) &
\end{array} \quad (2.19)$$

In this grammar, T, A, B, C, D and E are nonterminals; and *true*, *false*, *very*, *not*, *and*, *or*, (,) are terminals. Thus, a typical derivation yields

$$\begin{aligned} T &\Rightarrow A \Rightarrow A \textit{ and } B \Rightarrow B \textit{ and } B \Rightarrow \textit{not } C \textit{ and } B \Rightarrow \textit{not } E \textit{ and } B \\ &\Rightarrow \textit{not very } E \textit{ and } B \Rightarrow \textit{not very false and } B \Rightarrow \textit{not very false} \\ &\quad \textit{and not } C \Rightarrow \textit{not very false and not } D \Rightarrow \textit{not very false and} \\ &\quad \textit{not very } D \Rightarrow \textit{not very false and not very true}. \end{aligned} \tag{2.20}$$

If the syntactic rule for generating the elements of $\mathcal{T}$ is expressed as a context-free grammar, then the corresponding semantic rule may be conveniently expressed by a system of productions and relations in which each production in G is associated with a relation between the fuzzy subsets representing the meaning of the terminals and nonterminals [5].[4] For example, the production A → A *and* B induces the relation

$$A_L = A_R \cap B_R \tag{2.21}$$

where A_L, A_R, and B_R represent the meaning of A and B as fuzzy subsets of [0, 1] (the subscripts L and R serve to differentiate between the symbols on the left- and right-hand sides of a production), and ∩ denotes the intersection.[5] Thus, in effect, (2.21) defines the meaning of the connective *and*.

With this understanding, the dual system corresponding to (2.19) may be written as

$$\begin{array}{lcl} T \to A & : & T_L = A_R \\ T \to T \textit{ or } A & : & T_L = T_R \cup A_R \\ A \to B & : & A_L = B_R \\ A \to A \textit{ and } B & : & A_L = A_R \cap B_R \\ B \to C & : & B_L = C_R \\ B \to \textit{not } C & : & B_L = C'_R \\ C \to (T) & : & C_L = T_R \\ C \to D & : & C_L = D_R \\ C \to E & : & C_L = E_R \\ D \to \textit{very } D & : & D_L = (D_R)^2 \\ E \to \textit{very } E & : & E_L = (E_R)^2 \\ D \to \textit{true} & : & D_L = \textit{true} \\ E \to \textit{false} & : & E_L = \textit{false} \end{array} \tag{2.22}$$

This dual system is employed in the following manner to compute the meaning of a composite truth-value in $\mathcal{T}$.

1. The truth-value in question, e.g., *not very true and not very false*, is parsed by the use of an appropriate parsing algorithm for G [9], yielding a syntax tree such as shown in Figure 2. The leaves of this syntax tree are (a) primary terms whose meaning is specified a priori; (b) names of modifiers, connectives and negation; and (c) markers such as parentheses which serve as aids to parsing.

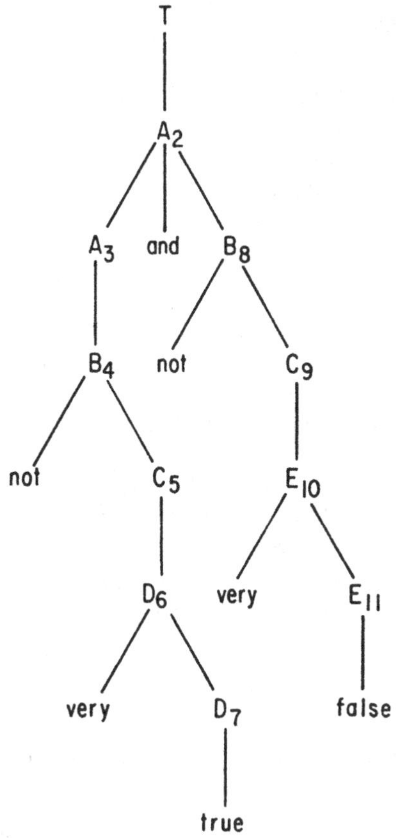

Fig. 2. Syntax tree for the linguistic truth-value *not very true and not very false*.

2. Starting from the bottom, the primary terms are assigned their meaning and, using the equations of (2.22), the meaning of nonterminals connected to the leaves is computed. Then, the subtrees which have these nonterminals as their roots are deleted, leaving the nonterminals in

question as the leaves of the pruned tree. This process is repeated until the meaning of the term associated with the root of the syntax tree is derived.[6]

In applying this procedure to the syntax tree shown in Figure 2, we first assign to *true* and *false* the meaning expressed by (2.6) and (2.12). Then, we obtain in succession

$$\begin{aligned}
D_7 &= true \\
E_{11} &= false \\
D_6 = D_7^2 &= true^2 \\
E_{10} = E_{11}^2 &= false^2 \\
C_5 = D_6 &= true^2 \\
C_9 = E_{10} &= false^2 \\
B_4 = C_5' &= (true^2)' \\
B_8 = C_9' &= (false^2)' \\
A_3 = B_4 &= (true^2)' \\
A_2 = A_3 \cap B_8 &= (true^2)' \cap (false^2)'
\end{aligned} \tag{2.23}$$

and finally,

$$\textit{not very true and not very false} = (true^2)' \cap (false^2)' \tag{2.24}$$

where $\mu_{true^2} = (\mu_{true})^2$ and likewise for μ_{false^2}. (See note 5.)

It should be noted that the truth-values in (2.18) involve just one modifier, *very*, whose meaning is characterized by (2.22). As defined by (2.22), *very* has the effect of squaring the compatibility function of its operand. This simple approximation should not be viewed, of course, as an accurate representation of the complex and rather varied ways in which *very* modifies the meaning of its operands in a natural language discourse.

In addition to *very*, the more important of the modifiers which may be of use in generating the linguistic truth-values in $\mathscr{T}$ are: *more or less*, *rather*, *quite*, *essentially*, *completely*, *somewhat*, and *slightly*. As in the case of *very*, the meaning of such modifiers may be defined – as a first approximation – in terms of a set of standardized operations on the fuzzy sets representing their operands.[7] Better approximations, however, would require the use of algorithmic techniques in which a definition is expressed as a fuzzy recognition algorithm which has the form of a branching questionnaire [12].

What is the rationale for using the linguistic truth-values of FL in preference to the numerical truth-values of L_1? At first glance, it may appear that we are moving in a wrong direction, since it is certainly easier to manipulate the real numbers in [0, 1] than the fuzzy subsets of [0, 1]. The answer is two-fold. First, the truth-value set of L_1 is a continuum whereas that of FL is a countable set. More importantly, in most applications to approximate reasoning, a small finite subset of the truth-values of FL would, in general, be sufficient because each truth-value of FL represents a fuzzy subset rather than a single element of [0, 1]. Thus, we gain by trading the large number of simple truth-values of L_1 for the small number of less simple truth-values of FL.

The second and related point is that approximate reasoning deals, for the most part, with propositions which are fuzzy rather than precise, e.g., 'Vera is *highly intelligent*', 'Douglas is *very inventive*', 'Berkeley is *close* to San Francisco', 'It is *very likely* that Jean-Paul will *succeed*', etc. Clearly, the fuzzy truth-values of FL are more commensurate with the fuzziness of such propositions than the numerical truth-values of L_1.

Operations on linguistic truth-values

So far, we have focused our attention on the structure of the truth-value set of FL. We turn next to some of the basic questions relating to the manipulation of linguistic truth-values which are lables of fuzzy subsets of [0, 1].

To extend the definitions of negation, conjunction, disjuction and implications in L_1 to those of FL, it is convenient to employ an extension principle for fuzzy sets which may be stated as follows [4].[8]

Let f be a mapping from V to W and let A be a fuzzy subset of V expressed as

$$A = \int_V \mu_A(v)/v \tag{2.25}$$

or, in the finite case, as

$$A = \mu_1 v_1 + \cdots + \mu_n v_n \tag{2.26}$$

where μ_A is the compatibility function of A, with $\mu_A(v)$ and μ_i denoting, respectively, the compatibilities of v and v_i, $i=1,\ldots,n$, with A.

Then, the image of A under f is a fuzzy subset, $f(A)$, of W defined by

$$f(A) = \int_W \mu_A(v)/f(v) \tag{2.27}$$

or, in the case of (2.26),

$$f(A) = \mu_1 f(v_1) + \cdots + \mu_n f(v_n) \tag{2.28}$$

where $w = f(v)$ is the image of v under f. In effect, (2.27) and (2.28) extend the domain of definition of f from points in V to fuzzy subsets of V.

More generally, let $*$ denote a mapping (or a relation) from the cartesian product $U \times V$ to W. Thus, expressed in infix form, we have

$$w = u * v, \quad u \in U, \quad v \in V, \quad w \in W \tag{2.29}$$

where w is the image of u and v under $*$.

Let A and B be fuzzy subsets of U and V, respectively, expressed as

$$A = \int_U \mu_A(u)/u \tag{2.30}$$

or

$$B = \int_V \mu_B(v)/v \tag{2.31}$$

$$A = \mu_1 u_1 + \cdots + \mu_m u_m \tag{2.32}$$

$$B = \nu_1 v_1 + \cdots + \nu_n v_n \tag{2.33}$$

Then, the image of $A \times B$ under $*$ is a fuzzy subset, $A * B$, of W defined by

$$A * B = \int_W (\mu_A(u) \wedge \mu_B(v))/(u*v) \tag{2.34}$$

or, in the case of (2.32) and (2.33),

$$A * B = \sum_{i,j} (\mu_i \wedge \nu_j)/u_i * v_j, \qquad i = 1, \ldots, m, \quad j = 1, \ldots, n \tag{2.35}$$

provided u and v are noninteractive [4] in the sense that the assignment of a value to u does not affect the values that may be assigned to v, and vice-versa. A convenient feature of (2.35) is that the expression for $A*B$ may be obtained quite readily through term by term multiplication of (2.32) and (2.33), and employing the identities

$$(\mu_i u_i)*(\nu_j v_j) = (\mu_i \wedge \nu_j)/u_i * v_j \tag{2.36}$$

and

$$\alpha_k w_k + \beta_k w_k = (\alpha_k \vee \beta_k)\, w_k \tag{2.37}$$

for combination and simplification.

To apply the extension principle to the definition of negation, conjunction, disjuction and implication in FL, it is expedient to use (2.8), since it is easy to extend the resulting definitions to the case where the truth-values are of the form (2.6).

Specifically, let p and q be fuzzy propositions whose truth-values are fuzzy sets of the form

$$v(p) = \mu_1 v_1 + \cdots + \mu_m v_m \tag{2.38}$$

$$v(q) = \nu_1 v_1 + \cdots + \nu_n v_n \tag{2.39}$$

For example, p might be 'Eugenia is *very kind*', with the truth-value of p being *very true*, while q might be 'Fania was *very healthy*', with the truth-value of q being *more or less true*.

Applying (2.28) to (2.38), the expression for the truth-value of the proposition *not p* is found to be

$$v(\textit{not } p) = \mu_1/(1 - v_1) + \cdots + \mu_m/(1 - v_m) \tag{2.40}$$

For example, if *true* is defined by (2.11) and $v(p) = \textit{very true}$, then

$$\textit{very true} = 0.09/0.6 + 0.25/0.7 + 0.49/0.8 + 0.81/0.9 + 1/1 \tag{2.41}$$

and

$$v(\textit{not } p) = 0.09/0.4 + 0.25/0.3 + 0.49/0.2 + 0.81/0.1 + 1/0 \tag{2.42}$$

which in view of (2.14) may be expressed as

$$v(\textit{not } p) = \textit{very false} \tag{2.43}$$

In this example, the truth-value of *not p* is an element of $\mathcal{T}$. In general, however, this will not be the case, so that a fuzzy truth-value, ϕ, obtained as a result of application of (2.28) or (2.35) would normally have to be approximated by a linguistic truth-value, ϕ^*, which is in $\mathscr{T}$. The relation between ϕ^* and ϕ will be expressed as

$$\phi^* = \text{LA}[\phi] \tag{2.44}$$

where LA is an abbreviation for *linguistic approximation.* Note that a linguistic approximation to a given ϕ will not, in general, be unique.[9]

At present, there is no simple or general technique for finding a 'good' linguistic approximation to a given fuzzy subset of V. In most cases, such an approximation has to be found by ad hoc procedures, without a precisely defined criterion of the 'goodness' of approximation. In view of this, the standards of precision in computations involving linguistic truth-values are, in general, rather low. This, however, is entirely consistent with the imprecise nature of fuzzy logic and its role in approximate reasoning.

Turning to the definitions of conjunction, disjunction and implication[10] in FL, we obtain on application of (2.35) to (2.2), (2.3) and (2.4)

$$\begin{aligned} v(p \text{ and } q) &= \text{LA}[v(p) \wedge v(q)] \\ &= \text{LA}[(\mu_1 u_1 + \cdots + \mu_m u_m) \wedge (v_1 v_1 + \cdots + v_n v_n)] \\ &= \text{LA}[\textstyle\sum_{i,j} (\mu_i \wedge v_j)/u_i \wedge v_j] \end{aligned} \tag{2.45}$$

$$\begin{aligned} v(p \text{ or } q) &= \text{LA}[v(p) \vee v(q)] \\ &= \text{LA}[(\mu_1 u_1 + \cdots + \mu_m u_m) \vee (v_1 v_1 + \cdots + v_n v_n)] \\ &= \text{LA}[\textstyle\sum_{i,j} (\mu_i \wedge v_j)/u_i \vee v_j] \end{aligned} \tag{2.46}$$

and similarly

$$v(p \Rightarrow q) = \text{LA}[\textstyle\sum_{i,j} (\mu_i \wedge v_j)/(1 \wedge (1 - (u_i - v_j)))]\,. \tag{2.47}$$

As an illustration, suppose that

$$v(p) = \textit{true} = 0.6/0.8 + 0.9/0.9 + 1/1 \tag{2.48}$$

and

$$v(q) = \textit{not true} = 1/(0 + 0.1 + \cdots + 0.7) + 0.4/0.8 + 0.1/0.9\,. \tag{2.49}$$

Then

$$v(\textit{not } p) = 0.6/0.2 + 0.9/0.1 + 1/0 \tag{2.50}$$

and

$$v(p \textit{ and } q) = \text{LA}\,[v(p) \wedge v(q)] \tag{2.51}$$
$$= \text{LA}\,[1/(0 + \cdots + 0.7) + 0.4/0.8 + 0.1/0.9]$$
$$= \textit{not true}.$$

Applying the same technique to the computation of the truth-value of the proposition *very p* (e.g., if $p \triangleq$ Evan is *very smart*, then *very* $p \triangleq$ Evan is *very very smart*), we have

$$v(\textit{very } p) = \text{LA}\,[v^2(p)]$$
$$= \text{LA}\,[(\mu_1 u_1 + \cdots + \mu_m u_m)^2]$$
$$= \text{LA}\,[\mu_1 u_1^2 + \cdots + \mu_m u_m^2] \tag{2.52}$$

and for the particular case where

$$v(p) = \textit{true}$$
$$= 0.6/0.8 + 0.9/0.9 + 1/1 \tag{2.53}$$

(2.52) yields

$$v(\textit{very } p) = \text{LA}\,[0.6/0.64 + 0.9/0.81 + 1/1] \tag{2.54}$$
$$\cong \textit{more or less true} \tag{2.55}$$

if the modifier *more or less* is defined by

$$\mu_{\textit{more or less } A} = (\mu_A)^{1/2} \tag{2.56}$$

where A is a fuzzy subset of U, and μ_A and $\mu_{\textit{more or less } A}$ are the compatibility functions of A and *more or less A*, respectively. It should be noted that the approximation of the bracketed expression in (2.54) by (2.55) is low in precision.

3. Approximate reasoning

It is rather illuminating as well as convenient to view the process of reasoning as the solution of a system of relational assignment equations. Specifically, consider a fuzzy proposition, p, of the form

$$p \triangleq u \text{ is } A \tag{3.1}$$

or, more concretely

$$p \triangleq \text{Mark is } \textit{tall} \tag{3.2}$$

in which A is a fuzzy subset of a universe of discourse U and u is an element of a possibly different universe V. Conventionally, p would be interpreted as 'u is a member of A', (e.g., 'Mark is a member of the class of *tall* men'). However, if A is a fuzzy rather than a nonfuzzy subset of U, then it is not meaningful to assert that u is a member of A – if 'is a member of' is interpreted in its usual mathematical sense.

We can get around this difficulty by interpreting 'u is A' as the assignment of a unary fuzzy relation A as the value of a variable which corresponds to an implied attribute of u. For example, 'Mark is *tall*', would be interpreted as the assignment equation

$$\text{Height(Mark)} = \textit{tall} \tag{3.3}$$

in which Height (Mark) is the name of a variable and *tall* is its assigned linguistic value. Similarly, the proposition

$$p \triangleq \text{Mark is } \textit{tall} \text{ and Jacob is } \textit{not heavy} \tag{3.4}$$

is equivalent to two assignment equations

$$\text{Height(Mark)} = \textit{tall} \tag{3.5}$$

and

$$\text{Weight(Jacob)} = \textit{not heavy} \tag{3.6}$$

in which both *tall* and *not heavy* are fuzzy subsets of the real line which may be characterized by their respective compatibility functions μ_{tall} and $\mu_{not\ heavy}$.

As a further example, consider the proposition

$$p \triangleq \text{Mark is } \textit{much taller} \text{ than Mac} \tag{3.7}$$

In this case, the relational assignment equation may be expressed as

$$(\text{Height(Mark), Height(Mac)}) = \textit{much taller than} \tag{3.8}$$

in which the linguistic value on the right-hand-side represents a binary fuzzy relation in $R \times R$ ($R \triangleq$ real line) which is assigned to the variable on the left-hand-side of (3.8).

More generally, let $U_1, \ldots, U_n$ be a collection of universes of discourse, and let $(u_1, \ldots, u_n)$ be an n-tuple in the cartesian product $U_1 \times \cdots \times U_n$. By a *restriction on* $(u_1, \ldots, u_n)$, denoted by $R(u_1, \ldots, u_n)$, is meant a fuzzy relation in $U_1 \times \cdots \times U_n$ which defines the compatibility with $R(u_1, \ldots, u_n)$ of values that are assigned to $(u_1, \ldots, u_n)$.[11] As a simple example, if u is a real number and $R(u)$ is the fuzzy set

$$R(u) = 1/0 + 1/1 + 0.8/2 + 0.5/3 + 0.2/4 \tag{3.9}$$

then 2 may be assigned as a value to u with compatibility 0.8.

Now if p is a proposition of the form

$$p \triangleq (u_1, \ldots, u_n) \text{ is } A \tag{3.10}$$

where A is an n-ary fuzzy relation in $U_1 \times \cdots \times U_n$, then (3.10) may be interpreted as the assignment equation

$$R(u_1, \ldots, u_n) = A \tag{3.11}$$

which for simplicity may be written as

$$(u_1, \ldots, u_n) = A. \tag{3.12}$$

In this sense, a collection of propositions of the form

$$p_i \triangleq (u_{i_1}, \ldots, u_{i_k}) \text{ is } A_i \tag{3.13}$$

where $(i_1, \ldots, i_k)$ is a subsequence of the index sequence $(1, \ldots, n)$, translates into a collection of assignment equations of the form

$$R(u_{i_1}, \ldots, u_{i_k}) = A_i, \quad i = 1, 2, \ldots \tag{3.14}$$

or more simply

$$(u_{i_1}, \ldots, u_{i_k}) = A_i. \tag{3.15}$$

For example, the propositions

$$p \triangleq u_1 \text{ is small} \tag{3.16}$$

and

$$q \triangleq u_1 \text{ and } u_2 \text{ are } \textit{approximately equal} \tag{3.17}$$

translate into the relational assignment equations

$$u_1 = \textit{small} \tag{3.18}$$

and

$$(u_1, u_2) = \textit{approximately equal}. \tag{3.19}$$

As was stated in the Introduction, the process of inference may be viewed as the solution of a system of relational assignment equations. In the case of (3.18) and (3.19), for example, solving these equations for u_2 yields

$$u_2 = \text{LA}\,[\textit{small} \circ \textit{approximately equal}] \tag{3.20}$$

where $\circ$ denotes the composition of fuzzy relations[12] and LA stands for linguistic approximation. Thus, if

$$\textit{small} = 1/1 + 0.6/2 + 0.2/3 \tag{3.21}$$

and

$$\begin{aligned}\textit{approximately equal} = {} & 1/((1,1) + (2,2) + (3,3) + (4,4)) + \\ & + 0.5/((1,2) + (2,1) + (2,3) + (3,2) \\ & + (3,4) + (4,3))\end{aligned} \tag{3.22}$$

then by expressing (3.20) as the max-min product of the relation matrices for *small* and *approximately equal*, we obtain

$$\begin{aligned} u_2 &= \text{LA}\,[1/1 + 0.6/2 + 0.5/3 + 0.2/4] \\ &\cong \textit{more or less small}\end{aligned} \tag{3.23}$$

as a rough linguistic approximation to the bracketed fuzzy set. This explains the way in which the consequent 'u_2 is *more or less small*', was inferred in the second example in the Introduction.

Stated in somewhat more general terms, the *compositional rule of inference* expressed by (3.18), (3.19) and (3.20) may be summarized as follows.[13]

$$\begin{array}{l} A_1 : u_1 \text{ is } A \\ \underline{A_2 : u_1 \text{ and } u_2 \text{ are } B} \\ A_3 : u_2 \text{ is LA}\,[A \circ B] \end{array} \tag{3.24}$$

and

$$\begin{array}{l} A_1 : u_1 \text{ and } u_2 \text{ are } A \\ \underline{A_2 : u_2 \text{ and } u_3 \text{ are } B} \\ A_3 : u_1 \text{ and } u_3 \text{ are LA}\,[A \circ B] \end{array} \tag{3.25}$$

where A and B are fuzzy relations expressed in linguistic terms and LA $[A \circ B]$ is a linguistic approximation to their composition.

The rationale for the compositional rule of inference can readily be understood by viewing the composition of A and B as the projection on

U_2 of the intersection of B with the cylindrical extension of A. More specifically, if $R(u_{i_1},\ldots,u_{i_k})$ is a fuzzy relation in $U_{i_1}\times\cdots\times U_{i_k}$, then its *cylindrical extension*, $\bar{R}(u_{i_1},\ldots,u_{i_k})$, is a fuzzy relation in $U_1\times\cdots\times U_n$ defined by

$$\bar{R}(u_{i_1},\ldots,u_{i_k})=R(u_{i_1},\ldots u_{i_k})\times U_{j_1}\times\cdots\times U_{j_l} \qquad (3.26)$$

where $(j_1,\ldots,j_l)$ is the index sequence complementary to $(i_1,\ldots i_k)$ (E.g., if $n=6$ and $(i_1,i_2,i_3,i_4)=(2,4,5,6)$, then $(j_1,j_2)=(1,3)$.)

Now suppose that we have translated a given set of propositions into a system of relational assignment equations each of which is of the form

$$(u_{r_1},\ldots,u_{r_s})=R_r \qquad (3.27)$$

where R_r is a fuzzy relation in $U_{r_1}\times\cdots\times U_{r_s}$. To solve this system for, say, $(u_{j_1},\ldots,u_{j_l})$, we form the intersection of the cylindrical extensions of the R_r and project[14] the resulting relation on $U_{j_1}\times\cdots\times U_{j_l}$. Thus, in symbols,

$$(u_{j_1},\ldots,u_{j_l})=\mathrm{Proj}_{U_{j_1}\times\ldots\times U_{j_l}}\bigcap_r \bar{R}_r \qquad (3.28)$$

which subsumes (3.24) and (3.25) as special cases. In this sense, as stated in the Introduction, the process of inference may be viewed as the solution of a system of relational assignment equations.

In the foregoing discussion, we have limited our attention to propositions of the form 'u is A'. How, then, could we treat nested propositions of the form

$$p_1 \triangleq (u \text{ is } A_1) \text{ is } \tau \qquad (3.29)$$

e.g., (Lisa is *young*) is *very true*, where A_1 is a fuzzy subset of U and τ is a linguistic truth-value?

It can readily be shown [12] that a proposition of the form (3.29) implies

$$p_2 \triangleq u \text{ is } A_2 \qquad (3.30)$$

where A_2 is given by the composition

$$A_2=\mu_{A_1}^{-1}\circ\tau$$

in which μ_{A_1} is the compatibility function of A_1 and $\mu_{A_1}^{-1}$ is its inverse (Figure 3). It is this relation between p_2 and p_1 that in conjunction with

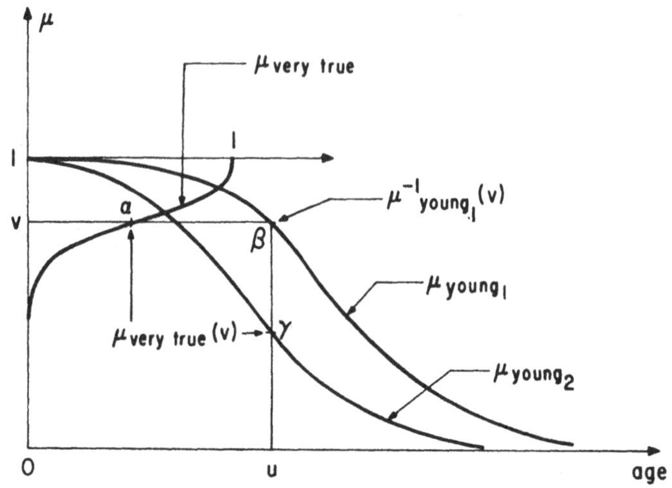

Fig. 3. The compatibility function associated with the nested proposition $p \triangleq$ (Lisa is *young*) is *very true*, where $\mu_{young_2} = \mu^{-1}_{young_1} \circ$ *very true*.

the compositional rule of inference provides the basis for the approximate inference

$$\begin{array}{l} (u_1 \text{ is } A) \text{ is } \tau_1 \\ (u_1 \text{ and } u_2 \text{ are } B) \text{ is } \tau_2 \\ \hline (u_2 \text{ is } C) \text{ is } \tau_3 \end{array} \tag{3.31}$$

where A, B, C, are fuzzy relations; τ_1, τ_2 and τ_3 are linguistic truth-values; and C and τ_3 satisfy the approximate equality

$$\mu_C^{-1} \circ \tau_3 \cong (\mu_A^{-1} \circ \tau_1) \circ (\mu_B^{-1} \circ \tau_2) \tag{3.32}$$

between the fuzzy set $\mu_C^{-1} \circ \tau_3$, on the one hand, and the composition of $\mu_A^{-1} \circ \tau_1$ and $\mu_B^{-1} \circ \tau_2$, on the other.

An illustration of (3.31) is provided by the last example in the Introduction.

4. Concluding remarks

In spirit as well as in substance, fuzzy logic and approximate reasoning represent a rather sharp departure from the traditional approaches to logic and the mathematization of human reasoning. Thus, in essence, fuzzy logic may be viewed as an attempt at accommodation with the pervasive reality of fuzziness and vagueness in human cognition. In this sense, fuzzy logic represents a retreat from what may well be an unrealizable objective, namely, the construction of a rigorous mathematical foundation for human reasoning and rational behavior.

In our brief discussion of fuzzy logic and approximate reasoning in the present paper, we have not considered many interesting as well as significant issues. Among these are inferences that are fuzzy-probabilistic in nature; the concept of a fuzzy 'proof' of a fuzzy assertion; modal logics with linguistic truth-values and fuzzy modal operators of the form *it is quite possible that, it is very necessary that*, etc.; and methods of translating a given complex fuzzy proposition into a system of relational assignment equations – a problem which is related to the case-grammar approach to deep structure and conceptual dependency [24]–[26].

University of California, Berkeley

NOTES

* Computer Science Division, Department of Electrical Engineering and Computer Sciences and the Electronics Research Laboratory, University of California, Berkeley, California 94720. This work was supported in part by the National Science Foundation under Grant GK-10656X3.

[1] If U is a universe of discourse and F is a fuzzy subset of U, then the *compatibility function* (or, equivalently, *membership function*) of F is a mapping $\mu_F: U \rightarrow [0,1]$ which associates with each $u \in U$ its compatibility (or *grade of membership*) $\leq \mu_F(u), 0 \leq 1$, [4].

[2] The symbol $\triangleq$ stands for 'is defined to be', or 'denotes'.

[3] The *support* of a fuzzy subset, A, of U is the set of points in U at which $\mu_A(u) > 0$. The *crossover* points of A are the points of U at which $\mu_A(u) = 0.5$.

[4] This technique is related to Knuth's method of synthesized attributes [6].

[5] If A and B are fuzzy subsets of $U = \{u\}$ with respective compatibility functions μ_A and μ_B, then the *complement*, A', of A is defined by $\mu_{A'}(u) = 1 - \mu_A(u)$; the *intersection* of A and B, $A \cap B$, is defined by $\mu_{A \cap B}(u) = \mu_A(u) \wedge \mu_B(u)$; the *union* of A and B (denoted by $A \cup B$ or $A + B$) is defined by $\mu_{A+B}(u) = \mu_A(u) \vee \mu_B(u)$; the *product* of A and B is defined by $\mu_{AB}(u) = \mu_A(u)\, \mu_B(u)$; and A^α is defined by $\mu_{A\alpha}(u) = (\mu_A(u))^\alpha$. If $A \subset U$ and $B \subset V$, then the Cartesian product of A and B, $A \times B$, is defined by $\mu_{A \times B}(u, v) = \mu_A(u) \wedge \mu_B(v)$ [7], [8].

[6] It should be noted that in the case of truth-values of the form (2.18), this process is similar to the familiar procedure for evaluating Boolean and arithmetic expressions.

[7] A more detailed discussion of linguistic modifiers and hedges may be found in [10], [11] and [4].

[8] In the context of operations on linguistic truth-values, this principle may be viewed

as an extension to fuzzy-set-valued logics of the expansion techniques used in quasi-truth-functional systems [3].

[9] It should be noted that the inexactness of the truth tables of FL is a consequence of the application of linguistic approximation to expressions of the form $v(p)*v(q)$, where $*$ is the tabulated operation on the linguistic truth-values of fuzzy propositions p and q.

[10] As defined here, these operations are tacitly assumed to be noninteractive. A more detailed discussion of interactivity of fuzzy variables may be found in [4] and [12].

[11] The concept of a restriction on a fuzzy variable may be viewed as a generalization of the concept of the range of a nonfuzzy variable. A more detailed discussion of this concept may be found in [4].

[12] The composition of a unary relation A with a binary relation B is defined by $\mu_{A \circ B}(u_2) \triangleq \vee_{u_1} \mu_A(u_1) \wedge \mu_B(u_1, u_2)$, where A and B are fuzzy subsets of U_1 and $U_1 \times U_2$, respectively, and $\vee_{u_1}$ is the supremum over $u_1 \in U_1$. If A and B are fuzzy subsets of $U_1 \times U_2$ and $U_2 \times U_3$, respectively, then $\mu_{A \circ B}(u_1, u_3) \triangleq \vee_{u_2} \mu_A(u_1, u_2) \wedge \mu_B(u_2, u_3)$, where μ_A and μ_B are the compatibility functions of A and B.

[13] As pointed out in [4], *modus ponens* may be viewed as a special case of (3.24).

[14] If R is a fuzzy relation in $U_1 \times \ldots \times U_n$, then its *projection on* $U_{j_1} \times \ldots \times U_{j_l}$ is a fuzzy relation in $U_{j_1} \times \ldots \times U_{j_l}$ defined by $\mu_{\text{Proj } R \text{ on } U_{j_1} \times \ldots \times U_{j_l}}(u_{j_1}, \ldots, u_{j_l}) = \vee_{u_{i_1}, \ldots u_{i_k}} \mu_R(u_1, \ldots u_n)$ where $(i_1, \ldots, i_k)$ and $(j_1, \ldots, j_l)$ are complementary index sequences, and $\vee_{u_{i_1}, \ldots, u_{i_k}}$ is the supremum over $(u_{i_1}, \ldots, u_{i_k}) \in U_{i_1} \times \ldots \times U_{i_k}$.

REFERENCES AND RELATED PUBLICATIONS

[1] J. Łukasiewicz, *Aristotle's Syllogistic*, Clarendon Press, Oxford, 1951.

[2] J. Hintikka and P. Suppes (eds.), *Aspects of Inductive Logic*, North-Holland Publ. Co., Amsterdam, 1966.

[3] N. Rescher, *Many-Valued Logic*, McGraw-Hill, New York, 1969.

[4] L. A. Zadeh, 'The Concept of a Linguistic Variable and Its Application to Approximate Reasoning', Memorandum No. ERL-M411, Electronics Research Lab., Univ. of Calif., Berkeley, Calif., October 1973.

[5] L. A. Zadeh, 'Quantitative Fuzzy Semantics', *Information Sciences* **3** (1971), 159–176.

[6] D. Knuth, 'Semantics of Context-Free Languages', *Math. Systems Theory* **2** (1968), 127–145.

[7] L. A. Zadeh, 'Fuzzy Sets', *Information and Control* **8** (1965), 338–353.

[8] A. Kaufmann, *Theory of Fuzzy Sets*, Masson, Paris, 1972.

[9] A. V. Aho and J. D. Ullman, *The Theory of Parsing, Translation and Compiling*, Prentice-Hall, Englewood Cliffs, N.J., 1973.

[10] L. A. Zadeh, 'A Fuzzy-Set-Theoretic Interpretation of Linguistic Hedges', *Jour. of Cybernetics* **2** (1972), 4–34.

[11] G. Lakoff, 'Hedges: A Study of Meaning Criteria and the Logic of Fuzzy Concepts', *Jour. of Philosophical Logic* **2** (1973), 458–508.

[12] L. A. Zadeh, 'A Fuzzy-Algorithmic Approach to the Definition of Complex or Imprecise Concepts', Memorandum No. ERL-M474, Electronics Research Lab., Univ. of Calif., Berkeley, Calif., 1974.

[13] M. Black, 'Reasoning with Loose Concepts', *Dialogue* **2** (1963), 1–12.

[14] J. A. Goguen, 'The Logic of Inexact Concepts', *Synthese* **19** (1969), 325–373.

[15] W. V. Quine, *From a Logical Point of View*, Harvard Univ. Press, Cambridge, 1953.

[16] K. Fine, 'Vagueness, Truth and Logic', this issue, pp. 265–300.
[17] B. C. van Fraassen, 'Presuppositions, Supervaluations and Free Logic', in *The Logical Way of Doing Things*, K. Lambert (ed.), Yale Univ. Press, New Haven, 1969.
[18] A. Tarski, *Logic, Semantics, Metamathematics*, Clarendon Press, Oxford, 1956.
[19] H. A. Simon and L. Siklossy (eds.), *Representation and Meaning Experiments with Information Processing Systems*, Prentice-Hall, Englewood Cliffs, N.J., 1972.
[20] J. Hintikka, J. Moravcsik, and P. Suppes (eds.), *Approaches to Natural Language*, D. Reidel Publ. Co., Dordrecht, 1973.
[21] J. A. Goguen, Jr., 'Concept Representation in Natural and Artificial Languages: Axioms, Extensions and Applications for Fuzzy Sets', *Inter. Jour. of Man-Machine Studies* **6** (1974), 513–561.
[22] G. Lakoff, 'Linguistic and Natural Logic', in *Semantics of Natural Languages*, D. Davidson and G. Harman (eds.), D. Reidel Publ. Co., Dordrecht, 1971.
[23] C. G. Hempel, 'Fundamentals of Concept Formation in Empirical Science', in *International Encyclopedia of Unified Science*, vol. 2, 1952.
[24] C. J. Fillmore, 'Toward A Modern Theory of Case', pp. 361–375 in *Modern Studies in English*, Reibel and Schane (eds.), Prentice-Hall, Toronto, 1969.
[25] W. A. Martin, 'Translation of English into MAPL Using Winogard's Syntax, State Transition Networks, and a Semantic Case Grammar', MIT APG Internal Memo 11, April 1973.
[26] R. C. Schank, 'Conceptual Dependency: A Theory of Natural Language Understanding', *Cognitive Psychology* **3** (1972), 552–631.

THE LINGUISTIC APPROACH AND ITS APPLICATION TO DECISION ANALYSIS†

L.A. Zadeh

Division of Computer Science
Department of Electrical Engineering and Computer Sciences
University of California, Berkeley, CA 94720

ABSTRACT

In a sharp departure from the conventional approaches to decision analysis, the linguistic approach abandons the use of numbers and relies instead on a systematic use of words to characterize the values of variables, the values of probabilities, the relations between variables, and the truth-values of assertions about them.

The linguistic approach is intended to be used in situations in which the system under analysis is too complex or too ill-defined to be amenable to quantitative characterization. It may be used, in particular, to define an objective function in linguistic terms as a function of the linguistic values of decision variables.

In cases in which the objective function is vector-valued, the linguistic approach provides a language for an approximate linguistic characterization of the trade-offs between its components. Such characterizations result in a fuzzy set of Pareto-optimal solutions, with the grade of membership of a solution representing the complement of the degree to which it is dominated by other solutions.

1. INTRODUCTION

The past two decades have witnessed many important theoretical

†Research sponsored by Naval Electronics Systems Command Contract N00039-76-C-0022, U.S. Army Research Office Contract DAHC04-75-G0056 and National Science Foundation Grant ENG74-06651-A01.

advances in decision theory [1-18] as well as in such related fields as mathematical programming, statistical analysis, system simulation, game theory and optimal control. And yet, there are many observers who would agree that it is by no means easy to find concrete examples of successful applications of decision theory in practice. What, then, is the reason for the paucity of practical applications of a wide-ranging theory that had its inception more than three decades ago?

Although this may not as yet be a widely accepted view, our belief is that the limited applicability of decision theory to real-world problems is largely due to the fact that decision theory -- like most other mathematical theories of rational behavior -- fails to come to grips with the pervasive fuzziness and imprecision of human judgment, perception and modes of reasoning.[1] Thus, based as it is on the foundations of classical mathematics, decision theory aims at constructing a model of rational decision-making which is quantitative, rigorous and precise. Unfortunately, this may well be an unrealizable objective, for real-world decision processes are, for the most part, far too complex and much too ill-defined to be dealt with in this spirit. Indeed, to be able to cope with real-world problems, the mathematical theories of human cognition and rational behavior may have to undergo an extensive restructuring -- a restructuring which would entail an abandonment of the unrealistically high standards of precision which have become the norm in the literature and an acceptance of modes of logical inference which are approximate rather than exact.

The linguistic approach outlined in the present paper may be viewed as a step in this direction. In a sharp break with deeply entrenched traditions in science, the linguistic approach abandons the use of numbers and precise models of reasoning, and adopts instead a flexible system of verbal characterizations which apply to the values of variables, the relations between variables and the truth-values as well as the probabilities of assertions about them. The rationale for this seemingly retrograde step of employing words in place of numbers is that verbal characterizations are intrinsically approximate in nature and hence are better suited for the description of systems and processes which are as complex and as ill-defined as those which relate to human judgment and decision-making.

It should be stressed, however, that the linguistic approach

[1]In fact, far from being a negative characteristic of human thinking -- as it is usually perceived to be -- fuzziness may well be the key to the human ability to cope with problems (e.g., language translation, summarization of information, etc.) which are too complex for solution by machines that lack the capability to operate in a fuzzy environment.

is not the traditional non-mathematical way of dealing with humanistic systems. Rather, it represents a blend between the quantitative and the qualitative, relying on the use of words when numerical characterizations are not appropriate and using numbers to make the meaning of words more precise [19,20].

The central concept in the linguistic approach is that of a linguistic variable, that is, a variable whose values are words or structured combinations of words whose meaning is defined by a semantic rule [20]. For example, Age is a linguistic variable if its values are assumed to be young, not young, very young, not very young, more or less young, etc., rather than the numbers 0,1,2,..., 100. The meaning of a typical linguistic value, say not very young, is assumed to be a fuzzy subset of a universe of discourse, e.g., U = [0,100], with the understanding that the meaning of not very young can be deduced from the meaning of young by the application of a semantic rule which is associated with the variable Age. In this sense, then, young is a primary term which plays a role akin to that of a unit of measurement. However, it is important to note that (a) the definition of young is purely subjective in nature; and (b) in contrast to the way in which the conventional units are used, the semantic rule involves nonlinear rather than linear operations on the meaning of the primary terms. These issues are discussed in greater detail in Section 2.

An important part of the linguistic approach relates to the treatment of truth as a linguistic variable with values such as true, very true, not very true, more or less true, etc. The use of such linguistic truth-values leads to what is called fuzzy logic [21] which provides a basis for approximate inference from possibly fuzzy premises whose validity may not be sharply defined. As an illustration, an approximate inference from (a) x is a small number, and (b) x and y are approximately equal, might be (c) y is more or less small. Similarly, an approximate inference from (a) (x is a small number) is very true, and (b) (x and y are approximately equal) is very true, might be (c) (y is more or less small) is true. In these assertions, small is assumed to be a specified fuzzy subset of the real line $R \triangleq (-\infty,\infty)$; approximately equal is a binary fuzzy relation in $R \times R$; and true and very true are fuzzy subsets of the unit interval [0,1].[2] Because of limitations on space, we shall not discuss the applications of fuzzy logic to decision analysis in the present paper.

[2] A brief exposition of the basic properties of fuzzy sets is contained in Appendix on p. 228. A more detailed discussion of various aspects of the theory of fuzzy sets and its applications may be found in [22]. The most comprehensive treatise on the theory of fuzzy sets is the five-volume work of A. Kaufmann [23]. Some of the applications of the theory of fuzzy sets to decision analysis are discussed in [24-32].

Insofar as decision analysis is concerned, the linguistic approach serves, in the main, to provide a language for an approximate characterization of those components of a decision process which are either inherently fuzzy or are incapable of precise measurement. For example, if the probability of an outcome of a decision is not known precisely, it may be described in linguistic terms as likely or not very likely or very unlikely or more or less likely, and so forth. Or, if the degree to which an alternative α is preferred to an alternative β is not well-defined, it may be assigned a linguistic value such as strong or very strong or mild or very weak, etc. Similarly, a fuzzy relation between two variables x and y may be described in linguistic terms as "x is much larger than y" or "If x is small then y is large else x is approximately equal to y," etc.

As will be seen in Section 2, a linguistic characterization such as "x is small" may be viewed as a fuzzy restriction on the values of x. What is important to realize is that the assertion "x is small" conveys no information concerning the probability distribution of x; what it means, merely, is that "x is small" induces an elastic constraint on the values that may be assigned to x. Thus, if small is a fuzzy set in R whose membership function takes the value, say, 0.6 at x = 8, then the degree to which the constraint "x is small" is satisfied when the value 8 is assigned to x, is 0.6.

In what follows, we shall outline the main features of the linguistic approach and indicate some of its possible applications to decision analysis. It should be stressed that such applications are still in an exploratory stage and experience in the use of the linguistic approach may well suggest substantive changes in its implementation.[3]

2. LINGUISTIC VARIABLES AND FUZZY RESTRICTIONS

As stated in the Introduction, a linguistic variable is a variable whose values are words or sentences which serve as names of fuzzy subsets of a universe of discourse. In more specific terms, a linguistic variable is characterized by a quintuple (X,T(X),U,G,M) in which X is the name of the variable, e.g., Age; T(X) is the term-set of X, that is, the collection of its linguistic

[3]The linguistic approach has been applied to various problems in situation calculus by Yu. Klikov, G. Pospelov, D. Pospelov, V. Pushkin, D. Shapiro and others at the Computing Center of the Academy of Sciences, Moscow, under the direction of N.N. Moyseev. Other types of applications of the linguistic approach have recently been reported by P. King and E. Mamdani [33], R. Assilian [34], G. Retherford and G. Bloore [35], F. Wenstop [36], L. Pun [37], V. Dimitrov, W. Wechler and P. Barnev [38], and others.

values, e.g., T(X) = {young, not young, very young, not very young, ...}; U is a universe of discourse, e.g., in the case of Age, the set {0,1,2,3,...}; G is a syntactic rule which generates the terms in T(X); and M is a semantic rule which associates with each term, x, in T(X) its meaning, M(x), where M(x) denotes a fuzzy subset of U. Thus, the meaning, M(x), of a linguistic value, x, is defined by a compatibility -- or, equivalently, membership -- function $\mu_x: U \to [0,1]$ which associates with each u in U its compatibility with x. For example, the meaning of young might be defined in a particular context by the compatibility function

$$\mu_{\text{young}}(u) = 1 \quad \text{for} \quad 0 \le u \le 20 \qquad (2.1)$$

$$= \frac{1}{1+\left(\frac{u-20}{10}\right)^2} \quad \text{for} \quad u \ge 20$$

which may be viewed as the membership function of the fuzzy subset young of the universe of discourse U = [0,∞). Thus, the compatibility of the age 27 with young is approximately 0.66, while that of 30 is 0.5. The variable u ε U is termed the base variable of X. The value of u at which $\mu_x(u) = 0.5$ is the cross-over point of x.

If X were a numerical variable, the assignment of a value, say a, to X would be expressed as

$$X = a . \qquad (2.2)$$

In the case of linguistic variables, the counterpart of the assignment equation (2.2) is the proposition "X is x," where x is a linguistic value of X. From this point of view, x may be regarded as a fuzzy restriction on the values of the base variable u. This fuzzy restriction, which is denoted by $R_x(u)$ (or simply R(u)), is identical with the fuzzy subset M(x) which is the meaning of x. Thus, the proposition "X is x" translates into the relational assignment equation[4].

$$R(u) = x \qquad (2.3)$$

which signifies that the proposition "X is x" may be interpreted as an elastic constraint on the values that may be assigned to u, with the membership function of x characterizing the compatibility, $\mu_x(u)$, of u with x.

As an illustration, consider the proposition "Edward is young." The translation of this proposition reads

---

[4] As will be seen later, a relational assignment equation involves, more generally, the assignment of a fuzzy relation to a fuzzy restriction on the values of a base variable [39].

$$R(Age(Edward)) = \underline{young} \tag{2.4}$$

where Age(Edward) is a numerical variable ranging over $[0,\infty)$, R(Age(Edward)) is a fuzzy restriction on its values, and young is a fuzzy subset of $[0,\infty)$ whose membership function is given by (2.1). To simplify the notation, a relational assignment equation such as (2.4) may be written as

$$Age(Edward) = \underline{young} \tag{2.5}$$

with the understanding that young is assigned not to the variable Age(Edward) but to the restriction on its values.

In this sense, each term, x, in the term-set of a linguistic variable X corresponds to a fuzzy restriction, R(u), on the values that may be assigned to the base variable u. A key idea behind the concept of a linguistic variable is that these fuzzy restrictions may be deduced from the fuzzy restrictions associated with the so-called primary terms in T(X). In effect, these fuzzy restrictions play the role of units which, upon calibration, make it possible to compute the meaning of the composite (that is non-primary) values of X from the knowledge of the meaning of the primary terms.

As an illustration of this technique, we shall consider an example in which $U = [0,\infty)$ and the term-set of X is of the form

$$T(X) = \{\underline{small}, \underline{not}\ \underline{small}, \underline{very}\ \underline{small}, \underline{very}\ (\underline{not}\ \underline{small}), \underline{not}\ \underline{very}\ \underline{small}, \underline{very}\ \underline{very}\ \underline{small}, \ldots\} \tag{2.6}$$

in which small is the primary term.

The terms in T(X) may be generated by a context-free grammar [40] $G = (V_T, V_N, S, P)$ in which the set of terminals, V_T, comprises (,), the primary term small and the linguistic modifiers very and not; the nonterminals are denoted by S, A and B and the production system is given by:

$$\begin{aligned} S &\to A \\ S &\to \underline{not}\ A \\ A &\to B \\ B &\to \underline{very}\ B \\ B &\to (S) \\ B &\to \underline{small} \end{aligned} \tag{2.7}$$

Thus, a typical derivation yields

$$S \to \underline{not}\ A \to \underline{not}\ B \Rightarrow \underline{not}\ \underline{very}\ B \Rightarrow \underline{not}\ \underline{very}\ \underline{very}\ B \Rightarrow \underline{not}\ \underline{very}\ \underline{very}\ \underline{small} \tag{2.8}$$

In this sense, the syntactic rule associated with X may be viewed as the process of generating the elements of T(X) by a succession of substitutions involving the productions in G.

As for the semantic rule, we shall assume for simplicity that if μ_A is the membership function of A then the membership functions of not A and very A are given respectively by[5]

$$\mu_{\underline{\text{not}}\ A} = 1 - \mu_A \tag{2.9}$$

and

$$\mu_{\underline{\text{very}}\ A} = (\mu_A)^2 \ . \tag{2.10}$$

Thus, (2.10) signifies that the modifier very has the effect of squaring the membership function of its operand.

Suppose that the meaning of small is defined by the compatibility (membership) function

$$\mu_{\underline{\text{small}}}(u) = (1 + (0.1u)^2)^{-1} \ , \quad u \geq 0 \ . \tag{2.11}$$

Then the meaning of very small is given by

$$\mu_{\underline{\text{very}}\ \underline{\text{small}}} = (1 + (0.1u)^2)^{-2} \tag{2.12}$$

while the meanings of not very small and very (not small) are expressed respectively by

$$\mu_{\underline{\text{not}}\ \underline{\text{very}}\ \underline{\text{small}}} = 1 - (1 + (0.1u)^2)^{-2} \tag{2.13}$$

and

$$\mu_{\underline{\text{very}}\ (\underline{\text{not}}\ \underline{\text{small}})} = (1 - (1 + (0.1u)^2)^{-1})^2 \ . \tag{2.14}$$

In this way, we can readily compute the expression for the membership function of any term in T(X) from the knowledge of the membership function of the primary term small.

In effect, a linguistic variable X may be viewed as a microlanguage whose syntax and semantics are represented, respectively, by the syntactic and semantic rules associated with X. The sentences of this language are the linguistic values of X, with the meaning of each sentence represented as a fuzzy restriction on the values that may be assigned to the base variable, $u \in U$, of X.

---

[5] A more detailed discussion of the effect of linguistic modifiers (hedges) may be found in [41], [42], and [43].

In the characterization of a decision process, we usually have to deal with a collection of interrelated linguistic variables. In this connection, it is helpful to have a set of rules for translating a proposition involving two or more linguistic variables into a set of relational assignment equations. The rules in question are as follows.[6]

Let X and Y be linguistic variables associated with possibly distinct universes of discourse U and V, and let P and Q be fuzzy subsets of U and V, respectively. Then, the conjunctive proposition p defined by

$$p \triangleq X \text{ is } P \text{ and } Y \text{ is } Q \tag{2.15}$$

translates into the relational assignment equation

$$R_p(u,v) = P \times Q \tag{2.16}$$

where R(u,v) is the restriction on the values that may be assigned to the ordered pair (u,v), $u \in U$, $v \in V$, and $P \times Q$ denotes the cartesian product of P and Q. Equivalently, (2.16) may be expressed as

$$R(u,v) = \bar{P} \cap \bar{Q} \tag{2.17}$$

where $\bar{P}$ and $\bar{Q}$ are the cylindrical extensions of P and Q, respectively, and $\bar{P} \cap \bar{Q}$ is their intersection. (See Appendix.)

Similarly, the disjunctive proposition

$$p \triangleq X \text{ is } P \text{ or } Y \text{ is } Q \tag{2.18}$$

translates into

$$R_p(u,v) = \bar{P} \cup \bar{Q} \tag{2.19}$$

where $\bar{P} \cup \bar{Q}$ is the union of the cylindrical extensions of P and Q.

The conditional proposition

$$p \triangleq \text{If } X \text{ is } P \text{ then } Y \text{ is } Q \tag{2.20}$$

translates into

$$R_p(u,v) = \bar{P}' \oplus \bar{Q} \tag{2.21}$$

[6] Such rules will be referred to as semantic rules of Type II when it is necessary to distinguish them from the semantic rules which apply to individual variables (i.e., semantic rules of Type I).

where $\bar{P}'$ is the complement of $\bar{P}$ and $\oplus$ denotes the bounded sum. (See A36). More generally, the conditional proposition

$$p \triangleq \text{If X is P then Y is Q else Y is R} \tag{2.22}$$

translates into

$$R_p(u,v) = (\bar{P}' \oplus \bar{Q}) \cap (\bar{P} \oplus R) \ . \tag{2.23}$$

Eq. (2.23) follows from (2.21) by the application of (2.15) and the fact that

$$p \triangleq \text{X is not P} \tag{2.24}$$

translates into

$$R_p(u) = P' \tag{2.25}$$

where P' is the complement of P.

In cases where a linguistic truth-value, τ, such as true, very true, more or less true, etc. is associated with a proposition, as in

$$p \triangleq \text{(X is small) is very true} \tag{2.26}$$

the following rule of truth-functional modification may be used to translate p into a relational assignment equation:

$$p \triangleq \text{(X is A) is } \tau \tag{2.27}$$

translates into

$$R_p(u) = \mu_A^{-1} * \tau \tag{2.28}$$

where μ_A^{-1} is the inverse of μ_A and $*$ denotes the composition of the binary relation μ_A^{-1} with the unary fuzzy relation τ. (See A60.) It can readily be verified that the membership function of $R_p(u)$ is given by

$$\mu_{R_p}(u) = \mu_\tau(\mu_A(u)) \ , \quad u \in U \tag{2.29}$$

where μ_τ is the membership function of the linguistic truth-value τ and μ_A is that of A.

The basic translation rules stated above may be employed, in combination, to translate more complex propositions involving relations between two or more variables. As an illustration, consider the following proposition:

$$\pi \triangleq X \text{ is } \underline{\text{large}} \text{ and } Y \text{ is } \underline{\text{small}} \text{ or } X \text{ is } \underline{\text{not}}\ \underline{\text{large}} \text{ and } Y \text{ is } \underline{\text{very}}\ \underline{\text{small}} \tag{2.30}$$

which may be regarded as a linguistic characterization of the table shown below:

(2.31)

X	Y
large	small
not large	very small

For simplicity we shall assume that U = V = {0,1,2,4} and that small and large are fuzzy sets defined by (see Appendix)

$$\underline{\text{small}} = 1/1 + 0.6/2 + 0.2/3 \ , \tag{2.32}$$

$$\underline{\text{large}} = 0.3/2 + 0.7/3 + 1/4 \ . \tag{2.33}$$

In this case, the application of (2.15) and (2.18) leads to the following expression for the restriction on (u,v) which is induced by the proposition in question:

$$R_p(u,v) = \underline{\text{large}} \times \underline{\text{small}} + \underline{\text{not}}\ \underline{\text{large}} \times \underline{\text{very}}\ \underline{\text{small}} \tag{2.34}$$

where × and + represent the cartesian product and the union, respectively. Now, from (2.9) and (2.10) it follows that

$$\underline{\text{not}}\ \underline{\text{large}} = 1/1 + 0.7/2 + 0.3/3 \tag{2.35}$$

$$\underline{\text{very}}\ \underline{\text{small}} = 1/1 + 0.36/2 + 0.04/3 \tag{2.36}$$

and hence

$$\begin{aligned} R_p(u,v) = {} & 0.3/(2,1) + 0.7/(3,1) + 1/(4,1) \\ & + 0.3/(2,2) + 0.6/(3,2) + 0.6/(4,2) \\ & + 0.2/(2,3) + 0.2/(3,3) + 0.2/(1,3) \end{aligned} \tag{2.37}$$

in which a term such as 0.6/(3,2) signifies that the compatibility of the assignments u = 3 and v = 2 with p is 0.6.

As a further illustration, consider the proposition

$$q \triangleq \text{If } (X \text{ is } \underline{\text{large}} \text{ and } Y \text{ is } \underline{\text{small}} \text{ or } X \text{ is } \underline{\text{not}}\ \underline{\text{large}} \text{ and } Y \text{ is } \underline{\text{very}}\ \underline{\text{small}}) \text{ then } Z \text{ is } \underline{\text{very}}\ \underline{\text{small}} \tag{2.38}$$

in which the proposition in parentheses is that of the preceding example and the universe of discourse associated with Z is assumed to be the same as U.

In this case, using (2.20), we have

$$R_q(u,v,w) = \bar{R}'_p(u,v) \oplus \overline{\underline{very}\ \underline{small}} \tag{2.39}$$

where

$$\begin{aligned}\bar{R}_p(u,v) = {} & 0.3/\big((2,1,1) + (2,1,2) + (2,1,3) + (2,1,4)\big) + \cdots \\ & + 0.2/\big((4,3,1) + (4,3,2) + (4,3,3) + (4,3,4)\big) \ ;\end{aligned} \tag{2.40}$$

$$\begin{aligned}\overline{\underline{very}\ \underline{small}} = {} & 1/\big((1,1,1) + (1,1,2) + (1,1,3) + (1,1,4) + \\ & + (1,2,1) + (1,2,2) + (1,2,3) + (1,2,4) + \\ & + (1,4,1) + (1,4,2) + (1,4,3) + (1,4,4)\big) + \cdots \\ & + 0.04/\big((3,1,1) + (3,1,2) + (3,1,3) + (3,1,4) + \\ & + (3,4,1) + (3,4,2) + (3,4,3) + (3,4,4)\big) \ ;\end{aligned} \tag{2.41}$$

$\bar{R}'_p(u,v)$ is the complement of $\bar{R}_p(u,v)$ and $\oplus$ is defined by (A36).

To illustrate the rule of truth-functional modification, consider the proposition

$$p \triangleq (X \text{ is } \underline{\text{small}}) \text{ is } \underline{\text{very}}\ \underline{\text{true}} \tag{2.42}$$

where small is defined by (2.32) and

$$\underline{\text{true}} \triangleq 0.2/0.6 + 0.5/0.8 + 0.8/0.9 + 1/1 \ . \tag{2.43}$$

In this case,

$$\underline{\text{very}}\ \underline{\text{true}} = 0.04/0.6 + 0.025/0.8 + 0.64/0.9 + 1/1 \tag{2.44}$$

and (2.29) yields

$$\begin{aligned}\mu_p(1) &= 1 \\ \mu_p(2) &= 0.2 \\ \mu_p(3) &= \mu_p(4) = 0\end{aligned} \tag{2.45}$$

which means that the compatibility of the assignment u = 2 with p is 0.2, while those of u = 3 and u = 4 are zero.

The above examples serve to illustrate one of the central features of the linguistic approach, namely, the mechanism for translating a proposition expressed in linguistic terms into a fuzzy restriction on the values which may be assigned to a set of base variables. Once the translation has been performed, the resulting fuzzy restrictions may be manipulated to yield the restrictions on whichever variables may be of interest. These restrictions, then, are translated into linguistic terms, yielding the final solution to the problem at hand.

In what follows, we shall illustrate this process by a few simple applications which are of relevance to decision analysis.

3. LINGUISTIC CHARACTERIZATION OF OBJECTIVE FUNCTIONS

In the literature of mathematical programming and decision analysis, it has become a universal practice to assume that the objective and utility functions are numerical functions of their arguments.

In most real-world problems, however, our perceptions of the consequences of a decision are not sufficiently precise or consistent to justify the assignment of numerical values to utilities or preferences. Thus, in most cases it would be more realistic to assume that the objective function is a linguistic function of the linguistic values of its arguments, and employ the techniques of the linguistic approach to assess the consequences of a particular choice of decision variables.

To be more specific, consider a simple case of a decision process in which the objective function $G(u_1,\ldots,u_n)$ takes values in a space V while the decision variables $u_1,\ldots,u_n$ take values in $U_1,\ldots,U_n$, respectively. To simplify the discussion, we shall assume that $U_1 = U_2 = \cdots = U_n = U$.

The linguistic values of decision variables as well as those of the objective function are assumed to be of the form {low, not low, very low, not very low, ..., medium, high, not high, very high, not very high, not low and not high, not very low and not very high, ...}. It can readily be verified that these linguistic values can be generated by a context-free grammar whose production system is given below:

$$
\begin{array}{llr}
S \to A & C \to \underline{\text{very}}\ C & (3.1) \\
S \to S\ \underline{\text{and}}\ A & D \to \underline{\text{very}}\ D & \\
A \to B & C \to \underline{\text{low}} & \\
A \to \underline{\text{not}}\ B & D \to \underline{\text{high}} & \\
B \to C & & \\
B \to D & & \\
B \to \underline{\text{medium}} & &
\end{array}
$$

in which S, A, B, C, D are non-terminals, S is the starting symbol, and and, not, very, low, medium and high are terminals, with low, medium and high playing the role of primary terms.

The simplicity of this grammar makes it possible to compute the meaning of various linguistic values by inspection. For example, the meaning of the value not very low and not high is given by

$$M(\text{not very low and not high}) = (\text{low}^2)' \cap (\text{high}') \qquad (3.2)$$

where low^2 is a fuzzy set whose membership function is the square of that of low, and ' and $\cap$ denote the complement and intersection, respectively.

It is important to note that the assumption that all of the decision variables and the objective function have the same term-set does not imply that the corresponding primary terms are also identical. Thus, low, for example, in the case of i-th decision variable need not have the same meaning as low for j-th decision variable ($j \neq i$) or G. To illustrate this point, suppose that $U = \{1,2,3,4\}$. Then low for u_1 might be defined as

$$\text{low} = 1/1 + 0.8/2 + 0.2/3 \qquad (3.3)$$

whereas low for u_2 may be

$$\text{low} = 1/1 + 0.6/2 + 0.1/3 \ . \qquad (3.4)$$

Typically, a tabulation of the linguistic values of G as a function of the linguistic values of the decision variables would have a form such as shown below ($\text{low}^2 \triangleq$ very low, med $\triangleq$ medium)

(3.5)

u_1	u_2	G
low	low	low^2
low	med	low
low	low^2	not low
--	--	--
high	high	high^2

It should be noted that, in general, not all of the possible combinations of the linguistic values of decision variables will appear in the tableau of G.

The definition of G by a tableau of the form (3.5) induces a fuzzy restriction on the values that may be assigned to the decision variables and G. More specifically, let ℓ_{ij} denote the linguistic value of j-th decision variable in the i-th row of the tableau, and let v_i be the corresponding linguistic value of the objective function. Then the fuzzy restriction in question is expressed by

$$R_G(u_1,\ldots,u_n,v) = \ell_{11}\times\cdots\times\ell_{1n}\times v_1 + \cdots + \ell_{m1}\times\cdots\times\ell_{mn}\times v_m \tag{3.6}$$

where m is the number of rows in the tableau, and × and + denote the cartesian product and union, respectively. The fuzzy restriction $R_G(u_1,\ldots,u_n,v)$ on the values of $u_1,\ldots,u_n$ and v may be viewed as the meaning of the tableau of G in the same sense as the translation rules (2.15-2.29) express the meaning of various propositions as fuzzy restrictions on the values of the base variables.[7]

As a very simple illustration of (3.6), assume that the tableau of G is given by

u_1	u_2	G
low	low	low^2
low	low'	low'

(3.7)

where low for u_1 and u_2 is defined by (3.3) and (3.4), respectively, and low for G has the same meaning as for u_2.

In this case, we have

$$\begin{aligned} R_G(u_1,u_2,v) &= (1/1+0.8/2+0.2/3)\times(1,1+0.6/2+0.1/3) \\ &\quad\times(1/1+0.36/2+0.01/3) \\ &\quad+(1/1+0.8/2+0.2/3)\times(0.4/2+0.9/3+1/4) \\ &\quad\times(0.4/2+0.9/3+1/4) \\ &= 1/(1,1,1)+0.6/(1,2,1)+0.36(1,1,2)+\cdots \\ &\quad+0.9/(1,3,3)+\cdots+1/(1,4,4)\ . \end{aligned} \tag{3.8}$$

Note that the restriction defined by (3.8) is a ternary fuzzy relation in $U_1\times U_2\times V$.

An important aspect of the linguistic definition of G is that it provides a basis for an interpolation of G for values of the decision variables which are not in the tableau. Thus, since the meaning of the tableau is provided by the fuzzy (n+1)-ary relation $R_G(u_1,\ldots,u_n,v)$, we can assert that the result of substitution of

[7] A more detailed discussion of this point may be found in [44].

arbitrary linguistic values $\bar{\ell}_{i1},\dots,\bar{\ell}_{in}$ for $u_1,\dots,u_n$ is the composition of R_G with $\bar{\ell}_{i1},\dots,\bar{\ell}_{in}$. This implies that the value of G corresponding to the prescribed values of $u_1,\dots,u_n$ is given by

$$G(\bar{\ell}_{i1},\dots,\bar{\ell}_{in}) = R_G(u_1,\dots,u_n,v)*\bar{\ell}_{i1}*\cdots*\bar{\ell}_{in} \qquad (3.9)$$

where * denotes the operation of composition.[8]

As a very simple illustration of (3.9), assume that $R_G(u_1,u_2,v)$ is expressed by (for simplicity, $U_1 = U_2 = V = \{1,2\}$)

$$\begin{aligned} R_G(u_1,u_2,v) &= 0.8/(1,1,1) + 0.9/(1,2,1) + 0.3/(2,1,1) \\ &\quad + 0.7/(2,2,1) + 0.3/(1,1,2) + 0.2/(1,2,2) \\ &\quad + 0.6/(2,1,2) + 0.5/(2,2,2) \end{aligned} \qquad (3.10)$$

and that

$$\bar{\ell}_1 = 0.3/1 + 0.5/2 \qquad (3.11)$$

$$\bar{\ell}_2 = 0.9/1 + 0.2/2 \ . \qquad (3.12)$$

The ternary fuzzy relation (3.10) may be represented as two matrices

$$A \triangleq \begin{bmatrix} 0.8 & 0.9 \\ 0.3 & 0.7 \end{bmatrix} \qquad B \triangleq \begin{bmatrix} 0.3 & 0.2 \\ 0.6 & 0.5 \end{bmatrix} \qquad (3.13)$$

Forming the max-min products of A and B with the row matrix [0.3 0.5] we obtain the matrix

$$C \triangleq \begin{bmatrix} 0.3 & 0.5 \\ 0.5 & 0.5 \end{bmatrix} \qquad (3.14)$$

and forming the max-min product of this matrix with the row matrix [0.9 0.2] we arrive at

$$D = [0.3 \quad 0.5] \qquad (3.15)$$

which implies that the interpolated value of G is

$$G(\bar{\ell}_1,\bar{\ell}_2) = 0.3/1 + 0.5/2 \ . \qquad (3.16)$$

[8] In the terminology of relational models of data, (3.9) may be viewed as an extension to fuzzy relations of the operation of disjunctive mapping [45].

To express this result in linguistic terms, it is necessary to approximate to the right-hand member of (3.16) by a linguistic value which belongs to the term-set of G. The issue of linguistic approximation is discussed in greater detail in [20] and [36].

In summary, if the objective function is defined in linguistic terms by a tableau of the form (3.5), the fuzzy restriction on the values of the decision variables which is induced by the definition is an (n+1)-ary fuzzy relation in $U_1 \times \cdots \times U_n \times V$ which is expressed by (3.6). By the use of this relation, the objective function may be interpolated for values of the decision variables which are not in the original tableau.

4. OPTIMIZATION UNDER MULTIPLE CRITERIA

The linguistic approach appears to be particularly well-adapted to the analysis of decision processes in which the objective function is vector- rather than scalar-valued.[9] The reason for this is that when more than one criterion of performance is involved, the trade-offs between the criteria are usually poorly defined. In such cases, then, linguistic characterizations of trade-offs or preference relations provide a more realistic conceptual framework for decision analysis than the conventional methods employing binary-valued preference relations.

A detailed exposition of the application of the linguistic approach to the optimization under multiple criteria will be presented in a separate paper. In what follows, we shall merely sketch very briefly the main ideas behind the method.

To simplify the notation, we shall assume that there are only two decision variables and two real-valued objective functions G_1 and G_2. The values of G_1 and G_2 at the points (u_1^1, u_2^1) and (u_1^2, u_2^2) are denoted by G_1^1 and G_2^2, respectively.

In the conventional formulation of the problem, the partial ordering defined by

$$(G_1^1, G_2^1) > (G_1^2, G_2^2) \Leftrightarrow G_1^1 \geq G_1^2 \text{ and } G_2^1 \geq G_2^2 \qquad (4.1)$$

induces a pre-ordering in $U_1 \times U_2$ defined by

$$(u_1^1, u_2^1) > (u_1^2, u_2^2) \Leftrightarrow (G_1^1, G_2^1) > (G_1^2, G_2^2) \ . \qquad (4.2)$$

[9] The literature on the optimization under multiple criteria is quite extensive. Of particular relevance to the discussion in this section are the references [46]-[48].

With each point (u_1^0, u_2^0) in $U_1 \times U_2$, we can associate the set of points $D(u_1^0, u_2^0)$ which dominate it; that is,

$$D(u_1^0, u_2^0) = \{(u_1, u_2) \mid (u_1, u_2) > (u_1^0, u_2^0)\} . \qquad (4.3)$$

If C is a constraint set in $U_1 \times U_2$, then a point (u_1^0, u_2^0) in C is undominated if and only if the intersection of C with $D(u_1^0, u_2^0)$ is the singleton $\{(u_1^0, u_2^0)\}$. The set of all undominated points in C is the set of Pareto-optimal solutions to the optimization under the objective functions G_1 and G_2.

Generally, additional assumptions are made to induce a linear ordering in the set of undominated points in C or, at least, to disqualify some of the points in this set from contention as solutions to the optimization problem. The main shortcoming of these techniques is that the assumptions needed to induce a linear ordering tend to be rather arbitrary and hard to justify.

In the linguistic approach to this problem, the Pareto-optimal set is fuzzified and its size is "reduced" by making use of whatever information might be available regarding the trade-offs between G_1 and G_2. Since the trade-offs are usually poorly defined, they are allowed to be expressed in linguistic terms. Generally, the trade-offs are assumed to be defined indirectly via fuzzy preference relations [49], although in some cases it may be possible to define an overall objective function directly as a linguistic function of the linguistic values of G_1 and G_2.

As a simple illustration, a linguistic characterization of a fuzzy preference relation might have the following form.

Assume that the strength of preference is a linguistic variable whose values are <u>strong</u>, <u>very strong</u>, <u>not strong</u>, <u>not very strong</u>, <u>weak</u>, <u>not very strong and not very weak</u>, ... in which the primary terms <u>strong</u> and <u>weak</u> are fuzzy subsets of the unit interval. The meaning of such linguistic values may be computed in exactly the same way as the meaning of the linguistic values of X in Example 2.6.

Let ρ denote the degree to which (u_1^1, u_2^1) is preferred to (u_1^2, u_2^2). Then, a partial linguistic characterization of ρ may be expressed as:

$$\text{If } (G_1^1 \text{ is } \underline{\text{much}}\ \underline{\text{larger}} \text{ than } G_1^2 \text{ and } G_2^1 \text{ is } \underline{\text{approximately}}\ \underline{\text{equal}} \text{ to } G_2^2 \text{ or } G_2^1 \text{ is } \underline{\text{much}}\ \underline{\text{larger}} \text{ than } G_2^2 \text{ and } G_1^1 \text{ is } \underline{\text{approximately}}\ \underline{\text{equal}} \text{ to } G_1^2) \text{ then } \rho \text{ is } \underline{\text{strong}}\ . \quad (4.4)$$

In this expression, the terms _much_ _larger_ and _approximately_ _equal_ play the role of linguistic values of a fuzzy binary relation in $V \times V$, while _strong_ is a linguistic value of ρ. By the use of appropriate semantic rules, the expression in question can be translated into a fuzzy restriction on 5-tuples of the form $(u_1^1, u_2^1, u_1^2, u_2^2, v)$. Combined with similar fuzzy restrictions resulting from whatever other linguistic characterizations of ρ might be available, (4.4) yields a fuzzy preference relation ρ in $U_1 \times U_2 \times U_1 \times U_2 \times V$ which provides a basis for fuzzifying the Pareto-optimal set and thereby reducing the degree to which some of the points in this set may be regarded as contenders for inclusion in the set of optimal solutions.

More specifically, let $u^0 \triangleq (u_1^0, u_2^0)$ be a point in $U_1 \times U_2$. Furthermore, let $D(u^0)$ be the fuzzy set of points in $U_1 \times U_2$ which results from setting u^1 equal to u^0 in the fuzzy preference relation ρ. As in (4.3), $D(u^0)$ is the fuzzy set of points which dominate u^0.

It will be recalled that when $D(u^0)$ is a non-fuzzy set, the point u^0 is undominated and hence an element of the Pareto-optimal set if and only if the intersection of $D(u^0)$ with the constraint set C is the singleton $\{u^0\}$. More generally, if $D(u^0)$ is a fuzzy set then the degree to which u^0 belongs to the fuzzy Pareto-optimal set, P, may be related to the height[10] of the fuzzy set $D(u^0) \cap C - \{u^0\}$ by the relation

$$\mu_P(u^0) = 1 - \sup_{u^1} \left(D(u^0) \cap C - \{u^0\} \right) . \quad (4.5)$$

In this sense, then, the Pareto-optimal set is fuzzified, with each point u^0 assigned a grade of membership in the fuzzy Pareto-optimal set by (4.5).

The fuzzification of the Pareto-optimal set has the effect of reducing the degree of contention for optimality of those points

[10] The height of a fuzzy set is the supremum of its membership function over the universe of discourse.

which have a low grade of membership in the set. In general, the extent to which the size of the Pareto-optimal set is reduced in this fashion depends on the linguistic information provided by the trade-offs. Thus, if the fuzzy restrictions which are associated with the translations of the linguistic statements about the trade-offs are only mildly restrictive -- which is equivalent to saying that they convey little information about the trade-offs -- then the reduction in the size of the Pareto-optimal set will, in general, be slight. By the same token, the opposite will be the case if the restrictions in question are highly informative -- that is, have the effect of assigning low grades of membership to most of the points in $U_1 \times U_2 \times V$.

In sketching the application of the linguistic approach to optimization under multiple criteria, we have side-stepped several non-trivial problems. In the first place, the preference relation ρ which results from translation of linguistic propositions of the form (4.4) is a fuzzy set of Type 2 (i.e., has a fuzzy-set-valued membership function), which makes it more difficult to find the intersection of $D(u_0)$ with the constraint set as well as to compute the grade of membership of u^0 in the fuzzy set of Pareto-optimal solutions. Secondly, the preference relation represented by ρ may not be transitive (in the sense defined in [49]), in which case it may be necessary to construct the transitive closure of ρ. And finally, it may not be a simple matter to apply linguistic approximation to $\mu_P(u^0)$. Notwithstanding these difficulties, the linguistic approach sketched above or some variants of it may eventually provide a realistic way of dealing with practical problems involving decision-making under multiple criteria.

5. CONCLUDING REMARKS

In the foregoing discussion, we have attempted to outline some of the main ideas behind the linguistic approach and point to its possible applications in decision analysis. The specific problems discussed in Sections 3 and 4 are representative -- but not exhaustive -- of such applications. In particular, we have not touched upon the important subject of the manipulation of linguistic probabilities in problems of stochastic control nor upon the problem of multistage decision processes and inference from fuzzy data.

At this juncture, the linguistic approach to decision analysis is in its initial stages of development. Eventually, it may become a useful aid in decision-making relating to real-world problems.

REFERENCES

1. L.J. Savage, The Foundations of Statistics, Wiley, New York, 1954.

2. R.D. Luce, Individual Choice Behavior, Wiley, New York, 1959.

3. G. Debreu, Theory of Value, Wiley, New York, 1959.

4. K.J. Arrow, Social Choice and Individual Values, Wiley, New York, 1963.

5. R.D. Luce and P. Suppes (eds.), Handbook of Mathematical Psychology, Wiley, New York, 1965.

6. R. Radner and J. Marschak (eds.), Economic Theory of Teams, Yale University Press, New Haven, 1972.

7. J. Marschak, "Decision Making: Economic Aspects," in Encyclopedia of Social Sciences, McMillan, New York, 1968.

8. M. Tribus, Rational Descriptions, Decisions and Designs, Pergamon Press, New York, 1969.

9. G. Menges (ed.), Information, Inference and Decision, Reidel, Dordrecht, 1974.

10. W. Edwards and A. Twersky (eds.), Decision Making: Selected Readings, Penguin Books, London, 1967.

11. D.V. Lindley, Making Decisions, Wiley, London, 1971.

12. H. Raiffa, Decision Analysis, Addison-Wesley, Reading, 1970.

13. R.L. Winkler, An Introduction to Bayesian Inference and Decision, Holt, Rinehart and Winston, New York, 1972.

14. H. Simon, "Theories of Bounded Rationality," in Decision and Organization, C.B. McGuire and R. Radner (eds.), North-Holland, 1972.

15. N. Rescher (eds.), The Logic of Decision and Action, Pittsburgh, 1967.

16. P.C. Fishburn, Mathematics of Decision Theory, Mouton, The Hague, 1974.

17. H.W. Gottinger, Bayesian Analysis, Probability and Decision, Vandenhoeck and Ruprecht, Gottingen, 1975.

18. P.C. Fishburn, "A Theory of Subjective Expected Utility with Vague Preferences," Theory and Decision 6, pp. 287-310, 1975.

19. L.A. Zadeh, "Outline of a New Approach to the Analysis of Complex Systems and Decision Processes," IEEE Trans. on Systems, Man and Cybernetics SMC-3, pp. 28-44, 1973.

20. L.A. Zadeh, "The Concept of a Linguistic Variable and its Application to Approximate Reasoning," Inf. Sciences, Part I, 8, pp. 199-249; Part II, 8, pp. 301-357; Part III, 9, pp. 43-80, 1975.

21. L.A. Zadeh, "Fuzzy Logic and Approximate Reasoning (In memory of Grigore Moisil)," Synthese 30, pp. 407-428, 1975.

22. L.A. Zadeh, K.S. Fu, K. Tanaka, M. Shimura (eds.), Fuzzy Sets and Their Applications to Cognitive and Decision Processes, Academic Press, New York, 1975.

23. A. Kaufmann, Introduction to the Theory of Fuzzy Subsets, vol. 1, Elements of Basic Theory, 1973; vol. 2, Applications to Linguistics, Logic and Semantics, 1975; vol. 3, Applications to Classification and Pattern Recognition, Automata and Systems, and Choice of Criteria, 1975, Masson and Co., Paris.

24. R.E. Bellman and L.A. Zadeh, "Decision-Making in a Fuzzy Environment," Management Sciences 17, B-141-B-164, 1970.

25. K. Tanaka, "Fuzzy Automata Theory and its Applications to Control Systems," Osaka University, Osaka, 1970.

26. R.M. Capocelli and A. De Luca, "Fuzzy Sets and Decision Theory, Information and Control 23, pp. 446-473, 1973.

27. L. Fung and K.S. Fu, "An Axiomatic Approach to Rational Decision Making Based on Fuzzy Sets," Purdue University, Lafayette, Indiana, 1973.

28. H.J. Zimmermann, "Optimization in Fuzzy Environments," Institute for Operations Research, Tech. Univ. of Aachen, Aachen, 1974.

29. T. Terano and M. Sugeno, "Microscopic Optimization by Using Conditional Fuzzy Measures," Tokyo Institute of Technology, Tokyo, 1974.

30. N. Tanaka, T. Okuda and K. Asai, "A Formalation of Decision Problems with Fuzzy Events and Fuzzy Information," Dept. of Industrial Eng., University of Osaka Prefecture, Osaka, 1975.

31. D.N. Jacobson, "On Fuzzy Goals and Maximizing Decisions in Stochastic Optimal Control," Nat. Res. Inst. for Math. Sci., Pretoria, 1975.

32. R.G. Woodhead, "On the Theory of Fuzzy Sets to Resolve Ill-Structured Marine Decision Problems," Dept. of Naval Architecture, University of Newcastle, 1972.

33. P.J. King and E.H. Mamdani, "The Application of Fuzzy Control Systems to Industrial Processes," Warren Spring Lab., Stevenage, and Dept. of Elec. Eng., Queen Mary College, London, 1975.

34. E.H. Mamdani and S. Assilian, "An Experiment in Linguistic Synthesis with a Fuzzy Logic Controller," Int. Jour. of Man-Mach. Studies **7**, pp. 1-13, 1975.

35. G. Retherford and G.C. Bloore," The Implementation of Fuzzy Algorithms for Control," Control Systems Center, University of Manchester, Manchester, 1975.

36. F. Wenstop, "Application of Linguistic Variables in the Analysis of Organizations," School of Bus. Ad., University of California, Berkeley, 1975.

37. L. Pun, "Experience in the Use of Fuzzy Formalism in Problems with Various Degrees of Subjectivity," University of Bordeaux, Bordeaux, 1975.

38. V. Dimitrov, W. Wechler and P. Barnev, "Optimal Fuzzy Control of Humanistic Systems," Inst. of Math. and Mechanics, Sofia, and Dept. of Math., Tech. Univ. Dresden, Dresden, 1974.

39. L.A. Zadeh, "Calculus of Fuzzy Restrictions," in Fuzzy Sets and Their Applications to Cognitive and Decision Processes, L.A. Zadeh, K.S. Fu, K. Tanaka and M. Shimura (eds.), Academic Press, New York, 1975.

40. A.V. Aho and J.D. Ullman, The Theory of Parsing, Translation and Compiling, Prentice-Hall, Englewood Cliffs, 1973.

41. L.A. Zadeh, "A Fuzzy-Set Theoretic Interpretation of Linguistic Hedges," Jour. of Cyber. **2**, pp. 4-34, 1972.

42. G. Lakoff, "Hedges: A Study in Meaning Criteria and the Logic of Fuzzy Concepts," Jour. of Phil. Logic **2**, pp. 458-508, 1973.

43. H.M. Hersh, "A Fuzzy Set Approach to Modifiers and Vagueness in Natural Language," Dept. of Psychology, The Johns Hopkins University, Baltimore, 1975.

44. L.A. Zadeh, "A Fuzzy-Algorithmic Approach to the Definition of Complex or Imprecise Concepts," Electronics Research Lab., University of California, Berkeley, 1974. (To appear in the Int. Jour. of Man-Machine Studies.)

45. R.F. Boyce, D.D. Chamberlin, M.M. Hammer and W.F. King III, "Specifying Queries as Relational Expressions," SIGPLAN Notices, ACM, No. 1, 1975.

46. J.L. Cochrane and M. Zeleny (eds.), Multiple Criteria Decision-Making, University of South Carolina Press, Columbia, 1973.

47. M. Zeleny, Linear Multiobjective Programming, Springer-Verlag, New York, 1974.

48. A.M. Geoffrion, "Proper Efficiency and the Theory of Vector Maximization," Jour. of Math. Anal. and Appl. **22**, pp. 618-630, 1968.

49. L.A. Zadeh, "Similarity Relations and Fuzzy Orderings," Inf. Sciences **3**, pp. 177-200, 1971.

R. E. BELLMAN* AND L. A. ZADEH**

LOCAL AND FUZZY LOGICS

ABSTRACT. Fuzzy logic differs from conventional logical systems in that it aims at providing a model for approximate rather than precise reasoning.

The fuzzy logic, FL, which is described in this paper has the following principal features. (a) The truth-values of FL are fuzzy subsets of the unit interval carrying labels such as *true*, *very true*, *not very true*, *false*, *more or less true*, etc.; (b) The truth-values of FL are *structured* in the sense that they may be generated by a grammar and interpreted by a semantic rule; (c) FL is a *local* logic in that, in FL, the truth-values as well as the connectives such as *and*, *or*, *if*... *then* have a variable rather than fixed meaning; and (d) The rules of inference in FL are approximate rather than exact.

The central concept in FL is that of a *fuzzy restriction*, by which is meant a fuzzy relation which acts as an elastic constraint on the values that may be assigned to a variable. Thus, a fuzzy proposition such as 'Nina is *young*' translates into a relational assignment equation of the form R(Age(Nina)) = *young* in which Age(Nina) is a variable, R(Age(Nina)) is a fuzzy restriction on the values of Age(Nina), and *young* is a fuzzy unary relation which is assigned as a value to R(Age(Nina)).

In general, a composite fuzzy proposition translates into a system of relational assignment equations. In this paper, translation rules are developed for propositions of four basic types: Type I, of the general form 'X is mF,' where X is the name of an object or a variable, m is a linguistic modifier, e.g., *not*, *very*, *more or less*, *quite*, etc., and F is a fuzzy subset of a universe of discourse. Type II, of the general form 'X is $F * Y$ is G' or 'X is in relation R to Y,' where * is a binary connective, e.g., *and*, *or*, *if*... *then*, etc., and R is a fuzzy relation, e.g., *much greater*. Type III, of the general form 'QX are F,' where Q is a fuzzy quantifier, e.g., *some*, *most*, *many*, *several*, etc., and F is a fuzzy subset of a universe of discourse. And, Type IV, of the general form 'X is F is τ,' where τ is a linguistic truth-value such as *true*, *very true*, *more or less true*, etc. These rules may be used in combination to translate composite propositions whose constituents are instances of some of the four types in question, e.g., '"*Most tall* men are *stronger* than *most short* men" is *more or less true*,' where the italicized words denote labels of fuzzy sets.

The translation rules for fuzzy propositions of Types I, II, III and IV induce corresponding truth valuation rules which serve to express the fuzzy truth-value of a fuzzy proposition in terms of the truth-values of its constituents. In conjunction with linguistic approximation, these rules provide a basis for approximate inference from fuzzy premises, several forms of which are described and illustrated by examples.

* Departments of Mathematics, Electrical Engineering and Medicine, University of Southern California, Los Angeles, CA 90007, U.S.A. Research partially supported by U.S. Army Research Office Contract DAHCO4-76-G-0027.

** Division of Computer Science, Department of Electrical Engineering and Computer Sciences and the Electronics Research Laboratory, University of California, Berkeley, CA 94720, U.S.A. Research partially supported by Naval Electronics Systems Command Contract NOOO39-76-C-0022 and U.S. Army Research Office Contract DAHC04-75-G0056 and National Science Foundation Grant ENG74-06651-A01.

1. INTRODUCTION

Traditionally, logical systems have aimed at the construction of exact models of exact reasoning – models in which there is no place for imprecision, vagueness or ambiguity.

In a sharp break with this deeply entrenched tradition, the model of reasoning embodied in *fuzzy logic* [1], [2], aims, instead, at an accommodation with the pervasive imprecision of human thinking and cognition. Clearly, we reason in approximate rather than precise terms when we have to decide on which route to take to a desired destination, where to find a space to park our car, or how to locate a lost object. Furthermore, we frequently use a mixture of precise and approximate reasoning in problem-solving situations, e.g., in looking for ways of proving a theorem, choosing a move in a game of chess, or trying to solve a puzzle. On the whole, however, it is evident that all but a small fraction of human reasoning is approximate in nature, and that such reasoning falls, in the main, outside of the domain of strict applicability of classical logic.

To provide an appropriate conceptual framework for approximate reasoning, fuzzy logic is based on the premise that human perceptions involve, for the most part, *fuzzy sets*, that is, classes of objects in which the transition from membership to non-membership is gradual rather than abrupt.[1] It is such sets – rather than sets in the traditional sense – that correspond to the italicized words in the propositions 'Nina is *very attractive*,' 'Mary is *extremely intelligent*,' '*Most* Swedes are *blond*,' 'It is *very true* that John is *much taller* than Betty,' '*Many tall* men are not *very agile*,' 'It is *quite likely* that it will be a *warm* day tomorrow,' etc. We shall refer to such assertions as *fuzzy propositions* in order to differentiate them from nonfuzzy propositions like 'All men are mortal,' 'x is larger than y,' 'Gisela has two sons,' etc.

A distinctive feature of fuzzy logic is that the meaning of such terms as *beautiful*, *tall*, *small*, *approximately equal*, *very true*, etc. is assumed to be not merely subjective but also *local* in the sense of having restricted validity in a specified domain of discourse. Thus, the definition of a *small* number, for example, as a fuzzy subset of the real line may hold only for a designated set of propositions and is allowed to vary from one such set to another. The same applies, more importantly, to the definition of the linguistic truth-values *true*, *very true*, etc. as well as the connectives *and*, *or* and *if ... then*. It is in this sense that fuzzy logic may be viewed as a local logic in which the meaning of propositions, connectives and truth-values is, in general, of local rather than universal validity.

An important consequence of the local validity of meaning is that the inference processes in fuzzy logic are semantic rather than syntactic in nature. By this we mean that the consequence of a given set of premises depends in an essential way on the meaning attached to the fuzzy sets which appear in these premises. As a simple illustration, the consequence of the premises 'X is a *small* number,' and 'X and Y are *approximately equal*,' depends on the meaning of *small* and *approximately equal* expressed as fuzzy subsets of the real line, R, and R^2, respectively. More specifically, the consequence in question may be expressed as 'Y is H,' where H is a fuzzy set which, as will be shown in Section 7, is given by the composition of the unary fuzzy relation *small* with the binary fuzzy relation *approximately equal*.

It is important to observe that *fuzzy logic*, in the sense used above, is a generic term which refers not to a unique logical system but to a collection of local logics in which the truth-values are fuzzy subsets of the truth-value set of an underlying multivalued logic. For example, if the underlying logic (i.e., *base logic*) is Łukasiewicz's L_{aleph_1} logic, then the truth-values of a fuzzy logic whose base logic is L_{aleph_1} would be fuzzy subsets of the unit interval.[2]

In this paper, our attention will be focussed on a particular fuzzy logic which, for convenience, will be referred to as FL [1]. The base logic for FL is L_{aleph_1} and its truth-value set is a countable collection of fuzzy subsets of the unit interval [0, 1], carrying labels of the form *true*, *very true*, *not very true*, *more or less true*, *not false and not true*, etc.

The principal feature that distinguishes FL from classical logics as well as other types of fuzzy logics is that its truth-values are (a) *linguistic* and (b) *structured* in the sense that such truth-values may be generated by a grammar and interpreted by a semantic rule. Thus, as will be seen in Section 4, with *true* playing the role of a *primary term*, the non-primary truth-values in the truth-value set of FL may be generated by a context-free grammar and related to fuzzy subsets of [0, 1] by an attributed grammar [1], [17], [110], [111].

The rationale for the use of linguistic truth-values in FL is the following. If p is a fuzzy proposition such as 'Frances is *very attractive*,' it would be inconsistent to attach a precise numerical truth-value to p, say 0.935, because the meaning of *very attractive* is not sharply defined. Thus, to be consistent, it would be logical to associate a fuzzy truth-value with p, that is, a fuzzy subset of [0, 1] rather than a point in this interval. But, if we allowed any fuzzy subset of [0, 1] to be a truth-value of FL, then the truth-value set of FL would be much too rich and much too difficult to manipulate. Thus, what suggests itself is the idea of allowing only a countable structured collection of fuzzy subsets of [0, 1] to be used as the truth-values of FL. In this way, we trade a continuum of simple truth-values of L_{aleph_1} for a countable – and actually, in most cases, a small – collection of more complex truth-values of FL and gain a significant advantage in the process.

As will be seen in Section 6, the linguistic truth-values of FL do not form a closed system under the operations of conjunction, disjunction and implication. Thus, if the truth-values of p and q are, say, *more or less true* and *not very true and not very false*, then the truth-value of the conjunction 'p and q' will not be, in general, a linguistic truth-value in the truth-value set of FL. Consequently, the use of linguistic truth-values in FL necessitates a *linguistic approximation* to fuzzy subsets of $[0, 1]$ by the linguistic truth-values of FL. The same applies, more generally, to the linguistic values for variables, relations and probabilities that might occur in fuzzy propositions, with the consequence that the inference processes in FL are, for the most part, approximate rather than exact. For example, as was stated earlier, the exact consequence of the premises 'X is a *small* number,' and 'X and Y are *approximately equal*' is 'Y is *small* ∘ *approximately equal*,' where ∘ denotes the operation of composition. A linguistic approximation to the fuzzy set *small* ∘ *approximately equal* might be taken to be *more or less small*,[3] in which case the conclusion 'Y is *more or less small*' becomes an approximate consequence of the premises in question.

In what follows, we shall begin our exposition of fuzzy logic with the introduction of the concept of a *fuzzy restriction*, by which is meant a fuzzy relation which acts as an elastic constraint on the values that may be assigned to a variable. In this capacity, a fuzzy restriction plays a basic role in FL which is somewhat similar to – and yet distinct from – that of a predicate in multivalued logic.

With the concept of a fuzzy restriction as a point of departure, the truth-value of a fuzzy proposition p may be defined as the degree of consistency of p with a reference proposition r. This, in turn, makes it possible to develop valuation rules for expressing the truth-value of a composite proposition in terms of the truth-values of its constituents. However, in FL, unlike the traditional logics, these rules are derived from translation rules which relate the fuzzy restriction associated with a composite fuzzy proposition to those associated with its constituents.

Translation and valuation rules in FL are divided into four categories depending on the form of the fuzzy propositions to which they apply. Thus, rules of Type I apply to propositions of the general form 'X is mF,' where X is the name of an object or a variable, F is a fuzzy subset of a universe of discourse and m is a modifier such as *not*, *very*, *more or less*, *quite*, *extremely*, etc. Examples of propositions of this form are: 'X is a *very small* number,' and 'Ruth is *highly intelligent*.'

Rules of Type II apply to composite propositions of the form (X is F) * (Y is G),' or, more generally, 'X is in relation R to Y,' where R is a fuzzy relation and * is a binary connective such as *and*, *or*, *if* ... *then* ..., etc. (In FL, the conjunction and disjunction are allowed to be *interactive* in the sense defined in Section 4.) Typical examples of such propositions are: 'X is *small* and Y is *very large*,' 'X is *much larger* than Y,' and 'X and Y are *approximately equal*.'

Rules of Type III apply to quantified fuzzy propositions of the form 'QX are F,' where Q is a fuzzy quantifier such as *most*, *many*, *several*, *few*, etc., as in '*Most* Swedes are *tall*.' As for rules of Type IV, they apply to qualified fuzzy propositions of the general form 'X is F is τ,' where τ is a linguistic truth-value. Examples of such propositions are: 'Sally is *very attractive* is *very true*,' and '*Most* Swedes are *tall* is *more or less true*.'

The basic rule of inference in fuzzy logic is the *compositional rule of inference* which may be represented as

$$\begin{array}{l} X \text{ is } F \\ X \text{ is in relation } G \text{ to } Y \\ \hline Y \text{ is } LA(F \circ G) \end{array}$$

where F and G are, respectively, unary and binary fuzzy relations, $F \circ G$ is their composition and $LA(F \circ G)$ is a linguistic approximation to the unary fuzzy relation $F \circ G$. As was stated earlier, in consequence of the use of linguistic approximation, the inference processes in fuzzy logic are, for the most part, approximate rather than exact.

Although fuzzy logic represents a significant departure from the conventional approaches to the formalization of human reasoning, it constitutes – so far at least – an extension rather than a total abandonment of the currently held views on meaning, truth and inference [79]–[108]. It should be stressed that, at this juncture, fuzzy logic is still in its infancy. Thus, our exposition of FL in the present paper should be viewed merely as a step toward the development of a logical system which may serve as a realistic model for human reasoning as well as a basis for a better understanding of the potentialities and limitations of machine intelligence.

2. THE CONCEPT OF A FUZZY RESTRICTION

The concept of a fuzzy restriction [32] plays a central role in fuzzy logic, providing a basis for the characterization of the meaning as well as the truth-value of composite propositions. In what follows, we shall outline some of the basic properties of such restrictions with a view to making use of these properties in later sections for the definition of linguistic truth-values and the formulation of rules of approximate inference from fuzzy premises.

Let X be a variable which takes values in a universe of discourse $U = \{u\}$. Informally, a *fuzzy restriction* is an elastic constraint on the values that may be assigned to X, expressed by a proposition of the form 'X is F,' where F is a fuzzy subset of U. For example, if X is a variable named *Temperature* and F is a fuzzy subset of the real line labeled *high*, then the fuzzy proposition '*Temperature* is *high*' may be interpreted as a fuzzy restriction on the values of *Temperature*.

If the fuzzy set *high* is characterized by its membership function $\mu_{high}: U \rightarrow [0, 1]$, which associates with each temperature, u, its grade of membership, $\mu_{high}(u)$, in the fuzzy set *high*, then $1 - \mu_{high}(u)$ represents the degree to which the elastic constraint expressed by '*Temperature* is *high*' must be stretched to accommodate the assignment of u to X. For example, if $\mu_{high}(100°) = 0.9$, then we shall write

$$Temperature = 100°:0.9 \tag{2.1}$$

to indicate that the assignment of 100° to *Temperature* is compatible to the degree 0.9 with the constraint '*Temperature* is *high*,' or, equivalently, that the constraint in question must be stretched to the degree 0.1 to accommodate the assignment of 100° to *Temperature*.

In more general terms, a variable, X, which takes values in $U = \{u\}$ is a *fuzzy variable* if the restriction on the values that may be assigned to X is a fuzzy subset of U.[4] In relation to X, then, a fuzzy subset F of U is a *fuzzy restriction* if it serves as an elastic constraint on the values of X in the sense that the assignment equation for X has the form

$$X = u:\mu_F(u) \tag{2.2}$$

where $\mu_F(u)$, the grade of membership of u in F, represents the *compatibility* of u with the fuzzy restriction F.

To express that F is a fuzzy restriction on the values of X, we write

$$R_X(u) = F \tag{2.3}$$

where $R_X(u)$ denotes a fuzzy restriction on the elements of U which is associated with the variable X.[5] Thus, the assignment equation (2.2) may be said to imply – or translate into – the assignment equation (2.3). To distinguish (2.3) from (2.2), the latter will be referred to as a *relational assignment equation.*

In general, a fuzzy proposition of the form 'X is F' translates not into

$$R(X) = F \tag{2.4}$$

but into

$$R(A(X)) = F \tag{2.5}$$

where A is an implied attribute of X. For example, the proposition 'Betty is *young*' translates into the relational assignment equation

$$R(Age(\text{Betty})) = young \tag{2.6}$$

where *Age* is an attribute of Betty which is implied by *young*; *Age*(Betty) is a fuzzy variable; and *young* is a fuzzy subset of the real line defined by, say,

$$\mu_{young}(u) = 1 - S(u; 20, 30, 40) \tag{2.7}$$

where the S-function, $S(u; 20, 30, 40)$, is expressed by (see A17)

$$\begin{aligned} S(u; 20, 30, 40) &= 0 && \text{for } u \leq 20 \\ &= 2\left(\frac{u-20}{20}\right)^2 && \text{for } 20 \leq u \leq 30 \\ &= 1 - 2\left(\frac{u-40}{20}\right)^2 && \text{for } 30 \leq u \leq 40 \\ &= 1 && \text{for } u \geq 40 \end{aligned} \tag{2.8}$$

In this definition of *young*, the age $u = 30$ is a *crossover point* in the sense that $\mu_{young}(30) = 0.5$. For $u = 25$, we have $\mu_{young}(25) = 0.875$, and hence 'Betty is *young*' implies

$$Age(\text{Betty}) = 25\colon 0.875 \tag{2.9}$$

In the foregoing discussion, we have restricted our attention to the case where X is a unary fuzzy variable with a base variable u ranging over a single universe of discourse U. In the more general case where X is an n-ary variable, $X = (X_1, \ldots, X_n)$, each of the n components of X is a fuzzy variable, X_i, $i = 1, \ldots, n$, whose base variable, u_i, ranges over a universe of discourse U_i. In this case, a fuzzy restriction on the values of X is an n-ary fuzzy relation, F, in the product space $U_1 \times \ldots \times U_n$, and the assignment equations (2.3) and (2.2) take the form

$$R_X(u_1, \ldots, u_n) = F \tag{2.10}$$

and

$$(X_1, \ldots, X_n) = (u_1, \ldots, u_n)\colon \mu_F(u_1, \ldots, u_n) \tag{2.11}$$

respectively. As an illustration, if X_1 and X_2 are real numbers, then the proposition 'X_2 is *much larger* than X_1' translates into the relational assignment equation

$$R(X_1, X_2) = \textit{much larger} \tag{2.12}$$

where *much larger* is a fuzzy relation in R^2 whose membership function may be defined as, say

$$\begin{aligned} \mu_{\textit{much larger}}(u_1, u_2) &= 0 \text{ for } u_2 \leq u_1 \\ &= \left(1 + \left(\frac{u_2 - u_1}{10}\right)^{-2}\right)^{-1}, u_2 > u_1 \end{aligned} \tag{2.13}$$

Correspondingly, for $u_1 = 2$ and $u_2 = 16$ we deduce

$$(X_1, X_2) = (2, 16)\colon 0.66 \tag{2.14}$$

An important concept that relates to n-ary fuzzy restrictions is that of *noninteraction*. Specifically, the components of an n-ary fuzzy variable are said to be *noninteractive* if and only if

$$R(X_1, \ldots, X_n) = R(X_1) \times \ldots \times R(X_n) \tag{2.15}$$

where $R(X_i)$ denotes the projection of $R(X_1, \ldots, X_n)$ on U_i and $\times$ denotes the cartesian product.[6] Equivalently, $X_1, \ldots, X_n$ are noninteractive if and only if the n-ary assignment equation

$$(X_1, \ldots, X_n) = (u_1, \ldots, u_n)\colon \mu_{R(X_1, \ldots, X_n)}(u_1, \ldots, u_n) \tag{2.16}$$

may be decomposed into n unary assignment equations

$$\begin{aligned} X_1 &= u_1 \colon \mu_{R(X_1)}(u_1) \\ &\cdots\cdots\cdots\cdots \\ X_n &= u_n \colon \mu_{R(X_n)}(u_n) \end{aligned} \tag{2.17}$$

What is implied by (2.15) is that, if $X_1, \ldots, X_n$ are noninteractive, then the assignment of values to any subset of the X_i has no effect on the fuzzy restrictions which apply to the remaining variables. For example, if X_1 and X_2 are noninteractive, then the assignment of a value, say u_1^0, to X_1 does not affect the fuzzy restriction on the values of X_2.[7] As we shall see in later sections, this property of noninteractive variables plays a basic role in the definition of logical connectives.

In the foregoing discussion of the concept of a fuzzy restriction, we have limited our attention to the translation of atomic fuzzy propositions of the form 'X is F.' In Section 4, we shall consider the more general problem of translation of composite propositions which are formed from atomic propositions through the use of logical connectives such as *and*, *or*, *if* ... *then* ..., and fuzzy quantifiers such as *most*, *many*, *few*, etc. As a preliminary, in the following section we shall define the concept of a linguistic variable and apply it to the characterization of the truth-values of fuzzy logic.

3. LINGUISTIC VARIABLES AND TRUTH-VALUES IN FUZZY LOGIC

As was pointed out in the Introduction, one of the important characteristics of fuzzy logic, FL, is that its truth-values are not points or sets but fuzzy subsets of the unit interval which are characterized by linguistic labels such as *true*, *very true*, *not very true*, etc.

To make the meaning of such truth-values more precise, we shall draw on the concept of a linguistic variable – a concept which plays a basic role in approximate reasoning and which, as will be seen in the sequel, bears a close relation to the concept of a fuzzy restriction.

Essentially, a linguistic variable, $\mathscr{X}$, is a nonfuzzy variable which ranges over a collection, $T(\mathscr{X})$, of structured fuzzy variables $X_1, X_2, X_3, \ldots$, with each fuzzy variable in $T(\mathscr{X})$ carrying a linguistic label, X_i, which characterizes the fuzzy restriction which is associated with X_i.

As an illustration, *Age* is a linguistic variable if its values are assumed to be the fuzzy variables labeled *young*, *not young*, *very young*, *not very young*, etc., rather than the numbers 0, 1, 2, 3, ... The *meaning* of a linguistic value of *Age*, say *very young*, is identified with the fuzzy restriction which is associated with the fuzzy variable labeled *very young*. Thus, if the base variable for *Age* (i.e., numerical age) is assumed to range over the universe $U = \{0, 1, \ldots, 100\}$, then the linguistic values of *Age* may be interpreted as the labels of fuzzy subsets of U.

More generally, a linguistic variable is characterized by a quintuple $(\mathscr{X}, T(\mathscr{X}), U, G, M)$, where $\mathscr{X}$ is the name of the variable, e.g., *Age*; $T(\mathscr{X})$ is the *term-set* of $\mathscr{X}$, that is, the collection of its linguistic values, e.g., $T(\mathscr{X}) = \{$*young*, *not young*, *very young*, *not very young*, ...$\}$; U is a universe of discourse, e.g., in the case of *Age*, the set $\{0, 1, 2, \ldots, 100\}$; G is a syntactic rule which generates the terms in $T(\mathscr{X})$; and M is a semantic rule which associates with each term, X_i, in $T(\mathscr{X})$ its *meaning*, $M(X_i)$, where $M(X_i)$ is a fuzzy subset of U which serves as a fuzzy restriction on the values of the fuzzy variable X_i.

A key idea behind the concept of a linguistic variable is that the fuzzy restriction associated with each X_i may be deduced from the fuzzy restrictions associated with the so-called *primary terms* in $T(\mathscr{X})$. In effect, these terms play the role of units which, upon calibration, make it possible to compute the meaning of the composite (i.e., non-primary) terms in $T(\mathscr{X})$ from the knowledge of the meaning of primary terms.

As an illustration, we shall consider an example in which $U = [0, \infty)$ and the term-set of $\mathscr{X}$ is of the form

$$T(\mathscr{X}) = \{\textit{small, not small, very small, very (not small), not very small, very very small}, \ldots\} \tag{3.1}$$

in which *small* is the primary term.

The terms in $T(\mathscr{X})$ may be generated by a context-free grammar $G = (V_T, V_N, S, P)$ in which the set of terminals, V_T, comprises (,), the primary term *small* and the linguistic modifiers *very* and *not*; the non-terminals are denoted by S, A and B, and the production system is given by:

$$\begin{aligned} S &\to A \\ S &\to not\ A \\ A &\to B \\ B &\to very\ B \\ B &\to (S) \\ B &\to small \end{aligned} \tag{3.2}$$

Thus, a typical derivation yields

$$S \to not\ A \to not\ B \to not\ very\ B \to not\ very\ very\ B \to not\ very\ very\ small. \tag{3.3}$$

In this sense, the syntactic rule associated with $\mathscr{X}$ may be viewed as the process of generating the elements of $T(\mathscr{X})$ by a succession of substitutions involving the productions in G.

As for the semantic rule, we shall assume for simplicity that if μ_A is the membership function of A then the membership functions of *not A* and *very A* are given respectively by

$$\mu_{not\ A} = 1 - \mu_A \tag{3.4}$$

and

$$\mu_{very\ A} = (\mu_A)^2. \tag{3.5}$$

Thus, (3.5) signifies that the modifier *very* has the effect of squaring the membership function of its operand.[8]

Suppose that the meaning of *small* is defined by the membership function

$$\mu_{small}(u) = \left(1 + (0.1u)^2\right)^{-1}, \quad u \geq 0. \tag{3.6}$$

Then the meaning of *very small* is given by

$$\mu_{very\ small} = \left(1 + (0.1u)^2\right)^{-2} \tag{3.7}$$

while the meanings of *not very small* and *very (not small)* are expressed respectively by

$$\mu_{not\ very\ small} = 1 - \left(1 + (0.1u)^2\right)^{-2} \tag{3.8}$$

and

$$\mu_{very\ (not\ small)} = \left(1 - \left(1 + (0.1u)^2\right)^{-1}\right)^2. \tag{3.9}$$

In this way, we can readily compute the expression for the membership function of any term in $T(\mathscr{X})$ from the knowledge of the membership function of the primary term *small*.

In summary, a linguistic variable $\mathscr{X}$ may be viewed, in effect, as a micro-language whose sentences are the linguistic values of $\mathscr{X}$, with the meaning of each sentence represented as a fuzzy restriction on the values of a base variable, u, in a universe of discourse, U. The syntax and semantics of this language are, respectively, the syntactic and semantic rules associated with $\mathscr{X}$.

In applying the concept of a linguistic variable to fuzzy logic, we assume that *Truth* is a linguistic variable with a term-set of the form[9]

$$T(Truth) = \{true, false, not\ true, very\ true, not\ very\ true, \\ very\ (not\ true), not\ very\ true\ and\ not\ very\ false, \ldots\} \tag{3.10}$$

in which the primary term is *true*.

In the case of FL, the universe of discourse, V, associated with *Truth* is assumed to be the unit interval $[0, 1]$, and the logical operations on the linguistic truth-values are fuzzy extensions – in the sense defined in Section 6 – of the corresponding operations in Lukasiewicz's logic L_{aleph_1} [109]. Thus, L_{aleph_1} serves as a *base logic* for FL, with the linguistic truth-values of FL being fuzzy subsets of the truth-value set of L_{aleph_1}.[10]

So far, we have not addressed ourselves to a basic issue, namely, what is the significance of associating a numerical or linguistic truth-value with a fuzzy proposition? What does it mean, for example, to assert that 'X is *small* is 0.8 true' or 'Gail is *highly intelligent* is *very true*?'

Informally, we shall adopt the view that a truth-value, numerical or linguistic, represents the degree of consistency of p with a reference proposition r. Thus, in symbols ($\triangleq$ denotes 'is defined to be')

$$v(p) \triangleq C(R(p), R(r)) \tag{3.11}$$

where $v(p)$ denotes the truth-value of p; $R(p)$ and $R(r)$ represent, respectively, the restrictions associated with p and r; and C is a *consistency function* which maps ordered pairs of restrictions into points in $[0, 1]$ or fuzzy subsets of $[0,1]$ and thereby defines the degree of consistency of p with r.

In general, r may be, like p, a fuzzy proposition. In the sequel, however, we shall take a more restricted point of view. Specifically, we shall assume that, if (a) p is a fuzzy proposition of the form

$$p \triangleq X \text{ is } F \tag{3.12}$$

which translates into

$$R(A(X)) = F \tag{3.13}$$

where $A(X)$ is an implied attribute of X, and (b) $v(p)$ is a numerical truth-value in $[0, 1]$, then the reference proposition r is a nonfuzzy proposition of the form

$$r \triangleq X \text{ is } u \tag{3.14}$$

where u is an element of U which represents a reference value of the variable $A(X)$.[11] Under these assumptions, then, the numerical truth-value of p is defined by

$$v(p) \triangleq t = C(F, u) \tag{3.15}$$

$$\triangleq \mu_F(u)$$

where $\mu_F(u)$ is the grade of membership of u in F. In effect, (3.15) implies that the truth-value of p is equated, by definition, to the grade of membership of u in F, where u is a reference value of the variable $A(X)$. As an illustration, consider the proposition $p \triangleq$ Ilka is *tall*, where *tall* is defined by

$$\mu_{tall}(u) = S(u; 160, 170, 180). \tag{3.16}$$

Then, if Ilka is, in fact, 172 cm tall and r is taken to be

$$r \triangleq \text{Ilka is 172 cm tall} \tag{3.17}$$

we have

$$v(\text{Ilka is } tall) = t = S(172; 160, 170, 180) \qquad (3.18)$$
$$= 0.68$$

which thus represents the numerical truth-value of the fuzzy proposition $p \triangleq$ Ilka is *tall*.

We are now in a position to extend the notion of a numerical truth-value to fuzzy truth-values by interpreting a linguistic truth-value, τ, as the degree of consistency of p with a fuzzy reference proposition r. Thus, if r is of the form

$$r \triangleq X \text{ is } G \qquad (3.19)$$

where G is a fuzzy subset of U, then a fuzzy truth-value, τ, may be associated formally with p by the expression

$$\tau = \mu_F(G) \qquad (3.20)$$

where μ_F, as in (3.15), represents the membership function of F.[12]

To make (3.20) meaningful, it is necessary to extend the domain of definition of μ_F from U to $\mathcal{F}(U)$, where $\mathcal{F}(U)$ is the set of fuzzy subsets of U. This can be done by using the *extension principle* (A70), which is a basic rule for extending the definition of a function defined on a space U to $\mathcal{F}(U)$. Specifically, in application to (3.20), let G be represented symbolically in the 'integral' form (see A8)

$$G = \int_U \mu_G(u)/u \qquad (3.21)$$

where the integral sign denotes the union of fuzzy singletons $\mu_G(u)/u$, with $\mu_G(u)/u$ signifying that the compatibility of u with G (or, equivalently, the grade of membership of u in G) is $\mu_G(u)$. Then, on invoking the extension principle and treating μ_F as a function from U to $[0, 1]$, we obtain

$$\mu_F(G) = \int_{[0,1]} \mu_G(u)/\mu_F(u) \qquad (3.22)$$

which means that μ_F(G) is the union of fuzzy singletons $\mu_G(u)/\mu_F$(u) in $[0, 1]$.

When we have to make explicit that an expression, E, has to be evaluated by the use of the extension principle, we shall enclose E in angular brackets. With this understanding, then, a linguistic truth-value, τ, may be expressed as

$$\tau = \langle \mu_F(G) \rangle = \int_{[0,1]} \mu_G(u)/\mu_F(u). \qquad (3.23)$$

Adopting the interpretation of τ which is defined by (3.23), let $\mu_\tau : V \rightarrow [0, 1]$ denote the membership function of τ. Then, the meaning of τ as a fuzzy subset of V may be expressed as

$$\tau = \int_0^1 \mu_\tau(v)/v \tag{3.24}$$

where $v \in V = [0, 1]$ is the base variable for the fuzzy variable τ, and the integral sign, as in (3.21), denotes the union of fuzzy singletons $\mu_\tau(v)/v$, with $\mu_\tau(v)/v$ signifying that the compatibility of the numerical truth-value v with the linguistic truth-value τ is $\mu_\tau(v)$.

If the support of τ, that is, the set of points in V at which $\mu_\tau(v) \neq 0$, is a finite subset $\{v_1, \ldots, v_n\}$ of V, and μ_i is the compatibility of v_i with τ, $i = 1, \ldots, n$, then τ may be expressed as

$$\tau = \mu_1/v_1 + \ldots + \mu_n/v_n \tag{3.25}$$

or more simply as the linear form

$$\tau = \mu_1 v_1 + \ldots + \mu_n v_n \tag{3.26}$$

when no confusion between μ_i and v_i in a term of the form $\mu_i v_i$ can arise. It should be noted that in (3.25) and (3.26) the plus sign – like the integral sign in (3.24) – should be interpreted as the union rather than the arithmetic sum.

As an illustration of (3.24), if the membership function of *true* is assumed to be expressed as an S-function (see A17)

$$\mu_{true}(v) = S(v; 0.5, 0.75, 1) \tag{3.27}$$

then the meaning of *true* is the fuzzy subset of V expressed as

$$true = \int_0^1 S(v; 0.5, 0.75, 1)/v. \tag{3.28}$$

If V is assumed to be the finite set $\{0, 0.1, 0.2, \ldots, 1\}$, then *true* may be defined as a fuzzy subset of V by, say,

$$true = 0.3/0.6 + 0.5/0.7 + 0.7/0.8 + 0.9/0.9 + 1/1. \tag{3.29}$$

In this expression, a term such as 0.7/0.8 signifies that the compatibility of the numerical truth-value 0.8 with the linguistic truth-value *true* is 0.7. It is important to note that the definition of *true* in (3.28) and (3.29) is entirely subjective as well as local in nature.

On occasion, we shall find it convenient to relate to a linguistic truth-value τ its *dual*, $D(\tau)$, which is defined by

$$\mu_{D(\tau)}(v) = \mu_\tau(1 - v), \quad v \in [0, 1]. \tag{3.30}$$

or, equivalently,

$$D(\tau) = 1 - \tau \tag{3.31}$$

where for simplicity we have suppressed the angular brackets in the right-hand member of (3.31). Thus, if *true*, for example, is defined by (3.29), then

$$D(true) = 0.3/0.4 + 0.5/0.3 + 0.7/0.2 + 0.9/0.1 + 1/0$$

and $D(true)$ will be assumed to be the meaning of *false*, i.e.,

$$false \triangleq D(true) \tag{3.32}$$

and conversely

$$true = D(false). \tag{3.33}$$

As shown in [1], the linguistic truth-values in $T(Truth)$ can be generated by a context-free grammar whose production system is given by

$$\begin{array}{ll}
S \to A & C \to D \\
S \to S \text{ or } A & C \to E \\
A \to B & D \to \text{very } D \\
A \to A \text{ and } B & E \to \text{very } E \\
B \to C & D \to \text{true} \\
B \to \text{not } C & E \to \text{false} \\
C \to (S) &
\end{array} \tag{3.34}$$

In this grammar, S, A, B, C, D, and E are nonterminals; and *true*, *false*, *very*, *not*, *and*, *or*, (,) are terminals. Thus, a typical derivation yields

$$\begin{aligned}
& S \to A \to A \text{ and } B \to B \text{ and } B \to \text{not } C \text{ and } B \to \\
& \quad \to \text{not } E \text{ and } B \to \text{not very } E \text{ and } B \to \text{not very false and } B \\
& \quad \to \text{not very false and not } C \to \text{not very false and not } D \\
& \quad \to \text{not very false and not very } D \\
& \quad \to \text{not very false and not very true}
\end{aligned} \tag{3.35}$$

If the syntactic rule for generating the elements of $T(Truth)$ is expressed as a context-free grammar, then the corresponding semantic rule may be conveniently expressed by a system of productions and relations in which each production in G is associated with a relation between the fuzzy subsets representing the meaning of the terminals and nonterminals.[13] For example, the production $A \rightarrow A \text{ and } B$ induces the relation

$$A_L = A_R \cap B_R \tag{3.36}$$

where A_L, A_R, and B_R represent the meaning of A and B as fuzzy subsets of $[0, 1]$ (the subscripts L and R serve to differentiate between the symbols on the left- and right-hand sides of a production), and $\cap$ denotes the intersection. Thus, in effect, (3.36) defines the meaning of the connective *and.*

Similarly, the production $B \rightarrow \text{not } C$ induces the relation

$$B_L = C'_R \tag{3.37}$$

where C'_R denotes the complement of the fuzzy set C_R (see A32), while $D \rightarrow \text{very } D$ induces

$$D_L = (D_R)^2 \tag{3.38}$$

which implies that the membership function of D_L is related to that of D_R by

$$\mu_{D_L} = (\mu_{D_R})^2. \tag{3.39}$$

With this understanding, the dual system corresponding to (3.34) may be written as

$$\begin{aligned}
&S \rightarrow A &&: S_L = A_R \\
&S \rightarrow S \text{ or } A &&: S_L = S_R \cup A_R \\
&A \rightarrow B &&: A_L = B_R \\
&A \rightarrow A \text{ and } B &&: A_L = A_R \cap B_R \\
&B \rightarrow C &&: B_L = C_R \\
&B \rightarrow \text{not } C &&: B_L = C'_R \\
&C \rightarrow S &&: C_L = S_R \\
&C \rightarrow D &&: C_L = D_R \\
&C \rightarrow E &&: C_L = E_R \\
&D \rightarrow \text{very } D &&: D_L = (D_R)^2
\end{aligned} \tag{3.40}$$

$$E \to very\ E \quad : E_L = (E_R)^2$$

$$D \to true \quad : D_L = true$$

$$E \to false \quad : E_L = false$$

where $\cup$ denotes the union.

To employ this dual system to compute the meaning of a term, τ, generated by G, it is necessary, in principle, to construct a syntax tree for τ. Then, by advancing from the leaves of the tree to its root and successively computing the meaning of each node by the use of (3.40), we eventually arrive at the expression for the membership function of τ in terms of the membership function of the primary term *true*.

In practice, however, the linguistic values of *Truth* that one would commonly employ to characterize the truth-value of a fuzzy proposition, e.g., 'Barbara is *very intelligent*,' are likely to be sufficiently simple to make it possible to compute their meaning by inspection. For example,[14]

$$not\ very\ true = (true^2)' \tag{3.41}$$

$$not\ very\ (not\ very\ true) = (((true^2)')^2)'. \tag{3.42}$$

$$true\ and\ not\ very\ true = true \cap (true^2)' \tag{3.43}$$

$$not\ very\ true\ and\ not\ very\ false = (true^2)' \cap (false^2)' \tag{3.44}$$

where $'$ denotes the complement and, in consequence of (3.32),

$$false = 1 - true \tag{3.45}$$

with (3.45) implying that the membership function of *false* is related to that of *true* by

$$\mu_{false}(v) = \mu_{true}(1 - v), \quad v \in [0, 1]. \tag{3.46}$$

Note that *false* $\neq$ *not true*, since

$$not\ true = true' \tag{3.47}$$

while *false* $= 1 -$ *true*. The reason for defining the meaning of *false* by (3.45) rather than by equating *false* to *not true* will become clear in Section 6.

In the following two sections, we shall turn our attention to a problem that occupies a central place in fuzzy logic, namely, that of translating a fuzzy proposition into one or more relational assignment equations. Then, from the rules governing such translations, we shall be able to derive a set of valuation rules for computing the truth-values of composite fuzzy propositions.

4. TRANSLATION RULES FOR FUZZY PROPOSITIONS—TYPES I AND II

As was stated in the Introduction, one of the basic problems in fuzzy logic is that of developing a set of rules for translating a given fuzzy proposition into a system of relational assignment equations.

In this section, we shall address ourselves to some of the simpler aspects of this problem, focusing our attention on what will be referred to as translation rules of Types I and II. In Section 5, we shall consider translation rules of Types III and IV, which apply to more complex propositions containing, respectively, quantifiers and truth-values. Implicit in all of these rules is Frege's principle [99], [112] that the meaning of a composite proposition is a function of the meanings of its constituents.

4.1. Translation Rules of Type I

Translation rules of this type apply to fuzzy propositions of the form $p \triangleq X$ is mF, where F is a fuzzy subset of $U = \{u\}$, m is a modifier such as *not*, *very*, *more or less*, *slightly*, *somewhat*, etc., and either X or $A(X)$ – where A is an implied attribute of X – is a fuzzy variable which takes values in U.

Translation rules of Type I may be subsumed under a general rule which, for convenience, will be referred to as the *modifier rule*. In essence, this rule asserts that the translation of a fuzzy proposition of the form $p \triangleq X$ is mF is expressed by

$$X \text{ is } mF \rightarrow R(A(X)) = mF \tag{4.1}$$

where m is interpreted as an operator which transforms the fuzzy set F into the fuzzy set mF.

In particular, if $m \triangleq$ *not*, then the *rule of negation* asserts that the translation of $p \triangleq X$ is *not* F is expressed by

$$X \text{ is } \textit{not } F \rightarrow X \text{ is } F' \rightarrow R(A(X)) = F' \tag{4.2}$$

where F' is the complement of F, i.e.,

$$\mu_{F'}(u) = 1 - \mu_F(u), \quad u \in U. \tag{4.3}$$

For example, if

$$\mu_{young}(u) = 1 - S(u; 20, 30, 40) \tag{4.4}$$

then $p \triangleq$ John is *not young* translates into

$$R(\text{Age(John)}) = young' \tag{4.5}$$

where, in the notation of (3.21),

$$young' = \int_0^\infty S(u; 20, 30, 40)/u. \tag{4.6}$$

In general, m may be viewed as a restriction modifier which acts in a specified way on its operand. For example, the modifier *very* may be assumed to act – to a first approximation – as a concentrator which has the effect of squaring the membership function of its operand [51]. Correspondingly, the *rule of concentration* asserts that the translation of the fuzzy proposition $p = X$ is *very* F is expressed by

$$X \text{ is } very\ F \rightarrow X \text{ is } F^2 \rightarrow R(A(X)) = F^2 \tag{4.7}$$

where

$$very\ F = F^2 = \int_U (\mu_F(u))^2/u \tag{4.8}$$

and $A(X)$ is an implied attribute of X.

As an illustration, on applying (4.7), we find that 'Sherry is *very young*' translates into

$$R(\text{Age(Sherry)}) = young^2 \tag{4.9}$$

where

$$young^2 = \int_0^\infty (1 - S(u; 20, 30, 40))^2/u. \tag{4.10}$$

Similarly, on combining (4.2) with (4.7), we find that 'Sherry is *not very very young*' translates into

$$R(\text{Age(Sherry)}) = (young^4)' \tag{4.11}$$

where

$$(young^4)' = \int_0^\infty (1 - (1 - S(u; 20, 30, 40))^4)/u. \tag{4.12}$$

The effect of the modifier *more or less* is less susceptible to simple approximation than that of *very*. In some contexts, *more or less* acts as a dilator, playing a role inverse to that of *very*. Thus, to a first approximation, we may assume that, in such contexts, *more or less* may be defined by

$$more\ or\ less\ F = \sqrt{F} \tag{4.13}$$

where

$$\sqrt{F} = \int_U (\mu_F(u))^{1/2}/u.$$

Based on this definition of *more or less*, the *rule of dilation* asserts that

$$X \text{ is } \textit{more or less } F \to X \text{ is } \sqrt{F} \to R(A(X)) = \sqrt{F} \tag{4.14}$$

where $A(X)$ is an implied attribute of X. For example, 'Doris is *more or less young*' translates into

$$R(\text{Age(Doris)}) = \sqrt{\textit{young}} = \int_0^\infty (1 - S(u; 20, 30, 40))^{1/2}/u \tag{4.15}$$

while 'Doris is *more or less* (*not very young*)' translates into

$$R(\text{Age(Doris)}) = ((\textit{young}^2)')^{1/2}. \tag{4.16}$$

In other contexts, *more or less* acts as a *fuzzifier* whose effect may be approximated by

$$\textit{more or less } F = \int_U \mu_F(u)\, K(u) \tag{4.17}$$

where $K(u)$ is a specified fuzzy subset of U which depends on u as a parameter, $\mu_F(u)\,K(u)$ is a fuzzy set whose membership function is the product of $\mu_F(u)$ and the membership function of $K(u)$, and $\int_U$ denotes the union of the fuzzy sets $\mu_F(u)\,K(u)$, $u \in U$. When *more or less* is defined as a fuzzifier by (4.17), the fuzzy set $K(u)$ in the right-hand member of (4.17) is referred to as the *kernel* of the fuzzifier. Note that (4.17) implies that $K(u)$ may be interpreted as the result of acting with *more or less* on the singleton $\{u\}$ [51].

As an illustration, suppose that

$$U = 1 + 2 + 3 + 4 \tag{4.18}$$

and that a fuzzy subset of U labeled *small* is defined by

$$\textit{small} = 1/1 + 0.6/2 + 0.2/3. \tag{4.19}$$

Furthermore, assume that the kernel of *more or less* is given by

$$\begin{aligned} K(1) &= 1/1 + 0.9/2 \\ K(2) &= 1/2 + 0.9/3 \\ K(3) &= 1/3 + 0.8/4 \end{aligned} \tag{4.20}$$

Then, on substituting (4.19) and (4.20) in (4.17), we obtain

$$\begin{aligned} \textit{more or less small} &= K(1) + 0.6K(2) + 0.2K(3) \\ &= 1/1 + 0.9/2 + 0.6/2 + 0.54/3 \\ &\quad + 0.2/3 + 0.16/4 \\ &= 1/1 + 0.9/2 + 0.54/3 + 0.16/4 \end{aligned} \tag{4.21}$$

whereas, had we used (4.14), we would have

$$\textit{more or less small} = 1/1 + 0.77/2 + 0.45/3. \tag{4.22}$$

When *more or less* is interpreted as a fuzzifier, the corresponding modifier rule will be referred to as the *rule of fuzzification*. In symbols, the statement of this rule reads:

$$X \text{ is } \textit{more or less } F \rightarrow R(A(X)) = \int_U \mu_F(u)\, K(u) \tag{4.23}$$

where $K(u)$ is the kernel of *more or less* and $A(X)$ is an implied attribute of X. For example, the application of this rule to the proposition 'X is *more or less small*,' in which *small* and *more or less* are defined by (4.19) and (4.20), yields

$$\begin{aligned} R(X) &= \textit{more or less small} \\ &= 1/1 + 0.9/2 + 0.54/3 + 0.16/4. \end{aligned} \tag{4.24}$$

By comparison, the application of the rule of dilation would yield

$$R(X) = 1/1 + 0.77/2 + 0.45/3. \tag{4.25}$$

In most practical applications, the difference between (4.24) and (4.25) would not be considered to be of significance.

Proceeding in a similar fashion, one can formulate, in principle, other concrete versions of the modifier rule for modifiers such as *slightly*, *quite*, *rather*, etc. In general, the definition of the effect of such modifiers presents many non-trivial problems which, at this stage of the development of the theory of fuzzy sets, are still largely unexplored [51]–[56].

4.2. Translation Rules of Type II

Translation rules of this type apply to composite fuzzy propositions which are generated from atomic fuzzy propositions of the form 'X is F' through the use of various kinds of binary connectives such as the conjunction, *and*, the disjunction, *or*, the conditional *if ... then ...*, etc.

More specifically, let $U = \{u\}$ and $V = \{v\}$ be two possibly different universes of discourse, and let F and G be fuzzy subsets of U and V, respectively.

Consider the atomic propositions 'X is F' and 'Y is G,' and let q be their conjunction 'X is F and Y is G.' Then, the rule of *noninteractive conjunctive composition* or, for short, the *rule of conjunctive composition* asserts that the translation of q is expressed by

$$X \text{ is } F \text{ and } Y \text{ is } G \rightarrow (X, Y) \text{ is } F \times G \rightarrow R(A(X), B(Y)) = F \times G \tag{4.26}$$

where $A(X)$ and $B(Y)$ are implied attributes of X and Y, respectively; $R(A(X), B(Y))$ is a fuzzy restriction on the values of the binary fuzzy variable $(A(X), B(Y))$; and $F \times G$ is the cartesian product of F and B. Thus, under this rule, the fuzzy proposition 'Keith is *tall* and Adrienne is *young*' translates into

$$R((\text{Height}(\text{Keith})), \text{Age}(\text{Adrienne})) = \textit{tall} \times \textit{young} \qquad (4.27)$$

where *tall* and *young* are fuzzy subsets of the real line.

To clarify the reason for qualifying the term 'conjunction' with the adjective 'noninteractive,' it is convenient to rewrite (4.26) in the equivalent form

$$X \text{ is } F \text{ and } Y \text{ is } G \rightarrow R(A(X), B(Y)) = \bar{F} \cap \bar{G} \qquad (4.28)$$

where $\bar{F}$ and $\bar{G}$ are the cylindrical extensions (see A59) of F and G, respectively, and $\bar{F} \cap \bar{G}$ is their intersection. In this form, the rule in question places in evidence the $1-1$ correspondence between the noninteractive conjunction of fuzzy propositions, on the one hand, and the intersection of fuzzy cylindrical extensions, on the other.

The rationale for identifying 'noninteraction' with set intersection is provided by the following lemma.[15]

LEMMA. Let $M = \{\mu\}$, $N = \{\nu\}$, and let c be a mapping from $M \times N$ to the unit interval $[0, 1]$. Then, under the following conditions on c:

(a) c is continuous in both arguments

(b) c is monotone non-decreasing in both arguments

(c) $c(\mu, 0) = c(0, \nu) = 0$ for all μ, ν in $[0, 1]$

(d) $c(\mu, \mu) = \mu$ for all μ in $[0, 1]$

(e) For all μ in $[0, 1]$, there do not exist $\alpha, \beta \in [0, 1]$ such that $\alpha > \mu, \beta < \mu$ (or $\alpha < \mu$ and $\beta > \mu$) and $c(\alpha, \beta) = c(\mu, \mu)$

c must necessarily be of the form

$$c = \min(\mu, \nu) = \mu \wedge \nu. \qquad (4.29)$$

Note that condition (e) signifies that an increase in the first argument of c cannot be compensated by, or traded for, a decrease in the second argument of c, or vice-versa.

Proof. The proof is immediate. Let $\alpha > \mu$ and assume that $c(\alpha, \mu) > c(\mu, \mu) = \mu$. Now, $c(\alpha, 0) = 0$ by (c) and hence from (a) it follows that there exists a β, $0 \leq \beta < \mu$, such that $c(\alpha, \beta) = \mu$. Since this contradicts (e), it follows that $c(\alpha, \mu) = \mu$ for $\alpha > \mu$ and hence that $c(\alpha, \mu) = \min(\alpha, \mu)$.

Q.E.D.

The main point of this lemma is that noncompensation implies and is implied by the form of dependence of c on μ and ν which is expressed by (4.29). Now, the intersection of $\bar{F}$ and $\bar{G}$ is defined by

$$\mu_{\bar{F} \cap \bar{G}}(u, v) = \mu_{\bar{F}}(u) \wedge \mu_{\bar{G}}(v) \tag{4.30}$$

and hence what we have called *noninteractive conjunction* – or simply *conjunction* – corresponds to noncompensation (in the sense of (e)) of the membership functions $\mu_{\bar{F}}$ and $\mu_{\bar{G}}$ which are associated with the operands of *and*.

To differentiate between noninteractive and interactive conjunction, the latter will be denoted by *and**. With this understanding, the rule of interactive conjunction, in its general form, may be expressed as

$$X \text{ is } F \text{ and* } Y \text{ is } G \rightarrow R(A(X), B(Y)) = F \otimes G \tag{4.31}$$

where $\otimes$ is a binary operation which maps F and G into a subset of $U \times V$ and thus provides a definition of *and** in a particular context.

A simple example of an interactive conjunction is provided by the translation rule

$$X \text{ is } F \text{ and* } Y \text{ is } G \rightarrow R(A(X), B(Y)) = FG \tag{4.32}$$

where

$$\mu_{FG} = \mu_F \mu_G. \tag{4.33}$$

Note that in this case, an increase in the grade of membership in F can be compensated for by a decrease in the grade of membership in G, and vice-versa.

It should be noted that while noninteractive conjunction is defined uniquely by (4.26), interactive conjunction is strongly application-dependent and has no universally valid definition. Thus, (4.33) constitutes but one of many ways in which interactive conjunction may be defined. In general, one would expect a definition of interactive conjunction to satisfy the conditions (a), (b), (c), and a weaker form of (d), namely, $c(\mu, \mu) \leq \mu$, but not (e).

The rules governing the translation of disjunctive propositions are dual of those of (4.26) and (4.31). Thus, the *rule of noninteractive disjunctive composition* – or simply the *rule of disjunctive composition* asserts that

$$X \text{ is } F \text{ or } Y \text{ is } G \rightarrow R(A(X), B(Y)) = \bar{F} + \bar{G} \tag{4.34}$$

where $\bar{F} + \bar{G}$ denotes the union of the cylindrical extensions of F and G. Correspondingly, the *rule of interactive disjunction* reads

$$X \text{ is } F \text{ or* } Y \text{ is } G \rightarrow R(A(X), B(Y)) = F \otimes G \tag{4.35}$$

where $\otimes$ is an operation on F, G which defines or*, with the' understanding that the conditions on or* are the same as on and*, except that 0 in (a) is replaced by 1.

Turning to conditional fuzzy propositions of the form 'If X is F then Y is G,' the translation rule for such propositions, which will be referred to as the *rule of conditional composition*, may be expressed as[16]

$$\text{If } X \text{ is } F \text{ then } Y \text{ is } G \rightarrow R(A(X), B(Y)) = \bar{F}' \oplus \bar{G} \tag{4.36}$$

where $\oplus$ denotes the bounded sum[17] and $\bar{F}'$ is the complement of the cylindrical extension of F.

As an illustration, assume that *tall* and *young* are defined by

$$tall = \int_U S(u; 160, 170, 180)/u \tag{4.37}$$

$$young = \int_V (1 - S(v; 20, 30, 40))/v \tag{4.38}$$

where U and V may be taken to be the real line and the height is assumed to be measured in centimeters. Then, the fuzzy proposition 'If Keith is *tall* then Adrienne is *young*' translates into

$$R(\text{Height(Keith)}, \text{Age(Adrienne)}) = \overline{tall'} \oplus \overline{young} \tag{4.39}$$

or, more explicitly,

$$\begin{aligned} &R(\text{Height(Keith)}, \text{Age(Adrienne)}) \\ &= \int_{U \times V} (1 \wedge (1 - \mu_{tall}(u) + \mu_{young}(v)))/(u, v) \\ &= \int_{U \times V} (1 \wedge (1 - S(u; 160, 170, 180) \\ &\quad + 1 - S(v; 20, 30, 40)))/(u, v) \end{aligned} \tag{4.40}$$

If the conditional fuzzy proposition 'If X is F then Y is G else Y is H' is interpreted as the conjunction of the propositions 'If X is F then Y is G' and 'If X is *not* F then Y is H,' then by using in combination the rule of negation (4.2), the rule of conjunctive composition (4.26), and the rule of conditional composition (4.36), the translation of the proposition in question is found to be expressed by

$$\begin{aligned} &\text{If } X \text{ is } F \text{ then } Y \text{ is } G \text{ else } Y \text{ is } H \rightarrow R(A(X), B(Y)) \\ &= (F' \oplus \bar{G}) \cap (\bar{F} \oplus \bar{H}) \end{aligned} \tag{4.41}$$

As a simple illustration, assume that $U = V = 1 + 2 + 3 + 4$,

$$F = small = 1/1 + 0.6/2 + 0.2/3 \tag{4.42}$$

$$G = large = 0.2/2 + 0.6/3 + 1/4 \tag{4.43}$$

and

$$H = very\ large = 0.04/2 + 0.36/3 + 1/4. \tag{4.44}$$

Then

$$F' = 0.4/2 + 0.8/3 + 1/4 \tag{4.45}$$

$$\begin{aligned} \bar{F}' = {} & 0.4/((2,1) + (2,2) + (2,3) + (2,4)) \\ & + 0.8/((3,1) + (3,2) + (3,3) + (3,4)) \\ & + 1/((4,1) + (4,2) + (4,3) + (4,4)) \end{aligned} \tag{4.46}$$

$$\begin{aligned} \bar{G} = {} & 0.2/((1,2) + (2,2) + (3,2) + (4,2)) \\ & + 0.6/((1,3) + (2,3) + (3,3) + (4,3)) \\ & + 1/((1,4) + (2,4) + (3,4) + (4,4)) \end{aligned} \tag{4.47}$$

$$\begin{aligned} \bar{F}' \oplus \bar{G} = {} & 0.2/(1,2) + 0.6/(1,3) + 1/(1,4) \\ & + 0.4/(2,1) + 0.6/(2,2) + 1/(2,3) + 1/(2,4) \\ & + 0.8/(3,1) + 1/(3,2) + 1/(3,3) + 1/(3,4) \\ & + 1/(4,1) + 1/(4,2) + 1/(4,3) + 1/(4,4) \end{aligned} \tag{4.48}$$

$$\begin{aligned} \bar{F} \oplus \bar{H} = {} & 1/(1,1) + 1/(1,2) + 1/(1,3) + 1/(1,4) \\ & + 0.6/(2,1) + 0.64/(2,2) + 0.96/(2,3) + 1/(2,4) \\ & + 0.2/(3,1) + 0.24/(3,2) + 0.56/(3,3) + 1/(3,4) \\ & + 0.04/(4,2) + 0.36/(4,3) + 1/(4,4) \end{aligned} \tag{4.49}$$

and hence the translation of 'If X is *small* then Y is *large else* Y is *very large*' becomes

$$\begin{aligned} R(X, Y) = {} & 0.2/(1,2) + 0.6/(1,3) + 1/(1,4) \\ & + 0.4/(2,1) + 0.6/(2,2) + 0.96/(2,3) + 1/(2,4) \\ & + 0.2/(3,1) + 0.24/(3,2) + 0.56/(3,3) + 1/(3,4) \\ & + 0.04/(4,2) + 0.36/(4,3) + 1/(4,4) \end{aligned} \tag{4.50}$$

As in the case of the preceding example, translation rules may be used in combination to yield the meaning of composite fuzzy propositions which contain modifiers, conjunctions, disjunctions and implications. For example, if X, Y and Z are associated with the universes of discourse U, V and W, respectively, then using (4.7), (4.26) and (4.36) in combination, we find

$$X \text{ is } \textit{very small} \text{ and (if } Y \text{ is } \textit{small} \text{ then } Z \text{ is } \textit{very large})$$
$$\rightarrow R(X, Y, Z) = small^2 \times (\overline{small'} \oplus \overline{large^2}) \tag{4.51}$$

where $\overline{small}$ and $\overline{large^2}$ are cylindrical extensions in $V \times W$ of *small* and $large^2$, respectively.

In addition to the rules discussed above, we shall regard as a rule of Type II the *relational rule*

$$X \text{ is in relation } F \text{ to } Y \rightarrow R(A(X), B(Y)) = F \tag{4.52}$$

or, equivalently,

$$X \text{ and } Y \text{ are } F \rightarrow R(A(X), B(Y)) = F \tag{4.53}$$

where F is a fuzzy relation in $U \times V$. For example, 'Naomi is *much taller* than Maria' translates into

$$R(\text{Height(Naomi)}, \text{Height(Maria)}) = \textit{much taller} \tag{4.54}$$

where *much taller* is a fuzzy relation in R^2 defined by, say,

$$\textit{much taller} = \int_{R^2} S(u - v; 0, 5, 10)/(u, v). \tag{4.55}$$

Similarly, the fuzzy proposition 'X and Y are *approximately equal*' translates into

$$R(X, Y) = \textit{approximately equal}$$

where *approximately equal* is a fuzzy relation in R^2 defined by, say,

$$\textit{approximately equal} = \int_{R^2} \left(1 + \left(\frac{u-v}{2}\right)^2\right)^{-1} \Big/ (u, v). \tag{4.56}$$

The rules and the examples given in the preceding discussion are intended merely to illustrate some of the basic ideas behind the characterization of the meaning of composite propositions by relational assignment equations. We proceed next to the somewhat more involved issues relating to the treatment of fuzzy quantification and truth-functional modification.

5. TRANSLATION RULES FOR FUZZY PROPOSITIONS—TYPES III AND IV

As was stated earlier, translation rules of Type III apply to fuzzy propositions of the general form 'QX are F,' where Q is a fuzzy quantifier such as *most, some, few, many, very many, not many*, etc.; and F is a fuzzy subset of a universe of discourse $U = \{u\}$. Typical examples of propositions of this type are: '*Most* Swedes are *tall*,' '*Not many* Italians are *blond*,' '*Some* X's are *large*,' etc.

Basically, what we are dealing with in cases of this type is not a single fuzzy proposition such as 'X is F,' but a fuzzy proposition concerning a collection of fuzzy or nonfuzzy propositions. More specifically, consider the proposition '*Most* Swedes are *tall*,' and let $S_1, \ldots, S_N$ be a population of Swedes, with μ_i, $i = 1, \ldots, N$, representing the grade of membership of S_i in the fuzzy set *tall*.

Now, if F is a fuzzy subset of a finite universe of discourse $U = \{u_1, \ldots, u_n\}$, then the cardinality (or the power) of F is expressed by [22], [2]

$$|F| \triangleq \mu_1 + \ldots + \mu_N \tag{5.1}$$

where μ_i is the grade of membership of μ_i in F and $+$ is the arithmetic sum.[18] Using (5.1), the proportion of Swedes who are *tall* may be expressed as

$$r_{tall} = \frac{\mu_1 + \ldots + \mu_N}{N} \tag{5.2}$$

and thus the proposition '*Most* Swedes are *tall*' translates into

$$R\left(\frac{\mu_1 + \ldots + \mu_N}{N}\right) = most \tag{5.3}$$

where *most* is a fuzzy subset of the unit interval defined by, say,

$$\mu_{most} = S(0.5, 0.75, 1). \tag{5.4}$$

Stated in more general terms, the *rule of quantification* asserts that the translation of 'QX are F' is given by

$$QX \text{ are } F \to R\left(\frac{\mu_1 + \ldots + \mu_N}{N}\right) = Q \tag{5.5}$$

or

$$QX \text{ are } F \to R(\mu_1 + \ldots + \mu_N) = Q \tag{5.6}$$

depending, respectively, on whether Q represents a fuzzy proportion (eg., *most*) or a fuzzy number (e.g., *several*). Thus, in (5.5) Q is a fuzzy subset of the unit interval, while in (5.6) Q is a fuzzy subset of the integers $\{0, 1, 2, \ldots\}$.

It is important to note that the relational assignment equations (5.5) and (5.6) define a fuzzy restriction not in U but in the N-cube $[0, 1]^N$. It is this restriction, then, that constitutes the meaning of the fuzzy proposition 'QX are F.' As a simple illustration, let $N = 4$ and $\mu_1 = 0.8$, $\mu_2 = 0.6$, $\mu_3 = 1$ and $\mu_4 = 0.4$. Then $r_{tall} = 0.7$ and, if *most* is defined by (5.4), $\mu_{most}(0.7) = 0.32$. Thus, the grade of membership of the point (0.8, 0.6, 1, 0.4) in the fuzzy restriction associated with the proposition '*Most* Swedes are *tall*' is 0.32.

Another point that should be noted is that the quantifier *some*, in the sense used in classical logic, may be viewed as the complement of *none*, where *none* is a subset of [0, 1] (or $\{0, 1, \ldots,\}$) defined by

$$\begin{aligned} \mu_{none}(u) &= 1 \quad \text{for } u = 0 \\ &= 0 \quad \text{elsewhere} \end{aligned} \tag{5.7}$$

Thus,

$$\begin{aligned} some &= none' \\ &= not\ none \end{aligned} \tag{5.8}$$

The dual (see (3.30)) of *none* is *all*, with the membership function of *all* expressed by

$$\begin{aligned} \mu_{all}(u) &= 1 \quad \text{for } u = 1 \\ &= 0 \quad \text{elsewhere} \end{aligned} \tag{5.9}$$

Thus,

$$D(none) = all \tag{5.10}$$

and hence

$$\begin{aligned} some &= not\ none \\ &= D(not\ all) \end{aligned} \tag{5.11}$$

In everyday discourse, however, *some* is usually used not in the non-fuzzy sense of (5.11), but in a fuzzy sense which may be approximated as

$$some = not\ none\ and\ not\ many \tag{5.12}$$

or, alternatively, as

$$some = D(most\ and\ not\ all). \tag{5.13}$$

Note that this interpretation of *some* as a fuzzy subset of [0, 1] differs substantially from the nonfuzzy definition expressed by (5.11).

When N is large, it is advantageous in many cases to use a limiting form of (5.5) as $N \to \infty$. Specifically, with reference to (5.1), let $\rho(u)\,du$ denote the proportion of Swedes whose height is in the interval $[u, u + du]$. Then, the proportion of Swedes who are *tall* is given by

$$r_{tall} = \int_U \rho(u)\,\mu_{tall}(u)\,du \tag{5.14}$$

where $\mu_{tall}(u)$ denotes the grade of membership of a Swede whose height is u in the fuzzy subset of U labeled *tall*. This implies that

$$\textit{Most}\text{ Swedes are }\textit{tall} \to R\left(\int_U \rho(u)\mu_{tall}(u)\,du\right) = \textit{most} \tag{5.15}$$

and, more generally, that the translation of 'QX are F' is given by

$$QX \text{ are } F \to R\left(\int_U \rho(u)\,\mu_F(u)\,du\right) = Q \tag{5.16}$$

where $\rho(u)\,du$ is the proportion of values of an implied attribute $A(X)$ which fall in the interval $[u, u + du]$.

As an illustration, suppose that *tall* and *most* are defined as fuzzy subsets of $U = [0, 200]$ and $V = [0, 1]$, respectively, by

$$\mu_{tall} = S(160, 170, 180) \tag{5.17}$$

and

$$\mu_{most} = S(0.5, 0.75, 1). \tag{5.18}$$

Then, the compatibility of a distribution ρ with the restriction induced by the fuzzy proposition $p \triangleq$ *Most* Swedes are *tall* is given by

$$\mu_p(\rho) = S\left(\int_0^{200} \rho(u)\,S(u; 160, 170, 180)\,du; 0.5, 0.75, 1\right). \tag{5.19}$$

Through this equation, the proposition in question defines a fuzzy set in the space of distributions $\{\rho\}$ in U, with the membership function of the set in question expressed by (5.19). This fuzzy set, then, may be viewed as a representation of the meaning of p.

Turning to translation rules of Type IV, let p be a fuzzy proposition and let p^* be a fuzzy proposition which is derived from p by truth-functional modification, that is,

$$p^* \triangleq p \text{ is } \tau \tag{5.20}$$

where τ is a linguistic truth-value. As an illustration, if $p \triangleq$ Andrea is *young*, then p^* might be

$$p^* \triangleq \text{Andrea is } young \text{ is } very\ true. \tag{5.21}$$

Similarly, if $p \triangleq X$ and Y are *approximately equal*, then p^* might be

$$p^* \triangleq X \text{ and } Y \text{ are } approximately\ equal \text{ is } more\ or\ less\ true. \tag{5.22}$$

For concreteness, we shall focus our attention on fuzzy propositions of the form $p \triangleq X$ is F, where F is a fuzzy subset of $U = \{u\}$. Let t, $t \in [0, 1]$, be a numerical truth-value of p. If we assume, as stated in Section 3, that t may be interpreted as the degree of consistency of the reference nonfuzzy proposition 'X is u' with the fuzzy proposition 'X is F,' then

$$t = \mu_F(u) \tag{5.23}$$

and hence

$$u = \mu_F^{-1}(t) \tag{5.24}$$

where μ_F^{-1} is a function (or, more generally, a relation) which is inverse to μ_F. As an illustration, if

$$F = young = \int_U (1 - S(u; 20, 30, 40))/u \tag{5.25}$$

and $t = 0.5$, then

$$\begin{aligned} u &= \mu_F^{-1}(0.5) \\ &= 30 \text{ years.} \end{aligned} \tag{5.26}$$

Thus, 'Andrea is *young* is 0.5 true' translates into 'Andrea is 30 years old,' and, more generally, 'X is F is t' translates into

$$X \text{ is } \mu_F^{-1}(t). \tag{5.27}$$

To extend (5.27) to linguistic truth-values, we may employ the extension principle in a manner similar to that of Section 3. Specifically, if g is a mapping from U to V and F is a fuzzy subset of U, then $g(F)$ is given by

$$\begin{aligned} g(F) &\triangleq \langle g(F) \rangle \\ &\triangleq \int_V \mu_F(u)/g(u) \end{aligned} \tag{5.28}$$

where the angular brackets signify that $\langle g(F) \rangle$ is to be evaluated by the use of the extension principle.[19] As a simple illustration, if

$$U = 0 + 0.1 + 0.2 + \dots + 0.9 + 1 \qquad (5.29)$$

and

$$F = 0.6/0.8 + 0.8/0.9 + 1/1 \qquad (5.30)$$

then for

$$g(u) = 1 - u \qquad (5.31)$$

we have

$$1 - (0.6/0.8 + 0.8/0.9 + 1/1) = 0.6/0.2 + 0.8/0.1 + 1/0 \qquad (5.32)$$

while for

$$g(u) = u^2 \qquad (5.33)$$

we obtain

$$(0.6/0.8 + 0.8/0.9 + 1/1)^2 = 0.6/0.64 + 0.8/0.81 + 1/1. \qquad (5.34)$$

Equivalently, by regarding g as a binary relation from U to V and F as a unary fuzzy relation in U, $g(F)$ may be expressed as the composition of F and g, that is (see A60)

$$\langle g(F) \rangle = F \circ g$$

In particular, if the mapping $g: U \rightarrow V$ is $1 - 1$, then (5.35) implies (through (5.28)) that

$$\mu_{F \circ g}(v) = \mu_F(u) \qquad (5.36)$$

where $v = g(u)$ is the image of u.

By applying these relations to (5.24), the *rule of truth-functional modification* may be expressed as the translation rule (of Type IV)

$$p^* = X \text{ is } F \text{ is } \tau \rightarrow q \triangleq X \text{ is } F^* \qquad (5.37)$$

where F is a fuzzy subset of U, τ is a linguistic truth-value and F^* is a fuzzy subset of U which is related to F and τ by

$$F^* = \langle \mu_F^{-1}(\tau) \rangle = \tau \circ \mu_F^{-1} \qquad (5.38)$$

where μ_F^{-1} is the inverse of the membership function of F and $\circ$ is the operation of composition. In more explicit terms, the membership function of F^* may be expressed as

$$\mu_{F^*}(u) = \mu_\tau(\mu_F(u)) \qquad (5.39)$$

where μ_τ is the membership function of τ.

On combining (5.37) with (5.38), the rule of truth-functional modification may be expressed as

$$X \text{ is } F \text{ is } \tau \rightarrow R(A(X)) = \tau \circ \mu_F^{-1} \tag{5.40}$$

where $A(X)$ is an implied attribute of X.

As a simple illustration, assume that $U = 1 + 2 + 3 + 4$ and consider the fuzzy proposition

$$p^* = X \text{ is } \textit{small} \text{ is } \textit{very true} \tag{5.41}$$

where *small* is defined by

$$\textit{small} = 1/1 + 0.8/2 + 0.4/3 \tag{5.42}$$

and

$$\textit{true} = 0.2/0.6 + 0.5/0.8 + 0.8/0.9 + 1/1. \tag{5.43}$$

From (5.43) and (4.8), it follows that

$$\textit{very true} = 0.04/0.6 + 0.25/0.8 + 0.64/0.9 + 1/1 \tag{5.44}$$

and hence by (5.39) the translation of (5.41) is given by

$$R(X) = 1/1 + 0.25/2 \tag{5.45}$$

which is approximately equivalent to

$$R(X) = \textit{very very small} \tag{5.46}$$

if

$$\textit{very very small} = 1/1 + 0.4/2 + 0.03/3 \tag{5.47}$$

is regarded as a linguistic approximation to the right-hand member of (5.45).

It is instructive to consider also a continuous version of this example. Assuming that $U = [0, \infty)$ and

$$\textit{small} = \int_0^\infty \left(1 + \left(\frac{u}{5}\right)^2\right)^{-1} \Big/ u \tag{5.48}$$

$$\textit{true} = \int_0^1 (1 + 16(1 - v)^2)^{-1}/v \tag{5.49}$$

and

$$\textit{very true} = \int_0^1 (1 + 16(1 - v)^2)^{-2}/v, \tag{5.50}$$

we obtain from (5.39) and (5.40) the translation

$$X \text{ is } \textit{small} \text{ is } \textit{very true}$$
$$\rightarrow R(X) = \int_0^\infty \left(1 + 16\left(1 - \left(1 + \left(\frac{u}{5}\right)^2\right)^{-1}\right)^2\right)^{-2} \bigg/ u. \tag{5.51}$$

By way of comparison, $u = 4$ is compatible to the degree 0.6 with 'X is *small*' and to the degree 0.08 with 'X is *small* is *very true*.'

An important conclusion that may be drawn from the rule of truth-functional modification is that the qualification of a fuzzy proposition p with a linguistic truth-value τ has the effect of transforming p^* into an unqualified fuzzy proposition q, with the fuzzy restriction associated with q related to that of p by (5.37). In this way, a qualified proposition such as 'X is *small* is *very true*' may be approximated to by an unqualified proposition such as 'X is *very very small*,' and, more generally, $p \triangleq X$ is F is τ may be replaced by $q \triangleq X$ is F^*.

It is important to recognize, however, that the rule of truth-functional modification rests in an essential way on the assumption that a numerical truth-value in a fuzzy proposition of the form $p^* = X$ is F is t serves as a measure of consistency of the nonfuzzy proposition $r \triangleq X$ is u with the fuzzy proposition $p \triangleq X$ is F. If this assumption is not valid, it might still be possible to assert that a qualified fuzzy proposition of the form $p^* \triangleq X$ is F is τ is equivalent to an unqualified fuzzy proposition of the form $q \triangleq X$ is F^*. However, the dependence of F^* on F and τ might not be correctly expressed by (5.38), since it is affected by the form of the reference proposition, r, as well as the criterion employed to define the consistency of p with r.

This concludes our discussion of translation rules of Types I, II, III and IV. As was stated earlier, these rules may be used in combination to yield translations of more complex composite fuzzy propositions, e.g., (If X is *large* is *true* and Y is *small* is *very true* then it is *more or less true* that *most* Z's are *small*) is *very true*. In general, the translations of such propositions assume the form of a system of relational assignment equations which, in graphical form, may be represented as a semantic network or a conceptual dependency graph [113]–[118].

6. TRUTH-VALUES OF COMPOSITE PROPOSITIONS

The translation rules stated in Sections 4 and 5 provide a means of determining the restriction associated with a composite proposition from the knowledge of the restrictions associated with its constituents. In an analogous fashion, the truth valuation rules given in this section provide a means of computing the truth-value of a composite proposition from the knowledge of the truth-values of its constituents.

As will be seen in the sequel, the rules for truth valuation may be inferred from the corresponding translation rules of Types I, II, III and IV. In what follows, we shall describe the basic idea behind this method and illustrate it by several examples.

Let p be a fuzzy proposition of the form 'X is F' and let $t = v(p)$ be its numerical truth-value in $V = [0, 1]$. We assume that F is a fuzzy subset of a universe of discourse $U = \{u\}$, and that $A(X)$, an implied attribute of X, is a fuzzy variable which takes values in U, with F representing a fuzzy restriction on the values of $A(X)$.

As was stated in Section 3, a proposition of the form 'X is F is t true,' e.g., 'Paule is *tall* is 0.8 true' means that the grade of membership of Paule in the class of *tall* women is 0.8, or, equivalently, that

$$\mu_{tall}(\text{Height}(\text{Paule})) = 0.8 \tag{6.1}$$

where μ_{tall} is the membership function of the fuzzy subset *tall* of the real line.

Now, if the truth-value of the proposition 'Paule is *tall*' is 0.8, then what is the truth-value of the proposition 'Paule is *very tall*?' If we assume that the effect of the modifier *very* is defined by (4.8), then it follows from the concentration rule (4.7) that the grade of membership of Height(Paule) in *very tall* – and hence the truth-value of the proposition $p \triangleq$ Paule is *very tall* – is given by

$$v(\text{Paule is } \textit{very tall}) = 0.8^2 \tag{6.2}$$

and, more generally,

$$\begin{aligned} v(\text{Paule is } \textit{very tall}) &= (v(\text{Paule is } \textit{tall}))^2 \\ &= t^2 \end{aligned} \tag{6.3}$$

where $v(p)$ stands for the truth-value of p. Thus, the rule for computing the numerical truth-value of a fuzzy proposition of the form 'X is *very* F' from the knowledge of the numerical truth-value of the proposition 'X is F,' may be expressed as

$$X \text{ is } F \text{ is } t \text{ true} \Rightarrow X \text{ is } \textit{very } F \text{ is } t^2 \text{ true} \tag{6.4}$$

where t is the numerical truth-value of the fuzzy proposition 'X is F.'

Now, having this rule for numerical truth-values, we can readily extend it to linguistic truth-values by the application of the extension principle, as we have done in Sections 3 and 5. Thus, for such values (6.4) becomes

$$X \text{ is } F \text{ is } \tau \Rightarrow X \text{ is } very\ F \text{ is } \langle \tau^2 \rangle \tag{6.5}$$

where the angular brackets indicate that the evaluation of $\langle \tau^2 \rangle$ is to be performed by the use of the extension principle.

In more specific terms, this means that, if

$$\begin{aligned} v(X \text{ is } F) &= \tau \\ &= \int_0^1 \mu_\tau(v)/v, \quad v \in V \end{aligned} \tag{6.6}$$

where μ_τ is the membership function of the linguistic truth-value τ, then

$$\begin{aligned} v(X \text{ is } very\ F) &= \langle \tau^2 \rangle \\ &= \int_0^1 \mu_\tau(v)/v^2 \end{aligned} \tag{6.7}$$

As a simple illustration, suppose that $V = 0 + 0.1 + \dots + 1$ and

$$v(\text{Paule is } tall) = very\ true \tag{6.8}$$

where

$$true = 0.6/0.8 + 0.9/0.9 + 1/1 \tag{6.9}$$

and

$$\begin{aligned} very\ true &= true^2 \\ &= 0.36/0.8 + 0.81/0.9 + 1/1. \end{aligned} \tag{6.10}$$

Then, by (6.7)

$$\begin{aligned} v(\text{Paule is } very\ tall) &= \langle (very\ true)^2 \rangle \\ &= \langle (0.36/0.8 + 0.81/0.9 + 1/1)^2 \rangle \\ &= 0.36/0.64 + 0.81/0.81 + 1/1 \end{aligned} \tag{6.11}$$

and, if *true* is taken to be a rough linguistic approximation to the right-hand member of (6.11), i.e.,

$$\begin{aligned} true &= 0.6/0.8 + 0.9/0.9 + 1/1 \\ &= LA(0.36/0.8 + 0.81/0.9 + 1/1), \end{aligned} \tag{6.12}$$

then we can infer from (6.11) that

$$v(\text{Paule is } very\ tall) \cong true. \tag{6.13}$$

More generally, let q be a fuzzy proposition of the form $q \triangleq X$ is mF where m is a modifier whose effect on F is described by the equation

$$\mu_{mF}(u) = g(\mu_F(u)), \quad u \in U \tag{6.14}$$

where g is a mapping from $[0, 1]$ to $[0, 1]$. Then, from the foregoing discussion it follows that

$$X \text{ is } F \text{ is } \tau \Rightarrow X \text{ is } mF \text{ is } \langle g(\tau) \rangle \tag{6.15}$$

where τ is the linguistic truth-value of $p \triangleq X$ is F, and

$$\langle g(\tau) \rangle = \int_0^1 \mu_\tau(v)/g(v) \tag{6.16}$$

where μ_τ is the membership function of τ. By analogy with (4.1), the rule expressed by (6.15) will be referred to as the *modifier rule* for truth valuation.

In particular, for the case where $m \triangleq$ *not*, (6.15) becomes

$$X \text{ is } F \text{ is } \tau \Rightarrow X \text{ is } \textit{not } F \text{ is } D(\tau) \tag{6.17}$$

where

$$D(\tau) = \langle 1 - \tau \rangle \tag{6.18}$$

is the dual of τ (see (3.30)). For example, if $\tau = \textit{true}$, then

$$D(\textit{true}) = \langle 1 - \textit{true} \rangle$$
$$= \textit{false}$$

and hence

$$X \text{ is } F \text{ is } \textit{true} \Rightarrow X \text{ is } \textit{not } F \text{ is } \textit{false} \tag{6.19}$$

where

$$\mu_{\textit{false}}(v) = \mu_{\textit{true}}(1 - v), \quad v \in V. \tag{6.20}$$

By analogy with (4.2), the rule expressed by (6.17) will be referred to as the *rule of negation* for truth valuation. It should be observed that the application of the rule of truth-functional modification to the left-hand member of (6.17) – and, more generally, (6.15) – yields the same restriction as its application to the right-hand member.

Turning to rules of Type II, consider the composite proposition $p \triangleq X$ is F and Y is G, and assume that the numerical truth-values of the constituent propositions are

$$v(X \text{ is } F) = s \tag{6.21}$$

and

$$v(Y \text{ is } G) = t. \tag{6.22}$$

Now, from the rule of conjunctive composition (4.26), it follows that p translates into

$$R(A(X), B(Y)) = F \times G \tag{6.23}$$

and consequently

$$\begin{aligned} &v(X \text{ is } F \text{ and } Y \text{ is } G) \\ &\quad = \text{grade of membership of } (A(X), B(Y)) \text{ in } F \times G \\ &\quad = \mu_F(A(X)) \wedge \mu_G(B(Y)) \end{aligned} \tag{6.24}$$

by the definition of $F \times G$ (A56).

On the other hand, we have (by (3.15))

$$v(X \text{ is } F) = \mu_F(A(X)) \tag{6.25}$$

$$v(Y \text{ is } G) = \mu_G(B(Y)) \tag{6.26}$$

and hence

$$\begin{aligned} v(X \text{ is } F \text{ and } Y \text{ is } G) &= v(X \text{ is } F) \wedge v(Y \text{ is } G) \\ &= s \wedge t \end{aligned} \tag{6.27}$$

or, equivalently,

$$\begin{aligned} &(X \text{ is } F \text{ is } s \text{ true}, Y \text{ is } G \text{ is } t \text{ true}) \\ &\quad \Rightarrow (X \text{ is } F \text{ and } Y \text{ is } G) \text{ is } s \wedge t \text{ true} \end{aligned} \tag{6.28}$$

As in the case of (6.15), we observe that

$$X \text{ is } F \text{ is } s \text{ true} \rightarrow X \text{ is } \mu_F^{-1}(s) \rightarrow A(X) = \mu_F^{-1}(s) \tag{6.29}$$

$$Y \text{ is } G \text{ is } t \text{ true} \rightarrow Y \text{ is } \mu_G^{-1}(t) \rightarrow B(Y) = \mu_G^{-1}(t) \tag{6.30}$$

and

$$\begin{aligned} &(X \text{ is } F \text{ and } Y \text{ is } G) \text{ is } s \wedge t \text{ true} \\ &\quad \rightarrow (A(X), B(Y)) \in \mu_{F \times G}^{-1}(s \wedge t). \end{aligned} \tag{6.31}$$

Thus, in this instance we obtain the inclusion relation

$$(\mu_F^{-1}(s), \mu_G^{-1}(t)) \subset \mu_{F \times G}^{-1}(s \wedge t) \tag{6.32}$$

rather than equality, as in (6.15).[20]

To extend (6.28) to linguistic truth-values, we can invoke the extension principle, as we have done in the case of the modifier rule (4.1). In this way, we are led to the *rule of conjunction* for truth valuation, which asserts that

$$v(X \text{ is } F \text{ and } Y \text{ is } G) = \langle v(X \text{ is } F) \wedge v(Y \text{ is } G)\rangle \qquad (6.33)$$

where the angular brackets signify that the evaluation is to be performed by the use of extension principle. Thus, if

$$v(X \text{ is } F) = \sigma \qquad (6.34)$$

and

$$v(X \text{ is } G) = \tau \qquad (6.35)$$

where σ and τ are linguistic truth-values with membership functions μ_σ and μ_τ, respectively, then (6.33) may be restated as

$$(X \text{ is } F \text{ is } \sigma,\ Y \text{ is } G \text{ is } \tau) \Rightarrow (X \text{ is } F \text{ and } Y \text{ is } G) \text{ is } \langle \sigma \wedge \tau \rangle \qquad (6.36)$$

where

$$\langle \sigma \wedge \tau \rangle = \int_0^1 \mu_\sigma(u) \wedge \mu_\tau(v)/u \wedge v, \quad u, v \in [0, 1]. \qquad (6.37)$$

In a similar fashion, the *rule of disjunction* for truth valuation is found to be expressed by

$$(X \text{ is } F \text{ is } \sigma,\ Y \text{ is } G \text{ is } \tau) \Rightarrow (X \text{ is } F \text{ or } Y \text{ is } G) \text{ is } \langle \sigma \vee \tau \rangle \qquad (6.38)$$

where

$$\langle \sigma \vee \tau \rangle = \int_0^1 \mu_\sigma(u) \wedge \mu_\tau(v)/u \vee v \qquad (6.39)$$

while the *rule of implication* reads

$$(X \text{ is } F \text{ is } \sigma,\ Y \text{ is } G \text{ is } \tau)$$
$$\Rightarrow (\text{If } X \text{ is } F \text{ then } Y \text{ is } G) \text{ is } \langle\!\langle 1 - \sigma\rangle \oplus \tau\rangle \qquad (6.40)$$

where $\oplus$ denotes the bounded sum (see A30) and [21]

$$\langle\!\langle 1 - \sigma\rangle \oplus \tau\rangle = \int_0^1 \mu_\sigma(u) \wedge \mu_\tau(v)/1 \wedge (1 - u + v). \qquad (6.41)$$

As an illustration, assume that

$$\sigma \triangleq \textit{true} = 0.6/0.8 + 0.9/0.9 + 1/1 \qquad (6.42)$$

$$\tau \triangleq \textit{not true} = 1/(0+0.1+\ldots+0.7)+0.4/0.8+0.1/0.9. \qquad (6.43)$$

Then

$$\langle \sigma \wedge \tau \rangle = 1/(0 + 0.1 + \ldots + 0.7) + 0.4/0.8 + 0.1/0.9$$
$$= \textit{not true} \tag{6.44}$$
$$\langle \sigma \vee \tau \rangle = \textit{true} \tag{6.45}$$

and

$$\langle\langle 1 - \sigma \rangle \oplus \tau \rangle = \langle \textit{false} \oplus \textit{not true} \rangle \tag{6.46}$$
$$= 1/(0 + 0.1 + \ldots + 0.7) + 0.9/0.8 + 0.6/0.9 + 0.4/1 \tag{6.47}$$
$$\cong \textit{not very very true} \tag{6.48}$$

where the right-hand member of (6.48) is a linguistic approximation to the right-hand member of (6.47).

Proceeding in a similar fashion, we can develop valuation rules for composite propositions of more complex types than those considered in the previous discussion. We shall not pursue this subject further in the present paper.

7. RULES OF INFERENCE IN FUZZY LOGIC

Stated informally, the rules of inference in fuzzy logic constitute a collection of propositions – some of which are precise and some are not – which serve to provide a means of computing the fuzzy restriction associated with a variable $(X_1, \ldots, X_m)$ from the knowledge of the fuzzy restrictions associated with some other variables $Y_1, \ldots, Y_n$.

A typical example of an inference process in fuzzy logic is the following. Consider the fuzzy propositions

$$p \triangleq X \text{ is } \textit{small} \tag{7.1}$$

and

$$q \triangleq X \text{ and } Y \text{ are } \textit{approximately equal} \tag{7.2}$$

where $U = V = 1 + 2 + 3 + 4$ and *small* and *approximately equal* are defined by

$$\textit{small} = 1/1 + 0.6/2 + 0.2/3$$

and

$$\textit{approximately equal} = 1/((1,1) + (2,2) + (3,3) + (4,4)) + 0.5/((1,2) + (2,1) + (2,3) + (3,2) + (3,4) + (4,3)). \tag{7.4}$$

By using (2.4) and (4.53), the translations of these propositions are found to be

$$R(X) = small \tag{7.5}$$

and

$$R(X, Y) = approximately\ equal. \tag{7.6}$$

Now, let us replace p by its cylindrical extension, $\bar{p}$, which reads

$$\bar{p} = X \text{ is } small \text{ and } Y \text{ is } unrestricted \tag{7.7}$$

and form the conjunctive composition of $\bar{p}$ and q, i.e.,

$$\bar{p} \text{ and } q = (X \text{ is } small\ and\ Y \text{ is } unrestricted)\ and$$
$$(X \text{ and } Y \text{ are } approximately\ equal) \tag{7.8}$$

which by (4.28) translates into

$$\bar{p} \text{ and } q \triangleq R^*(X, Y) = (small \times V) \cap (approximately\ equal) \tag{7.9}$$

implying that the membership function of the restriction defined by (7.9) is given by

$$\mu_{R^*}(u, v) = \mu_{small}(u) \wedge \mu_{approximately\ equal}(u, v). \tag{7.10}$$

From the restriction $R^*(X, Y)$ defined by (7.10), we can infer the fuzzy restriction associated with Y by projecting $R^*(X, Y)$ on the universe of discourse associated with X, that is

$$R(Y) = \text{Proj } R^*(X, Y) \text{ on } U \tag{7.11}$$

which, by the definition of projection (see (A58), (A60)) is equivalent to

$$R(Y) = R(X) \circ R(X, Y)$$
$$= small \circ approximately\ equal$$

where the right-hand member denotes the composition of the unary fuzzy relation *small* with the binary fuzzy relation *approximately equal.* Expressed in terms of membership functions of $R(Y)$, *small* and *approximately equal,* (7.12) reads

$$\mu_{R(Y)}(v) = V_u(\mu_{small}(u) \wedge \mu_{approximately\ equal}(u, v)) \tag{7.13}$$

where V_u denotes the supremum over $u \in U$.

To compute $\mu_{R(Y)}$ from (7.13), it is convenient to represent the right-hand member of (7.13) as the max-min product[22] of the relation matrices of *small* and *approximately equal*. In this way, we obtain

$$[1 \quad 0.6 \quad 0.2 \quad 0] \circ \begin{bmatrix} 1 & 0.5 & 0 & 0 \\ 0.5 & 1 & 0.5 & 0 \\ 0 & 0.5 & 1 & 0.5 \\ 0 & 0 & 0.5 & 1 \end{bmatrix} = [1 \quad 0.6 \quad 0.5 \quad 0.2] \qquad (7.14)$$

which implies that

$$R(Y) = 1/1 + 0.6/2 + 0.5/3 + 0.2/4. \qquad (7.15)$$

To approximate to the right-hand member of (7.15) by a linguistic value of Y, we note that if *more or less* is defined as a fuzzifier (see (4.17)) with

$$\begin{aligned} K(1) &= 1/1 + 0.7/2 \\ K(2) &= 1/2 + 0.7/3 \\ K(3) &= 1/3 + 0.7/4 \\ K(4) &= 1/4 \end{aligned} \qquad (7.16)$$

then *more or less small* becomes

$$\textit{more or less small} = 1/1 + 0.7/2 + 0.42/3 + 0.14/4 \qquad (7.17)$$

which is a reasonably close approximation to (7.15) in the sense that

$$\textit{more or less small} = LA(1/1 + 0.6/2 + 0.5/3 + 0.2/4). \qquad (7.18)$$

In this way, then, from the fuzzy propositions $p \triangleq X$ is *small* and $q \triangleq X$ and Y are *approximately equal* we can infer exactly the fuzzy proposition

$$Y \text{ is } 1/1 + 0.6/2 + 0.5/3 + 0.2/4 \qquad (7.19)$$

and approximately

$$Y \text{ is } \textit{more or less small}. \qquad (7.20)$$

The essential features of the procedure which we have employed in the above example may be summarized as follows.

Let p and q be fuzzy propositions of the form

$$p \triangleq X \text{ is } F \qquad (7.21)$$

$$q \triangleq X \text{ is in relation } G \text{ to } Y \qquad (7.22)$$

where F is a fuzzy subset of U and G is a fuzzy relation in $U \times V$. Then, from p and q we can infer exactly

$$r \triangleq Y \text{ is } F \circ G \tag{7.23}$$

and approximately

$$r \triangleq Y \text{ is } LA(F \circ G) \tag{7.24}$$

where $\circ$ is the operation of composition and LA stands for 'linguistic approximation.'[23] We shall refer to this rule as the *compositional rule of inference* [7], [1], [2]. It should be noted that this rule is an instance of a *semantic* rule in the sense that r depends on the meaning of F and G through the composition $F \circ G$.

A special but important case of the compositional rule of inference results when G is a function from U to V, with q having the form

$$q \triangleq Y \text{ is } g(X). \tag{7.25}$$

In this case, the composition of F and G yields

$$F \circ G = \langle g(F) \rangle \tag{7.26}$$

where the angular brackets signify that $\langle g(F) \rangle$ is to be evaluated by the use of the extension principle. Thus, the rule of inference which applies to this case may be expressed as

$$\frac{\begin{array}{l} p \triangleq X \text{ is } F \\ q \triangleq Y \text{ is } g(X) \end{array}}{r \triangleq Y \text{ is } \langle g(F) \rangle} \tag{7.27}$$

and we shall refer to it as the *transformational rule of inference.*[24]

As a simple illustration of (7.27), suppose that $U = V = 0 + 1 + 2 + 3 + \dots$,

$$F \triangleq \textit{small} \triangleq 1/0 + 1/1 + 0.8/2 + 0.6/3 + 0.4/4 + 0.2/5 \tag{7.28}$$

and g is the operation of squaring. Then,

$$\langle \textit{small}^2 \rangle = 1/0 + 1/1 + 0.8/4 + 0.6/9 + 0.4/16 + 0.2/25 \tag{7.29}$$

and, we have

$$\frac{\begin{array}{l} p \triangleq X \text{ is } \textit{small} \\ q \triangleq Y \text{ is } X^2 \end{array}}{r \triangleq Y \text{ is } 1/0 + 1/1 + 0.8/4 + 0.6/9 + 0.4/16 + 0.2/25}$$

Another important special case of (7.23) is the *rule of compositional modus ponens.* Specifically, for the case where q is of the form

$$q \triangleq \text{If } X \text{ is } F \text{ then } Y \text{ is } G \tag{7.30}$$

the translation rule of conditional composition (4.36) asserts that

$$\text{If } X \text{ is } G \text{ then } Y \text{ is } H \rightarrow (A(X), B(Y)) = \bar{G}' \oplus \bar{H} \tag{7.31}$$

where $\bar{G}'$ is the cylindrical extension of the complement of G, $\bar{H}$ is the cylindrical extension of H, $\oplus$ is the bounded sum, and $A(X)$ and $B(Y)$ are the implied attributes of X and Y, respectively.

On applying (7.31) to the case where q is of the form (7.30), we obtain the *rule of compositional modus ponens*, which reads

$$\begin{array}{l} p \triangleq X \text{ is } F \\ q \triangleq \text{If } X \text{ is } G \text{ then } Y \text{ is } H \\ \hline r \triangleq Y \text{ is } F \circ (\bar{G}' \oplus \bar{H}) \end{array} \tag{7.32}$$

or, as a linguistic approximation,

$$r \triangleq Y \text{ is } LA(F \circ (\bar{G}' \oplus \bar{H})). \tag{7.33}$$

As a simple example which does not involve linguistic values, assume that $U = V = 1 + 2 + 3 + 4$ and

$$F = 0.2/2 + 0.6/3 + 1/4, \tag{7.34}$$

$$G = 0.6/2 + 1/3 + 0.5/4, \tag{7.35}$$

$$H = 1/2 + 0.6/3 + 0.2/4. \tag{7.36}$$

Then

$$\bar{G}' \oplus \bar{H} = \begin{bmatrix} 1 & 1 & 1 & 1 \\ 0.4 & 1 & 1 & 0.6 \\ 0 & 1 & 0.6 & 0.6 \\ 0.5 & 1 & 1 & 0.7 \end{bmatrix} \tag{7.37}$$

and

$$F \circ (\bar{G}' \oplus \bar{H}) = [0 \quad 0.2 \quad 0.6 \quad 1] \circ \begin{bmatrix} 1 & 1 & 1 & 1 \\ 0.4 & 1 & 1 & 0.6 \\ 0 & 1 & 0.6 & 0.6 \\ 0.5 & 1 & 1 & 0.7 \end{bmatrix} \tag{7.38}$$

$$= [0.5 \quad 1 \quad 1 \quad 0.7]$$

from which we can infer that

$$Y \text{ is } 0.5/1 + 1/2 + 1/3 + 0.7/4. \tag{7.39}$$

As should be expected, the compositional rule of *modus ponens* reduces to the conventional rule of *modus ponens* when F is nonfuzzy and $F = G$. Thus, under these assumptions it can readily be verified that

$$F \circ (\bar{F}' \oplus G) = G. \tag{7.40}$$

When F is fuzzy, however, (7.40) does not hold true, except as an approximation. The explanation for this phenomenon [32] is that the implicit part of q, namely, 'If X is *not* F then Y is unrestricted' overlaps the explicit part, 'If X is F then Y is H' resulting in an 'interference' term which vanishes when F is nonfuzzy.

Underlying the rules of inference which we have formulated in the foregoing discussion is a basic principle – to which we shall refer as the *projection principle* – which asserts that if $R(X_1, \ldots, X_n)$ is a fuzzy restriction associated with an n-ary fuzzy variable $(X_1, \ldots, X_n)$ which takes values in $U_1 \times \ldots \times U_n$, then the restriction on $(X_{i_1}, \ldots, X_{i_k})$, where $(i_1, \ldots, i_k)$ is a subsequence of the index sequence $(1, 2, \ldots, n)$, is given by the projection of $R(X_1, \ldots, X_n)$ on $U_{i_1} \times \ldots \times U_{i_k}$. Thus if $(j_1, \ldots, j_m)$ is the sequence complementary to $(i_1, \ldots, i_k)$ (e.g., if $n = 5$ and $(i_1, i_2) = (1, 3)$, then $(j_1, j_2, j_3) = (2, 4, 5)$), then

$$R(X_{i_1}, \ldots, X_{i_k}) = \text{Proj } R(X_1, \ldots, X_n) \text{ on } U_{i_1} \times \ldots \times U_{i_k} \tag{7.41}$$

with

$$\mu_{R(X_{i_1}, \ldots, X_{i_k})}(u_{i_1}, \ldots, u_{i_k}) = \vee_{(u_{j_1}, \ldots, u_{j_m})} \mu_{R(X_1, \ldots, X_n)}(u_1, \ldots, u_n). \tag{7.42}$$

The rationale for the projection principle is that, by virtue of (7.42), the projection of $R(X_1, \ldots, X_n)$ on $U_{i_1} \times \ldots \times U_{i_k}$ yields the *maximal* (i.e., largest) restriction which is consistent with $R(X_1, \ldots, X_n)$. Thus, by employing the projection principle, we are, in effect, finding the largest restriction on the variables of interest which is consistent with the restrictions on the variables which enter into the premises.

We shall conclude our discussion of inference rules in fuzzy logic with an example of semantic inference from a quantified fuzzy proposition.

Specifically, let us consider the fuzzy proposition

$$p \triangleq \textit{Most} \text{ Swedes are } \textit{tall} \tag{7.43}$$

which by (5.3) translates into

$$R\left(\frac{\mu_1 + \ldots + \mu_N}{N}\right) = most \tag{7.44}$$

where μ_i, $i = 1, \ldots, N$, is the grade of membership of S_i in the fuzzy set *tall*.

Now, suppose that we wish to find the answer to the question 'How many Swedes are *very tall*?' To this end, we note that if μ_i is the grade of membership of S_i in *tall*, then the grade of membership of S_i in *very tall* is μ_i^2. Consequently, the numerical proportion of Swedes who are *very tall* is given by

$$r_{very\ tall} = \frac{\mu_1^2 + \ldots + \mu_N^2}{N} \tag{7.45}$$

The relational assignment equation (7.44) defines a fuzzy set D in $[0, 1]^N$ whose membership function is expressed by

$$\mu_D(\mu_1, \ldots, \mu_n) = \mu_{most}\left(\frac{\mu_1 + \ldots + \mu_N}{N}\right). \tag{7.46}$$

On the other hand, (7.45) defines a mapping from $[0, 1]^N$ to $[0, 1]$ which induces a fuzzy set $P_{very\ tall}$ in $[0, 1]$, with P standing for Proportion.

By the transformational rule of inference (7.27), the membership function of $P_{very\ tall}$ may be expressed as

$$\mu_P(r_{very\ tall}) = \max_{\mu_1 \ldots, \mu_N} \mu_{most}\left(\frac{\mu_1 + \ldots + \mu_N}{N}\right) \tag{7.47}$$

with the relation (7.45), i.e.,

$$r_{very\ tall} = \frac{\mu_1^2 + \ldots + \mu_N^2}{N} \tag{7.48}$$

playing the role of a constraint. Thus, the determination of $P_{very\ tall}$ reduces to the solution of a nonlinear program expressed by (7.47) and (7.45).

It is apparent by inspection that the maximizing values of $\mu_1, \ldots, \mu_N$ are given by

$$\mu_1 = \ldots = \mu_N = \sqrt{r_{very\ tall}} \tag{7.49}$$

and hence that

$$\mu_P(r_{very\ tall}) = \mu_{most}(\sqrt{r_{very\ tall}}) \tag{7.50}$$

which is equivalent to

$$P_{very\ tall} = \langle most^2 \rangle \tag{7.51}$$

where the angular brackets indicate that $\langle most^2 \rangle$ is to be evaluated by the use of the extension principle.[25]

To summarize, from

$$p \triangleq \textit{Most}\ \text{Swedes are}\ \textit{tall} \tag{7.52}$$

we can infer that

$$q \triangleq \langle \textit{Most} \rangle^2\ \text{Swedes are}\ \textit{very tall} \tag{7.53}$$

where

$$\langle Most^2 \rangle = \int_0^1 \mu_{most}(v)/v^2. \tag{7.54}$$

Thus, if *most* is defined by, say,

$$\mu_{most}(v) = S(v; 0.5, 0.75, 1), \quad v \in [0, 1] \tag{7.55}$$

where the S-function is expressed by (A17), then

$$\mu_{most^2}(v) = S(\sqrt{v}; 0.5, 0.75, 1). \tag{7.56}$$

In a similar fashion, from the premise '*Most* Swedes are *tall*,' we can obtain answers to such questions as 'How many Swedes are *very very tall*?', 'How many Swedes are *not very tall*?' and, more generally, 'How many Swedes are *m tall*?' where *m* is a modifier. As is typical of inference processes in fuzzy logic, the answers to such questions are fuzzy restrictions rather than points in or subsets of U. In this lies one of the basic differences between inference in fuzzy logic, which is inherently approximate in nature, and the traditional deductive processes in mathematics and its applications.

8. CONCLUDING REMARKS

Our exposition of fuzzy logic in the present paper has touched upon only a few of the many basic issues which arise in relation to this – as yet largely unexplored – conceptual model of human reasoning and perception.

Clearly, the problems, the aims and the concerns of fuzzy logic are substantially different from those which animate the traditional logical systems. Thus, axiomatization, decidability, completeness, consistency, proof procedures and other issues which occupy the center of the stage in such systems are, at best, of peripheral importance in fuzzy logic. In part, these differences stem from the use of linguistic variables in fuzzy logic but, more fundamentally, they reflect the fact that, in fuzzy logic, the conception of truth is local rather than universal and fuzzy rather than precise.

NOTES

[1] Relevant aspects of the theory of fuzzy sets are discussed in references [2]–[60]. For convenience of the reader, a summarized exposition is presented in Appendix on p. 228. Alternative approaches to vagueness and inexact reasoning are discussed in [61]–[78].

[2] In this sense, the conventional multivalued logics may be viewed as degenerate forms of fuzzy logics in which the fuzzy truth-values are singletons. Some authors, e.g., [23], [42], [47], [57] employ the term *fuzzy logic* in a more restricted sense, interpreting a fuzzy logic as a multivalued logic with nonfuzzy truth-values. A succinct discussion of fuzzy logics and their relation to probability logics may be found in papers by B. R. Gaines [58], [59], [60].

[3] As will be seen later, the effect of the modifier *more or less* on its operand may be characterized by a kernel function which represents the result of acting with *more or less* on a singleton.

[4] In some contexts it is convenient to regard u as a variable ranging over U rather than as a particular element of U. In such cases, u will be referred to as a *base variable* for X.

[5] For convenience, $R_X(u)$ will usually be abbreviated to R_X or $R(u)$ or $R(X)$, with the understanding that $R(u)$ and $R(X)$ are labels of a fuzzy set rather than functions of u and X, respectively.

[6] The membership function of the projection of $R(X_1, \dots, X_n)$ on U_i is defined by

$$\mu_{R(X_i)}(u_i) = \text{Sup}\, \mu_{R(X_1,\dots,X_n)}(u_1, \dots, u_n)$$

where the supremum is taken over $u_1, \dots, u_n$, excluding u_i. (See A58.)

If $F_1, \dots, F_n$ are fuzzy subsets of $U_1, \dots, U_n$, respectively, then the membership function of the cartesian product $F_1 \times \dots \times F_n$ is given by

$$\mu_{F_1 \times \dots \times F_n}(u_1, \dots, u_n) = \mu_{F_1}(u_1) \wedge \dots \wedge \mu_{F_n}(u_n)$$

where μ_{F_i} is the membership function of F_i and $\wedge$ stands for the infix form of min.

[7] A more detailed discussion of this aspect of noninteraction may be found in [2].

[8] A more detailed discussion of the effect of linguistic modifiers (hedges) may be found in [51], [52], [53], [54], [55] and [56].

[9] More generally, the truth-values in $T(Truth)$ could include, in addition to *very*, such linguistic modifiers (hedges) as *quite*, *more or less*, *essentially*, etc. As in the case of *very*, the meaning of these and other modifiers may be defined – as a first approximation – in terms of a set of standardized operations on the fuzzy sets which represent their operands.

[10] It should be stressed that, since *FL* is a local logic, the definitions of the logical connectives in *FL* may be context or application dependent. This applies, in particular, to the definitions of *and*, *or*, and *if ... then*.

[11] What we rule out here is the possibility that the degree of consistency of two fuzzy propositions be a numerical truth-value. This case is more complex than that discussed in the present paper.

[12] It should be noted that this interpretation of a fuzzy truth-value is contingent on the assumptions made in (3.15). Hence, a different set of assumptions concerning the consistency function C might lead to a different interpretation of τ.

[13] This technique is related to Knuth's method of synthesized attributes [1], [110].

[14] It should be noted that in (3.41)–(3.44) *true* plays the role of a label of a fuzzy set in the left-hand member and that of the set itself in the right-hand member.

[15] A thorough discussion of the rationale for the definitions of $\cap$ and $\cup$ for fuzzy sets may be found in [24].

[16] It is tacitly understood that the rule in question is noninteractive in nature. In the form defined by (4.36), it is consistent with the definition of implication in L_{aleph_1} logic. (See [1].) An alternative definition which is discussed in [2] is: If X is F then Y is $G \to R(A(X), B(Y)) = \bar{F}' + F \times G$. (See [109] and [121] for a discussion of implication in multivalued logics.)

[17] The bounded sum of F and G is defined by $\mu_{F \oplus G} = 1 \wedge (\mu_F + \mu_G)$, where $+$ denotes the arithmetic sum. (See also A30.)

[18] In some instances it may be necessary to modify (5.1) by introducing a cutoff such that the μ_i below the cutoff are excluded from the right-hand member of (5.1).

[19] The angular brackets may be suppressed whenever it is clear from the context that the evaluation is to be performed via the extension principle. If it is necessary to stipulate that the extension principle is *not* to be used, brackets of the form $\not< \; \not>$ may be used for this purpose.

[20] This touches upon some of the issues in fuzzy logic which are not as yet well understood.

[21] As shown in [1], this expression for *if ... then ...* may be derived alternatively by applying the extension principle to the definition of implication in Lukasiewicz's L_{aleph_1} logic.

[22] In this product, the operations of $+$ and product are replaced by $\vee$ and $\wedge$, respectively.

[23] Exposition of a least squares approach to linguistic appròximation may be found in [53].

[24] The transformational rule of inference is closely related to the rule for computing the membership function of a set induced by a mapping [3].

[25] For numerical values of $r_{very\ tall}$ and *most* it can readily be shown that $most^2 \leq r_{very\ tall} \leq most$. Extending these inequalities to fuzzy sets leads to the expression $r_{very\ tall} = (\geq \circ \langle most^2 \rangle) \cap (\leq \circ\, most)$ where $\geq \circ (most^2)$ denotes the composition of the nonfuzzy binary relation $\geq$ with the unary fuzzy relation $\langle most^2 \rangle$. Since $most \subset \langle most^2 \rangle$, this result is consistent with (7.51).

[26] This definition of convexity can readily be extended to fuzzy sets of type 2 by applying the extension principle (see (A70)) to (A26).

REFERENCES

[1] L. A. Zadeh, 'Fuzzy Logic and Approximate Reasoning (In Memory of Grigore Moisil)', *Synthese* **30** (1975), 407–428.

[2] L. A. Zadeh, 'The Concept of a Linguistic Variable and Its Application to Approximate Reasoning', *Information Sciences*, Part I, **8** (1975), 199–249; Part II, **8** (1975), 301–357; Part III, **9** (1975), 43–80.

[3] L. A. Zadeh, 'Fuzzy Sets', *Information and Control* **8** (1965), 338–353.

[4] A. Kaufmann, *Introduction to the Theory of Fuzzy Subsets*, vol. 1, Elements of Basic Theory, 1973; vol. 2, Applications to Linguistics, Logic and Semantics, 1975; vol. 3, Applications to Classification and Pattern Recognition, 1975, Masson and Co., Paris. Also, Academic Press, 1975.

[5] C. V. Negoita and D. A. Ralescu, *Applications of Fuzzy Sets to System Analysis*, Birkhauser Verlag, Basel, 1975.

[6] L. A. Zadeh, K. S. Fu, K. Tanaka, and M. Shimura (eds.), *Fuzzy Sets and Their Applications to Cognitive and Decision Processes*, Academic Press, New York, 1975.

[7] L. A. Zadeh, 'Outline of a New Approach to the Analysis of Complex Systems and Decision Processes', *IEEE Transactions on Systems, Man and Cybernetics* **SMC-3** (1973), 28–44.

[8] K. Tanaka, 'Fuzzy Automata Theory and Its Applications to Control Systems', Osaka University, Osaka, 1970.

[9] R. E. Bellman, R. Kalaba, and L. A. Zadeh, 'Abstraction and Pattern Classification', *J. Math. Analysis Applications* **13** (1966), 1–7.

[10] L. A. Zadeh, 'Shadows of Fuzzy Sets', *Probl. Transmission Inf.* (in Russian) **2** (1966), 37–44.

[11] J. Goguen, 'L-Fuzzy Sets', *J. Math. Analysis Applications* **18** (1967), 145–174.

[12] J. G. Brown, 'A Note on Fuzzy Sets', *Information and Control* **18** (1971), 32–39.

[13] L. A. Zadeh, 'Similarity Relations and Fuzzy Orderings', *Information Sciences* **3** (1971), 177–200.

[14] E. T. Lee and L. A. Zadeh, 'Note on Fuzzy Languages', *Information Sciences* **1** (1969), 421–434.

[15] L. A. Zadeh, 'Fuzzy Languages and Their Relation to Human and Machine Intelligence', in *Proc. Int. Conf. on Man and Computer*, Bordeaux, France, S. Karger, Basel, 1972, pp. 130–165.

[16] E. T. Lee, 'Fuzzy Languages and Their Relation to Automata', Dissertation, Department of Electrical Engineering and Computer Sciences, University of California, Berkeley, 1972.

[17] L. A. Zadeh, 'Quantitative Fuzzy Semantics', *Information Sciences* **3** (1971), 159–176.

[18] A. DeLuca and S. Termini, 'Algebraic Properties of Fuzzy Sets', *J. Math. Analysis Applications* **40** (1972), 377–386.

[19] L. A. Zadeh, 'Fuzzy Algorithms', *Information and Control* **12** (1968), 94–102.

[20] E. Santos, 'Fuzzy Algorithms', *Information and Control* **17** (1970), 326–339.

[21] S. S. L. Chang and L. A. Zadeh, 'Fuzzy Mapping and Control', *IEEE Transactions on Systems, Man and Cybernetics* **SMC-2** (1972), 30–34.

[22] A. DeLuca and S. Termini, 'A Definition of Non-probabilistic Entropy in the Setting of Fuzzy Set Theory', *Information and Control* **20** (1972), 201–312.

[23] R. C. T. Lee, 'Fuzzy Logic and the Resolution Principle', *J. Assoc. Comput. Mach.* **19** (1972), 109–119.

[24] R. E. Bellman and M. Giertz, 'On the Analytic Formalism of the Theory of Fuzzy Sets', *Information Sciences* **5** (1973), 149–156.

[25] R. E. Bellman and L. A. Zadeh, 'Decision-making in a Fuzzy Environment', *Management Science* **17** (1970), B-141-B-164.

[26] E. H. Mamdani and S. Assilian, 'An Experiment in Linguistic Synthesis with a Fuzzy Logic Controller', *Int. J. of Man-Machine Studies* **7** (1975), 1–13.

[27] R. Kling, 'Fuzzy Planner', Technical Report 168, Computer Science Department, University of Wisconsin, Madison, 1973.

[28] L. Pun, 'Experience in the Use of Fuzzy Formalism in Problems with Various Degrees of Subjectivity', University of Bordeaux, Bordeaux, 1975.

[29] V. Dimitrov, W. Wechler, and P. Barnev, 'Optimal Fuzzy Control of Humanistic Systems', Institute of Mathematics and Mechanics, Sofia and Department of Mathematics, Technical University Dresden, Dresden, 1974.

[30] L. A. Zadeh, 'Toward a Theory of Fuzzy Systems', in *Aspects of Network and System Theory*, R. Kalman and N. Declaris (eds.), Holt, Rinehart & Winston, London, 1971.

[31] M. A. Arbib and E. G. Manes, 'A Category-Theoretic Approach to Systems in a Fuzzy World', *Synthese* **30** (1975), 381–406.

[32] L. A. Zadeh, 'Calculus of Fuzzy Restrictions', in *Fuzzy Sets and Their Applications to Cognitive and Decision Processes*, L. A. Zadeh, K. S. Fu, K. Tanaka and M. Shimura (eds.), Academic Press, New York, 1975.

[33] T. Kitagawa, 'Fuzziness in Informative Logics', in *Fuzzy Sets and Their Applications to Cognitive and Decision Processes*, L. A. Zadeh, K. S. Fu, K. Tanaka, and M. Shimura (eds.), Academic Press, New York, 1975, pp. 97–124.

[34] S. Tamura and K..Tanaka, 'Learning of Fuzzy Formal Language', *IEEE Transactions on Systems, Man and Cybernetics* **SMC-3** (1973), 98–102.

[35] T. Terano and M. Sugeno, 'Conditional Fuzzy Measures and Their Applications', in *Fuzzy Sets and Their Applications to Cognitive and Decision Processes*, L. A. Zadeh, K. S. Fu, K. Tanaka, and M. Shimura (eds.), Academic Press, New York, 1975, pp. 151–170.

[36] M. Shimura, 'An Approach to Pattern Recognition and Associative Memories Using Fuzzy Logic', in *Fuzzy Sets and Their Applications to Cognitive and Decision Processes*, L. A. Zadeh, K. S. Fu, K. Tanaka, and M. Shimura (eds.), Academic Press, New York, 1975, pp. 449–476.

[37] Y. Inagaki and T. Fukumura, 'On the Description of Fuzzy Meaning of Context-Free Language', in *Fuzzy Sets and Their Applications to Cognitive and Decision Processes*, L. A. Zadeh, K. S. Fu, K. Tanaka, and M. Shimura (eds.), Academic Press, New York, 1975, pp. 301–328.

[38] C. L. Chang, 'Interpretation and Execution of Fuzzy Programs', in *Fuzzy Sets and Their Applications to Cognitive and Decision Processes*, L. A. Zadeh, K. S. Fu, K. Tanaka, and M. Shimura (eds.), Academic Press, New York, 1975, pp. 191–218.

[39] R. LeFaivre, 'Fuzzy: A Programming Language for Fuzzy Problem Solving', Technical Report 202, Department of Computer Science, University of Wisconsin, Madison, 1974.

[40] E. W. Chapin, Jr., 'Set-Valued Set Theory', *Notre Dame J. of Formal Logic*, Part I, **4** (1975), 619–634; Part II, **4** (1975), 255–267.

[41] E. Sanchez, 'Fuzzy Relations', Faculty of Medicine, University of Marseille, Marseille, 1974.

[42] P. N. Marinos, 'Fuzzy Logic and Its Application to Switching Systems', *IEEE Transactions on Electronic Computers* **18** (1969), 343–348.

[43] H. J. Zimmermann, 'Optimization in Fuzzy Environments', Institute for Operations Research, Technical University of Aachen, Aachen, 1974.

[44] P. K. Schotch, 'Fuzzy Modal Logic', *Proc. 1975 Int. Symp. on Multiple-Valued Logic*, 1975, pp. 176–182.

[45] R. Giles, 'Lukasiewicz Logic and Fuzzy Set Theory', *Proc. 1975 Int. Symp. on Multiple-Valued Logic*, 1975, pp. 197–211.

[46] F. P. Preparata and R. Yeh, 'Continuously Valued Logic', *J. Computer and System Sciences* **6** (1972), 397–418.

[47] A. Kandel, 'On Minimization of Fuzzy Functions', *IEEE Transactions on Computers* **C-22** (1973), 826–832.

[48] L. A. Zadeh, 'A Fuzzy-Algorithmic Approach to the Definition of Complex or Imprecise Concepts', Electronics Research Laboratory, University of California, Berkeley, 1974. (To appear in the *Int. J. of Man-Machine Studies*.)
[49] J. Meseguer and I. Sols, 'Fuzzy Semantics in Higher Order Logic and Universal Algebra', University of Zaragoza, Spain, 1975.
[50] A. N. Borisov, G. N. Wulf and J. J. Osis, 'Prediction of the State of a Complex System Using the Theory of Fuzzy Sets', *Kibernetika i Diagnostika* (1972), 79–84.
[51] L. A. Zadeh, 'A Fuzzy-Set Theoretic Interpretation of Linguistic Hedges', *J. of Cybernetics* **2** (1972), 4–34.
[52] G. Lakoff, 'Hedges: A Study in Meaning Criteria and the Logic of Fuzzy Concepts', *J. of Philosophical Logic* **2** (1973), 458–508.
[53] F. Wenstop, 'Application of Linguistic Variables in the Analysis of Organizations', School of Business Administration, University of California, Berkeley, 1975.
[54] H. M. Hersh and A. Caramazza, 'A Fuzzy Set Approach to Modifiers and Vagueness in Natural Language', *J. Exp. Psychology* **105** (1976), 254–276.
[55] W. Rödder, 'On "and" and "or" Connectives in Fuzzy Set Theory', Institute for Operations Research, Technical University of Aachen, Aachen, 1975.
[56] F. J. Damerau, 'On Fuzzy Adjectives', Memorandum RC 5340, IBM Research Laboratory, Yorktown Heights, New York, 1975.
[57] G. C. Moisil, *Lectures on Fuzzy Logic* (in Roumanian), Scientific and Encyclopedic Editions, Bucarest, 1975.
[58] B. R. Gaines, 'Foundations of Fuzzy Reasoning', *Int. J. Man-Machine Studies* **8** (1976), 623–668.
[59] B. R. Gaines, 'Stochastic and Fuzzy Logics', *Electronics Letters* **2** (1975), 188–189.
[60] B. R. Gaines, 'General Fuzzy Logics', Man-Machine Systems Laboratory, University of Essex, Colchester, U.K., 1976.
[61] L. Wittgenstein, 'Logical Form', *Proc. Aristotelian Soc.* **9** (1929), 162–171.
[62] M. Black, 'Vagueness', *Philosophy of Science* **4** (1937), 427–455.
[63] M. Black, 'Reasoning with Loose Concepts', *Dialogue* **2** (1963), 1–12.
[64] H. Khatchadourian', 'Vagueness, Meaning and Absurdity', *American Philosophical Quarterly* **2** (1965), 119–129.
[65] R. R. Verma, 'Vagueness and the Principle of Excluded Middle', *Mind* **79** (1970), 66–77.
[66] J. Goguen, 'The Logic of Inexact Concepts', *Synthese* **19** (1969), 325–373.
[67] E. Adams, 'The Logic of "Almost All"', *J. Philosophical Logic* **3** (1974), 3–17.
[68] E. H. Shortliffe and B. G. Buchanan, 'A Model of Inexact Reasoning in Medicine', *Math. Biosciences* **23** (1975), 351–379.
[69] N. Cliff, 'Adverbs as Multipliers', *Psychology Review* **66** (1959), 27–44.
[70] J. R. Ross, 'A Note on Implicit Comparatives', *Linguistic Inquiry* **1** (1970), 363–366.
[71] B. B. Rieger, 'Fuzzy Structural Semantics', German Institute, Technical University of Aachen, Aachen, 1976. (Third European Meeting on Cybernetics, Vienna.)
[72] K. F. Machina, 'Vague Predicates', *American Philosophical Quarterly* **9** (1972), 225–233.
[73] D. H. Sanford, 'Borderline Logic', *American Philosophical Quarterly* **12** (1975), 29–39.
[74] E. W. Adams and H. P. Levine, 'On the Uncertainties Transmitted from Premises to Conclusions in Deductive Inferences', *Synthese* **30** (1975), 429–460.
[75] S. C. Wheeler, 'Reference and Vagueness', *Synthese* **30** (1975), 367–380.
[76] C. Wright, 'On the Coherence of Vague Predicates', *Synthese* **30** (1975), 325–365.
[77] K. Fine, 'Vagueness, Truth and Logic', *Synthese* **30** (1975), 265–300.

[78] I. F. Carlstrom, 'Truth and Entailment for a Vague Quantifier', *Synthese* **30** (1975), 461–495.
[79] R. Carnap, *The Logical Syntax of Language*, Harcourt, Brace & World, New York, 1937.
[80] W. Quine, *Word and Object*, M.I.T. Press, Cambridge, Massachusetts, 1960.
[81] R. Carnap, *Meaning and Necessity*, University of Chicago Press, Chicago, 1956.
[82] Y. Bar-Hillel, *Language and Information*, Addison-Wesley, Reading, Massachusetts, 1964.
[83] J. A. Fodor and J. J. Katz (eds.), *The Structure of Language*, Prentice-Hall, Englewood Cliffs, New Jersey, 1964.
[84] J. J. Katz, *The Philosophy of Language*, Harper & Row, New York, 1966.
[85] S. Ullmann, *Semantics: An Introduction to the Science of Meaning*, Blackwell, Oxford, 1962.
[86] S. K. Shaumjan, *Structural Linguistics*, Nauka, Moscow, 1965.
[87] R. Jacobson (ed.), *On the Structure of Language and Its Mathematical Aspects*, American Mathematical Society, Providence, R.I., 1961.
[88] J. J. Katz, 'Recent Issues in Semantic Theory', *Found. Language* **3** (1967), 124–194.
[89] G. Lakoff, 'Linguistics and Natural Logic', in *Semantics of Natural Languages*, D. Davidson and G. Harman (eds.), D. Reidel, Dordrecht, The Netherlands, 1971.
[90] V. V. Nalimov, *Probabilistic Model of Language*, Moscow State University, Moscow, 1974.
[91] S. Kripke, 'Naming and Necessity', in *Semantics of Natural Languages*, D. Davidson and G. Harman (eds.), D. Reidel, Dordrecht, The Netherlands, 1971.
[92] D. K. Lewis, 'General Semantics', *Synthese* **22** (1970), 18–67.
[93] A. Tarski, 'The Concept of Truth in Formalized Languages', *Studia Philosophica* **1** (1936), 261–405. Translated in *Logics, Semantics and Metamathematics*, Clarendon Press, Oxford, 1956.
[94] W. V. Quine, *Philosophy of Logic*, Prentice-Hall, Englewood Cliffs, New Jersey, 1970.
[95] D. Greenwood, *Truth and Meaning*, Philosophical Library, New York, 1957.
[96] S. P. Stitch, 'Logical Form and Natural Language , *Philosophical Studies* **28** (December 1975), 397–418.
[97] C. G. Hempel, 'Inductive Inconsistencies', in *Logic and Language*, B. H. Kazemier and D. Vuysje (eds.), D. Reidel, Dordrecht, The Netherlands, 1962, pp. 128–158.
[98] R. Montague, *Formal Philosophy (Selected Papers)*, R. H. Thomason (ed.), Yale University Press, New Haven, 1974.
[99] M. J. Cresswell, *Logics and Languages*, Methuen and Co., London, 1973.
[100] D. Davidson, 'Truth and Meaning', *Synthese* **17** (1967), 304–323.
[101] W. C. Kneale, 'Propositions and Truth in Natural Languages', *Mind* **81** (1972), 225–243.
[102] K. Lambert and B. C. Van Fraassen, 'Meaning Relations, Possible Objects and Possible Worlds', in *Philosophical Problems in Logic*, K. Lambert (ed.), D. Reidel, Dordrecht, The Netherlands, 1970.
[103] C. Parsons, 'Informal Axiomatization, Formalization and the Concept of Truth', *Synthese* **27** (1974), 27–47.
[104] A. Sloman, 'Interactions Between Philosophy and Artificial Intelligence: The Role of Intuition and Nonlogical Reasoning in Intelligence', *Artificial Intelligence* **2** (1971), 209–225.
[105] H. A. Simon, 'The Structure of Ill Structured Problems', *Artificial Intelligence* **4** (1973), 181–201.
[106] W. V. Quine, 'Methodological Reflections on Current Linguistic Theory', *Synthese* **21** (1970), 387–398.

[107] J. Searle (ed.), *The Philosophy of Language*, Oxford University Press, Oxford, 1971.
[108] J. F. Staal, 'Formal Logic and Natural Languages', *Foundations of Language* **5** (1969), 256–284.
[109] N. Rescher, *Many-Valued Logic*, McGraw-Hill, New York, 1969
[110] D. E. Knuth, 'Semantics of Context-free Languages', *Math. Systems Theory* **2** (1968), 127–145.
[111] P. M. Lewis, D. J. Rosenkrantz, and R. E. Stearns, 'Attributed Translations', *J. Computer and System Science* **9** (1974), 279–307.
[112] G. Frege, *Translations from the Philosophical Writings of G. Frege*, P. T. Geach and M. Black (trans.), Blackwell, Oxford, 1952.
[113] R. F. Simmons, 'Semantic Networks, Their Computation and Use for Understanding English Sentences', in *Computer Models of Thought and Language*, R. Schank and K. Colby (eds.), Prentice-Hall, Englewood Cliffs, New Jersey, 1973, pp. 63–113.
[114] G. G. Hendrix, C. W. Thompson, and J. Slocum, 'Language Processing via Canonical Verbs and Semantic Models', *Proc. 3rd Joint Int. Conf. on Artificial Intelligence*, Stanford, 1973, pp. 262–269.
[115] R. C. Schank, 'Identification of Conceptualizations Underlying Natural Language', in *Computer Models of Thought and Language*, R. Schank and M. Colby (eds.), Prentice-Hall, Englewood Cliffs, New Jersey, 1973, pp. 187–247.
[116] D. Bobrow and A. Collins (eds.), *Representation and Understanding*, Academic Press, New York, 1975.
[117] W. A. Woods, 'What is a Link: Foundations for Semantic Networks', in *Representation and Understanding*, D. Bobrow and A. Collins (eds.), Academic Press, New York, 1975, pp. 35–82.
[118] D. A. Norman and D. E. Rumelhart (eds.), *Explorations in Cognition*, W. H. Freeman Co., San Francisco, 1975.
[119] C. J. Fillmore, 'Toward a Modern Theory of Case', in *Modern Studies in English*, Reibel and Schane (eds.), Prentice-Hall, Toronto, 1969, pp. 361–375.
[120] W. A. Martin, 'Translation of English into MAPL Using Winograd's Syntax, State Transition Networks, and a Semantic Case Grammar', M.I.T. APG Internal Memo 11, April 1973.
[121] G. Epstein, G. Frieder, and D. Rine, 'The Development of Multi-Valued Logic as Related to Computer Science', *Computer Magazine* (Sept., 1974), 20–32.
[122] I. Grattan-Guinness, 'Fuzzy Membership Mapped Onto Interval and Many-Valued Quantities', Middlesex Polytechnic, Enfield, U.K., 1974.
[123] P. Suppes, 'The Axiomatic Method in the Empirical Sciences', *Proc. Tarski Symp.*, Amer. Math. Soc., Providence, R.I., 1974.
[124] B. R. Gaines and L. J. Kohout, 'The Fuzzy Decade: A Bibliography of Fuzzy Systems and Closely Related Topics', *Int. J. of Man-Machine Studies* **9** (1977), 1–68.

L. A. ZADEH*

LINGUISTIC CHARACTERIZATION OF PREFERENCE RELATIONS AS A BASIS FOR CHOICE IN SOCIAL SYSTEMS

1. INTRODUCTION

In assessing the applicability of the theories of choice to social systems, one cannot escape the fact that such systems are generally much too complex and much too ill-defined to be susceptible of analysis in precise, quantitative terms. For example, as discussed in [1], [2], there is considerable uncertainty in the valuation of interpersonal as well as individual utilities among a collection of individuals. Another complicating factor is that the preference relations are frequently conditioned on variables whose values are unknown or, at least, not well-defined; in addition, they may be, and frequently are, interdependent in the sense that the preference relation of an individual may be affected by his or her perception of the preference relations of other members of the collection. Furthermore, the underlying decision processes are, in most cases, multi-stage processes with poorly defined horizons, uncertain dynamics and vague constraints. These are but a few of the many considerations which suggest that, in their present form, the mathematical theories of choice may well be excessively precise in relation to the overwhelming complexity of real-world social systems.

A less precise alternative to the conventional methods of quantitative analysis is provided by the so-called linguistic approach [3], [4], in which words rather than numbers are employed to characterize approximately the values of variables as well as the relations between them. As a matter of fact, we frequently resort to such characterizations in everyday discourse, e.g., when we describe the age of an individual by a label such as young, not young, very young, not very young, etc., rather than by a number in the set $U = \{0, 1, 2, \ldots, 100\}$. In this case, the labels in question

* Computer Science Division, Department of Electrical Engineering and Computer Sciences and the Electronics Research Laboratory, University of California, Berkeley, CA 94720. Research supported by the National Science Foundation Grants MCS76-06693 and ENG74-06651-A01.

Reprinted, with permission, from *Erkenntnis*, **11**(3), pp. 383–399 & 408–410.

may be interpreted as the names of fuzzy subsets of the set $U = [0, 100]$, with a fuzzy subset such as *young*, characterized by its membership (or compatibility) function $\mu_{\text{young}}: U \to [0, 1]$, which associates with each numerical age u the degree, $\mu_{\text{young}}(u)$, to which u is subjectively compatible (in a given context) with one's perception of the meaning of young.[1] For example, the value of the compatibility function μ_{young} at $u = 20$ might be 1; at $u = 25$: 0.9; at $u = 28$: 0.7; at $u = 30$: 0.5, etc., meaning that the subjective compatibilities of the numerical ages 20, 25, 28 and 30 with young are 1, 0.9, 0.7 and 0.5, respectively.

If *Age* is regarded as a *linguistic variable* whose *linguistic values* are young, not young, very young, etc., the meaning of each such value may be defined by specifying its compatibility function. However, a basic assumption behind the concept of a linguistic variable is that the meaning of its linguistic values may be computed in terms of the specified meaning of the *primary terms*, e.g., young in the case of *Age* [4]. For example, if the meaning of young is defined by its compatibility function μ_{young}, then the meaning of not young, very young and not very young would be expressed as

(1.1) $\mu_{\text{not young}} = 1 - \mu_{\text{young}}$

(1.2) $\mu_{\text{very young}} = \mu^2_{\text{young}}$

(1.3) $\mu_{\text{not very young}} = 1 - \mu^2_{\text{young}}$

in which the squaring operation has its usual meaning. Thus, if $\mu_{\text{young}}(28) = 0.7$, then $\mu_{\text{not young}}(28) = 0.3$; $\mu_{\text{very young}}(28) = 0.49$ and $\mu_{\text{not very young}}(28) = 0.51$.

To relate the linguistic approach to the characterization of preference relations in social systems, let $I = \{I_1, \ldots, I_N\}$ be a collection of individuals and let $A = \{a_1, \ldots, a_n\}$ be a set of alternatives. We assume that the preference relation for I_i, $i = 1, \ldots, N$, is a fuzzy relation R_i in A whose compatibility function, $\mu_i: A \times A \to [0, 1]$, defines the 'strength' of the preference of I_i for alternative a_k over alternative a_l, $k, l = 1, \ldots, n$.

Our basic premise is that the available information about the preference relations $R_1, \ldots, R_N$ is fuzzy in nature and that it is expressed as a collection of propositions exemplified by:

1. Preference of I_1 for a_5 over a_3 is strong.
2. Preference of I_1 for a_2 over a_5 is not very strong.
3. Preference of I_1 for a_2 over a_3 is weak.

4. Preference of I_1 for a_5 over a_4 is much stronger than the preference of I_1 for a_5 over a_3.
5. Preference of I_1 for a_5 over a_3 is very strong is more or less true.
6. Preference of I_1 for a_5 over a_3 is very strong is very probable.
7. Preference of I_1 for a_5 over a_3 is very strong is slightly possible.
8. Preference of most individuals for a_5 over a_3 is very strong.
9. If the preference of I_1 for a_5 over a_3 is strong then the preference of I_2 for a_5 over a_3 is very strong.
10. If the preference of many individuals for a_5 over a_3 is strong then the preference of I_3 for a_2 over a_3 is weak.

Examples 1, 2 and 3 are intended to indicate that in the linguistic characterization of preference relations the strength of preference is treated as a linguistic variable whose values are labeled strong, not strong, very strong, not very strong, weak, etc., with the understanding that each of these values denotes a fuzzy subset of the unit interval [0, 1]. Furthermore, among these values *strong* plays the role of the primary term. Thus, if the compatibility function of strong is $\mu_{\text{strong}}: [0, 1] \to [0, 1]$, then

$$\mu_{\text{not strong}} = 1 - \mu_{\text{strong}} \tag{1.4}$$

$$\mu_{\text{very strong}} = \mu^2_{\text{strong}} \tag{1.5}$$

$$\mu_{\text{not very strong}} = 1 - \mu^2_{\text{strong}} \tag{1.6}$$

and

$$\mu_{\text{weak}}(v) = \mu_{\text{strong}}(1 - v), \qquad v \in [0, 1] \tag{1.7}$$

where (1.7) signifies that weak is the antonym – rather than the negation – of strong.

Example 4 illustrates a linguistic characterization of a relative strength of preference for the same individual, with the understanding that similar comparisons may be made for different individuals.[2]

Examples 5, 6 and 7 illustrate, respectively, the truth qualification, probability qualification and possibility qualification of the proposition "Preference of I_1 for a_5 over a_3 is very strong".

Example 8 illustrates the use of linguistic quantifiers (e.g., most, few, many, all, some, not very many, etc.) to characterize the proportion of individuals who have a particular preference.

Example 9 illustrates the conditional composition of two propositions, namely, "Preference of I_1 for a_5 over a_3 is strong" and "Preference of I_2 for a_5 over a_3 is very strong".

Example 10, like Example 9, illustrates the conditional composition of two propositions, the first of which involves an assertion concerning the preference profile $\{R_1, \ldots, R_N\}$.

In aggregate, the above examples illustrate the manner in which the imprecise information concerning the preference relations of a collection of individuals may be expressed in the form of a set of linguistic propositions. The question, then, is: What is the meaning of such propositions and how can one infer other propositions from them?

To answer this question in general terms, it is necessary to specify, first, a grammar which can generate syntactically correct propositions of the type exemplified above. Second, a system of semantic rules for translating any proposition which can be generated by the grammar into a procedure for computing the compatibility function of the proposition in question. And third, a set of inference rules for deriving a consequent proposition from a set of premises.

In what follows, we shall employ a less formal approach which is adequate for the purposes of our analysis. As will be seen in the sequel, a key to the interpretation of linguistic propositions concerning preference relations and, more generally, fuzzy orderings, is provided by the concept of a *possibility distribution* of a fuzzy variable. We shall discuss this concept in Section 3, following a brief review of those aspects of fuzzy relations which will be needed in later sections.

The present paper has the limited objective of suggesting the possibility of applying the linguistic approach to the characterization of preference relations when the information about such relations is incomplete, imprecise or unreliable. We do not address ourselves to the important issue of how to derive a social preference relation from an imprecisely defined collection of linguistic preference relations, for this would require an extensive reformulation of the axiomatic basis of the theory of choice and collective behavior in the setting of the conceptual framework of fuzzy – rather than two-valued – logic [7].

2. FUZZY ORDERINGS

Our concern in this section is restricted to those aspects of fuzzy orderings which are of relevance to the linguistic characterization of preference relations. A more detailed discussion of the properties of various types of fuzzy orderings may be found in [8].

A fuzzy relation, R, in U is a fuzzy subset of $U \times U$. The membership (or compatibility) function of R is a mapping $\mu_R: U \times U \to [0, 1]$, with $\mu_R(u, v)$, $(u, v) \in U \times U$, representing the *strength* of the relation between u and v. In the following definitions, the symbols $\bigvee$ and $\bigwedge$ denote max (or Sup) and min (or Inf), respectively, and $\triangleq$ stands for "is defined to be" or "is equal by definition".

The *height* of R is defined by

$$\text{(2.1)} \qquad \text{Height}(R) \triangleq \bigvee_u \bigvee_v \mu_R(u, v).$$

A fuzzy relation, R, is *subnormal* if $\text{Height}(R) < 1$ and *normal* if $\text{Height}(R) = 1$.

If R and Q are fuzzy relations in U, their *composition*, or more specifically *max-min composition*, is denoted by $R \circ Q$ and is defined by

$$\text{(2.2)} \qquad \mu_{R \circ Q}(u, w) = \bigvee_v (\mu_R(u, v) \wedge \mu_Q(v, w)), \qquad u, v, w \in U.$$

Thus, if U is a finite set, $U = \{u_1, \ldots, u_n\}$ (e.g., $U \triangleq A$ = a finite set of alternatives) and R and Q are represented by their relation matrices in which the ijth elements are $\mu_R(u_i, u_j)$ and $\mu_Q(u_i, u_j)$, respectively, then the relation matrix for $R \circ Q$ is the max-min product of the relation matrices for R and Q. An n-fold composition of R with itself is denoted by R^n.

In some cases it is desirable to employ an operation $*$ other than $\wedge$ in the definition of the composition. Assuming that $*$ is associative and monotone nondecreasing in each of its arguments, the definition of max-star composition becomes

$$\text{(2.3)} \qquad \mu_{R \circ Q}(u, w) = \bigvee_v (\mu_R(u, v) * \mu_Q(v, w))$$

and, in particular, if $*$ is taken to be the product, we have

$$\text{(2.4)} \qquad \mu_{R \circ Q}(u, w) = \bigvee_v (\mu_R(u, v) \cdot \mu_Q(v, w)).$$

Unless stated to the contrary, it will be assumed that $\circ$ is defined by (2.2).

A fuzzy relation is *transitive* iff

$$\text{(2.5)} \qquad R \supset R \circ R,$$

where the containment of fuzzy relations is defined by (A27). In more intuitive terms, R is transitive iff for any u, v, w in U

(2.6) Strength of the relation between u and w
$\geqslant$ Strength of the relation between u and v or v and w.

In the case of max-product transitivity, however, (2.6) becomes

(2.7) Strength of the relation between u and w
$\geqslant$ Product of the strength of the relation between u and v and the strength of the relation between v and w.

Note that (2.7) is implied by (2.6).

The transitive closure, $\bar{R}$, of R is the smallest transitive relation which contains R. Equivalently, $\bar{R}$ may be expressed as

$$\bar{R} = R + R^2 + \cdots + R^n, \tag{2.8}$$

where + denotes the union. The well-known Warshall algorithm for the computation of the transitive closure of a nonfuzzy relation may readily be extended to the computation of the right-hand member of (2.8) [9], [10].

A fuzzy relation, R, is *reflexive* if

$$\mu_R(u, u) = 1, \qquad u \in U; \tag{2.9}$$

it is *symmetric* if

$$\mu_R(u, v) = \mu_R(v, u), \qquad u, v \in U; \tag{2.10}$$

and *antisymmetric* if

$$\mu_R(u, v) > 0 \quad \text{and} \quad \mu_R(v, u) > 0 \Rightarrow u = v, \qquad u, v \in U. \tag{2.11}$$

A fuzzy relation, R, is a *fuzzy ordering* if it is transitive. In particular, R is a *fuzzy preordering* if it is reflexive and transitive, and a *fuzzy partial ordering* if it is reflexive, transitive and antisymmetric. A fuzzy ordering is a *similarity* relation if it is reflexive, transitive and symmetric. A similarity relation may be viewed as a generalization to fuzzy relations of the concept of an equivalence relation.

It should be noted that if transitivity is interpreted in the max-product sense, a similarity relation may serve as an indifference relation without entailing the usual difficulties associated with the notion of transitivity of indifference relations [11], [12], [13]. For example, if U is the real line, a transitive indifference relation may be defined by [8]

$$\mu_R(u, v) = e^{-\beta|u-v|}, \tag{2.12}$$

where β is a positive constant.

In Section 3, our concern will be with preference relations in which the membership function ranges over the fuzzy subsets of [0, 1], that is, over fuzzy sets of Type 1 (see Appendix). Such subsets will be identified by the labels strong, not strong, very strong, not very strong, etc., and will be regarded as the values of the linguistic variable Strength. A simple example of a linguistic relation of this type is shown in Table I.

In this example, the entry in (1, 2) signifies that the strength of preference for a_2 over a_1 is strong. Similarly, the strength of preference for a_3 over a_1 is very strong.

In what sense can a relation of this type be said to be transitive? To extend the definition of transitivity to linguistic relations it is convenient to employ the *extension principle* (see Appendix), which allows the domain of definition of a function or a relation to be extended to the set of fuzzy subsets of the space on which it is defined. For example, if $U = \{u_1, \ldots, u_n\}$ is a subset of points on the real line, and F and G are fuzzy subsets of U defined by

$$F = \mu_1/u_1 + \cdots + \mu_k/u_k \tag{2.13}$$

$$G = \nu_1/u_1 + \cdots + \nu_k/u_k, \tag{2.14}$$

where the μ_i and ν_i are the grades of membership of u_i in F and G, respectively, then the extensions of $\bigwedge$ (min) and $\bigvee$ (max) to the fuzzy subsets of U may be expressed as

$$F \wedge G = \sum_{i,j} \mu_i \wedge \nu_j/u_i \wedge u_j \tag{2.15}$$

$$F \vee G = \sum_{i,j} \mu_i \wedge \nu_j/u_i \vee u_j. \tag{2.16}$$

TABLE I. RELATION MATRIX FOR A LINGUISTIC RELATION

R	a_1	a_2	a_3
a_1	1	strong	very strong
a_2	0	1	strong
a_3	0	0	1

These definitions entail the extension of the inequality $\geqslant$ which is expressed by

(2.17) $F \geqslant G$ iff $F \wedge G = G$.

In terms of (2.15) and (2.16), the composition of linguistic relations may be expressed, as before, by (2.2), with the understanding that the μ's in (2.2) are fuzzy sets and that $\wedge$ and $\vee$ are defined by (2.15) and (2.16), respectively. Likewise, the definitions of transitivity, (2.5) and (2.6), remain unchanged on the understanding that $\geqslant$ is defined by (2.17).

As a simple example, in the case of the linguistic relation defined by Table I, it is easy to verify that (see (3.20) for the expression for very strong)

(2.18) strong $\wedge$ very strong $=$ strong

and hence

(2.19) strong $\leqslant$ very strong.

Using (2.18) and (2.19) in forming the composition of R with itself, we find that $R^2 = R$ and hence that R, as defined by Table I, is transitive.

In a similar fashion, it is possible to extend to linguistic relations many of the other basic concepts pertaining to fuzzy relations in which the membership function takes values in the interval [0, 1]. We shall not dwell upon this subject, however, and, in the next section, will turn out attention to another important issue, namely, the translation of linguistic propositions concerning preference relations and their aggregates.

3. TRANSLATION RULES FOR LINGUISTIC PROPOSITIONS

Our main concern in this section is with the interpretation of linguistic propositions relating to a collection of fuzzy orderings. As was stated in the Introduction, a concept that plays a basic role in the translation of linguistic propositions is that of the possibility distribution of a fuzzy variable.[3] More specifically, let X be a variable which takes values in $U = \{u\}$ and let F be a fuzzy subset of U whose membership function is given by $\mu_F: U \rightarrow [0, 1]$. Then, a proposition, p, of the form

(3.1) X is F

has the effect of associating with X a *possibility distribution* Π_X which is equal to F, that is,

$$\Pi_X = F, \tag{3.2}$$

and a *possibility distribution function* π_X which is given by

$$\pi_X = \mu_F. \tag{3.3}$$

Thus, the proposition $p \triangleq X$ is F implies that the possibility that X can take a value $u \in U$ is $\mu_F(u)$, and, more generally, that the possibility that $X \in G$, where G is a subset of U, is given by

$$\text{Poss}\{X \in G\} = \sup_{u \in G} \mu_F(u). \tag{3.4}$$

When G is a fuzzy subset of U, it is not meaningful to speak of the possibility of X belonging to G. In this case, $X \in G$ is replaced by the proposition X is G, and (3.4) becomes

$$\text{Poss}\{X \text{ is } G\} = \sup_{u \in U} \mu_F(u) \wedge \mu_G(u), \tag{3.5}$$

where μ_G is the membership function of G. Thus, we have

$$\begin{aligned} X \text{ is } F \Rightarrow \text{Poss}\{X \text{ is } G\} &= \sup_{u \in U} \mu_F(u) \wedge \mu_G(u) \\ &= \text{Height}(F \cap G). \end{aligned} \tag{3.6}$$

As a simple illustration, let U be the universe of positive integers and let F be the fuzzy subset of small integers defined by

$$\text{small integer} = 1/1 + 1/2 + 0.8/3 + 0.6/4 + 0.4/5 + 0.2/6. \tag{3.7}$$

Then, the proposition $p \triangleq X$ is a small integer associates with X the possibility distribution

$$\Pi_X = 1/1 + 1/2 + 0.8/3 + 0.6/4 + 0.4/5 + 0.2/6 \tag{3.8}$$

in which a term such as 0.8/3 signifies that the possibility that X is 3, given that X is a small integer, is 0.8. Furthermore, the possibility that $X \in \{4, 5\}$ is 0.6 and the possibility that X is a very small integer is 1.

In essence, the possibility distribution, Π_X, which is associated with X may be interpreted as an elastic restraint on the values that may be assigned to X, with $\pi_X(u)$ representing the degree of ease with which X can take the value u. In this sense, a variable which is associated with a possibility distribution is a *fuzzy variable*, with Π_X playing the role of a fuzzy restriction on the values of X.

To clarify the distinction between possibility and probability distributions, assume that X is the number of passengers that can be put in a given car, say a VW. Then, by some specified or unspecified criterion, the possibilities associated with the values of X might be as follows:

$$\pi_X(1) = \pi_X(2) = \pi_X(3) = \pi_X(4) = 1;$$
$$\pi_X(5) = 0.8;$$
$$\pi_X(6) = 0.4;$$
$$\pi_X(7) = 0.2.$$

In general, the probability that X passengers might be carried in the car in question would be quite different from the possibility that X passengers could be put in it. For example, the probability that four passengers might be carried could be quite small, say 0.05, whereas the corresponding possibility is 1.

What is important about the concept of a possibility distribution is that much of human decision-making appears to be based on possibilistic rather that probabilistic information. In particular, as is pointed out in [14], the imprecision of natural languages is, for the most part, possibilistic in origin. Indeed, this is the main reason why the concept of a possibility distribution plays a basic role in the translation of linguistic propositions.

Translation Rules for Linguistic Propositions

Let X be a variable taking values in $U = \{u\}$, and let F be a fuzzy subset of U. By the *translation* of the proposition $p \triangleq X$ is F is meant the relation

(3.9) $\quad X \text{ is } F \rightarrow \Pi_X = F$

whose right-hand member is the possibility assignment equation (3.2). Thus, the translation of a proposition has the form of a possibility assignment equation or, more generally, a set of such equations.

As an illustration, consider the proposition

(3.10) $\quad p \triangleq$ Preference of I_1 for a_3 over a_5 is very strong

which for simplicity will be abbreviated to

(3.11) $\quad p \triangleq$ Strength is very strong

with Strength playing the role of a linguistic variable. Then by (3.9) the translation of p may be expressed as

(3.12) Strength is very strong $\to \Pi_{\text{Strength}}$ = very strong,

where very strong is a fuzzy subset of the unit interval $U = [0, 1]$.

The translation rules of interest to us are *conditional* in nature in the sense that they are of the form

(3.13) If $p \to \Pi_X = F$
then $M(p) \to M^+(\Pi_X = F)$,

where $M(p)$ is a modification of p and M^+ is a corresponding modification of the possibility assignment equation $\Pi_X = F$.

A basic rule of this type is the *modifier rule* [7], which may be stated as follows.

Modifier Rule

(3.14) If Strength is $F \to \Pi_{\text{Strength}} = F$
then Strength is $mF \to \Pi_{\text{Strength}} = F^+$,

where m is a modifier such as not, very, more or less, etc., and F^+ is a modification of F induced by m.[4] More specifically,

(3.15) If m = not, then $F^+ = F' \triangleq$ complement of F.
(3.16) If m = very, then $F^+ = F^2$.
(3.17) If m = more or less, then $F^+ = \sqrt{F}$.

As an illustration, assume that strong is a fuzzy subset of [0, 1] which is characterized by

(3.18) $\mu_{\text{strong}} = S(0.7, 0.8, 0.9)$,

where the S-function (with its argument suppressed) is defined by (A17). Then, by (3.16), we have

(3.19) If Strength is strong $\to \Pi_{\text{Strength}}$ = strong
then Strength is very strong $\to \Pi_{\text{Strength}} = \text{strong}^2$,

where

(3.20) $\mu_{\text{strong}^2} = (S(0.7, 0.8, 0.9))^2$.

The implication of this translation of the proposition $p \triangleq$ Strength is very strong is the following. On evaluating the right-hand member of (3.20) for, say, $v = 0.85$, we find

$$(3.21) \qquad \mu_{\text{strong}^2}(0.85) \cong 0.77,$$

which implies that the possibility that the strength of preference of I_1 for a_3 over a_5 is 0.85 is 0.77. It is in this sense, then, that the proposition in question translates into a possibility distribution over the numerical values of the strength of preference of I_1 for a_3 over a_5.

In a similar fashion, it is readily seen that in virtue of (1.7), we have

$$(3.22) \qquad \begin{array}{ll} \text{If} & \text{Strength is strong} \rightarrow \Pi_{\text{Strength}} = \text{strong} \\ \text{then} & \text{Strength is weak} \rightarrow \Pi_{\text{Strength}} = \text{strong}^{+}, \end{array}$$

where

$$(3.23) \qquad \mu_{\text{strong}^{+}} = 1 - S(0.1, 0.2, 0.3).$$

Thus, in this case the possibility that the strength of preference of I_1 for a_3 over a_5 is 0.85 is zero.

Compositional Rules

Compositional rules apply to the translation of a proposition p which is a composition of propositions q and r. The most commonly employed modes of composition are: conjunction, disjunction and implication. The translation rules for these modes of composition are as follows.

Let X and Y be variables taking values in U and V, respectively, and let F and G be fuzzy subsets of U and V. If

$$(3.24) \qquad X \text{ is } F \rightarrow \Pi_X = F$$

and

$$(3.25) \qquad Y \text{ is } G \rightarrow \Pi_Y = G$$

then

$$\text{(a) } (3.26) \qquad X \text{ is } F \text{ and } Y \text{ is } G \rightarrow \Pi_{(X,Y)} = F \times G$$

$$\text{(b) } (3.27) \qquad X \text{ is } F \text{ or } Y \text{ is } G \rightarrow \Pi_{(X,Y)} = \bar{F} + \bar{G}$$

and

$$\text{(c) } (3.28) \qquad \text{If } X \text{ is } F \text{ then } Y \text{ is } G \rightarrow \Pi_{(X,Y)} = \bar{F}' \oplus \bar{G},$$

where $\Pi_{(X,Y)}$ is the possibility distribution of the binary variable (X, Y). Furthermore, in the *conjunctive rule* expressed by (a) $F \times G$ denotes the Cartesian product of F and G (see (A56)); in the *disjunctive rule* expressed by (b) $\bar{F}$ and $\bar{G}$ are the cylindrical extensions (see (A59)) of F and G, respectively, and $+$ denotes the union; and in the *conditional rule* expressed by (c) $\bar{F}'$ is the cylindrical extension of the complement of F and $\oplus$ denotes the bounded sum (see (A30)).

As an illustration, by applying the modifier rule and the conjunctive rule in combination, we obtain the following result.

If

(3.29) $\quad$ Strength is strong $\rightarrow \Pi_{\text{Strength}} =$ strong

and

(3.30) $\quad$ Strength is weak $\rightarrow \Pi_{\text{Strength}} =$ weak

then

(3.31) $\quad$ Strength is not very strong and not very weak

$$\rightarrow \Pi_{\text{Strength}} = (\text{strong}^2)' \cap (\text{weak}^2)',$$

where weak is the antonym of strong (see (1.7)) and $\cap$ denotes the intersection.

As a further illustration, consider the proposition "If the preference of I_1 for a_3 over a_5 is strong then the preference of I_2 for a_2 over a_3 is very strong". On abbreviating this proposition to "If Strength$_1$ is strong then Strength$_2$ is very strong", and applying (3.28), we deduce as its translation the possibility assignment equation

(3.32)
$$\pi_{(\text{Strength}_1,\text{Strength}_2)}(v_1, v_2) = (1 - S(v_1; 0.7, 0.8, 0.9)) \oplus (S(v_2; 0.7, 0.8, 0.9))^2,$$

where $v_1, v_2 \in [0, 1]$, the S-function is defined by (A17), and $\pi_{(\text{Strength}_1,\text{Strength}_2)}$ denotes the possibility distribution function of the linguistic variables Strength$_1$ and Strength$_2$.

Quantifier Rule

The quantifier rule applies to propositions of the general form

(3.33) $\quad p = QX$ are F,

where Q is a linguistic quantifier (e.g., most, many, few, etc.), X is a variable taking values in U and F is a fuzzy subset of U. In the context of preference relations, a typical instance of (3.33) might be

(3.34) $p \triangleq$ Most individuals have very strong preference for a_5 over a_3,

which for simplicity will be abbreviated to

(3.35) $p \triangleq$ Most Strengths are very strong.

In general terms, let μ_Q be the membership function of Q and let μ_F be that of F. It should be observed that when Q relates to a proportion, as in the case of *most*, μ_Q is a mapping from [0, 1] to [0, 1], while μ_F is a mapping from U to [0, 1]. In the case of preference relations, however, $U = [0, 1]$ and thus μ_F, like μ_Q, is a mapping from [0, 1] to [0, 1].

Since a fuzzy set does not have sharply defined boundaries, the concept of the cardinality of a fuzzy set does not have a unique natural meaning. For many purposes, however, the concept of the *power* of a fuzzy set [19] may be used as a suitable measure of the number of elements in such a set. Thus, if $U = \{u_1, \ldots, u_N\}$, then the power of F is defined by

(3.36) $$|F| \triangleq \sum_{i=1}^{N} \mu_F(u_i),$$

where $\mu_F(u_i)$, $i = 1, \ldots, N$, is the grade of membership of u_i in F. For example, if

(3.37) $$F = 0.8/u_1 + 0.9/u_2 + 0.6/u_3 + 0.8/u_4$$

then

(3.38) $$|F| = 3.1.$$

For some applications, it is necessary to eliminate from the count those elements of F whose grade of membership falls below a specified threshold (which may be fuzzy). This is equivalent to replacing F in (3.36) with $F \cap \Gamma$, where Γ is a fuzzy or nonfuzzy set which induces the desired threshold.

Using (3.36), for simplicity, the quantifier rule may be expressed as follows.

(3.39) If $U = \{u_1, \ldots, u_N\}$ and X is $F \rightarrow \Pi_X = F$

then QX are $F \rightarrow \Pi_{|F|} = Q$;

and if Q is a proportional quantifier

(3.40) QX are $F \rightarrow \Pi_{|F|/N} = Q.$

As a simple illustration, consider the proposition

(3.41) $p \triangleq$ Most Strengths are very strong,

where

(3.42) $\mu_{\text{most}} = S(0.6, 0.7, 0.8)$

and

(3.43) $\mu_{\text{strong}} = S(0.7, 0.8, 0.9).$

On applying (3.40), (3.36) and (3.20), we obtain as the translation of (3.41)

(3.44) $\Pi_{(S^2(v_1:0.7,0.8,0.9)+\cdots+S^2(v_N:0.7,0.8,0.9))/N} = S(0.6, 0.7, 0.8),$

where $S^2(v_i; 0.7, 0.8, 0.9)$ is the compatibility of the strength of preference of I_i with very strong, $S(0.6, 0.7, 0.8)$ is the membership function of most and the argument of Π is the number of individuals whose preference is very strong.

Truth Qualification, Probability Qualification and Possibility Qualification

In natural languages, an important mechanism for the modification of the meaning of a proposition is provided by the adjunction of three types of qualifiers: (i) is τ, where τ is a linguistic truth-value, e.g., true, very true, more or less true, false, etc.; (ii) is λ, where λ is a linguistic probability-value (or likelihood), e.g., probable, very probable, very improbable, etc.; and (iii) is π, where π is a linguistic possibility-value, e.g., possible, quite possible, slightly possible, impossible, etc. The rules governing these qualifications may be stated as follows.

Truth qualification. If

(3.45) X is $F \rightarrow \Pi_X = F$

then

X is F is $\tau \rightarrow \Pi_X = F^+,$

where

(3.46) $\mu_{F^+}(u) = \mu_\tau(\mu_F(u)), \qquad u \in U;$

μ_τ and μ_F are the membership functions of τ and F, respectively, and U is the universe of discourse associated with X. As an illustration, if strong is defined by (3.18), $\tau \triangleq$ very true is defined by

(3.47) $\mu_{\text{very true}} = S^2(0.6, 0.8, 1)$

and

(3.48) Strength is strong $\rightarrow \Pi_{\text{Strength}} =$ strong

then

$$\mu_{\text{strong}^+}(u) = S^2(1 - S(u; 0.7, 0.8, 0.9); 0.6, 0.8, 1), \qquad u \in U.$$

Probability qualification. If

(3.49) X is $F \rightarrow \Pi_X = F$

then

(3.50) X is F is $\lambda \rightarrow \Pi_{\int_U p(u)\mu_F(u)\,du} = \lambda,$

where $p(u)\,du$ is the probability that the value of X falls in the interval $(u, u + du)$; the integral

(3.51) $\int_U p(u)\mu_F(u)\,du$

is the probability of the fuzzy event F [20]; and λ is a linguistic probability-value. Thus, (3.50) defines a possibility distribution of probability distributions, with the possibility of a probability density $p(\cdot)$ given by

(3.52) $\pi(p(\cdot)) = \mu_\lambda\left(\int_U p(u)\mu_F(u)\,du\right).$

As an illustration, consider the proposition $p \triangleq$ Strength is strong is very probable, in which strong is defined by (3.18) and

(3.53) $\mu_{\text{very probable}} = S^2(0.6, 0.8, 1).$

Then

(3.54) $\pi(p(\cdot)) = S^2\left(\int_0^1 p(u)(1 - S(u; 0.7, 0.8, 0.9))\,du; 0.6, 0.8, 1\right).$

Possibility qualification. If

(3.55) X is $F \rightarrow \Pi_X = F$

then

X is F is possible $\rightarrow \Pi_X = F^+$

in which

(3.56) $F^+ = F \oplus \text{II}$,

where II is a fuzzy set of Type 2 defined by

(3.57) $\mu_{\Pi}(u) = [0, 1], \quad u \in U,$

and $\oplus$ is the bounded sum defined by (A30). Equivalently,

(3.58) $\mu_{F^+}(u) = [\mu_F(u), 1], \quad u \in U,$

which defines μ_{F^+} as an interval-valued membership function [14].

In effect, the rule in question signifies that possibility qualification has the effect of weakening the proposition which it qualifies through the addition to F of a possibility distribution II which represents total indeterminacy in the sense that the degree of possibility which it associates with each point in U may be any number in the interval [0, 1].

The rules formulated above may be applied in combination, thus making it possible to translate fairly complex propositions regarding preference relations and their aggregates. More importantly, however, the translation of a linguistic proposition into a possibility assignment equation or a set of such equations provides a basis for inference from such propositions as well as the formulation of fuzzy algorithms or programs for the characterization of social welfare functions. These issues lie beyond the scope of the present paper and will not be considered here.

NOTES

[1] For convenience of the reader, a summary of the pertinent properties of fuzzy sets is presented in Appendix on p. 228. More detailed discussions may be found in the books by Kaufmann [5] and Negoita-Ralescu [6].

[2] The troublesome aspects of interpersonal comparisons are not at issue here [24].

[3] A more detailed discussion of the concept of a possibility distribution may be found in [14].

[4] A more detailed discussion of the effect of modifiers (or hedges) may be found in [15], [16], [17] and [18].

[5] This definition of convexity can readily be extended to fuzzy sets of Type 2 by applying the extension principle (see (A70)) to (A26).

REFERENCES

[1] Sen, A. K., *Collective Choice and Social Welfare*, Holden-Day, Inc., San Francisco (1970).

[2] Raiffa, H., *Decision Analysis*, Addison-Wesley, Reading (1970).

[3] Zadeh, L. A., 'Outline of a New Approach to the Analysis of Complex Systems and Decision Processes', *IEEE Trans. Systems, Man and Cybernetics SMC-3*, 28–44 (1973).

[4] Zadeh, L. A., 'The Concept of a Linguistic Variable and Its Application to Approximate Reasoning', Part I, *Information Sciences* **8**, 199–249 (1975); Part II, *Information Sciences* **8**, 301–357 (1975); Part III, *Information Sciences* **9**, 43–80 (1975).

[5] Kaufmann, A., *Introduction to the Theory of Fuzzy Subsets*, Vol. 1, *Elements of Basic Theory* (1973); Vol. 2, *Applications to Linguistics, Logic and Semantics* (1975); Vol. 3, *Applications to Classification and Pattern Recognition*, Masson and Co., Paris (1975). Also English trans. of Vol. 1, Academic Press, New York (1975).

[6] Negoita, C. V. and Ralescu, D. A., *Applications of Fuzzy Sets to Systems Analysis*, Birkhauser Verlag, Basel and Stuttgart (1975).

[7] Bellman, R. E. and Zadeh, L. A., 'Local and Fuzzy Logics', ERL Memo M-584, University of California, Berkeley (1976). To appear in G. Epstein (ed.), *Modern Uses of Multiple-Valued Logics*, D. Reidel, Dordrecht (1977).

[8] Zadeh, L. A., 'Similarity Relations and Fuzzy Orderings', *Information Sciences* **3**, 177–200 (1971).

[9] Robert, P. and Ferland, J., 'Generalization de l'algorithme de Warshall', *R.I.R.O.* **2**, 71–85 (1968).

[10] Chan, D., Lee, E. and Zadeh, L. A., 'A Generalization of Warshall's Algorithm', *Proc. Princeton Conf. on Inf. Sci. and Systems* (1969).

[11] May, K. O., 'Intransitivity, Utility and the Aggregation of Preference Patterns', *Econometrica* **22**, 1–13 (1954).

[12] Luce, R. D., 'Semiorders and a Theory of Utility Discrimination', *Econometrica* **24**, 178–191 (1956).

[13] Fishburn, P. C., *Mathematics of Decision Theory*, Mouton, The Hague (1972).

[14] Zadeh, L. A., 'Fuzzy Sets as a Basis for a Theory of Possibility', ERL Memo M77/12 (1977). To appear in the *International Journal for Fuzzy Sets and Systems*.

[15] Zadeh, L. A., 'A Fuzzy-set-theoretic Interpretation of Linguistic Hedges', *J. Cybernetics* **2**, 4–34 (1972).

[16] Lakoff, G., 'Hedges: A Study in Meaning Criteria and the Logic of Fuzzy Concepts', *J. Phil. Logic* **2**, 458–508 (1973).

[17] Hersh, H. M. and Caramazza, A., 'A Fuzzy Set Approach to Modifiers and Vagueness in Natural Language', *Journal of Experimental Psychology* **105**, 257–276 (1976).

[18] Wenstop, F., 'Deductive Verbal Models of Organization', *Int. J. Man-Machine Studies* **8**, 293–311 (1976).
[19] DeLuca, A. and Termini, S., 'A Definition of a Nonprobabilistic Entropy in the Setting of Fuzzy Sets Theory', *Inf. and Control* **20**, 301–312 (1972).
[20] Zadeh, L. A., 'Probability Measures of Fuzzy Events', *J. Math. Anal. Appl.* **23**, 421–427 (1968).
[21] Sen, A., 'Social Choice Theory: A Re-examination', *Econometrica* **45**, 53–89 (1977).
[22] Chipman, J. S., Hurwicz, L., Richter, M. K. and Sonnenschein, U. F., *Preference, Utility and Demand*, Harcourt, New York (1971).
[23] Intriligator, M., 'A Probabilistic Model of Social Choice', *Review of Economic Studies* **40**, 553–560 (1973).
[24] Harsanyi, J. C., 'Cardinal Welfare, Individualistic Ethics, and Interpersonal Comparisons of Utility', *J. of Polit. Economy* **63**, 309–321 (1955).
[25] Fishburn, P. C., 'A Probabilistic Model of Social Choice: Comment', *Review of Economic Studies* **42**, 297–301 (1975).
[26] Fishburn, P. C., 'A Theory of Subjective Expected Utility with Vague Preferences', *Theory and Decision* **6**, 287–310 (1975).

Manuscript received 14 April 1977

Fuzzy Sets and Their Application to Pattern Classification and Clustering Analysis

L. A. Zadeh

1. Introduction.

The development of the theory of fuzzy sets in the early sixties drew much of its initial inspiration from problems relating to pattern classification -- especially the analysis of proximity relations and the separation of subsets of R^n by hyperplanes. In a more fundamental way, however, the intimate connection between the theory of fuzzy sets and pattern classification rests on the fact that most real-world classes are fuzzy in nature -- in the sense that the transition from membership to nonmembership in such classes is gradual rather than abrupt. Thus, given an object x and a class F, the real question in most cases is not whether x is or is not a member of F, but the degree to which x belongs to F or, equivalently, the grade of membership of x in F.

There is, however, still another and as yet little explored connection between the theory of fuzzy sets and pattern classification. What we have in mind is the possibility of applying fuzzy logic and the so-called linguistic approach [1]-[4] to the definition of the basic concepts in pattern analysis as well as to the formulation of fuzzy algorithms for pattern recognition. The principal motivation for this approach is that most of the practical problems in pattern classification do not lend themselves to a precise mathematical formulation, with the consequence that the less precise methods based on the linguistic approach may well prove to be better matched to the imprecision which is intrinsic in such problems.

Although the literature of the theory of fuzzy sets contains a substantial number of papers dealing with various aspects of pattern

Reprinted, with permission, from *Classification and Clustering*, edited by J. Van Ryzin, pp. 251–282 & 292–299.

classification,[1] we do not, as yet, have a unified theory of pattern classification based on the theory of fuzzy sets. It is reasonable to assume that such a theory will eventually be developed, but its construction is likely to be a long-drawn task because it will require a complete reworking of the conceptual structure of the theory of pattern classification and radical changes in our formulation and implementation of pattern recognition algorithms.

In this perspective, the limited objective of the present paper is to outline a conceptual framework for pattern classification and cluster analysis based on the theory of fuzzy sets, and draw attention to some of the significant contributions by other investigators in which concrete pattern recognition and cluster analysis algorithms are described. For convenience of the reader, a brief exposition of the relevant aspects of the theory of fuzzy sets is presented in the Appendix.

2. Pattern Classification in a Fuzzy-Set-Theoretic Framework.

To place the application of the theory of fuzzy sets to pattern classification in a proper perspective, we shall begin with informal definitions of some of the basic terms which we shall employ in later analysis.

To begin with, it will be necessary for our purposes to differentiate between an object which is pointed to (or labeled) by a pointer (identifier) p , and a mathematical object, x , which may be characterized precisely by specifying the values of a finite (or, more generally, a countable) set of parameters. For example, in the proposition "Susan is very intelligent," Susan is a pointer to a person named Susan. The person in question, however, is not a mathematical object until a set of measurement procedures $\{M_1, \ldots, M_n\}$ is defined such that the application of $\{M_1, \ldots, M_n\}$ to the object p (or, more precisely, the object pointed to by p) yields an n-tuple of constants $(x_1, \ldots, x_n)$ which

[1] Some of the representative papers bearing on the application of fuzzy sets to pattern classification and cluster analysis are listed in the bibliography.

represent the feature-values (or attribute-values) of the object in question. The n-tuple $x \triangleq (x_1,\ldots,x_n)$, then, characterizes a mathematical object associated with p, expressed symbolically as[2]

$$x \triangleq M(p) \tag{2.1}$$

where $M = (M_1,\ldots,M_n)$. For example, M_1, M_2, M_3, M_4 could be, respectively, the procedures for measuring the height, weight and temperature, and determining the sex of the object in question. In this case, a 4-tuple of the form (5'7", 125, 98.6, F) would be a mathematical object associated with the person named Susan.

An important point that needs to be noted is that there are many -- indeed an infinity -- of mathematical objects that may be associated with p. In the first place, different combinations of attributes may be measured. And second, different mathematical objects result when the precision of measurement -- or, equivalently, the resolution level -- of an attribute is varied. Thus, to associate a mathematical object x with an object p it is necessary to specify, explicitly or implicitly, the resolution levels of the attributes of p. Usually this is done implicitly, rather than explicitly, which is the reason why the concept of a resolution level -- although important in principle -- does not play an overt role in pattern recognition.

Let U^o be a universe of objects, let U be the universe of associated mathematical objects, and let F be a fuzzy subset of U^o (or U). There are three distinct ways in which F may be characterized:

(a) Listing. If the support[3] of F is a finite set, then F may be defined by a listing of its elements together with their respective grades of membership in F. For example, if U^o is the set of persons pointed to by the labels John, Luise, Sarah and David, and F is the fuzzy subset labeled tall, then F may be characterized as the

[2] The symbol $\triangleq$ stands for "denotes" or "is equal to by definition."

[3] The support of a fuzzy set F is the set of elements of the universe of discourse whose grades of membership in F are positive.

collection of ordered pairs {(John, 0.9), (Luise, 0.8), (David, 0.7) and (Sarah, 0.8)}, which may be expressed more conveniently as the linear form (see A2)

(2.2) $\underline{\text{tall}} = 0.9\ \text{John} + 0.8\ \text{Luise} + 0.7\ \text{David} + 0.8\ \text{Sarah}$

where + denotes the union rather than the arithmetic sum.

(b) Recognition algorithm. Such an algorithm, when applied to an object p, yields the grade of membership of p in F. For example, if someone were to point to Luise and ask "What is the degree to which Luise is tall?" then a recognition algorithm applied to the object Luise would yield the answer 0.8.

(c) Generation algorithm. In this case, an algorithm generates those elements of U^o which belong to the support of F and associates with each such element its grade of membership in F. As a simple illustration, the recurrence relation

(2.3) $$x_n = x_{n-1} + x_{n-2}$$

with $x_0 = 0$, $x_1 = 1$ may be viewed as a nonfuzzy generation algorithm which defines the set of Fibonacci numbers {1,2,3,5,8,13,...}.[4] As an example of a generation algorithm which defines a fuzzy set, let U be the set of strings over a finite alphabet, say {a,b}, and let G be a fuzzy context-free grammer whose production system is given by

(2.4)
$$\begin{array}{llll} S \xrightarrow{0.8} bA & & B \xrightarrow{0.4} b \\ S \xrightarrow{0.6} aB & & A \xrightarrow{0.3} bSA \\ A \xrightarrow{0.2} a & & B \xrightarrow{0.5} aSB \end{array}$$

in which S, A, B are nonterminals and the number above a production indicates its "strength." The fuzzy language, L(G), generated by this grammar may be defined as follows. Let x be a terminal string derived from S by a sequence of substitutions in which the left-hand side of a production in G is replaced by its right-hand side member, e.g.,

[4] Many examples of nonfuzzy pattern generation algorithms may be found in the books by U. Grenander [5] and K. S. Fu [6].

(2.5) $S \xrightarrow{0.8} bA \xrightarrow{0.3} bbSa \xrightarrow{0.2} bbSa \xrightarrow{0.6} bbaBa \xrightarrow{0.4} bbaba$.

The strength of the derivation chain from S to x is defined to be the minimum of the strengths of constitutent productions in the chain, e.g., in the case of (2.5), the strength of the chain is $0.8 \wedge 0.3 \wedge 0.2 \wedge 0.6 \wedge 0.4 = 0.2$ (where $\wedge$ is the infix symbol for min). The grade of membership of x in L(G) is then defined as the strength of the strongest leftmost derivation[5] chain from S to x [7]. In the case of $x \triangleq bbaba$, there is just one leftmost derivation, namely,

(2.6) $S \xrightarrow{0.8} bA \xrightarrow{0.3} bbSA \xrightarrow{0.6} bbaBA \xrightarrow{0.4} bbabA \xrightarrow{0.2} bbaba$

whose strength is 0.2. Consequently, the grade of membership of the string $x \triangleq bbaba$ in the fuzzy set L(G) is 0.2. In this way, one can associate a grade of membership in L(G) with every string that may be generated by G, and thus the production system (2.4) together with the rule for computing the grade of membership of any string in U in L(G), constitutes a generation algorithm which characterizes the fuzzy subset, L(G), of U.

<u>Opaque vs. Transparent Algorithms.</u>

For the purposes of our analysis, it is necessary to differentiate between recognition algorithms which are opaque and those which are transparent. Informally, by an <u>opaque</u> recognition algorithm we mean an algorithm whose description is not known. For example, the user of a hand calculator may not know the algorithm which is employed in the calculator to perform exponentiation. Or, a person may not be able to articulate the algorithm which he/she uses to assign a grade of membership to a painting in the fuzzy set of beautiful paintings.

As its designation implies, a recognition algorithm is <u>transparent</u> if its description is known. For example, a parsing algorithm which

[5] In leftmost derivation, the leftmost nonterminal is replaced by the right-hand member of the corresponding production.

parses a string generated by a context-free grammar and thereby yields the grade of membership of the string in the fuzzy language generated by the grammar would be classified as a transparent algorithm.

Pattern Classification.

Within the framework of the theory of fuzzy sets, the problem of pattern classification may be viewed -- in its essential form -- as that of conversion of an opaque recognition algorithm into a transparent recognition algorithm. More specifically, let U^o be a universe of objects and let R_{op} be an opaque recognition algorithm which defines a fuzzy subset F of U^o. Then, pattern classification -- or, equivalently, pattern recognition -- may be defined as the process of converting an opaque recognition algorithm R_{op} into a transparent recognition algorithm R_{tr}.[6]

As an illustration of this formulation, consider the following typical problem. Suppose that U^o is the universe of handwritten letters and that when a letter, p, is presented to a person, P, that person -- by employing an opaque recongition algorithm R_{op} -- can specify the grade of membership, $\mu_F(p)$, of p in, say, the fuzzy set, F, of handwritten A's. Thus, in symbols,

(2.7) $$\mu_F(p) = R_{op}(p), \quad \text{for } p \text{ in } U$$

Usually, P is presented with a finite set of sample letters $p_1,\ldots,p_m$, so that the result of application of R_{op} to $p_1,\ldots,p_m$ is a set of ordered pairs $\{(p_1,\mu_F(p_1)),\ldots,(p_m,\mu_F(p_m))\}$ which in the notation of fuzzy sets may be expressed as the linear form

(2.8) $$S_F = \mu_F(p_1)p_1 + \ldots + \mu_F(p_m)p_m$$

where S_F stands for a fuzzy set of samples from F, and a term of the

[6] We assume for simplicity that only one fuzzy subset of U^o is defined by R_{op}. More generally, there may be a number of such subsets, say $F_1,\ldots,F_n$, with R_{op} yielding the grade of membership of p in each of these subsets.

form $\mu_F(p_i)p_i$, $i = 1,\ldots,m$, signifies that $\mu_F(p_i)$ is the grade of membership of p_i in F.

If, based on the knowledge of S_F, we could convert the opaque recognition algorithm R_{op} into a transparent recognition algorithm R_{tr}, then given any p we could deduce $\mu_F(p)$ by applying R_{tr} to p. Equivalently, we may view this as the process of interpolation of the membership function of F from the knowledge of the values which it takes at the points $p_1,\ldots,p_m$. It should be remarked that this is the way in which the problem of pattern classification was defined in [8], but the present formulation based on the conversion of R_{op} to R_{tr} appears to be more natural.

An important implicit assumption in pattern classification is that the recognition process must be automatic, in the sense that it must be performed by a machine rather than a human. This requires that the transparent recognition algorithm R_{tr} act on a mathematical object, $M(p)$, rather than on p itself, since an object must be well-defined in order to be capable of manipulation by a machine.

In more concrete terms, let U^o be a universe of objects and let M be a measurement procedure which associates with each object p in U^o a mathematical object $M(p)$ in U. Let F be a fuzzy subset of U^o which is defined by an opaque recognition algorithm R_{op} in the sense that

$$\mu_F(p) = R_{op}(p), \quad p \in U^o .$$

Denote by R_{tr} a transparent recognition algorithm which acting on the mathematical object $M(p)$ yields $\mu_F(p)$. Then, the problem of automatic (or machine) pattern recognition may be expressed in symbols as that of determining M and R_{tr} such that

$$\mu_F(p) = R_{op}(p) \tag{2.9}$$

$$R_{tr}(M(p)) = R_{op}(p) , \quad p \in U^o. \tag{2.10}$$

Thus, the problem of automatic pattern recognition involves two distinct subproblems: (a) conversion of the object p into a mathematical object M(p); and (b) conversion of the opaque recognition algorithm R_{op} which acts on p's into a transparent recognition algorithm which acts on M(p)'s. Of these, problem (a) is by far the more difficult. In the conventional nonfuzzy approach to pattern classification, it is closely related to the problem of feature analysis -- a problem which falls into the least well-defined and least well-developed area in pattern recognition [35]-[46].

It is important to observe that, from a practical point of view, it is desirable that (i) M(p) be defined by a small number of attributes, and (ii) that the measurement of these attributes be relatively simple. With these added considerations, then, the problem of pattern classification may be reformulated in the following terms.

Given an opaque recognition algorithm R_{op} which defines a fuzzy subset of objects p in U^o.

Problem I. Specify a preferably small set of preferably simple measurement procedures which convert an object p in U^o into a mathematical object M(p) = $\{M_1(p), \ldots, M_n(p)\}$ in U.

Problem II. Convert R_{op} into a transparent recognition algorithm R_{tr} which acts on M(p) and yields the grade of membership of p in F as defined by R_{op}.

In the above formulation, the problem of pattern classification is not mathematically well-defined. In part, this is due to the fact that, as pointed out earlier, the notion of an object does not admit of precise definition and hence the functions $M_1, \ldots, M_n$ cannot be regarded as functions in the accepted mathematical sense. In addition, since the desired equality

$$R_{tr}(M(p)) = R_{op}(p), \quad p \in U^o \tag{2.11}$$

cannot be realized precisely, the problem of pattern classification does not admit of exact solution. Furthermore, an added source of imprecision in pattern classification problems relates to the difficulty of assessing the goodness of a transparent recognition algorithm which may be offered as a solution to a given problem.

The main thrust of the above comments is that the problem of pattern classification is intrinsically incapable of precise mathematical formulation. For this reason, the conceptual structure of the theory of fuzzy sets may well provide a more natural setting for the formulation and approximate solution of problems in pattern classification than the more traditional approaches based on classical set theory, probability theory and two-valued logic [35]-[46].

3. The Linguistic Approach to Pattern Classification.

Most of the conventional approaches to pattern recognition are based on the tacit assumption that the mapping from the object space U^o to the feature space U has the property that if two mathematical objects $M(p)$ are "close" to one another in terms of some metric defined on U, then p and q are likely to be in the same class in U^o.[7] When F is a fuzzy set, this assumption may be expressed more concretely but not very precisely as the property of μ-continuity of M, namely: If p and q are objects in U^o and for almost all p and q $M(p)$ is close to $M(q)$ in terms of a metric defined on U, then the grade of membership of p in F, $\mu_F(p)$, is close to that of q, $\mu_F(q)$.

The importance of μ-continuity derives from the fact that it provides a basis for reducing Problem II to the interpolation of a "well-behaved" (i.e., smooth, slowly-varying) membership function. More significantly for our purposes, it makes it possible to employ the linquistic approach for describing the dependence of μ_F on the linguistic values of the attributes of an object.

[7] This assumption is implicit in perceptron-type approaches and is related to the notion of compactness in the potential function method of Aizerman, Braverman and Rozonoer [9]-[12].

More specifically, suppose that $M(p)$ has n components $x_1 \triangleq M_1(p), \ldots, x_n \triangleq M_n(p)$, with x_i, $i = 1, \ldots, n$, taking values in U_i. Let $\mu_F(p)$ denote the grade of membership of p in F. We assume that the dependence $\mu_F(p)$ on $x_1, \ldots, x_n$ is expressible as an $(n+1)$-ary fuzzy relation R in $U_1 \times \ldots \times U_n \times V$, where $V \triangleq [0,1]$. In what follows, R will be referred to as the relational tableau defining $\mu_F(p)$.

An essential assumption which motivates the linguistic approach is that our perception of the dependence of $\mu_F(p)$ on $x_1, \ldots, x_n$ is generally not sufficiently precise or well-defined to enable us to tabulate $\mu_F(p)$ as a function of the numerical values of $x_1, \ldots, x_n$. As a coarser and hence less precise characterization of this dependence, we allow the tabulated values of $x_1, \ldots, x_n$ and $\mu_F(p)$ to be linguistic rather than numerical, employing the techniques of the linguistic approach to enable us to interpolate R for the untabulated values of $x_1, \ldots, x_n$.

To be more specific, it is helpful to assume, as in [86], that a linguistic value of x_i, $i = 1, \ldots, n$, is an answer to the question Q_i : "What is the value of x_i ?" and that the corresponding linguistic value of $\mu_F(p)$ is the answer to the question Q: "If the answers to $Q_1, \ldots, Q_n$ are $r_1, \ldots, r_n$, respectively, then what is the value of $\mu_F(p)$?" A purpose of this interpretation of the values of $x_1, \ldots, x_n, \mu_F(p)$ is to express the recognition algorithm R_{tr} as a branching questionnaire, that is, a questionnaire in which the questions are asked sequentially, with the question asked at stage j depending on the answers to the previous questions. The conversion of a relational tableau to a branching questionnaire is discussed in greater detail in [86].

Typically, the entries in a relational tableau are of the form shown in Table 1, in which the rows correspond to different objects, with the entry under Q_i representing a linguistic value of x_i for a particular object. (For simplicity, we shall speak interchangeably of the values of x_i and Q_i.) The questions $Q_1, \ldots, Q_n$ will be referred to as the constituent questions of R (or Q).

Q_1	Q_2	Q_3	Q
true	small	wide	high
very true	very small	not wide	very high
not very true	medium	NA	not very high
borderline	very large	not wide	low
not true	not very small	not very wide	more or less low
true or not very true	small	not very wide	very low

Table 1. A relational tableau defining the dependence of Q on Q_1, Q_2, Q_3.

In this table, the entries in the column labeled Q_i constitute a subset of the term-set of Q_i (see A66), that is, the possible linguistic values that may be assigned to Q_i. For example, the term-set of Q_1 might be: {true, very true, not very true, borderline, very (not true), not true, not borderline, very very true,... }. The elements of the term-set of Q_i are assumed to be generated by a context-free grammar. For instance, the elements of the term-set of Q_1 can be generated by the grammar

$$
\begin{array}{llll}
 & S \rightarrow A & & C \rightarrow D \\
 & S \rightarrow S \text{ or } A & & C \rightarrow E \\
(3.1) & A \rightarrow B & & D \rightarrow \text{very } D \\
 & A \rightarrow A \text{ and } B & & E \rightarrow \text{very } E \\
 & B \rightarrow C & & D \rightarrow \text{true} \\
 & B \rightarrow \text{not } C & & E \rightarrow \text{borderline}
\end{array}
$$

in which S, A, B, C, D, E are nonterminals and "or," "and," "not," "very," "true" and "borderline" are terminals. Using the production system of this grammar, the linguistic value "true or not very true" may be derived from S by the chain of substitutions

$$
\begin{aligned}
&S \rightarrow S \text{ or } A \rightarrow A \text{ or } A \rightarrow B \text{ or } A \rightarrow C \text{ or } A \rightarrow D \text{ or } A \rightarrow \text{true or} \\
(3.2)\quad &A \rightarrow \text{true or } B \rightarrow \text{true or not } C \rightarrow \text{true or not } D \rightarrow \text{true or not} \\
&\text{very } D \rightarrow \text{true or not very true}
\end{aligned}
$$

The linguistic values of Q_i play the role of labels of fuzzy subsets of a universe of discourse which is associated with Q_i. For example, in the case of Q_1 the universe U_1 is the unit interval [0,1], and "true" is a fuzzy subset of U_1 whose membership function might be defined in terms of the S-function (see A17) by

$$\mu_{true}(v) = S(v;0.6,0.75,0.9), \quad v \in [0,1] \tag{3.3}$$

where $S(v;\alpha,\beta,\gamma)$ is an S-shaped function which vanishes to the left of α, is unity to the right of γ and takes the value 0.5 at $\beta = \frac{\alpha+\gamma}{2}$. Similarly, the membership function of the fuzzy subset labeled "borderline" may be defined in terms of the π-function (see A18) by

$$\mu_{borderline}(v) = \pi(v;0.3,0.5) \tag{3.4}$$

where $\pi(v;\beta,\gamma)$ is a bell-shaped function whose bandwidth is β and which achieves the value 1 at γ.

By the use of a semantic technique which is described in [2], it is possible to compute in a relatively straightforward fashion the membership function of the fuzzy set which plays the role of the meaning of a linguistic value in the term-set of Q_i. For example, the membership functions of "not true," "very true," "not very true" and "true or not very true" are related to that of "true" by the equations (in which the argument v is suppressed for simplicity)

$$\mu_{not\ true} = 1 - \mu_{true} \tag{3.5}$$

$$\mu_{very\ true} = (\mu_{true})^2 \tag{3.6}$$

$$\mu_{not\ very\ true} = 1 - (\mu_{true})^2 \tag{3.7}$$

$$\mu_{true\ or\ not\ very\ true} = \mu_{true} \vee (1 - (\mu_{true})^2) \tag{3.8}$$

where $(\mu_{true})^2$ denotes the square of the membership function of true and $\vee$ stands for the infix form of max.

A fuzzy set (or fuzzy sets) in terms of which the meaning of all other linguistic values in the term-set of Q_i may be computed is termed a primary fuzzy set (or sets). Thus, in the case of Q_1 the primary fuzzy set is labeled "true:" in the case of Q_2 the primary fuzzy sets are "small," "medium" and "large:" and in the case of Q the primary fuzzy sets are "high" and "medium," with "low" defined in terms of "high" by

$$\mu_{low}(v) = \mu_{high}(1-v), \qquad v \in [0,1] . \tag{3.9}$$

In effect, a primary fuzzy set plays a role akin to that of a unit whose meaning is context-dependent and hence must be defined a priori. The important point is that once the meaning of the primary terms is specified, the meaning of non-primary terms in the term-set of each Q_i may be computed by the application of the semantic rule which is associated with that Q_i.

The entry NA in Q_3 stands for "not applicable." What this means is that if the answer to Q_1 is, say, "not very true" and the answer to Q_2 is "medium," then Q_3 is not applicable to the object corresponding to the third row in the table. As a simple illustration of non-applicability, if the answer to the question "Is p a prime number?" is "true," then the question "What is the largest divisor of p other than 1?" is not applicable to p .

In the representation of R in the form of a relational tableau, it is helpful to divide the constituent questions into two categories: attributional and classificational. As its name implies, an attributional question is one which asks for the value of an attribute of p , e.g., Q_2 and Q_3 in Table 1 are attributional questions. A classificational question, on the other hand, relates to the degree to which a specified property is possessed by the object in question. Thus, the answer to a classificational question is either a truth-value, as in Q_1, or the grade of membership, as in Q . In both cases, the universe of discourse associated with a classificational question is assumed to be the interval [0,1]. Generally, we shall assume that "high" is equivalent to "true:" "medium" to "borderline:" and "low" to "false," where, by analogy with (3.9), "false" is defined by

(3.10) $$\mu_{false}(v) = \mu_{true}(1-v), \qquad v \in [0,1].$$

As an illustration of the above approach, assume that we wish to characterize the concept of an oval[8] contour, with U being the space of curved, smooth, simply-connected and non-self-intersecting contours in a plane.[9] To simplify the example, we assume that the constituent questions are limited to the following.

Classificational: $Q_1 \triangleq$ Does p have an axis of symmetry?

Classificational: $Q_2 \triangleq$ Does p have a second axis of symmetry?

Classificational: $Q_3 \triangleq$ Are the two axes of symmetry orthogonal?

Classificational: $Q_4 \triangleq$ Does p have more than two axes of symmetry?

Attributional: $Q_5 \triangleq$ What is the ratio of the lengths of the major and minor axes?

Calssificational: $Q_6 \triangleq$ Is p convex?

For simplicity, the answers to the classificational questions are allowed to be only <u>true</u>, <u>borderline</u> and <u>false</u>, abbreviated to t, b and f, respectively, with the membership functions of t, b and f expressed in terms of the S and π functions by (3.3), (3.4) and[10]

(3.11) $$\mu_f(v) = \mu_t(1-v)$$
$$= 1 - S(v;0.1,0.25,0.4).$$

Similarly, the term-set for Q_5 is assumed to be

$$T(Q_5) = \{\text{about } 1, \text{ about } 1.5, \text{ about } 2, \text{ about } 2.5, \text{ about } 3, \text{ about } 4, \text{ about } 5, > \text{about } 5\}$$

[8]For purposes of this example, by oval we mean a shape resembling that of an egg.

[9]Note that the point of departure in this example is U rather than U^o because we assume that a contour is a mathematical object.

[10]It should be understood that true and false in the present context do not have the same meaning as they do in classical logic. Rather, as in fuzzy logic [3], true in the sense of (3.3) means "approximately true," and likewise for "false".

where about α, $\alpha = 2,\ldots,5$, is defined by (with the arguments of π and S suppressed for simplicity)

(3.12) $$\text{about } \alpha = \pi(0.4,\alpha)$$

and

(3.13) $$\text{about } 1 = 1 - S(1,0.2,0.4) .$$

The answer to Q_6 is assumed to be provided by a subquestionnaire with an unspecified number of classificational constituent questions $Q_{61}, Q_{62}, \ldots$ which are intended to check on whether the slope of the tangent to the contour is a monotone function of the distance traversed along the contour by an observer. Thus, if an observer begins to traverse the contour in, say, the counterclockwise direction starting at a point a_0, and $a_1,\ldots,a_m$ are regularly spaced points on the contour, with $a_{m+1} = a_0$, then Q_{6i} would be the question

$Q_{6i} \overset{\Delta}{=}$ Is the slope of the tangent at a_i greater than that at a_{i-1}, $i = 1,2,\ldots,m+1$?

The answer to Q_6 is assumed to be true if and only if the answers to all of the constituent questions $Q_{61}, Q_{62}, \ldots$ are true.

In terms of the constituent questions defined above, the relational tableau characterizing an oval object may be expressed in a form such as shown in Table 2. For simplicity, only a few of the possible combinations of answers to these questions are exhibited in the table (NA stands for not applicable).

Q_1	Q_2	Q_3	Q_4	Q_5	Q_6	Q
t	t	t	f	about 1	t	b
t	t	t	f	about 1.5	t	t
f	f	t	f	about 1	t	f
t	f	NA	f	about 1	t	f
t	b	NA	f	about 1	t	b
t	b	NA	f	about 1.5	t	b

Table 2. Relational tableau characterizing an oval object

The first row in this table signifies that if the answer to Q_1 is t (i.e., p has one axis of symmetry); the answer to Q_2 is t (i.e., p has a second axis of symmetry; the answer to Q_3 is t (i.e., the two axes of symmetry are orthogonal); the answer to Q_4 is f (i.e., p has two and only two axes of symmetry); the answer to Q_5 is about 1 (i.e., the major and minor axes are about equal in length); and the answer to Q_6 is t (i.e., Q_6 is convex), with the answer to Q_6 provided by the subquestionnaire; then the answer to Q is b (i.e., p is an oval object to a degree which is approximately equal to 0.5, with "approximately equal to 0.5" defined by (3.4)).

Similarly, the fifth row in the table signifies that if the answer to Q_1 is t; the answer to Q_2 is b; the answer to Q_3 is NA; the answer to Q_4 is f; the answer to Q_5 is about 1 and the answer to Q_6 is t; then the answer to Q is b. Comparing the entries in row 5 with those of row 6, we note the answer to Q remains b when we change the answer to Q_5 from about 1 to about 1.5.

4. Translation Rules and the Interpolation of a Relational Tableau

Assuming that we have a characterization of M(p) in the form of a relational tableau R, the question that arises is: How can we deduce from R the grade of membership of an object p in F?

As a preliminary to arriving at an approximate answer to this question, we have to develop a way of converting R into an (n+1)-ary fuzzy relation in $U_1 \times \ldots \times U_n \times V$. To this end, we shall employ the translation rules of fuzzy logic -- rules which provide a basis for translating a composite fuzzy proposition into a system of so-called relational assignment equations [14].

More specifically, let p be a pointer to an object and let q be a proposition of the form

$$q \triangleq p \text{ is } F \tag{4.1}$$

where F is a fuzzy subset of U. For example, q may be

$$q \triangleq \text{Pamela is tall.} \tag{4.2}$$

Translation rule of Type I asserts that q translates into

(4.3) $$p \text{ is } F \rightarrow R(A(p)) = F$$

where $A(p)$ is an implied attribute of p and $R(A(p))$ is a <u>fuzzy restriction</u>[11] on the variable $A(p)$. Thus, (4.3) constitutes a relational assignment equation in the sense that the fuzzy set F -- viewed as a unary fuzzy relation in U -- is assigned to the restriction on $A(p)$. For example, in the case of (4.2), the rule in question yields

$$\text{Pamela is tall} \rightarrow R(\text{Height(Pamela)}) = \text{tall}$$

where R(Height(Pamela)) is a fuzzy restriction on the values that may be assigned to the variable Height(Pamela).

Now let us consider two propositions, say

(4.4) $$q_1 \stackrel{\Delta}{=} p_1 \text{ is } F_1$$

and

(4.5) $$q_2 \stackrel{\Delta}{=} p_2 \text{ is } F_2$$

where p_1 and p_2 are possibly distinct objects, and F_1 and F_2 are fuzzy subsets of U_1 and U_2, respectively. For example, q_1 and q_2 might be $q_1 \stackrel{\Delta}{=}$ X is large and $q_2 \stackrel{\Delta}{=}$ Y is small.

By (4.3), the translations of q_1 and q_2 are given by

(4.6) $$p_1 \text{ is } F_1 \rightarrow R(A_1(p_1)) = F_1$$

(4.7) $$p_2 \text{ is } F_2 \rightarrow R(A_2(p_2)) = F_2$$

where $A_1(p_1)$ and $A_2(p_2)$ are implied attributes of p_1 and p_2.

By the rule of conjunctive composition [4], the translation of the composite proposition q_1 and q_2 is given by

(4.8) $$q_1 \text{ and } q_2 \rightarrow R(A_1(p_1), A_2(p_2)) = F_1 \times F_2$$

where $F_1 \times F_2$ denotes the cartesian product of F_1 and F_2 (see A56)

---

[11] A fuzzy restriction is a fuzzy relation which acts as an elastic constraint on the values that may be assigned to a variable [2], [14].

which is assigned to the restriction on $A_1(p_1)$ and $A_2(p_2)$. Dually, by the rule of disjunctive composition, the translation of the composite composition q_1 or q_2 is given by

$$q_1 \text{ or } q_2 \rightarrow R(A_1(p_1), A_2(p_2)) = \bar{F}_1 + \bar{F}_2 \tag{4.9}$$

where $\bar{F}_1$ and $\bar{F}_2$ are the cylindrical extensions of F_1 and F_2 (see A59) and + denotes the union.

As we shall see presently, these two rules provide a basis for constructing a translation rule for relational tableaus. More specifically, consider a tableau of the form shown in Table 3

A_1	A_2	$\cdots$	A_n
r_{11}	r_{12}		r_{1n}
r_{21}	r_{22}	.	r_{2n}
$\vdots$	$\vdots$	$\vdots$	$\vdots$
r_{m1}	r_{m2}		r_{mn}

Table 3. A relational tableau

in which $A_1, \ldots, A_n$ are variables taking values in $U_1, \ldots, U_n$, and the r_{ij} are linguistic labels of fuzzy subsets of U_j. (In relation to Table 1, the A_j play the roles of Q_j and Q.)

Expressed in words, the meaning of the tableau in question may be stated as:

(4.10) A_1 is r_{11} and A_2 is r_{12} and ... and A_n is r_{1n}
or
A_1 is r_{21} and A_2 is r_{22} and ... and A_n is r_{2n}
or
:
.....
or
A_1 is r_{m1} and A_2 is r_{m2} and ... and A_n is r_{mn}

Regarding (4.9) as a composite proposition and applying (4.8) and (4.9) to (4.10), we arrive at the <u>tableau translation rule</u> which is expressed by

(4.11)

A_1	...	A_n
r_{11}	...	r_{1n}
.	...	.
r_{m1}	...	r_{mn}

$$\rightarrow R(A_1,\ldots,A_n) = r_{11}\times\ldots\times r_{1n}+\ldots + r_{m1}\times\ldots\times r_{mn}$$

where $r_{11}\times\ldots\times r_{1n}+\ldots+r_{m1}\times\ldots\times r_{mn}$ is an n-ary fuzzy relation in $U_1\times\ldots\times U_n$ which is assigned to the restriction $R(A_1,\ldots,A_n)$ on the values of the variables $A_1,\ldots,A_n$.

As a very simple illustration of the tableau translation rule, assume that the tableau of R is given by [86]

(4.12)

Q_1	Q_2	Q
t	t	vf
f	f	t

where t, f and vf are abbreviations for true, false and very false, respectively, and

(4.13) $$U_1 = U_2 = V = 0+0.2+0.4+0.6+0.8+1$$

(4.14) $$t = 0.6/0.8 + 1/1$$

(4.15) $$f = 1/0 + 0.6/0.2$$

and by (3.6)

(4.16) $$vf = 1/0 + 0.36/0.2\ .$$

Applying the translation rule (4.11) to the table in question, we obtain the ternary fuzzy relation in $V\times V\times V$:

(4.17) $R(Q_1,Q_2,Q) = t \times t \times vf + f \times f \times t$

$= (0.6/0.8+1/1)\times(0.6/0.8+1/1)\times(1/0+0.36/0.2)$

$+(1/0+0.6/0.2)\times(1/0+0.6/0.2)\times(0.6/0.8+1/1)$

$= 0.36/((0.8,0.8,0.2)+(0.8,1,0.2)+(1,0.8,0.2)$

$+(1,1,0.2))+0.6((0,0,0.8)+(0,0.2,0.8)+(0.2,0,0.8)$

$+(0.2,0.2,0.8) + (0,0.2,1)+(0.2,0.2,1))$

$+ 1/((0,0,1)+(1,1,0))$

as the expression for the meaning of the relational tableau (4.12).

The Mapping Rule

The translation rule expressed by (4.11) provides a basis for an interpolation of a relational tableau, yielding an approximate value for the answer to Q given the answers to $Q_1,\ldots,Q_n$ which do not appear in R.

Specifically, let $(r_{i1},\ldots,r_{in},r_i)$ denote the ith (n+1)-tuple in R and let $\tilde{R}$ denote the (n+1)-ary fuzzy relation in $U_1 \times \ldots \times U_n \times V$, $V \triangleq [0,1]$, expressed by

(4.13) $$\tilde{R} = r_{11} \times \ldots \times r_{1n} \times r_1 + \ldots + r_{m1} \times \ldots \times r_{mn} \times r_m$$

where, as in (4.11), $\times$ and $+$ denote the cartesian product and union, respectively.

Now suppose that $g_1,\ldots,g_n$ are given fuzzy subsets of $U_1,\ldots,U_n$, respectively, and that we wish to compute the value of Q given that the values of $Q_1,\ldots,Q_n$ are $g_1,\ldots,g_n$.

Let $R(g_1,\ldots,g_n)$ denote the result of the substitution and hence the desired value of Q, and let G denote the cartesian product

(4.14) $$G = g_1 \times \ldots \times g_n .$$

Then, the mapping rule may be expressed compactly as[12]

(4.15) $$R(g_1,\ldots,g_n) = \tilde{R} \circ G$$

[12] This mapping rule may be viewed as an extension to a fuzzy relation of the mapping rule employed in such query languages as SQUARE and SEQUEL [15], [16].

where $\circ$ denotes the composition (see A60) of the (n+1)-ary fuzzy relation $\tilde{R}$ with the n-ary fuzzy relation G.

In more explicit terms, the right-hand member of (4.15) is a fuzzy subset of U which may be computed as follows.

Assume for simplicity that $U_1,\ldots,U_n,V$ are finite sets which may be expressed in the form (+ denotes the union)

$$
\begin{aligned}
U_1 &= u_1^1 + \ldots + u_{k_1}^1 \\
U_2 &= u_1^2 + \ldots + u_{k_2}^2 \\
&\ldots\ldots\ldots\ldots \\
U_n &= u_1^n + \ldots + u_{k_n}^n \\
V &= v_1 + \ldots + v_k \quad .
\end{aligned}
\tag{4.16}
$$

Now suppose that the g_i are expressed as fuzzy subsets of the U_i by (see A6)

$$
\begin{aligned}
g_1 &= \gamma_1^1 u_1^1 + \ldots + \gamma_{k_1}^1 u_{k_1}^1 \\
&\ldots\ldots\ldots\ldots\ldots \\
g_n &= \gamma_1^n u_1^n + \ldots + \gamma_{k_n}^n u_{k_n}^n
\end{aligned}
\tag{4.17}
$$

so that

$$
G = \sum_I \gamma_{i_1}^1 \wedge \gamma_{i_2}^2 \wedge \ldots \wedge \gamma_{i_n}^n / u_{i_1}^1 u_{i_2}^2 \ldots u_{i_n}^n
\tag{4.18}
$$

where I denotes the index sequence $(i_1,\ldots,i_n)$, with $1 \le i_1 \le k_1$, $1 \le i_2 \le k_2,\ldots,1 \le i_n \le k_n$; $u_{i_1}^1 u_{i_2}^2 \ldots u_{i_n}^n$ is an abbreviation for the n-tuple $(u_{i_1}^1, u_{i_1}^2,\ldots,u_{i_n}^n)$, and $\gamma_{i_1}^1 \wedge \gamma_{i_2}^2 \wedge \ldots \wedge \gamma_{i_n}^n$ is the grade of membership of the n-tuple $u_{i_1}^1 u_{i_2}^2 \ldots u_{i_n}^n$ in the n-ary fuzzy relation G.

By the definition of composition, the composition of $\tilde{R}$ with G may be expressed as the projection on $U_1 \times \ldots \times U_n$ of the intersection of $\tilde{R}$ with the cylindrical extension of G. Thus,

(4.19) $$\tilde{R} \circ G = \operatorname*{Proj}_{U_1 \times \ldots \times U_n} (\tilde{R} \cap \bar{G})$$

where $\bar{G}$ is given by

(4.20) $$\bar{G} = \sum_{(I,i)} \gamma^1_{i_1} \wedge \gamma^2_{i_2} \wedge \ldots \wedge \gamma^n_{i_n} / u^1_{i_1} u^2_{i_2} \ldots u^n_{i_n} v_i .$$

In this expression, (I,i) denotes the index sequence $(i_1,\ldots,i_n,i)$, with $1 \leq i \leq k$, and $u^1_{i_1} u^2_{i_2} \ldots u^n_{i_n} v_i$ is an abbreviation for the $(n+1)$-tuple $(u^1_{i_1}, u^2_{i_2}, \ldots, u^n_{i_n}, v_i)$.

Now suppose that the computation of the right-hand member of (4.13) yields $\tilde{R}$ in the form

(4.21) $$\tilde{R} = \sum_{(I,i)} \mu_{(I,i)} / u^1_{i_1} u^2_{i_2} \ldots u^n_{i_n} v_i .$$

Then, the intersection of $\tilde{R}$ with $\bar{G}$ is given by

(4.22) $$\tilde{R} \cap \bar{G} = \sum_{(I,i)} \gamma^1_{i_1} \wedge \gamma^2_{i_2} \wedge \ldots \wedge \gamma^n_{i_n} \wedge \mu_{(I,i)} / u^1_{i_1} \ldots u^n_{i_n} v_i$$

and the projection[13] of $\tilde{R} \cap \bar{G}$ on $U_1 \times \ldots \times U_n$ -- and hence the composition of $\tilde{R}$ and G -- is expressed by

(4.23) $$\tilde{R} \circ G = \sum_{(I,i)} \gamma^1_{i_1} \wedge \gamma^2_{i_2} \wedge \ldots \wedge \gamma^n_{i_n} \wedge \mu_{(I,i)} / v_i$$

where, to recapitulate;

$R(g_1,\ldots,g_n) = \tilde{R} \circ G$

= result of substitution of g_i for Q_i, $i = 1,\ldots,n$, in R;

$G = g_1 \times \ldots \times g_n$;

$\gamma^\lambda_{i_\lambda}$ = grade of membership of u_{i_λ} in g_λ, $\lambda = 1,\ldots,n$;

$I \triangleq (i_1,\ldots,i_n)$

$(I,i) \triangleq (i_1,\ldots,i_n,i)$

---

[13] A convenient way of obtaining the projection is to set $u^1_{i_1} = \ldots = u^n_{i_n} = 1$ in the right-hand member of (4.22) and treat the $(n+1)$-tuple $(u^1_{i_1},\ldots,u^n_{i_n},v_i)$ as if it were an algebraic product of $u^1_{i_1},\ldots,u^n_{i_n},v_i$.

$$\mu_{(i,i)} \stackrel{\Delta}{=} \text{grade of membership of } (u^1_{i_1}, u^2_{i_2}, \ldots, u^n_{i_n}, v_i) \text{ in } \tilde{R}$$

$$\tilde{R} = r_{11} \times \ldots \times r_{1n} \times r_1 + \ldots + r_{m1} \times \ldots \times r_{mn} \times r_m .$$

It should be noted that we would obtain the same result by assigning $g_1, \ldots, g_n$ to $Q_1, \ldots, Q_n$ in sequence rather than simultaneously. This is a consequence of the identity

$$(4.24) \qquad \tilde{R} \circ G = (\ldots((\tilde{R} \circ g_1) \circ g_2) \ldots \circ g_n)$$

which in turn follows from the identity

$$(4.25) \qquad \sum_{(I,i)} \gamma^1_{i_1} \wedge \gamma^2_{i_2} \wedge \ldots \wedge \gamma^n_{i_n} \wedge \mu_{(I,i)}/v_i$$

$$= \sum_{(I,i)} [[[\gamma^1_{i_1} \wedge \mu_{(I,i)}/u^1_{i_1} u^2_{i_2} \ldots u^n_{i_n} v_i]_{u^1_{i_1}=1} \wedge \gamma^2_{i_2}]_{u^2_{i_2}=1} \wedge \ldots \wedge \gamma^n_{i_n}]_{u^n_{i_n}=1} .$$

As a very simple illustration of the mapping operation, assume that

$n = 2$;

$U_1 = U_2 = V = 0 + 0.2 + 0.4 + 0.6 + 0.8 + 1$;

$\tilde{R}$ is given by

$$(4.26) \quad \tilde{R} = 1/(0,0,0) + 0.8/(0,0,0.2) + 0.7/(0.2,0.2,0) + 0.6/(0.2,0,0) + 0.8/(0.4,0.6,0.4) + 0.8/(0.4,0.2,0) + 0.5/(0.4,0.2,0.4) + 0.6/(0.2,0.6,0.8) + 0.8(0.8,0.8,0.2) + 0.9/(0.8,0.8,1) + 0.8/(0.8,1,0.8) + 0.6/(0.2,0.8,1) + 0.8/(0.6,0.8,1)$$

and

$$(4.27) \qquad g_1 = 0.6/0.4 + 1/0.2$$

$$(4.28) \qquad b_2 = 1/0.6 + 0.8/0.2.$$

Then by (4.18)

$$(4.29) \qquad g = g_1 \times g_2 = 0.6/(0.4,0.6) + 0.6/(0.4,0.2) + 1/(0.2,0.6) + + 0.8/(0.2,0.2)$$

and thus

$$(4.30)\quad R(g_1, g_2) = \tilde{R} \circ g$$
$$= 0.6 \wedge 0.8/0.4 + 0.8 \wedge 0.6/0 + 0.5 \wedge 0.6/0.4 +$$
$$+ 0.6 \wedge 1/0.8 + 0.7 \wedge 0.8/0$$
$$= 0.6/0.4 + 0.7/0 + 0.6/0.8.$$

There are two points related to the computation of $\tilde{R} \circ g$ that are in need of comment. First, if $\tilde{R}$ is sparsely tabulated in the sense that many of the possible n-tuples of values of $Q_1, \ldots, Q_n$ are not in the table, then the interpolation of R by the use of (4.23) may not yield a valid approximation to the answer to Q. And second, the result of substitution of

$$g = r_{i1} \times \ldots \times r_{in}$$

in $\tilde{R}$ would not, in general, be exactly equal to r_i -- as one might expect to be the case. As pointed out in [14], the reason for this phenomenon is the interference between the rows of $\tilde{R}$, which in turn is due to the fact that the fuzzy sets which constitute a column of R are not, in general, disjoint, that is, do not have an empty intersection.

An important assumption that underlies the procedure described in this section is that one has or can obtain a relational tableau which characterizes the dependence of the grade of membership of an object on the linguistic values of its attributes and/or the degree to which it possesses specified properties. The main contribution of the linguistic approach is that it makes it possible to describe this dependence in an approximate manner, using words rather than numbers as values of the relevant variables.

5. Cluster Analysis.

Theory of fuzzy sets was first applied to cluster analysis by E. Ruspini [17]-[19]. More recently, J. Dunn and J. Bezdek have made a number of important contributions to this subject and have described effective algorithms for deriving optimal fuzzy partitions of a given set of sample points [20]-[32].

Viewed within the framework described in Section 2, cluster analysis differs from pattern classification in three essential respects.

First, the point of departure in cluster analysis is not -- as in pattern classification -- an opaque recognition algorithm in U^o which defines a fuzzy subset F of U^o, but a fuzzy similarity relation S^o which is a fuzzy subset of $U^o \times U^o$ and which is characterized by an opaque recognition algorithm R_{op}. Thus, when presented with two objects p and q in U^o, R_{op} yields the degree, $\mu_{S^o}(p,q)$, to which p and q are similar. The function $\mu_{S^o}: U^o \times U^o \rightarrow [0,1]$ is the membership function of the fuzzy relation S^o in U^o.

Second, the problem of cluster analysis includes as a subproblem the following problem in pattern classification.

Let p and q be objects in U^o and let $x \triangleq M(p)$ and $y \triangleq M(q)$ be their correspondents in the space of mathematical objects $U = \{M(p)\}$. The problem is to convert the opaque recognition algorithm R_{op} which acting on p and q yields

(5.1) $$R_{op}(p,q) = \mu_{S^o}(p,q) ,$$

into a transparent recognition algorithm R_{tr} which acting on x and y yields the same result as R_{op}, i.e.,

(5.2) $$R_{tr}(x,y) = R_{op}(p,q)$$
$$= \mu_{S^o}(p,q) .$$

It should be noted that this problem is of the same type as that formulated in Section 2, with the fuzzy subset S^o of $U^o \times U^o$ playing the role of F.

Third, assuming that we have R_{tr} -- which acts on elements of $U \times U$ -- the objective of cluster analysis is to derive from R_{tr} a number, say k, of transparent recognition algorithms $R_{tr_1}, \ldots, R_{tr_k}$ -- acting on elements of U -- such that the fuzzy subsets (fuzzy clusters)

$F_1, \ldots, F_k$ in U defined by $R_{tr_1}, \ldots, R_{tr_k}$, have a property which may be stated as follows.

Fuzzy Affinity Property

Let $x = M(p)$ and $y = M(q)$ be mathematical objects in U corresponding to the objects p and q in U^o. Let $\{F_1, \ldots, F_k\}$ be a collection of well-separated[14] fuzzy subsets of U with membership functions $\mu_1, \ldots, \mu_n$, respectively. Then the F_i are fuzzy clusters induced by S^o if they have the fuzzy affinity property defined below.

(a) Both x and y have high grades of membership in some F_r, $r = 1, \ldots, k \Rightarrow (x,y)$ has a high grade of membership in S (the similarity relation induced in U by S^o).

(b) x has a high grade of membership in some F_r, $r = 1, \ldots, k$ and y has a high grade of membership in F_t, $t \neq r \Rightarrow (x,y)$ does not have a high grade of membership in S .

Stated less formally, the fuzzy affinity property implies that (a) if x and y have a high degree of similarity then they have a high grade of membership in some cluster, and vice-versa; and (b) if x and y have high grades of membership in different clusters then they do not have a high degree of similarity. It should be noted that this property of fuzzy clusters is more demanding than that implicit in the conventional definitions in which the degree of similarity of objects which belong to the same cluster is merely required to be greater than the degree of similarity between objects which belong to different clusters. Another point that should be noted is that, if we assumed that the only alternative to the consequent of (b) is "(x,y) has a high grade of membership in S," then (b) would be implied by (a) since the latter consequent would imply that x and y have a high grade of membership in some F_r -- which contradicts the antecedent of (b). Thus, by stating (b) we are tacitly assuming that (x,y) is not restricted to having either "high" or "not high"

[14]By well-separated we mean that if F_r and F_t are distinct fuzzy sets in $\{F_1, \ldots, F_k\}$, then every point of U has a low grade of membership in $F_r \cap F_t$.

grades of membership in S. For example, the grade of membership in S could be "not high and not low."

An important implication of the fuzzy affinity property is the following. Suppose that x and y have high grades of membership in some fuzzy cluster F_r, and that z has a high grade of membership in a different fuzzy cluster, say F_t. Then, by (a) and (b), we have

(5.3) similarity of x and y is high
similarity of y and z is not high
similarity of x and z is not high

which implies that we could not have

(5.4) similarity of x and y is high
similarity of y and z is high
similarity of x and z is not high.

The inconsistency of the assertions in (5.4) is ruled out by the fuzzy transitivity of the similarity relation S which may be stated as[15]

(5.5) similarity of x and z is at least as great as the similarity of x and y or the similarity of y and z.

Thus, if S has the fuzzy transitivity property and the similarities of both x and y and y and z are high, then the similarity of x and z must also be high.

Another point that should be noted is that the fuzzy affinity property does not require that the fuzzy clusters $\{F_1, \dots, F_k\}$ form a fuzzy partition in the sense of Ruspini. However, the stronger assumption that the F_r form a fuzzy partition makes it possible for Dunn and Bezdek to construct an effective algorithm for deriving from a fuzzy similarity relation a family of fuzzy clusters which form a fuzzy partition.

---

[15] In more precise terms, the transitivity of a fuzzy relation R in U is defined by (see [13])

$$\mu_R(u,v) \geq \vee_w(\mu_R(u,w) \wedge \mu_R(w,v)), \qquad (u,v) \in U \times U$$

where $\mu_R(u,v)$ is the grade of membership of (u,v) in R, and $\vee_w$ is the supremum over $w \in U$.

As described in [26], the Dunn-Bezdek fuzzy ISODATA algorithm may be stated as follows.

Let $\mu_1,\ldots,\mu_k$ denote the membership functions of $F_1,\ldots,F_k$, where the F_i, $i = 1,\ldots,k$, are fuzzy subsets (clusters) of a finite subset, X, of points in U. The fuzzy clusters $F_1,\ldots,F_k$ form a fuzzy k-partition of X if and only if

(5.6) $$\mu_1(x) + \ldots + \mu_k(x) = 1, \quad x \in X$$

where + denotes the arithmetic sum. The goodness of a fuzzy partition is assumed to be assessed by the criterion functional

(5.7) $$J(\mu) = \min_v \sum_{i=1}^{k} \sum_{x \in X} (\mu_i(x))^2 \| x - v_i \|^2$$

where $\mu \triangleq (\mu_1,\ldots,\mu_k)$, $v = (v_1,\ldots,v_k)$, $v_i \in L$, and $L \triangleq$ vector space with inner product induced norm $\| \|$. Intuitively, the v_i represent the "centers" of $F_1,\ldots,F_k$ and $J(\mu)$ provides a measure of the weighted dispersion of points in X in the relation to the optimal locations of the centers $v_1,\ldots,v_k$.

Step 1: Choose a fuzzy partition $F_1,\ldots,F_k$ characterized by k nonempty membership functions $\mu = (\mu_1,\ldots,\mu_k)$, with $2 \le k \le n$.

Step 2: Compute the k weighted means (centers)

(5.8) $$v_i = \frac{\sum_{x \in X} (\mu_i(x))^2 x}{\sum_{x \in X} (\mu_i(x))^2}, \quad 1 \le i \le k$$

where $x \in X \subset L$.

Step 3: Construct a new partition, $\hat{F}_1,\ldots,\hat{F}_k$, characterized by $\hat{\mu} = (\hat{\mu}_1,\ldots,\hat{\mu}_k)$, according to the following rule.

Let $I(x) \triangleq \{1 \le i \le k \mid v_i = x\}$. If $I(x)$ is not empty let $\hat{i}$ be the least integer $I(x)$ and put

(5.9) $$\hat{\mu}_i(x) = 1 \quad \text{if} \quad i = \hat{i}$$
$$= 0 \quad \text{if} \quad i \ne \hat{i}$$

for $1 \le i \le k$. Otherwise, if $I(x)$ is empty (the usual case), set

$$\hat{\mu}_i(x) = \frac{\dfrac{1}{\|x-v_i\|^2}}{\sum_{j=1}^{k}\left(\dfrac{1}{\|x-v_i\|^2}\right)} \quad . \tag{5.10}$$

Step 4: Compute some convenient measure, δ, of the defect between μ and $\hat{\mu}$. If $\delta \leq \varepsilon \stackrel{\Delta}{=}$ a specified threshold, then stop. Otherwise go to Step 2.

In a number of papers [20]-[32], Bezdek and Dunn have studied the behavior of this and related algorithms and have established their convergence and other properties. Clearly, the work of Bezdek and Dunn on fuzzy clustering constitutes an important contribution to both the theory of cluster analysis and its practical applications.

Fuzzy Level-Sets

As was pointed out in [13], the conventional hierarchical clustering schemes [33] may be viewed as the resolution of a fuzzy similarity relation into a nested collection of nonfuzzy equivalence relations. To relate this result to the fuzzy affinity property, it is necessary to extend the notion of a level-set as defined in [13] to that of a fuzzy level-set. More specifically, let F be a fuzzy subset of U and let F_α, $0 \leq \alpha \leq 1$, be the α-level subset of U defined by

$$F_\alpha \stackrel{\Delta}{=} \{x \mid \mu_F(x) \geq \alpha\} \tag{5.11}$$

where μ_F is the membership function of F. We note that F_α -- which is a nonfuzzy set -- may be expressed equivalently as

$$F_\alpha = \mu_F^{-1}([\alpha,1]) \tag{5.12}$$

where μ_F^{-1} is the relation from [0,1] to U which is converse to μ_F, and F_α is the image of the interval $[\alpha,1]$ under this relation -- or, equivalently, multi-valued mapping -- μ_F^{-1}. It is easy to verify that in terms of the membership functions of F_α, F and $[\alpha,1]$, (5.12) translates into

(5.13) $$\mu_{F_\alpha}(x) = \mu_{[\alpha,1]}(\mu_F(x)), \quad x \in U$$

where μ_{F_α} and $\mu_{[\alpha,1]}$ denote the membership (characteristic) functions of the nonfuzzy sets F_α and $[\alpha,1]$, respectively.

Now suppose that α is a fuzzy subset of $[0,1]$ labeled, say, high, with μ_{high} defined by (see A17)

(5.14) $$\mu_{high}(v) = S(v;0.6,0.7,0.8), \qquad 0 \leq v \leq 1 .$$

When α is a fuzzy subset of $[0,1]$, the fuzzy set $\geq \alpha$ may be expressed as the composition of the nonfuzzy binary relation $\geq$ with the unary fuzzy relation α. Thus, if $\alpha \triangleq$ high, then

(5.15) $$\begin{aligned} \geq \alpha &= \geq \circ \alpha \\ &= \geq \circ \text{high} \\ &= \text{high} \end{aligned}$$

since the membership function of high is monotone nondecreasing in v. Correspondingly, the expression for the membership function of the fuzzy level set F_{high} becomes (see A73)

(5.16) $$\mu_{F_{high}}(x) = \mu_{high}(\mu_F(x)) .$$

To relate this result to the fuzzy affinity property, we note that if the objects x,y in U have a high degree of similarity, then the ordered pair (x,y) has a high grade of membership in the fuzzy similarity relation S. Thus, by analogy with (5.12), the set of pairs (x,y) in $U \times U$ which have a high grade of membership in S form a fuzzy level-set of S defined by

(5.17) $$S_{high} = \mu_S^{-1}(\mu_{high})$$

or, equivalently,

(5.18) $$\mu_{S_{high}}(x,y) = \mu_{high}(\mu_S(x,y)) .$$

This expression makes it possible to derive in a straight-forward fashion the fuzzy level-set S_{high} from the similarity relation S.

An important property of S_{high} may be stated as the

Proposition. If S is a transitive fuzzy relation, so is S_{high}. The validity of this proposition is readily established by observing that the transitivity of S means that (see (5.5))

$$\mu_S(x,y) \geq \vee_z \mu_S(x,z) \wedge \mu_S(z,y), \quad x, y, z \in U. \tag{5.19}$$

Now, (5.19) implies and is implied by

$$\forall z\, (\mu_S(x,y) \geq \mu_S(x,z) \wedge \mu_S(z,y)) \tag{5.20}$$

which in turn implies and is implied by

$$\forall z (\mu_S(x,y) \geq \mu_S(x,z) \text{ or } \mu_S(x,y) \geq \mu_S(z,y)). \tag{5.21}$$

Since μ_{high} is a monotone nondecreasing function, we have

$$\mu_S(x,y) \geq \mu_S(x,z) \Rightarrow \mu_{high}(\mu_S(x,y)) \geq \mu_{high}(\mu_S(x,z)) \tag{5.22}$$

and

$$\mu_S(x,y) \geq \mu_S(z,y) \Rightarrow \mu_{high}(\mu_S(x,y)) \geq \mu_{high}(\mu_S(z,y)) \tag{5.23}$$

and hence

$$\forall z (\mu_{S_{high}}(x,y) \geq \mu_{S_{high}}(x,z) \text{ or } \mu_{S_{high}}(x,y) \geq \mu_{S_{high}}(z,y)) \tag{5.24}$$

which by (5.21) and (5.20) leads to the conclusion that S_{high} is transitive.

Basically, the employment of fuzzy level-sets for purposes of clustering may be viewed as an application of a form of contrast intensification [34] to a fuzzy similarity relation which defines the degrees of similarity of mathematical objects in U. Thus, given a collection of such objects, we can derive S_{high} from S by the use of (5.18) and then apply a Dunn-Bezdek type of fuzzy clustering algorithm to group the given collection of objects into a set of fuzzy clusters $\{F_1, \ldots, F_k\}$.

6. Concluding Remarks.

In the foregoing discussion, we have touched upon only a few of the many basic issues which arise in the application of the theory of fuzzy sets to pattern classification and cluster analysis. Although this is not yet the case at present, it is very likely that in the years ahead it will be widely recognized that most of the problems in pattern classification and cluster analysis are intrinsically fuzzy in nature and that the conceptual framework of the theory of fuzzy sets provides a natural setting both for the formulation of such problems and their solution by fuzzy-algorithmic techniques.

References

1. L. A. Zadeh, Outline of a New Approach to the Analysis of Complex Systems and Decision Processes, IEEE Trans. on Systems, Man and Cybernetics SMC-3 (1973), 28-44.
2. L. A. Zadeh, The Concept of a Linguistic Variable and Its Application to Approximate Reasoning, Information Sciences, Part I, 8 (1975), 199-249; Part II, 8 (1975), 301-357; Part III, 9 (1975), 43-80.
3. L. A. Zadeh, Fuzzy Logic and Approximate Reasoning (In Memory of Grigore Moisil), Synthese 30 (1975), 407-428.
4. R. E. Bellman and L. A. Zadeh, Local and Fuzzy Logics, Memorandum No. ERL-M584, Electronics Research Laboratory, University of Califormia, Berkeley, 1976. (To appear in the Proceedings of the International Symposium on Multi-Valued Logic, University of Indiana, 1975).
5. U. Grenander, Pattern Synthesis: Lectures in Pattern Theory (vol. 1), Springer-Verlag, New York, 1976.
6. K. S. Fu, Syntactic Methods in Pattern Recognition, Academic Press, New York, 1974.
7. E. T. Lee and L. A. Zadeh, Note on Fuzzy Languages, Information Sciences 1 (1969), 421-434.
8. R. E. Bellman, R. Kalaba and L. A. Zadeh, Abstraction and Pattern Classification, J. Math. Anal. and Appl. 13 (1966), 1-7.
9. M. Minsky and S. Papert, Perceptrons, M.I.T. Press, Cambridge, 1969.

10. M. A. Aizerman, E. M. Braverman and L. I. Rozonoer, Method of Potential Functions in the Theory of Learning Machines, Science Press, Moscow, 1974.

11. A. G. Arkad'ev and E. M. Braverman, Computers and Pattern Recognition, Thompson Book Co., Washington, D. C., 1967.

12. V. H. Vapnik and A. Ya. Chervonenkis, Theory of Pattern Recognition, Science Press, Moscow. 1974.

13. L. A. Zadeh, Similarity Relations and Fuzzy Orderings, Information Sciences 3 (1971), 177-200.

14. L. A. Zadeh, Calculus of Fuzzy Restrictions, Proc. U. S.-Japan Seminar on Fuzzy Sets and Their Applications, L. A. Zadeh, K. S. Fu, K. Tanaka, M. Shimura (eds.), Academic Press, New York, 1975, 1-39.

15. R. F. Boyce, D. D. Chamberlin, W. F. King III and M. M. Hammer, Specifying Queries as Relational Expressions: SQUARE, IBM Research Report RJ129, 1973.

16. D. D. Chamberlin and R. F. Boyce, SEQUEL: A Structured English Query Language, Proc. ACM SIGFIDT Workshop on Data Description, Access and Control, 1975. (Also see IBM Research Report RJ1318, 1973.)

17. E. R. Ruspini, A New Approach to Clustering, Information and Control 15 (1969), 22-32.

18. E. R. Ruspini, Numerical Methods for Fuzzy Clustering, Information Sciences 2 (1970), 319-350.

19. E. R. Ruspini, New Experimental Results in Fuzzy Clustering, Information Sciences 6 (1973), 273-284.

20. J. C. Bezdek, Fuzzy Mathematics in Pattern Classification, Ph.D. Dissertation, Center for Applied Mathematics, Cornell University, Ithaca, New York, 1973.

21. J. C. Bezdek, Numerical Taxonomy with Fuzzy Sets, J. Math. Biology 1 (1974), 57-71.

22. J. C. Dunn, Some Recent Investigations of a Fuzzy Partitioning Algorithm and Its Application to Pattern Classification Problems, Center for Applied Mathematics, Cornell University, Ithaca, New York, 1974.

23. J. C. Dunn, A Fuzzy Relative of the ISODATA Process and Its Use in Detecting Compact Well Separated Clusters, J. of Cybernetics 3 (1974), 32-57.

24. J. C. Dunn, Well Separated Clusters and Optimal Fuzzy Partitions, Center for Applied Mathematics, Cornell University, Ithaca, New York, 1974.

25. J. C. Dunn, A Graph-Theoretic Analysis of Pattern Calssification via Tamura's Fuzzy Relation, IEEE Trans. on Systems. Man and Cybernetics SMC-4 (1974), 310-313.

26. J. C. Bezdek and J. C. Dunn, Optimal Fuzzy Partitions: A Heuristic for Estimating the Parameters in a Mixture of Normal Distributions, IEEE Trans. on Computers C-24 (1975), 835-838.

27. J. C. Bezdek, Cluster Validity with Fuzzy Sets, J. of Cybernetics 3 (1974), 58-73.

28. J. C. Bezdek and J. D. Harris, Convex Decompositions of Fuzzy Partitions, Departments of Mathematics, Utah State University, Logan, Utah and Marquette University, Milwaukee, Wisconsin, 1976.

29. J. C. Bezdek, A Physical Interpretation of Fuzzy ISODATA, IEEE Trans. on Systems, Man and Cybernetics SMC-6 (1976), 387-390.

30. J. C. Bezdek, Mathematical Models for Systematics and Taxonomy, Proc. 8th International Conference on Numerical Taxonomy, G. Estabrook (ed.) Freeman Co., San Francisco, 1975, 143-164.

31. J. C. Bezdek, Feature Selection for Binary Data: Medical Diagnosis with Fuzzy Sets, Proc. National Computer Conference, S. Winkler (ed.) AFIPS Press, Montvale, N.J., 1976, 1057-1058.

32. J. C. Bezdek and P. F. Castelaz, Prototype Classification and Feature Selection with Fuzzy Sets, Department of Mathematics Utah State University, Logan, Utah and Department of Electrical Engineering, Marquette University, Mulwaukee, Wisconsin, 1976.

33. S. C. Johnson, Hierarchical Clustering Schemes, Psychometrica 32 (1967), 241-254.

34. L. A. Zadeh, A Fuzzy-Set-Theoretic Interpretation of Linguistic Hedges, J. of Cybernetics 2 (1972), 4-34.

35. R. Sokal and P. Sneath, Principles of Numerical Taxonomy, Freeman Co., San Francisco, 1963.

36. Methodologies of Pattern Recognition, S. Watanabe (ed.), Academic Press, New York, 1969.

37. R. Jardine and R. Sibson, Mathematical Taxonomy, Wiley, New York, 1971.

38. K. Fukunaga, Introduction to Statistical Pattern Recognition, Academic Press, New York, 1972.

39. R. Duda and P. Hart, Pattern Classification and Scene Analysis, Wiley-Interscience, New York, 1973.

40. J. Tou and R. Gonzales, Pattern Recognition Principles, Addison-Wesley, Reading, Mass., 1974.

41. E. A. Patrick, Fundamentals of Pattern Recognition, Prentice-Hall, Englewood Cliffs, N.J., 1972.

42. L. M. Uhr, Pattern Recognition, Learning and Thought, Prentice-Hall, Englewood Cliffs, N.J., 1973.

43. W. Meisel, Computer-Oriented Approaches to Pattern Recognition, Academic Press, New York, 1972.

44. G. Nagy, State of the Art in Pattern Recognition, Proc. IEEE 56 (1969), 836-862.

45. Y. C. Ho and A. K. Agrawala, On Pattern Classification Algorithms: Introduction and Survey, Proc. IEEE 56 (1968), 2101-2114.

46. L. Kanal, Patterns in Pattern Recognition: 1968-1974, IEEE Trans. on Information Theory IT-20 (1974), 697-722.

47. A. Schroeder, Recognition of Components of a Mixture, Ph. D. Dissertation, University of Paris VI, 1974.

48. E. Diday, New Methods and New Concepts in Automatic Classification and Pattern Recognition, Ph. D. Dissertation, University of Paris VI, 1972.

49. V. I. Loginov, Probability Treatment of Zadeh's Membership Functions and Their Use in Pattern Recognition, Engineering Cybernetics (1966), 68-69.

50. C. L. Chang, Fuzzy Sets and Pattern Recognition, Ph. D. Dissertation, Department of Electrical Engineering, University of California, Berkeley, 1967.

51. W. G. Wee, On a Generalization of Adaptive Algorithms and Applications of the Fuzzy Set Concept to Pattern Calssification, Technical Report 67-7, Department of Electrical Engineering, 1967.

52. R. H. Flake and B. L. Turner, Numerical Classification for Taxonomic Problems, J. Theo. Biol. 20 (1968), 260-270.

53. A. N. Borisòv and E. A. Kokle, Recognition of Fuzzy Patterns by Feature Analysis, Cybernetics and Diagnostics, No. 4, Riga, U.S.S.R., 1970.

54. I. Gitman and M. D. Levine, An Algorithm for Detecting Unimodal Fuzzy Sets and Its Applications as a Clustering Technique, IEEE Trans. on Computers C-19 (1970), 583-593.

55. S. Otsuki, A Model for Learning and Recognizing Machine, Information Processing 11 (1970), 664-671.

56. S. K. Chang, Automated Interpretation and Editing for Fuzzy Line Drawings, Proc. Spring Joint Conf. (1971), 393-399.

57. S. Tamura, S. Niguchi and K. Tanaka, Pattern Classification Based on Fuzzy Relations, IEEE Trans. on Systems, Man and Cybernetics SMC-1 (1971), 937-944.

58. S. Tamura, Fuzzy Pattern Classification, Proc. Symp. on Fuzziness in Systems and Its Processing (1971), Tokyo.

59. E. T. Lee, Proximity Measures for the Classification of Geometric Figures, J. of Cybernetics 2 (1972), 43-59.

60. M. Shimura, Application of Fuzzy Functions to Pattern Calssification, Trans. IECE 55-d (1972), 218-225.

61. M. Sugeno, Evaluation of Similarity of Patterns by Fuzzy Integrals, Ann. Conf. Records of SICE, Tokyo, 1972.

62. K. Kotoh and K. Hiramatsu, A Representation of Pattern Classes Using the Fuzzy Sets, Trans. IECE 56-d (1973), 275-282.

63. L. E. Larsen, E. Ruspini, J. J. McNew, D. O. Walter and W. R. Adey, A Test of Sleep Staging Systems in the Unrestrained Chimpanzee, Brain Research 40 (1972), 319-343.

64. P. Siy, Fuzzy Logic and Hard-Written Character Recognition, Ph. D. Dissertation, Department of Electrical Engineering, University of Akron, Ohio, 1972.

65. R. K. Ragade, A Multiattribute Perception and Classification of Visual Similarities, Systems Res. and Planning Papers, S-001-73, Bell Northern Research, Canada, 1973.

66. C. C. Negoita, On the Application of the Fuzzy Sets Separation Theorem for Automatic Classification in Information Retrieval Systems, Information Sciences 5 (1973), 279-286.

67. M. Sugeno, Constructing Fuzzy Measure and Grading Similarity of Patterns by Fuzzy Integrals, Trans. SICE 9 (1973), 359-367.

68. Y. Noguchi, Pattern Recognition Systems Based on the Feature Extraction Technique, Report No. 739, Electrotechnical Laboratory, Tokyo, 1973.

69. B. Conche, A Method of Classification Based on the Use of a Fuzzy Automaton, University of Paris - Dauphine, 1973.

70. N. Malvache, Analysis and Identification of Visual Systems in Humans, Ph. D. Dissertation, University of Lille, Lille, 1973.

71. N. Okada and T. Tamachi, Automated Editing of Fuzzy Line Drawings for Picture Description, Trans. IECE 57-a (1974), 216-223.

72. M. Woodbury and J. Clive, Clinical Pure Types vs. A Fuzzy Partition, J. of Cybernetics 4 (1974), 111-120.

73. P. Siy and C. S. Cheu, Fuzzy Logic for Handwritten Numerical Character Recognition, IEEE Trans. on Systems, Man and Cybernetics SMC-4 (1974), 570-575.

74. M. G. Thomason, Finite Fuzzy Automata, Regular Fuzzy Languages, and Pattern Recognition, Department of Electrical Engineering, Duke University, Durham, N.C., 1974.

75. A. Kaufmann, Introduction to the Theory of Fuzzy Subsets (vol. III): Applications to Classification, Pattern Recognition, Automata and Systems, Masson, Paris, 1975.

76. C. V. Negoita and D. A. Ralescu, Theory of Fuzzy Sets and Its Applications, Wiley, New York, 1975.

77. T. Pavlidis, Fuzzy Representations as Means of Overcoming the Over-Commitment of Segmentation, Proc. Conf. On Computer Graphics, Pattern Recognition and Data Structures, Los Angeles, Calif., 1975.

78. A. Rosenfeld, Fuzzy Graphs, Proc. U.S.-Japan Seminar on Fuzzy Sets and Their Applications, L. A. Zadeh, K. S. Fu, K. Tanaka and M. Shimura (eds.), Academic Press, New York, 1975, 77-95.

79. E. T. Lee, Shape-Oriented Chromosome Identification, IEEE Trans. on Systems, Man and Cybernetics SMC-5 (1975) 629-632.

80. R. T. Yeh and S. Y. Band, Fuzzy Relations, Fuzzy Graphs, and Their Applications to Clustering Analysis, Proc. U.S.-Japan Seminar on Fuzzy Sets and Their Applications, L. A. Zadeh, K. S. Fu, K. Tanaka and M. Shimura (eds.), Academic Press, New York, 1975, 125-149.

81. G. F. DePalma and S. S. Yau, Fractionally Fuzzy Grammars with Application to Pattern Recognition, Proc. U.S.-Japan Seminar on Fuzzy Sets and Their Applications, L. A. Zadeh, K. S. Fu, K. Tanaka and M. Shimura (eds.), Academic Press, New York, 1975, 329-351.

82. M. Shimura, An Approach to Pattern Recognition and Associative Memories Using Fuzzy Logic, Proc. U.S.-Japan Seminar on Fuzzy Sets and Their Applications, L. A. Zadeh, K. S. Fu, K. Tanaka and M. Shimura (eds.), Academic Press, New York, 1975, 449-476.

83. R. L. Chang and T. Pavlidis, Fuzzy Decision Trees, Technical Report No. 203, Department of Electrical Engineering and Computer Science, Princeton University, Princeton, 1976.

84. S. Sugeno, Fuzzy Systems and Pattern Recognition, Workshop on Discrete Systems and Fuzzy Reasoning, Queen Mary College, University of London, 1976.

85. H. Bremermann, Pattern Recognition by Deformable Prototypes, in Structural Stability, the Theory of Catastrophes and Applications in the Sciences, Springer Notes in Mathematics 25 (1976), 15-57.

86. L. A. Zadeh, A Fuzzy-Algorithmic Approach to the Definition of Complex or Imprecise Concepts. Int. Jour. Man-Machine Studies 8 (1976), 249-291.

Research Supported by the U. S. Army Research Office Contract DAHCO4-75-G0056.

FUZZY SETS

The theory of fuzzy sets may be viewed as an attempt at developing a body of concepts and techniques for dealing in a systematic way with a type of imprecision which arises when the boundaries of a class of objects are not sharply defined. Among the very common examples of such classes are the classes of "bald men,"

[326]
FUZZY SETS

"young women," "small cars," "narrow streets," "short sentences," and "funny jokes." Membership in such classes or, as they are suggestively called, fuzzy sets, is a matter of degree rather than an all or nothing proposition. Thus, informally, a fuzzy set may be regarded as a class in which there is a graduality of progression from membership to nonmembership or, more precisely, in which an object may have a grade of membership intermediate between unity (full membership) and zero (nonmembership). In this perspective, then, a set in the conventional mathematical sense of the term may be viewed as a degenerate case of a fuzzy set—that is, a fuzzy set which admits of only two grades of membership: unity and zero.

Clearly, most of the classes of objects which we encounter in the real world are fuzzy sets in the informal sense defined above. And yet, the major focus of attention in mathematics, logic, and the "hard" sciences has been and continues to be centered on classes which are sets in the traditional sense. In the main, this is due to the misconception that fuzziness is a form of randomness and as such can be adequately treated by the tools provided by probability theory. However, as we develop a better understanding of the different varieties of imprecision, it is becoming increasingly clear that (a) fuzziness is fundamentally different from randomness; (b) that fuzziness plays a much more basic role in human cognition than randomness; and (c) that to deal with fuzziness effectively, we may have to abandon many long-held beliefs and attitudes, and develop radically new conceptual frameworks for the analysis of humanistic as well as mechanistic systems.

In speaking of the varieties of imprecision, a point that is in need of clarification relates to the distinction between fuzziness and vagueness. Although to some the terms are coextensive, it is more accurate to view vagueness as a particular form of fuzziness. More specifically, a fuzzy proposition, e.g., "Jill is quite tall" is fuzzy by virtue of the fuzziness of the class labeled quite tall. A vague proposition, on the other hand, is one which is (i) fuzzy and (ii) ambiguous—in the sense of providing insufficient information for a particular purpose. For example, the proposition "Jill is quite tall" may not be sufficiently specific for deciding what size jeans to buy for Jill. In this case, then, the proposition in question is both fuzzy and ambiguous—and hence is vague. On the other hand, "Jill is quite tall" may provide sufficient information for choosing a necklace for Jill, in which case the proposition is fuzzy but not vague. In effect, vagueness is an application-dependent or context-dependent characteristic of a proposition, whereas fuzziness is not.

To understand the distinction between fuzziness and randomness, it is helpful to interpret the grade of membership in a fuzzy set as a degree of compatibility (or possibility) rather than probability. As an illustration, consider the proposition "They got out of Roberta's car" (which is a Pinto). The question is: How many passengers got out of Roberta's car?—assuming for simplicity that the individuals involved have the same dimensions.

Let n be the number in question. Then, with each n we can associate two numbers μ_n and p_n representing, respectively, the possibility and the probability that n passengers got out of the car. For example, we may have for μ_n and p_n:

n	1	2	3	4	5	6	7
μ_n	0	1	1	1	0.7	0.2	0
p_n	0	0.6	0.3	0.1	0	0	0

in which μ_n is interpreted as the degree of ease with which n passengers can squeeze into a Pinto. Thus $\mu_5 = 0.7$ means that, by some specified or unspecified criterion, the degree of ease of squeezing 5 passengers into a Pinto is 0.7. On the other hand, the probability that Roberta may be carrying 5 passengers might be zero. Similarly, the possibility that a Pinto may carry 4 passengers is 1; by contrast, the corresponding probability in the case of Roberta might be 0.1.

This simple example brings out three important points. First, that possibility is not an all or nothing property and may be present to a degree. Two, that the degrees of possibility are not the same as probabilities. And three, that possibilistic[1] information is more elementary and less context-dependent than probabilistic information. But, what is most important as a motivation for the theory of fuzzy sets is that much, perhaps most, of human reasoning is based on information that is possibilistic rather than probabilistic in nature. This basic issue is discussed in greater detail at a later point, at which a connection between possibilities and probabilities is stated as a possibility/probability consistency principle.

The theory of fuzzy sets has two distinct branches at this juncture. In one, a fuzzy set is treated as a mathematical construct concerning which one can make provable assertions. This "nonfuzzy" theory of fuzzy sets is in the spirit of traditional mathematics and is typified by the rapidly growing literature on fuzzy topological spaces, fuzzy switching functions, fuzzy orderings, applications to system analysis, fuzzy measures, fuzzy clustering, etc. (See the Bibliography.)

The other branch may be viewed as a "fuzzy" theory of fuzzy sets in which fuzziness is introduced into the logic which underlies the rules of manipulation of fuzzy sets and assertions about them. The genesis of this branch of the theory is related to the introduction of the so-called linguistic approach [9, 10] which in turn has led to the development of fuzzy logic [1, 11]. In this logic, the truth-values as well as the rules of inference are allowed to be imprecise, with the result that the assertions about fuzzy sets based on this logic are not, in general, provable as propositions in two-valued logic. For example, the proposition "Helen is very intelligent" may be "more or less true," which in turn may be an approximate consequence of the truth-values of other fuzzy propositions. Although the "fuzzy" theory of fuzzy sets is still in its initial stages of development, it is important as a foundation for approximate, or, equivalently, fuzzy reasoning. Such reasoning permeates much of human thinking and is at the base of the remarkable human ability to attain imprecisely specified goals in an incompletely known environment.

In the following exposition of the theory of fuzzy sets, the accent is on the basic aspects of the theory. Expositions of such topics as the linguistic approach, fuzzy logic, fuzzy topological spaces, fuzzy languages, fuzzy algorithms and the applications to systems analysis, decision analysis, pattern classification, and other fields may be found in the papers listed in the Bibliography and in the comprehensive texts by Kaufmann [4] and Negoita and Ralescu [6].

[1]The term possibilistic in the sense close to that used here was coined by Gaines and Kohout in connection with their analysis of so-called possible automata [2].

[328]
FUZZY SETS

NOTATION, TERMINOLOGY, AND BASIC OPERATIONS

A fuzzy set is generally assumed to be imbedded in a nonfuzzy universe of discourse, which may be any collection of objects, concepts, or mathematical constructs. For example, a universe of discourse, U, may be the set of all real numbers; the set of integers 0, 1, 2, ..., 100; the set of all residents in a city; the set of all students in a course; the set of objects in a room; the set of all names in a telephone directory; etc. Universes of discourse are usually denoted by the symbols U, V, W, ..., with or without subscripts and/or superscripts. A fuzzy set in U or, equivalently, a fuzzy subset of U, is usually denoted by one of the uppercase symbols A, B, C, D, E, F, G, H, with or without subscripts and/or superscripts.

A fuzzy subset A of a universe of discourse U is characterized by a membership function $\mu_A: U \rightarrow [0, 1]$ which associates with each element u of U a number $\mu_A(u)$ in the interval [0, 1] (or, more generally, a point in a partially ordered set [3]), with $\mu_A(u)$ representing the grade of membership of u in A. The support of A is the set of points in U at which $\mu_A(u)$ is positive. The height of A is the supremum of $\mu_A(u)$ over A. A crossover point of A is the point in U whose grade of membership in A is 0.5. A is normal if its height is unity and subnormal if this is not the case.

Example. Let the universe of discourse be the interval [0, 100], with u interpreted as age. A fuzzy subset of U labeled old may be defined by a membership function such as

$$\begin{aligned} \mu_A(u) &= 0 && \text{for } 0 \leq u \leq 50 \\ &= \left(1 + \left(\frac{u - 50}{5}\right)^{-2}\right)^{-1} && \text{for } 50 \leq u \leq 100 \end{aligned} \tag{1}$$

In this case, the support of old is the interval [50, 100], the height of old is effectively unity, and the crossover point of old is 55.

It should be remarked that in many applications the grade of membership $\mu_A(u)$ may be interpreted as the degree of compatibility of u with the concept represented by A. (For example, in the case of the fuzzy set old as defined by (1), the degree to which the numerical age 60 is compatible with the concept of old is $\mu_{old}(60) = 0.8$.) In other cases, $\mu_A(u)$ may be interpreted as the degree of possibility of u given A. When $\mu_A(u)$ plays the role of a degree of compatibility or possibility, the function $\mu_A: U \rightarrow [0, 1]$ may be referred to as the compatibility function. The less specific term membership function is generally used in situations in which the interpretation of μ_A is unspecified.

It is important to note that the meaning attached to a particular numerical value of the membership function is purely subjective in nature. For example, in stating that the degree of ease with which 5 passengers may be squeezed into a Pinto is 0.7, one may or may not be able to explain how this figure is arrived at. In some instances, the meaning of an anchor (i.e., a reference) point on the scale may be explained and the meaning of others might be defined in relative terms. As will be seen later, what matters in most cases is not the meaning attached to the grades of membership in a particular context, but the manner in which the membership function of a fuzzy set is related to those of other fuzzy sets.

To simplify the representation of fuzzy sets, it is convenient to employ the following notation.

A nonfuzzy finite set such as

$$U = \{u_1, \ldots, u_n\}$$

is expressed as

$$U = u_1 + u_2 + \cdots + u_n \tag{2}$$

or

$$U = \sum_{i=1}^{n} u_i$$

with the understanding that (2) is a representation of U as the union of its constituent singletons, with + playing the role of the union rather than the arithmetic sum. Thus

$$u_i + u_j = u_j + u_i$$

and

$$u_i + u_i = u_i$$

for i, j = 1, ..., n.

As an extension of this notation, a finite fuzzy subset, A, of U is expressed as the linear form

$$A = \mu_1 u_1 + \cdots + \mu_n u_n \tag{3}$$

or

$$A = \sum_{i=1}^{n} \mu_i u_i$$

where μ_i, i = 1, ..., n, is the grade of membership of u_i in A. In cases where the u_i are numbers, there might be some ambiguity regarding the identity of the μ_i and u_i components of the string $\mu_i u_i$. In such cases, it is convenient to employ a separator symbol such as / for disambiguation, writing

$$A = \mu_1/u_1 + \cdots + \mu_n/u_n \tag{4}$$

or

$$A = \sum_{i=1}^{n} \mu_i/u_i$$

Example. Let U = {a, b, c, d} or, equivalently,

[330]
FUZZY SETS

$$U = a + b + c + d$$

In this case, a fuzzy subset A of U may be represented unambiguously as

$$A = 0.3a + b + 0.9c + 0.5d$$

On the other hand, if

$$U = 1 + 2 + \cdots + 100$$

then A should be expressed as

$$A = 0.3/25 + 0.9/3$$

in order to avoid ambiguity.

Example. In the universe of discourse comprising the integers 1, 2, ..., 10, i.e.,

$$U = 1 + 2 + \cdots + 10$$

the fuzzy subset labeled several may be defined as

$$\underline{\text{several}} = 0.5/3 + 0.8/4 + 1/5 + 1/6 + 0.8/7 + 0.5/8 \tag{5}$$

Example. In the case of the countable universe of discourse

$$U = 0 + 1 + 2 + \cdots$$

the fuzzy set labeled small may be expressed as

$$\underline{\text{small}} = \sum_{0}^{\infty} \left(1 + \left(\frac{u}{10}\right)^2\right)^{-1} \tag{6}$$

Like (2), (3) may be interpreted as a representation of a fuzzy set as the union of its constituent fuzzy singletons $\mu_i u_i$ (or μ_i/u_i). From the definition of the union (see (26)), it follows that if in the representation of A we have $u_i = u_j$, then we can make the substitution expressed by

$$\mu_i u_i + \mu_j u_i = (\mu_i \vee \mu_j) u_i \tag{7}$$

where $\vee$ is the symbol for max.

For example,

$$A = 0.3a + 0.8a + 0.5b$$

may be rewritten as

$$\begin{aligned} A &= (0.3 \vee 0.8)a + 0.5b \\ &= 0.8a + 0.5b \end{aligned}$$

Consistent with the representation of a finite fuzzy set as a linear form in the u_i, an arbitrary fuzzy subset of U may be expressed in the form of an integral

$$A \triangleq \int_U \mu_A(u)/u \tag{8}$$

with the understanding that $\mu_A(u)$ is the grade of membership of u in A, and the integral denotes the union of the fuzzy singletons $\mu_A(u)/u$, $u \in U$. (The symbol $\triangleq$ stands for "is defined to be.")

Example. In the universe of discourse consisting of the interval [0, 100], with u = age, the fuzzy subset labeled old (whose membership function is given by (1)), may be expressed as

$$\underline{\text{old}} = \int_{50}^{100} \left(1 + \left(\frac{u - 50}{5}\right)^{-2}\right)^{-1} / u \tag{9}$$

In many cases it is convenient to express the membership function of a fuzzy subset of the real line in terms of a standard function whose parameters may be adjusted to fit a specified membership function in an approximate fashion. Two such functions, the S-function and the π-function, are defined below.

$$\begin{aligned} S(u; \alpha, \beta, \gamma) &= 0 && \text{for } u \leq \alpha \\ &= 2\left(\frac{u - \alpha}{\gamma - \alpha}\right)^2 && \text{for } \alpha \leq u \leq \beta \\ &= 1 - 2\left(\frac{u - \gamma}{\gamma - \alpha}\right)^2 && \text{for } \beta \leq u \leq \gamma \\ &= 1 && \text{for } u \geq \gamma \end{aligned} \tag{10}$$

$$\begin{aligned} \pi(u; \beta, \gamma) &= S(u; \gamma - \beta, \gamma - \frac{\beta}{2}, \gamma) && \text{for } u \leq \gamma \\ &= 1 - S(u; \gamma, \gamma + \frac{\beta}{2}, \gamma + \beta) && \text{for } u \geq \gamma \end{aligned} \tag{11}$$

In $S(u; \alpha, \beta, \gamma)$, the parameter β, $\beta = (\alpha + \gamma)/2$, is the crossover point. In $\pi(u; \beta, \gamma)$, β is the bandwidth, that is, the separation between the crossover points of π, while γ is the point at which π is unity.

In some cases, the assumption that μ_A is a mapping from U to [0, 1] may be too restrictive, and it may be desirable to allow μ_A to take values in a lattice or, more particularly, in a Boolean algebra. For most purposes, however, it is sufficient to deal with the first two of the following hierarchy of fuzzy sets.

Definition. A fuzzy subset, A, of U is of Type 1 if its membership function, μ_A, is a mapping from U to [0, 1]; and A is of Type n, n = 2, 3, ..., if μ_A is a mapping from U to the set of fuzzy subsets of Type n - 1. For simplicity, it will always be understood that A is of Type 1 if it is not specified to be of a higher type.

Example. Suppose that U is the set of all nonnegative integers and A is a fuzzy subset of U labeled small integers. Then A is of Type 1 if the grade of membership of a generic element u in A is a number in the interval [0, 1], e.g.,

[332]
FUZZY SETS

$$\mu_{\underline{\text{small integers}}}(u) = \left(1 + \left(\frac{u}{5}\right)^2\right)^{-1}, \quad u = 0, 1, 2, \ldots \tag{12}$$

On the other hand, A is of Type 2 if for each u in U, $\mu_A(u)$ is a fuzzy subset of [0, 1] of Type 1, e.g., for u = 10,

$$\mu_{\underline{\text{small integers}}}(10) = \underline{\text{low}} \tag{13}$$

where low is a fuzzy subset of [0, 1] whose membership function is defined by, say,

$$\mu_{\underline{\text{low}}}(v) = 1 - S(v; 0, 0.25, 0.5), \quad v \in [0, 1] \tag{14}$$

which implies that

$$\underline{\text{low}} = \int_0^1 (1 - S(v; 0, 0.25, 0.5)/v \tag{15}$$

Containment

A fuzzy subset of U may be a subset of another fuzzy or nonfuzzy subset of U. More specifically, A is a subset of B or is contained in B if and only if $\mu_A(u) \leq \mu_B(u)$ for all u in U. In symbols,

$$A \subset B \Leftrightarrow \mu_A(u) \leq \mu_B(u), \quad u \in U \tag{16}$$

Example. If u = a + b + c + d and

$$A = 0.5a + 0.8b + 0.3d$$

$$B = 0.7a + b + 0.3c + d$$

then $A \subset B$.

Level-Sets of a Fuzzy Set

If A is a fuzzy subset of U, then an α-level-set of A is a nonfuzzy set denoted by A_α which comprises all elements of U whose grade of membership in A is greater than or equal to α. In symbols

$$A_\alpha = \{u \mid \mu_A(u) \geq \alpha\} \tag{17}$$

A fuzzy set A may be decomposed into its level-sets through the resolution identity [7, 10]

$$A = \int_0^1 \alpha A_\alpha \tag{18}$$

or

$$A = \sum_\alpha \alpha A_\alpha \tag{19}$$

where αA_α is the product of a scalar α with the set A_α (in the sense of (3)) and $\int_0^1$ $\left(\text{or } \sum_\alpha\right)$ is the union of the A_α, with α ranging from 0 to 1.

The resolution identity may be viewed as the result of combining together those terms in (3) which fall into the same level-set. More specifically, suppose that A is represented in the form

$$A = 0.1/2 + 0.3/1 + 0.5/7 + 0.9/6 + 1/9 \tag{20}$$

Then by using (7), A can be rewritten as

$$\begin{aligned} A = 0.1/2 + 0.1/1 + 0.1/7 + 0.1/6 + 0.1/9 \\ + 0.3/1 + 0.3/7 + 0.3/6 + 0.3/9 \\ + 0.5/7 + 0.5/6 + 0.5/9 \\ + 0.9/6 + 0.9/9 \\ + \quad 1/9 \end{aligned}$$

or

$$\begin{aligned} A = \; & 0.1(1/2 + 1/1 + 1/7 + 1/6 + 1/9) \\ & + 0.3(1/1 + 1/7 + 1/6 + 1/9) \\ & + 0.5(1/7 + 1/6 + 1/9 \\ & + 0.9(1/6 + 1/9) \\ & + 1/9 \end{aligned} \tag{21}$$

which is in the form (19), with the level-sets given by

$$\begin{aligned} A_{0.1} &= 2 + 1 + 7 + 6 + 9 \\ A_{0.3} &= 1 + 7 + 6 + 9 \\ A_{0.5} &= 7 + 6 + 9 \\ A_{0.9} &= 6 + 9 \\ A_1 &= 9 \end{aligned} \tag{22}$$

As will be seen in later sections, the resolution identity—in combination with the extension principle—provides a convenient way of generalizing various concepts associated with nonfuzzy sets to fuzzy sets. As an illustration, if U is a linear vector space, then A is <u>convex</u> if and only if for all $\lambda \in [0, 1]$ and all u_1, u_2 in U,

$$\mu_A(\lambda u_1 + (1 - \lambda)u_2) \geq \min(\mu_A(u_1), \mu_A(u_2)) \tag{23}$$

In terms of the level-sets of A, A is convex if and only if the A_α are convex for all $\alpha \in (0, 1]$. Dually, A is <u>concave</u> if and only if

$$\mu_A(\lambda u_1 + (1 - \lambda)u_2) \leq \max(\mu_A(u_1), \mu_A(u_2)) \tag{24}$$

[334]
FUZZY SETS

Operations on Fuzzy Sets

Among the basic operations which can be performed on fuzzy sets are the following. (A, B are fuzzy subsets of U.)

1. The complement of A is denoted by A' and is defined by

$$A' \triangleq \int_U (1 - \mu_A(u))/u \tag{25}$$

2. The union of fuzzy sets A and B is denoted by A + B (or, more conventionally, by A ∪ B) and is defined by

$$A + B \triangleq \int_U (\mu_A(u) \vee \mu_B(u))/u \tag{26}$$

where ∨ is the symbol for max.

3. The intersection of A and B is denoted by A ∩ B and is defined by

$$A \cap B \triangleq \int_U (\mu_A(u) \wedge \mu_B(u))/u \tag{27}$$

where ∧ is the symbol for min.

4. The product of A and B is denoted by AB and is defined by

$$AB \triangleq \int_U \mu_A(u)\mu_B(u)/u \tag{28}$$

Thus, A^α, where α is any positive number, should be interpreted as

$$A^\alpha \triangleq \int_U (\mu_A(u))^\alpha/u \tag{29}$$

Similarly, if α is any nonnegative real number such that $\alpha \sup_u \mu_A(u) \leq 1$, then

$$\alpha A \triangleq \int_U \alpha\mu_A(u)/u \tag{30}$$

As a special case of (29), the operation of concentration is defined as

$$\text{CON}(A) \triangleq A^2 \tag{31}$$

while that of dilation is expressed by

$$\text{DIL}(A) \triangleq A^{0.5} \tag{32}$$

5. The bounded-sum of A and B is denoted by A ⊕ B and is defined by

$$A \oplus B \triangleq \int_U 1 \wedge (\mu_A(u) + \mu_B(u))/u \tag{33}$$

where + is the arithmetic sum.

6. The bounded-difference of A and B is denoted by A ⊖ B and is defined by

$$A \ominus B \triangleq \int_U 0 \vee (\mu_A(u) - \mu_B(u))/u \tag{34}$$

where - is the arithmetic difference.

7. The left-square of A is denoted by ${}^2A$ and is defined by

$${}^2A \triangleq \int_V \mu_A(u)/u^2 \tag{35}$$

where $V \triangleq \{u^2 | u \in U\}$. More generally,

$$^{\alpha}A \triangleq \int_V \mu_A(u)/u^{\alpha} \tag{36}$$

where $V \triangleq \{u^{\alpha} | u \in U\}$.

Example. If

$$U = 1 + 2 + \cdots + 10$$

$$A = 0.8/3 + 1/5 + 0.6/6$$

$$B = 0.7/3 + 1/4 + 0.5/6$$

then

$$\begin{aligned}
A' &= 1/1 + 1/2 + 0.2/3 + 1/4 + 0.4/6 + 1/7 + 1/8 + 1/9 + 1/10 \\
A + B &= 0.8/3 + 1/4 + 1/5 + 0.6/6 \\
A \cap B &= 0.7/3 + 0.5/6 \\
AB &= 0.56/3 + 0.3/6 \\
A^2 &= 0.64/3 + 1/5 + 0.36/6 \\
0.4A &= 0.32/3 + 0.4/5 + 0.24/6 \\
\mathrm{CON}(B) &= 0.49/3 + 1/4 + 0.25/6 \\
\mathrm{DIL}(B) &= 0.84/3 + 1/4 + 0.7/6 \\
A \oplus B &= 1/3 + 1/4 + 1/5 + 1/6 \\
A \ominus B &= 0.1/3 + 1/5 + 0.1/6 \\
{}^2A &= 0.8/9 + 1/25 + 0.6/36 \\
{}^3A &= 0.8/27 + 1/125 + 0.6/216
\end{aligned} \tag{37}$$

8. If $A_1, \ldots, A_n$ are fuzzy subsets of U, and $w_1, \ldots, w_n$ are nonnegative weights adding up to unity, then a convex combination of $A_1, \ldots, A_n$ is a fuzzy set A whose membership function is expressed by

$$\mu_A = w_1 \mu_{A_1} + \cdots + w_n \mu_{A_n} \tag{38}$$

where + denotes the arithmetic sum. The concept of a convex combination is useful in the representation of linguistic modifiers such as essentially and typically, which modify the weights associated with the components of a fuzzy set [8].

9. If $A_1, \ldots, A_n$ are fuzzy subsets of $U_1, \ldots, U_n$, respectively, the Cartesian product of $A_1, \ldots, A_n$ is denoted by $A_1 \times \cdots \times A_n$ and is defined as a fuzzy subset of $U_1 \times \cdots \times U_n$ whose membership function is expressed by

$$\mu_{A_1 \times \cdots \times A_n}(u_1, \ldots, u_n) = \mu_{A_1}(u_1) \wedge \cdots \wedge \mu_{A_n}(u_n) \tag{39}$$

Equivalently,

[336]
FUZZY SETS

$$A_1 \times \cdots \times A_n = \int_{U_1 \times \cdots \times U_n} (\mu_{A_1}(u_1) \wedge \cdots \wedge \mu_{A_n}(u_n))/(u_1, \ldots, u_n) \tag{40}$$

Example. If $U_1 = U_2 = 3 + 5 + 7$, $A_1 = 0.5/3 + 1/5 + 0.6/7$, and $A_2 = 1/3 + 0.6/5$, then

$$A_1 \times A_2 = 0.5/(3,3) + 1/(5,3) + 0.6/(7,3) + 0.5/(3,5) + 0.6/(5,5) + 0.6/(7,5) \tag{41}$$

Fuzzy Relations

If U is the Cartesian product of n universes of discourse $U_1, \ldots, U_n$, then an n-ary fuzzy relation, R, in U is a fuzzy subset of U. As in (8), R may be expressed as the union of its constituent fuzzy singletons $\mu_R(u_1, \ldots, u_n)/(u_1, \ldots, u_n)$, i.e.,

$$R = \int_{U_1 \times \cdots \times U_n} \mu_R(u_1, \ldots, u_n)/(u_1, \ldots, u_n) \tag{42}$$

where μ_R is the membership function of R.

Common examples of (binary) fuzzy relations are: much greater than, resembles, is relevant to, and is close to. For example, if $U_1 = U_2 = (-\infty, \infty)$, the relation is close to may be defined by

$$\text{is close to} \triangleq \int_{U_1 \times U_2} e^{-a|u_1-u_2|}/(u_1, u_2) \tag{43}$$

where a is a scale factor. Similarly, if $U_1 = U_2 = 1 + 2 + 3 + 4$, then the relation much greater than may be defined by the relation matrix

R	1	2	3	4
1	0	0.3	0.8	1
2	0	0	0	0.8
3	0	0	0	0.3
4	0	0	0	0

(44)

in which the (i, j)-th element is the value of $\mu_R(u_1, u_2)$ for the i-th value of u_1 and the j-th value of u_2.

If R is a relation from U to V (or, equivalently, a relation in U × V) and S is a relation from V to W, then the composition of R and S is a fuzzy relation from U to W denoted by R ∘ S and defined by

$$R \circ S = \int_{U \times W} \vee_v (\mu_R(u, v) \wedge \mu_S(v, w))/(u, w) \tag{45}$$

If U, V, and W are finite sets, then the relation matrix for R ∘ S is the max-min product of the relation matrices for R and S. For example, the max-min product of the relation matrices on the left-hand side of (46) is given by the right-hand member of (46):

$$\overset{R}{\begin{pmatrix} 0.3 & 0.8 \\ 0.6 & 0.9 \end{pmatrix}} \circ \overset{S}{\begin{pmatrix} 0.5 & 0.9 \\ 0.4 & 1 \end{pmatrix}} = \overset{R \circ S}{\begin{pmatrix} 0.4 & 0.8 \\ 0.5 & 0.9 \end{pmatrix}} \tag{46}$$

Projections and Cylindrical Fuzzy Sets

If R is an n-ary fuzzy relation in $U_1 \times \cdots \times U_n$, then its projection (shadow) on $U_{i_1} \times \cdots \times U_{i_k}$ is a k-ary fuzzy relation R_q in U which is defined by

$$\begin{aligned} R_q &\triangleq \text{Proj } R \text{ on } U_{i_1} \times \cdots \times U_{i_k} \triangleq P_q R \\ &\triangleq \int_{U_{i_1} \times \cdots \times U_{i_k}} (\vee_{u_{(q')}} \mu_R(u_1, \ldots, u_n))/(u_{i_1}, \ldots, u_{i_k}) \end{aligned} \tag{47}$$

where q is the index sequence $(i_1, \ldots, i_k)$; $u_{(q)} \triangleq (u_{i_1}, \ldots, u_{i_k})$; q' is the complement of q; and $\vee_{u_{(q')}}$ is the supremum of $\mu_R(u_1, \ldots, u_n)$ over the u's which are in $u_{(q')}$.

Example. For the fuzzy relation defined by the relation matrix (44), we have

$$R_1 = 1/1 + 0.8/2 + 0.3/3 \tag{48}$$

and

$$R_2 = 0.3/2 + 0.8/3 + 1/4 \tag{49}$$

It is clear that distinct fuzzy relations in $U_1 \times \cdots \times U_n$ can have identical projections on $U_{i_1} \times \cdots \times U_{i_k}$. However, given a fuzzy relation R_q in $U_{i_1} \times \cdots \times U_{i_k}$, there exists a unique largest relation $\bar{R}_q$ in $U_1 \times \cdots \times U_n$ whose projection on $U_{i_1} \times \cdots \times U_{i_k}$ is R_q. In consequence of (47), the membership function of $\bar{R}_q$ is given by

$$\mu_{\bar{R}_q}(u_1, \ldots, u_n) = \mu_{R_q}(u_{i_1}, \ldots, u_{i_k}) \tag{50}$$

with the understanding that (50) holds for all $u_1, \ldots, u_n$ such that the $i_1, \ldots, i_k$ arguments in $\mu_{\bar{R}_q}$ are equal, respectively, to the first, second, ..., k-th arguments in μ_{R_q}. This implies that the value of $\mu_{\bar{R}_q}$ at the point $(u_1, \ldots, u_n)$ is the same as that at the point $(u'_1, \ldots, u'_n)$ provided that $u_{i_1} = u'_{i_1}, \ldots, u_{i_k} = u'_{i_k}$. For this reason, $\bar{R}_q$ is referred to as the cylindrical extension of R_q, with R_q constituting the base of $\bar{R}_q$.

[338]
FUZZY SETS

Suppose that R is an n-ary relation in $U_1 \times \cdots \times U_n$, R_q is its projection on $U_{i_1} \times \cdots \times U_{i_k}$, and $\bar{R}_q$ is the cylindrical extension of R_q. Since $\bar{R}_q$ is the largest relation in $U_1 \times \cdots \times U_n$ whose projection on $U_{i_1} \times \cdots \times U_{i_k}$ is R_q, it follows that R_q satisfies the containment relation

$$R \subset \bar{R}_q \tag{51}$$

for all q, and hence

$$R \subset \bar{R}_{q_1} \cap \bar{R}_{q_2} \cap \cdots \cap \bar{R}_{q_r} \tag{52}$$

for arbitrary $q_1, \ldots, q_r$ (index subsequences of (1, 2, ..., n)).

In particular, if we set $q_1 = 1, \ldots, q_r = n$, then (52) reduces to

$$R \subset \bar{R}_1 \cap \bar{R}_2 \cap \cdots \cap \bar{R}_n \tag{53}$$

where $R_1, \ldots, R_n$ are the projections of R on $U_1, \ldots, U_n$, respectively, and $\bar{R}_1, \ldots, \bar{R}_n$ are their cylindrical extensions. But, from the definition of the Cartesian product (see (40)), it follows that

$$\bar{R}_1 \cap \cdots \cap \bar{R}_n = R_1 \times \cdots \times R_n$$

which leads to the containment relation

$$R \subset R_1 \times \cdots \times R_n \tag{54}$$

The concept of a cylindrical extension can also be used to provide an intuitively appealing interpretation of the composition of fuzzy relations. Thus, suppose that R and S are binary fuzzy relations in $U_1 \times U_2$ and $U_2 \times U_3$, respectively. Let $\bar{R}$ and $\bar{S}$ be the cylindrical extensions of R and S in $U_1 \times U_2 \times U_3$. Then, from the definition of $R \circ S$ (see (45)), it follows that

$$R \circ S = \text{Proj } \bar{R} \cap \bar{S} \text{ on } U_1 \times U_3 \tag{55}$$

The Extension Principle

The extension principle for fuzzy sets is in essence a basic identity which allows the domain of the definition of a mapping or a relation to be extended from points in U to fuzzy subsets of U. More specifically, suppose that f is a mapping from U to V and A is a fuzzy subset of U expressed as

$$A = \mu_1 u_1 + \cdots + \mu_n u_n \tag{56}$$

Then, the extension principle asserts that

$$f(A) = f(\mu_1 u_1 + \cdots + \mu_n u_n) \equiv \mu_1 f(u_1) + \cdots + \mu_n f(u_n) \tag{57}$$

Thus the image of A under f can be deduced from the knowledge of the images of $u_1, \ldots, u_n$ under f. When it is necessary to signify that f(A) is to be evaluated by the use of (57), f(A) is enclosed in angular brackets. Thus

$$\langle f(A)\rangle \triangleq f(A) \triangleq \mu_1 f(u_1) + \cdots + \mu_n f(u_n) \tag{58}$$

Example. Let

$$U = 1 + 2 + \cdots + 10$$

and let f be the operation of squaring. Let small be a fuzzy subset of U defined by

$$\underline{small} = 1/1 + 1/2 + 0.8/3 + 0.6/4 + 0.4/5 \tag{59}$$

Then, in consequence of (57) and (35), we have

$$^2\underline{small} = \langle \underline{small}^2\rangle = 1/1 + 1/4 + 0.8/9 + 0.6/16 + 0.4/25 \tag{60}$$

If the support of A is a continuum, that is

$$A = \int_U \mu_A(u)/u \tag{61}$$

then the statement of the extension principle assumes the following form

$$f(A) \triangleq f\left(\int_U \mu_A(u)/u\right) \triangleq \int_V \mu_A(u)/f(u) \tag{62}$$

with the understanding that f(u) is a point in V and $\mu_A(u)$ is its grade of membership in f(A), which is a fuzzy subset of V.

In some applications it is convenient to use a modified form of the extension principle which follows from (62) by decomposing A into its constituent level-sets rather than its fuzzy singletons (see the resolution identity (18)). Thus, on writing

$$A = \int_0^1 \alpha A_\alpha \tag{63}$$

where A_α is an α-level-set of A, the statement of the extension principle assumes the form

$$f(A) = f\left(\int_0^1 \alpha A_\alpha\right) \equiv \int_0^1 \alpha f(A_\alpha) \tag{64}$$

when the support of A is a continuum, and

$$f(A) = f\left(\sum_\alpha \alpha A_\alpha\right) = \sum_\alpha \alpha f(A_\alpha) \tag{65}$$

when either the support of A is a countable set or the distinct level-sets of A form a countable collection.

In many applications of the extension principle, one encounters the following problem. We have an n-ary function f, which is a mapping from a Cartesian product $U_1 \times \cdots \times U_n$ to a space V, and a fuzzy set (relation) A in $U_1 \times \cdots \times U_n$ which is characterized by a membership function $\mu_A(u_1, \ldots, u_n)$, with u_i, $i = 1, \ldots, n$, denoting a generic point in U_i. A direct application of the extension principle (62) to this case yields

[340]
FUZZY SETS

$$f(A) = f\left(\int_{U_1\times\cdots\times U_n} \mu_A(u_1, \ldots, u_n)/(u_1, \ldots, u_n)\right)$$

$$= \int_V \mu_A(u_1, \ldots, u_n)/f(u_1, \ldots, u_n) \qquad (66)$$

However, in many instances what we know is not A but its projections $A_1, \ldots, A_n$ on $U_1, \ldots, U_n$, respectively (see (47)). The question that arises, then, is: What expression for μ_A should be used in (66)?

In such cases, unless otherwise specified, it is assumed that the membership function of A is expressed by

$$\mu_A(u_1, \ldots, u_n) = \mu_{A_1}(u_1) \wedge \mu_{A_2}(u_2) \wedge \cdots \wedge \mu_{A_n}(u_n) \qquad (67)$$

where μ_{A_i}, $i = 1, \ldots, n$, is the membership function of A_i. In view of (39), this is equivalent to assuming that A is the Cartesian product of its projections, i.e.,

$$A = A_1 \times \cdots \times A_n$$

which in turn implies that A is the largest set whose projections on $U_1, \ldots, U_n$ are $A_1, \ldots, A_n$, respectively.

Example. Suppose that

$$U_1 = U_2 = 1 + 2 + 3 + \cdots + 10$$

and

$$A_1 = \underset{\sim}{2} \triangleq \underline{\text{approximately}}\ 2 = 1/2 + 0.6/1 + 0.8/3 \qquad (68)$$

$$A_2 = \underset{\sim}{6} \triangleq \underline{\text{approximately}}\ 6 = 1/6 + 0.8/5 + 0.7/7 \qquad (69)$$

and

$$f(u_1, u_2) = u_1 \times u_2 = \text{arithmetic product of } u_1 \text{ and } u_2$$

Using (67) and applying the extension principle as expressed by (66) to this case, we have

$$\underset{\sim}{2} \times \underset{\sim}{6} = (1/2 + 0.6/1 + 0.8/3) \times (1/6 + 0.8/5 + 0.7/7)$$

$$= 1/12 + 0.8/10 + 0.7/14 + 0.6/6 + 0.6/5 + 0.6/7 + 0.8/18 + 0.8/15 + 0.7/21$$

$$= 0.6/5 + 0.6/6 + 0.6/7 + 0.8/10 + 1/12 + 0.7/14 + 0.8/15 + 0.8/18 + 0.7/21 \qquad (70)$$

Thus the arithmetic product of the fuzzy numbers approximately 2 and approximately 6 is a fuzzy number given by (70).

More generally, let $*$ be a binary operation defined on $U \times V$ with values in W. Thus, if $u \in U$ and $v \in V$, then

$$w = u * v, \quad w \in W$$

Now suppose that A and B are fuzzy subsets of U and V, respectively, with

$$A = \mu_1 u_1 + \cdots + \mu_n u_n \tag{71}$$

and

$$B = \nu_1 v_1 + \cdots + \nu_m v_m$$

By using the extension principle under the assumption (67), the operation * may be extended to fuzzy subsets of U and V by the defining relation

$$\begin{aligned} A * B &= \left(\sum_i \mu_i u_i\right) * \left(\sum_j \nu_j v_j\right) \\ &= \sum_{i,j} (\mu_i \wedge \nu_j)(u_i * v_j) \end{aligned} \tag{72}$$

It is easy to verify that for the case where $A = \underset{\sim}{2}$, $B = \underset{\sim}{6}$, and $* = \times$, the application of (72) yields the expression for $\underset{\sim}{2} \times \underset{\sim}{6}$.

Fuzzy Sets with Fuzzy Membership Functions

Fuzzy sets with fuzzy membership functions play an important role in the linguistic approach [9, 10] in which the values of variables are not numbers but words or sentences in a natural or synthetic language. For example if Age is treated as a linguistic variable, its values might be: young, not young, very young, more or less young, not very young, old, not old, not very young and not very old, etc. Each of these values represents a label of a fuzzy subset of a universe of discourse which is associated with Age—e.g., the interval [0, 100]. A fuzzy set which corresponds to a linguistic value of Age, say not very young, constitutes the meaning of not very young. The meaning of each possible value of a linguistic variable is defined by the semantic rule which is associated with the variable [10].

Frequently, the grade of membership in a fuzzy set is not well-defined. In such cases it is natural to treat the grade of membership as a linguistic variable with the linguistic values: low, not low, very low, more or less low, medium, high, not high, very high, more or less high, not low and not high, etc. Each of these values represents a fuzzy subset of the interval [0, 1], e.g.,

$$\mu_{\underline{low}}(v) = 1 - S(v; 0, 0.25, 0.5), \quad v \in [0, 1] \tag{73}$$

$$\mu_{\underline{very\ low}}(v) = (1 - S(v; 0, 0.25, 0.5))^2 \tag{74}$$

$$\mu_{\underline{medium}}(v) = \pi(v; 0.5, 0.2) \tag{75}$$

$$\mu_{\underline{high}}(v) = \mu_{\underline{low}}(1 - v) \tag{76}$$

where S and π are the S- and π-functions defined by (10) and (11).

The fuzzy sets in question are of Type 2 (see (13)). Consequently, to manipulate the linguistic grades of membership, it is necessary to extend to fuzzy sets of Type 2 the definitions of complementation, intersection, union, product, etc. which were stated earlier for fuzzy sets of Type 1 (see (25)-(36)). The method used for this purpose is illustrated in the sequel by application to the computation of the intersection of fuzzy sets of Type 2. The same technique can be used to define other types of operations on fuzzy sets with fuzzy membership functions [5] and, in

[342]
FUZZY SETS

particular, to characterize the operations of negation, conjunction, disjunction, and implication in fuzzy logic [1].

To extend the definition of intersection to fuzzy sets of Type 2, it is natural to make use of the extension principle. It is convenient, however, to accomplish this in two stages: First, by extending the Type 1 definition to fuzzy sets with interval-valued membership functions; and second, generalizing from intervals to fuzzy sets by the use of the level-set form of the extension principle (see (64)). More specifically, it will be recalled that the expression for the membership function of the intersection of A and B, where A and B are fuzzy subsets of Type 1, is given by

$$\mu_{A\cap B}(u) = \mu_A(u) \wedge \mu_B(u), \quad u \in U \tag{77}$$

Now if $\mu_A(u)$ and $\mu_B(u)$ are intervals in [0, 1] rather than points in [0, 1], that is, for a fixed u

$$\mu_A(u) = [a_1, a_2]$$

$$\mu_B(u) = [b_1, b_2]$$

where a_1, a_2, b_1, and b_2 depend on u, then the application of the extension principle (64) to the function $\wedge$ (min) yields

$$[a_1, a_2] \wedge [b_1, b_2] = [a_1 \wedge b_1, a_2 \wedge b_2] \tag{78}$$

Thus, if A and B have interval-valued membership functions, then their intersection is an interval-valued function whose value for each u is given by (78).

Next, consider the case where, for each u, $\mu_A(u)$ and $\mu_B(u)$ are fuzzy subsets of the interval [0, 1]. For simplicity, we shall assume that these subsets are <u>convex</u>, that is, have intervals as level-sets. In other words, we shall assume that, for each α in (0, 1], the α-level-sets of μ_A and μ_B are interval-valued membership functions.

By applying the level-set form of the extension principle (64) to the α-level sets of μ_A and μ_B, we are led to the following definition of the intersection of fuzzy sets of Type 2.

<u>Definition</u>. Let A and B be fuzzy subsets of Type 2 of U such that, for each $u \in U$, $\mu_A(u)$ and $\mu_B(u)$ are convex fuzzy subsets of Type 1 of [0, 1], which implies that, for each α in (0, 1], the α-level-sets of the fuzzy membership functions μ_A and μ_B are interval-valued membership functions μ_A^α and μ_B^α.

Let the α-level-set of the fuzzy membership function of the intersection of A and B be denoted by $\mu_{A\cap B}^\alpha$, with the α-level-sets μ_A^α and μ_B^α defined for each u by

$$\mu_A^\alpha \triangleq \{v \mid \nu_A(v) \geq \alpha\} \tag{79}$$

$$\mu_B^\alpha \triangleq \{v \mid \nu_B(v) \geq \alpha\} \tag{80}$$

where $\nu_A(v)$ denotes the grade of membership of a point v, $v \subset [0, 1]$, in the fuzzy set $\mu_A(u)$, and likewise for μ_B. Then, for each u,

$$\mu^{\alpha}_{A\cap B} = \mu_A^{\alpha} \wedge \mu_B^{\alpha} \tag{81}$$

In other words, the α-level-set of the fuzzy membership function of the intersection of A and B is the minimum (in the sense of (78)) of the α-level-sets of the fuzzy membership functions of A and B. Thus, using the resolution identity (18), we can express $\mu_{A\cap B}$ as

$$\mu_{A\cap B} = \int_0^1 \alpha(\mu_A^{\alpha} \wedge \mu_B^{\alpha}) \tag{82}$$

For the case where μ_A and μ_B have finite supports, that is, μ_A and μ_B are of the form

$$\mu_A = \alpha_1 v_1 + \cdots + \alpha_n v_n, \quad v_i \in [0, 1], \quad i = 1, \ldots, n \tag{83}$$

and

$$\mu_B = \beta_1 w_1 + \cdots + \beta_m w_m, \quad w_j \in [0, 1], \quad j = 1, \ldots, m \tag{84}$$

where α_i and β_j are the grades of membership of v_i and w_j in μ_A and μ_B, respectively, the expression for $\mu_{A\cap B}$ can readily be derived by employing the extension principle in the form (72). Thus, by applying (72) to the operation $\wedge$, we obtain at once

$$\begin{aligned}\mu_{A\cap B} &= \mu_A \wedge \mu_B \\ &= (\alpha_1 v_1 + \cdots + \alpha_n v_n) \wedge (\beta_1 w_1 + \cdots + \beta_m w_m) \\ &= \sum_{i,j} (\alpha_i \wedge \beta_j)(v_i \wedge w_j)\end{aligned} \tag{85}$$

as the desired expression for $\mu_{A\cap B}$.

THE CONCEPT OF A FUZZY RESTRICTION AND TRANSLATION RULES FOR FUZZY PROPOSITIONS

The concept of a fuzzy restriction plays a basic role in the applications of the theory of fuzzy sets to logic, approximate reasoning, pattern classification, and many other fields. In what follows, a brief discussion of the basic aspects of this concept is presented and its application to the formulation of translation rules for fuzzy propositions is outlined.

Informally, by a fuzzy restriction is meant a fuzzy relation which acts as an elastic constraint on the values that may be assigned to a variable. More specifically, if X is a variable that takes values in a universe of discourse U, then a fuzzy restriction R(X) on the values that may be assigned to X is a fuzzy relation in U such that the assignment of a value u to X requires a stretch of the restriction expressed by

[344]
FUZZY SETS

degree of stretch $= 1 - \mu_{R(X)}(u)$ (86)

where $\mu_{R(X)}(u)$ is the grade of membership of u in R(X). In symbols, this is expressed as the assignment equation

$$x = u\colon \mu_{R(X)}(u) \qquad (87)$$

where x denotes a generic value of X and $\mu_{R(X)}(u)$ is the "degree of ease" with which u may be assigned to X.

As a simple illustration, suppose that $U = 0 + 1 + 2 + \cdots$ and that X is a variable labeled "small integer." Assume that the fuzzy set small integer is defined by

$$\text{small integer} = 1/0 + 1/1 + 0.8/2 + 0.6/3 + 0.4/4 + 0.2/5 \qquad (88)$$

Then, if x is a generic value of the variable "small integer" and we assign the value 3 to this variable, we have

$$x = 3\colon 0.6 \qquad (89)$$

which implies that the fuzzy restriction labeled small integer must be stretched to the degree 0.4 to allow the assignment of the value 3 to the variable "small integer."

More generally, if $X = (X_1, \ldots, X_n)$ is an n-ary variable taking values in the Cartesian product space

$$U = U_1 \times \cdots \times U_n$$

then an n-ary fuzzy relation $R(X_1, \ldots, X_n)$ in U is a fuzzy restriction if it acts as an elastic constraint on the values that may be assigned to X. An n-ary variable which is associated with a fuzzy restriction on the values that may be assigned to it is said to be an n-ary fuzzy variable.

The concept of a fuzzy restriction provides a basis for the formulation of translation rules for fuzzy propositions; that is, propositions which contain names of fuzzy sets. Common examples of such propositions are the following. (Names of fuzzy sets are underscored.)

Karl is very intelligent.
Anneliese is rather emotional.
John is tall and Pat is very kind.
If X is large then Y is small.
X is much smaller than Y.
Most tall women are well-built.
X is small is true.
X is small is likely.
X is small is possible.
If X is small is true then Y is large is very likely.

By a translation of a fuzzy proposition is meant a representation of the meaning of a fuzzy proposition as a system of relational assignment equations; that is, a set of assignment equations whose right-hand members are fuzzy relations which are assigned to fuzzy restrictions on the variables associated with the proposition in question.

[345]
FUZZY SETS

As a simple illustration, the translation of the proposition "John is tall" has the form

$$\text{John is } \underline{\text{tall}} \rightarrow R(\text{Height}(\text{John})) = \underline{\text{tall}} \tag{90}$$

where Height(John) is a variable, R(Height(John)) is a fuzzy restriction on the values that may be assigned to this variable, and tall is a unary fuzzy relation which is assigned to the fuzzy restriction R(Height(John)). More generally, the translation of a fuzzy proposition has the form

$$\begin{aligned} p \rightarrow R(X_1) &= F_1 \\ R(X_2) &= F_2 \\ &\cdots\cdots \\ R(X_n) &= F_n \end{aligned} \tag{91}$$

where $X_1, \ldots, X_n$ are variables which are implicit or explicit in p, $R(X_1), \ldots, R(X_n)$ are the fuzzy restrictions on these variables, and $F_1, \ldots, F_n$ are fuzzy relations which are assigned to $R(X_1), \ldots, R(X_n)$, respectively. For brevity, the system of relational assignment equations associated with p is denoted by R(p).

Example. The translation of "Brian is tall and blond" may be expressed as

$$\begin{aligned} \text{Brian is } \underline{\text{tall}} \text{ and } \underline{\text{blond}} \rightarrow R(\text{Color}(\text{Hair}(\text{Brian}))) &= \underline{\text{blond}} \\ R(\text{Height}(\text{Brian})) &= \underline{\text{tall}} \end{aligned}$$

To deduce the translation of a given fuzzy proposition p, it is convenient to treat p as the result of a sequence of operations on a set of kernel fuzzy propositions which play the role of generators. For example, attributional modification of the kernel propositions

Mike is intelligent

Zene is charming

results in

Mike is very intelligent

Zene is extremely charming

which upon conjunctive composition yield the composite fuzzy proposition

Mike is very intelligent and Zene is extremely charming

which upon truth-qualification results in

(Mike is very intelligent and Zene is extremely charming) is very true

With each operation is associated a translation rule which describes the effect of the operation on the relational assignment equations associated with the operand proposition. Thus, for example, if M(p) is the result of applying a modification M to a fuzzy proposition p and $\tilde{M}(R(p))$ is the modification induced by M in R(p), then the associated translation rule has the general form

[346]
FUZZY SETS

$$\text{If} \quad p \to R(p) \tag{92}$$
$$\text{then} \quad M(p) \to \tilde{M}(R(p))$$

which implies that R, viewed as a mapping, is a homomorphism.

In what follows, the translation process is described in greater detail for (i) a type of attributional modification (Type I), (ii) conjunctive composition (Type II), and (iii) likelihood and possibility-qualifications.

Translation Rules of Type I

Translation rules of this type pertain to operations involving attribute modification; more specifically, they apply to fuzzy propositions of the form $p \triangleq X$ is mF, where F is a fuzzy subset of $U = \{u\}$; m is a modifier such as not, very, more or less, slightly, and somewhat; and either X or A(X)—where A is an implied attribute of X—is a fuzzy variable which takes values in U.

Translation rules of Type I may be subsumed under a general rule which, for convenience, is referred to as the modifier rule. In essence, this rule asserts that the translation of a fuzzy proposition of the form $p \triangleq X$ is mF is expressed by

$$X \text{ is } mF \to R(A(X)) = mF \tag{93}$$

where m is interpreted as an operator which transforms the fuzzy set F into the fuzzy set mF.

In particular, if $m \triangleq$ not, then the rule of negation asserts that the translation of $p \triangleq X$ is not F is expressed by

$$X \text{ is } \underline{\text{not}}\ F \to X \text{ is } F' \to R(A(X)) = F' \tag{94}$$

where F' is the complement of F, i.e.,

$$\mu_{F'}(u) = 1 - \mu_F(u), \qquad u \in U$$

For example, if

$$\mu_{\underline{\text{young}}}(u) = 1 - S(u; 20, 30, 40) \tag{95}$$

then $p \triangleq$ John is not young translates into

$$R(\text{Age(John)}) = \underline{\text{young}}' \tag{96}$$

where, in the notation of (25),

$$\underline{\text{young}}' = \int_0^\infty S(u; 20, 30, 40)/u \tag{97}$$

In general, m may be viewed as a restriction modifier which acts in a specified way on its operand. For example, the modifier very may be assumed to act—to a first approximation—as a concentrator which has the effect of squaring the membership function of its operand. Correspondingly, the rule of concentration asserts that the translation of the fuzzy proposition p = X is very F is expressed by

$$X \text{ is } \underline{\text{very}}\ F \to X \text{ is } F^2 \to R(A(X)) = F^2 \tag{98}$$

where

$$\underline{\text{very}}\ F = F^2 = \int_U (\mu_F(u))^2/u \tag{99}$$

and A(X) is an implied attribute of X.

As an illustration, on applying (98) one finds that "Jennifer is very young" translates into

$$R(\text{Age(Jennifer)}) = \underline{\text{young}}^2 \tag{100}$$

where

$$\underline{\text{young}}^2 = \int_0^\infty (1 - S(u; 20, 30, 40))^2/u \tag{101}$$

The effect of the modifier more or less is less susceptible to simple approximation than that of very. In some contexts, more or less acts as a dilator, playing a role inverse to that of very. Thus, to a first approximation, we may assume that, in such contexts, more or less may be defined by

$$\underline{\text{more or less}}\ F = \sqrt{F} \tag{102}$$

where

$$\sqrt{F} = \int_U (\mu_F(u))^{\frac{1}{2}}/u$$

Based on this definition of more or less, the rule of dilation asserts that

$$X \text{ is } \underline{\text{more or less}}\ F \rightarrow X \text{ is } \sqrt{F} \rightarrow R(A(X)) = \sqrt{F} \tag{103}$$

where A(X) is an implied attribute of X. For example, "Pat is more or less young" translates into

$$R(\text{Age(Pat)}) = \sqrt{\underline{\text{young}}} = \int_0^\infty (1 - S(u; 20, 30, 40))^{\frac{1}{2}}/u \tag{104}$$

Translation Rules of Type II

Translation rules of this type apply to composite fuzzy propositions which are generated from fuzzy propositions of the form "X is F" through the use of various kinds of binary connectives such as the conjunction, and, the disjunction, or, and the conditional if ... then ....

More specifically, let U = {u} and V = {v} be two possibly different universes of discourse, and let F and G be fuzzy subsets of U and V, respectively.

Consider the propositions "X is F" and "Y is G," and let q be their conjunction "X is F and Y is G." Then the rule of noninteractive conjunctive composition or, for short, the rule of conjunctive composition asserts that the translation of q is expressed by

$$X \text{ is } F \text{ and } Y \text{ is } G \rightarrow (X, Y) \text{ is } F \times G \rightarrow R(A(X), B(Y)) = F \times G \tag{105}$$

where A(X) and B(Y) are implied attributes of X and Y, respectively; R(A(X), B(Y)) is a fuzzy restriction on the values of the binary fuzzy variable (A(X), B(Y)); and F × G is the Cartesian product of F and G. Thus, under this rule, the fuzzy proposition "Eugene is tall and Kathleen is young" translates into

[348]
FUZZY SETS

$$R(\text{Height(Eugene)}),\ \text{Age(Kathleen)}) = \underline{\text{tall}} \times \underline{\text{young}} \tag{106}$$

where tall and young are fuzzy subsets of the real line.

To differentiate between noninteractive and interactive conjunction, the latter is denoted by and*. With this understanding, the rule of interactive conjunction, in its general form, may be expressed as

$$X \text{ is } F \text{ and* } Y \text{ is } G \rightarrow R(A(X),\ B(Y)) = F \otimes G \tag{107}$$

where $\otimes$ is a binary operation which maps F and G into a subset of $U \times V$ and thus provides a definition of and* in a particular context.

A simple example of an interactive conjunction is provided by the translation rule

$$X \text{ is } F \text{ and* } Y \text{ is } G \rightarrow R(A(X),\ B(Y)) = FG \tag{108}$$

where

$$\mu_{FG} = \mu_F \mu_G \tag{109}$$

Note that, in this case, an increase in the grade of membership in F can be compensated for by a decrease in the grade of membership in G, and vice versa.

In general, interactive conjunction is strongly application-dependent and has no universally applicable definition.

The translation rule for conditional fuzzy propositions of the form "If X is F then Y is G" is referred to as the rule of conditional composition and may be expressed as

$$\text{If } X \text{ is } F \text{ then } Y \text{ is } G \rightarrow R(A(X),\ B(Y)) = \bar{F}' + \bar{G} \tag{110}$$

where $\oplus$ denotes the bounded sum and $\bar{F}'$ is the complement of the cylindrical extension of F.

As an illustration, assume that tall and young are defined by

$$\underline{\text{tall}} = \int_U S(u;\ 160,\ 170,\ 180)/u$$

$$\underline{\text{young}} = \int_V (1 - S(v;\ 20,\ 30,\ 40))/v$$

where U and V may be taken to be the real line and the height is assumed to be measured in centimeters. Then, the fuzzy proposition "If Eugene is tall then Kathleen is young" translates into

$$R(\text{Height(Eugene)},\ \text{Age(Kathleen)}) = \overline{\underline{\text{tall}}'} \oplus \overline{\underline{\text{young}}} \tag{111}$$

or, more explicitly,

$$\begin{aligned} &R(\text{Height(Eugene)},\ \text{Age(Kathleen)}) \\ &\quad = \int_{U\times V} \Big(1 \wedge (1 - \mu_{\underline{\text{tall}}}(u) + \mu_{\underline{\text{young}}}(v))\Big)\Big/(u,v) \\ &\quad = \int_{U\times V} \Big(1 \wedge (1 - S(u;\ 160,\ 170,\ 180) + 1 - S(v;\ 20,\ 30,\ 40))\Big)\Big/(u,v) \end{aligned} \tag{112}$$

If the conditional fuzzy proposition "If X is F then Y is G else Y is H" is interpreted as the conjunction of the propositions "If X is F then Y is G" and "If X is not

F then Y is H," then by using in combination the rule of negation (94), the rule of conjunctive composition (105), and the rule of conditional composition (110), the translation of the proposition in question is found to be expressed by

$$\text{If X is F then Y is G else Y is H} \rightarrow R(A(X), B(Y)) = (\bar{F}' \oplus \bar{G}) \cap (\bar{F} \oplus \bar{H}) \tag{113}$$

Translation Rules for Likelihood- and Possibility-Qualified Propositions

An important mechanism for effecting a modification in a proposition p involves the use of a qualifier following or preceding p. In ordinary discourse, the most commonly used qualifiers are truth-values, likelihood-values, and possibility-values. For example, if p $\triangleq$ X is small, then as modifications of p we may have propositions such as

X is small is quite true

X is small is very likely

X is small is possible

A discussion of translation rules for truth-qualified fuzzy propositions of the form "X is F is τ," where τ is a linguistic truth-value such as true, quite true, very true, and not very true, may be found in Ref. 1. The translation rules for likelihood-qualified propositions of the form "X is F is λ," where λ is a linguistic likelihood-value such as likely, unlikely, and very likely, are quite similar to the rules described in Ref. 1 which apply to quantified propositions of the form "QX are F," where Q is a fuzzy quantifier such as most, many, and few.

As was stated earlier, the concept of possibility differs in essential ways from that of probability. Reflecting these differences, the translation rules for likelihood-qualified propositions are very different from the corresponding rules for possibility-qualified propositions. More specifically, the translation rule for a likelihood-qualified fuzzy proposition of the form "X is F is λ" is expressed by

$$\text{X is F is } \lambda \rightarrow R\left(\int_U p_{A(X)}(u)\, \mu_F(u)\, du\right) = \lambda \tag{114}$$

where $p_{A(X)}(u)\, du$ is the probability that the value of the implied attribute A(X) falls in the interval (u, u + du), and μ_F is the membership function of F as a subset of U. For example,

$$\text{Laura is young is likely} \rightarrow R\left(\int_0^{100} p_{age}(u)\, \mu_{young}(u)\, du\right) = likely \tag{115}$$

where likely is a fuzzy subset of the unit interval [0, 1]. In effect, (115) defines a fuzzy set of probability density functions $p_{age}(\cdot)$ which is induced by the proposition in question.

By contrast, the translation rule for the possibility-qualified fuzzy proposition "X is F is possible" is expressed by

$$\text{X is F is possible} \rightarrow R(A(X)) = F^+ \tag{116}$$

where A(X) is an implied attribute of X and F^+ is a fuzzy set of Type 2 which is related to F by

[350]
FUZZY SETS

$$\mu_{F^+}(u) = [\mu_F(u), 1] \tag{117}$$

which signifies that μ_{F^+} is interval-valued, with the value of μ_{F^+} at u being the interval expressed by the right-hand member of (117).

As a simple illustration of (116), consider the nonfuzzy proposition "X is in [a, b]" where X is a real-valued variable. Applying (116) to this proposition, we obtain the translation

$$X \text{ is in } [a, b] \text{ is possible} \rightarrow R(X) = [a, b]^+ \tag{118}$$

which implies that

$$\begin{aligned} \mu_{R(X)}(u) &= 1 && \text{for } a \leq u \leq b \\ &= [0, 1] && \text{elsewhere} \end{aligned} \tag{119}$$

Intuitively, (118) signifies that, whereas "X is in [a, b]" implies that the degree of possibility that X is outside of the interval [a, b] is zero, "X is in [a, b] is possible" implies that the degree of possibility that X is outside of the interval [a, b] is unknown, i.e., is the interval [0, 1].

An interesting point that is worthy of note is that (118) provides a justification for an intuitively plausible implication, namely,

$$X \text{ is in } [a, b] \text{ is possible} \Rightarrow X \text{ is in } [c, d] \text{ is possible} \tag{120}$$

where

$$[a, b] \subset [c, d] \tag{121}$$

which is consistent with

$$X \text{ is in } [a, b] \Rightarrow X \text{ is in } [c, d] \tag{122}$$

To verify (121) and (122), it is sufficient to demonstrate that the restriction associated with the antecedent is a subset of the restriction associated with the consequent. This is obvious in the case of (122) and is an immediate consequence of (118) in the case of (120).

What is particularly important about the concept of possibility is that much of the knowledge on which human decision-making is based is in reality possibilistic rather than probabilistic in nature. Thus if X is a variable which takes the values $x_1, \ldots, x_n$ with respective probabilities $p_1, \ldots, p_n$ and possibilities $\mu_1, \ldots, \mu_n$, then, in practice, one is much more likely to know—or be given—the μ's rather than the p's. In many cases the distinction between the two is not clearly understood, so that any collection of data, regardless of whether it is possibilistic or probabilistic, is treated as if it were probabilistic in nature. However, as the foregoing analysis shows, the manipulation of possibilities calls for rules that are quite different from those that apply to probabilities. Thus, in any realistic application of decision analysis, it is essential to differentiate between probabilities and possibilities and treat them by different methods.

Although in principle there is no connection between probabilities and possibilities, in practice the knowledge of possibilities conveys some information about the probabilities but not vice versa. Certainly, if an event is impossible, then it is also improbable. However, it is not true that an event which is possible is also probable. This rather weak connection between the two may be stated more precisely in the form of the possibility/probability consistency principle, namely: If X is a variable which takes the values $x_1, \ldots, x_n$ with probabilities $p_1, \ldots, p_n$ and possibilities $\mu_1, \ldots, \mu_n$, respectively, then the degree of consistency of the probabilities $p_1, \ldots, p_n$ with the possibilities $\mu_1, \ldots, \mu_n$ is given by

$$\rho = \mu_1 p_1 + \mu_2 p_2 + \cdots + \mu_n p_n \tag{123}$$

Intuitively, (123) means that, in order to be consistent with μ's, high probabilities should not be assigned to those values of X which are associated with low degrees of possibility.

REFERENCES

1. Bellman, R. E., and L. A. Zadeh, Local and Fuzzy Logics, ERL Memo M-584, University of California, Berkeley, 1976; also in Modern Uses of Multiple-Valued Logics (D. Epstein, ed.), Reidel, Dordrecht, 1977.
2. Gaines, B. R., and L. J. Kohout, Possible automata, in Proceedings of the International Symposium on Multiple-Valued Logic, Indiana University, Bloomington, 1975, pp. 183-196.
3. Goguen, J. A., L-fuzzy sets, J. Math. Anal. Appl. 18, 145-173 (1967).
4. Kaufmann, A., Introduction to the Theory of Fuzzy Subsets, Vol. 1. Elements of Basic Theory, Masson, Paris, 1973; Vol. 2. Applications to Linguistics, Logic and Semantics, Masson, Paris, 1975; Vol. 3. Applications to Classification and Pattern Recognition, Automata and Systems, and Choice of Criteria, Masson, Paris, 1975. Also English translation of Vol. 1, Academic, New York, 1975.
5. Mizumoto, M., and K. Tanaka, Some properties of fuzzy sets of type 2, Inf. Control 31, 312-340 (1976).
6. Negoita, C. V., and D. A. Ralescu, Applications of Fuzzy Sets to Systems Analysis, Birkhauser, Basel, 1975.
7. Zadeh, L. A., Similarity relations and fuzzy orderings, Inf. Sci. 3, 177-200 (1971).
8. Zadeh, L. A., A fuzzy-set-theoretic interpretation of linguistic hedges, J. Cybern. 2, 4-34 (1972).
9. Zadeh, L. A., Outline of a new approach to the analysis of complex systems and decision processes, IEEE Trans. Syst., Man Cybern. SMC-3, 28-44 (1973).
10. Zadeh, L. A., The concept of a linguistic variable and its application to approximate reasoning, Part I, Inf. Sci. 8, 199-249 (1975); Part II, Inf. Sci. 8, 301-357 (1975); Part III, Inf. Sci. 9, 43-80 (1975).
11. Zadeh, L. A., Fuzzy logic and approximate reasoning (in memory of Grigore Moisil), Synthese 30, 407-428 (1975).

BIBLIOGRAPHY

Adams, E. W., Elements of a theory of inexact measurement, Philos. Sci. 32, 205-228 (1968).

Adams, E. W., The logic of 'almost all,' J. Philos. Logic 3, 3-17 (1974).

[352]
FUZZY SETS

Adams, E. W., and H. P. Levine, On the uncertainties transmitted from premises to conclusions in deductive inferences, Synthese 30, 429–460 (1975).

Aizerman, M. A., Fuzzy sets, fuzzy proofs and certain unsolved problems in the theory of automatic control, Avtom. Telemokh. 9, 171-177 (1976).

Albin, M., Fuzzy Sets and Their Application to Medical Diagnosis, Ph.D. Thesis, Department of Mathematics, University of California, Berkeley, 1975.

Arbib, M. A., and E. G. Manes, Fuzzy morphisms in automata theory, in Proceedings of the 1st International Symposium on Category Theory Applied to Computation and Control, University of Massachusetts, Amherst, 1974, pp. 98–105.

Arbib, M. A., and E. G. Manes, A category-theoretic approach to systems in a fuzzy world, Synthese 30, 381–406 (1975).

Asai, K., and S. Kitajima, A method for optimizing control of multimodal systems using fuzzy automata, Inf. Sci. 3, 343–353 (1971).

Asai, K., and H. Tanaka, On fuzzy mathematical programming, in Proceedings of the 3rd IFAC Symposium on Identification and System Parameter Estimation, Part II, North Holland, Amsterdam, 1973.

Aubin, J. P., Fuzzy Games (MRC Technical Summary Report 1480), Mathematics Research Center, University of Wisconsin-Madison, Madison, 1974.

Auray, J. P., and G. Duru, Introduction to the Theory of Multifuzzy Spaces, Institute of Mathematical Economics, University of Dijon, France, 1976.

Baas, S. M., and H. Kwakernaak, Rating and Ranking of Multiple-Aspect Alternatives Using Fuzzy Sets (Memo 73), Department of Applied Mathematics, Twente University of Tech., Enschede, The Netherlands, 1975.

Barnev, P., V. Dimitrov, and V. Stanchev, Fuzzy System Approach to Decision-Making Based on Public Opinion Investigation through Questionnaires, Institute of Mathematics and Mechanics, Bulgarian Academy of Sciences, Sofia, Bulgaria, 1974.

Barthelmy, J. P., D. Boichut, X. Luong, and J. P. Massonie (eds.), Notes of the University Seminar on Fuzzy Sets, University of Bezancon, Bezancon, France, 1976.

Bellman, R. E., and M. Giertz, On the analytic formalism of the theory of fuzzy sets, Inf. Sci. 5, 149–156 (1973).

Bellman, R. E., R. Kalaba, and L. A. Zadeh, Abstraction and pattern classification, J. Math. Anal. Appl. 13, 1–7 (1966).

Bellman, R. E., and L. A. Zadeh, Decision-making in a fuzzy environment, Manage. Sci. 17, B141–B164 (1970).

Bellman, R. E., and L. A. Zadeh, Local and Fuzzy Logics (ERL Memo M–584), University of California, Berkeley, 1976; also in Modern Uses of Multiple-Valued Logics (D. Epstein, ed.), Reidel, Dordrecht, 1977.

Bezdek, J. C., Fuzzy Mathematics in Pattern Classification, Ph.D. Thesis, Center for Applied Mathematics, Cornell, 1973.

Bezdek, J. C., Numerical taxonomy with fuzzy sets, J. Math. Biol. 1, 57–71 (1974).

Bezdek, J. C., Mathematical models for systematics and taxonomy, in Proceedings of the 8th International Conference on Numerical Taxonomy (G. Estabrook, ed.), Freeman, San Francisco, 1975.

Bezdek, J. C., and J. C. Dunn, Optimal fuzzy partitions: A heuristic for estimating the parameters in a mixture of normal distributions, IEEE Trans. Comput. C-24, 835–838 (1975).

Black, M., Vagueness, Philos. Sci. 4, 427–455 (1937).

[353]
FUZZY SETS

Black, M., Reasoning with loose concepts, Dialogue 2, 1-12 (1963).
Blin, J. M., Fuzzy relations in group decision theory, J. Cybern. 4, 17-22 (1974).
Borisov, A. N., and E. A. Kokle, Recognition of fuzzy patterns by feature analysis, Cybern. Diagn. (Riga) 4, 135-147 (1970).
Borisov, A. N., G. N. Wulf, and J. J. Osis, Prediction of the state of a complex system using the theory of fuzzy sets, Kibern. Diagn. 5, 79-84 (1972).
Bouchon, B., Une application informationelle de la theorie des questionnaires, in Colloquium on Information Theory, Keszthely, Hungary, 1975.
Bremermann, H. J., Cybernetic functionals and fuzzy sets, IEEE Symp. Record, Syst., Man Cybern. 71C46SMC, 248-253 (1971).
Brown, J. G., A note on fuzzy sets, Inf. Control 18, 32-39 (1971).
Capocelli, R. M., and A. DeLuca, Fuzzy sets and decision theory, Inf. Control 23, 446-473 (1973).
Carlstrom, I. F., Truth and entailment for a vague quantifier, Synthese 30, 461-495 (1975).
Chang, C. L., Fuzzy Sets and Pattern Recognition, Ph.D. Thesis, Department of Electrical Engineering, University of California, Berkeley, 1967.
Chang, C. L., Fuzzy topological spaces, J. Math. Anal. Appl. 24, 182-190 (1968).
Chang, C. L., Interpretation and execution of fuzzy programs, in Fuzzy Sets and Their Applications to Cognitive and Decision Processes (L. A. Zadeh, K. S. Fu, K. Tanaka, and M. Shimura, eds.), Academic, New York, 1975, pp. 191-218.
Chang, R. L. P., and T. Pavlidis, Fuzzy decision trees, in Proceedings of the International Conference on Cybernetics and Society, Washington, D.C., 1976, pp. 564-567.
Chang, S. K., On the execution of fuzzy programs using finite state machines, IEEE Trans. Comp. C-21, 241-253 (1972).
Chang, S. K., and J. S. Ke, Database Skeleton and Its Application to Fuzzy Query Translation, Department of Information Engineering, University of Illinois, Chicago Circle, Chicago, 1976.
Chang, S. S. L., Fuzzy mathematics, man and his environment, IEEE Trans. Syst., Man Cybern. SMC-2, 92-93 (1972).
Chang, S. S. L., Application of fuzzy set theory to economics, in Proceedings of the International Conference on Cybernetics and Society, Washington, D.C., 1976, pp. 556-558.
Chang, S. S. L., and L. A. Zadeh, On fuzzy mapping and control, IEEE Trans. Syst., Man and Cybern. SMC-2, 30-34 (1972).
Chapin, E. W., An axiomatization of the set theory of Zadeh, Not. Am. Math. Soc. (687-02-4), 753 (1971).
Chapin, E. W., Set-valued set theory, Notre Dame J. Formal Logic, Part I, 15, 619-634 (1974); Part II, 16, 255-267 (1975).
Cochrane, J. L., and M. Zeleny (eds.), Multiple Criteria Decision-Making, University of South Carolina Press, Columbia, 1973.
Conche, B., Eléments d'une méthode de classification par utilisation d'un automate flou, J.E.E.F.L.N., University of Paris-Dauphine, France, 1973.
Cools, M., and M. Peteau, STIM 5: Un programme de stimulation inventive utilisant la théorie des sous-ensembles flous, IMAGO Discussion Paper, Universite Catholique de Louvain, Belgium, 1973.
Coppo, M., and L. Saitta, Semantic support for a speech understanding system based on fuzzy relation, in Proceedings of the International Conference on Cybernetics and Society, Washington, D.C., 1976, pp. 520-524.

[354]
FUZZY SETS

Dal Cin, M., Fuzzy-State Automata, Their Stability and Fault-Tolerance, Institute of Science, University of Tubingen, Germany, 1973.
Davio, M., and A. Thayse, Representation of fuzzy functions, Philips. Res. Rep. 28, 93-106 (1973).
DeLuca, A., and S. Termini, Algebraic properties of fuzzy sets, J. Math. Anal. Appl. 40, 373-386 (1972).
DeLuca, A., and S. Termini, A definition of a nonprobabilistic entropy in the setting of fuzzy sets theory, Inf. Control 20, 301-312 (1972).
DeLuca, A., and S. Termini, Entropy of L-fuzzy sets, Inf. Control 24, 55-73 (1974).
DePalma, G. F., and S. S. Yau, Fractionally fuzzy grammars with application to pattern recognition, in Fuzzy Sets and Their Applications to Cognitive and Decision Processes (L. A. Zadeh, K. S. Fu, K. Tanaka, and M. Shimura, eds.), Academic, New York, 1975, pp. 329-351.
Dimitrov, V. D., GMDH algorithms on fuzzy sets of Zadeh, Sov. Autom. Control 3, 40-45 (1970).
Dimitrov, V. D., Efficient Governing Humanistic Systems by Fuzzy Instructions, presented at 3rd International Congress of General Systems and Cybernetics, Bucharest, 1975.
Dunn, J. C., A fuzzy relative of the ISODATA process and its use in detecting compact well-separated clusters, J. Cybern. 3, 32-57 (1974).
Dunn, J. C., A graph theoretic analysis of pattern classification via Tamura's fuzzy relation, IEEE Trans. Syst., Man and Cybern. SMC-4, 310-313 (1974).
Engel, A. B., and V. Buonomano, Towards a General Theory of Fuzzy Sets I, Inst. de Mat., Univ. Estadual de Campinas, Brazil, 1973.
Esogbue, A. O., and V. Ramesh, Dynamic Programming and Fuzzy Allocation Processes (Technical Memo No. 202), Department of Operations Research, Case Western Reserve University, Cleveland, 1970.
Fellinger, W. L., Specifications for a Fuzzy System Modeling Language, Ph.D. Thesis, Oregon State University, Corvallis, 1974.
Fine, K., Vagueness, truth and logic, Synthese 30, 265-300 (1975).
Fu, K. S., and T. J. Li, Formulation of learning automata and automata games, Inf. Sci. 1, 237-256 (1969).
Gaines, B. R., Fuzzy and Stochastic Metric Logics, Department of Electrical Engineering Science, University of Essex, Colchester, Essex, England, 1975.
Gaines, B. R., Multivalued Logics and Fuzzy Reasoning, Lecture Notes of AISB Summer School, Cambridge, England, 1975, pp. 100-112.
Gaines, B. R., Stochastic and fuzzy logics, Electron. Lett. 11, 188-189 (1975).
Gaines, B. R., Fuzzy reasoning and the logic of uncertainty, in Proceedings of the International Symposium on Multiple-Valued Logic, Utah State University, Logan, 1976, pp. 179-188.
Gaines, B. R., General Fuzzy Logics, Man-Machine Systems Laboratory, University of Essex, Colchester, Essex, England, 1976.
Gaines, B. R., Multi-Valued Logics and Fuzzy Reasoning, Workshop on Discrete Systems and Fuzzy Reasoning, Department of Electrical Engineering Science, University of Essex, Colchester, Essex, England, 1976.
Gaines, B. R., and L. J. Kohout, Possible automata, in Proceedings of the International Symposium on Multiple-Valued Logic, Indiana University, Bloomington, 1975, pp. 183-196.
Gaines, B. R., and L. J. Kohout, The fuzzy decade: A bibliography of fuzzy systems and closely related topics, Int. J. Man-Mach. Stud. 9, 1-68 (1977).

[355]
FUZZY SETS

Gale, S., Inexactness, fuzzy sets, and the foundations of behavioral geography, Geogr. Anal. 4, 337-349 (1972).

Giles, R., Lukasiewicz logic and fuzzy set theory, Int. J. Man-Mach. Stud. 8, 313-327 (1976).

Gitman, I., and M. D. Levine, An algorithm for detecting unimodal fuzzy sets and its applications as a clustering technique, IEEE Trans. Comput. C-19, 583-593 (1970).

Gluss, B., Fuzzy multi-stage decision-making, fuzzy state and terminal regulators and their relationship to non-fuzzy quadratic state and terminal regulators, Int. J. Control 17, 177-192 (1973).

Goguen, J. A., L-fuzzy sets, J. Math. Anal. Appl. 18, 145-173 (1967).

Goguen, J. A., Categories of Fuzzy Sets: Applications of non-Cantorian Set Theory, Ph.D. Thesis, Department of Mathematics, University of California, Berkeley, 1968.

Goguen, J. A., The logic of inexact concepts, Synthese 19, 325-373 (1969).

Goguen, J. A., The fuzzy Tychonoff theorem, J. Math. Anal. Appl. 43, 734-742 (1973).

Goguen, J. A., Concept representation in natural and artificial languages: Axioms, extensions and applications for fuzzy sets, Int. J. Man-Mach. Stud. 6, 513-561 (1974).

Gottinger, H. W., Toward a fuzzy reasoning in the behavioral science, Cybernetica [2] 16, 113-135 (1973).

Gottwald, S., Fuzzy topology: Product and quotient theorem, J. Math. Anal. Appl. 45, 512-521 (1974).

Gottwald, S., Ein kumulatives system mehrwertiger mengen, Karl-Marx University, Leipzig, Germany, 1975.

Gupta, M. M., IFAC report: Round table discussion on estimation and control in fuzzy environments, Automatica 11, 209-212 (1975).

Gusev, L. A., and I. M. Smirnova, Fuzzy sets: Theory and application (a survey), Avtom. Telemekh. 5, 66-85 (1973).

Halpern, J., Set adjacency measures in fuzzy graphs, J. Cybern. 5, 77-88 (1975).

Harris, J. I., Fuzzy Implication—Comments on a Paper by Zadeh, DOAE Research Working Paper, Ministry of Defense, Byfleet, Surrey, England, 1974.

Harris, J. I., Fuzzy Sets: How to be Imprecise Precisely, DOAE Research Working Paper, Ministry of Defense, Byfleet, Surrey, England, 1974.

Hendry, W. L., Fuzzy Sets and Russell's Paradox, Los Alamos Scientific Laboratory, University of California, Los Alamos, New Mexico, 1972.

Hersch, H. M., and A. Caramazza, A fuzzy set approach to modifiers and vagueness in natural languages, J. Exp. Psychol. 105, 254-276 (1976).

Hirai, H., K. Asai, and S. Kitajima, Fuzzy automata and their application to learning control systems, Mem. Fac. Eng., Osaka City Univ. 10, 67-73 (1968).

Hutton, B., Normality in fuzzy topological spaces, J. Math. Anal. Appl. 50, 74-79 (1975).

Hutton, B., and J. L. Reilly, Separation Axioms in Fuzzy Topological Spaces, University of Auckland, New Zealand, 1974.

Inagaki, Y., and T. Fukumura, On the description of fuzzy meaning of context-free language, in Fuzzy Sets and Their Applications to Cognitive and Decision Processes (L. A. Zadeh, K. S. Fu, K. Tanaka, and M. Shimura, eds.), Academic, New York, 1975, pp. 301-328.

[356]
FUZZY SETS

Itzinger, O., Aspects of axiomatization of behavior: Towards an application of Rasch's measurement model to fuzzy logic, COMPSTAT 1974, in Proceedings of the Symposium on Computational Statistics, University of Vienna, Austria (G. Bruckman, F. Ferschl, and L. Schmetterer, eds.), Physica-Verlag, 1974, pp. 173-182.

Jakubowski, R., and A. Kasprzak, Application of fuzzy programs to the design of machining technology, Bull. Pol. Acad. Sci. 21, 12-33 (1973).

Jouault, J. P., and P. M. Luan, Application des concepts flous a la programmation en languages quasi-naturels, Inst. Inf. d'Entreprise, C.N.A.M., Paris, 1975.

Kalmanson, D., and H. F. Stegall, Recherche cardiovasculaire et théorie des ensembles flous, Nouv. Presse Med. 41, 2757-2760 (1973); also in Am. J. Cardiol. 35, 80-84 (1975).

Kandel, A., Comment on an algorithm that generates fuzzy prime implicants by Lee and Chang, Inf. Control 22, 279-282 (1973).

Kandel, A., On minimization of fuzzy functions, IEEE Trans. Comput. C-22, 826-832 (1973).

Kandel, A., Codes over languages, IEEE Trans. Syst. Man Cybern. SMC-4, 135-138 (1974).

Kandel, A., On the minimization of incompletely specified fuzzy functions, Inf. Control 26, 141-153 (1974).

Kaufmann, A., Introduction to the Theory of Fuzzy Subsets, Vol. 1. Elements of Basic Theory, Masson, Paris, 1973; Vol. 2. Applications to Linguistics, Logic and Semantics, Masson, Paris, 1975; Vol. 3. Applications to Classification and Pattern Recognition, Automata and Systems, and Choice of Criteria, Masson, Paris, 1975; also English translation of Vol. 1, Academic, New York, 1975.

Kaufmann, A., M. Cools, and T. Dubois, Stimulation inventive dans un dialogue homme-machine utilisant la méthode des morphologies et la théorie des sous-ensembles flous, IMAGO Discussion Paper 6, Universite Catholique de Louvain, Belgium, 1973.

Khatchadourian, H., Vagueness, meaning and absurdity, Am. Philos. Q. 2, 119-129 (1965).

Kickert, W. J. M., and H. R. van Nauta Lemke, Application of a fuzzy controller in a warm water plant, Control Laboratory, Department of Electrical Engineering, Delft University of Technology, The Netherlands, 1975; also in Automatica 12, 301-308 (1976).

Kitawaga, T., Fuzziness in informative logics, in Fuzzy Sets and Their Applications to Cognitive and Decision Processes (L. A. Zadeh, K. S. Fu, K. Tanaka, and M. Shimura, eds.), Academic, New York, 1975, pp. 97-124.

Klaua, D., Uber einen ansatz zur mehrwertigen mengenlehre, Monatsber. Dtsch. Akad. Wiss. Berlin 7, 859-876 (1965).

Klaua, D., Uber einen zweiten ansatz zur mehrwertigen mengenlehre, Monatsber. Dtsch. Akad. Wiss. Berlin 8, 161-177 (1966).

Kling, R., Fuzzy Planner (Technical Report 168), Computer Science Department, University of Wisconsin, Madison, 1973.

Knopfmacher, K., On measures of fuzziness, J. Math. Anal. Appl. 49, 529-534 (1975).

Kochen, M., On the Precision of Adjectives Which Denote Fuzzy Sets, University of Michigan Mental Health Research Institute, Ann Arbor, 1974.

Koczy, L. T., and M. Hajnal, A new fuzzy calculus and its application as a pattern recognition technique, in Proceedings of the 3rd International Congress of WOGSC, Bucharest, 1975.

[357]
FUZZY SETS

Kotoh, K., and K. Hiramatsu, A representation of pattern classes using the fuzzy sets, Trans. IECE 56-d, 275-282 (1973).

Lake, J., Fuzzy Sets and Bald Men, Department of Mathematics, Polytechnic of the South Bank, London, England, 1974.

Lake, J., Sets, Fuzzy Sets, Multi-Sets and Functions, Department of Mathematics, Polytechnic of the South Bank, London, England, 1974; also J. London Math. Soc. 12, 323-326 (1976).

Lakoff, G., Hedges: A study in meaning criteria and the logic of fuzzy concepts, J. Philos. Logic 2, 458-508 (1973); also paper presented at 8th Regional Meeting of Chicago Linguistics Society, 1972, and in Contemporary Research in Philosophical Logic and Linguistic Semantics (D. Hockney, W. Harper, and B. Freed, eds.), Reidel, The Netherlands, 1975, pp. 221-271.

Lakoff, G., Fuzzy grammar and the performance/competence terminology game, Proc. Meet. Chicago Linguistics Soc., pp. 271-291 (1973).

Lee, E. T., Fuzzy Languages and Their Relation to Automata, Ph.D. Thesis, Department of Electrical Engineering and Computer Sciences, University of California, Berkeley, 1972.

Lee, E. T., Shape-oriented chromosome identification, IEEE Trans. Syst., Man Cybern. SMC-5, 629-632 (1975).

Lee, E. T., An application of fuzzy sets to the classification of geometric figures and chromosome images, Inf. Sci. 10, 95-114 (1976).

Lee, E. T., and L. A. Zadeh, Note on fuzzy languages, Inf. Sci. 1, 421-434 (1969).

Lee, R., and C. L. Chang, Some properties of fuzzy logic, Inf. Control 19, 417-431 (1971).

Lee, R. C. T., Fuzzy logic and the resolution principle, J. ACM 19, 109-119 (1972).

Lee, S. C., and E. T. Lee, Fuzzy sets and neural networks, J. Cybern. 4, 83-103 (1974).

Le Faivre, R., FUZZY: A Programming Language for Fuzzy Problem Solving (Technical Report 202), Department of Computer Science, University of Wisconsin, Madison, 1974.

Lientz, B., On time-dependent fuzzy sets, Inf. Sci. 4, 367-376 (1972).

Longo, G., Fuzzy sets, graphs and source coding, in New Directions in Signal Processing in Communications and Control (J. K. Swirzynski, ed.), Noordhoff, Leyden, 1975, pp. 27-33.

Lowen, P., A Theory of Fuzzy Topologies, Ph.D. Thesis, Department of Mathematics, Free University of Brussels, Belgium, 1974.

Lowen, P., Topologie flous, C. R. Acad. Sci., Paris 278, 925-928 (1974).

Machina, K. F., Vague predicates, Am. Philos. Q. 9, 225-233 (1972).

Mamdani, E. H., Applications of fuzzy algorithms for control of simple dynamic plant, Proc. IEE 121, 1585-1588 (1974).

Mamdani, E. H., Application of fuzzy logic to approximate reasoning using linguistic synthesis, in Proceedings of the 6th International Symposium on Multiple-Valued Logic, Utah State University, Logan, 1976, pp. 196-202.

Mamdani, E. H., and S. Assilian, An experiment in linguistic synthesis with a fuzzy logic controller, Int. J. Man-Mach. Stud. 7, 1-13 (1975).

Marinos, P. N., Fuzzy logic and its application to switching systems, IEEE Trans. Comput. C-18, 343-348 (1969).

Maurer, W. D., Input-Output Correctness and Fuzzy Correctness, George Washington University, Washington, D.C., 1974.

[358]
FUZZY SETS

Meseguer, J., and I. Sols, Automata in semimodule categories, in Proceedings of the 1st International Symposium on Category Theory Applied to Computation and Control, University of Massachusetts, Amherst, 1974, pp. 196-202.

Mizumoto, M., Fuzzy Automata and Fuzzy Grammars, Ph.D. Thesis, Faculty of Engineering Science, Osaka University, Osaka, Japan, 1971.

Mizumoto, M., and K. Tanaka, Algebraic properties of fuzzy numbers, in Proceedings of the International Conference on Cybernetics and Society, Washington, D.C., 1976, pp. 559-564.

Mizumoto, M., and K. Tanaka, Some properties of fuzzy sets of type 2, Inf. Control 31, 312-340 (1976).

Mizumoto, M., J. Toyoda, and K. Tanaka, Some considerations on fuzzy automata, J. Comput. Syst. Sci. 3, 409-422 (1969).

Mizumoto, M., J. Toyoda, and K. Tanaka, Examples of formal grammars with weights, Inf. Proc. Lett. 2, 74-78 (1973).

Mizumoto, M., J. Toyoda, and K. Tanaka, N-fold fuzzy grammars, Inf. Sci. 5, 25-43 (1973).

Moisil, G. C., Essais sur les logiques non-chrysippiennes, Romanian Academy of Sciences, Bucharest, Romania, 1972.

Moisil, G. C., Lectures on the Logic of Fuzzy Reasoning, Scientific Editions, Bucharest, 1975.

Nahmias, S., Discrete Fuzzy Random Variables, University of Pittsburgh, Pittsburgh, Pennsylvania, 1974.

Nalimov, V. V., Probabilistic Model of Language, Moscow State University, Moscow, 1974.

Nasu, M., and N. Honda, Fuzzy events realized by finite probabilistic automata, Inf. Control 12, 284-303 (1968).

Nazaroff, G. J., Fuzzy topological polysystems, J. Math. Anal. Appl. 41, 478-485 (1973).

Negoita, C. V., Information Retrieval Systems, Ph.D. Thesis, Polytechnic Institute, Bucharest, 1969 (in Romanian).

Negoita, C. V., On the application of the fuzzy sets separation theorem for automatic classification in information retrieval systems, Inf. Sci. 5, 279-286 (1973).

Negoita, C. V., On the decision process in information retrieval, Stud. Cercet. Doc., pp. 369-381 (1973).

Negoita, C. V., Fuzzy models for social processes, in Symposium on Social Processes Modelling, Bucharest, 1975.

Negoita, C. V., and D. A. Ralescu, Fuzzy systems and artificial intelligence, Kybernetes 3, 173-178 (1974).

Negoita, C. V., and D. A. Ralescu, Applications of Fuzzy Sets to Systems Analysis, Birkhauser, Basel, 1975.

Negoita, C. V., and D. A. Ralescu, Representation theorems for fuzzy concepts, Kybernetes 4 (1975).

Nguyen, H. T., Information fonctionelle et ensembles flous, in Seminar on Questionnaires, University of Paris 6, Paris, 1975.

Nguyen, H. T., On Fuzziness and Linguistic Probabilities (Memo ERL M-595), University of California, Berkeley, 1976.

Nguyen, H. T., A Note on the Extension Principle for Fuzzy Sets (Memo ERL M-611), University of California, Berkeley, 1976.

[359]
FUZZY SETS

Noguchi, K., M. Umano, M. Mizumoto, and K. Tanaka, Implementation of Fuzzy Artificial Intelligence Language FLOU, Technical Report on Automation and Language of IECE, 1976.

Nurminen, M., On Fuzziness in the Analysis of Information Systems, University of Turku, Finland, 1976.

Ostegaard, J. J., Fuzzy Logic Control of a Heat Exchanger Process (Publ. No. 7601), Technical University of Denmark, Lyngby, 1976.

Pavlidis, T., Fuzzy representations as means of overcoming the over-commitment of segmentation, in Proceedings of a Conference on Computer Graphics, Pattern Recognition and Data Structures, Los Angeles, 1975.

Paz, A., Fuzzy star functions, probabilistic automata and their approximation by nonprobabilistic automata, J. Comput. Syst. Sci. 1, 371-390 (1967).

Preparata, F. P., and R. Yeh, Continuously-valued logic, J. Comput. Syst. Sci. 6, 397-418 (1972).

Prugovecki, E., Fuzzy sets in the theory of measurement of incompatible observables, Found. Phys. 4, 9-18 (1974).

Prugovecki, E., Probability measures on fuzzy events in phase space, J. Math. Phys. 17, 517-523 (1976).

Prugovecki, E., Quantum two-particle scattering in fuzzy phase space, J. Math. Phys. 17, 1673-1681 (1976).

Pun, L., Experience in the Use of Fuzzy Formalism in Problems with Various Degrees of Subjectivity, University of Bordeaux, Bordeaux, 1975; also presented at Special Interest Discussion Session on Fuzzy Automata and Decision Processes, 6th IFAC World Congress, Boston, 1975.

Ragade, R. K., On Some Aspects of Fuzziness in Communication, I. Fuzzy Entropies, Systems Research and Planning, Systems Engineering, Bell-Northern Research, Canada, 1973.

Ragade, R. K., Fuzzy Games in the Analysis of Options, Department of Systems Design, University of Waterloo, Waterloo, Canada, 1976.

Rajasethupathy, K. S., and S. Lakshmivarahan, Connectedness in Fuzzy Topology, Department of Mathematics, Vivekanandha College, Madras, India, 1974.

Reisinger, L., On fuzzy thesauri, in Proceedings of the Symposium on Computational Statistics, University of Vienna, Austria (G. Bruckman, F. Ferschl, and L. Schmetterer, eds.), Physica-Verlag, 1974, pp. 119-127.

Rescher, N., Many-Valued Logic, McGraw-Hill, New York, 1969.

Rieger, B. B., Fuzzy Structural Semantics, German Institute, Technical University of Aachen, Aachen, 1976; also 3rd European Meeting on Cybernetics, Vienna.

Rödder, W., On "and" and "or" Connectives in Fuzzy Set Theory, Institute for Operations Research, Technical University of Aachen, Aachen, 1975.

Rosenfeld, A., Fuzzy groups, J. Math. Anal. Appl. 35, 512-517 (1971).

Ruspini, E. H., Numerical methods for fuzzy clustering, Inf. Sci. 2, 319-350 (1970).

Ruspini, E. H., New experimental results in fuzzy clustering, Inf. Sci. 6, 273-284 (1973).

Rutherford, G., and G. C. Bloore, The Implementation of Fuzzy Algorithms for Control, Control Systems Center, University of Manchester, Manchester, England, 1975.

Saaty, T., Measuring the fuzziness of sets, J. Cybern. 4, 53-61 (1974).

Sanchez, E., Equations de relations flous, Ph.D. Dissertation, Department of Human Biology, Faculty of Medicine, Marseille, France, 1974.

[360]
FUZZY SETS

Santos, E. S., Maximin automata, Inf. Control 13, 363-377 (1968).

Santos, E. S., Fuzzy algorithms, Inf. Control 17, 326-339 (1970).

Santos, E. S., Context-free fuzzy languages, Inf. Control 26, 1-11 (1974).

Santos, E. S., and W. G. Wee, General formulation of sequential machines, Inf. Control 12, 5-10 (1968).

Schotch, P. K., Fuzzy modal logic, in Proceedings of the International Symposium on Multiple-Valued Logic, Indiana University, Bloomington, 1975, pp. 176-182.

Schwede, G., N-variable fuzzy maps with application to disjunctive decomposition of fuzzy switching functions, in Proceedings of the International Symposium on Multiple-Valued Logic, Utah State University, Logan, 1976, pp. 203-216.

Shapiro, D. I., Mathematical Methods in Decision Analysis, Committee on Cybernetics, Academy of Sciences of USSR, 1974.

Shimura, M., Applications of fuzzy functions to pattern classification, Trans. IECE 55-d, 218-225 (1972).

Shimura, M., Fuzzy sets concept in rank-ordering objects, J. Math. Anal. Appl. 43, 717-733 (1973).

Shimura, M., An approach to pattern recognition and associative memories using fuzzy logic, in Fuzzy Sets and Their Applications to Cognitive and Decision Processes (L. A. Zadeh, K. S. Fu, K. Tanaka, and M. Shimamura, eds.), Academic, New York, 1975, pp. 449-476.

Siy, P., and C. S. Chen, Minimization of fuzzy functions, IEEE Trans. Comput. C-21, 100-102 (1972).

Siy, P., and C. S. Chen, Fuzzy logic for handwritten numerical character recognition, IEEE Trans. Syst., Man Cybern. SMC-4, 570-575 (1974).

Skala, H. J., On the Problem of Imprecision, Dordrecht, The Netherlands, 1974.

Smith, P. E., Measure Theory on Fuzzy Sets, Thesis, University of Saskatchewan, Saskatoon, Canada, 1970.

Sols, I., Topology in Complete Lattices and Continuous Fuzzy Relations, Facultad de Ciencias, Zaragoza University, Zaragoza, Spain, 1975.

Stephanou, H. E., and G. N. Saridis, Hierarchical control in a fuzzy environment, in Proceedings of the International Conference on Cybernetics and Society, Washington, D.C., 1976, pp. 568-572.

Sugeno, M., Constructing fuzzy measure and grading similarity of patterns by fuzzy integrals, Trans. SICE 9, 359-367 (1973).

Sugeno, M., Theory of Fuzzy Integrals and Its Applications, Ph.D. Thesis, Tokyo Institute of Technology, Tokyo, 1974.

Sugeno, M., Fuzzy Systems with Underlying Deterministic Systems (Publ. No. 1525), Laboratoire d'Automatique et d'Analyse des Systemes, Toulouse, France, 1976.

Sundstrom, D. E., Regulatory Control and Modeling of Responsive Behavior in Autonomous Systems, Ph.D. Thesis, Southern Methodist University, 1973.

Tahani, V., Fuzzy Sets in Information Retrieval, Ph.D. Thesis, Department of Electrical Engineering and Computer Sciences, University of California, Berkeley, 1971.

Tamura, S., S. Higuchi, and K. Tanaka, Pattern classification based on fuzzy relations, IEEE Trans. Syst., Man Cybern. SMC-1, 61-65 (1971).

Tamura, S., and K. Tanaka, Learning of fuzzy formal languages, IEEE Trans. Syst., Man Cybern. SMC-3, 98-102 (1973).

[361]
FUZZY SETS

Tanaka, K., Fuzzy Automata Theory and Its Applications to Control Systems, Osaka University, Osaka, 1970.

Tanaka, K., T. Okuda, and K. Asai, On fuzzy mathematical programming, J. Cybern. 3, 37–46 (1974).

Terano, T. (ed.), Summary of Papers on General Fuzzy Problems, The Working Group on Fuzzy Systems, Tokyo, 1975.

Terano, T., and M. Sugeno, Conditional fuzzy measures and their applications, in Fuzzy Sets and Their Applications to Cognitive and Decision Processes (L. A. Zadeh, K. S. Fu, K. Tanaka, and M. Shimura, eds.), Academic, New York, 1975, pp. 151-170.

Thomason, M. G., Finite Fuzzy Automata, Regular Fuzzy Languages, and Pattern Recognition, Department of Electrical Engineering, Duke University, Durham, North Carolina, 1974.

Thomason, M. G., Fuzzy syntax-directed translations, J. Cybern. 4, 87-94 (1974).

Thomason, M. G., and P. N. Marinos, Deterministic acceptors of regular fuzzy languages, IEEE Trans. Syst., Man Cybern. SMC-4, 228-230 (1974).

Tsichritzis, D., Fuzzy Properties and Almost Solvable Problems (Technical Report 70), Department of Electrical Engineering, Princeton University, Princeton, New Jersey, 1969.

Tsuji, H., M. Mizumoto, J. Toyoda, and K. Tanaka, Interaction between random environments and fuzzy automata with variable structures, Trans. IECE 55-d, 143-144 (1973).

Uhr, L., Toward integrated cognitive systems, which must make fuzzy decisions about fuzzy problems, in Fuzzy Sets and Their Applications to Cognitive and Decision Processes (L. A. Zadeh, K. S. Fu, K. Tanaka, and M. Shimura, eds.), Academic, New York, 1975, pp. 353-393.

Umano, M., M. Mizumoto, and K. Tanaka, Implementation of Fuzzy Sets Manipulation Systems, Technical Report on Automation and Language of IECE, 1976.

Van Velthoven, G. D., Application of Fuzzy Sets Theory to Criminal Investigation, Ph.D. Thesis, University of Louvain, Belgium, 1974.

Van Velthoven, G. D., Fuzzy models in personnel management, in Proceedings of the 3rd International Congress on Cybernetics and Systems, Bucharest, 1975.

Verma, R. R., Vagueness and the principle of the excluded middle, Mind 79, 66-77 (1970).

Vincke, P., Une application de la theorie des graphes flous, Free University of Brussels, Belgium, 1973.

Warren, R. H., Neighborhoods, Bases and Continuity in Fuzzy Topological Spaces, Applied Mathematics Research Laboratory, Wright-Patterson AFB, Ohio, 1974.

Wechler, W., R-Fuzzy Grammars, Technical University of Dresden, Dresden, Germany, 1974.

Wechler, W., and V. D. Dimitrov, R-fuzzy automata, in Proceedings of the IFIPS Congress on Information Processing 74, North Holland, Amsterdam, 1974, pp. 657-660.

Wechsler, H., Applications of fuzzy logic to medical diagnosis, in Proceedings of the International Symposium on Multiple-Valued Logic, Indiana University, Bloomington, pp. 162-174.

Wee, W. G., On a Generalization of Adaptive Algorithms and Applications of the Fuzzy Set Concept to Pattern Classification (Technical Report 67-7), Department of Electrical Engineering, Purdue University, Lafayette, Indiana, 1967.

[362]
FUZZY SETS

Wee, W. G., and K. S. Fu, A formulation of fuzzy automata and its application as a model of learning systems, IEEE Trans. Syst. Sci. Cybern. SSC-5, 215-223 (1969).

Weiss, M. D., Fixed points, separation, and induced topologies for fuzzy sets, J. Math. Anal. Appl. 50, 142-150 (1975).

Wenstop, F., Applications of Linguistic Variables in the Analysis of Organizations, Ph.D. Thesis, School of Business Administration, University of California, Berkeley, 1975.

Wenstop, F., Deductive verbal models of organization, Int. J. Man-Mach. Stud. 8, 293-311 (1976).

Wheeler, S. C., Reference and vagueness, Synthese 30, 367-380 (1975).

Wong, C. K., Covering properties of fuzzy topological spaces, J. Math. Anal. Appl. 43, 697-704 (1973).

Wong, C. K., Fuzzy points and local properties of fuzzy topology, J. Math. Anal. Appl, 46, 316-328 (1974).

Wong, C. K., Fuzzy topology: Product and quotient theorems, J. Math. Anal. Appl. 45, 513-521 (1974).

Woodbury, M., and J. Clive, Clinical pure types vs. a fuzzy partition, J. Cybern. 4, 111-120 (1974).

Wright, C., On the coherence of vague predicates, Synthese 30, 325-366 (1975).

Yeh, R. T., and S. Y. Bang, Fuzzy Relations, Fuzzy Graphs, and Their Applications to Clustering Analysis (Report SESLTC-3), Institute of Computer Science and Computer Applications, University of Texas at Austin, 1974; also in Fuzzy Sets and Their Applications to Cognitive and Decision Processes (L. A. Zadeh, K. S. Fu, K. Tanaka, and M. Shimura, eds.), Academic, New York, 1975, pp. 125-149.

Zadeh, L. A., Fuzzy sets, Inf. Control 8, 338-353 (1965).

Zadeh, L. A., Fuzzy algorithms, Inf. Control 12, 94-102 (1968).

Zadeh, L. A., Probability measures of fuzzy events, J. Math. Anal. Appl. 23, 421-427 (1968).

Zadeh, L. A., Quantitative fuzzy semantics, Inf. Sci. 3, 159-176 (1971).

Zadeh, L. A., Similarity relations and fuzzy orderings, Inf. Sci. 3, 177-200 (1971).

Zadeh, L. A., Toward a theory of fuzzy systems, in Aspects of Networks and Systems Theory (R. E. Kalman and N. DeClaris, eds.), Holt, Rinehart and Winston, New York, 1971, pp. 469-490.

Zadeh, L. A., On Fuzzy Algorithms (ERL Memo M-325), University of California, Berkeley, 1972.

Zadeh, L. A., Fuzzy languages and their relation to human and machine intelligence, in Proceedings of the International Conference on Man and Computer, Bordeaux, France, Karger, Basel, 1972, pp. 130-165.

Zadeh, L. A., A fuzzy-set-theoretic interpretation of linguistic hedges, J. Cybern. 2, 4-34 (1972).

Zadeh, L. A., Outline of a new approach to the analysis of complex systems and decision processes, IEEE Trans. Syst., Man Cybern. SMC-3, 28-44 (1973).

Zadeh, L. A., Calculus of fuzzy restrictions, in Fuzzy Sets and Their Applications to Cognitive and Decision Processes (L. A. Zadeh, K. S. Fu, K. Tanaka, and M. Shimura, eds.), Academic, New York, 1975, pp. 1-39.

Zadeh, L. A., The concept of a linguistic variable and its application to approximate reasoning, Part I, Inf. Sci. 8, 199-249 (1975); Part II, Inf. Sci. 8, 301-357 (1975); Part III, Inf. Sci. 9, 43-80 (1975).

[363]
GAME THEORY

Zadeh, L. A., Fuzzy logic and approximate reasoning (in memory of Grigore Moisil), Synthese 30, 407–428 (1975).
Zadeh, L. A., A fuzzy-algorithmic approach to the definition of complex or imprecise concepts, Int. J. Man-Mach. Stud. 8, 249–291 (1976).
Zadeh, L. A., Fuzzy Sets and Their Application to Pattern Classification and Cluster Analysis (ERL Memo M-607), University of California, Berkeley, 1976.
Zadeh, L. A., The linguistic approach and its application to decision analysis, in Directions in Large Scale Systems (Y. C. Ho and S. K. Mitter, eds.), Plenum, New York, 1976, pp. 339–370.
Zadeh, L. A., K. S. Fu, K. Tanaka, and M. Shimura (eds.), Fuzzy Sets and Their Applications to Cognitive and Decision Processes, Academic, New York, 1975.
Zeleny, M., Linear Multiobjective Programming, Springer, New York, 1974.
Zimmermann, H. J., Optimization in Fuzzy Environments, Institute for Operations Research, Technical University of Aachen, Aachen, 1974.

Lotfi A. Zadeh

FUZZY SETS AND INFORMATION GRANULARITY*

L.A. Zadeh

Computer Science Division
Department of Electrical Engineering and Computer Sciences
and the Electronics Research Laboratory
University of California at Berkeley

1. Introduction

Much of the universality, elegance and power of classical mathematics derives from the assumption that real numbers can be characterized and manipulated with infinite precision. Indeed, without this assumption, it would be much less simple to define what is meant by the zero of a function, the rank of a matrix, the linearity of a transformation or the stationarity of a stochastic process.

It is well-understood, of course, that in most real-world applications the effectiveness of mathematical concepts rests on their robustness, which in turn is dependent on the underlying continuity of functional dependencies [1]. Thus, although no physical system is linear in the idealized sense of the term, it may be regarded as such as an approximation. Similarly, the concept of a normal distribution has an operational meaning only in an approximate and, for that matter, not very well-defined sense.

There are many situations, however, in which the finiteness of the resolving power of measuring or information gathering devices cannot be dealt with through an appeal to continuity. In such cases, the information may be said to be granular in the sense that the data points within a granule have to be dealt with as a whole rather than individually.

Taken in its broad sense, the concept of information granularity occurs under various guises in a wide variety of fields. In particular, it bears a close relation to the concept of aggregation in economics; to decomposition and partition--in the theory of automata and system theory; to bounded uncertainties--in optimal control [2], [3]; to locking granularity--in the analysis of concurrencies in data base management systems [4]; and to the manipulation of numbers as intervals--as in interval analysis [5]. In the present paper, however, the concept of information granularity is employed in a stricter and somewhat narrower sense which is defined in greater detail in Sec. 2. In effect, the main motivation for our approach is to define the concept of information granularity in a way that relates it to the theories of evidence of Shafer [6], Dempster [7], Smets [8], Cohen [9], Shackle [10] and others, and provides a basis for the construction of more general theories in which the evidence is allowed to be fuzzy in nature.

More specifically, we shall concern ourselves with a type of information granularity in which the data granules are characterized by propositions of the general form

$$g \triangleq X \text{ is } G \text{ is } \lambda \qquad (1.1)$$

---

*To Professor J. Kampe de Feriet.
Research supported by Naval Electronic Systems Command Contract N00039-78-G0013 and National Science Foundation Grant ENG-78-23143.

in which X is a variable taking values in a universe of discourse U, G is a fuzzy subset of U which is characterized by its membership function μ_G, and the qualifier λ denotes a fuzzy probability (or likelihood). Typically, but not universally, we shall assume that U is the real line (or R^n), G is a convex fuzzy subset of U and λ is a fuzzy subset of the unit interval. For example:

$g \triangleq$ X is small is likely

$g \triangleq$ X is not very large is very unlikely

$g \triangleq$ X is much larger than Y is unlikely

We shall not consider data granules which are characterized by propositions in which the qualifier λ is a fuzzy possibility or fuzzy truth-value.

In a general sense, a <u>body of evidence</u> or, simply, <u>evidence</u>, may be regarded as a collection of propositions. In particular, the evidence is <u>granular</u> if it consists of a collection of propositions,

$$E = \{g_1,\ldots,g_N\} \ , \tag{1.2}$$

each of which is of the form (1.1). Viewed in this perspective, Shafer's theory relates to the case where the constituent granules in (1.2) are crisp (nonfuzzy) in the sense that, in each g_i, G_i is a nonfuzzy set and λ_i is a numerical probability, implying that g_i may be expressed as

$$g_i \triangleq \text{"Prob}\{X \in G_i\} = p_i\text{"} \tag{1.3}$$

where p_i, $i = 1,\ldots,N$, is the probability that the value of X is contained in G. In the theories of Cohen and Shackle, a further restriction is introduced through the assumption that the G_i are nested, i.e., $G_1 \subset G_2 \subset \cdots \subset G_N$. As was demonstrated by Suppes and Zanotti [11] and Nguyen [12], in the analysis of evidence of the form (1.3) it is advantageous to treat E as a random relation.

Given a collection of granular bodies of evidence $E = \{E_1,\ldots,E_K\}$, one may ask a variety of questions the answers to which depend on the data resident in E. The most basic of these questions--which will be the main focus of our attention in the sequel--is the following:

Given a body of evidence $E = \{g_1,\ldots,g_N\}$ and an arbitrary fuzzy subset Q of U, what is the probability--which may be fuzzy or nonfuzzy--that X is Q? In other words, from the propositions

$$\begin{array}{l} g_1 \triangleq X \text{ is } G_1 \text{ is } \lambda_1 \\ - - - - - - - - \\ g_N \triangleq X \text{ is } G_N \text{ is } \lambda_N \end{array} \tag{1.4}$$

we wish to deduce the value of $?\lambda$ in the question

$$q \triangleq X \text{ is } Q \text{ is } ?\lambda \tag{1.5}$$

As a concrete illustration, suppose that we have the following granular information concerning the age of Judy ($X \triangleq$ Age(Judy))

$$\begin{array}{l} g_1 \triangleq \text{Judy is very young is unlikely} \\ g_2 \triangleq \text{Judy is young is likely} \\ g_3 \triangleq \text{Judy is old is very unlikely} \end{array} \tag{1.6}$$

The question is: What is the probability that Judy is not very young; or, equivalently: What is the value of $?\lambda$ in

$q \triangleq$ Judy is not very young is $?\lambda$

In cases where E consists of two or more distinct bodies of evidence, an important issue relates to the manner in which the answer to (1.5)--based on the information resident in E --may be composed from the answers based on the information resident in each of the constituent bodies of evidence $E_1,\ldots,E_K$. We shall consider this issue very briefly in Sec. 3.

In the theories of Dempster and Shafer, both the evidence and the set Q in (1.5) are assumed to be crisp, and the question that is asked is: What are the bounds on the probability λ that $X \in Q$? The lower bound, λ_*, is referred to as the lower probability and is defined by Shafer to be the degree of belief that $X \in Q$, while the upper bound, λ^*, is equated to the degree of plausibility of the proposition $X \in Q$. An extension of the concepts of lower and upper probabilities to the more general case of fuzzy granules will be described in Sec. 3.

As will be seen in the sequel, the theory of fuzzy sets and, in particular, the theory of possibility, provides a convenient conceptual framework for dealing with information granularity in a general setting. Viewed in such a setting, the concept of information granularity assumes an important role in the analysis of imprecise evidence and thus may aid in contributing to a better understanding of the complex issues arising in credibility analysis, model validation and, more generally, those problem areas in which the information needed for a decision or system performance evaluation is incomplete or unreliable.

2. Information Granularity and Possibility Distributions

Since the concept of information granularity bears a close relation to that of a possibility distribution, we shall begin our exposition with a brief review of those properties of possibility distributions which are of direct relevance to the concepts introduced in the following sections.

Let X be a variable taking values in U, with a generic value of X denoted by u. Informally, a possibility distribution, Π_X, is a fuzzy relation in U which acts as an elastic constraint on the values that may be assumed by X. Thus, if π_X is the membership function of Π_X, we have

$$\mathrm{Poss}\{X = u\} = \pi_X(u) \ , \quad u \in U \tag{2.1}$$

where the left-hand member denotes the possibility that X may take the value u and $\pi_X(u)$ is the grade of membership of u in Π_X. When used to characterize Π_X, the function π_X: $U \to [0,1]$ is referred to as a possibility distribution function.

A possibility distribution, Π_X, may be induced by physical constraints or, alternatively, it may be epistemic in nature, in which case Π_X is induced by a collection of propositions--as described at a later point in this section.

A simple example of a possibility distribution which is induced by a physical constraint is the number of tennis balls that can be placed in a metal box. In this case, X is the number in question and $\pi_X(u)$ is a measure of the degree of ease (by some specified mechanical criterion) with which u balls can be squeezed into the box.

As a simple illustration of an epistemic possibility distribution, let X be a real-valued variable and let p be the proposition

$$p \triangleq a \le X \le b$$

where [a,b] is an interval in R^1. In this case, the possibility distribution

[1]A more detailed discussion of possibility theory may be found in [13]-[15].

induced by p is the uniform distribution defined by

$$\pi_X(u) = 1 \quad \text{for} \quad a \leq u \leq b$$
$$= 0 \quad \text{elsewhere.}$$

Thus, given p we can assert that

$$\text{Poss}\{X = u\} = 1 \quad \text{for } u \text{ in } [a,b]$$
$$= 0 \quad \text{elsewhere.}$$

More generally, as shown in [16], a proposition of the form

$$p \triangleq N \text{ is } F \tag{2.2}$$

where F is a fuzzy subset of the cartesian product $U = U_1 \times \cdots \times U_n$ and N is the name of a variable, a proposition or an object, induces a possibility distribution defined by the possibility assignment equation

$$N \text{ is } F \longrightarrow \Pi_{(X_1,\ldots,X_n)} = F \tag{2.3}$$

where the symbol $\longrightarrow$ stands for "translates into," and $X \triangleq (X_1,\ldots,X_n)$ is an n-ary variable which is implicit or explicit in p. For example,

(a) $$X \text{ is small} \longrightarrow \Pi_X = \text{SMALL} \tag{2.4}$$

where SMALL, the denotation of small, is a specified fuzzy subset of $[0,\infty)$. Thus, if the membership function of SMALL is expressed as μ_{SMALL}, then (2.4) implies that

$$\text{Poss}\{X = u\} = \mu_{\text{SMALL}}(u) \ , \quad u \in [0,\infty) \ . \tag{2.5}$$

More particularly, if--in the usual notation--

$$\text{SMALL} = 1/0 + 1/1 + 0.8/2 + 0.6/3 + 0.5/4 + 0.3/5 + 0.1/6 \tag{2.6}$$

then

$$\text{Poss}\{X = 3\} = 0.6$$

and likewise for other values of u.

Similarly,

(b) $$\text{Dan is tall} \longrightarrow \Pi_{\text{Height(Dan)}} = \text{TALL} \tag{2.7}$$

where the variable Height(Dan) is implicit in the proposition "Dan is tall" and TALL is a fuzzy subset of the interval [0,220] (with the height assumed to be expressed in centimeters).

(c) $$\text{John is big} \longrightarrow \Pi_{(\text{Height(John)},\text{Weight(John)})} = \text{BIG} \tag{2.8}$$

where BIG is a fuzzy binary relation in the product space $[0,220] \times [0,150]$ (with height and weight expressed in centimeters and kilograms, respectively) and the variables $X_1 \triangleq \text{Height(John)}$, $X_2 \triangleq \text{Weight(John)}$ are implicit in the proposition "John is big."

In a more general way, the translation rules associated with the meaning representation language PRUF [16] provide a system for computing the possibility distributions induced by various types of propositions. For example

$$X \text{ is not very small} \longrightarrow \Pi_X = (\text{SMALL}^2)' \tag{2.9}$$

where $SMALL^2$ is defined by

$$\mu_{SMALL^2} = (\mu_{SMALL})^2 \tag{2.10}$$

and ' denotes the complement. Thus, (2.10) implies that the possibility distribution function of X is given by

$$\pi_X(u) = 1 - \mu_{SMALL}^2(u) \ . \tag{2.11}$$

In the case of conditional propositions of the form $p \triangleq$ If X is F then Y is G, the possibility distribution that is induced by p is a conditional possibility distribution which is defined by[2]

$$\text{If X is F then Y is G} \longrightarrow \Pi_{(Y|X)} = \bar{F}' \cup \bar{G} \tag{2.12}$$

where $\Pi_{(Y|X)}$ denotes the conditional possibility distribution of Y given X, F and G are fuzzy subsets of U and V, respectively, $\bar{F}$ and $\bar{G}$ are the cylindrical extensions of F and G in $U \times V$, $\cup$ is the union, and the conditional possibility distribution function of Y given X is expressed by

$$\pi_{(Y|X)}(v|u) = \left(1 - \mu_F(u)\right) \vee \mu_G(v) \ , \quad u \in U, \ v \in V \tag{2.13}$$

where μ_F and μ_G are the membership functions of F and G, and $\vee \triangleq \max$. In connection with (2.12), it should be noted that

$$\pi_{(Y|X)}(v|u) = \text{Poss}\{Y = v | X = u\} \tag{2.14}$$

whereas

$$\pi_{(X,Y)}(u,v) = \text{Poss}\{X = u, \ Y = v\} \ . \tag{2.15}$$

A concept which is related to that of a conditional possibility distribution is the concept of a conditional possibility measure [13]. Specifically, let Π_X be the possibility distribution induced by the proposition

$$p \triangleq X \text{ is } G \ ,$$

and let F be a fuzzy subset of U. Then, the conditional possibility measure of F with respect to the possibility distribution Π_X is defined by

$$\text{Poss}\{X \text{ is } F | X \text{ is } G\} = \sup_u \left(\mu_F(u) \wedge \mu_G(u)\right) \ . \tag{2.16}$$

It should be noted that the left-hand member of (2.16) is a set function whereas $\Pi_{(Y|X)}$ is a fuzzy relation defined by (2.12).

The foregoing discussion provides us with the necessary background for defining some of the basic concepts relating to information granularity. We begin with the concept of a fuzzy granule.

Definition. Let X be a variable taking values in U and let G be a fuzzy subset of U. (Usually, but not universally, $U = R^n$ and G is a convex fuzzy subset of U.) A fuzzy granule, g, in U is induced (or characterized) by a proposition of the form

$$g \triangleq X \text{ is } G \text{ is } \lambda \tag{2.17}$$

---

[2] There are a number of alternative ways in which $\Pi_{(Y|X)}$ may be defined in terms of F and G [17], [18], [19]. Here we use a definition which is consistent with the relation between the extended concepts of upper and lower probabilities as described in Sec. 3.

where λ is a fuzzy probability which is characterized by a possibility distribution over the unit interval. For example, if $U = R^1$, we may have

$$g \triangleq X \text{ is small is not very likely} \tag{2.18}$$

where the denotation of small is a fuzzy subset SMALL of R^1 which is characterized by its membership function μ_{SMALL}, and the fuzzy probability not very likely is characterized by the possibility distribution function

$$\pi(v) = 1 - \mu^2_{LIKELY}(v) \ , \quad v \in [0,1] \tag{2.19}$$

in which μ_{LIKELY} is the membership function of the denotation of likely and v is a numerical probability in the interval [0,1].

If the proposition $p \triangleq X$ is G is interpreted as a fuzzy event [20], then (2.17) may be interpreted as the proposition

$$\text{Prob}\{X \text{ is } G\} \text{ is } \lambda$$

which by (2.3) translates into

$$\Pi_{\text{Prob}\{X \text{ is } G\}} = \lambda \ . \tag{2.20}$$

Now, the probability of the fuzzy event $p \triangleq X$ is G is given by [20]

$$\text{Prob}\{X \text{ is } G\} = \int_U p_X(u)\mu_G(u)du \tag{2.21}$$

where $p_X(u)$ is the probability density associated with X. Thus, the translation of (2.17) may be expressed as

$$g \triangleq X \text{ is } G \text{ is } \lambda \longrightarrow \pi(p_X) = \mu_\lambda\left(\int_U p_X(u)\mu_G(u)du\right) \tag{2.22}$$

which signifies that g induces a possibility distribution of the probability distribution of X, with the possibility of the probability density p_X given by the right-hand member of (2.22). For example, in the case of (2.18), we have

$$X \text{ is small is not very likely} \longrightarrow \pi(p_X) = 1 - \mu^2_{LIKELY}\left(\int_U p_X(u)\mu_{SMALL}(u)du\right). \tag{2.23}$$

As a special case of (2.17), a fuzzy granule may be characterized by a proposition of the form

$$g \triangleq X \text{ is } G \tag{2.24}$$

which is not probability-qualified. To differentiate between the general case (2.17) and the special case (2.24), fuzzy granules which are characterized by propositions of the form (2.17) will be referred to as πp-granules (signifying that they correspond to possibility distributions of probability distributions), while those corresponding to (2.24) will be described more simply as π-granules.

A concept which we shall need in our analysis of bodies of evidence is that of a conditioned π-granule. More specifically, if X and Y are variables taking values in U and V, respectively, then a conditioned π-granule in V is characterized by a conditional proposition of the form

$$g \triangleq \text{If } X = u \text{ then } Y \text{ is } G \tag{2.25}$$

where G is a fuzzy subset of V which is dependent on u. From this definition it follows at once that the possibility distribution induced by g is defined by the possibility distribution function

$$\pi_{(Y|X)}(v|u) \triangleq \text{Poss}\{Y=v|X=u\} = \mu_G(v) \quad . \tag{2.26}$$

An important point which arises in the characterization of fuzzy granules is that the same fuzzy granule may be induced by distinct propositions, in which case the propositions in question are said to be semantically equivalent [16]. A particular and yet useful case of semantic equivalence relates to the effect of negation in (2.17) and may be expressed as ($\leftrightarrow$ denotes semantic equivalence)

$$X \text{ is } G \text{ is } \lambda \leftrightarrow X \text{ is not } G \text{ is ant } \lambda \tag{2.27}$$

where ant λ denotes the antonym of λ which is defined by

$$\mu_{\text{ant }\lambda}(v) = \mu_\lambda(1-v) \ , \quad v \in [0,1] \ . \tag{2.28}$$

Thus, the membership function of ant λ is the mirror image of that of λ with respect to the midpoint of the interval [0,1].

To verify (2.27) it is sufficient to demonstrate that the propositions in question induce the same fuzzy granule. To this end, we note that

$$\begin{aligned} X \text{ is not } G \text{ is ant } \lambda \rightarrow \pi(p_X) &= \mu_{\text{ant }\lambda}\left(\int_U p_X(u)(1-\mu_G(u))du\right) \\ &= \mu_{\text{ant }\lambda}\left(1-\int_U p_X(u)\mu_G(u)du\right) \\ &= \mu_\lambda\left(\int_U p_X(u)\mu_G(u)du\right) \end{aligned} \tag{2.29}$$

which upon comparison with (2.22) establishes the semantic equivalence expressed by (2.27).

In effect, (2.27) indicates that replacing G with its negation may be compensated by replacing λ with its antonym. A simple example of an application of this rule is provided by the semantic equivalence

$$X \text{ is small is likely} \leftrightarrow X \text{ is not small is unlikely} \tag{2.30}$$

in which unlikely is interpreted as the antonym of likely.

A concept that is related to and is somewhat weaker than that of semantic equivalence is the concept of semantic entailment [16]. More specifically, if g_1 and g_2 are two propositions such that the fuzzy granule induced by g_1 is contained in the fuzzy granule induced by g_2, then g_2 is semantically entailed by g_1 or, equivalently, g_1 semantically entails g_2. To establish the relation of containment it is sufficient to show that

$$\pi_1(p_X) \le \pi_2(p_X) \ , \quad \text{for all } p_X \tag{2.31}$$

where π_1 and π_2 are the possibilities corresponding to g_1 and g_2, respectively.

As an illustration, it can readily be established that ($\mapsto$ denotes semantic entailment)

$$X \text{ is } G \text{ is } \lambda \mapsto X \text{ is very } G \text{ is } {}^2\lambda \tag{2.32}$$

or, more concretely,

$$X \text{ is small is likely} \mapsto X \text{ is very small is } {}^2\text{likely} \tag{2.33}$$

where the left-square of λ is defined by

$$\mu_{2_\lambda}(v) = \mu_\lambda(\sqrt{v}) \ , \qquad v \in [0,1]$$

and μ_λ is assumed to be monotone nondecreasing. Intuitively, (2.32) signifies that an intensification of G through the use of the modifier very may be compensated by a dilation (broadening) of the fuzzy probability λ.

To establish (2.32), we note that

$$X \text{ is } G \text{ is } \lambda \longrightarrow \pi_1(p_X) = \mu_\lambda\left(\int_U p_X(u)\mu_G(u)du\right) \tag{2.34}$$

$$X \text{ is very } G \text{ is } {}^2\lambda \longrightarrow \pi_2(p_X) = \mu_{2_\lambda}\left(\int_U p_X(u)\mu_G^2(u)du\right) \tag{2.35}$$

$$= \mu_\lambda\left(\sqrt{\int_U p_X(u)\mu_G^2(u)du}\right) \ .$$

Now, by Schwarz's inequality

$$\sqrt{\int_U p_X(u)\mu_G^2(u)du} \geq \int_U p_X(u)\mu_G(u)du \tag{2.36}$$

and since μ_λ is monotone nondecreasing, we have

$$\pi_1(p_X) \leq \pi_2(p_X)$$

which is what we wanted to demonstrate.

3. Analysis of Granular Evidence

As was stated in the introduction, a body of evidence or, simply, evidence, E, may be regarded as a collection of propositions

$$E = \{g_1,\ldots,g_N\} \ . \tag{3.1}$$

In particular, evidence is granular if its constituent propositions are characterizations of fuzzy granules.

For the purpose of our analysis it is necessary to differentiate between two types of evidence which will be referred to as evidence of the first kind and evidence of the second kind.

Evidence of the first kind is a collection of fuzzy πp-granules of the form

$$g_i \triangleq Y \text{ is } G_i \text{ is } \lambda_i \ , \qquad i = 1,\ldots,N \tag{3.2}$$

where Y is a variable taking values in V, $G_1,\ldots,G_N$ are fuzzy subsets of V and $\lambda_1,\ldots,\lambda_N$ are fuzzy probabilities.

Evidence of the second kind is a probability distribution of conditioned π-granules of the form

$$g_i \triangleq Y \text{ is } G_i \ . \tag{3.3}$$

Thus, if X is taken to be a variable which ranges over the index set $\{1,\ldots,N\}$, then we assume to know (a) the probability distribution $P_X = \{p_1,\ldots,p_N\}$, where

$$p_i \triangleq \text{Prob}\{X = i\} \ , \qquad i = 1,\ldots,N \tag{3.4}$$

and (b) the conditional possibility distribution $\Pi_{(Y|X)}$, where

$$\Pi_{(Y|X=i)} = G_i \ , \qquad i = 1,\ldots,N \ . \tag{3.5}$$

In short, we may express evidence of the second kind in a symbolic form as

$$E = \{P_X, \Pi_{(Y|X)}\}$$

which signifies that the evidence consists of P_X and $\Pi_{(Y|X)}$, rather than P_X and $P_{(Y|X)}$ (conditional probability distribution of Y given X), which is what is usually assumed to be known in the traditional probabilistic approaches to the analysis of evidence. Viewed in this perspective, the type of evidence considered in the theories of Dempster and Shafer is evidence of the second kind in which the G_i are crisp sets and the probabilities $p_1,\ldots,p_n$ are known numerically.

In the case of evidence of the first kind, our main concern is with obtaining an answer to the following question. Given E, find the probability, λ, or, more specifically, the possibility distribution of the probability λ, that Y is Q, where Q is an arbitrary fuzzy subset of V.

In principle, the answer to this question may be obtained as follows.

First, in conformity with (2.20), we interpret each of the constituent propositions in E,

$$g_i \triangleq Y \text{ is } G_i \text{ is } \lambda_i \ , \quad i = 1,\ldots,N \tag{3.6}$$

as the assignment of the fuzzy probability λ_i to the fuzzy event $q_i \triangleq Y$ is G_i. Thus, if $p(\cdot)$ is the probability density associated with Y, then in virtue of (2.22) we have

$$\pi_i(p) = \mu_{\lambda_i}\left(\int_V p(v)\mu_{G_i}(v)dv\right) \tag{3.7}$$

where $\pi_i(p)$ is the possibility of p given g_i, and μ_{λ_i} and μ_{G_i} are the membership functions of λ_i and G_i, respectively.

Since the evidence $E = \{g_1,\ldots,g_N\}$ may be regarded as the conjunction of the propositions $g_1,\ldots,g_N$, the possibility of $p(\cdot)$ given E may be expressed as

$$\pi(p) = \pi_1(p) \wedge \cdots \wedge \pi_N(p) \tag{3.8}$$

where $\wedge \triangleq \min$. Now, for a p whose possibility is expressed by (3.8), the probability of the fuzzy event $q \triangleq X$ is Q is given by

$$\rho(p) = \int_V p(v)\mu_Q(v)dv \ . \tag{3.9}$$

Consequently, the desired possibility distribution of $\rho(p)$ may be expressed in a symbolic form as the fuzzy set [21]

$$\lambda = \int_{[0,1]} \pi(p)/\rho(p) \tag{3.10}$$

in which the integral sign denotes the union of singletons $\pi(p)/\rho(p)$.

In more explicit terms, (3.10) implies that if ρ is a point in the interval [0,1], then $\mu_\lambda(\rho)$, the grade of membership of ρ in λ or, equivalently, the possibility of ρ given λ, is the solution of the variational problem

$$\mu_\lambda(\rho) = \operatorname{Max}_p(\pi_1(p) \wedge \cdots \wedge \pi_N(p)) \tag{3.11}$$

subject to the constraint

$$\rho = \int_V p(v)\mu_Q(v)dv \ . \tag{3.12}$$

In practice, the solution of problems of this type would, in general, require both discretization and approximation, with the aim of reducing (3.11) to a computationally feasible problem in nonlinear programming. In the longer run, however, a more effective solution would be a "fuzzy hardware" implementation which would yield directly a linguistic approximation to λ from the specification of q and E.

It should be noted that if we were concerned with a special case of evidence of the first kind in which the probabilities λ_i are numerical rather than fuzzy, then we could use as an alternative to the technique described above the maximum entropy principle of Jaynes [22] or its more recent extensions [23]-[26]. In application to the problem in question, this method would first yield a probability density $p(\cdot)$ which is a maximum entropy fit to the evidence E, and then, through the use of (3.12), would produce a numerical value for λ.

A serious objection that can be raised against the use of the maximum entropy principle is that, by constructing a unique $p(\cdot)$ from the incomplete information in E, it leads to artificially precise results which do not reflect the intrinsic imprecision of the evidence and hence cannot be treated with the same degree of confidence as the factual data which form a part of the database. By contrast, the method based on the use of possibility distributions leads to conclusions whose imprecision reflects the imprecision of the evidence from which they are derived and hence are just as credible as the evidence itself.

Turning to the analysis of evidence of the second kind, it should be noted that, although there is a superficial resemblance between the first and second kinds of evidence, there is also a basic difference which stems from the fact that the fuzzy granules in the latter are π-granules which are conditioned on a random variable. In effect, what this implies is that evidence of the first kind is conjunctive in nature, as is manifested by (3.8). By contrast, evidence of the second kind is disjunctive, in the sense that the collection of propositions in E should be interpreted as the disjunctive statement: g_1 with probability λ_1 or g_2 with probability λ_2 or ... or g_N with probability λ_N.

As was stated earlier, evidence of the second kind may be expressed in the equivalent form

$$E = \{P_X, \Pi_{(Y|X)}\}$$

where X is a random variable which ranges over the index set $U = \{1,\ldots,N\}$ and is associated with a probability distribution $P_X = \{p_1,\ldots,p_N\}$; and $\Pi_{(Y|X)}$ is the conditional possibility distribution of Y given X, where Y is a variable ranging over V and the distribution function of $\Pi_{(Y|X)}$ is defined by

$$\pi_{(Y|X)}(v|i) \triangleq \text{Poss}\{Y=v|X=i\}\ , \quad i \in U,\ v \in V\ . \tag{3.13}$$

For a given value of X, X = i, the conditional possibility distribution $\Pi_{(Y|X)}$ defines a fuzzy subset of V which for consistency with (3.2) is denoted by G_i. Thus,

$$\Pi_{(Y|X=i)} = G_i\ , \quad i = 1,\ldots,N \tag{3.14}$$

and more generally

$$\Pi_{(Y|X)} = G_X\ . \tag{3.15}$$

As was pointed out earlier, the theories of Dempster and Shafer deal with a special case of evidence of the second kind in which the G_i and Q are crisp sets and the probabilities $p_1,\ldots,p_N$ are numerical. In this special case, the event $q \triangleq Y \in Q$ may be associated with two probabilities: the lower probability λ_* which is defined--in our notation--as

$$\lambda_* \triangleq \text{Prob}\{\Pi_{(Y|X)} \subset Q\} \tag{3.16}$$

and the upper probability λ^* which is defined as[3]

$$\lambda^* \triangleq \text{Prob}\{\Pi_{(Y|X)} \cap Q \neq \theta\} \quad (\theta \triangleq \text{empty set}) . \tag{3.17}$$

The concepts of upper and lower probabilities do not apply to the case where the G_i and Q are fuzzy sets. For this case, we shall define two more general concepts which are related to the modal concepts of necessity and possibility and which reduce to λ_* and λ^* when the G_i and Q are crisp.

For our purposes, it will be convenient to use the expressions sup F and inf F as abbreviations defined by[4]

$$\sup F \triangleq \sup_v \mu_F(v) , \quad v \in V \tag{3.18}$$

$$\inf F \triangleq \inf_v \mu_F(v) , \quad v \in V \tag{3.19}$$

where F is a fuzzy subset of V. Thus, using this notation, the expression for the conditional possibility measure of Q given X may be written as (see (2.16))

$$\begin{aligned} \text{Poss}\{Y \text{ is } Q|X\} &= \text{Poss}\{Y \text{ is } Q|Y \text{ is } G_X\} \\ &= \sup(Q \cap G_X) \end{aligned} \tag{3.20}$$

Since X is a random variable, we can define the expectation of Poss{Y is Q|X} with respect to X. On denoting this expectation by $E\Pi(Q)$, we have

$$\begin{aligned} E\Pi(Q) &\triangleq E_X \text{ Poss}\{Y \text{ is } Q|X\} \\ &= \sum_i p_i \sup(Q \cap G_i) \end{aligned} \tag{3.21}$$

We shall adopt the expected possibility, $E\Pi(Q)$, as a generalization of the concept of upper probability. Dually, the concept of lower probability may be generalized as follows.

First, we define the conditional certainty (or necessity) of the proposition $q \triangleq Y$ is Q given X by

$$\text{Cert}\{Y \text{ is } Q|X\} \triangleq 1 - \text{Poss}\{Y \text{ is not } Q|X\} . \tag{3.22}$$

Next, in view of the identities

$$\begin{aligned} 1 - \sup(F \cap G) &= \inf((F \cap G)') \\ &= \inf(F' \cup G') \\ &= \inf(G \Rightarrow F') \end{aligned} \tag{3.23}$$

where the implication $\Rightarrow$ is defined by (see (2.13))

$$G \Rightarrow F' \triangleq G' \cup F' \tag{3.24}$$

we can rewrite the right-hand member of (3.22) as

[3]It should be noted that we are not normalizing the definitions of λ_* and λ^*--as is done in the papers by Dempster and Shafer--by dividing the right-hand members of (3.16) and (3.17) by the probability that $\Pi_{(Y|X)}$ is not an empty set. As is pointed out in [27], the normalization in question leads to counterintuitive results.

[4]The definitions in question bear a close relation to the definitions of universal and existential quantifiers in L_{Aleph_1} logic [28].

$$\mathrm{Cert}\{Y \text{ is } Q|X\} = \inf(G_X \Rightarrow Q) \ . \tag{3.25}$$

Finally, on taking the expectation of both sides of (3.22) and (3.25), we have

$$\begin{aligned} EC(Q) &\triangleq E_X \, \mathrm{Cert}\{Y \text{ is } Q|X\} \\ &= \sum_i p_i \inf(G_i \Rightarrow Q) \\ &= 1 - E\Pi(Q') \end{aligned} \tag{3.26}$$

As defined by (3.26), the expression EC(Q), which represents the expected certainty of the conditional event (Y is $Q|X$), may be regarded as a generalization of the concept of lower probability.

The set functions $E\Pi(Q)$ and EC(Q) may be interpreted as fuzzy measures. However, in general, these measures are neither normed nor additive. Instead, $E\Pi(Q)$ and EC(Q) are, respectively, superadditive and subadditive in the sense that, for any fuzzy subsets Q_1 and Q_2 of V, we have

$$EC(Q_1 \cup Q_2) \geq EC(Q_1) + EC(Q_2) - EC(Q_1 \cap Q_2) \tag{3.27}$$

and

$$E\Pi(Q_1 \cup Q_2) \leq E\Pi(Q_1) + E\Pi(Q_2) - E\Pi(Q_1 \cap Q_2) \ . \tag{3.28}$$

It should be noted that these inequalities generalize the superadditive and subadditive properties of the measures of belief and plausibility in Shafer's theory.

The inequalities in question are easy to establish. Taking (3.28), for example, we have

$$\begin{aligned} E\Pi(Q_1 \cup Q_2) &= \textstyle\sum_i p_i \sup_v \Big((\mu_{Q_1}(v) \vee \mu_{Q_2}(v)) \wedge \mu_{G_i}(v) \Big) \\ &= \sum_i p_i \sup_v (\mu_{Q_1}(v) \wedge \mu_{G_i}(v) \vee \mu_{Q_2}(v) \wedge \mu_{G_i}(v)) \\ &= \sum_i p_i \Big(\sup_v (\mu_{Q_1}(v) \wedge \mu_{G_i}(v)) \vee \sup_v (\mu_{Q_2}(v) \wedge \mu_{G_i}(v)) \Big) \end{aligned} \tag{3.29}$$

Now, using the identity (a,b $\triangleq$ real numbers)

$$a \vee b = a + b - a \wedge b \tag{3.30}$$

the right-hand member of (3.29) may be rewritten as

$$\begin{aligned} E\Pi(Q_1 \cup Q_2) = \sum_i p_i \Big[& \sup_v (\mu_{Q_1}(v) \wedge \mu_{G_i}(v)) + \sup_v (\mu_{Q_2}(v) \wedge \mu_{G_i}(v)) \\ & - \big(\sup_v (\mu_{Q_1}(v) \wedge \mu_{G_i}(v)) \wedge \sup_v (\mu_{Q_2}(v) \wedge \mu_{G_i}(v)) \big) \Big] \end{aligned} \tag{3.31}$$

Furthermore, from the min-max inequality

$$\sup_v f(v) \wedge \sup_v g(v) \geq \sup_v (f(v) \wedge g(v)) \tag{3.32}$$

it follows that

$$\begin{aligned} & \sup_v (\mu_{Q_1}(v) \wedge \mu_{G_i}(v)) \ \wedge \ \sup_v (\mu_{Q_2}(v) \wedge \mu_{G_i}(v)) \\ & \geq \sup_v (\mu_{Q_1}(v) \wedge \mu_{Q_2}(v) \wedge \mu_{G_i}(v)) \end{aligned} \tag{3.33}$$

and hence that

$$E\Pi(Q_1 \cup Q_2) \leq \sum_i p_i \sup_v (\mu_{Q_1}(v) \wedge \mu_{G_i}(v)) + \sum_i p_i \sup_v (\mu_{Q_2}(v) \wedge \mu_{G_i}(v)) - \sum_i p_i \sup_v (\mu_{Q_1}(v) \wedge \mu_{Q_2}(v) \wedge \mu_{G_i}(v)) \quad (3.34)$$

Finally, on making use of (3.21) and the definition of $Q_1 \cap Q_2$, we obtain the inequality

$$E\Pi(Q_1 \cup Q_2) \leq E\Pi(Q_1) + E\Pi(Q_2) - E\Pi(Q_1 \cap Q_2) \quad (3.35)$$

which is what we set out to establish.

The superadditive property of $EC(Q)$ has a simple intuitive explanation. Specifically, because of data granularity, if Q_1 and Q_2 are roughly of the same size as the granules $G_1, \dots, G_N$, then $EC(Q_1)$ and $EC(Q_2)$ are likely to be small, while $E(Q_1 \cup Q_2)$ may be larger because the size of $Q_1 \cup Q_2$ is likely to be larger than that of $G_1, \dots, G_N$. For the same reason, with the increase in the relative size of Q_1 and Q_2, the effect of granularity is likely to diminish, with $EC(Q)$ tending to become additive in the limit.

In the foregoing analysis, the probabilities $p_1, \dots, p_N$ were assumed to be numerical. This, however, is not an essential restriction, and through the use of the extension principle [21], the concepts of expected possibility and expected certainty can readily be generalized, at least in principle, to the case where the probabilities in question are fuzzy or linguistic. Taking the expression for $E\Pi(Q)$, for example,

$$E\Pi(Q) = \sum_i p_i \sup(Q \cap G_i) \quad (3.36)$$

and assuming that the p_i are characterized by their respective possibility distribution functions $\pi_1, \dots, \pi_N$, the determination of the possibility distribution function of $E\Pi(Q)$ may be reduced to the solution of the following variational problem

$$\pi(z) \triangleq \operatorname{Max}_{p_1, \dots, p_N} \pi_1(p_1) \wedge \cdots \wedge \pi_N(p_N) \quad (3.37)$$

subject to

$$z = p_1 \sup(Q \cap G_1) + \cdots + p_N \sup(Q \cap G_N)$$

$$p_1 + \cdots + p_N = 1$$

which upon solution yields the possibility, $\pi(z)$, of a numerical value, z, of $E\Pi(Q)$. Then, a linguistic approximation to the possibility distribution would yield an approximate value for $\Pi_{E\Pi(Q)}$ expressed as, say, <u>not very high</u>.

As was alluded to already, a basic issue in the analysis of evidence relates to the manner in which two or more distinct bodies of evidence may be combined. In the case of evidence of the second kind, for example, let us assume for simplicity that we have two bodies of evidence of the form

$$\mathcal{E} = \{\mathcal{E}_1, \mathcal{E}_2\} \quad (3.38)$$

in which

$$\mathcal{E}_1 = \{P_{X_1}, \Pi_{(Y|X_1)}\} \quad (3.39)$$

$$\mathcal{E}_2 = \{P_{X_2}, \Pi_{(Y|X_2)}\} \quad (3.40)$$

where Y takes values in V; while X_1 and X_2 range over the index sets $U_1 = \{1, \dots, N_1\}$ and $U_2 = \{1, \dots, N_2\}$, and are associated with the joint probability distribution $P_{(X_1, X_2)}$ which is characterized by

$$p_{ij} \triangleq \operatorname{Prob}\{X_1 = i,\ X_2 = j\} . \quad (3.41)$$

For the case under consideration, the expression for the expected possibility of the fuzzy event $q \triangleq Y$ is Q given E_1 and E_2 becomes

$$E\Pi(Q) = E_{(X_1,X_2)}\ \mathrm{Poss}\{Y \text{ is } Q|(X_1,X_2)\} \tag{3.42}$$
$$= \sum_{i,j} p_{ij}\ \sup(Q \cap G_i \cap H_j)$$

where

$$\Pi_{(Y|X_1=i)} \triangleq G_i \tag{3.43}$$

and

$$\Pi_{(Y|X_2=j)} \triangleq H_j\ . \tag{3.44}$$

The rule of combination of evidence developed by Dempster [7] applies to the special case of (3.42) in which the sets G_i and H_j are crisp and X_1 and X_2 are independent. In this case, from the knowledge of $E\Pi(Q)$ (or $EC(Q)$) for each of the constituent bodies of evidence and $Q \subset V$, we can determine the probability distributions of X_1 and X_2 and then use (3.42) to obtain $E\Pi(Q)$ for the combined evidence. Although simple in principle, the computations involved in this process tend to be rather cumbersome. Furthermore, as is pointed out in [27], there are some questions regarding the validity of the normalization employed by Dempster when

$$G_i \cap H_j = \theta \tag{3.45}$$

for some i, j, and the probability of the event "Y is θ" is positive.

4. Concluding Remarks

Because of its substantial relevance to decision analysis and model validation, analysis of evidence is likely to become an important area of research in the years ahead.

It is a fact of life that much of the evidence on which human decisions are based is both fuzzy and granular. The concepts and techniques outlined in this paper are aimed at providing a basis for a better understanding of how such evidence may be analyzed in systematic terms.

Clearly, the mathematical problems arising from the granularity and fuzziness of evidence are far from simple. It may well be the case that their full solution must await the development of new types of computing devices which are capable of performing fuzzy computations in a way that takes advantage of the relatively low standards of precision which the results of such computations are expected to meet.

References and Related Papers

1. A.N. Tikhonov and V. Ya. Arsenin, Methods of Solution of Ill-Posed Problems, Nauka, Moscow, 1974.

2. S. Gutman, "Uncertain dynamical systems--a Lyapounov min-max approach," IEEE Trans. on Automatic Control, AC-24, 437-443, 1979.

3. F. Schlaepfer and F. Schweppe, "Continuous-time state estimation under distrubances bounded by convex sets," IEEE Trans. on Automatic Control, AC-17, 197-205, 1972.

4. D.R. Ries and M.R. Stonebraker, "Locking granularity revisited," ERL Memorandum M78/71, Electronics Research Laboratory, University of California, Berkeley, 1978.

5. R.E. Moore, Interval Analysis, Prentice-Hall, Englewood Cliffs, N.J., 1966.

6. G. Shafer, A Mathematical Theory of Evidence, Princeton University Press, 1976.

7. A.P. Dempster, "Upper and lower probabilities induced by a multivalued mapping," Ann. Math. Statist. 38, 325-329, 1967.

8. P. Smets, "Un modele mathematico-statistique simulant le processus du diagnostic medicale," Free University of Brussels, 1978.

9. L.J. Cohen, The Implications of Induction, Methuen, London, 1970.

10. G.L.S. Shackle, Decision, Order and Time in Human Affairs, Cambridge University Press, Cambridge, 1961.

11. P. Suppes and M. Zanotti, "On using random relations to generate upper and lower probabilities," Synthese 36, 427-440, 1977.

12. H.T. Nguyen, "On random sets and belief functions," J. Math. Anal. Appl. 65, 531-542, 1978.

13. L.A. Zadeh, "Fuzzy sets as a basis for a theory of possibility," Fuzzy Sets and Systems 1, 3-28, 1978.

14. H.T. Nguyen, "On conditional possibility distributions," Fuzzy Sets and Systems 1, 299-309, 1978.

15. E. Hisdal, "Conditional possibilities: independence and noninteraction," Fuzzy Sets and Systems 1, 283-297, 1978.

16. L.A. Zadeh, "PRUF--a meaning representation language for natural languages," Int. J. Man-Machine Studies 10, 395-460, 1978.

17. M. Mizumoto, S. Fukame and K. Tanaka, "Fuzzy reasoning methods by Zadeh and Mamdani, and improved methods," Proc. Third Workshop on Fuzzy Reasoning, Queen Mary College, London, 1978.

18. B.S. Sembi and E.H. Mamdani, "On the nature of implication in fuzzy logic," Proc. 9th International Symposium on Multiple-Valued Logic, Bath, England, 143-151, 1979.

19. W. Bandler and L. Kohout, "Application of fuzzy logics to computer protection structures," Proc. 9th International Symposium on Multiple-Valued Logic, Bath, England, 200-207, 1979.

20. L.A. Zadeh, "Probability measures of fuzzy events," J. Math. Anal. Appl. 23, 421-427, 1968.

21. L.A. Zadeh, "The concept of a linguistic variable and its application to approximate reasoning, Part I," Information Sciences 8, 199-249, 1975; Part II, Information Sciences 8, 301-357, 1975; Part III, Information Sciences 9, 43-80, 1975.

22. E.T. Jaynes, "Information theory and statistical mechanics," Parts I and II, Physical Review 106, 620-630; 108, 171-190, 1957.

23. S. Kullback, Information Theory and Statistics, John Wiley, New York, 1959.

24. M. Tribus, Rational Descriptions, Decisions and Designs, Pergamon Press, New York, 1969.

25. J.E. Shore and R.W. Johnson, "Axiomatic derivation of the principle of maximum entropy and the principle of minimum cross-entropy," NRL Memorandum Report 3-898, Naval Research Laboratory, Washington, D.C., 1978.

26. P.M. Williams, "Bayesian conditionalization and the principle of minimum information," School of Mathematical and Physical Sciences, The University of Sussex, England, 1978.

27. L.A. Zadeh, "On the validity of Dempster's rule of combination of evidence," Memorandum M79/24, Electronics Research Laboratory, University of California, Berkeley, 1979.

28. N. Rescher, Many-Valued Logic, McGraw-Hill, New York, 1969.

29. J. Kampé de Feriet and B. Forte, "Information et probabilité," Comptes Rendus Acad. Sci. A-265, 110-114, 142-146, 350-353, 1967.

30. M. Sugeno, "Theory of fuzzy integrals and its applications," Tokyo Institute of Technology, 1974.

31. T. Terano and M. Sugeno, "Conditional fuzzy measures and their applications," in Fuzzy Sets and Their Application to Cognitive and Decision Processes (L.A. Zadeh, K.S. Fu, K. Tanaka and M. Shimura, eds.), 151-170, 1975.

32. E. Sanchez, "On possibility-qualification in natural languages," Memorandum M77/28, Electronics Research Laboratory, University of California, Berkeley, 1977.

33. P.M. Williams, "On a new theory of epistemic probability (review of G. Shafer: A Mathematical Theory of Evidence)," Brit. J. for the Philosophy of Science 29, 375-387, 1978.

34. P. Suppes, "The measurement of belief," J. Roy. Statist. Soc. B 36, 160-175, 1974.

35. K.M. Colby, "Simulations of belief systems," in Computer Models of Thought and Language (R.C. Schank and K.M. Colby, eds.), W. Freeman, San Francisco, 1973.

36. B.C. Bruce, "Belief systems and language understanding," N.I.H. Report CBM-TR-41, Rutgers University, 1975.

37. R.P. Abelson, "The structure of belief systems," in Computer Models of Thought and Language (R.C. Schank and K.M. Colby, eds.), W. Freeman, San Francisco, 1973.

38. R.D. Rosenkrantz, Inference, Method and Decision, D. Reidel, Dordrecht, 1977.

39. N. Rescher, Plausible Reasoning, Van Gorcum, Amsterdam, 1976.

40. A. Tversky and D. Kahneman, "Judgment under uncertainty: heuristics and biases," Science 185, 1124-1131, 1974.

41. G. Banon, "Distinctions between several types of fuzzy measures," Proc. Int. Colloquium on the Theory and Applications of Fuzzy Sets, University of Marseille, Marseille, 1978.

42. I.J. Good, "Subjective probability as the measure of a non-measurable set," in Logic, Methodology and Philosophy of Science: Proceedings of the 1960 International Congress (E. Nagel, P. Suppes and A. Tarski, eds.), Stanford University Press, 1962.

LIAR'S PARADOX AND TRUTH-QUALIFICATION PRINCIPLE*

by

L.A. Zadeh

1. Introduction. Stated in its "naked" and most elementary form, Liar's paradox arises as a result of a self-referential definition of a proposition p by the assertion

$$(1) \qquad p \triangleq p \text{ is false}$$

where the symbol $\triangleq$ stands for "is defined to be."

There is a voluminous literature dealing with various issues relating to self-referential definitions of the form (1). The analyses of Liar's paradox which are particularly relevant to that presented in this note are those of Bochvar [1], van Fraassen [13], Skyrms [11], Kearns [7], Herzberger [5], Martin [8], Chihara [2], Pollock [9], Swiggart [12] and Haack [4].

Our approach to Liar's paradox is in the spirit of approaches employing three-valued logic, but is more general in that (1) is treated as a special case of a self-referential definition in fuzzy logic, FL, [14], [15], [16], [3] having the form

$$(2) \qquad p \triangleq p \text{ is } \tau$$

where τ is a truth-value whose denotation is a fuzzy subset of the set of truth-values of Lukasiewicz's L_{Aleph_1} logic,[1] and p is a proposition whose meaning is characterized by a possibility distribution -- which is induced by p -- over a universe of discourse U. The manner in which the concept of a possibility distribution may be employed to characterize the meaning of p is described in **2**.

*Research supported by the National Science Foundation Grant MCS77-07568.

The principle of truth-qualification in fuzzy logic serves to provide a mechanism for the computation of the possibility distribution induced by the proposition "p is τ" from the knowledge of the possibility distributions induced by p and τ. By employing this principle, the self-referential definition (2) may be translated into a fixed-point equation which upon solution yields the possibility distribution of p for a given τ. As shown in 2, this solution is not, in general, an admissible proposition in two-valued logic. Furthermore, for certain τ, the solution does not exist, leading in the special case of (1) to Liar's paradox.

The transformation of a self-referential definition of the form (2) into a fixed-point equation whose solution is the possibility distribution of p has the effect of clarifying the basic issues arising in Liar's paradox and, perhaps, supplies its resolution. The basic ideas of the method by which (2) is transformed into a fixed-point equation are described in the following section.

2. Possibility distributions, truth-qualification principle and Liar's paradox

Our analysis of Liar's paradox is based in an essential way on the concept of a possibility distribution.[2] Informally, if X is a variable taking values in a universe of discourse U, then by a possibility distribution, Π_X, which is associated with X, is meant a fuzzy subset of U which plays the role of an elastic constraint on the values that may be assumed by X. Thus, if u is a point in U and $\mu_X(u)$ is the grade of membership of u in Π_X, then the possibility that X may take the value u is a number in the interval [0,1], denoted by $\pi_X(u)$, which is numerically equal to $\mu_X(u)$. The function $\pi_X: U \rightarrow [0,1]$ is termed the possibility distribution function, and a variable which is associated with a possibility distribution is called a fuzzy variable. Thus, if X is a fuzzy variable, we have, by definition,

$$\text{Poss}\{X = u\} = \pi_X(u) \tag{3}$$

where π_X is the possibility distribution function which characterizes Π_X.

The elastic constraint on the values of X may be physical or epistemic in nature. For example, if X represents the number of tennis balls that may be squeezed into a metal box, then Π_X is determined by physical constraints. On the other hand, if X is characterized by the proposition "X is small," where, SMALL, the denotation of small, is a fuzzy subset of the interval $[0,\infty)$, then Π_X is an epistemic possibility distribution such that $\pi_X(u)$ -- the degree of possibility or, simply, the possibility that $X = u$ -- is equal to $\mu_{SMALL}(u)$, the grade of membership of u in SMALL. More generally, if p is a proposition of the form

$$p \triangleq X \text{ is } F$$

where X takes values in U and F is a fuzzy subset of U, then we write

$$X \text{ is } F \rightarrow \Pi_X = F \tag{4}$$

where the arrow stands for "translates into" and the right-hand member of (4) constitutes a possibility assignment equation. Equation (4) implies that Π_X is induced by the proposition "X is F" and that

$$\pi_X(u) \triangleq \text{Poss}\{X = u\} = \mu_F(u) \tag{5}$$

where $\mu_F: U \rightarrow [0,1]$ is the membership function which characterizes F.

4

In our analysis of Liar's paradox, we shall be concerned with propositions of the general form $p \triangleq N$ is F, where F is a fuzzy subset of the cartesian product $U_1 \times \cdots \times U_n$ of a collection of universes of discourse $U_1, \ldots, U_n$, and N is the name of an object, a variable or a proposition. In this case, the translation of p assumes the more general form

$$(6) \qquad N \text{ is } F \rightarrow \Pi_{(X_1,\ldots,X_n)} = F$$

where $X = (X_1,\ldots,X_n)$ is an n-ary variable which is implicit or explicit in N, with X_i taking values in U_i, $i = 1,\ldots,n$. To illustrate:

$$(7) \qquad \text{Naomi is young} \rightarrow \Pi_{\text{Age(Naomi)}} = \text{YOUNG}$$

where the variable Age(Naomi) is implicit in the left-hand member of (7) and YOUNG is a fuzzy subset of the interval [0,100]. Similarly,

$$(8) \qquad \text{John is big} \rightarrow \Pi_{(\text{Height(John)},\text{Weight(John)})} = \text{BIG}$$

where the variables Height(John) and Weight(John) are implicit, and BIG is a fuzzy subset of the product space $[0,200] \times [0,100]$ (with the height and weight assumed to be expressed in centimeters and kilograms, respectively). In general, then, a proposition of the form $p \triangleq N$ is F induces a possibility distribution of a variable $X = (X_1,\ldots,X_n)$ which is implicit or explicit in N, with F defining the distribution in question. In this sense, the meaning of the proposition "N is F" is defined by the possibility assignment equation (6), which is an instance of an expression in the meaning representation language PRUF.[3]

An important aspect of fuzzy logic relates to the ways in which the meaning of a proposition may be modified through the employment of (a) modifiers such as not, very, more or less, somewhat, etc.; and (b) qualifiers exemplified by true, false, quite true, very likely, quite possible, etc. In particular, in the case of modifiers, the pertinent rule may be stated as follows:

If m is a modifier and the translation of $p \triangleq N$ is F is of the form

(9) $$N \text{ is } F \rightarrow \Pi_X = F$$

then the translation of the modified proposition $p^\dagger = N$ is mF is given by

(10) $$N \text{ is } mF \rightarrow \Pi_X = F^\dagger$$

where $F^\dagger$ is a modification of F. In particular,

(a) if $m \triangleq$ not then

(11) $$F^\dagger = F' = \text{complement of } F ,$$

(12) i.e., $$\mu_{F'}(u) = 1 - \mu_F(u) , \quad u \in U$$

(b) if $m \triangleq$ very then[4]

(13) $$F^\dagger = F^2 ,$$

(14) i.e., $$\mu_{F^\dagger}(u) = (\mu_F(u))^2 , \quad u \in U$$

and (c) if $m =$ more or less, then

(15) $$F^\dagger = \sqrt{F} ,$$

(16) i.e., $$\mu_{F^\dagger}(u) = \sqrt{\mu_F(u)} , \quad u \in U .$$

6

The main point at issue in the case of Liar's paradox is the manner in which the meaning of a proposition is affected by truth-qualification. In this connection, let τ denote a linguistic truth-value, e.g., true, false, very true, not quite true, more or less true, etc., with the understanding that (a) the denotation of τ is a possibility distribution Π_τ over the unit interval [0,1], and (b) once Π_{true} is specified, the denotation of τ may be computed in terms of the denotation of true through the application of a semantic rule [16]. For example, if the denotation of true is Π_{true}, then the denotation of not very true is expressed by

(17) $$\Pi_{not\ very\ true} = (\Pi^2_{true})'$$

Similarly, the denotation of false, which is the antonym of true, is defined by

(18) $$\pi_{false}(v) = \pi_{true}(1-v)\ , \quad 0 \leq v \leq 1$$

where π_{false} and π_{true} are the possibility distribution functions of false and true, respectively.

Within the conceptual framework of fuzzy logic, the notion of truth-value serves, in the main, to provide a measure of the compatibility of possibility distributions. More specifically, if (p,r) is an ordered pair of propositions such that p and r induce the possibility distributions Π^p and Π^r, respectively, then the truth-value of p relative to the reference proposition r is defined as the compatibility of Π^p with Π^r, which in turn is defined by the equation

(19) $$\mathrm{Comp}(\Pi^p/\Pi^r) = \pi_p(\Pi^r)$$

7

where π_p is the possibility distribution function characterizing Π^p and the right-hand member of (19) expresses a possibility distribution whose possibility distribution function is given by [15]

$$\pi_\tau(v) = \mathrm{Sup}_u\ \pi_r(u)\ , \quad u \in U \tag{20}$$

subject to

$$v = \pi_p(u)\ , \quad v \in [0,1]\ .$$

The content of the definitions expressed by (19) and (20) may be stated more transparently in the form of an assertion which for convenience will be referred to as the truth-qualification principle. More specifically, let π_τ denote the possibility distribution function of a truth-value τ, and let Π^p be the possibility distribution induced by a proposition p over a universe of discourse U.[5] Then the truth-qualification principle asserts that:

(a) The possibility distribution, Π^q, induced by the truth-qualified proposition q,

$$q \triangleq p \text{ is } \tau\ , \tag{21}$$

is given by

$$\pi_q(u) = \pi_\tau(\pi_p(u))\ , \quad u \in U \tag{22}$$

where π_p and π_q are the possibility distribution functions of Π^p and Π^q, respectively.

(b) Proposition q is semantically equivalent[6] to the reference proposition r, that is,

8

(23) $$p \text{ is } \tau \leftrightarrow r$$

where r is the proposition with respect to which the truth-value of p is τ.

As a simple illustration of (22) and (23), consider the propositions:

$p \triangleq$ Susan is young

$p \triangleq$ Susan is young is very true

where young and true are defined by

(24) $$\pi_{young}(u) = (1 + (\frac{u}{25})^2)^{-1}, \quad u \geq 0$$

(25) $$\pi_{true}(v) = (1 + (\frac{1-v}{0.3})^2)^{-1}, \quad 0 \leq v \leq 1$$

Then by (14)

(26) $$\pi_{very\ true}(v) = (\pi_{true}(v))^2$$

and by (22)

(27) $$\pi_q(u) = (1 + (\frac{1 - (1 + (\frac{u}{25})^2)^{-1}}{0.3})^2)^{-2}$$

which may be roughly approximated as

(28) $$\pi_q(u) \cong (\pi_{young}(u))^2$$

Thus, the proposition "Susan is young" has the truth-value very true with respect to the reference proposition r whose possibility distribution function is expressed by (27) and which is approximately semantically equivalent to "Susan is very young."

To apply the truth-qualification principle to Liar's paradox, consider a proposition p which is defined self-referentially as

(29) $$p \triangleq p \text{ is } \tau$$

with the understanding that the denotation of the truth-value τ is a possibility distribution over the unit interval, and that p induces a possibility distribution Π^p over a universe of discourse U.

On applying (22) to (29), we find that the possibility distribution functions associated with p and τ must satisfy the identity

(30) $$\pi_p(u) = \pi_\tau(\pi_p(u)) \ , \quad u \in U$$

which implies that π_p is a fixed point of the mapping $\pi_\tau : [0,1] \rightarrow [0,1]$.

From (30) it follows at once that when

(31) $$\pi_\tau(v) = v \ , \quad v \in [0,1]$$

we have, for all p,

(32) $$p \text{ is } \tau \leftrightarrow p$$

The possibility distribution described by (31) defines a <u>unitary</u> truth-value which is denoted as u-true. Then,

(33) $$p \text{ is u-true} \leftrightarrow p$$

which in two-valued logic corresponds to

(34) $$p \text{ is true} \leftrightarrow p$$

The antonym of u-true is u-false, which is defined by

(35) $$\pi_{\text{u-false}}(v) = 1 - v \ , \quad v \in [0,1] \ .$$

We are now ready to raise the question "What is the proposition which is defined self-referentially by

(36) $$p \triangleq p \text{ is u-false ? "}$$

On applying (30) to (36), we have

(37) $$\pi_p(u) = 1 - \pi_p(u) \ , \quad u \in U$$

which implies that

(38) $$\pi_p(u) = 0.5 \ , \quad u \in U \ .$$

Thus, the proposition which satisfies the self-referential definition of Liar's paradox is characterized by a uniform possibility distribution which is expressed by (38). It should be noted that p is not a proposition in two-valued logic.

In a similar vein, we may consider propositions which are defined self-referentially by strengthened or weakened forms of (36), e.g.,

(39) (a) $$p \triangleq p \text{ is very u-false}$$

(40) (b) $$q \triangleq q \text{ is more or less u-false}$$

In this case, on making use of (14), (16) and (30), we deduce

(41) $$\pi_p(u) = (1 - \pi_p(u))^2$$

and

(42) $$\pi_q(u) = \sqrt{1 - \pi_q(u)}$$

which lead, respectively, to the solutions

(43) $$\pi_p(u) = \frac{3-\sqrt{5}}{2}, \quad u \in U$$
$$\cong 0.38$$

and

(44) $$\pi_q(u) = \frac{-1+\sqrt{5}}{2}, \quad u \in U$$
$$\cong 0.62$$

More generally, if in (29) we set

$$\tau \triangleq \text{false}$$

where <u>false</u> is interpreted as a specified possibility distribution over the unit interval, then (29) becomes

(45) $$p \triangleq p \text{ is false}$$

and the corresponding fixed-point equation reads

(46) $$\pi_p(u) = \pi_{false}(\pi_p(u)), \quad u \in U,$$

where π_{false} is the possibility distribution function which characterizes <u>false</u>.

Sufficient conditions for (45) to have a non-null solution are: (i) $\pi_{false}(0) > 0$ and (ii) π_{false} is continuous. Furthermore, if π_{false} is monotone non-increasing -- which is a property that the denotation of <u>false</u> would normally be expected to have -- the solution of (45) is unique. In general, this unique solution does not define an admissible proposition in two-valued logic.

It is easy to construct a truth-value, τ, for which the fixed-point equation (30) does not have a solution other than the null solution

(47) $$\pi_p(u) \equiv 0 \ , \quad u \in U$$

For example,

(48) $$\pi_\tau(v) = v^2 \ , \quad 0 \leq v \leq 0.5$$
$$= (1-v)^2 \ , \quad 0.5 < v < 1$$

or, more compactly,

(49) $$\pi_\tau(v) = \mathrm{Min}(v^2,(1-v)^2) \ , \quad 0 \leq v \leq 1$$

which represents the linguistic truth-value

(50) $$\tau = \text{very u-true and very u-false}$$

In this case, the only solution of (30) is the null solution (47). Furthermore, (30) has no solution when π_τ is discontinuous at, say, $v = \beta$, $0 < \beta < 1$, and

$$\pi_\tau(v) > v \ , \quad 0 \leq v < \beta$$
$$\pi_\tau(v) < v \ , \quad \beta < v \leq 1$$

In such cases, then, it is the non-existence of a solution of the fixed-point equation (30) that leads to paradoxes of the Liar and strengthened Liar types.

In summary, the application of truth-qualification principle to a self-referential definition of the form

$$p \triangleq p \text{ is } \tau$$

where τ is a truth-value whose denotation is a possibility distribution over [0,1], leads to the result that π_p, the possibility distribution function which is induced by p, is a solution of the fixed-point equation

(52) $$\pi_p(u) = \pi_\tau(\pi_p(u)) \ , \quad u \in U$$

13

In general, the solution of this equation is a uniform possibility distribution characterized by a possibility distribution function of the form

$$\pi_p(u) = \alpha , \quad u \in U$$

where α is a constant in the interval [0,1] which is determined by τ. For some τ, however, (52) does not have a solution, in which case p does not exist, leading to the Liar and related paradoxes.

Notes

[1]More generally, the denotation of a truth-value in fuzzy logic may be a fuzzy subset of the set of truth-values of a multi-valued logic which serves as a base logic for the fuzzy logic [16].

[2]In contrast to the concept of possibility in modal logic and possible world semantics [6],[10], the possibilities associated with a possibility distribution take values in the interval [0,1] or, more generally, in a partially ordered set. The theory of possibility which is based on the concept of a possibility distribution parallels the theory of probability but, unlike the latter, is not rooted in repeated experimentation or subjective perception of likelihood. A preliminary exposition of possibility theory may be found in [18].

[3]PRUF is a relation-manipulating language which is based on the theory of fuzzy sets and, more particularly, the theory of possibility [17]. An expression in PRUF is, in general, a procedure which computes a possibility distribution or a fuzzy relation. One of the important uses of PRUF relates to the precisiation of meaning of utterances in a natural language. As a language, PRUF is considerably more expressive than first-order predicate calculus and, in particular, allows the use of fuzzy quantifiers exemplified

by many, most, few, several, etc.; fuzzy truth-values, e.g., very true, more or less true, quite false, etc.; fuzzy probabilities, e.g., likely, unlikely, very unlikely, etc.; and fuzzy possibilities, e.g., quite possible, almost impossible, etc.

[4]The expressions for $F^{\dagger}$ corresponding to m = very and m = more or less should be regarded as default definitions, i.e. standardized definitions which, when necessary, may be replaced by other more elaborate or context-dependent characterizations of $F^{\dagger}$ as a function of F.

[5]In the special case where τ is a numerical truth-value, say $\tau = \alpha$, $\alpha \in [0,1]$, the possibility distribution of τ is expressed as $\pi_{\tau}(v) = 1$ for $v = \alpha$, $\pi_{\tau}(v) = 0$ for $v \neq \alpha$. In this case, it is not merely possible but certain that α is the value of τ.

[6]Semantic equivalence of q and r, denoted as $q \leftrightarrow r$, implies and is implied by the equality $\Pi^q = \Pi^r$.

References

[1] Bochvar, D. A., "On a three-valued calculus and its application in the analysis of the paradoxes of the extended functional calculus," *Matematicheskii Sbornik*, n.s. 4, vol. 46 (1938), pp. 287-308.

[2] Chihara, C. S., "A diagnosis of the Liar and other semantical vicious circle paradoxes," in: G. Roberts (ed.), *The Work of Bertrand Russell*, Allen and Unwin, London (1976).

[3] Gaines, B. R., "Foundations of fuzzy reasoning," *Int. J. of Man-Machine Studies*, vol. 6 (1975), pp. 623-668.

[4] Haack, S., *Philosophy of Logics*, Cambridge University Press, Cambridge (1978).

[5] Herzberger, H. G., "Truth and modality in semantically closed languages," in: R. L. Martin (ed.), *The Paradox of the Liar*, Yale University Press, New Haven (1970), pp. 25-46.

[6] Hughes, G. E. and M. J. Cresswell, *An Introduction to Modal Logic*, Methuen, London (1968).

15

[7] Kearns, J. T., "Some remarks prompted by van Fraassen's paper," in: R. L. Martin (ed.), *The Paradox of the Liar*, Yale University Press, New Haven (1970), pp. 47-58.

[8] Martin, R. L., "A category solution to the Liar," in R. L. Martin (ed.), *The Paradox of the Liar*, Yale University Press, New Haven (1970), pp. 91-111.

[9] Pollock, J. L., "The truth about truth: A reply to Brian Skyrms," in: R. L. Martin (ed.), *The Paradox of the Liar*, Yale University Press, New Haven (1970), pp. 79-89.

[10] Rescher, N., *A Theory of Possibility*, University of Pittsburgh Press, Pittsburgh.

[11] Skyrms, B., "Return of the Liar: Three-valued logic and the concept of truth," *American Philosophical Quarterly*, vol. 7 (1970), pp. 153-161.

[12] Swiggart, P., "Domain restrictions in standard deductive logic," *Notre Dame Journal of Formal Logic*, vol. 20 (1979), pp. 115-129.

[13] van Fraassen, B. C., "Truth and paradoxical consequences," in R. L. Martin (ed.), *The Paradox of the Liar*, Yale University Press, New Haven (1970), pp. 13-23.

[14] Zadeh, L. A., "Fuzzy logic and approximate reasoning (in memory of Grigore Moisil)," *Synthese*, vol. 30 (1975), pp. 407-428.

[15] Zadeh, L. A., "The concept of a linguistic variable and its application to approximate reasoning. Part I," *Information Sciences*, vol. 8 (1975), pp. 119-249; Part II, *Information Sciences*, vol. 8 (1975), pp. 301-357; Part III, *Information Sciences*, vol. 9 (1975), pp. 43-80.

[16] Zadeh, L. A., "Local and fuzzy logics" (with R. E. Bellman), in: J. M. Dunn and G. Epstein (eds.), *Modern Uses of Multiple-Valued Logic*, D. Reidel, Dordrecht (1977), pp. 103-165.

[17] Zadeh, L. A., "PRUF--a meaning representation language for natural languages," *Int. J. of Man-Machine Studies*, vol. 10 (1978), pp. 395-460.

[18] Zadeh, L. A., "Fuzzy sets as a basis for a theory of possibility," *Fuzzy Sets and Systems*, vol. 1 (1978), pp. 3-28.

University of California
Berkeley, California

FUZZY SYSTEMS THEORY: *A Framework for the Analysis of Humanistic Systems*

Lotfi A. Zadeh

During the past decade the focus of research in systems theory has shifted increasingly toward the analysis of large-scale systems in which human judgment, perception, and emotions play an important role. Such *humanistic* systems are typified by socioeconomic systems, transportation systems, environmental control systems, food production systems, education systems, health care-delivery systems, criminal justice systems, information dissemination systems, and the like. The growing involvement of systems theorists in the analysis of large-scale systems—a trend that became discernible in the early sixties (Zadeh, 1962)—is a logical consequence of two concurrent developments: (1) the increasing interdependence of all sectors of modern industrial society and (2) the advent of powerful computers that make it possible to quantify, simulate, and analyze the behavior of systems involving hundreds and even thousands of interrelated variables.

Despite the widespread use of systems-theoretic methods in the modeling of large-scale systems, serious questions have been raised regarding the applicability of systems theory to the analysis of humanistic and, especially, socioeconomic

Research for this paper was supported by the National Science Foundation, Grants ENG76-84522 and MC76-06693.

Reprinted, with permission, from *Systems Methodology in Social Science Research*, edited by R. Cavallo, pp. 25–41. 25

systems. Hoos (1962), Berlinski (1976), and others have argued that systems analysis techniques are frequently misapplied, and that the armamentarium of system theorists has little, if anything, that is of value in attacking the extremely complex problems that arise in the analysis of large-scale systems that are imbued with uncertainty and imprecision.

As is frequently the case, the debate between systems theorists and their critics is not susceptible of definitive resolution. Personally, I tend to sympathize with the critics when they attack the mystique of systems analysis and deflate its exaggerated claims. On the other hand, I believe that, intrinsically, systems theory is a discipline of great potential importance and that, in the years to come, it will develop an effective body of concepts and techniques not only for the analysis of mechanistic systems—as it has done in the past—but, more important, for the analysis of humanistic systems in which the relations between system variables are too complex for description by differential, integral, or differential equations.

The systems theory of the future—the systems theory that will be applicable to the analysis of humanistic systems—is certain to be quite different in spirit as well as in substance from systems theory as we know it today. I will take the liberty of referring to it as *fuzzy systems theory* because I believe that its distinguishing characteristic will be a conceptual framework for dealing with a key aspect of humanistic systems—namely, the pervasive fuzziness of almost all phenomena that are associated with their external as well as internal behavior.

A rudimentary sketch of a conceptual framework for fuzzy systems theory has been presented in Zadeh (1973). A semantic point that is in need of clarification at this juncture is that fuzzy systems theory is not merely a theory of fuzzy systems, as described in Zadeh (1971), Negoita and Ralescu (1975), and other papers in the literature. Rather, it is a theory that allows an assertion about a system to be a fuzzy proposition (e.g., "System S is slightly nonlinear"). In this sense, then, fuzzy systems theory is not so much a precise theory of fuzzy systems as it is a fuzzy theory of both fuzzy and nonfuzzy systems. What this implies is that an assertion in fuzzy systems theory is normally not a theorem but a proposition that has a high degree of truth and, in addition, is informative in relation to a stated question.

At this juncture, fuzzy systems theory is not as yet an existing theory whose exposition can be found in the literature. What we have at present are merely the foundations for such a theory and a rough sketch of its structure. In what follows I shall attempt to convey my perception of some of the basic ideas that underlie fuzzy systems theory—ideas that, on further development, may eventually lead to a unified body of concepts and techniques for the analysis of humanistic systems.

BASIC CONCEPTS

Two related concepts are likely to play important roles in fuzzy systems theory: (1) the concept of a linguistic variable (Zadeh, 1973, 1975*a*) and (2) the concept of a fuzzy number (Zadeh, 1975*a*; Mizumoto and Tanaka, 1976; Nahmias, 1976; Jain, 1976*a*; Dubois and Prade, 1978). As its name implies, a *linguistic variable* is a variable whose values are expressed not as numbers but as words or sentences in a natural or synthetic language. For example, when the height of a person is characterized as not very tall, *not very tall* may be viewed as a linguistic value of the linguistic variable *Height.* Similarly, *quite high* is a linguistic value of the linguistic variable *Intelligence,* and *quite attractive* is a linguistic value of the linguistic variable *Appearance.*

Clearly, the use of words in place of numbers implies a low degree of precision in the characterization of the value of a variable. In some instances we elect to be imprecise because we do not need a higher degree of precision. In most cases, however, the imprecision is forced on us by the fact that there are no units of measurement for the attributes of an object and no quantitative criteria for representing the values of such attributes as points on an anchored scale.

Viewed in this perspective, the concept of a linguistic variable may be regarded as a device for systematizing the use of words or sentences in a natural or synthetic language for the purpose of characterizing the values of variables and describing their interrelations. In this role the concept of a linguistic variable serves a basic function in fuzzy systems theory, both in the representation of values of variables and in the characterization of truth-values of fuzzy propositions.

For the purpose of a brief exposition of the concept of a linguistic variable, we can conveniently focus our attention on a particular linguistic variable, say, Age, which may be viewed both as a numerical variable ranging over, say, the interval [0,150], and as a linguistic variable that can take the values *young, not young, very young, not very young, quite young, old, not very young and not very old,* and so forth. Each of these values may be interpreted as a label of a fuzzy subset of the universe of discourse $U = [0,150]$, whose base variable, u, is the generic numerical value of Age.

Typically, the values of a linguistic variable such as Age are built up of one or more *primary terms,* which are the labels of *primary fuzzy sets,*[1] together with a collection of modifiers and connectives that allow a composite linguistic value to be generated from the primary terms. Usually, the number of such terms is two, with one being an antonym of the other. For example, in the case of Age, the primary terms are *young* and *old,* with *old* being the antonym of *young.*

A basic assumption underlying the concept of a linguistic variable is that the meaning of the primary terms is context dependent, while the meaning of the modifiers and connectives is not. Furthermore, once the meaning of the primary terms is specified (or "calibrated") in a given context, the meaning of composite terms such as *not very young, not very young and not very old,* and so on, may be computed by the application of a semantic rule.

Typically, the *term set*—that is, the set of linguistic values of a linguistic variable—comprises the values generated from each of the primary terms, together with the values generated from various combinations of the primary terms. For example, in the case of Age, the following is a partial list of the linguistic values of Age:

young	old	not young nor old
not young	not old	not very young and not very old
very young	very old	young or old
not very young	not very old	not young or not old
quite young	quite old	etc.
more or less young	more or less old	
extremely young	extremely old	
etc.	etc.	

What is important to observe is that most linguistic variables have the same basic structure as Age. For example, on replacing *young* with *tall* and *old* with *short,* we obtain the list of linguistic values of the linguistic variable Height. The same applies to the linguistic variables Weight (*heavy* and *light*), Appearance (*beautiful* and *ugly*), Speed (*fast* and *slow*), Truth (*true* and *false*), and so forth, with the words in parentheses representing the primary terms.

As is shown in Zadeh (1975*a*), a linguistic variable may be characterized by an attributed grammar (Knuth, 1968; Lewis, Rosenkrantz, and Stearns, 1976) that generates the term set of the variable and provides a simple procedure for computing the meaning of a composite linguistic value in terms of the primary fuzzy sets that appear in its constituents. For example, if the meaning of *young* is characterized by a membership function such as

$$\mu_{\text{young}}(u) = \left[1 + \left(\frac{u}{30}\right)^2\right]^{-1}, \qquad u \in [0, 150],$$

then the meaning of the linguistic value *not very young* can readily be computed to be

$$\begin{aligned}\mu_{\text{not very young}} &= 1 - \mu^2_{\text{young}}(u)\\ &= 1 - \left[1 + \left(\frac{u}{30}\right)^2\right]^{-2}.\end{aligned}$$

Similarly, the meaning of any linguistic value of *Age* may be expressed in terms of the membership functions of the primary fuzzy sets *young* and *old*.

The concept of a linguistic variable plays a particularly important role in fuzzy logic (Zadeh, 1975*b*; Bellman and Zadeh, 1977), where it serves to give an approximate characterization of the truth-value of a proposition (e.g., as *true, not true, very true, not very true,* and so on) or as the value of a quantifier (e.g., *many, most, few, almost all,* and so on). We shall have more to say about this application at a later point.

A concept that is closely related to that of a linguistic variable is the concept of a *fuzzy number* (Zadeh, 1975*a*), which is usually taken to be a convex fuzzy subset of the real line, R'. Fuzzy arithmetic—which may be viewed as a generalization of interval arithmetic (Moore, 1966)—is beginning to emerge as an important area of research within the theory of fuzzy sets (Mizumoto and Tanaka, 1976; Nahmias, 1976; Jain, 1976*a*; Dubois and Prade, 1978) and is likely to become a basic tool in the analysis of fuzzy systems in the years ahead.

Briefly, if x and y are fuzzy numbers and $*$ is a binary operation such as addition (+), subtraction (-), multiplication (×), division (/), max (∨), min (∧), and so forth, then by the application of the extension principle (Zadeh, 1975*a*), it can readily be shown that the fuzzy number z defined by

$$z = x * y$$

is given (as a fuzzy set) by

$$\mu_z(w) = V_{u,v}\mu_x(u) \wedge \mu_y(v), \qquad u, v, w \in R',$$

subject to the constraint

$$w = u * v,$$

where μ_x, μ_y, and μ_z denote the membership functions of x, y, and z, respectively, and $V_{u,v}$ denotes the supremum over u,v.

A basic property of fuzzy numbers, which has the effect of greatly simplifying operations on them, is that of ***shape invariance.*** This property was discovered by Nahmias (1976, 1978) and Misumoto and Tanaka (1976) and generalized by Dubois and Prade (1978).

As a simple illustration, if both x and y are ***triangular*** fuzzy numbers (i.e., μ_x and μ_y have the form of triangles) and $z = x + y$, then z will likewise be a triangular fuzzy number. Thus, if a triangular fuzzy number x is characterized by a triple $x = (x_1, x_2, x_3)$, in which x_1, x_2, and x_3 are the abscissae of the three vertices of the triangle [i.e., $\mu(x_1) = \mu(x_3) = 0, \mu(x_2) = 1$], then

$$x + y = (x_1, x_2, x_3) + (y_1, y_2, y_3)$$

is given by

$$x + y = (x_1 + y_1, x_2 + y_2, x_3 + y_3).$$

Similarly, if x and y are π-numbers (Zadeh, 1975*a*) (i.e., have piecewise-quadratic membership functions) characterized as ordered pairs $x = (\bar{x}, \beta_x)$, $y = (\bar{y}, \beta_y)$, where $\bar{x}$ and $\bar{y}$ are the abscissae of the peaks of x and y, and β_x and β_y are their respective bandwidths (i.e., the separations between the crossover points at which $\mu = 0.5$), then their sum, $x + y$, is a π-number characterized by

$$x + y = (\bar{x} + \bar{y}, \beta_x + \beta_y),$$

while their product, $x \times y$, is a fuzzy number characterized by

$$x \times y = (\bar{x} \times \bar{y}, \sigma_x + \sigma_y + \sigma_x \sigma_y),$$

where $\sigma_x = \beta_x/\bar{x}$ and $\sigma_y = \beta_y/\bar{y}$ denote the normalized bandwidths. Furthermore, for small σ_x and σ_y, $x \times y$ is, approximately, a π-number characterized by

$$x \times y \cong (\bar{x} \times \bar{y}, \sigma_x + \sigma_y).$$

The property of shape invariance, which holds exactly for addition and subtraction and approximately for other operations, makes it possible to represent fuzzy numbers in parametric form and thus translate various operations on fuzzy numbers into corresponding arithmetic operations on their parameters. This idea is developed at length in the recent work of Dubois and Prade (1978) and has the potential for many significant applications to the approximate analysis of both fuzzy and nonfuzzy systems.

Of particular note among the applications of linguistic variables and fuzzy numbers that have already been reported in the literature is the work of Wenstop (1975, 1976, 1977) on organization theory. Also of note is the rapidly expanding work on so-called fuzzy logic controllers (Mamdani, 1976; Mamdani and Assilian, 1975; Kickert and van Nauta Lemke, 1976; Jain, 1976*b*; Kickert and Mamdani, 1978; King and Mamdani, 1977; Rutherford and Carter, 1976; Ostergaard, 1977; Tong, 1976, 1977). What is surprising about the latter work is that fuzzy logic controllers have found considerable success not in the realm of humanistic systems—which motivated the conception of a linguistic variable and fuzzy logic—but in the very practical area of industrial process control.

Basic to the applications of linguistic variables and fuzzy numbers is the concept of a *linguistic fuzzy-relational* representation of dependencies in both fuzzy and nonfuzzy systems. Such representations are closely related to the concept of a branching questionnaire (Zadeh, 1976*b*) and subsume the rule-based systems (Winston, 1977) that are widely employed in artificial intelligence and related fields.

Typically, if $X_1, \ldots, X_n$ and Y are variables taking values in $U_1, \ldots, U_n$, and V, respectively, and R is a fuzzy relation from $U_1, \ldots, U_n$ to V, then a linguistic fuzzy-relational representation of R has the form of a tableau such as shown in Table 3.1, in which the r_{ij} and r_i are labels of fuzzy subsets of $U_1, \ldots, U_n, V$. In general, the r_{ij} and r_i are fuzzy numbers or the linguistic values of attributes, grades of membership, truth-values, probability-values, or possibility-values. Thus, typically, a row of R may contain entries exemplified by the following: (150,5) (a fuzzy number with peak value 150 and bandwidth 5 representing an approximate value of an attribute, say, Weight); *not very young* (a linguistic value of Age); *very low* (a linguistic value of the grade of membership in a fuzzy set, e.g., the class of creative people); *quite true* (a linguistic value of the fuzzy predicate Healthy); *not very likely* (a linguistic value of the probability of a fuzzy or nonfuzzy event, e.g., inheriting a fortune); (0.4, 0.1) (a fuzzy number representing the probability of, say, living beyond the age of 60); and *quite possible* (a linguistic value of the possibility of, say, carrying seven passengers in a five-passenger car).

As shown in Zadeh (1977*a, b*), a tableau of the form shown in Table 3.1 *translates* into an $(n+1)$-ary fuzzy relation expressed by

$$\begin{aligned}\tilde{R} = & r_{11} \times r_{12} \times \cdots \times r_{1n} \times r_1 + \\ & r_{21} \times r_{22} \times \cdots \times r_{2n} \times r_2 + \cdots + \\ & r_{m1} \times r_{m2} \times \cdots \times r_{mn} \times r_m, \end{aligned} \tag{3.1}$$

where + denotes the union of fuzzy sets, which for fuzzy subsets A, B of U is defined by

$$\mu_{A+B}(u) = \mu_A(u) \vee \mu_B(u), \qquad u \in U,$$

while $\times$ is the Cartesian product, defined by

$$\mu_{A \times B}(u, v) = \mu_A(u) \wedge \mu_B(v), \qquad u \in U, \qquad v \in V.$$

Thus, through the use of (3.1), a relation R, whose elements are fuzzy numbers

Table 3.1. Tableau of R

X_1	X_2		X_n	Y
r_{11}	r_{12}	$\cdots$	r_{1n}	r_1
r_{21}	r_{22}	$\cdots$	r_{2n}	r_2
$\vdots$	$\vdots$		$\vdots$	$\vdots$
r_{m1}	r_{m2}	$\cdots$	r_{mn}	r_m

and/or the values of linguistic variables, may be translated into a fuzzy relation $\tilde{R}$, whose elements are $(n+1)$-tuples in $U_1 \times U_2 \times \cdots \times U_n \times V$.

We speak of the *translation* of R into $\tilde{R}$ because $\tilde{R}$ defines the meaning of R as a fuzzy $(n+1)$-ary relation in $U_1 \times U_2 \times \cdots \times U_n \times V$. Having $\tilde{R}$, we can define the effect of various operations that may be performed on R. In particular, the knowledge of $\tilde{R}$ provides a basis for an interpolation of R for values of $X_1, \ldots, X_n$ that are not tabulated in the tableau of R. More specifically, assume that we wish to find the value of Y corresponding to the linguistic values $X_1 = s_1$, $X_2 = s_2, \ldots, X_n = s_n$, where the n-tuple $(s_1, \ldots, s_n)$ does not appear as a row in the tableau of R. To this end, compute the Cartesian product

$$S = s_1 \times \cdots \times s_n$$

as a fuzzy relation in $U_1 \times \cdots \times U_n$. Then, as shown in Zadeh (1977*a*), the corresponding value of Y is given approximately by the formula

$$Y = \tilde{R} \circ S, \tag{3.2}$$

where $\circ$ denotes the operation of composition.[2] If necessary, the value of Y yielded by (3.2) may be approximated by a linguistic value of Y through the use of linguistic approximation (Zadeh, 1975*a*; Wenstop, 1976; Procyk, 1976).

Linguistic fuzzy-relational representations are particularly relevant to the definition of complex concepts (Zadeh, 1976*a*), characterization of control strategies (Mamdani and Assilian, 1978; Tong, 1977), pattern classification (Zadeh, 1977*a*), and diagnostics (Sanchez, 1977). Furthermore, they provide a basis for the characterization of dependencies in which the sources of imprecision comprise both fuzzy and random variables. In such cases the tableau of R may be expressed in the canonical form shown in Tables 3.2*a* and 3.2*b*, in which the r_i are pointers to relations of the form shown in Table 3.2*b*, with $F_1, \ldots, F_k$ representing specified fuzzy sets and p_r, $r = 1, \ldots, \ell$, denoting a linguistic probability that an object characterized by the rth row of R has the grade of membership μ_{r1} in F_1, μ_{r2} in $F_2, \ldots, \mu_{rk}$ in F_k, with $\mu_{r1}, \ldots, \mu_{rk}$ expressed as fuzzy subsets of the unit interval.

As an elementary illustration,[3] assume that $X_1, \ldots, X_n$ represent a set of symptoms (e.g., $X_1 \triangleq$ body temperature, $X_2 \triangleq$ pulse rate, $X_3 \triangleq$ presence of pain); $F_1, \ldots, F_k$ are possible illnesses corresponding to the symptoms in question (e.g., flu and bronchitis); and p_r is the probability that a person has the illnesses $F_1, \ldots, F_k$ to the degrees $\mu_{r1}, \ldots, \mu_{rk}$ simultaneously, given the linguistic values of the symptoms $X_1, \ldots, X_n$. In this case, Tables 3.2*a* and 3.2*b* may have the form shown in Tables 3.3*a*, *b*, and *c*. Thus, if the temperature is *high* (with *high* regarded as a primary term of the linguistic variable Temperature), the pulse rate is given approximately by the fuzzy number (80,5), and the truth-value of the fuzzy predicate Pain is *not true*, where *true* is a primary term

Table 3.2. Tableau of R and the Pointer r_i

a

R	X_1	X_2	$\cdots$	X_n	Y_1
	r_{11}	r_{12}	$\cdots$	r_{1n}	r_1
	r_{21}	r_{22}	$\cdots$	r_{2n}	r_2
	$\vdots$	$\vdots$		$\vdots$	$\vdots$
	r_{m1}	r_{m2}	$\cdots$	r_{mn}	r_m

b

r_i	F_1	F_2	$\cdots$	F_k	P
	μ_{11}	μ_{12}	$\cdots$	μ_{1k}	p_1
	μ_{21}	μ_{22}	$\cdots$	μ_{2k}	p_2
	$\vdots$	$\vdots$		$\vdots$	$\vdots$
	$\mu_{\ell 1}$	$\mu_{\ell 2}$	$\cdots$	$\mu_{\ell k}$	p_ℓ

Note: $i = 1, \ldots, m$ (i as a subscript or superscript is implicit in all of the entries in the tableau of r_i).

of the linguistic variable Truth; then with linguistic probability *very likely,* the diagnosis is "flu to the degree *low* and bronchitis to the degree *high*"; with linguistic probability *unlikely,* the diagnosis is "flu to the degree *high* and bronchitis to the degree *low*"; and, with probability *unlikely,* the diagnosis is "flu to the degree *low* and bronchitis to the degree *low*." In these expressions, *low* is a primary term for the linguistic variable Grade, *high* is the antonym of *low*; *likely* is a primary term for the linguistic variable Probability, and *unlikely* is the antonym of likely.[4]

In the foregoing discussion, we have restricted our attention to the representation of attribute dependencies in the case of a single object. In systems analysis, however, our main concern is with the representation of the collective behavior of a group of interacting objects rather than with the behavior of a single object. Thus, the question is, How can the fuzzy-relational representation of the constituents of a system be combined to form a fuzzy-relational representation of the system as a whole? Although some aspects of this problem have been studied and reported in the literature (Zadeh, 1973, 1971; Negoita and Ralescu, 1975; Kaufmann, 1975), it remains, at this juncture, a largely unexplored basic issue in fuzzy systems theory.

Table 3.3. Tableau of R, the Pointer r_1, and the Pointer r_2

a

Temp.	*Pulse*	*Pain*	*Y*
High	(80,5)	Not true	r_1
High	(70,5)	True	r_2
·	·	·	·
Normal	(60,5)	False	r_m

b

r_1	*Flu*	*Bronchitis*	*P*
	Low	High	Very likely
	High	Low	Unlikely
	·	·	·
	Low	Low	Unlikely

c

r_2	*Flu*	*Bronchitis*	*P*
	Low	High	Unlikely
	High	Low	Very likely
	·	·	·
	High	High	Unlikely

FUZZY SYSTEMS THEORY AND FUZZY LOGIC

An essential distinction between classical systems theory, on the one hand, and fuzzy systems theory, on the other, relates to a basic difference in their underlying logics. Thus, classical systems theory, like most other mathematical theories, rests on the foundation of two-valued logic, which implies that the propositions asserted in classical systems theory are either true—in which case they are theorems—or false.

In contrast, fuzzy systems theory is based on *fuzzy logic* (Zadeh, 1975*b*, 1977*c*; Bellman and Zadeh, 1977)—that is, on a logic with fuzzy truth-values and rules of inference that are approximate rather than exact. In this logic a fuzzy proposition is usually associated with a fuzzy truth-value (e.g., the truth-value of the proposition "X is much larger than Y" may be *not very true*). Thus, what matters in fuzzy logic are not theorems but propositions that, though fuzzy, are informative and have a high degree of truth. Such propositions are, in general, inferences drawn from fuzzy premises, and their degree of truth is determined in an approximate manner by the linguistic truth-values of the premises from which they are inferred.

A concept that plays a basic role in fuzzy logic is that of a *possibility distribution* (Zadeh, 1978).[5] Thus, if X is a variable taking values in a universe of discourse, U, then a possibility distribution, Π_X, associated with X, is a fuzzy subset F of U such that the *possibility* that X may take a value $u \in U$ is numerically equal to the grade of membership of u in F, that is,

$$\begin{aligned}\text{poss}\{X = u\} &= \pi_X(u), \qquad u \in U \\ &= \mu_F(u), \end{aligned} \tag{3.3}$$

where μ_F is the membership function of F and $\pi_X(u)$ is termed the *possibility distribution function* associated with Π_X.

Given the possibility distribution of X, the possibility of X taking a value in a specified subset A of U is given by

$$\text{poss}\{X \in A\} = V_u \pi_X(u), \qquad u \in U, \tag{3.4}$$

and, if A is a fuzzy subset characterized by its membership function μ_A, then

$$\text{poss}\{X \text{ is } A\} = V_u \pi_X(u) \wedge \mu_A(u), \qquad u \in U. \tag{3.5}$$

As an illustration, if *small* is a specified fuzzy subset of the real line, then the proposition "X is small" translates into what is called a *possibility assignment equation*

$$\Pi_X = \text{small},$$

which implies that

$$\text{poss}\{X = u\} = \mu_{\text{small}}(u), \qquad u \in (-\infty, \infty).$$

Furthermore, if we know that X is small, then, by (3.5), the possibility that X is not very small is given by

$$\text{poss}\{X \text{ is not very small}\} = V_u \{\pi_{\text{small}}(u) \wedge [1 - \mu^2_{\text{small}}(u)]\}. \tag{3.6}$$

More generally, a proposition of the form "X is F," where X is a variable taking values in U, and F is a fuzzy subset of U, translates into a possibility assignment equation of the form

$$\Pi_X = F; \tag{3.7}$$

which implies that

$$\text{poss}\{X = u\} = \mu_F(u), \qquad u \in U.$$

The concept of a possibility distribution provides a basis for the translation of propositions expressed in a natural language into expressions in a synthetic meaning representation language called PRUF (Zadeh, 1977*b*). Thus, an expression in PRUF is, in general, a procedure that acts on a collection of relations in a data base and returns a possibility distribution. For example, given the definition of *small* as a fuzzy subset of the real line, the translation of the proposition "X is not very small" may be expressed as ($\rightarrow$ stands for "translates into")

$$X \text{ is not very small} \rightarrow \Pi_X = 1 - (\text{small}^2),$$

which means that the proposition in question induces a possibility distribution of X that may be obtained from the fuzzy set small by squaring small (i.e., squaring its membership function) and forming its complement (i.e., subtracting the resulting membership function from unity). It should be noted that it is this translation of the proposition "X is not very small" that is employed in (3.6) to compute the possibility that X is not very small.

Another example of a basic translation rule in PRUF is the *rule of conjunctive composition,* which asserts that if

$$X \text{ is } F \rightarrow \Pi_X = F, \quad F \subset U$$

and

$$Y \text{ is } G \rightarrow \Pi_Y = G, \quad G \subset V,$$

then

$$X \text{ is } F \text{ and } Y \text{ is } G \rightarrow \Pi_{(X,Y)} = F \times G, \tag{3.8}$$

where $\Pi_{(X,Y)}$ is the joint possibility distribution of the variables X and Y, and $F \times G$ is the Cartesian product of the fuzzy sets F and G. Similarly, the *rule of conditional composition* states:

$$\text{If } X \text{ is } F, \text{ then } Y \text{ is } G \rightarrow \Pi_{Y(X)} = \bar{F}' \oplus \bar{G}, \tag{3.9}$$

where $\Pi_{Y(X)}$ is the conditional possibility of Y given X, and the fuzzy set $\bar{F}' \oplus \bar{G}$ is defined by Zadeh (1975*a*):

$$\mu_{\bar{F}' \oplus \bar{G}}(u, v) = 1 \wedge [1 - \mu_F(u) + \mu_G(v)], \quad u \in U, \quad v \in V. \tag{3.10}$$

When a proposition is qualified by a truth-value, as in "X is small is very true," its translation is governed by the *rule of truth qualification,* which asserts:

$$\text{If } X \text{ is } F \rightarrow \Pi_X = F,$$

then

$$X \text{ is } F \text{ is } \tau \rightarrow \Pi_X = F^+, \tag{3.11}$$

where τ is a linguistic truth-value, μ_F and μ_T are the membership functions of F and τ, respectively, and

$$\mu_{F^+}(u) = \mu_\tau[\mu_F(u)], \quad u \in U. \tag{3.12}$$

Thus, the association of a truth-value, τ, with a proposition of the form "X is F," has the effect of modifying the possibility distribution of X in the manner defined by (3.12).

Our brief discussion of some of the elementary translation rules in fuzzy logic is intended to illustrate the basic principles by which a fairly complex composite proposition describing a relation between two or more variables may be translated into an assertion concerning the joint or conditional possibility distribution of the variables in question. For example, if the relation between X, Y, and Z is described by the proposition

"If X is small and Y is large, then Z is very small," (3.13)

then, by the use of (3.8) and (3.9), the proposition in question may be translated into a possibility assignment equation that expresses the conditional possibility distribution $\Pi_{Z(X,Y)}$ as a function of the primary fuzzy sets *small* and *large*. Given this distribution, then, we can find the possibility distribution of Z from a specification of the possibility distributions of X and Y.

More generally, if Y is the output of a system, S, if $X_1, \ldots, X_n$ are the inputs to S, and if the dependence of Y on $X_1, \ldots, X_n$ is described by a collection of propositions of the form (3.13), then, by the application of translation rules of fuzzy logic, we can compute the possibility distribution of Y as a function of the possibility distributions of $X_1, \ldots, X_n$.

In the foregoing exposition we have limited our attention to those aspects of fuzzy logic that are of relevance to the analysis of fuzzy systems—that is, systems that are characterized by fuzzy input-output relations. What should be recognized, however, is that, counter to what one might expect, fuzzy logic also has an important role to play in the analysis of nonfuzzy systems. In this role it provides (1) a language (PRUF) for an approximate characterization of nonfuzzy input-output relations and (2) a method for assessing the consistency of such characterizations with the data resident in a data base.

As a very simple illustration of this application, suppose that S is a memoryless system with input X and output Y, and that we have a tabulation of Y as a function of X. Assume that the dependence of Y on X is expressed in a summarized form by the proposition

"If X is small then Y is large, and if X is not small then
Y is not very large." (3.14)

By using the translation rules (3.8) and (3.9), the proposition in question translates into the possibility assignment equation (Zadeh, 1978)

$$\Pi_{Y(X)} = [\overline{\text{small}'} \oplus \overline{\text{large}}] \cap [\overline{\text{small}} \oplus \overline{(\text{large}^2)'}], \qquad (3.15)$$

which implies that the conditional possibility distribution function of Y given X is expressed by

$$\pi_{Y(X)}(u, v) = [1 - \mu_{\text{small}}(u) + \mu_{\text{large}}(v)] \wedge [\mu_{\text{small}}(u) + 1 - \mu^2_{\text{large}}(v)]. \qquad (3.16)$$

Now let (x_i, y_i) be the entry in the ith row of the tabulation of Y as a function of X. Substituting this pair into (3.16), we obtain its consistency, γ_i, with the given proposition—that is,

$$\gamma_i = \pi_{Y(X)}(x_i, y_i). \qquad (3.17)$$

Then, using (3.17), a conservative assessment of the degree of consistency between the given tabulation of Y as a function of X and its summary as expressed by (3.16) may be defined as

$$\gamma = \min_i \pi_{Y(X)}(x_i, y_i), \qquad (3.18)$$

with i ranging over the rows of the tabulation. It is understood, of course, that other, less conservative, measures of consistency may be preferable in some applications.

In summary, fuzzy logic serves three essential functions in fuzzy systems theory. First, it provides a language (PRUF) for the characterization of input-output relations of both fuzzy and nonfuzzy systems. Second, it provides a system for drawing approximate conclusions from imprecise data. And finally, it provides a method for assessing the goodness of a model or, equivalently, a summary of the behavior of a system that is too complex or too ill-defined to be susceptible to analysis by conventional techniques.

CONCLUDING REMARKS

Fuzzy systems theory, as outlined in our exposition, represents a rather sharp break with the tradition of precision and exactitude in classical systems theory. Based as it is on fuzzy rather than two-valued logic, fuzzy systems theory does not aim at the discovery of precise assertions about the behavior of complex systems. Rather, it aims at an accommodation with the pervasive imprecision of real-world systems by abandoning the unattainable goals of classical systems theory and adopting instead a conceptual framework that is tolerant of imprecision and partial truths.

Fuzzy systems theory is not as yet an existing theory. What we have at present are merely parts of its foundation. Nevertheless, even at this very early stage of its development, fuzzy systems theory casts some light on the processes of approximate reasoning in human decision making, planning, and control. Furthermore, in the years ahead, it is likely to develop into an effective body of concepts and techniques for the analysis of large-scale humanistic as well as mechanistic systems.

NOTES

1. In the case of humanistic systems, primary fuzzy sets play a role that is somewhat analogous to that of physical units in the case of mechanistic systems.

2. Equation (3.2) implies that, in terms of the membership functions of $\tilde{R}$ and S, the membership function of Y is given by

$$\mu_Y(v) = V_{u_1, \ldots, u_n} [\mu_{\tilde{R}}(u_1, \ldots, u_n, v) \wedge \mu_S(u_1, \ldots, u_n)],$$

where $V_{u_1, \ldots, u_n}$ denotes the supremum over $u_1 \in U_1, \ldots, u_n \in U_n$.

3. Needless to say, this example does not pretend to be a realistic representation of the relation between the symptoms in question and the corresponding diseases.

4. If A is a fuzzy subset of the unit interval, as is true of both *low* and *likely*, then the membership function of the antonym of A is related to that of A by

$$\mu_{\mathrm{ant}(A)}(v) = \mu_A(1 - v), \qquad v \in [0,1].$$

5. Intuitively, *possibility* relates to feasibility, ease of attainment, and compatibility, whereas *probability* relates to likelihood, frequency, and strength of belief. In contrast to the concept of probability, the concept of possibility is nonstatistical in nature.

REFERENCES

Bellman, R.E., and L.A. Zadeh, 1977. "Local and Fuzzy Logics." In J.M. Dunn and G. Epstein, eds. *Modern Uses of Multiple-Valued Logic.* Dordrecht, The Netherlands: Reidel.

Berlinski, D. 1976. *On Systems Analysis.* Cambridge, Mass.: MIT Press.

Dubois, D., and H. Prade. 1978. "Fuzzy Algebra, Analysis, Logics." Technical Report 78-13, Purdue University, School of Electrical Engineering.

Hoos, I. 1962. *Systems Analysis in Public Policy.* Berkeley: University of California Press.

Jain, R. 1976*a*. "Tolerance Analysis Using Fuzzy Sets." *International Journal of Systems Science* 7:1393–1401.

——. 1976*b*. "Outline of an Approach for the Analysis of Fuzzy Systems." *International Journal of Control* 23:627–40.

Kaufmann, A. 1975. *Introduction to the Theory of Fuzzy Subsets,* vol. 3.:

Applications to Classification and Pattern Recognition, Automata and Systems, and Choice of Criteria. Paris: Masson.

Kickert, W.J.M., and E.H. Mamdani. 1978. "Analysis of a Fuzzy Logic Controller." *Fuzzy Sets and Systems* 1:29–44.

Kickert, W.J.M., and H.R. van Nauta Lemke. 1976. "Application of a Fuzzy Controller in a Warm Water Plant." *Automatica* 12:301–08.

King, P.J., and E.H. Mamdani. 1975. "The Application of Fuzzy Control Systems to Industrial Processes." *Proceedings of the 6th IFAC World Congress*, Boston. (Also in *Automatica* 13(1977):235–42.)

Knuth, D.E. 1968. "Semantics of Context-Free Languages." *Mathematical Systems Theory* 2:127–45.

Lewis, P.M., D.J. Rosenkrantz, and R.E. Stearns. 1976. "Attributed Translations." *Journal of Computer and System Sciences* 9:279–307.

Mamdani, E.H. 1976. "Advances in the Linguistic Synthesis of Fuzzy Controllers." *International Journal of Man-Machine Studies* 8:669–78.

Mamdani, E.H., and S. Assilian. 1975. "An Experiment in Linguistic Synthesis with a Fuzzy Logic Controller." *International Journal of Man-Machine Studies* 7:1–13.

Mizumoto, M., and K. Tanaka. 1976. "Algebraic Properties of Fuzzy Numbers." *Proceedings of the International Conference on Cybernetics and Society*, Washington, D.C.

Moore, R.E. 1966. *Interval Analysis*. Englewood Cliffs, N.J.: Prentice-Hall.

Nahmias, S. 1976. "Fuzzy Variables." Technical Report 33, University of Pittsburgh, Department of Industrial Engineering, Systems Management Engineering and Operations Research.

——. 1978. "Fuzzy Variables." *Fuzzy Sets and Systems* 1:97–110.

Negoita, C.V., and D.A. Ralescu. 1975. *Applications of Fuzzy Sets to Systems Analysis*. Basel: Birkhauser Verlag.

Ostergaard, J.-J. 1977. "Fuzzy Logic Control of a Heat Exchanger Process." In M.M. Gupta, G.N. Saridis, and B.R. Gaines, eds. *Fuzzy Automata and Decision Processes*. New York: North-Holland.

Procyk, T.J. 1976. "Linguistic Representation of Fuzzy Variables." Queen Mary College, Fuzzy Logic Working Group, London.

Rutherford, D., and G.A. Carter. 1976. "A Heuristic Adaptive Controller for a Sinter Plant." *Proceedings of the 2nd IFAC Symposium on Automation in Mining, Mineral and Metal Processing*, Johannesburg.

Sanchez, E. 1977. "Solutions in Composite Fuzzy Relation Equations: Application to Medical Diagnosis in Brouwerian Logic." In M.M. Gupta, G.N. Saridis, and B.R. Gaines, eds. *Fuzzy Automata and Decision Processes*. New York: North-Holland.

Tong, R.M. 1976. "Analysis of Fuzzy Control Algorithms Using the Relation Matrix." *International Journal of Man-Machine Studies* 8:679–86.

——. 1977. "A Control Engineering Review of Fuzzy Systems." *Automatica* 13: 559–69.

Wenstøp, F. 1975. "Application of Linguistic Variables in the Analysis of Organizations." Ph.D. thesis, University of California, Berkeley, School of Business Administration.

——. 1976. "Deductive Verbal Models of Organizations." *International Journal of Man-Machine Studies* 8:293–311.

——. 1977. "Fuzzy Sets and Decision-Making." *California Engineer* 16:20–24.

Winston, P.H. 1977. *Artificial Intelligence.* Reading, Mass.: Addison-Wesley.

Zadeh, L.A. 1962. "From Circuit Theory to System Theory." *Proceedings of the IRE* 50:856–65.

——. 1971. "Toward a Theory of Fuzzy Systems." In R.E. Kalman and N. DeClaris, eds. *Aspects of Networks and Systems Theory.* New York: Holt, Rinehart & Winston.

——. 1973. "Outline of a New Approach to the Analysis of Complex Systems and Decision Processes." *IEEE Transactions on Systems, Man and Cybernetics,* SMC-3:28–44.

——. 1975*a*. "The Concept of a Linguistic Variable and Its Application to Approximate Reasoning." Part I, *Information Sciences* 8:199–249; Part II, *Information Sciences* 8:301–57.

——. 1975*b*. "Fuzzy Logic and Approximate Reasoning (In Memory of Grigore Moisil)." *Synthese* 30:407–28.

——. 1976*a*. "The Concept of a Linguistic Variable and Its Application to Approximate Reasoning." Part III, *Information Sciences* 9:43–80.

——. 1976*b*. "A Fuzzy-Algorithmic Approach to the Definition of Complex or Imprecise Concepts." *International Journal of Man-Machine Studies* 8:249–91.

——. 1977*a*. "Fuzzy Sets and Their Application to Pattern Classification and Clustering Analysis." In J. Van Ryzin, ed. *Classification and Clustering.* New York: Academic Press.

——. 1977*b*. "PRUF–A Meaning Representation Language of Natural Languages." Memorandum 77/61, University of California, Berkeley, Electronics Research Laboratory.

——. 1977*c*. "A Theory of Approximate Reasoning." Memorandum M77/58, University of California, Berkeley, Electronics Research Laboratory.

——. 1978. "Fuzzy Sets as a Basis for a Theory of Possibility." *Fuzzy Sets and Systems* 1:3–28.

Lotfi A. Zadeh

3. Possibility Theory and Soft Data Analysis

Abstract

A thesis advanced in this paper is that much of the uncertainty which is associated with soft data is nonstatistical in nature. Based on this premise, an approach to the representation and manipulation of soft data--in which the recently developed theory of possibility plays a central role--is described and illustrated with examples.

1. Introduction

The term *soft data* does not have a universally agreed upon meaning. Some use it to characterize data that are imprecise or uncertain, while others attach the label "soft" to data whose credibility is open to question.

In dealing with soft data of the type encountered in such diverse fields as psychology, sociology, anthropology, medicine, economics, management science, operations research, pattern classification and systems analysis, it is a standard practice to rely almost entirely on the techniques provided by probability theory and statistics, especially in applications relating to parameter estimation, hypothesis testing and system identification. It can be argued, however, as we

---

To Professor Brian R. Gaines.

Supported by Naval Electronic Systems Command Contract N00039-78-C-0013 and National Science Foundation Grant ENG78-23143.

do in the present paper, that such techniques cannot cope effectively with those problems in which the softness of data is nonstatistical in nature--in the sense that it relates, in the main, to the presence of fuzzy sets rather than to random measurement errors or data variability.

Needless to say, the inability of conventional statistical techniques to deal with problems of this type would not matter much if the predominance of fuzziness in softness were a rare phenomenon. In reality, the opposite is the case; for, upon closer examination, it becomes clear that much of the softness in data analysis is nonstatistical in the sense explicated above. Moreover, the same is true of most of the linguistic information that humans manipulate through an implicit use of what might be called *approximate* (or *fuzzy*) *reasoning* based on fuzzy rather than standard logic.

To make the latter point more concretely, it will be helpful to list--and subsequently analyze in greater detail--several typical examples of everyday type of questions which cannot be handled effectively by conventional probability-based methods. In these questions, the soft data are expressed as propositions appearing above the horizontal line; the italicized words are the labels of fuzzy sets; and the answers are expected to be in the form of a fuzzy proposition, that is, a proposition whose constituents may have a fuzzy denotation. Specifically:

(a) X is a *large number*
Y is *much larger* than X
———
How large is Y?

(b) *Most* Frenchmen are not *tall*
Elie is a Frenchman
———
How tall is Elie?

(c) It is *unlikely* that Andrea is very *young*
It is *likely* that Andrea is *young*
It is *very unlikely* that Andrea is *old*

How likely is it that Andrea is not old?

(d) It is *true* that Hans is not very *tall*
It is *very true* that Hans is not *short*

How tall is Hans?

(e) Brian is *much taller* than *most* of his *close friends*

How tall is Brian?

(f) If Bernadette lives in Versailles then she is *very rich*
If Bernadette lives in Monmartre then she is *poor*
It is *likely* that Bernadette lives in Versailles
It is *very unlikely* that Bernadette lives in Monmartre

How likely is it that Bernadette is not rich?

As will be seen in the sequel, our approach to the analysis of soft data of the type illustrated by the above examples is based on *fuzzy logic* [7,22,89] rather than on a combination of classical logic and probability-based methods --as is true of the conventional approaches to soft data analysis. In essence, our rationale for the use of fuzzy logic for soft data analysis rests on the premise that the denotations of imprecise terms which occur in a soft database are, for the most part, fuzzy sets rather than probability distributions. For example, in a proposition such as

$$p \triangleq X \text{ is a } \textit{large number} \qquad (1.1)$$

the softness of data is due to the fuzziness of the denotation of *large number*. Similarly, in the proposition

$$p \triangleq \text{It is } \textit{likely} \text{ that Andrea is } \textit{young} \qquad (1.2)$$

softness is due to: (a) the fuzziness of the denotation of

young; and (b) the fuzziness of the term *likely*, which characterizes the probability of the fuzzy event "Andrea is young" [71,86]. As we shall see presently, the imprecision in (1.1) is possibilistic in nature, whereas in (1.2) it is partly probabilistic and partly possibilistic. Viewed in this perspective, then, a *soft datum* may be regarded, in general, as a proposition in which the uncertainty is due to a combination of probabilistic and possibilistic constituents.

When it is necessary to differentiate between a term and its denotation, the latter will be expressed in uppercase symbols. To illustrate, in (1.1) the term *large number* (or, simply, *large*) has as its denotation a fuzzy subset, LARGE, of the interval $U \triangleq [0,\infty)$. This subset is characterized by its membership function $\mu_{LARGE}: U \to [0,1]$ which associates with each number $u \in U$ the grade of membership of u in LARGE. For example, the grade of membership of $u = 100$ in LARGE might be 0.2 while that of 400 might be 0.9.

A basic aspect of a fuzzy proposition such as "X is small" is that it does not provide a precise characterization of the value of X. Instead, it defines a *possibility distribution* [92] of values of X which associates with each nonnegative real number u a number in the interval [0,1] which represents the *possibility* that X could take u as a value given the proposition "X is small." To express this in a symbolic form, we write

$$X \text{ is small} \to \Pi_X = \text{SMALL} \tag{1.3}$$

which signifies that the proposition "X is small" translates into the assignment of the fuzzy set SMALL to the possibility distribution of X, Π_X. Equivalently, the proposition "X is small" will be said to *induce* the possibility distribution Π_X, with the right-hand member of (1.3) constituting a *possibility assignment equation*. For notational convenience, we shall write

$$\text{Poss}\{X = u\} \triangleq \pi_X(u) \tag{1.4}$$

where the function $\pi_X: U \longrightarrow [0,1]$ is the *possibility distribution function* and U is the domain of X.

Essentially, the possibility distribution of X is the collection of possible values of X, with the understanding that possibility is a matter of degree, so that the possibility that X could take u as a value may be any number in the interval [0,1] or, more generally, a point in a partially ordered set.

In general, a possibility distribution may be induced by a physical constraint or, alternatively, may be epistemic in origin. To illustrate the difference, let X be the number of passengers that can be carried in Carole's car, which is a five passenger Mercedes. In this case, by identifying $\pi_X(u)$ with the degree of ease with which u passengers can be put in Carole's car, the tabulation of π_X may assume the following form in which an entry such as (7,0.6) signifies that, by

X	1	2	3	4	5	6	7	8	9	10
π_X	1	1	1	1	1	0.8	0.6	0.9	0	0

some explicit or implicit criterion, the degree of ease with which 7 passengers can be carried in Carole's car is 0.6.

In the above example, the possibility distribution of X is induced by a physical constraint on the number of passengers that can be carried in Carole's car. To illustrate the case where the possibility distribution of X is epistemic in origin, i.e., reflects the state of knowledge about X, let X be Carole's age and let the information about Carole's age be conveyed by the proposition

$$p \triangleq \text{Carole is young} \tag{1.5}$$

where young is the label of a specified fuzzy subset of the

interval [0,100] which is characterized by its membership function μ_{YOUNG}, with $\mu_{YOUNG}(u)$ representing the degree to which a person who is u years old is young in a specified context.

The connection between π_X and μ_{YOUNG} is provided by the so-called *possibility postulate* of possibility theory [92,93] which asserts that, in the absence of any information about X other than that supplied by the proposition p $\triangleq$ Carole is young, the possibility that X = u is numerically equal to the grade of membership of u in YOUNG. Thus

$$\text{Poss}\{X=u\} = \pi_X(u) = \mu_{YOUNG}(u) \ , \quad u \in [0,100] \qquad (1.6)$$

or, equivalently,

$$\Pi_{Age(Carole)} = YOUNG \qquad (1.7)$$

with the understanding that the possibility assignment equation (1.7) is the translation of (1.5), i.e.,

$$\text{Carole is young} \longrightarrow \Pi_{Age(Carole)} = YOUNG \ . \qquad (1.8)$$

It is in this sense, then, that the epistemic possibility distribution of Carole's age is induced by the proposition p $\triangleq$ Carole is young.

What is the difference between probability and possibility? As the above examples indicate, the concept of possibility is an abstraction of our intuitive perception of ease of attainment or degree of compatibility, whereas the concept of probability is rooted in the perception of likelihood, frequency, proportion or strength of belief. Furthermore, as we shall see in Section 2, the rules governing the manipulation of possibilities are distinct from those which apply to probabilities.

An important aspect of the connection between probabilities and possibilities relates to the fact that they are *independent* characterizations of uncertainty in the sense that from the knowledge of the possibility distribution of a variable X we cannot deduce its probability distribution, and vice-versa. For example, from the knowledge of the possibility distribution of the number of passengers in Carole's car we cannot deduce its probability distribution. Nor can we deduce the possibility distribution from the probability distribution of the number of passengers. However, we can make a weaker assertion to the effect that if the possibility that $X=u$ is small, then it is likely that the probability that $X=u$ is also small. However, from this it does not follow that high possibility implies high probability, as is reflected in the commonly used statements of the form "It is possible but not probable that... ."[1].

In the present paper, we shall focus our attention on only a few of the basic aspects of possibility theory and its applications to the analysis of soft data. Thus, our main concern will be with the representation of soft data in linguistic form and with approximate inference from such data. In addition, we shall touch upon the issue of data granularity and its relation to the theory of evidence. We shall not consider, however, an issue that is of considerable relevance to the analysis of soft data, namely, the representation of imprecise relational dependencies in the form of linguistic decision tables and branching questionnaires [10, 97].

---

[1]It was brought to the author's attention by John E. Shively (Lawrence Berkeley Laboratory) that an interesting case of an interplay between probability and possibility occurs in the historical letter from Einstein to Roosevelt (dated August 2, 1939). In a passage in this letter, Einstein writes:

> In the course of the last four months it has been made probable--through the work of Joliot in France as well as Fermi and Szilard in America--that it may become possible to set up nuclear chain reactions in a large mass of uranium, by which vast amounts of power and large quantities of new radium-like elements would be generated. Now it appears almost certain that this could be achieved in the immediate future.

2. Basic Properties of Possibility Distributions

As we have indicated in the preceding section, the concept of a possibility distribution plays a central role in our approach to the representation and manipulation of soft data. In what follows, we shall discuss some of the basic properties of possibility distributions[2] and lay the groundwork for their application to soft data analysis in later sections.

Possibility Measure

Consider a variable X which takes values in a universe of discourse U, and let Π_X be the possibility distribution induced by a proposition of the form

$$p \triangleq X \text{ is } G \tag{2.1}$$

where G is a fuzzy subset of U which is characterized by its membership function μ_G. In consequence of the possibility postulate, we can assert that

$$\Pi_X = G \tag{2.2}$$

which implies that

$$\pi_X(u) = \mu_G(u) \ , \quad u \in U \tag{2.3}$$

where π_X is the possibility distribution function of X.

Now if F is a fuzzy subset of U, then the *possibility measure* of F is defined by the expression

$$\Pi(F) = \sup(F \cap G) \tag{2.4}$$

or, more explicitly,

$$\Pi(F) = \sup_U \big(\mu_F(u) \wedge \mu_G(u)\big) \tag{2.5}$$

where the supremum is taken over $u \in U$ and $\wedge$ represents the min operation. The number $\Pi(F)$, which ranges in value from 0

[2] In our exposition of the basic properties of possibility distributions and related concepts we shall draw on some of the definitions and examples in [91,94,98].

to 1, may be interpreted as the possibility that X is F given that X is G. Thus, in symbols,

$$\Pi(F) = \mathrm{Poss}\{X \text{ is } F \mid X \text{ is } G\} = \sup(F \cap G) \tag{2.6}$$

In particular, if F is a nonfuzzy set A, then

$$\mu_A(u) = 1 \quad \text{if} \quad u \in A$$
$$= 0 \quad \text{if} \quad u \notin A$$

and hence

$$\Pi(A) = \mathrm{Poss}\{X \text{ is } A \mid X \text{ is } G\} = \sup_A(G) \tag{2.7}$$
$$= \sup_A\left(\mu_G(u)\right), \quad u \in U$$

An important immediate consequence of (2.4) is the F-additivity of possibility measures expressed by

$$\Pi(F \cup H) = \Pi(F) \vee \Pi(H) \tag{2.8}$$

where F and H are arbitrary fuzzy subsets of U and $\vee$ is the max operation. By contrast, the probability measures of F and H have the additive property expressed by

$$P(F \cup H) = P(F) + P(H) - P(F \cap H) \tag{2.9}$$

The fact that possibility measures are F-additive but not additive in the usual sense constitutes one of the basic differences between the concepts of possibility and probability [92].

As a simple illustration of (2.6), assume that the proposition "X is G" has the form

$$p \triangleq X \text{ is small} \tag{2.10}$$

where SMALL is a fuzzy set defined by[3]

$$\text{SMALL} = 1/0 + 0.8/2 + 0.6/3 + 0.4/4 + 0.25 \tag{2.11}$$

---

[3] The notation $F = \mu_1/u_1 + \cdots + \mu_n/u_n$ signifies that F is a collection of fuzzy singletons μ_i/u_i, $i = 1, \ldots, n$, with μ_i representing the grade of membership of u_i in F. More generally, F may be expressed as $F = \sum_i \mu_i/u_i$ or $F = \int_U \mu_F(u)/u$.

In this case, the possibility distribution induced by p is given by

$$\Pi_X = 1/0 + 0.8/2 + 0.6/3 + 0.4/4 + 0.1/5$$

and if the proposition X is F has the form

$$q \triangleq X \text{ is large} \tag{2.12}$$

where LARGE is defined by

$$\text{LARGE} \triangleq 0.2/4 + 0.4/5 + 0.6/6 + 0.8/7 + 1/8 + \cdots ,$$

then

$$\text{SMALL} \cap \text{LARGE} = 0.2/4 + 0.1/5$$

and hence

$$\text{Poss}\{X \text{ is large} | X \text{ is small}\} = 0.2$$

Joint, Marginal and Conditional Possibility Distributions

Let $X \triangleq (X_1,\ldots,X_n)$ be an n-ary variable which takes values in a universe of discourse $U = U_1 \times \cdots \times U_n$, with X_i, $i = 1,\ldots,n$, taking values in U_i. Furthermore, let F be an n-ary fuzzy relation in U which is characterized by its membership function μ_F. Then, the proposition

$$p \triangleq X \text{ is } F \tag{2.13}$$

induces an n-ary joint possibility distribution

$$\Pi_X \triangleq \Pi_{(X_1,\ldots,X_n)} \tag{2.14}$$

which is given by

$$\Pi_{(X_1,\ldots,X_n)} = F \tag{2.15}$$

Correspondingly, the possibility distribution function of X is expressed by

$$\pi_{(X_1,\ldots,X_n)}(u_1,\ldots,u_n) = \mu_F(u_1,\ldots,u_n) \ , \quad u \triangleq (u_1,\ldots,u_n) \in U$$
$$= \text{Poss}\{X_1 = u_1,\ldots,X_n = u_n\}$$

As in the case of probabilities, we can define marginal and conditional possibilities. Thus, let $s \triangleq (i_1,\ldots,i_k)$ be a subsequence of the index sequence $(1,\ldots,n)$ and let s' denote the complementary subsequence $s' \triangleq (j_1,\ldots,j_m)$ (e.g., for $n = 5$, $s = (1,3,4)$ and $s' = (2,5)$). In terms of such sequences, a k-tuple of the form $(A_{i_1},\ldots,A_{i_k})$ may be expressed in an abbreviated form as $A_{(s)}$. In particular, the variable $X_{(s)} = (X_{i_1},\ldots,X_{i_k})$ will be referred to as a k-ary *subvariable* of $X \triangleq (X_1,\ldots,X_n)$, with $X_{(s')} = (X_{j_1},\ldots,X_{j_m})$ being a subvariable complementary to $X_{(s)}$.

The *projection* of $\Pi_{(X_1,\ldots,X_n)}$ *on* $U_{(s)} \triangleq U_{i_1} \times \cdots \times U_{i_k}$ is a k-ary possibility distribution denoted by

$$\Pi_{X_{(s)}} \triangleq \mathrm{Proj}_{U_{(s)}} \Pi_{(X_1,\ldots,X_n)} \tag{2.16}$$

and defined by

$$\pi_{X_{(s)}}(u_{(s)}) \triangleq \sup_{u_{(s')}} \pi_X(u_1,\ldots,u_n) \tag{2.17}$$

where $\pi_{X_{(s)}}$ is the possibility distribution function of $\Pi_{X_{(s)}}$. For example, for $n = 2$,

$$\pi_{X_1}(u_1) \triangleq \sup_{u_2} \pi_{(X_1,X_2)}(u_1,u_2)$$

is the expression for the possibility distribution function of the projection of $\Pi_{(X_1,X_2)}$ on U_1. By analogy with the concept of a marginal probability distribution, $\Pi_{X_{(s)}}$ will be referred to as a *marginal possibility distribution*.

As a simple illustration, assume that $n = 3$, $U_1 = U_2 = U_3 = a + b$ or, more conventionally, $\{a,b\}$, and $\Pi_{(X_1,X_2,X_3)}$ is expressed as a linear form

$$\Pi_{(X_1,X_2,X_3)} = 0.8aaa + 1aab + 0.6baa + 0.2bab + 0.5bbb \tag{2.18}$$

in which a term of the form 0.6baa signifies that

$$\mathrm{Poss}\{X_1 = b,\ X_2 = a,\ X_3 = a\} = 0.6$$

To derive $\Pi_{(X_1,X_2)}$ from (2.18), it is sufficient to replace the value of X_3 in each term in (2.18) by the null string Λ. This yields

$$\Pi_{(X_1,X_2)} = 0.8aa + 1aa + 0.6ba + 0.2ba + 0.5bb$$
$$= 1aa + 0.6ba + 0.5bb$$

and similarly

$$\Pi_{X_1} = 1a + 0.6b + 0.5b$$
$$= 1a + 0.6b$$

An *n*-ary possibility distribution is *particularized* by forming the conjunction of the propositions "X is F" and "$X_{(s)}$ is G," where $X_{(s)}$ is a subvariable of X. Thus,

$$\Pi_X[\Pi_{X_{(s)}} = G] \triangleq F \cap \bar{G} \qquad (2.19)$$

where the right-hand member denotes the intersection of F with the cylindrical extension of G, i.e., a cylindrical fuzzy set defined by

$$\mu_{\bar{G}}(u_1,\ldots,u_n) = \mu_G(u_{i_1},\ldots,u_{i_k}) , \qquad (2.20)$$
$$(u_1,\ldots,u_n) \in U_1 \times \cdots \times U_n .$$

As a simple illustration, consider the possibility distribution defined by (2.18), and assume that

$$\Pi_{(X_1,X_2)} = 0.4aa + 0.9ba + 0.1bb .$$

In this case,

$$\bar{G} = 0.4aaa + 0.4aab + 0.9baa + 0.9bab + 0.1bba + 0.1bbb$$
$$F \cap \bar{G} = 0.4aaa + 0.4aab + 0.6baa + 0.2bab + 0.1bbb$$

and hence

$$\Pi_{(X_1,X_2,X_3)}[\Pi_{(X_1,X_2)} = G]$$
$$= 0.4aaa + 0.4aab + 0.6baa + 0.2bab + 0.1bbb .$$

There are many cases in which the operations of particularization and projection are combined. In such cases it is convenient to use the simplified notation

$$_{X_{(r)}}\Pi[\Pi_{X_{(s)}} = G] \qquad (2.21)$$

to indicate that the particularized possibility distribution (or relation) $\Pi[\Pi_{X_{(s)}} = G]$ is projected on $U_{(r)}$, where r, like s, is a subsequence of the index sequence (1,...,n). For example,

$$X_1 \times X_3 \, \Pi[\Pi_{(X_3,X_4)} = G]$$

would represent the projection of $\Pi[\Pi_{(X_3,X_4)} = G]$ on $U_1 \times U_3$. Informally, (2.21) may be interpreted as: Constrain the $X_{(s)}$ by $\Pi_{X_{(s)}} = G$ and read out the $X_{(r)}$. In particular, if the values of $X_{(s)}$--rather than their possibility distribution--are set equal to G, then (2.21) becomes

$$X_{(r)} \, \Pi[X_{(s)} = G] \ .$$

We shall make use of (2.21) and its special cases in Section 3.

As we shall see in Section 3, if X and Y are variables taking values in U and V, respectively, then the *conditional possibility distribution* of Y given X is induced by a proposition of the form "If X is F then Y is G" and is expressed as $\Pi_{(Y|X)}$, with the understanding that

$$\pi_{(Y|X)}(v|u) \triangleq \text{Poss}\{Y = v | X = u\} \tag{2.22}$$

where (2.21) defines the conditional possibility distribution function of Y given X.

If we know the distribution function of X and the conditional distribution function of Y given X, then we can construct the joint distribution function of X and Y by forming the conjunction ($\wedge \triangleq \min$)

$$\pi_{(X,Y)}(u,v) = \pi_X(u) \wedge \pi_{(Y|X)}(v|u) \ . \tag{2.23}$$

However, unlike the identity that holds in the case of probabilities, we can also obtain $\pi_{(X,Y)}(u,v)$ by forming the conjunction of $\pi_{(X|Y)}(u|v)$ and $\pi_{(Y|X)}(v|u)$:

$$\pi_{(X,Y)}(u,v) = \pi_{(X|Y)}(u|v) \wedge \pi_{(Y|X)}(v|u) \ . \tag{2.24}$$

In yet another deviation from parallelism with probabilities, the marginal possibility distribution function of X may be expressed in more than one way in terms of the joint and conditional possibility distribution functions. More specifically, we may have

(a) $$\pi_X(u) = \vee_v \pi_{(X,Y)}(u,v) \qquad (2.25)$$

where $\vee_v$ denotes the supremum over $v \in V$;

(b) $$\pi_X(u) = \vee_v \pi_{(X|Y)}(u|v) \qquad (2.26)$$

and

(c) $$\pi_X(u) = \pi_{(X|Y)}(u,\tilde{v}(u)) \qquad (2.27)$$

where, for a given u, $\tilde{v}(u)$ is the value of v at which $\pi_{(Y|X)}(v|u) = 1$, if $\tilde{v}(u)$ is defined for every $u \in U$.

Intuitively, (a) represents the possibility of assigning a value to X as perceived by an observer ((X,Y) observer) who observes the joint possibility distribution $\Pi_{(X,Y)}$. Similarly, (b) represents the perception of an observer ((X|Y) observer) who observes only the conditional possibility distribution $\Pi_{(X|Y)}$ and is unconcerned with or unaware of $\Pi_{(Y|X)}$. And (c) expresses the perception of an observer who assumes that v is assigned that value, if it exists, which makes $\pi_{(Y|X)}(v|u)$ equal to unity.

As will be seen in Section 3, the concept of a conditional possibility distribution plays a basic role in the formulation of a generalized form of *modus ponens* and in defining a measure of belief. What is as yet an unsettled issue revolves around the question of how to derive $\pi_{(X|Y)}$ and $\pi_{(Y|X)}$ from $\pi_{(X,Y)}$. Somewhat different answers to this question are presented in [92], [57] and [33]. It may well turn out to be the case that, in contrast to probabilities, there does not exist a unique solution to the problem and that, in general, the answer depends on the perspective of the observer.

The Extension Principle

Let f be a function from U to V. The extension principle--as its name implies--serves to extend the domain of definition of f from U to the set of fuzzy subsets of U. In particular, if F is a finite fuzzy subset of U expressed as

$$F = \mu_1/u_1 + \cdots + \mu_n/u_n$$

then f(F) is a finite fuzzy subset of V defined as

$$\begin{aligned} f(F) &= f(\mu_1/u_1 + \cdots + \mu_n/u_n) \\ &= \mu_1/f(u_1) + \cdots + \mu_n/f(u_n) \ . \end{aligned} \qquad (2.28)$$

More generally, if the support of F is a continuum, i.e.,

$$F = \int_U \mu_F(u)/u \qquad (2.29)$$

then

$$f(F) = \int_U \mu_F(u)/f(u) \ . \qquad (2.30)$$

Furthermore, if U is a cartesian product of $U_1,\ldots U_n$ and f is a mapping from $U_1 \times \cdots \times U_n$ to V, then

$$f(F) = \int_U \mu_F(u_1,\ldots,u_n)/f(u_1,\ldots,u_n) \ . \qquad (2.31)$$

In connection with (2.31), it should be noted that there are many cases in which we have only partial information about μ_F, e.g., the knowledge of its projections on $U_1,\ldots,U_n$, which implies that the available information consists of the marginal membership functions $\mu_1,\ldots,\mu_n$, where

$$\mu_i(u_i) = \sup_{u_1,\ldots,u_{i-1},u_{i+1},\ldots,u_n} \mu_F(u_1,\ldots,u_n) \ , \quad i = 1,\ldots,n \ .$$

In such cases, the extension of the domain of definition of f is expressed by

$$f(F) = \int_U \mu_1(u_1) \wedge \cdots \wedge \mu_n(u_n)/f(u_1,\ldots,u_n) \qquad (2.32)$$

with the understanding that, in replacing $\mu_F(u_1,\ldots,u_n)$ with

$\mu_1(u_1) \wedge \cdots \wedge \mu_n(u_n)$, we are tacitly invoking the principle of maximal restriction [95], which asserts that, in the absence of complete information about Π_X, we should equate Π_X to the maximal (i.e., least restrictive) possibility distribution which is consistent with the partial information about Π_X.

In applying the extension principle to the analysis of soft data, it is frequently convenient to employ a more explicit representation of f(F) which is equivalent to (2.32). Specifically, on denoting the membership function of f(F) by μ, we have

$$f(F) = \int_V \mu(v)/v \tag{2.33}$$

where

$$\mu(v) \triangleq \mathrm{Max}_{u_1,\ldots,u_n}\ \mu_1(u_1) \wedge \cdots \wedge \mu_n(u_n) \tag{2.34}$$

subject to the constraint

$$v = f(u_1,\ldots,u_n) \ .$$

In this form, the extension principle will be employed in Section 4 to reduce the problem of inference from soft data to the solution of a variational problem in mathematical programming.

An important aspect of our approach to the analysis of soft data is the flexibility afforded by the assumption that the variables are allowed to be *linguistic* [90], that is, are allowed to have values that are represented as sentences in a natural or synthetic language, with each such value defining a possibility distribution in the domain of the variable. For example, if *Age* is a linguistic variable, its linguistic values might be of the form:

young	old
not young	not old
very young	very old
not very young	not very old
more or less young	more or less old
quite young	quite old
rather young	rather old
- - - - -	- - - - -

not young and not old
not very young and not very old
- - - - - - - - - - - - - - - - -

where *young* is a primary term which has to be calibrated in a specified context and *old* is its antonym. As we shall see in Section 3, the translation rules for propositions expressed in a natural language provide a method for computing the possibility distribution induced by a proposition of the form "X is ℓ," where ℓ is a linguistic value of X, from the knowledge of the membership functions of the primary term and its antonym.

3. Translation Rules and Meaning Representation

When soft data are represented in the form of propositions in a natural language, it is necessary to have, first, a system for translating such propositions into a more precise form; and second, a set of rules of inference which apply to the translated propositions and which may be employed to arrive at answers to questions regarding the data.

A meaning representation language which is well-suited for this purpose is PRUF [93]. In what follows, we shall state some of the relevant translation rules in PRUF and outline the associated rules of inference.

The translation rules in PRUF serve the purpose of facilitating the composition of the meaning of a complex proposition from the meanings of its constituents. For convenience, the rules in question are categorized into four basic types: Type 1: Rules pertaining to modification; Type II: Rules pertaining to composition; Type III: Rules pertaining to quantification; and Type IV: Rules pertaining to qualification.

Following a discussion of these rules and the associated rules of inference, we shall outline a general translation principle which forms the basis for PRUF, and sketch a general question-answering technique which reduces the problem of inference to the solution of a variational problem in mathematical programming.

Translation Rules

Modifier rule (Type I). Let X be a variable which takes values in a universe of discourse U and let F be a fuzzy subset of U. Consider the proposition

$$p \triangleq X \text{ is } F \tag{3.1}$$

or, more generally,

$$p = N \text{ is } F \tag{3.2}$$

where N is a variable, an object or a proposition. For example,

$$p \triangleq \text{Mary is young} \tag{3.3}$$

which may be expressed in the form (3.1), i.e.,

$$p \triangleq \text{Age(Mary) is young} \tag{3.4}$$

by identifying X with the variable Age(Mary).

Now, if in a particular context the proposition X is F translates into

$$X \text{ is } F \longrightarrow \Pi_X = F \tag{3.5}$$

then in the same context

$$X \text{ is } mF \longrightarrow \Pi_X = F^+ \tag{3.6}$$

where m is a modifier such as *not*, *very*, *more or less*, etc., and F^+ is a modification of F induced by m. More specifically: If m = not, then $F^+ = F'$ = complement of F, i.e.,

$$\mu_{F^+}(u) = 1 - \mu_F(u) \ , \quad u \in U \ . \tag{3.7}$$

If m = very, then $F^+ = F^2$, i.e.,

$$\mu_{F^+}(u) = \mu_F^{\ 2}(u) \ , \quad u \in U \ . \tag{3.8}$$

If m = more or less, then $F^+ = \sqrt{F}$, i.e.,

$$\mu_{F^+}(u) = \sqrt{\mu_F(u)} \ , \quad u \in U \ . \tag{3.9}$$

As a simple illustration of (3.8), if SMALL is defined as in (2.11), then

$$\text{X is very small} \longrightarrow \Pi_X = F^2 \tag{3.10}$$

where

$$F^2 = 1/0 + 1/1 + 0.64/2 + 0.36/3 + 0.16/4 + 0.04/5 \ .$$

It should be noted that (3.7), (3.8) and (3.9) should be viewed as default rules which may be replaced by other translation rules in cases in which some alternative interpretations of the modifiers *very* and *more or less* are more appropriate.

Conjunctive, Disjunctive and Implicational Rules (Type II). If

$$\text{X is F} \longrightarrow \Pi_X = F \quad \text{and} \quad \text{Y is G} \longrightarrow \Pi_Y = G \tag{3.11}$$

where F and G are fuzzy subsets of U and V, respectively, then

(a) $$\text{X is G and Y is G} \longrightarrow \Pi_{(X,Y)} = F \times G \tag{3.12}$$

where

$$\mu_{F \times G}(u,v) \triangleq \mu_F(u) \wedge \mu_G(v) \ . \tag{3.13}$$

(b) $$\text{X is F or Y is G} \longrightarrow \Pi_{(X,Y)} = \bar{F} \cup \bar{G} \tag{3.14}$$

where

$$\bar{F} \triangleq F \times V \ , \quad \bar{G} \triangleq U \times G \tag{3.15}$$

and

$$\mu_{\bar{F} \cup \bar{G}}(u,v) = \mu_F(u) \vee \mu_G(v) \ . \tag{3.16}$$

(c) $$\text{If X is F then Y is G} \longrightarrow \Pi_{(Y|X)} = \bar{F}' \oplus \bar{G} \tag{3.17}$$

where $\Pi_{(Y|X)}$ denotes the conditional possibility distribution of Y given X, and the bounded sum $\oplus$ is defined by

$$\mu_{\bar{F}' \oplus \bar{G}}(u,v) = 1 \wedge (1 - \mu_G(u) + \mu_G(v)) \ . \tag{3.18}$$

In stating the implicational rule in the form (3.17), we have merely chosen one of several alternative ways in which the conditional possibility distribution $\Pi_{(Y|X)}$ may be defined, each of which has some advantages and disadvantages depending on the application. Among the more important of these are the following [5,49,66]:

(c_2) If X is F then Y is G $\rightarrow \Pi_{(Y|X)} = \bar{F}' \cup G$ (3.19)

(c_3) If X is F then Y is G $\rightarrow \Pi_{(Y|X)} = F \times G \cup F' \times V$ (3.20)

(c_4) If X is F then Y is G $\rightarrow \pi_{(Y|X)}(v|u)$ (3.21)

$$= 1 \text{ if } \mu_G(v) \geq \mu_F(u)$$

$$= \frac{\mu_G(v)}{\mu_F(u)} \text{ otherwise}$$

(c_5) If X is F then Y is G $\rightarrow \pi_{(Y|X)}(v|u)$ (3.22)

$$= 1 \text{ if } \mu_G(v) \geq \mu_F(u)$$

$$= \mu_G(v) \text{ otherwise}$$

As simple illustrations of (3.12), (3.14) and (3.17), if

$$F \triangleq \text{SMALL} = 1/1 + 0.6/2 + 0.1/3$$

$$G \triangleq \text{LARGE} = 0.1/1 + 0.6/2 + 1/3$$

then

X is small and Y is large $\rightarrow \Pi_{(X,Y)}$

$$= 0.1/(1,1) + 0.6/(1,2) + 1/(1,3) + 0.1(2,1) + 0.6/(2,2) + 0.6/(2,3) + 0.1/(3,1) + 0.1/(3,2) + 0.1/(3,3)$$

X is small or Y is large $\rightarrow \Pi_{(X,Y)}$

$$= 1/(1,1) + 1/(1,2) + 1/(1,3) + 0.6/(2,1) + 0.6/(2,2) + 1/(2,3) + 0.1/(3,1) + 0.6/(3,2) + 1/(3,3)$$

and

If X is small then Y is large $\rightarrow \Pi_{(Y|X)}$

$$= 0.1/(1,1) + 0.6/(1,2) + 1/(1,3) + 0.5/(2,1) + 1/(2,2) + 1/(2,3) + 1/(3,1) + 1/(3,2) + 1/(3,3) .$$

<u>Quantification Rule (Type III)</u>. If $U = \{u_1, \ldots, u_N\}$, Q is a quantifier such as *many*, *few*, *several*, *all*, *some*, *most*, etc., and

$$X \text{ is } F \longrightarrow \Pi_X = F \tag{3.23}$$

then the proposition "QX is F" (e.g., "many X's are large") translates into

$$\Pi_{\text{Count}(F)} = Q \tag{3.24}$$

where Count(F) denotes the number (or the proportion) of elements of U which are in F. By the definition of cardinality of F [90], if the fuzzy set F is expressed as

$$F = \mu_1/u_1 + \mu_2/u_2 + \cdots + \mu_N/u_N \tag{3.25}$$

then

$$\text{Count}(F) = \sum_{i=1}^{N} \mu_i \tag{3.26}$$

where the right-hand member is understood to be rounded-off to the nearest integer. As a simple illustration of (3.24), if the quantifier *several* is defined as

$$\text{SEVERAL} \triangleq 0/1 + 0.4/2 + 0.6/3 + 1/4 + 1/5 + 1/6 + 0.6/7 + 0.2/8 \tag{3.27}$$

then

$$\text{Several X's are large} \longrightarrow \Pi_{\sum_{i=1}^{N} \mu_{\text{LARGE}}(u_i)} \tag{3.28}$$

$$= 0/1 + 0.4/2 + 0.6/3 + 1/4 + 1/5 + 1/6 + 0.6/7 + 0.2/8$$

where $\mu_{\text{LARGE}}(u_i)$ is the grade of membership of the ith value of X in the fuzzy set LARGE.

Alternatively, and perhaps more appropriately, the cardinality of F may be defined as a fuzzy number, as is done in [91]. Thus, if the elements of F are sorted in descending order, so that $\mu_n \leq \mu_m$ if $n \geq m$, then the truth-value of the proposition

$$p \triangleq F \text{ has at least } n \text{ elements} \tag{3.29}$$

is defined to be equal to μ_n, while that of q,

$$q \triangleq F \text{ has at most } n \text{ elements} , \tag{3.30}$$

is taken to be $1-\mu_{n+1}$. From this, then, it follows that the truth-value of the proposition r,

$$r \triangleq F \text{ has exactly } n \text{ elements }, \tag{3.31}$$

is given by $\mu_n \wedge (1-\mu_{n+1})$.

Let F↓ denote F sorted in descending order. Then (3.29) may be expressed compactly in the equivalent form

$$\text{FGCount}(F) = F{\downarrow} \tag{3.32}$$

which signifies that if the fuzzy cardinality of F is defined in terms of (3.29), with G standing for *greater than*, then the fuzzy count of elements in F is given by F↓, with the understanding that F↓ is regarded as a fuzzy subset of {0,1,2,...}. In a similar fashion, (3.30) leads to the definition

$$\text{FLCount}(F) = (F{\downarrow})' - 1 \tag{3.33}$$

where L stands for *less than* and subtraction should be interpreted as translation to the left, while (3.31) leads to

$$\text{FECount}(F) = (F{\downarrow}) \cap ((F{\downarrow})'-1)$$

where E stands for *equal to*. For convenience, we shall refer to FGCount, FLCount and FECount as the FG cardinality, FL cardinality and FE cardinality, respectively. The concept of FG cardinality will be illustrated in Example 9, Section 5.

Remark. There may be some cases in which it may be appropriate to normalize the definition of FECount in order to convey a correct perception of the count of elements in a fuzzy set. In such cases, we may employ the definition

$$\text{FENCount}(F) = \frac{\text{FECount}(F)}{\text{Max}_n(\mu_n \wedge (1-\mu_{n+1}))} . \tag{3.34}$$

<u>Truth Qualification Rule (Type IV)</u>. Let τ be a linguistic truth-value, e.g., *very true*, *quite true*, *more or less*, *true*, etc. Such a truth-value may be regarded as a fuzzy

subset of the unit interval which is characterized by a membership function $\mu_\tau: [0,1] \rightarrow [0,1]$.

A truth-qualified proposition, e.g., "It is τ that X is F," is expressed as "X is F is τ." As shown in [89], the translation rule for such propositions is given by

$$X \text{ is } F \text{ is } \tau \longrightarrow \Pi_X = F^+ \tag{3.35}$$

where

$$\mu_{F^+}(u) = \mu_\tau(\mu_F(u)) \ . \tag{3.36}$$

As an illustration, consider the truth-qualified proposition

Yolanda is young is very true

which by (3.35), (3.36) and (3.8) translates into

$$\Pi_{Age(Yolanda)} = \mu_{TRUE^2}(\mu_{YOUNG}(u)) \ . \tag{3.37}$$

Now, if we assume that

$$\mu_{YOUNG}(u) = \left(1 + \left(\frac{u}{25}\right)^2\right)^{-1} \ , \quad u \in [0,100] \tag{3.38}$$

and

$$\mu_{TRUE}(v) = v^2 \ , \quad v \in [0,1]$$

then (3.36) yields

$$\Pi_{Age(Yolanda)} = \left(1 + \left(\frac{u}{25}\right)^2\right)^{-4}$$

as the possibility distribution of the age of Yolanda.

Probability Qualification Rule (Type IV). This rule applies to propositions of the general form "X is F is λ," where X is a real-valued variable, F is a linguistic value of X, and λ is a linguistic value of likelihood (or probability), e.g., "X is small is not very likely." Unless stated to the contrary, λ is assumed to be a fuzzy subset of the unit interval [0,1] which is characterized by its membership function μ_λ, and the probability distribution of X is characterized by its probability density function p, i.e.,

$$\text{Prob}\{X \in [u, u+du]\} = p(u)\,du\ . \tag{3.39}$$

As shown in [93], the translation rule for probability-qualified propositions is expressed by

$$X \text{ is } F \text{ is } \lambda \longrightarrow \pi(p) = \mu_\lambda\left(\int_U \mu_F(u)\,p(u)\,du\right) \tag{3.40}$$

where $\pi(p)$ denotes the possibility that the probability density function of X is p, and the integral in the right-hand member of (3.40) represents the probability of the fuzzy event [86] "X is F." Thus, in the case of probability-qualified propositions, the proposition "X is F is λ" induces a possibility distribution of the probability density function of X.

As a simple illustration, consider the proposition

$$q \triangleq \text{Yolanda is young is very likely}\ . \tag{3.41}$$

In this case, $X \triangleq \text{Age(Yolanda)}$ and the right-hand member of (3.40) becomes

$$\pi(p) = \mu^2_{LIKELY}\left(\int_0^{100} \mu_{YOUNG}(u)\,p(u)\,du\right)\ . \tag{3.42}$$

Used in combination, the translation rules stated above provide a system for the determination of the possibility distributions induced by a fairly broad class of composite propositions. For example, by the use of (3.7), (3.8), (3.9), (3.12) and (3.18), the proposition

If X is not very large and Y is more or less small then Z is very very large.

can readily be found to induce the conditional possibility distribution described by

$$\pi_{(Z|X,Y)}(w|u,v) = 1 \wedge \left(1 - \left(1 - \mu^2_{LARGE}(u)\right) \wedge \mu^{0.5}_{SMALL}(v) + \mu^4_{LARGE}(w)\right)\ .$$

It is of interest to note that translation rules like those described above have found practical applications in the design of fuzzy logic controllers in steel plants, cement kilns and other types of industrial process control applications in which instructions expressed in a natural language are transformed into control signals [45,46,39,79].

A more general type of translation process in PRUF which subsumes the translation rules given above is the following.

Let $\mathcal{D} = \{D\}$ denote a collection of databases, with D representing a generic element of $\mathcal{D}$. For the purposes of our analysis, D will be assumed to consist of a collection of possibly time-varying relations. If R is a constituent relation in D, then by the *frame* of R is meant the name of R together with the names of its columns (i.e., attributes). For example, if a constituent of D is a relation labeled POPULATION whose tableau is comprised of columns labeled Name and Height then the frame of POPULATION is represented as POPULATION‖Name|Height| or, equivalently, as POPULATION[Name;Height].

If p is a proposition in a natural language, its translation into PRUF can assume one of three--essentially equivalent--forms.[4]

(a) p → a possibility assignment equation

(b) p → a procedure which yields for each D in $\mathcal{D}$ the possibility of D given p, i.e., Poss{D|p}

(c) p → a procedure which yields for each D in $\mathcal{D}$ the truth-value of p relative to D, i.e., Tr{p|D}

Remark. An important implicit assumption about the procedures involved in (b) and (c) is that they have a high degree of what might be called *explanatory effectiveness*, by

[4] It should be noted that (b) and (c) are in the spirit of truth-conditional semantics and possible-world semantics, respectively [15,34]. In their conventional form, however, these semantics have no provision for fuzzy propositions and hence are not suitable for the analysis of soft data.

which is meant a capability to convey the meaning of p to a human (or a machine) who is conversant with the meaning of the constituent terms in p but not with the meaning of p as a whole. For example, a procedure which merely tabulates the possibility of each D in $\mathcal{D}$ would, in general, have a low degree of explanatory effectiveness if it does not indicate in sufficient detail the way in which that possibility is arrived at. On the other extreme, a procedure which is excessively detailed and lacking in modularity would also have a low degree of explanatory effectiveness because the meaning of p might be obscured by the maze of unstructured steps in the body of the procedure.

The equivalence of (b) and (c) is a consequence of the way in which the concept of truth is defined in fuzzy logic

Thus, it can readily be shown that, under mildly restrictive assumptions on D, we have

$$\mathrm{Tr}\{p|D\} = \mathrm{Poss}\{D|p\}$$

which implies the equivalence of (b) and (c).

To illustrate (b) and show how (a) may be derived from (b), we shall consider first the relatively simple proposition

$$p \triangleq \text{Madan is not very tall .} \qquad (3.43)$$

In this case, it is convenient to assume that D contains two relations whose frames are:

POPULATION‖Name|Height|

TALL‖Height|μ|

In the relation TALL, each value of height is associated with the degree to which a person having that height is tall. In effect, then, the relation TALL defines the fuzzy set TALL.

The desired procedure involves the following steps.

1. Find Madan's height, h. In symbols, h is given by the expression (see (2.21))

$$h = {}_{\text{Height}}\ \text{POPULATION[Name} = \text{Madan]}\ .$$

2. Find the degree, δ, to which Madan is not very tall in D. Using the expression obtained in the preceding step, the answer is:

$$\delta = 1 - ({}_{\mu}\text{TALL[Height} = {}_{\text{Height}}\ \text{POPULATION[Name} = \text{Madan]]})^2\ .$$

3. Equate the possibility of D to δ. This yields the desired translation of p into PRUF, namely

$$\pi(D) = 1 - ({}_{\mu}\text{TALL[Height} = {}_{\text{Height}}\ \text{POPULATION[Name=Madan]]})^2 \tag{3.44}$$

To find the possibility distribution of Madan's height from (3.41), it is sufficient to observe that, for a fixed relation TALL, $\pi(D)$ depends only on Madan's height. From this it follows at once that

$$\Pi_{\text{Height(Madan)}} = (\text{TALL}^2)' \tag{3.45}$$

or, equivalently,

$$\pi_{\text{Height(Madan)}}(u) = 1 - \mu^2_{\text{TALL}}(u) \tag{3.46}$$

where u is a generic value of the variable Height. What should be noted is that the possibility assignment equation (3.45) could be obtained directly by applying to p the translation rules (3.7) and (3.8). Furthermore, the explanatory effectiveness of (3.45) is higher than that of (3.44).

Remark. In PRUF, it is important to differentiate between the meaning of a proposition and the information that is conveyed by it. Thus, if p is a proposition, then the procedure, P, into which it translates represents the meaning of p or, equivalently, its intension [15,41]. On the other hand, the possibility distribution which is induced by p constitutes the information, I(p), which is conveyed by p. Thus, in the foregoing example the possibility distribution defined by (3.45) represents the information conveyed by the proposition p $\triangleq$ Madan is not very tall. The meaning of p, then, is the procedure described by the right-hand member of (3.45).

If p and q are propositions such that

$$I(p) = I(q) \tag{3.47}$$

then p and q are *semantically equivalent* [93], which is expressed as

$$p \leftrightarrow q \; . \tag{3.48}$$

On the other hand, if

$$I(p) \leq I(q) \tag{3.49}$$

then p *semantically entails* q [93], i.e.,

$$p \mapsto q \tag{3.50}$$

As we shall see in the next section, the concepts of semantic equivalence and semantic entailment play an important role in inference from soft data.

4. Inference from Soft Data and Mathematical Programming

By interpreting a soft datum as a fuzzy proposition, the problem of inference from soft data may be reduced to the problem of inference from a collection of fuzzy propositions.

Suppose that $E = \{p_1,\ldots,p_n\}$ (with E standing for *evidence*) is a collection of fuzzy propositions and let p be a proposition that is inferred from E. At this point, it is natural to raise two basic questions. First, what does it mean to say that p is inferred from E; and second, by what methods can p be inferred from E.

To answer the first question, it is convenient to make use of the concept of information, as defined in Section 3. More specifically, let $I(p_1 \wedge \cdots \wedge p_n)$ be the information conveyed by the conjunction of propositions $p_1,\ldots,p_n$ or, equivalently, the possibility distribution induced by

$p_1 \wedge \cdots \wedge p_n$, and let $I(p_1 \wedge \cdots \wedge p_n \wedge p_n)$ be the information conveyed by the conjunction of $p_1 \wedge \cdots \wedge p_n$ and p. Then, we shall say, informally, that p may be *inferred from* $E = \{p_1, \ldots, p_n\}$ if

$$I(p_1 \wedge \cdots \wedge p_n) = I(p_1 \wedge \cdots \wedge p_n \wedge p) \ . \qquad (4.1)$$

In other words, p is inferrable from E if the addition of p to the evidence, E, does not affect the information conveyed by E.

As shown in [91], the above definition implies that the possibility distribution induced by the conjunction of $p_1, \ldots, p_n$ is contained in that induced by p. It is this containment property that underlies the *entailment principle* [91,93] which serves as a basis for the rules of inference stated in the sequel.

Remark. In speaking of entailment, it is necessary to differentiate between the entailment which obtains for particular denotations of the labels of fuzzy sets in $p_1, \ldots, p_n, p$, and *strong entailment*, which results when (4.1) holds for all denotations. As an illustration, if *very* is interpreted as a squaring operation, then the proposition

$$p \triangleq \text{Veronica is intelligent}$$

is strongly entailed by

$$p_1 \triangleq \text{Veronica is very intelligent}$$

since

$$\text{INTELLIGENT}^2 \subset \text{INTELLIGENT}$$

regardless of the way in which INTELLIGENT, the denotation of *intelligent*, is defined. On the other hand, in the case of the propositions

$$\begin{array}{l} p_1 \triangleq \text{John is not young} \\ \underline{p_2 \triangleq \text{John is not old}} \\ p \triangleq \text{John is middle-aged} \end{array}$$

the conjunction of p_1 and p_2 may be expressed as (see (3.12))

$$p_1 \wedge p_2 \triangleq \text{John is not young and not old .} \qquad (4.2)$$

Consequently, if the denotations of *young*, *old* and *middle-aged* are such that the containment condition

$$\text{YOUNG}' \cap \text{OLD}' \subset \text{MIDDLE-AGED} \qquad (4.3)$$

is satisfied, then p is entailed by p_1 and p_2. However, since the question of whether or not (4.2) is satisfied depends on the denotations of the labels of fuzzy sets in p_1, p_2 and p, it follows that p is not strongly entailed by p_1 and p_2.

Remark. In some ways, the entailment principle appears to be counterintuitive because we generally expect a conclusion, p, to be sharper than the totality of data on which it is based. However, the reason for the apparent sharpness is that, in general, p involves only a small subset of the variables present in $p_1,\ldots,p_n$. More specifically, as we shall see in the sequel, in the process of inference we usually focus our attention on a small number of functionals defined on $\mathcal{D}$ and preceive the higher degree of focusing as a manifestation of sharpness of p. An example illustrating this and other aspects of the entailment principle is described in Section 5.

Rules of Inference

For purposes of inference from a collection of fuzzy propositions, it is convenient to have at one's disposal a system of basic rules which may be used singly or in combination to infer a fuzzy proposition p from a body of evidence $E = \{p_1,\ldots,p_n\}$. Several such rules, which constitute a subset of the inference rules in fuzzy logic, FL [89], are stated in a summary form in the following.

1. Projection Principle. Consider a fuzzy proposition whose translation is expressed as

$$p \rightarrow \Pi_{(X_1,\ldots,X_n)} = F \tag{4.4}$$

and let $X_{(s)}$ denote a subvariable of the variable $X \triangleq (X_1,\ldots,X_n)$, i.e.,

$$X_{(s)} = (X_{i_1},\ldots,X_{i_k}) \tag{4.5}$$

where the index sequence $s \triangleq (i_1,\ldots,i_k)$ is a subsequence of the sequence $(1,\ldots,n)$.

Furthermore, let $\Pi_{X_{(s)}}$ denote the marginal possibility distribution of $X_{(s)}$; that is,

$$\Pi_{X_{(s)}} = \mathrm{Proj}_{U_{(s)}} F \tag{4.6}$$

where U_i, $i = 1,\ldots,n$, is the universe of discourse associated with X_i;

$$U_{(s)} = U_{i_1} \times \cdots \times U_{i_k} \tag{4.7}$$

and the projection of F on $U_{(s)}$ is defined by the possibility distribution function (see (2.17))

$$\pi_{X_{(s)}}(u_{i_1},\ldots,u_{i_k}) = \sup_{u_{j_1},\ldots,u_{j_m}} \mu_F(u_1,\ldots,u_n) \tag{4.8}$$

where $s' \triangleq (j_1,\ldots,j_m)$ is the index subsequence which is complementary to s, and μ_F is the membership function of F.

Now let q be a retranslation (i.e., reverse translation) of the possibility assignment equation

$$\Pi_{X_{(s)}} = \mathrm{Proj}_{U_{(s)}} F\ . \tag{4.9}$$

Then, the projection rule asserts that q may be inferred from p. In a schematic form, this assertion may be expressed more transparently as

$$\begin{array}{c} p \longrightarrow \Pi_{(X_1,\ldots,X_n)} = F \\ \downarrow \\ q \longleftarrow \Pi_{X_{(s)}} = \mathrm{Proj}_{U_{(s)}} F \end{array} \tag{4.10}$$

As was indicated in Section 2, the rule of inference represented by (4.10) is easy to apply when Π_X is expressed as a linear form. As an illustration, assume that $U_1 = U_2 = \{a,b\}$, and

$$\Pi_{(X_1,X_2)} = 0.8aa + 0.6ab + 0.4ba + 0.2bb$$

in which a term of the form 0.6ab signifies that

$$\mathrm{Poss}\{X_1 = a,\ X_2 = b\} = 0.6\ .$$

To obtain the projection of Π_X on, say, U_2 it is sufficient to replace the value of X_1 in each term by the null string Λ. Thus

$$\mathrm{Proj}_{U_2} \Pi_{(X_1,X_2)} = 0.8a + 0.6b + 0.4a + 0.2b = 0.8a + 0.6b$$

and hence from the proposition

$$(X_1,X_2) \text{ is } 0.8aa + 0.6ab + 0.4ba + 0.2bb$$

we can infer by (4.10) that

$$X_2 \text{ is } 0.8a + 0.6b\ .$$

2. Conjunction Rule. Consider a proposition p which is an assertion concerning the possible values of, say, two variables X and Y which take values in U and V, respectively. Similarly, let q be an assertion concerning the possible values of the variables Y and Z, taking values in V and W. With these assumptions, the translations of p and q may be expressed as

$$\begin{array}{l} p \longrightarrow \Pi^{p}_{(X,Y)} = F \\ q \longrightarrow \Pi^{q}_{(Y,Z)} = G \end{array} \ . \tag{4.11}$$

Let $\bar{F}$ and $\bar{G}$ be, respectively, the cylindrical extensions of F and G in $U \times V \times W$. Thus,

$$\bar{F} = F \times W \tag{4.12}$$

and

$$\bar{G} = U \times G \ . \tag{4.13}$$

Using the conjunction rule, we can infer from p and q a proposition which is defined by the following scheme:

$$\begin{array}{l} r \longrightarrow \Pi^{p}_{(X,Y)} = F \\ q \longrightarrow \Pi^{q}_{(Y,Z)} = G \\ \hline r \longleftarrow \Pi_{(X,Y,Z)} = \bar{F} \cap \bar{G} \end{array} \tag{4.14}$$

On combining the projection and conjunction rules, we obtain the *compositional rule of inference* (4.17) which includes the classical *modus ponens* as a special case.

More specifically, on applying the projection rule to (4.14), we obtain the following inference scheme

$$\begin{array}{l} p \longrightarrow \Pi^{p}_{(X,Y)} = F \\ q \longrightarrow \Pi^{q}_{(Y,Z)} = G \\ \hline r \longleftarrow \Pi^{r}_{(X,Z)} = F \circ G \end{array} \tag{4.15}$$

where the composition of F and G is defined by

$$\mu_{F \circ G}(u,w) = \sup_{v} \left(\mu_F(u,v) \wedge \mu_G(v,w) \right) \ . \tag{4.16}$$

In particular, if p is a proposition of the form "X is F" and q is a proposition of the form "If X is G then Y is H," then (4.15) becomes

$$\begin{array}{l} p \longrightarrow \Pi_{X} = F \\ q \longrightarrow \Pi_{(Y|X)} = \bar{G}' \oplus \bar{H} \\ \hline r \longleftarrow \Pi_{(Y)} = F \circ (\bar{G}' \oplus \bar{H}) \end{array} \tag{4.17}$$

The rule expressed by (4.17) may be viewed as a generalized

form of *modus ponens* which reduces to the classical *modus ponens* when F = G and F, G, H are nonfuzzy sets.

Stated in terms of possibility distributions, the generalized *modus ponens* places in evidence the analogy between probabilistic and possibilistic inference. Thus, in the case of probabilities, we can deduce the probability distribution of Y from the knowledge of the probability distribution of X and the conditional probability distribution of Y given X. Similarly, in the case of possibility distributions, we can infer the possibility distribution of Y from the knowledge of the possibility distribution of X and the conditional possibility distribution of Y given X.

It is important to note that the generalized *modus ponens* as expressed by (4.17) may be used to enlarge significantly the area of applicability of rule-based systems of the type employed in MYCIN and other expert systems. This is due primarily to two aspects of (4.17) which are not present in conventional rule-based systems: (a) in the propositions "X is F" and "If X is G then Y is H," F, G and H may be fuzzy sets; and (b) F and G need not be identical. Thus, as a result of (a) and (b), a rule-based system employing (4.17) may be designed to have an interpolative capability [88,97].

In addition to the rules described above, there is an important method of inference through which the deduction of p is reduced to the solution of a variational problem in mathematical programming.

In general terms, suppose that we have a database D and that we wish to answer a question q which relates to the data resident in D. For example, we may have a database which contains a relation with the frame

POPULATION	Name	Age

and q may be: What is the average age of individuals in POPULATION?

In PRUF, the translation of q is expressed as the translation of the answer to q, with a symbol of the form $?\alpha$ identifying the variable whose value is to be determined. As an illustration, for the example under discussion the proposition to be inferred from D may be expressed as

p ≜ The average age of individuals in POPULATION is ?f

where f is a function of the entries in D, say $X_1,\ldots,X_m$. Thus, to answer q we must compute the value of $f(X_1,\ldots,X_m)$ from whatever information is available about D.

To link the method under discussion to our earlier formulation of the problem of inference, we shall assume that the available information about D consists of the evidence $E = \{p_1,\ldots,p_n\}$, in which the p_i are fuzzy propositions.

Our definition of translation in Section 3 implies that each of the p_i in E induces a possibility distribution over $\mathcal{D}$. Thus, letting $\pi_i(X_1,\ldots,X_m)$ denote the possibility of D given p_i, we can assert that the possibility of D given $p_1,\ldots,p_n$ is given by the conjunction

$$\pi(D) \triangleq \pi_1(X_1,\ldots,X_m) \wedge \cdots \wedge \pi_n(X_1,\ldots,X_m) \qquad (4.18)$$

Thus, $\pi(D)$, as expressed by (4.18), may be viewed as an elastic constraint on D which is induced by the evidence $E \triangleq \{p_1,\ldots,p_n\}$.

From the knowledge of $\pi(D)$ we can infer the possibility distribution of the function

$$z = f(X_1,\ldots,X_m) \qquad (4.19)$$

by invoking the extension principle, as shown in Section 3. In this way, the determination of the possibility distribution of f reduces, in principle, to the solution of the following variational problem in mathematical programming.

$$\mu(z) \triangleq \operatorname{Max}_{X_1,\ldots,X_m} \pi_1(X_1,\ldots,X_m) \wedge \cdots \wedge \pi_n(X_1,\ldots,X_m) \qquad (4.20)$$

subject to

$$z = f(X_1, \ldots, X_m) \ .$$

In terms of $\mu(z)$, the possibility distribution of f may be expressed in the form

$$\Pi_f = \int_V \mu(z)/z \qquad (4.21)$$

where V is the range of z. An example illustrating the application of this technique will be discussed in Section 5.

As a further example, consider the proposition which occurs in Example (e), Section 1, namely:

$p \triangleq$ Brian is much taller than most of his close friends

For the purpose of representing the meaning of p, it is expedient to assume that D is comprised of the relations

POPULATION ‖ Name | Height |

FRIENDS ‖ Name1 | Name2 | μ |

MUCH TALLER ‖ Height1 | Height2 | μ |

MOST ‖ ρ | μ |

In the relation FRIENDS, μ represents the degree to which an individual whose name is Name2 is a friend of Name1. Similarly, in the relation MUCH TALLER, μ represents the degree to which an individual whose height is HEIGHT1 is much taller than one whose height is HEIGHT2. In MOST, μ represents the degree to which a proportion, ρ, fits the definition of MOST as a fuzzy subset of the unit interval.

To represent the meaning of p we shall translate p--in the spirit of (c) (Section 3)--into a procedure which computes the truth-value of p relative to a given D. The procedure--as described below--may be viewed as a sequence of computations which, in combination, yield the truth-value of p.

1. Obtain Brian's height from POPULATION. Thus,

$$\text{Height(Brian)} =_{\text{Height}} \text{POPULATION}[\text{Name} = \text{Brian}]$$

2. Determine the fuzzy set, MT, of individuals in POPULATION in relation to whom Brian is much taller.

Let Name_i be the name of the ith individual in POPULATION. The height of Name_i is given by

$$\text{Height}(\text{Name}_i) =_{\text{Height}} \text{POPULATION}[\text{Name} = \text{Name}_i]$$

Now the degree to which Brian is much taller than Name_i is given by

$$\delta_i =_{\mu} \text{MUCH TALLER}[\text{Height}(\text{Brian}), \text{Height}(\text{Name}_i)]$$

and hence MT may be expressed as

$$\text{MT} = \sum_i \delta_i/\text{Name}_i \ , \qquad \text{Name}_i \in_{\text{Name}} \text{POPULATION}$$

where ${}_{\text{Name}}\text{POPULATION}$ is the list of names of individuals in POPULATION, δ_i is the grade of membership of Name_i in MT, and $\sum_i$ is the union of singletons δ_i/Name_i (see footnote 3).

3. Determine the fuzzy set, CF, of individuals in POPULATION who are close friends of Brian.

To form the relation CLOSE FRIENDS from FRIENDS we intensify FRIENDS by squaring it (i.e., by replacing μ with μ^2). Then, the fuzzy set of close friends of Brian is given by

$$\text{CF} =_{\mu\times\text{Name2}} \text{FRIENDS}^2[\text{Name1} = \text{Brian}]$$

4. Form the count of elements of CF:

$$\text{Count}(\text{CF}) = \sum_i \mu_{\text{CF}}(\text{Name}_i)$$

where $\mu_{\text{CF}}(\text{Name}_i)$ is the grade of membership of Name_i in CF and $\sum_i$ is the arithmetic sum. More explicitly

$$\text{Count}(\text{F}) = \sum_i \mu^2_{\text{FRIENDS}}(\text{Brian}, \text{Name}_i)$$

5. Form the intersection of CF and MT, that is, the fuzzy set of those close friends of Brian in relation to whom he is much taller.

$$H \triangleq CF \cap MT$$

6. Form the count of elements of H.

$$\text{Count}(H) = \sum_i \mu_H(\text{Name}_i)$$

where $\mu_H(\text{Name}_i)$ is the grade of membership of Name_i in H and $\sum_i$ is the arithmetic sum.

7. Form the ratio

$$r = \frac{\text{Count}(MT \cap CF)}{\text{Count}(CF)}$$

which represents the proportion of close friends of Brian in relation to whom he is much taller.

8. Compute the grade of membership of r in MOST

$$\tau = {}_{\mu}\text{MOST}[\rho = r]$$

The value of τ is the desired truth-value of p with respect to D and, equivalently, the possibility of D given p. In terms of the membership functions of FRIENDS, MUCH TALLER and MOST, the value of τ is given explicitly by the expression

$$\tau = \mu_{MOST}\left(\frac{\sum_i \mu_{MT}(\text{Height(Brian)},\text{Height}(\text{Name}_i)) \wedge \mu_{CF}(\text{Brian},\text{Name}_i)}{\sum_i \mu_{CF}(\text{Brian},\text{Name}_i)}\right) \quad (4.22)$$

In summary, the procedure in question serves to represent the meaning of p by describing the operations that must be performed on D in order to compute the truth-value of p with respect to D. Thus, viewed as an expression in PRUF, (4.22) is in effect a mathematical description of a procedure which defines τ as a function of D. However, as was stressed in Section 3, the meaning of p is the procedure itself rather than the value of τ which it returns for a given D.

5. Examples of Inference from Soft Data

To illustrate the application of some of the techniques

described in the preceding sections, we shall consider several simple examples, including Examples (a), (b), (c) and (e) of Section 2. As is generally the case in inference from soft data, the chains of inference in these examples are short.

Example 1 (Example (a), Section 1).

X is a large number
Y is much larger than X
―――――――――――――
How large is Y?

Solution. On applying the compositional rule of inference (4.15), we obtain the following expression for the possibility distribution of Y

$$\Pi_Y = \text{LARGE} \circ \text{MUCH LARGER} \tag{5.1}$$

or, more explicitly,

$$\pi_Y(v) = \sup_u (\mu_{\text{LARGE}}(u) \wedge \mu_{\text{MUCH LARGER}}(u,v)) \tag{5.2}$$

where LARGE and MUCH LARGER are the fuzzy denotations of *large* and *much larger*, respectively.

Example 2.

X is small
Y is approximately equal to X
Z is much larger than both X and Y
―――――――――――――
How large is Z?

Solution. Proceeding as in Example 1, we obtain the following expression for the possibility distribution of Z

$$\Pi_Z = (\text{MUCH LARGER THAN} \circ \text{APPROXIMATELY EQUAL} \circ \text{SMALL}) \cap \text{MUCH LARGER THAN} \circ \text{SMALL} \tag{5.3}$$

in which the intersection implies that Z is much larger than X, and Z is much larger than Y.

Example 3 (Example (b), Section 1).

Most Frenchmen are not tall
Elie is a Frenchman

How tall is Elie?

Solution. First, we interpret the question as follows:

Most Frenchmen are not tall
Elie is a Frenchman picked at random

What is the probability that Elie is tall?

Second, we assume that the database consists of a single relation of the form

POPULATION‖Name|μ|

in which μ_i is the degree to which Name_i is tall, and i ranges from 1 to N.

Now, the constraint on the database induced by the proposition

$$p \triangleq \text{Most Frenchmen are not tall}$$

gives rise to the possibility distribution expressed by

$$\pi_p(\text{POPULATION}) = \mu_{\text{MOST}}(\frac{1}{N}\sum_i(1-\mu_i)) \tag{5.4}$$

in which the argument of μ_{MOST} represents the proportion of Frenchmen who are not tall.

Furthermore, if a Frenchman is chosen at random, then the probability that he is tall is given by (see (3.40))

$$\text{Prob}\{\text{Frenchman is tall}\} = \frac{1}{N}\sum_i \mu_i \ . \tag{5.5}$$

Thus, the proposition (in which λ is a linguistic probability)

$$q \triangleq \text{The probability that a Frenchman is tall is } \lambda$$

induces the possibility distribution

$$\pi_q(\text{POPULATION}) = \mu_\lambda(\frac{1}{N}\sum_i \mu_i) \ . \tag{5.6}$$

To apply the entailment principle to the problem in hand, we have to find a λ such that

$$\mu_\lambda(\tfrac{1}{N}\textstyle\sum_i \mu_i) \geq \mu_{MOST}(\tfrac{1}{N}\sum_i \mu_i) \ . \tag{5.7}$$

Furthermore, to be as informative as possible, the λ in q should be as small as possible in the sense that there should be no λ' such that

$$\lambda'(v) \leq \lambda(v) \tag{5.8}$$

for all v in [0,1] and $\lambda'(v) < \lambda(v)$ for at least some v in [0,1].

With this as our objective, we first note that (5.4) may be rewritten as

$$\begin{aligned}\pi_p(\text{POPULATION}) &= \mu_{MOST}(1 - \tfrac{1}{N}\textstyle\sum_i \mu_i) \\ &= \mu_{ANT\ MOST}(\tfrac{1}{N}\textstyle\sum_i \mu_i)\end{aligned} \tag{5.9}$$

where ANT MOST stands for the denotation of the antonym of *most*, i.e.,

$$\mu_{ANT\ MOST}(v) = \mu_{MOST}(1-v) \ , \quad v \in [0,1] \tag{5.10}$$

which signifies that the membership function of ANT MOST is the mirror image of that of MOST.

At this juncture, then, we can assert that

$$\begin{aligned}p &\triangleq \text{Most Frenchmen are not tall} \\ &\rightarrow \pi_p(\text{POPULATION}) = \mu_{ANT\ MOST}(\tfrac{1}{N}\textstyle\sum_i \mu_i)\end{aligned} \tag{5.11}$$

while

$$\begin{aligned}r &\triangleq \text{Prob\{Frenchman is tall\} is } \gamma \\ &\rightarrow \pi_r(\text{POPULATION}) = \mu_\gamma(\tfrac{1}{N}\textstyle\sum_i \mu_i)\end{aligned} \tag{5.12}$$

where γ is a linguistic probability.

On comparing (5.11) with (5.12), we note that if the fuzzy set LIKELY is defined to be equal to MOST, i.e.,

$$\mu_{LIKELY}(v) = \mu_{MOST}(v) \ , \ v \in [0,1] \tag{5.13}$$

so that

$$\mu_{UNLIKELY}(v) = \mu_{ANT\ LIKELY}(v) = \mu_{ANT\ MOST}(v) \qquad (5.14)$$

then we can infer from (5.11) and (5.12) the semantic equivalence (3.48)

$$p \triangleq \text{Most Frenchmen are not very tall} \leftrightarrow$$
$$r \triangleq \text{Prob\{Frenchman is tall\} is unlikely}$$

Consequently, as the answer to the posed question, we have

Most Frenchmen are not tall
Elie is a Frenchman
___
It is unlikely that Elie is tall

In essence, then, what we have shown is that, under the assumption that the fuzzy sets MOST and LIKELY are equal, we can infer from the premise

$$p \triangleq \text{Most Frenchmen are not tall}$$

the semantically equivalent proposition

$$r \triangleq \text{It is unlikely that a Frenchman picked at random is tall}$$

from which it follows that "It is unlikely that Elie is tall."

Example 4.

Most Swedes are tall
___
How many Swedes are very tall?

Solution. Suppose that the answer is of the form

$$r \triangleq Q \text{ Swedes are very tall}$$

where Q is a fuzzy quantifier. Then, proceeding as in Example 3, we have

$$p \triangleq \text{Most Swedes are tall} \rightarrow \pi_p(\text{POPULATION}) = \mu_{MOST}\left(\frac{1}{N}\sum_i \mu_i\right) \qquad (5.15)$$

and

$$r \triangleq Q \text{ Swedes are very tall} \longrightarrow \pi_r(\text{POPULATION}) = \mu_Q(\frac{1}{N}\sum_i \mu_i^2) \tag{5.16}$$

Consequently, what we have to find is the "smallest" Q such that

$$\mu_Q(\frac{1}{N}\sum_i \mu_i^2) \geq \mu_{MOST}(\frac{1}{N}\sum_i \mu_i) \ . \tag{5.17}$$

It can easily be verified that such a Q is given by[5]

$$Q = {}^2\text{MOST} \tag{5.18}$$

where the "left-square" of MOST is defined by

$$\mu_{{}^2\text{MOST}}(F) = \mu_{MOST}(\sqrt{v}) \ , \quad v \in [0,1] \ . \tag{5.19}$$

For, from the elementary inequality

$$\sqrt{1/N\, \Sigma_i\, \mu_i^2} \geq \frac{1}{N}\sum_i \mu_i \tag{5.20}$$

and the monotonicity of μ_{MOST} it follows that

$$\mu_{MOST}(\sqrt{1/N\, \Sigma_i\, \mu_i^2}) \geq \mu_{MOST}(\frac{1}{N}\sum_i \mu_i) \tag{5.21}$$

which, in view of (5.19), implies that

$$\mu_{{}^2\text{MOST}}(\frac{1}{N}\sum_i \mu_i^2) \geq \mu_{MOST}(\frac{1}{N}\sum_i \mu_i) \tag{5.22}$$

and hence that the proposition

$p \triangleq$ Most Swedes are tall

entails

$q \triangleq {}^2$Most Swedes are very tall

Example 5.

Naomi is not very tall is true

How true is it that Naomi is tall?

Solution. Suppose that the answer to the question is expressed as a proposition q:

$q \triangleq$ Naomi is tall is τ

---

[5] If MOST is interpreted as a fuzzy number [90,18,20] then ^{2}MOST may be expressed as the product of MOST with itself.

where τ is a linguistic truth-value, e.g., very true, more or less true, etc.

To determine τ, we set q semantically equal to p (see (3.49)), i.e., we assert that the possibility distributions induced by p and q are equal. Now, by (3.8) and (3.36), we have

$$\text{Naomi is not very tall is true} \rightarrow \Pi_{\text{Height(Naomi)}} = F \tag{5.23}$$

where

$$\mu_F(u) = \mu_{\text{TRUE}}(1 - \mu^2_{\text{TALL}}(u)) \tag{5.24}$$

and

$$\text{Naomi is tall is } \tau \rightarrow \mu_\tau(\mu_{\text{TALL}}(u)) \tag{5.25}$$

where μ_{TALL} and μ_{TRUE} are the membership functions of TALL and TRUE, respectively. Consequently, for all u in the domain of the variable Height(Naomi), we have

$$\mu_{\text{TRUE}}(1 - \mu^2_{\text{TALL}}(u)) = \mu_\tau(\mu_{\text{TALL}}(u)) \tag{5.26}$$

from which it follows that the membership function of τ is given by

$$\mu_\tau(v) = 1 - v^2 , \quad v \in [0,1] . \tag{5.27}$$

Thus, if μ_{TRUE} is defined by

$$\mu_{\text{TRUE}}(v) = v^2 \tag{5.28}$$

then

$$\mu_\tau(v) = 1 - \mu_{\text{TRUE}}(v) \tag{5.29}$$

and hence

$$\tau = \text{not true} . \tag{5.30}$$

On the other hand, if

$$\mu_{\text{TRUE}}(v) = v \tag{5.31}$$

then

$$\mu_\tau(v) = 1 - \mu^2_{\text{TRUE}}(v) \tag{5.32}$$

and

$$\tau = \text{not very true} . \tag{5.33}$$

Example 6 Marvin lives near MIT

Lucia lives near MIT

What is the distance between the residences of Marvin and Lucia?

Solution. Let (X_M,Y_M) and (X_L,Y_L) be the coordinates of the residences of Marvin and Lucia, respectively. Furthermore, let $\Pi_{(X_M,Y_M)}$ and $\Pi_{(X_L,Y_L)}$ be the possibility distributions induced by p and q, that is, derived from the definition of the binary fuzzy relation NEAR.

Now, the distance between the residences of Marvin and Lucia is expressed by

$$d = \sqrt{(X_M-X_L)^2 + (Y_M-Y_L)^2} \ . \qquad (5.34)$$

Using (5.34) and applying the extension principle (2.34), the possibility distribution function of d is found to be given by

$$\pi_d(w) = \sup_{u_1,v_1,u_2,v_2}\left(\pi_{(X_M,Y_M)}(u_1,v_1) \wedge \pi_{(X_L,Y_L)}(u_2,v_2)\right) \qquad (5.35)$$

subject to

$$w = \sqrt{(u_1-u_2)^2 + (v_1-v_2)^2} \qquad (5.36)$$

where the supremum is taken over all possible values of X_M, Y_M, X_L and Y_L subject to the constraint (5.36). Generally, π_d as defined by (5.35) will be a monotone decreasing function of w, with $\pi_d(w) = 1$ for sufficiently small values of w.

Example 7 (Example (c), Section 1).

$p_1 \triangleq$ It is unlikely that Andrea is very young

$p_2 \triangleq$ It is likely that Andrea is young

$p_3 \triangleq$ It is very unlikely that Andrea is old

$q \triangleq$ How likely is it that Andrea is not old?

Solution. To find the answer to the posed question, we shall reduce the stated problem to the solution of a mathematical program, as described in Section 4.

First, each of the premises is translated into a constraint on the probability density, p, of Andrea's age. Thus, using (3.8), (5.14) and (3.40), we have

$p_1 \triangleq$ It is unlikely that Andrea is very young $\rightarrow$

$$\pi_1(p) = \mu_{LIKELY}\left(1 - \int_0^{100} \mu^2_{YOUNG}(u)p(u)du\right) \tag{5.37}$$

$$\pi_2(p) = \mu_{LIKELY}\left(\int_0^{100} \mu_{YOUNG}(u)p(u)du\right) \tag{5.38}$$

$$\pi_3(p) = \mu^2_{LIKELY}\left(1 - \int_0^{100} \mu_{OLD}(u)p(u)du\right) \tag{5.39}$$

where $\int_0^{100} \mu_{YOUNG}(u)p(u)du$ represents the probability of the fuzzy event "Andrea is young," with the understanding that the range of the variable Age(Andrea) is the interval [0,100].

Next, we must translate the answer to the posed question, which we assume to be of the form "It is λ that Andrea is not old," where λ is a linguistic probability. Thus

$$q \rightarrow \pi_q(p) = \mu_\lambda\left(\int_0^{100} \left(1 - \mu_{OLD}(u)\right)p(u)du\right) \tag{5.40}$$

where μ_λ is the unknown membership function of λ.

Finally, by using (4.20), the problem in question is reduced to the solution of the variational problem

$$\begin{aligned} \mu_\lambda(\gamma) & \\ \triangleq \max_p & \left\{\left[\mu_{LIKELY}\left(1 - \int_0^{100} \mu^2_{YOUNG}(u)p(u)du\right)\right.\right. \\ & \wedge \mu_{LIKELY}\left(\int_0^{100} \mu_{YOUNG}(u)p(u)du\right) \\ & \left.\left. \wedge \mu^2_{LIKELY}\left(1 - \int_0^{100} \mu_{OLD}(u)p(u)du\right)\right]\right\} \end{aligned} \tag{5.41}$$

subject to

$$\gamma = \int_0^{100} \left(1 - \mu_{OLD}(u)\right)p(u)du$$

where γ is the numerical probability of the fuzzy event "Andrea is not old."

Example 8 (Example (e), Section 1).

Brian is much taller than most of his close friends

How tall is Brian?

Solution. Let x denote Brian's height. In section 4, we have found that, relative to a given database D, the truth of p is given by

$$\tau = \mu_{MOST}\left(\frac{\sum_i \mu_{MT}(x,\text{Height}(\text{Name}_i)) \wedge \mu_{CF}(\text{Brian},\text{Name}_i)}{\sum_i \mu_{CF}(\text{Brian},\text{Name}_i)}\right) \tag{5.42}$$

where $\mu_{MT}(x,\text{Height}(\text{Name}_i))$ is the degree to which Brian is much taller than Name_i and μ_F is the degree to which Name_i is Brian's close friend.

Now, for a given value of x and a given D, the value of τ may be interpreted as the possibility of x given D. Thus, the possibility distribution function of Brian's height is given by the same expression as τ, and hence

$$\text{Poss}\{\text{Height}(\text{Brian}) = x\} = \mu_{MOST}\left(\frac{\sum_i \mu_{MT}(x,\text{Height}(\text{Name}_i)) \wedge \mu_{CF}(\text{Brian},\text{Name}_i)}{\sum_i \mu_{CF}(\text{Brian},\text{Name}_i)}\right) \tag{5.43}$$

Example 9. Find the consistency of the proposition

$p \triangleq$ Sharon has more than a few good friends

with the database

$$GF_{Sharon} = \text{Mary} + 0.9\text{Valya} + 0.9\text{Doris} + 0.8\text{John} + 0.7\text{Chris} + 0.6\text{Pat} + 0.5\ \text{Denise} + \cdots \tag{5.44}$$

$$FEW = 0.8/1 + 0.9/2 + 1/3 + 1/4 + 0.8/5 + 0.5/6 + 0.2/7 \tag{5.45}$$

where GF_{Sharon} is the fuzzy set of Sharon's good friends (arranged in order of decreasing degree of friendship) and FEW is the fuzzy denotation of *few*.[6]

Solution. If FEW is defined by (5.45), then *at least few* is expressed by

$$\underline{>}\circ FEW = 0.8/1 + 0.9/2 + 1/3 + 1/4 + \cdots \quad (5.46)$$

where $\underline{>}\circ FEW$ is the composition of the binary relation $\underline{>}$ with the unary relation FEW

The FG cardinality of the fuzzy set GF_{Sharon} is given by

$$FGCount(GF_{Sharon}) = 1/1 + 0.9/2 + 0.9/3 + 0.8/4 + 0.7/5 + 0.6/6 + 0.5/7 + \cdots \quad (5.47)$$

and hence the degree of consistency of p with the database is given by

$$\begin{aligned}\gamma &= \sup(FGCount(GF_{Sharon}) \cap \underline{>}\circ FEW) \quad (5.48)\\ &= \sup(0.8/1 + 0.9/2 + 0.9/3 + 0.8/4 + \cdots)\\ &= 0.9\end{aligned}$$

6. Evidence, Certainty and Possibility

An important issue that arises in the analysis of soft data relates to the need for a way of assessing the degree of credibility of a conclusion which is inferred from a body of evidence.

For our purposes, it will be convenient to regard a body of evidence--or simply evidence, E--as a collection of fuzzy propositions, $E = \{g_1, \ldots, g_n\}$. Furthermore, we shall assume that the evidence is *granular* in nature, that is, each g_i, $i = 1, \ldots, n$, is a granule of the form[7]

(a) $g_i \triangleq Y$ is G_i is λ_i (6.1)

and/or

(b) $g_i \triangleq$ If X is F_i then Y is G_i (6.2)

[6] A fuller discussion of problems of this type may be found in [11].

[7] A more detailed discussion of the concept of information granularity may be found in [94].

and/or

(c) $g_i \triangleq$ If X is F_i then Y is G_j is λ_j, $j = 1,\ldots,m$ (6.3)

and/or

(d) $g_i \triangleq$ X is F_i is p_i (6.4)

where X and Y are variables taking values in U and V, respectively; F_i, $i = 1,\ldots,n$ and G_j, $j = 1,\ldots,m$, are fuzzy subsets of U and V; and p_i and λ_j are linguistic probabilities.

Although E may comprise a mixture of granules of the form (a), (b), (c) and (d), there are two special cases which are typical of the problems encountered in practice. In one, which we shall label Type I, all of the granules in E are of the form (a), and E may be regarded as the conjunction of $g_1,\ldots,g_n$. In the other, all of the granules in E are of the form (b) and (d), and the evidence is said to be of Type II. In the latter case, we shall assume for simplicity that X ranges over a finite set which for convenience may be taken to be the set of integers $\{1,\ldots,n\}$.

As a simple illustration of evidence of Type I, assume that we are interested in Penny's age and that the available evidence about her age is comprised of the following soft data granules:

(a) $g_1 \triangleq$ Penny is very young is unlikely
$g_2 \triangleq$ Penny is young is very likely
$g_3 \triangleq$ Penny is not young is unlikely

As an illustration of evidence of Type II, we may have, as in Example (f) in Section 1:

(b) $g_1 \triangleq$ If Penny is an undergraduate student, then she is very young
$g_2 \triangleq$ If Penny is a graduate student, then she is young

$g_3 \triangleq$ If Penny is a doctor then she is not very young

$g_4 \triangleq$ Penny is an undergraduate student is unlikely

$g_5 \triangleq$ Penny is a graduate student is likely

$g_6 \triangleq$ Penny is a doctor is not likely

Given a collection of data granules such as those appearing in (a) and (b), we wish to infer from E an answer to a question of the general form:

$$q \triangleq Y \text{ is } Q \text{ is } ?\alpha \qquad (6.5)$$

where Q is a specified fuzzy subset of V and $?\alpha$ is the desired linguistic probability. For example:

$$q \triangleq \text{Penny is not very young is } ?\alpha \qquad (6.6)$$

to which the answer might be, say,

$$?\alpha \triangleq \text{not very likely} .$$

In the case of evidence of Type I, an answer to a question of the form (6.5) may be obtained, in principle, by using the mathematical programming technique employed in Example 7, Section 5. In the case of evidence of Type II, however, we shall use a different approach involving a replacement of the posed question with a *surrogate* question, q_s, that is, a question which, unlike q, may be answerable based on the information contained in E. Such a question in the case of (6.6), for example, might be

$q_s \triangleq$ What is the degree of certainty that Penny is not very young?

or

$q_s \triangleq$ What is the degree of possibility that Penny is not very young?

The approach described in the sequel is based on a generalization of the concepts of upper and lower probabilities [17,29] which serve as a point of departure for Shafer's theory of evidence [67]. Viewed from the perspective of our approach, the latter theory is concerned with the special case where (a) the evidence is of Type II; (b) the G_i and Q are nonfuzzy sets; and (c) the p_i are numerical probabilities.

Assuming, first, that the G_i are fuzzy sets but the p_i are numerical probabilities, we define the *conditional possibility* and the *conditional certainty* of the proposition "Y is Q" (or, equivalently, the event "Y is Q") given that "Y is G_i" as follows:

$$\text{Poss}\{Y \text{ is } Q | Y \text{ is } G_i\} = \sup(Q \cap G_i) \tag{6.7}$$

$$\text{Cert}\{Y \text{ is } Q | Y \text{ is } G_i\} = \inf(G_i \Rightarrow Q) \tag{6.8}$$

where

$$\sup(Q \cap G_i) = \sup_V(\mu_Q(v) \wedge \mu_{G_i}(v)) , \quad v \in V \tag{6.9}$$

$$\inf(G_i \Rightarrow Q) = \inf_V((1 - \mu_{G_i}(v)) \vee \mu_Q(v)) \tag{6.10}$$

and μ_Q and μ_{G_i} are the membership functions of Q and G_i, respectively.

In effect, the right-hand members of (6.7) and (6.8) serve as measures of the degree to which the proposition "Y is G_i" influences one's belief in the proposition "Y is Q." In particular, (6.7) serves as a measure of the degree of possibility while (6.8) plays the same role in relation to the degree of certainty. Note that when Q and G_i are nonfuzzy, we have

$$\begin{aligned} \sup(Q \cap G_i) &= 1 \text{ if } Q \cap G_i \text{ is nonempty} \\ &= 0 \text{ if } Q \cap G_i = \theta \end{aligned} \tag{6.11}$$

and

$$\begin{aligned} \inf(G_i \Rightarrow Q) &= 1 \text{ if } G_i \subset Q \\ &= 0 \text{ otherwise} \end{aligned} \tag{6.12}$$

Now since X is assumed to be a random variable which takes the values 1,...,n with respective probabilities

$p_1,\ldots,p_n$, the conditional possibility and conditional certainty of the proposition "Y is $\dot{Q}$" are also random variables whose respective expectations are given by

$$E\Pi(Q) = \sum_i p_i \sup(Q \cap G_i) = \sum_i p_i \sup_v (\mu_Q(v) \wedge \mu_{G_i}(v)) \tag{6.13}$$

$$EC(Q) = \sum_i p_i \inf(G_i \Rightarrow Q) = \sum_i p_i \inf_v ((1-\mu_{G_i}(v)) \vee \mu_Q(v)) = 1 - E\Pi(Q') \tag{6.14}$$

We shall refer to $E\Pi(Q)$ and $EC(Q)$ as the *expected possibility* and the *expected certainty*, respectively, of the proposition "Y is Q." When Q and $G_1,\ldots,G_n$ are nonfuzzy, EC(Q) and $E\Pi(Q)$ reduce to the Shafer's *degree of belief* and *degree of plausibility*, respectively, which correspond to the lower and upper probabilities in Dempster's work [17].[8] Our feeling is that Shafer's identification of "degree of belief" with the lower rather than the upper probability (or, more generally, with E(Q) rather than $E\Pi(Q)$) is open to question, since there is no particular reason for singling out EC(Q) or $E\Pi(Q)$ or, for that matter, any convex combination of them as a universal measure of the degree of belief.

Having defined the concepts of expected certainty and expected possibility, we are in a position to see the rationale for employing the technique of surrogate questions in the case of evidence of Type II. Taking for simplicity the case where the G_i and Q are nonfuzzy and the p_i are numerical probabilities, the evidence can be expressed in the form

[8] It should be remarked that EC(Q) and $E\Pi(Q)$ are not normalized--as are the lower and upper probabilities in the work of Dempster and Shafer. As is pointed out in [95], the normalization in question leads to counterintuitive results in application to combination of bodies of evidence.

$$g_1 \triangleq Y \in G_1 \text{ or } g_2 \triangleq Y \in G_2 \text{ or } \cdots \text{ or } g_n \triangleq Y \in G_n$$

$$\text{Prob}\{g_1\} = p_1 \text{ and } \text{Prob}\{g_2\} = p_2 \text{ and } \cdots \text{ and } \text{Prob}\{g_n\} = p_n$$

Now let us assume that the original question is: What is the numerical probability that $Y \in Q$? It is easy to see that the granularity of available evidence makes it infeasible to answer questions of this type for arbitrary Q. Thus, we are compelled to replace the original unanswerable question with a surrogate answerable question which in some sense is close to the original question. In the case under discussion, such questions would be:

(a) What is the expected certainty (or, equivalently, the degree of belief (Shafer) or the lower probability (Dempster)) that $Y \in Q$?

(b) What is the expected possibility (or, equivalently, the degree of plausibility (Shafer) or the upper probability (Dempster)) that $Y \in Q$?

Based on the available evidence, the answers to (a) and (b) are:

$$EC(Q) = \sum_i p_i \inf(G_i \Rightarrow Q) \ , \quad i = 1,\ldots,n$$

and

$$E\Pi(Q) = \sum_i p_i \sup(G_i \cap Q)$$

where (see (6.11) and (6.12))

$$\begin{aligned} \inf(G_i \Rightarrow Q) &= 1 \text{ if } G_i \subset Q \\ &= 0 \text{ otherwise} \end{aligned}$$

and

$$\begin{aligned} \sup(G_i \cap Q) &= 1 \text{ if } G_i \cap Q = \theta \\ &= 0 \text{ otherwise} \end{aligned}$$

A serious shortcoming of the Shafer-Dempster approach is that if G_i and Q are nonfuzzy and the condition

$$G_i \subset Q$$

is not satisfied exactly, then no matter how small the error might be the contribution of the term $p_i \inf(G_i \Rightarrow Q)$ to the value of EC(Q) in the summation

$$EC(Q) = \sum_i p_i \inf(G_i \Rightarrow Q)$$

would be zero. In intuitive terms, what this means is that a piece of evidence will be disregarded so long as there is the slightest doubt about its perfect validity. We avoid this extreme degree of conservatism in our approach by (a) allowing the G_i and Q to be fuzzy; and (b) fuzzifying the concept of containment, with the expression $\inf(G_i \Rightarrow Q)$ in (6.14) representing, in effect, the degree to which G_i is contained in Q. Thus, if G is regarded as a random variable which takes the values $G_1,\ldots,G_n$ with respective probabilities $p_1,\ldots,p_n$, then we can write

$$EC(Q) = \text{Prob}\{G \subset Q\} \tag{6.15}$$

with the understanding that $G \subset Q$ is a fuzzy event [86] and that the degree to which $G \subset Q$ is satisfied is expressed by

$$\text{degree}\{G \subset Q\} = \inf(G \Rightarrow Q) \;.$$

Viewed in this perspective, (6.15) may be regarded as a natural generalization of Dempster's lower probability and Shafer's degree of belief.

For the purpose of illustration, we shall conclude this section by describing the application of our approach to Example (b). In this example, the G_i and Q are fuzzy and the p_i are linguistic probabilities. More specifically, we have

$$G_1 \triangleq \text{YOUNG}^2$$
$$G_2 \triangleq \text{YOUNG}$$
$$G_2 \triangleq (\text{YOUNG}^2)'$$
$$Q \triangleq \text{YOUNG}'$$
$$p_1 \triangleq \text{UNLIKELY} = \text{ANT LIKELY}$$
$$p_2 \triangleq \text{LIKELY}$$
$$p_3 \triangleq (\text{LIKELY})'$$

where YOUNG is the denotation of *young*, YOUNG^2 is the denotation of *very young*, ANT is the antonym, i.e., (see (3.40))

$$\mu_{\text{ANT LIKELY}}(v) = \mu_{\text{LIKELY}}(1-v) , \quad v \in [0,1] \quad (6.16)$$

and the prime represents the complement.

Now let

$$\alpha_1 = \sup(\text{YOUNG}^2 \cap \text{YOUNG}') \quad (6.17)$$

$$\alpha_2 = \sup(\text{YOUNG} \cap \text{YOUNG}') \quad (6.18)$$

$$\alpha_3 = \sup((\text{YOUNG}^2)' \cap \text{YOUNG}') \quad (6.19)$$

where the α_i are numbers in the interval [0,1]. (From (6.18) it follows that $\alpha_2 = 0.5$ but we shall not make use of this fact.) Then, using (6.13) we can express $E\Pi(Q)$ as

$$E\Pi(Q) = \alpha_1\text{UNLIKELY} \oplus \alpha_2\text{LIKELY} \oplus \alpha_3\text{LIKELY}' \quad (6.20)$$

where $\oplus$ denotes the sum of fuzzy numbers [90,50,18].

To compute $E\Pi(Q)$ as a fuzzy number, we have to take into consideration the fact that the numerical probabilities must sum up to unity. Thus, on denoting these probabilities by v_1, v_2, and v_3, and applying the extension principle (4.20), the determination of the membership function of $E\Pi(Q)$ is reduced to the solution of the following variational problem:

$$\mu(z) \triangleq \max_{v_1,v_2,v_3}(\mu_{\text{LIKELY}}(1-v_1) \wedge \mu_{\text{LIKELY}}(v_2) \wedge (1-\mu_{\text{LIKELY}}(v_3)) \quad (6.21)$$

subject to

$$z = \alpha_1 v_1 + \alpha_2 v_2 + \alpha_3 v_3 \quad (6.22)$$

$$1 = v_1 + v_2 + v_3$$

Thus, expressed as a fuzzy set, we have

$$E\Pi(Q) = \int_{[0,1]} \mu(z)/z \quad (6.23)$$

where $\mu(z)$ is given by (6.21). To compute $EC(Q)$, then, we can make use of the identity (6.14)

$$EC(Q) = 1 - E\Pi(Q') \quad (6.24)$$

From our definitions of $E\Pi(Q)$ and $EC(Q)$ it is a simple matter to derive a basic rule of conditioning which may be regarded as a generalization of those given by Dempster and Shafer. Specifically, assume that the evidence has the form:

$$\text{If } X = i \text{ then } Y \text{ is } G_i, \quad i = 1,\ldots,n$$
$$\text{Prob}\{X = i\} = p_i$$

and, in addition, we know that

$$g_0 \triangleq Y \text{ is } G_0$$

where G_0 is a given fuzzy subset of V.

Clearly, the available evidence may be expressed in the equivalent form:

$$\text{If } X = i \text{ then } Y \text{ is } G_i \cap G_0, \quad i = 1,\ldots,n$$
$$\text{Prob}\{X = i\} = p_i$$

which implies that

$$E\Pi(Q) \text{ conditioned on "Y is } G_0\text{"} = E\Pi(Q \cap G_0) \tag{6.25}$$

and correspondingly

$$EC(Q) \text{ conditioned on "Y is } G_0\text{"} = 1 - E\Pi(Q' \cup G_0') \tag{6.26}$$

Remark. The connection between the definition of expected possibility--as expressed by (6.13)--with that of the upper probability in [17] and [67]--may be made more transparent by interpreting $E\Pi(Q)$ as the probability of a fuzzy event--in the manner of (6.15). More specifically, if $\sup(G \cap Q)$ is regarded as the degree of occurrence of the fuzzy event $G \cap Q$?, in which the question mark serves to signify that we are concerned with the degree to which G intersects Q rather than with the intersection of G and Q, then we can write

$$E\Pi(Q) = \text{Prob}\{G \cap Q?\} \tag{6.27}$$

with the understanding that G is a random variable which

takes the values $G_1,\ldots,G_n$ with respective probabilities $p_1,\ldots,p_n$.

In summary, then, the expected possibility and expected certainty may be expressed in the form

$$E\Pi(Q) = \text{Prob}\{G \cap Q?\} \tag{6.28}$$

and

$$EC(Q) = \text{Prob}\{G \subset Q\} \tag{6.29}$$

which clarifies the sense in which $E\Pi(Q)$ and $EC(Q)$ may be viewed, respectively, as generalizations of the concepts of upper and lower probabilities--concepts which are defined in [17] and [67] under the assumption that the G_i and Q are nonfuzzy sets.

7. Concluding Remark

The approach to the analysis of soft data described in this paper represents a substantive departure from the conventional probability-based methods.

The main thesis underlying our approach is that, in general, the uncertainty which is intrinsic in soft data is a mixture of probabilistic and possibilistic constituents and, as such, must be dealt with by a combination of probabilistic and possibilistic methods. We have indicated, in general terms, how this can be done through the use of the concept of a possibility distribution and the related concepts of a linguistic variable, semantic entailment, semantic equivalence, and the extension principle. Finally, we have shown how the concepts of expected possibility and expected certainty relate to the important issue of credibility analysis, and indicated a way of reducing many of the problems in inference from soft data to the solution of nonlinear programs.

The issues associated with soft data analysis are varied and complex. Clearly, we have--at this juncture--only a partial understanding of the basic problem of inference from soft data and the associated problem of credibility assessment. What is likely, however, is that, in the years to come, our understanding of these and related problems will be enhanced through a further development of possibility-based methods for the representation and manipulation of soft data.

8. References and Related Papers

1. B. Adams, *Math. Biosci.* 32, 177 (1976).
2. J. F. Baldwin, Report EM/FS 10, University of Bristol (1978).
3. J. F. Baldwin, N. C. F. Guild and B. W. Pilsworth, Report EM/FS 5, University of Bristol (1978).
4. J. F. Baldwin and B. W. Pilsworth, Report EM/FS 9, University of Bristol (1978).
5. W. Bandler and L. Kohout, *Proc. 9th Int. Symp. on Multiple-Valued Logic*, 200 (1979).
6. G. Banon, *Proc. Int. Colloq. Theory Appl. of Fuzzy Sets* (1978).
7. R. E. Bellman and L. A. Zadeh, in *Modern Uses of Multiple-Valued Logic*, J. M. Dunn, G. Epstein, Eds. (D. Reidel, Dordrecht-Holland, 1977), p. 103.
8. M. Black, *Dialogue* 2, 1 (1963).
9. D. Bobrow and A. Collins, *Representation and Understanding* (Academic Press, New York, 1975).
10. B. Bouchon, to appear in *Fuzzy Sets and Systems*, 1979.
11. B. Cerny, Doctoral Dissertation, Dept. of Educ. Psych., Univ. of Calif., Berkeley, 1978.
12. L. J. Cohen, *The Implications of Induction* (Methuen, London, 1970).
13. A. Collins, *Proc. TINLAP-2*, 194 (1978).
14. A. Collins, E. Warnock, N. Aiello and M. Miller, in *Representation and Understanding*, D. Bobrow, A. Collins, Eds. (Academic Press, New York, 1975).
15. M. J. Cresswell, *Logics and Languages* (Methuen, London, 1973).
16. D. Davidson, *Synthese* 17, 304 (1967).
17. A. P. Dempster, *Ann. Math. Statist.* 38, 325 (1967).
18. D. Dubois and H. Prade, *Int. J. System Sci.* 9, 613 (1979).
19. D. Dubois and H. Prade, *Fuzzy Sets and Systems* (Academic Press, New York, 1980).
20. R. Duda et al., Ann. Report SRI International, Nos. 5821, 6415 (1977).
21. K. Fine, *Synthese* 30, 265 (1975).
22. B. R. Gaines, *Int. J. Man-Machine Studies* 6, 623 (1975).
23. B. R. Gaines, *Proc. 6th Int. Symp. on Multiple-Valued Logic* IEEE76CH 1111-4C, 179 (1976).

24. B. R. Gaines and L. J. Kohout, *Proc. Int. Symp. on Multiple-Valued Logic*, 183 (1975).
25. B. R. Gaines and L. J. Kohout, *Int. J. Man-Machine Studies* 9, 1 (1977).
26. R. Giles, *Int. J. Man-Machine Studies* 8, 313 (1976).
27. J. A. Goguen, *Synthese* 19, 325 (1969).
28. J. A. Goguen, *Int. J. Man-Machine Studies* 6, 513 (1974).
29. I. J. Good, in *Logic, Methodology and Philosophy of Science: Proceedings of the 1960 International Congress*, E. Nagel, P. Suppes, A. Tarski, Eds. (Stanford University Press, Stanford, 1962).
30. S. Haack, *Philosophy of Logics* (Cambridge University Press, Cambridge, 1978).
31. I. Hacking, *The Emergence of Probability* (Cambridge University Press, Cambridge, 1975).
32. H. M. Hersh and A. Caramazza, *J. Exp. Psych.* 105, 254 (1976).
33. E. Hisdal, *Fuzzy Sets and Systems* 1, 283 (1978).
34. G. E. Hughes and M. J. Cresswell, *An Introduction to Modal Logic* (Methuen, London, 1968).
35. E. T. Jaynes, *Phys. Rev.* 106, 620 (1957); 108, 171 (1957).
36. A. Joshi, in *Pattern Directed Inference*, F. Hays-Roth, D. Waterman, Eds. (Academic Press, New York, 1978).
37. J. Kampé de Feriet and B. Forte, *Comptes Rendus Acad. Sci.* A-265, 110, 142, 350 (1967).
38. A. Kaufmann, *Introduction to the Theory of Fuzzy Subsets* (Masson and Co., Paris, 1975).
39. W. J. M. Kickert and H. R. van Nauta Lemke, *Automatica* 12, 301 (1976).
40. S. Kullback, *Information Theory and Statistics* (John Wiley, New York, 1959).
41. H. E. Kyburg, *Synthese* 36, 87 (1977).
42. G. Lakoff, *J. Phil. Logic* 2, 458 (1973). Also in *Contemporary Research in Philosophical Logic and Linguistic Semantics*, D. Hockney, W. Harper, B. Freed, Eds. (D. Reidel, The Netherlands, 1973), p. 221.
43. R. A. LeFaivre, *J. Cybernetics* 4, 57 (1974).
44. R. C. Lyndon, *Notes on Logic* (D. van Nostrand, New York, 1966).
45. M. Mamdani, in *Fuzzy Automata and Decision Processes*, M. M. Gupta, G. N. Saridis, B. R. Gaines, Eds. (Elsevier North-Holland, New York, 1977).
46. E. H. Mamdani and S. Assilian, *Int. J. Man-Machine Studies* 7, 1 (1975).
47. G. A. Miller and P. N. Johnson-Laird, *Language and Perception* (Harvard University Press, Cambridge, 1976).
48. M. Minsky, in *The Psychology of Computer Vision*, P. Winston, Ed. (McGraw-Hill, New York, 1975), p. 211.
49. M. Mizumoto, S. Fukame and K. Tanaka, *Proc. 3rd Workshop on Fuzzy Reasoning* (1978).

50. M. Mizumoto and K. Tanaka, *Proc. Int. Conf. on Cybernetics and Society* (1976).
51. G. C. Moisil, Lectures on the logic of fuzzy reasoning, *Scientific Editions* (Bucharest, 1975).
52. R. E. Moore, *Interval Analysis* (Prentice-Hall, Englewood Cliffs, N.J., 1966).
53. S. Nahmias, *Fuzzy Sets and Systems* 1, 97 (1978).
54. C. V. Negoita and D. A. Ralescu, *Applications of Fuzzy Sets to Systems Analysis* (Birkhauser Verlag, Basel, 1975).
55. A. Newell and H. A. Simon, *Human Problem Solving* (Prentice-Hall, Englewood Cliffs, N. J., 1972).
56. H. T. Nguyen, *J. Math. Anal. Appl.* 65, 531 (1978).
57. H. T. Nguyen, *Fuzzy Sets and Systems* 1, 283 (1978).
58. J. J. Ostergaard, Pub. 7601, Technical University of Denmark, Lyngby (1976).
59. T. J. Procyk, Fuzzy Logic Working Group, Queen Mary College, London (1976).
60. N. Rescher, *Plausible Reasoning* (Van Gorcum, Amsterdam, 1976).
61. C. Rieger, *Proc. Georgetown University Linguistics Roundtable* (1976).
62. R. D. Rosenkrantz, *Inference, Method and Decision* (D. Reidel, Dordrecht, 1977).
63. E. Sanchez, Fuzzy relations, University of Marseille (1974).
64. E. Sanchez, M77/28, Univ. of Calif. Berkeley (1977).
65. R. C. Schank, *Conceptual Information Processing* (Academic Press, New York, 1975).
66. B. S. Sembi and E. H. Mamdani, *Proc. 9th Int. Symp. on Multiple-Valued Logic*, 143 (1979).
67. G. Shafer, *A Mathematical Theory of Evidence* (Princeton University Press, Princeton, 1976).
68. J. E. Shore and R. W. Johnson, NRL Memo 3-898, Naval Research Laboratory (1978).
69. E. Shortliffe, *MYCIN: Computer-Based Medical Consultations* (American Elsevier, New York, 1976).
70. E. H. Shortliffe and B. G. Buchanan, *Math. Biosci.* 23, 351 (1975).
71. P. Smets, Un modele mathematico-statistique simulant le processus du diagnostic medicale, Free University of Brussels (1978).
72. M. Sugeno, Ph.D. Dissertation, Tokyo Institute of Technology (1974).
73. P. Suppes, *J. Roy. Statist. Soc. B* 36, 160 (1974).
74. P. Suppes and M. Zanotti, *Synthese* 36, 427 (1977).
75. R. G. Swinburne, *An Introduction to Confirmation Theory* (Methuen, London, 1973).
76. P. Szolovits, L. B. Hawkinson and W. A. Martin, LCS Memo, M.I.T. (1977).

77. A. Tarksi, *Logic, Semantics, Metamathematics* (Clarendon, Press, London, 1956).
78. T. Terano and M. Sugeno, in *Fuzzy Sets and Their Applications to Cognitive and Decision Processes*, L. A. Zadeh, K. S. Fu, K. Tanaka, M. Shimura, Eds. (Academic Press, New York, 1975), p. 151.
79. R. M. Tong, *Int. J. General Systems* 4, 143 (1978).
80. M. Tribus, *Rational Descriptions, Decisions and Designs* (Pergamon Press, New York, 1969).
81. A. Tversky and D. Kahneman, *Science* 185, 1124 (1974).
82. S. Watanabe, *Information and Control* 15, 1 (1969).
83. H. Wechsler, *Proc. Int. Symp. on Multiple-Valued Logic*, 162 (1975).
84. F. Wenstop, *Int. J. Man-Machine Studies* 8, 293 (1976).
85. P. M. Williams, Bayesian conditionalization and the principle of minimum information, University of Sussex (1978).
86. L. A. Zadeh, *J. Math. Anal. Appl.* 23, 421 (1968).
87. L. A. Zadeh, *J. Cybernetics* 2, 4 (1972).
88. L. A. Zadeh, *IEEE Trans. Systems, Man and Cybernetics* SMC-3, 28 (1973).
89. L. A. Zadeh, *Synthese* 30, 407 (1975).
90. L. A. Zadeh, *Information Sciences* 8, 199 (1975); 8, 301 (1975); 9, 43 (1975).
91. L. A. Zadeh, Memo M77/58, Univ. of Calif. Berkeley (1977).
92. L. A. Zadeh, *Fuzzy Sets and Systems* 1, 3 (1978).
93. L. A. Zadeh, *Int. J. Man-Machine Studies* 10, 395 (1978).
94. L. A. Zadeh, in *Advances in Fuzzy Sets Theory and Applications*, M. Gupta, R. Ragade, R. Yager, Eds. (North-Holland, Amsterdam, 1979).
95. L. A. Zadeh, M79/24, Univ. of Calif. Berkeley (1979).
96. L. A. Zadeh, K. S. Fu, K. Tanaka and M. Shimura, *Fuzzy Sets and Their Application to Cognitive and Decision Processes* (Academic Press, New York, 1975).
97. L. A. Zadeh, *Int. J. Man-Machine Studies* 8, 249 (1976).
98. L. A. Zadeh, M79/32, Univ. of Calif. Berkeley (1979).

TEST-SCORE SEMANTICS FOR NATURAL LANGUAGES AND MEANING REPRESENTATION VIA PRUF

L. A. ZADEH*

1. Introduction

There are some philosophers of language who believe, as Montague did,[75] that the construction of a rigorous mathematical theory of natural languages is an attainable objective. An opposing point of view, which is articulated in the present paper, is that no mathematical theory based on two-valued logic is capable of mirroring the elasticity, ambiguity and context-dependence which set natural languages so far apart from the synthetic models associated with formal syntax and set-theoretic semantics.

The basis for our contention is that almost everything associated with natural languages is a matter of degree. This applies, in particular, to the issue of grammaticality and, even more so, to the notion of meaning. Thus, any logical system in which there are no gradations of truth and membership is *ipso facto* unsuitable as a framework for a comprehensive theory of natural languages and, especially, for the representation of meaning, knowledge and strength of belief. As an alternative to the approaches based on two-valued logic, we have proposed in[139] a meaning-representation language PRUF[a] in which an essential use is made of what may be described as *possibility theory*.[138,140] This theory — which is distinct from the bivalent theories of possibility related to modal logic and possible-world semantics[47,92] — is based on the concept of a *possibility distribution*, which in turn is analogous to, and yet distinct from, that of a probability distribution. In effect, the basic idea underlying PRUF is that the concept of a possibility distribution provides a natural mechanism for the representation of much of the imprecision and lack of specificity which is intrinsic in communication between humans.

To Professor Max Black

*Computer Science Division, Department of Electrical Engineering and Computer Sciences and the Electronics Research Laboratory, University of California, Berkeley, CA 94720. This paper was written while the author was a visiting member of the Artificial Intelligence Center, SRI International, Menlo Park, CA 94025. Research supported in part by the NSF Grants MCS 79-06543 and IST-801896.

[a]Actually PRUF is not just a language but a meaning-representation system, which includes a language as one its components.

As will be seen in the sequel, the expressive power of PRUF is substantially greater than that of predicate calculus, Montague grammar, semantic networks, conceptual dependency, and other types of meaning-representation systems that are currently in use.[27,68,70,101] In particular, PRUF makes it possible to represent the meaning of propositions which contain (a) fuzzy quantifiers, e.g., *many, most, few, almost all*, etc.; (b) modifiers such as *very, more* or *less, quite, rather, extremely*, etc.; and (c) fuzzy qualifiers such as *quite true, not very likely, almost impossible*, etc. However, the price of being able to translate almost any proposition in a natural language into PRUF is the difficulty of establishing a homomorphic connection between syntax and semantics — as is done in Montague grammar for fragments of English, and in Knuth semantics and attributed grammars for programming languages.[57] What this implies is that, although it is relatively easy to teach a human subject to translate from a natural language into PRUF, it would be very hard to write a program that could perform similarly without human assistance or intervention.

The semantics underlying PRUF is what we shall refer to as *test-score semantics* — a semantics in which the concept of aggregation of test scores plays a central role. Test-score semantics subsumes most of semantical systems which have been proposed for natural languages and, in particular, includes as limiting cases both truth-conditional and possible-world semantics.[70,68,18]

The basic idea behind test-score semantics may be summarized as follows. An entity in linguistic discourse, e.g., a predicate, a proposition, a question or a command, has, in general, the effect of inducing elastic constraints on a set of objects or relations in a universe of discourse. The meaning of such an entity, then, may be defined by (a) identifying the constraints which are induced by the entity; (b) describing the tests that must be performed to ascertain the degree to which each constraint is satisfied; and (c) specifying the manner in which the degrees in question or, equivalently, the partial test scores are to be aggregated to yield an overall test score. Viewed in this perspective, then, the meaning of a linguistic entity in a natural language may be identified with the testing of elastic constraints which are implicit or explicit in the entity in question.

We shall begin our exposition of PRUF and test-score semantics with a brief review of some of the basic notions in possibility theory which will be needed in later sections. A more detailed exposition of possibility theory may be found in Refs. 26, 45, 83, 130, 138, 140.[b]

2. The Concept of Possibility Distribution

Informally, let X be a variable which takes values in a set U. Then, the *possibility distribution* of X, denoted by Π_X, is the fuzzy set of possible values of X, with the understanding that possibility is a matter of degree. Thus, if U is a possible value

[b]Some of the definitions and examples in Sec. 2 are drawn from Refs. 137 and 140.

of X, we shall write

$$\text{Poss}\,\{X = u\} = a \tag{2.1}$$

to indicate that the possibility that X can take u as its value is a, where a is a number in the interval $[0, 1]$.

The function $\pi_X : U \to [0, 1]$ which associates with each $u \in U$ the possibility that X can take u as its value is called the *possibility distribution function.* Thus

$$\text{Poss}\,\{X = U\} = \pi_X(u)\,, \quad u \in U\,, \tag{2.2}$$

where U is the domain of X. In effect, the possibility distribution function π_X is the membership function of the possibility distribution Π_X.

In general, a possibility distribution may be induced by a physical constraint or, alternatively, may be epistemic in origin. To illustrate the difference, let X be the number of passengers that can be carried in Suppes' car, which is a five passenger Mercedes. In this case, by identifying $\pi_X(u)$ with the degree of ease with which u passengers can be put in Suppes' car, the tabulation of π_X may assume the following form:

X	1	2	3	4	5	6	7	8	9	10
π_X	1	1	1	1	1	0.8	0.6	0.2	0	0

in which an entry such as $(7, 0.6)$ signifies that, by some explicit or implicit criterion, the degree of ease with which 7 passengers can be carried in Suppes' car is 0.6.

In the above example, the possibility distribution of X is induced by a physical constraint on the number of passengers that can be carried in Suppes' car. To illustrate the case where the possibility distribution of X is epistemic in origin, i.e., reflects the state of knowledge about X, let X be Suppes' height and let the information about Suppes' height be conveyed by the proposition

$$p \triangleq \text{Suppes is tall}\,, \tag{2.3}$$

where tall is the label of a specified fuzzy subset of the interval [0, 250 cm] which is characterized by its membership function μ_{TALL}, with $\mu_{\text{TALL}}(u)$ representing the degree to which a person whose height is u cm is tall in a specified context.

The connection between the variable $X \triangleq$ Height (Suppes), the proposition $p \triangleq$ Suppes is tall, and the fuzzy set TALL[c] is provided by the so-called *possibility postulate* of possibility theory,[137,139] which for the example under consideration implies that, in the absence of any information about X other than that supplied by p, the possibility that $X = u$ is numerically equal to the grade of membership of u in TALL. Thus

$$\text{Poss}\,\{X = u\} = \pi_X(u) = \mu_{\text{TALL}}(u)\,, \quad u \in [0, 250] \tag{2.4}$$

[c]We use uppercase letters to represent fuzzy sets and fuzzy relations.

or, equivalently,

$$\Pi_{\mathbf{Height(Suppes)}} = \text{TALL}\,, \tag{2.5}$$

where (2.5) is referred to as the *possibility assignment equation.* In summary, we shall say that p *translates into the possibility assignment equation* (2.5), i.e.,

$$\text{Suppes is tall} \longrightarrow \Pi_{\mathbf{Height(Suppes)}} = \text{TALL}\,, \tag{2.6}$$

where the arrow $\rightarrow$ should be read as "translates into".

More generally, a central idea in PRUF is that any proposition in a natural language that may be put into the canonical form

$$p \triangleq N \text{ is } F\,, \tag{2.7}$$

where N is the name of an object, a variable or a proposition, may be interpreted as a characterization of the joint possibility distribution of a collection of variables $X_1, \ldots, X_n$ which are implicit or explicit in p. Thus, in symbols, N is F translates into

$$N \text{ is } F \longrightarrow \Pi_{(X_1,\ldots,X_n)} = F\,. \tag{2.8}$$

The variables $X_1, \ldots, X_n$ which are constrained by the possibility assignment equation will be referred to as the *base variables* of p.

Example. Consider the proposition

Nils has a large office

which may be expressed as

$$p \triangleq \text{Nils' office is large}\,.$$

In this case, the implicit base variables are:

$$X_1 = \text{Length(Office(Nils))}$$

$$X_2 = \text{Width(Office(Nils))}$$

and the possibility assignment equation assumes the form

$$\Pi_{\mathbf{(Length(Office(Nils)),Width(Office(Nils)))}} = \text{LARGE}\,, \tag{2.9}$$

where LARGE is a fuzzy set or, equivalently, a fuzzy binary relation in the product space LENGTH $\times$ WIDTH. Thus, (2.9) implies that

$$\text{Poss}\,\{\text{Length(Office(Nils))} = u\,,\ \text{Width(Office(Nils))} = v\} = \mu_{\text{LARGE}}(u, v)\,,$$

where $\mu_{\text{LARGE}}(u, v)$ is the degree to which an office which is u long and v wide is defined to be large in a specified context.

What is the difference between probability and possibility? As the above examples indicate, the concept of possibility is an abstraction of our intuitive perception of ease of attainment or the degree of compatibility, whereas the concept of probability is rooted in the perception of likelihood, frequency, proportion or strength of belief. Furthermore, as we shall see in Sec. 3, the rules governing the manipulation of possibilities are distinct from those which apply to probabilities.

An important aspect of the connection between probabilities and possibilities relates to the fact that, in principle, they are independent characterizations of uncertainty in the sense that, from the knowledge of the possibility distribution of a variable X, we cannot deduce its probability distribution, and vice-versa. For example, from the knowledge of the possibility distribution of the number of passengers in Suppes' car we cannot deduce its probability distribution; nor can we deduce the possibility distribution from the probability distribution of the number of passengers. In general, however, we can make a vague assertion to the effect that, if the possibility that $X = u$ is small, then it is likely that the probability that $X = u$ is also small. However, from this it does not follow that high possibility implies high probability, as is reflected in the commonly used statements of the form "It is possible but not probable that ...."

If the translation of a proposition p in a natural language is taken to be a possibility assignment equation as represented (2.8), then a question that naturally arises is: How can the base variables $X_1, \ldots, X_n$ and their joint possibility distribution $\Pi_{(X_1,\ldots,X_n)}$ be determined from p?

At this juncture in the development of PRUF, we do not have an algorithm for identifying the base variables in a given proposition. However, experience has shown that it is not difficult for a human subject to acquire a facility for translating any proposition within a broad class of propositions into a possibility assignment equation. What is difficult, as we alluded to already, is mechanizing this process completely, so that the translation represented by (2.8) could be accomplished without any human assistance.

In PRUF, the translation of a proposition may be either *focused*[d] or *unfocused*, with the focused translation leading, in general, to a possibility assignment equation. The unfocused translation — of which the focused translation is a special case — is based on test-score semantics and has the form of (i) a collection of tests which are performed on the database induced by the proposition; and (ii) a set of rules for aggregating the partial test scores into a overall test score which represents the compatibility of the given proposition with the database. In what follows, we shall present a condensed exposition of test-score semantics and illustrate its use in PRUF by a number of examples.

[d]The concept of focusing in test-score semantics differs from that introduced by B. Grosz[37] in the context of partitioned semantic networks.

3. Test-Score Semantics: Nature of Tests

To simplify our exposition of test-score semantics, it will be convenient to focus our attention on the representation of the meaning of propositions, with the understanding that the basic ideas underlying test-score semantics are equally applicable to predicates, questions, commands and most other types of linguistic entities.

As will be seen in the sequel, the conceptual framework of test-score semantics is rooted — like that of truth-conditional semantics — in our intuitive perception of meaning as a collection of criteria for relating a linguistic entity to its designation. More specifically, suppose that we wish to test whether or not a human subject, H, understands the meaning of a proposition p, e.g., $p \triangleq$ Laura is dancing with Irwin. A natural way of doing this would be to present H with a variety of scenes (or worlds) depicting a joint activity of Laura and Irwin, and ask H to indicate, for each scene or world W, the degree, $c(W)$, to which W corresponds to or is compatible with H's perception of the meaning of p. If H can do this correctly for each W, then we may conclude that H understands the meaning of p. And, more importantly, if H can articulate the tests which H performs on W to arrive at $c(W)$, then H not only understands what p means ostensively, but can also precisiate the meaning of p by a concretization of the test procedure.

In truth-conditional and possible-world semantics, the degree of compatibility, $c(W)$, is allowed to have one of two possible values: {true, false} or, equivalently, {pass, fail}. By contrast, in test-score semantics, $c(W)$ can be any point in a linear or partially ordered set—which for simplicity is usually taken to be the unit interval $[0, 1]$. Furthermore, $c(W)$ is also allowed to be a probability or possibility distribution over the unit interval or, more generally, a composition of probability and possibility distributions.

Instead of dealing with scenes or worlds directly, it is simpler and more effective to deal with their characterizations in the form of state descriptions (Carnap[17]) or, equivalently, as databases. In essense, then, we assume that H is presented, on the one hand, with a proposition p and, on the other, with a database D, and that H performs a test, T, on D which yields a test score, τ. In symbols,

$$\begin{aligned} \tau &= T(D) \\ &= \text{Comp}\,(p, D)\,, \end{aligned} \tag{3.1}$$

where the test T may be viewed as a representation of the meaning of p, and its test score, τ, as a measure of the compatibility of p and D. Furthermore, viewed from the perspective of truth-conditional semantics, τ may be interpreted as the truth-value of p given D, i.e.,

$$\tau = \text{Tr}\,\{p|D\}\,. \tag{3.2}$$

Alternatively, p may be interpreted — in the spirit of possible-world semantics — as the possibility of D given p, i.e.,

$$\tau = \text{Poss}\,\{D|p\}\,. \tag{3.3}$$

In general, a test, T, is composed of a number of constituent tests, $T_1, \ldots T_n$, and the overall test score, τ, is the result of aggregation of constituent test scores $\tau_1, \ldots \tau_n$, where τ_i, $i = 1, \ldots, n$, is the test score associated with T_i. In test-score semantics, the process of aggregation need not be carried to the extreme of yielding a single test score, i.e., a number in the interval $[0, 1]$. Thus, more generally, the aggregated test score τ may be a vector, $\tau = (\tau_\alpha, \ldots, \tau_\gamma)$, in which each of the components is a number in the interval [0, 1] or a probability/possibility distribution over the unit interval. In particular, the analysis of presuppositions requires the use of vector test scores to differentiate the results of tests performed on presuppositions from those performed on other constituents of the proposition under analysis.[e]

Notational preliminaries

We shall assume that a database consists of a collection of relations, each of which is represented by (a) its relational frame, i.e., the name of the relation and the names of variables (columns); and (b) the data, i.e., the entries in the table. For example, the relational frame of the relation named POPULATION:

POPULATION	Name	Age	Height (cm)
	Minker	38	170
	Rieger	36	182
	Sanchez	36	175

may be expressed as *POPULATION* || *Name* | *Age* | *Height* || or equivalently as POPULATION [Name; Age; Height].

Generally, we shall be dealing with fuzzy relations of the form:[f]

R	X_1	X_2	$\cdots$	X_n	μ
	.	.	.	.	.
	r_{t1}	r_{t2}	.	r_{tn}	μ_t
	.	.	.	.	.

in which r_{tk}, $k = 1, \ldots, n$, is the entry in tth row and column X_k, and μ_t is the grade of membership of the n-tuple $r_t \triangleq r_{t1} \cdots r_{tn}$ (or $(r_{t1}, \ldots, r_{tn})$) in the fuzzy

[e]The idea of a vector truth-value was suggested earlier by the author (see Ref. 60). The concept of a vector test score as defined in this paper provides a more general framework for the analysis of presuppositions than that of two-dimensional languages (Herzberger,[43] McCawley,[68] Bergmann[11]).

[f]Here and elsewhere in the paper, the subscripts on variables are raised for typographical convenience.

relation R. For example, in the relation BIG

BIG	Length (cm)	Width (cm)	μ
	35	28	0.7
	45	39	0.9

the entries in the second row signify that an object which is 45 cm long and 39 cm wide is defined to be big to the degree 0.9. In effect, R may be viewed as an elastic constraint on the n-ary variable $X \triangleq (X_1, \ldots, X_n)$, with $\mu_t \triangleq \mu_R(r_{t1}, \ldots, r_{tn})$ representing the degree to which an n-tuple $(r_{t1}, \ldots, r_{tn})$ of values of $X_1, \ldots, X_n$ satisfies the constraint in question. When it is desirable to place in evidence that R is a constraint on X, we shall express R as R_X or, more explicitly, as $R_{(X_1,\ldots,X_n)}$.

Let $s \triangleq (i_1, \ldots, i_k)$ be a subsequence of the index sequence $(1, \ldots, n)$, and let s' denote the complementary subsequence $s' \triangleq (j_1, \ldots, j_m)$ (e.g., for $n = 5$, $s = (1, 3, 4)$ and $s' = (2, 5)$). In terms of such sequences, a k-tuple of the form $(r_{i_1}, \ldots, r_{i_k})$, where r is an arbitrary symbol, may be expressed in an abbreviated form as $r_{(s)}$ (or $r(s)$). Expressed in this notation, the variable $X_{(s)} \triangleq (X_{i_1}, \ldots, X_{i_k})$ will be referred to as a k-ary *subvariable* of $X \triangleq (X_1, \ldots, X_n)$, with $X_{(s')} \triangleq (X_{j_1}, \ldots, X_{j_m})$ being a subvariable complementary to $X_{(s)}$.

Projection

An operation which plays a basic role in the manipulation of fuzzy relations and possibility distributions is that of *projection*. Specifically, assume that X_i, $i = 1, \ldots, n$, takes values in the universe of discourse $U_i(X_i) \triangleq U_i$. Then, the projection of R on the domain $U(s) \triangleq U_{i_1} \times \cdots \times U_{i_k}$ is expressed as[g]:

$$\begin{aligned} \mathrm{Proj}_{U(s)} R &\triangleq {}_{X_{i_1} \times \cdots \times X_{i_k}} R \\ &\triangleq {}_{X(s)} R\,. \end{aligned} \tag{3.4}$$

The grade of membership of a k-tuple $u(s) \triangleq (u_{i_1}, \ldots, u_{i_k})$ in ${}_{X(s)}R$ is defined by

$$\mu_{X(s)} R(u_{i_1}, \ldots, u_{i_k}) \triangleq \sup_{u(s')} \mu_R(u_1, \ldots, u_n)\,, \tag{3.5}$$

where the notation $\sup_{u(s')}$ signifies that the supremum is taken over the domain of the complementary subvariable $u(s') \triangleq (u_{j_1}, \ldots, u_{j_m})$. Stated more simply, the operation of projection on $U_{i_1} \times \cdots \times U_{i_k}$ has the effect of deleting the components $u_{j_1}, \ldots, u_{j_m}$ in the n-tuple $(u_1, \ldots, u_n)$ and associating with the resulting k-tuple the

[g]This notation for projections is patterned after the notation employed in the query language SQUARE.[14]

highest grade of membership among all n-tuples in R in which $X_{i_1} = u_{i_1}, \ldots, X_{i_k} = u_{i_k}$. To illustrate, if R is given as

R	$X1$	$X2$	$X3$	μ
	a	a	a	0.7
	a	a	b	0.8
	a	b	a	0.2
	a	b	b	1
	b	a	a	0.4
	b	b	a	0.6

then the projections of R on $U_1 \times U_2$ and U_3 are:

${}_{X_1 \times X_2}R$	$X1$	$X2$	μ
	a	a	0.8
	a	b	1
	b	a	0.4
	b	b	0.6

${}_{X_3}R$	$X3$	μ
	a	0.7
	b	1 .

Note that, from the definition of projection (3.5), it follows at once that

$$ {}_{X(\alpha)}R \equiv {}_{X(\alpha)}\left({}_{X(\beta)}R\right) $$

provided every variable that is in the index sequence α is also in the index sequence β.

Particularization

A basic operation on fuzzy relations which plays an important role in test-score semantics is that of *particularization.*[h] More specifically, assume that R is an n-ary relation which represents a constraint on an n-ary variable $X \triangleq (X_1, \ldots, X_n)$. Now suppose that we impose an additional constraint, G, on a subvariable of X, say $X(s) \triangleq (X_{i_1}, \ldots, X_{i_k})$. Then, the additional constraint on X may be viewed as a *particularization* of R, expressed in symbols as

$$ R[X(s) \text{ is } G] \tag{3.6} $$

[h]In the case of nonfuzzy relations, particularization reduces to what is commonly referred to as restriction or selection.

or, equivalently, in virtue of (2.8), as

$$R[\Pi_{X(s)} = G] , \tag{3.7}$$

where $\Pi_{X(s)}$ is the possibility distribution of the subvariable $X(s)$.

Remark. In some cases it is necessary to differentiate between two different interpretations of propositions of the form "X is F". In what we shall refer to as the *possibilistic* (or *disjunctive*) interpretation, the translation of "X is F" is $\Pi_X = F$. On the other hand, in the *conjunctive* interpretation, "X is F" is interpreted as $X = F$, which in turn means that if F is a fuzzy set expressed as[i]

$$F = \mu_1/u_1 + \cdots + \mu_N/u_N \tag{3.8}$$

or, equivalently, as

$$F = \Sigma_i \ \mu_i/u_i \tag{3.9}$$

then each u_i is a value of X to the degree μ_i.

On occasion, to differentiate between the disjunctive and conjunctive interpretations, we shall employ the more explicit notation

$$X = \text{dis}(F) \qquad \text{in place of } \Pi_X = F \tag{3.10}$$

and

$$X = \text{con}(F) \qquad \text{in place of } X = F \tag{3.11}$$

with the understanding that, unless stated to the contrary, "X is F" should be interpreted as $X = \text{dis}(F)$. An example illustrating the difference between disjunctive and conjunctive interpretations is given in Ref. 139.

To give a concrete meaning to (3.7), it is convenient to employ the concept of a *row test*. Specifically, let $r_r(u_{1t}, \ldots, u_{nt}, \mu_t)$ be the tth row of R, where $u_{1t}, \ldots, u_{nt}, \mu_t$ are the values of $X_1, \ldots, X_n, \mu$ respectively. Furthermore, let μ_G be the membership function of the fuzzy set G which appears in (3.7), and let ν_t be the grade of membership of $r_{t(s)}$ in G, i.e.,

$$\nu_t = \mu_G(r_{t(s)}) . \tag{3.12}$$

In terms of the parameters just defined, the row test in question may be described as follows. First, determine the degree to which $r_{t(s)}$ satisfies the particularizing constraint "$X(s)$ is G" by setting the test score equal to ν_t; and second, combine μ_t and ν_t by employing the min operator $\wedge$, yielding the aggregated test score

$$\tau_t = \mu_t \wedge \nu_t . \tag{3.13}$$

[i]In this notation, μ_i/u_i signifies that μ_i is the grade of membership of u_i in F, and $+$ denotes the union rather than the arithmetic sum.

Remark. The aggregation operator $\wedge$ (min) should be viewed as a default choice when no alternative is specified. When an aggregation operator $*$ other than min is specified (e.g., arithmetic mean, product, geometric mean, etc.[j]) the expression for τ_t becomes

$$\tau_t = \mu_t * \nu_t \,. \tag{3.14}$$

Once the aggregated test score is found for each row in R, the particularized relation $R[\Pi_{X(s)} = G]$ is readily constructed by replacing μ_t in r_t by τ_t, resulting in the modified $(n+1)$-tuple

$$r_t^* = (u_{1t}, \ldots, u_{nt}, \tau_t)\,,$$

which represents the tth row of $R^* \triangleq R[\Pi_{X(s)} = G]$ and in which τ_t is expressed by (3.13) or, more generally, by (3.14).

A row test is *compartmentalized* when more than one particularizing constraint is involved, as in:

$$R[X(s) \text{ is } F;\ X(v) \text{ is } G]\,, \tag{3.15}$$

where $X(s)$ and $X(v)$ are not necessarily disjoint subvariables of X. In this case, let $\nu_t^{(F)}$ and $\nu_t^{(G)}$ be the test scores associated with the row tests "$X(s)$ is F" and "$X(v)$ is G," respectively. Then, using the default definition of the aggregation operator $*$, the aggregated test score for r_t may be expressed as

$$\tau_t = \mu_t \wedge \nu_t^{(F)} \wedge \nu_t^{(G)} \,. \tag{3.16}$$

Example. Consider a relation R defined by the table

R	X_1	X_2	X_3	μ
	a	a	a	1
	a	b	a	0.8
	b	a	a	0.6
	b	b	b	0.3

which is particularized by the constraints

$$(X_1, X_2) \text{ is } F$$

$$(X_2, X_3) \text{ is } G\,,$$

[j]The closely related issue of various ways in which operations on fuzzy sets may be defined has received considerable attention in the literature. See, in particular, Refs. 25, 56, 131 and 142.

where F and G are defined by

$$F = 1/(a,a) + 0.6/(b,a) + 0.2/(b,b)$$
$$G = 0.3/(a,a) + 0.9/(a,b) + 0.7/(b,a) + 0.4/(b,b)$$

with the understanding that a term such as $0.6/(b,a)$ in F signifies that the grade of membership of the tuple (b,a) in F is 0.6.

Applying the compartmentalized row test to the rows of R, we obtain successively

$$\nu_1(F) = 1;\ \nu_1(G) = 0.3;\ \tau_1 = 1 \wedge 1 \wedge 0.3 = 0.3$$
$$\nu_2(F) = 0;\ \nu_2(G) = 0.7;\ \tau_2 = 0.8 \wedge 0 \wedge 0.7 = 0$$
$$\nu_3(F) = 0.6;\ \nu_3(G) = 0.3;\ \tau_3 = 0.6 \wedge 0.6 \wedge 0.3 = 0.3$$
$$\nu_4(F) = 0.2;\ \nu_4(G) = 0.4;\ \tau_4 = 0.3 \wedge 0.2 \wedge 0.4 = 0.2$$

and hence $R^* \triangleq R[\Pi_{(X_1,X_2)} = F;\ \Pi_{(X_2,X_3)} = G]$ is given by the table

R^*	X_1	X_2	X_3	τ
	a	a	a	0.3
	b	a	a	0.3
	b	b	b	0.2

In the foregoing discussion, we have discussed the concepts of projection and particularization in the context of operations on relations. Inasmuch as a possibility distribution is a relation which acts as a disjunctive constraint on the values of a variable, the operations of projection and particularization apply equally well to possibility distributions. For example, we may write

$$\Pi_1 = \Pi\big[\Pi_{(X_1,X_2)} = F;\ \Pi_{(X_2,X_4)} = G\big] \tag{3.17}$$

to indicate that Π_1 is a possibility distribution which results from particularizing the possibility distribution Π with the constraints "(X_1, X_2) is F" and "(X_2, X_4) is G."

Particularization/projection (transduction)

In test-score semantics, we usually deal with relations or possibility distributions which are both particularized and projected. For example:

$$_{X(w)}R[X(s) \text{ is } F;\ X(v) \text{ is } G] \tag{3.18}$$

which should be interpreted as a fuzzy relation R which is first particularized and then projected. It should be noted, however, that if $s \subset w$ and $v \subset w$, then

(3.18) could also be interpreted as a relation R which is first projected and then particularized. It is easy to show that the latter interpretation leads to the same result by virtue of the distributivity of $\wedge$ (min) over $\vee$ (max).

In what follows, we shall employ the suggestive term *transduction* to refer to the combination of particularization and projection. In essence, transduction may be viewed as a generalization of the familiar operation of finding the value of a function for a given value of its argument. In this light, (3.18) may be read as "substitute F for $X(s)$, G for $X(v)$ and get $X(w)$", with the understanding that the substitution of F for $X(s)$ and G for $X(v)$ involves in actuality the substitution of F and G for the possibility distributions of $X(s)$ and $X(v)$, and reading the possibility distribution of $X(w)$. In particular, in the special case of relations of the form

$$_{X_{i_1}\times\cdots\times X_{i_m}\times\mu}R[X_{j_1}=a_1;\ldots;X_{j_\ell}=a_\ell] \tag{3.19}$$

in which $a_1,\ldots,a_\ell$ are specified values of the variables $X_{j_1},\ldots,X_{j_\ell}$, what is read is a fuzzy subset of $U_{i_1}\times\cdots\times U_{i_m}$ which is a "section" of R with the planes $X_{j_1}=a_1,\ldots,X_{j_\ell}=a_\ell$. More particularly, an expression of the form

$$_{\mu}R[X_1=a_1;\ldots;X_n=a_n] \tag{3.20}$$

should be interpreted as "Read (or get or obtain) the grade of membership of the n-tuple $(a_1,\ldots,a_n)$ in the fuzzy relation R".

As an illustration, the following expressions should be interpreted as indicated:

(a) $_{\text{Age}}$POPULATION[Name = Barbara].
Obtain Barbara's age from the relation POPULATION which includes Name and Age among its variables. In this case, Barbara is transduced into her age.

(b) $_{\text{Name2}\times\mu}$FRIEND[Name1 = Maria].
Obtain the fuzzy set of Maria's friends from the fuzzy relation FRIEND in which μ is the degree to which Name2 is a friend of Name1. In this example, Maria is transduced into the fuzzy set of her friends.

(c) $_{\mu}$FRIEND[Name1 = Lucia; Name2 = Richard].
Obtain from the relation FRIEND the degree to which Richard is a friend of Lucia. Here Lucia and Richard are transduced into their grade of friendship.

(d) $_{\text{Name}\times\mu}$POPULATION[Π_{Age} = YOUNG].
Obtain from POPULATION the fuzzy set of names of those who are young. In this case, the fuzzy set YOUNG is transduced into a fuzzy subset of the nonfuzzy set $_{\text{Name}}$POPULATION. A point that should be noted is that even though the relation POPULATION is nonfuzzy and has no μ attribute, the particularized relation POPULATION[Π_{Age} = YOUNG] is fuzzy and has a μ attribute which is the attribute referred to in Name $\times$ μ.

Cardinality of fuzzy sets

How many lakes are there in California? What is the proportion of tall men among fat men? What is the meaning of "Brian is much taller than most of Mildred's friends?" What is the denotation of *several red apples*? The answer to questions of this type hinge on the concept of *cardinality* of fuzzy sets or, more generally, on the concept of *measure*. In what follows, we shall give a definition of cardinality which serves to provide a basis for testing the elastic constraints induced by fuzzy quantifiers such as *many, most, several, few, almost all*, etc. The tests in question will be described in Secs. 4 and 5.

As should be expected, the concept of cardinally of a fuzzy set is an extension of the count of elements of a crisp, i.e., nonfuzzy, set. Specifically, assume, for simplicity, that A is a fuzzy set expressed as

$$A = \mu_1/u_1 + \cdots + \mu_n/u_n\,, \tag{3.21}$$

where the u_i, $i = 1,\ldots,n$, are elements of a universe of discourse U. A simple way of extending the concept of cardinality which was suggested by DeLuca and Termini[24] and which is related to the notion of the probability measure of a fuzzy event[132] is to form the arithmetic sum of the grades of membership. We shall refer to this sum, with or without a round-off to the nearest integer, as the *sigma count* or, equivalently, as *nonfuzzy cardinality* of A. Thus, by definition,

$$\Sigma\text{Count}(A) \triangleq \sum_{i=1}^{n} \mu_i\,. \tag{3.22}$$

For example

$$\Sigma\text{Count}\ (0.6/a + 0.9/b + 1/c + 0.6/d + 0.2/e) = 3\,.$$

A less simple but perhaps more natural extension which was suggested in Ref. 137 expresses the cardinality of a fuzzy set as a fuzzy number. Thus, let A be the α-level-set of A, i.e., the nonfuzzy set defined by

$$A_\alpha \triangleq \{u_i | \mu_A(u_i) \geq \alpha\}\,,\quad 0 < \alpha \leq 1\,,\quad u_i \in U\,,\ i = 1,\ldots,n\,, \tag{3.23}$$

where $\mu_i \triangleq \mu_A(u_i)\,,\ i = 1,\ldots,n$, is the grade of membership of u_i in A. Then, as shown in Ref. 133, A may be expressed in terms of the A_α by the identity

$$A = \sum_\alpha \alpha A_\alpha\,, \tag{3.24}$$

where Σ stands for the union and αA_α is a fuzzy set whose membership function is defined by

$$\begin{aligned} \mu_{\alpha A_\alpha}(u) &= \alpha \qquad \text{for } u \in A_\alpha \\ &= 0 \qquad \text{elsewhere}\,. \end{aligned} \tag{3.25}$$

For example, if $U = \{a, b, c, d, e, f\}$ and

$$A = 0.6/a + 0.9/b + 1/c + 0.6/d + 0.2/e \tag{3.26}$$

then

$$\begin{aligned} A_1 &= \{c\} \\ A_{0.9} &= \{b, c\} \\ A_{0.6} &= \{a, b, c, d\} \\ A_{0.2} &= \{a, b, c, d, e\} \end{aligned}$$

and (3.24) becomes

$$A = 1/c + 0.9/(b + c) + 0.6/(a + b + c + d) + 0.2/(a + b + c + d + e)\,.$$

Now, let Count(A_α) denote the count of elements of the nonfuzzy set A_α. Then, the FGCount of A, where F stands for *fuzzy* and G stands for *greater than*, is defined as the fuzzy number

$$\mathrm{FGCount}(A) \triangleq \sum_{\alpha} /\mathrm{Count}(A_\alpha) \tag{3.27}$$

with the understanding that any gap in the Count(A_α) may be filled by a lower count with the same α. For example, for A defined by (3.26), we have

$$\begin{aligned} \mathrm{FGCount}(A) &= 1/1 + 0.9/2 + 0.6/4 + 0.2/5 \\ &= 1/1 + 0.9/2 + 0.6/3 + 0.6/4 + 0.2/5\,. \end{aligned} \tag{3.28}$$

It is of some help in understanding the significance of (3.27) to interpret a term such as 0.6/4 in (3.28) as the assertion:

The truth-value of the assertion that A contains at least four elements is 0.6.

More generally, let p_m, q_m and r_m be the propositions:

$$\begin{aligned} p_m &\triangleq A \text{ contains at least } m \text{ elements} \\ q_m &\triangleq A \text{ contains at most } m \text{ elements} \end{aligned}$$

and

$$r_m \triangleq A \text{ contains no more and no less than } m \text{ elements}\,.$$

Furthermore, assume that the elements of A are sorted in descending order, so that $\mu_m \le \mu_k$ if $m \ge k$. Then, the truth-values of p_m, q_m and r_m are given by Ref. 140

$$\mathrm{Tr}\{p_m\} = \mu_m \tag{3.29}$$

$$\mathrm{Tr}\{q_m\} = 1 - \mu_{m+1} \tag{3.30}$$

$$\mathrm{Tr}\{r_m\} = \mu_m \wedge (1 - \mu_{m+1}) \tag{3.31}$$

These expressions provide a rationale for defining FGCount, FLCount (L standing for *less than*), and FECount (E standing for *equal to*) as follows.

Let $A\!\downarrow$ denote A sorted in descending order and let $NA\!\downarrow$ denote the fuzzy number resulting from replacing the mth element in $A\!\downarrow$ by μ_m/m and adding the element 1/0. For example, if

$$A = 0.6/a + 0.9/b + 1/c + 0.6/d + 0.2/e \tag{3.32}$$

then

$$A\!\downarrow = 1/c + 0.9/b + 0.6/a + 0.6/d + 0.2/e \tag{3.33}$$

$$NA\!\downarrow = 1/0 + 1/1 + 0.9/2 + 0.6/3 + 0.6/4 + 0.2/5\,. \tag{3.34}$$

In terms of this notation, the definition of FGCount (A) stated earlier (3.27) may be expressed more succinctly as

$$\text{FGCount}(A) = NA\!\downarrow\ . \tag{3.35}$$

In a similar vein, the definitions of FLCount(A) and FECount(A) may be expressed as

$$\text{FLCount}(A) = (NA\!\downarrow)' \ominus 1 \tag{3.36}$$

and

$$\text{FECount}(A) = \text{FGCount}(A) \cap \text{FLCount}(A)\,, \tag{3.37}$$

where $(NA\!\downarrow)'$ denotes the complement of $NA\!\downarrow$, $\ominus$ represents fuzzy subtraction [136], [76], [26], and $\cap$ is the operation of intersection.

A basic identity which relates the fuzzy cardinalities of A, B, $A \cap B$ and $A \cup B$ may be expressed as

$$\text{FGCount}(A \cup B) \oplus \text{FGCount}(A \cap B) = \text{FGCount}(A) \oplus \text{FGCount}(B)\,, \tag{3.38}$$

where $\oplus$ denotes fuzzy addition. For example, if

$$A = 0.4/2 + 1/3 + 0.2/4$$
$$B = 0.5/3 + 1/4 + 0.3/5$$

then

$$\begin{aligned}
A \cup B &= 0.4/2 + 1/3 + 1/4 + 0.3/5\\
A \cap B &= 0.5/3 + 0.2/4\\
\text{FGCount}(A) &= 1/0 + 1/1 + 0.4/2 + 0.2/3\\
\text{FGCount}(B) &= 1/0 + 1/1 + 0.5/2 + 0.3/3 \qquad (3.39)\\
\text{FGCount}(A) \oplus \text{FGCount}(B) &= 1/0 + 1/1 + 1/2 + 0.5/3 + 0.4/4 + 0.3/5 + 0.2/6\\
\text{FGCount}(A \cup B) &= 1/0 + 1/1 + 1/2 + 0.4/3 + 0.3/4\\
\text{FGCount}(A \cap B) &= 1/0 + 0.5/1 + 0.2/2
\end{aligned}$$

and

$$\text{FGCount}(A \cup B) \oplus \text{FGCount}(A \cap B) = 1/0 + 1/1 + 1/2 + 0.5/3 + 0.4/4 + 0.3/5 + 0.2/6$$

in agreement with (3.39).

In fomulating tests for cardinality in Secs. 4 and 5, we shall be employing for the most part the definitions of ΣCount and FGCount. Although the definitions of fuzzy cardinality expressed by (3.27) and (3.35) are not simple enough to be obvious on first exposure, the examples presented in Sec. 5 suggest that the concept of fuzzy cardinality is a natural extension of the corresponding concept for crisp sets.

4. Test-Score Semantics: Meaning Representation

In the preceding section, we have discussed some of the basic concepts which underlie the testing of fuzzy relations in a relational database. In this and the following section our attention will be focused on the principal issues relating to the representation of the meaning of a proposition by the testing of constraints which are induced by it.

Let p be a proposition whose meaning we wish to represent. The first question that arises is: What is the collection of relational databases which should be used as the object of testing? Once the answer to this question is arrived at, the next question is: What are the tests to be performed and how should their test scores be aggregated?

With respect to the first question, the position we shall take is that the choice of the test bed should be goal-oriented, that is, should depend on the state of knowledge of the actual or composite addressee of the meaning-representation process. In plain language, what this means is that in representing the meaning of p we should be influenced by our perception of the concepts and variables which are explicit or implicit in p and whose meaning is known to the addressee. Generally, these are tacitly assumed to be the concepts whose labels appear in p, together with the attributes with which they are associated. However, in test score semantics, this is a flexible rather than a rigid desideratum.

As an illustration, consider the proposition $p \triangleq$ Overeating causes obsesity, and assume that the intended interpretation of p is

$$q \triangleq \text{Most of those who overeat are obese}. \tag{4.1}$$

Furthermore, assume that the addressee knows, in principle, the meaning of the terms *most, overeat* and *obese*, so that the objective of the meaning-representation process is a *precisiation* of the meaning of p. In this event, an appropriate set of relational frames for the database might be:

$$DF1 \triangleq \text{POPULATION[Name; Age; Weight; Height; Consumption]}$$
$$+ \text{OBESE[Age; Height, Weight; } \mu] + \text{ OVEREAT[Consumption; } \mu]$$
$$+ \text{MOST}[r;\ \mu]\,, \tag{4.2}$$

where DF stands for *database frame* and + denotes the union.

The first relation, labeled POPULATION, lists the names of individuals, together with the values of the attributes Age, Weight, Height and Consumption, with the latter expressed as the ratio of the level of food consumption to what would be considered to be the normal level of consumption for an individual of that age, weight and height.

The relation OBESE defines the grade of membership of an individual, μ, in the fuzzy set of obese individuals as a function of the attributes Age, Weight, and Height. The relation OVEREAT defines the grade of membership of an individual, μ, in the fuzzy set of those who overeat, as a function of Consumption. The last relation, MOST, defines the fuzzy quantifier *most* as a fuzzy subset of the unit interval, with r representing a numerical proportion.

Alternatively, and more simply, we could assume that DF consists of the following relations:

$$DF2 \triangleq \text{POPULATION[Name]}$$
$$+ \text{OBESE[Name; } \mu] + \text{OVEREAT[Name; } \mu] + \text{MOST}[r;\ \mu]\,. \tag{4.3}$$

In this case, the fuzzy subsets OBESE and OVEREAT of POPULATION are defined directly rather than through the intermediary of the numerically-valued attributes Age, Weight and Height. As should be expected, the representation of the meaning of p as a test on the database represented by (4.3) would be less informative than a test on (4.2).

As was alluded to already, the test on a database, D, depends on the choice of relational frames, DF. As an illustration, for the database frame $DF2$ defined by (4.3), the compatibility test for p and D may be described as follows.

1. Count the number of individuals in POPULATION who overeat. To this end, let Name_i denote the name of ith individual in POPULATION. Using the expression for the ΣCount as defined by (3.22), we have

$$\Sigma\text{Count(OVEREAT)} = \Sigma_i({}_\mu\text{OVEREAT [Name} = \text{Name}_i])\,. \tag{4.4}$$

2. Count the number of individuals in POPULATION who are obese and overeat. In this case, we have to compute the ΣCount of the intersection of fuzzy sets OVEREAT and OBESE. The grade of membership of Name_i in the intersection is given by (See Ref. 139)

$$\mu_{\text{OVEREAT} \cap \text{OBESE}}(\text{Name}_i) = \mu_{\text{OVEREAT}}(\text{Name}_i) \wedge \mu_{\text{OBESE}}(\text{Name}_i) \tag{4.5}$$

where

$$\mu_{\text{OVEREAT}}(\text{Name}_i) = {}_{\mu}\text{OVEREAT}[\text{Name} = \text{Name}_i] \tag{4.6}$$

and

$$\mu_{\text{OBESE}}(\text{Name}_i) = {}_{\mu}\text{OBESE}[\text{Name} = \text{Name}_i]\,. \tag{4.7}$$

Consequently, the ΣCount of individuals who are obese and overeat is given by

$$\begin{aligned}\Sigma\text{Count}(\text{OVEREAT} \cap \text{OBESE}) = \Sigma_i\,(({}_{\mu}\text{OVEREAT}[\text{Name} = \text{Name}_i]) \\ \wedge({}_{\mu}\text{OBESE}[\text{Name} = \text{Name}_i]))\,.\end{aligned} \tag{4.8}$$

3. Compute the proportion of those who are obese among the fuzzy subset of those who overeat. Using (4.6) and (4.8), we find

$$\begin{aligned}\gamma &\triangleq \frac{\Sigma\text{Count}(\text{OVEREAT} \cap \text{OBESE})}{\Sigma\text{Count}(\text{OVEREAT})} \\ &= \frac{\Sigma_i(({}_{\mu}\text{OVEREAT}[\text{Name} = \text{Name}_i]) \wedge ({}_{\mu}\text{OBESE}[\text{Name} = \text{Name}_i]))}{\Sigma_i({}_{\mu}\text{OVEREAT}[\text{Name} = \text{Name}_i])}\,.\end{aligned} \tag{4.9}$$

4. Compute the test score corresponding to the degree to which the proportion γ expressed by (4.9) satisfies the constraint induced by the fuzzy quantifier *most.* Using (4.9), the test score for this constraint is found to be given by

$$\tau = {}_{\mu}\text{MOST}[r = \gamma]\,. \tag{4.10}$$

This test score, then, may be interpreted as the truth of p given D or, equivalently, as the possibility of D given p.

There are several important observations relating to this example that are of general validity.

(a) The meaning of p is represented by the test which yields the test score τ.
(b) The description of the test involves only the relational frames in the assumed database and not the data. In other words, the test represents the intension of p.[139]
(c) The structure of the test depends on the choice of relational frames. Thus, the description of the test would be different for $DF1$ (defined by (4.2)). Furthermore, for the same choice of relational frames, different tests would be required to accommodate different definitions of cardinality. This point is discussed in greater detail in Example 4, Sec. 5.
(d) The choice of DF affects the *explanatory effectiveness* of meaning representation in test-score semantics. More specifically, lessening the degree of detail in DF has the effect of lowering the degree of explanatory effectiveness. For example, in the case of $DF1$ and $DF2$, $DF2$ is less detailed than $DF1$. Correspondingly, the test procedure associated with $DF2$ conveys less information about the meaning of p than that associated with $DF1$.

The simplest possible DF for the proposition $p \triangleq$ *Overeating causes obesity* is

$$DF = \text{CAUSE[Cause; Effect]}. \tag{4.11}$$

For this DF, the test reduces to the containment condition

$$\text{(Overeat, Obese)} \subset \text{CAUSE}$$

which signifies that the tuple (Overeat, Obese) belongs to the relation CAUSE. Equivalently, the test may be represented as

$$\text{CAUSE[Cause = Overeat; Effect = Obese]} \tag{4.12}$$

which is similar in form to the conventional semantic-network representation of the meaning of p.

It is of interest to observe that the DF represented by (4.11) is insufficiently detailed to allow a differentiation between the meanings of the propositions

$$p \triangleq \text{Overeating causes obesity}$$

and

$$p' \triangleq \text{Obesity is caused by overeating}$$

with the latter interpreted as

$$q' \triangleq \text{Most of those who are obese overeat}. \tag{4.13}$$

It can readily be verified that the test score corresponding q' is given by

$$\tau = {}_{\mu}\text{MOST}\left[r = \frac{\Sigma\text{Count(OBESE} \cap \text{OVEREAT)}}{\Sigma\text{Count(OBESE)}}\right] \tag{4.14}$$

which differs from (4.9) in the denominator of r.

As a further example consider the proposition

$$p \triangleq \text{Dana is very young and Tandy is not much older than Dana}.$$

In this case, we shall assume that the database frame is[k]:

$$DF \triangleq \text{POPULATION[Name; Age]} + \text{YOUNG[Age; } \mu]$$
$$+ \text{MUCH·OLDER[Age1; Age2; } \mu]. \tag{4.15}$$

In the last relation, μ is the degree to which Age1 is much older than Age2.

The proposition under consideration induces two elastic constraints: (a) a constraint on the age of Dana, and (b) a constraint on the age of Tandy relative to that of Dana. To test these constraints, we proceed as follows.

[k]To place in evidence that a sequence of words is a label of a relation, we employ the convention of inserting periods between the words.

1. Find the ages of Dana and Tandy. Using (4.15), we have

$$\text{Age(Dana)} = {}_{\text{Age}}\text{POPULATION[Name = Dana]} \tag{4.16}$$

$$\text{Age(Tandy)} = {}_{\text{Age}}\text{POPULATION[Name = Tandy]}\,. \tag{4.17}$$

2. Test the constraint on the age of Dana. Denoting the test score for this constraint by τ_1, we have

$$\tau_1 = ({}_{\mu}\text{YOUNG[Age = Age(Dana)]})^2\,, \tag{4.18}$$

where Age(Dana) is given by (4.16) and the squaring accounts for the effect of the modifier *very* (see (4.31)).

3. Test the constraint on the age of Tandy relative to that of Dana. The test score for this constraint is given by

$$\tau_2 = 1 - {}_{\mu}\text{MUCH OLDER[Age1 = Age(Tandy)};\quad \text{Age2 = Age(Dana)]}\,, \tag{4.19}$$

where the subtraction of the second term from unity accounts for the effect of the negation *not* in the relation "not much older". (See (4.30).)

4. Aggregate the test scores τ_1 and τ_2. Using the product for aggregate (instead of the usual min), we arrive at the overall test score

$$\tau = \tau_1\tau_2 \tag{4.20}$$

as a measure of the compatibility of p with the database.

Focused translation

In general, the test score τ for a given test T depends not on the entire database D but on a subset of it. Typically, if $X_1, \ldots, X_m$ are the variables involved in D (i.e., the designations of entries in relations in D), then τ may depend on a proper subset of the X_i, say $X_{i_1}, \ldots, X_{i_k}$. To take a simple example, if the database, D, consists of two relations, say POPULATION[Name; Age; Weight; Height] and YOUNG[Age; μ], then the compatibility of the proposition

$$p \triangleq \text{Lillian is young}$$

with D depends only on Lillian's age — which is an entry under Age in POPULATION — and the degree to which Lillian's age satisfies the constraint induced by *young* — which is an entry under μ in the relation YOUNG.

More generally, a subset $F(D,p)$ of D will be said to be a *focus of D relative to* p if

(a) The compatibility of p with D is identical with the compatibility of p with $F(D,p)$

and

(b) $F(D,p)$ is *minimal*, i.e., there is no proper subset of $F(D,p)$ with property (a).

The notion of a focus provides a natural point of departure for introducing the concept of a *focused translation*. Specifically, given p and D, let $F(D,p)$ be the focus of D relative to p and let $X_{i_1},\ldots,X_{i_k}$ or, more simply, $X_1,\ldots,X_n$, be the variables which enter into $F(D,p)$. Then, using unfocused translation, we can compute for each D — and hence for each n-tuple $(u_1,\ldots,u_n)$ of values of $X_1,\ldots,X_n$ — the compatibility, τ, of p with $\{X_1 = u_1,\ldots,X_n = u_n\}$. Now, if we interpret τ as the possibility of the n-tuple $(u_1,\ldots,u_n)$, i.e.,

$$\tau = \text{Poss}\,\{X_1 = u_1,\ldots,X_n = u_n\}\,, \tag{4.21}$$

then the *focused translation* of p may be expressed symbolically as

$$p \rightarrow \Pi_{(X_1,\ldots,X_n)} = F\,, \tag{4.22}$$

where τ defines the membership function of F; $\Pi_{(X_1,\ldots,X_n)}$ represents the possibility distribution of the n-ary variable $(X_1,\ldots,X_n)$; the variables $X_1,\ldots,X_n$ are the *base variables* in p; and the right-hand member of (4.22) is what we have referred to in Sec. 2 as the *possibility assignment equation.*

As a simple illustration of the concept of a focused translation, consider the proposition

$$p \triangleq \text{Brian is much taller than Mildred}\,. \tag{4.23}$$

Assuming that DF consists of the relational frames

$$\begin{aligned} DF = {} & \text{POPULATION[Name; Height]} \\ & + \text{MUCH·TALLER[Height 1; Height 2; } \mu]\,, \end{aligned}$$

the unfocused translation of p is characterized by the following test:

1. Determine the height of Brian and Mildred:

$$\text{Height(Brian)} = {}_{\text{Height}}\text{POPULATION[Name = Brian]}$$

$$\text{Height(Mildred)} = {}_{\text{Height}}\text{POPULATION[Name = Mildred]}\,.$$

2. Test the constraint induced by the fuzzy relation MUCH·TALLER. The test score for this constraint is given by

$$\begin{aligned} \tau = {}_{\mu}\text{MUCH·TALLER[Height1} &= \text{Height(Brian)}\,; \\ \text{Height2} &= \text{Height(Mildred)]}\,. \end{aligned} \tag{4.24}$$

Since p induces just one constraint, no aggregation is necessary and τ as expressed by (4.24) defines the compatibility of p with D.

Correspondingly, the focused translation of p may be expressed compactly as

$$p \to \Pi_{(\text{Height(Brian)}, \text{ Height(Mildred)})} = \text{MUCH·TALLER}\,. \tag{4.25}$$

In this form, the translation of p signifies that the base variables in p are $X_1 =$ Height(Brian) and $X_2 =$ Height(Mildred), and that the focused translation of p defines the meaning of p as an assignment statement which assigns the fuzzy relation MUCH·TALLER to the joint possibility distribution of X_1 and X_2.

Additional examples of both unfocused and focused translations will be presented in Sec. 5. What is important to note at this juncture is that, as its name implies, a focused translation serves the purpose of placing in evidence the base variables in p and focuses the translation process on the determination of the joint possibility distribution of these variables. In general, a focused translation has the advantage of greater transparency in the case of relatively simple propositions, but becomes rather unwieldy in the case of propositions whose DF's involve more than a few relational frames.

When focusing is employed in the translation of a complex proposition, it is frequently advantageous to (a) decompose it into simpler propositions; (b) translate separately the constituent propositions; and (c) compose the results. In this connection, it is convenient to have a collection of translation rules which may be employed — when this is possible — to compose the meaning of a proposition from the meanings of its constituents. Among the basic translation rules in PRUF which serve this purpose are the rules of Type I, Type II, Type III and Type IV.[1] For convenient reference, these rules are summarized in the following.

Translation rules

Modifier rule (Type I). Let X be a variable which takes values in a universe of discourse U, and let F be a fuzzy subset of U. Consider the proposition

$$p \triangleq X \text{ is } F \tag{4.26}$$

or, more generally,

$$p \triangleq N \text{ is } F\,, \tag{4.27}$$

where N is a variable, an object or a proposition.

Now, if, in a particular context, the proposition X is F translates into

$$X \text{ is } F \to \Pi_X = F \tag{4.28}$$

then in the same context

$$X \text{ is } mF \to \Pi_X = F^+\,, \tag{4.29}$$

where m is a modifier such as *not, very, more or less*, etc., and F^+ is a modification of F induced by m. More specifically: If $m = not$, then $F^+ \triangleq F' \triangleq$ complement

[1]A more detailed discussion of these rules may be found in Ref. 139.

of F, i.e.,

$$\mu_{F^+}(u) = 1 - \mu_F(u)\,, \quad u \in U\,. \tag{4.30}$$

If $m = very$, then $F^+ = F^2$, i.e.,

$$\mu_{F^+}(u) = \mu_F^2(u)\,, \qquad u \in U\,. \tag{4.31}$$

If $m = more\ or\ less$, then $F^+ = \sqrt{F}$, i.e.,

$$\mu_{F^+}(u) = \sqrt{\mu_F(u)}\quad , \quad u \in U\,. \tag{4.32}$$

As a simple illustration of (4.31), if SMALL is defined as

$$\text{SMALL} = 1/0 + 1/1 + 0.8/2 + 0.6/3 + 0.4/4 + 0.2/5$$

then

$$x \text{ is very small} \to \Pi_X = F^2\,, \tag{4.33}$$

where

$$F^2 = 1/0 + 1/1 + 0.64/2 + 0.36/3 + 0.16/4 + 0.04/5\,.$$

It should be noted that (4.30), (4.31) and (4.32) should be viewed as default rules which may be replaced by other translation rules in cases in which some alternative interpretations of the modifiers *not very* and *more or less* are more appropriate.

Conjunctive, disjunctive and implicational rules (Type II). If

$$X \text{ is } F \to \Pi_X = F \ \text{ and } \ Y \text{ is } G \to \Pi_Y = G\,, \tag{4.34}$$

where F and G are fuzzy subsets of U and V, respectively, then

(a)
$$X \text{ is } F \ \text{ and } \ Y \text{ is } G \to \Pi_{(X,Y)} = F \times G\,, \tag{4.35}$$

where

$$\mu_{F\times G}(u,v) \triangleq \mu_F(u) \wedge \mu_G(v)\,. \tag{4.36}$$

(b)
$$X \text{ is } F \text{ or } Y \text{ is } G \to \Pi_{(X,Y)} = \bar{F} \cup \bar{G}\,, \tag{4.37}$$

where

$$\bar{F} \triangleq F \times V\,, \quad \bar{G} \triangleq U \times G \tag{4.38}$$

and

$$\mu_{\bar{F}\cup\bar{G}}(u,v) = \mu_F(u) \vee \mu_G(v)\,. \tag{4.39}$$

(c)
$$\text{If } X \text{ is } F \text{ then } Y \text{ is } G \to \Pi_{(Y|X)} = \bar{F}' \oplus \bar{G}\,, \tag{4.40}$$

where $\Pi_{(Y|X)}$ denotes the conditional possibility distribution of Y given X, and the bounded sum $\oplus$ is defined by

$$\mu_{\bar{F}'\oplus\bar{G}}(u,v) = 1 \wedge (1 - \mu_F(u) + \mu_G(v))\,. \tag{4.41}$$

Note. In stating the implicational rule in the form (4.40), we have merely chosen one of the several alternative ways in which the conditional possibility distribution $\Pi_{(Y|X)}$ may be defined, each of which has some advantages and disadvantages depending on the application. A detailed discussion of this issue can be found in Refs. 5, 72 and 105.

As simple illustrations of (4.35), (4.37) and (4.40), if

$$F \triangleq \text{SMALL} = 1/1 + 0.6/2 + 0.1/3$$
$$G \triangleq \text{LARGE} = 0.1/1 + 0.6/2 + 1/3$$

then

$$\begin{aligned}\text{X is small and Y is large} &\rightarrow \Pi_{(X,Y)}\\ &= 0.1/(1,1) + 0.6/(1,2) + 1/(1,3) + 0.1/(2,1)\\ &\quad + 0.6/(2,2) + 0.6/(2,3) + 0.1/(3,1) + 0.1/(3,2) + 0.1/(3,3)\,.\end{aligned}$$

$$\begin{aligned}\text{X is small or Y is large} &\rightarrow \Pi_{(X,Y)}\\ &= 1/(1,1) + 1/(1,2) + 1/(1,3) + 0.6/(2,1) + 0.6/(2,2)\\ &\quad + 1/(2,3) + 0.1/(3,1) + 0.6/(3,2) + 1/(3,3)\end{aligned}$$

and

$$\begin{aligned}\text{If X is small then Y is large} &\rightarrow \Pi_{(Y|X)}\\ &= 0.1/(1,1) + 0.6/(1,2) + 1/(1,3) + 0.5/(2,1)\\ &\quad + 1/(2,2) + 1/(2,3) + 1/(3,1) + 1/(3,2) + 1/(3,3)\,.\end{aligned}$$

Quantification rule (Type III). If $U = \{u_1, \ldots, u_N\}$, Q is a fuzzy quantifier such as *many, few, several, all, some, most,* etc., and

$$X \text{ is } F \rightarrow \Pi_X = F\,, \tag{4.42}$$

then the proposition "QX are F" (e.g., "many X's are large") translates into

$$QX \text{ are } F \rightarrow \Pi_{\Sigma\text{Count}(F)} = Q \tag{4.43}$$

if the concept of nonfuzzy cardinality is employed. (See (3.22).) As a simple example, if the quantifier *several* is defined as

$$\text{SEVERAL} = 0.4/2 + 0.6/3 + 1/4 + 1/5 + 1/6 + 0.7/7 + 0.2/8 \tag{4.44}$$

then

$$\text{SEVERAL } X\text{'s are large} \rightarrow \Pi_{\Sigma_i \mu_{\text{LARGE}}(u_i)} = \text{SEVERAL}\,. \tag{4.45}$$

Examples in the which the concept of fuzzy cardinality is employed will be considered in Sec. 5.

Truth qualification rule (Type IV). Let τ be a linguistic truth-value, e.g., *very true, quite true, more or less true*, etc. Such a truth-value may be regarded as a fuzzy subset of the unit interval which is characterized by a membership function $\mu_\tau : [0, 1] \to [0, 1]$.

A truth-qualified proposition, e.g., "It is τ that X is F", is expressed as "X is F is τ." As shown in Ref. 10, the translation rule for such propositions is given by

$$X \text{ is } F \text{ is } \tau \to \Pi_X = F^+ , \tag{4.46}$$

where

$$\mu_{F^+}(u) = \mu_\tau(\mu_F(u)) . \tag{4.47}$$

As an illustration, consider the truth-qualified proposition

Teresa is young is very true

which by (4.46), (4.47) and (4.31) translates into

$$\Pi_{\text{Age(Teresa)}} = \mu_{\text{TRUE}^2}(\mu_{\text{YOUNG}}) . \tag{4.48}$$

Now, if we assume that

$$\mu_{\text{YOUNG}}(u) = \left(1 + \left(\frac{u}{25}\right)^2\right)^{-1} , \qquad u \in [0, 100] \tag{4.49}$$

and

$$\mu_{\text{TRUE}}(v) = v^2 , \qquad v \in [0, 1]$$

then (4.47) yields

$$\mu_{\text{Age(Teresa)}} = \left(1 + \left(\frac{u}{25}\right)^2\right)^{-4}$$

as the possibility distribution of the age of Teresa.

Probability qualification rule (Type IV). This rule applies to propositions of the general form "X is F is λ," where X is a real-valued variable, F is a linguistic value of X, and λ is a linguistic value of likelihood (or probability), e.g., "X is small is not very likely." Unless stated to the contrary, λ is assumed to be a fuzzy subset of the unit interval $[0, 1]$ which is characterized by its membership function μ_λ, and the probability distribution of X is characterized by its probability density function p, i.e.,

$$\text{Prob}\{X \in [u, u + du]\} = p(u)\, du . \tag{4.50}$$

As shown in Ref. 139, the translation rule for probability-qualified propositions is expressed by

$$X \text{ is } F \text{ is } \lambda \rightarrow \pi(p) = \mu_\lambda \left(\int_U \mu_F(u)p(u)du \right), \tag{4.51}$$

where $\pi(p)$ denotes the possibility that the probability density function of X is p, and the integral in the right-hand member of (4.51) represents the probability of the fuzzy event[132] "X is F." Thus, in the case of probability-qualified propositions, the proposition "X is F is λ" induces a possibility distribution of the probability density function of X.

As a simple illustration, consider the proposition

$$q \triangleq \text{Vickie is young is very likely}. \tag{4.52}$$

In this case, $X \triangleq$ Age(Vickie) and the right-hand member of (4.51) becomes

$$\pi(p) = \mu^2_{\text{LIKELY}} \left(\int_0^{100} \mu_{\text{YOUNG}}(u)p(u)du \right). \tag{4.53}$$

The translation rules stated above may be used in combination. For example, consider the proposition

$$p \triangleq \text{If } X \text{ is not very large and } Y \text{ is more or less small then}$$
$$Z \text{ is very very large}.$$

In this case, by the application of (4.30), (4.31), (4.32), (4.35) and (4.40), we find that p induces a conditional possibility distribution of Z given X and Y, i.e., $\Pi_{(Z|X,Y)}$. The possibility distribution function of this distribution is given by

$$\pi_{(Z|X,Y)}(w|u,v) = 1 \wedge \left[1 - \left(1 - \mu^2_{\text{LARGE}}(u)\right) \wedge \mu^{0.5}_{\text{SMALL}}(v) + \mu^4_{\text{LARGE}}(w)\right] \tag{4.54}$$

where μ_{LARGE} and μ_{SMALL} denote, respectively, the membership functions of the denotations of *large* and *small* in p.

Vector test scores and presuppositions

Since an agregated test score is basically a summary, it would be natural to expect that in some cases the degree of summarization which is associated with a single overall test score might be excessive. In such cases, then, a vector test score might be required to convey the meaning of a proposition correctly.

Among the cases which fall into this category are propositions with false presuppositions, as in the classical example $p \triangleq$ The King of France is bald. In this case, an attempt to associate a single test score or truth-value with p leads to difficulties which have been discussed at length in the literature.[68] In our view, a natural way of dealing with these difficulties is provided by the concept of a vector test score —

a concept which furnishes a general framework for the analysis of presuppositions and related issues.

Let p be a given proposition and let $p*$ be a presupposition which is associated with p. Usually, but not necessarily, $p*$ asserts the existence of an object which is characterized by p. In a departure from the conventional point of view, we shall assume that existence is a matter of degree and hence that $p*$ is a *fuzzy presupposition*, i.e., a proposition whose compatibility with a database may be a number other than 0 or 1.

As a simple illustration, consider the proposition

$$p \triangleq \text{By far the richest man in France is bald}\,. \tag{4.55}$$

In this case,

$$p* \triangleq \text{There exists by far the richest man in France} \tag{4.56}$$

is a fuzzy presupposition by virtue of the fuzziness of the predicate *by far the richest man*.

To apply test-score semantics to this proposition, assume that the DF contains the following relational frames

$$\begin{aligned} DF \triangleq\ & \text{POPULATION[Name; Wealth; } \mu\text{Bald]} \\ & + \text{BY·FAR·RICHEST[Wealth; Wealth2; } \mu]\,. \end{aligned} \tag{4.57}$$

In the first relation in (4.57), Wealth is interpreted as the net worth of Name and μBald is the degree to which Name is bald. In the second relation, Wealth2 is the wealth of the second richest man, and μ is the degree to which Wealth and Wealth2 qualify the richest man in France (who is assumed to be unique) to be regarded as by far the richest man in France.

To compute the compatibility of p with the database, we perform the following test.

1. Sort POPULATION in descending order of Wealth. Denote the result by POPULATION↓ and let Name_i be the ith name in POPULATION↓.
2. Determine the degree to which the richest man in France is bald:

$$\tau_1 \triangleq {}_{\mu\text{Bald}}\text{POPULATION}[\text{Name} = \text{Name}_1]\,. \tag{4.58}$$

3. Determine the wealth of the richest and second richest men in France:

$$\begin{aligned} w_1 &\triangleq {}_{\text{Wealth}}\text{POPULATION}\downarrow[\text{Name} = \text{Name}_1] \\ w_2 &\triangleq {}_{\text{Wealth}}\text{POPULATION}\downarrow[\text{Name} = \text{Name}_2]\,. \end{aligned}$$

4. Determine the degree to which the richest man in France is by far the richest man in France:

$$\tau_2 \triangleq {}_{\mu}\text{BY FAR RICHEST}[\text{Wealth} = w_1;\ \text{Wealth2} = w_2]\,. \tag{4.59}$$

5. The overall test score is taken to be the ordered pair

$$\tau = (\tau_1, \tau_2)\,. \tag{4.60}$$

Thus, instead of aggregating τ_1 and τ_2 into a single test score, we maintain their separate identities in the overall test score. We do this because the aggregated test score

$$\tau = \tau_1 \wedge \tau_2$$

would be creating a misleading impression when τ_1 is small, that is, when the test score for the constraint on the existence of "by far the richest man in France" is low.

In the simple case which we have used as an example, the overall test score as expressed by (4.60) has only two components. In general, however, a proposition p may have a multiplicity of fuzzy presuppositions each of which may have to be represented by a component test score in the overall test score for p. For example, the proposition

$p \triangleq$ By far the richest man in France is much taller than most of his close friends

has at least two fuzzy presuppositions

$p_1^* \triangleq$ There exists by far the richest man in France

$p_2^* \triangleq$ By far the richest man in France has close friends

and hence the overall test score for p will have to have at least three components.

It is important to observe that the fuzzy presuppositions $p_1^*, p_2^*, \ldots, p_m^*$ which are associated with a proposition p depend in an essential way on the formulation of the test of compatibility of p with the database. For example, consider the proposition

$p \triangleq$ By far the richest man in France is by far the tallest man in Paris.

In this case, depending on the way in which the test procedure is formulated, either one of the following propositions could be regarded as a fuzzy presupposition of p:

$p_1^* =$ There exists by far the richest man in France

$p_2^* =$ There exists by far the tallest man in Paris.

The issue of vector test scores has many ramifications which extend beyond the scope of the present paper. In what follows, we shall confine ourselves to a discussion of examples in which the fuzzy presuppositions are tacitly assumed to have perfect test scores and hence need not be considered in the computation of compatibility.

5. Examples of Translation

The examples considered in this section are intended to clarify some of the aspects of test-score semantics which were discussed in general terms in Secs. 3 and 4. The examples are relatively simple and, for the most part, involve propositions. When appropriate, both focused and unfocused translations are presented.

1. *Margaret is slim and very attractive.*

Assume that

$$\begin{aligned} DF \triangleq\ & \text{POPULATION[Name; Weight; Height]} \\ & + \text{SLIM[Weight; Height; } \mu] \\ & + \text{ATTRACTIVE[Name; } \mu]\,. \end{aligned} \tag{5.1}$$

The steps in the test procedure are:

(i) Find Margaret's height and weight:

$$a \triangleq \text{Weight(Margaret)} = {}_{\text{Weight}}\text{POPULATION[Name = Margaret]}$$

$$b \triangleq \text{Height(Margaret)} = {}_{\text{Height}}\text{POPULATION[Name = Margaret]}\,.$$

(ii) Test the constraint induced by SLIM:

$$\tau_1 \triangleq {}_{\mu}\text{SLIM[Weight} = a;\ \text{Height} = b]\,. \tag{5.2}$$

(iii) Test the constraint induced by ATTRACTIVE:

$$\tau_2 \triangleq {}_{\mu}\text{ATTRACTIVE[Name = Margaret]}\,. \tag{5.3}$$

(iv) Modify τ_2 to account for the modifier *very*:

$$\tau_3 \triangleq \tau_2^2\,. \tag{5.4}$$

(v) Aggregate τ_1 and τ_3:

$$\tau = \tau_1 \wedge \tau_3\,. \tag{5.5}$$

The aggregated test score given by (5.5) represents the compatibility of the proposition in question with the database whose DF is expressed by (5.1).

2. *Ellen resides in a small city near Oslo.*

Unfocused translation. Assume that

$$\begin{aligned} DF \triangleq\ & \text{RESIDENCE[Name; City·Name]} \\ & + \text{POPULATION[City·Name; Population]} \\ & + \text{SMALL[Population; } \mu] + \text{NEAR[City Name1; City·Name2; } \mu]\,. \end{aligned} \tag{5.6}$$

(i) Find the name of the residence of Ellen:

$$a \triangleq {}_{\text{City·Name}}\text{RESIDENCE}[\text{Name} = \text{Ellen}]\,.$$

(ii) Find the population of the residence of Ellen:

$$b \triangleq {}_{\text{Population}}\text{POPULATION}[\text{City·Name} = a]\,.$$

(iii) Test the constraint induced by SMALL:

$$\tau_1 \triangleq {}_{\mu}\text{SMALL}[\text{Population} = b]\,. \tag{5.7}$$

(iv) Test the constraint induced by NEAR:

$$\tau_2 = {}_{\mu}\text{NEAR}[\text{City·Name1} = \text{Oslo, City·Name2} = a]\,. \tag{5.8}$$

(v) Aggregate τ_1 and τ_2:

$$\tau = \tau_1 \wedge \tau_2\,. \tag{5.9}$$

Focused translation. Suppose that we are interested in the location of residence of Ellen and that the relation RESIDENCE does not contain Ellen's name. Then, if the base variable implicit in the proposition under consideration is taken to be $X \triangleq$ Location (Residence(Ellen)), the proposition translates into the possibility assignment equation

$$\begin{aligned}\Pi_{\text{Location(Residence(Ellen))}} = &\ ({}_{\text{City·Name2}\times\mu}\text{NEAR}[\text{City·Name1} = \text{Oslo}])\\ &\cap ({}_{\text{City·Name}\times\mu}\text{POPULATION}[\Pi_{\text{Population}}\\ &= \text{SMALL}])\,.\end{aligned} \tag{5.10}$$

In effect, (5.10) conveys the information that the possibility distribution of X is the intersection of two possibility distributions: the first reflects the constraint that the residence of Ellen is near Oslo while the second reflects the constraint that it is a small city.

3. ***Gary earns much more than his youngest brother***

Assume that

$$\begin{aligned}DF \triangleq &\ \text{POPULATION}[\text{Name; Income; Age}]\\ &+ \text{BROTHER}[\text{Name1; Name2}]\\ &+ \text{MUCH·MORE}[\text{Income1; Income2; }\mu]\,.\end{aligned} \tag{5.11}$$

(i) Find Gary's income:

$$a \triangleq {}_{\text{Income}}\text{POPULATION}[\text{Name} = \text{Gary}]\,.$$

(ii) Determine the set of Gary's brothers:

$$b \triangleq {}_{\text{Name1}}\text{BROTHER}[\text{Name2} = \text{Gary}]\,.$$

(iii) Restrict POPULATION to brothers of Gary:

$$c \triangleq \text{POPULATION}[\text{Name} = \text{con}(b)]\,,$$

where the prefix con indicates that b should be interpreted as a conjunctive fuzzy set (see (3.11)).

(iv) Find the income of Gary's youngest brother:

$$d \triangleq {}_{\text{Income}}\text{Min}\,{}_{\text{Age}}(c)\,, \tag{5.12}$$

where the operation ${}_{\text{Income}}\text{Min}_{\text{Age}}$ finds the tuple in c which minimizes the value of Age and reads the Income value in this tuple.

(v) Test the constraint induced by MUCH·MORE:

$$\tau = {}_{\mu}\text{MUCH·MORE}[\text{Income1} = a;\ \text{Income2} = d]\,. \tag{5.13}$$

This value of τ is the desired compatibility of the proposition with the database.

4. *Several large balls*

In this case, the problem is to determine the compatibility of the description $d \triangleq$ *several large balls* with an object, D, which consists of a collection of n balls of various sizes represented by the DF

$$DF \triangleq \text{BALL}[\text{Identifier; Size}] + \text{LARGE}[\text{Size}; \mu] + \text{SEVERAL}[N; \mu]\,. \tag{5.14}$$

In (5.14), the first relation has n rows and is a listing of the identifiers of the balls and their respective sizes. In SEVERAL, μ is the degree to which an integer N fits the definition of *several.*

The description $d \triangleq$ *several large balls* is susceptible of different interpretations. In one, which we shall analyze first, the interpretation is *compartmentalized* in the sense that the constraints induced by LARGE and SEVERAL are tested separately. In another interpretation, which will be referred to as *integrated*, the tests are not separated. To differentiate between these interpretations, we shall write [*several*] [*large*] *balls* and [*several large*] balls to represent the first and second interpretations, respectively.

In an expanded form, the compartmentalized interpretation of d may be expressed as:

$$\text{[several][large] balls} \Leftrightarrow \text{the object consists of several balls and all of the balls are large}\,. \tag{5.15}$$

The test procedure corresponding to this interpretation is the following.

(i) Test the constraint induced by SEVERAL:

$$\tau_1 \triangleq {}_{\mu}\text{SEVERAL}[N = n] .$$

(ii) Find the size of the smallest ball:

$$a \triangleq {}_{\text{Size}}\text{Min}_{\text{Size}}(\text{BALL}) .$$

(iii) Test the constraint induced by LARGE by finding the degree to which the smallest ball is large:

$$\tau_2 \triangleq {}_{\mu}\text{LARGE}[\text{Size} = a] .$$

(iv) Aggregate the test scores:

$$\tau = \tau_1 \wedge \tau_2 . \tag{5.16}$$

In the case of the integrated interpretation, the expanded form of d is assumed to be expressed as:

$$d \Leftrightarrow \text{at least several large balls and at most several large balls} . \tag{5.17}$$

Furthermore, we shall employ the FGCount and the FLCount to count the elements of D.

At a first step in the translation of d, we represent d as a conjunction of d_1 and d_2, where

$$d_1 \triangleq \text{at least several large balls} \tag{5.18}$$

and

$$d_2 \triangleq \text{at most several large balls} . \tag{5.19}$$

Consider the particularized fuzzy set (see (3.11))

$$D_L = \text{BALL}[\text{Size} = \text{LARGE}] \tag{5.20}$$

which represents the restriction of the set BALL to large balls. The FGCount of this set is obtained by sorting D_L in order of decreasing μ and replacing the ith element by i (see (3.35)). Thus,

$$\text{FGCount}(D_L) = ND_L \downarrow . \tag{5.21}$$

Now the quantifier *at least several* may be expressed as the composition of the binary relation $\geq$ with SEVERAL. Thus, if

$$\text{SEVERAL} = 0.5/3 + 1/4 + 1/5 + 1/6 + 0.5/7$$

then

$$\geq \circ\ \text{SEVERAL} = 0.5/3 + 1/4 + 1/5 + \cdots$$

and similarly, for *at most several*, we have

$$\leq \circ \text{SEVERAL} = 1/0 + \cdots + 1/6 + 0.5/7,$$

where $\circ$ denotes the composition operator (see Ref. 133).

In terms of FGCount(D_L), FLCount(D_L) and the quantifiers $\geq \circ$ SEVERAL and $\leq \circ$ SEVERAL, the test scores for the constraints induced by d_1 and d_2 may be expressed as[h]

$$\tau_1 \triangleq \sup(\text{FGCount}(D_L) \cap (\geq \circ \text{SEVERAL})) \tag{5.22}$$

and

$$\tau_2 \triangleq \sup(\text{FLCount}(D_L) \cap (\leq \circ \text{SEVERAL})) \,. \tag{5.23}$$

The aggregated test score, then, is given by

$$\tau = \tau_1 \wedge \tau_2 \,. \tag{5.24}$$

Note. It may be argued that (5.18) and (5.19) should not be treated as independent propositions, that is, as propositions in which the base variables are not jointly constrained. If we constrain the base variables to have the same value, the expression for the aggregated test score becomes

$$\tau = \sup(\text{FECount}(D_L) \cap \text{SEVERAL}) \tag{5.25}$$

in which the FECount (D_L) (see (3.37)) may be normalized by scaling its membership function by the reciprocal of sup(FECount(D_L)).

(v) Let G be a given set of balls of various sizes. The proposition, p, which we wish to translate is related to the description considered in the preceding example. Specifically,

$$p \triangleq G \text{ contains several large balls} \,.$$

In this case, DF is assumed to be:

$$DF \triangleq G[\text{Identifier; Size}] + \text{LARGE}[\text{Size}; \ \mu] + \text{SEVERAL}[N; \ \mu] \,. \tag{5.26}$$

(i) Form the fuzzy subset of large balls in G:

$$a \triangleq G[\text{Size} = \text{LARGE}] \,.$$

(ii) Determine the FGCount of a:

$$b \triangleq \text{FGCount}(a) \,.$$

[h] If F is a fuzzy set, sup(F) is its height, i.e., the supremum of $\mu_F(u)$ over U. (See Ref. 141)

(iii) The test score for the constraint induced by SEVERAL and the relation of containment is given by (as in (5.22)).

$$\tau = \sup(b \cap (\geq \circ \text{SEVERAL})) . \tag{5.27}$$

5. *Patricia has many acquaintances and a few close friends most of whom are highly intelligent*

The database frame is assumed to be:

$$\begin{aligned} DF \triangleq\ & \text{ACQUAINTANCE [Name1; Name2; } \mu] \\ & + \text{FRIEND [Name1; Name2; } \mu] \\ & + \text{INTELLIGENT [Name; } \mu] \\ & + \text{MANY } [N;\ \mu] \\ & + \text{FEW } [N;\ \mu] \\ & + \text{MOST } [\rho;\ \mu] . \end{aligned} \tag{5.28}$$

In ACQUAINTANCE, μ is the degree to which Name2 is an acquaintance of Name1, and likewise for FRIEND. In INTELLIGENT, μ is the degree to which Name is intelligent. *Highly intelligent* will be interpreted as INTELLIGENT^3 and *close friend* as FRIEND^2, where the exponent represents the power to which μ is raised. For simplicity, we shall employ the sigma-count for the representation of the meaning of MANY, FEW and MOST.

(i) Find the fuzzy set of Patricia's acquaintances:

$$a \triangleq {}_{\text{Name2} \times \mu}\text{ACQUAINTANCE[Name1 = Patricia]} .$$

(ii) Count the number of Patricia's acquaintances. Using the sigma count, we have:

$$b \triangleq \Sigma\text{Count}(a) .$$

(iii) Find the test score for the constraint induced by MANY:

$$\tau_1 = {}_{\mu}\text{MANY } [N = b] .$$

(iv) Find the fuzzy set of friends of Patricia:

$$c \triangleq {}_{\text{Name2} \times \mu}\text{FRIEND [Name1 = Patricia]} .$$

(v) Find the set of close friends by intensifying FRIEND:

$$d = c^2 .$$

(vi) Determine the count of d:

$$e \triangleq \Sigma\text{Count}(c^2)\,.$$

(vii) Find the test score for the constraint induced by FEW:

$$\tau_2 \triangleq {}_{\mu}\text{FEW}\ [N = e]\,.$$

(viii) Find the set of close friends of Patricia who are highly intelligent:

$$f = d \cap \text{INTELLIGENT}^3\,.$$

(ix) Determine the count of f:

$$g = \Sigma\text{Count}(f)\,.$$

(x) Form the proportion of those who are highly intelligent among the close friends of Patricia:

$$r = \frac{\Sigma\text{Count}(f)}{\Sigma\text{Count}(d)} = \frac{g}{e}\,.$$

(xi) Find the test score for the constraint induced by MOST:

$$\tau_3 = {}_{\mu}\text{MOST}\ [p = r]\,.$$

(xii) The aggregated test score for the proposition under consideration is given by

$$\tau = \tau_1 \wedge \tau_2 \wedge \tau_3\,. \tag{5.29}$$

6. *During the past few months three large tankers carried a total of 500,000 tons of oil to Naples*

The database frame is assumed to be:

$$DF \triangleq \text{TANKER [Name; Displacement; Cargo; Weight; Destination; Time·Arrival]}$$
$$+ \text{ LARGE [Displacement; } \mu] + \text{ FEW·MONTHS } [t;\ \mu]\ 500{,}000\ [N;\ \mu]\,. \tag{5.30}$$

The inclusion of the relation 500,000 $[N; \mu]$ in the database reflects the assumption that the number 500,000 should be interpreted in an approximate rather than exact sense. Thus, the relation in question defines the degree to which a real number N fits the description "500,000." In the relation FEW·MONTHS, t stands for the time-difference between the present time and the time of arrival.

(i) Particularize TANKER by specifying the displacement, cargo and destination. Thus (see (3.10)),

$$\text{TANKER1} \triangleq \text{TANKER [Displacement} = \text{dis(LARGE)};\ \text{Cargo} = \text{Oil; Destination} = \text{Naples]}\,.$$

(ii) To take into consideration the constraint induced by the number of tankers, we pick an arbitrary three-element subset of tankers, say

$$T3 = \{\text{Name}_i,\ \text{Name}_j,\ \text{Name}_k\}$$

and restrict TANKER1 to T3. Thus

$$\text{TANKER2} \triangleq \text{TANKER1 [Name} = T3]\,.$$

(iii) For each tanker in TANKER2 find the time of arrival and weight of cargo:

$$t_i \triangleq {}_{\text{Time}\cdot\text{Arrival}}\text{TANKER2[Name} = \text{Name}_i]$$
$$c_i \triangleq {}_{\text{Weight}}\text{TANKER2[Name} = \text{Name}_i]$$

and likewise for Name_j and Name_k.

(iv) Determine the test score for the constraint induced by 500,000:

$$\tau_1 = {}_{\mu}500,000[N = c_i + c_j + c_k]\,.$$

(v) For each tanker in $T3$ determine the test score for the temporal constraint induced by FEW ($t_0 \triangleq$ present time):

$$\tau_{i2} = \mu\text{FEW}[t = t_0 - t_i]$$

and likewise for t_j and t_k.

(vi) Aggregate the test scores determined in (v):

$$\tau_2 = \tau_{i2} \wedge \tau_{j2} \wedge \tau_{k2}\,.$$

(vii) Aggregate τ_1 and τ_2:

$$\tau_3 = \tau_1 \wedge \tau_2\,. \tag{5.31}$$

(viii) The test score expressed by (5.31) represents the compatibility of the given proposition with the subset TANKER2. To find the compatibility with the whole database, it is necessary to maximize τ_3 over all three-element subsets of TANKER1, finding that subset which yields the best fit of the proposition to the database. Thus, the overall test score for the proposition in question is given by

$$\tau = \text{Max}_{i,j,k}\tau_3\,. \tag{5.32}$$

7. *Our last example involves a command rather than a proposition*

Specifically, what we wish to translate is:

$$c \triangleq \text{Keep under refrigeration}\,,$$

in which the underlying assumption is that an item A (say a carton of milk) must be stored in a refrigerator when not in use. We assume that A is taken out of the refrigerator at times $t_1, \ldots, t_n$, with $[t_i, t_i + d_i]$ representing the ith time-interval during which A is not under refrigeration. The ambient temperature during the time-interval $[t_i, t_i + d_i]$, $i = 1, \ldots, n$, is assumed to be a_i.

In general, to translate a command, c, it is necessary to identify the *compliance criterion*, cc, which is implicit in c, and devise a procedure for testing the constraints induced by cc. To this end, assume that ed_i, $i = 1, \ldots, n$, is the effective duration of noncompliance which takes into consideration the ambient temperature a_i. Thus

$$ed_i = g(d_i, a_i)\,,$$

where g is a specified function.

The compliance criterion, cc, is assumed to be expressed by the proposition:

$$cc \triangleq \text{Total effective duration of nonrefrigeration is not much longer than } K\,,$$

where K is a specified length of time, and

$$\text{Total effective duration} \triangleq ted \triangleq ed_1 + \ldots + ed_n\,. \tag{5.33}$$

To translate cc, we assume that

$$DF \triangleq \text{PROCESS[Effective·Duration]} + \text{MUCH·LONGER}[T;\ \mu]\,, \tag{5.34}$$

in which the relation PROCESS lists the effective duration of noncompliance at times $t_1, \ldots, t_n$, and MUCH·LONGER defines the degree to which T is much longer than K.

To compute the test score associated with cc we proceed as follows.

(i) Obtain from the relation PROCESS the total effective duration:

$$ted = \Sigma_i\ (\text{Effective·Duration}_i)\,.$$

(ii) Compute the test score:

$$\tau = 1 - {}_\mu\text{MUCH·LONGER}[T = ted]\,. \tag{5.35}$$

This test score, then, represents the degree to which an execution sequence defined by the relation PROCESS complies with the instruction $c \triangleq$ *Keep under refrigeration*.

Concluding Remark

To give an adequate idea of the applicability of test-score semantics to the problem of meaning representation in natural languages would require a far greater number of diverse examples than could be included in the present paper. In particular, with a few exceptions, we have not considered linguistic entities other than propositions and have not illustrated the use of truth-qualification, probability-qualification and possibility-qualification. Furthermore, we have not touched upon (a) the important issue of nesting of linguistic entities, and (b) the concepts of semantic equivalence and entailment. In sum, what we have attempted to convey is a general idea of the conceptual framework of test-score semantics and to articulate the conviction that a comprehensive theory of natural languages cannot be constructed without coming to grips with the issues of imprecision, elasticity and lack of specificity — issues which are intimately related to the necessity for gradation of truth, membership and possibility.

References

1. J. R. Abrial, "Data semantics," in *Data Management Systems*, eds. J. W. Klimbie and K. L. Koffeman (North-Holland, Amsterdam, 1974), pp. 1–60.
2. C. Alsina, E. Trillas and L. Valverde, "On nondistributive logical connectives for fuzzy set theory," *BUSEFAL* **3** (1980), pp. 18–29.
3. J. D. Atlas, "How linguistics matters to philosophy: presupposition truth, and meaning," in *Syntax and Semantics 11: Presupposition*, eds. C-K. Oh and D. Dinneen (Academic Press, New York, 1979), pp. 265–281.
4. J. F. Baldwin and B. W. Pilsworth, "Axiomatic approach to implication for approximate reasoning using a fuzzy logic," Rep. No. EM/FS9, Dept. of Eng. Math., Univ. of Bristol, 1978.
5. W. Bandler and L. J. Kohout, "Semantics of implication operators and fuzzy relational products," *Int. J. Man-Machine Studies* **12** (1980), pp. 89–116.
6. W. Bandler and L. Kohout, "Fuzzy power sets and fuzzy implication operators," *Fuzzy Sets and Systems* **4** (1980), pp. 13–30.
7. A. Barr and E. Feigenbaum (eds.), *The Handbook of Aritificial Intelligence* (Kaufmann, Los Altos, 1981).
8. R. Bartsch and T. Vennemann, *Semantic Structures* (Attenaum Verlag, Frankfurt, 1972).
9. R. Bellman and M. Giertz, "On the analytic formalism of the theory of fuzzy sets," *Inf. Sciences* **5** (1973), pp. 149–156.
10. R. E. Bellman and L. A. Zadeh, "Local and fuzzy logics," in *Modern Uses of Multiple-Valued Logic*, ed. G. Epstein (D. Reidel, Dordrecht, 1977), pp. 103–165.
11. M. Bergmann, "Presupposition and two-dimensional logic," *J. of Philos. Logic* **10** (1981), pp. 27–53.
12. M. Black, "Reasoning with loose concepts," *Dialogue* **2** (1963), pp. 1–12.
13. D. Bobrow and A. Collins (eds.), *Representation and Understanding* (Academic Press, New York, 1975).
14. R. F. Boyce, D. D. Chamberlin, W. F. King III and M. M. Hammer, "Specifying queries as relational expressions," in *Data Base Management* eds. J. W. Klimbie and K. L. Koffeman (North-Holland, Amsterdam, 1974), pp. 211–223.

15. R. J. Brachman, "What's in a concept: structural foundations for semantic networks," *Int. J. Man-Machine Studies* **9** (1977), pp. 127–152.
16. V. M. Briabrin and G. V. Senin, "Natural language processing within a restricted context," in *Proc. Int. Workshop on Natural Language for Interactions with Data Bases*, IIASA, Vienna, 1977.
17. R. Carnap, *Meaning and Necessity* (University of Chicago Press, Chicago, 1952).
18. W. S. Cooper, *Logical Linguistics* (D. Reidel, Dordrecht, 1978).
19. N. Chomsky, "Deep structure, surface structure, and semantic interpretation," in *Semantics: An Interdisciplinary Reader in Philosophy, Linguistics and Psychology*, eds. D. D. Steinberg and L. A. Jakobovits (Cambridge University Press, Cambridge, 1971).
20. M. J. Cresswell, *Logics and Languages* (Methuen, London, 1973).
21. F. J. Damerau, "On fuzzy adjectives," Memorandum RC 5340, IBM Research Laboratory, Yorktown Heights, New York, 1975.
22. D. Davidson, "Truth and meaning," *Synthese* **17** (1967), pp. 304–323.
23. D. Davidson and N. Gilbert, *Semantics of Natural Language* (D. Reidel, Dordrecht, 1972).
24. A. DeLuca and S. Termini, "A definition of a non-probabilistic entropy in the setting of fuzzy sets theory," *Information and Control* **20** (1972), pp. 301–312.
25. D. Dubois and H. Prade, "New results about properties and semantics of fuzzy-set-theoretic operators," in *Fuzzy Sets: Theory and Applications to Policy Analysis and Information Systems*, eds. P. P. Wang and S. K. Chang (1980), pp. 59–75.
26. D. Dubois and H. Prade, *Fuzzy Sets and Systems: Theory and Applications* (Academic Press, New York, 1980).
27. N. V. Findler (ed.), *Associative Networks* (Academic Press, New York, 1979).
28. K. Fine, "Vagueness, truth and logic," *Synthese* **30** (1975), pp. 265–300.
29. C. Frederiksen, "Representing logical and semantic structure of knowledge acquired from discourse," *Cognitive Psychology* **7** (1975), pp. 371–458.
30. B. R. Gaines, Logical foundations for database systems," *Int. J. Man-Machine Studies* **11** (1979), pp. 481–500.
31. B. R. Gaines and L. J. Kohout, "The fuzzy decade: A bibliography of fuzzy systems and closely related topics," *Int. J. Man-Machine Studies* **9** (1977), pp. 1–68.
32. H. Gallaire and J. Minker (eds.), *Logic and Data Bases* (Plenum Press, New York, 1978).
33. G. Gazdar, *Pragmatics: Implicature, Presupposition, and Logical Form* (Academic Press, New York, 1979).
34. J. A. Goguen, "Concept representation in natural and artificial languages: axioms, extensions and applications for fuzzy sets," *Int. J. Man-Machine Studies* **6** (1974), pp. 513–561.
35. H. P. Grice, "Utterer's meaning, sentence-meaning and word-meaning," *Foundations of Language* **4** (1968), pp. 225–242.
36. R. Grishman and L. Hirschman, "Question answering from natural language medical databases," *Artificial Intelligence* **11** (1978), pp. 25–43.
37. B. J. Grosz, "Focusing and description in natural language dialogues," Tech. Note, AI Center, SRI International, Menlo Park, Calif., 1979.
38. S. Haack, *Philosophy of Logics* (Cambridge University Press, Cambridge, 1978).
39. P. K. Halvorsen, "An interpretation procedure for functional structures," Cognitive Science Center, MIT, Cambridge, Mass., 1981.
40. H. Hamacher, "On logical connectives of fuzzy statements and their affiliated truth functions," in *Proceedings of the Third European Meeting on Cybernetics and Systems Research*, Vienna, 1976.

41. G. G. Hendrix, "Encoding knowledge in partitioned networks," in *Associative Networks*, ed. N. V. Findler (Academic Press, New York, 1979), pp. 51–92.
42. H. M. Hersh and A. Caramazza, "A fuzzy set approach to modifiers and vagueness in natural language," *J. Experimental Psychology* **105** (1976), pp. 254–276.
43. H. G. Herzberger, "Dimensions of truth," *J. of Philos. Logic* **2** (1973), pp. 535–556.
44. J. Hintikka, *Logic, Language-Games, and Information* (Claredon Press, Oxford, 1973).
45. E. Hisdal, "Conditional possibilities: independence and noninteraction," *Fuzzy Sets and System* **1** (1978), pp. 283–297.
46. J. R. Hobbs, "Making computational sense of Montague's intensional logic," *Artificial Intelligence* **9** (1978), pp. 287–306.
47. G. E. Hughes and M. J. Cresswell, *An Introduction to Modal Logic* (Methuen, London, 1968).
48. J. M. Janas and C. B. Schwind, "Extensional semantic networks: their representation, application and generation," in *Associative Networks* ed. N. V. Findler (Academic Press, New York, 1979), pp. 267–305.
49. P. N. Johnson-Laird, "Procedural semantics," *Cognition* **5** (1977), pp. 189–214.
50. J. Kampé de Feriet and B. Forte, "Information et probabilité," *Comptes Rendus, Academy of Sciences (Paris)* **265A** (1967), pp. 142–146, 350–353.
51. L. Karttunen and P. S. Peters, "Requiem for presupposition," in *Proc. 3rd Meeting Berkeley Linguistics Society* (1977), pp. 360–371.
52. J. J. Katz, *The Philosophy of Language* (Harper & Row, New York, 1966).
53. A. Kaufmann, *Introduction to the Theory of Fuzzy Subsets, Vol. 2. Applications to Linguistics, Logic and Semantics* (Masson and Co., Paris, 1975).
54. R. Kempson, *Presupposition and the Delimitation of Semantics* (Cambridge University Press, Cambridge, 1975).
55. H. Khatchadourian, "Vagueness, meaning and absurdity," *Amer. Phil. Quarterly* **2** (1965), pp. 119–129.
56. E. P. Klement, "An axiomatic theory of operations on fuzzy sets," Institut fur Mathematik, Johannes Kepler Universitat Linz, Institutsbericht 159, 1981.
57. D. Knuth, "Semantics of context-free languages," *Mathematical Systems Theory* **2** (1968), pp. 127–145.
58. S. Kripke, "Naming and necessity," *Semantics of Natural Languages*, ed. D. Davidson and G. Harman (D. Reidel, Dordrecht, 1971).
59. W. Labov, "The boundaries of words and their meanings," in *New Ways of Analyzing Variation in English, Vol. 1*, eds. C.-J. N. Bailey and R. W. Shuy (Georgetown University Press, Washington, 1973).
60. G. Lakoff, "Hedges: A study in meaning criteria and the logic of fuzzy concepts," *J. Phil. Logic* **2** (1973), pp. 458–508. Also in *Contemporary Research in Philosophical Logic and Linguistic Semantics*, eds. D. Jockney, W. Harper and B. Freed (D. Riedel, Dordrecht, 1973), pp. 221–271.
61. G. Lakoff, "Fuzzy grammar and the performance/competence terminology game," in *Proc. Meeting of Chicago Linguistics Society* (1973), pp. 271–291.
62. K. Lambert and B. C. van Fraassen, "Meaning relations, possible objects and possible worlds," *Philosophical Problems in Logic* (1970), pp. 1–19.
63. W. Lehnert, "Human and computational question answering," *Cognitive Science* **1** (1977), pp. 47–73.
64. H. Levesque and J. Mylopoulos, "A procedural semantics for semantic networks," in *Associative Networks*, ed. N. V. Findler (Academic Press, New York, 1979), pp. 93–121.
65. D. Lewis, "General semantics," *Synthese* **22** (1970), pp. 18–67.
66. J. N. Martin, "Karttunen on possibility," *Linguistic Inquiry* **6** (1975), pp. 339–341.

67. J. McCarthy and P. Hayes, "Some philosophical problems from the standpoint of artificial intelligence," in *Machine Intelligence* **4**, eds. D. Michie and B. Meltzer (Edinburgh University Press, Edinburgh, 1969), pp. 463–502.
68. J. D. McCawley, *Everything that Linguists Have Always Wanted to Know about Logic* (The University of Chicago Press, Chicago, 1981).
69. J. R. McSkimin and J. Minker, "A predicate calculus based semantic network for deductive searching," in *Associative Networks*, ed. N. V. Findler (Academic Press, New York, 1979), pp. 205–238.
70. G. A. Miller and P. N. Johnson-Laird, *Language and Perception* (Harvard University Press, Cambridge, 1976).
71. M. Minsky, "A framework for representing knowledge," in *The Psychology of Computer Vision*, ed. P. Winston (McGraw-Hill, New York, 1975), pp. 211–277.
72. M. Mizumoto, S. Fukame and K. Tanaka, "Fuzzy reasoning methods by Zadeh and Mamdani, and improved methods," in *Proc. Third Workshop on Fuzzy Reasoning*, Queen Mary College, London, 1978.
73. M. Mizumoto, M. Umano and K. Tanaka, "Implementation of a fuzzy-set-theoretic data structure system," in *Third Int. Conf. on Very Large Data Bases*, Tokyo, 1977.
74. G. C. Moisil, *Lectures on the Logic of Fuzzy Reasoning* (Scientific Editions, Bucharest, 1975).
75. R. Montague, *Formal Philosophy* (Selected Papers), ed. R. Thomason (Yale University Press, New Haven, 1974).
76. M. Mizumoto and K. Tanaka, "Some properties of fuzzy numbers," in *Advances in Fuzzy Set Theory and Applications*, eds. M. M. Gupta, R. K. Ragade and R. R. Yager (North Holland, Amsterdam, 1979), pp. 153–164.
77. R. C. Moore, "Reasoning about knowledge and actions," Tech. Note 191, AI Center, SRI International, Menlo Park, Calif., 1981.
78. N. N. Nalimov, "Probability distribution functions as a means of characterization of fuzzy sets. Outline of a meta theory (discussion of the work of L. A. Zadeh)," *Automatika* **6** (1979), pp. 80–87.
79. A. S. Naranyani, "Methods of modeling incompleteness of data in knowledge bases," in *Knowledge Representation and Modeling of Processes of Understanding* (Novosibirsk, Siberian Academy of Sciences, 1980), pp. 153–162.
80. C. V. Negoita and D. A. Ralescu, *Applications of Fuzzy Sets to Systems Analysis* (Birkhäuser Verlag, Stuttgart, 1975).
81. A. Newell and H. A. Simon, *Human Problem Solving* (Prentice-Hall, N.J., 1972).
82. H. T. Nguyen, "On conditional possibility distributions," *Fuzzy Sets and Systems* **1** (1978), pp. 299–309.
83. H. T. Nguyen, "Toward a calculus of the mathematical notion of possibility," in *Advances in Fuzzy Set Theory and Applications*, eds. M. M. Gupta, R. K. Ragade and R. R. Yager (North Holland, Amsterdam, 1979), pp. 235–246.
84. K. Noguchi, M. Umano, M. Mizumoto and K. Tanaka, "Implementation of fuzzy artificial intelligence language FLOU," Technical Report on Automation and Language of IECE, 1976.
85. D. Norman and D. E. Rumelhart, *Explorations in Cognition* (Freeman, San Francisco, 1975).
86. B. Partee, *Montague Grammar* (Academic Press, New York, 1976).
87. P. Peterson, "On the logic of *few, many* and *most*," *Notre Dame J. of Formal Logic* **20** (1979), pp. 155–179.
88. M. Platts (ed.), *Reference, Truth and Reality* (Routledge and Kegan Paul, London, 1980).

89. H. Prade, "Unions and intersections of fuzzy sets," *BUSEFAL* **3** (1980), pp. 58–61.
90. H. Putnam, "The meaning of 'meaning'," in *Language, Mind and Knowledge*, ed. K. Gunderson (University of Minnesota Press, Minn., 1975).
91. N. Rescher, *The Coherence Theory of Truth* (Oxford University Press, Oxford, 1973).
92. N. Rescher, *Theory of Possibility* (Pittsburgh University Press, Pittsburgh, 1975).
93. N. Rescher, *Plausible Reasoning* (Van Gorcum, Amsterdam, 1976).
94. B. Rieger, "Fuzzy structural semantics," in *Proc. Third European Meeting on Cybernetics and Systems Research*, Vienna, 1976.
95. C. Rieger, "An organization of knowledge for problem solving and language comprehension," *Artificial Intelligence* **7** (1976), pp. 89–127.
96. A. E. Robinson, D. E. Appelt, B. J. Grosz, G. G. Hendrix and J. Robinson, "Interpreting natural-language utterances in dialogs about tasks," Tech. Note 210, AI Center, SRI International, Menlo Park, Calif., 1980.
97. J. Sadock, "Truth and approximations," in *Proc. Third Meeting Berkeley Linguistics Society* (1977), pp. 430–439.
98. N. Sager, "Natural language analysis and processing," in *Encyclopedia of Computer Science and Technology*, eds. J. Belzer, A. G. Holtzman and A. Kent (Marcel Dekker, New York, 1978), pp. 152–169.
99. E. J. Sandewall, "Representing natural language information in predicate calculus," *Machine Intelligence* **6**, eds. B. Meltzer and D. Michie (American Elsevier, New York, 1971), pp. 255-277.
100. E. Sanchez, "On possibility qualification in natural languages," Electronics Research Laboratory Memorandum M77/28, University of California, Berkeley, 1977.
101. R. C. Schank (ed.), *Conceptual Information Processing* (North-Holland, Amsterdam, 1975).
102. L. K. Schubert, "Extending the expressive power of semantic networks," *Artificial Intelligence* **2** (1972), pp. 163–198.
103. L. K. Schubert, R. G. Goebel and N. Cercone, "The structure and organization of a semantic net for comprehension and inference," in *Associative Networks*, ed. N. V. Fundler (Academic Press, New York, 1979), pp. 122–178.
104. J. Searle (ed.), *The Philosophy of Language* (Oxford University Press, Oxford, 1971).
105. B. S. Sembi and E. H. Mamdani, "On the nature of implication in fuzzy logic," in *Proc. 9th Int. Symp. on Multiple-Valued Logic*, Bath, England (1979), pp. 143–151.
106. R. Simmons, "Semantic networks: their computation and use for understanding English sentences," in *Computer Models of Thought and Language*, eds. R. C. Schank and K. Colby (Freeman, San Francisco, 1973), pp. 63–113.
107. H. A. Simon, "The structure of ill structured problems," *Artificial Intelligence* **4** (1973), pp. 181–201.
108. J. F. Staal, "Formal logic and natural languages," *Foundations of Language* **5** (1969), pp. 256–284.
109. R. Stalnaker, "Presuppositions," *J. of Philosophical Logic* **2** (1973), pp. 447–456.
110. S. P. Stitch, "Logical form and natural language," *Phil. Studies* **28** (1975), pp. 397–418.
111. P. F. Strawson, *Introduction to Logical Theory* (Methuen, London, 1952).
112. O. M. Sugeno, "Fuzzy measures and fuzzy integrals: a survey," in *Fuzzy Automata and Decision Processes*, eds. M. M. Gupta, G. N. Saridis and B. R. Gaines (North Holland, Amsterdam, 1977), pp. 89–102.
113. P. Suppes, "Elimination of quantifiers in the semantics of natural languages by use of extended relation algebras," *Revue Internationale de Philosophie* (1976), pp. 117–118, 243–259.

114. P. Szolovits, L. B. Hawkinson and W. A. Martin, "An overview of OWL, a language for knowledge representation," MIT/LCS/TM-86, MIT, Cambridge, Mass., 1977.
115. A. Tarski, *Logic, Semantics, Metamathematics* (Clarendon Press, Oxford, 1956).
116. T. Terano and M. Sugeno, "Conditional fuzzy measures and their applications," in *Fuzzy Sets and Their Applications to Cognitive and Decision Processes*, eds. L. A. Zadeh, K. S. Fu, K. Tanaka and M. Shimura (Academic Press, New York, 1975), pp. 151–170.
117. U. Thole, H. J. Zimmermann and P. Zysno, "On the suitability of minimum and product operator for the intersection of fuzzy sets," *Fuzzy Sets and System* **2** (1979), pp. 167–180.
118. R. Thomason, *Semantics, Pragmatics, Conversation, Presupposition* Department of Philosophy, University of Pittsburgh (1973).
119. B. C. van Fraassen, "Singular terms, truth-value gaps, and free logic," *J. of Philos.* **63** (1966), pp. 481–495.
120. B. C. van Fraassen, *Formal Semantics and Logic* (Macmillan, New York, 1971).
121. W. Wahlster, W. V. Hahn, W. Hoeppner and A. Jameson, "The anatomy of the natural language dialog system HAM-RPM," in *Natural Language Computer Systems*, ed. L. Bolc (Hanser/Macmillan, Munchen, 1980).
122. D. Waltz, "Natural language interfaces," *SIGART Newsletter* **61** (1977), pp. 16–65.
123. P. D. Wang and S. K. Chang (eds.), *Fuzzy Sets* (Plenum Press, New York, 1980).
124. F. Wenstop, "Deductive verbal models of organizations," *Int. J. Man-Machine Studies* **8** (1976), pp. 293–311.
125. Y. Wilks, "Philosophy of language," in *Computational Linguistics*, eds. E. Charniak and Y. Wilks (North Holland, Amsterdam, 1976), pp. 205–233.
126. T. Winograd, *Understanding Natural Language* (Academic Press, New York, 1972).
127. T. Winogard, "Towards a procedural understanding of semantics, "SAIL Memo AIM-292. Stanford University, Stanford, Calif., 1976.
128. T. Winograd, "Language as a cognitive process," Department of Computer Science, Stanford University, 1981.
129. W. A. Woods, "What is in a link: foundations for semantic networks," in *Representation and Understanding*, eds. D. B. Bobrow and A. Collins (Academic Press, New York, 1975), pp. 35–82.
130. R. R. Yager, "A foundation for a theory of possibility," *J. Cybernetics* **10** (1980), pp. 177–204.
131. R. R. Yager, "On a general class of fuzzy connectives," *Fuzzy Sets and Systems* **4** (1980), pp. 235–242.
132. L. A. Zadeh, "Probability measures of fuzzy events," *J. Math. Anal. Appl.* **23** (1968), pp. 421–427.
133. L. A. Zadeh, "Similarity relations and fuzzy orderings," *Inf. Sci.* **3** (1971), pp. 177–200.
134. L. A. Zadeh, "Fuzzy languages and their relation to human and machine intelligence," in *Proc. Int. Conf. on Man and Computer*, Bordeaux, France (S. Karger, Basel, 1972), pp. 130–165.
135. L. A. Zadeh, "Fuzzy logic and approximate reasoning (in memory of Grigore Moisil)," *Synthese* **30** (1975), pp. 407–428.
136. L. A. Zadeh, "The concept of a linguistic variable and its application to approximate reasoning," Part I, *Inf. Sci.* **8** (1975), pp. 199–249; Part II, *Inf. Sci.* **8** (1975), pp. 301–357; Part III, *Inf. Sci.* **9** (1975), pp. 43–80.
137. L. A. Zadeh, "A theory of approximate reasoning," Electronics Research Laboratory Memorandum M77/58, University of California, Berkeley, 1977; also in *Machine Intelligence* **9** eds. J. E. Hayes, M. Michie and L. I. Kulich (Wiley, New York, 1979), pp. 149–194.

138. L. A. Zadeh, "Fuzzy sets as a basis for a theory of possibility," *Fuzzy Sets and Systems* **1** (1978), pp. 3–28.
139. L. A. Zadeh, "PRUF — A meaning representation language for natural languages," *Int. J. Man-Machine Studies* **10** (1978), pp. 395–460.
140. L. A. Zadeh, "Possibility theory and soft data analysis," Electronics Research Laboratory Memorandum M79/59, University of California, Berkeley, 1979; also in *Mathematical Frontiers of the Social and Policy Sciences*, eds. L. Cobb and R. M. Thrall (Westview Press, Boulder, 1981), pp. 69–129.
141. L. A. Zadeh, "Fuzzy sets and information granularity," in *Advances in Fuzzy Set Theory and Applications*, eds. M. M. Gupta, R. K. Ragade and R. R. Yager (North Holland, Amsterdam, 1979), pp. 3–18.
142. H.-J. Zimmermann and P. Zysno, "Latent connectives in human decision making," *Fuzzy Sets and Systems* **4** (1980), pp. 37–52.

A note on prototype theory and fuzzy sets

L. A. ZADEH*
University of California, Berkeley

In a recent paper, Osherson and Smith (1981) present an insightful critique of some of the contending approaches to prototype theory and arrive at the conclusion that the theory of fuzzy sets does not provide a satisfactory solution to the problems that stand in the way of constructing an adequate theory of prototypes.

In what follows, the issues raised by Osherson and Smith are commented upon and an alternative definition of the concept of a prototype is proposed. In contrast to some of the conventional definitions, the proposed definition does not associate with a given set A a unique prototypical element of A. Rather, the prototypes of A constitute a fuzzy set, PT(A), whose elements, in general, are not elements of A. Viewed in this perspective, the concept of a prototype is a fuzzy concept, and the theory of fuzzy sets provides an appropriate framework for its formulation and applications.

The first issue raised by Osherson and Smith relates to the observation that, in the case of conjunctive concepts, e.g., a *striped apple*, the rules of combination of fuzzy sets lead to a contradiction when an object is more prototypical of a conjunction than of its constituents.

The same point was raised earlier by Paul Kay (1975), who observed that, in some cases, the grade of membership of an object, u, in the intersection of two fuzzy sets A and B may be greater than its grade of membership in A (or B).

In explaining this phenomenon (Zadeh, 1978), it was pointed out that when (a) the intersection of A and B is a subnormal fuzzy set (i.e., a fuzzy set whose maximal grade of membership is less than unity); and (b) we focus our attention on $A \cap B$ by giving it a label, say C, we are, in effect, tacitly normalizing C by relativizing the grades of membership in C with respect to the maximal grade of membership in $A \cap B$. By so doing, we are generating a normalized fuzzy set Norm $(A \cap B)$ which is *not* a subset of A and B. Consequently, an object, u, may have a higher grade of membership in Norm $(A \cap B)$ than in A or B.

---

*Research supported in part by the NSF Grant IST-8018196 and DARPA Contract N00039-82-C-0235. Reprint requests should be sent to L. A. Zadeh, Computer Science Division, Department of Electrical Engineering and Computer Sciences and the Electronics Research Laboratory, University of California, Berkeley, CA 94720, U.S.A.

Reprinted, with permission, from *Cognition*, 12(3), pp. 291–297.

Another point that relates to this issue is that, in the theory of fuzzy sets, the conjunctive combination is defined via the min operator when the combination is *noninteractive* (Zadeh, 1978). It is widely agreed at this juncture that no single formula for conjunction could model the wide variety of ways in which conjunction enters into concept formation and meaning representation. A number of papers in the literature of fuzzy sets discuss this issue from both theoretical and experimental points of view (Dubois and Prade, 1980).

Also of relevance to what appears to be a failure of compositionality in the case of the concept of a *striped apple* is the fact that in natural languages the denotation of a phrase of the form AN, where N is a noun (e.g., *apple*) and A is a descriptor of N, (e.g., *striped*), is not, in general, the intersection of the denotations of N and A, no matter how the intersection is defined. The reason for it is that in many cases A is not a descriptor of N but an operator which transforms the denotation of N into the denotation of AN. As an illustration, in the case of the concept of a *model car*, its denotation is the result of acting with the operator *model* on the denotation of *car*, rather than the intersection of the denotations of *model* and *car*. Thus, what appears to be a failure of compositionality in this case is, in fact, the result of interpreting *model* as a descriptor of *car*, while in reality it is an operator whose operand is *car*.

An aspect of the theory of fuzzy sets which Osherson and Smith find objectionable is that, in the theory, the union of A and its complement, A', is not, in general, the whole universe of discourse. This relates, of course, to the long-standing controversy regarding the validity of the *principle of the excluded middle* (Haack, 1978, 1980; Muir, 1981). The principle of the excluded middle is not accepted as a valid axiom in the theory of fuzzy sets because it does not apply to situations in which one deals with classes which do not have sharply defined boundaries.

In their discussion of disjunctive concepts, Osherson and Smith suggest that the theory of fuzzy sets leads to counterintuitive results in the case of the example considered in their paper. The source of the difficulty lies in their definition of wealth as a disjunction of liquidity and investment—a definition which fails to mirror our intuitive perception of the relation between these variables. A suitably formulated relational type of definition in the spirit of those given in Zadeh (1976) would avoid the inconsistencies noted by the authors.

Another issue raised by the authors relates to the concept of inclusion of fuzzy sets. Specifically, Osherson and Smith consider the proposition 'All grizzly bears are inhabitants of North America', and note that it would be falsified—counterintuitively—by the existence of a squirrel on Mars.

The source of the difficulty in this case is not the concept of inclusion but the fact that in a natural language the quantifier *all* is usually not meant in its strict logical sense. Thus, in general, *all* in a proposition in a natural language should be interpreted as a fuzzy proportion which is close to unity. With this understanding, employment of the concept of cardinality of fuzzy sets (Zadeh, 1978), and use of a threshold which eliminates from the count those objects whose grade of membership falls below the threshold, resolves the difficulty noted by Osherson and Smith. An alternative way of resolving the difficulty is to fuzzify the concept of inclusion, as is done in the papers by Bandler and Kohout (1980), Gottwald (1979) and Wilmott (1981). Their approach may be viewed as a concretization of a suggestion made by Osherson and Smith with regard to partial falsification.

In sum, the difficulties noted by Osherson and Smith can readily be resolved in the manner described above. By contrast, the shortcomings of the standard version of prototype theory as summarized by Osherson and Smith are much more serious. In particular, in the standard version, the prototype is (a) assumed to be a member of the class of objects, A, which it represents; and (b) the closer an object is to its prototype, the more characteristic it is of the concept. In the first place, it may be argued that, in general, a prototype is *not* a member of the class in question. And second, an object may be far from the prototype in terms of a given metric and yet have full membership in A.

How, then, could a satisfactory definition of a prototype be formulated? I believe that, in order to have a valid claim to adequacy, a definition should be compatible with the following postulates:

1. A prototype is not a single object or even a group of objects in A. Rather, it is a fuzzy schema for generating a set of objects which is roughly coextensive with A.
2. Prototypicality is a matter of degree, which implies that the concept of a prototype is a fuzzy concept.
3. The concept of a prototype is an opaque[1] concept in the sense that even though we may be able to define it ostensively[2] or by exemplification, we may not be capable of formulating explicit operational criteria for assessing the degree to which a schema qualifies as a prototype.

---

[1]Commonplace examples of opaque concepts are: summary, parody, introduction, caricature, funny, interesting, beautiful, relevant, delicious, etc.

[2]In the case of a fuzzy set, A, an ostensive definition has the form of a finite collection of ordered pairs of the form $\{(\mu_1,e_1),...(\mu_n,e_n)\}$, in which $e_1,...,e_n$ are exemplars and $\mu_1,...,\mu_n$ are their respective grades of membership.

What these postulates imply is that the goal of formalizing the concept of a prototype within the framework of standard theory is, for all practical purposes, unrealizable. Thus, it may be necessary to accept a fuzzier type of definition in which the gain in information is achieved by defining the opaque concept of a prototype in terms of a more elementary opaque concept, namely, the concept of a summary. Such a definition—a definition which employs the concept of a *σ-summary*, that is, a succession of summaries, to generate a collection of prototypes for a given population of objects—is sketched in the sequel. The definition in question is merely a partial precisiation of the process by which the concept of a prototype is formed and is more or less in the spirit of definitions based on the concept of a probabilistic summary (Smith and Medin, 1981).

The point of departure in our construction is a population, A, of not necessarily distinct objects $u_1,\ldots,u_n$ which is represented as a fuzzy multiset[3]

(1) $A = \mu_1/u_1 + \mu_2/u_2 + \ldots + \mu_n/u_n$

which means, in words, that A consists of u_1 with grade of membership μ_1 and u_2 with grade of membership μ_2 and ... and u_n with grade of membership μ_n. To place in evidence the identical elements, A may be expressed as

(2) $A = \mu_1/m_1 \times u_1 + \ldots + \mu_n/m_n \times u_n$

where m_i, $i = 1,\ldots, n$, is a real number—usually an integer—which represents the *multiplicity* of u_i.

As a simple illustration, assume that A is a population of station wagons. Then, a term of the form $0.6/5 \times u_3$ would signify that the population under consideration contains five identical cars with the common descriptor u_3, and that the degree of compatibility of each u_3 car with the concept labeled *station wagon* is 0.6. Each descriptor is assumed to consist of an N-tuple of named slots (features) and slot values (feature values). For example, the name of one of the slots might be *passenger capacity* and its value might be *9*. A slot value indicated as * means that it may be any element of a specified set. In words, this would be interpreted as 'does not matter so long as it is within certain bounds'.

The motivation behind our assumption that A is a fuzzy multiset is the following: First, as a *multiset* A provides information about the distribution of elements of A—a factor which certainly influences our perception of prototypicality. And, second, as a *fuzzy* multiset, the representation (2) defines the degree to which each object u_i fits A as a concept. These degrees,

[3] A multiset differs from a set in that it may contain identical elements.

serving as clues to features which distinguish good exemplars from bad ones, play an important role in the prototype formation process.

For our purposes, it will be convenient to *stratify* the representation of A by grouping together terms which have the same, or nearly the same, grades of membership, and quantizing the grades into a small number of levels, say three or four. In this way, A may be represented as (for three quantization levels):

$$A = \text{High}/A_{\text{Good}} + \text{Medium}/A_{\text{Borderline}} + \text{Low}/A_{\text{Poor}}$$

in which A_{Good}, $A_{\text{Borderline}}$ and A_{Poor} are multisets of good, borderline and poor exemplars, respectively, and High, Medium and Low are fuzzy numbers which represent the corresponding fuzzy grades of membership.

From this point on, each of the groups of exemplars in A is processed separately, as follows. However, the lower the grade of membership associated with a stratum, the less weight it has in the prototype generation process.

Starting with A_{Good}, each of the exemplars in A_{Good} is partially summarized by eliminating one or more features in its characterization. For example, if the descriptor u_5, say, is of the form

$$\begin{array}{ccccc} u_5 & F1 & F2 & F3 & F4 \\ & v_1 & v_2 & v_3 & v_4 \end{array}$$

where v_i, $i = 1, 2, 3, 4$, is the value of feature F_i, then a partially summarized representation of u_5 might be

$$\begin{array}{ccccc} s(u_5) & F1 & F2 & F3 & F4 \\ & * & v_2 & v_3 & v_4 \end{array}$$

in which $s(u_5)$ denotes a summary of u_5 and the "don't care" value * indicates that, within bounds, the value of feature F1 does not affect the goodness of u_5 as an exemplar.

As a result of partial summarization—which is associated with a reduction in the degree of detail—some of the nonidentical elements in A_{Good} become identical—or nearly identical. On grouping such elements together, their multiplicities will necessarily increase and, correspondingly, the number of distinct objects in A_{Good} will decrease. On iterating this process, we may eventually arrive at a maximally summarized object $PT(A_{\text{Good}})$ which may be regarded as a *prototype* of A_{Good}. Proceeding in a similar fashion in the case of $A_{\text{Borderline}}$, A_{Poor} and other strata, if they are defined, we may arrive at their respective prototypes—or, more generally, groups of prototypes —$PT(A_{\text{Borderline}})$, $PT(A_{\text{Poor}})$, etc. The *prototype* of A, then, is the fuzzy set

$$PT(A) = High/PT(A_{Good}) + Medium/PT(A_{Borderline}) + Low/PT(A_{Poor})$$

and it is in this sense that the prototype of A may be regarded as an object which is a σ-summary of the exemplars in the initially given population.

It should be noted that the summarization process sketched above is closely related to the compactification algorithm which is described in Zadeh (1976), and which in turn is related to the Quine-McCluskey algorithm (McCluskey, 1965) for the minimization of switching functions. The σ-summary is a *fuzzy schema* for generating the exemplars in A in the sense that by filling out the details in $PT(A_{Good})$, $PT(A_{Borderline})$ and $PT(A_{Poor})$, we can reconstruct, in an approximate fashion, the strata of exemplars in A.

The schema may also be used for purposes of recognition. Specifically, given an object, u, we may determine, roughly, its grade of membership in A by generating A_{Good}, $A_{Borderline}$ and A_{Poor} from their respective prototypes and finding that stratum which contains u as a member. The grade of membership associated with the stratum will be approximately the grade of membership of u in A and may be interpreted as the degree of *compatibility* of u with PT(A). In this sense, the concept of compatibility plays a role that is somewhat analogous to that of distance in standard theory.

A prototype, in our definition, is a fuzzy set rather than a single object. However, when we form a mental image of a prototype in our mind, our inability to visualize simultaneously a collection of objects forces us to imagine a single summarized object which may be regarded as a prototype $PT(A_{Good})$ with some instantiated features. What is understood, however, is that the instantiated feature values are examples whose choice reflects the multiplicities of exemplars in A_{Good}. It is this understanding that links the definition of a prototype as a fuzzy set with our intuitive perception of a prototype as a single summarized object.

In essence, then, we define a prototype as a fuzzy schema for generating or recognizing the elements of a population of objects. Our definition does not incorporate any precise criteria of prototypicality because it mirrors the intrinsic imprecision in our intuitive perception of a prototype, and it leads to a fuzzy set of prototypes rather than a unique prototypical object. Furthermore, the definition does not guarantee that, given a fuzzy multiset A, there will always exist a non-vacuous prototype PT(A). In particular, a prototype will not, in general, exist if A is the union of dissimilar classes, e.g., birds and cows. This is likely to happen in the case of strata with low grades of membership, and it is for this reason that we have to allow for groups of distinct prototypes in $A_{Borderline}$ and A_{Poor}.

In conclusion, the difficulties noted by Osherson and Smith by no means disqualify the theory of fuzzy sets as a basis for a theory of prototypes. On the contrary, it is very unlikely that an adequate theory of prototypes could be constructed without an explicit use of fuzzy sets and related concepts.

References

Bandler, W. and Kohout, L. J. (1980) Fuzzy power sets and fuzzy implication operators. *Fuzzy Sets and Systems, 4*, 13–30.

Coleman, L. and Kay, P. (1980) Prototype semantics: The English verb *lie. Lang., 57*, 26–44.

Dubois, D. and Prade, H. (1980) *Fuzzy Sets and Systems: Theory and Applications.* New York, Academic Press.

Goguen, J. A. (1974) Concept representation in natural and artificial languages: axioms, extensions and applications for fuzzy sets. *Inter. J. Man-Machine Studies, 6*, 513–561.

Gottwald, S. (1979) Set theory for fuzzy sets of higher order. *Fuzzy Sets and Systems, 2*, 125–151.

Haack, S. (1978) *Philosophy of Logics.* Cambridge, Cambridge University Press.

Haack, S. (1980) Is truth flat or bumpy?. In D. H. Mellor (ed.), *Prospects for Pragmatism.* New York, Academic Press.

Kay, P. (1975) A model-theoretic approach to folk taxonomy. *Soc. Sci. Inf., 14*, 151–166.

McCluskey, E. J. (1965) *Introduction to the Theory of Switching Circuits.* New York, McGraw-Hill.

Muir, A. (1981) Fuzzy sets and probability. *Kybernetes, 10*, 197–200.

Osherson, D. N. and Smith, E. E. (1981) On the adequacy of prototype theory as a theory of concepts. *Cog., 9*, 59–72.

Rosch, E. (1978) Principles of categorization. In E. Rosch and B. B. Lloyd (eds.), *Cognition and Categorization.* Hillsdale, NJ, Erlbaum.

Smith, E. E. and Medin, D. L. (1981) *Categories and Concepts.* Cambridge, Harvard University Press.

Wilmott, R. (1981) Mean measures of containment and equality between fuzzy sets. *Proc. 11th Inter. Symp. on Multiple-Valued Logic*, Norman, Oklahoma, 183–190.

Yager, R. (1981) Prototypical values for fuzzy subsets. *Kybernetes, 10*, 135–139.

Zadeh, L. A. (1976) A fuzzy-algorithmic approach to the definition of complex or imprecise concepts. *Inter. J. Man-Machine Studies, 8*, 249–291.

Zadeh, L. A. (1978) PRUF—A meaning representation language for natural languages. *Inter. J. Man-Machine Studies, 10*, 395–460.

A FUZZY-SET-THEORETIC APPROACH TO THE COMPOSITIONALITY OF MEANING: PROPOSITIONS, DISPOSITIONS AND CANONICAL FORMS*

L.A. Zadeh

Abstract

In its traditional interpretation, Frege's principle of compositionality is not sufficiently flexible to have a wide applicability to natural languages. In a fuzzy-set-theoretic setting which is outlined in this paper, Frege's principle is modified and broadened by allowing the meaning of a proposition, p, *to be composed not from the meaning of the constituents of* p, *but, more generally, from the meaning of a collection of fuzzy relations which form a so-called* explanatory database *that is associated with* p. *More specifically, through the application of test-score semantics, the meaning of* p *is represented as a procedure which tests, scores and aggregates the elastic constraints which are implicit in* p. *The employment of fuzzy sets in this semantics allows* p *to contain fuzzy predicates such as* tall, kind, much richer, *etc.; fuzzy quantifiers such as* most, several, few, usually *etc.; modifiers such as* very, more or less, quite somewhat, *etc.; and other types of semantic entities which cannot be dealt with within the framework of classical logic.*

The approach described in the paper suggests a way of representing the meaning of dispositions, e.g., Overeating causes obesity, Icy roads are slippery, Young men like young women, *etc. Specifically, by viewing a disposition,* d, *as a proposition with implicit fuzzy quantifiers, the problem of representing the meaning of* d *may be decomposed into (a) restoring the suppressed fuzzy quantifiers and/or fuzzifying the nonfuzzy quantifiers in the body of* d; *and (b) representing the meaning of the resulting dispositional proposition through the use of test-score semantics.*

To place in evidence the logical structure of p *and, at the same time, provide a high-level description of the composition process,* p *may be expressed in the canonical form* "X is F" *where* $X=(X_1,\ldots,X_n)$ *is an explicit n-ary variable which is constrained by* p, *and* F *is a fuzzy n-ary relation which may be interpreted as an elastic constraint on* X. *This canonical form and the meaning-composition process for propositions and dispositions are illustrated by several examples among which is the proposition* p $\triangleq$ Over the past few years Naomi earned far more than most of her close friends.

Reprinted, with permission, from *J. of Semantics*, 2(3/4), pp. 253–272. 253

L.A. ZADEH

1. Introduction

It is widely agreed at this juncture that Frege's principle of compositionality has a rather limited validity in application to the natural languages (Hintikka (1982)). However, as is well known, its applicability may be extended, as it is done in Montague semantics (Partee (1976)), by the employment of higher-order type-theoretical constructs.

A different approach which is described in this paper is based on a broader interpretation of compositionality which allows the meaning of a proposition to be composed not from the meaning of its constituents, but, more generally, from the meaning of a collection of fuzzy relations in what is referred to as an *explanatory database*. With this interpretation of compositionality, Frege's principle regains much of its validity and, in its modified form, provides a basis for representing the meaning of complex propositions and other types of semantic entities. In particular, it may be used to represent the meaning of propositions containing fuzzy predicates exemplified by *tall*, *kind*, *much younger*, *close friend*, etc.; fuzzy quantifiers such as *most*, *many*, *few*, *several*, *not very many*, *frequently*, *rarely*, *mostly*, etc.; modifiers such as *very*, *quite*, *more or less*, *somewhat*, etc.; and qualifiers such as *quite true*, *very unlikely*, *almost impossible* , etc.

An especially important application of the approach described in this paper relates to the representation of the meaning of *dispositions*, that is, propositions with implicit fuzzy quantifiers. For example, the disposition *Overeating causes obesity* may be viewed as a result of suppressing the fuzzy quantifier *most* in the proposition *Most of those who overeat are obese*. Similarly, the disposition *Young men like young women* may be interpreted as an abbreviation of the proposition *Most young men like mostly young women*. On the other hand, the proposition *Anne tells a lie very rarely* may be interpreted as the *dispositional* proposition *Anne tells a lie very rarely*, in which the fuzzy quantifier *very rarely* may be viewed as a fuzzified version of the nonfuzzy quantifier *never*. In general, a disposition may have a number of different interpretations and the restoration or explicitation of fuzzy quantifiers is an interpretation-dependent process.

2. Test-Score Semantics

The modified Frege's principle underlies a fuzzy-set-based meaning-representation system termed *test-score semantics* (Zadeh (1981)). In this system, a semantic entity such as a proposition, predicate, predicate-modifier, quantifier, qualifier, command, etc., is regarded as a system of elastic constraints whose domain is a collection of fuzzy relations in a database - a database which describes a state of affairs, a possible world, or more generally, a set of objects or derived objects in a universe of discourse. The meaning of a semantic entity, then, is represented as a test which when applied to the database yields a collection of partial test scores. Upon aggregation, these test scores lead to an overall vector test score, τ, whose components are numbers in the unit interval, with τ serving as a measure of the compatibility of the semantic entity with the database. In this respect, test-score semantics subsumes both truth-conditional and possible-world semantics as limiting cases in which the partial and overall test scores are restricted to {pass, fail} or, equivalently, { true, false } or {1, 0}.

In more specific terms, the process of meaning representation in test-score semantics involves three distinct phases. In Phase 1, an *explanatory database frame* or *EDF*, for short, is constructed. *EDF* consists of a collection of relational frames, i.e., names of relations, names of attributes and attribute domains whose meaning is assumed to be known. In consequence of this assumption, the choice of *EDF* is not unique and is strongly influenced by the knowledge profile of the addressee of the representation process as well as by the objective of explanatory effectiveness. For example, in the case of the proposition $p \triangleq$ *Over the past few years Naomi earned far more than most of her close friends*, the *EDF* might consist of the following relations: *INCOME [Name: Amount; Year]*, which lists the income of each individual identified by his/her name as a function of the variable *Year; FRIEND [Name,*μ*]*, where μ is the degree to which *Name* is a friend of Naomi; *FEW [Number;*μ*]*, where μ is the degree to which *Number* is compatible with the fuzzy number *few;MOST [Proportion;*μ*]* in which μ is the degree to which *Proportion* is compatible with the fuzzy quantifier *most*; and *FAR MORE [Income 1; Income 2;*μ*]* where μ is the degree to which *Income 1* fits the fuzzy predicate *far more* in relation to *Income 2*. Each of these relations is interpreted as an elastic constraint on the variables which are associated with it.

In Phase 2, a test procedure is constructed which acts on the relations in the explanatory database and yields the test scores which represent the degree to which the elastic constraints induced by the constituents of the semantic entity are satisfied. For example, in the case of p, the test procedure would yield the test scores for the constraints induced by the relations *FRIEND*, *FEW*, *MOST* and *FAR MORE*.

In Phase 3, the partial test scores are aggregated into an overall test score, τ, which, in general, is a vector which serves as a measure of the compatibility of the semantic entity with an instantiation of *EDF*. As was stated earlier, the components of this vector are numbers in the unit interval or, more generally, possibility/probability distributions over this interval. In particular, in the case of a proposition, p, for which the overall test score is a scalar, τ may be interpreted as the degree of truth of p with respect to the explanatory database *ED*(i.e., an instantiation of *EDF*). It is in this sense that test-score semantics may be viewed as a generalization of truth-conditional and model-theoretic semantics.

In summary, the process described above may be regarded as a test which assesses the compatibility of a given proposition, p, with an explanatory database, ED. What is important to note is that the meaning of p is the test itself rather than the overall test score, τ, which it yields.

In effect, the test in question may be viewed as the process by which the meaning of a proposition is composed from the meaning of the constituent relations in the associated explanatory database. As was stated earlier, the essential difference between this approach to compositionality and that of Frege is that, in general, the meaning of a proposition, p, is composed not from the meaning of the constituents of p but from those of a database, EDF, which is constructed for the explicit purpose of explaining or representing the meaning of p in terms of fuzzy relations whose meaning is assumed to be known to the addressee of the representation process.

In some instances, the names of constituent relations in the explanatory database may bear a close relation to the constituents or the proposition. In general, however, the connection may be implicit rather than explicit.

In testing the constituent relations in EDF, it is helpful to have a collection of standardized rules for computing the aggregated test score of a combination of elastic constraints $C_1, \ldots, C_k$ from the knowledge of the test scores of each constraint considered in isolation. For the most part, such rules are *default rules* in the sense that they are intended to be used in the absence of alternative rules supplied by the user.

In test-score semantics, the elementary rules of this type are the following:[1]

Rules pertaining to unary modification

If the test score for an elastic constraint C in a specified context is τ, then in the same context the test score for
(a) *not C* is $1 - \tau$ (negation).
(b) *very C* is τ^2 (intensification or concentration).
(c) *more or less C* is $\tau^{\frac{1}{2}}$ (diffusion or dilation).

Rules pertaining to composition

If the test scores for elastic constraints C_1 and C_2 in a specified context are τ_1 and τ_2, respectively, then in the same context the test score for
(a) C_1 and C_2 is $\tau_1 \wedge \tau_2$, where $\wedge \triangleq$ min (conjunction).
(b) C_1 *or* C_2 is $\tau_1 \vee \tau_2$ where $\vee \triangleq$ max (disjunction).
(c) *If* C_1 *then* C_2 is $1 \wedge (1 - \tau_1 + \tau_2)$ (implication)

Rules pertaining to quantification

Let Q be a fuzzy quantifier (i.e., a fuzzy number) which is characterized by its membership function μ_Q.

Let A and B be fuzzy subsets of a universe of discourse $U = \{u_1, \ldots, u_n\}$, with respective membership functions μ_A and μ_B .

Define the *sigma-count* (i.e., the cardinality) of A as the real number

$$\Sigma\, Count\ (A) \triangleq \Sigma_i \mu_A(u_i)$$

where $\mu_A(u_i)$, $i = 1,\ldots, n$, is the grade of membership of u_i in A. [2]

Define the *relative sigma-count* of B in A as the ratio

$$\Sigma\, Count\ (B/A) = \frac{\Sigma\, Count\ (A \cap B)}{\Sigma\, Count\ (A)}$$

$$= \frac{\Sigma_i \mu_A(u_i) \wedge \mu_B(u_i)}{\Sigma_i \mu_A(u_i)}$$

Then, the overall test score for the generic proposition

$$p \triangleq Q\ A\text{'s are } B\text{'s},$$

where A's and B's are generic names of the elements of A and B , is given by

$$\tau = \mu_Q(\ Count\ (B/A))$$

In effect, this expression indicates that the compatibility of p with the denotations of A and B is equal to the degree to which the proportion of B's in A - or, more generally, the degree of containment of A in B - fits the denotation of Q.

As an illustration of the use of some of these rules in test-score semantics, consider the proposition cited earlier, namely, $p \triangleq$ *Over the past few years Naomi earned far more than most of her close friends.* In this case, we shall assume, as was done earlier, that the constituent relations in the explanatory database are:

EDF $\triangleq$ *INCOME [Name; Amount; Year] +*
FRIEND [Name; μ*] +*
FEW [Number; μ*] +*
FAR MORE [Income 1; Income 2; μ*] +*
MOST [Proportion; μ*] .*

Note that some of these relations are explicit in p; some are not; and that most of the constituent words in p do not appear in *EDF*.

In what follows, we shall describe the process by which the meaning of p may be composed from the meaning of the constituent relations in *EDF*. Basically, this process is a test procedure which tests, scores and aggregates the elastic constraints which are induced by p.

1. Find Naomi's income, IN_i, in $Year_i$, $i=1,2,3,\ldots$, counting backward from present. In symbols,

$$IN_i \triangleq {}_{Amount} INCOME\ [Name=Naomi; Year=Year_i]$$

which signifies that *Name* is bound to Naomi, *Year* to $Year_i$, and the resulting relation is projected on the domain of the attribute *Amount*, yielding the value of *Amount* corresponding to the values assigned to the attributes *Name* and *Year*.

2. Test the constraint induced by *FEW*:

$$\mu_i \triangleq {}_{\mu}FEW\ [Year=Year_i],$$

which signifies that the variable *Year* is bound to $Year_i$ and the corresponding value of μ is read by projecting on the domain of μ.

3. Compute Naomi's total income during the past few years:

$$TIN=\Sigma_i \mu_i IN_i,$$

in which the play the role of weighting coefficients. Thus, we are tacitly asuming that the total income earned by Naomi during a fuzzily specified interval of time is obtained by weighting Naomi's income in year $Year_i$ by the degree to which $Year_i$ satisfies the constraint induced by *FEW* and summing up the weighted incomes.

4. Compute the total income of each $Name_j$ (other than Naomi) during the past few years:

$$TIName_j=\Sigma_i \mu_i IName_{ji},$$

where $IName_{ji}$ is the income of $Name_j$ in $Year_i$.

5. Find the fuzzy set of individuals in relation to whom Naomi earned far more. The grade of membership of $Name_j$ in this set is given by

$$\mu_{FM}(Name_j)= {}_{\mu}FAR\ MORE[Income1=TIN;\ Income\ 2=TIName_j\ ].$$

6. Find the fuzzy set of close friends of Naomi by intensifying (Zadeh (1978)) the relation *FRIEND* :

$$CF \triangleq CLOSE\ FRIEND \triangleq {}^{2}FRIEND.$$

which implies that

$$\mu_{CF}(Name_j)=({}_{\mu}FRIEND[Name=Name_j])^2,$$

where the expression

$${}_{\mu}FRIEND[Name=Name_j]$$

represents $\mu_F(Name_j)$, that is, the grade of membership of $Name_j$ in the set of Naomi's friends.

7. Count the number of close friends of Naomi. On denoting the count in question by $\Sigma Count$ (CF), we have:

$$\Sigma Count(CF) = \Sigma_j \mu^2_{FRIEND}(Name_j)$$

8. Find the intersection of FM with CF. The grade of membership of $Name$ in the intersection is given by

$$\mu_{FM \cap CF}(Name_j) = \mu_{FM}(Name_j) \wedge \mu_{CF}(Name_j),$$

where the min operator signifies that the intersection is defined as to the conjunction of its operands.

9. Compute the sigma-count of $FM \cap CF$:

$$\Sigma Count(FM \cap CF) = \Sigma_j \mu_{FM}(Name_j) \wedge \mu_{CF}(Name_j).$$

10. Compute the relative sigma-count of FM in CF, i.e., the proportion of individuals in $FM \cap CF$ who are in CF:

$$\rho \triangleq \frac{\Sigma Count\ (FM \cap CF)}{\Sigma Count\ (CF)}$$

11. Test the constraint induced by $MOST$:

$$\tau = \mu_{MOST}[Proportion = \rho],$$

which expresses the overall test score and thus represents the compatibility of p with the explanatory database.

In general, the relations in EDF are context-dependent. As an illustration, consider the proposition

$$p \triangleq Both\ are\ tall,$$

in which the standards of tallness are assumed to be class-dependent, e.g., depend on whether an individual is male or female. To reflect this, we may express the EDF for p in the following form:

$$\begin{aligned} EDF \triangleq\ & POPULATION\ [Name;\ Height;\ Sex;] + \\ & Indexical \rightarrow Name_\alpha + \\ & Indexical \rightarrow Name_\beta + \\ & TALL\ [Height;\ Sex;\ \mu], \end{aligned}$$

in which the notation $Indexical \rightarrow Name_\alpha$ indicates that $Name_\alpha$ is an *indexical* object,. i.e., is pointed to by the context. More specifically, we assume (a) that $Name_\alpha$ and $Name_\beta$ are the names of two individuals in $POPULATION$ who are pointed to by the context in which p is asserted; and (b) that the relation *TALL* is sex-dependent, with μ representing the degree to which an individual whose height is *Height* and whose sex is *Sex* is *tall.*

For the *EDF* in question, the steps in the test procedure which leads to the overall test score and thereby represents the meaning of p may be described as follows:

1. Find the height and sex of $Name_\alpha$ and $Name_\beta$:

   $Height\ (Name_\alpha)$ $POPULATION\ [Name=Name_\alpha]$
   $Sex\ (Name_\alpha)$ $POPULATION\ [Name=Name_\alpha]$
   $Height\ (Name_\beta)$ $POPULATION\ [Name=Name_\beta]$
   $Sex\ (Name_\beta)$ $POPULATION\ [Name=Name_\beta]$

2. Find the degrees to which *Name* and *Name* are tall:

   $\tau_\alpha \triangleq \mu\, TALL\ [Height=Height\ (Name_\alpha);\ Sex=Sex\ (Name_\alpha)],$
   $\tau_\beta \triangleq \mu\, TALL\ [Height=Height\ (Name_\beta);\ Sex=Sex\ (Name_\beta)]$

3. Aggregate the test scores found in 2:

$$\tau = \tau_\alpha \wedge \tau_\beta$$

   in which we use the min operator ($\wedge$) to combine the test scores τ_α and τ_β into the overall test score τ.

As an illustration of the compositionality of meaning in the case of dispositions, we shall consider, first, the following simple disposition:

$d \triangleq$ *Claudine is a better tennis player than Michael.*

For concreteness, d will be assumed to have the interpretation expressed by the proposition

$p \triangleq$ *When Claudine* and *Michael play tennis, Claudine usually wins.*

The *EDF* for p is assumed to consist of the relations

$$EDF \triangleq PLAY\ TENNIS\ [Outcome] + USUALLY\ [Proportion; \mu].$$

The relation *PLAY TENNIS* represents a tally of the outcomes of n plays between Claudine and Michael, with the variable *Outcome* ranging over the set {*Win, Lose*}, and with *Win* implying that Claudine won the game. The relation *USUALLY* is a temporal fuzzy quantifier with μ representing the degree to which a numerical value of *Proportion* fits the intended meaning of *USUALLY*.

The steps in the test procedure are as follows.

1. Find the proportion of plays won by Claudine:

$$p = \frac{1}{n} Count\ (PLAY\ TENNIS\ [Outcome=Win]).$$

2. Test the constraint induced by *USUALLY*:

$\tau = {}_{\mu}USUALLY\ [Proportion=\rho]$.

This expression for τ represents the overall test score for d. We can make use of the above result to represent the meaning of a more complex disposition, namely,

$d \triangleq$ *Men are better tennis players than women.*

which will be assumed to be interpreted as the proposition

$p \triangleq$ *Most men are better tennis players than most women,*

with the associated *EDF* consisting of the relations

EDF $\triangleq$ *POPULATION [M. Name; F. Name;* μ*]+*
MOST [Proportion; μ*].*

For simplicity, we assume that there are n men and n women in *POPULATION*, with μ representing the degree - computed as in the above example - to which *M. Name* is a better tennis player than *F. Name*. (More specifically, μ_{ij} is the degree to which *M. Name*$_i$ is a better tennis player than *F. Name*$_j$, $i,j=1,...,n$.)

The steps in the test procedure are as follows:

1. For each *M. Name*$_i$, find the proportion (i.e. the relative sigma-count) of women tennis players in relation to whom *M. Name*$_i$ is a better tennis player:

$$\rho_i \triangleq \frac{1}{n}\Sigma_j \mu_{ij}$$

2. For each *M. Name*$_i$, find the degree to which *M. Name*$_i$ is a better tennis player than most women:

$$\tau_i \triangleq {}_{\mu}MOST\ [Proportion=\rho_i].$$

3. Compute the proportion of men who are better tennis players than most women:

$$\rho = \frac{1}{n}\Sigma_i \tau_i$$

4. Compute the test score for the constraint induced by *MOST*:

$$\tau = {}_{\mu}MOST\ [Proportion=\rho].$$

This τ represents the overall test score for d.

As an additional illustration, consider the disposition

$d \triangleq$ *Young men like young women*

which, as stated earlier, may be interpreted as the proposition

$p \triangleq$ *Most young men like mostly young women.*

The candidate *EDF* for p is assumed to consist of the following relations:

EDF $\triangleq$ *POPULATION [Name; Sex; Age]+*
LIKE [Name 1; Name 2; μ*]+*

MOST [Proportion;μ],

in which μ in *LIKE* is the degree to which *Name 1* likes *Name 2.*

To represent the meaning of p, it is expedient to replace p with the semantically equivalent proposition

$q \triangleq$ *Most young men are P,*

where P is the fuzzy *dispositional* predicate

$P \triangleq$ *likes mostly young women.*

In this way, the representation of the meaning of p is decomposed into two simpler problems, namely, the representation of the meaning of P, and the representation of the meaning of q knowing the meaning of P.

The meaning of P is represented by the following test procedure.

1. Divide *POPULATION* into the population of males, *M. POPULATION*, and population of females, *F. POPULATION*:

   $M.\ POPULATION \triangleq {}_{Name,Age}POPULATION\ [\ Sex=Male\ ]$
   $F.\ POPULATION \triangleq {}_{Name,Age}POPULATION\ [\ Sex=Female\ ],$

   where ${}_{Name,Age}POPULATION$ denotes the projection of *POPULATION* on the attributes *Name* and *Age.*
2. For each $Name_j$, $j=1,\ldots,l$, in *F. POPULATION*, find the age of $Name_j$:

   $A_j \triangleq {}_{Age}F.\ POPULATION\ [Name=Name_j].$
3. For each $Name_j$, find the degree to which $Name_j$ is young:

   $\alpha_i \triangleq {}_{\mu}YOUNG\ [Age=A_j],$

   where α_i may be interpreted as the grade of membership of $Name_j$ in the fuzzy set, *YW*, of young women.
4. For each $Name_i$, $i=1,\ldots,k$, in *M. POPULATION*, find the age of $Name_i$:

   $B_i \triangleq {}_{Age}M.\ POPULATION\ [Name=Name_i].$
5. For each $Name_i$, find the degree to which $Name_i$ is young:

   $\delta_i \triangleq {}_{\mu}YOUNG\ [Age=B_i],$

   where δ_i may be interpreted as the grade of membership of $Name_i$ in the fuzzy set, *YM*, of young men.
6. For each $Name_j$, find the degree to which $Name_i$ likes $Name_j$:

   $\beta_{ij} \triangleq {}_{\mu}LIKE\ [Name\ 1=Name_i\ ;\ Name\ 2=Name_j],$

   with the understanding that β_{ij} may be interpreted as the grade of membership of $Name_j$ in the fuzzy set, WL_i, of women whom $Name_i$ likes.
7. For each $Name_j$ find the degree to which $Name_i$ likes $Name_j$ and $Name_j$ is young:

$$\gamma_{ij} \triangleq \alpha_j \wedge \beta_{ij}$$

Note: As in previous examples, we employ the aggregation operator min ($\wedge$) to represent the effect of conjunction. In effect, γ_{ij} is the grade of membership of *Name* in the intersection of the fuzzy sets WL_i and YW.

8. Compute the relative sigma-count of young women among the women whom $Name_i$ likes:

$$\rho_i \triangleq \Sigma Count\ (YW/WL_i)$$

$$= \frac{\Sigma Count\ (YW \cap WL_i)}{\Sigma Count\ (WL_i)}$$

$$= \frac{\Sigma_i\ \gamma_{ij}}{\Sigma_j\ \beta_{ij}} = \frac{\Sigma_j\ \alpha_j \wedge \beta_{ij}}{\Sigma_j\ \beta_{ij}}$$

9. Test the constraint induced by *MOST*:

$$\tau_i \triangleq \mu MOST\ [Proportion{=}\rho_i].$$

This test score, then, represents the degree to which $Name_i$ has the property expressed by the predicate

$$P \triangleq likes\ mostly\ young\ women$$

Continuing the test procedure, we have:

10. Compute the relative sigma-count of men who have property P among young men:

$$\rho \triangleq \Sigma Count\ (P/YM)$$

$$= \frac{\Sigma Count\ (P \cap YM)}{\Sigma Count\ (YM)}$$

$$= \frac{\Sigma_i\ \tau_i \wedge \delta_i}{\Sigma_i\ \delta_i}$$

11. Test the constraint induced by *MOST*:

$$\tau = \mu MOST\ [Proportion{=}\ \rho]$$

This test score represents the overall test score for the disposition *Young men like young women.*

3. *Canonical Form*

The test procedures described in the preceding section provide, in effect, a characterization of the process by which the meaning of a proposition, p, may be composed from the meaning of the constituent relations in the *EDF* which is associated with p. However, the details of the test procedure tend to obscure the higher-level features of the process of composition and thus make it difficult to discern its underlying modularity and hierarchical structure.

The concept of a *canonical form* of p, which plays an important role in PRUF (Zadeh (1978)), provides a way of displaying the logical structure of p and thereby helps to place in a clearer perspective the role of the consecutive steps in the test procedure in the representation of meaning of p. Specifically, as was stated earlier, a proposition, p, may be viewed as a system of elastic constraints whose domain is the collection of fuzzy relations in the explanatory database. In more concrete terms, this implies that p may be represented in the *canonical form*

$$p \rightarrow X \text{ is } F$$

where $X=(X_1,\ldots,X_n)$ is an n-ary **base variable** whose components $X_1,\ldots,X_n$ are the variables which are constrained by p; and F- which is a fuzzy subset of the universe of discourse $U=U_1\times\ldots\times U_n$, where U_i, $i=1,\ldots,n$, denotes the domain of X_i - plays the role of elastic constraint on X. In general, both the base variables and F are implicit rather than explicit in p.

As a simple illustration, consider the proposition

$$p \triangleq \textit{Virginia is slim.}$$

In this case, the base variables are $X_1 \triangleq$ *Height (Virginia)*, $X_2 \triangleq$ *Weight (Virginia)*; the constraint set is *SLIM*; and hence the canonical form of p may be expressed as

(Height (Virginia), Weight (Virginia)) is SLIM,

where *SLIM* is a fuzzy subset of the rectangle $U_1 \times U_2$, with $U_1 \triangleq [0,200cm]$ and $U_2 \triangleq [0,100\,kg]$.

If the assertion "X *is* F" is interpreted as an elastic constraint on the possible values of X, then the canonical form of p may be expressed as the *possibility assignment equation* (Zadeh (1978))

$$\Pi_{(X_1,\ldots,X_n)} = F,$$

in which $\Pi_{(X_1,\ldots,X_n)}$ denotes the *joint possibility distribution* of $X_1,\ldots,X_n$. In more concrete terms, this equation implies that the possibility that the variables $X_1,\ldots,X_n$ may take the values $u_1,\ldots,u_n$, respectively, is equal to the grade of membership of the n-tuple $(u_1,\ldots,u_n)$ in F, that is,

$$Poss\,\{X_1=u_1,\ldots,X_n=u_n\} = \mu_F\,(u_1,\ldots,u_n),$$

where μ_F denotes the membership function of F.

As an illustration, consider the disposition

$d \triangleq$ *Fat men are kind,*

which may be interpreted as an abbreviation of the proposition

$p \triangleq$ *Most fat men are kind.*

A FUZZY-SET-THEORETIC APPROACH

Let *FAT* and *KIND* denote the fuzzy sets of *fat men* and *kind men*, respectively, in *U*. Now, the fuzzy quantifier *most* in *p* may be interpreted as a fuzzy characterization of the relative sigma-count of *kind men* in *fat men*. From this, it follows that the canonical form of *p* may be expressed as

$$\Sigma Count\ (KIND/FAT)\ is\ MOST$$

or, equivalently, as the possibility assignment equation

$$\Pi_X = MOST$$

where

$$X = \Sigma Count\ (KIND/FAT),$$

and *MOST* is a fuzzy subset of the unit interval [0,1].

Along the same lines, consider the proposition

$p \triangleq$ *Most big men are not very agile.*

As in the previous example, *BIG* will be assumed to be a fuzzy subset of the rectangle [0,200 cm] x [0,100 kg]. As for the fuzzy predicate *not very agile*, its denotation may be expressed as

$$not\ very\ agile \rightarrow ({}^2AGILE)'$$

where ${}^2AGILE$ represents the denotation of *very agile* and ' denotes the complement. More concretely, the membership function of ${}^2AGILE$ is given by

$$\mu_{{}^2AGILE} = (\mu_{AGILE})^2$$

and thus

$$\mu_{({}^2AGILE)'} = 1 - (\mu_{AGILE})^2$$

By relating the denotation of *not very agile* to that of *agile* , the canonical form of *p* may be expressed compactly as

$$p \rightarrow \Sigma Count\ (({}^2AGILE)'/BIG)\ is\ MOST$$

As expected, this canonical form places in evidence the manner in which the meaning of *p* may be composed from the meaning of the fuzzy relations *AGILE*, *BIG* and *MOST*.

As a further example, consider the proposition

$p \triangleq$ *Peggy lives in a small city near San Francisco,*

with which we associate the *EDF*

EDF $\triangleq$ *RESIDENCE [Name; City]+*
SMALL CITY [City;μ]+
NEAR [City 1; City 2;μ].

In *RESIDENCE*, *City* is the city in which *Name* lives; in *SMALL CITY*, μ is the degree to which *City* is small; and in *NEAR*, μ is the degree to which *City 1* is near *City 2*.

The fuzzy set of *cities which are near San Francisco* may be expressed as

$$CNSF \triangleq {}_{City_1}NEAR\ [City\ 2{=}San\ Francisco],$$

and hence the fuzzy set of *small cities which are near San Francisco* is given by the intersection

$$SCNSF \triangleq SMALL.\ \ CITY \cap CNSF,$$

which is, in effect, the fuzzy constraint set F in the canonical form "*X is F*." In terms of this set, then, the canonical form of p may be expressed as

$$p \rightarrow Location\ (Residence\ (Peggy))\ is$$

$$SMALL\ CITY \cap_{City_1}NEAR\ [City\ 2{=}San\ Francisco].$$

To illustrate a different aspect of canonical forms, consider the proposition

$$p \triangleq Mia\ had\ high\ fever.$$

In this case, we have to assume that the base variable

$$X\ (t) \triangleq Temperature\ (Mia,\ t)$$

$$\triangleq Temperature\ of\ Mia\ at\ time\ t$$

is time-dependent. Furthermore, the verb *had* induces a fuzzy or, equivalently, elastic constraint on time which may be expressed as

$$had \Rightarrow t\ is\ PAST$$

with the understanding that *PAST* is a fuzzy subset of the interval ($-\infty$, present time) which is *indexical* in the sense that it is characterized more specifically by the context in which p is aserted. Using this interpretation of *PAST* , the canonical form of p may be written as

$$p \rightarrow Temperature\ (Mia,\ t\ is\ PAST)\ is\ HIGH$$

To conclude our examples, we shall construct canonical forms for two of the propositions considered in Section 2. We begin with the proposition

$$p \triangleq Most\ young\ men\ like\ mostly\ young\ women.$$

As before, we represent p as the proposition

$$p \triangleq Most\ young\ men\ are\ P,$$

where P is the dispositional predicate *likes mostly young women.* In this way, the canonical form of p may be expressed as

$$\Sigma Count\ (P/YM)\ is\ MOST,$$

where P is the fuzzy set which represents the denotation of *likes mostly young women* in *M. POPULATION*, and *YM* is the fuzzy subset of *young men* in *M. POPULATION*.

A FUZZY-SET-THEORETIC APPROACH

To complete the construction of the canonical form, we must show how to construct P. To this end, we shall express in the canonical form the proposition

$$p_i \triangleq Name_i \text{ is } P,$$

where *Name* is the name of *i*th man in *M. POPULATION.*

As before, let WL_i and YW denote, respectively, the fuzzy set of women whom $Name_i$ likes and the fuzzy set of young women in *F. POPULATION.* Then, the canonical form of p_i may be represented as

$$Name_i \text{ is } P \rightarrow \Sigma Count\ (YW/WL_i) \text{ is } MOST.$$

In the above analysis, we have employed a two-stage process to represent the meaning of p through the construction of two canonical forms. Alternatively, we can subsume the second form in the first, as follows.

First, we note that, for each $Name_i$, the relative sigma-count $\Sigma Count\ (YW/WL_i)$ is a number in the interval [0,1]. Let R denote a fuzzy subset of *M. POPULATION* such that

$$\mu_R(Name_i) = \Sigma Count\ (YW/WL\ ).$$

Then, the fuzzy set of *men who like mostly young women* may be represented as

$$P \triangleq MOST\ (R),$$

with the understanding that *MOST (R)* should be evaluated through the use of the extension principle (Zadeh (1978)). This implies that the grade of membership of $Name_i$ in P is related to the grade of membership of $Name_i$ in R through the composition

$$\mu_P(Name_i) = \mu_{MOST}(\mu_R(Name_i)),\ i=1,\ldots,k.$$

Using this representation of P, the canonical form of p may be expressed more compactly as

$$p \rightarrow \Sigma Count\ (MOST\ (R)/YM) \text{ is } MOST.$$

Using the same approach, the canonical form of the proposition

$$p \triangleq \text{Over the past few years Naomi earned far more than most of her close friends}$$

may be constructed as follows.

First, we construct the canonical form

$$p \rightarrow \Sigma Count\ (FM/{}^2F) \text{ is } MOST,$$

where

$$CF \triangleq {}^2F \triangleq \text{fuzzy set of close friends of Naomi}$$

and

$$FM \triangleq \text{fuzzy set of individuals in relation to whom Naomi earned}$$

far more during the past few years.

Second, we construct the canonical form for the proposition which defines *FM*. Thus,

$$Name_j \text{ is } FM \rightarrow (TIN, TIName_j) \text{ is } FAR\ MORE,$$

in which the base variables are defined by

$$TIN \triangleq \text{total income of Naomi during the past few years.}$$
$$= \Sigma_i \mu_{FEW}(i) IN$$

and

$$TIName_j \triangleq \text{ total income of } Name_j \text{ during the past few years.}$$
$$\triangleq \Sigma_i \mu_{FEW}(i) IName_{ji},$$

where IN_i is Naomi's income in year $Year_i$, $i=1,2,3,\ldots$, and $IName_{ji}$ is $Name_j$'sincome in $Year_i$.

It is possible, as in the previous example, to absorb the second canonical form in the first form. The complexity of the resulting form, however, would make it more difficult to perceive the modularity of the meaning-representation process.

Concluding Remark

The fuzzy-set-theoretic approach outlined in the preceding sections is intended to provide a framework for representing the meaning of propositions and dispositions which do not lend themselves to semantic analysis by conventional techniques. The principal components of this framework are (a) the explanatory database which consists of a collection of fuzzy relations; (b) the procedure which tests, scores and aggregates the elastic constraints, and thereby characterizes the process by which the meaning of a proposition is composed from the meaning of the constituent relations in the explanatory database; and (c) the canonical form which represents a proposition as a collection of elastic constraints on a set of base variables which are implicit in the proposition.

Notes

*To Walter and Sally Sedelow.

Research supported in part by the NSF Grants ECS-8209679 and IST-8018196.

1. A more detailed discussion of the rules in question may be found in Zadeh (1978).

2. The concept of cardinality is treated in greater detail in Zadeh (1982 b).

3. To obtain the projection in question, all columns other than *Name* and *Age* in the relation *POPULATION [Sex=Female]* should be deleted.

References and related publications

1. Adams, E.W., 1974: The logic of "almost all". *Journal of Philosophical Logic* 3; 3-17.
2. Bartsch, R. and Vennemann,T., 1972: *Semantic Structures.* Athenäum Verlag, Frankfurt.
3. Barwise, J. and Cooper, R., 1981: Generalized quantifiers and natural language. *Linguistics and Philosophy* 4; 159-219.
4. Blanchard, N., 1981: Theories cardinales et ordinales des ensembles flou: les multiensembles. Thesis, University of Claude Bernard, Lyon.
5. Carlstrom, I.F., 1975: Truth and entailment for a vague quantifier. *Synthese 30*; 461-495.
6. Carnap, R., 1952: *Meaning and Necessity.* University of Chicago Press, Chicago.
7. Chomsky, N., 1980: *Rules and Representations.* Columbia U. Press, New York.
8. Cooper, W.S., 1978: *Foundations of Logico-Linguistics.* Reidel, Dordrecht.
9. Cresswell, M.J., 1973: *Logic and Languages.* Methuen, London.
10. Cushing, S., 1982: *Quantifier Meanings. A Study in the Dimensions of Semantic Competence.* North-Holland, Amsterdam.
11. DeLuca, A. and Termini, S., 1972: A definition of non-probabilistic entropy in the setting of fuzzy sets theory. *Information and Control* 20; 301-312.
12. Dubois, D. and Prade, H., 1980: *Fuzzy Sets and Systems: Theory and Applications.* Academic Press, New York.
13. Gallin, D., 1975: *Intensional and Higher-Order Modal Logic.* North-Holland, Amsterdam.
14. Goguen, J.A., 1969: The logic of inexact concepts. *Synthese 19;* 325-373.
15. Groenendijk, J., Janssen, T. and Stokhoff, M. (eds.), 1981: *Formal Methods in the Study of Language.* Mathematical Centre, Amsterdam.

L.A. ZADEH

16. Hersh, H.M. and Caramazza, A., 1976: A fuzzy set approach to modifiers and vagueness in natural language. *J. Experimental Psychology 105*; 254-276.

17. Higginbotham, J. and May, R., 1981: Questions, quantifiers and crossing, *The Linguistic Review* 1; 41-80.

18. Hintikka, J.K., 1973: *Logic, Language-Games, and Information; Kantian Themes in the Philosophy of Logic*. Oxford University Press, Oxford.

19. Hintikka, J., 1982: Game-theoretical semantics: insights and prospects. *Notre Dame Journal of Formal Logic 23*; 219-241.

20. Janssen, T., 1980: On Problems Concerning the Quantification Rules in Montague Grammar. In: C. Rohrer (ed.), *Time, Tense and Quantifiers*. Niemeyer, Tübingen.

21. Jansen, T., 1981: Relative Clause Constructions in Montague Grammar and Compositional Semantics. In: J. Groenendijk, T. Janssen and M. Stokhof (eds.), *Formal Methods in the Study of Language*, Mathematical Centre, Amsterdam.

22. Keenan, E.L., 1971: Quantifier structures in English, *Foundations of Language 7*; 255-336.

23. Klement, E.P., 1981: An axiomatic theory of operations on fuzzy sets. Institut fur Mathematik, Johannes Kepler Universität Linz, Institutsbericht 159.

24. Lakoff, G., 1973: A study in meaning criteria and the logic of fuzzy concepts. *J. Phil. Logic* 2; 458-508. Also in: *Contemporary Research in Philosophical Logic and Linguistic Semantics*. Jockney, D., Harper, W. and Freed, B., (eds.). Dordrecht: Reidel, 221-271, 1973.

25. Lambert, K. and van Fraassen, B.C., 1970: Meaning relations, possible objects and possible worlds, *Philosophical Problems in Logic*; 1-19.

26. Mamdani, E.H. and Gaines, B.R., 1981: *Fuzzy Reasoning and its Applications*. Academic Press, London.

27. McCarthy, J., 1980: Circumscription: A non-monotonic inference rule. *Artificial Intelligence 13*; 27-40.

28. McCawley, J.D., 1981: *Everything that Linguists have Always Wanted to Know about Logic*. University of Chicago Press, Chicago.

29. McDermott, D.V. and Doyle, J., 1980: Non-monotonic logic I. *Artificial Intelligence 13*; 41-72.

30. McDermott, D.V., 1982: Nonmonotonic logic II: Nonmonotonic modal theories. *Jour. Assoc. Comp. Mach. 29*; 33-57.

31. Miller, G.A. and Johnson-Laird, P.N., 1976: *Language and Perception*. Harvard University Press, Cambridge.

32. Mizumoto, M. and Tanaka, K., 1979: Some properties of fuzzy numbers. In: *Advances in Fuzzy Set Theory and Applications*, Gupta, M.M., Ragade, R.K. and Yager, R.R. (eds.). Amsterdam: North-Holland, 153-164.

33. Moisil, G.C., 1975: *Lectures on the Logic of Fuzzy Reasoning*. Scientific Editions, Bucarest.

34. Montague, R., 1974: *Formal Philosophy*. In: *Selected Papers*, Thomason, R., (ed.). New Haven: Yale University Press.

35. Morgenstern, C.F., 1979: The measure quantifier. *Journal of Symbolic Logic 44*; 103-108.

36. Mostowski, A., 1957: On a generalization of quantifiers. *Fundamenta Mathematicae 44*; 17-36.

37. Osherson, D.N. and Smith, E.E., 1982: Gradedness and conceptual combination. *Cognition 12R*; 299-318.

38. Partee, B., 1976: *Montague Grammar*. Academic Press, New York.

39. Peterson, P., 1979: On the logic of *few* , *many* and *most*. *Notre Dame J. of Formal Logic 20*;155-179.

40. Peterson, P.L., 1980: Philosophy of Language. *Social Research 47*; 749-774.

41. Rescher, N., 1976: *Plausible Reasoning*. Van Gorcum, Amsterdam.

42. Schubert, L.K., Goebel, R.G. and Cercone, N., 1979: The structure and organization of a semantic net for comprehension and inference. In: *Associative Networks*, Findler, N.V., (ed.). New York: Academic Press, 122-178.

43. Scheffler, I., 1981: *A Philosophical Inquiry into Ambiguity, Vagueness and Metaphor in Language*. Routledge & Kegan Paul, London.

44. Searle, J. (ed.), 1971: *The Philosophy of Language*. Oxford University Press, Oxford.

45. Suppes, P., 1976: Elimination of quantifiers in the semantics of natural languages by use of extended relation algebras. *Revue Internationale de Philosophie*; 117-118; 243-259.

46. Terano, T. and Sugeno, M., 1975: Conditional fuzzy measures and their applications. In: *Fuzzy Sets and Their Applications to Cognitive and Decision Processes*, Zadeh, L.A., Fu, K.S., Tanaka, K. and Shimura, M. (eds), New York: Academic Press, 151-170.

47. Yager, R.R., 1980: Quantified propositions in a linguistic logic. In: *Proceedings of the 2nd International Seminar on Fuzzy Set Theory*, Klement, E.P., (ed.). Johannes Kepler University, Linz, Austria.

48. Yager, R.R., 1982: Some procedures for selecting fuzzy-set-theoretic operators. *Inter. Jour. of General Systems 8;* 115-124.

L.A. ZADEH

49. Zadeh, L.A., 1975: The concept of a linguistic variable and its application to approximate reasoning. *Information Sciences 8 and 9*; 199-249; 301-357; 43-80.

50. Zadeh, L.A., 1978: PRUF - a meaning representation language for natural languages. *Int. J. Man-Machine Studies 10*; 395-460.

51. Zadeh, L.A., 1981: Test-score semantics for natural languages and meaning-representation via PRUF. *Tech. Note 247, AI Center, SRI International*, Menlo Park, CA. Also in *Empirical Semantics*, Rieger, B.B. (ed.). Bochum: Brockmeyer, 281-349.

52. Zadeh, L.A., 1982: Test-score semantics for natural languages. In: *Proceedings of the Ninth International Conference on Computational Linguistics* Prague, 425-430.

53. Zadeh, L.A., 1982: A Computational Approach to Fuzzy Quantifiers in Natural Languages. Memorandum no. UCB/ERL M82/36. University of California, Berkeley. To appear in *Computers and Mathematics*.

54. Zimmer, A., 1982: Some experiments concerning the fuzzy meaning of logical quantifiers. In: *General Surveys of Systems Methodology*, Troncoli, L. (ed.). Louisville: Society for General Systems Research, 435-441.

55. Zimmermann, H.-J. and Zysno, P., 1980: Latent connectives in human decision making. *Fuzzy Sets and Systems 4*; 37-52.

L.A. Zadeh
Division of Computer Science
University of California
Berkeley Ca. 94720

L. A. ZADEH*

PRECISIATION OF MEANING VIA TRANSLATION INTO PRUF

ABSTRACT. It is suggested that communication between humans – as well as between humans and machines – may be made more precise by the employment of a meaning representation language PRUF which is based on the concept of a possibility distribution. A brief exposition of PRUF is presented and its application to precisiation of meaning is illustrated by a number of examples.

1. INTRODUCTION

Of the many ways in which natural languages differ from synthetic languages, one of the most important relates to ambiguity. Thus, whereas synthetic languages are, for the most part, unambiguous, natural languages are *maximally ambiguous* in the sense that the level of ambiguity in human communication is usually near the limit of what is disambiguable through the use of an external body of knowledge which is shared by the parties in discourse.

Although vagueness and ambiguity[1] can and do serve a number of useful purposes, there are many cases in which there is a need for a precisiation of meaning not only in communication between humans but also between humans and machines. In fact, the need is even greater in the latter case because it is difficult, in general, to provide a machine with the extensive contextual knowledge base which is needed for disambiguation on the syntactic and semantic levels.

The traditional approach to the precisiation of meaning of utterances in a natural language is to translate them into an unambiguous synthetic language – which is usually a programming language, a query language or a logical language such as predicate calculus. The main limitation of this approach is that the available synthetic languages are nowhere nearly as expressive as natural languages. Thus, if the target language is the first order predicate calculus, for example, then only a small fragment of a natural language would be amenable to translation, since the expressive power of first order predicate calculus is extremely limited in relation to that of a natural language.

To overcome this limitation, what is needed is a synthetic language whose expressive power is comparable to that of natural languages. A candidate for such a language is PRUF [81] – which is a meaning representation language for natural languages based on the concept of a possibility distribution [80].

Reprinted, with permission, from *Cognitive Constraints on Communication*, edited by L. Vaina and J. Hintikka, pp. 373–402.

In essence, a basic assumption underlying PRUF is that the imprecision which is intrinsic in natural languages is possibilistic rather than probabilistic in nature. With this assumption as the point of departure, PRUF provides a system for translating propositions or, more generally, utterances in a natural language into expressions in PRUF. Such expressions may be viewed as procedures which act on a collection of relations in a database – or, equivalently, a possible world – and return possibility distributions which represent the information conveyed by the original propositions.[2]

In what follows, we shall outline some of the main features of PRUF and exemplify its application to precisiation of meaning. As a preliminary, we shall introduce the concept of a possibility distribution and explicate its role in PRUF.[3]

2. POSSIBILITY AND MEANING

A randomly chosen sentence in a natural language is almost certain to contain one or more words whose denotations are fuzzy sets, that is, classes of objects in which the transition from membership to nonmembership is gradual rather than abrupt. For example:

> Hourya is very *charming* and *intelligent.*
>
> It is *very unlikely* that *inflation* will end *soon.*
>
> In *recognition* of his *contributions*, Mohammed is *likely* to be *promoted* to a *higher position*

in which the italics signify that a word has a fuzzy denotation in the universe of discourse.

For simplicity, we shall focus our attention for the present on canonical propositions of the form "N is F," where N is the name of an object, a variable or a proposition, and F is a fuzzy subset of a universe of discourse U. For example:

(2.1) $p \triangleq$ John is very tall
$q \triangleq X$ is small
$r \triangleq$ (John is very tall) is not quite true

where:

In p, $N \triangleq$ John, and *very tall* is a fuzzy subset of the interval [0, 200] (with the height assumed to be measured in centimeters).

In q, $N \triangleq X$ and *small* is a fuzzy subset of the real line.

In r, $N \triangleq$ John is very tall, and *not quite true* is a linguistic truth-value [77] whose denotation is a fuzzy subset of the unit interval.

Now if X is a variable taking values in U, then by the *possibility distribution* of X, denoted by Π_X, is meant the fuzzy set of possible values of X, with the *possibility distribution function* π_X: $U \to [0, 1]$ defining the possibility that X can assume a value u. Thus,

$$\text{(2.2)} \qquad \pi_X(u) \triangleq \text{Poss}\,\{X = u\}$$

with $\pi_X(u)$ taking values in the interval $[0, 1]$.

The connection between possibility distributions and fuzzy sets is provided by the

Possibility Postulate. In the absence of any information about X other than that conveyed by the proposition

$$\text{(2.3)} \qquad p \triangleq X \text{ is } F,$$

the possibility distribution of X is given by the *possibility assignment equation*

$$\text{(2.4)} \qquad \Pi_X = F.$$

This equation implies that

$$\text{(2.5)} \qquad \pi_X(u) = \mu_F(u)$$

where $\mu_F(u)$ is the grade of membership of u in F, i.e., the degree to which u fits one's subjective perception of F.

As a simple illustration, consider the proposition

$$\text{(2.6)} \qquad p \triangleq X \text{ is SMALL}$$

where SMALL is a fuzzy set defined by[4]

$$\text{(2.7)} \qquad \text{SMALL} = 1/0 + 0.8/2 + 0.6/3 + 0.4/4 + 0.2/5.$$

In this case, the possibility assignment equation corresponding to (2.5) may be expressed as

$$\text{(2.8)} \qquad \Pi_X = 1/0 + 0.8/2 + 0.6/3 + 0.4/4 + 0.2/5$$

with Π_X representing the possibility distribution of X. In this case – and more generally – the proposition $p \triangleq N$ is F will be said to *translate* into the possibility assignment equation

$$\Pi_X = F$$

where X is a variable that is explicit or implicit in N. To express this connection between p and the corresponding possibility assignment equation, we shall write

(2.10) $N \text{ is } F \rightarrow \Pi_X = F.$

When X is implicit rather than explicit in N, the possibility assignment equation serves, first, to identify X and, second, to characterize its possibility distribution. For example, in the proposition

(2.11) $p \triangleq$ Clara has dark hair

X may be expressed as

$$X = \text{Color (Hair (Clara))}$$

and the possibility assignment equation reads

(2.12) $\Pi_{\text{Color (Hair (Clara))}} = \text{DARK}.$

Before proceeding further in our discussion of the relation between possibility and meaning, it will be necessary to establish some of the basic properties of possibility distributions. A brief exposition of these properties is presented in the following.

Joint, Marginal and Conditional Possibility Distributions

In the preceding discussion, we have assumed that X is a unary variable such as color, height, age, etc. More generally, let $X \triangleq (X_1, \ldots, X_n)$ be an n-ary variable which takes values in a universe of discourse $U = U_1 \times \ldots \times U_n$, with X_i, $i = 1, \ldots, n$, taking values in U_i. Furthermore, let F be an n-ary fuzzy relation in U which is characterized by its membership function μ_F. Then, the proposition

(2.13) $p \triangleq X \text{ is } F$

induces an n-ary joint possibility distribution

(2.14) $\Pi_X \triangleq \Pi_{(X_1, \ldots, X_n)}$

which is given by

(2.15) $\Pi_{(X_1, \ldots, X_n)} = F.$

Correspondingly, the possibility distribution function of X is expressed by

$$\pi_{(X_1,\ldots,X_n)}(u_1,\ldots,u_n)=\mu_F(u_1,\ldots,u_n),\quad u\triangleq(u_1,\ldots,u_n)\in U$$
$$=\text{Poss}\,\{X_1=u_1,\ldots,X_n=u_n\}.$$

As in the case of probabilities, we can define marginal and conditional possibilities. Thus, let $s \triangleq (i_1,\ldots,i_k)$ be a subsequence of the index sequence $(1,\ldots,n)$ and let s' denote the complementary subsequence $s' \triangleq (j_1,\ldots,j_m)$ (e.g., for $n = 5$, $s = (1, 3, 4)$ and $s' = (2, 5)$). In terms of such sequences, a k-tuple of the form $(A_{i_1},\ldots,A_{i_k})$ may be expressed in an abbreviated form as $A_{(s)}$. In particular, the variable $X_{(s)} = (X_{i_1},\ldots,X_{i_k})$ will be referred to as a k-ary *subvariable of* $X \triangleq (X_1,\ldots,X_n)$, with $X_{(s')} = (X_{j_1},\ldots,X_{j_m})$ being a subvariable complementary to $X_{(s)}$.

The *projection* of $\Pi_{(X_1,\ldots,X_n)}$ on $U_{(s)} \triangleq U_{i_1}\times\ldots\times U_{i_k}$ is a k-ary possibility distribution denoted by

(2.16) $\Pi_{X_{(s)}} \triangleq \text{Proj}_{U_{(s)}}\,\Pi_{(X_1,\ldots,X_n)}$

and defined by

(2.17) $\pi_{X_{(s)}}(u_{(s)}) \triangleq \sup_{u_{(s')}} \pi_X(u_1,\ldots,u_n)$

where $\pi_{X_{(s)}}$ is the possibility distribution function of $\Pi_{X_{(s)}}$. For example, for $n = 2$,

$$\pi_{X_1}(u_1) \triangleq \sup_{u_2} \pi_{(X_1,X_2)}(u_1,u_2)$$

is the expression for the possibility distribution function of the projection of $\Pi_{(X_1,X_2)}$ on U_1. By analogy with the concept of a marginal probability distribution, $\Pi_{X_{(s)}}$ will be referred to as a *marginal possibility distribution.*

As a simple illustration, assume that $n = 3$, $U_1 = U_2 = U_3 = a + b$ or, more conventionally, $\{a, b\}$, and $\Pi_{(X_1,X_2,X_3)}$ is expressed as a linear form

(2.18) $\Pi_{(X_1,X_2,X_3)} = 0.8aaa + 1aab + 0.6baa + 0.2bab + 0.5bbb$

in which a term of the form $0.6baa$ signifies that

$$\text{Poss}\,\{X_1 = b, X_2 = a, X_3 = a\} = 0.6.$$

To derive $\Pi_{(X_1,X_2)}$ from (2.18), it is sufficient to replace the value of X_3 in each term in (2.18) by the null string Λ. This yields

$$\Pi_{(X_1,X_2)} = 0.8aa + 1aa + 0.6ba + 0.2ba + 0.5bb$$
$$= 1aa + 0.6ba + 0.5bb;$$

and similarly

$$\Pi_{X_1} = 1a + 0.6b + 0.5b$$
$$= 1a + 0.6b.$$

An *n-ary* possibility distribution is *particularized* by forming the conjunction of the propositions "X is F" and "$X_{(s)}$ is G," where $X_{(s)}$ is a subvariable of X. Thus,

$$(2.19) \quad \Pi_X [\Pi_{X_{(s)}} = G] \triangleq F \cap \bar{G}$$

where the right-hand member denotes the intersection of F with the cylindrical extension of G, i.e., a cylindrical fuzzy set defined by

$$(2.20) \quad \mu_{\bar{G}} (u_1, \ldots, u_n) = \mu_G (u_{i_1}, \ldots, u_{i_k}),$$
$$(u_1, \ldots, u_n) \in U_1 \times \ldots \times U_n.$$

As a simple illustration, consider the possibility distribution defined by (2.18), and assume that

$$\Pi_{(X_1, X_2)} = 0.4aa + 0.9ba + 0.1bb.$$

In this case,

$$\bar{G} = 0.4aaa + 0.4aab + 0.9baa + 0.9bab + 0.1bba + 0.1bbb$$
$$F \cap \bar{G} = 0.4aaa + 0.4aab + 0.6baa + 0.2bab + 0.1bbb;$$

and hence

$$\Pi_{(X_1, X_2, X_3)} [\Pi_{(X_1, X_2)} = G]$$
$$0.4aaa + 0.4aab + 0.6baa + 0.2bab + 0.1bbb.$$

There are many cases in which the operations of particularization and projection are combined. In such cases it is convenient to use the simplified notation

$$(2.21) \quad X_{(r)} \,\Pi\, [\Pi_{X_{(s)}} = G]$$

to indicate that the particularized possibility distribution (or relation) $\Pi\, [\Pi_{X_{(s)}} = G]$ is projected on $U_{(r)}$, where r, like s, is a subsequence of the index sequence $(1, \ldots, n)$. For example,

$$X_1 \times X_3 \,\Pi\, [\Pi_{(X_3, X_4)} = G]$$

would represent the projection of $\Pi\, [\Pi_{(X_3, X_4)} = G]$ on $U_1 \times U_3$. Informally, (2.21) may be interpreted as: Constrain the $X_{(s)}$ by $\Pi_{X_{(s)}} = G$ and read out the $X_{(r)}$. In particular, if the values of $X_{(s)}$ – rather than their possibility distributions – are set equal to G, then (2.21) becomes

$$X_{(r)}\ \Pi\ [X_{(s)} = G].$$

We shall make use of (2.21) and its special cases in Section 3.

If X and Y are variables taking values in U and V, respectively, then the *conditional possibility distribution* of Y given X is induced by a proposition of the form "If X is F then Y is G" and is expressed as $\Pi_{(Y|X)}$, with the understanding that

(2.22) $\pi_{(Y|X)}(v|u) \triangleq \text{Poss}\{Y = v | X = u\}$

where (2.22) defines the conditional possibility distribution function of Y given X. If we know the distribution function of X and the conditional distribution function of Y given X, then we can construct the joint distribution function of X and Y by forming the conjunction ($\wedge \triangleq \min$)

(2.23) $\pi_{(X,Y)}(u, v) = \pi_X(u) \wedge \pi_{(Y|X)}(v|u)$.

Translation Rules. The translation rules in PRUF serve the purpose of facilitating the composition of the meaning of a complex proposition from the meanings of its constituents. For convenience, the rules in question are categorized into four basic types: Type 1: Rules pertaining to modification; Type II: Rules pertaining to composition; Type III: Rules pertaining to quantification; and Type IV: Rules pertaining to qualification.

Remark. Translation rules as described below relate to what might be called *focused* translations, that is, translation of p into a possibility assignment equation. More generally, a translation may be *unfocused*, in which case it is expressed as a procedure which computes the possibility of a database, D, given p or, equivalently, the truth of p relative to D. A more detailed discussion of these issues will be presented at a later point in this section.

Modifier rule (Type I). Let X be a variable which takes values in a universe of discourse U and let F be a fuzzy subset of U. Consider the proposition

(2.24) $p \triangleq X$ is F

or, more generally,

(2.25) $p = N$ is F

where N is a variable, an object or a proposition. For example,

(2.26) $p \triangleq$ Lucia is young

which may be expressed in the form (2.24), i.e.,

(2.27) $p \triangleq$ Age (Lucia) is young

by identifying X with the variable Age (Lucia).

Now, if in a particular context the proposition X is F translates into

(2.28) $X \text{ is } F \rightarrow \Pi_X = F$

then in the same context

(2.29) $X \text{ is } mF \rightarrow \Pi_X = F^+$

where m is a modifier such as *not, very, more or less*, etc., and F^+ is a modification of F induced by m. More specifically: If m = not, then $F^+ = F' =$ complement of F, i.e.,

(2.30) $\mu_{F^+}(u) = 1 - \mu_F(u),\ u \in U.$

If m = very, then $F^+ = F^2$, i.e.,

(2.31) $\mu_{F^+}(u) = \mu_{F^2}(u), u \in U.$

If m = more or less, then $F^+ = \sqrt{F}$, i.e.,

(2.32) $\mu_{F^+}(u) = \sqrt{\mu_F(u)}, u \in U.$

As a simple illustration of (2.31), if SMALL is defined as in (2.7), then

(2.33) $X \text{ is very small} \rightarrow \Pi_X = F^2$

where

$$F^2 = 1/0 + 1/1 + 0.64/2 + 0.36/3 + 0.16/4 + 0.04/5.$$

It should be noted that (2.30), (2.31) and (2.32) should be viewed as default rules which may be replaced by other translation rules in cases in which some alternative interpretations of the modifiers *not, very* and *more or less* may be more appropriate.

Conjunctive, Disjunctive and Implicational Rules (Type II).

If

(2.34) $X \text{ is } F \rightarrow \Pi_X = F \text{ and } Y \text{ is } G \rightarrow \Pi_Y = G$

where F and G are fuzzy subsets of U and V, respectively, then

(2.35) (a) $X \text{ is } F \text{ and } Y \text{ is } G \rightarrow \Pi_{(X,Y)} = F \times G$

where

(2.36) $\mu_{F \times G}(u, v) \triangleq \mu_F(u) \wedge \mu_G(v).$

(2.37) (b) X is F or Y is $G \to \Pi_{(X,Y)} = \bar{F} \cup \bar{G}$

where

(2.38) $\bar{F} \triangleq F \times V, \bar{G} \triangleq U \times G$

and

(2.39) $\mu_{\bar{F} \cup \bar{G}}(u,v) = \mu_F(u) \vee \mu_G(v)$.

(2.40) (c) If X is F then Y is $G \to \Pi_{(Y|X)} = \bar{F}' \oplus \bar{G}$

where $\Pi_{(Y|X)}$ denotes the conditional possibility distribution of Y given X, and the bounded sum $\oplus$ is defined by

(2.41) $\mu_{\bar{F}' \oplus \bar{G}}(u,v) = 1 \wedge (1 - \mu_F(u) + \mu_G(v))$.

In stating the implicational rule in the form (2.40), we have merely chosen one of several alternative ways in which the conditional possibility distribution $\Pi_{(Y|X)}$ may be defined, each of which has some advantages and disadvantages depending on the application. Among the more important of these are the following [1], [41], [62]:

(2.42) (c_2) If X is F then Y is $G \to \Pi_{(Y|X)} = \bar{F}' \cup G$;

(2.43) (c_3) If X is F then Y is $G \to \Pi_{(Y|X)} = F \times G \cup F' \times V$;

(2.44) (c_4) If X is F then Y is $G \to \pi_{(Y|X)}(v|u) = 1$ if $\mu_G(v) \geqslant \mu_F(u)$,

$$= \frac{\mu_G(v)}{\mu_F(u)} \text{ otherwise;}$$

(2.45) (c_5) If X is F then Y is $G \to \pi_{(Y|X)}(v|u) = 1$ if $\mu_G(v) \geqslant \mu_F(u)$,

$$= \mu_G(v) \text{ otherwise.}$$

Quantification Rule (Type III). If $U = \{u_1, \ldots, u_N\}$, Q is a quantifier such as *many, few, several, all, some, most,* etc., and

(2.46) X is $F \to \Pi_X = F$

then the proposition "QX is F" (e.g., "many X's are large") translates into

(2.47) $\Pi_{\text{Count}(F)} = Q$

where Count (F) denotes the number (or the proportion) of elements of U which are in F. By the definition of cardinality of F, if the fuzzy set F is expressed as

(2.48) $F = \mu_1/u_1 + \mu_2/u_2 + \ldots + \mu_N/u_N$

then

(2.49) $\text{Count}(F) = \sum_{i=1}^{N} \mu_i$

where the right-hand member is understood to be rounded-off to the nearest integer. As a simple illustration of (2.47), if the quantifier *several* is defined as

(2.50) $\text{SEVERAL} \triangleq 0/1 + 0.4/2 + 0.6/3 + 1/4 + 1/5 + 1/6 + 0.6/7 + 0.2/8$

then

(2.51) $\text{Several } X\text{'s are large} \to \Pi_{\sum_{i=1}^{N} \mu_{\text{LARGE}}(u_i)}$

$$= 0/1 + 0.4/2 + 0.6/3 + 1/4 + 1/5 + 1/6 + 0.6/7 + 0.2/8$$

where $\mu_{\text{LARGE}}(u_i)$ is the grade of membership of the ith value of X in the fuzzy set LARGE.

Alternatively, and perhaps more appropriately, the cardinality of F may be defined as a fuzzy number, as is done in [79]. Thus, if the elements of F are sorted in descending order, so that $\mu_n \leqslant \mu_m$ if $n \geqslant m$, then the truth-value of the proposition

(2.52) $p \triangleq F$ has at least n elements

is defined to be equal to μ_n, while that of q,

(2.53) $q \triangleq F$ has at most n elements,

is taken to be $1 - \mu_{n+1}$. From this, then, it follows that the truth-value of the proposition r,

(2.54) $r \triangleq F$ has exactly n elements,

is given by $\mu_n \wedge (1 - \mu_{n+1})$.

Let $F\!\downarrow$ denote F sorted in descending order. Then (2.52) may be expressed compactly in the equivalent form

(2.55) $FG\text{Count}(F) = F\!\downarrow$

which signifies that if the fuzzy cardinality of F is defined in terms of (2.52), with G standing for *greater than*, then the fuzzy count of elements in F is given by $F\!\downarrow$, with the understanding that $F\!\downarrow$ is regarded as a fuzzy subset of $\{0, 1, 2, \ldots\}$. In a similar fashion, (2.53) leads to the definition

(2.56) $FL\text{Count}(F) = (F\downarrow)' - 1$

where L stands for *less than* and subtraction should be interpreted as translation to the left, while (2.54) leads to

$$FE\text{Count}(F) = (F\downarrow) \cap ((F\downarrow)' - 1)$$

where E stands for *equal to*. For convenience, we shall refer to FGCount, FLCount and FECount as the FG cardinality, FL cardinality and FE cardinality, respectively. The concept of FG cardinality will be illustrated in Example 9, Section 3.

Remark. There may be some cases in which it may be appropriate to normalize the definition of FECount in order to convey a correct perception of the count of elements in a fuzzy set. In such cases, we may employ the definition

(2.57) $$FEN\text{Count}(F) = \frac{FE\text{Count}(F)}{\text{Max}_n(\mu_n \wedge (1 - \mu_{n+1}))}.$$

Truth Qualification Rule (Type IV). Let τ be a linguistic truth-value. e.g., *very true, quite true, more or less true*, etc. Such a truth-value may be regarded as a fuzzy subset of the unit interval which is characterized by a membership function μ_T: $[0, 1] \to [0, 1]$.

A truth-qualified proposition, e.g., "It is τ that X is F," is expressed as "X is F is τ." As shown in [79], the translation rule for such propositions is given by

(2.58) X is F is $\tau \to \Pi_X = F^+$

where

(2.59) $\mu_{F^+}(u) = \mu_T(\mu_F(u))$.

As an illustration, consider the truth-qualified proposition

Susana is young is very true

which by (2.58), (2.59) and 2.31) translates into

(2.60) $\pi_{\text{Age (Susana)}} = \mu_{\text{TRUE}^2}(\mu_{\text{YOUNG}}(u))$.

Now, if we assume that

(2.61) $\mu_{\text{YOUNG}}(u) = (1 + (\frac{u}{25})^2)^{-1}, u \in [0, 100]$

and

$$\mu_{\text{TRUE}}(\nu) = \nu^2, \nu \in [0, 1]$$

then (2.60) yields

$$\pi_{\text{Age (Susana)}} = (1 + (\frac{u}{25})^2)^{-4}$$

as the possibility distribution function of the age of Susana.

A more general type of translation process in PRUF which subsumes the translation rules given above is the following.

Let $\mathscr{D} = \{D\}$ denote a collection of databases, with D representing a generic element of $\mathscr{D}$. For the purposes of our analysis, D will be assumed to consist of a collection of possibly time-varying relations. If R is a constituent relation in D, then by the *frame* of R is meant the name of R together with the names of its columns (i.e., attributes). For example, if a constituent of D is a relation labeled POPULATION whose tableau is comprised of columns labeled Name and Height, then the frame of POPULATION is represented as *POPULATION* ‖*Name*|*Height*| or, more simply, as POPULATION [Name; Height].

If p is a proposition in a natural language, its translation into PRUF can assume one of three – essentially equivalent – forms.[5]

(a) $p \to$ a possibility assignment equation;

(b) $p \to$ a procedure which yields for each D in $\mathscr{D}$ the possibility of D given p, i.e., Poss $\{D|p\}$;

(c) $p \to$ a procedure which yields for each D in $\mathscr{D}$ the truth-value of p relative to D, i.e., Tr $\{p|D\}$.

Remark. An important implicit assumption about the procedures involved in (b) and (c) is that they have a high degree of what might be called *explanatory effectiveness*, by which is meant a capability to convey the meaning of p to a human (or a machine) who is conversant with the meaning of the constituent terms in p but not with the meaning of p as a whole. For example, a procedure which merely tabulates the possibility of each D in $\mathscr{D}$ would, in general, have a low degree of explanatory effectiveness if it does not indicate in sufficient detail the way in which that possibility is arrived at. On the other extreme, a procedure which is excessively detailed and lacking in modularity would also have a low degree of explanatory effectiveness because the meaning of p might be obscured by the maze of unstructured steps in the body of the procedure.

The equivalence of (b) and (c) is a consequence of the way in which the concept of truth is defined in fuzzy logic [77], [2]. Thus, it can readily be shown that, under mildly restrictive assumptions on D, we have

$$\text{Tr}\ \{p|D\} = \text{Poss}\ \{D|p\},$$

which implies the equivalence of (b) and (c).

The restricted subset of PRUF which we have discussed so far is adequate for illustrating some of the simpler ways in which it may be applied to the precisiation of meaning. We shall do this in the following section.

3. PRECISIATION OF MEANING – EXAMPLES

There are two distinct and yet interrelated ways in which PRUF provides a mechanism for a precisiation of meaning of propositions. First, by expressing the meaning of a proposition as an explicitly defined procedure which acts on the fuzzy denotations of its constituents; and second, by disambiguation – especially in those cases in which what is needed is a method of differentiation between the nuances of meaning.

In what follows, we shall illustrate the techniques which may be employed for this purpose by several representative examples, of which Examples 6, 7, 8 and 9 relate to cases in which a proposition may have two or more distinct readings. Whenever appropriate, we consider both focused and unfocused translations of the given proposition.

EXAMPLE 1

(3.1) $p \triangleq$ John is very rich.

Assume that the database, D, consists of the following relations

(3.2) POPULATION [Name; Wealth]
RICH [Wealth; μ]

in which the first relation, POPULATION, tabulates the wealth, Wealth_i, of each individual, Name_i, while the second relation, RICH, tabulates the degree, μ_i, to which an individual whose wealth is Wealth_i is rich.

Unfocused translation: First, we find John's wealth, which is given by

(3.3) Wealth (John) = ${}_{\text{Wealth}}$POPULATION [Name = John].

Second, we intensify RICH to account for the modifier *very* by squaring

RICH,[6] and substitute Wealth (John) into RICH^2 to find the degree, δ, to which John is very rich. This yields

(3.4) $\delta = ({}_{\mu}\text{RICH [Wealth} = {}_{\text{Wealth}}\text{POPULATION [Name} = \text{John]]})^2$.

Finally, on equating δ to the possibility of the database, we obtain

(3.5) John is very rich
$\rightarrow \pi(D) = ({}_{\mu}\text{RICH [Wealth} = {}_{\text{Wealth}}\text{POPULATION [Name} = \text{John]]})^2$.

Focused translation: On interpreting the given proposition as a characterization of the possibility distribution of the implicit variable Wealth(John), we are led to the possibility assignment equation

(3.6) John is very rich $\rightarrow \Pi_{\text{Wealth(John)}} = \text{RICH}^2$

which implies that

(3.7) $\text{Poss}\,\{\text{Wealth (John)} = \mu\} = (\mu_{\text{RICH}}(u))^2$

where μ_{RICH} is the membership function of the fuzzy set RICH, with u ranging over the domain of Wealth.

EXAMPLE 2

(3.8) $p \triangleq$ Hans is much richer than Marie.

We assume that the database, D, consists of the relations

(3.9) POPULATION [Name; Wealth]

and

MUCH RICHER [Wealth1; Wealth2; μ]

in which μ is the degree to which an individual who has Wealth1 is much richer than one who has Wealth2.

Unfocused translation: Proceeding as in Example 1, we arrive at

(3.10) Hans is much richer than Marie $\rightarrow$
$\pi(D) = {}_{\mu}\text{MUCH RICHER [}{}_{\text{Wealth}}\text{POPULATION [Name} = \text{Hans]; } {}_{\text{Wealth}}\text{POPULATION [Name} = \text{Marie]]}$.

Focused translation:

(3.11) Hans is much richer than Marie $\rightarrow$
$\Pi_{(\text{Wealth (Hans), Wealth (Marie)})} = \text{MUCH RICHER}$

which implies that

(3.12) $\text{Poss}\{\text{Wealth (Hans)} = u_1, \text{Wealth (Marie)} = u_2\} = \mu_{\text{MUCH RICHER}}(u_1, u_2)$.

EXAMPLE 3

(3.13) $p \triangleq$ Vera is very kind.

In this case, we assume that kindness is not a measurable characteristic like height, weight, age, wealth, etc. However, we also assume that it is possible to associate with each individual his/her index of kindness on the scale from 0 to 1, which is equivalent to assuming that the class of kind individuals is a fuzzy set KIND, with the index of kindness corresponding to the grade of membership in KIND.

Unfocused translation: Assume that D consists of the single relation

(3.14) KIND [Name; μ]

in which μ is the degree of kindness of Name. Then

(3.15) Vera is very kind $\to \pi(D) = ({}_{\mu}\text{KIND [Name = Vera]})^2$.

Focused translation: A special type of possibility distribution which we need in this case is the *unitor*, $\perp$, which is defined as

(3.16) $\pi_{\perp}(\nu) = \nu, \quad 0 \leqslant \nu \leqslant 1$.

In terms of the unitor, then, we have

(3.17) Vera is very kind $\to \Pi_{\text{Kindness (Vera)}} = \perp^2$

which implies that

(3.18) $\text{Poss}\{\text{Kindness (Vera)} = \nu\} = \nu^2, \quad 0 \leqslant \nu \leqslant 1$.

This follows at once from (3.15), since

(3.19) Kindness (Vera) $= {}_{\mu}\text{KIND [Name = Vera]}$.

EXAMPLE 4

(3.20) $p \triangleq$ Brian is much taller than most of his close friends.

Unfocused translation: For the purpose of representing the meaning of p, we shall assume that D is comprised of the relations

(3.21) POPULATION [Name; Height]
FRIENDS [Name1; Name2; μ]
MUCH TALLER [Height1; Height2; μ]
MOST [ρ; μ].

In the relation FRIENDS, μ represents the degree to which an individual whose name is Name2 is a friend of Name1. Similarly, in the relation MUCH TALLER, μ represents the degree to which an individual whose height is Height1 is much taller than one whose height is Height2. In MOST, μ represents the degree to which a proportion, ρ, fits the definition of MOST as a fuzzy subset of the unit interval.

To represent the meaning of p we shall express the translation of p as a procedure which computes the possibility of D given p. The sequence of computations in this procedure is as follows.

1. Obtain Brian's height from POPULATION. Thus,

$$\text{Height (Brian)} = {}_{\text{Height}}\text{POPULATION [Name = Brian]}.$$

2. Determine the fuzzy set, MT, of individuals in POPULATION in relation to whom Brian is much taller.

Let Name_i be the name of the ith individual in POPULATION. The height of Name_i is given by

$$\text{Height (Name}_i) = {}_{\text{Height}}\text{POPULATION [Name = Name}_i].$$

Now the degree to which Brian is much taller than Name_i is given by

$$\delta_i = {}_{\mu}\text{MUCH TALLER [Height (Brian), Height (Name}_i)]$$

and hence MT may be expressed as

$$\text{MT} = \Sigma_i \delta_i/\text{Name}_i, \text{Name}_i \in {}_{\text{Name}}\text{POPULATION}$$

where ${}_{\text{Name}}$POPULATION is the list of names of individuals in POPULATION, δ_i is the grade of membership of Name_i in MT, and Σ_i is the union of singletons δ_i/Name_i. ($\text{Name}_i \neq$ Brian.)

3. Determine the fuzzy set, CF, of individuals in POPULATION who are close friends of Brian.

To form the relation CLOSE FRIENDS from FRIENDS we intensify FRIENDS by squaring, as in Example 1. Then, the fuzzy set of close friends of Brian is given by

$$\text{CF} = {}_{\mu \times \text{Name2}}\text{FRIENDS}^2 \text{ [Name1 = Brian]}.$$

4. Form the count of elements of CF:

$$\text{Count(CF)} = \Sigma_i \mu_{\text{CF}}(\text{Name}_i)$$

where $\mu_{\text{CF}}(\text{Name}_i)$ is the grade of membership of Name_i in CF and Σ_i is the arithemetic sum. More explicitly

$$\text{Count}(F) = \Sigma_i \mu^2_{\text{FRIENDS}}(\text{Brian}, \text{Name}_i).$$

5. Form the intersection of CF and MT, that is, the fuzzy set of those close friends of Brian in relation to whom he is much taller

$$H \triangleq \text{CF} \cap \text{MT}.$$

6. Form the count of elements of H

$$\text{Count}(H) = \Sigma_i \mu_H(\text{Name}_i)$$

where $\mu_H(\text{Name}_i)$ is the grade of membership of Name_i in H and Σ_i is the arithmetic sum.

7. Form the ratio

$$r = \frac{\text{Count (MT} \cap \text{CF)}}{\text{Count (CF)}}$$

which represents the proportion of close friends of Brian in relation to whom he is much taller.

8. Compute the grade of membership of r in MOST

$$\delta = {}_{\mu}\text{MOST } [\rho = r].$$

The value of δ is the desired possibility of D given p. In terms of the membership functions of FRIENDS, MUCH TALLER and MOST, the value of δ is given explicitly by the expression

$$(3.22) \quad \delta = \mu_{\text{MOST}} \left[\frac{\Sigma_i \mu_{\text{MT}}(\text{Height(Brian)}, \text{Height (Name}_i)) \wedge \mu^2_{\text{CF}}(\text{Brian}, \text{Name}_i)}{\Sigma_i \mu^2_{\text{CF}}(\text{Brian}, \text{Name}_i)} \right].$$

Thus,

$$(3.23) \quad \text{Brian is much taller than most of his close friends} \rightarrow \pi(D) = \delta$$

where δ is given by (3.22).

Focused translation: From (3.23) it follows at once that

$$(3.24) \quad p \rightarrow \pi_{\text{Height (Brian)}}(u) \triangleq \text{Poss } \{\text{Height (Brian)} = u\} = \mu_{\text{MOST}} \left[\frac{\Sigma_i \mu_{\text{MT}}(u, \text{Height (Name}_i)) \wedge \mu^2_{\text{CF}}(\text{Brian}, \text{Name}_i)}{\Sigma_i \mu^2_{\text{CF}}(\text{Brian}, \text{Name}_i)} \right].$$

EXAMPLE 5

(3.25) $p \triangleq$ Lane resides in a small city near Washington.

Unfocused translation: Assume that the database consists of the relations

(3.26) RESIDENCE [P.Name; C.Name; Population]
SMALL [Population; μ]
NEAR [C.Name1; C.Name2; μ].

In RESIDENCE, P.Name stands for Person Name, C.Name for City Name, and Population for population of C.Name. In SMALL, μ is the degree to which a city whose population figure is Population is small. In NEAR, μ is the degree to which C.Name1 and C.Name2 are near one another.

The population of the city in which Lane resides is given by

(3.27) $_{\text{Population}}$RESIDENCE [P.Name = Lane]

and hence the degree, δ, to which the city is small may be expressed as

(3.28) $\delta_1 = {}_{\mu}$SMALL [$_{\text{Population}}$RESIDENCE [P. Name = Lane]].

Now the degree to which the city in which Lane resides is near Washington is given by

(3.29) $\delta_2 = {}_{\mu}$NEAR [C.Name1 = Washington;
C.Name 2 = $_{\text{C.Name}}$RESIDENCE [P.Name = Lane]].

On forming the conjunction of (3.28) and (3.29), the possibility of D – and hence the translation of p – is found to be expressed by ($\wedge \triangleq$ min)

(3.30) Lane resides in a small city near Washington $\to \pi(D) = \delta_1 \wedge \delta_2$

where δ_1 and δ_2 are given by (3.28) and (3.29).

Focused translation: The implicit variable in this case may be expressed as

(3.31) $X \triangleq$ Location (Residence (Lane)).

Thus, the goal of the focused translation in this case is the computation of the possibility distribution of the location of residence of Lane.

To illustrate the effect of choosing different databases on the translation of p, we shall consider two cases each of which represents a particular assumption concerning the relations in D.

First, we consider the simpler case in which the constituent relations in D are assumed to be:

(3.32) SMALL [C.Name; μ]
(3.33) NEAR [C.Name1; C.Name2; μ].

In SMALL, μ is the degree to which the city whose name is C.Name is small. In NEAR, μ is the degree to which cities named C.Name1 and C.Name2 are near each other.

From NEAR, the fuzzy set of cities which are near Washington is found to be given by

$$_{\text{C.Name1}} \times_{\mu} \text{NEAR [C.Name2 = Washington]}.$$

Consequently, the fuzzy set of cities which are near Washington and, in addition, are small is given by the intersection

$$\text{SMALL} \cap {}_{\text{C.Name1}} \times_{\mu} \text{NEAR [C.Name2 = Washington]}.$$

With this expression in hand, the focused translation of p may be expressed as

(3.34) Lane resides in a small city near Washington $\rightarrow$
$\Pi_{\text{Location (Residence (Lane))}} = \text{SMALL} \cap {}_{\text{C.Name1}} \times_{\mu}$
NEAR [C.Name2 = Washington].

In the case to be considered next, the relations in D are assumed to be less directly related to the denotations of words in p than the relations expressed by (3.32) and (3.33). More specifically, we assume that D consists of the relations

(3.35) LIST [C.Name; Population]
DISTANCE [C.Name1; C.Name2; Distance]
SMALL [Population; μ]
NEAR [Distance; μ].

In LIST, Population is the population of C.Name. In DISTANCE, Distance is the distance between C.Name1 and C.Name2. In NEAR, μ is the degree to which two cities whose distance from one another is Distance are near each other. As for SMALL, it has the same meaning as in (3.32).

For our purposes, we need a relation which tabulates the degree to which each city in LIST is small. To this end, we form the composition[7] of LIST and SMALL, which yields the relation

(3.36) $G \triangleq$ SMALL [C.Name; μ] $\triangleq$ LIST [C.Name; Population] $\circ$
SMALL [POPULATION; μ]

in which μ is the degree to which C.Name is small. Actually, since LIST and SMALL are functions, we can write

(3.37) $\mu_G(\text{C.Name}) = \mu_{\text{SMALL}}(\text{Population (C.Name)})$

in which the right-hand member of (3.37) expresses the degree to which a city whose population is Population (C.Name) is small.

Now from DISTANCE we can find the distances of cities in LIST from Washington. These distances are yielded by the relation

(3.38) $\text{DC} \triangleq {}_{\text{C.Name1} \times \text{Distance}}\text{DISTANCE [C.Name2 = Washington]}$.

Furthermore, on forming the composition of this relation with NEAR, we obtain the relation

(3.39) $H\ [\text{C.Name}; \mu] \triangleq \text{NEAR [Distance}; \mu] \circ$
$${}_{\text{C.Name1} \times \text{Distance}}\text{DISTANCE [C.Name2 = Washington]}.$$

In H [C.Name; μ], μ represents the degree to which C.Name is near Washington. More explicitly:

$$\mu_H(\text{C.Name}) = \mu_{\text{NEAR}}(\text{Distance of C.Name from Washington})$$

in which the distance of C.Name from Washington is obtained from DC by expressing the distance as a function of C.Name.

At this point, we have constructed from the given database the relations which were given initially in the previous case. With these relations in hand, the translation of p may be expressed compactly as

(3.40) $\Pi_{\text{Location (Residence (Lane))}} = G \cap H$

where G and H are defined by (3.36) and (3.39), respectively.

EXAMPLE 6

(3.41) $p \triangleq$ Vivien is over thirty.

The literal reading of p may be expressed as

$$p_1 \triangleq \text{Age of Vivien is greater than thirty}$$

which translates into

(3.42) $p_1 \rightarrow \text{Age (Vivien)} > 30$.

In many cases, however, the intended meaning of p would be

$$p_2 \triangleq \text{Vivien is over thirty but not much over thirty.}$$

In this case, the translation of p_2 into PRUF would be expressed as

(3.43) $\Pi_{\text{Age (Vivien)}} = (30, 100] \cap {}_{\text{Age1}} \times_{\mu} \text{MUCH OVER}' \; [\text{Age2} = 30]$

in which (30, 100] is the age interval $30 < u \leqslant 100$; MUCH OVER [Age1; Age2; μ] is a relation in which μ is the degree to which Age1 is much over Age 2; and MUCH OVER$'$ is the complement of MUCH OVER. More explicitly, (3.43) implies that

(3.44) $$\begin{aligned} \text{Poss}\,\{\text{Age (Vivien)} = u\} &= 0 && \text{for } u \leqslant 30 \\ &= 1 - \mu_{\text{MUCH OVER}}(u, 30), && \text{for } u > 30. \end{aligned}$$

EXAMPLE 7

(3.45) $p \triangleq$ John is not very smart.

Assuming that D consists of the relation

SMART [Name; μ]

in which μ is the degree to which Name is smart, the literal translation of p may be expressed as (see Example 3)

(3.46) $p \to \Pi_X = (\perp^2)'$

where

$$X = {}_{\mu}\text{SMART [Name = John]}$$

and $(\perp^2)'$ is the complement of the square of the unitor.

However, if the intended meaning of p is

(3.47) $p_1 \triangleq$ John is very (not smart).

then the translation of p into PRUF would be

(3.48) $\Pi_X = (\perp')^2$.

Note that (3.48) implies that

(3.49) $\text{Poss}\,\{X = \nu\} = 1 - \nu^2$

whereas (3.46) implies that

(3.50) $\text{Poss}\,\{X = \nu\} = (1 - \nu)^2$.

EXAMPLE 8

(3.51) $p \triangleq$ Naomi has a young daughter.

There are three distinct readings of p:

$p_1 \triangleq$ Naomi has only one daughter and her daughter is young;
$p_2 \triangleq$ Naomi has one or more daughters of whom only one is young;
$p_3 \triangleq$ Naomi has one or more daughters of whom one or more are young.

Assume that D consists of the relation

$$\text{DAUGHTER [M.Name; D.Name; } \mu_{DY}]$$

in which M.Name and D.Name stand for Mother's name and Daughter's name, respectively, and μ_{DY} is the degree to which D.Name is young.

The translations of p_1, p_2 and p_3 may be expressed as follows

$$(3.52) \quad p_1 \to \pi(D) = \delta_1 \wedge \mu_1$$

where

$$\delta_1 = 1 \text{ if Naomi has only one daughter, i.e., if } \text{Count } ({}_{\text{D.Name}}\text{DAUGHTER [M.Name = Naomi]}) = 1$$

and $\delta_1 = 0$ otherwise;

and

$\mu_1 \triangleq$ the degree to which Naomi's daughter is young, i.e.,

$$\mu_1 = {}_{\mu_{DY}}\text{DAUGHTER [M.Name = Naomi]}.$$

Turning to p_2 and p_3, let the set of daughters of Naomi be sorted in descending order according to the degree of youth. For this set, then, let

$\mu_i \triangleq$ degree of youth of ith youngest daughter of Naomi.

Now applying the concept of fuzzy cardinality (see (2.52)) to the set in question, we obtain at once

$$(3.53) \quad p_2 \to \pi(D) = \mu_1 \wedge (1 - \mu_2)$$

and

$$(3.54) \quad p_3 \to \pi(D) = \mu_1 .$$

EXAMPLE 9

(3.55) $p \triangleq$ Naomi has several young daughters.

In this case, we assume that D consists of the relations

DAUGHTER [M.Name; D.Name; μ_{DY}]

and

SEVERAL [N; μ]

in which the first relation has the same meaning as in Example 8, and μ in SEVERAL is the degree to which an integer N fits one's perception of *several.* Furthermore, we assume that p should be read as p_3 in Example 8.

With these assumptions, the translation of p may be expressed compactly as

$$(3.56)\quad p \to \pi(D) = \sup\,((\geqslant \circ \text{SEVERAL}) \cap \\ FG\text{Count}\,({}_{\text{D. Name}} \times_{\mu} \text{DAUGHTER [M.Name = Naomi]}))$$

where FGCount is defined by (2.55); sup F is defined by

$$(3.57)\quad \sup F \triangleq \sup_{u \in U} \mu_F(u)$$

where F is a fuzzy subset of U and μ_F is its membership function; and $\geqslant \circ$ SEVERAL is the composition of the relations $\geqslant$ and SEVERAL, i.e., (see note 7)

$$\mu_{\geqslant \circ \text{SEVERAL}}(u) = \mu_{\text{SEVERAL}}(n) \quad \text{for } n \leqslant n_{\max}$$
$$= 1 \quad \text{for } n \geqslant n_{\max}$$
$$n_{\max} \triangleq \text{smallest value of } n \text{ at which } \mu_{\text{SEVERAL}}(u) = 1.$$

Intuitively, the composition of $\geqslant$ and SEVERAL serves to precisiate the count expressed in words as "at least several." The intersection of ($\geqslant \circ$ SEVERAL) and the FGCount of the daughters of Naomi serves to define the conjunction of "at least several" with the FGCount of daughters of Naomi; and the supremum of the intersection provides a measure of the degree of consistency of "at least several" with the FGCount in question.

As a concrete illustration of (3.56), assume that the fuzzy relation SEVERAL is defined as

$$(3.59)\quad \text{SEVERAL} \triangleq 0.5/2 + 0.8/3 + 1/4 + 1/5 + 0.8/6 + 0.5/0.7.$$

Then

$$(3.60)\quad \geqslant \circ\, \text{SEVERAL} = 0.5/2 + 0.8/3 + 1/4 + 1/5 + 1/6 + \ldots.$$

Furthermore, assume that

$$(3.61)\quad {}_{\text{D.Name}} \times_{\mu} \text{DAUGHTER [M. Name = Naomi]} = \\ 1/\text{Eva} + 0.8/\text{Lisa} + 0.6/\text{Ruth}$$

so that

(3.62) $FG\text{Count}\,({}_{\text{D.Name}} \times {}_{\mu}\text{DAUGHTER [M.Name = Naomi]}) = 1/1 + 0.8/2 + 0.6/3.$

From (3.60) and (3.62), we deduce that

(3.63) $(\geqslant \circ \text{SEVERAL}) \cap FG\text{Count}\,({}_{\text{D.Name}} \times {}_{\mu}\text{ DAUGHTER [M.Name = Naomi]}) = 0.5/2 + 0.6/3$

and since

$$\sup\,(0.5/2 + 0.6/3) = 0.6$$

we arrive at

(3.64) $\pi(D) = 0.6$

which represents the possibility of the given database given the proposition p.

4. CONCLUDING REMARK

The above examples are intended to illustrate the manner in which PRUF may be employed to precisiate the meaning of propositions expressed in a natural language. Such precisiation may be of use not only in communication between humans, but also – and perhaps more importantly – in communication between humans and machines.

University of California at Berkeley

NOTES

* Computer Science Division, Department of Electrical Engineering and Computer Sciences and the Electronics Research Laboratory, University of California, Berkeley, California 94720. Research supported by the National Science Foundation Grants IST8018196 and MCS79-06543.

[1] As is pointed out in [81], ambiguity, vagueness and fuzziness are not coextensive concepts. Specifically, a proposition, p, is *fuzzy* if it contains words with fuzzy denotations, e.g., $p \triangleq$ Ruth has *dark* skin and owns a *red* Porsche. A proposition, p, is *vague* if it is both fuzzy and ambiguous in the sense of being insufficiently specific. For example, the proposition $p \triangleq$ Ruth lives *somewhere near* Berkeley is vague if it does not characterize the location of residence of Ruth with sufficient precision. Thus, a proposition may be fuzzy without being vague, and ambiguous without being fuzzy or vague.

[2] As will be seen in Section 2 and 3, PRUF is a language in a somewhat stretched sense of the term. Basically, it is a *translation system* in which only the simpler procedures

may be represented as expressions in PRUF. For the description of complex procedures, PRUF allows the use of any suitable mathematically oriented language.

[3] In our exposition of the concept of a possibility distribution and the relevant parts of PRUF we shall draw on the definitions and examples in [79], [81] and [82].

[4] We use uppercase symbols to differentiate between a term, e.g., small, and its denotation, SMALL. The notation

$$(2.9) \qquad F = \mu_1/u_1 + \ldots + \mu_n/u_n$$

which is employed in (2.7) signifies that F is a collection of fuzzy singletons μ_i/u_i, $i = 1, \ldots, n$, with μ_i representing the grade of membership of u_i in F. More generally, F may be expressed as $F = \Sigma_i \mu_i/u_i$ or $F = \int_U \mu_F(u)/u$. (See [78] for additional details.)

[5] It should be noted that (b) and (c) are in the spirit of possible-world semantics and truth-conditional semantics, respectively. In their conventional form, however, these semantics have no provision for fuzzy propositions and hence do not provide a sufficiently expressive system for our purposes.

[6] If the frame of RICH is RICH [Wealth; μ] then the frame of RICH^2 is RICH^2 [Wealth; μ^2], which signifies that each μ in RICH is replaced by μ^2. This representation of *very rich* is a consequence of the translation rule (2.31).

[7] If the membership functions of R $[X; Y]$ and S $[Y; Z]$ are expressed as $\mu_R(x, y)$ and $\mu_S(y, z)$, respectively, then the membership function of the composition of R and S with respect to Y is given by

$$\mu_{R \circ S}(x, z) = \sup_y (\mu_R(x, y) \wedge \mu_S(y, z)).$$

REFERENCES

Bandler, W. and Kohout, L.: 1978, 'Fuzzy relational products and fuzzy implication operation,' *Proc. Third Workshop on Fuzzy Reasoning*, Queen Mary College, London.

Bellman, R. E. and Zadeh, L. A.: 1977, 'Local and fuzzy logics,' *Modern Uses of Multiple-Valued Logic* (G. Epstein, ed.), D. Reidel, Dordrecht, 103–165.

Black, M.: 1963, 'Reasoning with loose concepts,' *Dialogue* **2**, 1–12.

Bobrow, D. and Collins, A. (eds.): 1975, *Representation and Understanding*, Academic Press, New York.

Boyce, R. F., Chamberlin, D. D., King III, W. F., and Hammer, M. M.: 1974, 'Specifying queries as relational expressions,' *Data Base Management* (J. W. Klimbie and K. L. Koffeman, eds.), North-Holland, Amsterdam, 21–223.

Brachman, R. J.: 1977, 'What's in a concept: structural foundations for semantical networks,' *Int. J. Man-Machine Studies* **9**, 127–152.

Briabrin, V. M. and Senin, G. V.: 1977, 'Natural language processing within a restricted context,' *Proc. Int. Workshop on Natural Language for Interactions with Data Bases*, IIASA, Vienna.

Chomsky, N.: 1971, 'Deep structure, surface structure, and semantic interpretation,' *Semantics: An Interdisciplinary Reader in Philosophy, Linguistics and Psychology*, (D. D. Steinberg and L. A. Jakobovits, eds.), Cambridge University Press, Cambridge.

Cresswell, M. J.: 1973, *Logics and Languages*, Methuen, London.

10. Damerau, F. J.: 1975, 'On fuzzy adjectives,' *Memorandum RC 5340*, IBM Research Laboratory, Yorktown Heights, New York.
11. Davidson, D.: 1967, 'Truth and meaning,' *Synthese* **17**, 304–323.
12. Deluca, A. and Termini, S.: 1972, 'A definition of a non-probabilistic entropy in the setting of fuzzy sets theory,' *Information and Control* **20**, 301–312.
13. Fine, K.: 1975, 'Vagueness, truth and logic,' *Synthese* **30**, 265–300.
14. Frederiksen, C.: 1975, 'Representing logical and semantic structure of knowledge acquired from discourse,' *Cognitive Psychology* **7**, 371–458.
15. Gaines, B. R.: 1976, 'Foundations of fuzzy reasoning,' *Int. J. Man-Machine Studies* **6**, 623–668.
16. Gaines, B. R., and Kohout, L. J.: 1977, 'The fuzzy decade: a bibliogrpahy of fuzzy systems and closely related topics,' *Int. J. Man-Machine Studies* **9**, 1–68.
17. Goguen, J. A.: 1974, 'Concept representation in natural and artificial languages: axioms, extension and applications for fuzzy sets,' *Int. J. Man-Machine Studies* **6**, 513–561.
18. Grice H. P.: 1968, 'Utterer's meaning, sentence-meaning and word-meaning,' *Foundations of Language* **4**, 225–242.
19. Haack, S.: 1978, *Philosophy of Logics*, Cambridge University Press, Cambridge.
20. Harris, J. I.: 1974, 'Fuzzy sets: how to be imprecise precisely,' DOAE Research Working Paper, Ministry of Defense, Byfleet, Surrey, United Kingdom.
21. Hersh, H. M., and Caramazza, A.: 1976, 'A fuzzy approach to modifiers and vagueness in natural language,' *J. Experimental Psychology* **105**, 254–276.
22. Hisdal, E.: 1978, 'Conditional possibilities: independence and non-interaction,' *Fuzzy Sets and Systems* **1**, 283–297.
23. Hughes, G. E., and Cresswell, M. J.: 1968, *An Introduction to Modal Logic*, Methuen, London.
24. Jouault, J. P. and Luan, P. M.: 1975, 'Application des concepts flous à la programmation en langages quasi-naturels,' Inst. Inf. d'Entreprise, C.N.A.M., Paris.
25. Kampé de Feriet, J. and Forte, B.: 1967, 'Information et probabilité,' *Comptes Rendus*, Academy of Sciences, Paris, **265A**, 152–146, 350–353.
26. Katz, J. J.: 1966, *The Philosophy of Language*, Harper & Row, New York.
27. Kaufmann, A.: 1975, 'Introduction to the Theory of Fuzzy Subsets,' *Applications to Linguistics, Logic and Semantics* **2**, Masson and Co., Paris.
28. Khatchadourian, H.: 1965, 'Vagueness, meaning and absurdity,' *Amer. Phil. Quarterly* **2**, 119–129.
29. Labov, W.: 1973, 'The boundaries of words and their meanings,' *New Ways of Analyzing Variation in English* **1**, (C. J. N. Bailey and R. W. Shuy, eds.), Georgetown University Press, Washington.
30. Lakoff, G.: 1973, 'Hedges: a study in meaning criteria and the logic of fuzzy concepts," *J. Phil. Logic* **2**, 458–508. Also in *Contemporary Research in Philosophical Logic and Linguistic Semantics*, (D. Dockney, W. Harper and B. Freed, eds.), D. Reidel, Dordrecht, 221–271.
31. Lakoff, G.: 1973, 'Fuzzy grammar and the performance/competence terminology game,' *Proc. Meeting of Chicago Linguistics Society*, 271–291.
32. Lambert, K. and van Fraassen, B. C.: 1970, 'Meaning relations, possible objects and possible worlds,' *Philosophical Problems in Logic*, 1–19.
33. Lehnert, W.: 1977, 'Human and computational question answering,' *Cognitive Science* **1**, 47–73.

34. Lewis, D.: 1970, 'General semantics,' *Synthese* **22**, 18–67.
35. Linsky, L.: 1971, *Reference and Modality*, Oxford University Press, London.
36. Lyndon, R. C.: 1976, *Notes on Logic*, d. Van Nostrand, New York.
37. Machina, K. F.: 1972, 'Vague predicates,' *Amer. Phil. Quarterly* **9**, 225–233.
38. Mamdani, E. H., and Assilian, S.: 1975, 'An experiment in linguistic synthesis with a fuzzy logic controller,' *Int. J. Man-Machine Studies* 7, 1–13.
39. McCarthy, J. and Hayes, P.: 1969, 'Some philosophical problems from the standpoint of artificial intelligence,' *Machine Intelligence* **4**, (D. Michie and B. Meltzer, eds), Edinburgh University Press, Edinburgh, 463–502.
40. Miller, G. A. and Johnson-Laird, P. N.: 1976, *Language and Perception*, Harvard University Press, Cambridge.
41. Mizumoto, M., Fukame, S., and Tanaka, K.: 1978, 'Fuzzy reasoning methods by Zadeh and Mamdani, and improved methods,' *Proc. Third Workshop on Fuzzy Reasoning*, Queen Mary College, London.
42. Mizumoto, M., Umano, M. and Tanaka, K.: 1977, 'Implementation of a fuzzy-set-theoretic data structure system,' *Third Int. Conf. on Very Large Data Bases*, Tokyo.
43. Moisil, G. C.: 1975, 'Lectures on the logic of fuzzy reasoning,' *Scientific Editions*, Bucarest.
44. Montague, R.: 1974, *Formal Philosophy* (Selected Papers), Yale University Press, New Haven.
45. Montgomery, C. A.: 1972, 'Is natural language an unnatural query language?,' *Proc. ACM National Conf.*, New York, 1075–1078.
46. Nalimov, V. V.: 1974, *Probabilistic Model of Language*, Moscow State University, Moscow.
47. Negoita, C. V., and Ralescu, D. A.: 1975, *Applications of Fuzzy Sets to Systems Analysis*, Birkhauser Verlag, Basel, Stuttgart.
48. Newell, A. and Simon, H. A.: 1972, *Human Problem Solving*, Prentice-Hall, Englewood Cliffs, N.J.
49. Nguyen, H. T.: 1978, 'On conditional possibility distributions,' *Fuzzy Sets and Systems* **1**, 299–309.
50. Noguchi, K., Umano, M., Mizumoto, M., and Tanaka, K.: 1976, 'Implementation of fuzzy artificial intelligence language FLOU,' *Technical Report on Automation and Language of IECE.*
51. Partee, B.: 1976, *Montague Grammar*, Academic Press, New York.
52. Putnam, H.: 1975, 'The meaning of 'meaning',' *Language, Mind and Knowledge* (K. Gunderson, ed.), University of Minnesota Press, Minneapolis.
53. Quine, W. V.: 1970, *Philosophy of Logic*, Prentice-Hall, Englewood Cliffs, N.J.
54. Rescher, N.: 1973, *The Coherence Theory of Truth*, Oxford University Press, Oxford.
55. Rieger, B.: 1976, 'Fuzzy structural semantics,' *Proc. Third European Meeting on Cybernetics and Systems Research*, Vienna.
56. Sanchez, E.: 1977, 'On possibility qualification in natural languages,' *Electronics Re-Search Laboratory Memorandum M77/28*, University of California, Berkeley.
57. Sanford, D. H.: 1975, 'Borderline logic,' *Amer. Phil. Quarterly* **12**, 29–39.
58. Schank, R. C. (ed.): 1975, *Conceptual Information Processing*, North-Holland, Amsterdam.
59. Schotch, P. K.: 1975, 'Fuzzy modal logic,' *Proc. Int. Symp. on Multiple-Valued Logic*, University of Indiana, Bloomington, 176–182.

60. Schubert, L. K.: 1972, 'Extending the expressive power of semantic networks,' *Artificial Intelligence* **2**, 163–198.
61. Searle, J. (ed.): 1971, *The Philosophy of Language*, Oxford University Press, Oxford.
62. Sembi, B. S., and Mamdani, E. H.: 1979, 'On the nature of implication in fuzzy logic,' *Proc. 9th Int. Symp. on Multiple-Valued Logic*, Bath, England, 143–151.
63. Simon, H. A.: 1973, 'The structure of ill structured problems,' *Artificial Intelligence* **4**, 181–201.
64. Staal, J. F.: 1969, 'Formal logic and natural languages,' *Foundations of Language* **5**, 256–284.
65. Stitch, S. P.: 1975, 'Logical form and natural language,' *Phil. Studies* **28**, 397–418.
66. Sugeno, M.: 1974, 'Theory of fuzzy integrals and its application,' Ph.D. thesis, Tokyo Institute of Technology, Japan.
67. Suppes, P.: 1976, 'Elimination of quantifiers in the semantics of natural languages by use of extended relation algebras,' *Revue Internationale de Philosophie*, 117–118, 243–259.
68. Tarski, A.: 1956, *Logic, Semantics, Metamathematics*, Clarendon Press, Oxford.
69. Terano, T., and Sugeno, M.: 1975, 'Conditional fuzzy measures and their applications,' *Fuzzy Sets and Their Applications to Cognitive and Decision Processes*, (L. A. Zadeh, K. S. Fu, K. Tanaka and M. Shimura, eds.), Academic Press, New York, 151–170.
70. van Fraassen, B. C.: 1971, *Formal Semantics and Logic*, Macmillan, New York.
71. Wenstop, F.: 1976, 'Deductive verbal models of organizations,' *Int. J. Man-Machine Studies* **8**, 293–311.
72. Wheeler, S. C.: 1975, 'Reference and vagueness,' *Synthese* **30**, 367–380.
73. Woods, W. A.: 1975, 'What is in a link: foundations for semantic networks,' *Representation and Understanding* , (D. B. Bobrow and A. Collins, eds.), Academic Press, New York, 35–82.
74. Zadeh, L. A.: 1972, 'Fuzzy languages and their relation to human and machine intelligence,' *Proc. Int. Conf. on Man and Computer*, Bordeaux, France, S. Karger, Basel, 130–165.
75. Zadeh, L. A.: Jan. 1973, 'Outline of a new approach to the analysis of complex systems and decision processes,' *IEEE Trans. Systems, Man and Cybernetics SMC-3*, 28–44.
76. Zadeh, L. A.: 1975, 'Calculus of fuzzy restrictions,' *Fuzzy Sets and Their Applications to Cognitive and Decision Processes*, (L. A. Zadeh, K. S. Fu, K. Tanaka and M. Shimura, eds.), Academic Press, New York, 1–39.
77. Zadeh, L. A.: 1975, 'Fuzzy logic and approximate reasoning (in memory of Grigore Moisil),' *Synthese* **30**, 407–428.
78. Zadeh, L. A.: 1975, 'The concept of a linguistic variable and its application to approximate reasoning,' *Inf. Sci.* **8**, Part I, 199–249; *Inf. Sci.* **8**, Part II, 301–357; *Inf. Sci.* **9**, part III, 43–80.
79. Zadeh, L. A.: 1977, 'A theory of approximate reasoning,' *Electronics Research Laboratory Memorandum M77/58*, University of California, Berkeley. Also in *Machine Intelligence* 9, (J. E. Hayes, D. Michie and L. I. Kulich, eds.), Wiley, New York, 149–194.
80. Zadeh, L. A.: 1978, 'Fuzzy sets as a basis for a theory of possibility,' *Fuzzy Sets and Systems* **1**, 3–28.
81. Zadeh, L. A.: 1978, 'PRUF – a meaning representation language for natural language,' *Int. J. Man-Machine Studies* **10**, 394–460.

82. Zadeh, L. A.: 1979, 'Possibility theory and soft data analysis,' *Mathematical Frontiers of the Social and Policy Sciences*, (L. Cobb and R. M. Thrall, eds.), Westview Press, Boulder, 69–129.
83. Zadeh, L. A.: 1981, 'Test-score semantics for natural languages and meaning-representation via PRUF,' *Empirical Semantics*, (B. B. Rieger, ed.), Brockmeyer, Bochum, 281–349.
84. Zadeh, L. A.: 1983, 'A computational approach to fuzzy quantifiers in natural languages,' *Computers and Mathematics* 9, 149–184.

FUZZY PROBABILITIES

LOTFI A. ZADEH†
Computer Science Division, Department of Electrical Engineering and Computer Sciences and the Electronics Research Laboratory, University of California, Berkeley, CA 94720, U.S.A.

Abstract—The conventional approaches to decision analysis are based on the assumption that the probabilities which enter into the assessment of the consequences of a decision are known numbers. In most realistic settings, this assumption is of questionable validity since the data from which the probabilities must be estimated are usually incomplete, imprecise or not totally reliable.

In the approach outlined in this paper, the probabilities are assumed to be fuzzy rather than real numbers. It is shown how such probabilities may be estimated from fuzzy data and a basic relation between joint, conditional and marginal fuzzy probabilities is established. Manipulation of fuzzy probabilities requires, in general, the use of fuzzy arithmetic, and many of the properties of fuzzy probabilities are simple generalizations of the corresponding properties of real-valued probabilities.

1. INTRODUCTION

Computer-assisted decision analysis is likely to play an increasingly important role in applications—such as command and control—in which vast amounts of information in the database exceed the capacity of the unassisted human mind to assess the consequences of various alternatives and choose that action which is optimal with respect to a set of specified criteria.

An issue which complicates the determination of an optimal action is that in most realistic settings the information which is available to the decision maker is imprecise, incomplete or not totally reliable. In the conventional approaches to decision analysis, uncertain information is treated probabilistically, with probabilities assumed to be known in numerical form. In an alternative approach which is described in this paper, a more realistic assumption is made, namely, that probabilities are known imprecisely as fuzzy rather than crisp numbers. Such probabilities—which will be referred to as *fuzzy probabilities*—are exemplified by the perceptions of likelihood which are commonly labeled as *very likely*, *unlikely*, *not very likely*, etc. [29].

The concept of fuzzy probability is distinct from that of second-order probability (i.e. a probability-value which is characterized by its probability distribution) and contains that of interval-valued probability as a special case. As will be seen in the sequel, in our formulation of the concept of fuzzy probability, the uncertainty in probability is characterized by a possibility[26] rather than probability distribution. In our view, the use of possibility rather than probability in this context leads to a more effective way of dealing with uncertain probabilities and provides a basis for a natural generalization of classical probability theory.

2. THE CONCEPT OF FUZZY PROBABILITY

Theories of subjective probability provide ways of eliciting probability judgments but do not have much to say about the processes by which such judgments are formed. To relate this issue to the concept of fuzzy probability, it is instructive to consider an elementary example of a situation in which an imprecise perception of probability is formed and in which the underlying uncertainty is possibilistic rather than probabilistic in nature. Specifically, consider the following question, in which the italicized words have a fuzzy

† Research supported by NSF Grant IST-8320416 and NESC Contract N0039-83-C-0243.

Reprinted, with permission, from *Information Processing and Management*, **20**(3), pp. 363–372.

meaning: An urn contains *approximately n* balls of various sizes, of which *several* are *large*. What is the probability that a ball drawn at random is *large*?

If the information-bearing terms in the question, namely, *approximately n*, *several* and *large* were real numbers, the answer to the question would be a numerical probability. But, since these terms are fuzzy rather than real numbers, it should be expected that the desired probability, like the data on which it is based, is a fuzzy number, i.e. a fuzzy probability.

This conclusion may be stated more succinctly as a principle, namely: *Fuzzy information induces fuzzy probabilities*. What is important to note is that this principle is at variance with the traditional Bayesian point of view which implies that probabilities are real numbers regardless of the nature of the underlying data.

To support our principle, we have to be able to demonstrate how fuzzy probabilities may be computed from fuzzy data. To this end, it is necessary, first, to provide a mechanism for counting the number of elements in a fuzzy set, i.e. for determining its cardinality or, more generally, its measure. We need this mechanism to precisiate the meaning of fuzzy descriptions such as *several large balls* and to be able to answer fuzzy questions like, "How many *combat-ready* ships are there in the *vicinity* of the Persian Gulf?"

In what follows, we shall limit our discussion of the cardinality of fuzzy sets to what is needed to enable us to define fuzzy probabilities in more concrete terms than we have done so far. A more detailed discussion of related issues may be found in [25, 27 and 28].

Consider a fuzzy set A which is represented as

$$A = \mu_1/u_1 + \ldots + \mu_n/u_n \tag{1.1}$$

where μ_i, $i = 1, \ldots, n$, is an element of a universe of discourse U, μ_i is the grade of membership of u_i in A, and + denotes the union rather than the arithmetic sum.

Strictly speaking, it is not meaningful to ask for a count of the elements of U which are in A, since some of the elements of U may be in A "to a degree." Nevertheless, it is useful to have one or more extensions of the conventional concept of cardinality which make it meaningful to speak of the "count" of elements of a fuzzy set. One such extension, which was suggested by DeLuca and Termini[3], is the power of A, which is defined as the arithmetic sum of the grades of membership in A of all elements of U. For our purposes, it is preferable to refer to this count as the sigma-count of A and write

$$\Sigma\,\text{Count}\,(A) \overset{\Delta}{=} \Sigma_i \mu_i \tag{1.2}$$

with the understanding that, when appropriate, the right-hand member of (1.2) may be rounded to the nearest integer.

Example: Assume that U is comprised of the elements a, b, c, d, e and f. Then

$$\Sigma\,\text{Count}\,(0.8/a + 0.3/b + 0.8/c + 1/d + 0.2/e) = 3.$$

An alternative extension which was suggested in [25] defines the count of A as a fuzzy number. More specifically, let A_α be the α-level-set of A, i.e. the nonfuzzy set defined by [24]

$$A_\alpha \overset{\Delta}{=} \{u_i | \mu_A(u_i) \geq \alpha\}\ 0 > \alpha \geq 1,\ u_i \in U,\ i = 1, \ldots, n, \tag{1.3}$$

where $\mu_i \overset{\Delta}{=} \mu_A(u_i)$, $i = 1, \ldots, n$, is the grade of membership of u_i in A. Then, as shown in [24], A may be expressed in terms of the A_α by the relation

$$A = \Sigma_\alpha \alpha A_\alpha, \tag{1.4}$$

where Σ stands for the union, and αA_α is a fuzzy set whose membership function is defined by

$$\mu_{\alpha A_\alpha}(u) = \alpha \quad \text{for } u \in A_\alpha$$
$$= 0 \text{ elsewhere.} \qquad (1.5)$$

For example, if $U = \{a, b, c, d, e, f\}$ and

$$A = 0.8/a + 0.3/b + 0.8/c + 1/d + 0.2/e \qquad (1.6)$$

then

$A_1 = \{d\}$; $A_{0.8} = \{a, c, d\}$; $A_{0.3} = \{a, b, c, d\}$; $A_{0.2} = \{a, b, c, d, e\}$ and (1.4) becomes

$$A = 1/d + 0.8/(a + c + d) + 0.3/(a + b + c + d) + 0.2/(a + b + c + d + e). \qquad (1.7)$$

Now, let Count(A_α) denote the count of elements of the nonfuzzy set A_α. Then, the *FG*Count of A, where F stands for *fuzzy* and G stands for greater than, is defined as the fuzzy number

$$FG\text{Count}(A) \stackrel{\Delta}{=} \Sigma_\alpha \alpha/\text{Count}(A_\alpha) \qquad (1.8)$$

with the understanding that any gap in the Count (A_α) may be filled by a lower count with the same α. For example, for A defined by (1.6), we have

$$FG\text{Count}(A) = 1/1 + 0.8/3 + 0.6/4 + 0.2/5$$
$$= 1/0 + 1/1 + 0.8/2 + 0.8/3 + 0.6/4 + 0.2/5. \qquad (1.9)$$

Let $A\downarrow$ denote A sorted in descending order and let $NA\downarrow$ denote the fuzzy number resulting from replacing the mth element in $A\downarrow$ by μ_m/m and adding the element 1/0. For example, if

$$A = 0.6/a + 0.9/b + 1/c + 0.6/d + 0.2/e \qquad (1.10)$$

then

$$A\downarrow = 1/c + 0.9/b + 0.6/a + 0.6/d + 0.2/e \qquad (1.11)$$

$$NA\downarrow = 1/0 + 1/1 + 0.9/2 + 0.6/3 + 0.6/4 + 0.2/5. \qquad (1.12)$$

In terms of this notation, then, the definition of *FG*Count (A) stated earlier (1.8) may be expressed more succinctly as

$$FG\text{Count}(A) = NA\downarrow. \qquad (1.13)$$

To illustrate the use of the concepts defined above, we shall show how to arrive at an answer to a question raised earlier, namely, "How many combat-ready ships are there in the vicinity of the Persian Gulf?"

Assume that in the database we have a relation LIST [Name; μCR; μProx] which lists the name of each ship; its degree of combat-readiness, μCR; and its degree of proximity to the Persian Gulf, μProx.

Furthermore, we assume that only those ships are to be considered whose degree of proximity to the Persian Gulf exceeds a specified threshold, say 0.6.

From the relation LIST we can derive another relation LIST[Name; μCR $\wedge$ μProx], in which μCR $\wedge$ μProx denotes the combined degree of combat-readiness and proximity to the Persian Gulf. For example, if the degrees of combat-readiness and proximity of a ship S1 are 0.8 and 0.7, respectively, then the combined degree will be assumed to be the smaller of the two degrees, i.e. 0.7. More generally, in place of $\wedge$ (min) any desired mode of aggregation may be employed to express the combined degree as a function of its constituents.

To be specific, assume that the relation LIST[Name; μCR/μProx] reads

LIST	Name	μCR $\wedge$ μProx
	S1	0.9
	S2	1
	S3	0.6
	S4	0.7
	S5	0.8
	S6	0.7
	S7	0.9
	S8	1
	S9	0.8

Upon using (1.2), the Σ-count of LIST is found to be given by:

$$\Sigma\text{Count (LIST)} = 8.$$

On the other hand, using the definition of *FG*Count, we obtain the fuzzy number

$$FG\text{Count (LIST)} = 1/0 + 1/1 + 1/2 + 0.9/4 + 0.8/5$$
$$0.8/6 + 0.7/7 + 0.7/8 + 0.6/9.$$

A constituent such as 0.8/6 in this number signifies that there are six ships whose combined degree of combat-readiness and proximity to the Persian Gulf is greater than or equal to 0.8.

In addition to providing a basis for answering questions of the form "How many objects are there which satisfy a set of specified fuzzy criteria?", the concept of cardinality serves also as a means of precisiation of descriptions of the form *QAO*, where *Q* is a fuzzy quantifier, e.g. *several, many, few*, etc.; *A* is a fuzzy adjective, e.g. *tall, combat-ready, blue, young*, etc.; and *O* is the description of an object, e.g. *ball, ship, car, man*, etc. As will be seen in the sequel, the ability to precisiate the meaning of such expressions plays an essential role in the computation of fuzzy probabilities.

As a concrete illustration, consider the description

$$d \triangleq \text{several large balls}. \tag{1.14}$$

Using test-score semantics[28], the meaning of *d* may be defined as a test procedure which yields the degree of compatibility of *d* with a database which consists of a collection $D = \{b_1, \ldots, b_m)$ of *m* balls of various sizes. More specifically, let $\mu_{\text{LARGE}}(b_i)$ be the degree to which a ball, b_i, $i = 1, \ldots, m$, is large. Furthermore, let μ_{SEVERAL} denote the membership function of the fuzzy quantifier *several*. Then, on employing the Σ-count of large balls, we have

$$\Sigma\text{Count (LARGE BALL)} = \Sigma_{i=1}^{m} \mu_{\text{LARGE}}(b_i) \tag{1.15}$$

and hence the degree to which this count satisfies the constraint induced by the quantifier *several* is given by

$$\tau = \mu_{\text{SEVERAL}}(\Sigma_i^m \mu_{\text{LARGE}}(b_i)). \tag{1.16}$$

As shown in [27], the degree of compatibility, τ, may be interpreted as the possibility of the database, *D*, given the description $d \triangleq$ *several large balls*.

Alternatively, the compatibility of *d* with *D* may be computed by using the *FG*Count.

Thus, let τ_1

$$\tau_1 \stackrel{\Delta}{=} \mu_{\text{LARGE}}(b_1) \wedge \ldots \wedge \mu_{\text{LARGE}}(b_m)$$

represent the degree to which the constraint on the size of the balls is satisfied. Now, the degree to which the constraint on the number of balls is satisfied is given by

$$\tau_2 = \mu_{\text{SEVERAL}}(m) \tag{1.17}$$

and hence the degree to which both constraints are satisfied may be expressed as

$$\begin{aligned} \tau &= \tau_1 \wedge \tau_2 \\ &= \mu_{\text{SEVERAL}}(m) \wedge \mu_{\text{LARGE}}(b_1) \wedge \ldots \wedge \mu_{\text{LARGE}}(b_m), \end{aligned} \tag{1.18}$$

where $\wedge$ denotes the min operator in infix form. This expression for the compatibility of d and D corresponds to what is referred to in [28] as a *compartmentalized* interpretation of the description $d \stackrel{\Delta}{=}$ *several large balls*.

The foregoing analysis provides us with a means of precisiating the meaning of descriptions of the general form QAO, of which $d \stackrel{\Delta}{=}$ *several large balls* is a typical instance. With this means, then, we can address the issue of computing fuzzy probabilities when the underlying data contain fuzzy descriptions.

As a concrete illustration, we shall consider a slightly simplified version of a question that was posed earlier. Specifically:

An urn contains m balls of various sizes, of which several are large. What is the probability that a ball drawn at random is large?

The simplification—which is not essential—is that the number of balls in the urn is assumed to be m rather than *approximately* m. Furthermore, in the representation of the meaning of *several large balls* we shall employ the ΣCount rather than the *FG*Count.

Assume that the urn, U, consists of the balls $b_1, \ldots, b_m$, with $\mu_{\text{LARGE}}(b_i)$, $i = 1, \ldots m$, representing the grade of membership of b_i in the fuzzy set LARGE. Now from (1.16) it follows that the possibility of U given the datum "The urn contains several large balls" is

$$\tau = \mu_{\text{SEVERAL}}(\Sigma_{i=1}^{m} \mu_{\text{LARGE}}(b_i)).$$

On the other hand, if a ball is chosen at random, the probability of the fuzzy event "The chosen ball is large" is given by (see [23])

$$q \stackrel{\Delta}{=} \text{Prob}\{\text{ball is large}\} = \frac{1}{m} \Sigma_{i=1}^{m} \mu_{\text{LARGE}}(b_i). \tag{1.19}$$

Consequently, the possibility that Prob{ball is large} may take a value, say, v, is

$$\text{Poss}\{q = v\} = \mu_{\text{SEVERAL}}(mv) \tag{1.20}$$

or equivalently,

$$\Pi_q = \frac{\text{SEVERAL}}{m}, \tag{1.21}$$

where Π_q denotes the possibility distribution of q [25] and SEVERAL is interpreted as a fuzzy number. For example, if $m = 10$ and

$$\text{SEVERAL} = 0.4/3 + 0.8/4 + 1/5 + 1/6 + 0.6/7 + 0.3/8 \tag{1.22}$$

then

$$\Pi_q = 0.4/0.3 + 0.8/0.4 + 1/0.5 + 1/0.6 + 0.6/0.7 + 0.3/0.8 \qquad (1.23)$$

is the possibility distribution of the fuzzy number which represents the fuzzy probability that a ball drawn at random is large.

As was pointed out earlier, the fuzziness in the probability of drawing a large ball is induced by the fuzziness in our knowledge of the number of large balls in the urn. In this connection, it should be noted that, if instead of being given the ΣCount of large balls we were given the *FG*Count of large balls, the expression for fuzzy probability would become

$$F\text{Prob}\{\text{ball is large}\} = \frac{FG\text{Count(LARGE)}}{m}, \qquad (1.24)$$

where *F*Prob identifies the probability in question as a fuzzy probability which is the ratio of the fuzzy number *FG*Count (LARGE) and the nonfuzzy number m. Stated in this form, the fuzzy probability *F*Prob{ball is large} becomes closely related to the probability distribution function of the random variable which is associated with the membership function of LARGE.

Remark. There is a significant difference between the results expressed by (1.21) and (1.24) that is in need of clarification.

In the case of (1.21), it is tacitly assumed that the probability of drawing a large ball is a real number whose possibility distribution is expressed by (1.21). In the case of (1.24), on the other hand, the probability is assumed to be a fuzzy rather than a real number. To differentiate between these interpretations, the probabilities expressed by (1.21) and (1.24) will be referred to as *disjunctive fuzzy probability* and *conjunctive fuzzy probability*, respectively. We shall rely on the context to indicate whether a fuzzy probability should be interpreted in a disjunctive or conjuctive sense.

To view the computation of fuzzy probability from a broader perspective, let $U = \{u_1, \ldots, u_m\}$ be a finite universe of discourse and let X be a variable which takes the values $u_1, \ldots, u_m$ with a uniform probability $(1/m)$. Now if A is a nonfuzzy subset of U, the probability of the proposition or, equivalently, of the event

$$p \triangleq X \in A \qquad (1.25)$$

is given by

$$\text{Prob}\{X \in A\} = \frac{\text{Count}(A)}{m}. \qquad (1.26)$$

More generally, if A is a fuzzy subset of U then the probability of the fuzzy proposition or, equivalently, of the fuzzy event

$$p \triangleq X \text{ is } A \qquad (1.27)$$

may be expressed in two distinct ways: (a) as a nonfuzzy probability

$$\text{Prob}\{X \text{ is } A\} \triangleq \frac{\Sigma\text{Count}(A)}{m} \qquad (1.28)$$

and (*b*) as a fuzzy probability

$$F\text{Prob}\{X \text{ is } A\} \triangleq \frac{FG\text{Count}(A)}{m} \qquad (1.29)$$

with the understanding that (1.29) is implied by

$$\text{Prob}\{X \in A_\alpha\} = \frac{\text{Count}(A_\alpha)}{m} \qquad (1.30)$$

where A_3 is the α-level-set of A.

Furthermore, if A and B are fuzzy subsets of U, then the joint fuzzy probability of the fuzzy events $p \triangleq X$ is A and $q \triangleq X$ is B is given by

$$F\text{Prob}\{X \text{ is } A,\ X \text{ is } B\} = \frac{FG\text{Count}(A \cap B)}{m}. \tag{1.31}$$

Correspondingly, the conditional fuzzy probability of p given q may be defined as the fuzzy number

$$F\text{Prob}\{X \text{ is } A | X \text{ is } B\} = \Sigma_\alpha \alpha \Big/ \frac{\text{Count}(A_\alpha \cap B_\alpha)}{\text{Count}(B_\alpha)} \tag{1.32}$$

where Σ stands for the union rather than the arithmetic sum and $\text{Count}(B_\alpha) \neq 0$.

From (1.31) and (1.32), we can deduce the basic identity for fuzzy probabilities:

$$F\text{Prob}\{X \text{ is } A,\ X \text{ is } B\} = F\text{Prob}\{X \text{ is } A\} \otimes F\text{Prob}\{X \text{ is } B\} \tag{1.33}$$

where $\otimes$ is the product of fuzzy numbers[4, 14]. This identity may be viewed as a natural generalization of the familiar relation:

$$\text{Prob}\{X \in A,\ X \in B\} = \text{Prob}\{X \in B\}\ \text{Prob}\{X \in A | X \in B\} \tag{1.34}$$

which holds when A and B are nonfuzzy probabilities of fuzzy events defined via the ΣCount as in (1.28).

In the foregoing discussion, we have assumed that the probability distribution on U is uniform. More generally, if $\text{Prob}(u_i) \triangleq p_i$, $i = 1, \ldots, m$, and $p_1 + \ldots + p_m = 1$, then (1.29) becomes

$$F\text{Prob}\{X \text{ is } A\} = \Sigma_\alpha \alpha / \text{Prob}(A_\alpha), \tag{1.35}$$

where

$$\text{Prob}(A_\alpha) \triangleq \text{Prob}\{X \in A_\alpha\}. \tag{1.36}$$

Similarly, if X and Y take values in $U = \{u_1, \ldots, u_m\}$ and $V = \{v_1, \ldots, v_n\}$, respectively, and

$$\text{Prob}(u_i, v_j) \triangleq p_{ij}, \quad i = 1, \ldots, m, \quad j = 1, \ldots, n$$

then

$$F\text{Prob}\{X \text{ is } A,\ Y \text{ is } B\} = \Sigma_\alpha \alpha / \text{Prob}\{X \in A_\alpha,\ Y \in B_\alpha\} \tag{1.37}$$

$$F\text{Prob}\{X \text{ is } A | Y \text{ is } B\} = \Sigma_\alpha \alpha / \text{Prob}\{X \in A_\alpha | Y \in B_\alpha\} \tag{1.38}$$

and

$$F\text{Prob}\{X \text{ is } A,\ Y \text{ is } B\} = F\text{Prob}\{Y \text{ is } B\} \otimes F\text{Prob}\{X \text{ is } A | Y \text{ is } B\}, \tag{1.39}$$

which reduces to (1.33) when $X = Y$. By analogy with numerical probabilities, the fuzzy events X is A and Y is B will be said to *independent* if

$$F\text{Prob}\{X \text{ is } A | Y \text{ is } B\} = F\text{Prob}\{X \text{ is } A\}, \tag{1.40}$$

which implies that

$$F\text{Prob}\{X \text{ is } A,\ Y \text{ is } B\} = F\text{Prob}\{X \text{ is } A\} \otimes F\text{Prob}\{Y \text{ is } B\}. \tag{1.41}$$

In addition to the cases discussed above, there is another important way in which fuzzy information induces fuzzy probabilities. More specifically, consider the case where an individual, I, is faced with the decision of whether or not to insure his or her car. To find that choice which maximizes the expected utility, it is necessary to know, among other parameters, the probability that I's car may be stolen. How could this probability be determined?

Just a little reflection makes it clear that the desired probability cannot be deduced from the statistics of car thefts, since I's car—and the way in which it is driven, parked and garaged—is unique. Furthermore, there is no way in which I can obtain the desired probability by experimentation. What we see in this case is a paradigm of a well known paradox in probability theory which raises serious questions with regard to the meaningfulness of the concept of probability in application to unique events.

One way of getting around the difficulty with uniqueness is to relate probability to similarity, with similarity viewed as a fuzzy relation [24]. Thus, suppose that we wish to estimate the probability that an object, a, which is an element of a finite universe of discourse U, belongs to A, a subset of U. To this end, let S be a fuzzy similarity relation which associates with each element $u \in U$ its degree of similarity to a, $\mu_S(u, a)$. Then, $\mu_S(u, a)$ may be regarded as the membership function of a fuzzy set, $S(a)$, of objects which are similar to a.

In terms of the similarity relation S, the probability Prob $\{a \in A\}$ may be defined via the ΣCount or the FGCount of the intersection of $S(a)$ and A. Thus

$$\text{Prob}\,\{a \in A\} \stackrel{\Delta}{=} \frac{\Sigma\text{Count}\,(S(a) \cap A)}{\text{Count}\,(U)} \tag{1.42}$$

or, alternatively,

$$\text{Prob}\,\{a \in A\} \stackrel{\Delta}{=} \frac{FG\text{Count}\,(S(a) \cap A)}{\text{Count}\,(U)} \tag{1.43}$$

where $S(a) \cap A$ denotes the intersection of the fuzzy set $S(a)$ with A [23].

If the similarity relation were known precisely, (1.42) would yield a numerical value for the probability of a belonging to A. But, in general, this would not be the case, with the result that the expression for Prob $\{a \in A\}$ would be a fuzzy number. In this sense, then, estimates of probability based on similarity will, in general, be fuzzy rather than real numbers.

To make the point more concretely, assume that the imprecision in S is modeled by treating S as a fuzzy relation of type 2 [26], which implies that the degree of similarity of a and u, $\mu_S(a, u)$, is taken to be a fuzzy number. More specifically, assume that $\mu_S(a, u)$ is a fuzzy number ϕ whose membership function μ_ϕ is a π-function [25], that is,

$$\begin{aligned}
\pi\,(u\ \delta,\ \gamma)\ &= o \text{ for } u \le \gamma - \delta \\
&= 2\left(\frac{u-\gamma+\delta}{\delta}\right)^2 \text{ for } \gamma - \delta \le \gamma - \frac{\delta}{2} \\
&= 1 - 2\left(\frac{\mu-\gamma}{\delta}\right)^2 \text{ for } \gamma - \frac{\delta}{2} \le u \le \gamma \\
&= 1 - 2\left(\frac{\gamma-u}{\delta}\right)^2 \text{ for } \gamma \le u \le \gamma + \frac{\delta}{2} \\
&= 2\left(\frac{\gamma+\delta-u}{\delta}\right)^2 \text{ for } \gamma + \frac{\delta}{2} \le u \le \gamma + \delta \\
&= 0 \text{ for } u \ge \gamma + \delta
\end{aligned} \tag{1.44}$$

where γ is the peak of ϕ and δ is its bandwidth. Then, as shown in [4], the sum of fuzzy numbers of this form is a number of the same form whose peak and bandwidth are, respectively, the arithmetic sums of the peaks and bandwidths of their summands. In this way, the numerator of (1.42) evaluates to a fuzzy number which upon division by the count of U yields the fuzzy probability of a belonging to A.

Since the principle of maximization of expected utility plays a central role in decision analysis, it is important to be able to evaluate fuzzy expectations of the general form

$$E = (g_1 \otimes p_1) \oplus (g_2 \otimes p_2) \oplus \cdots \oplus (g_n \otimes p_n), \tag{1.45}$$

where $\otimes$ and $\oplus$ represent fuzzy multiplication and addition, respectively; $p_1, \ldots, p_n$ are fuzzy probabilities; and $g_1, \ldots, g_n$ are fuzzy gains (or utilities). Expressions of the form (1.45) can readily be computed by the use of fuzzy arithmetic. This and related issues are discussed in greater detail in [1, 2, 4, 5, 7, 8, 11, 14, 15, 18, 19, 20, 22] and other papers in the literature.

3. CONCLUDING REMARK

The main point which we have attempted to convey in this paper is that in most realistic applications of decision analysis the underlying probabilities are fuzzy rather than real numbers. In general, fuzzy probabilities are induced by fuzzy data and may be determined by (a) employing the concept of cardinality of fuzzy sets, and (b) using fuzzy arithmetic to compute the ratios, products and sums of counts of elements in such sets.

REFERENCES

[1] J. M. Adamo, Fuzzy decision trees, *Fuzzy Sets and Systems* 1980 **4** 207–219.

[2] S. J. Baas and H. Kwakernaak, Rating and ranking of multi-aspect alternatives using fuzzy sets, *Automatica* 1977 **13** 47–58.

[3] A. DeLuca and S. Termini, A definition of non-probabilistic entropy in the setting of fuzzy sets theory, *Information and Control* 1972 **20** 301–312.

[4] D. Dubois and H. Prade, Operations on fuzzy numbers, *Int. J. Syst. Sci.* 1978 **9** 613–626.

[5] D. Dubois and H. Prade, Decision-making under fuzziness. In *Advances in Fuzzy Set Theory and Applications* (Edited by M. M. Gupta, R. K. Ragade and R. R. Yager) North-Holland, Amsterdam, 279–302, 1979.

[6] D. Dubois and H. Prade, *Fuzzy Sets and Systems: Theory and Applications*. Academic Press, New York, 1980.

[7] J. Efstathiou and V. Rajkovic, Multiattribute decision-making using a fuzzy heuristic approach, *IEEE Trans. Syst. Man, Cybern,* 1979 **SMC-9** 326–333.

[8] J. Efstathiou and R. M. Tong, Ranking fuzzy sets using linguistic preference relations, *Proc. 10th Int. Symp. Multiple-Valued Logic*, Northwestern Univ., Evanston, IL, 1980.

[9] T. Fine, *Theories of Probability*. Academic Press, New York, 1973.

[10] P. C. Fishburn, *Mathematics of Decision Theory*. Mouton, The Hague, 1973.

[11] R. Jain, Decision-making in the presence of fuzzy variables, *IEEE Trans. on Systems, Man and Cybern.* 1976 **SMC-6**, 698–703.

[12] R. L. Keeney and R. Raiffa, *Decisions with Multiple Objectives: Preferences and Value Trade-offs*. Wiley, New York, 1976.

[13] W. J. M. Kickert, *Fuzzy Theories on Decision Making: A Critical Review*. Martinus Nijhoff, Leiden, Netherlands, 1978.

[14] M. Mizumoto and K. Tanaka, Some properties of fuzzy numbers, in *Advances in Fuzzy Set Theory and Applications* (Edited by M. M. Gupta, R. K. Ragade and R. R. Yager). North-Holland, Amsterdam, 153–164, 1979.

[15] H. T. Nguyen, On fuzziness and linguistic probabilities, *J. Math. Anal. and Appl.* 1977 **61**, 658–671.

[17] R. I. Savage, *Statistics: Uncertainty and Behavior*. Houghton–Mifflin, Boston, 1968.

[18] J. Tanaka, T. Okuda and K. Asai, Fuzzy information and decision in statistical model, In *Advances in Fuzzy Set Theory and Applications* (Edited by M. M. Gupta, R. K. Ragade and R. R. Yager), 300–320. North–Holland, Amsterdam, 1979.

[19] R. M. Tong and P. P. Bonissone, A linguistic approach to decision-making with fuzzy sets, *IEEE Trans. on Systems, Man, and Cybernetics* 1980 **SMC-10** 716–723.

[20] S. R. Watson, J. J. Weiss and M. L. Donell, Fuzzy decision analysis, *IEEE Trans. Syst. Man, Cybern,* 1979 **SMC-9** 1–9.

[21] J. W. WILCOX, A Method for Measuring Decision Assumptions. MIT Press, Cambridge, 1972.
[22] R. R. YAGER, Fuzzy sets, probabilities and decision, *J. Cybernetics*, 1980 **10** 1–18.
[23] L. A. ZADEH, Probability measures of fuzzy events, *J. Math. Anal. Appl.* 1968 **23** 421–427.
[24] L. A. ZADEH, *Similarity relations and fuzzy orderings, Inf. Sci.* 1971 **3** 177–200.
[25] L. A. ZADEH, A Theory of approximate reasoning, *Electronics Research Laboratory Memorandum M* 77/58, University of California, Berkeley, 1977. Also in *Machine Intelligence* 9 (Edited by J. E. Hayes, M. Michie and L. I. Kulich). 149–194, Wiley, New York, 1979.
[26] L. A. ZADEH, Fuzzy sets as a basis for a theory of possibility, *Fuzzy Sets and Systems*, 1978 **1** 3–28.
[27] L. A. ZADEH, Possibility theory and soft data analysis, *Electronics Research Laboratory Memorandum M79/58*, University of California, Berkeley, 1979. Also in *Mathematical Frontiers of the Social and Policy Sciences* (Edited by L. Cobb and R. M. Thrall) 69–120, Boulder, Westview Press, 1981.
[28] L. A. ZADEH, Test-score semantics and meaning representation via PRUF, Tech. Note 247, AI Center, SRI International, Menlo Park, 1981. Also in *Empirical Semantics* (Edited by B. B. Rieger). Bochum: Brockmeyer, 281–349, 1982.
[29] L. A. ZADEH, The concept of a linguistic variable and its application to approximate reasoning, Part I, *Inf. Sci.* 1975, **8**, 199–249; Part II, *Inf. Sci.* 1975, **8**, 301–357; Part III, *Inf. Sci.* 1975, **9**, 43–80.

A Formalization of Commonsense Reasoning Based on Fuzzy Logic*

L.A. Zadeh

Computer Science Division
University of California
Berkeley, CA 94720

Abstract

The basic idea underlying the approach outlined in this paper is that commonsense knowledge may be regarded as a collection of dispositions, that is, propositions which are preponderantly, but not necessarily always, true. Technically, a disposition may be interpreted as a proposition with implicit fuzzy quantifiers, e.g., *most, almost all, usually, often*, etc. For example, a disposition such as *Swedes are blond* may be interpreted as *most Swedes are blond*. For purposes of inference from commonsense knowledge, the conversion of a disposition into a proposition with explicit fuzzy quantifiers sets the stage for an application of syllogistic reasoning in which the premises are allowed to be of the form *Q A's are B's*, where *A* and *B* are fuzzy predicates and *Q* is a fuzzy quantifier. In general, the conclusion yielded by such reasoning is a proposition which may be converted into a disposition through the suppression of fuzzy quantifiers.

1. Introduction

In recent years, it has become increasingly clear that further advances in AI require a better understanding of how to represent and infer from commonsense knowledge. The problem with such knowledge - exemplified by *snow is white, a loaf of bread costs about a dollar, students are young*, etc. - is that it does not lend itself to representation within the framework of traditional logical systems, although some progress toward this end has been achieved through the employment of variants of predicate logic involving circumscription (6), default reasoning (12), truth-maintenance (1), non-monotonic reasoning (8) and related techniques.

In an alternative approach which is outlined in this paper,* a key idea is that commonsense knowledge may be viewed as a collection of dispositions, that is, propositions which are preponderantly, but not necessarily always, true. Commonplace examples of dispositions are: *glue is sticky, slimness is attractive, overeating causes* obesity, Maria is very straightforward, big planes are safer than small planes, etc.

Techically, a disposition may be interpreted as a proposition which contains implicit fuzzy quantifiers such as *most, almost always, usually, often*, etc. For example, *Mary is very straightforward* may be interpreted as *usually Maria is very straightforward*. The process of conversion of a disposition into a proposition is referred to as *explicitation*. An important aspect of explicitation is that it is interpretation-dependent in the sense that the manner in which the suppressed quantifiers in a disposition are restored is determined by the intended meaning of the disposition. For example, *slimness is attractive* may be understood as *most of the slim are attractive*, but it may also be interpreted as *most of the attractive are slim*. Similarly, *heavy smoking causes lung cancer* may be interpreted in many ways, among them: *most of the heavy smokers develop lung cancer, most of those who have lung cancer are heavy smokers*, and *among those who have lung cancer, the number of heavy smokers is much larger than the number of non-smokers*.

Explicitation sets the stage for the representation of the meaning of a disposition through the use of fuzzy logic and, more specifically, test-score semantics (16). A brief exposition of test-score semantics is presented in the following.

2. Test Score Semantics

In test-score semantics, a proposition is regarded as a collection of elastic, or, equivalently, fuzzy constraints. For example, the proposition *Kathryn is tall* represents an elastic constraint on the height of Kathryn. Similarly, the proposition *Charlotte is blonde* represents an elastic constraint on the color of Charlotte's hair. And, the proposition *most tall men are not very agile* represents an elastic constraint on the proportion of men who are not very agile among tall men.

In more concrete terms, representing the meaning of a proposition, p, through the use of test-score semantics involves the following steps.

1. Identification of the variables $X_1, \ldots, X_n$ whose values are constrained by the proposition. Usually, these variables are implicit rather than explicit in p.
2. Identification of the constraints $C_1, \ldots, C_m$ which are induced by p.
3. Characterization of each constraint, C_i, by describing a testing procedure which associates with C_i a test score τ_i representing the degree to which C_i is satisfied. Usually τ_i is expressed as a number in the interval $[0,1]$. More generally, however, a test score may be a probability/possibility distribution over the unit interval.
4. Aggregation of the partial test scores $\tau_1, \ldots, \tau_m$ into a smaller number of test scores $\bar{\tau}_1, \ldots, \bar{\tau}_k$, which are represented as an *overall vector test score* $\tau = (\bar{\tau}_1, \ldots, \bar{\tau}_k)$. In most cases $k = 1$, so that the overall test scores is a scalar. We shall assume that this is the case unless an explicit statement to the contrary is made.

It is important to note that, in test-score semantics, the meaning of p is represented not by the overall test score τ but by the procedure which leads to it. Viewed in this perspective, test-score semantics may be regarded as a generalization of truth-conditional, possible-world and model-theoretic semantics. However, by providing a computational framework for dealing with uncertainty and dispositionality — which the conventional semantical systems disregard — test-score semantics achieves a

Research supported by NASA Grant NCC2-275 and NSF Grant IST-8420416.

* A more detailed exposition of fuzzy logic and its application to commonsense reasoning may be found in (18).

much higher level of expressive power and thus provides a basis for representing the meaning of a much wider variety of propositions in a natural language.

In test-score semantics, the testing of the constraints induced by p is performed on a collection of fuzzy relations which constitute an *explanatory database*, or *ED* for short. A basic assumption which is made about the explanatory database is that it is comprised of relations whose meaning is known to the addressee of the meaning-representation process. In an indirect way, then, the testing and aggregation procedures in test-score semantics may be viewed as a description of a process by which the meaning of p is composed from the meanings of the constituent relations in the explanatory database. It is this explanatory role of the relations in *ED* that motivates its description as an *explanatory database*.

As will be seen in the sequel, in describing the testing procedures we need not concern ourselves with the actual entries in the constituent relations. Thus, in general, the description of a test involves only the frames of the constituent relations, that is, their names, their variables (or attributes) and the domain of each variable. When this is the case, the explanatory database will be referred to as the *explanatory database frame*, or *EDF* for short.

As a simple illustration of the concept of a test procedure, consider the proposition $p \triangleq$ *Maria is young and attractive*. The *EDF* in this case will be assumed to consist of the following relations:

$$EDF \triangleq POPULATION\ [Name;\ Age;\ \mu Attractive\ ] + YOUNG\ [Age;\ \mu]\ , \tag{2.1}$$

in which + should be read as "and."

The relation labeled *POPULATION* consists of a collection of triples whose first element is the name of an individual; whose second element is the age of that individual; and whose third element is the degree to which the individual in question is attractive. The relation *YOUNG* is a collection of pairs whose first element is a value of the variable *Age* and whose second element is the degree to which that value of *Age* satisfies the elastic constraint characterized by the fuzzy predicate *young*. In effect, this relation serves to calibrate the meaning of the fuzzy predicate *young* in a particular context by representing its denotation as a fuzzy subset, *YOUNG*, of the interval [0,100].

With this *EDF*, the test procedure which computes the overall test score may be described as follows:

1. Determine the age of Maria by reading the value of *Age* in *POPULATION*, with the variable *Name* bound to Maria. In symbols, this may be expressed as

   $$Age\ (Maria) = {}_{Age}\ POPULATION\ [Name\ =\ Maria]\ .$$

   In this expression, we use the notation $_Y R[X = a]$ to signify that X is bound to a in R and the resulting relation is projected on Y, yielding the values of Y in the tuples in which $X = a$.

2. Test the elastic constraint induced by the fuzzy predicate *young*:

   $$\tau_1 = {}_{\mu}\ YOUNG[Age\ =\ Age\,(Maria)]\ .$$

3. Determine the degree to which Maria is attractive:

   $$\tau_2 = {}_{\mu Attractive}\ POPULATION[Name\ =\ Maria]\ .$$

4. Compute the overall test score by aggregating the partial test scores τ_1 and τ_2. For this purpose, we shall use the min operator $\wedge$ as the aggregation operator, yielding

   $$\tau = \tau_1 \wedge \tau_1\ . \tag{2.2}$$

which signifies that the overall test score is taken to be the smaller of the operands of $\wedge$. The overall test score, as expressed by (2.2), represents the compatibility of $p \triangleq$ *Maria is young and attractive* with the data resident in the explanatory database.

In testing the constituent relations in *EDF*, it is helpful to have a collection of standardized translation rules for computing the test score of a combination of elastic constraints $C_1, \ldots, C_k$ from the knowledge of the test scores of each constraint considered in isolation. For the most part, such rules are *default* rules in the sense that they are intended to be used in the absence of alternative rules supplied by the user.

For purposes of commonsense knowledge representation, the principal rules of this type are the following.**

Rules pertaining to modification

If the test score for an elastic constraint C in a specified context is τ, then in the same context the test score for

(a) *not* C *is* $1-\tau$ (*negation*)

(b) *very* C *is* τ^2 (*concentration*)

(c) *more or less* C *is* $\tau^{\frac{1}{2}}$ (*diffusion*) .

Rules pertaining to composition

If the test scores for elastic constraints C_1 and C_2 in a specified context are τ_1 and τ_2, respectively, then in the same context the test score for

(a) C_1 *and* C_2 *is* $\tau_1 \wedge \tau_2$ (*conjunction*), where $\wedge \triangleq min$.

(b) C_1 *or* C_2 *is* $\tau_1 \vee \tau_2$ (*disjunction*), where $\vee \triangleq max$.

(c) *If* C_1 *then* C_2 *is* $1 \wedge (1-\tau_1+\tau_2)$ (*implication*) .

Rules pertaining to quantification

The rules in question apply to propositions of the general form *Q A's are B's* , where *Q* is a fuzzy quantifier, e.g., *most*, *many*, *several*, *few*, etc, and *A* and *B* are fuzzy sets, e.g., *tall men*, *intelligent men*, etc. As was stated earlier, when the fuzzy quantifiers in a proposition are implied rather than explicit, their suppression may be placed in evidence by referring to the proposition as a *disposition*. In this sense, the proposition *overeating causes obesity* is a disposition which results from the suppression of the fuzzy quantifer *most* in the proposition *most of those who overeat are obese*.

To make the concept of a fuzzy quantifer meaningful, it is necessary to define a way of counting the number of elements in a fuzzy set or, equivalently, to determine its cardinality.

There are several ways in which this can be done (15). For our purposes, it will suffice to employ the concept of a *sigma-count*, which is defined as follows.

Let F be a fuzzy subset of $U = \{u_1, \ldots, u_n\}$ expressed symbolically as

$$F = \mu_1/u_1 + \ldots + \mu_n/u_n = \Sigma_i \mu_i/u_i$$

or, more simply, as

$$F = \mu_1 u_1 + \ldots + \mu_n u_n\ ,$$

in which the term μ_i/u_i, $i = 1, \ldots, n$, signifies that μ_i is the grade of membership of u_i in F, and the plus sign represents the union.

The sigma-count of F is defined as the arithmetic sum of the μ_i , i.e.,

$$\Sigma Count\,(F) \triangleq \Sigma_i \mu_i\ ,\ i = 1, \ldots, n\ ,$$

** A more detailed discussion of such rules in the context of PRUF may be found in (16).

with the understanding that the sum may be rounded, if need be, to the nearest integer. Furthermore, one may stipulate that the terms whose grade of membership falls below a specified threshold be excluded from the summation. The purpose of such an exclusion is to avoid a situation in which a large number of terms with low grades of membership become count-equivalent to a small number of terms with high membership.

The *relative sigma-count*, denoted by $\Sigma Count(F/G)$, may be interpreted as the proportion of elements of F which are in G. More explicitly,

$$\Sigma Count(F/G) = \frac{\Sigma Count(F \cap G)}{\Sigma Count(G)},$$

where $F \cap G$, the intersection of F and G, is defined by

$$\mu_{F \cap G}(u) = \mu_F(u) \wedge \mu_G(u) \ , \ u \in U \ .$$

Thus, in terms of the membership functions of F and G, the relative sigma-count of F in G is given by

$$\Sigma Count(F/G) = \frac{\Sigma_i \mu_F(u_i) \wedge \mu_G(u_i)}{\Sigma_i \mu_G(u_i)} \ .$$

The concept of a relative sigma-count provides a basis for interpreting the meaning of propositions of the form *Q A's are B's*, e.g., *most young men are healthy*. More specifically, if the focal variable (ie., the constrained variable) in the proposition in question is taken to be the proportion of *B's* in *A's*, then the corresponding translation rule may be expressed as

$$Q\ A\text{'s are } B\text{'s} \to \Sigma Count(B/A) \text{ is } Q$$

As will be seen in the following section, the quantification rule together with the other rules described in this section provide a basic conceptual framework for the representation of commonsense knowledge. We shall illustrate the representation process through the medium of several examples in which the meaning of a disposition is represented as a test on a collection of fuzzy relations in an explanatory database.

3. Representation of Meaning of Dispositions

To clarify the difference between the conventional approaches to meaning representation and that described in the present paper, we shall consider as our first example the disposition

$$d \triangleq \textit{snow is white} \ .$$

The first step in the representation process involves a restoration of the suppressed quantifiers in d. We shall assume that the intended meaning of d is conveyed by the proposition

$$p \triangleq \textit{usually snow is white} \ ,$$

and, as an *EDF*, we shall use

$$EDF \triangleq WHITE[Sample;\mu] + USUALLY[Proportion;\mu] \ .$$

.PPLet (3.1)

τ_i, $i = 1, \ldots, m$, denote the degree to which the color of S_i matches white. Thus, τ_i may be interpreted as the test score for the constraint on the color of S_i which is induced by *WHITE*.

Using this notation, the steps in the testing procedure may be described as follows:

1. Find the proportion of samples whose color is white:

$$\rho = \frac{\Sigma Count\,(WHITE)}{m} = \frac{\tau_1 + \ldots + \tau_m}{m}$$

2. Compute the degree to which ρ satisfies the constraint induced by *USUALLY*:

$$\tau = {}_{\mu} USUALLLY[Proportion = \rho] \ . \qquad (3.2)$$

In (3.2), τ represents the overall test score and the right-hand member signifies that the relation *USUALLY* is particularized by setting Proportion equal to ρ and projecting the resulting relation on μ. The meaning of d, then, is represented by the test procedure which leads to the value of τ.

To illustrate the use of translation rules relating to modification, we shall consider the disposition

$$d \triangleq \textit{Frenchmen are not very tall} \ .$$

After explicitation, the intended meaning of d is assumed to be represented by the proposition

$$p \triangleq \textit{most Frenchmen are not very tall} \ .$$

To represent the meaning of p, we shall employ an *EDF* whose constituent relations are:

$$EDF \triangleq POPULATION[Name;\ Height] +$$
$$TALL[Height;\ \mu] +$$
$$MOST[Proportion;\ \mu] \ .$$

The relation *POPULATION* is a tabulation of *Height* as a function of *Name* for a representative group of Frenchmen. In *TALL*, μ is the degree to which a value of *Height* fits the description *tall*; and in *MOST*, μ is the degree to which a numerical value of *Proportion* fits the intended meaning of *most*.

The test procedure which represents the meaning of p involves the following steps:

1. Let $Name_i$ be the name of ith individual in *POPULATION*. For each $Name_i$, $i = 1, \ldots, m$, find the height of $Name_i$:

$$Height\ (Name_i) \triangleq {}_{Height} POPULATION[Name = Name_i$$

2. For each $Name_i$, compute the test score for the constraint induced by *TALL*:

$$\tau_i = {}_{\mu}TALL[Height = Height(Name_i)] \ .$$

3. Using the translation rules, compute the test score for the constraint induced by *NOT.VERY.TALL*:

$$\tau'_i = 1 - \tau_i^2 \ .$$

4. Find the relative sigma-count of Frenchmen who are not very tall:

$$\rho \triangleq \Sigma Count(NOT.VERY.TALL/POPULATION) = \frac{\Sigma_i \tau'_i}{m} \ .$$

5. Compute the test score for the constraint induced by *MOST*:

$$\tau = {}_{\mu}MOST[Proportion = \rho] \ . \qquad (3.3)$$

The test score given by (3.3) represents the overall test score for d, and the test procedure which yields τ represents the meaning of d.

4. Inference

In what follows, we shall restrict our attention to dispositions which, after explicitation, are expressible in the canonical form *QA's* are *B's*, where *Q is a fuzzy quantifier*, e.g., *most*, *almost all*, *usually*, etc., and *A* and *B* are fuzzy predictes sub as *small*, *tall*, *slim*, *young*, etc.* Fuzzy logic provides a basis for inference from dispositions of this type through the use of *fuzzy syllogistic seasoning* (19). As its name implies, fuzzy syllogistic seasoning is an extension of classical syllogistic seasoning to fuzzy predicates and fuzzy quantifiers. In

* A more general treatment of inference in fuzzy logic may be found in (15).

its generic form, a fuzzy syllogism may be expressed as the inference schema

$$\frac{\begin{array}{l} Q_1 A\text{'s are } B\text{'s} \\ Q_2 C\text{'s are } D\text{'s} \end{array}}{Q_3 E\text{'s are } F\text{'s}} \qquad (4.1)$$

in which A, B, C, D, E and F are interrelated fuzzy predicates and Q_1, Q_2 and Q_3 are fuzzy quantifiers.

The interrelations between A, B, C, D, E and F provide a basis for a classification of fuzzy syllogisms. The more important of these syllogisms are the following. ($\wedge \triangleq$ conjunction, $\vee \triangleq$ disjunction).

(*a*) *Intersection/product syllogism*: $C = A \wedge B$, $E = A$, $F = C \wedge D$

(*b*) *chaining syllogism*: $C = B$, $E = A$, $F = D$

(*c*) *Consequent conjunction syllogism*: $A = C = E$, $F = B \wedge D$

(*d*) *Consequent disjunction syllogism*: $A = C = E$, $F = B \vee D$

(*e*) *Antecedent conjunction syllogism*: $B = D = F$, $E = A \wedge C$

(*f*) *Antecedent disjunction syllogism*: $B = D = F$, $E = A \vee C$.

In the context of expert systems, these and related syllogisms provide a set of inference rules for combining evidence through conjunction, disjunction and chaining (17).

One of the basic problems in fuzzy syllogistic seasoning is the following. Given A, B, C, D, E and F, find the maximally specific (i.e., most restrictive) fuzzy quantifier Q_3 such that the proposition Q, *E's are F's* is entailed by the premises. In the case of (a), (b) and (c), this leads to the following syllogisms.

Intersection/product syllogism

$$\frac{\begin{array}{l} Q_1 A\text{'s are } B\text{'s} \\ Q_2 (A \text{ and } B)\text{'s are } C\text{'s} \end{array}}{(Q_1 \otimes Q_2) A\text{'s are } (B \text{ and } C)\text{'s}} \qquad (4.2)$$

where $\otimes$ denotes the product in fuzzy arithmetic (4). It should be noted that (4.2) may be viewed as an analog of the basic probabilistic identity

$$p(B,C/A) = p(B/A)p(C/A,B) \; .$$

A concrete example of the intersection/product syllogism is the following

most students are young (4.3)

<u>*most young students are single*</u>

most^2 *students are young* and *single* ,

where *most*^{2} denotes the product of the fuzzy quantifier *most* with itself.

Chaining syllogism

$$\frac{\begin{array}{l} Q_1 A\text{'s are } B\text{'s} \\ Q_2 B\text{'s are } C\text{'s} \end{array}}{(Q_1 \otimes Q_2) A\text{'s are } C\text{'s}} \qquad (4.4)$$

This syllogism may be viewedas a special case of the intersection produced syllogism. It results when $B \subset A$ and Q_1 and Q_2 are monotone increasing, i.e., $\geq Q_1 = Q_1$, and $\geq Q_2 = Q_2$, where $\geq Q_1$ should be read as *at least* Q_1, and likewise for Q_2. A simple example of the chaining syllogism is the following:

most students are undergraduates

<u>*most undergraduates are single*</u>

most^2 *students are single*

Note that *undergraduates* $\subset$ *students* and that in the conclusion F = *single*, rather than *young and single*, as in (4.3).

Consequent conjunction syllogism

The consequent conjunction syllogism is an example of a basic syllogism which is not a derivative of the intersection/product syllogism. Its statement may be expressed as follows:

$$\frac{\begin{array}{l} Q_1 A\text{'s are } B\text{'s} \\ Q_2 A\text{'s are } C\text{'s} \end{array}}{Q A\text{'s are } (B \text{ and } C)\text{'s}} \; , \qquad (4.5)$$

where Q is a fuzzy quantifier which is defined by the inequalities

$$0 \circledcirc (Q_1 \oplus Q_2 \ominus 1) \leq Q \leq Q_1 \circledcirc Q_2 \qquad (4.6)$$

in which $\circledcirc$, $\circledcirc$, $\oplus$ and $\ominus$ are the operations of $\vee$ (max), $\wedge$ (min), + and - in fuzzy arithmetic.

An illustration of (4.5) is provided by the example

most students are young

<u>*most students are single*</u>

Q students are single and *young*

where

$$2most \ominus 1 \leq Q \leq most \; . \qquad (3.17)$$

This expression for Q follows from (4.6) by noting that

$$most \circledcirc most = most$$

and

$$0 \circledcirc (2most \ominus 1) = 2most \ominus 1 \; .$$

The three basic syllogisms stated above are merely examples of a collection of fuzzy syllogisms which may be developed and employed for purposes of inference from commonsense knowledge. In addition to its application to commonsense reasoning, fuzzy syllogistic reasoning may serve to provide a basis for the development of a system of rules for combining uncertain evidence in expert systems (17).

REFERENCES AND RELATED PUBLICATIONS

[1] J. Doyle, "A truth-maintenance system," *Artificial Intelligence 12*, pp. 231-272, 1979.

[2] D. Dubois and H. Prade, *Fuzzy Sets and Systems: Theory and Applications*. New York:Academic Press, 1980.

[3] J.A. Goguen, "The logic of inexact concepts," *Synthese 19*, pp. 325-373, 1969.

[4] A. Kaufmann and M.M. Gupta, *Introduction to Fuzzy Arithmetic*. New York:Van Nostrand, 1985.

[5] E.H. Mamdani and B.R. Gaines, *Fuzzy Reasoning and its Applications*. London:Academic Press, 1981.

[6] J. McCarthy, "Circumscription: A non-monotonic inference rule," *Artificial Intelligence 13*, pp. 27-40, 1980.

[7] D.V. McDermott and J. Doyle, "Non-monotonic logic, I," *Artificial Intelligence 13*, pp. 41-72, 1980.

[8] D.V. McDermott, "Non-monotonic logic, II: non-monotonic modal theories," *J. Assoc. Comp. Mach. 29*, pp. 33-57, 1982.

[9] R.C. Moore and J.R. Hobbs, (eds.), *Formal Theories of the Commonsense World*. Harwood, NJ:Ablex Publishing, 1984.

[10] C.V. Negoita, *Expert Systems and Fuzzy Systems*. Menlo Park:Benjamin/Cummings, 1985.

[11] N. Nilsson, *Probabilistic logic*, SRI Tech. Note 321, Menlo Park, CA, 1984.

[12] R. Reiter and G. Criscuolo, "Some representational issues in default reasoning," *Computers and Mathematics 9*, pp. 15-28, 1983.

[13] M. Sugeno, "Fuzzy measures and fuzzy integrals: a survey," in *Fuzzy Automata and Decision Processes*, M.M. Gupta, G.N. Saridis and B.R. Gaines, (eds.), Amsterdam:North-Holland, pp. 89-102, 1977.

[14] R.R. Yager, "Quantified propositions in a linguistic logic," in: *Proceedings of the 2nd International Seminar on Fuzzy Set Theory*. E.P. Klement, (ed.), Johannes Kepler University, Linz, Austria, 1980.

[15] L.A. Zadeh, "A theory of approximate reasoning," *Electronics Research Laboratory Memorandum M77/58*, University of California, Berkeley, 1977. Also in: *Machine Intelligence 9*. J.E. Hayes. D. Michie and L.I. Kulich, (eds.), New York:Wiley, pp. 149-194, 1979.

[16] L.A. Zadeh, "Test-score semantics for natural languages and meaning-representation via PRUF," *Tech. Note 247, AI Center, SRI International*, Menlo Park, CA, 1981. Also in *Empirical Semantics*. B.B. Rieger, (ed.), Bochum:Brockmeyer, pp. 281-349, 1981.

[17] L.A. Zadeh, "The role of fuzzy logic in the management of uncertainty in expert systems," *Fuzzy Sets and Systems 11*, pp. 199-227, 1983.

[18] L.A. Zadeh, "A theory of commonsense knowledge," in *Issues of Vagueness*. H.J. S. Skala Termini and E. Trillas, (eds.), pp. 257-296, Dordrecht:Reidel, 1984.

[19] L.A. Zadeh, "Syllogistic reasoning in fuzzy logic and its application to usuality and reasoning with dispositions," to appear in the *IEEE Trans. on Systems, Man and Cybernetics*, 1985.

[20] M. Zemankova-Leech and A. Kandel, *Fuzzy Relational Data Bases - A Key to Expert Systems*. Cologne: Verlag TUV Rheinland, 1984.

MANAGEMENT OF UNCERTAINTY IN EXPERT SYSTEMS

L. A. ZADEH*

Computer Science Division, Department of Electrical Engineering and Computer Science, University of California Berkeley, CA 94720

ABSTRACT

During the past several years, the question of how to deal with uncertainty in the context of expert systems has attracted a great deal of attention because much of the information which is resident in the knowledge base of a typical expert system is imprecise, incomplete or not totally reliable.

The existing approaches to the management of uncertainty in expert systems are based for the most part on probability theory or its variants. However, it may be argued, as it is done in this paper, that probability theory is not sufficiently expressive as a language of uncertainty to represent the meaning of the imprecise facts and rules that form the knowledge base of a typical expert system. In an alternative approach which is outlined in this paper, fuzzy logic forms the basis for both meaning representation and inference. In particular, syllogistic reasoning is used to formulate a collection of rules for combination of evidence, with fuzzy quantifiers replacing probabilities and certainty factors as indicators of the degree of uncertainty.

1. Introduction

The issue of uncertainty plays an important role in the design and operation of expert systems because much of the information which is resident in the knowledge base of a typical expert system is imprecise, incomplete or not totally reliable.

The traditional probability-based methods of dealing with uncertainty do not work well in the case of expert systems because in practice it is usually infeasible to determine all of probability distributions which are needed to compute the conditional probability of a hypothesis given the evidence. This makes it necessary to employ ad hoc techniques of analysis in which many implicit and hard-to-verify assumptions regarding the underlying probability distributions are made.

Among the best known systems for dealing with uncertainty in the context of expert systems are those of MYCIN[11] and PROSPECTOR.[18] In MYCIN, for example, a typical rule is associated with a *certainty factor*, CF, which is a number in the interval $[-1, 1]$. If positive, this number serves as a measure of the relative increase in the probability of a hypothesis given the evidence. If negative, its magnitude measures the relative decrease in the probability of the hypothesis given the

*Research supported in part by NASA Grant NCC2-275 and National Science Foundation Grant ECS-82 09679.

evidence. The MYCIN rules of combination provide a system for computing the certainty factor of the conclusion from the certainty factors of the primary sources of evidence.

Although the MYCIN system works reasonably well in practice, it has a number of serious shortcomings which are analyzed in detail in a recent paper by Heckerman.[23] In his paper, Heckerman proposes several modifications to the MYCIN system which make it much less ad hoc and are more solidly based on probability theory. However, there are some important sources of uncertainty in expert systems which are not addressed by the techniques based on probability theory and first-order logic. Among the more important of these sources are the following.[52]

(1) The fuzziness of antecedents and/or consequents in rules of the form

(a) If X is A then Y is B,
(b) If X is A then Y is B with $\mathrm{CF} = \alpha$,

where the antecedent, X is A, and the consequent, X is B, are fuzzy propositions, and α is a numerical value of the certainty factor, CF. For example[11]

(a) If the search space is *moderately small* then *exhaustive* search is *feasible.*
(b) If a piece of code is called *frequently* then it is *worth optimizing.*
(c) If *large* oil spill or *strong* acid spill then *emergency* is *strongly* suggested.
(d) If X is *small* then Y is *large* with $\mathrm{CF} = 0.8$.
(e) If the route of the administration of the penicillin is oral, and there is a gastro-intestinal factor which *may interfere* with the *absorption* of penicillin, then there is *suggestive evidence* (0.6) that the route of administration of the penicillin is not *adequate.*

In these rules, the *italicized* words are labels of fuzzy predicates (e.g., *small, large, emergency*) or fuzzy predicate modifiers (e.g., *moderately*). This implies that the antecedents and consequents in the rules in question are fuzzy propositions or, equivalently, fuzzy events.

In the existing expert systems, the fuzziness of antecedents and consequents is ignored or treated incorrectly because neither probability-based methods nor bivalent logical systems provide a computational framework for dealing with it. As a consequence, fuzzy facts and rules are generally manipulated as if they were nonfuzzy, leading to conclusions of doubtful validity.

To illustrate this point, consider a rule of the general form[52]:

If X is A then Y is B with probability β,

where X and Y are variables, A and B are fuzzy predicates and β is a fuzzy probability expressed as a fuzzy number, e.g., *about* 0.8, or as a linguistic probability, e.g., *very likely.* For example

If Mary is young then Mary is healthy is likely,

where $X \doteq$ Age(Mary), $Y \doteq$ Health(Mary), $A \doteq$ young, $B \doteq$ healthy and $\beta \doteq$ likely.

Expressed as a conditional probability, the rule in question may be written as

$$\Pr\{Y \text{ is } B|X \text{ is } A\} \text{ is } \beta. \tag{1.1}$$

In the existing expert systems, such a rule would be treated as an ordinary conditional probability, from which it would follow that

$$\Pr\{Y \text{ is not } B|X \text{ is } A\} \text{ is } 1-\beta. \tag{1.2}$$

However, as shown in Ref. 52, this conclusion is, in general, incorrect if A is a fuzzy set. The correct conclusion is weaker than (1.2), namely,

$$\Pr\{Y \text{ is not } B|X \text{ is } A\} + \Pr\{Y \text{ is } B|X \text{ is } A\} \geq 1\,, \tag{1.3}$$

with the understanding that the probabilities in question may be fuzzy numbers.

The above example points to two essential shortcomings of classical probability theory as a tool for dealing with uncertainty in expert systems. First, it makes no provision for fuzzy events; and second, it does not provide a mechanism for computing with fuzzy probabilities. Thus the problem with the use of probability theory as a basis for the management of uncertainty in expert systems stems not from any flaws in its axiomatic foundations but from its lack of expressive power in representing the meaning of facts and rules which contain fuzzy predicates and/or fuzzy probabilities (or, equivalently, fuzzy quantifiers). Thus, viewed as a language, probability theory does not offer an appropriate framework for inference from propositions of the general form X is A, if X is A then Y is B, X is A is λ, if X is A then Y is B is λ, and QA's are B's, where A and B are fuzzy predicates (e.g., *small, tall*), λ is a fuzzy probability (e.g., *likely, very unlikely*), and Q is a fuzzy quantifier (e.g., *most, many*).

A view articulated in Ref. 52 is that the expressiveness of probability theory and predicate logic may be enhanced through the employment of fuzzy logic — a logical system which allows the use of fuzzy predicates and fuzzy quantifiers and thus subsumes both probability theory and predicate logic. In particular, through the use of fuzzy syllogisms, fuzzy logic provides an effective framework for the formulation of rules of construction of evidence in expert systems. In what follows, we shall present a summary of the basic concepts in fuzzy logic based on Refs. 50, 52, 53 and outline the rules of inference which are needed for dealing with uncertain facts and rules in the knowledge base of an expert system.

2. Fuzzy Logic

Like most logical systems, fuzzy logic has two components: (1) a *representational component* which deals with the representation of meaning of predicates, connectives, predicate modifiers and propositions; and (2) an *inferential component*, which, as its name implies, is concerned with the deduction of a conclusion from a set of premises. The representational component is based on PRUF[46] and test-score semantics,[51] while the inferential component involves, for the most part, the manipulation of possibility distributions and fuzzy quantifiers.

More specifically, the first step in inference in fuzzy logic involves a translation of the premises $p_1, \ldots, p_n$ into PRUF — a meaning representation language which is based on the concept of a possibility distribution.[46,49] Thus, if p is a proposition and P is its translation into PRUF,

$$p \rightarrow P, \tag{2.1}$$

then P may be viewed as a procedure which acts on a collection of relations in a database — or, equivalently, a possible world — and returns a possibility distribution which represents the information conveyed by p.

If X is a variable taking values in U, then the *possibility distribution* of X, denoted by Π_X, is the fuzzy set of possible values of X. The membership function of Π_X is referred to as the *possibility distribution function* and is defined by

$$\Pi_X(u) = \text{Poss}\{X = u\} \tag{2.2}$$

where the right-hand member of (2.2) should be read as: "The possibility that X can take u as a value," with the understanding that $0 \leq \Pi_X(u) \leq 1$. More generally, if X is an n-ary variable

$$X = (X_1, \ldots, X_n) \tag{2.3}$$

where X_i takes values in U_i, $i = 1, \ldots, n$, then $\Pi_{(X_1,\ldots,X_n)}$ is a fuzzy subset of the cartesian product $U \doteq U_1 \times \cdots \times U_n$, and the projection of $\Pi_{(X_1,\ldots,X_n)}$ on $U_{(s)} \doteq U_{i_1} \times \cdots \times U_{i_k}$ is defined by the possibility distribution function

$$\begin{aligned} &{}_{(X_{i_1}\ldots X_{i_k})}\Pi_{(X_1,\ldots,X_n)}(u_{i_1}, \ldots, u_{i_k}) \\ &= \sup_{u_{j_1},\ldots,u_{j_\ell}} \Pi_{(X_1,\ldots,X_n)}(u_1 \ldots, u_n) \end{aligned} \tag{2.4}$$

where $X_{(s)} \doteq (X_{i_1}, \ldots, X_{i_k})$ is a subvariable of $X \doteq (X_1, \ldots, X_n)$ and $X_{(s')} \doteq (X_{j_1}, \ldots, X_{j_\ell})$ is the complementary subvariable, i.e., $\{j_1, \ldots, j_\ell\} = \{1, \ldots, n\} - \{i_1, \ldots, i_k\}$.

An n-ary possibility distribution is *particularized* by forming the conjunction of the proposition "X is F" and "$X_{(s)}$ is G," where $X_{(s)}$ is a subvariable of X and F and G are fuzzy subsets of U. Thus,

$$\Pi_X[\Pi_{X_{(s)}} = G] \doteq F \cap \bar{G} \tag{2.5}$$

where the right-hand member denotes the intersection of F with the cylindrical extension of G, i.e., a cylindrical fuzzy set defined by

$$\mu_{\bar{G}}(u_1, \ldots, u_n) = \mu_G(u_{i_1}, \ldots, u_{i_k}), \quad (u_1, \ldots, u_n) \in U_1 \times \cdots \times U_n \tag{2.6}$$

where μ_G denotes the membership function of G.

There are many cases in which the operations of particularization and projection are combined. In such cases it is convenient to use the simplified notation

$$_{(X_{i_1}\cdots X_{i_k})}\Pi[\Pi_{X_{(s)}} = G] \tag{2.7}$$

to indicate that the particularized possibility distribution (or relation) $\Pi[\Pi_{X_{(s)}} = G]$ is projected on $U_{i_1} \times \cdots \times U_{i_k}$. For example,

$$_{(X_1,X_3)}\Pi[\Pi_{(X_s,X_4)} = G] \tag{2.8}$$

would represent the projection of $\Pi[\Pi_{(X_3,X_4)} = G]$ on $U_1 \times U_3$. Informally, (2.7) may be interpreted as: Constrain the $X_{(s)}$ by $\Pi_{X_{(s)}} = G$ and read out the X_i. In particular, if the value of $X(s)$ — rather than its possibility distribution — is set equal to G, then (2.7) becomes

$$_{(X_{i_1},\ldots,X_{i_k})}\Pi[X_{(s)} = G]\,. \tag{2.9}$$

Now let p be a proposition of the form

$$p \doteq N \text{ is } F \tag{2.10}$$

where N is the name of an object, a variable or a proposition, and F is a fuzzy subset of a universe of discourse U. For example:

$p \doteq$ Sheila is very intelligent

$q \doteq X$ is small

$r \doteq (X$ is small) is more or less true.

A translation of p may be *focused* or *unfocused.* By a focused translation in PRUF is meant a translation of the form

$$p \to \Pi_{(X_1,\ldots,X_n)} = F \tag{2.11}$$

where the X_i are variables which are explicit or implicit in N and F is a fuzzy subset of $U_1 \times \cdots \times U_n$. A translation of this form serves to (a) identify the variables in N whose possibility distribution is determined by p, and (b) specify the possibility distribution in question. To reflect this aspect of the translation process, the right-hand member of (2.11) is referred to as the *possibility assignment equation*, with F representing the possibility distribution induced by p.

As a simple illustration of (2.11), consider the proposition

$$p \doteq \text{Mary has blue eyes.} \tag{2.12}$$

In this case, (2.11) becomes

$$\text{Mary has blue eyes} \to \Pi_{\text{Color(Eyes(Mary))}} = BLUE \tag{2.13}$$

in which $X \doteq$ Color(Eyes(Mary)) and BLUE, the denotation of blue, is the fuzzy subset of colors which are perceived as blue.

Turning to the concept of an unfocused translation, let $\mathcal{D} = \{D\}$ denote a collection of databases, with D representing a generic element of $\mathcal{D}$. For the purposes of our analysis, D will be assumed to consist of a collection of possibly time-varying relations. If R is a constituent relation in D, then by the *frame* of R is meant the name of R together with the names of its columns (i.e., attributes). For example, if a constituent of D is a relation labeled POPULATION whose tableau is comprised of columns labeled Name and Height, then the frame of POPULATION is represented as POPULATION[Name, Height].

In relation to $\mathcal{D}$, the unfocused translation of p can assume one of two equivalent forms[a]:

(a) $p \to$ a procedure which yields for each D in $\mathcal{D}$ the possibility of D given p, i.e., $\text{Poss}\{D|p\}$

(b) $p \to$ a procedure which yields for each D in $\mathcal{D}$ the truth-value of p relative to D, i.e., $\text{Tr}\{p|D\}$

The equivalence of (a) and (b) is a consequence of the way in which the concept of truth is defined in fuzzy logic.[53] Thus, it can readily be shown that, under mildly restrictive assumptions on D, we have

$$\text{Tr}\{p|D\} = \text{Poss}\{D|p\} \tag{2.14}$$

which implies the equivalence of (a) and (b). Furthermore, it should be noted that (2.11) is a special case of (a), so that the concept of a focused translation is subsumed by that of an unfocused translation. In essence, our motivation for introducing the concept of a focused translation is to provide a mechanism for enhancing the *explanatory effectiveness* of a translation. In the case of a focused translation, this is accomplished by focusing on those and only those variables in D whose possibility distribution is constrained by the meaning of p.

If Π^p and Π^q are the possibility distributions induced by p and q, respectively, then p and q are semantically equivalent if and only if $\Pi^p = \Pi^q$.[b]
In symbols

$$p \leftrightarrow q \text{ iff } \Pi^p = \Pi^q \,. \tag{2.15}$$

For example, it can readily be shown that

$$X \text{ is small is true} \leftrightarrow X \text{ is not small is false}$$

provided the linguistic truth-value *false* is taken to be the antonym of *true*, i.e.,

$$\mu_{\text{false}}(v) = \mu_{\text{true}}(1-v)\,, \quad 0 \le v \le 1 \tag{2.16}$$

[a]It should be noted that (a) and (b) are in the spirit of possible-world semantics and truth-conditional semantics, respectively. In their conventional form, however, these semantics have no provision for fuzzy propositions and hence are not suitable for use in fuzzy logic.

[b]To be more precise, we have to differentiate between the concepts of semantic equivalence and strong semantic equivalence. The latter concept reduces to that of semantic equivalence in predicate logic when p and q are nonfuzzy propositions.

where μ_{false} and μ_{true} are the membership functions of *false* and *true*, respectively. More generally, q is *semantically entailed* by p if and only if $\Pi^p \subset \Pi^q$. In symbols

$$p \mapsto q \text{ iff } \Pi^p \subset \Pi^q\,. \tag{2.17}$$

For example,

$$X \text{ is very small} \mapsto X \text{ is small} \tag{2.18}$$

if *very* is defined by

$$\mu_{\text{very small}}(u) = [\mu_{\text{small}}(u)]^2\,, \quad u \in U\,. \tag{2.19}$$

We shall make use of the concept of semantic entailment is Sec. 3.

An essential component of a fuzzy logic is the set of translation rules, which may be categorized into four basic types: Type I — rules pertaining to modification; Type II — rules pertaining to composition; Type III — rules pertaining to quantification; and Type IV — rules pertaining to qualification. For our purposes, it will suffice to state the rules of Type II, which are:

$$\text{If } X \text{ is } F \to \Pi_X = F \text{ and } Y \text{ is } G \to \Pi_Y = G \tag{2.20}$$

where F and G are fuzzy subsets of U and V, respectively, then

$$\text{(a) } X \text{ is } F \text{ and } Y \text{ is } G \to \Pi_{(X,Y)} = F \times G \tag{2.21}$$

where

$$\mu_{F\times G}(u,v) = \mu_F(u) \wedge \mu_G(v)\,. \tag{2.22}$$

$$\text{(b) } X \text{ is } F \text{ or } Y \text{ is } G \to \Pi_{(X,Y)} = \bar{F} \cup \bar{G} \tag{2.23}$$

where

$$\bar{F} \doteq F \times V\,, \quad \bar{G} \doteq U \times G \tag{2.24}$$

and

$$\mu_{\bar{F}\cup\bar{G}}(u,v) = \mu_F(u) \vee \mu_G(v)\,. \tag{2.25}$$

$$\text{(c) If } X \text{ is } F \text{ then } Y \text{ is } G \to \Pi_{(Y|X)} = \bar{F}' \oplus \bar{G} \tag{2.26}$$

where $\Pi_{(Y|X)}$ denotes the conditional possibility distribution of Y given X, and the bounded sum $\oplus$ is defined by

$$\mu_{\bar{F}'\oplus\bar{G}}(u,v) = 1 \wedge [1 - \mu_F(u) + \mu_G(v)]\,. \tag{2.27}$$

It should be noted that the compositional rules in fuzzy logic are defined in a way that makes them consistent with the valuation rules in Lukasiewicz's L_{Aleph1} logic. In particular, if $X = Y$ then it follows at once from (2.27) that the proposition

$$r \doteq \text{If } X \text{ is } F \text{ then } X \text{ is } G \tag{2.29}$$

conveys no information concerning X (i.e., is a tautology) if and only if $F \subset G$. This conclusion serves as a basis for the entailment principle which is stated in the following section.

3. Rules of Inference

The rules of inference in fuzzy logic are semantic rather than syntactic in nature and are based, in the main, on two principles: (a) the entailment principle, and (b) the extension principle.

The entailment principle, which is based in turn on (2.28), may be expressed in a schematic form as

$$\frac{p \rightarrow \Pi_X^p = F}{q \leftarrow \Pi_X^q = G\colon\ F \subset G} \tag{3.1}$$

which means that if the possibility distribution induced by p is contained in that induced by q, then q may be inferred from p. (The symbol $\leftarrow$ stands for "retranslation.") In other words, from p we can infer any proposition which is semantically equivalent to p or, more generally, semantically entailed by p.

To state the extension principle, let f be a function from U or V and let F be a finite fuzzy subset of U expressed as

$$F = \mu_1/u_1 + \cdots + \mu_n/u_n\,. \tag{3.2}$$

Then, the extension of f to the set of fuzzy subsets of U is defined by[c]

$$\begin{aligned} f(F) &= f\,(\mu_1/u_1 + \cdots + \mu_n/u_n) \\ &= \mu_1/f(u_1) + \cdots + \mu_n/f(u_n)\,. \end{aligned} \tag{3.3}$$

More generally, if the support of F is a continuum, i.e.,

$$F = \int_U \mu_F(u)/u \tag{3.4}$$

then

$$f(F) = \int_U \mu_F(u)/f(u)\,. \tag{3.5}$$

Furthermore, if U is a cartesian product of $U_1, \ldots, U_n$ and f is a mapping from $U_1 \times \cdots \times U_n$ to V, then

$$f(F) = \int_U \mu_F(u_1, \ldots, u_n)/f(u_1, \ldots, u_n)\,. \tag{3.6}$$

In particular, if we have only partial information about μ_F, e.g., the knowledge of its projections on $U_1, \ldots, U_n$, then

[c] The notation $F = \mu_1/u_1 + \cdots + \mu_n/u_n$ signifies that F is a collection of fuzzy singletons μ_i/u_i, $i = 1, \ldots, n$, with μ_i representing the grade of membership of u_i in F. More generally, F may be expressed as $F = \Sigma_i\, \mu_i/u_i$ or $F = \int_U \mu_F(u)/u$.

$$f(F) = \int_U \mu_1(u_1) \wedge \cdots \wedge \mu_n(u_n) / f(u_1, \ldots, u_n) \tag{3.7}$$

where μ_i, $i = 1, \ldots, n$, is the membership function of the projection of F on U_i.

A more explicit representation of $f(F)$ which is equivalent to (3.7) is the following. ($\mu \doteq$ membership function of $f(F)$.)

$$f(F) = \int_V \mu(v)/v \tag{3.8}$$

where

$$\mu(v) \doteq \max_{u_1,\ldots,u_n} \mu_1(u_1) \wedge \cdots \wedge \mu_n(u_n) \tag{3.9}$$

subject to the constraint

$$v = f(u_1, \ldots, u_n) .$$

In this form, the extension principle serves to reduce an inference process to the determination of the solution of a variational problem in nonlinear programming.

Among the rules of inference which are based on the entailment principle are the following.

Projection rule. Stated in a schematic form, this rule may be expressed as

$$\frac{p \rightarrow \Pi^p_{(X_1,\ldots,X_n)} = F}{q \leftarrow \Pi^q_{(X_{i_1},\ldots,X_{i_k})} = {}_{(X_{i_1},\ldots,X_{i_k})}F} \tag{3.10}$$

where ${}_{(X_{i_1},\ldots,X_{i_k})}F$ denotes the projection of F on $U_{i_1} \times \cdots \times U_{i_k}$ (see (2.4)). In other words, (3.10) asserts that if p induces the possibility distribution $\Pi^p_{(X_1,\ldots,X_n)}$, then from p we can infer any proposition q which induces the projection of Π^p on $U_{i_1} \times \cdots \times U_{i_k}$.

As a simple illustration of (3.10), consider the proposition

$$p \doteq \text{John is big}$$

and assume that BIG, the denotation of big, is a binary fuzzy relation which may be represented as the cartesian product of the unary fuzzy relations TALL and FAT. Then

$$\text{TALL} = {}_{\text{Height}}\text{BIG}$$

and hence we can assert that

$$\frac{\text{John is big}}{\text{John is tall}}$$

Conjunction rule. Let X, Y and Z take values in U, V and W, respectively; let F and G be fuzzy subsets of $U \times V$ and $V \times W$; and let $\bar{F}$ and $\bar{G}$ be the cylindrical extensions of F and G in $U \times V \times W$. Thus,

$$\bar{F} = F \times W$$

and

$$\bar{G} = U \times G\,.$$

The conjunction rule is defined by the following scheme:

$$\begin{array}{l} p \rightarrow \Pi^{p}_{(X,Y)} = F \\ q \rightarrow \Pi^{q}_{(Y,Z)} = G \\ \hline r \leftarrow \Pi_{(X,Y,Z)} = \bar{F} \cap \bar{G}\,. \end{array} \tag{3.11}$$

In particular, in the special case where

$$\begin{array}{l} p \rightarrow \Pi^{p}_{X} = F \\ q \rightarrow \Pi^{q}_{X} = G \end{array} \tag{3.12}$$

(3.11) implies that from p and q we can infer r, where

$$\Pi^{r}_{X} = F \cap G\,.$$

Compositional rule. On combining the projection and conjunction rules, we obtain the *compositional rule of inference* (3.13) which includes the classical *modus ponens* as a special case.

More specifically, on applying the projection rule to (3.11), we obtain the following inference scheme

$$\begin{array}{l} p \rightarrow \Pi^{p}_{(X,Y)} = F \\ q \rightarrow \Pi^{q}_{(Y,Z)} = G \\ \hline r \leftarrow \Pi^{r}_{(X,Z)} = F \circ G \end{array} \tag{3.13}$$

where the composition of F and G is defined by

$$\mu_{F \circ G}(u, w) = \sup_{v} [\mu_F(u, v) \wedge \mu_G(v, w)]\,. \tag{3.14}$$

In particular, if p is a proposition of the form "X is F" and q is a proposition of the form "If X is G then Y is H," then (3.13) becomes

$$\begin{array}{l} p \rightarrow \Pi_{X} = F \\ q \rightarrow \Pi_{(Y|X)} = \bar{G}' \oplus \bar{H} \\ \hline r \leftarrow \Pi_{Y} = F \circ (\bar{G}' \oplus \bar{H}) \end{array} \tag{3.15}$$

The rule expressed by (3.15) may be viewed as a generalized form of *modus ponens* which reduces to the classical *modus ponens* when $F = G$ and F, G, H are nonfuzzy sets.

Semantic equivalence. An immediate consequence of the entailment principle is that from p we can infer any proposition q which is semantically equivalent to p.

An important special case of this rule is embodied in the *truth-qualification principle* which may be stated as follows.

Let τ be a linguistic truth-value which is characterized by its membership function μ_τ and assume that

$$p \doteq X \text{ is } F\,.$$

Then

$$X \text{ is } F \leftrightarrow X \text{ is } G \text{ is } \tau \tag{3.16}$$

where the membership functions of F, G and τ are related by

$$\mu_F(u) = \mu_\tau[\mu_G(u)]\,. \tag{3.17}$$

Thus, from the proposition $q \doteq X$ is G is τ we can infer $p \doteq X$ is F, and vice-versa, with the understanding that μ_F is given by the composition of μ_τ and μ_G.

As an illustration, consider the proposition

$$p \doteq \text{Lynn is young is very true}$$

in which

$$\mu_{\mathbf{young}}(u) = \left[1 + \left(\frac{u}{20}\right)^2\right]^{-1}, \quad u \in [0, 100]$$

and

$$\mu_{\mathbf{true}}(v) = v^2\,, \quad v \in [0,1]\,.$$

Then, we can infer from p that

$$\pi_{\mathbf{Age(Lynn)}}(u) = \left[1 + \left(\frac{u}{20}\right)^2\right]^{-4}$$

which upon retranslation may be expressed as

$$q \doteq \text{Lynn is very very young}\,.$$

Transformational rule. This rule is implied by the extension principle and may be expressed in a schematic form as

$$\begin{array}{l} p \doteq X \text{ is } F \\ q \doteq Y \text{ is } f(X) \\ \hline r \doteq Y \text{ is } f(F) \end{array} \tag{3.18}$$

where F is a fuzzy subset of U, f is a mapping from U to V, and $f(F)$ is a fuzzy subset of V defined by (3.8).

As a simple illustration of (3.18), assume that X is a fuzzy number which is expressed as "approximately 5" or, more explicitly,

$$X = 0.2/2 + 0.5/3 + 0.8/4 + 1/5 + 0.8/6 + 0.6/7 + 0.2/8$$

and $Y = X^2$. Then

$$Y = 0.2/4 + 0.5/9 + 0.8/16 + 1/25 + 0.8/36 + 0.6/49 + 0.2/64\,.$$

4. Syllogistic Reasoning

In addition to the rules described in the preceding section, there is a class of rules of inference in fuzzy logic which are of particular relevance to the combination of evidence in expert systems. The rules in question may be viewed as fuzzy syllogisms[54] in which the premises are propositions of the form QA's are B's, where A and B are fuzzy predicates and Q is a fuzzy quantifier.

In its generic form, a fuzzy syllogism may be expressed as the inference schema

$$\begin{array}{l} Q_1A\text{'s are }B\text{'s} \\ Q_2C\text{'s are }D\text{'s} \\ \hline Q_3E\text{'s are }F\text{'s} \end{array} \tag{4.1}$$

in which A, B, C, D, E and F are interrelated fuzzy predicates and Q_1, Q_2 and Q_3 are fuzzy quantifiers.

The interrelations between A, B, C, D, E and F provide a basis for a classification of fuzzy syllogisms. The more important of these syllogisms are the following. ($\wedge \doteq$ conjunction, $\vee \doteq$ disjunction).

(a) Intersection/product syllogism: $C = A \wedge B$, $E = A$, $F = C \wedge D$
(b) Chaining syllogism: $C = B$, $E = A$, $F = D$
(c) Consequent conjunction syllogism: $A = C = E$, $F = B \wedge D$
(d) Consequent disjunction syllogism: $A = C = E$, $F = B \vee D$
(e) Antecedent conjunction syllogism: $B = D = F$, $E = A \wedge C$
(f) Antecedent disjunction syllogism: $B = D = F$, $E = A \vee C$.

In the context of expert systems, these and related syllogisms provide a set of inference rules for combining evidence through conjunction, disjunction and chaining.[52]

One of the basic problems in fuzzy syllogistic reasoning is the following: Given A, B, C, D, E and F, find the maximally specific (i.e., most restrictive) fuzzy quantifier Q_3 such that the proposition Q_3E's are F's is entailed by the premises. In the case of (a), (b) and (c), this leads to the following syllogisms.

Intersection/product syllogism

$$\begin{array}{l} Q_1\ A\text{'s are }B\text{'s} \\ Q_2(A\text{ and }B)\text{'s are }C\text{'s} \\ \hline (Q_1 \otimes Q_2)\ A\text{'s are }(B\text{ and }C)\text{'s} \end{array} \tag{4.2}$$

where $\otimes$ denotes the product in fuzzy arithmetic.[25] It should be noted that (4.2) may be viewed as an analog of the basic probabilistic identity $p(B, C/A) = p(B/A)p(C/A, B)$.

A concrete example of the intersection/product syllogism is the following:

$$\begin{array}{l} \text{most students are young} \\ \text{most young students are single} \\ \hline \text{most}^2 \text{ students are young and single}, \end{array} \tag{4.3}$$

where *most*^{2} denotes the product of the fuzzy quantifier *most* with itself.

Chaining syllogism

$$\begin{array}{l} Q_1\ A\text{'s are } B\text{'s} \\ Q_2\ B\text{'s are } C\text{'s} \\ \hline (Q_1 \otimes Q_2)\ A\text{'s are } C\text{'s}. \end{array} \tag{4.4}$$

This syllogism may be viewed as a special case of the intersection/product syllogism. It results when $B \subset A$ and Q_1 and Q_2 are monotone increasing, i.e., $\geq Q_1 = Q_1$, and $\leq Q_2 = Q_2$, where $\geq Q_1$ should be read as *at least* Q_1, and likewise for Q_2. A simple example of the chaining syllogism is the following:

$$\begin{array}{l} \text{most students are undergraduates} \\ \text{most undergraduates are single} \\ \hline \text{most}^2 \text{ students are single}, \end{array}$$

Note that *undergraduates* $\subset$ *students* and that in the conclusion $F =$ *single*, rather than *young and single*, as in (4.3).

Consequent conjunction syllogism. The consequent conjunction syllogism is an example of a basic syllogism which is not a derivative of the intersection/product syllogism. Its statement may be expressed as follows:

$$\begin{array}{l} Q_1\ A\text{'s are } B\text{'s} \\ Q_2\ A\text{'s are } C\text{'s} \\ \hline Q\ A\text{'s are } (B \text{ and } C)\text{'s}, \end{array} \tag{4.5}$$

where Q is a fuzzy quantifier which is defined by the inequalities

$$0 \circledvee (Q_1 \oplus Q_2 \ominus 1) \leq Q \leq Q_1 \circledwedge Q_2 \tag{4.6}$$

in which $\circledvee$, $\circledwedge$, $\oplus$ and $\ominus$ are the operations of $\vee$ (max), $\wedge$ (min), $+$ and $-$ in fuzzy arithmetic.

An illustration of (4.5) is provided by the example

$$\begin{array}{l} \text{most students are young} \\ \text{most students are single} \\ \hline Q \text{ students are single and young}, \end{array}$$

where

$$2\text{most} \ominus 1 \leq Q \leq \text{most}\,. \tag{4.7}$$

This expression for Q follows from (4.6) by noting that

$$\text{most} \oslash \text{most} = \text{most}$$

and

$$0 \oslash (2\text{most} \ominus 1) = 2\text{most} \ominus 1\,.$$

The three basic syllogisms described above are representative of a class of rules of inference in fuzzy logic in which fuzzy quantifiers play a role analogous to that of probabilities in probabilistic reasoning. Through the use of such rules, probabilistic reasoning becomes a part of fuzzy logic. In this way, it becomes possible to employ a single conceptional framework for the management of uncertainty in expert systems in which both probability theory and possibility theory play central roles.

References and Related Publications

1. K. P. Adlassnig, "A survey of medical diagnosis and fuzzy subsets," in *Approximate Reasoning in Decision Analysis* eds. M. M. Gupta and E. Sanchez (North-Holland, Amsterdam, 1982), pp. 203–217.
2. J. F. Baldwin, "A new approach to approximate reasoning using a fuzzy logic," *Fuzzy Sets and Systems* **2** (1979), pp. 302–325.
3. W. Bandler, "Representation and manipulation of knowledge in fuzzy expert systems," *Proc. Workshop on Fuzzy Sets and Knowledge-Based Systems*, Queen Mary College, University of London (1983).
4. A. Barr and E. W. Feigenbaum, *The Handbook of Artificial Intelligence*, Vols. 1, 2 and 3 (Kauffmann, Los Altos, 1982).
5. J. Barwise and R. Cooper, "Generalized quantifiers and natural language," *Linguistics and Philosophy* **4** (1981), pp. 159–219.
6. R. E. Bellman and L. A. Zadeh, "Local and fuzzy logics," in *Modern Uses of Multiple-Valued Logic*, ed. G. Epstein (Reidel, Dordrecht, 1977), pp. 103–165.
7. M. Ben-Bassat *et al.*, "Pattern-based interactive diagnosis of multiple disorders: The MEDAS system," *IEEE Trans. Pattern Anal. Machine Intell.* (1980), pp. 148–160.
8. J. Bezdek, *Pattern Recognition with Fuzzy Objective Function Algorithms* (Plenum Press, New York, 1981).
9. P. P. Bonissone and R. M. Tong (eds.), *Special Issue on Reasoning with Uncertainty in Expert Systems, Int. J. Man-Machine Studies* **22** (1985).
10. R. J. Brachman and B. C. Smith, *Special Issue on Knowledge Representation, SIG ART* **70** (1980).
11. B. B. Buchanan and E. H. Shortliffe, *Rule-Based Expert Systems: The MYCIN Experiment of the Standard Heuristic Programming Project* (Addison-Wesley, Reading, MA, 1984).
12. P. Cheeseman and J. Lemmer (eds.), *Proceedings of Workshop on Certainty and Probability in Artificial Intelligence*, UCLA, Los Angeles (1985).
13. M. S. Cohen, D. A. Schum, A. N. S. Freeling and J. O. Chinnis, "On the art and science of hedging a conclusion: alternative theories of uncertainty in intelligence analysis," Tech. Rep. 84-6, Decision Science Consortium, Falls Church, VA, 1984.
14. R. Davis and D. B. Lenat, *Knowledge-Based Systems in Artificial Intelligence* (McGraw-Hill, New York, 1982).

15. A. DeLuca and S. Termini, "A definition of non-probabilistic entropy in the setting of fuzzy sets theory," *Inform. and Control* **20** (1972), pp. 301–312.
16. D. Dubois and H. Prade, *Fuzzy Sets and Systems: Theory and Applications* (Academic Press, New York, 1980).
17. D. Dubois and H. Prade, "On several representations of an uncertain body of evidence," in *Fuzzy Information and Decision Processes*, eds. M. M. Gupta and E. Sanchez (North-Holland, Amsterdam, 1982), pp. 167–181.
18. R. O. Duda, P. E. Hart, K. Konolige, and R. Reboh, "A computer-based consultant for mineral exploration," Final Tech. Report, SRI International, Menlo Park, CA (1979).
19. E. A. Feigenbaum, "The art of artificial intelligence: Themes and case studies in knowledge engineering," *Proc. IJCAI5* (1977).
20. B. R. Gaines, "Logical foundations for database systems," *Int. J. Man-Machine Studies* **11** (1979), pp. 481–500.
21. T. Garvey and J. Lowrance, "Evidential reasoning: implementation for multisensor integration," SRI International Tech. Rep. 307, Menlo Park, CA (1983).
22. J. A. Goguen, "The logic of inexact concepts," *Synthese* **19** (1959), pp. 325–373.
23. D. Heckerman, "Probabilistic interpretations for MYCIN's certainty factors," *Proc. Workshop on Certainty and Probability in Artificial Intelligence*, UCLA, Los Angeles (1985), pp. 9–20.
24. M. Ishizuka, K. S. Fu and J. T. P. Yao, "A rule-based inference with fuzzy set for structural damage assessment," in *Fuzzy Information and Decision Processes*, eds. M. Gupta and E. Sanchez (North-Holland, Amsterdam, 1982).
25. A. Kaufmann and M. M. Gupta, *Introduction to Fuzzy Arithmetic* (Van Nostrand Reinhold, New York, 1985).
26. C. A. Kulikowski, "AI methods and systems for medical consultation," *IEEE Trans. Pattern Anal. Machine Intell.* (1980), pp. 464–476.
27. E. H. Mamdani and B. R. Gaines, *Fuzzy Reasoning and its Applications* (Academic Press, London, 1981).
28. J. McCarthy, "Circumscription: A non-monotonic inference rule," *Artificial Intelligence* **13** (1980), pp. 27–40.
29. R. Michalski, J. G. Carbonell and T. M. Mitchell, *Machine Learning* (Tioga Press, Palo Alto, 1983).
30. M. Mizumoto, S. Fukami and K. Tanaka, "Fuzzy reasoning methods by Zadeh and Mamdani, and improved methods," *Proc. Third Workshop on Fuzzy Reasoning*, Queen Mary College, London (1979).
31. D. Nau, "Expert computer systems," *IEEE Computer* **16** (1983), pp. 63–85.
32. C. V. Negoita, *Expert Systems and Fuzzy Systems* (The Benjamin/Cummings Publishing Co., Menlo Park, 1985).
33. N. Nilsson, "Probabilistic Logic," SRI Tech. Note 321, Menlo Park, CA (1984).
34. A. I. Orlov, *Problems of Optimization and Fuzzy Variables* (Znaniye, Moscow, 1980).
35. H. Prade, "Lipski's approach to incomplete information data bases restated and generalized in the setting of Zadeh's possibility theory," *Information Systems* **9** (1984), pp. 27–42.
36. R. Reiter and G. Criscuolo, "Some representational issues in default reasoning," *Computers and Mathematics* **9** (1983), pp. 15–28.
37. N. Rescher, *Plausible Reasoning* (Van Gorcum, Amsterdam, 1976).
38. E. Sanchez, "Medical diagnosis and composite fuzzy relations," in *Advances in Fuzzy Set Theory and Applications*, eds. M. M. Gupta, R. K. Ragade and R. Yager (North-Holland, Amsterdam, 1979), pp. 437–444.

39. G. Shafer, *A Mathematical Theory of Evidence* (Princeton University Press, Princeton, 1976).
40. E. H. Shortliffe and B. Buchanan, "A model of inexact reasoning in medicine," *Mathematical Biosciences* **23** (1975), pp. 351–379.
41. P. Szolovits and S. G. Pauker, "Categorical and probabilistic reasoning in medical diagnosis," *Artificial Intelligence* **11** (1978), pp. 115–144.
42. L. Wesley, J. Lowrance and T. Garvey, "Reasoning about control: an evidential approach," SRI International Tech. Rep. 324, Menlo Park, CA (1984).
43. R. R. Yager, "Quantified propositions in a linguistic logic," in *Proc. 2nd Int. Seminar on Fuzzy Set Theory*, ed. E. P. Klement, Johannes Kepler University, Linz, Austria (1980).
44. L. A. Zadeh, "Outline of a new approach to the analysis of complex systems and decision processes," *IEEE Trans. Systems Man Cybernet.* **3** (1973), pp. 28–44.
45. L. A. Zadeh, "The concept of a linguistic variable and its application to approximate reasoning," *Inform. Sci.* **8** (1975), pp. 199–249, 301–357; **9**, pp. 43–80.
46. L. A. Zadeh, "PRUF — a meaning representation language for natural languages," *Internat. J. Man-Machine Studies* **10** (1978), pp. 395–460.
47. L. A. Zadeh, "Fuzzy sets and information granularity," in *Advances in Fuzzy Set Theory and Applications*, eds. M. Gupta, R. Ragade and R. Yager (North-Holland, Amsterdam, 1979), pp. 3–18.
48. L. A. Zadeh, "A theory of approximate reasoning," Electronics Research Laboratory Memorandum M77/58, University of California, Berkeley (1977); also in *Machine Intelligence* **9**, eds. J. E. Hayes, D. Michie and L. I. Kulich (Wiley, New York, 1979), pp. 149–194.
49. L. A. Zadeh, "Fuzzy sets as a basis for a theory of possibility," *Fuzzy Sets and Systems* **1** (1978), pp. 3–28.
50. L. A. Zadeh, "Inference in fuzzy logic," *Proc. 1980 ISMUL*, Northwestern University, Evanston (1980).
51. L. A. Zadeh, "Test-score semantics for natural languages and meaning-representation via PRUF," Tech. Note 247, AI Center, SRI International, Menlo Park, CA (1981); also in *Empirical Semantics*, eds. B. B. Rieger (Brockmeyer, Bochem, 1981), pp. 281–349.
52. L. A. Zadeh, "A computational approach to fuzzy quantifiers in natural languages," *Computers and Mathematics* **9** (1983), pp. 149–184.
53. L. A. Zadeh, "Formalization of common sense reasoning based on fuzzy logic," *Proc. AIAA*, long Beach (1985).
54. L. A. Zadeh, "Syllogistic reasoning in fuzzy logic and its application to usuality and reasoning with dispositions," *IEEE Trans. on Systems, Man and Cybernetics* (1985).
55. M. Zemankova-Leech and A. Kandel, "Fuzzy Relational Databases — A Key to Expert Systems," Interdisciplinary Systems Research, Verlag TUV Rhineland, Cologne (1984).
56. A. Zimmer, "Some experiments concerning the fuzzy meaning of logical quantifiers," in *General Surveys of Systems Methodology*, ed. L. Troncoli (Society for General Systems Research, Louisville, 1982), pp. 435–441.
57. H.-J. Zimmermann and P. Zysno, "Latent connectives in human decision making," *Fuzzy Sets and Systems* **4** (1980), pp. 37–52.

A Simple View of the Dempster-Shafer Theory of Evidence and its Implication for the Rule of Combination

Lotfi A. Zadeh

Computer Science Division, University of California, Berkeley, California 94720

The emergence of expert systems as one of the major areas of activity within AI has resulted in a rapid growth of interest within the AI community in issues relating to the management of uncertainty and evidential reasoning. During the past two years, in particular, the Dempster-Shafer theory of evidence has attracted considerable attention as a promising method of dealing with some of the basic problems arising in combination of evidence and data fusion. To develop an adequate understanding of this theory requires considerable effort and a good background in probability theory. There is, however, a simple way of approaching the Dempster-Shafer theory that only requires a minimal familiarity with relational models of data. For someone with a background in AI or database management, this approach has the advantage of relating in a natural way to the familiar framework of AI and databases. Furthermore, it clarifies some of the controversial issues in the Dempster-Shafer theory and points to ways in which it can be extended and made useful in AI-oriented applications.[1]

The Basic Idea

The basic idea underlying the approach in question is that in the context of relational databases the Dempster-Shafer theory can be viewed as an instance of inference from second-order relations, that is, relations in which the entries are first-order relations.[2] To clarify this point, let us first consider a standard example of retrieval from a first-order relation, such as the relation EMPLOYEE1 (or EMP1, for short) that is tabulated in the following:

EMP1	Name	Age
	1	23
	2	28
	3	21
	4	27
	5	30

As a point of departure, consider a simple example of a range query: What fraction of employees are between 20 and 25 years old, inclusively? In other words,

Abstract

During the past two years, the Dempster-Shafer theory of evidence has attracted considerable attention within the AI community as a promising method of dealing with uncertainty in expert systems. As presented in the literature, the theory is hard to master. In a simple approach that is outlined in this paper, the Dempster-Shafer theory is viewed in the context of relational databases as the application of familiar retrieval techniques to second-order relations, that is, relations in which the data entries are relations in first normal form. The relational viewpoint clarifies some of the controversial issues in the Dempster-Shafer theory and facilitates its use in AI-oriented applications.

Research sponsored by the NASA Grant NCC-2-275, NESC Contract NOOO39-84-C-0243, and NSF Grant IST-8420416.

[1]The approach described in this article is derived from the application of the concepts of possibility and certainty (or necessity) to information granularity and the Dempster-Shafer model of uncertainty (Zadeh, 1979a, 1981). Extensive treatments of the concepts of possibility and necessity and their application to retrieval from incomplete databases can be found in recent papers by Dubois and Prade (1982, 1984).

[2]In the terminology of relational databases, a first-order relation is a relation which is in first normal form, that is, a relation whose elements are atomic rather than set-valued.

what fraction of employees satisfy the condition Age(i) ε Q, i = 1,. . . ,5, where Q is the query set $Q = [20,25]$. Counting those i's which satisfy the condition, the answer is 2/5.

Next, let us assume that the age of i is not known with certainty. For example, the age of 1 might be known to be in the interval [22,26]. In this case, the EMP1 relation becomes a second-order relation, for example:

EMP2	Name	Age
	1	[22,26]
	2	[20,22]
	3	[30,35]
	4	[20,22]
	5	[28,30]

Thus, in the case of 1, for example, the interval-valued attribute [22, 26] means that the age of 1 is known to be an element of the set $\{22, 23, 24, 25, 26\}$. In effect, this set is the set of possible values of the variable Age(1) or, equivalently, the *possibility distribution* of Age(1). Viewed in this perspective, the data entries in the column labeled Age are the possibility distributions of the values of Age. Similarly, the query set Q can also be regarded as a possibility distribution. In this sense, the information resident in the database and the queries about it can be described as *granular* (Zadeh, 1979a, 1981), with the data and the queries playing the roles of *granules.*

When the attribute values are not known with certainty, tests of set membership such as Age(i) ε Q cease to be applicable. In place of such tests then, it is natural to consider the *possibility* of Q given the possibility distribution of Age(i). For example, if Q = [20, 25] and Age(1) ε [22, 26], it is *possible* that Age(1) ε Q; in the case of 3, it is *not possible* that Age(3) ε Q; and in the case of 4, it is *certain (or necessary)* that Age(4) ε Q; more generally:

(a) *Age(i)εQ* is *possible*, if the possibility distribution of Age(i) intersects Q; that is, $D_i \cap Q \neq \Theta$ where D_i denotes the possibility distribution of Age(i) and Θ is the empty set.

(b) Q is *certain (or necessary)* if the possibility distribution of Age(i) is contained in Q, that is, $D_i \subset Q$.

(c) Q is *not possible* if the possibility distribution of Age(i) does not intersect Q or, equivalently, is contained in the complement of Q. This implies that—as in modal logic—possibility and necessity are related by

$$\text{necessity of } Q = \text{not (possibility of complement of } Q).$$

In the case of EMP2, the application of these tests to each row of the relation yields the following results for $Q = [20, 25]$:

EMP2	Name	Age	Test
	1	[22,26]	poss
	2	[20,22]	cert
	3	[30,35]	¬ poss
	4	[20,22]	cert
	5	[28,30]	¬ poss

(In the Test column, poss, cert, and ¬ poss, are abbreviations for possible, certain, and not possible, respectively.)

We are now in a position to construct a surrogate answer to the original question: What fraction of employees are between 20 and 25 years old, inclusively? Clearly, the answer will have to be in two parts, one relating to the certainty (or necessity) of Q and the other to its possibility; in symbols:

$$Resp(Q) = (N(Q); \Pi(Q)), \tag{1}$$

where Resp(Q), $N(Q)$, and $\Pi(Q)$ denote, respectively, the response to Q, the certainty (or necessity) of Q, and the possibility of Q. For the example under consideration, counting the test results in EMP2 leads to the response:

$$\text{Resp}[20, 25] = (N([20, 25]) = 2/5; \Pi([20, 25]) = 3/5),$$

with the understanding that *cert* counts also as *poss* because certainty implies possibility. Basically, a two-part response of this form, that is, *certainly α and possibly β*, where α and β are absolute or relative counts of objects with a specified property, is characteristic of responses based on incomplete information; for example, *certainly 10% and possibly 30%* in response to: How many households in Palo Alto own a VCR?

The first constituent in Resp(Q) is what is referred to as the measure of *belief* in the Dempster-Shafer theory, and the second constituent is the measure of *plausibility*. Seen in this perspective then, the measures of belief and plausibility in the Dempster-Shafer theory are, respectively, the certainty (or necessity) and possibility of the query set Q in the context of retrieval from a second-order relation in which the data entries are possibility distributions.

There are two important observations that can be made at this point. First, assume that EMP is a relation in which the values of Age are singletons chosen from the possibility distributions in EMP2. For such a relation, the response to Q would be a number, say, alpha. Then, it is evident that the values of $N(Q)$ and $\Pi(Q)$ obtained for Q (that is, 2/5 and 3/5) are the *lower* and *upper bounds*, respectively, on the values of alpha. This explains why in the Dempster-Shafer theory the measures of belief and plausibility are interpreted, respectively, as the *lower* and *upper probabilities* of Q.

Second, because the values of $N(Q)$ and $\Pi(Q)$ represent the result of averaging of test results in EMP2, what matters is the ***distribution*** of test results and not their association with particular employees. Viewing this distribution as a summary of EMP2, this implies that $N(Q)$ and $\Pi(Q)$ are computable from a summary of EMP2 which specifies the fraction of employees whose ages fall in each of the interval-valued entries in the Age column.

More specifically, assume that in a general setting EMP2 has n rows, with the entry in row $i, i = 1, \ldots, n$, under Age being D_i. Furthermore, assume that the D_i are comprised of k distinct sets $A_1, \ldots. A_K$ so that (a) each D is one of the $A_s, s = 1, \ldots, k$. For example, in the case of EMP2,

$$\begin{array}{lll} n = 5, & & k = 4 \\ D_1 = [22,26] & & A_1 = [22,26] \\ D_2 = [20,22] & & A_2 = [20,22] \\ D_3 = [30,35] & & A_3 = [30,35] \\ D_4 = [20,22] & & A_4 = [28,30] \\ D_5 = [28,30] & & \end{array}$$

Viewing EMP2 as a *parent relation*, its summary can be expressed as a *granular distribution*, Δ, of the form

$$\Delta = \{(A_1, p_1), (A_2, p_2), \ldots, (A_k, p_k)\},$$

in which $p_s, s = 1, \ldots k$,[3] is the fraction of D's that are A_s. Thus, in the case of EMP2, we have

$$\begin{aligned} \Delta = \{&([22, 26], 1/5), \\ &([20, 22], 2/5), \\ &([30, 35], 1/5), \\ &([28, 30], 1/5)\}. \end{aligned} \quad (2)$$

As is true of any summary, a granular distribution can have a multiplicity of parents, because Δ is invariant under permutations of the values of Name. At a later point, we see that this observation has an important bearing on the so-called Dempster-Shafer rule of combination of evidence.

In summary, given a query set Q, the response to Q has two components, $N(Q)$ and $\Pi(Q)$. In terms of the granular distribution $\Delta, N(Q)$ and $\Pi(Q)$ can be expressed as

$$N(Q) = \sum_s p_s \text{ such that } (A_s \subset Q, \; s = 1, \ldots, k)$$

$$\Pi(Q) = \sum_s p_s \text{ such that } (A_s \cap Q \neq \Theta, \; s = 1, \ldots, k.) \quad (3)$$

[3]The relative counts $p_1, \ldots p_k$ are referred to as the *basic probability numbers* in the Dempster-Shafer theory.

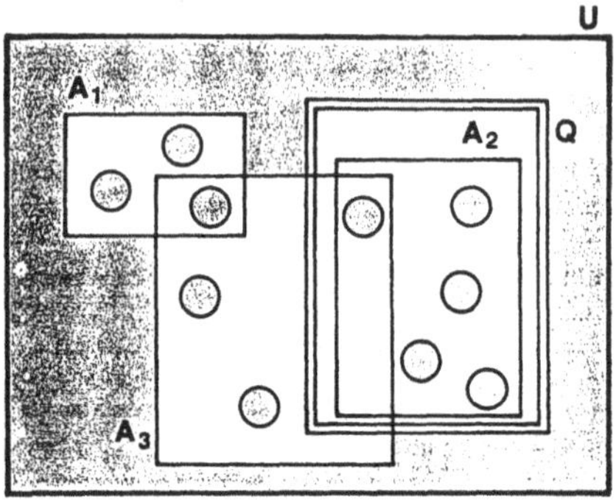

Figure 1

These expressions for the necessity and possibility of Q are identical with the expressions for belief and plausibility in the Dempster-Shafer theory.

The Ball-Box Analogy

The relational model of the Dempster-Shafer theory has a simple interpretation in terms of what might be called the *ball-box analogy*.

Specifically, assume that, as shown in Figure 1, we have n unmarked steel balls which are distributed among k boxes $A_1, \ldots, A_k$, with p_i representing the fraction of balls put in A_i. The boxes are placed in a box U and are allowed to overlap. The position of each ball within the box in which it is placed is unspecified. In this model, the granular distribution Δ describes the distribution of the balls among the boxes. (Note that the number of balls put in A_i, is unrelated to that put in A_j. Thus, if $A_i \subset A_j$, the number of balls put in A_i can be larger than the number of balls put in A_j. It is important to differentiate between the number of balls put in A_i and the number of balls in A_i. The need for differentiation arises because the A_i might overlap, and the boundary of each box is penetrable, except that a ball put in A_i is constrained to stay in A_i.)

Now, given a region Q in U, we can ask the question: How many balls are in Q? To simplify visualization, we assume that, as in Figure 1, the boxes as well as Q are rectangular.

Because the information regarding the position of each ball is incomplete, the answer to the question will, in general, be interval-valued. The upper bound can readily be found by visualizing Q as an attractor, for example, a magnet. Under this assumption, it is evident that the proportion of balls drawn into Q is given by

$$\Pi(Q) = \textstyle\sum_s p_s, \qquad A_s \cap Q \neq \Theta, \qquad s = l, \dots, k,$$

which is the expression for plausibility in the Dempster-Shafer theory. Similarly, the lower bound results from visualizing Q as a repeller. In this case, the lower bound is given by

$$N(Q) = \textstyle\sum_s p_s, \qquad A_s \subset Q, \qquad s = 1, \dots, k,$$

which coincides with the expression for belief in the Dempster-Shafer theory. Note that making Q an attractor is equivalent to making Q' (the complement of Q) a repeller. From this it follows at once that

$$\Pi(Q) = 1 - N(Q'),$$

which has already been cited as one of the basic identities in the Dempster-Shafer theory.

The ball-box analogy has the advantage of providing a pictorial—and, thus, easy to grasp–interpretation of the Dempster-Shafer model. As a simple illustration of its use, consider the following problem. There are 20 employees in a department. Five are known to be under 20, 3 are known to be over 40 and the rest are known to be between 25 and 45. How many are over 30? The answer that is yielded at once by the analogy is between 3 and 15.

The Issue of Normalization

A controversial issue in the Dempster-Shafer theory relates to the normalization of upper and lower probabilities and its role in the Dempster-Shafer rule of combination of evidence.

To view this issue in the context of relational databases, assume that the attribute tabulated in the EMP2 relation is not the employee's age but the age of the employee's car, Age(Car(i)), i = 1,..., 5, with the understanding that Age(Car(i)) = 0 means the car is brand new and that Age(Car(i)) = Θ, where Θ is the empty set (or, equivalently, a null value) means i does not have a car. For convenience in reference, an attribute is said to be *definite* if it cannot take a null value and *indefinite* if it can. In these examples, Age is definite, whereas Age (Car) is not.

The question that arises is: How should the null values be counted? Questions of this type arise, generally, when the referent in a proposition does not exist. In the theory of presuppositions, for example, a case in point is the proposition "The King of France is bald," with the question being: What is the truth-value of this proposition if the King of France does not exist? Closer to AI, similar issues arise in the literature on cooperative responses to database queries (Joshi, 1982; Joshi & Webber, 1982; Kaplan, 1982) and the treatment of null values in relational models of data (Biskup, 1980).

In the Dempster-Shafer theory, the null values are not counted, giving rise to what is referred to as *normalization.*[4] However, it is easy to see that normalization can lead to a misleading response to a query. Consider, for example, the relation EMP3 shown in the following:

EMP3	Name	Age(Car)
	1	[3,4]
	2	Θ
	3	[2,3]
	4	Θ
	5	Θ

For the query set $Q \triangleq [2, 4]$, normalization would lead to the unqualified conclusion that *all* employees have a car that is two to four years old.

Such misleading responses can be avoided, of course, by not allowing normalization or, better, by providing a relative count of all the null values. As an illustration, in the example under consideration, avoiding normalization would lead to the response $N(Q) = \Pi(Q) = 2/5$. Adding the information about the null values would result in a response with three components: $N(Q) = 2/5; \Pi(Q) = 2/5; RC\Theta = 3/5$, where RC denotes the relative count of the null values.

As pointed out in Zadeh (1979b), normalization can lead to serious problems in the case of what has come to be known as the *Dempster-Shafer rule of combination.* As is seen in the following section, this rule has a simple interpretation in the context of retrieval from relational databases—an interpretation that serves to clarify the implications of normalization and points to ways in which the rule can be made useful.

The Dempster-Shafer Rule

In the examples considered so far, we have assumed that there is just one source of information concerning the attribute Age. What happens when there are two or more sources, as in the relation EMP4 tabulated below?

[4]In Shafer's theory (Shafer, 1976), null values are not allowed in the definition of belief functions but enter the picture in the rule of combination of evidence.

EMP4	Name	Age 1	Age 2
	1	[22,23]	[22,24]
	2	[19,21]	[20,21]
	3	[20,21]	[19,20]
	4	[21,22]	[19,20]
	5	[22,23]	[19,21]

Because the entries in Age 1 and Age 2 are possibility distributions, it is natural to combine the sources of information by forming the intersection (or, equivalently, the conjunction) of the respective possibility distributions for each i, resulting in the relation EMP5

EMP5	Name	Age 1 * Age 2
	1	[22,23]
	2	[20,21]
	3	20
	4	Θ
	5	Θ

in which the aggregation operator * has the meaning of intersection.

Using the combined relation to compute the nonnormalized response to the query set $Q = [20, 25]$, leads to

$$\text{Resp}(Q) = (N(Q) = 3/5; \Pi(Q) = 3/5; \text{RC}\Theta = 2/5).$$

With normalization, the response is given by

$$\text{Resp}(Q) = (N(Q) = 1; \Pi(Q) \doteq 1). \qquad (4)$$

Note the normalized response suppresses the fact that in the case of 4 and 5 the two sources are flatly contradictory.

Next, consider the case where we know the distribution of the possibility distributions associated with the two sources but not their association with particular employees. Thus, in the case of Age 1, the information conveyed by source 1 is that the possibility distributions of the Age variable and their relative counts in Age1 are given by the granular distribution

$$\Delta_1 = \{(A_1^1, p_1), \ldots, (A_k^1, p_k)\}$$

and in the case of Age 2, the corresponding granular distribution is

$$\Delta_2 = \{(A_1^2, q_1), \ldots, (A_m^2, q_m)\}.$$

Because we do not know the association of A's with particular employees, to combine the two sources we have to form all possible intersections of A^1's and A^2's. As a result, in the combined column Age 1 * Age 2, the data entries will be of the form

$$A_s^1 \cap A_t^2, s = 1, \ldots, k, t = 1, \ldots, m,$$

and the relative count of $A_s^1 \cap A_t^2$'s will be $p_s q_t$.

The result of the combination then is the following granular distribution:

$$\Delta_{1,2} = \{(A_s^1 \cap A_t^2, p_s q_t);\ s = 1, \ldots, k,\ t=1,\ \ldots,\ m\} (5)$$

Knowing $\Delta_{1,2}$, we can compute the responses to Q using (3) and (4) with or without normalization. It is the first choice that leads to the Dempster-Shafer rule.

As a simple illustration, assume that we wish to combine the following granular distributions:

$$\Delta_1 = \{([20, 21], 0.8), ([22, 24], 0.2)\}$$

$$\Delta_2 = \{([19, 20], 0.6), ([20, 23], 0.4)\}.$$

In this case, (5) becomes

$$\Delta_{1,2} = \{(20, 0.48), ([20, 21], 0.32), ([22, 23], 0.08), (\Theta, 0.12)\},$$

and if Q is assumed to be given by $Q = [20,22]$, the nonnormalized and normalized responses can be expressed as

$$\text{Resp}(Q) = (N(Q) = 0.8; \Pi(Q) = 0.88; RC\Theta = 0.12)$$

$$\text{Norm. Resp}(Q) = (N(Q) = 0.8/0.88; \Pi(Q) = 1).$$

If we are dealing with a definite attribute, that is, an attribute which is not allowed to take null values, then it is reasonable to reject the null values in the combined distribution. However, if the attribute is indefinite, such rejection can lead to counterintuitive results.

The relational point of view leads to an important conclusion regarding the validity of the Dempster-Shafer rule. Specifically, if we assume that the attribute is definite, then the intersection of the attributes associated with any entry cannot be empty, that is, the relation must be *conflict-free*. Now, if we are given two granular distributions Δ_1 and Δ_2, then there must be at least one parent relation for Δ_1 and Δ_2 that is conflict-free. In this case, we say that Δ_1 and Δ_2 are *combinable.*

What this implies is that in the case of a definite attribute one cannot, in general, combine two arbitrarily specified granular distributions. In more specific terms, this conclusion can be stated as the following conjecture:

> In the case of definite attributes, the Dempster-Shafer rule of combination of evidence is not applicable unless the underlying granular distributions are combinable, that is, have at least one parent relation which is conflict-free.

An obvious corollary of this conjecture is the following:

> If there exists a granule A_s in Δ_1 that is disjoint from all granules A_t in Δ_2, or vice-versa, then Δ_1 and Δ_2 are not combinable.

An immediate consequence of this corollary is that distinct probability distributions are not combinable and, hence, that the Dempster-Shafer rule is not applicable to such distributions. This explains why the example given in Zadeh (1979b, 1984) leads to counterintuitive results.

Concluding Remarks

The relational view of the Dempster-Shafer theory that is outlined here exposes the basic ideas and assumptions underlying the theory and makes it much easier to understand. Furthermore, it points to extensions of the theory for use in various AI-oriented applications and, especially, in expert systems. Among such extensions, which are discussed in Zadeh (1979a), is the extension to second-order relations in which (1) the data entries are not restricted to crisp sets and (2) the distributions of data entries are specified imprecisely. This extension provides a three-way link between the Dempster-Shafer theory, the theory of information granularity (Zadeh, 1979a, 1981) and the theory of fuzzy relational databases (Zemankova-Leech and Kandel, 1984). Another important extension relates to the combination of sources of information with unequal credibility indexes. Extension to such sources necessitates the use of graded possibility distributions in which possibility, like probability, is a matter of degree rather than a binary choice between perfect possibility and complete impossibility.

As far as the validity of the Dempster-Shafer rule is concerned, the relational point of view leads to the conjecture that it cannot be applied until it is ascertained that the bodies of evidence are not in conflict; that is, there exists at least one parent relation which is conflict-free. In particular, under this criterion, it is not permissible to combine distinct probability distributions—which is allowed in the current versions of the Dempster-Shafer theory.

References

Barnett, J. A. (1981) *Computational methods for a mathematical theory of evidence.* IJCAI 7: 868-875.

Biskup, J. (1980) A formal approach to null values in database relations. In H. Gallaire & J. M. Nicolas (Eds.) *Formal bases for data bases.* New York: Plenum Press.

Dempster, A. P. (1967) Upper and lower probabilities induced by a multivalued mapping. *Annals Mathematics Statistics* (38)325-339.

Dillard, R., (1983) Computing confidences in tactical rule-based systems by using Dempster-Shafer theory. Tech. Doc. 649, Naval Ocean Systems Center.

Dubois, D., & Prade, H. (1982) On several representations of an uncertain body of evidence. In M. M. Grupta & E. Sanchez, (Eds.) *Fuzzy information and processes.* Amsterdam: North Holland, 167-181.

Garvey, T., & Lowrance, J. (1983) Evidential reasoning: implementation for multisensor integration. Tech. Rep. 305, SRI International Artificial Intelligence Center.

Gordon, J. & Shortliffe, E. (1983) The Dempster-Shafer theory of evidence. In B. Buchanan, B. & E. Shortliffe, (Eds.) *Rule based systems.* Menlo Park, Calif.: Addison-Wesley.

Joshi, A. K., & Webber, B. L., (1982) *Taking the initiative in natural language database interactions.* European Artificial Intelligence Conference, Paris.

Joshi, A. K. (1982) Varieties of cooperative responses in a question-answer system. In F. Kiefer, (Ed.) *Questions & answers.* Dordrecht, Netherlands: Reidel, 229-240.

Kaplan, S. J. (1982) Cooperative responses for a portable natural language query system. *Artificial Intelligence* 19: 165-187.

Kempson, R. M. (1975) *Presupposition and the delimitation of semantics.* Cambridge: Cambridge University Press.

Nguyen, H. T. (1978) On random sets and belief functions. *Journal of Mathematical Analysis and Applications* (65): 531-542.

Prade, H., (1984) Lipski's approach to incomplete information data bases restated and generalized in the setting of Zadeh's possibility theory. *Information Systems* 9(1): 27-42.

Shafer, G. (1976) *A mathematical theory of evidence.* Princeton, N.J.: Princeton University Press.

Wesley, L., Lowrance, J., & Garvey T. (1984) Reasoning about control: an evidential approach. Tech. Rep. 324, SRI International Artificial Intelligence Center.

Zadeh, L. A. (1979a) Fuzzy sets and information granularity. In M. M. Gupta, R. Ragade, and R. Yager, (Eds.) *Advances in fuzzy set theory and applications.* Amsterdam: North Holland, 3-18.

Zadeh, L. A. (1979b) On the validity of Dempster's rule of combination of evidence. ERL Mem. M79/24, Department of EECS, University of California at Berkeley.

Zadeh, L. A. (1981) Possibility theory and soft data analysis. In L. Cobb & R. M. Thrall, (Eds.) *Mathematical frontiers of the social and policy sciences.* Boulder, Colo: Westview Press, 69-129.

Zadeh, L. A. (1984) Review of Shafer's a mathematical theory of evidence. *AI Magazine* 5(3): 81-83.

Zemankova-Leech, M. & Kandel, A. (1984) *Fuzzy relational databases—a key to expert systems.* Cologne, West Germany: Verlag TUV, Interdisciplinary Systems Research.

Outline of a Computational Approach to Meaning and Knowledge Representation Based on the Concept of a Generalized Assignment Statement*

L.A. Zadeh
Computer Science Division
University of California
Berkeley, CA 94720

1. Introduction

The concept of an assignment statement plays a central role in programming languages. Could it play a comparable role in the representation of knowledge expressed in a natural language? In our paper, we generalize the concept of an assignment statement in a way that makes it a convenient point of departure for representing the meaning of propositions in a natural language. Furthermore, it can be shown – though we do not stress this issue in the present paper -- that the concept of a generalized assignment statement provides an effective computational framework for a system of inference with propositions expressed in a natural language. In some ways, this system is simpler and more direct than predicate-logic-based systems in which it is the concept of a logical form – rather than a generalized assignment statement – that plays a central role [7,16,23,24,25,26,28,30,31].

The approach described in the present paper may be viewed as an evolution of our earlier work on test-score semantics and canonical forms [36,38,41]. In test-score semantics, a proposition, *p*, is viewed as a collection of elastic constraints, and its meaning is represented as a procedure which tests, scores, and aggregates the constraints associated with *p*, yielding a vector test score which serves as a measure of compatibility between *p* and what is referred to as an *explanatory database*. The main advantage of test-score semantics over the classical approaches to meaning representation such as truth-conditional semantics, possible-world semantics and model-theoretic semantics [3,8,17,20,21,30,31], lies in its greater expressive power and, in particular, its ability to deal with fuzzy predicates such as *young*, *intelligent*, *near*, etc. [2,5,11,18,22,32,36,44]; fuzzy quantifiers exemplified by *most*, *several*, *few*, *often*, *usually*, etc. [10,33,40]; predicate modifiers such as *very*, *more or less*, *quite*, *extremely*, etc. [35,44]; and fuzzy truth-values exemplified by *quite true*, *almost true*, and *mostly false* [36].

---

*Research supported in part by NASA Grant NCC-2-275 and NSF Grant IST-8320416.

The concept of a generalized assignment statement serves to place in a sharper focus the representation of a proposition in a natural language as a collection of elastic constraints. More specifically, in its generic form, the generalized assignment statement may be expressed as

$$X \textit{ isr } \Omega\,, \tag{1.1}$$

where X is the constrained variable; Ω is the constraining object, usually an n-ary predicate; and *isr* is a copula in which r is a variable which defines the role of Ω in relation to X. The usual values of r are: d, standing for *disjunctive*; c, standing for *conjunctive*; p, standing for *probabilistic*; g, standing for *granular*; and h, standing for *hybrid*. Since in most cases the value of r is d, it is convenient to adopt the convention that *isd* may be written more simply as *is*.

In (1.1), the generalized assignment statement is unconditioned. More generally, the statement may be *conditioned*, in which case it may be expressed as

$$X \textit{ isr1 } \Omega 1 \textit{ if } Z \textit{ isr2 } \Omega 2\,, \tag{1.2}$$

in which Z is a conditioning variable; $\Omega 2$ is an object which constrains Z; and *r1* and *r2* are variables which define the roles of $\Omega 1$ and $\Omega 2$ in relation to X and Z, respectively. In general, both X and Z may be vector-valued.

Disjunctive and Conjunctive Constraints[1]

As a simple illustration of a disjunctive constraint, if X is a variable which takes values in a universe of discourse U and Ω is a subset, A, of U, then the generalized assignment statement

$$X \textit{ is } A \tag{1.3}$$

signifies that the value of X is one of the elements of A. In this sense, A may be interpreted as the *possibility distribution* of X, that is, the set of its possible values [11,36,39].

More concretely, consider the proposition

p: Mary left home sometime between four and five in the afternoon.

In this case, if X is taken to be the time at which Mary left home, the meaning of p may be represented as the generalized assignment statement

$$X \textit{ isd } [4pm, 5pm]\,, \tag{1.4}$$

[1] The discussion of disjunctive and conjunctive constraints in the present paper is based on earlier discussions in [36,38]. Recent results may be found in [34].

or more simply, as

$$X \text{ is } [4pm, 5pm] ,$$

in which the interval [4pm, 5pm] plays the role of a unary predicate.

As an illustration of a conjunctive constraint, consider the proposition

p: Mary was at home from four to five in the afternoon.

In this case, if X is taken to be the time at which Mary was at home, the meaning of p may be represented as:

$$X \text{ isc } [4pm, 5pm]. \qquad (1.5)$$

Note that in this case X takes *all* values in the interval [4pm, 5pm].

The assignment statements (1.4) and (1.5) differ from conventional assignment statements in that the assignment is set-valued rather than point-valued. Furthermore, although the assigned sets are identical in (1.4) and (1.5), they play different roles in relation to X. The possibility that the same constraining object may constrain X in different ways is the principal motivating reason for employing in (1.1) a copula of the form *isr* in which the variable r specifies the role of Ω in relation to X.

In the examples considered so far, the constraint induced by Ω is inelastic in the sense that there are only two possibilities: either the constraint is satisfied or it is not, which is characteristic of constraints associated with assignment statements in programming languages. In the case of natural languages, however, the constraints are usually elastic rather than inelastic, which implies that Ω is a fuzzy predicate. As a simple example, in the case of the proposition

p: Mary is young

the constrained variable, X, is the age of Mary, and the predicate *young* may be interpreted as an elastic constraint on X characterized by the function μ_{young}: [0, 100] → [0, 1], which associates which each numerical value, u, of the variable *Age* the degree to which u fits the definition of *young* in the context in which p is asserted. In this sense, $1 - \mu_{young}(u)$ may be interpreted as the degree to which the predicate *young* must be stretched to fit u.

Probabilistic Constraints

As was alluded to already, a proposition p may have different generalized assignment statement representations depending on the intended meaning of p. For example, the proposition

$$p\text{: } Madeleine \text{ is } tall \tag{1.6}$$

may be represented as a disjunctive statement

$$X \text{ is } TALL \ , \tag{1.7}$$

in which $X \triangleq Height(Madeleine)$ and $TALL$ is a unary fuzzy relation which is the denotation of the fuzzy predicate *tall*.[2] The fuzzy relation $TALL$ is characterized by its membership function μ_{TALL}, which associates with each numerical value of height, h, the degree, $\mu_{TALL}(h)$, to which h fits the intended meaning of *tall*. Equivalently, $TALL$ may be interpreted as the possibility distribution, Π_X, of X. In this interpretation, (1.7) may be represented as

$$\Pi_X = TALL \ , \tag{1.8}$$

with the understanding that the possibility that X can take h as a value is given by

$$\pi_X(h) \triangleq Poss\,\{X = h\} = \mu_{TALL}(h) \ , \tag{1.9}$$

where π_X represents the *possibility distribution function* of X.

Alternatively, the proposition *Madeleine is tall* may be interpreted as a characterization of the probability distribution of the variable *Height(Madeleine)*. If this is the intended meaning of (1.6), then the corresponding generalized assignment statement would be probabilistic, i.e.,

$$X \text{ isp } TALL \ , \tag{1.10}$$

in which $r = p$ and $TALL$ is a probability distribution. Thus, if P_X is the probability distribution of X, then (1.10) may be represented as

$$P_X = TALL \tag{1.11}$$

It should be noted that in the absence of a specification of the value of the copula variable r, the proposition

$$p\text{: } Madeleine \text{ is } tall$$

may be interpreted as a possibilistic constraint on $X \triangleq Height\,(Madeleine)$, as in (1.7), or as a probabilistic constraint, as in (1.10). We shall assume that, unless it is specifically stated that the intended interpretation of a proposition, p, is probabilistic or conjunctive, p should be interpreted as a possibilistic, i.e., disjunctive constraint. This understanding reflects the assumption that in natural languages the constraints implicit in propositions are preponderantly possibilistic in nature.

---

[2] Here and in the sequel, denotations of predicates are expressed in uppercase symbols. The symbol $\triangleq$ stands for *is defined to be*.

A related point that should be noted is that in the possibilistic interpretation of (1.6), the value of $\pi_X(h)$ or, equivalently, $\mu_{TALL}(h)$, may be interpreted as the conditional probability of the truth of the proposition *Madeleine is tall* for a given h. In the context of a voting model, this is equivalent to viewing $\mu_{TALL}(h)$ as the proportion of voters who would vote that *Madeleine is tall* given that her height is h [13,14]. Although these interpretations are of help in developing a better understanding of the properties of the membership function, it is simplest to regard $\mu_{TALL}(h)$ as the degree to which h fits the predicate *tall* in a given context, or, equivalently, as $1 - \sigma$, where σ is the degree to which the predicate *tall* must be stretched to fit h.

Granular Constraints

In the case of a granular constraint, the generalized assignment statement assumes the form

$$X \ isg \ G \ , \tag{1.12}$$

where X is an n-ary variable $X = (X_1, ..., X_n)$, and G is a *granular distribution* expressed as

$$G = \{(p_1, G_1), ..., (p_k, G_k)\} \ , \tag{1.13}$$

in which $p_1, ..., p_k$ are positive numbers in the interval [0,1] which add up to unity,[3] and the $G_j, j=1,...,k$, are distinct fuzzy subsets of a universe of discourse U.

The generalized assignment statement (1.12) may be interpreted as a summary of n possibilistic assignment statements, each of which involves a component of X, i.e.,

$$X_1 \ is \ G_{j_1} \tag{1.14}$$

$$\cdots$$

$$X_n \ is \ G_{j_k} \ ,$$

in which each G_{j_s}, $s = 1, ..., k$, is one of the G_j. In this collection of statements, p_j is the proportion of X's which are G_j.

As an illustration, consider the following proposition

> *p: There are twenty residents in an apartment house; seven are old, five are young and the rest are middle-aged.* (1.15)

In this case, X_i *is the age of ith resident*, $i = 1, ..., 20$; $n = 20$; $k = 3$; $G_1 \triangleq OLD$; $G_2 \triangleq YOUNG$; $G_3 \triangleq MIDDLEAGED$; $p_1 = 7/20$; $p_2 = 5/20$; and $p_3 = 8/20$.

[3] A more detailed discussion of the concept of a granular constraint and its role in the Dempster-Shafer theory of evidence may be found in [37].

Hybrid Constraints

A hybrid constraint is associated with a generalized assignment statement of the form

$$X \ \mathit{ish} \ \Omega \ , \tag{1.16}$$

and may be viewed as the result of combination of two or more generalized assignment statements of different types, e.g.,

$$\begin{array}{l} X \ \mathit{isr1} \ \Omega_1 \\ \underline{X \ \mathit{isr2} \ \Omega_2} \\ X \ \mathit{ish} \ \Omega \ . \end{array}$$

An important special case of a hybrid constraint is associated with the concept of a hybrid number [19]. In this case, the constraint on X is characterized by two generalized assignment statements of the form

$$\begin{array}{l} Y \ \mathit{is} \ A \\ Z \ \mathit{isp} \ P \end{array} \tag{1.17}$$

and the relation

$$X = Y + Z \ .$$

in which A and P are, respectively, possibility and probability distributions, and X is defined to be the sum of Y and Z. In terms of A and P, the constraining object Ω in (1.16) may be viewed equivalently as a *probabilistic set* [15], a random fuzzy set [14], or a fuzzy random variable [27].

2. Meaning Representation

As was stated already, the basic idea underlying test-score semantics is that a proposition in a natural language may be interpreted as a collection of elastic constraints. Thus, by expressing the meaning of a proposition, p, in the form of a generalized assignment statement, we are, in effect, answering two basic questions: (a) What is the constrained variable X in p; and (b) What is the constraint, Ω, to which X is subjected?

In more concrete terms, the process of representing the meaning of a proposition, p, in the form of a generalized assignment statement, X *isr* A, involves three basic steps.[4]

1. Constructing a collection of relations $\{R_1, \ldots, R_k\}$ in terms of which the meaning of p is to be represented. The meaning of each of these relations is assumed to be known, and each relation is assumed to be characterized by its name, the names of its attributes and the domain of each attribute. For our purposes, it is convenient to

[4] For simplicity, our discussion of these steps is limited to the possibilistic case.

refer to the collection $\{R_1, \ldots, R_k\}$ as an *explanatory database* or *ED* for short, and to regard each relation as an elastic constraint on the values of its attributes. It should be noted that the concept of an explanatory database is related, but is not identical, to that of a collection of possible worlds [8,17,29,21,31].

2. Identifying the variable X which is constrained by p and constructing a defining procedure which computes X for a given explanatory database.
3. Constructing a procedure which computes the constraint A as a function of ED.

To illustrate this process, consider the proposition

> *p: Over the past few years Naomi earned far more than all of her close friends put together.*

To represent the meaning of this proposition, assume that the explanatory database consists of the following relations (+ should be read as *and*):

$$ED = INCOME\ [Name;\ Amount;\ Year] + \tag{2.1}$$
$$FRIEND\ [Name1;\ Name2;\ \mu] +$$
$$FEW\ [Number;\ \mu] +$$
$$FAR.MORE\ [Income1;\ Income2;\ \mu]\ .$$

In this database, the relation *INCOME* associates with each $Name_j$, $j = 1,\ldots,n$, $Name_j$'s income in year $Year_i$, $i = 1, 2, 3, \ldots$, counting backward from the present; in *FRIEND*, μ is the degree to which *Name1* is a friend of *Name2*; in *FEW*, μ is the degree to which the value of the attribute *Number* fits the definition of *few*; and in *FAR.MORE*, μ is the degree to which *Income1* is far more than *Income2*.

Next, we have to construct a procedure for computing the constrained variable X. Assume that X is the total income of Naomi over the past few years. Then, the following procedure will compute X.

1. Find Naomi's income, IN_i, in $Year_i$, i = 1, 2, 3,..., counting backward from present. In symbols,

$$IN_i = {}_{Amount}\, INCOME[Name = Naomi; Year = Year_i]\ , \tag{2.2}$$

which signifies that *Name* is bound to Naomi, *Year* to $Year_i$, and the resulting relation is projected on the domain of the attribute *Amount*, yielding the value of *Amount* corresponding to the values assigned to the attributes *Name* and *Year*.

2. Test the constraint induced by *FEW*:

$$\mu_i = {}_{\mu}FEW[Year = Year_i]\ , \tag{2.3}$$

which signifies that the variable *Year* is bound to $Year_i$ and the corresponding value of μ is read by projecting on the domain of μ.

3. Compute Naomi's total income, X, during the past few years:

$$X = \Sigma_i \mu_i IN_i, \tag{2.4}$$

in which the μ_i plays the role of weighting coefficients. Thus, we are tacitly assuming that the total income earned by Naomi during a fuzzily specified interval of time is obtained by (a) weighting Naomi's income in year $Year_i$ by the degree to which $Year_i$ satisfies the constraint induced by FEW, and (b) summing the weighted incomes.

The last step in the meaning representation process involves the computation of A. In words, A may be expressed as *far more than the combined income of Naomi's close friends over the past few years*. The expression for A is yielded by the following procedure.

1. Compute the total income of each $Name_j$ (other than Naomi) during the past few years:

$$TIName_j = \Sigma_i \mu_i IName_{ji}, \tag{2.5}$$

where $IName_{ji}$ is the income of $Name_j$ in $Year_i$.

2. Find the fuzzy set of close friends of Naomi by intensifying the relation $FRIEND$ [35]:

$$CF = CLOSE.FRIEND = {}^2FRIEND, \tag{2.6}$$

which implies that

$$\mu_{CF}(Name_j) = ({}_{\mu}FRIEND[Name = Name_j])^2,$$

where the expression

$${}_{\mu}FRIEND[Name = Name_j]$$

represents $\mu_F(Name_j)$, that is, the grade of membership of $Name_j$ in the set of Naomi's friends.

3. Compute the combined income of Naomi's close friends:

$$CI = \Sigma_j \mu_{CF}(Name_j) TIName_j\ , \tag{2.7}$$

which implies that in computing the combined income, the total income of $Name_j$ is weighted with the degree to which $Name_j$ is a close friend of Naomi.

4. The desired expression for A is obtained by substituting CI for $Income2$ in $FAR.MORE$ and projecting the result on $Income1$ and μ. Thus

$$A = {}_{\mu,\, Income1}FAR.MORE\ [Income2 = CI]\ . \tag{2.8}$$

In summary, the meaning of p may be represented as the possibilistic assignment statement (1.3) in which the constrained variable, X, is given by (2.4), and the elastic constraint on X is expressed by (2.8). In essence, the possibilistic assignment statement (1.3) defines the possibility distribution of X given p. What this means is that A, as expressed by (1.8), associates with each numerical value of *Income1*, the possibility that it could be far more than the combined income of Naomi's close friends over the past few years.

The same basic technique may be applied to the representation of the meaning of a wide variety of propositions in a natural language. In the following, we present in a summarized form a few representative examples.

Example 1.

$$p\text{: } \textit{Richard is blond} \ . \tag{2.9}$$

In this case

$$p \rightarrow \textit{Color}(\textit{Hair}(\textit{Richard})) \text{ is } \textit{BLOND} \ , \tag{2.10}$$

where → stands for *translates into*.

Example 2.

$$p\text{: } \textit{Brian is much taller than Mildred} \ . \tag{2.11}$$

Here X is a binary variable (X_1, X_2) whose components are

$$X_1 = \textit{Height}(\textit{Brian})$$

and

$$X_2 = \textit{Height}(\textit{Mildred}) \ .$$

The elastic constraint on $X = (X_1, X_2)$ is characterized by the fuzzy relation *MUCH.TALLER*. Thus,

$$p \rightarrow (\textit{Height}(\textit{Brian}), \textit{Height}(\textit{Mildred})) \text{ is } \textit{MUCH.TALLER}$$

is the possibilistic assignment statement which represents the meaning of (2.11).

Example 3.

$$p\text{: } \textit{most Swedes are blond} \ . \tag{2.12}$$

In this case, the constrained variable X is the proportion of blond Swedes among the Swedes. More specifically,

$$X = \Sigma\, \textit{Count}(\textit{BLOND}/\textit{SWEDE}) \ , \tag{2.13}$$

where the right-hand member expresses the *relative sigma-count* [40] of blond Swedes among the Swedes. Thus, if the individuals in a sample population in Sweden are labeled *Name1*, ..., *Namen*, then

$$\Sigma\, \textit{Count}(\textit{BLOND}/\textit{SWEDE}) = \frac{\Sigma_i\, \mu_{BLOND}(\textit{Name}_i) \wedge \mu_{SWEDE}(\textit{Name}_i)}{\Sigma_i\, \mu_{SWEDE}(\textit{Name}_i)} \tag{2.14}$$

in which $\mu_{BLOND}(Name_i)$ and $\mu_{SWEDE}(Name_i)$ represent, respectively, the degrees to which $Name_i$, $i = 1, \ldots, n$, is *blond* and Swedish, and the conjunctive connective $\wedge$ yields the minimum of its arguments.

The elastic constraint on X is characterized by the possibility distribution of the fuzzy quantifier *most*, which is a fuzzy number *MOST*. From (2.13) and (2.14), it follows that the possibilistic assignment statement which represents the meaning of (2.12) may be expressed as

$$p \to \Sigma\, Count(BLOND/SWEDE) \text{ is } MOST \ , \tag{2.15}$$

in which the constrained variable is given by (2.14).

3. Inference

One of the important advantages of employing the concept of a generalized assignment statement for purposes of meaning representation is that the process of deductive retrieval from a knowledge base is greatly facilitated when the propositions in the knowledge base are represented as generalized assignment statements. This is a direct consequence of the fact that a generalized assignment statement places in evidence the variable which is constrained and the constraint to which it is subjected.

Viewed in this perspective, a knowledge base may be equated to a collection of generalized assignment statements, and a query may be interpreted as a question regarding the value of a specified variable. Equivalently, a knowledge base may be regarded as a specification of elastic constraints on a collection of knowledge base variables $X_1, \ldots, X_n$; the answer to a query as the induced constraint on the variable in the query; and the inference process as the computation of the induced constraint on the query variable as a function of the given constraints on the knowledge base variables. In this view, the inference process resembles this solution of a nonlinear program [42,44].

In the following, our discussion of the problem of inference will be limited in scope. More specifically, we shall restrict our attention to disjunctive (i.e., possibilistic) assignment statements, since the inference rules for conjunctive statements can readily be derived by dualization, that is, replacing $\subset$ (is contained in) with $\supset$ (contains), and $\cap$ (intersection) with $\cup$ (union). Furthermore, we shall state only the principal rules of inference and will omit proofs.

In the rules stated below, $X, Y, Z, \ldots$, are the constrained variables and $A, B, C, \ldots$, are the constraining possibility distributions.

Entailment principle

$$\frac{\begin{array}{c} X \text{ is } A \\ A \subset B \end{array}}{X \text{ is } B} \ . \tag{3.1}$$

Unary conjunctive rule

$$\frac{\begin{array}{c} X \text{ is } A \\ X \text{ is } B \end{array}}{X \text{ is } A \cap B} \quad (3.2)$$

In the conclusion, $A \cap B$ denotes the intersection of A and B, which is defined by

$$\mu_{A \cap B}(u) = \mu_A(u) \wedge \mu_B(u), \quad u \in U. \quad (3.3)$$

Binary conjunctive rule

$$\frac{\begin{array}{c} X \text{ is } A \\ Y \text{ is } B \end{array}}{(X,Y) \text{ is } A \times B}, \quad (3.4)$$

where $A \times B$ denotes the cartesian product of A and B, defined by

$$\mu_{A \times B}(u,v) = \mu_A(u) \wedge \mu_B(v), \quad u \in U, \quad v \in V, \quad (3.5)$$

where U and V are the domains of X and Y, respectively.

Cylindrical extension rule

$$\frac{X \text{ is } A}{(X,Y) \text{ is } A \times V}, \quad (3.6)$$

where V is the domain of Y.

Projective rule

$$\frac{(X,Y) \text{ is } A}{X \text{ is } {}_X A}, \quad (3.7)$$

where ${}_X A$ denotes the projection A on the domain of X. The membership function of ${}_X A$ is defined by

$$\mu(u) = \vee_v (\mu_A(u,v)), \quad (3.8)$$

where $\vee_v$ denotes the suprenum over $v \in V$.

Compositional rule

$$\frac{\begin{array}{c} X \text{ is } A \\ (X,Y) \text{ is } B \end{array}}{Y \text{ is } A \circ B}, \quad (3.9)$$

where $A \circ B$ denotes the composition of A and B, defined by

$$\mu_{A \circ B}(v) = \vee_u \mu_A(u) \wedge \mu_B(u,v). \quad (3.10)$$

The compositional rule may be viewed as a corollary of the cylindrical extension rule, the binary conjunctive rule and the projective rule.

Extension principle

$$\frac{X \text{ is } A}{f(X) \text{ is } f(A)}, \tag{3.11}$$

where f is a function from U to V, and $f(A)$ is a possibility distribution defined by

$$\mu_{f(A)}(v) = \vee_u \mu_A(u), \quad \text{over all } u \text{ such that } v = f(u). \tag{3.12}$$

A more general version of the extension principle which follows from (3.4) and (3.11) is

$$\begin{array}{c} X \text{ is } A \\ \underline{Y \text{ is } B} \\ f(X,Y) \text{ is } f(A,B) \end{array}. \tag{3.13}$$

Generalized modus ponens

$$\begin{array}{c} X \text{ is } A \\ \underline{\text{if } X \text{ is } B \text{ then } Y \text{ is } C} \\ Y \text{ is } A \circ (B' \oplus C) \end{array}, \tag{3.14}$$

in which B' is the complement of B and $\oplus$ is the bounded sum, defined by

$$\mu_{B' \oplus C}(v) = 1 \vee (1 - \mu_B(v) + \mu_C(v)), \tag{3.15}$$

where $\vee$ = max. The inference rule expressed by (3.14) follows from the compositional rule of inference (3.9) and the assumption that the meaning of the conditional assignment statement which is the second premise in (3.14) is expressed by [36]

$$\text{if } X \text{ is } B \text{ then } Y \text{ is } C \rightarrow \pi_{(Y|X)}(u,v) = 1 \vee (1 - \mu_A(u) + \mu_B(v)), \tag{3.16}$$

where $\pi_{(Y|X)}$ denotes the conditional possibility distribution function of Y given X.

REFERENCES AND RELATED PUBLICATIONS

1. Ballmer, T.T., and Pinkal, M. (eds.), *Approaching Vagueness*. Amsterdam: North-Holland, 1983.
2. Bandler, W., Representation and manipulation of knowledge in fuzzy expert systems, *Proc. Workshop on Fuzzy Sets and Knowledge-Based Systems*, Queen Mary College, University of London, 1983.
3. Bartsch, R. and Vennenmann, T., *Semantic Structures*. Frankfurt: Attenaum Verlag, 1972.
4. Barwise, J. and Cooper, R., Generalized quantifiers and natural language, *Linguistics and Philosophy* 4 (1981) 159-219.
5. Bonissone, P.P., A survey of uncertainty representation in expert systems, in *Proc. Second Workshop of the North-American Fuzzy Information Processing Society*, General Electric Corporate Research and Development, Schenectady, NY, 1983.

210

6. Bosch, P., Vagueness, ambiguity and all the rest, in: *Sprachstruktur, Individuum und Gesselschaft*, Van de Velde, M., and Vandeweghe, W. (eds.). Tubingen: Niemeyer, 1978.
7. Brachman, R.J., What is-a is and isn't, *Computer 16* (1983).
8. Cresswell, M.J., *Logic and Languages*. London: Methuen, 1973.
9. Czogala, E., *Probabilistic Sets in Decision Making and Control*. Rhineland: Verlag TUV, 1984.
10. Dubois, D., and Prade, H., Fuzzy cardinality and the modeling of imprecise quantification, *Fuzzy Sets and Systems 16* (1985) 199-230.
11. Dubois, D., and Prade, H., *Théorie des Possibilité's*, Paris: Masson, 1985.
12. Fox, M.S., On inheritance in knowledge representation, *Proc. IJCAI* (1979) 282-284.
13. Giles, R., Foundations for a theory of possibility, in: *Fuzzy Information and Decision Processes*, Gupta, M.M. and Sanchez, E. (eds.). Amsterdam: North-Holland, 183-195.
14. Goodman, I.R., and Nguyen, H.T., *Uncertainty Models for Knowledge-Based Systems*. Amsterdam: North-Holland, 1985.
15. Hirota, K., and Pedrycz, W., Analysis and synthesis of fuzzy systems by the use of probabilistic sets, *Fuzzy Sets and Systems 10* (1983) 1-13.
16. Israel, D., The role of logic in knowledge representation, *Computer 16* (1983) 37-41.
17. Kamp, H., A theory of truth and semantic representation, in *Formal Methods in the Study of Language*, Groenendijk, J.A. et al, (eds.), Mathematical Centre, Amsterdam, Tract 135, 1981.
18. Kandel, A., *Fuzzy Mathematical Techniques with Applications*. Reading: Addison-Wesley, 1986.
19. Kaufmann, A. and Gupta, M., *Introduction to Fuzzy Arithmetic*. New York: Van Nostrand, 1985.
20. Keenan, E., (ed.). *Formal Semantics of Natural Language*. Cambridge: Cambridge University Press, 1975.
21. Lambert, K., and van Fraassen, B.C., Meaning relations, possible objects and possible worlds, *Philosopical Problems in Logic* (1970) 1-19.
22. Mamdani, E.H., and Gaines, B.R., *Fuzzy Reasoning and its Applications*. London: Academic Press, 1981.
23. McDermott, D., and Cherniak, E., *Introduction to Artificial Intelligence*. Reading: Addison-Wesley, 1985.
24. Moore, R.C., *Problems in Logical Form*, SRI Tech. Report 241, Menlo Park, 1981.
25. Moore, R.C., The role of logic in knowledge representation and commonsense reasoning, *Proc. AAAI* (1982) 428-433.
26. Nilsson, N., *Principles of Artificial Intelligence*, Palo Alto: Tioga Press, 1980.
27. Ralescu, D., Toward a general theory of fuzzy variables, *Journ. Math. Analysis and Appl. 86* (1982) 176-193.
28. Rich, C., Knowledge representation languages and predicate calculus: how to save your cake and eat it too, *Proc. AAAI* (1982) 192-196.
29. Scheffler, I., *A Philosophical Inquiry into Ambiguity, Vaguenss and Metaphor in Language*. London: Routledge & Kegan Paul, 1981.
30. Tarski, A., *Logic, Semantics, Metamathematics*. Oxford: Clarendon Press, 1956.
31. van Fraassen, B.C., *Formal Semantics and Logic*. New York: Macmillan, 1971.
32. Wahlster, W., Hahn, W.V., Hoeppner, W., and Jameson, A., The anatomy of the natural language dialog system HAM-RPM, in: *Natural Language Computer Systems*, Bolc, L., (ed.). Amsterdam: North-Holland, 205-233, 1976.

33. Yager, R., Reasoning with fuzzy quantified statements - I, *Kybernetes 14* (1985) 233-240.

34. Yager, R., *Set Based Representation of Conjunctive and Disjunctive Knowledge*, Machine Intelligence Institute Tech. Rep. #M11-604, Iona College, New Rochelle, NY, 1986.

35. Zadeh, L.A., A fuzzy-set-theoretic interpretation of linguistic hedges, *Journal of Cybernetics 2* (1972) 4-34.

36. Zadeh, L.A., PRUF -- a meaning representation language for natural languages, *Int. J. Man-Machine Studies 10 (1978) 395-460.*

37. Zadeh, L.A., Fuzzy sets and information granularity, in *Advances in Fuzzy Set Theory and Applications* (Gupta, M., Ragade, R. and Yager, R., eds.). Amsterdam: North-Holland, 3-18, 1979.

38. Zadeh, L.A., Test-score semantics for natural languages and meaning-representation via PRUF, *Tech. Note 247, AI Center, SRI International*, Menlo Park, CA, 1981. Also in: *Empirical Semantics*, Rieger, B.B., (ed.). Bochum: Brockmeyer, 281-349, 1981.

39. Zadeh, L.A., Possibility theory as a basis for meaning representation, in: *Proc. of the Sixth Wittgenstein Symposium*, Leinfellner, W., et al, (eds.), Kirchberg, 253-261, 1982.

40. Zadeh, L.A., A Computational Approach to Fuzzy Quantifiers in Natural Languages, *Computers and Mathematics 9* (1983) 149-184.

41. Zadeh, L.A., A fuzzy-set-theoretic approach to the compositionality of meaning: Propositions, dispositions and canonical forms, *Journal of Semantics 3* (1983) 253-272.

42. Zadeh, L.A., The role of fuzzy logic in the management of uncertainty in expert systems, *Fuzzy Sets and Systems 11* (1983) 199-227.

43. Zadeh, L.A., Syllogistic reasoning in fuzzy logic and its application to usuality and reasoning with dispositions, *IEEE Transactions on Systems, Man and Cybernetics SMC-15* (1985) 754-763.

44. Zimmermann, J., *Fuzzy Set Theory - and its Applications*. Boston: Kluwer, 1985.

Outline of a Theory of Usuality Based on Fuzzy Logic

L.A. Zadeh*
University of California, Berkeley

Abstract.

The concept of *usuality* relates to propositions which are usually true or, more precisely, to events which have a high probability of occurrence. For example, *usually Cait is very cheerful, usually a TV set weighs about fifty pounds*, etc. Such propositions are said to be *usuality-qualified*. A usuality-qualified proposition may be expressed in the form *usually (X is F)*, in which X is a variable taking values in a universe of discourse U and F is a fuzzy subset of U which may be interpreted as a *usual value* of X. In general, a usual value of variable, X, is not unique, and any fuzzy subset of U qualifies to a degree to be a usual value of X. A usuality-qualified proposition in which *usually* is implicit rather than explicit is said to be a *disposition*. Simple examples of dispositions are *snow is white, a cup of coffee costs about fifty cents* and *Swedes are taller than Italians*.

In this paper, we outline a theory of usuality in which the point of departure is a method of representing the meaning of usuality-qualified propositions. Based on this method, a system of inference for usuality-qualified propositions may be developed. As examples, a dispositional version of the Aristotelian Barbara syllogism as well as a dispositional version of the *modus ponens* are described. Such dispositional rules of inference are of direct relevance to commonsense reasoning and, in particular, to commonsense decision analysis. A potentially important application area for the theory of usuality is the management of uncertainty in expert systems.

1. Introduction

Theory of usuality, as its name suggests, is concerned with what is usual or, more precisely, with events of high probability.

Usuality plays a pervasive role in human activity. Indeed, most of our actions are based in one way or another on our knowledge of the usual values of various variables. For example, when we get up in the morning, we know how long it usually takes to dress and have breakfast; we know the usual duration of travel to our place of work; we know how much it usually costs to have lunch at our favorite restaurant; and so on, until we retire at night. Viewed in this perspective, the concept of usuality underlies much of what is commonly referred to as commonsense knowledge [25, 27], and governs most of our decision-making in the course of a day.

*Computer Science Division, University of California, Berkeley, CA 94720. Research supported in part by NSF Grants ECS-8209679 and IST-8320416 and NASA Grant NCC2-275. To Professor Arnold Kaufmann.

79

Reprinted, with permission, from *Fuzzy Sets Theory and Applications*, edited by A. Jones *et al.*, pp. 79–97.

As a point of departure for our theory of usuality, we shall focus our attention on usuality-qualified propositions of the form

$$\textit{usually}\ (X\ \textit{is}\ F)\,, \tag{1.1}$$

where X is a variable taking values in a universe of discourse U, F is a fuzzy subset of U and *usually* is a fuzzy quantifier which we shall presently define in greater detail. As a simple illustration, consider the proposition

$$p\text{: } \textit{a loaf of bread usually costs about a dollar.} \tag{1.2}$$

In p, X is the cost of a loaf of bread, U is an interval of prices, and F is a fuzzy subset of U described by the label *about a dollar* (Figure 1). We shall refer to F as a *usual value* of X, and will denote it as $U(X)$. In symbols, this may be expressed as

$$\textit{usually}\ (X\ \textit{is}\ F) \leftrightarrow U(X) = F\,, \tag{1.3}$$

where $\rightarrow$ may be interpreted either as *implies* or *translates into*. A usuality-qualified proposition in which *usually* is implicit, e.g., *a loaf of bread costs about a dollar*, will be referred to as a *disposition*.

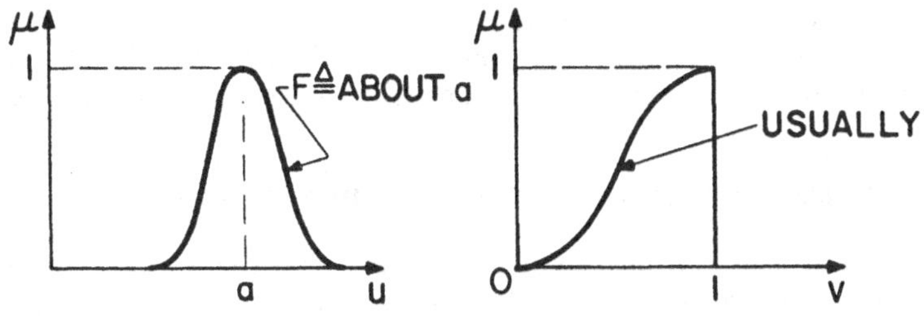

Figure 1. Representation of *usually (X is about a)*.

There are several concepts which are related to that of a usual value. Among these are: *expected value, typical value,* and *default value*. The differences between these concepts will be discussed in Section 3.

The concept of usuality gives rise to a number of basic questions relating to meaning representation, inference and decision analysis. Among the more important of these are the following.

1. How can the meaning of usuality-qualified propositions be represented? For example, what is the meaning of the proposition *usually it is cold and foggy in San Francisco during the early part of summer*? How can the usual value of a variable be computed?
2. How can the usual values of two or more variables be combined? For example, if $Z = X + Y$, and one is given the usual values of X and Y, what will be the usual value of Z?
3. How can one construct an inference system for reasoning with usuality-qualified propositions? For example if A, B, and C are fuzzy sets, then what will be the value of the fuzzy quantifier Q in the inference schema

$$\begin{array}{l} \textit{usually}\ (A \subset B) \\ \underline{\textit{usually}\ (B \subset C)} \\ Q\ (A \subset C)\,. \end{array} \tag{1.4}$$

4. How can rational decisions be made in an environment in which knowledge is usuality-qualified, i.e., one knows the usual values of probabilities, costs and payoff's?

In what follows, we shall restrict our attention to the issues of meaning representation and inference, and will outline how some of the basic questions relating to these issues may be answered, at least tentatively. It is our belief that, when it is more fully developed, the theory of usuality may prove to be of use in many problem-areas in which knowledge is imprecise, incomplete or not totally reliable. In particular, it may find important applications in the management of uncertainty in expert systems and, more generally, in the design of decision-support systems in which commonsense knowledge plays an important role.

2. Meaning Representation of Usuality-Qualified Propositions

In our approach to usuality, *usually* is interpreted as a fuzzy quantifier which plays the role of a fuzzy proportion (Figure 2). To make this more specific, it is necessary to define a way of counting the number of elements in a fuzzy set or, equivalently, to determine its cardinality.

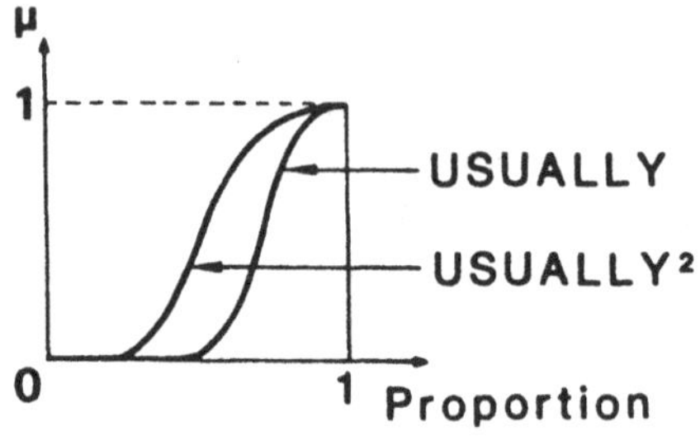

Figure 2. Representation of *usually* and *usually*^{2}.

There are several ways in which this can be done [21]. For our purposes, it will suffice to employ the concept of a *sigma-count*, which is defined as follows.

Let F be a fuzzy subset of $U = \{u_1, \ldots, u_n\}$

expressed symbolically as

$$F = \mu_1/u_1 + \ldots + \mu_n/u_n = \Sigma_i \mu_i/u_i \tag{2.1}$$

or, more simply, as

$$F = \mu_1 u_1 + \ldots + \mu_n u_n \ , \tag{2.2}$$

in which the term μ_i/u_i, $i = 1, \ldots, n$, signifies that μ_i is the grade of membership of u_i in F, and the plus sign represents the union.

The sigma-count of F is defined as the arithmetic sum of the μ_i , i.e.,

$$\Sigma Count(F) \triangleq \Sigma_i \mu_i \, , \; i = 1, \ldots, n \ , \tag{2.3}$$

with the understanding that the sum may be rounded, if need be, to the nearest integer. Furthermore, one may stipulate that the terms whose grade of membership falls below a specified threshold be excluded from the summation. The purpose of such an exclusion is to avoid a situation in which a large number of terms with low grades of membership become count-equivalent to a small number of terms with high membership.

The *relative sigma-count*, denoted by $\Sigma Count(F/G)$, may be interpreted as the proportion of elements of F which are in G. More explicitly,

$$\Sigma Count(F/G) = \frac{\Sigma Count(F \cap G)}{\Sigma Count(G)} \ , \tag{2.4}$$

where $F \cap G$, the intersection of F and G, is defined by

$$\mu_{F \cap G}(u) = \mu_F(u) \wedge \mu_G(u) \ , \quad u \in U \ .$$

Thus, in terms of the membership functions of F and G, the relative sigma-count of F in G is given by

$$\Sigma Count(F/G) = \frac{\Sigma_i \mu_F(u_i) \wedge \mu_G(u_i)}{\Sigma_i \mu_G(u_i)} \ . \tag{2.5}$$

The concept of a relative sigma-count provides a basis for interpreting the meaning of propositions of the form Q *A's are B's*, e.g., *most young men are healthy*. More specifically, if the focal variable (ie., the constrained variable) in the proposition in question is taken to be the proportion of *B's* in *A's*, then the corresponding translation rule may be expressed as

$$Q\ A\text{'s are } B\text{'s} \rightarrow \Sigma Count(B/A) \text{ is } Q\ . \tag{2.6}$$

In what follows, we shall use this translation rule to represent the meaning of (1.1).

In defining the meaning of *usually*, it is important to differentiate between those cases in which *usually* acts as an unconditioned quantifier and those in which it is conditioned on the values of a so-called *conditioning variable*.

More specifically, assume that X takes a sequence of values $u_1, \ldots, u_n$ in U. Then, *usually* is an *unconditioned* quantifier if

$$usually\ (X \text{ is } F) \rightarrow most\ u\text{'s are } F. \tag{2.7}$$

Now, using (2.3) and (2.6), the right-hand member of (2.7) may be expressed as

$$most\ u\text{'s are } F \rightarrow \frac{1}{n}\Sigma_i \mu_F(u_i) \text{ is } MOST\ , \tag{2.8}$$

where $\mu_F(u_i)$, i = 1,...,n, is the grade of membership of u_i in F and $MOST$ is the fuzzy number which represents the fuzzy quantifier *most.*[1]

For a given sequence $u_1, \ldots, u_n$ and a specified F, the degree, τ, to which the right-hand member of (2.8) is satisfied is given by

$$\tau = \mu_{MOST}\left[\frac{1}{n}\Sigma_i \mu_F(u_i)\right], \tag{2.9}$$

where μ_{MOST} is the membership function of $MOST$. This expression provides a basis for defining the meaning of (1.1) in the framework of test-score semantics [18, 20, 21].

In test-score semantics, a proposition is viewed as a collection of elastic constraints and its meaning is described by a procedure which computes the overall test score for any given explanatory database. In application to (1.1), the explanatory database consists of the u_i, μ_F and μ_{MOST}; the meaning-representation procedure is represented by the right-hand member of (2.9), and the overall test score is given by τ. In this sense, then, the meaning of (1.1) in the unconditioned case may be expressed as

$$usually\ (X \text{ is } F) \rightarrow \tau = \mu_{MOST}\left[\frac{1}{n}\Sigma_i \mu_F(u_i)\right]. \tag{2.10}$$

1. Here and elsewhere in this paper we employ uppercase symbols to represent a fuzzy set which plays the role of a denotation or extension of a term in a proposition.

As was stated earlier, the assertion *usually (X is F)* implies that F is a usual value of X. Based on (2.10), we can formulate what might be called a *qualificational definition* of a usual value of X, as follows.

Definition. Any given fuzzy subset, F, of U qualifies, to the degree τ, to be called a *usual value* of X, where τ is expressed by (2.9), i.e.,

$$\tau = \mu_{MOST}\left[\frac{1}{n}\Sigma_i \mu_F(u_i)\right] . \tag{2.11}$$

What this definition implies is that, in general, a usual value of X is not unique. Thus, any fuzzy subset of U qualifies to a degree to be a usual value of X, with the degree of qualification given by (2.11). It should be noted that, in the same setting, the expected, i.e., the average, value of X is given by

$$E(X) = \frac{1}{n}\Sigma_i u_i , \tag{2.12}$$

and is unique, if it exists.

In the foregoing discussion, we have defined the meaning of (1.1) in terms of a sequence of values of X. If X is taken to be a random variable, the meaning of (1.1) and the definition of a usual value of X may be expressed in terms of the probability distribution of X. Thus, if p_i is the probability of X taking u_i as its value, then

$$usually\ (X\ is\ F) \rightarrow \tau = \mu_{MOST}[\Sigma_i p_i \mu_F(u_i)] \tag{2.13}$$

or equivalently,

$$usually\ (X\ is\ F) \rightarrow \tau = \mu_{MOST}\left[E\ [\mu_F(X)]\right] , \tag{2.14}$$

where $E\ [\mu_F(X)]$ is the expected value of the random variable $\mu_F(X)$.

From (2.14), it follows that any given F qualifies as a usual value of X to the degree

$$\tau = \mu_{MOST}\left[E[\mu_F(X)]\right] . \tag{2.15}$$

An interesting aspect of usuality which is a consequence of (2.11) and (2.14) is that the expected value of a variable is a point in U whereas a usual value is usually a fuzzy subset of U as a result of an imprecise specification of the probability or the $\Sigma Count$ of F. In this sense, fuzziness is an intrinsic characteristic of usuality. As a case in point, it would sound odd to say *a cup of coffee usually costs fifty cents* rather than *a cup of coffee usually costs about fifty cents*. Likewise odd would be *usually it takes thirty minutes to drive from Berkeley to San Francisco*, unless *thirty* is interpreted as an interval or a fuzzy number.

As a simple illustration of (2.10), consider the proposition

$$p\text{: } \textit{usually a cup of coffee costs about fifty cents}, \tag{2.16}$$

which may be expressed more explicitly as the usuality-qualified proposition

$$p\text{: } \textit{usually}(\textit{Cost}(\textit{Cup}(\textit{Coffee})) \textit{ is } \textit{ABOUT.FIFTY.CENTS}), \tag{2.17}$$

in which $X \triangleq Cost(Cup(Coffee))$ and $F \triangleq ABOUT.FIFTY.CENTS$.[2]

Now assume that in the explanatory database we have a record of instances of cups of coffee $C_1, \ldots, C_n$ and their respective costs $c_1, \ldots, c_n$. Then, the degree to which *ABOUT.FIFTY.CENTS* qualifies to be a usual value of the cost of a cup of coffee may be expressed as

$$\tau = \mu_{MOST}\left[\frac{1}{n}\Sigma_i \mu_{ABOUT.FIFTY.CENTS}(c_i)\right]. \tag{2.18}$$

We are now in a position to consider the case where *usually* is a conditioned quantifier. In this case, in the expression

$$\textit{usually } (X \textit{ is } F) \leftrightarrow U(X) = F, \tag{2.19}$$

the degree to which F qualifies to be a usual value of X is conditioned on a proposition of the form Z *is* R, where Z is a *conditioning variable* and R is a fuzzy predicate which serves to characterize a set of *normal* or, equivalently, *non-exceptional* conditions which circumscribe the validity of the usuality-qualified proposition *usually (X is F)*. Thus, in the conditioned case, the meaning of (2.19) may be expressed as

$$\textit{usually } (X \textit{ is } F) \rightarrow \textit{in most instances } (\textit{if } Z \textit{ is } R \textit{ then } X \textit{ is } F) \tag{2.20}$$

and the expression for the degree to which F qualifies as a usual value of X becomes

$$\tau = \mu_{MOST}\,(\Sigma Count\,(F/R)) \tag{2.21}$$

or, more explicitly,

2. The symbol $\triangleq$ stands for *denotes* or *is equal to by definition*.

$$\tau = \mu_{MOST}\left[\frac{\Sigma_i \mu_F(u_i) \wedge \mu_R(v_i)}{\Sigma \mu_R(v_i)}\right], \tag{2.22}$$

in which u_i and v_i are, respectively, the values of X and Z asociated with C_i, $i = 1,...,n$.

As an illustration, assume that *usually* in (2.17) is conditioned on the rating of the eating establishment where the coffee is served, so that $Z \triangleq$ *Rating* and $R \triangleq$ *NOT.HIGH*. Then (2.20) becomes

usually(Cost(Cup(Coffee)) is ABOUT.FIFTY.CENTS) → *in most instances*

(if Rating is NOT.HIGH then Cost(Cup(Coffee)) is ABOUT.FIFTY.CENTS) .

On applying (2.22) to this expression, we obtain

$$\tau = \mu MOST\left[\frac{\Sigma_i \mu_{ABOUT.FIFTY.CENTS}(c_i) \wedge [1 - \mu_{HIGH}(r_i)]}{\Sigma_i [1 - \mu_{HIGH}(r_i)]}\right] \tag{2.23}$$

as the degree to which *about fifty cents* qualifies as a conditioned usual value of the cost of a cup of coffee. In (2.23), r_i is the rating of the eating establishment in which C_i is served, μ_{HIGH} is the membership function of *HIGH*, and $(1 - \mu_{HIGH})$ is the membership function of *NOT.HIGH*.

Remark. It should be noted that the concept of conditioned usuality may be defined in more than one way. For example, if in the right-hand member of (2.20), the *if...then* proposition is interpreted as an implication in fuzzy logic, then one possible interpretation of it might be expressed as [18]

$$\tau_i = 1 \wedge [1 - \mu_F(u_i) + \mu_R(v_i)] , \tag{2.24}$$

where τ_i is the test score for $X = u_i$ and $Z = v_i$, $i = 1,...,n$. In terms of (2.24), the overall test score for the proposition

$$\textit{in most instances (if Z is R then X is F)} \tag{2.25}$$

is given by

$$\tau = \mu_{MOST}\left[\frac{1}{n}\Sigma_i(1 \wedge [1 - \mu_F(u_i)+\mu_R(v_i)])\right] . \tag{2.26}$$

This test score, then, defines the degree to which F qualifies as a usual value of X when (2.20) is interpreted via (2.24).

Another possible interpretation of conditioned usuality may be expressed as

$$\textit{usually } (X \textit{ is } F) \rightarrow \textit{ is } Z \textit{ is } R \textit{ then in most instances } X \textit{ is } F. \tag{2.27}$$

In this case, the degree to which F would qualify as a usual value of X would depend on the value assumed by Z. Thus, if $Z = v_i$, then

$$\tau_i = 1 \wedge \left[1 - \mu_R(v_i) + \mu_{MOST}[\frac{1}{n}\Sigma_j \mu_F(u_j)]\right] \tag{2.28}$$

expresses the degree to which F qualifies as a usual value of X when $Z = v_i$, $i = 1,...,n$.

In what follows, it will be assumed, unless stated to the contrary, that conditioned usuality is defined by (2.20) and (2.22).

3. Relation to Default and Typical Values

As was alluded to earlier, the concepts of a usual value, default value, and a typical value are distinct but not unrelated. Thus, a default value, unlike a usual value, is generally a singleton, e.g., *fifty cents* might be a default value of the cost of a cup of coffee. In many cases, but not always, such a singleton would be a crisp approximation to a fuzzy value, e.g., *about fifty cents*. An example of a default value which is not a crisp approximation to a usual value is the value of X yielded by the following rule: if X is known to lie in the interval [a,b], then choose as its default value, $D(X)$, $D(X) = \frac{1}{2}(a + b)$.

The difference between usuality and typicality is more subtle and depends, of course, on the way in which the concept of typicality is defined. In what follows, we shall make use of the definition and the analysis presented in [19] and [24].

In [24], typicality is defined in terms of *similarity* [17]. More specifically, let A be a fuzzy set in U (e.g., $U \triangleq$ *cars* and $A \triangleq$ *station wagons*). The definition of a *typical* element of A may be expressed in verbal terms as follows:

t is a *typical* element of A if and only if (a) t has a high grade of membership in A , (3.1)

and (b) most elements of A are similar to t.

It should be remarked that this definition should be viewed as a *dispositional definition*, in the sense that it may fail, in some cases, to reflect our intuitive perception of the meaning of typicality.[3] Furthermore, in (3.1), A plays a role similar to that of R in the definition of a usual value (2.22).

3. It should be noted that most dictionary definitions are dispositional in nature. E.g., a lake is a body of water of considerable size surrounded by land; a spinster is an unmarried woman beyond the usual age of marriage.

To put the verbal definition expressed by (3.1) into a more precise form, let S be a similarity relation defined on U which associates with each element u in U the degree to which u is similar to t. Furthermore, let $S(t)$ be the *similarity class* of t, i.e., the fuzzy set of elements of U which are similar to t. What this means is that the grade of membership of u in $S(t)$ is equal to $\mu_S(t,u)$, the degree to which u is similar to t [24]. (Figure 3.)

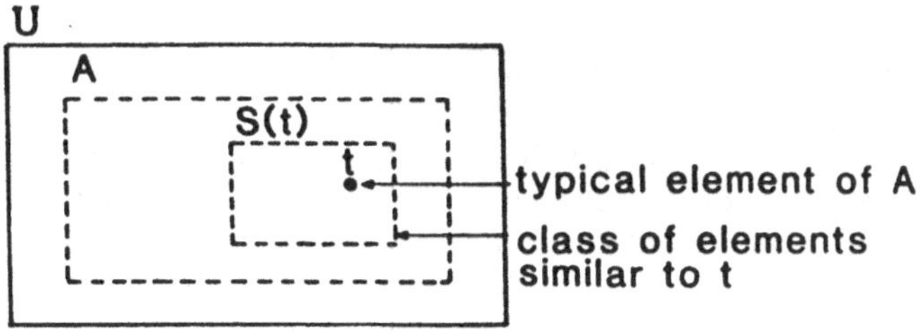

Figure 3. Definition of typicality.

Let *HIGH* denote the fuzzy subset of the unit interval which is the denotation of the fuzzy predicate *high*. Then, the verbal definition (3.1) may be expressed more precisely in the form:

t is a *typical* element of A if (a) $\mu_A(t)$ is *HIGH*, and (b) $\Sigma Count(S(t)/A)$ is *MOST*. (3.2)

An important implication of this definition is that typicality, like usuality, is a matter of degree. Thus, it follows at once from (3.2) that the degree, τ, to which t is typical or, equivalently, the grade of membership of t in the fuzzy set of typical elements of A, is given by

$$\tau = \mu_{HIGH}(\mu_A(t)) \wedge \mu_{MOST}\left[\frac{\Sigma_u\, \mu_S(t,u) \wedge \mu_A(u)}{\Sigma_u\, \mu_A(u)}\right], \tag{3.3}$$

where μ_{HIGH}, μ_{MOST}, μ_S and μ_A are the membership functions of *HIGH*, *MOST*, S and A, respectively, and the summation Σ_u extends over the elements of U.

It is of interest to observe that if $\mu_A(t) = 1$ and

$$\mu_S(t,u) = \mu_A(u)\,, \tag{3.4}$$

that is, the grade of membership of u in A is equal to the degree of similarity of u to t, then the degree of typicality of t is unity. This is reminiscent of definitions of prototypicality in which the grade of membership of an object in a category is assumed to be inversely related to its "distance" from the prototype.

As was stated earlier, in our formulation of the concept of typicality the notion of a typical value is distinct from that of a usual value. However, there is a close connection between the two which is brought out by the following result.

Assume for simplicity that $\mu_A(t) = 1$. Then, the degree to which t is a typical element of A is given by

$$\tau = \mu_{MOST}\,[\Sigma Count(S(t)/A)]\ . \qquad (3.5)$$

Comparing this expression with (3.1), we note that if we equate Z to X, R to A, and F to $S(t)$, the expression for the degree to which F is a usual value of X becomes identical with (3.5). Consequently, we can assert that

the degree to which t is a typical element of A = (3.6)

the degree to which S(t) is a usual value of X.

In other words, the similarity class of a typical element of A may be interpreted as a usual value of the variable which ranges over U and is conditioned on A.

4. Reasoning with Usuality-Qualified Propositions

As was stated earlier, one of the basic issues in the theory of usuality relates to inference from usuality-qualified propositions. A generic example of a problem of this type is the following: Suppose that p and q are propositions from which we can infer a proposition r. The question is: What can be inferred from the usuality-qualified propositions *usually p* and *usually q*?

An instance of this problem which is the Barbara syllogism of Aristotelian logic may be expressed in the schematic form

$$\begin{array}{ll} A \subset B & usually\ (A \subset B) \\ \underline{B \subset C} & \underline{usually\ (B \subset C)} \\ A \subset C & (0 \vee (2\ usually \ominus 1))(A \subset C) \end{array} \qquad (4.1)$$

where $\vee$ = max, A, B, C are possibly fuzzy sets, the fuzzy quantifier *usually* is interpreted as a fuzzy proportion, and $0 \vee (2\ usually \ominus 1)$ is a fuzzy proportion which is computed from *usually* through the use of fuzzy arithmetic [4] (Figure 4). We shall refer to the syllogism on the right as *usuality-qualified Barbara* or, equivalently, as *dispositional Barbara*.

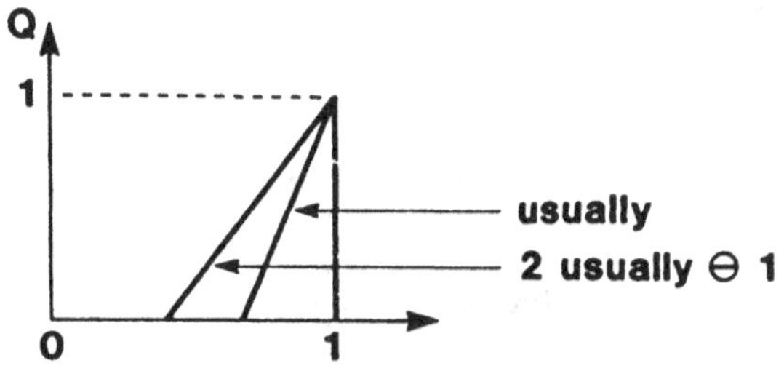

Figure 4. Triangular representations of *usually* and *2 usually* $\ominus$ *1*.

To establish the validity of dispositional Barbara, we first note that, in the usuality-qualified proposition *usually* $(A \subset B)$, *usually* is a *second-order* quantifier in the sense that the objects which it counts are sets (actually pairs of sets) rather than points, as in *usually (X is A)*.

With this understanding, let r, s and t be three binary random variables defined as follows:

$$\begin{aligned} r &= 1 \quad \text{if } A \subset B \\ &= 0 \quad \textit{otherwise} \\ s &= 1 \quad \text{if } B \subset C \\ &= 0 \quad \textit{otherwise} \\ t &= 1 \quad \text{if } A \subset C \\ &= 0 \quad \textit{otherwise} \end{aligned} \tag{4.2}$$

From these definitions, it follows at once that

$$Prob\ \{t = 1\} \geq Prob\ \{r = 1, s = 1\} \tag{4.3}$$

since $A \subset C$ is implied by $A \subset B$ and $B \subset C$.

Employing the type of arguments used in inductive logic and probabilistic reasoning, let the joint probability distribution of r and s be denoted as $p(r,s)$. Then

$$Prob\{A \subset B\} = Prob\{r = 1\} = p(1,0) + p(1,1) \tag{4.4}$$

$$Prob\{B \subset C\} = Prob\{s = 1\} = p(0,1) + p(1,1) \tag{4.5}$$

$$p(0,0) + p(0,1) + p(1,0) + p(1,1) = 1 . \tag{4.6}$$

Now, if we assume that

$$Prob\{r = 1\} \geq \alpha \tag{4.7}$$

$$Prob\{s = 1\} \geq \alpha ,$$

then on adding (4.4) and (4.5), we obtain

$$p(1,0) + p(1,1) + p(0,1) + 2p(1,1) \geq 2\alpha , \tag{4.8}$$

which in view of (4.6) leads to the inequality

$$p(1,1) \geq O \vee (2\alpha - 1)$$

and consequently to the conclusion that

$$Prob\{A \subset C\} \geq O \vee (2\alpha - 1) . \tag{4.9}$$

We are now in a position to extend this conclusion to fuzzy probabilities--and hence to fuzzy quantifiers--by employing the quantifier extension principle [21]. The application of this principle to (4.9) leads to the inequality

$$Prob\{A \subset C\} \geq O \vee (2 usually \ominus 1) , \tag{4.10}$$

which may be expressed as the equality

$$Prob\{A \subset C\} = O \vee (2 usually \ominus 1) \tag{4.11}$$

if *usually* is assumed to be monotonic [1, 21], i.e., $\geq$ *usually* = *usually*. Finally, on interpreting the probability in the left-hand member of (4.11) as a quantifier Q, we are led to the conclusion that

$$Q = O \vee (2 \; usually \ominus 1) , \tag{4.12}$$

which establishes the validity of the deduction represented by the dispositional Barbara syllogism (4.1).

Many results of a similar nature may be deduced from the intersection-product syllogism [21]

$$\begin{array}{l} Q_1\ A\text{'s are } B\text{'s} \\ \underline{Q_2\ B\text{'s are } C\text{'s}} \\ (Q_1 \otimes Q_2)\ A\text{'s are } (B \text{ and } C)\text{'s,} \end{array} \tag{4.13}$$

where A, B and C are fuzzy sets, Q_1 and Q_2 are fuzzy quantifiers, and $Q_1 \otimes Q_2$ is the product of Q_1 and Q_2 in fuzzy arithmetic (Figure 5). As an illustration, we can derive from this syllogism a version of the so-called *dispositional modus ponens* [26, 27] which may be expressed as

$$\begin{array}{l} usually\ (X \text{ is } F) \\ \underline{usually\ (\text{if } X \text{ is } F \text{ then } Y \text{ is } G)} \\ usually^2\ (Y \text{ is } G)\ , \end{array} \tag{4.14}$$

where F and G are fuzzy sets and $usually^2$ is the product of *usually* with itself in fuzzy arithmetic (Figure 2).

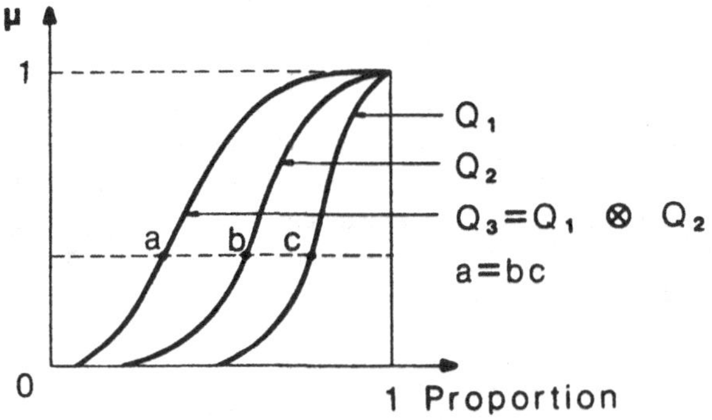

Figure 5. Multiplication of fuzzy quantifiers.

To do so, we make use of the representations

$$usually\ (X \text{ is } F) \rightarrow \Sigma Count(F) \text{ is } USUALLY \tag{4.15}$$

$$usually\ (\text{if } X \text{ is } F \text{ then } Y \text{ is } G) \rightarrow \Sigma Count(G/F) \text{ is } USUALLY\ , \tag{4.16}$$

where *USUALLY* is a fuzzy number which represents the denotation of *usually*.

On making use of (4.15) and (4.16), we obtain

$$\Sigma Count(G \cap F) \text{ is } USUALLY^2 , \tag{4.17}$$

and since

$$\Sigma Count(G) \geq \Sigma Count(G \cap F) \tag{4.18}$$

it follows that

$$\Sigma Count(G) \geq USUALLY^2 \tag{4.19}$$

and hence

$$\Sigma Count(G) = USUALLY^2 \tag{4.20}$$

in view of the monotonicity of *usually*. Finally, upon retranslation of (4.20), we obtain the conclusion

$$usually^2(Y \text{ is } G) , \tag{4.21}$$

which is what we wanted to establish.

In the formalization of rules of inference for usuality-qualified propositions, it is important to bear in mind that such propositions may admit of a multiplicity of interpretations. For example, in our discussion of dispositional Barbara, we have interpreted *usually* in *usually* $(A \subset B)$ as a second-order quantifier. Alternatively, we could employ the interpretation

$$usually\ (A \subset B) \rightarrow usually\ (\text{if } X \text{ is } A \text{ then } Y \text{ is } B) , \tag{4.22}$$

in which case *usually* would act as a first-order quantifier. In this event, we would have

$$\begin{array}{l} usually\ (\text{if } X \text{ is } A \text{ then } Y \text{ is } B) \\ \underline{usually\ (\text{if } Y \text{ is } B \text{ then } Z \text{ is } C)} \\ [0,1]\ (\text{if } X \text{ is } A \text{ then } Z \text{ is } C) , \end{array} \tag{4.23}$$

in which [0,1] is the vacuous quantifier *never-to-always* or *none-to-all*. This implies that under the interpretation in question nothing can be said about the validity of the conclusion *if X is A then Z is C*.

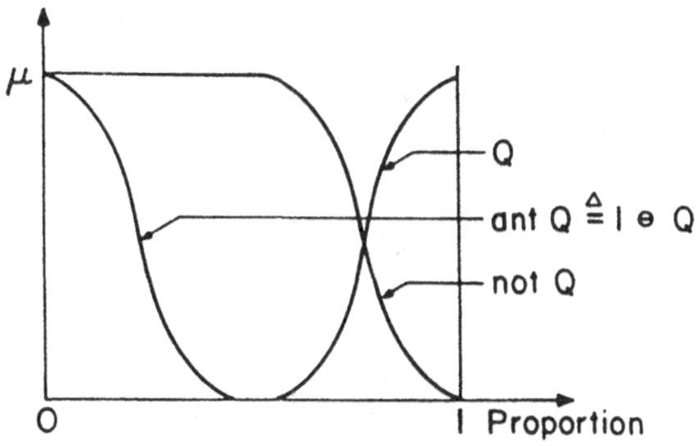

Figure 6. Representation of *Q*, *not Q* and *ant Q*.

In dealing with usuality in the context of commonsense reasoning, it is important to be able to deal not only with what is usual, but also with what is unusual. In this connection, we shall establish the following identity (Figure 6):

$$usually\ (X\ is\ F) \leftrightarrow unusually\ (X\ is\ not\ F)\ , \tag{4.24}$$

in which *unusually* (or *rarely*) is the antonym of *usually*, that is,

$$UNUSUALLY\ = 1 \ominus USUALLY \tag{4.25}$$

or, equivalently,

$$\mu_{UNUSUALLY}\,(v) = \mu_{USUALLY}\,(1 - v),\ \ 0 \le v \le 1. \tag{4.26}$$

To this end, it is sufficient to show that the overall test scores for the two members of (4.24) are identical. Thus, for the left-hand member we have

$$\tau_e = \mu_{USUALLY}\,[\frac{1}{n}\Sigma_i\mu_F(u_i)]\ , \tag{4.27}$$

while for the right-hand member the corresponding expression is

$$\tau_r = \mu_{UNUSUALLY}\left[\frac{1}{n}\Sigma_i[1 - \mu_F(u_i)]\right]. \tag{4.28}$$

From (4.28), it follows at once that $\tau_e = \tau_r$, which is what we wanted to establish.

What happens when *usually* is conditioned? In this case it does not follow from

$$usually\ (if\ Z\ is\ R\ then\ X\ is\ F)$$

that

$$unusually\ (if\ Z\ is\ R\ then\ X\ is\ not\ F)\ .$$

However, we can establish a weaker rule [21], namely

$$\frac{unusually\ (if\ Z\ is\ R\ then\ X\ is\ not\ F)}{usually\ (if\ Z\ is\ R\ then\ X\ is\ F)}\ . \qquad (4.29)$$

In a similar fashion, one can readily establish a variety of rules of inference which apply to usuality-qualified propositions. Several additional examples of such rules may be found in [24].

Concluding Remark

In this brief outline of the theory of usuality, we have focused our attention on only a few of the basic issues. Further progress in our understanding of the concept of usuality may provide a basis for the development of more effective approaches to commonsense reasoning and, more generally, for constructing a systematic framework for deduction in knowledge-based systems in which some of the information is imprecise, incomplete or not totally reliable.

REFERENCES AND RELATED PUBLICATIONS

1. Barwise, J. and Cooper, R., Generalized quantifiers and natural language, *Linguistics and Philosophy* 4 (1981) 159-219.
2. Buchanan, B.G. and Shortliffe, E.H., *Rule-Based Expert Systems. Reading: Addison-Wesley, 1984.*
3. Dubois, D. and Prade, H., *Fuzzy Sets and Systems: Theory and Applications.* New York: Academic Press, 1980.
4. Kaufmann, A. and Gupta, M., *Introduction to Fuzzy Arithmetic.* New York: Van Nostrand, 1985.
5. Mamdani, E.H., and Gaines, B.R., *Fuzzy Reasoning and its Applications.* London: Academic Press, 1981.
6. Mellor, D.H., *Matter of Chance.* Cambridge: Cambridge University Press, 1971.
7. Mellor, D.H., *Science, Belief and Behavior.* Cambridge: Cambridge University Press, 1980.
8. Miller, G.A. and Johnson-Laird, P.N., *Language and Perception.* Cambridge: Harvard University Press, 1976.
9. Moore, R.E., *Interval Analysis.* Englewood Cliffs: Prentice-Hall, 1966.
10. Osherson, D.N. and Smith, E.E., On the adequacy of prototype theory as a theory of concepts, *Cognition 9* (1981) 59-72.
11. Peterson, P., On the logic of *few, many* and *most, Notre Dame J. Formal Logic 20* (1979) 155-179.
12. Reiter, R. and Criscuolo, G., Some representational issues in default reasoning, *Computers and Mathematics 9* (1983) 15-28.
13. Rescher, N., *Plausible Reasoning.* Amsterdam: Van Gorcum, 1976.
14. Smith, E. and Medin, D.L., *Categories and Concepts.* Cambridge: Harvard University Press, 1981.
15. Yager, R.R., Quantified propositions in a linguistic logic, in: *Proceedings of the 2nd International Seminar on Fuzzy Set Theory,* Klement, E.P., (ed.). Johannes Kepler University, Linz, Austria, 1980.
16. Yager, R.R., Reasoning with fuzzy quantified statements - I, *Kybernetes 14* (1985) 233-240.
17. Zadeh, L.A., Similarity relations and fuzzy orderings, *Information Sciences 3* (1971) 177-200.
18. Zadeh, L.A., PRUF -- A meaning representation language for natural languages, *Inter. J. Man-Machine Studies 10* (1978) 395-460.
19. Zadeh, L.A., A note on prototype theory and fuzzy sets, *Cognition 12* (1982) 291-297.
20. Zadeh, L.A., Test-score semantics for natural languages and meaning-representation via PRUF, *Proc. COLING 82*, Prague, 425-430, 1982. Full text in: *Empirical Semantics*, Rieger, B.B., (ed.). Bochum: Brockmeyer, 281-349, 1982.

21. Zadeh, L.A., A computational approach to fuzzy quantifiers in natural languages, *Computers and Mathematics 9* (1983) 149-184.

22. Zadeh, L.A., A fuzzy-set-theoretic approach to the compositionality of meaning: Propositions, dispositions and canonical forms, *Journal of Semantics 3* (1983) 253-272.

23. Zadeh, L.A., Fuzzy logic as a basis for the management of uncertainty in expert systems, *Fuzzy Sets and Systems 11* (1983) 199-227.

24. Zadeh, L.A., A computational theory of dispositions, in *Proceedings of the 1984 Conference on Computational Linguistics*, Stanford, CA, 312-318, 1984.

25. Zadeh, L.A., A theory of commonsense knowledge, in *Aspects of Vagueness*, (H.J. Skala, S. Termini and E. Trillas, eds.), Dordrecht: Reidel, 257-296, 1984.

26. Zadeh, L.A., Syllogistic reasoning in fuzzy logic and its application to usuality and reasoning with dispositions, *IEEE Transactions on Systems, Man and Cybernetics SMC-15* (1985) 754-763.

27. Zadeh, L.A., Fuzzy sets, usuality and commonsense reasoning, *Berkeley Cognitive Science Report No. 32*, University of California, Berkeley, CA, 1985. To appear in *Matters of Intelligence*, L. Vaina, ed. Dordrecht: Reidel, 1986.

A Computational Theory of Dispositions*

Lotfi A. Zadeh
Computer Science Division, University of California, Berkeley, CA 94720

A *disposition* may be interpreted as a proposition which is preponderantly, but not necessarily always, true. In this sense, *birds can fly* is a disposition, as are the propositions *Swedes are blond*, *snow is white*, and *slimness is attractive*. An idea which underlies the theory described in this article is that a disposition may be viewed as a proposition with implicit fuzzy quantifiers which are approximations to *all* and *always*, e.g., *almost all*, *almost always*, *most*, *frequently*, *usually*, etc. For example, *birds can fly* may be interpreted as the result of suppressing the fuzzy quantifier *most* in the proposition *most birds can fly*. Similarly, *young men like young women* may be read as *most young men like mostly young women*. The process of transforming a disposition into a proposition with explicit fuzzy quantifiers is referred to as *explicitation* or *restoration*. Explicitation sets the stage for representing the meaning of a disposition through the use of test-score semantics [see L.A. Zadeh: *International J. Man–Machine Studies*, **10** 395–460 (1978); *Empirical Semantics*, 281–349 (1982)]. In this approach to semantics, a proposition, p, is viewed as a collection of interrelated elastic constraints, and the meaning of p is represented as a procedure which tests, scores and aggregates the constraints which are induced by p. The article closes with a description of an approach to reasoning with dispositions which is based on the concept of a fuzzy syllogism. Syllogistic reasoning with dispositions has an important bearing on commonsense reasoning as well as on the management of uncertainty in expert systems. As a simple application of the techniques described in this article, we formulate a definition of *typicality* and establish a connection between the typical and usual values of a variable.

I. INTRODUCTION

Informally, a disposition is a proposition which is preponderantly, but not always necessarily always, true. Simple examples of dispositions are: *Snow is white, exercise is good for your health, long sentences are more difficult to parse than short sentences, a cup of coffee costs about fifty cents, slimness is attractive, a bachelor is an unmarried man*, etc. Dispositions play a central role in human reasoning, since much of human knowledge and, especially, commonsense knowledge, may be viewed as a collection of dispositions.

The concept of a disposition gives rise to a number of related concepts among which is the concept of a *dispositional predicate*. Familiar examples of unary predicates of this type are: *healthy*, *honest*, *optimist*, *safe*, etc., with binary dispositional predicates exemplified by: *taller than* in *Swedes are taller than Frenchmen*, *like* in *Italians are like Spaniards*, *like* in *young men like young women*, *smokes* in *Ron smokes cigarettes*, and *relevant* in *age is relevant to health*.

*To Henri Prade and Didier Dubois. This research was supported in part by NASA Grant No. NCC-2-275, and NSF Grants Nos. IST-8320416 and DCR-8513139.

Reprinted, with permission, from *Intern. J. of Intelligent Systems*, **2**(1), pp. 39–63.

Another related concept is that of a *dispositional definition* which is exemplified by: *a spinster is an unmarried woman past the common age for marrying, an island is a tract of land surrounded by water*, etc. It is of interest to note that most of the definitions found in a dictionary are dispositional definitions in the sense that it is almost always possible to find (1) examples of objects that satisfy the definition and yet do not fit the concept, or (2) fit the concept but do not satisfy the definition.

The basic idea underlying the approach described in this article is that a disposition may be viewed as a proposition with suppressed, or, more generally, implicit fuzzy quantifiers such as *most*, *almost all*, *almost always*, *usually*, *rarely*, *much of the time*, etc.*

To illustrate, the disposition *a cup of coffee costs about fifty cents* may be viewed as the result of suppression of the fuzzy quantifier *usually* in the proposition *usually a cup of coffee costs about fifty cents*. Similarly, the disposition *young men like young women* may be interpreted as *most young men like mostly young women*. It should be stressed, however, that *restoration* (or *explicitation*)—viewed as the inverse of suppression—is an interpretation-dependent process in the sense that, in general, a disposition may be interpreted in different ways depending on the manner in which the fuzzy quantifiers are restored and defined. For example, *slimness is attractive* may be interpreted in a number of ways, among them: (1) *most slim people are attractive*; (2) *most attractive people are slim*; and (3) *the proportion of attractive people in the population of slim people is substantially larger than in the general population*.

The implicit presence of fuzzy quantifiers stands in the way of representing the meaning of dispositional concepts through the use of conventional methods based on truth-conditional, possible-world or model-theoretic semantics.[5–7] In the computational approach which is described in this article, a fuzzy quantifier is manipulated as a fuzzy number. This idea serves two purposes. First, it provides a basis for representing the meaning of dispositions; and second, it opens a way of reasoning with dispositions through the use of a collection of syllogisms. This aspect of the concept of a disposition is of relevance to default reasoning and nonmonotonic logic.[8–11]

To illustrate the manner in which fuzzy quantifiers may be manipulated as fuzzy numbers, assume that, after restoration, two dispositions d_1 and d_2 may be expressed as propositions of the form

$$p_1 = Q_1 A\text{s are } B\text{s} \tag{1}$$

$$p_2 = Q_2 B\text{s are } C\text{s}, \tag{2}$$

*In the literature of linguistics, logic and philosophy of languages, fuzzy quantifiers are usually referred to as *vague* or *generalized* quantifiers.[1,2] In the approach described in this paper, a fuzzy quantifier is interpreted as a fuzzy number which provides an approximate characterization of absolute or relative cardinality. Fuzzy numbers may be manipulated through the use of fuzzy arithmetic,[3] which is a generalization of interval arithmetic.[4]

in which Q_1 and Q_2 are fuzzy quantifiers, and A, B, and C are fuzzy predicates. For example,

$$p_1 = \textit{most students are undergraduates} \tag{3}$$

$$p_2 = \textit{most undergraduates are young.}$$

By treating p_1 and p_2 as the minor and major premises in a syllogism, the following *chaining* syllogism may be established if $B \subset A$:[12–14]

$$\begin{array}{c} Q_1 \text{ As are Bs} \\ \underline{Q_2 \text{ Bs are Cs}} \\ \geqslant (Q_1 \otimes Q_2) \text{ As are Cs,} \end{array} \tag{4}$$

in which $Q_1 \otimes Q_2$ represents the product of the fuzzy numbers Q_1 and Q_2 (Fig. 1), and $\geqslant (Q_1 \otimes Q_2)$ should be read as "at least $Q_1 \otimes Q_2$." As shown in Figure 1, Q_1 and Q_2 are defined by their respective possibility distributions, which means that if the value of Q_1 at the point u is α, then α represents the possibility that the proportion of As in Bs is u.

In the special case where p_1 and p_2 are expressed by Eq. (3), the chaining syllogism yields

most students are undergraduates

most undergraduates are young

most^2 *students are young*

where *most*^{2} represents the product of the fuzzy number *most* with itself (Fig. 2).

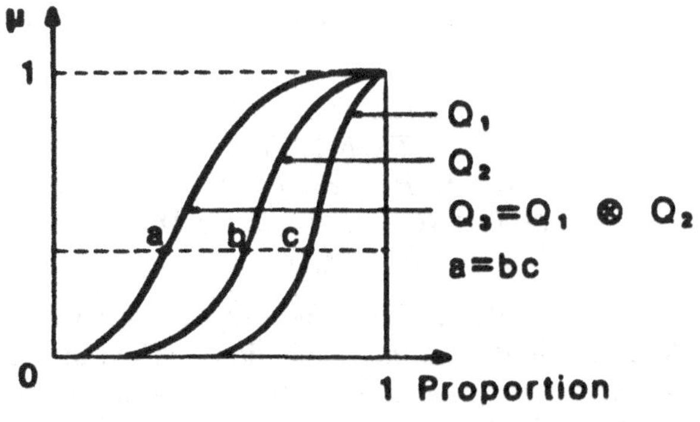

Figure 1. Multiplication of fuzzy quantifiers.

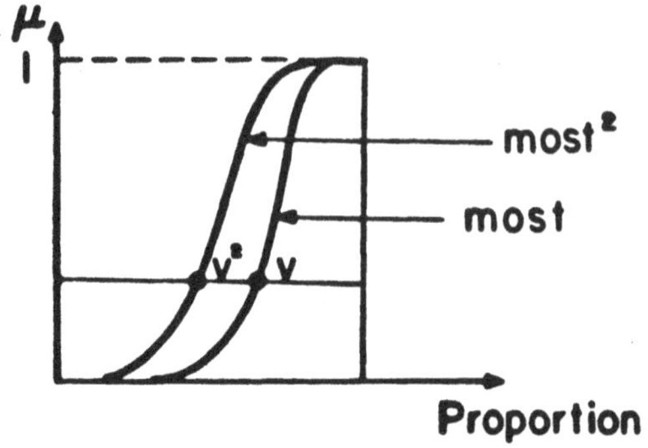

Figure 2. Representation of *most* and *most*^{2}.

II. MEANING REPRESENTATION AND TEST-SCORE SEMANTICS

To represent the meaning of a disposition, d, we employ a two-stage process. First, the suppressed fuzzy quantifiers in d are restored, resulting in a fuzzily quantified proposition p. Then, the meaning of p is represented—through the use of test-score semantics[15–17]—as a procedure which acts on a collection of relations in an explanatory database and returns a test score which represents the degree of compatibility of p with the database. In effect, this implies that p may be viewed as a collection of elastic constraints which are tested, scored, and aggregated by the meaning-representation procedure. In test-score semantics, these elastic constraints play a role which is analogous to that of truth-conditions in truth-conditional semantics.[5]

In more specific terms, the process of meaning representation in test-score semantics involves three distinct phases. In Phase 1, an *explanatory database frame* or *EDF*, for short, is constructed. *EDF* consists of a collection of relational frames, i.e., names of relations, names of attributes and attribute domains whose meaning is assumed to be known. For example, in the case of the proposition

$$p = \textit{Carol lives in a small city near San Francisco}, \tag{5}$$

the *EDF* may consist of the following relations (in which "+" should be read as *and*):

$$\begin{aligned} EDF = {} & RESIDENCE\ [Name;\ City] + \\ & POPULATION\ [City;\ Population] + \\ & SMALL\ [Population;\ \mu] + \\ & DISTANCE\ [City1;\ City2;\ Distance] + \\ & NEAR\ [Distance;\ \mu]. \end{aligned} \tag{6}$$

In *RESIDENCE*, the attribute *City* is the name of the city in which *Name* resides; in *POPULATION*, *Population* is the population of *City*; in *SMALL*, μ is the degree to which a city whose population is the value of the attribute *Population*, is small; in *DISTANCE*, *Distance* is the distance between *City1* and *City2*; and in *NEAR*, μ is the degree to which two cities whose distance from one another is the value of *Distance*, are near each other. The relations in question may be interpreted as constraints on the attribute variables which are associated with them. In the case of the relations *SMALL* and *NEAR*, the constraints are elastic; in the case of *RESIDENCE*, *POPULATION*, and *DISTANCE*, the constraints are inelastic. In essence, the role played by the concept of an explanatory database frame in test-score semantics is similar to that of a collection of possible worlds in truth-conditional and possible-world semantics. In this sense, an explanatory database *ED* which is an instantiation of *EDF*, may be interpreted as a possible world, i.e., an instantiation of a collection of possible worlds. The main difference between the two concepts is that the elasticity of constraints plays a central role in test-score semantics and is ignored in truth-conditional and possible-world semantics.

The testing of elastic constraints constitutes Phase 2 of the meaning representation process. More specifically, in Phase 2 a test procedure is constructed which acts on the relations in *EDF* and yields the test scores which represent the degrees to which the elastic constraints are satisfied. For example, in the case of *p*, the test procedure would yield the test scores for the constraints induced by *RESIDENCE*, *POPULATION*, *SMALL*, *DISTANCE*, and *NEAR*. Normally, the test scores are numbers in the unit interval [0,1]. More generally, the test scores may be elements of a partially ordered set or possibility/probability distributions.

In Phase 3, the partial test scores are aggregated into an overall test score, τ, which, in general, is a vector which serves to represent the degree of compatibility of *p* with *ED*, that is, an explanatory database which is an instantiation of *EDF*. As is the case of partial test scores, the components of τ are numbers in the unit interval or, more generally, possibility/probability distributions over the interval. When τ is a single number, which is usually the case, it may be interpreted as the truth value of *p* with respect to *ED* or, equivalently, as the degree of possibility of *ED* given *p*.

As a simple illustration of the application of test-score semantics, consider the proposition expressed by Eq. (5). In this case, for the *EDF* defined by Eq. (6), the test procedure which computes the overall test score may be described as follows:

(1) Determine the city in which Carol resides:

$$City(Carol) = {}_{City}RESIDENCE\ [Name = Carol].$$

In this expression, we use the notation ${}_{Y}R[X = a]$ to signify that X is bound to a in R and the resulting relation is projected on Y, yielding the values of Y in the tuples in which $X = a$. If there is only one such tuple, then ${}_{Y}R[X = a]$ is simply the value of Y corresponding to $X = a$.

(2) Determine the popoulation of the city in which Carol resides:

$$P = {}_{Population}POPULATION\ [City = City(Carol)].$$

(3) Determine the distance between San Francisco and the city in which Carol resides:

$$D = {}_{Distance}DISTANCE\ [City1 = SF;\ City2 = City(Carol)].$$

(4) Test the elastic constraint induced by the fuzzy predicate *small*:

$$\tau_1 = {}_{\mu}SMALL\ [Population = P].$$

(5) Test the elastic constraint induced by the fuzzy predicate *near*:

$$\tau_2 = {}_{\mu}NEAR\ [Distance = D].$$

(6) Compute the overall test score by aggregating the partial test scores τ_1 and τ_2. For this purpose, we shall use the min operator $\wedge$ as the aggregation operator, yielding

$$\tau = \tau_1 \wedge \tau_1, \tag{7}$$

which signifies that the overall test score is taken to be the smaller of the operands of *and*. The overall test score, as expressed by Eq. (7), represents the compatibility of p = *Carol lives in a small town near San Francisco* with the data resident in the explanatory database.

In testing the constituent relations in *EDF*, it is helpful to have a collection of standardized aggregation rules for computing the test score of a combination of elastic constraints $C_1, \ldots, C_k$ from the knowledge of the test score of each constraint considered in isolation. For the most part, such rules are default rules in the sense that they are intended to be used in the absence of alternative rules supplied by the user. This applies, in particular, to the rules pertaining to such modifiers as *very* and *more or less*.

In test-score semantics, the basic aggregation rules are the following.

Rules Pertaining to Modification

If the test score for an elastic constraint C in a specified context is τ, then in the same context the test score for

(*a*) *not* C is $1 - \tau$ (negation)

(*b*) *very* C is τ^2 (concentration)

(*c*) *more or less* C is $\tau^{1/2}$. (diffusion)

Rules Pertaining to Composition

If the test scores for elastic constraints C_1 and C_2 in a specified context are τ_1 and τ_2, respectively, then in the same context the test score for

(*a*) C_1 *and* C_2 is $\tau_1 \wedge \tau_2$ (conjunction)

(*b*) C_1 *or* C_2 is $\tau_1 \vee \tau_2$ (disjunction)

(*c*) *If* C_1 *then* C_2 is $1 \wedge (1 - \tau_1 + \tau_2)$, (implication)

where $\wedge$ = min and $\vee$ = max.

Rules Pertaining to Quantification

The rules in question apply to propositions of the general form *Q As are Bs*, where Q is a fuzzy quantifier, e.g., *most*, *many*, *several*, *few*, etc.

To make the concept of a fuzzy quantifier meaningful, it is necessary to define a way of counting the number of elements in a fuzzy set or, equivalently, to determine its cardinality. There are several ways in which this can be done.[12] For our purposes, it will suffice to employ the concept of a *sigma-count*, which is defined as follows.

Let F be a fuzzy subset $U = \{u_1, \ldots, u_n\}$

expressed symbolically as

$$F = \mu_1/u_1 + \ldots + \mu_n/u_n = \Sigma_i \mu_i/u_i,$$

in which the term μ_i/u_i, $i = 1, \ldots, n$, signifies that μ_i is the grade of membership of u_i in F, and the plus sign represents the union.

The *sigma-count* of F is defined as the arithmetic sum of the μ_i, i.e.,

$$\Sigma Count(F) = \Sigma_i \mu_i,\ i = 1, \ldots, n, \tag{8}$$

with the understanding that the sum may be rounded if necessary to the nearest integer. Furthermore, one may stipulate that terms with grades of membership below a specified threshold be excluded from the summation in order to keep a large number of terms with low grades of membership from becoming count-equivalent to a small number of terms with high membership.

The *relative sigma-count*, denoted by $\Sigma Count(F/G)$, may be interpreted as the proportion of elements of F which are in G. More explicitly,

$$\Sigma Count(F/G) = \frac{\Sigma Count(F \cap G)}{\Sigma Count(G)}, \tag{9}$$

where $F \cap G$, the intersection of F and G, is defined by

$$\mu_{F \cap G}(u) = \mu_F(u) \wedge \mu_G(u),\ u \in U.$$

Thus, in terms of the membership functions of F and G, the relative sigma-count of F and G is given by

$$\Sigma Count(F/G) = \frac{\Sigma_i \mu_F(u_i) \wedge \mu_G(u_i)}{\Sigma_i \mu_G(u_i)}. \tag{10}$$

The concept of a relative sigma-count provides a basis for representing the meaning of a proposition of the general form

$$p = Q \text{ } As \text{ } are \text{ } Bs, \tag{11}$$

where Q is a fuzzy quantifier, and A and B are fuzzy predicates. More specifically, assume that the *EDF* associated with p consists of three relations:

$$EDF = Q[v; \mu] + A[u; \mu] + B[w; \mu], \tag{12}$$

in which v is a point in the unit interval, and μ in Q is the grade of membership of v in the fuzzy number which represents Q; μ in A is the grade of membership of u in

A; and μ in B is the grade of membership of w in B, with u and w representing points in the domains of A and B, respectively.

With the *EDF* defined by Eq. (12), the overall test score for p may be expressed as the translation rule

$$p \rightarrow \tau = {}_{\mu}Q\ [v = \Sigma Count(B/A)], \tag{13}$$

in which the right-hand member is the test procedure which computes the value of τ and thus represents the meaning of p.

As an illustration of translation rule (13), consider the proposition

$$p = \textit{most physicians are more affluent than all but a few musicians}, \tag{14}$$

with which we associate the *EDF*:

$$\begin{aligned} EDF = {} & PHYSICIAN\ [Name;\ Income] + \\ & MUSICIAN\ [Name;\ Income] + \\ & MUCH\ MORE\ [Income1;\ Income2;\ \mu] + \\ & MOST\ [Proportion;\ \mu] + \\ & FEW\ [Proportion;\ \mu]. \end{aligned}$$

The steps in the test procedure which lead to the overall test score may be described as follows.

(1) Let $Name_i$ be the name of the ith individual in *PHYSICIAN*. For each $NAME_i$, $i = 1, \ldots, m$, find his/her income:

$$IP_i = {}_{Income}PHYSICIAN\ [Name = Name_i].$$

(2) For each $Name_j$, $j = 1, \ldots n$, in *MUSICIAN*, find his/her income:

$$IM_j = {}_{Income}MUSICIAN\ [Name = Name_j].$$

(3) For each pair ($Name_i$, $Name_i$) find the degree to which $Name_i$ is much more affluent than $Name_j$ (assuming that affluence is measured by income):

$$A_{ij} = {}_{\mu}MUCH\ MORE\ [Income1 = IP_i;\ Income2 = IM_j].$$

(4) For each $Name_i$, compute the relative sigma-count of musicians in relation to whom $Name_i$, is much more affluent:

$$P_i = \frac{1}{n}\,\Sigma_j A_{ij}.$$

(5) Test the constraint on P_i induced by the fuzzy quantifier *all but a few*:

$$\tau_i = 1 - {}_{\mu}FEW\ [Proportion = P_i].$$

(6) Compute the relative sigma-count of physicians who satisfy the constraint *much more affluent than all but a few musicians*:

$$\sigma = \frac{1}{m}\,\Sigma_i \tau_i$$

(7) Compute the test score for the constraint on σ induced by the fuzzy quantifier *most*:

$$\tau = {}_{\mu}MOST\,[Proportion = \sigma]. \tag{16}$$

The value of τ expressed by Eq. (16) represents the overall test score which defines the compatibility of p (14) with the explanatory database. The meaning of p is defined by the test procedure which computes τ.

III. THE SCOPE OF A FUZZY QUANTIFIER

In dealing with the conventional quantifiers *all* and *some* in first-order logic, the scope of a quantifier plays an essential role in defining its meaning. In the case of a fuzzy quantifier which is characterized by a relative sigma-count, what matters is the identity of the sets which enter into the relative sigma-count. Thus, if the sigma-count is of the form $\Sigma Count(B/A)$, which should be read as the proportion of Bs in As, then B and A will be referred to as the *n-set* (with n standing for numerator) and *b-set* (with b standing for base), respectively. The ordered pair {*n*-set, *b*-set}, then, may be viewed as a generalization of the concept of the scope of a quantifier. Note, however, that, in this sense, the scope of a fuzzy quantifier is a semantic rather than syntactic concept.

As a simple illustration, consider the proposition p = *most students are undergraduates*. In this case, the *n*-set of *most* is *undergraduates*, the *b*-set is *students*, and the scope of *most* is the pair {*undergraduates*, *students*}.

As an additional illustration of the interaction between scope and meaning, consider the disposition

$$d = young\ men\ like\ young\ women. \tag{17}$$

Among the possible interpretations of this disposition, we shall focus our attention on the following (the symbol *rd* denotes a restoration of a disposition):

$$rd_1 = most\ young\ men\ like\ most\ young\ women$$

$$rd_2 = most\ young\ men\ like\ mostly\ young\ women.$$

To place in evidence the difference between rd_1 and rd_2, it is expedient to express them in the form

$$rd_1 = most\ young\ men\ P_1$$

$$rd_2 = most\ young\ men\ P_2,$$

where P_1 and P_2 are the fuzzy predicates

$$P_1 = likes\ most\ young\ women$$

and

$$P_2 = likes\ mostly\ young\ women,$$

with the understanding that, for grammatical correctness, *likes* in P_1 and P_2 should be replaced by *like* when P_1 and P_2 act as constituents of rd_1 and rd_2.

In more explicit terms, P_1 and P_2 may be expressed as

$$P_1 = P_1\ [Name;\ \mu] \qquad (18)$$
$$P_2 = P_2\ [Name;\ \mu],$$

in which *Name* is the name of a male person and μ is the degree to which the person in question satisfies the predicate. (Equivalently, μ is the grade of membership of the person in the fuzzy set which represents the extension of the predicate.)

To represent the meaning of P_1 and P_2 through the use of test-score semantics, we assume that the *EDF* consists of the following relations:[13]

$$\begin{aligned} EDF = {} & POPULATION\ [Name;\ Age;\ Sex] + \\ & LIKE\ [Name1;\ Name2;\ \mu] + \\ & YOUNG\ [Age;\ \mu] + \\ & MOST\ [Proportion;\ \mu]. \end{aligned}$$

In *LIKE*, μ is the degree to which *Name*1 likes *Name*2; and in *YOUNG*, μ is the degree to which a person whose age is *Age* is young.

First, we shall represent the meaning of P_1 by the following test procedure.

(1) Divide *POPULATION* into the population of males, *M.POPULATION*, and the population of females, *F.POPULATION*:

$$M.POPULATION = {}_{Name,Age}POPULATION\ [Sex = Male]$$
$$F.POPULATION = {}_{Name,Age}POPULATION\ [Sex = Female],$$

where ${}_{Name,Age}POPULATION$ *denotes the projection of POPULATION* on the attributes *Name* and *Age*.

(2) For each $Name_j$, $j = 1, \ldots, L$, in *F.POPULATION*, find the age of $Name_j$:

$$A_j = {}_{Age}F.POPULATION\ [Name = Name_j].$$

(3) For each $Name_j$, find the degree to which $Name_j$ is young:

$$\alpha_j = {}_{\mu}YOUNG\ [Age = A_j],$$

where α_j may be interpreted as the grade of membership of $Name_j$ in the fuzzy set, *YW*, of young women.

(4) For each $Name_i$, $i = 1, \ldots, K$, in *M.POPULATION*, find the age of $Name_i$:

$$B_i = {}_{Age}M.POPULATION\ [Name = Name_i].$$

(5) For each $Name_j$, find the degree to which $Name_i$ likes $Name_j$:

$$\beta_{ij} = {}_{\mu}LIKE\ [Name1 = Name_i;\ Name2 = Name_j],$$

with the understanding that β_{ij} may be interpreted as the grade of membership of $Name_j$ in the fuzzy set, WL_i, of women whom $Name_i$ likes.

(6) For each $Name_j$ find the degree to which $Name_i$ likes $Name_j$ and $Name_j$ is young:

$$\gamma_{ij} = \alpha_j \wedge \beta_{ij}.$$

Note: As in previous examples, we employ the aggregation operator min ($\wedge$) to represent the meaning of conjunction. In effect, γ_{ij} is the grade of membership of $Name_j$ in the intersection of the fuzzy sets WL_i and *YW*.

(7) Compute the relative sigma-count of women whom $Name_i$ likes among young women:

$$\begin{aligned} \rho_i &= \Sigma Count(WL_i/YW) \qquad (19)\\ &= \frac{\Sigma Count(WL_i \cap YW)}{\Sigma Count(YW)} \\ &= \frac{\Sigma_j \gamma_{ij}}{\Sigma \alpha_j} \\ &= \frac{\Sigma_j \alpha_j \wedge \beta_{ij}}{\Sigma_j \alpha_j} . \end{aligned}$$

(8) Compute the test score for the constraint induced by *MOST*:

$$\tau_i = {}_{\mu}MOST\ [Proportion = \rho_i]. \qquad (20)$$

This test score way be interpreted as the degree to which $Name_i$ satisfies P_1, i.e.,

$$\tau_i = {}_{\mu}P_1\ [Name = Name_i].$$

The test procedure described above represents the meaning of P_1. In effect, it tests the constraint expressed by the proposition

$$\Sigma Count(WL_i/YW) \text{ is } MOST$$

and implies that the *n*-set and the *b*-set for the quantifier *most* in P_1 are given by:

$$n\text{-}set = WL_i = {}_{Name2}LIKE\ [Name\ 1 = Name_i] \cap F.POPULATION$$

and

$$b\text{-}set = YW = YOUNG \cap F.POPULATION.$$

By contrast, in the case of P_2, the identities of the *n*-set and the *b*-set are interchanged, i.e.,

$$n\text{-}set = YW$$

and

$$b\text{-}set = WL_i,$$

which implies that the constraint which defines P_2 is expressed by

$$\Sigma Count(YW/WL_i) \text{ is } MOST.$$

Thus, whereas the scope of the quantifier *most* in P_1 is $\{WL_i, YW\}$, the scope of *mostly* in P_2 is $\{YW, WL_i\}$.

Having represented the meaning of P_1 and P_2, it becomes a simple matter to represent the meaning of rd_1 and rd_2. Taking rd_1, for example, we have to add the following steps to the test procedure which defines P_1.

(9) For each $Name_i$, find the degree to which $Name_i$ is young:

$$\delta_i = {}_{\mu}YOUNG\,[Age = B_i],$$

where δ_i may be interpreted as the grade of membership of $Name_i$ in the fuzzy set, YM, of young men.

(10) Compute the relative sigma-count of men who have property P_1 among young men:

$$\rho = \Sigma Count(P_1/YM) = \frac{\Sigma Count(P_1 \cap YM)}{\Sigma Count(YM)} = \frac{\Sigma_i \tau_i \wedge \delta_i}{\Sigma_i \delta_i}.$$

(11) Test the constraint induced by $MOST$:

$$\tau = {}_{\mu}MOST\,[Proportion = \rho]. \qquad (21)$$

The test score expressed by Eq. (21) represents the overall test score for the disposition

$$d = \textit{young men like young women}$$

if d is interpreted as rd_1. If d is interpreted as rd_2, which is a more likely interpretation, then the procedure is unchanged except that τ_i in Eq. (20) should be replaced by

$$\tau_i = {}_{\mu}MOST\,[Proportion = \sigma_i],$$

where

$$\sigma_i = \Sigma Count(YW/WL_i) = \frac{\Sigma_j \alpha_j \wedge \beta_{ij}}{\Sigma_j \beta_{ij}}.$$

IV. REPRESENTATION OF DISPOSITIONAL COMMANDS

A *dispositional command*, *dc*, is an imperative exemplified by *avoid overeating*, *be honest*, *keep under refrigeration*, *do not exert yourself if you feel tired*, etc.

Any command, whether dispositional or not, may be defined through its propositional content[18] or, equivalently, its compliance criterion.[15,17] Naturally, if a command is dispositional, so is its defining compliance criterion. For example, the dispositional command

$$dc = \textit{avoid overeating}, \tag{22}$$

is associated with the dispositional compliance criterion

$$dcc = \textit{A avoids overeating}, \tag{23}$$

where A is an indexical representing the addressee of the command.

As an illustration, consider the conditional dispositional command

$$dc = \textit{do not go late to bed if you feel tired}, \tag{24}$$

which is assumed to be defined by the dispositional compliance criterion

$$dcc = \textit{A does not go late to bed when he/she feels tired}. \tag{25}$$

As a first step in representing the meaning of the dispositional command (24), we have to make explicit the implicit fuzzy quantifiers in Eq. (25). We assume that the intended meaning of Eq. (25) is defined by prefixing Eq. (25) with the fuzzy quantifier *most of the time*:

$$cc = \textit{most of the time A does not go late bed when he/she feels tired}. \tag{26}$$

To represent the meaning of Eq. (26), we associate with the explicit compliance criterion (26) the *EDF*

$$\begin{aligned} EDF = {} & RECORD\,[Day;\ Time;\ \mu Tired] + \\ & LATE\,[Time;\ \mu] + \\ & MOST\,[Proportion;\ \mu]. \end{aligned} \tag{27}$$

In Eq. (27) *RECORD* may be interpreted as a diary—kept during the period of interest—in which *DAY* ranges over successive days; *TIME* is the time of going to bed; and $\mu Tired$ is the degree to which A feels tired. In *LATE*, μ is the degree to which the value of *Time* fits the description *late*; and in *MOST*, μ is the degree to which the value of *Proportion* fits the fuzzy quantifier *most*.

The steps in the test procedure which represent the meaning of Eq. (26) may be described as follows.

(1) Let Day_i denote the ith day in the Diary, $i = 1, \ldots, m$. For each Day_i determine the time of going to bed, and the degree to which A felt tired:

$$t_i = {}_{Time}RECORD\,[Day = Day_i] \tag{28}$$

$$\mu_i = {}_{\mu Tired}RECORD\,[Day = Day_i]. \tag{29}$$

(2) Find the test score for the elastic constraint induced by the predicate *late*:

$$\tau_i = {}_{\mu}LATE\,[Time = t_i]. \tag{30}$$

(3) Find the relative sigma-count of days when A did not go late to bed when A felt tired:

$$\sigma = \frac{\Sigma_i \mu_i \wedge (1 - \tau_i)}{\Sigma \mu_i} \tag{31}$$

(4) Compute the test score for the elastic constraint induced by the fuzzy quantifier *most*:

$$\tau = {}_{\mu}MOST\ [Proportion = \sigma]. \tag{32}$$

The value of compatability expressed by Eq. (32) represents the overall test score yielded by the test procedure which represents the meaning of the conditional dispositional command (24).

It is of interest to note that maxims and, more generally, rules of conduct of a proverbial nature may be viewed as special cases of the concept of a dispositional command. In many cases, such rules of conduct result from the application of a dispositional version of *modus ponens* [see Eq. (57)] to a disposition. As an illustration, from the disposition *regular exercise is good for your health* we can infer through the application of *modus ponens* the maxim *to be in good health, exercise regularly*.

In summary, representation of the meaning of a dispositional command involves three basic steps. First, the meaning of the command is defined by a dispositional compliance criterion. Second, the implicit fuzzy quantifiers in the dispositional compliance criterion are made explicit. And third, the meaning of the resulting compliance criterion is represented by a test procedure which computes the overall score of compliance in relation to an explanatory database which contains a record of executions of the given command.

The Concept of a Subdisposition

Among the examples of dispositions cited in the preceding sections there are some which may be described more precisely as *subdispositions*.

A subdisposition, as its name suggests, is a weaker variant of a disposition in the sense that it connotes an increase in relative cardinality or probability without implying that their values are close to unity. In this sense, *slimness is attractive* is a subdisposition if its intended reading is (c) (see Section I) *the proportion of attractive people in the population of slim people is substantially larger than in the general population*, rather than (a) *most slim people are attractive* or (b) *most attractive people are slim*.

We shall employ the sentence *slimness is attractive* to illustrate how the meaning of a subdisposition may be represented. Specifically, let U be a universe of discourse (a collection of persons), and let S and A be, respectively, the fuzzy subsets of U representing slim and attractive people, respectively.

In terms of these sets, the proportion of attractive people in the general population is expressed by the relative sigma-count $\Sigma Count(A/U)$, while the proportion of attractive people among the slim is given by the relative sigma-count $\Sigma Count(A/S)$.

By viewing the relative sigma-count $\Sigma Count(A/U)$ as a reference point in the unit interval [0,1], the relative sigma-count $\Sigma Count(A/S)$ may be represented as a point in the interval $[\Sigma Count(A/U), 1]$ which is a convex combination of its end-points. More specifically,

$$\Sigma Count(A/S) = \rho + (1 - \rho)\Sigma Count(A/U), \tag{33}$$

where ρ is a number in the unit interval which, as a weighting coefficient, serves as a measure of the closeness of the point $\Sigma Count(A/S)$ to unity. In this sense, ρ plays a role which is similar to that of the measure of increased belief in confirmation theory and, in particular, in its applications to the management of uncertainty in expert systems.[19]

In terms of ρ, the subdisposition *slimness is attractive* may be represented as a proposition which provides a fuzzy characterization of its value, i.e.,

$$\textit{slimness is attractive} \rightarrow \rho \textit{ is MEDIUM}, \tag{34}$$

where *MEDIUM* is a fuzzy number which for simplicity may be assumed to have a triangular membership function as shown in Figure 3. By contrast, if *slimness is attractive* were interpreted as a disposition in the sense of (a), then in terms of ρ its meaning would be represented by

$$\textit{slimness is attractive} \rightarrow \rho \textit{ is HIGH}, \qquad (34)$$

where *HIGH* is a fuzzy number which, as an approximation, may be assumed to be triangular (Fig. 3).

As an illustration of the use of Eq. (33) in commonsense reasoning, consider the following premises and a related question:

slimness is attractive (35)

Carol is slim

Carol is?

The answer to the question may be deduced from Eqs. (33) and (34) as follows. Let α be a fuzzy number which characterizes the relative sigma-count of

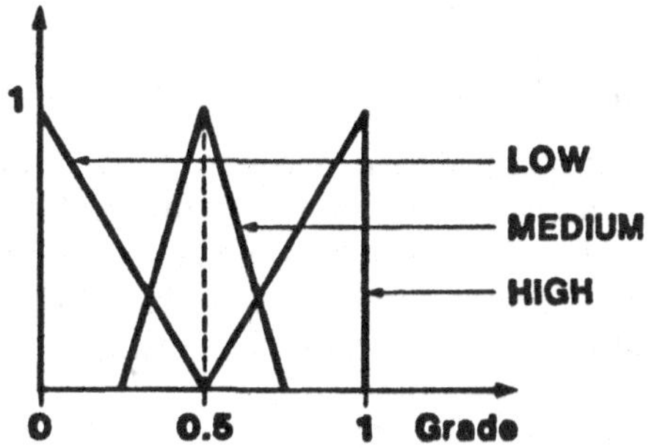

Figure 3. Representation of *HIGH*, *MEDIUM*, and *LOW* as triangular possibility distributions.

attractive people in the general population, i.e.,

$$\Sigma Count(A/U) \text{ is } \alpha. \tag{36}$$

Furthermore, let β be the fuzzy number *MEDIUM*. Then from Eq. (33) it follows that the relative sigma-count $\Sigma Count(A/S)$ is characterized by a fuzzy number γ which is related to α and β by the expression

$$\gamma = \beta \oplus (1 \ominus \beta) \otimes \alpha, \tag{37}$$

where $\oplus$, $\ominus$, and $\otimes$ represent, respectively, addition, subtraction, and multiplication in fuzzy arithmetic.[3] If this number is interpreted as a fuzzy probability,[20] then the answer to the question may be stated as follows:

(a) If it is not known that Carol is slim, then the fuzzy probability that she is attractive is α. (38)
(b) If it is known in addition that there is a relationship between slimness and attractiveness which is expressed by the subdisposition *slimness is attractive*, then the fuzzy probability that Carol is attractive increases to γ, as expressed by Eq. (37).

V. DISPOSITIONAL VALUATIONS—TYPICAL AND USUAL VALUES

Qualified propositions of the form *usually p* and *typically p*, where *p* is a proposition, play a basic role in human reasoning, especially in commonsense reasoning, default reasoning,[11] and concept formation.[21]

The concept of a disposition provides a natural framework for representing the meaning of such propositions and constructing an inferential system for commonsense reasoning in which the premises are allowed to be of the form *usually p*.[14,22] In this connection, what is of particular relevance is a variant of the concept of a disposition which will be referred to as a *dispositional valuation*.

As its name implies, a dispositional valuation is a dispositional statement regarding the values of a variable. For example:

(a) *a cup of coffee costs about fifty cents*
(b) *it takes about an hour to drive from Berkeley to Stanford*
(c) *a typical TV set weighs about fifty pounds*.

In (a), the variable is the price of a cup of coffee and its dispositional value is *about fifty cents*; in (b), the variable is the duration of driving from Berkeley to Stanford and its dispositional value is *about an hour*; and in (c), the variable is the weight of a typical TV set and its dispositional value is *about fifty pounds*.

In more general terms, in the case of dispositional valuations of the form

usually (*X is F*)

typically (*X is G*)

F and G play, respectively, the roles of *usual* and *typical* values of the variable X. Thus,

$$\textit{usual value of } X = U(X) = F \tag{39}$$

$$\textit{typical value of } X = T(X) = G = \{t\} \tag{40}$$

with the understanding that usually F is a fuzzy subset of the universe of discourse, U, in which X takes its values, while G is a singleton $\{t\}$. What this implies is that (1) with each fuzzy subset, F, of U we can associate the degree to which F qualifies to be regarded as a usual value of X; and (2) with each element, t, of U we can associate the degree to which t qualifies to be regarded as a typical value of X. In this sense, $T(X)$ and $U(X)$ are, respectively, first- and second-order predicates defined on U.

To define what is meant by a usual value it is necessary to define the meaning of the qualified proposition *usually* (X *is* F). Viewed as a fuzzy quantifier, *usually* may be interpreted as a *conditioned* quantifier whose definition involves a *conditioning variable* whose role is to characterize a set of *normal* or, equivalently, *nonexceptional* conditions which circumscribe the validity of a dispositional valuation. More concretely,

$$\textit{usually } (X \textit{ is } F) \rightarrow \text{if } Z \textit{ is } R \text{ then } \textit{most Xs are } F, \tag{41}$$

where Z is the conditioning variable and R is a prescribed set which is the complement of the set of exceptions. From this definition, it follows that if X takes the successive values $x_1, \ldots, x_n$ in U, then the meaning of *usually* (X *is* F) may be represented by the test procedure

$$\tau = {}_{\mu}MOST\ [Proportion = \Sigma Count(F/R)], \tag{42}$$

which computes the overall test score τ. If there is no conditioning variable or, equivalently, if $R = U$, then *usually* is an *unconditioned* quantifier defined by

$$\textit{usually } (X \textit{ is } F) \rightarrow \textit{most Xs are } F. \tag{43}$$

As an illustration, consider the disposition *snow is white*. Assume that its intended interpretation is *usually* (*snow is white*), in which *usually* is a fuzzy quantifier conditioned on the freshness of snow, i.e.,

$$\textit{snow is white} \rightarrow \textit{usually } (\textit{if snow is fresh } \text{then } \textit{it is white})$$

If in the explanatory database the successive samples of snow, say $s_1, \ldots, s_n$, are fresh to the degree $f_1, \ldots, f_n$ and white to the degree $w_1, \ldots, w_n$, respectively, then from Eqs. (42) and (43), it follows that

$$\tau = \mu MOST\ [\Sigma_i f_i \wedge w_i / \Sigma_i f_i]. \tag{44}$$

This expression defines the meaning of *snow is white* as a test procedure which computes its compatibility, τ, with a given explanatory database.

Turning to the concept of a typical value, we note that it is a common practice to treat *typical* and *usual* as almost synonymous notions. In what follows, we define a typical element (or value) in a way that sets it apart from the concept of a usual value. However, we also show that the concepts are related and exhibit the relation between them.

Let A be a fuzzy set in U (e.g., U = *cars* and A = *station wagons*). The definition of a typical element of A may be expressed in verbal terms as follows:*

> t is a *typical* element of A if and only if (a) t has a high grade of membership in A, and (b) most elements of A are similar to t. (45)

It should be remarked that this definition should be viewed as a *dispositional definition*, in the sense that it may fail, in some cases, to reflect our intuitive perception of the meaning of typicality. Furthermore, in Eq. (45), A plays a role similar to that of R in the definition of a usual value (41).

To put the verbal definition expressed by Eq. (45) into a more precise form, let S be a similarity relation defined on U which associates with each element u in U the degree to which u is similar to t. Furthermore, let $S(t)$ be the *similarity class* of t, i.e., the fuzzy set of elements of U which are similar to t. What this means is that the grade of membership of u in $S(t)$ is equal to $\mu_S(t,u)$, the degree to which u is similar to t (Fig. 4).[23]

Let *HIGH* denote the fuzzy subset of the unit interval which is the extension of the fuzzy predicate *high*. Then, the verbal definition (45) may be expressed more precisely in the form of Figure 4. t is a *typical* element of A if (a) $\mu_A(t)$ is *HIGH*, and (b) $\Sigma Count(S(t)/A)$ is *MOST*. (46)

The fuzzy predicate *high* may be characterized by its membership function μ_{HIGH} or, equivalently, as the fuzzy relation *HIGH* [*Grade*; μ], in which *Grade* is a number in the interval [0,1] and μ is the degree to which the value of *Grade* fits the intended meaning of *high*.

An important implication of this definition is that typicality is a matter of degree. Thus, it follows at once from Eq. (46) that the degree, τ, to which t is

*For consistency with the definition of A, S must be such that if u and u' have a high degree of similarity, then their grades of membership in A should be close in magnitude.

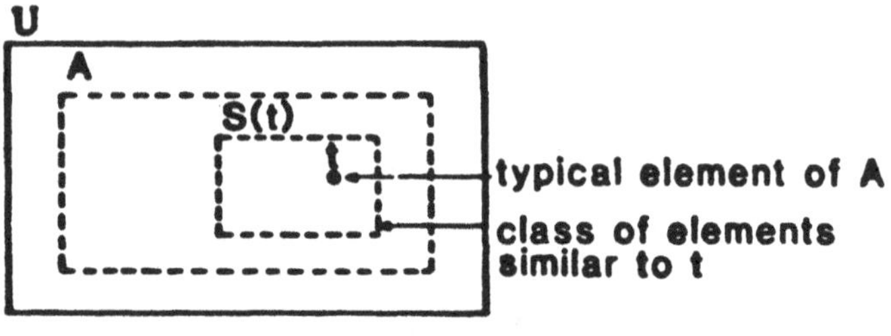

Figure 4. Definition of typicality.

typical or, equivalently, the grade of membership of t in the fuzzy set of typical elements of A, is given by

$$\tau = {}_{\mu}HIGH\ [Grade = \mu_A(t)] \wedge {}_{\mu}MOST\ [Proportion = \Sigma Count(S(t)/A)]. \quad (47)$$

In terms of the membership functions of $HIGH$, $MOST$, S, and A, Eq. (47) may be written as

$$\tau = \mu_{HIGH}(\mu_A(t)) \wedge \mu_{MOST}\left[\frac{\Sigma_u \mu_S(t,u) \wedge \mu_A(u)}{\Sigma_u \mu_A(u)}\right], \quad (48)$$

where μ_{HIGH}, μ_{MOST}, μ_S, and μ_A are the membership functions of $HIGH$, $MOST$, S, and A, respectively, and the summation Σ_u extends over the elements of U.

It is of interest to observe that if $\mu_A(t) = 1$ and

$$\mu_S(t,u) = \mu_A(u), \quad (49)$$

that is, the grade of membership of u in A is equal to the degree of similarity of u to t, then the degree of typicality of t is unity. This is reminiscent of definitions of prototypicality[24] in which the grade of membership of an object in a category is assumed to be inversely related to its "distance" from the prototype.

Another point of interest is that in the definition of prototypicality given in Zadeh,[16] a prototype is interpreted as a so-called σ-summary. In relation to the definition of typicality expressed by Eq. (45), we may say that a prototype is a σ-summary of typical elements of A. In this sense, a prototype is *not*, in general, an element of U, whereas a typical element of A is, by definition, an element of U. As a simple illustration of this difference, assume that U is a collection of movies, and A is the fuzzy set of Western movies. A prototype of A is a summary of the summaries (i.e., plots) of Western movies, and thus is not a movie. A typical Western movie, on the other hand, is a movie and thus is an element of U.

As was stated earlier, in our formulation of the concept of typicality the notion of a typical value is distinct from that of a usual value. However, there is a close connection between the two which is brought out by the following result.

Assume for simplicity that $\mu_A(t) = 1$. Then, the degree to which t is a typical element of A is given by

$$\tau = {}_{\mu}MOST\ [Proportion = \Sigma Count(S(t/A))]. \quad (50)$$

Comparing this expression with Eq. (42), we note that if we equate Z to X, R to A, and F to $S(t)$, the expression for the degree to which F is a usual value of X becomes identical with Eq. (50). Consequently, we can assert that

the degree to which t is a typical element of A = (51)

the degree to which S(t) is a usual value of X.

In other words, the similarity class of a typical element of A may be interpreted as a usual value of the variable which ranges over U and is conditioned on A.

VI. FUZZY SYLLOGISMS

A concept which plays an essential role in reasoning with dispositions is that of a *fuzzy syllogism*.[25] As a general inference schema, a fuzzy syllogism may be expressed in the form

$$\frac{\begin{array}{c} Q_1 \text{ } As \text{ } are \text{ } Bs \\ Q_2 \text{ } Cs \text{ } are \text{ } Ds \end{array}}{Q_3 \text{ } Es \text{ } are \text{ } Fs,} \tag{52}$$

where Q_1 and Q_2 are given fuzzy quantifiers, Q_3 is fuzzy quantifier which is to be determined, and A, B, C, D, E, and F are interrelated fuzzy predicates.

In what follows, we shall present a brief discussion of two basic types of fuzzy syllogisms. A more detalied description of these and other fuzzy syllogisms may be found in Refs. 14 and 25.

The *intersection/product syllogism* may be viewed as an instance of Eq. (52) in which

$$C = A \text{ } and \text{ } B$$

$$E = A$$

$$F = B \text{ } and \text{ } D \text{ },$$

and $Q_3 = Q_1 \otimes Q_2$, i.e., Q_3 is the product of Q_1 and Q_2 in fuzzy arithmetic. Thus, we have as the statement of the syllogism:

$$\frac{\begin{array}{c} Q_1 \text{ } As \text{ } are \text{ } Bs \\ Q_2 \text{ } (A \text{ } and \text{ } B)s \text{ } are \text{ } Cs \end{array}}{(Q_1 \otimes Q_2) \text{ } As \text{ } are \text{ } (B \text{ and } C)s.} \tag{53}$$

In particular, if B is contained in A, i.e., $\mu_B \leqslant \mu_A$, where μ_A and μ_B are the membership functions of A and B, respectively, then A and $B = B$, and Eq. (53) becomes

$$\frac{\begin{array}{c} Q_1 \text{ } As \text{ } are \text{ } Bs \\ Q_2 \text{ } Bs \text{ } are \text{ } Cs \end{array}}{(Q_1 \otimes Q_2) \text{ } As \text{ } are \text{ } (B \text{ } and \text{ } C)s.} \tag{54}$$

Since *B and C* implies *C*, it follows at once from Eq. (54)

$$\frac{\begin{array}{c} Q_1 \text{ } As \text{ } are \text{ } Bs \\ Q_2 \text{ } Bs \text{ } are \text{ } Cs \end{array}}{\geqslant (Q_1 \otimes Q_2) \text{ } As \text{ } are \text{ } Cs,} \tag{55}$$

which is the *chaining syllogism* expressed by Eq. (4). Furthermore, if the quantifiers Q_1 and Q_2 are monotone increasing, i.e., $\geqslant Q_1 = Q_1$ and $\geqslant Q_2 = Q_2$, then Eq. (55) becomes the *product syllogism*

$$\frac{\begin{array}{l} Q_1 \ As \ are \ Bs \\ Q_2 \ Bs \ are \ Cs \end{array}}{(Q_1 \otimes Q_2) \ As \ are \ Cs.} \tag{56}$$

An important special case of the product syllogism which obtains when $A = U$ and $Q_1 = Q_2 = usually$, is a variant of the *dispositional modus ponens*. On observing that the proposition *Q As are Bs* may be expressed as if *X is A* then Q Xs *are B*, the variant in question may be stated as the syllogism

$$\frac{\begin{array}{l} usually \ (X \ is \ B) \\ usually \ (if \ X \ is \ B \ \text{then} \ X \ is \ C) \end{array}}{usually^2 \ (X \ is \ C)} \tag{57}$$

when $usually^2$ is the product of the fuzzy number *usually* with itself.

In the case of the *consequent conjuction syllogism*, we have

$$C = A$$

$$E = A$$

$$F = B \ and \ D.$$

In this case, the statement of the syllogism is:

$$\frac{\begin{array}{l} Q_1 \ As \ are \ Bs \\ Q_2 \ As \ are \ Cs \end{array}}{Q_3 \ As \ are \ (B \ and \ C)s,} \tag{58}$$

where Q_3 is a fuzzy number (or interval) defined by the inequalities

$$0 \oslash (Q_1 \oplus Q_2 \ominus 1) \leq Q_3 \leq Q_1 \oslash Q_2, \tag{59}$$

where $\oplus$, $\ominus$, $\oslash$, and $\oslash$ are the operations of addition, subtraction, min, and max in fuzzy arithmetic.

As a simple illustration, consider the dispositions

$$d_1 = students \ are \ young$$

$$d_2 = students \ are \ single.$$

Upon restoration, these dispositions become the quantified propositions

$$p_1 = most \ students \ are \ young$$

$$p_2 = most \ students \ are \ single.$$

Then, applying the consequent conjunction syllogism to p_1 and p_2, we can infer that

$$Q \text{ students are single and young}$$

where

$$2\ most \ominus 1 \leqslant Q \leqslant most. \tag{60}$$

Thus, from the dispositions in question we can infer the disposition

$$d = \text{students are single and young}$$

on the understanding that the implicit fuzzy quantifier in d is expressed by Eq. (60).

VII. NEGATION OF DISPOSITIONS

In dealing with dispositions, it is natural to raise the question: What happens when a disposition is acted upon with an operator, T, where T might be the operation of negation, active-to-passive transformation, etc.? More generally, the same question may be asked when T is an operator which is defined on pairs or n-tuples of dispositions.

As an illustration, we shall focus our attention on the operation of negation. More specifically, the question which we shall consider briefly is the following: Given a disposition, d, what can be said about the negation of d, *not d*? For example, what can be said about *not* (*birds can fly*) or *not* (*young men like young women*).

For simplicity, assume that, after restoration, d may be expressed in the form

$$rd = Q\ As\ are\ Bs. \tag{61}$$

Then,

$$not\ d = not\ (Q\ As\ are\ Bs). \tag{62}$$

Now, using the semantic equivalence established in Ref. 15, we may write

$$not\ (Q\ As\ are\ Bs) \equiv (not\ Q)\ As\ are\ Bs, \tag{63}$$

where *not Q* is the negation of the fuzzy quantifier Q in the sense that the membership function of *not Q* is given by

$$\mu_{not\ Q}(u) = 1 - \mu_Q(u), \quad 0 \leqslant u \leqslant 1. \tag{64}$$

Furthermore, the following inference rule can readily be established:[12]

$$\frac{Q\ As\ are\ Bs}{\geqslant (ant\ Q)\ As\ are\ not\ Bs}\ , \tag{65}$$

where *ant Q* denotes the *antonym* of Q, defined by (Fig. 5)

$$\mu_{antQ}(u) = \mu_Q(1-u), 0 \leqslant u \leqslant 1. \tag{66}$$

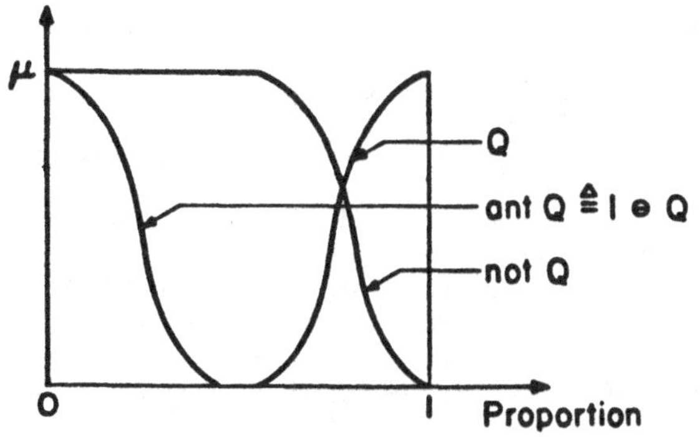

Figure 5. Representation of Q, *not* Q, and *ant* Q.

On combining Eqs. (63) and (65), we are led to the following result:

$$\textit{not}\ (Q\ \text{As}\ \textit{are}\ B\text{s}) = \geqslant (\textit{ant}\ (\text{not Q}))\ \text{As}\ \textit{are not}\ B\text{s} \qquad (67)$$

which reduces to

$$\textit{not}\ (Q\ \text{As}\ \textit{are}\ B\text{s}) = (\textit{ant}\ (\textit{not}\ Q))\ \text{As}\ \textit{are not}\ B\text{s} \qquad (68)$$

if Q is monotone increasing (e.g., Q = *most*).

As an illustration, if d = *birds can fly* and Q = *most*, then Eq. (68) yields

$$\textit{not (birds can fly)} = (\textit{ant (not most)})\ \textit{birds cannot fly}. \qquad (69)$$

It should be observed that if Q is an approximation to *all*, then *ant* (*not* Q) is an approximation to *some*. For the right-hand member of Eq. (69) to be a disposition, *most* must be an approximation to *at least a half*. In this case *ant* (*not most*) will be an approximation to *most*, and consequently the right-hand member of Eq. (69) may be expressed—upon the suppression of *most*—as the disposition *birds cannot fly*.

References

1. J. Barwise and R. Cooper, "Generalized quantifiers and natural language." *Linguistics and Philosophy*, **4** 159–219 (1981).
2. P. Peterson, "On the logic of *few*, *many*, and *most*," *Notre Dame J. Formal Logic*, **20**, 155–179 (1979).
3. A. Kaufmann and M. Gupta, *Introduction to Fuzzy Arithmetic*, Van Nostrand, New York, 1985.
4. R.E. Moore, *Interval Analysis*, Prentice-Hall, Englewood Cliffs, 1966.
5. M.J. Cresswell, *Logic and Languages*. Methuen, London, 1973.
6. J.D. McCawley, *Everything that Linguists have Always Wanted to Know about Logic*, University of Chicago Press, Chicago, 1981.
7. G.A. Miller and P.N. Johnson-Laird, *Language and Perception*, Harvard University Press, Cambridge, MA, 1976.
8. J. McCarthy, "Circumscription: A non-monotonic inference rule," *Artificial Intelligence*, **13**, 27–40 (1980).

9. D.V. McDermott, and J. Doyle, "Non-monotonic logic, I.," *Artificial Intelligence*, **13**, 41–72 (1980).
10. D.V. McDermott, "Non-monotonic logic, II., non-monotonic modal theories," *J. Assoc. Comp. Mach.*, **29**, 33–57 (1982).
11. R. Reiter and G. Criscuolo, Some representational issues in default reasoning, *Computers and Mathematics*, **9**, 15–28 (1983).
12. L.A. Zadeh, "A computational approach to fuzzy quantifiers in natural languages," *Computers and Mathematics*, **9**, 149–184 (1983a).
13. L.A. Zadeh, "A fuzzy-set-theoretic approach to the compositionality of meaning: Propositions, dispositions and canonical forms," *Journal of Semantics*, **3**, 253–272 (1983b).
14. L.A. Zadeh, "Fuzzy logic as a basis for the management of uncertainty in expert systems," *Fuzzy Sets and Systems*, **11**, 199–227 (1983c).
15. L.A. Zadeh, "PRUF—A meaning representation language for natural languages," *Int. J. Man–Machine Studies*, **10**, 395–460 (1978).
16. L.A. Zadeh, "A note on prototype theory and fuzzy sets," *Cognition*, **12**, 291–297 (1982).
17. L.A. Zadeh, "Test-score semantics for natural languages and meaning-representation via PRUF," In *Proc. COLING 82*, Prague, 1982, pp. 425–430. Full text in: *Empirical Semantics*, B.B. Rieger (Ed.), Brockmeyer, Bochum, 1982, pp. 281–349.
18. J. Searle, *Expression and Meaning*, Cambridge University Press, Cambridge, 1979.
19. B.G. Buchanan and E.H. Shortliffe, *Rule-Based Expert Systems*, Addison-Wesley, Reading, MA, 1984.
20. L.A. Zadeh, "A theory of commonsense knowledge," In *Aspects of Vagueness*, H.J. Skala, S. Termini, and E. Trillas (Eds.), Reidel, Dordrecht, 1984.
21. E. Smith and D.L. Medin, *Categories and Concepts*, Harvard University Press, Cambridge, MA, 1981.
22. L.A. Zadeh, "Fuzzy sets, usuality and commonsense reasoning," *Berkeley Cognitive Science Report No. 32*, 1985. To appear in *Matters of Intelligence*, L. Vaina, (Ed.), Reidel, Dordrecht, 1986.
23. L.A. Zadeh, "Similarity relations and fuzzy orderings," *Information Sciences*, **3**, 177–200 (1971).
24. E. Rosch, "Principles of categorization," In *Cognition and Categorization*, E. Rosch and B.B. Lloyd (Eds.),Erlbaum, Hillsdale, NJ, 1978.
25. L.A. Zadeh, "Syllogistic reasoning in fuzzy logic and its application to reasoning with dispositions," *IEEE Trans. on Systems, Man and Cybernetics*, **SMC-15**, 754–763 (1985).
26. R.E. Bellman and L.A. Zadeh, "Local and fuzzy logics, In *Modern Uses of Multiple-Valued Logic*, G. Epstein (Ed.), Reidel, Dordrecht, 1977, pp. 103–165.
27. R.J. Brachman and B.C. Smith, *Special Issue on Knowledge Representation*, SIGART 70, 1980.
28. R. Carnap, "The methodological character of theoretical concepts," In *Minnesota Studies in the Philosophy of Science*, H. Fiegl and M. Scriven (Eds.), 1956, pp. 38–76.
29. S. Cushing, *Quantifier Meanings—A Study in the Dimensions of Semantic Competence*, North-Holland, Amsterdam, 1982.
30. D. Dubois and H. Prade, *Fuzzy Sets and Systems: Theory and Applications*, Academic, New York, 1980.
31. J.A. Goguen, "The logic of inexact concepts," *Synthese*, **19**, 325–373 (1969).
32. I. Hacking, *Logic of Statistical Inference*, Cambridge University Press, Cambridge, 1965.
33. C.G. Hempel, "Maximal specificity and lawlikeness," *Philosophy of Science*, **35**, 116–133 (1968).
34. J. Hintikka, "Statistics, induction and lawlikeness." *Synthese*, **20**, 72–83 (1969).
35. R.C. Jeffrey, *The Logic of Decision*, McGraw-Hill, New York, 1965.

36. E.L. Keenan, "Quantifier structures in English," *Foundations of Language*, **7**, 255–336 (1971).
37. H.E. Kyburg, *Probability and Inductive Logic*, Macmillan, New York, 1970.
38. E.H. Mamdani and B.R. Gaines, *Fuzzy Reasoning and its Applications*, Academic, London, 1981.
39. D.H. Mellor, *Matter of Chance*, Cambridge University Press, Cambridge, 1971.
40. D.H. Mellor, *Science, Belief and Behavior*, Cambridge University Press, Cambridge, 1980.
41. D.N. Osherson and E.E. Smith, "On the adequacy of prototype theory as a theory of concepts," *Cognition*, **9**, 59–72 (1983).
42. N. Rescher, *Plausible Reasoning*, Van Gorcum, Amsterdam, 1976.
43. P. Suppes, *A Probabilistic Theory of Causality*, North-Holland, Amsterdam, 1970.
44. R.R. Yager, "Quantified propositions in a linguistic logic," In *Proceedings of the 2nd International Seminar on Fuzzy Set Theory*, E.P. Klement (Ed.), Linz, Austria, Johannes Kepler University, 1980.
45. R.R. Yager, "Reasoning with fuzzy quantified statements—I," *Kybernetes*, **14**, 233–240 (1985).
46. L.A. Zadeh, "Fuzzy sets and their application to pattern classification and clustering analysis," In *Classification and Clustering*, J. Ryzin (Ed.), Academic, New York, 1977, pp. 251–299.

Fuzzy Sets, Usuality and Commonsense Reasoning

Lotfi A. Zadeh

12.1 Introduction

Although fascination with the mechanization of human reasoning goes back to Leibnitz and Pascal, serious interest in artificial intelligence became manifest with the arrival of the computer age in the late forties. Since then, computers have become vastly more powerful and AI has become the subject of almost daily articles in the popular press. While it may be true that such articles are creating unrealistic expectations—as they have done throughout the history of AI—it should be borne in mind, as Jules Verne noted at the turn of the century, that scientific progress is driven by exaggerated expectations.[1]

[1]As an example of such expectations, the opening paragraph of my paper, entitled "Thinking Machines–A New Field in Electrical Engineering," which appeared in the January 1950 issue of *Columbia Engineering Quarterly*, reads: 'Psychologists Report Memory is Electrical,' 'Electronic Brain Able to Translate Foreign Languages is Being Built,'

289

Reprinted, with permission, from *Matters of Intelligence*, edited by L. M. Vaina, pp. 289–309.

Whether exaggerated or not, what is clear is that modern technology has entered a new phase whose dominant theme is the conception of machines which can imitate human reasoning and perform nontrivial cognitive tasks exemplified by recognition of speech, diagnosis of faults, understanding of images, summarization of knowledge. etc. What is also clear is that, in order to be able to design machines which can perform such tasks more impressively than the machines we have at present, it will be necessary to develop a much better understanding of commonsense reasoning and, especially, the ability of the human mind to reason with information which is imprecise, incomplete or not totally reliable.

The quest for a better understanding of commonsense reasoning is in conflict with one of the fundamental tenets of modern science, which is that a phenomenon cannot be claimed to be well understood until it can be described and analyzed in quantitative terms. As stated succinctly by Lord Kelvin in 1883:

> "In physical science, a first essential step in the direction of learning any subject is to find principles of numerical reckoning and practicable methods for measuring some quality connected with it. I often say that when you can measure what you are speaking about and express it in numbers, you know something about it; but when you cannot measure it, when you cannot express it in numbers, your knowledge is of a meager and unsatisfactory kind; it may be the beginning of knowledge, but you have scarcely, in your thoughts, advanced to the state of *science*, whatever the matter may be."

In sharp contrast to most of the reasoning in physical sciences, commonsense reasoning is predominantly qualitative in nature. Consider, for example, the reasoning that guides our search for a parking space or for the fastest way to get to our place of work in heavy traffic. Or, more generally,

'Electronic Brain Does Research,' 'Scientists Confer on Electronic Brain,'–these are some of the headlines that were carried in newspapers throughout the nation during the past year. What is behind these headlines? How will 'electronic brains' or 'thinking machines' affect our way of living? What is the role played by electrical engineers in the design of these devices? These are some of the questions that we shall try to answer in this article." Many more examples may be found in H. Dreyfus, *What Computers Can't Do: A Critique of Artificial Intelligence*, 2nd edition, Harper and Row, New York, 1979.

the reasoning which shapes our behavior and underlies our beliefs, desires and aspirations. Or, on a lower level, the reasoning which enables us to recognize speech, decipher sloppy handwriting, estimate the age of a person or identify the composer of a piece which we have never heard before. It is evident that the concepts which enter into such reasoning are, for the most part, imprecise. To put it in more technical terms, the denotations of such concepts are *fuzzy sets*, that is, classes with fuzzy boundaries in which the transition from membership to nonmembership is gradual rather than abrupt. For example, the class of *bald men* is a fuzzy set, as is the class of *intelligent women.* In these classes, there is no sharp dividing line between those individuals who are bald (or intelligent) and those who are not. What this means is that, in general, membership in a fuzzy set is a matter of degree, so that an individual could be a member of the fuzzy set of bald men, for example, to a degree which may be represented as a number between zero (nonmember) and one (full member).

In short, our everyday, commonsense reasoning involves, for the most part, fuzzy concepts exemplified by *small*, *short*, *slightly*, *above*, *pink*, *bitter*, *fast*, *much taller than*, etc. By contrast, essentially all concepts in mathematics are crisp. Thus, a number is either *prime* or *nonprime*; a matrix is either *symmetrical* or *nonsymmetrical*, and a system is either *stable* or *unstable*. Furthermore, the meaning of these concepts is the same in New York as in Paris, London and Moscow. This is not true of fuzzy concepts such as *small*, *tall*, *fast*, etc., which, in general, are both subjective and context-dependent.

In its quest for the ultimate in precision and universality, mathematics has become intolerant of imprecision and partial truths. The price of this intolerance is the inability of mathematics and, by extension, classical logical systems, to provide a framework for representing commonsense knowledge and reasoning with it. Thus, one cannot represent in any of the standard logical systems the meaning of propositions expressing commonsense knowledge, e.g., *glue is sticky*, *overeating causes obesity*, *icy roads are slippery*, *winters are cold*, etc. And as a consequence, one cannot employ such logical systems to assess the validity of a conclusion drawn from a commonsense knowledge base, e.g., the conclusion that *icy roads are dangerous* from the knowledge that *icy roads are slippery* and *slippery roads are dangerous.*

The ineffectiveness of classical logical systems in dealing with commonsense knowledge lies at the root of the slow progress made by artificial intelligence in such problem areas as speech recognition, machine translation, image understanding and, in particular, nonstereotypical story summarization. Whether based on classical logic or not, most of the AI techniques which are in vogue today provide no methods for dealing with fuzzy concepts. As a result, such techniques lack the capability to represent commonsense knowledge and infer from it. For the same reason, the standard logical systems and probability-based methods do not provide a satisfactory framework for the management of uncertainty in expert systems.

Viewed in this perspective, the main motivation for the concept of a fuzzy set is to extend the applicability of mathematical methods to imprecise problem domains which cannot be dealt with effectively through the use of conventional methods based on probability theory and predicate logic. Commonsense reasoning is an important instance of a domain of this type.

There are three basic concepts in the theory of fuzzy sets which relate in an essential way to commonsense reasoning. These are: (a) the concept of a *linguistic variable*, which provides a basis for qualitative analysis and characterization of complex systems; (b) the concept of *dispositionality*, which makes it possible to deal with propositions such as *glue is sticky*, *Swedes are blond*, etc., which are preponderantly, but not necessarily always true; and (c) the concept of *usuality*, which is closely related to that of dispositionality and serves to provide a systematic basis for *dispositional valuations*, i.e., dispositions exemplified by *a cup of coffee costs about fifty cents*, *it takes about an hour to drive from Berkeley to Stanford*, etc.

In what follows, we shall present a brief exposition of these and related concepts, and explain their relevance to commonsense reasoning.[2] As will be seen in the sequel, the concept of a fuzzy set plays an essential role in our approach.

[2]A more detailed exposition of these concepts may be found in L. A. Zadeh, "The concept of a linguistic variable and its application to approximate reasoning," *Information Sciences*, **8** and **9**, 199-249, 301-357, 43-80, 1975; L. A. Zadeh, "A computational approach to fuzzy quantifiers in natural languages," *Computers and Mathematics*, **9**, 149-194, 1983a; L. A. Zadeh, "A theory of commonsense knowledge," in: *Issues of Vagueness*, H. Skala, S. Termini and E. Trillas, eds., Reidel, Dordrecht, 257-296, 1983b.

12.2 Fuzzy sets and linguistic variables

As was stated already, a fuzzy set—as its name implies—is a class with fuzzy boundaries, e.g., the class of *expensive cars*, *small numbers*, *high mountains*, *blonde women*, etc. Such a class, say F, may be characterized by associating with each object u in a universe of discourse U the *grade of membership* of u in F. For example, suppose that the universe of discourse consists of the members of the American Ballet Theater (ABT) and F is the fuzzy set of *young* dancers. Then, if Eric is a member of ABT and his age is 30, his grade of membership in F may be, say, 0.6. Expressing F as *young*, the fuzzy set *young*, then, is defined by its *membership function* μ_{young} which associates with each member of ABT his or her grade of membership in *young*.

This informal definition raises several questions. First, how is the grade of membership arrived at? Second, is it necessary to express it as a number? And third, what is the difference between the grade of membership and probability?

Basically, the grade of membership is subjective in nature, and is a matter of definition rather than measurement. Thus, the number 0.6 in the case of Eric may be viewed as a response to the question: Eric is 30 years old and is a member of the ABT corps. To what degree (on the scale from 0 to 1) does the label *young member* of ABT apply to him?

In a way that is not well understood at present, humans have a remarkable ability to assign a grade of membership to a given object without a conscious understanding of the way in which the grade is arrived at. For example, a student in a course would have no difficulty in assigning a grade of membership in the class of, say, *good teachers*, to his professor. The same would apply to assigning a grade of membership to an individual in the fuzzy set of *handsome men*. And yet, in both cases, the assignment would usually be arrived at almost instantaneously without any analysis of the factors which enter into the assessment of the grade of membership in a given class.

In the theory of fuzzy sets, a number of attempts have been made to put the assignment of the grade of membership on a more rational basis. In one such approach, a method based on betting is employed which is somewhat similar to the approach used in defining subjective probabilities.[3]

[3] R. Giles, "Foundations for a theory of possibility," in: *Fuzzy Information and Decision*

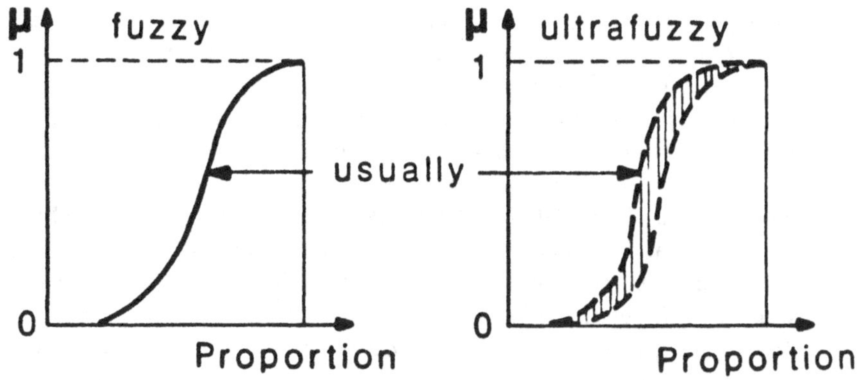

Figure 12.1: Fuzzy and ultrafuzzy representations of the temporal quantifier *usually*.

In another approach, the grade of membership is interpreted as a measure of consensus. This approach is closely related to the representation of a fuzzy set as an arithmetic average of its so-called level sets.[4]

Since the grade of membership is both subjective and context-dependent, there is not much point in treating it as a precise number. Thus, in many applications, it is sufficient to represent the grade of membership as a *fuzzy number*, expressed as, say, *close to* 0.8, *approximately* 0.6, *quite high*, *very low*, etc. A fuzzy set whose membership function takes fuzzy values is said to be *ultrafuzzy*. As an illustration, Figure 12.1 shows the fuzzy and ultra-fuzzy representations of the fuzzy set labeled *usually* in which the abscissa is the numerical frequency and the ordinate is the corresponding grade of membership.

What is the relationship, if any, between the grade of membership and

Processes, M. M. Gupta and E. Sanchez, eds., Amsterdam, North-Holland, 183-195, 1981.

[4]See Zadeh, 1975.

probability? Basically, the grade of membership is a measure of the compatibility of an object with the concept represented by a fuzzy set (e.g., 0.6 is the compatibility of Eric with the fuzzy set of young members of ABT). Thus, 0.6 is *not* the probability that Eric is a young member of ABT. However, it is possible to establish a connection between the number 0.6 and the arithmetic average of the level-sets of the fuzzy set *young*.[5]

A concept which plays an important role in applications of fuzzy sets is that of a *linguistic variable*.[6] The motivation for this concept derives from the observation that in most of our commonsense reasoning, we employ words rather than numbers to describe the values of variables. For example, the age of an individual may be described as *young*, height as *tall*, intelligence as *extremely high*, health as *not very good*, etc., with each linguistic value representing a fuzzy set. (See Figure 12.2.) In general, the values of a linguistic variable are generated from a *primary term* and its *antonym* (e.g., *young* and *old* in the case of the linguistic variable *Age*) through the use of various modifiers and connectives. For example, the linguistic values of the variables *Age* and *Health* may be tabulated as in Table 12.1.

One of the most important characteristics of a linguistic variable is that the meaning of any of its linguistic values may be deduced from the meaning of the primary terms from which it is generated. For example, if Maria is stated to be young, and the linguistic value *young* is defined by a membership function which assigns the grade 0.8 to age 34, then the grade of membership of 34 in the fuzzy set *not very young* may be expressed as $1 - (0.8)^2 = 0.36$, in which the effect of the modifier *very* is represented by the squaring operation, while the negation is accounted for by the subtraction of $(0.8)^2$ from 1. This simple example is an instance of a general technique[7] for computing the values of a linguistic variable which is analogous to the method underlying Knuth semantics and attributed

[5]This issue is discussed in greater detail in I. R. Goodman, "Fuzzy sets as equivalence classes of random sets," in: *Recent Developments in Fuzzy Set and Possibility Theory*, R. R. Yager, ed., London, Pergamon Press, 327-343, 1981.

[6]L. A. Zadeh, "Outline of a new approach to the analysis of complex systems and decision processes", *IEEE Trans. on Systems, Man and Cybernetics*, **SMC-3**, 28-44, 1973; A. Borisov, A. V. Alekseev, O. A. Krumberg, G. V. Merkur'eva and V. A. Popov, *Models of Decision-Making Based on the Concept of a Linguistic Variable*, Riga, Zinatne, 1982.

[7]See Zadeh, 1975.

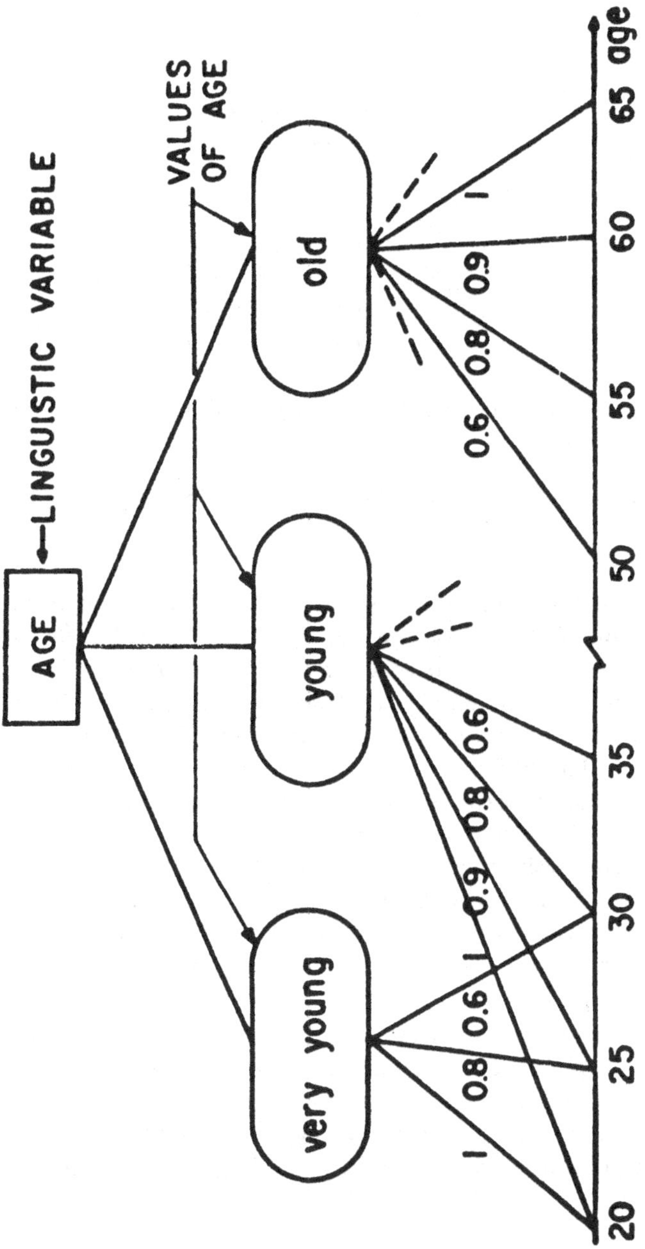

Figure 12.2: Hierarchical representation of the linguistic variable *Age*.

Age	Health
young	good
not young	not good
very young	very good
not very young	not very good
more or less young	more or less good
...	...
old	poor
not old	not poor
very old	very poor
not very old	not very poor
more or less old	more or less poor
...	...
not very old and not very young	not very good and not very poor
...	...

Table 12.1: Linguistic Values of the Variables *Age* and *Health.*

grammars.

What makes it possible to apply the attributed grammar technique to the computation of the values of a linguistic variable is the fact that the context-dependent constituents of a linguistic value are the primary terms rather than the modifiers and connectives. Thus, a primary term plays a role akin to that of a *unit of measurement* which, like any unit, is in need of calibration. Once the primary term is calibrated, the meaning of any linguistic value may be expressed as a function of the primary terms. This function is determined, in turn, by the context-independent meaning of the modifiers and connectives and the way in which they operate on the primary terms. As an illustration, Figure 12.3 shows the membership functions of the primary terms *young* and *old*, and those of several representative linguistic values which have these terms as their constituents.

Another important characteristic of linguistic variables is the universality of their structure. For example, the variables *Age* and *Health* have the same structure in the sense that their respective linguistic values have the same form and differ only in the primary terms. This implies that the meaning of the linguistic values of any linguistic variable may be computed by a general procedure which applies to all linguistic variables. Another

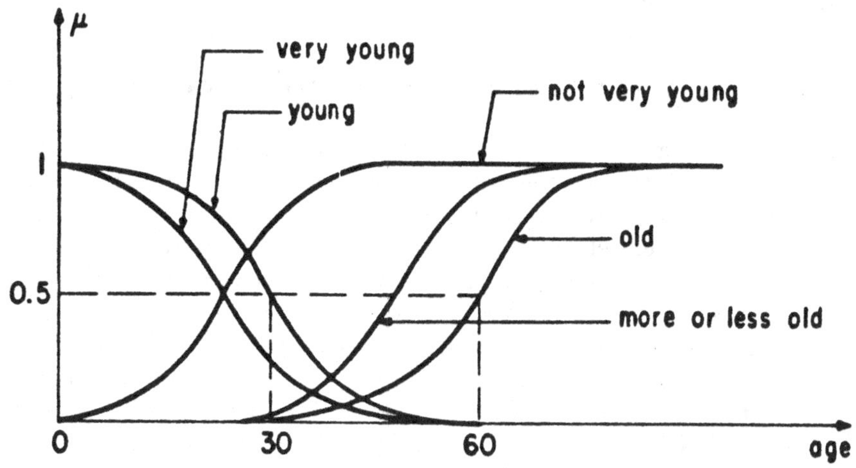

Figure 12.3: Representation of the linguistic values of *Age*.

point that should be noted is that the concept of a linguistic variable subsumes that of quantized variables, and, in particular, the concept of a three-valued variable which takes the values (*negative*, *zero*, *positive*). Such variables play a central role in qualitative process theory.[8]

12.3 Representation of complex concepts

The concept of a linguistic variable has found a number of applications in such diverse fields as industrial process control, medical diagnosis, assessment of credit worthiness, risk analysis, etc. An immediate application which suggests itself relates to the characterization of criteria which define a complex system, a condition, an event or a level of performance, e.g., the criteria which define a hierarchical system, decentralized system, traffic congestion, recession, atherosclerosis, vulnerability, instability, fault tolerance, etc. As an illustration, consider the concept of recession. Technically, the economy is considered to be in a state of recession if it is preceded by a decline in GNP in two successive quarters. But it is clear that a simple definition of this type cannot capture the complexity of a concept such as the concept of recession which has a multiplicity of dimensions of which the decline in GNP is but one of many. On the other hand, it would be too difficult to express the degree to which the economy is in a state of recession as a *numerical* function of more than a very small number of *numerical* criteria. In such cases, the concept of a *linguistic* variable provides a way of tabulating the linguistic values of the degree of recession as a function of the linguistic values of the relevant variables.

As an illustration, assume that the principal determinants of the seriousness of a recession are (a) the decline in GNP; (b) the level of unemployment; (c) the increase in bankruptcies; and (d) the decline in the Dow-Jones average. This implies that we are viewing the concept of a recession as a predicate whose arguments are (a), (b), (c) and (d). To define the predicate then, we have to characterize its dependence on its arguments. In terms of linguistic values, this may be done in the form of a table, as shown below.

In this table, the second row, for example, means that if the decline in GNP is *moderate*, the level of unemployment is *low*, the increase in bankruptcies is *small*, and the decline in Dow-Jones average is *small*, then

[8] See the special issue on *Qualitative Reasoning, Artificial Intelligence*, **24**, 1-492, 1984.

GNP↓	UNEMP	BANKR↑	D-J↓	RECESSION
small	low	small	small	not true
moderate	low	small	small	not true
large	low	small	small	not very true
.	.	.	.	.
large	moderate	moderate	large	quite true
large	high	high	large	very true

Table 12.2: *Recession*: Linguistic Relational Representation

the truth-value of *recession* is *not true*, and likewise for other rows. Furthermore, the linguistic values in each column are fuzzy sets which are defined as illustrated in Figure 12.4, with the understanding that the meaning of a primary term is local to the column in which it appears, i.e., the meaning of *small* in the column labeled *increase in bankruptcies* is not the same as in the column labeled *decline in Dow-Jones*. Another point that should be noted is that a row in a relational representation may be interpreted as an if-then rule, e.g., **IF** *the decline in GNP is large* and *the level of unemployment is moderate* and *the increase in bankruptcies is moderate* and *the decline in Dow-Jones is large* **THEN** *recession is quite true*.

As shown in Zadeh,[9] a linguistic definition of a concept may be converted into a branching questionnaire which, through a succession of answers to questions, leads to a linguistic value of the dependent variable. In this way, it becomes possible to deal in a systematic way with concepts such as relevance, vulnerability, etc. which are too complex or insufficiently well-defined to be susceptible to definition by conventional methods. Furthermore, the linguistic approach provides a basis for interpolating the defining table and computing the linguistic value of the dependent variable for linguistic values of independent variables which are not in the table. The ability to interpolate plays a particularly significant role in the case of rule-based expert systems in which the number of rules is not large enough to account for every possible combination of values of knowledge-base variables.

[9] L. A. Zadeh, "A fuzzy-algorithmic approach to the definition of complex or imprecise concepts," *Int. J. Man-Machine Studies*, **8**, 249-291, 1976.

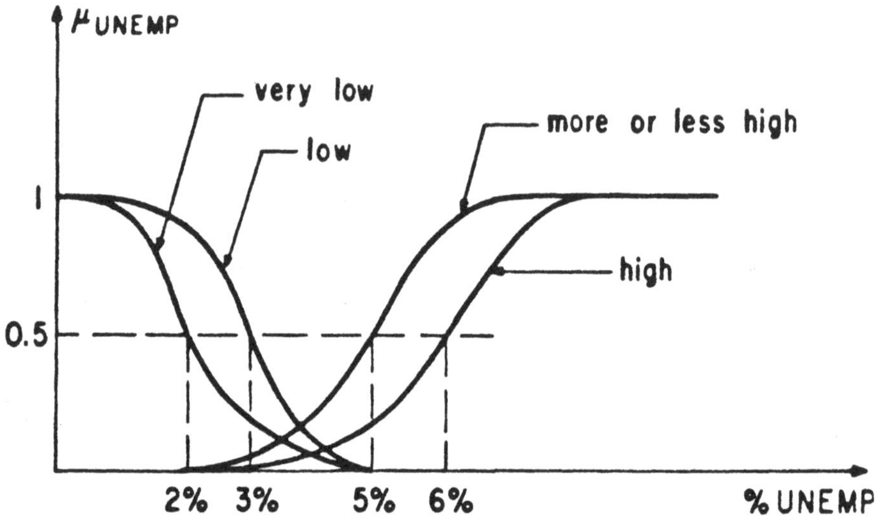

Figure 12.4: Representation of the linguistic values of the linguistic variable *Unemployment*.

12.4 Fuzzy logic control

An important application of the concept of a linguistic variable was pioneered by Mamdani and Assilian.[10] In the intervening years, fuzzy logic control has been applied successfully in many industrial process control systems. One of the most significant examples of work in this area is the cement kiln control system developed by Ostergaard and his colleagues at the F. L. Smidth Co. in Denmark.[11] In this system, as in most rule-based expert systems, the control rules imitate the actions that would be taken by an experienced human operator when the system under control is in a specified state. For example, a typical control rule in the Smidth system is: **IF** the oxygen percentage is *low* **THEN** a *medium-negative* change in coal is required. In this rule, oxygen percentage and coal feed play the role of linguistic variables whose linguistic values are *low* and *medium-negative*. Through the use of fuzzy logic control in this and related applications, significant improvements in the efficiency and uniformity of control processes have been achieved. Another application area in which fuzzy logic control may prove to be very effective is that of automobile engine control. Some work in this direction has been done by Murakami at Kyushu University in Japan.[12]

12.5 Reasoning with commonsense knowledge

As was stated earlier, classical logic does not provide an appropriate framework for reasoning with commonsense knowledge. In fuzzy logic, such knowledge is treated as a collection of *dispositions*, that is, propositions which are preponderantly—but not necessarily always—valid.[13] In this sense, *overeating causes obesity* is a disposition because it is usually, but not always, true.

[10]E. H. Mamdani and S. Assilian, "An experiment in linguistic synthesis with a fuzzy logic controller," *Int. J. Man-Machine Studies*, **7**, 1-13, 1975.

[11]E. H. Mamdani and B. R. Gaines, eds., *Fuzzy Reasoning and its Applications*, London, Academic Press, 1981.

[12]S. Murakami, "Application of fuzzy controller to automobile speed control system," in: *Proc. IFAC Conference on Fuzzy Information, Knowledge Representation and Decision Analysis*, E. Sanchez and M. M. Gupta, eds., Oxford, Pergamon Press, 1983.

[13]See L. A. Zadeh, 1983b.

Much of the information which resides in the knowledge base of a typical expert system consists of a collection of dispositions. For this reason, the application of fuzzy logic to commonsense reasoning is of considerable relevance to the development of rules for combination of evidence in expert systems, and more generally, to the management of uncertainty in such systems.[14] The basic idea underlying the use of fuzzy logic in commonsense reasoning may be summarized as follows:

Technically, a disposition in a knowledge base may be viewed as a proposition in which there are implicit fuzzy quantifiers such as *most*, *almost always*, *usually*, etc. Thus, as a first step in the reasoning process, the implicit quantifiers must be made explicit. For example,

overeating causes obesity → *usually overeating causes obesity*
athletes are healthy → *most athletes are healthy.*

In fuzzy logic, fuzzy quantifiers are treated as fuzzy numbers which represent in an imprecise way the absolute or relative count of elements in a fuzzy set.[15] Thus, the proposition *most A's are B's* means that the proportion of elements of B in A is represented by the fuzzy number *most*. (See Figure 12.5.)

Once the fuzzy quantifiers are made explicit, various syllogisms in fuzzy logic may be employed to arrive at a conclusion. For example, the so-called *intersection/product syllogism* leads to the following reasoning chain:[16]

most students are undergraduates
most undergraduates are young
―――――――――――――――
most^2 *students are young*

where *most*^{2} represents the product of the fuzzy number *most* with itself (Figure 12.5) in fuzzy arithmetic.[17] As should be expected, the quantifer *most*^{2} in the conclusion is less specific than the quantifier *most* in the premises.

---

[14] L. A. Zadeh, "The role of fuzzy logic in the management of uncertainty in expert systems," *Fuzzy Sets and Systems*, **11**, 199-227, 1983c.

[15] See Zadeh, 1983a.

[16] L. A. Zadeh, "Syllogistic reasoning in fuzzy logic and its applications to usuality and reasoning with dispositions," *IEEE Trans. Systems, Man and Cybernetics* **SMC-15**, 754-763, 1985.

[17] A. Kaufmann and M. M. Gupta, *Introduction to Fuzzy Arithmetic*, New York, Van Nostrand, 1985.

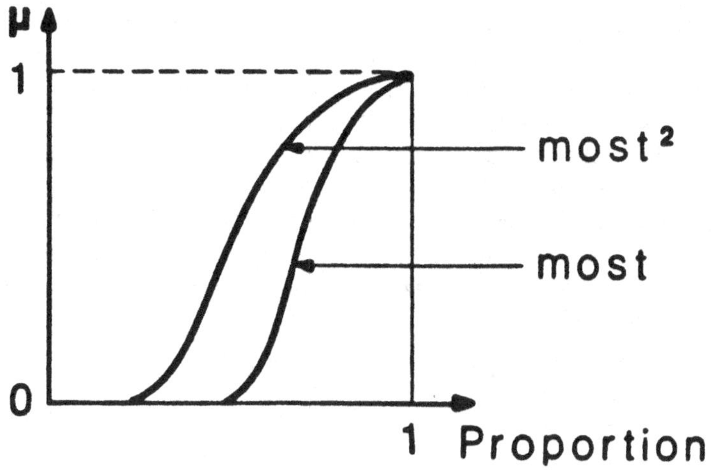

Figure 12.5: Representation of the fuzzy quantifiers *most* and *most*^{2}.

More generally, the use of fuzzy logic for reasoning with commonsense knowledge reduces the determination of the answer to a question to solving a nonlinear program.[18] The solution of such programs could be greatly simplified if we knew how to take advantage of the tolerance for imprecision in computing a solution. This is an open problem at this juncture.

12.5.1 Usuality

As was stated earlier, the concept of usuality is closely related to that of dispositionality and, more specifically, to the concept of a *dispositional valuation.* For example, *a cup of coffee costs about fifty cents,* is a dispositional valuation in the sense that it can be interpreted as the proposition *usually a cup of coffee costs about fifty cents,* in which *usually* acts as a fuzzy quantifier, and *about fifty cents* is a fuzzy number which represents the *usual value* of the cost of a cup of coffee.

The concept of usuality plays a central role in commonsense reasoning because most of the facts which underlie such reasoning relate to our

[18]See L. A. Zadeh, 1983c.

knowledge of the usual values of decision variables. For example, we use our knowledge of such values to decide where to look for a place to park a car, buy a suit, rent an apartment, etc. In what follows, we shall sketch briefly our approach to a formalization of the notion of usuality within the conceptual structure of fuzzy logic.[19]

To begin with, consider a dispositional valuation of the form X *is* F, where X is a variable taking values in a universe of discourse U, and F is a fuzzy subset of U which is characterized by its membership function μ_F. In referring to the statement X *is* F as a dispositional valuation, we imply that it contains an implicit fuzzy quantifier *usually*, so that its meaning may be interpreted as

$$X \text{ is } F \rightarrow \text{usually } (X \text{ is } F),$$

with the understanding that, in this formulation, F plays the role of a *usual value* of X.

What is the *usual value* of X? In contrast to the expected value of a variable, it is generally neither crisp nor unique. Thus, any fuzzy subset of U qualifies to a degree as a usual value of X. In this sense, the definition of a usual value of X is a procedure which for any given F computes the degree to which F qualifies as a usual value of X.

To formulate the procedure in question, it is necessary to have a means of computing the cardinality of a fuzzy set. In the theory of fuzzy sets, there are several ways in which this can be done.[20] The simplest involves the concept of a *sigma-count* which is defined as follows:

Let F be a fuzzy subset of $U = \{u_1, \ldots, u_n\}$

expressed symbolically as

$$F = \mu_1/u_1 + \ldots + \mu_n/u_n = \Sigma_i \mu_i/u_i$$

or, more simply, as

$$F = \mu_1 u_1 + \ldots + \mu_n u_n,$$

---

[19]See Zadeh, 1985.

[20]See Zadeh, 1983a; D. Dubois and H. Prade, "Fuzzy cardinality and the modeling of imprecise quantification," *Fuzzy Sets and Systems*, **16**, 199-230, 1985.

in which the term μ_i/u_i $i = 1, \ldots, n$, signifies that μ_i is the grade of membership of u_i, in F, and the plus sign represents the union.

The sigma-count of F is defined as the arithmetic sum of the μ_i, i.e.,

$$\Sigma\mathrm{Count}(F) = \Sigma_i \mu_i, i = 1, \ldots, n,$$

with the understanding that the sum may be rounded if need be to the nearest integer. Furthermore, one may stipulate that the terms whose grade of membership falls below a specifies threshold be excluded from the summation. The purpose of such an exclusion is to avoid a situation in which a large number of terms with low grades of membership become count-equivalent to a small number of terms with high membership.

The *relative sigma-count*, denoted by $\Sigma\mathrm{Count}(F/G)$, may be interpreted as the proportion of elements of F which are in G. More explicitly,

$$\Sigma\mathrm{Count}(F/G) = \frac{\Sigma\mathrm{Count}\ (F \cap G)}{\Sigma\mathrm{Count}(G)},$$

where $F \cap G$, the intersection of F and G, is defined by

$$\mu_{F \cap G}(u) = \mu_F(u) \wedge \mu_G(u), u \epsilon U.$$

Thus, in terms of the membership functions of F and G, the relative sigma-count of F in G is given by

$$\Sigma\mathrm{Count}(F/G) = \frac{\Sigma_i \mu_F(u_i) \wedge \mu_G(u_i)}{\Sigma_i \mu_G(u_i)}.$$

The concept of a relative sigma-count provides a basis for interpreting the meaning of propositions of the form *QA's are B's*, e.g., *most young men are healthy*, and thus leads to a way of defining the meaning of *usually (X is F)*.

More specifically, the translation of *QA's are B's* may be expressed as

$$QA\text{'s are } B\text{'s} \rightarrow \Sigma\ \mathrm{Count}\ (B/A) \text{ is } Q,$$

which signifies that the fuzzy quantifier Q characterizes the fuzzy proportion of B's in A's. Thus, for any given A, B and Q, the degree of compatibility or, equivalently, the truth-value, ρ, of the proposition *QA's are B's*, is given by

$$\rho = \mu_Q\,(\Sigma\mathrm{Count}(B/A))\,,$$

where μ_Q is the membership function of the fuzzy number Q.

Turning to the definition of *usually*, assume that X takes the values $u_{1,\ldots,}u_n$ in U. Then, if we interpret the statement *usually (X is F)* as *most u's are F*, it follows from the definition of *QA's are B's* that, with Q set equal to *MOST*, we have

$$\textit{usually (X is F)} \rightarrow \Sigma\mathrm{Count}\ \textit{(F/U) is MOST},$$

where *MOST* is a fuzzy number which represents the fuzzy quantifier *most* and $\Sigma\mathrm{Count}(F/U)$ is the relative sigma-count of F in the universe of discourse U. Based on this interpretation of the proposition *usually (X is F)*, the degree ρ to which F qualifies as a usual value of X may be expressed as

$$\rho = \mu_{MOST}\,(\Sigma\mathrm{Count}(F/U))\,.$$

Equivalently, if X is a random variable whose probability density is $p(u)$, then from the definition of the measure of a fuzzy event[21] it follows that

$$\rho = \mu_{MOST}\left(\int_U \mu_F(u)p(u)du\right)$$

where μ_F is the membership function of F.

It is natural to raise the question: Is the concept of a *usual* value different from that of a *typical* value? To answer this question,we must first define what is meant by a typical value of a variable. Based on the definition given in Zadeh,[22] t is a typical value of X if it is representative of the values which X can take. More specifically, let μ_S denote the membership function of a similarity relation, S, such that $\mu_S(t,u)$ is the degree to which t and u are similar. Furthermore, let $p(u)$ denote the probability density of X, Then the degree to which t qualifies to be regarded as a typical value of X is expressed by

[21]L. A. Zadeh, "Probability measures of fuzzy events," *J. Math. Anal. and Appl.*, **23**, 421-427, 1968.

[22]L. A. Zadeh, "A computational theory of dispositions," in *Proceedings of the 1984 International Conference on Computational Linguistics*, Stanford University, CA., 312-318, 1984.

$$\sigma = \mu_{MOST}\left(\int_U \mu_S(t,u)p(u)du\right)$$

where the argument of μ_{MOST} is the sigma-count of values of X which are similar to t.

Now the membership function, $\mu_S(t,u)$, of the similarity relation S may be interpreted as the membership function of $S(t)$, the *similarity class* of t, that is, the fuzzy set of points in U which are similar to t. With this interpretation, the expression for S may be rewritten as

$$\sigma = \mu_{MOST}\left(\int_U \mu_{S(t)}(u)p(u)du\right)$$

and, on comparing this expression with the corresponding expression for ρ, we are led to the following result:

The degree to which t is a typical value of **X** *is equal to the degree to which S(t) is a usual value of* **X**.

This result establishes a connection between the concepts of a typical and usual value. At the same time, it shows that the concepts are distinct. In particular, a usual value is in general fuzzy, whereas a typical value is not.

In application to commonsense reasoning, the concept of usuality provides a basis for what might be called *dispositional rules of inference.* An example of a basic rule of this type is the *dispositional modus ponens*

$$\frac{\begin{array}{c}\textit{usually } (X \textit{ is } f)\\ \textit{if } X \textit{ is } F \textit{ then usually } (Y \textit{ is } G)\end{array}}{\textit{usually}^2\ (Y \textit{ is } G)}$$

where F and G are usual values of X and Y, respectively, and $usually^2$ is the product of the fuzzy number *usually* with itself in fuzzy arithmetic.[23]

Another important application of usuality relates to rules of inference in which an assumption, e.g., $F \subset G$, is assumed to hold usually, but not necessarily always. For example, the so-called *entailment principle* is fuzzy logic which may be expressed as the inference rule

$$\begin{array}{c} X \textit{ is } F \\ \underline{F \subset G} \end{array}$$

[23]See Kaufmann and Gupta, 1985.

$$X \textit{ is } G$$

which means that from the proposition X *is* F, we can always infer a less specific proposition X *is* G. Now, if the assumption $F \subset G$ is assumed to hold usually, then the entailment principle becomes the ***dispositional entailment principle***

$$\frac{\begin{array}{c} X \textit{ is } F \\ \textit{usually } (F \subset G) \end{array}}{\textit{usually } (X \textit{ is } G)}$$

in which the conclusion defines G as a usual value of X.

Still another way in which the concept of usuality enters into commonsense reasoning relates to what might be called the ***calculus of usual values.*** For example, if we know the usual values of X and Y, what can be said about the usual values of, say, $X+Y$ and XY? Qualitative questions of this type arise in one guise or another in much of human decision-making and play a major role in commonsense reasoning. However, at this juncture, the development of the theory of usuality has not progressed far enough to provide us with complete answers to general questions of this nature.

Acknowledgements: I would like to acknowledge stimulating discussions with Professor Lucia Vaina. This research was supported in part by a grant from NASA, Grant Number NCC-2-275, and in part by an NSF grant, number ECS-8209679.

[*Lotfi A. Zadeh, Ph.D., is a member of the Department of Electrical Engineering and Computer Science, University of California, Berkeley, California 94230.*]

Dispositional Logic

L. A. Zadeh*

1. Introduction

Mathematical analysis as we know it today is based almost entirely on two-valued logical systems in which every proposition is either true or false, with no gradation of truth allowed. However, this restriction is mitigated to some extent by allowing probability qualification, that is, assertions of the form: *The probability that proposition p is true is α, where α is a number in the interval* [0, 1].

The successes of mathematical analysis in science have led to an almost unquestioned assumption that the combination of two-valued logic and probability theory is all that is needed, especially in those branches of science, e.g., physics, chemistry, astronomy, analytical mechanics, control theory, etc., in which the systems under analysis are well-defined in the sense that their behavior may be described by a family of integro-differential or difference equations in which the stochastic components, if any, have known or measurable probability distributions. But what is questionable is the adequacy of two-valued-logic-based mathematics for the social sciences and, more generally, for the analysis of systems in which human judgment, perception, and emotions play an important role. The problem with such systems is that they are much too ill-defined to admit of characterization within any mathematical framework which is based on two-valued logic. This holds, in particular, for systems encountered in such fields as economics, psychology, sociology, medicine, etc. It is true that even in these fields, as in most fields of science, respect and recognition is accorded to those who create quantitative theories within the classical paradigm. But the extent to which such theories are relevant to real-world problems is a debatable thesis which cannot be supported in the affirmative if one expects a theory to have a predictive value.

Viewed against this background, fuzzy logic may be regarded as an alternative to two-valued logical systems—an alternative which aims at providing a model for modes of reasoning which are approximate rather than exact. Thus, in fuzzy logic, which is basically a generalization of multivalued logic, truth is not only a matter of degree—as it is in multivalued logic—but, more importantly, a fuzzy degree. The same applies to quantifiers, probabilities, possibilities and, more generally, to everything else. In this way, that is, by abandoning the concept of two-valuedness, fuzzy logic acquires the capability to model cognitive phenomena which are too complex or too ill-defined to be amenable to analysis by traditional means.

There is a branch of fuzzy logic, namely, ***dispositional logic***, which is of particular relevance to the commonsense mode of reasoning which underlies our ability to communicate and make rational decisions in an environment of uncertainty and imprecision. Since classical predicate logic is not effective in such environments, a number of attempts have been made during the past decade to extend it in ways which would make it possible to address at least some of the problems which are associated with commonsense reasoning and, in particular, the problem of exceptions. The best known of the methods in this spirit are circumscription (3), nonmonotonic reasoning (4), and default reasoning (5).

The methods in question have played an important role in improving our understanding of commonsense reasoning and knowledge representation. However, based as they are on two-valued logic, they do not provide a framework for inference when the premises are fuzzy and/or are

Computer Science Division, University of California, Berkeley, CA 94720. Research supported in part by NASA Grant NCC-2-275 and NSF Grant DCR-8513139.

95

Reprinted, with permission, from *Appl. Math. Lett.*, 1(1), pp. 95–99.

associated with fuzzy probabilities—which is characteristic of the premises representing commonsense knowledge. In this setting, dispositional logic provides an alternative system of inference based on fuzzy logic which is capable of addressing the issues of uncertainty and imprecision in the context of commonsense reasoning and knowledge representation. In what follows, we shall outline the conceptual structure of dispositional logic and provide a sketch of some of its main features. A more detailed exposition of a related theory of dispositions may be found in (7).

2. Dispositionality and Usuality

The point of departure in dispositional logic is the concept of a *disposition*, that is, a proposition which is preponderantly but not necessarily always true. For example, *birds can fly* is a disposition, as are the propositions *smoking is harmful*, *Swedes are blond*, *flying is safe*, *young men like young women*, and *it takes about an hour to drive from Berkeley to Stanford*. Most dispositions are of the form *A is B* or *A's are B's*, where A and B are fuzzy predicates, as in *smoking is harmful* and *Swedes are blond*. (Note that to be a Swede is a matter of degree.) Expressed in these forms, a disposition signifies that the conditional probability of B given A is high, where high should be interpreted as a fuzzy probability.

In more concrete terms, a disposition may be expressed in one of two canonical forms:

(a) *unconditional*:

$$\text{usually } (X \text{ is } A) \tag{1}$$

and (b), *conditional*:

$$\text{usually } (X \text{ is } A \text{ if } Y \text{ is } B), \tag{2}$$

where X and Y are variables, A and B are fuzzy predicates, and *usually* is a fuzzy quantifier which may be represented as a fuzzy number in the interval [0, 1]. In (1), A is a *usual value* of X, while in (2) B is a usual value of X conditioned on *Y is B*. Propositions of the form (1) and (2) are said to be *usuality-qualified*. In most cases, the quantifier *usually* in such propositions is implicit rather than explicit. As an illustration, the disposition *snow is white* may be represented in an unconditional form as

usually (Color (Snow) is white).

Similarly, the conditional proposition *snow is white if it is fresh* may be expressed as

usually (Color (Snow) is white if Snow is fresh),

where *Color (Snow)* plays the role of X; *white* the role of A; *Snow* the role of Y; and *fresh* the role of B. Note that in this case X is a function of Y.

The meaning of a disposition which is expressed in its unconditional form may be defined as follows (6). Assume for simplicity that X is a random variable which takes the values $u_1, \ldots, u_n$ with respective probabilities $p_1, \ldots, p_n$. Then, (1) may be interpreted as a constraint on the vector $p = (p_1, \ldots, p_n)$, with the degree, τ, to which p satisfies the constraint given by

$$\tau = \mu_{usually}\left(\textstyle\sum_i p_i \mu_A(u_i)\right), \quad i = 1, \ldots, n\,, \tag{3}$$

in which $\mu_{usually}$ is the membership function of the fuzzy number *usually*.

More generally, in the case of a conditional disposition, let p_{ij} and p_j denote, respectively, the joint probability that $X = u_i$ and $Y = v_j$, and the probability that $Y = v_j$, $i,j = 1, \ldots, n$. Then, the degree, τ, to which the constraint on p_{ij} and p_i is satisfied is given by

$$\tau = \mu_{usually}\left[\frac{\sum_{i,j} p_{ij}\,(\mu_A(u_i) \wedge \mu_B(v_j))}{\sum_j p_j \mu_B(v_j)}\right], \tag{4}$$

in which the argument of $\mu_{usually}$ is the conditional probability of the fuzzy event *X is A* given the fuzzy event *Y is B*.

Another important concept in dispositional logic is that of a ***subdisposition***, exemplified by ***slimness is attractive***. In this case, it would not be correct to interpret the proposition in question as ***most of those who are slim are attractive***. A more accurate interpretation would be that the conditional probability that a slim person is attractive is significantly higher than the unconditional probability that a person is attractive. More specifically, if a subdisposition is expressed as a conditional proposition of the form *X is A* if *Y is B*, then the relative increase, ρ, in the conditional probability of A given B may be expressed as

$$\rho = \frac{P(A \mid B) - P(A)}{1 - P(A)}. \tag{5}$$

To say that the conditional probability $P(A \mid B)$ is significantly higher than $P(A)$ is roughly equivalent to saying that the ratio ρ in (5) is a fuzzy number which is greater than or equal to ***medium***, which in turn is a fuzzy number close to 0.5. Under this assumption, the degree, τ, to which a given subdisposition constrains p_{ij} and p_j may be expressed as

$$\tau = \mu_\rho\left[\frac{p(A \mid B) - P(A)}{1 - P(A)}\right], \tag{6}$$

in which $P(A \mid B)$ and $P(A)$ are given by

$$P(A \mid B) = \frac{\sum_{i,j} p_{ij}\,(\mu_A(u_i) \wedge \mu_B(v_j))}{\sum_j p_j \mu_B(vu_j)} \tag{7}$$

and

$$P(A) = \sum_i p_i \mu_A(u_i), \quad i = 1, \ldots, n,$$

where p_i is the probability that $X = u_i$.

In dispositional logic, the concepts of a disposition and subdisposition as defined above provide a point of departure for the construction of a system of inference from commonsense knowledge. In this system, the techniques of fuzzy logic are employed to express commonsense knowledge in the form of usuality-qualified propositions exemplified by (1) and (2). Then, the deductive apparatus of both dispositional and fuzzy logic is called upon to provide answers to queries relating to the information stored in a database containing dispositions, subdispositions, and possibly other types of factual data.

The form of inference rules in dispositional logic may be illustrated by two basic rules: (a) the dispositional conjunctive rule; and (b) the dispositional *modus ponens*. These rules may be stated as follows.

The dispositional conjunctive rule

$$\frac{\begin{array}{c} usually\ (X\ is\ A) \\ usually\ (X\ is\ B) \end{array}}{(2\ usually \ominus 1)\ (X\ is\ A \cap B)}, \tag{8}$$

where $A \cap B$ denotes the intersection (or conjunction) of A and B, and the fuzzy quantifier $2\ usually \ominus 1$ is a fuzzy arithmetic expression in which $\ominus$ denotes the operation of subtraction in fuzzy arithmetic (2). As is generally true of deductions in dispositional logic, the fuzzy quantifier in the conclusion is less specific than the fuzzy quantifiers in premises. (What this means is that, viewed as a fuzzy subset of the unit interval, the fuzzy number *usuall* is a subset of $2\ usually \ominus 1$.)

The dispositional modus ponens

$$\frac{\begin{array}{c} usually\ (X\ is\ A) \\ usually\ (Y\ is\ B\ \text{if}\ X\ is\ A) \end{array}}{usually^2\ (Y\ is\ B)}, \tag{9}$$

where $usually^2$ is the product of *usually* with itself in fuzzy arithmetic. As in the case of the dispositional conjunctive rule, the fuzzy quantifier $usually^2$ is less specific than *usually*.

Simple examples of (8) and (9) are the following:

$$\frac{\begin{array}{c} usually\ (Age\ (Professor)\ is\ not\ very\ young) \\ usually\ (Age\ (Professor)\ is\ not\ very\ old) \end{array}}{(2\ usually \ominus 1)\ (Age\ (Professor)\ is\ not\ very\ young\ and\ not\ very\ old)}$$

$$\frac{\begin{array}{c} usually\ (Pressure\ is\ high) \\ usually\ (Volume\ is\ low\ if\ Pressure\ is\ high) \end{array}}{usually^2\ (Volume\ is\ low)}$$

Concluding remark. Although we have focused our attention in this note on the concept of dispositionality in the context of commonsense reasoning, its implications are much broader. Indeed, as we develop a better understanding of human reasoning we may discover that dispositionality—in its diverse manifestations—plays a key role in the remarkable human ability to make rational decisions in an environment of uncertainty and imprecision.

References and Related Publications

1. P.R. Cohen and E.A. Feigenbaum (Eds.), *Handbook of Artificial Intelligence,* Kaufmann, Los Altos, CA, 1982.
2. A. Kaufmann and M. Gupta, *Introduction to Fuzzy Arithmetic*, Van Nostrand, New York, 1985.
3. J. McCarthy, "Circumscription: A non-monotonic inference rule," *Artificial Intelligence,* **13**, 27-40 (1980).
4. D.V. McDermott and J. Doyle, "Non-monotonic logic, I.," *Artificial Intelligence,* **13**, 41-72 (1980).
5. R. Reiter and G. Criscuolo, "Some representational issues in default reasoning," *Computers and Mathematics,* **9**, 15-28 (1983).
6. L.A. Zadeh, "Test-score semantics as a basis for a computational approach to the representation of meaning," *Literary and Linguistic Computing,* **1**, 24-35 (1986b).
7. L.A. Zadeh, "A computational theory of dispositions," *Int. J. of Intelligent Systems,* **2**, 39-63 (1987).

Knowledge Representation in Fuzzy Logic

LOTFI A. ZADEH, FELLOW, IEEE

(Invited Paper)

Abstract—The conventional approaches to knowledge representation, e.g., semantic networks, frames, predicate calculus, and Prolog, are based on bivalent logic. A serious shortcoming of such approaches is their inability to come to grips with the issue of uncertainty and imprecision. As a consequence, the conventional approaches do not provide an adequate model for modes of reasoning which are approximate rather than exact. Most modes of human reasoning and all of common sense reasoning fall into this category.

Fuzzy logic, which may be viewed as an extension of classical logical systems, provides an effective conceptual framework for dealing with the problem of knowledge representation in an environment of uncertainty and imprecision. Meaning representation in fuzzy logic is based on test-score semantics. In this semantics, a proposition is interpreted as a system of elastic constraints, and reasoning is viewed as elastic constraint propagation. Our paper presents a summary of the basic concepts and techniques underlying the application of fuzzy logic to knowledge representation and describes a number of examples relating to its use as a computational system for dealing with uncertainty and imprecision in the context of knowledge, meaning, and inference.

Index Terms—Approximate reasoning, fuzzy logic, knowledge representation.

I. Introduction

KNOWLEDGE representation is one of the most basic and actively researched areas of AI [4], [5], [30], [31], [36], [37], [39], [46], [47]. And yet, there are many important issues underlying knowledge representation which have not been adequately addressed. One such issue is that of the representation of knowledge which is lexically imprecise and/or uncertain.

As a case in point, the conventional knowledge representation techniques do not provide effective tools for representing the meaning of or inferring from the kind of everyday type facts exemplified by the following.

1) *Usually* it takes *about an hour* to drive from Berkeley to Stanford in *light* traffic.

2) Unemployment is *not likely* to undergo a *sharp* decline during the next *few* months.

3) *Most* experts believe that the likelihood of a *severe* earthquake in the *near* future is *very low*.

The italicized words in these assertions are the labels of fuzzy predicates, fuzzy quantifiers, and fuzzy probabilities. The conventional approaches to knowledge representation lack the means for representing the meaning of fuzzy concepts. As a consequence, the approaches based on first-order logic and classical probability theory do not provide an appropriate conceptual framework for dealing with the representation of common sense knowledge, since such knowledge is by its nature both lexically imprecise and noncategorical [36], [37], [63].

The development of fuzzy logic was motivated in large measure by the need for a conceptual framework which can address the issues of uncertainty and lexical imprecision. The principal objective of this paper is to present a summary of some of the basic ideas underlying fuzzy logic and to describe their application to the problem of knowledge representation in an environment of uncertainty and imprecision. A more detailed discussion of these ideas may be found in Zadeh [59], [60], [65], [67] and other references.

II. Essentials of Fuzzy Logic

Fuzzy logic, as its name suggests, is the logic underlying modes of reasoning which are approximate rather than exact. The importance of fuzzy logic derives from the fact that most modes of human reasoning—and especially common sense reasoning—are approximate in nature. It is of interest to note that, despite its pervasiveness, approximate reasoning falls outside the purview of classical logic largely because it is a deeply entrenched tradition in logic to be concerned with those and only those modes of reasoning which lend themselves to precise formulation and analysis.

Some of the essential characteristics of fuzzy logic relate to the following.

In fuzzy logic, exact reasoning is viewed as a limiting case of approximate reasoning.

In fuzzy logic, everything is a matter of degree.

Any logical system can be fuzzified.

In fuzzy logic, knowledge is interpreted as a collection of elastic or, equivalently, fuzzy constraint on a collection of variables.

Inference is viewed as a process of propagation of elastic constraints.

Fuzzy logic differs from traditional logical systems both in spirit and in detail. Some of the principal differences are summarized in the following [62].

Truth: In bivalent logical systems, truth can have only two values: true or false. In multivalued systems, the truth value of a proposition may be an element of: a) a finite set; b) an interval such as [0, 1]; or c) a boolean algebra. In fuzzy logic, the truth value of a proposition may be a

Manuscript received March 1, 1989. This work was supported in part by NASA under Grant NCC-2-275 and by the Air Force Office of Scientific Research under Grant 89-0084.

The author is with the Computer Science Division, Department of Electrical Engineering and Computer Science, University of California, Berkeley, CA 94720.

IEEE Log Number 8928831.

Reprinted, with permission, from *IEEE Trans. on Knowledge and Data Engineering,* 1(1), pp. 89–99.

fuzzy subset of any partially ordered set, but usually it is assumed to be a fuzzy subset of the interval [0, 1] or, more simply, a point in this interval. The so-called *linguistic* truth values expressed as *true, very true, not quite true*, etc., are interpreted as labels of fuzzy subsets of the unit interval.

Predicates: In bivalent systems, the predicates are crisp, e.g., *mortal, even, larger than*. In fuzzy logic, the predicates are fuzzy, e.g., *tall, ill, soon, swift, much larger than*. It should be noted that most of the predicates in a natural language are fuzzy rather than crisp.

Predicate Modifiers: In classical systems, the only widely used predicate modifier is the negation, *not*. In fuzzy logic, there is a variety of predicate modifiers which act as hedges, e.g., *very, more or less, quite, rather, extremely*. Such predicate modifiers play an essential role in the generation of the values of a linguistic variable, e.g., *very young, not very young, more or less young*, etc. [57].

Quantifiers: In classical logical systems there are just two quantifiers: *universal* and *existential*. Fuzzy logic admits, in addition, a wide variety of fuzzy quantifiers exemplified by *few, several, usually, most, almost always, frequently, about five*, etc. In fuzzy logic, a fuzzy quantifier is interpreted as a fuzzy number or a fuzzy proportion [61].

Probabilities: In classical logical systems, probability is numerical or interval-valued. In fuzzy logic, one has the additional option of employing linguistic or, more generally, fuzzy probabilities exemplified by *likely, unlikely, very likely, around 0.8, high*, etc. [65]. Such probabilities may be interpreted as fuzzy numbers which may be manipulated through the use of fuzzy arithmetic [24].

In addition to fuzzy probabilities, fuzzy logic makes it possible to deal with fuzzy events. An example of a fuzzy event is: *tomorrow will be a warm day*, where *warm* is a fuzzy predicate. The probability of a fuzzy event may be a crisp or fuzzy number [56].

It is important to note that from the frequentist point of view there is an interchangeability between fuzzy probabilities and fuzzy quantifiers or, more generally, fuzzy measures. In this perspective, any proposition which contains labels of fuzzy probabilities may be expressed in an equivalent form which contains fuzzy quantifiers rather than fuzzy probabilities.

Possibilities: In contrast to classical modal logic, the concept of possibility in fuzzy logic is graded rather than bivalent. Furthermore, as in the case of probabilities, possibilities may be treated as linguistic variables with values such as *possible, quite possible, almost impossible*, etc. Such values may be interpreted as labels of fuzzy subsets of the real line.

A concept which plays a central role in fuzzy logic is that of a possibility distribution [59], [8], [28]. Briefly, if X is a variable taking values in a universe of discourse U, then the *possibility distribution* of X, Π_X, is the fuzzy set of all possible values of X. More specifically, let $\pi_X(u)$ denote the possibility that X can take the value u, $u \in U$. Then the membership function of X is numerically equal to the *possibility distribution function* $\pi_X(u)$: $U \to [0, 1]$, which associates with each element $u \in U$ the possibility that X may take u as its value. More about possibilities and possibility distributions will be said at a later point in this paper.

It is important to observe that in every instance fuzzy logic adds to the options which are available in classical logical systems. In this sense, fuzzy logic may be viewed as an extension of such systems rather than as a system of reasoning which is in conflict with the classical systems.

Before taking up the issue of knowledge representation in fuzzy logic, it will be helpful to take a brief look at some of the principal modes of reasoning in fuzzy logic. These are the following, with the understanding that the modes in question are not necessarily disjoint.

1) Categorical Reasoning: In this mode of reasoning, the premises contain no fuzzy quantifiers and no fuzzy probabilities. A simple example of categorical reasoning is:

Carol is slim
Carol is very intelligent

Carol is slim and very intelligent

In the premises, *slim* and *very intelligent* are assumed to be fuzzy predicates. The fuzzy predicate in the conclusion, *slim and very intelligent*, is the conjunction of *slim* and *very intelligent*.

Another example of categorical reasoning is:

Mary is young
John is much older than Mary

John is (much older ∘ *young).*

where (*much_older* ∘ *young*) represents the composition of the binary fuzzy predicate *much_older* with the unary fuzzy predicate *young*. More specifically, let π_{much_older} and π_{young} denote the possibility distribution functions associated with the fuzzy predicates *much_older* and *young*, respectively. Then, the possibility distribution function of John's age may be expressed as [59]

$$\pi_{Age(John)}(u) = \vee_v(\pi_{much\_older}(u, v) \wedge \pi_{young}(v))$$

where $\vee$ and $\wedge$ stand for max and min, respectively.

2) Syllogistic Reasoning: In contrast to categorical reasoning, syllogistic reasoning relates to inference from premises containing fuzzy quantifiers [64], [11]. A simple example of syllogistic reasoning is the following:

most Swedes are blond
most blond Swedes are tall

---

most^2 Swedes are blond and tall

where the fuzzy quantifier *most* is interpreted as a fuzzy proportion and *most*^{2} is the square of *most* in fuzzy arithmetic [24].

3) Dispositional Reasoning: In dispositional reasoning the premises are dispositions, that is, propositions which are preponderantly but necessarily always true [66]. An example of dispositional reasoning is:

heavy smoking is a leading cause of lung cancer

---

to avoid lung cancer avoid heavy smoking

Note that in this example the conclusion is a maxim which may be interpreted as a dispositional command. Another example of dispositional reasoning is:

usually the probability of failure is not very low
usually the probability of failure is not very high

(2 *usually* $\ominus$ 1) *the probability of failure is not very low and not very high*

In this example, *usually* is a fuzzy quantifier which is interpreted as a fuzzy proportion and 2 *usually* $\ominus$ 1 is a fuzzy arithmetic expression whose value may be computed through the use of fuzzy arithmetic. ($\ominus$ denotes the operation of subtraction in fuzzy arithmetic.) It should be noted that the concept of *usuality* plays a key role in dispositional reasoning [64], [66], and is the concept that links together the dispositional and syllogistic modes of reasoning. Furthermore, it underlies the theories of nonmonotonic and default reasoning [33], [34], [35], [45].

4) Qualitative Reasoning: In fuzzy logic, the term *qualitative reasoning* refers to a mode of reasoning in which the input-output relation of a system is expressed as a collection of fuzzy if-then rules in which the antecedents and consequents involve linguistic variables [58], [69]. In this sense, qualitative reasoning in fuzzy logic bears some similarity to—but is not coextensive with—qualitative reasoning in AI [6], [14], [29].

A very simple example of qualitative reasoning is:

volume is small if pressure is high
volume is large if pressure is low

---

volume is ($w1 \wedge$ *high* $+$ $w2 \wedge$ *large*) *if pressure is medium*

where + should be interpreted as infix max; and

$$w1 = sup(high \wedge medium)$$

and

$$w2 = sup(low \wedge medium)$$

are weighting coefficients which represent, respectively, the degrees to which the antecedents *high* and *low* match the input *medium*. In $w1$, the conjunction *high* $\wedge$ *medium* represents the intersection of the possibility distributions of *high* and *low*, and the supremum is taken over the domain of *high* and *medium*. The same applies to $w2$.

Qualitative reasoning underlies many of the applications of fuzzy logic in the realms of control and systems analysis [48], [42], [50]. In this connection, it should be noted that fuzzy Prolog provides an effective knowledge representation language for qualitative reasoning [1], [2], [38], [69].

III. Meaning and Knowledge Representation

In a general setting, knowledge may be viewed as a collection of propositions, e.g.,

Mary is young
Pat is much taller than Mary
overeating causes obesity
most Swedes are blond
tomatoes are red unless they are unripe
usually high quality goes with high price
if pressure is high then volume is low

To constitute knowledge, a proposition must be understood. In this sense, meaning and knowledge are closely interrelated. In fuzzy logic, meaning representation—and thus knowledge representation—is based on test-score semantics [60], [65].

A basic idea underlying test-score semantics is that a proposition in a natural language may be viewed as a collection of elastic or, equivalently, fuzzy constraints. For example, the proposition *Mary is tall* represents an elastic constraint on the height of Mary. Similarly, the proposition *Jean is blonde* represents an elastic constraint on the color of Jean's hair. And, the proposition *most tall men are not very agile* represents an elastic constraint on the proportion of men who are not very agile among tall men.

In more concrete terms, representing the meaning of a proposition p through the use of test-score semantics involves the following steps.

1) Identification of the variables $X_1, \cdots, X_n$ whose values are constrained by the proposition. Usually, these variables are implicit rather than explicit in p.

2) Identification of the constraints $C_1, \cdots, C_m$ which are induced by p.

3) Characterization of each constraint C_i by describing a testing procedure which associates with C_i a test score τ_i representing the degree to which C_i is satisfied. Usually τ_i is expressed as a number in the interval $[0, 1]$. More generally, however, a test score may be a probability/possibility distribution over the unit interval.

4) Aggregation of the partial test scores $\tau_1, \cdots, \tau_m$ into a smaller number of test scores $\bar{\tau}_1, \cdots, \bar{\tau}_k$, which are represented as an *overall vector test score* $\tau = (\bar{\tau}_1, \cdots, \bar{\tau}_k)$. In most cases $k = 1$, so that the overall test score is a scalar. We shall assume that this is the case unless an explicit statement to the contrary is made.

It is important to note that, in test-score semantics, the meaning of p is represented not by the overall test score τ but by the procedure which leads to it. Viewed in this perspective, test-score semantics may be regarded as a generalization of truth-conditional, possible-world, and model-theoretic semantics. However, by providing a computational framework for dealing with uncertainty and dispositionality—which the conventional semantical systems disregard—test-score semantics achieves a much higher level of expressive power and thus provides a basis for representing the meaning of a much wider variety of propositions in a natural language.

In test-score semantics, the testing of the constraints induced by p is performed on a collection of fuzzy relations which constitute an *explanatory database*, or *ED* for short. A basic assumption which is made about the explanatory database is that it is comprised of relations whose meaning is known to the addressee of the meaning-representation process. In an indirect way, then, the testing and aggregation procedures in test-score semantics may be viewed as a description of a process by which the meaning of p is composed from the meanings of the constituent relations in the explanatory database. It is this explanatory role of the relations in *ED* that motivates its description as an *explanatory database*.

As will be seen in the sequel, in describing the testing procedures we need not concern ourselves with the actual entries in the constituent relations. Thus, in general, the description of a test involves only the frames of the constituent relations, that is, their names, their variables (or attributes), and the domain of each variable.

As a simple illustration of the concept of a test procedure, consider the proposition $p \triangleq$ *Maria is young and attractive*. The *ED* in this case will be assumed to consist of the following relations:

$$ED \triangleq POPULATION\,[Name;\ Age;\ \mu Attractive] + YOUNG\,[Age;\ \mu] \tag{3.1}$$

in which + should be read as "and," and $\triangleq$ stands for "denotes."

The relation labeled *POPULATION* consists of a collection of triples whose first element is the name of an individual, whose second element is the age of that individual, and whose third element is the degree to which the individual in question is attractive. The relation *YOUNG* is a collection of pairs whose first element is a value of the variable *Age* and whose second element is the degree to which that value of *Age* satisfies the elastic constraint characterized by the fuzzy predicate *young*. In effect, this relation serves to calibrate the meaning of the fuzzy predicate *young* in a particular context by representing its denotation as a fuzzy subset, *YOUNG*, of the interval [0, 100].

With this *ED*, the test procedure which computes the overall test score may be described as follows.

1) Determine the age of Maria by reading the value of *Age* in *POPULATION*, with the variable *Name* bound to Maria. In symbols, this may be expressed as

$$Age(Maria) = {}_{Age}POPULATION\,[Name = Maria].$$

In this expression, we use the notation ${}_{Y}R[X = a]$ to signify that X is bound to a in R and the resulting relation is projected on Y, yielding the values of Y in the tuples in which $X = a$.

2) Test the elastic constraint induced by the fuzzy predicate *young*:

$$\tau_1 = {}_{\mu}YOUNG[Age = Age(Maria)].$$

3) Determine the degree to which Maria is attractive:

$$\tau_2 = {}_{\mu Attractive}POPULATION[Name = Maria].$$

4) Compute the overall test score by aggregating the partial test scores τ_1 and τ_2. For this purpose, we shall use the min operator $\wedge$ as the aggregation operator, yielding

$$\tau = \tau_1 \wedge \tau_1 \tag{3.2}$$

which signifies that the overall test score is taken to be the smaller of the operands of $\wedge$. The overall test score, as expressed by (3.2), represents the compatibility of $p \triangleq$ *Maria is young and attractive* with the data resident in the explanatory database.

In testing the constituent relations in *ED*, it is helpful to have a collection of standardized translation rules for computing the test score of a combination of elastic constraints $C_1, \cdots, C_k$ from the knowledge of the test scores of each constraint considered in isolation. For the most part, such rules are *default* rules in the sense that they are intended to be used in the absence of alternative rules supplied by the user.

For purposes of knowledge representation, the principal rules of this type are the following.

1) Rules Pertaining to Modification: If the test score for an elastic constraint C in a specified context is τ, then in the same context the test score for

(*a*) *not C* is $1 - \tau$ (*negation*)
(*b*) *very C* is τ^2 (*concentration*)
(*c*) *more or less C* is $\tau^{1/2}$ (*diffusion*).

2) Rules Pertaining to Composition: If the test scores for elastic constraints C_1 and C_2 in a specified context are τ_1 and τ_2, respectively, then in the same context the test score for

(*a*) C_1 *and* C_2 is $\tau_1 \wedge \tau_2$ (*conjunction*), where $\wedge \triangleq$ *min*.
(*b*) C_1 *or* C_2 is $\tau_1 \vee \tau_2$ (*disjunction*), where $\vee \triangleq$ *max*.
(*c*) *If* C_1 *then* C_2 is $1 \wedge (1 - \tau_1 + \tau_2)$ (*implication*).

3) Rules Pertaining to Quantification: The rules in question apply to propositions of the general form *Q A's are B's*, where Q is a fuzzy quantifier, e.g., *most, many, several, few*, etc., and A and B are fuzzy sets, e.g., *tall men, intelligent men*, etc. As was stated earlier, when the fuzzy quantifiers in a proposition are implied rather than explicit, their suppression may be placed in evidence by referring to the proposition as a *disposition*. In this sense, the proposition *overeating causes obesity* is a disposition which results from the suppression of the fuzzy quantifier *most* in the proposition *most of those who overeat are obese*.

To make the concept of a fuzzy quantifier meaningful, it is necessary to define a way of counting the number of elements in a fuzzy set or, equivalently, to determine its cardinality.

There are several ways in which this can be done [60], [9], [52]. For our purposes, it will suffice to employ the concept of a *sigma-count*, which is defined as follows.

Let F be a fuzzy subset of $U = \{u_1, \cdots, u_n\}$ expressed symbolically as

$$F = \mu_1/u_1 + \cdots + \mu_n/u_n = \Sigma_i \mu_i/u_i$$

or, more simply, as

$$F = \mu_1 u_1 + \cdots + \mu_n u_n$$

in which the term μ_i/u_i, $i = 1, \cdots, n$ signifies that μ_i is the grade of membership of u_i in F, and the plus sign represents the union.

The sigma-count of F is defined as the arithmetic sum of the μ_i, i.e.,

$$\Sigma Count(F) \triangleq \Sigma_i \mu_i, \qquad i = 1, \cdots, n$$

with the understanding that the sum may be rounded, if need be, to the nearest integer. Furthermore, one may stipulate that the terms whose grade of membership falls below a specified threshold be excluded from the summation. The purpose of such an exclusion is to avoid a situation in which a large number of terms with low grades of membership become count-equivalent to a small number of terms with high membership.

The *relative sigma-count*, denoted by $\Sigma Count(F/G)$, may be interpreted as the proportion of elements of F which are in G. More explicitly,

$$\Sigma Count(F/G) = \frac{\Sigma Count(F \cap G)}{\Sigma Count(G)}$$

where $F \cap G$, the intersection of F and G, is defined by

$$\mu_{F \cap G}(u) = \mu_F(u) \wedge \mu_G(u), \qquad u \in U.$$

Thus, in terms of the membership functions of F and G, the relative sigma-count of F in G is given by

$$\Sigma Count(F/G) = \frac{\Sigma_i \mu_F(u_i) \wedge \mu_G(u_i)}{\Sigma_i \mu_G(u_i)}.$$

The concept of a relative sigma-count provides a basis for interpreting the meaning of propositions of the form *Q A's are B's*, e.g., *most young men are healthy*. More specifically, if the focal variable (i.e., the constrained variable) in the proposition in question is taken to be the proportion of *B's* in *A's*, then the corresponding translation rule may be expressed as

$$Q\ A\text{'s are } B\text{'s} \rightarrow \Sigma Count(B/A) \text{ is } Q.$$

As an illustration, consider the proposition $p \triangleq$ *over the past few years Naomi earned far more than most of her close friends*. In this case, we shall assume that the constituent relations in the explanatory database are:

$ED \triangleq$ *INCOME [Name; Amount; Year]* +
FRIEND [Name; μ] +
FEW [Number; μ] +
FAR.MORE [Income1; Income2; μ] +
MOST [Proportion; μ].

Note that some of these relations are explicit in p; some are not; and that most of the constituent words in p do not appear in *ED*.

In what follows, we shall describe the process by which the meaning of p may be composed from the meaning of the constituent relations in *ED*. Basically, this process is a test procedure which tests, scores, and aggregates the elastic constraints which are induced by p.

1) Find Naomi's income, IN_i, in $Year_i$, $i = 1, 2, 3, \cdots$, counting backward from present. In symbols,

$$IN_i \triangleq {}_{Amount}INCOME[Name = Naomi;\ Year = Year_i]$$

which signifies that *Name* is bound to Naomi, *Year* to $Year_i$, and the resulting relation is projected on the domain of the attribute *Amount*, yielding the value of *Amount* corresponding to the values assigned to the attributes *Name* and *Year*.

2) Test the constraint induced by *FEW*:

$$\mu_i \triangleq {}_{\mu}FEW\,[Year = Year_i]$$

which signifies that the variable *Year* is bound to $Year_i$ and the corresponding value of μ is read by projecting on the domain of μ.

3) Compute Naomi's total income during the past few years:

$$TIN \triangleq \Sigma_i \mu_i IN_i$$

in which the μ_i play the role of weighting coefficients. Thus, we are tacitly assuming that the total income earned by Naomi during a fuzzily specified interval of time is obtained by weighting Naomi's income in year $Year_i$ by the degree to which $Year_i$ satisfies the constraint induced by *FEW* and summing the weighted incomes.

4) Compute the total income of each $Name_j$ (other than Naomi) during the past few years:

$$TIName_j = \Sigma_i \mu_i IName_{ji}$$

where $IName_{ji}$ is the income of $Name_j$ in $Year_i$.

5) Find the fuzzy set of individuals in relation to whom Naomi earned far more. The grade of membership of $Name_j$ in this set is given by

$$\mu_{FM}(Name_j) = {}_{\mu}FAR.MORE[Income1 = TIN;\ Income2 = TIName_j].$$

6) Find the fuzzy set of close friends of Naomi by intensifying [59] the relation *FRIEND*:

$$CF \triangleq CLOSE.FRIEND \triangleq {}^2FRIEND$$

which implies that

$$\mu_{CF}(Name_j) = ({}_{\mu}FRIEND[Name = Name_j])^2$$

where the expression

$${}_{\mu}FRIEND[Name = Name_j]$$

represents $\mu_F(Name_j)$, that is, the grade of membership of $Name_j$ in the set of Naomi's friends.

7) Count the number of close friends of Naomi. On denoting the count in question by $\Sigma Count(CF)$, we have:

$$\Sigma Count(CF) = \Sigma_j \mu^2_{FRIEND}(Name_j).$$

8) Find the intersection of *FM* with *CF*. The grade of membership of $Name_j$ in the intersection is given by

$$\mu_{FM \cap CF}(Name_j) = \mu_{FM}(Name_j) \wedge \mu_{CF}(Name_j)$$

where the min operator $\wedge$ signifies that the intersection is defined as the conjunction of its operands.

9) Compute the sigma-count of $FM \cap CF$:

$$\Sigma Count(FM \cap CF) = \Sigma_j \mu_{FM}(Name_j) \wedge \mu_{CF}(Name_j).$$

10) Compute the relative sigma-count of *FM* in *CF*, i.e., the proportion of individuals in $FM \cap CF$ who are in *CF*:

$$\rho \triangleq \frac{\Sigma Count(FM \cap CF)}{\Sigma Count(CF)}.$$

11) Test the constraint induced by *MOST*:

$$\tau \triangleq {}_{\mu}MOST[Proportion = \rho]$$

which expresses the overall test score and thus represents the compatibility of *p* with the explanatory database.

In application to the representation of dispositional knowledge, the first step in the representation of the meaning of a disposition involves the process of *explicitation*, that is, making explicit the implicit quantifiers. As a simple example, consider the disposition

$$d \triangleq \textit{young men like young women}$$

which may be interpreted as the proposition

$$p \triangleq \textit{most young men like mostly young women.}$$

The candidate *ED* for *p* is assumed to consist of the following relations:

$$ED \triangleq POPULATION[Name; Sex; Age] + LIKE[Name1; Name\ 2; \mu] + MOST[Proportion; \mu],$$

in which μ in *LIKE* is the degree to which *Name1* likes *Name2*.

To represent the meaning of *p*, it is expedient to replace *p* with the semantically equivalent proposition

$$q \triangleq \textit{most young men are } P$$

where *P* is the fuzzy *dispositional* predicate

$$P \triangleq \textit{likes mostly young women.}$$

In this way, the representation of the meaning of *p* is decomposed into two simpler problems, namely, the representation of the meaning of *P*, and the representation of the meaning of *q* knowing the meaning of *P*.

The meaning of *P* is represented by the following test procedure.

1) Divide *POPULATION* into the population of males, *M.POPULATION*, and population of females, *F.POPULATION*:

$$M.POPULATION \triangleq {}_{Name,Age}POPULATION[Sex = Male]$$

$$F.POPULATION \triangleq {}_{Name,Age}POPULATION[Sex = Female]$$

where ${}_{Name,Age}POPULATION$ denotes the projection of *POPULATION* on the attributes *Name* and *Age*.

2) For each $Name_j$, $j = 1, \cdots, K$, in *F.POPULATION*, find the age of $Name_j$:

$$A_j \triangleq {}_{Age}F.POPULATION[Name = Name_j].$$

3) For each $Name_j$, find the degree to which $Name_j$ is young:

$$\alpha_i \triangleq {}_{\mu}YOUNG[Age = A_j]$$

where α_i may be interpreted as the grade of membership of $Name_j$ in the fuzzy set *YW* of young women.

4) For each $Name_i$, $i = 1, \cdots, k$, in *M.POPULATION*, find the age of $Name_i$:

$$B_i \triangleq {}_{Age}M.POPULATION[Name = Name_i].$$

5) For each $Name_i$, find the degree to which $Name_i$ is young:

$$\delta_i \triangleq {}_{\mu}YOUNG[Age = B_i]$$

where δ_i may be interpreted as the grade of membership of $Name_i$ in the fuzzy set *YM* of young men.

6) For each $Name_j$, find the degree to which $Name_i$ likes $Name_j$:

$$\beta_{ij} \triangleq {}_{\mu}LIKE[Name1 = Name_i; Name2 = Name_j]$$

with the understanding that β_{ij} may be interpreted as the grade of membership of $Name_j$ in the fuzzy set WL_i of women whom $Name_i$ likes.

7) For each $Name_j$ find the degree to which $Name_i$ likes $Name_j$ and $Name_j$ is young:

$$\gamma_{ij} \triangleq \alpha_j \wedge \beta_{ij}.$$

Note: As in previous examples, we employ the aggregation operator min ($\wedge$) to represent the effect of conjunction. In effect, γ_{ij} is the grade of membership of $Name_j$ in the intersection of the fuzzy sets WL_i and *YW*.

8) Compute the relative sigma-count of young women among the women whom $Name_i$ likes:

$$\rho_i \triangleq \Sigma Count(YW/WL_i) = \frac{\Sigma Count(YW \cap WL_i)}{\Sigma Count(WL_i)} = \frac{\Sigma_j \gamma_{ij}}{\Sigma_j \beta_{ij}} = \frac{\Sigma_j \alpha_j \wedge \beta_{ij}}{\Sigma_j \beta_{ij}}.$$

9) Test the constraint induced by *MOST*:

$$\tau_i \triangleq {}_{\mu}MOST[Proportion = \rho_i].$$

This test score, then, represents the degree to which $Name_i$ has the property expressed by the predicate

$$P \triangleq \textit{likes mostly young women.}$$

Continuing the test procedure, we have the following.

10) Compute the relative sigma-count of men who have property P among young men:

$$\rho \triangleq \Sigma Count(P/YM) = \frac{\Sigma Count(P \cap YM)}{\Sigma Count(YM)} = \frac{\Sigma_i \tau_i \wedge \delta_i}{\Sigma_i \delta_i}.$$

11) Test the constraint induced by *MOST*:

$$\tau = {}_{\mu}MOST[Proportion = \rho].$$

This test score represents the overall test score for the disposition *young men like young women*.

IV. The Concept of a Canonical Form and Its Application to the Representation of Meaning

When the meaning of a proposition p is represented as a test procedure, it may be hard to discern in the description of the procedure the underlying structure of the process through which the meaning of p is constructed from the meanings of the constituent relations in the explanatory database.

A concept which makes it easier to perceive the logical structure of p, and thus to develop a better understanding of the meaning representation process, is that of a canonical form of p, abbreviated as $cf(p)$ [60], [65].

The concept of a canonical form relates to the basic idea which underlies test-score semantics, namely, that a proposition may be viewed as a system of elastic constraints whose domain is a collection of relations in the explanatory database. Equivalently, let $X_1, \cdots, X_n$ be a collection of variables which are constrained by p. Then, the canonical form of p may be expressed as

$$cf(p) \triangleq X \text{ is } F \tag{4.1}$$

where $X = (X_1, \cdots, X_n)$ is the constrained variable which is usually implicit in p, and F is a fuzzy relation, likewise implicit in p, which plays the role of an elastic (or fuzzy) constraint on X. The relation between p and its canonical form will be expressed as

$$p \to X \text{ is } F \tag{4.2}$$

signifying that the canonical form may be viewed as a representation of the meaning of p.

In general, the constrained variable X in $cf(p)$ is not uniquely determined by p, and is dependent on the focus of attention in the meaning-representation process. To place this in evidence, we shall refer to X as the *focal* variable.

As a simple illustration, consider the proposition

$$p \triangleq \textit{Anne has blue eyes.} \tag{4.3}$$

In this case, the focal variable may be expressed as

$$X \triangleq Color\,(Eyes\,(Anne))$$

and the elastic constraint is represented by the fuzzy relation *BLUE*. Thus, we can write

$$p \to Color(Eyes(Anne)) \text{ is } BLUE. \tag{4.4}$$

As an additional illustration, consider the proposition

$$p \triangleq \textit{Brian is much taller than Mildred.} \tag{4.5}$$

Here, the focal variable has two components, $X = (X_1, X_2)$, where

$$X_1 = Height(Brian)$$
$$X_2 = Height(Mildred);$$

and the elastic constraint is characterized by the fuzzy relation $MUCH.TALLER\ [Height1;\ Height2;\ \mu]$, in which μ is the degree to which *Height*1 is *much taller* than *Height*2. In this case, we have

$$p \to (Height(Brian),\ Height(Mildred)) \text{ is } MUCH.TALLER. \tag{4.6}$$

In terms of the possibility distribution of X, the canonical form of p may be interpreted as the assignment of F to Π_X. Thus, we may write

$$p \to X \text{ is } F \to \Pi_X = F \tag{4.7}$$

in which the equation

$$\Pi_X = F \tag{4.8}$$

is termed the *possibility assignment equation* [60]. In effect, this equation signifies that the canonical form $cf(p) \triangleq X \text{ is } F$ implies that

$$Poss\,\{X = u\} = \mu_F(u), \qquad u \in U \tag{4.9}$$

where μ_F is the membership function of F. It is in this sense that F, acting as an elastic constraint on X, restricts the possible values which X can take in U. An important implication of this observation is that a proposition p may be interpreted as an implicit assignment statement which characterizes the possibility distribution of the focal variable in p.

As an illustration, consider the disposition

$$d \triangleq \textit{overeating causes obesity} \tag{4.10}$$

which upon explicitation becomes

$$p \triangleq \textit{most of those who overeat are obese.} \tag{4.11}$$

If the focal variable in this case is chosen to be the relative sigma-count of those who are obese among those who overeat, the canonical form of p becomes

$$\Sigma Count(OBESE/OVEREAT) \text{ is } MOST \tag{4.12}$$

which in virtue of (4.9) implies that

$$Poss\{\Sigma Count(OBESE/OVEREAT) = u\} = \mu_{MOST}(u) \tag{4.13}$$

where μ_{MOST} is the membership function of *MOST*. What is important to note is that (4.13) is equivalent to the assertion that the overall test score for p is expressed by

$$\tau = \mu_{MOST}(\Sigma Count(OBESE/OVEREAT)) \quad (4.14)$$

in which *OBESE*, *OVEREAT*, and *MOST* play the roles of the constituent relations in *ED*.

It is of interest to observe that the notion of a semantic network may be viewed as a special case of the concept of a canonical form. As a simple illustration, consider the proposition

$$p \triangleq \textit{Richard gave Cindy a red pin.} \quad (4.15)$$

As a semantic network, this proposition may be represented in the standard form:

$$Agent(GIVE) = Richard$$
$$Recipient(GIVE) = Cindy$$
$$Time(GIVE) = Past$$
$$Object(GIVE) = Pin$$
$$Color(Pin) = Red. \quad (4.16)$$

Now, if we identify X_1 with *Agent*(*GIVE*), X_2 with *Recipient*(*GIVE*), etc., the semantic network representation (4.16) may be regarded as a canonical form in which $X = (X_1, \cdots, X_5)$, and

$$X_1 = Richard$$
$$X_2 = Cindy$$
$$X_3 \text{ is } Past$$
$$X_4 \text{ is } Pin$$
$$X_5 \text{ is } Red. \quad (4.17)$$

More generally, since any semantic network may be expressed as a collection of triples of the form (Object, Attribute, Attribute Value), it can be transformed at once into a canonical form. However, since a canonical form has a much greater expressive power than a semantic network, it may be difficult to transform a canonical form into a semantic network.

V. Inference

The concept of a canonical form provides a convenient framework for representing the rules of inference in fuzzy logic. Since the main concern of this paper is with knowledge representation rather than with inference, our discussion of the rules of inference in fuzzy logic in this section has the format of a summary.

In the so-called categorical rules of inference, the premises are assumed to be in the canonical form *X is A* or the conditional canonical form *X is A if Y is B*, where *A* and *B* are fuzzy predicates (or relations). In the syllogistic rules, the premises are expressed as *Q A's are B's*, where *Q* is a fuzzy quantifier and *A* and *B* are fuzzy predicates (or relations).

The rules in question are the following.

Categorical rules

$X, Y, Z, \cdots \triangleq$ variables taking values in $U, V, W,$

Examples

$X \triangleq Age(Mary)$, $Y \triangleq Distance(P1, P2)$
$A, B, C, \cdots \triangleq$ fuzzy predicates (relations)

Examples

$A \triangleq small$, $B \triangleq much\ larger$

Entailment rule

X is A
$A \subset B \rightarrow \mu_A(u) \leq \mu_B(u), u \in U$

X is B

Example

Mary is very young
very young $\subset$ *young*

Mary is young

Conjunction rule

X is A
X is B

X is $A \cap B \rightarrow \mu_{A \cap B}(u) = \mu_A(u) \wedge \mu_B(u)$
$\cap$ = intersection (conjunction)

Example

pressure is not very high
pressure is not very low

---

pressure is not very high and not very low

Disjunction rule

X is A
or *X is B*

X is $A \cup B \rightarrow \mu_{A \cup B}(u) = \mu_A(u) \vee \mu_B(u)$
$\cup$ = union (disjunction)

Projection rule

(X, Y) is R

X is ${}_XR \rightarrow \mu_{{}_XR}(u) = sup_v \mu_R(u, v)$
${}_XR \triangleq$ projection of R on U

Example

(X, Y) is close to (3, 2)

X is close to 3

Compositional rule

(X, Y) is R → *binary predicate*
Y is B

X is $A \circ R \rightarrow \mu_{A \circ R}(u) = sup_v(\mu_R(u, v) \wedge \mu_B(v))$

Example

X is much larger than Y
Y is large

X is much larger $\circ$ *large*

Negation rule

not (X is A)

$$X \text{ is } \neg A \rightarrow \mu_{\neg A}(u) = 1 - \mu_A(u)$$

$\neg \triangleq$ negation

Example

not (Mary is young)

Mary is not young

Extension principle

$$\frac{X \text{ is } A}{f(X) \text{ is } f(A)}$$

$$A = \mu_1/u_1 + \mu_2/u_2 + \cdots + \mu_n/u_n$$

$$f(A) = \mu_1/f(u_1) + \mu_2/f(u_2) + \cdots + \mu_n/f(u_n)$$

Example

X is small

X^2 *is* ^{2}*small*

$$^2small \triangleq very\ small,\ \mu_{very\ small} = (\mu_{small})^2$$

It should be noted that the use of the canonical form in these rules stands in sharp contrast to the way in which the rules of inference are expressed in classical logic. The advantage of the canonical form is that it places in evidence that inference in fuzzy logic may be interpreted as a propagation of elastic constraints. This point of view is particularly useful in the applications of fuzzy logic to control and decision analysis (*Proc. of the 2nd IFSA Congress, 1987; Proc. of the International Workshop*, Iizuka, 1988).

As was pointed out already, it is the qualitative mode of reasoning that plays a key role in the applications of fuzzy logic to control. In such applications, the input–output relations are expressed as collections of fuzzy if-then rules [32].

For example, if X and Y are input variables and Z is the output variable, the relation between X, Y, and Z may be expressed as

Z *is* C_1 if X *is* A_1 and Y *is* B_1

Z *is* C_2 if X *is* A_2 and Y *is* B_2

Z *is* C_n if X *is* A_n and Y *is* B_n

where C_i, A_i, and B_i, $i = 1, \cdots, n$ are fuzzy subsets of their respective universes of discourse. For example,

Z is small if X is large and Y is medium
Z is not large if X is very small and Y is not large

Given a characterization of the dependence of Z on X and Y in this form, one can employ the compositional rule of inference to compute the value of Z given the values of X and Y. This is what underlies the Togai–Watanbe fuzzy logic chip [50] and the operation of fuzzy logic controllers in industrial process control [48].

In general, the applications of fuzzy logic in systems and process control fall into two categories. First, there are those applications in which, in comparison to traditional methods, fuzzy logic control offers the advantage of greater simplicity, greater robustness, and lower cost. The cement kiln control pioneered by the F. L. Smidth Company falls into this category.

Second, are the applications in which the traditional methods provide no solution. The self-parking fuzzy car conceived by Sugeno [48] is a prime example of what humans can do so easily and is so difficult to emulate by the traditional approaches to systems control.

Syllogistic Rules: In its generic form, a fuzzy syllogism may be expressed as the inference schema

Q_1A*'s are* B*'s*

Q_2C*'s are* D*'s*

Q_3E*'s are* F*'s*

in which A, B, C, D, E, and F are interrelated fuzzy predicates and Q_1, Q_2, and Q_3 are fuzzy quantifiers.

The interrelations between A, B, C, D, E, and F provide a basis for a classification of fuzzy syllogisms. The more important of these syllogisms are the following.

a) *Intersection/Product Syllogism:*

$$C = A \wedge B,\ E = A,\ F = C \wedge D.$$

b) *Chaining Syllogism:*

$$C = B,\ E = A,\ F = D.$$

c) *Consequent Conjunction Syllogism:*

$$A = C = E,\ F = B \wedge D.$$

d) *Consequent Disjunction Syllogism:*

$$A = C = E,\ F = B \vee D.$$

e) *Antecedent Conjunction Syllogism:*

$$B = D = F,\ E = A \wedge C.$$

f) *Antecedent Disjunction Syllogism:*

$$B = D = F,\ E = A \vee C.$$

In the context of expert systems, these and related syllogisms provide a set of inference rules for combining evidence through conjunction, disjunction, and chaining [62].

One of the basic problems in fuzzy syllogistic reasoning is the following: given A, B, C, D, E, and F, find the maximally specific (i.e., most restrictive) fuzzy quantifier Q_3 such that the proposition Q_3E*'s are* F*'s* is entailed by the premises. In the case of a), b), and c), this leads to the following syllogisms.

Intersection/Product Syllogism:

Q_1*A's are B's*

Q_2(*A* and *B*)*'s are C's*

$(Q_1 \otimes Q_2)$*A's are* (*B* and *C*)*'s* (5.1)

where $\otimes$ denotes the product in fuzzy arithmetic [24]. It should be noted that (5.1) may be viewed as an analog of the basic probabilistic identity

$$p(B, C/A) = p(B/A)\,p(C/A, B).$$

A concrete example of the intersection/product syllogism is the following:

most students are young

most young students are single

---

most^2 *students are young* and *single* (5.2)

where *most*^{2} denotes the product of the fuzzy quantifier *most* with itself.

Chaining Syllogism:

Q_1*A's are B's*

Q_2*B's are C's*

$(Q_1 \otimes Q_2)$*A's are C's*

This syllogism may be viewed as a special case of the intersection product syllogism. It results when $B \subset A$ and Q_1 and Q_2 are monotone increasing, that is, $\geq Q_1 = Q_1$, and $\geq Q_2 = Q_2$, where $\geq Q_1$ should be read as *at least* Q_1. A simple example of the chaining syllogism is the following:

most students are undergraduates

most undergraduates are single

---

most^2 *students are single*

Note that *undergraduates* $\subset$ *students* and that in the conclusion F = *single*, rather than *young and single*, as in (5.2).

Consequent Conjunction Syllogism: The consequent conjunction syllogism is an example of a basic syllogism which is not a derivative of the intersection/product syllogism. Its statement may be expressed as follows:

Q_1*A's are B's*

Q_2*A's are C's*

Q *A's are* (*B* and *C*)*'s* (5.3)

where Q is a fuzzy quantifier which is defined by the inequalities

$$0 \circledvee (Q_1 \otimes Q_2 \ominus 1) \leq Q \leq Q_1 \circledwedge Q_2 \qquad (5.4)$$

in which $\circledvee$, $\circledwedge$, $\oplus$, and $\ominus$ are the operations of $\vee$ (max), $\wedge$ (min), +, and − in fuzzy arithmetic.

An illustration of (5.3) is provided by the example

most students are young

most students are single

Q *students are single* and *young*

where

$$2most \circledvee 1 \leq Q \leq most.$$

This expression for Q follows from (5.4) by noting that

$$most \circledvee most = most$$

and

$$0 \circledvee (2most \ominus 1) = 2most \ominus 1.$$

The three basic syllogisms stated above are merely examples of a collection of fuzzy syllogisms which may be developed and employed for purposes of inference from common sense knowledge. In addition to its application to common sense reasoning, fuzzy syllogistic reasoning may serve to provide a basis for combining uncertain evidence in expert systems [62].

VI. Concluding Remarks

One of the basic aims of fuzzy logic is to provide a computational framework for knowledge representation and inference in an environment of uncertainty and imprecision. In such environments, fuzzy logic is effective when the solutions need not be precise and/or it is acceptable for a conclusion to have a dispositional rather than categorical validity. The importance of fuzzy logic derives from the fact that there are many real world applications which fit these conditions, especially in the realm of knowledge-based systems for decision-making and control.

References

[1] J. F. Baldwin, "FRIL—A fuzzy relational inference language," *Fuzzy Sets Syst.*, vol. 14, pp. 155-174, 1984.

[2] J. F. Baldwin, T. P. Martin, and B. W. Pilsworth, "Implementation of FPROG—A fuzzy Prolog interpreter," *Fuzzy Sets and Syst.*, vol. 23, pp. 119-129, 1987.

[3] J. C. Bezdek, Ed., *Analysis of Fuzzy Information—Vol. 1, 2, and 3: Applications in Engineering and Science.* Boca Raton, FL: CRC, 1987.

[4] R. J. Brachman and H. J. Levesque, *Readings in Knowledge Representation.* Los Altos, CA: Morgan Kaufmann, 1985.

[5] R. J. Brachman, "The basics of knowledge representation and reasoning," *AT&T Tech. J.*, vol. 67, pp. 25-40, 1988.

[6] J. de Kleer and J. Brown, "A qualitative physics based on confluences," *Artificial Intell.*, vol. 24, pp. 7-84, 1984.

[7] J. Doyle, "A truth-maintenance system," *Artificial Intell.*, vol. 12,

pp. 231-272, 1979.
[8] D. Dubois and H. Prade, *Fuzzy Sets and Systems: Theory and Applications.* New York: Academic, 1980.
[9] —, "Fuzzy cardinality and the modeling of imprecise quantification," *Fuzzy Sets Syst.*, vol. 16, pp. 199-230, 1985.
[10] —, *Possibility Theory—An Approach to Computerized Processing of Uncertainty.* New York: Plenum, 1988.
[11] —, "On fuzzy syllogisms," *Comput. Intell.*, vol. 14, pp. 171-179, 1988.
[12] —, "The treatment of uncertainty in knowledge-based systems using fuzzy sets and possibility theory," *Int. J. Intell. Syst.*, vol. 3, pp. 141-165, 1988.
[13] H. Farreny and H. Prade, "Dealing with the vagueness of natural languages in man-machine communication," in *Applications of Fuzzy Set Theory in Human Factors*, W. Karvowski and A. Mital, Eds. New York: Elsevier, 1986, pp. 71-85.
[14] K. Forbus, "Qualitative physics: Past, present, and future," in *Exploring Artificial Intelligence*, H. Shrobe, Ed. Los Altos, CA: Morgan Kaufman, 1989.
[15] Fujitec, "Artificial intelligence type elevator group control system," *JETRO*, vol. 26, 1988.
[16] J. A. Goguen, "The logic of inexact concepts," *Synthese*, vol. 19, pp. 325-373, 1969.
[17] I. R. Goodman and H. T. Nguyen, *Uncertainty Models for Knowledge-Based Systems.* Amsterdam, The Netherlands: North-Holland, 1985.
[18] M. M. Gupta and T. Yamakawa, Eds., *Fuzzy Logic in Knowledge-Based Systems.* Amsterdam, The Netherlands: North-Holland, 1988.
[19] C. Isik, "Inference engines for fuzzy rule-based control," *Int. J. Approximate Reasoning*, vol. 2, pp. 122-187, 1988.
[20] P. N. Johnson-Laird, "Procedural semantics," *Cognition*, vol. 5, pp. 189-214, 1987.
[21] J. Kacprzyk and R. R. Yager, *Management Decision Support Systems Using Fuzzy Sets and Possibility Theory*, (Interdisciplinary Systems Research Series, Vol. 83). New York: Springer-Verlag, 1985.
[22] J. Kacprzyk and S. A. Orlovski, Eds., *Optimization Models Using Fuzzy Sets and Possibility Theory.* Dordrecht, The Netherlands: Reidel, 1987.
[23] Y. Kasai and Y. Morimoto, "Electronically controlled continuously variable transmission," in *Proc. Int. Congress on Transportation Electron.*, Dearborn, MI, 1988.
[24] A. Kaufmann and M. M. Gupta, *Introduction to Fuzzy Arithmetic.* New York: Van Nostrand, 1985.
[25] —, *Fuzzy Mathematical Models with Applications to Engineering and Management Science.* Amsterdam, The Netherlands: North-Holland, 1988.
[26] M. Kinoshita and T. Fukuzaki, T. Satoh, and M. Miyake, "An automatic operation method for control rods in BWR plants," in *Proc. Specialists' Meet. In-core Instrument. Reactor Core Assessment*, Cadarache, France, 1988.
[27] J. B. Kiszka, M. M. Gupta, and P. N. Nikiforuk, "Energetistic stability of fuzzy dynamic systems," *IEEE Trans. Syst., Man, Cybern.*, vol. SMC-15, 1985.
[28] G. J. Klir and T. A. Folger, *Fuzzy Sets, Uncertainty and Information.* Englewood Cliffs, NJ: Prentice-Hall, 1988.
[29] P. Kuipers, "Qualitative simulation," *Artificial Intell.*, vol. 29, pp. 289-338, 1986.
[30] H. J. Levesque, "Knowledge representation and reasoning," *Annual Reviews of Computer Science 1*, Annual Review, Inc., Palo Alto, CA, pp. 255-287.
[31] H. J. Levesque and R. Brachman, "Expressiveness and tractability in knowledge representation and reasoning," *Comput. Intell.*, vol. 3, pp. 78-93, 1987.
[32] E. H. Mamdani and B. R. Gaines, Eds., *Fuzzy Reasoning and Its Applications.* New York: Academic, 1981.
[33] J. McCarthy, "Circumscription: Non-monotonic inference rule," *Artificial Intell.*, vol. 13, pp. 27-40, 1980.
[34] D. V. McDermott, "Non-monotonic logic, I," *Artificial Intell.*, vol. 13, pp. 41-72, 1980.
[35] —, "Non-monotonic logic, II: Non-monotonic modal theories," *J. Ass. Comput. Mach.*, vol. 29, pp. 33-57, 1982.
[36] R. C. Moore, "The role of logic in knowledge representation and commonsense reasoning," in *Proc. Nat. Conf. Artificial Intell.*, 1982, pp. 428-433.
[37] R. C. Moore and J. C. Hobbs, Eds., *Formal Theories of the Commonsense World.* Harwood, NJ: Ablex, 1984.
[38] M. Mukaidono, Z. Shen, and L. Ding, "Fuzzy prolog," in *Proc. 2nd IFSA Congress*, Tokyo, Japan, 1987, pp. 452-455.
[39] C. V. Negoita, *Expert Systems and Fuzzy Systems.* Menlo Park, CA: Benjamin/Cummings, 1985.
[40] N. Nilsson, "Probabilistic logic," *Artificial Intell.*, vol. 20, pp. 71-87, 1986.
[41] P. Peterson, "On the logic of few, many, and most," *Notre Dame J. Formal Logic*, vol. 20, pp. 155-179, 1979.
[42] G. S. Pospelov, "Fuzzy set theory in the USSR," *Fuzzy Sets Syst.*, vol. 22, pp. 1-24, 1987.
[43] *Proc. 2nd Congress Int. Fuzzy Syst. Assoc.*, Tokyo, Japan, 1987.
[44] *Proc. Int. Workshop Fuzzy Syst. Appl.*, Kyushu Inst. Technol., Iizuka, Japan, 1988.
[45] R. Reiter and G. Criscuolo, "Some representational issues in default reasoning," *Comput. Math.*, vol. 9, pp. 15-28, 1983.
[46] J. C. Shapiro, Ed., *Encyclopedia of Artificial Intelligence.* New York: Wiley, 1987.
[47] S. L. Small, G. W. Cottrell, and M. K. Tanenhaus, Eds., *Lexical Ambiguity Resolution.* Los Altos, CA: Morgan Kaufman, 1988.
[48] M. Sugeno, Ed., *Industrial Applications of Fuzzy Control.* Amsterdam, The Netherlands: North-Holland, 1985.
[49] C. J. Talbot, "Scheduling TV advertising: An expert systems approach to utilizing fuzzy knowledge," in *Proc. 4th Australian Conf. Appl. Expert Syst.*, Sydney, Australia, 1988.
[50] M. Togai and H. Watanabe, "Expert systems on a chip: An engine for real-time approximate reasoning," *IEEE Expert*, vol. 1, pp. 55-62, 1986.
[51] R. Wilensky, "Some problems and proposals for knowledge representation," Comput. Sci. Division, Univ. California, Berkeley, Tech. Rep. 87/351, 1987.
[52] R. R. Yager, "Quantified propositions in a linguistic logic," in *Proc. 2nd Int. Seminar Fuzzy Set Theory*, E. P. Klement, Ed., Johannes Kepler Univ., Linz, Austria, 1980.
[53] —, "Reasoning with fuzzy quantified statements—I," *Kybernetes*, vol. 14, pp. 233-240, 1985.
[54] S. Yasunobu and G. Hasegawa, "Evaluation of an automatic container crane operation system based on predictive fuzzy control," *Contr. Theory Advanced Technol.*, vol. 2, no. 3, 1986.
[55] S. Yasunobu and S. Myamoto, "Automatic train operation by predictive fuzzy control," in *Industrial Applications of Fuzzy Control*, M. Sugeno, Ed. Amsterdam, The Netherlands: North-Holland, 1985.
[56] L. A. Zadeh, "Probability measures of fuzzy events," *J. Math. Anal. Appl.*, vol. 23, pp. 421-427, 1968.
[57] —, "Outline of a new approach to the analysis of complex systems and decision processes," *IEEE Trans. Syst., Man, Cybern.*, vol. SMC-3, pp. 28-44, 1973.
[58] —, "The concept of a linguistic variable and its application to approximate reasoning, Part I," *Inf. Sci.*, vol. 8, pp. 199-249; Part II, *Inf. Sci.*, vol. 8, pp. 301-357; Part III, *Inf. Sci.*, vol. 9, pp. 43-80, 1975.
[59] —, "Fuzzy sets as a basis for a theory of possibility," *Fuzzy Sets Syst.*, vol. 1, pp. 3-28, 1978.
[60] —, "PRUF—A meaning representation language for natural languages," *Int. J. Man—Mach. Studies*, vol. 10, pp. 395-460, 1978.
[61] —, "A fuzzy-set-theoretic approach to fuzzy quantifiers in natural languages," *Comput. Math.*, vol. 9, pp. 149-184, 1983.
[62] —, "The role of fuzzy logic in the management of uncertainty in expert systems," *Fuzzy Sets Syst.*, vol. 11, pp. 199-227, 1983.
[63] —, "A theory of commonsense knowledge," in *Aspects of Vagueness*, H. J. Skala, S. Termini, and E. Trillas, Eds. Dordrecht, The Netherlands: Reidel, 1984.
[64] —, "Syllogistic reasoning in fuzzy logic and its application to reasoning with dispositions," *IEEE Trans. Syst., Man, Cybern.*, vol. SMC-15, pp. 754-763, 1985.
[65] —, "Test-score semantics as a basis for a computational approach to the representation of meaning," *Literary Ling. Comput.*, vol. 1, pp. 24-35, 1986.
[66] —, "A computational theory of dispositions," *Int. J. Intell. Syst.*, vol. 2, pp. 39-63, 1987.
[67] —, "Fuzzy logic," *Computer*, vol. 1, pp. 83-93, 1988.
[68] —, "Dispositional logic," *Appl. Math. Lett.*, pp. 95-99, 1988.
[69] —, "QSA/FL—Qualitative systems analysis based on fuzzy logic," in *Proc. AAAI Symp.*, Stanford Univ., Stanford, CA, 1989.
[70] M. Zemankova-Leech and A. Kandel, *Fuzzy Relational Data Bases—A Key to Expert Systems.* Cologne: Verlag TUV Rheinland, 1984.

Fuzzy Logic, Neural Networks, and **Soft Computing**

LOTFI A. ZADEH

In retrospect, the year 1990 may well be viewed as the beginning of a new trend in the design of household appliances, consumer electronics, cameras, and other types of widely used consumer products. The trend in question relates to a marked increase in what might be called the Machine Intelligence Quotient (MIQ) of such products compared to what it was before 1990. Today, we have microwave ovens and washing machines that can figure out on their own what settings to use to perform their tasks optimally; cameras that come close to professional photographers in picture-taking ability; and many other products that manifest an impressive capability to reason, make intelligent decisions, and learn from experience.

There are many factors that underlie the marked increase in MIQ. It is the author's opinion that the most important factor is the use of what might be referred to as *soft computing*—and, in particular, fuzzy logic—to mimic the ability of the human mind to effectively employ modes of reasoning that are approximate rather than exact.

In traditional—hard—computing, the prime desiderata are precision, certainty, and rigor. By contrast, the point of departure in soft computing is the thesis that precision and certainty carry a cost and that computation, reasoning, and decision making should exploit—wherever possible—the tolerance for imprecision and uncertainty.

A case in point is the problem of parking an automobile. Most people are able to park an automobile quite easily because the final position of the vehicle and its orientation are not specified precisely. If they were, the difficulty of parking would grow geometrically with the increase in precision and eventually would become unmanageable for humans. What is important to observe is that the problem of parking is easy for humans when it is formulated imprecisely and difficult to solve by traditional methods because such methods do not exploit the tolerance for imprecision.

The exploitation of the tolerance for imprecision and uncertainty underlies the remarkable human ability to understand distorted speech, decipher sloppy handwriting, comprehend nuances of natural language, summarize text, recognize and classify images, drive a vehicle in dense traffic and, more generally, make rational decisions in an environment of uncertainty and imprecision. In effect, in raising the banner of "Exploit the tolerance for imprecision and uncertainty," soft computing uses the human mind as a role model and, at the same time, aims at a formalization of the cognitive processes humans employ so effectively in the performance of daily tasks.

As was observed earlier, the year 1990 may be viewed as a turning point in the evolution of the MIQ of consumer products. The basis for this observation are the following facts.

The industrial applications of fuzzy logic starting in the early 1980s—of which the prime examples are the F.L. Smidth cement kiln and the Sendai subway system designed by Hitachi—laid the groundwork for the use of fuzzy logic in the design and production of high-MIQ consumer products. The first such product—a fuzzy-logic-controlled shower head—was announced by Matsushita in 1987. This was followed by the first fuzzy-logic-based washing machine—also designed by Matsushita—in 1989.

In 1990, high-MIQ consumer products employing fuzzy logic began to grow in number and visibil-

Reprinted, with permission, from *Communications of the ACM*, 37(3), pp. 77–84.

ity. Somewhat later, neural network techniques combined with fuzzy logic began to be employed in a wide variety of consumer products, endowing such products with the capability to adapt and learn from experience. Such neurofuzzy products are likely to become ubiquitous in the years ahead. The same is likely to happen in the realms of robotics, industrial systems, and process control.

It is from this perspective that the year 1990 may be viewed as a turning point in the evolution of high-MIQ products and systems. Underlying this evolution was an acceleration in the employment of soft computing—and especially fuzzy logic—in the conception and design of intelligent systems that can exploit the tolerance for imprecision and uncertainty, learn from experience, and adapt to changes in the operating conditions.

At this juncture, the principal constituents of soft computing are fuzzy logic (FL), neural network theory (NN), and probabilistic reasoning (PR), with the latter subsuming belief networks, genetic algorithms, parts of learning theory, and chaotic systems. In the triumvirate of FL, NN, and PR, FL is primarily concerned with imprecision, NN with learning, and PR with uncertainty. What is important to note is that although there are substantial areas of overlap between FL, NN, and PR, in general FL, NN, and PR are complementary rather than competitive. For this reason, it is frequently advantageous to employ FL, NN, and PR in combination rather than exclusively. A case in point is the growing number of so-called neurofuzzy (NF) consumer products employing a combination of fuzzy logic and neural network techniques. Most NF products are fuzzy rule-based systems in which NN techniques are used for purposes of learning and/or adaptation.

The Meaning of Fuzzy Logic

When discussing fuzzy logic, there is a semantic issue which requires clarification. The term *fuzzy logic* is currently used in two different senses. In a narrow sense, fuzzy logic is a logical system that aims at a formalization of approximate reasoning. As such, it is rooted in multivalued logic, but its agenda is quite different from that of traditional multivalued logical systems, e.g., Lukasiewicz's logic. In this connection, what should be noted is that many of the concepts which account for the effectiveness of fuzzy logic as a logic of approximate reasoning are not a part of traditional multivalued logical systems. Among these are the concept of a linguistic variable, canonical form, fuzzy if-then rule, fuzzy quantifiers, and such modes of reasoning as interpolative reasoning, syllogistic reasoning, and dispositional reasoning.

In a broad sense, fuzzy logic is almost synonymous with fuzzy set theory. Fuzzy set theory, as its name suggests, is basically a theory of classes with unsharp boundaries. Fuzzy set theory is much broader than fuzzy logic in its narrow sense and contains the latter as one of its branches. Among the other branches of fuzzy set theory are, for example, fuzzy arithmetic, fuzzy mathematical programming, fuzzy topology, fuzzy graph theory, and fuzzy data analysis. What is important to recognize is that any crisp theory can be fuzzified by generalizing the concept of a set within that theory to the concept of a fuzzy set. Indeed, it is very likely that eventually most theories will be fuzzified in this way. The impetus for the transition from a crisp theory to a fuzzy one derives from the fact that both the generality of a theory and its applicability to real-world problems are substantially enhanced by replacing the concept of a set with that of a fuzzy set.

Today, the growing tendency is to use the term *fuzzy logic* in its broad sense. In part this reflects the fact that fuzzy set theory sounds less euphonious than fuzzy logic.

Linguistic Variables, Data Compression, and Granulation

A concept that plays a central role in the applications of fuzzy logic is that of a linguistic variable [29, 31]. The concept of a linguistic variable has become sufficiently well understood to make it unnecessary to dwell upon it here. There is, however, one basic aspect of the concept of a linguistic variable which is worthy of note since it is at the heart of its utility.

Specifically, consider a linguistic variable such as *Age* whose linguistic values are *young*, *middle-aged*, and *old*, with *young* defined by a membership function such as shown in Figure 1.

Clearly, a numerical value such as 25 is simpler than the function *young*. But *young* represents a choice of one out of three possible values whereas 25 is a choice of one out of, say, 100 values. The point of this simple example is that the use of linguistic values may be viewed as a form of data compression. It is suggestive to refer to this form of data compression as *granulation*.

The same effect can be achieved, of course, by conventional quantization. But in the case of quantization, the values are intervals whereas in the case of granulation the values are overlapping fuzzy sets. The advantages of granulation over quantization are a) it is more general; b) it mimics the way in which humans interpret linguistic values (i.e., as fuzzy sets rather than intervals); and c) the transition from one linguistic value to a contiguous linguistic value is gradual rather than abrupt, resulting in continuity and robustness.

Calculi of Fuzzy Rules and Fuzzy Graphs

The concept of a linguistic variable serves as a point of departure for other concepts in fuzzy logic whose use results in data compression. Among these are the concepts of a fuzzy if-then rule—or simply fuzzy rule—and fuzzy graph. There is a close relation between these concepts, and both may be interpreted as granular representations of functional dependencies and relations. Viewed from this perspective, fuzzy rules and fuzzy graphs bear the same relation to numerically-valued dependencies that linguistic variables bear to numerically-valued variables.

Like the concept of a linguistic variable, the concept of a fuzzy rule is sufficiently well understood to make it unnecessary to dwell upon it here. In what follows, we shall confine our attention to the less well-developed concept of a fuzzy graph.

The concept of a fuzzy graph was initially introduced in 1971 [32] and, in a more explicit form, in 1974 [28, 30]. In an implicit form, the concept of a fuzzy graph underlies the seminal work of Mamdani and Assilian

[14] on fuzzy control. In what follows, we shall assume for notational simplicity that mappings are from R to R.

As shown in Figure 2, a fuzzy graph f^*, of a functional dependence $f: X \rightarrow Y$, where X and Y are linguistic variables in U and V, respectively, serves to provide an approximate, compressed representation of f in the form

$$f^* = A_1 \times B_1 + A_2 \times B_2 + \ldots + A_n \times B_n$$

or more compactly,

$$f^* = \sum_{i=1}^{n} A_i \times B_i$$

where the A_i and B_i, $i = 1, \ldots, n$, are contiguous fuzzy subsets of U and V, respectively; $A_i \times B_i$ is the cartesian product of A_i and B_i; and + is the operation of disjunction, which is usually taken to be the union. Expressed more explicitly in terms of membership functions of f^*, A_i and B_i, we have

$$\mu_{f^*}(u, v) = V_i(\mu_{A_i}(u) \wedge \mu_{B_i}(v)),$$

where $\wedge = min$, $\vee = max$, $u \in U$, and $v \in V$. In a more general setting, in place of $\wedge$ and $\vee$ we may employ t-norms and s-norms [35].

Alternatively, a fuzzy graph may be represented as a fuzzy relation f^*

f^*	A	B
	A_1	B_1
	A_2	B_2
	.	.
	.	.
	.	.
	A_n	B_n

or a collection of fuzzy if-then rules

f^* if X is A_1 then Y is B_1
if X is A_2 then Y is B_2
...
if X is A_n then Y is B_n

with the understanding that the fuzzy if-then rule

if X is A_i then Y is B_i, $i = 1, \ldots, n$

is interpreted as the joint constraint on X and Y defined by

$$(X, Y) \text{ is } A_i \times B_i.$$

For example, with this understanding the fuzzy rule set

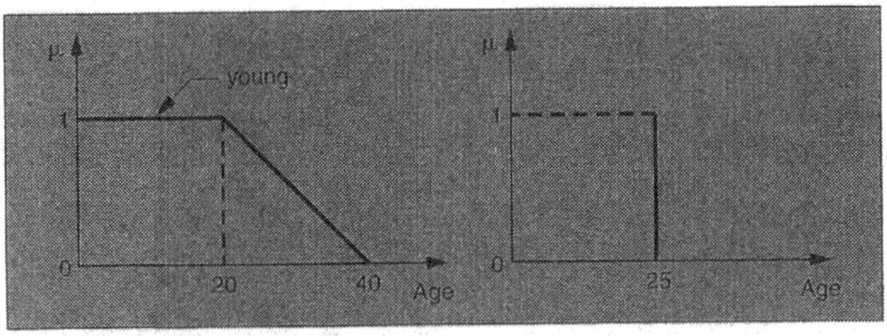

Figure 1. Linguistic and numerical values of *young*

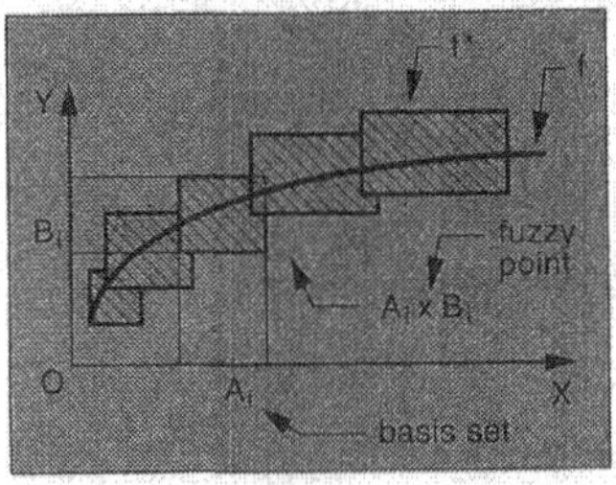

Figure 2. Representation of a function and its fuzzy graph

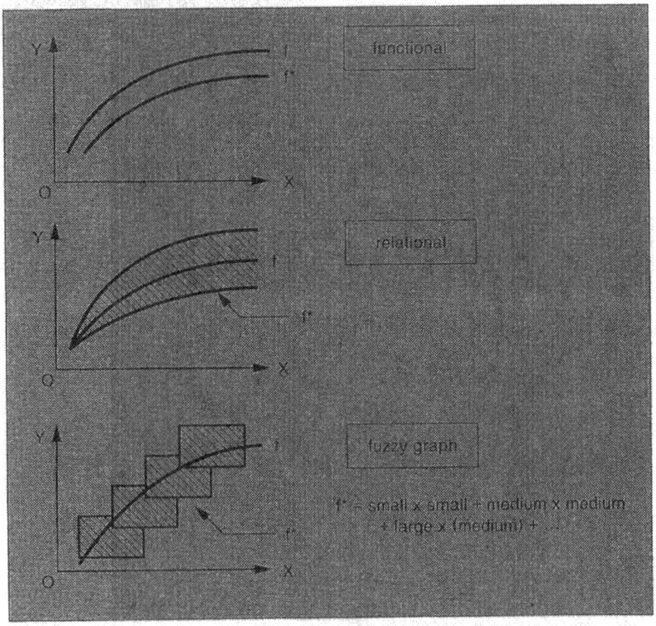

Figure 3. Types of approximation: functional, relational, and fuzzy graph

f^* if X is *small* then Y is *large*
if X is *medium* then Y is *medium*
...
if X is *large* then Y is *small*

may be represented equivalently as the fuzzy graph

$$f^* = small \times large + medium \times medium + \ldots + large \times small.$$

In effect, a fuzzy graph approximation to a given function combines a relational approximation with data compression (see Figure 3).

Central to the applications of the concept of a fuzzy graph is the fact that any type of function or relation can be represented by a fuzzy graph (see Figure 4).

Furthermore, fuzzy graph representations may be employed to approximate to probability distributions and membership functions (see Figure 5). Such representations play a particularly important role in qualitative decision analysis and fault diagnosis.

Operations on Fuzzy Graphs

A key issue in the calculus of fuzzy graphs relates to the development of computational methods for performing various basic operations on fuzzy graphs. The operations in question are generalizations of the corresponding operations on crisp (nonfuzzy) functions and relations. Some of the basic operations of this type are shown in Figure 6.

In dealing with this issue, it turns out that the necessary computations can be greatly simplified if an operation, $*$, is monotonically nondecreasing, i.e., if a, b, a', and b' are real numbers, then

$$a' \geq a,\ b' \geq b \rightarrow a' * b' \geq a * b$$
$$a' \leq a,\ b' \leq b \rightarrow a' * b' \leq a * b.$$

For such operations, it can readily be shown that $*$ distributes over $\vee$ (max) and $\wedge$ (min). Thus

$$a * (b \vee c) = a * b \vee a * c$$
$$a * (b \wedge c) = a * b \wedge a * c.$$

This implies that if

$$f^* = \sum_i A_i \times B_i$$

is a fuzzy graph and C is a fuzzy set then

$$C * \Big(\sum_i A_i \times B_i\Big) = \sum_i C * (A_i \times B_i).$$

As an illustration, consider the problem of finding the intersection of fuzzy graphs f^* and g^* (Figure 7), where

$$f^* = \sum_i A_i \times B_i$$

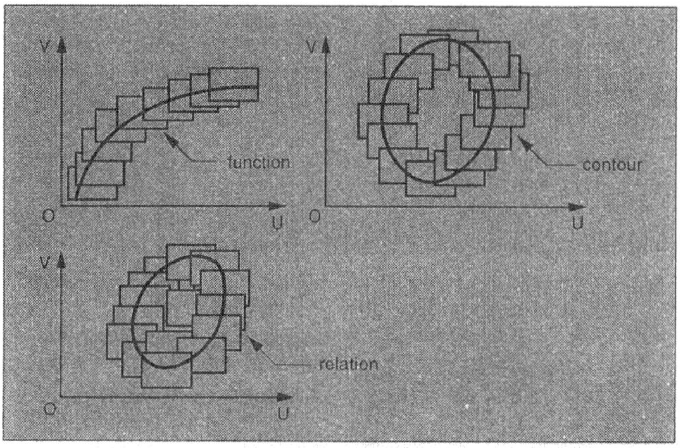

Figure 4. Fuzzy graph approximations to functions, contours, and relations

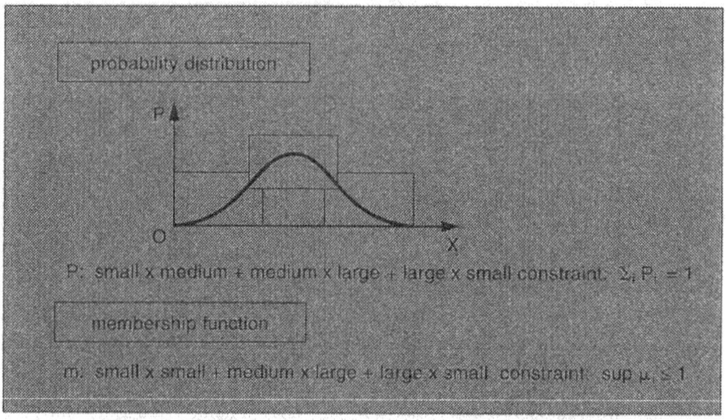

Figure 5. Fuzzy graph approximate representations of probability distributions and membership functions

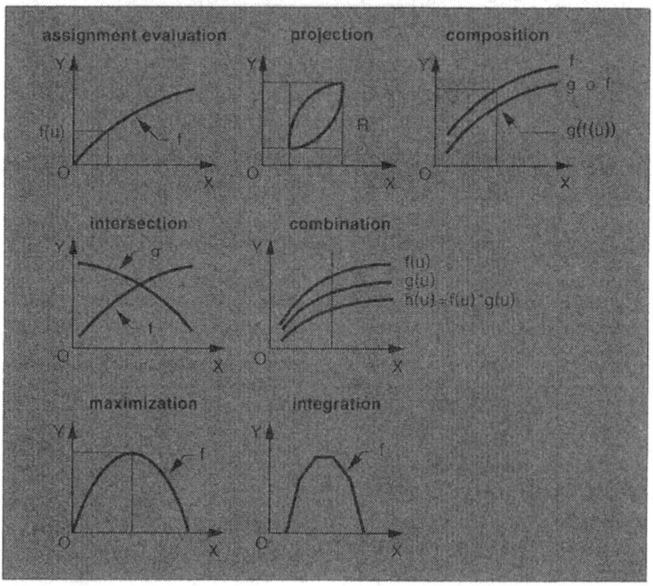

Figure 6. Basic operators on functions and relations

and

$$g^* = \sum_j C_j \times D_j.$$

In this case, we have

$$f^* \cap g^* = \sum_{i,j} (A_i \times B_i) \cap (C_j \times D_j)$$

which in the view of the distributivity of $\cap$ reduces to

$$f^* \cap g^* = \sum_{i,j} (A_i \cap C_j) \times (B_i \cap D_j).$$

This result has an immediate application to the interpolation of fuzzy if-then rules, a problem which plays a key role in fuzzy control.

More specifically, the problem of interpolation may be expressed as an inference query

$$\begin{array}{l} (X, Y) \text{ is } \Sigma_i A_i \times B_i \\ \underline{X \text{ is } A \qquad\qquad} \\ Y \text{ is } ?B \end{array}$$

On representing the major premise in the query as a fuzzy graph $f^* = \Sigma_i A_i \times B_i$ and the minor premise as a cylindrical extension, $\overline{A}$, of the fuzzy set A (see Figure 8), the computation of ?B reduces to that of finding the intersection of f^* and $\overline{A}$ and projecting the resulting fuzzy set on V, the domain of Y.

Thus,

$$B = projV(\overline{A} \cap (\sum_i A_i \times B_i)$$

which reduces to

$$B = projV(\sum_i (A \cap A_i) \times B_i)$$

or, more compactly,

$$B = \sum_i m_i \wedge B_i$$

where

$$m_i = sup(A \cap A_i)$$

represents the degree of match between A and A_i (see Figure 9).

It should be noted that in a different guise this technique of interpolation was employed in the seminal paper of Mamdani and Assilian [14] and is currently used in most rule-based control systems.

As a further example, consider the problem of combining f^* and g^* through the minimum operator. Thus, if

$$f^* = \sum_i A_i \times B_i$$

and

$$g^* = \sum_i A_i \times C_i$$

and *min* is the minimum operator, then

$$f^* \text{ min } g^* = \sum_i A_i \times (B_i \text{ min } C_i)$$

where $B_i$minC_i is the minimum of B_i and C_i computed through the extension principle [29]. This result makes it possible to compute the intersection, $F \cap G$, of fuzzy sets F and G whose membership functions μ_F and μ_G are represented qualitatively in the form of fuzzy if-then rules (see Figure 10),

F: if X is A_i then μ_F is B_i $\quad i = 1, \ldots, n$

G: if X is A_i then μ_G is C_i $\quad i = 1, \ldots, n.$

An important practical application of the fuzzy graph representation of the intersection $F \cap G$ relates to the case where F and G represent two conflicting goals and $F \cap G$ a maximizing decision [1].

The concept of a fuzzy graph has an important connection with the representation of fuzzy relations. Thus, if R is a fuzzy relation with attributes which take linguistic values (see Figure 11) then R may be represented as a fuzzy graph

$$R = R_{11} \times R_{12} \times R_{13} + R_{21} \times R_{22} \times R_{23} + R_{31} \times R_{32} \times R_{33}.$$

The representation of a fuzzy relation as a fuzzy graph may be applied to the representation of diagnostic tableaus (see Figure 12) in which the entries are linguistic values of tests and corresponding faults.

Thus, if the result of tests T_1, T_2, and T_3 are L, L, and M, respectively, then the degrees to which the faults F_1 and F_2 are present are L and Z,

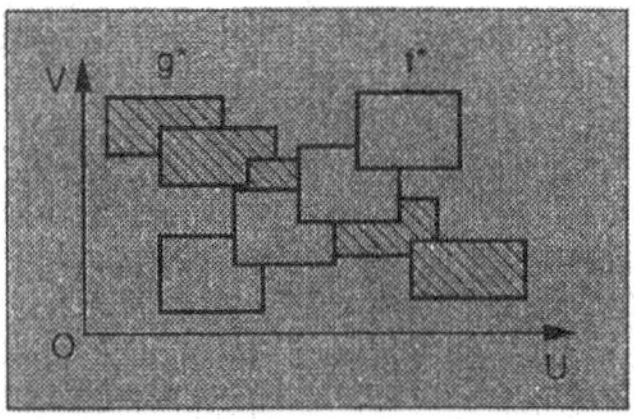

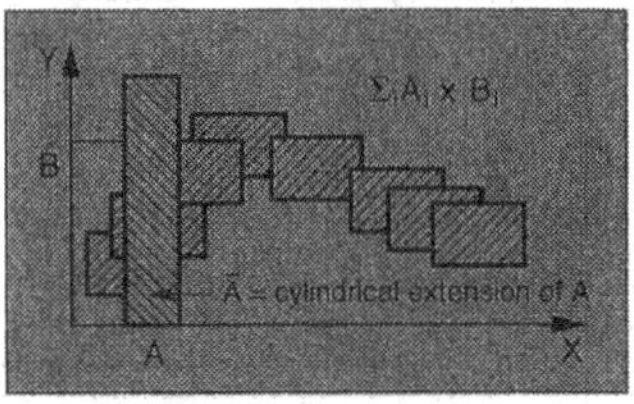

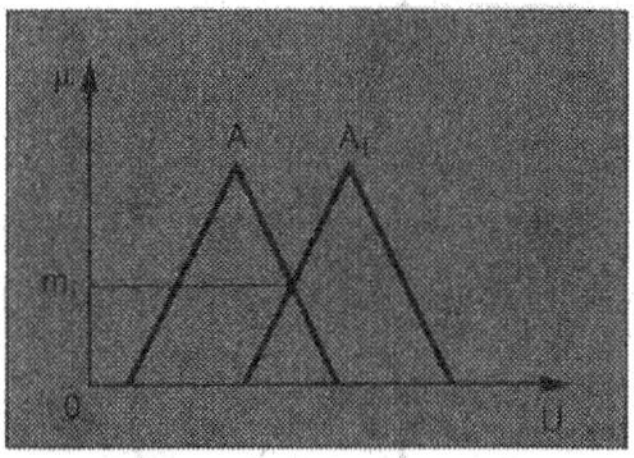

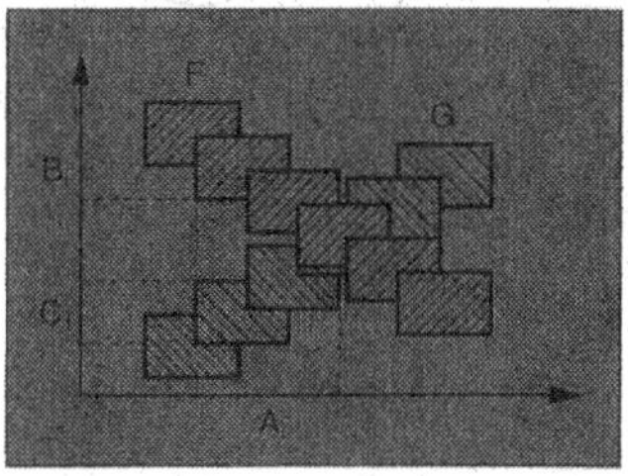

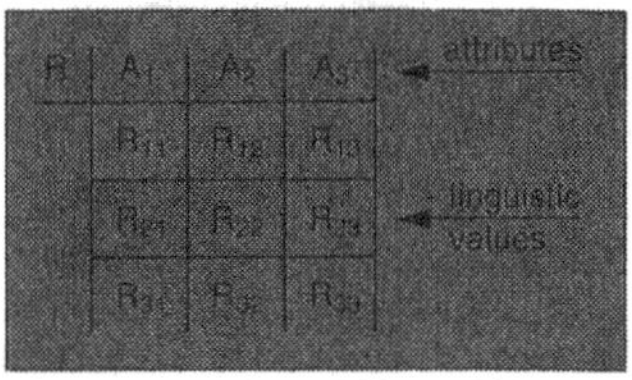

Figure 7. Intersection of fuzzy graphs f^* and g^*

Figure 8. Intersection of f^* and $\overline{A}$

Figure 9. The meaning of the degree of match between A and A_i

Figure 10. Intersection of fuzzy sets F and G whose membership functions are represented as fuzzy graphs

Figure 11. A relation with fuzzy-valued attributes

DT	T_1	T_2	T_3	F_1	F_2
	L	L	M	L	Z
	M	H	L	M	Z
	H	L	L	H	L

Figure 12. Diagnostic tableau. L = low; M = medium; H = high; Z = zero

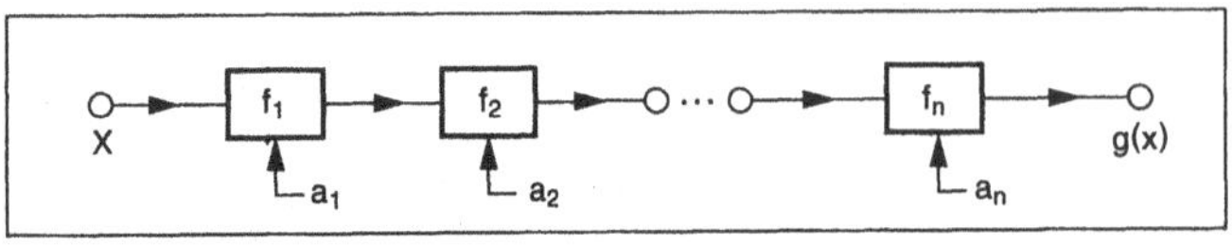

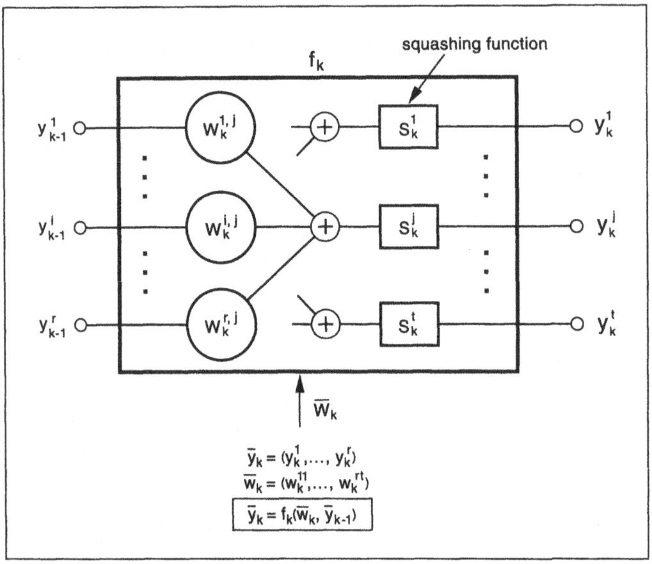

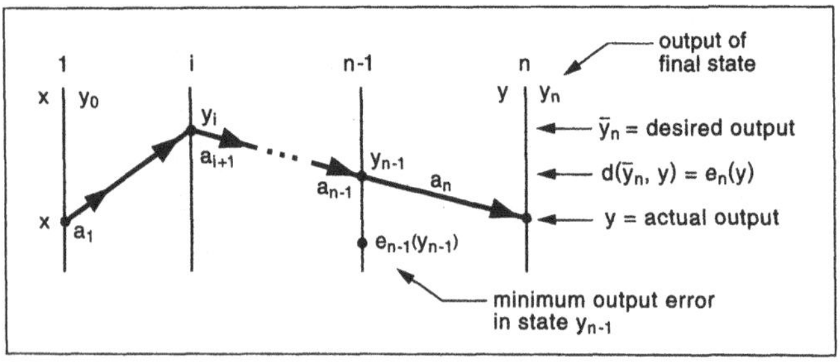

Figure 13. Multilayer feedforward architecture with adjustable parameters

Figure 14. Structure of a layer. $\overline{w}_k$ plays the role of the parameter vector a_k

Figure 15. Graphical representation of dynamic programming

respectively. If the results of tests are not in the tableau, then the degrees of F_1 and F_2 may be computed through the use of interpolation applied to the fuzzy graph

$$DT = L \times L \times M \times L \times Z + M \times H \times L \times M \times Z + H \times L \times L \times H \times L.$$

Fuzzy Probabilities Expressed as Fuzzy Graphs

An important application area for the calculus of fuzzy graphs relates to computation with fuzzy probabilities in the context of qualitative decision analysis. In more specific terms, assume that X and Y are random variables whose probability distributions on finite sets are described in linguistic terms. For example,

$p(X)$: probability is low if X is small
probability is high if X is medium
probability is low if X is large
$q(Y|X)$: probability is high if X is small and Y is large

. . .

where $q(Y \mid X)$ is the conditional probability distribution of Y given X. The problem is to compute the probability distribution of Y in the form of a fuzzy graph.

Representing $p(X)$ and $q(Y \mid X)$ in the form of fuzzy graphs

$$p(X) = \sum_i A_i \times B_i$$

and

$$q(Y \mid X) = \sum_{i,j} A_i \times C_j \times E_{i,j}$$

where the A_i are fuzzy subsets of u, the B_i are fuzzy subsets of [0, 1], the C_j are fuzzy subsets of V, and the $E_{i,j}$ are fuzzy subsets of [0, 1], the problem is to find the fuzzy graph of the joint probability distribution

$$h(X, Y) = p(X)q(Y \mid X).$$

To this end, we use a general rule of combination of fuzzy graphs which may be stated as follows.

Assume that $f(X)$ and $g(Y)$ are functions which may be represented as fuzzy graphs

$$f(X) = \sum_i (F_i \times F_i')$$

and

$$g(Y) = \sum_j (G_j \times G_j').$$

Then, if $f(X)$ and $g(Y)$ are combined through a binary operation $*$ (e.g., multiplication or addition), then the resulting function may be expressed as

$$h(X, Y) = f(X) * g(Y),$$

and the fuzzy graph representing $h(X, Y)$ is given by

$$h(X, Y) = \sum_{i,j} (F_i \times G_j) \times (F_i' * G_j').$$

This result provides the basis for computation with imprecisely known probabilities which are expressed as fuzzy graphs or equivalently as collections of fuzzy if-then rules involving linguistic probabilities. In the case of such probabilities, we have

$$p(X) = \Sigma_i (P_i \times P_i')$$
$$q(Y \mid X) = \Sigma_j (Q_j \times Q_j')$$
$$r(X, Y) = p(X)\, q(Y \mid X)$$

and

$$r(X, Y) = \sum_{i,j} (P_i \times Q_j) \times (P_i' * Q_j')$$

where $*$ represents the operation of multiplication of fuzzy probabilities P_i' and Q_j'.

Dynamic and Gradient Programming

A basic problem in the calculi of fuzzy rules and fuzzy graphs is that of the induction of rules from input/output data. For this purpose, it is expedient to employ the techniques of dynamic programming and gradient programming—which have been developed for multistage optimization—to identify parameters in multilayer structures employing feedforward architecture of the form shown in Figure 13.

In this architecture, $a_1, \ldots, a_n$ are vector parameters which play the role of weights in a neural network or parameters of membership functions in a fuzzy rule-based system; x is the input; y is the output, and $f_1, \ldots, f_n$ are functions defining the layers of the feedforward structure. In the case of a neural network, the structure of f_k, $k = 1, \ldots, n$, is shown in Figure 14, with $\overline{w}_k$ playing the role of the parameter vector a_k.

If $\bar{y}_n$ is the target output when the input is $x = x_0$, then $d(\bar{y}_n, y)$ is the distance between the output y and the target output $\bar{y}_n$ (see Figure 15). In effect, $d(\bar{y}_n, y)$ is the error, $e_n(y)$, at the output of the nth layer. Using dynamic programming and letting $e_i(y_i)$ denote the minimum output error achievable when the input to f_{i+1} is y_i and $a_{i+1}, \ldots, a_n$ are optimal, the recurrence equations for $e_i(y_i)$ may be written as

$$e_{n-1}(y_{n-2}) = \min_{a_n}(e_n(f_n(a_n, y_{n-1})))$$
$$e_{n-2}(y_{n-2}) = \min_{a_{n-1}}(e_{n-1}(f_{n-1}(a_{n-1}, y_{n-2})))$$
$$\ldots$$
$$e_1(y_1) = \min_{a_2}(e_2(f_2(a_2, y_1)))$$
$$e_0(y_0) = \min_{a_1}(e_1(f_1(a_1, y_0)))$$
$$y_0 = x_0$$

Thus, setting $y_0 = x_0$, we can successively compute optimal $a_1, \ldots, a_n$ and thereby determine the parameter vectors which minimize the output error. In these computations, x and y can be treated as vectors representing the input and output data sets.

To approximate to the solution of recurrence equations, we can employ gradient programming, which involves the use of chain differentiation. More specifically, in the case of the feedforward structure shown in Figure 13, we can write

$$\frac{\delta e_n(y_n)}{\delta a_n} = \frac{\delta e_n(y_n)}{\delta y_n} \cdot \frac{\delta y_n}{\delta a_n}$$
$$\frac{\delta e_n(y_n)}{\delta a_{n-i}} = \frac{\delta e_n(y_n)}{\delta y_{n-i}} \cdot \frac{\delta y_{n-i}}{\delta a_{n-i}}$$
$$\frac{\delta e_n(y_n)}{\delta y_{n-i}} = \frac{\delta y_n}{\delta y_{n-i+1}} \cdot \frac{\delta y_{n-i+1}}{\delta y_{n-i}}.$$

It is of interest to note that, on applying these equations to the structure shown in Figure 15, we arrive at the familiar recurrence equations associated with the backpropagation algorithm [3].

Alternatively, applying the equations in question to multilayer structures representing fuzzy rule-based systems, one obtains recursive algorithms for the computation of parameters of membership functions. More detailed expositions of methods of this type may be found in important contributions of Takagi, Sugeno, and Kang [19, 21], Jang [4, 5], Wang [24], Lee and Lin [13], among others.

Concluding Remarks

In this brief article we have attempted to summarize some of the basic ideas underlying soft computing and its relation to fuzzy logic, neural network theory, and probabilistic reasoning. The principal aim of soft computing is to achieve tractability, robustness, low solution cost, and high MIQ through the exploitation of the tolerance for imprecision and uncertainty. Insofar as fuzzy logic is concerned, its principal contribution to this aim centers on the concept of granulation, the concept of a linguistic variable, and the calculi of fuzzy rules and fuzzy graphs. Through these concepts and methods, fuzzy logic provides a model for modes of reasoning which are approximate rather than exact. The role model for fuzzy logic is the human mind. ■

References

1. Bellman, R.E and Zadeh, L.A. Decision-making in a fuzzy environment. *Manage. Sci. 17,* (1970), B-141–B-164.
2. Berenji, H.R. Fuzzy logic controllers. In *An Introduction to Fuzzy Logic Applications in Intelligent Systems.* Kluwer Academic Publishers, Boston, 1991, 69–96.
3. Hertz, J., Krogh, A. and Palmer, R. *Introduction to the Theory of Neural Computation.* Addison-Wesley, Reading, Mass., 1991.
4. Jang, J.-S.R. ANFIS: Adaptive-network-based fuzzy inference systems. *IEEE Trans. Syst. Man Cybernet. 23,* 3 (May 1992).
5. Jang, J.-S.R. Self-learning fuzzy controller based on temporal back-propagation. *IEEE Trans. Neural Netw. 3,* 5 (Sept. 1992), 714–723.
6. Karr, C. Genetic algorithms for fuzzy controllers. *AI Exp. 6,* (1991), 26–33.
7. Kaufmann, A. and Gupta, M.M. *Fuzzy Mathematical Models in Engineering and Management Science.* North Holland, Amsterdam, 1988.
8. Kaufmann, A. and Gupta, M.M. *Introduction to Fuzzy Arithmetic.* Van Nostrand, New York, 1985.
9. Kosko, B. *Neural Networks and Fuzzy Systems: A Dynamical Systems Approach to Machine Intelligence.* Prentice-Hall, Englewood Cliffs, N.J., 1991.
10. Langari, R. and Berenji, H.R. Fuzzy logic in control engineering. In *Handbook of Intelligent Control.* Van Nostrand, New York, 1992.

11. Lee, C.C. Fuzzy logic in control systems: Fuzzy logic controller. Part I and Part II. *IEEE Trans. Syst. Man Cybernet. 20,* (1990).

12. Lee, M.A. and Takagi, H. Integrating design stages of fuzzy systems using genetic algorithms. In *Proceedings of the Second International Conference on Fuzzy Systems (FUZZ-IEEE '93)* (Mar. 28-Apr. 1, 1993). IEEE, New York, 1993, pp. 612–617.

13. Lin, C.-T. and Lee, C.S.G. Neural-network-based fuzzy logic control and decision system. *IEEE Trans. Comput. 40,* 12 (Dec. 1991), 1320–1336.

14. Mamdani, E.H. and Assilian, S. An experiment in linguistic synthesis with a fuzzy logic controller. *Int. J. Man-Machine Stud. 7,* (1975).

15. Mamdani, E.H. and Gaines, B.R., Eds. *Fuzzy Reasoning and Its Applications.* Academic Press, London, 1981.

16. Negoita, C. *Expert Systems and Fuzzy Systems.* Benjamin Cummings, Menlo Park, Calif., 1985.

17. Pedrycz, W. *Fuzzy Control and Fuzzy Systems.* John Wiley, New York, 1989.

18. Sugeno, M. *Industrial Applications of Fuzzy Control.* Elsevier Science Publishers B.V., Amsterdam, 1985.

19. Sugeno, M. and Kang, G.T. Structure identification of fuzzy model. *Fuzzy Sets Syst. 28,* (1988), 15–33.

20. Takagi, H. and Hayashi, I. NN-driven fuzzy reasoning. *Int. J. Approx. Reason.* (1991), 191–212.

21. Takagi, T. and Sugeno, M. Fuzzy identification of systems and its applications to modeling and control. *IEEE Trans. Syst. Man Cybernet.* (1985), 116–132.

22. Togai, M. and Watanabe, H. An inference engine for real-time approximate reasoning: Toward an expert system on a chip. *IEEE Exp. 1,* (1986), 55–62.

23. Turksen, I.B. Approximate reasoning for production planning. *Fuzzy Sets Syst. 26,* (1988), 23–37.

24. Wang, L.-X. Stable adaptive fuzzy control of nonlinear systems. *IEEE Trans. Fuzzy Syst. 1,* 1 (Feb. 1993).

25. Yager, R.R. and Zadeh, L.A., Eds. *An Introduction to Fuzzy Logic Applications in Intelligent Systems.* Kluwer Academic Publishers, Boston, 1991.

26. Yasunobu, S. and Myamoto, S. Automatic train operation by predictive fuzzy control. In *Industrial Applications of Fuzzy Control.* North Holland, Amsterdam, 1985.

27. Zadeh, L.A. The calculus of fuzzy if-then rules. *AI Exp. 7,* 3 (Mar. 1992), 22–27.

28. Zadeh, L.A. A fuzzy-algorithmic approach to the definition of complex or imprecise concepts. Electronics Res. Lab. Rep. ERL-M474, Univ. of California, Berkeley. 1974. Also in *Int. J. Man-Machine Stud. 8,* (1976), 249–291.

29. Zadeh, L.A. The concept of a linguistic variable and its application to approximate reasoning—I. *Inf. Sci. 8,* (1975), 199–249.

30. Zadeh, L.A. On the analysis of large scale systems. In *Systems Approaches and Environment Problems.* Vandenhoeck and Ruprecht, Gottingen, Germany, 1974, 23–37.

31. Zadeh, L.A. Outline of a new approach to the analysis of complex systems and decision processes. *IEEE Trans. Syst. Man Cybernet. SMC-3,* (1973), 28–44.

32. Zadeh, L.A. Toward a theory of fuzzy systems. In *Aspects of Network and System Theory.* Rinehart and Winston, New York, 1971, 469–490.

33. Zadeh, L.A. Thinking machines—a new field in electrical engineering. *Columbia Eng. 3,* (1950), 12–13, 30, 31.

34. Zadeh, L.A. and Yager, R.R., Eds. *Uncertainty in Knowledge Bases.* Springer-Verlag, Berlin, 1991.

35. Zimmerman, H.J. *Fuzzy Set Theory and Its Applications.* 2d ed. Kluwer-Nijhoff, 1990.

About the Author:
LOTFI A. ZADEH is Professor Emeritus and Director of the Berkeley Initiative in Soft Computing (BISC) in the Computer Science Division at the University of California at Berkeley. Current research interests include fuzzy logic, soft computing, and intelligent systems. **Author's Present Address:** Computer Science Division, University of California at Berkeley, Berkeley, CA 94720; email: zadeh@cs.berkeley.edu

Research supported by NASA Grant NCC 2-275, EPRI Agreement RP 8010-34, MICRO State Program No. 90-191 and the BISC (Berkeley Initiative in Soft Computing) program.

The role of fuzzy logic in modeling, identification and control

LOTFI A. ZADEH†

Keywords: *Fuzzy logic; fuzzy control; fuzzy modeling.*

In the nearly four decades which have passed since the launching of the Sputnik, great progress has been achieved in our understanding of how to model, identify and control complex systems. However, to be able to design systems having high MIQ (Machine Intelligence Quotient), a profound change in the orientation of control theory may be required. More specifically, what may be needed is the employment of soft computing—rather than hard computing—in systems analysis and design. Soft computing—unlike hard computing—is tolerant of imprecision, uncertainty and partial truth.

At this juncture, the principal constituents of soft computing are fuzzy logic, neurocomputing and probabilistic reasoning. In this paper, the focus is on the role of fuzzy logic. The basic ideas underlying fuzzy logic and its applications to modeling, identification and control are described and illustrated by examples. The role model for fuzzy logic is the human mind.

1. Introduction—A personal perspective

The origins of modern control theory go back to the days of World War II when the analysis and design of servomechanisms played a central role in the conception and construction of electromechanical systems which could transform low-power inputs into high-power outputs.

As a student at MIT—and later a professor at Columbia University—I witnessed the evolution of control theory from a simplistic, frequency-based theory of linear control systems into a mathematically sophisticated theory of linear/nonlinear systems based on the theory of differential equations and dynamical systems.

It was, above all, the advent of the space age in 1957 that changed the orientation and spirit of control theory. The competition in space—and the challenges posed by the complexity of control problems related to the guidance of space vehicles—attracted to control theory a number of prominent mathematicians, most notably L. S. Pontryagin in the USSR and R. E. Bellman in the United States. As a result, the level of mathematical sophistication of the theory began to grow very rapidly, swinging the pendulum all the way from the low-brow approaches of the forties and fifties to the high-brow mathematical formalism of the seventies, eighties and nineties.

In the fifties and early sixties, my interests centred not on control but on a more general theory—system theory—a theory which was aimed at the development of a

---

Received 31 March 1994.

†Computer Science Division and the Electronics Research Laboratory, Department of EECS, University of California, Berkeley, CA 94720; Tel: 510-642-4959; Fax: 510-642-8271, 510-642-5775; Email: zadeh@cs.berkeley.edu.

Research supported in part by the BISC Program, NASA Grant NCC2-275, EPRI Agreement RP 8010-34 and MICRO State Program No. 92-180.

better understanding of how abstract systems behave and how they could be designed to perform in a specified way.

As a mathematically oriented system theorist, I had been conditioned to believe that the analytical tools based on set theory and two-valued logic were all that was needed to build a framework for a precise, rigorous and effective body of concepts and techniques for the analysis of almost any kind of man-made or natural system, including control systems. Then, in 1961–1963, in the course of writing a book on system theory with C. A. Desoer, I began to feel that highly complex systems—typified by economic and biological systems—cannot be dealt with effectively by the use of conventional approaches. My feeling derived, in the main, from a realization that system description languages based on classical mathematics are not sufficiently expressive to serve as a means of characterization of complex input output relations in an environment of imprecision and uncertainty.

The culprit as I saw it was the universally made assumption that classes have sharply defined boundaries. They do in classical mathematics, but in the real world that we live in the opposite is the case, that is, almost all classes are fuzzy in the sense that the transition from membership to nonmembership in such classes is gradual rather than abrupt. Accepting this fact, the obvious thing to do is to assume that membership in a class is a matter of degree. This assumption is the genesis of the theory of fuzzy sets.

After I wrote my first paper on fuzzy sets in 1965, my aims as a system theorist underwent a marked shift. I came to the conclusion that not just control theory and systems analysis, but, more generally, most or all scientific methodologies will have to undergo a critical reexamination and move toward the replacement of their crisp foundations with foundations based on fuzzy set theory and fuzzy logic (Zadeh 1971, 1972), aiming at greater generality and better approximation to reality. In the realm of control, in particular, the replacement of crisp logic with fuzzy logic could make it possible to design systems with a much higher MIQ (Machine Intelligence Quotient) compared to those which can be designed by traditional methods. In what follows, I will attempt to describe very briefly the basis for my conclusion.

2. Fuzzy logic, linguistic variables and granulation

Fuzzy logic has been and still is somewhat controversial. In part, the controversy relates to the fact that the term fuzzy logic is used in two different senses. In a narrow sense, fuzzy logic (FLn) is a logical system which aims at a formalization of approximate reasoning. As such, it is rooted in multivalued logic but its agenda is quite different from that of traditional multivalued logical systems, e.g., Lukasiewicz's logic. In this connection, it should be noted that many of the concepts which account for the effectiveness of fuzzy logic as a logic of approximate reasoning are not a part of traditional multivalued logical systems. Among these are the concepts of a linguistic variable, canonical form, fuzzy rule, fuzzy graph, fuzzy quantifiers and such modes of reasoning as interpolative reasoning, syllogistic reasoning and dispositional reasoning.

In a broad sense, fuzzy logic (FLw) is almost synonymous with fuzzy set theory. Fuzzy set theory is much broader than fuzzy logic in its narrow sense and contains the latter as one of its branches. Among the other branches of fuzzy set theory are fuzzy arithmetic, fuzzy mathematical programming, fuzzy topology, fuzzy graph theory, possibility theory, etc. What is important to recognize is that any crisp theory can be fuzzified by generalizing the concept of a set within that theory to the concept of a fuzzy set. Indeed, it is very likely that eventually most theories will be fuzzified in this way. As was alluded to earlier, the impetus for transition from a crisp theory to a fuzzy one derives from the fact that both the generality of a theory and its applicability to real world problems are substantially enhanced by replacing the concept of a set with that of a fuzzy set.

Today, the growing tendency is to use the term fuzzy logic (FL) in its broad sense. In part this reflects the fact that fuzzy logic sounds more euphonious than fuzzy set theory.

A concept which plays a central role in the applications of fuzzy logic is that of a linguistic variable (Zadeh 1973, 1975). A linguistic variable, as its name suggests, is a variable whose values are words rather than numbers. For example, age is a linguistic variable if its values are: young, old, not very old, etc. Each linguistic value is interpreted as a label of a fuzzy set in its universe of discourse and each such set, e.g., old, is defined by its membership function, $\mu_{old}(u)$, which associates with each numerical value, u, of age the degree to which n fits one's subjective, context-dependent perception of the meaning of old. The grade of membership is assumed to take values in the interval [0, 1].

In current practice, in most applications to control, the membership functions of linguistic values are assumed to be trapezoidal or triangular in shape (Fig. 1). The number of linguistic values is usually in the range of three to seven, and the values are labeled positive small (PS), negative large (NL), zero (Z), etc.

There is a basic aspect of the concept of a linguistic variable which is at the heart of its utility. Specifically, consider a linguistic variable such as age whose linguistic values are young, middle-aged, and old, with young defined by a membership function such as shown in Fig. 2.

Clearly, a numerical value such as 25 is simpler than the function young. But young represents a choice of one out of three possible values whereas 25 is a choice of one out of, say, 100 values. The point of this simple example is that the use of linguistic values may be viewed as a form of data compression. It is suggestive to refer to this form of data compression as fuzzy granulation or simply granulation.

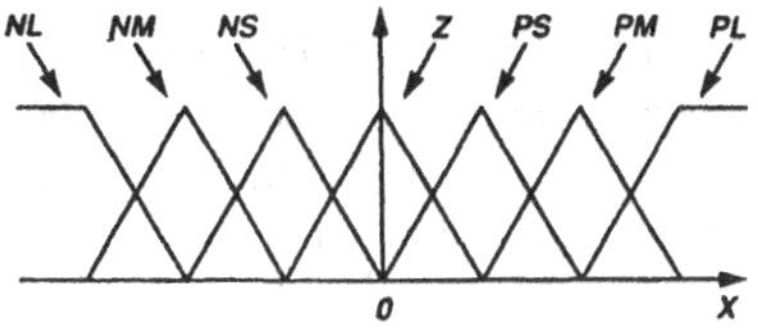

Figure 1. Triangular linguistic values.

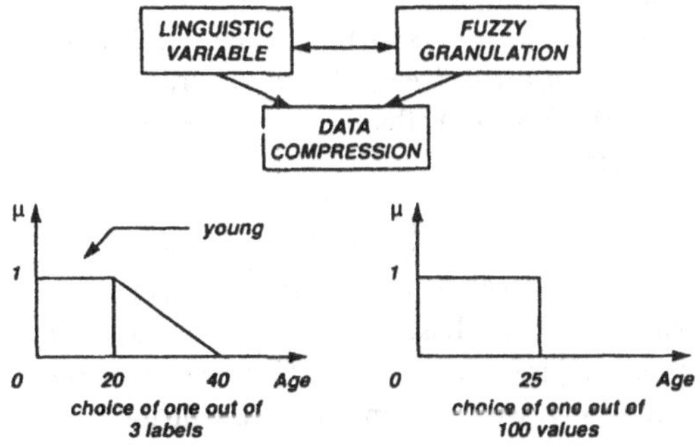

Figure 2. Granulation and data compression.

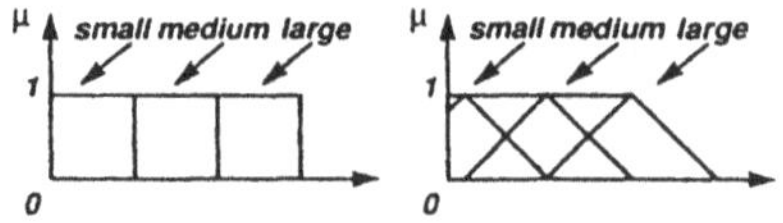

Figure 3. Quantization vs. granulation.

The same effect can be achieved, of course, by conventional quantization. But in the case of quantization, the values are crisp intervals whereas in the case of granulation the values are overlapping fuzzy intervals (Fig. 3), resulting in a gradual rather than abrupt transition from one value to another.

The graduality of transition mimics the way in which humans perceive linguistic values. More importantly—as will be seen later—it provides a basis for interpolative reasoning. Such reasoning plays a central role in learning from experience.

3. Fuzzy rules

In fuzzy logic, the concept of a linguistic variable serves as a point of departure for the construction of a language, referred to as FDCL (Fuzzy Dependency and Command Language), which provides a framework for the description of imprecise dependencies and commands through the use of fuzzy if-then rules or simply fuzzy rules. In what follows, we shall sketch some of the basic ideas underlying FDCL.

Like any language, FDCL is characterized by its syntax and semantics. The syntax and semantics of FDCL define, respectively, the form of rules and their meaning.

Simple examples of the rules in FDCL are the following.

(*a*) if pressure is high then volume is small
(*b*) if pressure is high and temperature is low then volume is very small
(*c*) if pressure is high then lower temperature slightly
(*d*) if pressure is high then volume is small unless temperature is high
(*e*) if pressure is high then usually volume is small.

In these examples, pressure, volume and temperature are linguistic variables and small, low and high are their linguistic values. All of the rules except (*c*) represent dependencies, with (*c*) representing a command. All of the rules except (*d*) and (*e*) are categorical. Rules (*d*) and (*e*) are qualified, with (*d*) qualified through an exception and (*e*) through usuality. (*e*) exemplifies what is referred to as a dispositional rule. All of the rules except for (*b*) involve a single variable in the antecedent. A real-world example of rules used in Honda's fuzzy logic transmission is shown in Fig. 4.

Assuming that small, low, high, usually and whatever other linguistic values may be involved are defined by their membership functions, as in Fig. 4, a question of semantics is: What is the meaning of a rule? And, more generally: What is the meaning of a collection of rules? We shall examine these questions very briefly in the context of basic generic rules of the form

$$\text{if } X \text{ is } A \text{ then } Y \text{ is } B, \tag{1}$$

where A and B are linguistic values of X and Y, respectively.

In fuzzy logic, the answers to these questions are not unique. In what has become a standard interpretation, (1) is interpreted as a fuzzy (elastic) constraint on the variables X and Y. More specifically, with $\rightarrow$ representing translation, we have

$$\text{if } X \text{ is } A \text{ then } Y \text{ is } B \rightarrow (X, Y) \text{ is } A \times B, \tag{2}$$

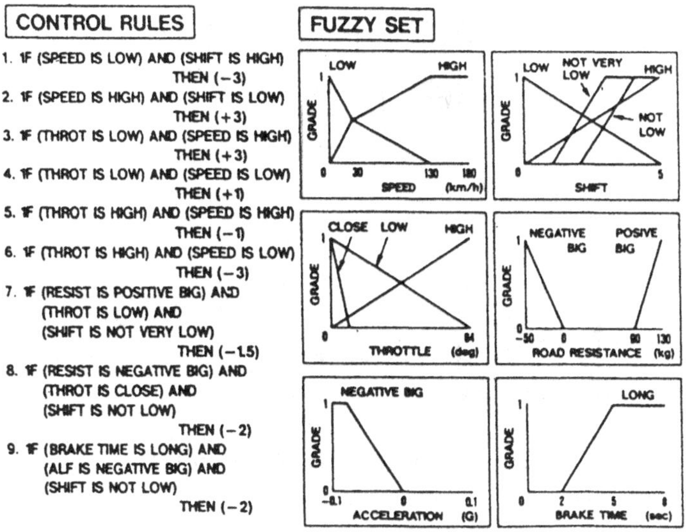

Figure 4. Fuzzy rules employed in Honda's fuzzy logic transmission.

where A × B is the cartesian product of A and B. $A \times B$ is defined by

$$\mu_{A\times B}(u, v) = \mu_A(u) \wedge \mu_B(v),\ u \in U,\ v \in V,$$

where μ_A and μ_B are the membership functions of A and B, respectively; U and V are the universes of discourse of X and Y; and $\wedge$ is the operation of conjunction, which is usually defined as min but, more generally, can be any t-norm (Zimmermann 1990).

More generally, if the dependence of Y on X is characterized by a collection of n rules of the form (1), that is:

$$\text{if } X \text{ is } A_i \text{ then } Y \text{ is } B_i,\ i = 1, \ldots, n, \tag{3}$$

then the meaning of the collection in question is defined by

$$\text{if } X \text{ is } A_i \text{ then } Y \text{ is } B_i,\ i = 1, \ldots, n \rightarrow (X, Y) \text{ is } A_1 \times B_1 + \ldots + A_n \times B_n, \tag{4}$$

where + denotes disjunction. Usually the disjunction is defined as max but, more generally, could be any t-conorm. For convenience, the right-hand member of (4) can be written as

$$(X, Y) \text{ is } \Sigma_i A_i \times B_i.$$

If f is a crisp function of X, $Y = f(X)$, the expression

$$f^* = \Sigma_i A_i \times B_i \tag{5}$$

constitutes the fuzzy graph of f (Zadeh 1971, 1973/74a, 1974b/76). More generally, if $Y = f(X_1, \ldots, X_n)$ is defined via n fuzzy rules of the form

$$\text{Y is } B_i \text{ if } X_1 \text{ is } A_i^1 \text{ and} \ldots \text{and } X_k \text{ is } A_i^k,\ i = 1, \ldots, n \tag{6}$$

then the fuzzy graph, f^*, is expressed as

$$f^* = \Sigma_i B_i \times A_i^1 \times \ldots \times A_i^k,\ i = 1, \ldots, n.$$

As shown in Fig. 5, f^* may be interpreted as a coarse relational approximation to f.

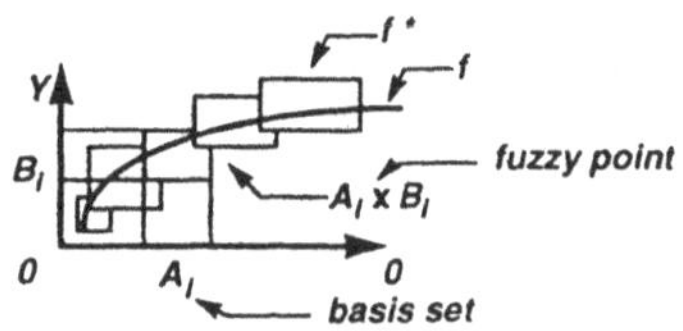

Figure 5. Fuzzy graph approximation to f.

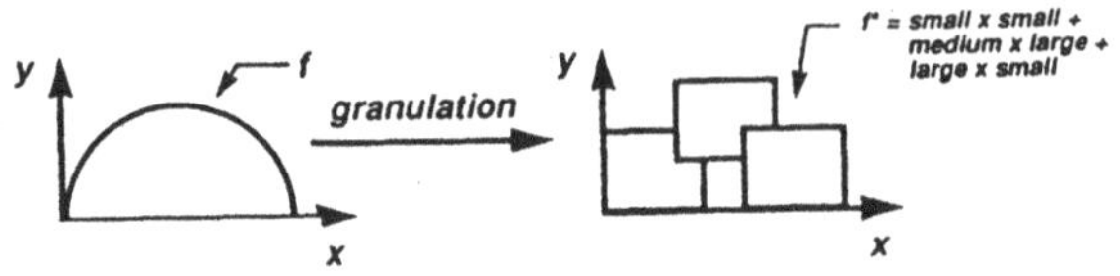

Figure 6. Granulation and data compression.

What is important to note is that f^* serves to represent the dependence of Y on X in a data-compressed form. For example, in the case of the function shown in Fig. 6, the fuzzy graph

$$f^* = \text{small} \times \text{small} + \text{medium} \times \text{large} + \text{large} \times \text{small}$$

may be interpreted as a compressed representation of f.

Manipulation of compressed representations expressed as fuzzy graphs is the province of the calculus of fuzzy graphs (CFG) (Zadeh 1994). Most of the applications of fuzzy logic in the realms of systems analysis and control are in reality applications of CFG.

The importance of CFG derives from the fact that it provides a simple and yet effective way of representing imprecise dependencies. What should be stressed is that CFG does not replace the traditional calculi of differential equations, difference equations, matrices, etc. Rather, it adds to the collection of tools for systems analysis a body of concepts and techniques which are effective in dealing with dependencies which are imprecise to begin with or can be treated imprecisely to achieve tractability, robustness or low solution cost.

4. Fuzzy modeling and control

In an idealized sense, a system S has a model M(S) if M(S) makes it possible to predict the response of S to any given input. In reality, the response of M(S) is usually an approximation to the response of S—an approximation which holds for a restricted set of inputs.

In traditional approaches to systems analysis, M(S) is generally represented as a collection of differential or difference equations. In fuzzy-logic-based approaches, M(S) is represented as a collection of fuzzy if-then rules or, more particularly, as a collection of fuzzy rules of the form (6). In this sense, M(S) is a fuzzy model if through the use of the calculi of fuzzy rules or fuzzy graphs the knowledge of M(S) makes it possible to predict the response of S to any given fuzzy input.

The role of fuzzy logic

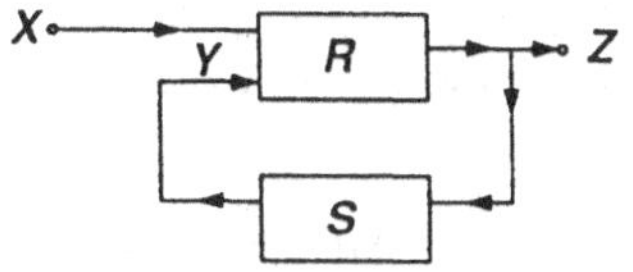

Figure 7. Example of a fuzzy model.

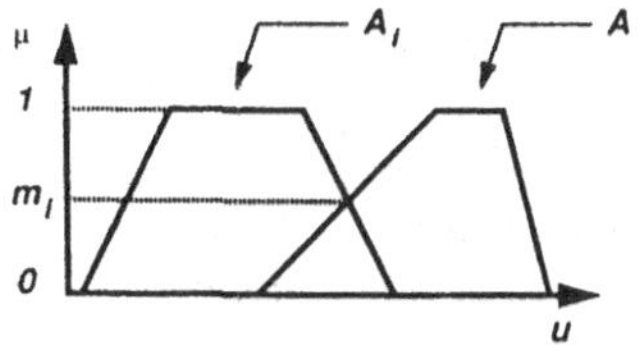

Figure 8. The meaning of the degree of match between A and A_i.

An example of a fuzzy model is shown in Fig. 7. In this model, R and S are assumed to be characterized by the fuzzy rules

$$R\begin{cases}\text{Z is large if X is small and Y is medium}\\ \text{Z is small if X is medium and Y is not very small}\\ \ldots\ldots\ldots\ldots\end{cases}$$

$$S\begin{cases}\text{Y is small if Z is large}\\ \text{Y is medium if Z is not very large}\\ \ldots\ldots\ldots\ldots\end{cases}$$

The calculus of fuzzy graphs provides a computationally simple method of computing the response of S to any given fuzzy input through the use of fuzzy interpolation. The basis for the computation in question is the interpolation rule

$$\begin{array}{c}(X, Y) \text{ is } \Sigma_i A_i \times B_i\\ X \text{ is } A\\ \hline Y \text{ is } \Sigma_i m_i \wedge B_i\end{array} \tag{7}$$

where m_i represents the degree to which the value of X, A, matches the antecedent of ith rule. More specifically

$$m_i = \sup_u(\mu_A(u) \wedge \mu_{A_i}(u)), \tag{8}$$

where the supremum is taken over all $u \in U$ (Fig. 8).

The interpolation rule (7) is a derivative of the compositional rule of inference (Zadeh 1973); it was described in Zadeh (1974a, 1974/76b) and was employed independently by Mamdani and Assilian in their seminal work on fuzzy control (Mamdani 1975). Today, the interpolation rule and its variants play a central role in most of the applications of fuzzy logic to control and systems analysis.

In the foregoing discussion, we have tacitly restricted our attention to static fuzzy systems. However, as shown in some of our early work (Zadeh 1971, 1974), the method in question can readily be extended to dynamic fuzzy systems.

More specifically, let X_t, Y_t and S_t denote the fuzzy input, fuzzy output and fuzzy state at time t, $t=0, 1, 2, \ldots$, of a finite-state fuzzy system S. Then, the state equations of S may be expressed as

$$\begin{aligned} S_{t+1} &= f(S_t, X_t),\ t=0,\ 1,\ 2,\ldots \\ Y_t &= g(S_t, X_t). \end{aligned} \tag{9}$$

Expressed in FDCL, the state equations can be represented as a collection of fuzzy rules of the form

$$\begin{aligned} &\text{if } X_t \text{ is } A_i \text{ and } S_t \text{ is } B_i \text{ then } S_{t+1} \text{ is } C_i,\ i=1,\ldots,n \\ &\text{if } X_t \text{ is } A_i \text{ and } S_t \text{ is } B_i \text{ then } Y_t \text{ is } D_i, \end{aligned} \tag{10}$$

where A_i, B_i and C_i are linguistic values of X_t, S_t and Y_t, respectively.

Equivalently, the state equations can be represented as fuzzy graphs

$$\begin{aligned} f^* &= \Sigma_i A_i \times B_i \times C_i \\ g^* &= \Sigma_i A_i \times B_i \times D_i. \end{aligned} \tag{11}$$

As a simple illustration, assume that the linguistic values of X_t, S_t and Y_t are S (small), M (medium) and L (large), respectively, with the understanding that the membership functions of S, M and L are not necessarily the same for X_t, S_t and Y_t. Expressed in tabular form, the state equation may have, as an example, the form shown in Table 1.

In cases where the spaces of states, inputs and outputs are continua rather than finite sets it may be convenient to represent S_{t+1} in incremental form, that is,

$$S_{t+1} = S_t + \delta S_t.$$

As an illustration, in the case of an inverted pendulum, $S_t = (\theta_t, \dot{\theta}_t)$, where θ_t is the vertical inclination and θ_t is the time-derivative of θ_t, with both θ_t and θ_t interpreted as linguistic variables with linguistic values Z (zero), PS (positive small), NS (negative small), etc. In this case, an entry in the state transition table may be expressed as a fuzzy rule exemplified by

$$\text{if } S_t \text{ is } (Z,\ PS) \text{ and } X_t \text{ is } PS \text{ then } \delta S_t \text{ is } (NS,\ Z).$$

Knowledge of a fuzzy model of S in a direct or incremental form provides a basis for the formulation and solution of various types of generic control problems centring on S. One such problem is the following.

Table 1. State equations of a finite-state fuzzy system.

transition table (columns: current state; rows: current input; entries: next state)

current input \ current state	S	M	L
S	M	L	S
M	S	L	M
L	L	M	S

output table (columns: current state; rows: current input; entries: current output)

current input \ current state	S	M	L
S	M	L	S
M	S	L	M
L	L	M	S

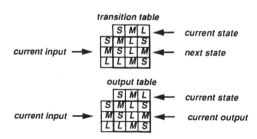

Given an initial state S_I and a goal state S_G in the state space of S find a policy function π,

$$X_t = \pi(S_t),$$

which would take S from the initial state at time $t=0$ to a state at time $t=N$ which is nearest to S_G.

Problems of this type can be solved through the use of fuzzy dynamic programming (Bellman and Zadeh 1970). More specifically, assume that the error at time N is defined as the distance, d, between S_N and S_G, i.e.,

$$e_N(S_N) = d(S_N, S_G).$$

Using backward iteration, we can write

$$\begin{aligned} e_{N-1}(S_{N-1}) &= \min_{X_{N-1}}(d(f(S_{N-1}, X_{N-1}), S_G)) \qquad (12)\\ &= \text{minimum error at } t=N \\ &\quad \text{achievable from } S_{N-1} \\ e_{N-2}(S_{N-2}) &= \min_{X_{N-2}}(e_{N-1}(f(S_{N-2}, X_{N-2}))) \\ &= \text{minimum error at } t=N \\ &\quad \text{achievable from } S_{N-2} \\ &\ldots \\ e_0(S_0) &= \min X_0(e_1(f(S_0, X_0))). \end{aligned}$$

Then, proceeding in the forward direction we can determine the policy function by successively minimizing the error at times $t=0, \ldots, N$.

At this juncture, fuzzy-logic-based control is used extensively in a wide variety of consumer products and industrial systems ranging from cameras and washing machines to cement kilns and subways. In such applications, a fuzzy model of the system is not known. Instead, the point of departure is the designer's or operator's perception of the fuzzy rules which should be used to achieve a desired objective. Viewed in this perspective, in most of its current applications fuzzy control involves a representation of what is basically a human solution in the form of fuzzy if-then rules expressed in FDCL.

It should be realized, however, that a human solution is implicitly rooted in a fuzzy model of the system under control. Thus, the main difference between the prescriptive fuzzy-model-based approach described earlier and the descriptive 'model-free' approach which is employed in current practice reduces to the question of whether the fuzzy model is explicit or implicit. At this juncture, our understanding of how fuzzy models can be constructed and dealt with is still rather rudimentary. In coming years, as our understanding of fuzzy models improves, prescriptive approaches to fuzzy control are likely to gain in importance and visibility.

5. Fuzzy system identification and induction of rules from observations

In dealing with fuzzy rules, it is important to differentiate between the surface structure and the deep structure of a fuzzy rule.

The surface structure of a rule is the rule expressed in a symbolic form, e.g.,

$$\text{if X is A then Y is B.} \qquad (13)$$

The deep structure of a rule is its surface structure together with the definitions of linguistic values which appear in its antecedent and consequent. In the case of the rule represented by (13), the deep structure is the rule itself together with a specification of the membership functions of A and B.

The concepts of surface and deep structure provide a convenient point of departure for the formulation of the identification problem in the context of fuzzy rule-based systems.

The basic identification problem has two variants. In the first variant, the starting point is the knowledge of the surface structure of a system, *S*, which is the object of identification. The problem is to approximate to the deep structure of S based on given input–output data, that is, a collection of input–output pairs.

The second variant is considerably more difficult than the first. In this variant, the problem is the same but the surface structure is not known initially. A seminal contribution to the solution of this problem was made by Takagi and Sugeno (1985). Today, there is a fairly extensive literature on the problem in question but a definitive solution is not yet in hand. In what follows, we shall discuss very briefly the simpler (first variant) of the identification problem.

As is typical of standard approaches to the identification problem, the point of departure is the postulated structure of a fuzzy system modulo the parameters of linguistic variables in the fuzzy if-then-rules.

Many of the approaches described in the literature are based on variants of the Takagi–Sugeno–Kang (TSK) architecture, which is illustrated in Fig. 9. In this architecture, the input X is assumed to have k components $X_1, \ldots, X_k$ and the consequent of rule R^i is assumed to be a linear combination of the constituents of X. The output, Y, is a convex combination of the consequents, with the weight, w_i, being the conjunction of the grades of membership of $X_1, \ldots, X_k$ in the antecedents $A_1^i, \ldots, A_k^i$, respectively. In a frequently employed variant of this architecture, $\wedge$ is replaced with * (product) and the membership functions are assumed to be triangular or trapezoidal. In

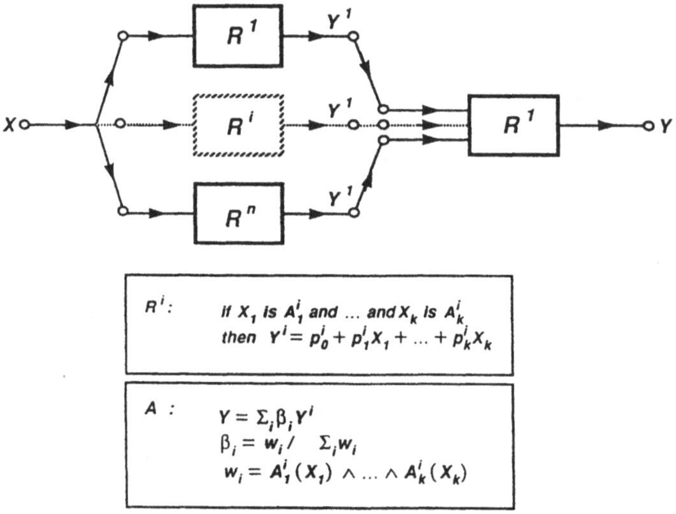

Figure 9. Takagi–Sugeno–Kang architecture.

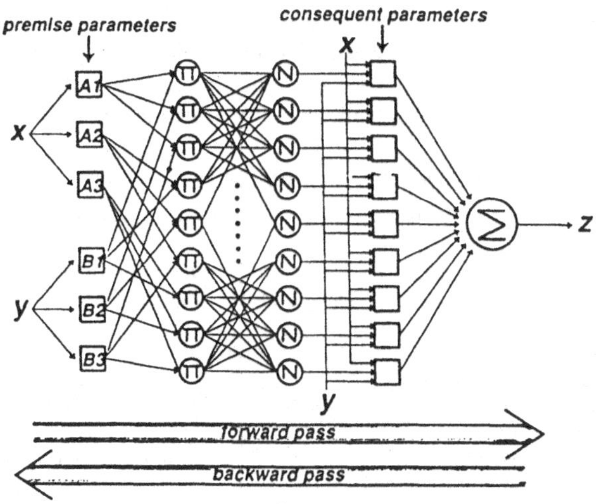

Figure 10. The Jang architecture. In the illustrated system, there are two inputs, x and y, and three rules.

other variants, the membership functions are assumed to be gaussian. This assumption leads to methods which are similar to the radial basis function approaches used in neurocomputing (Warwick *et al.* 1992).

A basic idea underlying the approaches described in the literature is that a fuzzy system based on the TSK architecture can be represented as a multilayer feedforward network. In the Jang approach (Jang 1992), for example, the system is represented as shown in Fig. 10. The circles with Π and N represent multipliers and normalizers, respectively.

Representing a fuzzy system as a multilayer structure lays the groundwork for the application of neurocomputing techniques and, in particular, the backpropagation algorithm (Hertz *et al.* 1991) to the determination of parameters of membership functions. In a more basic way, the techniques in question are rooted in dynamic programming (Werbos 1974) and, more particularly, in gradient programming, which through chain differentiation leads to the backpropagation algorithm (Zadeh 1994). More detailed expositions of these methods may be found in (Jang 1992, Lin and Lee 1991, Wang 1993 and Takagi 1991).

In addition to the use of techniques borrowed from neurocomputing, there are many promising approaches based on reinforcement learning (Berenji 1993) and genetic algorithms (Lee and Takagi 1994). Important progress had been made in our understanding of the identification problem in the context of fuzzy systems, but many difficult problems remain to be addressed.

6. Concluding remarks

In coming years, a significant paradigm shift in systems analysis and control is likely to take place. The shift in question involves a move toward the replacement of crisp foundations of modern control theory and systems analysis by a foundation based on fuzzy logic and soft computing—a collection of computing methodologies which are tolerant of imprecision, uncertainty and partial truth.

In my perception, the shift in question will have an invigorating effect on control theory and systems analysis. It will open the door to the development of systems which will have a much higher MIQ (Machine Intelligence Quotient) than those which could be conceived and designed through the use of traditional methods.

References and Related Papers

Bellman, R. E., and Zadeh, L. A. (1970). Decision-making in a fuzzy environment, *Management Science*, **17**, B141–B164.

Berenji, H. R. (1991). Fuzzy logic controllers, In *An Introduction to Fuzzy Logic Applications in Intelligent Systems*, edited by R. R. Yager and L. A. Zadeh (Kluwer Academic Publishers), pp. 69–96.

Chang, S. S. L., and Zadeh, L. A. (1972). On fuzzy mapping and control, *IEEE Trans. Systems, Man, and Cybernetics*, **2**, 30–34.

Driankov, D., Hellendoorn, H., and Reinfrank, M. (1993). *An Introduction to Fuzzy Control* (Springer-Verlag, Berlin).

Dubois, D., Prade, H., and Yager, R. (Eds.) (1993). *Readings in Fuzzy Sets for Intelligent Systems* (Morgan Kaufmann, San Mateo).

Hertz, J., Krogh, A., and Palmer, R. (1991). *Introduction to the theory of neural computation* (Addison Wesley).

Jamshidi, M., Vadiee, N. and Ross, T. (Eds.) (1993). *Fuzzy Logic and Control* (Prentice Hall, Englewood Cliffs, NJ).

Jang, J.-S. R. (1992). Self-learning fuzzy controller based on temporal back-propagation. *IEEE Trans. on Neural Networks*, **3**, 714–723.

Kandel, A., and Langholz, G. (Eds.) (1994). *Fuzzy Control Systems* (CRC Press, Boca Raton).

Karr, C. (1991). Genetic algorithms for fuzzy controllers. *AI Expert*, **6**, 26–33.

Kosko, B. (1991). *Neural Networks and Fuzzy Systems: A Dynamical Systems Approach to Machine Intelligence* (Englewood Cliffs, Prentice-Hall).

Lee, C. C. (1990). Fuzzy logic in control systems: Fuzzy logic controller, Part I and Part II, *IEEE Trans. Systems, Man and Cybernetics*, **20**, 404–418.

Lee, M. A. and Takagi, H. (1993). Integrating design stages of fuzzy systems using genetic algorithms. *2nd International Conference on Fuzzy Systems* (*FUZZ-IEEE '93*), pp. 612–617, March 28–April 1.

Lin, C.-T. and George Lee, C. S. (1991). Neural-network-based fuzzy logic control and decision system. *IEEE Transactions on Computers*, **40**, 1320–1336.

Mamdani, E. H. and Assilian, S. (1975). An experiment in linguistic synthesis with a fuzzy logic controller. *Int. J. Man-Machine Studies*, **7**, 1–13.

Pedrycz, W. (1989). *Fuzzy Control and Fuzzy Systems* (John Wiley, New York).

Sugeno, M. and Kang, G. T. (1988). Structure identification of fuzzy model. *Fuzzy Sets and Systems*, **28**, 15–33.

Terano, T., Asai, K. and Sugeno, M. (1992). *Fuzzy Systems Theory and its Applications* (Academic Press).

Takagi, T. and Sugeno, M. (1985). Fuzzy identification of systems and its applications to modeling and control, *IEEE Trans. Systems, Man and Cybernetics*, **15**, 116–132.

Wang, L.-X. (1994). *Adaptive Fuzzy Systems and Control: Design and Stability Analysis* (PTR Prentice Hall, Englewood Cliffs, New Jersey).

Warwick, K., Irwin, G. W. and Hunt, K. J. (1992). *Neural networks for control and systems* (London, Peter Peregrinus Ltd.).

Werbos, P. J. (1974). *Beyond Regression: New Tools for Prediction and Analysis in the Behaviour Sciences*, Ph.D. Thesis, Harvard University, Committee on Applied Mathematics.

Zadeh, L. A. (1971). Toward a theory of fuzzy systems, In *Aspects of Network and System Theory*, R. E. Kalman and N. DeClaris (eds.) (New York: Rinehart & Winston), 469–490.

Zadeh, L. A. (1972). A rationale for fuzzy control, *J. Dynamic Systems, Measurement and Control* *94*, Series G, 3–4.

Zadeh, L. A. (1973). Outline of a new approach to the analysis of complex systems and decision processes, *IEEE Trans. Systems, Man and Cybernetics*, **3**, 28–44.

Zadeh, L. A. (1974a). On the analysis of large scale systems, In *Systems Approaches and Environment Problems*, H. Gottinger (ed.), 23–27 (Gottingen, Vandenhoeck and Ruprecht).

ZADEH, L. A. (1974b). A fuzzy-algorithmic approach to the definition of complex or imprecise concepts, Electronics Research Laboratory Report ERL-M474, University of California, Berkeley, (also published in *Int. Man-Machine Studies*, **8**, 249–291, 1976).

ZADEH, L. A. (1975). The concept of a linguistic variable and its applications to approximate reasoning, I, *Information Sciences*, **8**, 199–249.

ZADEH, L. A. (1994). Fuzzy Logic, Neural Networks and Soft Computing, *Comm. ACM*, **37**, 77–84.

ZIMMERMAN, H. J. (1990). *Fuzzy Set Theory and Its Applications*, second edition (Kluwer-Nijhoff).

Soft Computing and Fuzzy Logic

LOTFI A. ZADEH, *University of California at Berkeley*

◆ *Soft computing is a collection of methodologies that aim to exploit the tolerance for imprecision and uncertainty to achieve tractability, robustness, and low solution cost. Its principal constituents are fuzzy logic, neurocomputing, and probabilistic reasoning. Soft computing is likely to play an increasingly important role in many application areas, including software engineering. The role model for soft computing is the human mind.*

One of the deepest traditions in science is that of according respectability to what is quantitative, precise, rigorous, and categorically true. It is a fact, however, that we live in a world that is pervasively imprecise, uncertain, and hard to be categorical about. It is also a fact that precision and certainty carry a cost. Driven by our quest for respectability, we tend to close our eyes to these facts and thereby lose sight of the steep price we must pay for high precision and low uncertainty. Another visible concomitant of the quest for respectability is that in much of the scientific literature elegance takes precedence over relevance.

A case in point is the traveling salesman problem, which is frequently used as a testbed for assessing the effectiveness of various methods of solution. What is striking about this problem is the steep rise in computing time as a function of precision of solution. As the data in Table 1 show, lowering the accuracy to 3.50 percent reduces the computing time by an order of magnitude for a ten-fold increase in the number of cities.

A more familiar example that illustrates the point is the problem of parking a car. We find it relatively easy to park a car because the final position of the car is not specified precisely. If it were, the difficulty of parking would increase geometrically with the increase in precision, and eventually parking would become impossible.

Guiding principle. These and many similar examples lead to the basic premises and the guiding principle of *soft computing*.

The basic premises of soft computing are

♦ The real world is pervasively imprecise and uncertain.

Reprinted, with permission, from *IEEE Software*, **11**(6), pp. 48–56. Copyright © 1994 by IEEE.

♦ Precision and certainty carry a cost.

The guiding principle of soft computing is

♦ Exploit the tolerance for imprecision, uncertainty, and partial truth to achieve tractability, robustness, and low solution cost.

The label soft computing is growing in use. What does it mean? Where does it stand today and where is it headed? And what is the role of fuzzy logic in soft computing?

Sample application. Some of the most striking examples of the application of the guiding principle of soft computing are the data-compression techniques that play a key role in high-definition television and audio recording and reproduction.

For example, in NHK's Muse system, a motion-compensating technique determines the outline, direction, and speed of the moving body, then shifts the moving image without waiting to receive all the pixel data. The resulting moving image does not have the resolution of the still picture. Muse exploits the fact that the human eye cannot grasp the details of moving objects with the same precision as still objects. Even more impressive is what is achieved in the recently developed digital HDTV systems. For example, the General Instrument system, instead of transmitting data for every color dot in a blue sky, sends an instruction to paint the sky. The compression ratio this system achieves is on the order of 60 to 1. In audio recording and reproduction, similar ideas are embodied in Sony's MD-1 system and Philips' DCC.

In its current incarnation, the concept of soft computing has links to many earlier influences, among them my 1965 paper on fuzzy sets;[1] 1973 paper on the use of linguistic variables in the analysis and control of complex systems;[2] and 1979 report (1981 paper) on possibility theory and soft data analysis.[3]

Unlike traditional hard computing, soft computing is aimed at accommodating the pervasive imprecision of the real world. Although soft computing has not as yet had a visible impact on software engineering, it is likely to do so in the years ahead. Among the areas in which it is likely to be applied are programming languages, computer security, database management, user-friendly interfaces, automated programming, fault diagnosis, and networking.

In this article, I will focus on some of the basic ideas that underlie soft computing and relate them to its guiding principle.

SOFT COMPUTING AND FUZZY LOGIC

Basically, soft computing is not a homogeneous body of concepts and techniques. Rather, it is a partnership of distinct methods that in one way or another conform to its guiding principle. At this juncture, the dominant aim of soft computing is to exploit the tolerance for imprecision and uncertainty to achieve tractability, robustness, and low solution cost. The principal constituents of soft computing are fuzzy logic, neurocomputing, and probabilistic reasoning, with the latter subsuming genetic algorithms, belief networks, chaotic systems, and parts of learning theory. In the partnership of fuzzy logic, neurocomputing, and probabilistic reasoning, fuzzy logic is mainly concerned with imprecision and approximate reasoning; neurocomputing with learning and curve-fitting; and probabilistic reasoning with uncertainty and belief propagation.

In large measure, fuzzy logic, neurocomputing, and probabilistic reasoning are complementary, not competitive. It is becoming increasingly clear that in many cases it is advantageous to combine them. A case in point is the growing number of "neurofuzzy" consumer products and systems that use a combination of fuzzy logic and neural-network techniques.

TABLE 1
SOLUTIONS FOR TRAVELING SALESMAN PROBLEM

Number of cities	Accuracy	Computing time
100,000	1.00%	two days
100,000	0.75%	seven months
1,000,000	3.50%	3.5 hours

Source: New York Times, March 12, 1991.

In this article, I focus on fuzzy logic.

FUZZY LOGIC CONCEPTS

As one of the principal constituents of soft computing, fuzzy logic is playing a key role in what might be called high MIQ (machine intelligence quotient) systems.

Two concepts within fuzzy logic play a central role in its applications.

♦ The first is a *linguistic variable;* that is, a variable whose values are words or sentences in a natural or synthetic language.[2]

♦ The other is a *fuzzy if-then rule*, in which the antecedent and consequents are propositions containing linguistic variables.[2]

The essential function of linguistic variables is that of granulation of variables and their dependencies. In effect, the use of linguistic variables and fuzzy if-then rules results — through granulation — in lossy data compression. In this respect, fuzzy logic mimics the remarkable ability of the human mind to summarize data and focus on decision-relevant information.

With regard to fuzzy logic, there is an issue of semantics that is in need of clarification. Specifically, it is frequently not recognized that the term fuzzy logic is actually used in two different senses. In a narrow sense, fuzzy logic (*FLn*) is a logical system — an extension of multivalued logic that is intended to serve as a logic of approximate reasoning. In a wider sense, fuzzy

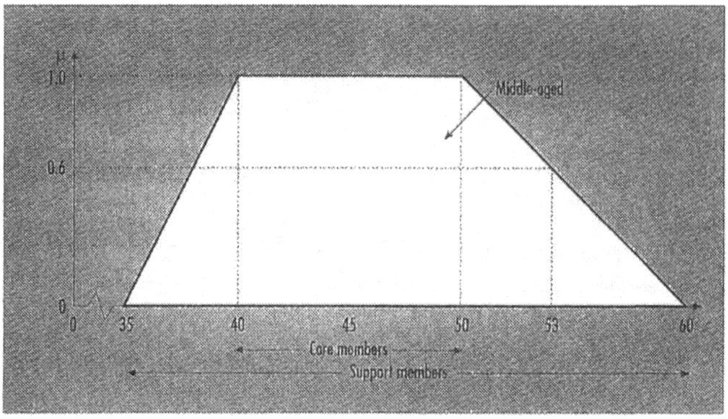

Figure 1. *Interpretation of middle-aged as a linguistic value.*

logic (*FLw*) is more or less synonymous with fuzzy set theory; that is, the theory of classes with unsharp boundaries. In this perspective, *FL* = *FLw*, and *FLn* is merely a branch of *FL*. What is important to recognize is that today the term fuzzy logic is used predominantly in its wider sense. It is in this sense that any field *X* can be "fuzzified" — and hence generalized — by replacing the concept of a crisp set in *X* by a fuzzy set. In application to basic fields such as set theory, arithmetic, topology, graph theory, probability theory, and logic, fuzzification leads to fuzzy set theory, fuzzy arithmetic, fuzzy topology, fuzzy graph theory, and fuzzy logic in its narrow sense.

Similarly, in application to applied fields like neurocomputing, stability theory, pattern recognition and mathematical programming, fuzzification leads to fuzzy neurocomputing, fuzzy stability theory, fuzzy pattern recognition, and fuzzy mathematical programming. What is gained through fuzzification is greater generality, higher expressive power, an enhanced ability to model real-world problems, and — most important — a methodology for exploiting the tolerance for imprecision, a methodology that fits the guiding principle of soft computing and thus serves to achieve tractability, robustness, and low solution cost.

Linguistic variables. A concept in fuzzy logic that plays a key role in exploiting the tolerance for imprecision is the linguistic variable. A linguistic variable, as its name suggests, is a variable whose values are words or sentences in a natural or synthetic language. For example, *age* is a linguistic variable if its *linguistic values* are *young, old, middle-aged, very old, not very young*, and so on. A linguistic variable is interpreted as a label of a fuzzy set that is characterized by a *membership function*, as illustrated in Figure 1. Thus, if u is a numerical age, say 53, then $\mu_{middle\text{-}aged}(53)$ is the *grade of membership* of 53 in *middle-aged*. Subjectively, you may interpret $\mu_{middle\text{-}aged}(u)$ as the degree to which u fits your perception of middle-aged in a specified context.

In a general setting, a linguistic variable, V, can be viewed as a microlanguage with context-free grammar and attributed-grammar semantics. The context-free grammar defines the legal values of V. For example, in the case of *age*, the legal values are *young, not young, not very young, quite old, middle-aged*, and so on. The attributed-grammar semantics provides a mechanism for computing the membership function of any value of V from the knowledge of the membership functions of the so-called *primary terms* — *young* and *old*, for example. A primary term plays the role of a generator whose meaning (its membership function) must be calibrated in context. For example, the meaning of *not very young* might be computed as

$$\mu_{not\ very\ young}(u) = 1 - (\mu_{young}(u))^2$$

where *very* plays the role of an intensifier and *young* is a primary term whose membership function is specified in context.

Most current applications of fuzzy logic employ a simpler framework, illustrated in Figure 2. Specifically, the membership functions are assumed to be triangular or trapezoidal, and the number of linguistic values is usually in the range of three to seven.

The concept of a linguistic variable plays a central role in the applications of fuzzy logic because it goes to the heart of the way in which humans perceive, reason, and communicate. Quintessentially, the use of words may be viewed as a form of data compression that exploits the tolerance for imprecision to achieve tractability, robustness, and economy of communication. This fits almost precisely the guiding principle of soft computing.

Granulation. In a related sense, the use of words may be viewed as a form of fuzzy quantization or more generally as *granulation*, as Figure 3 shows.

Basically, granulation involves a replacement of a constraint of the form

$$X = a$$

with a constraint of the form

$$X \text{ is } A$$

where A is a fuzzy subset of U, the universe of X. For example,

$$X = 2$$

might be replaced with

$$X \text{ is } small$$

In fuzzy logic, X is a is interpreted as a

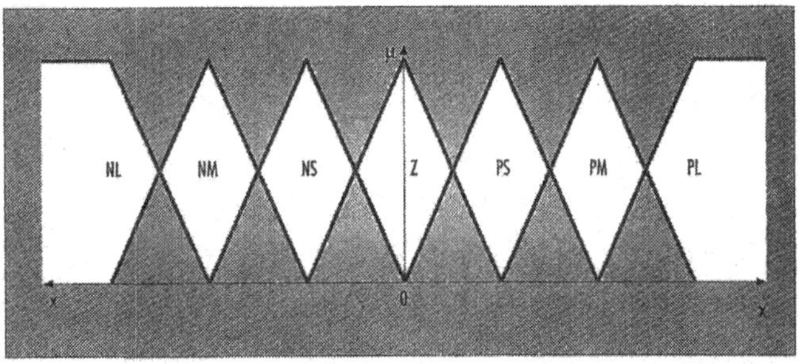

Figure 2. Triangular linguistic values, usually ranging from negative large, negative medium, and negative small (NL, NM, and NS) to zero (Z) to positive small, positive medium, and positive large (PS, PM, and PL).

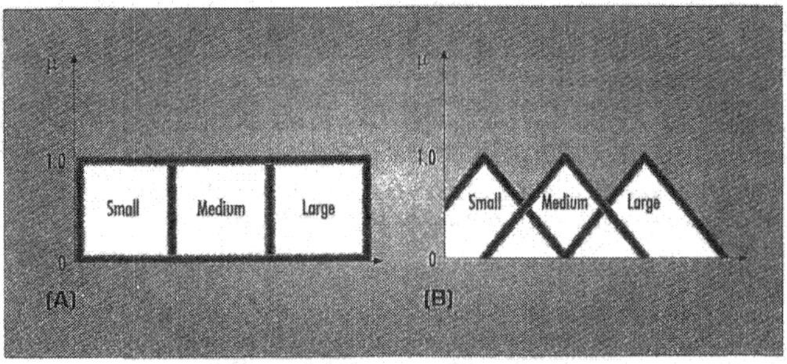

Figure 3. (A) Quantization versus (B) granulation (fuzzy quantization).

characterization of the possible values of X, with A representing a possibility distribution. Thus, the possibility that X can take a value u is given by

$$Poss\{X = u\} = \mu A(u)$$

It is in this sense that X is $\mu A(u)$, with possibility interpreted as ease of attainment or assignment, may be interpreted as an elastic constraint on X.

Fuzzy rules and fuzzy graphs. The concept of a linguistic variable serves as a point of departure for what might be called the Fuzzy Dependency and Command Language.[4] As its name suggests, FDCL provides a system for representing and manipulating fuzzy dependencies and commands. Central to FDCL are the concepts of a *fuzzy rule* and *fuzzy graph* and the concomitant calculi of fuzzy rules and fuzzy graphs.[4,5] Employed in an informal way, these calculi have played and continue to play a key role in most of the applications of fuzzy logic.

To view the calculi of fuzzy rules and fuzzy graphs in a proper perspective, it is necessary to note that the representation and manipulation of dependencies is an essential part of the scientific method. Mathematics provides us with several calculi to do this, among them the calculi of differential equations, difference equations, matrices, linear and nonlinear mappings, and probabilistic dependencies. These calculi are effective when the dependencies are well-defined and amenable to numerical analysis. When they are not, the calculi of fuzzy rules and fuzzy graphs provide an alternative methodology aimed at results that are in the spirit of the guiding principle of soft computing.

More specifically, the use of the calculi of fuzzy rules and fuzzy graphs is indicated when the dependencies are

♦ ill-defined or too complex for conventional methods, or

♦ well-defined, but it is advantageous to use linguistic variables to exploit the tolerance for imprecision, thereby lowering the solution cost and achieving a higher MIQ.

Interestingly, the development of fuzzy-set theory was motivated by the first situation, but today most applications of fuzzy logic in the realm of consumer products are motivated by the second.

FDCL has many facets. Here, I shall sketch some of the basic ideas that underlie FDCL and the calculi of fuzzy rules and fuzzy graphs.

Like any language, FDCL is characterized by its syntax and semantics. The syntax of FDCL is concerned with the form of admissible fuzzy rules; the semantics is concerned with their meaning. It is important to note that FDCL is not a "fuzzified" version of a standard programming language, as is true of Fuzzy Prolog.[6]

Fuzzy rules. FDCL allows the use of a wide variety of fuzzy if-then rules, or simply fuzzy rules. A typical fuzzy rule relates m antecedent variables $X_1,\ldots,X_m$ to n consequent variables, $Y_1,\ldots,Y_n$ and has the form:

if X_1 is A_1 and ... X_m is A_m
then Y_1 is B_1 and ... Y_n is B_n

where $X = (X_1,\ldots,X_m)$ and $Y = (Y_1,\ldots,Y_n)$ are linguistic variables and $(A_1,\ldots,A_n)$ and $(B_1,\ldots,B_n)$ their respective linguistic values. For example:

if *Pressure* is *high* and *Temperature* is *high* then *Volume* is *small*

For simplicity, I will discuss only rules in which $m = n = 1$.

A rule can have a *surface structure* or a *deep structure*. The *surface structure* is the rule in its symbolic form:

if X is A then Y is B

Such a rule is said to be *uncalibrated*, which means that the membership functions of A and B are not specified.

The *deep structure* is the surface structure together with a characterization of the membership functions of linguistic values of variables. In this case, the rule is said to be *calibrated*.

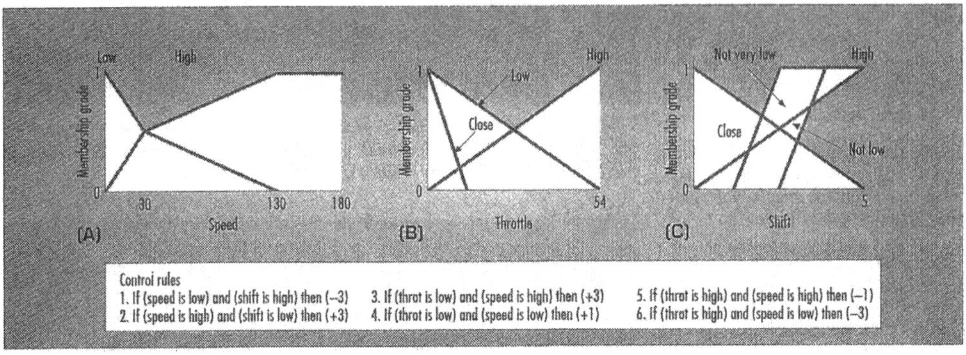

Figure 4. *Fuzzy rules used in Honda's fuzzy-logic transmission. Here, the meaning of the numeric values associated with the rules is not important; they only illustrate how rules are calibrated*

Figure 4 shows an example of the calibrated fuzzy rules used in Honda's fuzzy-logic transmission. As I explain later, one of the central problems in the applications of fuzzy logic is that of deriving the deep structure of a set of fuzzy rules from I/O data.

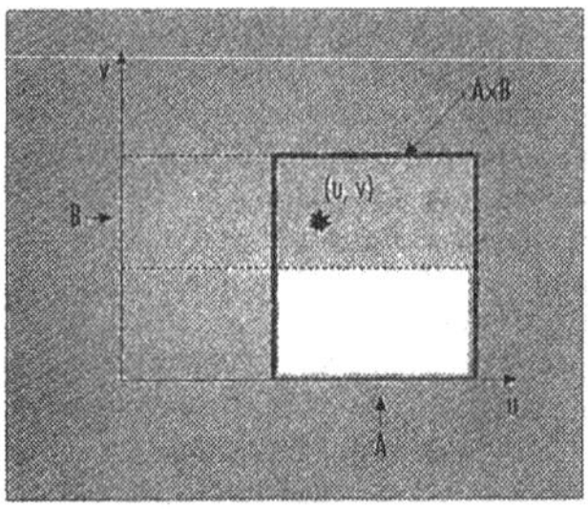

Figure 5. *$A \times B$ interpreted as a fuzzy point or a granule.*

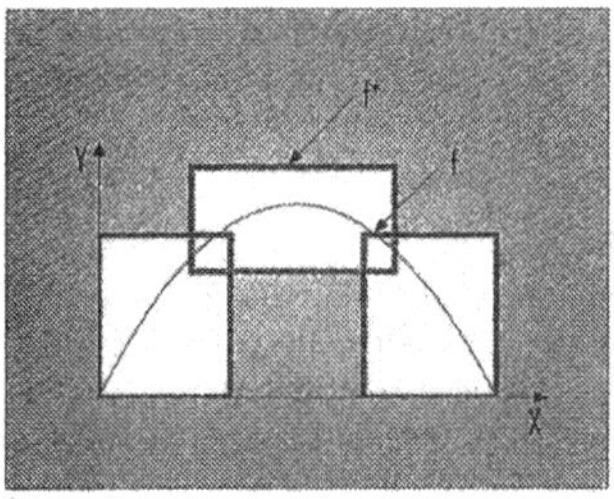

Figure 6. *Interpretation of a collection of fuzzy rules as a fuzzy graph.*

DERIVING RULES AND GRAPHS

In the semantics of FDCL, the basic questions are, what is the meaning of a single rule and what is the meaning of a collection of rules?

Deriving rules. Consider the simplest type of rule:

$$\text{if } X \text{ is } A \text{ then } Y \text{ is } B$$

where A and B are linguistic values of X and Y, respectively. The question is, what is the meaning of this rule given the membership functions of A and B?

In fuzzy logic, the meaning of a proposition p is expressed as a *canonical form*

$$p \to Z \text{ is } C$$

where $\to$ means "translates into," Z is the constrained variable, and C is an fuzzy relation that plays the role of a fuzzy constraint on Z. What this implies is that the meaning of p is expressed as a fuzzv — or, equivalently, elastic — constraint on a designated variable. To illustrate, the meaning of the proposition *Mary is young* might be expressed as

$$\textit{Mary is young} \to \textit{Age(Mary)} \text{ is } \textit{young}$$

where *Age(Mary)* is the focal variable and *young* is a fuzzy constraint on *Age(Mary)*.

Applying this concept of meaning representation to the fuzzy rule

$$\text{if } X \text{ is } A \text{ then } Y \text{ is } B$$

we can express the meaning of the rule in question as a fuzzy constraint on the joint variable (X,Y). More specifically,

$$\text{if } X \text{ is } A \text{ then } Y \text{ is } B \to (X,Y) \text{ is } A \times B,$$

where $A \times B$ is the Cartesian product of A and B. The membership function of $A \times B$ is given by

$$\mu_{A\times B}(u,v) = \mu_A(u) \wedge \mu_B(u)$$

where $\wedge$ is the conjunction operator, usually defined as min. $A \times B$ may be interpreted as a *fuzzy point* or a *granule*, as shown in Figure 5.

Deriving graphs. In the case of a collection of rules expressed as

$$\text{if } X \text{ is } A_i \text{ then } Y \text{ is } B_i,\ i = 1, \ldots, n$$

and the meaning of the collection is defined as

$$\text{if } X \text{ is } A_i \text{ then } Y \text{ is } B_i,$$
$$(i = 1,\ldots,n) \to (X,Y) \text{ is}$$

$$(A_1 \times B_1 + \ldots + A_n \times B_n)$$

where + is used in place of ∨ to denote the disjunction operator, which is usually defined as max. For simplicity, the right-hand member of the collection may be written as

$$(X,Y) \text{ is } (\Sigma_i A_i \times B_i)$$

The expression $\Sigma_i A_i \times B_i$ may be viewed as a superposition of fuzzy points or granules, as illustrated in Figure 7. In effect, it represents a coarse — or, equivalently, compressed — characterization of the dependency and for this reason it is called a *fuzzy graph*.[5] Thus, a collection of fuzzy rules is represented as a fuzzy graph. For example:

if X is *small* then Y is *small*
if X is *medium* then Y is *large*
if X is *large* then Y is *small*

is a coarse characterization of the dependency illustrated in Figure 6.

INTERPOLATION

If we interpret a collection of rules as a coarse representation of the functional dependence of Y on X, the *problem of interpolation* may be defined as that of computing the value of Y given a value of X that may not be a perfect match with any of the antecedent variables in the collection. More specifically, this problem can be expressed as the inference schema

$$(X,Y) \text{ is } (\Sigma_i A_i \times B_i)$$
$$\frac{X \text{ is } A}{Y \text{ is} ?B}$$

in which $?B$ signifies that B is the object of computation. In graphical terms, as shown in Figure 8, the problem may be viewed as that of assigning a linguistic value to X and computing the corresponding linguistic value of Y.

In fuzzy logic, computation of B is carried out through the basic rule of inference, called the *compositional rule* of inference.[2] The rule in question reads

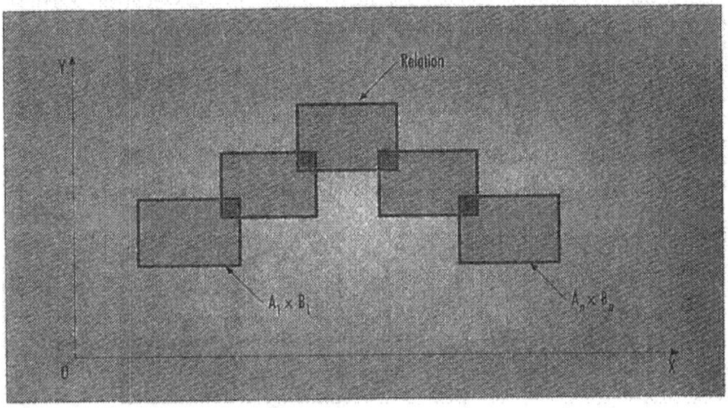

***Figure** 7. Representing a collection of fuzzy rules as a fuzzy graph, f^*, which approximates to f.*

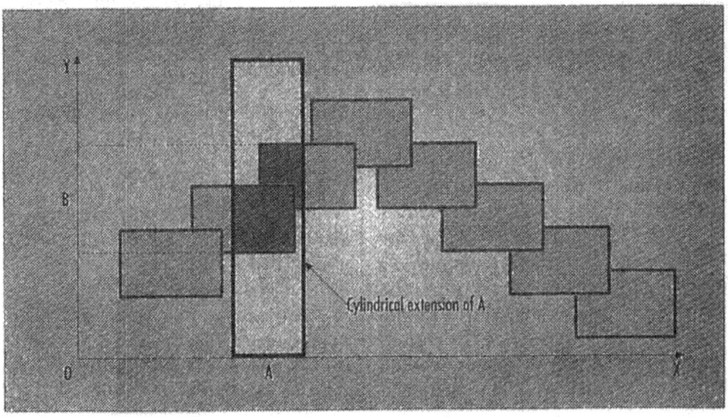

***Figure** 8. Interpolation of a fuzzy graph. The value of Y may be interpreted as the projection of the intersection of the fuzzy graph with the cylindrical extension of A.*

$$(X,Y) \text{ is } R$$
$$\frac{X \text{ is } A}{Y \text{ is } R \bullet A}$$

in which the composition operation is defined by

$$\mu_{R \bullet A}(v) = sup_u(\mu_R(u,v) \wedge \mu_A(u))$$

in which $\mu_R(u,v)$ and $\mu_A(u)$ are, respectively, the membership functions of R and A.

In the example considered earlier, R is given by

$$R = (\Sigma_i A_i \times B_i)$$

in which

$$\mu_R(u,v) = \Sigma_i \mu_A(u) \wedge \mu_B(v)$$

Then

$$\mu_B(v) = \Sigma_i \mu_i \wedge \mu_B(v)$$

or, equivalently,

$$B = \Sigma_i \mu_i \wedge B_i$$

in which

$$\mu_i = (\mu_{A_i}(u) \wedge \mu_A(u))$$

The sequence of computations that leads to B is standard in most fuzzy logic applications and is usually implemented in software or hardware. In some implementations, called max-product implementations, the conjunction ∧ is interpreted as the arithmetic product.

Interpolation lies at the heart of the utility of fuzzy rule-based systems because it makes it possible to employ a relatively small number of fuzzy rules to characterize a complex relationship between two or more variables. In a typical application in a consumer

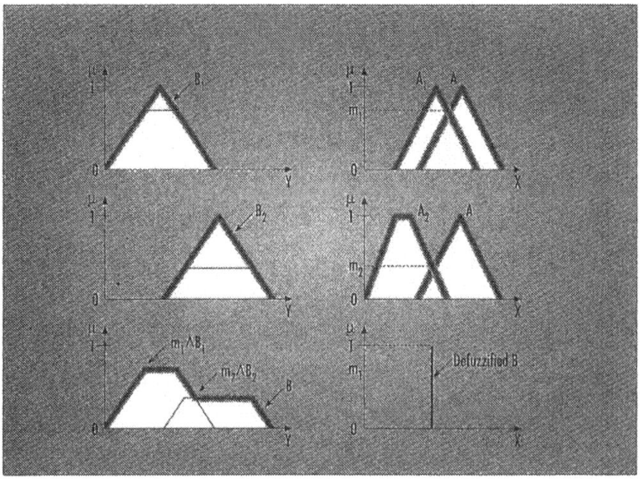

Figure 9. Interpolation of two rules and defuzzification.

product or industrial-control system, the number of rules is on the order of 10 to 20.[7,8]

In applications in which B plays the role of a control variable (an input to a motor, for example), B must be "defuzzified" — converted to a singleton — before it is applied. In current practice, the center-of-gravity method is generally used to achieve defuzzification. Figure 9 shows a simple example of interpolation and defuzzification.

In this figure, the rules are

if X is A_1 then Y is B_1
if X is A_2 then Y is B_2

and the input is

X is A

m_1 and m_2 are, respectively, the degrees to which A matches A_1 and A_2. The expression for the output is

$$\mu_B(v) = \Sigma_i \mu_i \wedge \mu_{Bi}(v)$$

which upon center-of-gravity defuzzification leads to a numerical value of B.

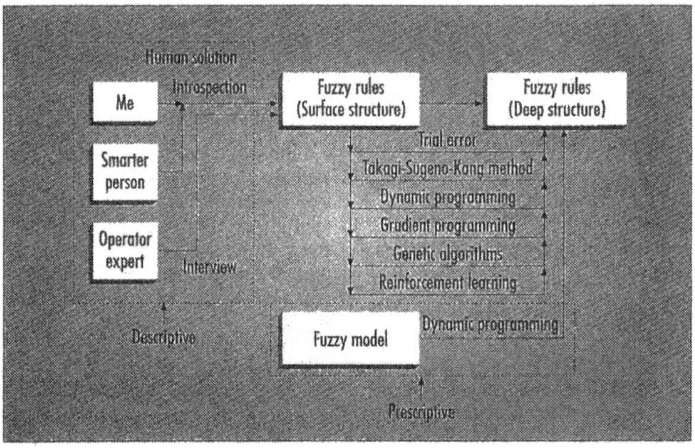

Figure 10. Summary of alternative methods to deduce the deep structures of a set of rules.

INDUCING RULES FROM OBSERVATION

One of the central problems in the applications of fuzzy logic relates to the question, how can rules be inferred from observations; that is, from the knowledge of a collection of I/O pairs? In the context of self-organizing systems, this problem was first formulated and analyzed by T.J. Procyk and E.H. Mamdani. Later, a seminal paper by T. Takagi and M. Sugeno made a major contribution.[9]

During the past several years, researchers have made important advances toward at least a partial solution to the problem by applying neural-network techniques or, more generally, dynamic and gradient programming,[7,10-11] Other promising approaches involve the use of genetic algorithms[12,13] and reinforcement learning.[14] Figure 10 summarizes the ways to derive the deep structure of a set of rules from the surface structure.

A basic idea underlying these approaches involves representing a fuzzy rule-based system as a multilayered structure, such as that shown in Figure 11.[11] In a simple version of this architecture[11] that is rooted in the Takagi-Sugeno-Kang approach,[9] the rules are assumed to be of the form

(if X_1 is A_{1i} and ... and X_m is A_{mi} then $Y = b_i$), $i = 1,\ldots,n$

where b_i are constants (singleton consequents). If the numerical values of X_1, ... X_m are u_{1i}, ... u_{mi}, respectively, and the grades of membership of u_{1i}, ... u_{mi}, in A_{1i}, ... A_{mi} are $\mu_{1i}(u_{1i})$,... $\mu_{mi}(u_{mi})$, then the combined degree to which the input n-tuple $X(u_{1i}, \ldots u_{mi})$ matches the antecedents is taken to be the product

$$m_i = \mu_{1i}(u_{1i}),\ldots \mu_{mi}(u_{mi}),$$

Then, defining the normalized weight w_i as

$$w_i = m_i / m_1 + \ldots + m_m$$

the output is expressed as

$$Y = \Sigma_i w_i b_i$$

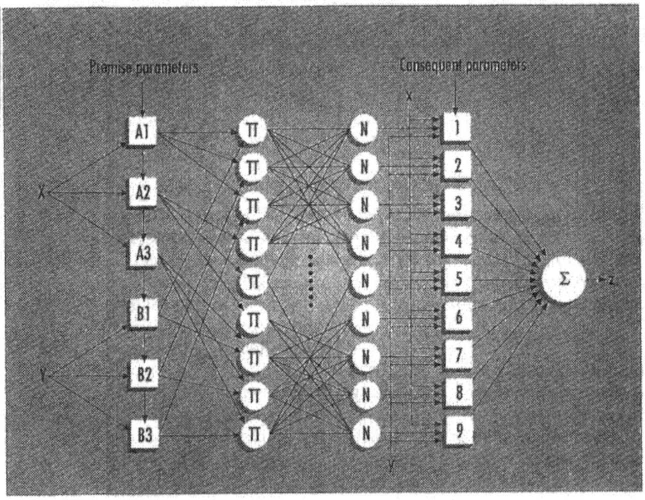

Figure 11. Representing a fuzzy system as a multilayered structure. Π and N denote multipliers and normalizers, respectively.

Note that in this architecture there is no defuzzifier because the inputs X_1, ... X_m are assumed to be singletons.

In the application of gradient programming to this architecture, the membership functions of A_{1i}, ... A_{mi} are assumed to be triangular, trapezoidal, or Gaussian in form. Then, using backward iteration, the values of membership-function parameters are computed from right to left.[10-11] In this way, from the knowledge of I/O pairs we can compute the values of parameters and thereby induce the rules from observations.

The approach sketched here is one way the methodologies of fuzzy rule-based systems and neural networks can be combined, leading to "neurofuzzy" systems. Such systems are growing in number and visibility and are illustrative of the advantages derived from combining soft computing's constituent methodologies. In this context, it is important to note that interpolation and induction of rules from observations are key issues in both fuzzy logic and neurocomputing.

FUZZY BALL AND BEAM PROBLEM

An interesting problem that serves as a testbed for fuzzy logic is a variation on the ball and beam problem. The ball and beam problem, shown in Figure 12, is to transfer the ball from some initial position to a point in a specified positional set-interval and keep it in that interval.

Initially, the ball is placed in the notch at the center of the beam. The purpose of the notch is to constrain the initial value of Θ to be above a specified threshold. The same purpose would be served by a notch at each end of the beam.

In the fuzzy version of the problem, we want to transfer the ball from the notch to a point in a specified positional set-interval $[a_1, a_2]$ and keep it in that interval. Clearly, no approach that is model-dependent — in the sense of requiring a formulation of equations governing system behavior — can be employed because we do not know how to model a ball rolling or sliding on a rug-like surface. This rules out the use of classical control theory as well as any approach that requires simulation.

The set-interval may be viewed as a disjunctive goal. This feature makes it difficult to employ neural-network techniques.

By contrast, the problem is easy to solve with fuzzy logic because it is relatively easy for a human. In fact, the presence of a fuzzy layer makes the ball-and-beam problem easy for humans and difficult or impossible for alternative methodologies. As in most fuzzy-logic applications, the solution is in effect a translation of a human solution into FDCL. A human solution would normally involve seven steps:

1. Compile uncalibrated fuzzy or crisp rules from knowledge of natural laws, to govern the behavior of the ball and beam. For example

   if Θ is negative
    then $\ddot{Y}$ is positive
   if Θ is positive
    then $\ddot{Y}$ is negative
   the more negative Θ,
    the more positive $\ddot{Y}$
   the more positive Θ,
    the more negative $\ddot{Y}$

2. Construct a plan of action (an algorithm), expressed in terms of uncalibrated fuzzy rules of the form

   if *State* is *A* then *Action* is *B*

3. Test the system without trying to solve the problem
4. Calibrate the fuzzy rules in step 2 using metarules, rules that modify other rules
5. Test the algorithm constructed in step 2.
6. Refine the calibrated fuzzy rules derived in step 5.
7. Iterate steps 5 and 6 until the ball stays in the set-interval.

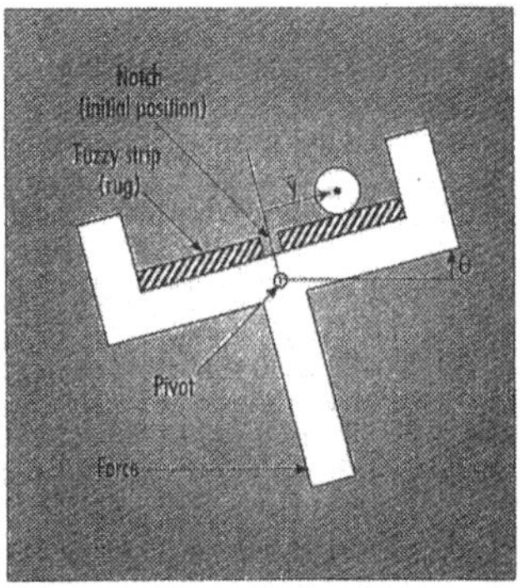

Figure 12. Fuzzy ball and beam problem.

Translating these steps into a collection of fuzzy rules expressed in FDCL is by no means a trivial problem. This is particularly true of the so-called gradual rules[15] of the form

the more X is A the more Y is B

because such rules describe the global behavior of a functional dependency rather than its local properties. However, what is important is that, though it is not easy, it is feasible to translate a human solution into FDCL, whereas it is not feasible to translate it into analytical techniques.

Now suppose you wanted the ball to reach the set interval at some time t and stay there. This is significantly more difficult for a human because it involves a conjunction of two goals:

♦ confine the motion of the ball to the prescribed set-interval $[a_1, a_2]$, and

♦ enter the set-interval at a time t which is constrained to lie in a prescribed temporal set-interval $[t_1, t_2]$.

In this case, formulating a human solution and translating it into FDCL is a real challenge. We do not yet completely understand how to apply fuzzy logic to problems like this. But it is evident that fuzzy logic — used alone or in combination with neurocomputing and probabilistic reasoning — is the methodology of choice when analytic models are impossible or hard to formulate.

Although soft computing is still in its initial stages of evolution, it is rapidly growing in importance and visibility. In the years ahead, soft computing and its principal constituents — fuzzy logic, neurocomputing, and probabilistic reasoning — are likely to emerge as essential tools for the conception, analysis, and design of high MIQ systems. In the final analysis, the role model for soft computing is the human mind. ◆

ACKNOWLEDGMENTS

This research was supported in part by the BISC Program, NASA Grant NCC 2-275, EPRI Agreement RP 8010-34 and MICRO State Program No. 92-180.

REFERENCES

1. L.A. Zadeh, "Fuzzy Sets," *Information and Control*, June 1965, pp. 338-353.
2. L.A. Zadeh, "Outline of a New Approach to the Analysis of Complex Systems and Decision Processes," *IEEE Trans. Systems, Man and Cybernetics*, 1973, pp. 28-44.
3. L.A. Zadeh, "Possibility Theory and Soft Data Analysis," *Mathematical Frontiers of the Social and Policy Sciences*, L. Cobb and R. M. Thrall, eds., Westview Press, Boulder, Colo., 1981, pp.69-129.
4. L.A. Zadeh, "Fuzzy Logic, Neural Networks and Soft Computing," *Comm. ACM*, Mar. 1994, pp. 77-84.
5. L.A. Zadeh, "On the Analysis of Large-Scale Systems," in *Systems Approaches and Environment Problems*, H. Gottinger, ed., Vandenhoeck and Ruprecht, Gottingen, 1974, pp. 23-37.
6. M. Mukaidono, Z.L. Shen, and L. Ding, "Fundamentals of Fuzzy Prolog," *Int'l J. Approximate Reasoning*, No. 3, 1989, pp. 179-193.
7. B. Kosko, *Neural Networks and Fuzzy Systems: A Dynamical Systems Approach to Machine Intelligence*, Prentice-Hall, Englewood Cliffs, N.J., 1991.
8. T. Terano, K. Asai, and M. Sugeno, "Fuzzy Systems Theory and Its Applications," Academic Press, San Diego, Calif., 1992.
9. T. Takagi and M. Sugeno, "Fuzzy Identification of Systems and its Applications to Modeling and Control," *IEEE Trans. Systems, Man, and Cybernetics 15*, 1985, pp. 116-132.
10. C.-T. Lin and C.S. George Lee, "Neural-Network-Based Fuzzy Logic Control and Decision System," *IEEE Trans. Computers*, Dec. 1991, pp. 1320-1336.
11. J.-S.R. Jang, "Self-Learning Fuzzy Controller Based on Temporal Back-Propagation," *IEEE Trans. Neural Networks*, May 1992, pp. 714-723.
12. C.C. Lee, "Fuzzy Logic in Control Systems: Fuzzy Logic Controller, Part I and Part II," *IEEE Trans. Systems, Man, and Cybernetics 20*, 1990, pp. 404-418.
13. C. Karr, "Genetic Algorithms for Fuzzy Controllers," *AI Expert*, Nov. 1991, pp. 26-33.
14. M.A. Lee and H. Takagi, "Integrating Design Stages of Fuzzy Systems Using Genetic Algorithms," *Proc. Int'l Conf. on Fuzzy Systems*, IEEE Press, New York, 1993, pp. 612-617.
15. D. Dubois and H. Prade, "Gradual Inference Rules in Approximate Reasoning," *Information Sciences*, 1992, pp. 103-122.

Lotfi A. Zadeh is professor emeritus of electrical engineering and computer sciences at the University of California, Berkeley, where he is director of the Berkeley Initiative in Soft Computing. His research interests are the theory of fuzzy sets and its applications to artificial intelligence, linguistics, logic, decision analysis, expert systems, and neural networks.

Zadeh is a graduate of the University of Teheran, MIT, and Columbia University. He has received honorary doctorates from the Paul-Sabatier University, France, the State University of New York at Binghamton, Dortmund University, Germany; and the University of Granada and Oviedo, Spain, in recognition of his development of the theory of fuzzy sets. He is a fellow of the IEEE, AAAS, ACM, and AAAI and a member of the National Academy of Engineering and the Russian Academy of Natural Sciences.

Address questions about this article to Zadeh at the CS Div., Dept. of EECS, University of California, Berkeley, Berkeley, Calif. 94720; zadeh@cs.berkeley.edu

Discussion: Probability Theory and Fuzzy Logic Are Complementary Rather Than Competitive

Lotfi A. Zadeh

Computer Science Division
Department of EECS
University of California
Berkeley, CA 94720-1776

The relationship between probability theory and fuzzy logic has long been an object of discussion and some controversy. The position articulated in this article is that probability theory by itself is not sufficient for dealing with uncertainty and imprecision in real-world settings. To enhance its effectiveness, probability theory needs an infusion of concepts and techniques drawn from fuzzy logic—especially the concept of a linguistic variable and the calculus of fuzzy if–then rules. In the final analysis, probability theory and fuzzy logic are complementary rather than competitive.

Traditionally, probability theory has been viewed as the methodology of choice for dealing with uncertainty and imprecision. It is this view that has been called into question by the advent of fuzzy set theory or, as it is commonly referred to today, fuzzy logic.

The central point at issue is the sufficiency of probability theory. The core of the position put forth in this article is that probability theory by itself is not sufficient and that it must be used in concert with fuzzy logic to enhance its effectiveness. In this perspective, probability theory and fuzzy logic are complementary rather than competitive.

What are the connections between fuzzy logic and probability theory? Is fuzzy logic subsumed by probability theory or vice versa? Is there anything that can be done with fuzzy logic that cannot be done equally well or better by probability theory? Is fuzzy logic a disguised form of probability theory? What are the shortcomings of probability theory as a methodology for dealing with uncertainty? What can be done with fuzzy logic that cannot be done with probability theory? These are some of the questions that have been discussed at length in the literature (Buoncristiani 1980; Dubois and Prade 1993; Freeling 1981; Klir 1989; Kosko 1990; Nguyen 1977; Nurmi 1977; Rapoport, Walsten, and Cox 1985; Stallings 1977; Sugeno 1977; Viertl 1987; Yager 1984; Zadeh 1968, 1980, 1981, 1983, 1984, 1988) since the appearance of the first article on fuzzy sets (Zadeh 1965).

The earliest article to consider a connection between fuzzy sets and probabilities was authored by Loginov (1966). In his article, Loginov suggested that the membership function of a fuzzy set may be interpreted as a conditional probability. Similar suggestions were made later by Hisdal (1986), Cheeseman (1986), and many others. In this article, I shall return to Loginov's suggestion at a later point.

In many of the works dealing with the questions just cited, one finds assertions that reflect a lack of familiarity with fuzzy logic or a misunderstanding of what it has to offer. This does not apply to the article by Laviolette, Seaman, Barrett, and Woodall [1995] discussed here. The authors of the article under discussion offer seasoned arguments and carefully worked out examples. Nevertheless there are many significant issues that are not addressed in their article. These issues affect the validity of their analysis and lead to conclusions that are quite different from those arrived at by the authors.

In what follows, I will argue briefly that (a) probability theory and fuzzy logic are distinct, (b) that probability theory is not sufficient by itself for dealing with uncertainty and imprecision, and (c) that probability theory and fuzzy logic are complementary rather than competitive.

1. CONNECTIONS BETWEEN PROBABILITY THEORY AND FUZZY LOGIC

Among the connections and points of tangency between probability theory and fuzzy logic, the principal one is centered on Loginov's suggestion and the closely related viewpoints involving voting and consensus models, random sets, and the plausibility measure of the Dempster–Shafer theory. These connections do not imply that fuzzy logic is subsumed by probability theory or vice versa. In fact, probability theory and fuzzy logic have distinct agendas and different domains of applicability.

Let us start with Loginov's suggestion, which is closely related to the approach used in the article under discussion.

Consider a fuzzy set A in a universe of discourse U—for example, the fuzzy set *young* in the interval $U = [0, 100]$. A is characterized by its membership function $\mu_A: U \rightarrow [0, 1]$, with $\mu_A(u)$ representing the grade of

Reprinted, with permission, from *Technometrics*, 37(3), pp. 271–276. 271

membership of u in A. For example, in the case of *young*, we may have $\mu_{young}(25) = .8$. It is understood that μ_A is context-dependent.

Let X be a random variable that can take the values A and A' (not A), with A and A' interpreted as symbols. In essence, Loginov's suggestion is to interpret $\mu_A(u)$ as the conditional probability, $\Pr(A \mid u)$, that $X = A$ for a given u. More concretely, assume that we have a collection of voters $V = \{V_1, \ldots, V_n\}$, with each V_i voting on whether a given u should be classified as A or not A. Then, $\Pr(A \mid u)$ may be interpreted as the probability that a voter picked at random would classify u as A. In this sense, $\mu_{young}(25) = .8$ means that the probability that a voter picked at random would classify 25 as *young* is .8. Equivalently, .8 may be equated to the proportion of voters in V who classify 25 as *young*. It is this voting—or consensus—model that may be viewed as an interpretation of Loginov's suggestion.

Loginov's suggestion (or interpretation) has serious drawbacks. In the first place, it is unnatural to force a voter to choose either A or not A when A is a fuzzy concept in which the transition from membership to nonmembership is gradual rather than abrupt. More importantly, the consensus model does not make sense when subjective judgment is involved. For example, if the designer of a system states the rule "If pressure is high, then volume is low," how could the meaning of *high* and *low* be determined by consensus? How could the underlying probabilities "be determined subjectively or estimated by observation of human operators"(p. 000), as suggested in the article under discussion? How would one give a probabilistic answer to the question "In your perspective, what is the degree to which Mary is tall?" or "What is the degree to which Mary resembles Cindy?" What must be considered is that for humans it is generally much easier to estimate grades of membership or degrees of possibility rather than probabilities. This is one of the reasons why Loginov's interpretation—though known for a long time—has found little use in applications of fuzzy logic.

An interpretation of the membership function that is closely related to Loginov's involves the concept of a random set—that is, a set-valued random variable. More specifically, in the context of the voting model, assume that a voter V_i classifies u as A if u falls in an interval A_i. For example, 25 is classified as *young* if $25 \in [0, 30]$.

In this way, the collection of voters $\{V_1, \ldots, V_N\}$ induces a collection of intervals $\{A_1, \ldots, A_N\}$. It follows that to say (a) that V_i classifies u as A is equivalent to saying that $u \in A_i$ and (b) that picking a voter at random from $\{V_1, \ldots, V_N\}$ is equivalent to picking an interval at random from $\{A_1, \ldots, A_N\}$.

Because the A_i may not be distinct, the uniform probability distribution on $\{V_1, \ldots, V_N\}$ induces, in general, a nonuniform probability distribution $(p_1, \ldots, p_K)$ on the subset of distinct intervals, say $\{A_1^*, \ldots, A_K^*\}$, of $\{A_1, \ldots, A_N\}$. Then, the set-valued random variable $\{(A_1^*, p_1), \ldots, (A_K^*, p_K)\}$ may be viewed as a random set. In terms of this random set, $\mu_A(u)$ may be interpreted as the probability of coverage of u by $\{A_1^*, \ldots, A_K^*\}$. More specifically, if

$$\begin{aligned} a_j &= 1 \quad \text{if } u \in A_j^* \\ &= 0 \quad \text{if } u \notin A_j^*, \end{aligned}$$

then $\mu_A(u) = a_1 p_1 + \cdots + a_K p_K$.

In a more general approach, which was developed in detail by Orlov (1980), Goodman and Nguyen (1985), Wang and Sanchez (1982), and others, the random set is generated by the α cuts (or level sets) of A. More specifically, an α cut, A_α, of A is a nonfuzzy set defined by $A_\alpha = \{u \mid \mu_A(u) \geq \alpha\}, 0 \leq \alpha \leq 1$. The α cuts are taken to be the constituents of a random set, with α assumed to be uniformly distributed over the interval [0, 1].

In this way, a fuzzy set A may be derived from a random set. In actuality, however, the same result can be achieved without bringing randomness into the picture. More specifically, it is well known that a fuzzy set can be generated from its α cuts both disjunctively and additively. To show this, let $\mu_{A_\alpha}(u)$ denote the membership function of A_α—which, because A_α is nonfuzzy, coincides with the characteristic function of A_α. Then, the membership function of A may be expressed in terms of the membership functions of the A_α (a) disjunctively as $\mu_A(u) = \sup_\alpha(\alpha \wedge \mu_{A_\alpha}(u)), 0 \leq \alpha \leq 1$, where $\wedge$ denotes min, and (b) additively as

$$\mu_A(u) = \int_0^1 \mu_{A_\alpha}(u)\, d\alpha.$$

The additive representation is illustrated in Figures 1 and 2.

The random set representation of a fuzzy set is of substantial theoretical interest. It has not played a significant role in the applications of fuzzy logic largely because of the difficulty of dealing with random sets.

In another direction, the random set representation underlies the connection between the concept of possibility

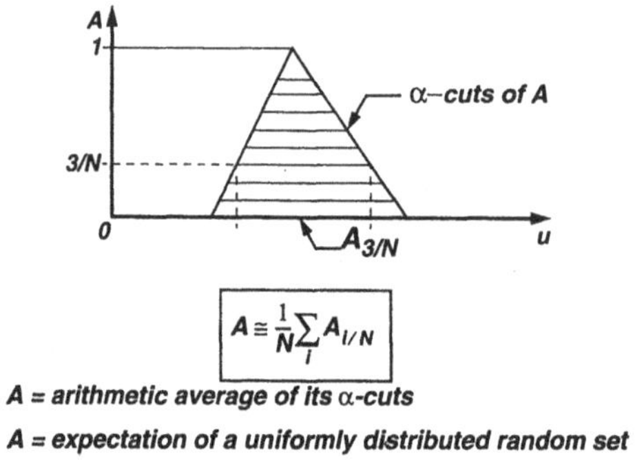

Figure 1. Additive Decomposition of a Fuzzy Set. The α cuts are discretized.

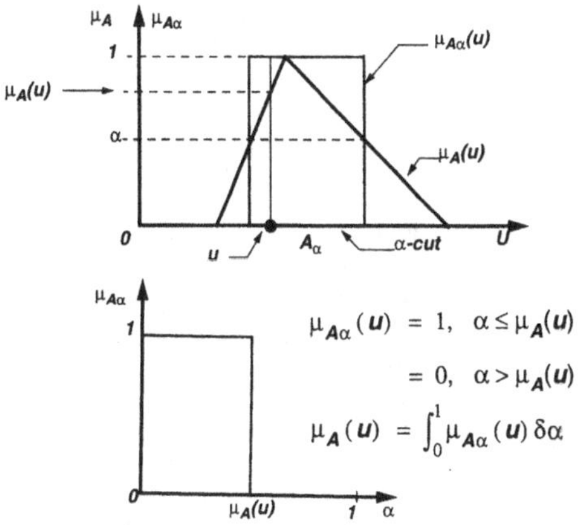

$$\mu_{A\alpha}(u) = 1, \quad \alpha \le \mu_A(u)$$
$$= 0, \quad \alpha > \mu_A(u)$$
$$\mu_A(u) = \int_0^1 \mu_{A\alpha}(u)\,\delta\alpha$$

Figure 2. Additive Decomposition of a Fuzzy Set. The α cuts form a continuum.

measure in fuzzy logic and the concept of plausibility measure in the Dempster–Shafer theory (Shafer 1976). Specifically, the two concepts coincide when the focal sets in the Dempster–Shafer theory are consonant—that is, nested. In this case, the focal sets may be regarded as the α cuts of a fuzzy set, and the Dempster–Shafer structure may be viewed as a random set whose constituents are the focal sets. As in the case of the random set representation of a fuzzy set, however, randomness in the Dempster–Shafer theory may be replaced by an additive representation (Zadeh 1986).

In summary, it is possible, in a restricted way, to represent a fuzzy set as a random set or as a disjunctive or additive combination of nonfuzzy sets. This is illustrated in Figure 3. The important point to note is that the connection between fuzzy sets and random sets in no way implies that fuzziness and randomness are identical concepts or that fuzzy logic and probability theory have the same foundation and similar agendas.

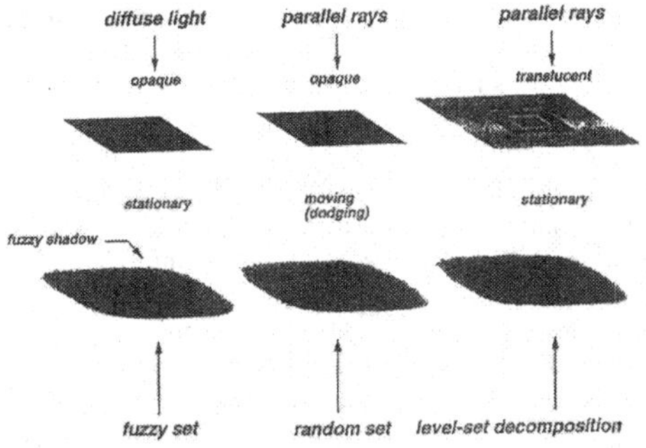

Figure 3. Optical Generation of a Fuzzy Set by a Random Set and Additive Decomposition.

2. LIMITATIONS OF PROBABILITY THEORY

In the article under discussion, it is suggested that (a) probability theory can do anything that can be done with fuzzy logic and (b) that there would be many more applications of probability theory in areas in which fuzzy logic has been used with success if probabilists and statisticians were more adept at "selling" their tools.

In reality, the applications of fuzzy logic are growing rapidly in number and variety largely because fuzzy logic fills a definite need for ways of dealing with problems in which the sources of imprecision and uncertainty do not lend themselves to analysis by conventional methods. In essence, what fuzzy logic offers—and what is clearly a useful offering—is a methodology for computing with words rather than numbers.

In this perspective, let us examine—as was done by Zadeh (1986)—the reasons why classical probability theory falls short of providing a comprehensive methodology for dealing with uncertainty and imprecision.

1. Probability theory does not support the concept of a fuzzy event. Simple examples of propositions involving fuzzy events are as follows: tomorrow will be a warm day; there will be a strong earthquake in the near future; the prices will stabilize in the long run.

The incapability of dealing with fuzzy events places a roadblock to applying probability theory to inference from fuzzy premises that represent real-world knowledge. In this connection, it is important to note that in the case of propagation of probabilities in belief networks a problem that arises is that the events associated with nodes are fuzzy rather than crisp. For example a node labeled *arthritis* may be linked to nodes labeled *swollen joints* and *painful joints*. It is a common practice to associate conditional numerical probabilities with such links. But the question is: What is the meaning of such probabilities? A related question is: How can the independence of fuzzy events be defined? These questions are not raised—much less answered—in the theory of Bayesian belief networks.

2. Probability theory offers no techniques for dealing with fuzzy quantifiers like *many, most, several, few*.

3. Probability theory does not provide a system for computing with fuzzy probabilities expressed as *likely, unlikely, not very likely*, and so forth. Such probabilities are not second-order probabilities.

4. Probability theory does not provide methods for estimating fuzzy probabilities. Subjective probability theory serves the purposes of elicitation rather than estimation. It provides no answers to questions exemplified by "What is the probability that my car may be stolen?" In this connection, it should be noted that, in most instances, subjective probabilities are rooted in fuzzy perceptions of frequency-based probabilities.

5. Probability theory is not sufficiently expressive as a meaning-representation language. For example, what is the meaning of "It is not likely that there will be a sharp increase in the price of oil in the near future"?

6. The limited expressive power of probability theory makes it difficult to analyze problems in which the data are described in fuzzy terms. Consider, for example, the following questions:

a. An urn contains approximately 20 balls of various sizes of which several are large, a few are small, and the rest are of medium size. What is the probability that a ball drawn at random is neither large nor small?
b. A variable X can take the values *small, medium*, and *large* with respective probabilities *low, high*, and *low*. What is the expected value of X? What is the probability that X is *not large*?

Turning to the applications in control, in the article under discussion the authors consider a very simple example in which the rules are of the form if X is A then Y is B. In most practical applications, however, the rules are of the more general form if X_i is A_{ij} and ... and X_n is A_{in}, then Y is B_i, $i = 1, 2, \ldots, m$. In this setting, the problem of interpolation is that of computing B in Y is B when X_1 is $A_1, \ldots, X_n$ is A_n.

How would the authors solve this problem? How would they treat problems in which conjunction and disjunction are specified t norms and s norms rather than min and max?

In general, probability theory is not an appropriate tool to use in the solution of deterministic control problems. A case in point is the parallel-parking problem. How would the authors solve this problem? A more difficult dynamic motion-planning problem is the fuzzy ball-and-beam problem (Zadeh 1994a), which is illustrated in Figure 4. In this case, the problem is to transfer the ball from an initial position at the center to a point in a specified interval $[a_1, a_2]$ on the beam at a time t, which is specified to be in an interval $[t_1, t_2]$. The beam is covered with a strip of fuzzy felt to complicate the formulation of equations of motion and thereby preclude the possibility of simulation.

Going beyond control, one of the principal tools in the tool chest of fuzzy logic is a language for manipulating a wide variety of both categorical (i.e., unqualified)

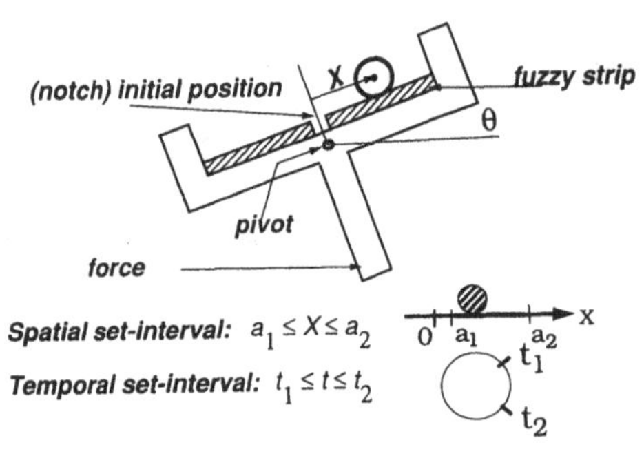

Figure 4. The Fuzzy Ball-and-Beam Problem. The ball rolls/slides on a fuzzy strip, which is attached to a beam.

and qualified rules. The latter rules may be probability-qualified, as in if X is A then it is likely that Y is B; possibility-qualified, as in if X is A then it is possible that Y is B; truth-qualified, as in (if X is A then Y is B) is quite true; usuality-qualified as in usually (if X is A then Y is B); or with exceptions, as in if X is A then Y is B unless Z is C.

The question is: How can the authors process rules of this form using standard probability theory? For example, how can they infer an answer to the following question:

usually (X is not very small)
usually (X is not very large)

X is?

These and many other questions that could be posed are intended to make the point that classical probability theory has definite limitations—limitations that stem for the most part from an avoidance of issues and problems in which fuzziness lies at the center rather than on the periphery. What has to be recognized is that in real-world settings such issues and problems are the rule rather than the exception.

3. COMPLEMENTARITY OF PROBABILITY THEORY AND FUZZY LOGIC

In the article under discussion, the authors take the position that fuzzy logic does not have much to add to what can be done through the use of standard probability-based techniques. The thrust of our arguments is that this is not the case.

Clearly, classical probability theory has been and continues to be employed with remarkable success in those fields in which the systems are mechanistic, and human reasoning, perceptions, and emotions do not play a significant role. Such is the case in statistical mechanics, theories of turbulence, quantum mechanics, communication systems, evolutionary programming, and related fields.

What should be recognized, however, is that classical probability theory is much less effective in those fields in which the dependencies between variables are not well defined, the knowledge of probabilities is imprecise and/or incomplete, the systems are not mechanistic, and human reasoning, perceptions, and emotion do play an important role. This is the case, in varying degrees, in economics, pattern recognition, group decision analysis, speech and handwriting recognition, expert systems, weather and earthquake forecasting, and analysis of evidence.

To enhance its effectiveness in dealing with systems of this kind, probability theory needs an infusion of fuzzy logic. Such an infusion serves to fuzzify—and hence generalize—some of the most basic concepts of probability theory. Among such concepts are those of probability, event, random sample, causality, independence, stationarity, similarity, and convergence. This is the sense in which the complementarity of probability theory and fuzzy logic should be understood.

In a reverse direction, the concepts of measure, cardinality, and probability have played and are certain to play an increasingly important role in fuzzy logic. This is particularly true of the concepts of usuality and dispositionality, especially in the context of common-sense reasoning and expert systems.

Today, the most visible applications of fuzzy logic are related to control, especially in the realms of consumer products and industrial systems. In such applications, what fuzzy logic offers is an effective methodology for exploiting the tolerance for imprecision, uncertainty, and partial truth to achieve tractability, robustness, and low solution cost. The key concept in this methodology is that of a linguistic variable—that is, a variable whose values are words rather than numbers (Zadeh 1973). The concept of a linguistic variable is the point of departure for the development of the calculus of fuzzy if–then rules.

In coming years, the concept of a linguistic variable and the calculus of fuzzy if–then rules are likely to play key roles in the symbiosis of probability theory and fuzzy logic. The development of a symbiotic relationship between probability theory and fuzzy logic should be an important objective for all of us.

4. CONCLUDING REMARKS

I should like to compliment the authors of the article under discussion for arguing with conviction and cogency their case for the sufficiency of standard probability theory and statistical methods.

What has to be recognized, however, is that in science as in other domains of human activity there is a tendency to be nationalistic—to embrace a particular methodology and take a skeptical view of the other methodologies that are asking for a place at the table.

In many cases there is more to be gained from cooperation than from arguments over which methodology is best. A case in point is the concept of *soft computing* (Zadeh 1994b). Soft computing is not a methodology—it is a partnership of methodologies that function effectively in an environment of imprecision and/or uncertainty and are aimed at exploiting the tolerance for imprecision, uncertainty, and partial truth to achieve tractability, robustness, and low solution costs. At this juncture, the principal constituents of soft computing are fuzzy logic, neurocomputing, and probabilistic reasoning, with the latter subsuming genetic algorithms, evidential reasoning, and parts of learning and chaos theories.

Although the article under discussion argues in favor of sufficiency of probability theory, it is in fact a significant contribution to the development of a better understanding of how probability theory and fuzzy logic can act in concert. In this sense, it is consistent with the aims of soft computing.

A final note—a minor matter of semantics: In the article under discussion, the authors employ interchangeably the terms *fuzzy* and *vague*. In fact, fuzzy and vague are distinct concepts, as was pointed out by Zadeh (1979). More specifically, a proposition is fuzzy if it contains terms that are labels of fuzzy sets. For example, "I will be back in a few minutes" is a fuzzy proposition by virtue of the fuzziness of *few*.

A proposition is vague if it is insufficiently specific for a specified purpose. For example, "I will be back sometime" is vague if it is insufficiently specific. An example of a common vague proposition is "Use with adequate ventilation." Vagueness is a property of propositions rather than predicates and, in most cases, is purpose dependent. Note that a proposition may be vague without being fuzzy. Usually a vague proposition is fuzzy, but the converse is not generally true.

ACKNOWLEDGMENTS

Research was supported in part by NASA Grant NCC 2-275, EPRI Agreement RP 8010-34, and the BISC (Berkeley Initiative in Soft Computing) Program.

REFERENCES

Buoncristiani, J. (1980), *Probability on Fuzzy Sets*, unpublished Ph.D. thesis, Boston University, Dept. of Mathematics.

Cheeseman, P. (1986), "Probability Versus Fuzzy Reasoning," in *Uncertainty in Artificial Intelligence*, eds. L. N. Kanal and L. F. Lemmer, Amsterdam: Elsevier, pp. 85–102.

Dubois, D., and Prade, H. (1993), "Fuzzy Sets and Probability: Misunderstandings, Bridges, and Gaps," in *Second IEEE International Conference on Fuzzy Systems (FUZZ-IEEE '93)*, Piscataway, NJ: Institute of Electrical and Electronic Engineers, pp. 1059–1068.

Freeling, A. N. S. (1981), *Possibilities Versus Fuzzy Probabilities—Two Alternative Decision Aids*, Tech. Report 81–6, Decision Science Consortium Inc., Washington, DC.

Goodman, I. R., and Nguyen, H. T. (1985), *Uncertain Models for Knowledge-Based Systems*, Amsterdam: North-Holland.

Hisdal, E. (1986), "Infinite-Valued Logic Based on Two-Valued Logic and Probability, Part 1.1. Difficulties With Present-Day Fuzzy Set Theory and Their Resolution in the TEE Model," *International Journal of Man-Machine Studies*, 25, 89–111.

Klir, G. J. (1989), "Is There More to Uncertainty Than Some Probability Theorists Might Have Us Believe?" *International Journal of General Systems*, 15, 347–378.

Kosko, B. (1990), "Fuzziness Vs. Probability," *International Journal of General Systems*, 17, 211–240.

Laviolette, M., J. W. Seaman, Jr., Barrett, J. D., and Woodall, W. H. (1995), *Technometrics*, 37, 249–259.

Loginov, V. J. (1966), "Probability Treatment of Zadeh Membership Functions and Their Use in Pattern Recognition," *Engineering Cybernetics*, 68–69.

Nguyen, H. T. (1977), "On Fuzziness and Linguistic Probabilities," *Journal of Mathematical Analysis and Applications*, 61, 658–671.

Nurmi, H. (1977), "Probability and Fuzziness: Some Methodological Considerations," unpublished paper presented at the *Sixth Research Conference on Subjective Probability, Utility, and Decision Making*, Warszawa.

Orlov, A. I. (1980) *Problems of Optimization and Fuzzy Variables*, Moscow: Znaniye.

Rapoport, A., Wallsten, T., and Cox, J. (1985), "Direct and Indirect Scaling of Membership Function of Probability Phrases," Tech. Report 174, University of North Carolina, Psychometric Laboratory.

Shafer, G. (1976), *A Mathematical Theory of Evidence*, Princeton, NJ: Princeton University Press.

Stallings, W. (1977), "Fuzzy Set Theory Versus Bayesian Statistics," *IEEE Transactions on Systems, Man and Cybernetics*, SMC-7, 216–219.

Sugeno, M. (1977), "Fuzzy Measures and Fuzzy Integrals: A Survey," in *Fuzzy Automata and Decision Processes*, eds. M. M. Gupta, G. N. Saridis, and B. R. Gaines, Amsterdam: North-Holland, pp. 89–102.

Viertl, R. (1987), "Is It Necessary to Develop a Fuzzy Bayesian Inference?" in *Probability and Bayesian Statistics*, ed. R. Viertl, New York: Plenum, pp. 471–475.

Wang, P. Z., and Sanchez, E. (1982), "Treating a Fuzzy Subset as a Projectable Random Set," in *Fuzzy Information and Decision Processes*, eds. M. M. Gupta and E. Sanchez, Amsterdam: North-Holland, pp. 213–220.

Yager, R. R. (1984), "Probabilities From Fuzzy Observations," *Information Sciences*, 32, 1–31.

Zadeh, L. A. (1965), "Fuzzy Sets," *Information and Control*, 8, 338–353.

_____ (1968), "Probability Measures of Fuzzy Events," *Journal of Mathematical Analysis and Applications*, 23, 421–427.

_____ (1973), "Outline of a New Approach to the Analysis of Complex System and Decision Processes," *IEEE Transactions on Systems, Man, and Cybernetics*, SMC-3, 28–44.

_____ (1979), "PRUF—A Meaning Representation Language for Natural Languages," *International Journal of Man-Machines Studies*, 10, 395–460.

_____ (1980), "Fuzzy Sets vs. Probability" (correspondence item), *Proceedings of the IEEE*, 68, 421.

_____ (1981), "Fuzzy Probabilities and Their Role in Decision Analysis," *Proceedings of the MIT/ONR Workshop on* C^3, Cambridge, MA: MIT.

_____ (1983), "Is Possibility Different From Probability?" Human Systems Management, 3, 253–254.

_____ (1984), "Fuzzy Probabilities," *Information Processing and Management*, 19, 148–153.

_____ (1986), "A Simple View of the Dempster–Shafer Theory of Evidence and Its Implications for the Rule of Combination of Evidence," *AI Magazine*, 7, 85–90.

_____ (1988), "On the Treatment of Uncertainty in AI," *The Knowledge Engineering Review*, 2, Pt. I, 81–85.

_____ (1994a), "Soft Computing and Fuzzy Logic," *IEEE Software*, 11, 48–56.

_____ (1994b), "Fuzzy Logic, Neural Networks and Soft Computing," *Communications of the ACM*, 37, 77–84.

Zwick R. (1985), "Fuzzy Probabilities," unpublished paper presented at the *18th Annual Mathematical Psychology Meeting*, La Jolla, CA.

The Birth and Evolution of Fuzzy Logic (FL), Soft Computing (SC) and Computing with Words (CW): A Personal Perspective

Lotfi A. Zadeh

Computer Science Division, Department of EECS
University of California
Berkeley, CA 94720-1776

Text of a lecture presented on the occasion of the award of Doctorate Honoris Causa, University of Oviedo, Spain.

Right Honourable and most distinguished Rector, most worthy officers of the University, dear professors, researchers, and students, Ladies and Gentlemen,

It is a great honor for me to stand here today as a recipient of the Doctorate Honoris Causa. The award of the Doctorate Honoris Causa has a special significance for me. First, because Spain is a country in which the theory of fuzzy sets and its concomitants have been embraced by many prominent mathematicians, scientists and engineers; and second, because Spain and Spanish people have always occupied a very warm spot in my heart. One cannot but admire the richness of Spanish culture and its intellectual traditions. Spain has produced and it continuing to produce men and women who have contributed and are contributing so much to arts, music, literature, and science. But what touches me most is the warmth and generosity of the Spanish people. In today's world of turbulence and conflict, these are qualities that are in short supply.

In my lecture, I should like to sketch my perception of the events which have shaped the birth and evolution of fuzzy logic and its conceptual offsprings — soft computing and computing with words. Let me begin by clarifying the meaning of fuzzy logic, since there are many misconceptions about what it is and how it relates to other methodologies which, like fuzzy logic, address the issues of imprecision, uncertainty and approximate reasoning.

The term fuzzy logic has two different meanings. In its narrow sense, fuzzy logic, or FLn for short, is a logical system which is aimed at a formalization of modes of reasoning which are approximate rather than exact. In this sense, fuzzy logic is an extension of multivalued logical systems, but its agenda is quite different both in spirit and in substance.

In its wide sense, fuzzy logic, or FLw for short, is coextensive with the theory of fuzzy sets, that is, a theory of classes with unsharp boundaries. FLw is much broader than FLn and contains the latter as one of its branches. Today, the term *fuzzy logic* is used for the most part in its wide sense. This is the sense in which fuzzy logic, or FL for short, it will be used in the sequel.

The basic ideas underlying fuzzy logic were described in my first paper on fuzzy sets which was published in 1965. This paper and my subsequent papers on fuzzy sets drew a mixed reaction. Some academics and especially the late mathematicians Richard Bellman and Grigori Moisil, greeted my ideas with enthusiasm. For the most part, however, what I encountered was skepticism and , on occasion, downright hostility. Today, thirty years later, the controversy surrounding fuzzy logic is still with us, though not to the same degree. The numerous applications of fuzzy logic are too visible to be ignored. However, there are still some who remain unconvinced that fuzzy logic has something important to offer. The Cartesian tradition of respect for what is quantitative and precise, and disdain for what is qualitative and imprecise is too deep-seated to be abandoned without a fight. The basic tenet of this tradition was stated succinctly by Lord Kelvin — one of the outstanding intellects of the 19th century — in 1883. He wrote, "In physical science a first essential step in the direction of learning any subject is to find principles of numerical reckoning and practicable methods for measuring some quality connected with it. I often say that when you can measure what you are speaking about and express it in numbers, you know something about it; but when you cannot measure it, when you cannot express it in numbers, your knowledge is of a meagre and unsatisfactory kind: it may be the beginning of knowledge but you have scarcely, in your thoughts, advanced to the state of science, whatever the matter may be."

Reflecting this tradition, Professor Rudolf Kalman — one of the foremost contributors to system theory and control — had this to say about my work in 1972.

> "I would like to comment briefly on Professor Zadeh's presentation. His proposals could be severely, ferociously, even brutally criticized from a technical point view. This would be out of place here. But a blunt question remains: Is Professor Zadeh presenting important ideas or is he indulging in wishful thinking?
>
> No doubt Professor Zadeh's enthusiasm for fuzziness has been reinforced by the prevailing political climate in the U.S. — one of unprecedented permissiveness. 'Fuzzification' is a kind of scientific permissiveness; it tends to result in socially appealing slogans unaccompanied by the discipline of hard scientific work and patient observation.
>
> Let me say quite categorically that there is no such thing as a fuzzy scientific concept, in my opinion."

In a similar vein, a colleague of mine, Professor William Kahan, commented in 1975:

> "Fuzzy theory is wrong, wrong, and pernicious. I can not think of any problem that could not be solved better by ordinary logic. What Zadeh is saying is the same sort of things 'Technology got us into this mess and now it can't get us out.' Well, technology did not get us into this mess. Greed and weakness and ambivalence got us into this mess. What we need is more logical thinking, not less. The danger of fuzzy theory is that it will encourage the sort of imprecise thinking that has brought us so much trouble."

Despite the skepticism and hostility, there is, today, a rapidly growing international community of mathematicians, scientists and engineers who are actively engaged in the development of fuzzy logic and its applications.

To cite just one statistic, the number of papers on fuzzy logic and its applications published worldwide was approximately 600 in 1988, 1,200 in 1991, and is close to 2400 at this juncture. Of these papers, about 1500 relate to fuzzy control. I will have more to say about fuzzy control at a later point.

The country in which fuzzy logic and fuzzy-logic-based products have highest visibility is Japan. In Japan, interest in fuzzy logic goes back to 1968, when Professors K. Asai, K. Tanaka, T. Terano and their students began to publish papers on fuzzy automata and learning systems. By 1972, there were regular meetings of scientists and engineers who were working on fuzzy logic and its applications. A landmark event was the USA-Japan Seminar on Fuzzy Sets and their Applications which took place in Berkeley in 1974. After that, the tempo of advancement of fuzzy logic and its applications began to accelerate, culminating in the IFSA (International Fuzzy Systems Association) Congress in Tokyo in 1987. At that Congress, Matsushita announced the first consumer product using fuzzy logic — a showerhead. Simultaneously, but in another realm, the Sendai Subway System, which employed a fuzzy logic controller designed and built by Hitachi, began to operate. The Sendai Subway System is widely regarded as one of the most successful applications of fuzzy logic.

In Europe, interest in fuzzy logic became visible in the early 70's. A landmark event was the seminal work on fuzzy control by Professor E. H. Mamdani and his students at Queen Mary College in London. This work led to the first important industrial application — the cement kiln control — which was developed by Dr. H. Ostergaard in association with the F.L.Smidth Co. in Copenhagen in the late 70's.

Although there were some important practical applications made in Europe starting in the middle and late 70's, the major contributions were in the realm of foundations and theory. In this context, I should like to pay my tribute to the late Professor Arnold Kaufmann whose seminal books on fuzzy logic have had a profound impact.

There is another man that I should like to pay my tribute to; that is Professor Enric Trillas who is serving as Secretario General del Plan Nacional de Investigacion Cientifica y Desarrollo Tecnologico and who in 1977, when I first met him, was a Professor of Mathematics at the School of Architecture, Polytechnic University of Barcelona. Professor Trillas initiated research on fuzzy logic and its applications in Spain and it is his vision and support that made Spain one of the leading centers of fuzzy-logic-oriented activity in Europe. Today, there are many mathematicians, scientists, and engineers in Spain who through their contributions to fuzzy logic and its applications have achieved national and international prominence. It gives me great satisfaction to be able to say that some of them have spent time at Berkeley as Visiting Scholars under my sponsorship. Professor Maria Gil, who is here at the University of Oviedo, is a member of this group, and was an active participant in fuzzy-logic-related research at Berkeley. We miss her presence very much.

What are the basic ideas underlying fuzzy logic, soft computing and computing with words? What are their potentialities and limitations? These are some of the issues which I should like to focus on in my lecture.

First, a bit of history. Although I am an electrical engineer by training, I have always been a strong believer in the power of mathematics. To me, it was an article of faith that to almost any problem there is a mathematical solution. Like many other workers in systems analysis, information analysis and control, I was driven by a quest for precision, rigor and mathematical sophistication. There was no doubt in my mind that this was the right path to follow.

However, in the course of writing a book with Professor Charles Desoer on linear system theory, I began to realize that there are many concepts in system theory that do not lend themselves to precise definition. For example, one can give a precise definition of a linear system, a stable system, a time-invariant system, etc. But how can one define what is meant by a decentralized system, a slowly-varying system, a reliable system, etc.?

In trying to formulate such definitions, I began to realize that the problem lay in the Aristotelian framework of classical mathematics — a framework which is intolerant of imprecision and partial truth. In essence, a basic assumption in classical mathematics is that a concept must admit of precise definition which partitions the class of all objects into two classes: (i) those objects which are instances of the concept; and (ii)those which are not, with no borderline cases allowed. For example, a function is either continuous or discontinuous; it cannot be continuous to a degree. Similarly, a matrix is either symmetric or not symmetric; it cannot be somewhat symmetric or more or less symmetric or symmetric to a degree. By the same token, a paper published in a mathematical journal is expected to contain precisely stated definitions, assumptions and theorems. Generally, a paper would not be acceptable for publication if its conclusions are stated as assertions which are not unequivocally true.

In sharp contrast to the idealized world of mathematics, our perception of the real world is pervaded by concepts which do not have sharply defined boundaries, e.g., *tall, fat, many, most, slowly, old, familiar, relevant, much larger than, kind*, etc. A key assumption in fuzzy logic is that the denotations of such concepts are fuzzy sets, that is, classes of objects in which the transition from membership to non-membership is gradual rather than abrupt. Thus, if A is a fuzzy set in a universe of discourse U, then every member of U has a grade of membership in A which is usually taken to be a number between 0 and 1, with 1 and 0 representing full membership and non-membership, respectively. The function which associates with each object its grade of membership in A is called the *membership function of* A. This function defines A as a fuzzy subset of U.

It is important to observe that there is an intimate connection between fuzziness and complexity. Thus, a basic characteristic of the human brain, a characteristic shared in varying degrees with all information processing systems, is its limited capacity to handle classes of very high cardinality, that is, classes having a very large number of members. Consequently, when we are presented with a class of very high cardinality, we tend to group its elements together into subclasses in such a way as to reduce the complexity of the information processing task involved. When a point is reached where the cardinality of the class of subclasses exceeds the information handling capacity of the human brain, the boundaries of subclasses are forced to become imprecise and fuzziness becomes a manifestation of this imprecision. This is the reason why the limited vocabulary we have for the description of colors makes it necessary that the names of colors such as red, green blue, purple, etc., be in effect, names of fuzzy rather than non-fuzzy sets. This is also why natural languages, which are much higher in level than programming languages, are fuzzy whereas programming languages are not.

I use the term *granulation* to refer to the process of forming fuzzy classes of objects which are drawn together by similarity. Granulation is one of the most basic facets of human cognition. As was alluded to above, granulation is necessitated by the limited ability of humans to resolve and/or store details. In this perspective, fuzziness and granulation are concomitants of complexity and play a pivotal role in exploiting the tolerance for imprecision to achieve tractability, robustness and low solution cost.

An important implication of this observation is that with the rapid increase in the complexity of information processing tasks which computers are called upon to perform, we are reaching a point where computers will have to be designed for processing of fuzzy information. In fact, it is the capability to manipulate fuzzy concepts that distinguishes human intelligence from machine intelligence of current generation computers. Without such capability, we cannot build machines that can summarize non-stereotypical stories, translate well from one natural language to another, or perform many other tasks that humans can do with ease because of their ability to granulate and manipulate the resulting fuzzy concepts.

To be able to say more about fuzzy logic and its applications, I will have to clarify some of the issues underlying the concept of a fuzzy set. For this purpose, let us consider a concept, say *kind person*, which does not admit of a precise definition in terms of a collection of necessary and sufficient conditions. Such a concept may be defined extensionally by associating with each individual who is a member of a universe of discourse U, his or her grade of membership in the fuzzy set of kind persons.

For example, the grade of membership of Arnold might be 0.6, while that of Carol might be 0.9. These numbers would be elicited from an observer by asking the question "On the scale from 0 to 1, to what degree is Carol kind?" What is important to note is that the numbers in question are subjective in nature. In the case of Carol, for example, the number 0.9 would not be interpreted as a measure of consensus, that is, as the proportion of individuals who when asked if Carol is kind would respond in the affirmative; nor would 0.9 be interpreted as the probability or the belief that Carol is kind. In this connection, it should be noted that, in general, it is much easier for humans to estimate numerical grades of membership than to estimate numerical probabilities.

In the case of a quantifiable concept, the membership function may be represented as a function of one or more measurable attributes. For example, in the case of a *young person*, the attribute in question would be *Age*. In this case, the universe of discourse may be taken to be the interval [0,120], and the grade of membership in the class of young people of a person who is, say, 35 years old might be 0.6.

Clearly, the concepts *kind* person and *young* person are both context-dependent and subjective. Some concepts are more context-dependent than others. For example, *many* is more context-dependent than *several*, and *small* is more context-dependent than *circular*. As will be seen at a later point, in the theory of fuzzy sets context-dependence plays a key role in the concept of so-called linguistic variable.

It should be noted that grade of membership may be interpreted as the truth value of a predicate in multivalued logic. For example, the grade of membership of Carol in the class of kind persons may be equated to the truth value of the proposition "Carol is kind." However, the development of the theory fuzzy sets and fuzzy logic has followed a path quite different from that of multivalued logic. As an illustration, in the context of the theory of fuzzy sets it is natural to ask the question "What is a convex fuzzy set, or what is meant by the convex hull of a fuzzy set?" This would not be a natural question in multivalued logic. In a more general setting, the theory of fuzzy sets has stimulated the development of a new branch of topology called *fuzzy topology*, which is a sophisticated mathematical theory in the classical tradition. The conceptual framework of fuzzy topology is related to that of the theory of fuzzy sets but not to multivalued logic.

Fuzzy topology may be viewed as an instance of a characteristic of fuzzy logic which may be referred to as *fuzzifiability*. More specifically, any theory, X, may be fuzzified by replacing the concept of a set in X by the more general concept of a fuzzy set. In this way, topology can be generalized to fuzzy topology; algebra to fuzzy algebra; mathematical programming to fuzzy mathematical programming; logic to fuzzy logic (in its narrow sense); control to fuzzy control, and so on. What is gained by fuzzification is, in the main, greater generality and better rapport with reality. It may not be an exaggeration to expect that eventually most theories and concepts will be fuzzified in this manner.

By providing a body of computationally-oriented concepts and techniques for dealing with uncertainty and imprecision, fuzzy logic comes much closer to serving as a descriptive model of human reasoning than traditional logical systems. In this way, fuzzy logic opens the door to many applications which fall beyond the reach of conventional logic-based methods as well as methods based on classical probability theory. I will not attempt to be more specific at this point by listing the many important applications of fuzzy logic which have been made over the past few years in many countries, including Spain. But I should like to comment on a point mentioned earlier, namely, the preponderance of papers dealing with fuzzy control.

When I wrote my 1965 paper on fuzzy sets, my expectation was that most of the applications of fuzzy set theory will relate to fields in which the systems are complex and ill-defined, e.g., economic systems, linguistics, psychology, biomedical systems, social systems, etc. By 1970, I could see that fuzzy logic could be applied to control, and described my views in a 1972 paper entitled "A Rationale for Fuzzy Control." I could not have predicted, however, that, twenty years later, control would be the most visible application-area for fuzzy logic.

There are several reasons why fuzzy control is a rapidly growing field encompassing theory, development and implementation. In the first place, applications of fuzzy logic to control are easy to make since they involve not much more than the use of fuzzy if-then rules for the manipulation of dependencies and commands.

Second, the point of departure in fuzzy control is a human solution. Thus, in most instances, fuzzy control is used in a descriptive mode to describe what is basically a human solution in the language of fuzzy if-then rules — FDCL(Fuzzy Dependency and Command Language).

Third, fuzzy controllers are simple and robust. But, perhaps most importantly, fuzzy control makes it possible to perform tasks, such as parking a car, which do not lend themselves to solution by conventional methods. Much of the classical theory of control is set-point oriented and has little to say about problems which relate to task-oriented control. Such problems are certain to gain in importance in the years ahead.

Taking a retrospective view of my own research, I should like to comment briefly on my first paper on possibility theory entitled "Fuzzy Sets as a Basis for a Theory of Possibility," which was published in 1978. The key idea advanced in that paper was that there is a need for differentiation between probability and possibility, with the latter based on fuzzy logic. Thus, possibility may be viewed as a measure of ease of attainment or degree of compatibility, whereas probability has to do with chance and random behavior. Since the publication of my 1978 paper, possibility theory has blossomed in various directions and found many applications, especially in the realm of knowledge-based and decision-support systems. Among the many contributions to the development of possibility theory, particularly noteworthy is the work of D. Dubois and H. Prade in France. The many fundamental contributions to the advancement of fuzzy logic and possibility theory made by Dubois and Prade have generated and are continuing to generate a deep and wide-ranging impact.

It should be noted that there was, and still is, some controversy relating to the connection between probability theory, on the one hand, and fuzzy logic and possibility theory, on the other. Within the probability community, there are some who claim that there is nothing that can be done with fuzzy logic and possibility theory that could not be done equally well or better through the use of probability-based methods. To me, such claims reflect a lack of familiarity with fuzzy logic and a misunderstanding of what it has to offer. I have no doubt that eventually the skeptics within the probability community will realize that probability theory and possibility theory are complementary rather than competitive and that probability theory needs an infusion of fuzzy concepts to enhance its effectiveness in dealing with real-world problems.

Another direction in my research that is likely to gain more recognition in the years ahead, relates to the concept of *usuality* as a basis for what I call *dispositional logic.* In dispositional logic, propositions are assumed to be usuality-qualified, e.g., "usually it is cold and foggy in San Francisco during the summer" and "usually what is rare is expensive". In natural languages, usuality-qualification is generally implicit rather than explicit; thus, "overeating causes obesity" should be interpreted as "usually overeating causes obesity." The importance of usuality-qualification derives from the fact that much of commonsense knowledge consists of dispositions, that is, usuality-qualified propositions. In this perspective, dispositional logic may be viewed as the logic of commonsense knowledge and commonsense reasoning.

The emergence of neurocomputing and genetic algorithms — in the middle 80's — as highly effective methodologies for the conception and design of learning, adaptive and self-organizing systems — had a significant impact on the development of fuzzy logic. It became increasingly clear that the complementarity of probability theory and fuzzy logic applies also to the methodologies of neurocomputing and genetic algorithms. This led me to suggest the concept of *soft computing* as a consortium or partnership of fuzzy logic, neurocomputing and probabilistic reasoning, with the latter subsuming genetic algorithms, evidential reasoning and chaotic systems. In this partnership, the main contribution of fuzzy logic is a methodology for dealing with imprecision, approximate reasoning and computing with words; that of neurocomputing is a methodology for learning, adaptation and system identification; and that of probabilistic reasoning are methodologies for evidential reasoning and systematized random search. In the latter, the methodology of genetic algorithms plays a pivotal role.

What is important about soft computing is that it suggests the possibility of employing fuzzy logic, neurocomputing and genetic algorithms in combination rather than in isolation. A combination that has the highest visibility at this juncture is that of neuro-fuzzy systems. Most such systems are basically fuzzy rule-based systems in which neural network techniques are employed for purposes of tuning and optimization. However, we are also beginning to see neural systems in which fuzzy if-then rules are employed to improve the performance of basic algorithms such as the back-propagation algorithm. Eventually, hybrid systems employing a combination of fuzzy logic, neurocomputing and genetic algorithms are likely to become ubiquitous.

The growing use of soft computing has made an important contribution to the conception, design and deployment of intelligent systems. The time is approaching when we will need a way of measuring the intelligence of man-made systems. By analogy with IQ, a measure of intelligence of such systems may be referred to as MIQ (Machine Intelligence Quotient). In this perspective, one of the major aims of soft computing is to provide a body of concepts and techniques for the conception and design of systems with high MIQ. The Berkeley Initiative in Soft Computing (BISC), was launched in 1991 to serve this purpose.

Much of my current research is focused on what I call Computing with Words, or CW for short. Based on fuzzy logic, CW provides a conceptual framework for computing and reasoning with words rather than numbers. The basic idea underlying CW is that, in general, information is conveyed by constraining the values which a variable can take. The point of departure in CW is the assumption that the given information is represented as a collection of propositions expressed in a natural language. Each proposition is viewed as an implicit constraint on an implicit variable. For purposes of computation, it is necessary to make such constraints explicit. This leads to the concept of a *canonical form* which serves to make explicit the variable which is constrained and the constraining relation.

Once the implicit constraints in the premise propositions are made explicit through the use of canonical forms, the rules of inference in fuzzy logic can be employed to propagate fuzzy constraints from premises to conclusions. Finally, the induced constraints are translated into a natural language. This is the basic idea which underlies computing with words.

Computing with words serves three important purposes. First, to provide a methodology for computing and reasoning when the available information is not precise enough to justify the use of numbers. Second, to exploit the tolerance for imprecision to achieve tractability, robustness, low solution cost and better rapport with reality. And third, to provide a foundation for the development of programming languages which could approximate to natural languages in appearance and expressive power.

I believe that eventually computing with words will become a methodology in its own right with a wide-ranging impact on both basic and applied levels. In the final analysis, the role model for computing with words is the human mind.

I should like to conclude my talk with an optimistic forecast. We are entering an era of intelligent systems which will have a profound — and hopefully positive — impact on ways in which we communicate, make decisions and use machines. I believe that fuzzy logic — in concert with its partners in soft computing — will play a major role in making the era of intelligent systems a reality.

SUBJECT INDEX